THE LIBRARY

OF

LITERARY CRITICISM

OF

ENGLISH AND AMERICAN AUTHORS

VOLUME I
680 - 1638

EDITED BY CHARLES WELLS MOULTON
ASSISTED BY A CORPS OF ABLE CONTRIBUTORS

GLOUCESTER, MASS.
PETER SMITH
1959

To

Professor Thomas Raynesford Lounsbury, LL. D., L. H. D.

PREFACE.

IN OFFERING to the public "THE LIBRARY OF LITERARY CRITICISM OF ENGLISH AND AMERICAN AUTHORS," the editor feels that an extended Preface would be superfluous. The scope and usefulness of this work will be apparent to all who have occasion to consult its pages. The arrangement is in chronological order; and this volume brings the work down to 1638. Each volume will contain an alphabetical Table of Contents, and in the last volume copious indexes will follow the regular text.

Each author is treated chronologically,—in most cases beginning with contemporary criticism and ending with some living authority. Under the head of Geoffrey Chaucer, the first articles are by Deschamps and Gower, written in the twelfth century, and the concluding criticisms are by Lounsbury, Courthope, Pollard, Corson, Saintsbury, and Skeat, of the last decade, whose co-operation is much appreciated.

In every instance it has been the editor's aim to fix the date of each article by giving either the date the article was written or the date of its publication. In cases like the "History of English Literature" by H. A. Taine, although published in France in 1864, the date of its first appearance in English, 1871, as translated by Mr. Van Laun with M. Taine's corrections, has been adopted. Where accurate information was not obtainable, an approximate date has been given. Where several editions of a work have been published, the last edition has generally been consulted. With few exceptions the quotations have been collated with the original text, and over five thousand volumes have been consulted in compiling this volume.

Acknowledgments are due to so many individuals and firms that it is impossible to enumerate my obligations here. There is not an important publishing house in America or Great Britain that has not contributed to this LIBRARY. To the many laymen and scholars who have lent their helpful assistance and counsel in the preparation of the following pages I gratefully acknowledge my indebtedness.

CHARLES WELLS MOULTON.

BUFFALO, NEW YORK, January 30, 1901.

INTRODUCTION.

A man will turn over half a library to make one book.—JOHNSON, SAMUEL, 1775, *Life by Boswell.*

Adam scriveyn, if ever it thee bifalle
Boece or Troilus to wryten newe,
Under thy lokkes thou most have the scalle
But after my making thou wryte trewe.
So ofte a daye I mot thy werk renewe,
Hit to correcte and eek to rubbe and scrape;
And al is through thy negligence and rape.

—CHAUCER, GEOFFREY, C 1390, *Wordes unto Adam, his Owne Scriveyn, Chaucer's Works, ed. Skeat, vol.* I, *p.* 379.

Say worthy doctors and Clerkes curious:
What moves you of Bokes to have such a number,
Syn divers doctrines through way contrarious
Doth mans minde distract and sore encomber;
Alas, blind men awake, out of your slomber,
And if ye will needs your books multiply
With diligence endeavour you some to occupy.

—BARCLAY, ALEXANDER, 1509, *The Shyp of Folys.*

Give me leave
To enjoy myself; that place that does contain
My books, the best companions, is to me
A glorious court, where hourly I converse
With the old sages and philosophers;
And sometimes, for variety, I confer
With kings and emperors, and weigh their ounsels;
Calling their victories, if unjustly got,
Unto a strict account, and, in my fancy,
Deface their ill-placed statues. Can I then
Part with such constant pleasures, to embrace
Uncertain vanities? No, be it your care
To augment your heap of wealth; it shall be mine
To increase in knowledge.—Lights there, for my study!

—FLETCHER, JOHN, C 1625, *The Elder Brother, Act I., Sc.* 2.

As good almost kill a man as kill a good book: who kills a man kills a reasonable creature, God's image; but he who destroys a good book, kills reason itself, kills the image of God, as it were, in the eye. Many a man lives a burden to the earth; but a good book is the precious life-blood of a master-spirit, embalmed and treasured up on purpose to a life beyond life.—MILTON, JOHN, 1644, *Areopagitica, Works, Bohn ed., vol.* II, *p.* 55.

Books are the depositary of every thing that is most honourable to man. Literature, taken in all its bearings, forms the grand line of demarcation between the human and the animal kingdoms. He that loves reading, has every thing within his reach. He has but to desire; and he may possess himself of every species of wisdom to judge, and power to perform.—GODWIN, WILLIAM, 1797, *Of an Early Taste for Reading, The Enquirer, p.* 31.

At no hour of your life will the love of letters ever oppress you as a burden, or fail you as resource. In the vain and foolish exultation of the heart, which the brighter prospects of life will sometimes excite, the pensive portress of science shall call you to the sober pleasures of her holy cell. In the mortifications of disappointment, her soothing voice shall whisper serenity and peace. In social converse with the mighty dead of ancient days, you will never smart under the galling sensation of dependence upon the mighty living of the present age; and in your struggles with the world, should a crisis ever occur, when even friendship may deem it prudent to desert you; when even your country may seem ready to abandon herself and you; when, even priest and levite shall come and look on you, and pass by on the other side; seek refuge, my unfailing friends, and be assured you will find it, in the friendships of Lælius and Scipio; in the patriotism of Cicero, Demosthenes, and Burke; as well as in the precepts and example of Him, whose law is love, and who taught us to remember injuries only to forgive them.—ADAMS, JOHN QUINCY, 1809, *Lectures on Rhetoric and Oratory, vol.* II, *p.* 196.

We can select our companions from among the most richly gifted of the sons of God, and they are companions who will not desert us in poverty, or sickness, or disgrace; when everything else fails,—when fortune frowns, and friends cool, and health forsakes us,—when this great world of forms and shows appears a "two-edged lie, which *seems* but *is* not,"—when all our earth-clinging hopes and ambitions melt away into nothingness,

"Like snow-falls on a river,
One moment white, then gone forever,"—

we are still not without friends to animate and console us,—friends, in whose immortal countenances, as they look out upon us from books, we can discern no change; who will dignify low fortunes and humble life with their kingly presence; who will people solitude with shapes more glorious than ever glittered in palaces; who will consecrate sorrow and take the sting from care; and who, in the long hours of despondency and weakness, will send healing to the sick heart, and energy to the wasted brain.—WHIPPLE, EDWIN PERCY, 1846–71, *Literature and Life, p.* 40.

In that great social organ which, collectively, we call literature, there may be distinguished two separate offices that may blend, and often *do* so, but capable, severally, of a severe insulation, and naturally fitted for a reciprocal repulsion. There is, first, the literature of *knowledge;* and, secondly, the literature of *power.* The function of the first is—to *teach;* the function of the second is—to *move:* the first is a rudder; the second, an oar or a sail. The first speaks to the *mere* discursive understanding; the second speaks ultimately, it may happen, to the higher understanding or reason, but always *through* affections of pleasure and sympathy.—DE QUINCEY, THOMAS, 1848–58, *The Poetry of Pope, De Quincey's Works, ed. Masson, vol.* XI, *p.* 54.

It is the relation to universal humanity which constitutes literature; it matters not how elevated, whether it be history, philosophy, or poetry, in its highest aspirations; or how humble, it may be the simplest rhyme or story that is level to the unquestioning faith and untutored intellect of childhood: let it but be addressed to our common human nature, it is literature in the true sense of the term.—REED, HENRY, 1855, *Lectures on English Literature, p.* 30.

Words afford a more delicious music than the chords of any instrument; they are susceptible of richer colors than any painter's palette; and that they should be used merely for the transportation of intelligence, as a wheelbarrow carries brick, is not enough. The highest aspect of literature assimilates it to painting and music. Beyond and above all the domain of use lies beauty, and to aim at this makes literature an art.—HIGGINSON, THOMAS WENTWORTH, 1867–71, *Literature as an Art, Atlantic Essays, p.* 28.

When the conceptions of an individual mind are expressed in a permanent form of words, we get literature. The sum total of all the permanent forms of expression in one language make up the literature of that language; and if no one has given his conceptions a form which has been preserved, the language is without a literature. There are then two things essential to a literary work: first, the conceptions of an individual mind; second, a permanent form of expression. Hence it follows that the domain of literature is distinct from the domain of natural or mathematical science. Science does not give us the conceptions of an individual mind, but it tells us what every rational person who studies the subject must think. And science is entirely independent of any form of words: a proposition of Euclid is science; a sonnet of Wordsworth's is literature. . . . So great is the difference between science and literature, that in literature, as the first Lord Lytton said, the best books are generally the oldest; in science they are the newest —QUICK, ROBERT HEBERT, 1868-90, *Essays on Educational Reformers, pp.* 5, 6.

We may aver with confidence, that English literature furnishes the amplest, the most varied, and the most interesting materials for the critic, of any whether ancient or modern.—PORTER, NOAH, 1870, *Books and Reading, p.* 285.

Literature is the greatest of all sources of refined pleasure.—HUXLEY, THOMAS HENRY, 1870, *Lay Sermons, p.* 52.

What is your first remark on turning over the great, stiff leaves of a folio, the yellow sheets of a manuscript,—a poem, a code of laws, a declaration of faith? This, you say, was not created alone. It is but a mould, like a fossil shell, an imprint, like one of those shapes embossed in stone by an animal, which lived and perished. Under the shell there was an animal, and behind the document there was a man. Why do you study the shell, except to represent to yourself the animal? So do you study the document only in order to know the man. The shell and the document are lifeless wrecks, valuable only as a clue to the entire and living existence. We must reach back to this existence, endeavour to re-create it. It is a mistake to study the document, as if it were isolated. This were to treat things like a simple pedant, to fall into the error of the bibliomaniac. Behind all, we have neither mythology nor languages, but only men, who arrange words and imagery according to the necessities of their organs and the original bent of their intellects. A dogma is nothing in itself; look at the people who have made it,—a portrait, for instance, of the sixteenth century, the stern and energetic face of an English archbishop or martyr. Nothing exists except through some individual man; it is this individual with whom we must become acquainted. When we have established the parentage of dogmas, or the classification of poems, or the progress of constitutions, or the modification of idioms, we have only cleared the soil: genuine history is brought into existence only when the historian begins to unravel, across the lapse of time, the living man, toiling, impassioned, entrenched in his customs, with his voice and features, his gestures and his dress, distinct and complete as he from whom we have just parted in the street.—TAINE, H. A., 1871, *History of English Literature, tr. Van Laun, Introduction, vol.* I, *p.* 1.

Let no beginner think that when he has read this book, or any book, or any number of books for any number of years, he will have thoroughly learned English Literature. We can but study faithfully and work on from little to more, never to much. . . . No labour of this kind is intended to save any one the pains of reading good books for himself. It is useful only when it quickens the desire to come into real contact with great minds of the past, and gives the kind of knowledge that will lessen distance between us and them.—MORLEY, HENRY, 1873, *A First Sketch of English Literature, Preface.*

Our high respect for a well-read man is praise enough of literature.—EMERSON, RALPH WALDO, 1876, *Letters and Social Aims, p.* 170.

Every one knows how much is added to our understanding of an author's works when we become acquainted with his biography. We thus discover what qualities he has inherited, what others have been developed through the vicissitudes of his life, and what have been attained by labor and aspiration. This is equally true to the literature of a race. It has its pedigree, its birth and childhood, its uncertain youth, and its varying fortunes through the ages, before it reaches a mature and permanent character. Although it grows in grace and variety of expression, and charms us most when it gives large and lofty utterance to the thought and feeling of our own times, we none the less need to turn back and listen to the prattle of its infancy.—TAYLOR, BAYARD, 1878, *Studies in German Literature, p.* 1.

Literature is that part of thought that is wrought out in the name of the beautiful. . . . A poem, like that of Homer, or an essay upon Milton or Dante or Cæsar from a Macaulay, a Taine or a Froude, is created in the name of beauty, and is a fragment in literature, just as a Corinthian capital is a fragment in art. When truth, in its forward flow, joins beauty, the two rivers make a new flood called "Letters." It is an Amazon of broad bosom, resembling the sea. — SWING, DAVID, 1881, *Club Essays, pp.* 166, 167.

Literature consists of a whole body of classics in the true sense of the word. . . Literature consists of all the books —and they are not so many—where moral truth and human passion are touched with a certain largeness, sanity, and attraction of form. My notion of the literary student is one who through books explores the strange voyages of man's moral reason, the impulses of the human heart, the chances and changes that have overtaken human ideals of virtue and happiness, of conduct and manners, and the shifting fortunes of great conceptions of truth and virtue. Poets, dramatists, humorists, satirists, masters of fiction, the great preachers, the character-writers, the maxim-writers, the great political orators—they are all literature in so far as they teach us to know man and to know human nature. This is what makes literature, rightly sifted and selected and rightly studied, not the mere elegant trifling that it is so often and so erroneously supposed to be, but a proper instrument for a systematic training of the imagination and sympathies, and of a genial and varied moral sensibility.—MORLEY, JOHN, 1887, *On the Study of Literature, pp.* 38, 39.

Literature, more especially poetic and dramatic literature, is the expression in letters of the spiritual, coöperating with the intellectual, man, the former being the primary, dominant coëfficient.—CORSON, HIRAM, 1895, *The Aims of Literary Study, p.* 24.

Such words as *literature,* as also, for other examples, *beauty, poetry, imagination, idealism,* are used by us all without any attempt to define for ourselves precisely what we mean by them. We find they designate accurately enough the most of the things associated with them in our thought, and we do not trouble ourselves if there be, so to speak, a ragged fringe on either side of the line of their meaning. It is only when we try to define such terms that we realize how vague and careless is our use of them. We find it difficult to make out with precision the limits of meaning we ourselves would assign to them; and when we have done that, we find our neighbor has assigned quite different ones; so that we are often driven to one of two or three makeshifts. We may give to such a word a signification so wide as to cover all its uses, but of little value because too vague to fix the essential quality that the word ought to signify; or we may give the word several meanings, showing, if we can, what they have in common; or we may arbitrarily fix on a meaning, and confine our own use to it, recognizing that others use the word in other senses.—WINCHESTER, C. T., 1899, *Some Principles of Literary Criticism, p.* 34.

If we would broaden ourselves and increase our capacity for appreciating the manifold sides of the life of the spirit, we must become familiar with the thoughts and ideals of those who have given us our inspiring literature. For nearly fifteen hundred years the Anglo-Saxon race has been producing the greatest of all literatures. The most boastful of other nations make no claim to having a Shakspeare on the list of their immortals.—HALLECK, REUBEN POST, 1900, *History of English Literature, p.* 11.

CONTENTS.

ENGRAVINGS.

The
Library of Literary Criticism
of
English and American Authors

VOLUME I

Beowulf

The Beowulf MS. (Cotton Vitellius A. xv.) was one of those collected by Sir Robert Cotton. It was in Little Deans Yard, Westminster, when the fire which, in 1731, destroyed so many manuscripts took place, and was fortunately among those which were not fatally injured. In 1753, having spent some time in the old dormitory at Westminster, it was transferred to the British Museum. In 1705 Wanley, employed by Hickes, the Anglo-Saxon scholar, to make a catalogue of the old northern books in the kingdom, discovered the poem of Beowulf in the Cottonian library and calls it a *tractatus nobilissimus poeticè scriptus*. It is a parchment codex, and the handwriting of the two copyists is of the beginning of the tenth century. Thorkelin, a Danish scholar, had two copies of it made in 1786, and published the whole of it for the first time in 1815. This edition made the poem known, and it was discussed in English and foreign reviews. Meantime, in 1805, Sharon Turner gave the first account of the poem in his history of the Anglo-Saxons. Turner again, in 1823, and Conybeare, in 1826, filled up that account and translated portions of "Beowulf" into English verse, and in 1833 and 1837 John M. Kemble edited, with historical prefaces, and translated the whole of the poem. This scholarly book increased the interest of foreign scholars in the poem; and, since then, a great number of editions and translations have been published, while the essays, dissertations, articles, and notices on the poem and the subjects contained in it, fill a long list, and are written by English, French, German, Dutch, Danish, and American scholars.—BROOKE, STOPFORD A., 1892, *The History of Early English Literature, p.* 12.

The plan . . . is sufficiently simple. The characters, as far as they are developed, are well sustained, and their speeches usually natural and well appropriated. The narrative is by no means so encumbered with repetitions as that of the reputed Cædmon; nor is the style so ambitious and inflated. Over the almost unintelligible rhapsodies of the Edda (for these are the fairest points of comparison) it possesses a decided superiority; nor are there many among the metrical romances of the more polished Normans, with which it may not fairly abide a competition.—CONYBEARE, JOHN JOSIAS, 1826, *Illustrations of Anglo-Saxon Poetry, p.* 81.

Is probably a Translation or Rifacciamento of some older Lay originally written in the antient Language of Denmark.—WHEATON, HENRY, 1831, *History of the Northmen, p.* 130.

If antiquaries still wander among shadows, the poet cannot err. Beowulf may be a god or a nonentity; but the poem which records his exploits must at least be true,—true in the manners it paints and the emotions which the poet reveals,—the emotions of his contemporaries.—DISRAELI, ISAAC, 1841, *Beowulf: The Hero-Life, Amenities of Literature.*

One of the oldest and most important remains of Anglo-Saxon literature is the epic poem of "Beowulf." Its age is unknown; but it comes from a very distant and hoar antiquity; somewhere between the seventh and tenth centuries. It is like a piece of ancient armor; rusty and battered, and yet strong. From within comes a voice sepulchral, as if the ancient armor spoke, telling a simple, straight-forward narrative; with here and there the boastful speech of a rough old Dane, reminding one of those made by the heroes of Homer. The style, likewise, is simple,—perhaps one should say, austere. The bold metaphors, which characterize nearly all the Anglo-Saxon poems we have read, are for the most part wanting in this. The author seems mainly bent upon telling us, how his Sea-Goth slew the Grendel and the Fire-drake. He is too much in earnest to multiply epithets and gorgeous figures. At times he is tedious; at times obscure; and he who undertakes to read the original will find it no easy task.—LONGFELLOW, HENRY WADSWORTH, 1845, *The Poets and Poetry of Europe*, p. 4.

The Beowulf's-Lay, then, appears to me to have as good a Claim to be considered an original Work in its Present State as the Æneid of Virgil or indeed any Epic Poem in Existence. I conceive then that the Author was a Christian of this Country, and from the little Bits of Preaching that one meets with every here and there, and his References to the Sacred Volumes, I think it probable that he may have been an Ecclesiastic. . . . The Language of the Poem, again, does not appear to me to differ so much from that of King Ælfred, or of Ceadmon, as to warrant our placing a very long Interval between the Productions: but it appears to forbid our considering it as belonging to the later Danish Dynasty of Cnut.—WACKERBARTH, A. DIEDRICH, 1847, *ed. Beowulf, Introduction*, p. xlv.

With respect to this the oldest heroic poem in any Germanic tongue, my opinion is, that it is not an original production of the Anglo-Saxon muse, but a metrical paraphrase of an heroic Saga composed in the south-west of Sweden, in the old common language of the North, and probably brought to this country during the sway of the Danish dynasty. . . From the allusions to Christianity contained in the poem, I do not hesitate to regard it as a Christian paraphrase of a heathen Saga, and those allusions as interpolations of the paraphrast, whom I conceive to have been a native of England of Scandinavian parentage. As a monument of language the poem of Beowulf is highly valuable, but far more valuable is it as a vivid and faithful picture of old Northern manners and usages, as they existed in the halls of the kingly and the noble at the remote period to which it relates. In this respect, where are we to look for its like?—THORPE, BENJAMIN, 1855, *The Anglo-Saxon Poems of Beowulf, etc., Preface*, pp. viii, ix.

In the higher excellences of poetry, the celebrated epic, Beowulf, ranks perhaps first among the monuments of Anglo-Saxon literature, but in subject, plan, and treatment, it differs so widely from the general character of the versified compositions in the language, that it cannot be considered as a product of the same genius or the same influences which have given form and spirit to the other literary efforts of that people. . . . In its machinery, it has many points of resemblance to Scandinavian mythic poetry, and though there exists no Old-Northern poem of very similar character, there are prose sagas—generally indeed of much later date—which in tone and treatment are not unlike the story of Beowulf.—MARSH, GEORGE P., 1862, *The Origin and History of the English Language and of the Early Literature it Embodies*, p. 101.

Fiction as yet is not far removed from fact: the man breathes manifest under the hero. Rude as the poetry is, its hero is grand; he is so, simply by his deeds. Faithful, first to his prince, then to his people, he went alone, in a strange land, to venture himself for the delivery of his fellow-men; he forgets himself in death, while thinking only that it profits others. "Each one of us," he says in one place, "must abide the end of his present life." Let, therefore, each do justice, if he can, before his death. Compare with him the monsters whom he destroys, the last traditions of the ancient wars against inferior races, and of the primitive religion; think of his life of danger, nights upon the waves, man's efforts against the brute creation, the indomitable breast crushing the breasts of beasts, powerful muscles which, when exerted, tear the flesh of the monsters: you will see through the mist of legends, and under the light of poetry, the valiant men who, amid the furies of war and the raging of their own mood, began to settle a people and to found a state.—TAINE, H. A., 1871, *History of English Literature, tr. Van Laun, vol.* I, *p.* 41.

If "Beowulf" is no national poem and no epos in the strict sense, taking matter and composition into account, yet as regards style and tone, character and customs, it is both in a high degree; and it is not without significance that a poem stands at the head of English literature whose subject is the struggle with the waves, and which is permeated by a vivid perception of the sea and of sea life. A great wealth of poetic feeling is revealed in this poem. We are charmed by pictures of external things and actions delineated with most realistic freshness, and epic minuteness.—TEN BRINK, BERNHARD, 1877–83, *History of English Literature, (To Wiclif) tr. Kennedy, p.* 28.

Although much of the poem of Beowulf is at best only legendary, and a great deal of it purely fabulous, there can be no doubt, I think, that we have, imbedded in the marvels and wild fancies of the story, a dim and vague but authentic record of the doings of our ancestors some fourteen centuries ago. . . . Its real value—considered as an historical authority merely—lies in the vivid picture it gives us of the life, the manners, and the habits of thought and speech of our forefathers in that "dark backward and abysm of time." We have it here at first hand, "proving," in Chapman's words,

"—how firm truth builds in poet's
feigning;"

and it is scarcely an exaggeration to say that we may live with our ancestors and know them—which surely is the chief end of history—better in this poem than in all the bulky volumes of professed historians. —LUMSDEN, LIEUT.-COL. H. W., 1881, *ed. Beowulf, Introduction, p.* v.

Even if the poem were composed in the first half of the eighth century, the life depicted is that of two centuries earlier, unless the writer transfers to those times the manners and customs of his own day. —GARNETT, JAMES M., 1882, *ed. Beowulf, Introduction, p.* xviii.

The heroic tale of "Beowulf" is worth a thousand Ossians. Not one falsetto note, not one sham-antique sentiment or image, not one grotesque anachronism stains its primitive beauty and simplicity.—ROSS, JOHN MERRY, 1884, *Scottish History and Literature to the Period of the Reformation, ed. Brown, p.* 44.

There is speech from beginning to end; there is music; the minstrel sitting on the mead bench sings several noble lays. Our ears are deafened with the roar of talk; there are long orations; there is dramatic dialogue canto after canto. The very silence of the poem is a thunder, for through it we hear the tread of the dragon; the very darkness of it is like a vivid flash, for out of it leaps the figure of Grendel. Even the raven tells the eagle "how he joyed him in the feast when with the wolf he plundered the slain" (3027). The "storm of arrows," the "shower of iron," the din and friction of clashing weapons, horns and trumpets blowing their blasts, bring sharply before us more than a sound: they evoke a picture. All three fights with the dragons are tempests in words. All the people are loud-voiced; there are joyous welcomes and partings; the "glee-beam," the "music-wood" soften or stir the hearts of the feasting watchers as they keep the vigil. There is no noiseless wassailing or shadow-drinking in pantomine.—HARRISON, JAMES A., 1884, *Old Teutonic Life in Beowulf, Overland Monthly, 2nd S., vol.* 4, *p.* 21.

It does not show the imaginative character of the Edda. There was never with the Saxon any such epic cycle as with the Scandinavian. It is a grand torso. But it is the very image of the time and the men.—WASHBURN, EMELYN W., 1884, *Studies in Early English Literature, p.* 5.

The general sense of the poem is this. There is work for the age of Blood and Iron, but such an age must yield to a better. Force is not the supreme and final arbiter of human destiny; above and behind Might is enthroned the diviner genius of Right. In this idea we recognize the essential thought of Civilization, the clue to emergence out of barbarism. And even further back, as if in barbarism itself, we see a germ of culture and the gentler forms of life. The honoured position of woman, which here rests upon ancestral custom, is full of promise for the development of the nobler instincts of Society.—EARLE JOHN, 1892, *ed. The Deeds of Beowulf, Introduction, p.* lxxxviii.

If we want to feel whether "Beowulf" is good poetry or not, let us place ourselves in the hall as evening draws on, when the benches are filled with warriors and seamen, and the chief sits in the high seat, and the fires flame in the midst, and the cup goes round—and then hear the Shaper strike the harp. With gesture, with the beat of his voice and of the hand upon his instrument at each alliterative word of the saga, he sings of the great fight with Grendel or the dragon, of Hrothgar's giving, of the sea-voyage, to men who had themselves fought against desperate odds, to sailors who knew the storms, to the fierce rovers of the deep, to great ealdormen who ruled their freemen, to thegns who followed their kings to battle and would die rather than break the bond of comradeship. Then as we image this, and read the accented verse, sharply falling and rising with the excitement of the thing recorded, we understand how good the work is, how fitted for its time and place, how national, how full of noble pleasure.—BROOKE, STOPFORD A., 1892, *The History of Early English Literature, p.* 73.

Beowulf crushes all he touches; in his fights he upsets monsters, in his talks he tumbles his interlocutors headlong. His retorts have nothing winged about them; he does not use the feathered arrow, but the iron hammer. Hunferth taunts him with not having had the best in a swimming match. Beowulf replies by a strong speech, which can be summed up in few words: liar, drunkard, coward, murderer! It seems an echo from the banqueting hall of the Scandinavian gods; in the same manner Loki and the goddesses played with words. For the assembled warriors of Hrothgar's court Beowulf goes in nowise beyond bounds; they are not indignant, they would rather laugh. So did the gods. —JUSSERAND, J. J., 1895, *A Literary History of the English People, p.* 55.

The poem of "Beowulf" has been sorely tried; critics have long been at work on the body of it, to discover how it is made. It gives many openings for theories of agglutination and adulteration. Many things in it are plainly incongruous. . . . However the result was obtained, "Beowulf" is, at any rate, the specimen by which the Teutonic epic poetry must be judged. It is the largest monument extant. There is nothing beyond it, in that kind, in respect of size and completeness. If the old Teutonic epic is judged to have failed, it must be because "Beowulf" is a failure.—KER, W. P., 1897, *Epic and Romance, pp.* 182, 183.

The manuscript itself, the handwriting of which is probably of the tenth century, affords, apart from that fact, no presumption as to the date of the poem. It is a bad transcript of a work the language of which the scribe seems to have imperfectly understood, and hence to have in many places hopelessly misrepresented; and the interval in time between the transcript and the original composition may have been indefinitely great. . . . Briefly summarised, the views here suggested as to the authorship of "Beowulf" may be stated thus: Sagas, either in the Danish dialect or in that of the Geatas—more probably the latter—were current in the Scandinavian countries in the seventh century. Among these Sagas, that of Beowulf the Geat must have had a prominent place; others celebrated Hygelac his uncle, Hnæf the Viking, the wars of the Danes and the Heaðobards, of the Danes and the Swedes, etc., etc. About the end of the century missioners from England are known to have been busy in Friesland and Denmark, endeavouring to convert the natives to Christianity. Some one of these, whose mind had a turn for literature, and dwelt with joy among the traditions of the past, collected or learnt by heart a number of these Sagas, and taking that of Beowulf as a basis, and weaving many others into his work, composed an epic poem of upwards of three thousand lines, to which, although it contains the record of two, or rather of three adventures, the heroic scale of the figure who accomplishes them all imparts a real unifying epic interest. The poet who, returning to England, gave this work to his countrymen, cannot at present be identified. It was not Cynewulf; style, tone, and tendency are all so different, that this solution, in my opinion at least, must be decisively rejected. Nor was it, for the reasons that have been given, the author of "Andreas;" nor, most certainly, was it the author of "Guðlac." A fresh, searching examination of the entire mass of Anglo-Saxon poetry, with a view to the solution of this one question—Who wrote "Beowulf"?—must be made, before the problem can be put aside as insoluble. Such an examination, if not undertaken in England, will doubtless be ultimately carried out by some scholar of a Swedish or German university.—ARNOLD, THOMAS, 1898, *Notes on Beowulf*, *pp.* 3, 129.

If we take into consideration the fact, which is all but a certain fact, that "Beowulf" is the very oldest poem of any size and scope in any modern language, that it has no known predecessors, and has the whole literature of romance for successors—then without attributing to it merits which it cannot claim, or muddling it up with myths which simply minish its interest, we shall see that it is a very venerable document indeed, well worth the envy of the nations to whom it does not belong. Even if it were no older than its MS., "Beowulf" would be the senior of the "Chanson de Roland" by nearly a century, the senior of the "Poema del Cid" by two, the senior of the "Nibelungen Lied" by two or three. In reality it is possibly the elder of the eldest of these by half a millennium. Some of those who love England least have been fain to admit that we have the best poetry in Europe; it is thanks mainly to "Beowulf" that our poetry can claim the oldest lineage, and poetical coat-armour from the very first. —SAINTSBURY, GEORGE, 1898, *A Short History of English Literature*, *p.* 6.

Cædmon

C. 680

The poetical works which now bear Cædmon's name received that name from Junius, the first editor, in 1655, on the ground of the general agreement of the subjects with Bede's description of Cædmon's works. In this book we find a first part containing the most prominent narratives from the books of Genesis, Exodus, and Daniel; and a second part containing the Descent of Christ into Hades and the delivery of the patriarchs from their captivity, according to the apocryphal Gospel of Nicodemus and the constant legend of the Middle Ages. This comprises a kind of Paradise Lost and Paradise Regained. Of all this, the part which has attracted most notice is a part of which the materials are found neither in Scripture nor in any known Apocrypha. The nearest approximation yet indicated is in the hexameters of Avitus.—EARLE, JOHN, 1884, *Anglo-Saxon Literature*, *p.* 111.

The original MS. of the poem, preserved in the Bodleian Library, is a small parchment volume in folio, containing two hundred and twenty-nine pages; the first two hundred and twelve of which are written in a fair, though not elegant hand, apparently of the tenth century. The remaining seventeen pages, forming a Second Book, are in an inferior handwriting: and as the orthography used in this part of the poem is less pure, and the language less grammatical than in the first part, it is perhaps to be considered as less ancient. Of the history of this MS. nothing more, I believe, is known, than that it was the property of Archbishop Usher, who presented it to Junius, by whom, with the rest of his MSS., it was bequeathed to the Bodleian Library. This work . . . was first given to the world by the learned foreigner above named, in a small quarto, printed at Amsterdam in 1655, containing the Saxon text, unaccompanied by translation or notes.—THORPE, BENJAMIN, 1832, *Cædmon's Metrical Paraphrase, Translator's Preface*, *p.* ix.

There was in this abbess's* monastery a certain brother, particularly remarkable for the grace of God, who was wont to make pious and religious verses, so that whatever was interpreted to him out of Scripture, he soon after put the same into poetical expressions of much sweetness and humility, in English, which was his native language. By his verses the minds of many were often excited to despise the world, and to aspire to heaven. Others after him attempted, in the English nation, to compose religious poems, but none could ever compare with him, for he did

*Hilda.

not learn the art of poetry from men, but from God; for which reason he never could compose any trivial or vain poem, but only those which relate to religion suited his religious tongue.—BEDE, 731, *Ecclesiastical History, bk.* iv, *ch.* xxiv, (*A. D.* 680), *ed. Giles.*

Cedmon's memory remained in great veneration, not only at Streanshalh, but also through the whole kingdom of Northumberland, where his name was long honorably used as an appellative or proper name, and after the conquest was adopted as a surname; so that there yet remain to these our days some families in Whitby and its neighborhood that are known by the name of Cedmon or Sedman; a name with us the most honorable and ancient of all others.—CHARLTON, LIONEL, 1779, *History of Whitby and Whitby Abbey, vol.* I, *p.* 17.

The obscurity attending the origin of the Cædmonian poems will perhaps increase the interest excited by them. Whoever may have been their author, their remote antiquity is unquestionable. In poetical imagery and feeling they excel all the other early remains of the North. —PALGRAVE, FRANCIS, 1832, *Observations on the History of Cædmon, Archaeologia, vol.* 24, *p.* 343.

Cædmon, of whom we have heard so much, was one of those gifted men, who have stamped deeply and lastingly upon the literature of their country, the impress of their own mind and feelings. He was the first Englishman—it may be, the first individual of Gothic race—who exchanged the gorgeous images of the old mythology for the chaster beauties of Christian poetry. From the sixth to the twelfth century, he appears to have been the great model, whom all imitated, and few could equal. For upwards of five centuries, he was the father of English poetry; and when his body was discovered in the reign of John, it seems to have excited no less reverence than those of the kings and saints by which it was surrounded. Nothing shows more clearly the influence which this extraordinary man exerted upon our national modes of thought and expression, than a comparison between the Anglo-Saxon and early Icelandic literatures. So striking is the contrast, both as to style and subject, that Rask has even ventured to maintain they were radically distinct. A better knowledge of the Anglo-Saxon would have shown him his mistake. But though it might easily be proved, that our fathers had poems on almost all the subjects which were once thought peculiar to the Eddas, yet the remains of them are so scanty, or the allusions to them so ambiguous, as rather to baffle criticism, than to enlighten it. The revolution effected by Cædmon appears to have been complete.—GUEST, EDWIN, 1838, *A History of English Rhythms, vol.* II, *p.* 23.

We dare not place "the Milton of our forefathers" by the side of the only Milton whom the world will recognize. We would not compare our Saxon poetry to Saxon art, for that was too deplorable; but to place Cædmon in a parallel with Milton, which Plutarch might have done (for he was not very nice in his resemblances), we might as well compare the formless forms and the puerile inventions of the rude Saxon artist, profusely exhibited in the drawings of the original manuscript of Cædmon, with the noble conceptions and the immortal designs of the Sistine Chapel.—DISRAELI, ISAAC, 1841, *Cædmon and Milton, Amenities of Literature.*

The type of the Anglo-Saxon religious poetry was Cædmon, who, according to the legend, received miraculously in a dream the gift of song. We are far from believing, as some have wished to explain the matter, that this miracle really occurred, and that it may be accounted for naturally, on the presumption of the simple and easy construction of Anglo-Saxon verse. On the contrary, that Cædmon's poems were exceedingly beautiful we have Bede's own testimony, a man well skilled in and much attached to the poetry of his forefathers; and that they were by no means easy to compose, we may be convinced by a comparison of the older religious poetry with that which was certainly written at a later period, (when the minstrel, though he still existed, was no more the same personage he had been,) such as the metrical translations from Boethius attributed to King Alfred. The terms in which Bede speaks of the miracle, show how extraordinary it appeared to those who lived at the time, that one who had not been taught the profession of poetry, should be able to compose like a regular bard. All, indeed, that we are justified in concluding from this story is, that Cædmon was considered to be so far superior to his contemporaries in the same art, that it required (as has often been the case under similar circumstances) the formation of a particular legend to account for it.—WRIGHT, THOMAS, 1842, *Biographia Britannica Literaria, vol.* I, *p.* 19.

Cædmon was treated as one inspired. He could not read, he did not understand Latin. But when any passage of the Bible was interpreted to him, or any of the sublime truths of religion unfolded, he sate for some time in quiet rumination, and poured it all forth in that brief alliterative verse, which kindled and enchanted his hearers. Thus was the whole history of the Bible, and the whole creed of Christianity, in the imaginative form which it then wore, made at once accessible to the Anglo-Saxon people. Cædmon's poetry was their bible, no doubt far more effective in awakening and changing the popular mind than a literal translation of the Scriptures could have been. He chose, by the natural test of his own kindred sympathies, all which would most powerfully work on the imagination, or strike to the heart of a rude yet poetic race.—MILMAN, HENRY HART, 1854, *History of Latin Christianity, vol.* II, *p.* 95.

His style not unfrequently is meagre and flat; his epithets have the Homeric vagueness of idea, and precision of application, which belong to an early literature; the reflections are often commonplace. . . . The style of Milton is no doubt unapproachable; but the mere story, as told by Cædmon, has been less hampered by theological difficulties, and is freer and grander than the Puritan poem.—PEARSON, CHARLES H., 1867, *History of England During the Early and Middle Ages, vol.* I, *pp.* 298, 300.

We must not forget that the poems which Cædmon made were written down from his dictation, and that we have not even the original manuscript thus written. In all such cases it is absurd to expect perfect literal accuracy; and, indeed, where religious people have had to deal with such matters, we shall generally find that they have been somewhat unscrupulous in their treatment of their original; they have been ready to make it coincide with their ideas of what it ought to be. I have no doubt that much which is not Cædmon's has been interpolated, and that he had little to do with the so-called second book.—WATSON, ROBERT SPENCE, 1875, *Cædmon the First English Poet, p.* 32.

Drawing epic, lyrical, didactic matter into its domain Cædmon's poetry seems, according to Beda's account, to have embraced all classes, and most of the range of material to which the Old English religious poetry is in any sense congenial. The question is pertinent if, of the numerous works of Cædmon, nothing besides that short hymn is preserved; if among the considerable remnants of the older ecclesiastical literature, the majority of which have reached us without the names of their authors, one or more are not to be traced to Cædmon. To this inquiry there is no satisfactory answer. It has been customary, since the time of Junius, to connect the poems contained in the Bodleian manuscript, Jun. XI., with Cædmon's name, but belief in the authority for this has been more and more abandoned. In the course of time an ever greater variety of elements and diversity of style have been discovered in the contents of that codex; and at present hardly any one feels justified in ascribing even a part of it to the most ancient Christian poet of England.—TEN BRINK, BERNHARD, 1877–83, *History of English Literature,* (*To Wiclif*) *tr. Kennedy, p.* 40.

Ground can be found . . . on which to raise an opinion that, although the poem—a poem, and a noble one—exists, and cannot itself be explained out of existence, yet at least there never was a man named Cædmon by whom it could have been written. If so, we should lose little, having the poem. Somebody wrote it, and for want of other name Cædmon will serve to represent him; or them, if we walk in the new paths of criticism and distribute the work in fragments among a little company of authors, and allot the shares due to the several members of the firm of Cædmon and Co.—MORLEY, HENRY, 1888, *English Writers, vol.* II, *p.*80.

With this fine passage close the poems that bear the name of Cædmon. Whatever their several dates be, they are a noble beginning to English song. Whoever be their several writers, they owe their impulse to the man who on that night took care of the cattle in the monastery of Hild. Honour from all the English race, from all the poets, greatest of the English race, is due to his name. He was the first (and I borrow some of Ebert's phrases) who, like a Scôp singing heroic tales, sang to the people in their own tongue the tales of the Old Testament and the subject-matters of Christianity. He showed how this new material might be assimilated by the genius of the people. He made the bridge which led to the artistic poetry which begins, after him, to handle the same subjects. The old singers of heathendom, crossing it, became the new singers of Christianity.—BROOKE, STOPFORD A., 1892, *The History of Early English Literature, p.* 331.

He could compose nothing but religious poetry, but in this he stood supreme. "Others after him strove to compose religious poems, but none could compete with him, for he learnt the art of poetry, not from men, but from God." One is loath to cast a doubt upon so sweet a story, which Bede repeated, as it was generally current in his own day; but it bears a suspicious resemblance to stories which are told of others who possessed, what no art can teach, the divine gift of poesy. But there can be no reasonable doubt that he *was* a poet—born, not made—and that he exercised his gift on the highest of all subjects, and thus was a glory of the Church of his day.—OVERTON, JOHN HENRY, 1897, *The Church in England, vol.* I, *p.* 96.

In regard of his origin and idiosyncrasy Cædmon is rather the prototype of a modern people-poet like Burns: the one summoned from the oxstall, the other from the plough, to tell of the things of the spirit; both humble in birth and occupation, and with distinct folk-traits and sympathies. The Whitby poet sings in strong, sweet speech of the Israelitish quest of the Promised Land, or of such stirring happenings as those which centre around Judith as protagonist. And throughout his Bible-inspired epics it is curious to see the moody earnestness of the Saxon merged in the solemn, mystic-dreamy, or jubilant joy of the neophyte; this blend of character and influence coloring the touches of nature as it does other phases of the work. His verses are paraphrase in the broadest, freest sense. When so the singer wills, he expands, interpolates, introduces so much of local color that the composition comes to have independent and creative worth.—BURTON, RICHARD, 1898, *Literary Likings, p.* 206.

Aldhelm

C. 640–709

The eighth century produced no English poet, whose name has reached us, unless we may refer Aldhelm to this period. Aldhelm, nephew of Ina, King of the West-Sexe, was taught Latin at Malmesbury by Maildulf the Scot, and Greek Dialectics and Rhetoric at Canterbury, by Archbishop Theodore, and the celebrated Adrian, abbot of St. Austin's. He was shorn in Maildulf's monastery, of which he became the second abbot; and when the diocese of Winchester was divided A. D. 705, he was made first bishop of Shireburn. His abbot's robe, his psalter, and his silver altar, were long kept as relics at Malmesbury, and were shown to Leland, when he visited that monastery. He is said to have written many English songs, interspersed with notices of Scripture. One of these was still sung by the people, in the days of Malmesbury; and many of them are probably extant in the vast mass of devotional poetry, which lies unowned, and we may add unread, in our Anglo-Saxon MSS.—GUEST, EDWIN, 1838, *A History of English Rhythms, vol.* II, *p* 400.

He was a great imitator of the ancients; he was a celebrated Greek scholar, and he filled his writings with foreign words and clumsy compounds; he was also a lover and composer of Anglo-Saxon verse, and he shows a deeply rooted taste for alliteration and pompous diction; and in addition to these defects we see in his writings generally a bad choice of words, with harsh sentences, and a great deficiency in true delicacy and harmony. In a word, Aldhelm's writings, popular as they once were, exhibit a very general want of good taste.—WRIGHT, THOMAS, 1842, *Biographia Britannica Literaria, vol.* I, *p.* 45.

The style of his Latin poems, as might be expected from his other compositions, is more characteristic of the Saxon gleeman than of the classic scholar: alternately pompous and homely; occasionally delighting the reader with the beauty of its imagery, often offending him by the utter absence of grace or dignity. His countrymen, however, looked up to him with admiration; nor was his fame confined to the Anglo-Saxons; it quickly spread itself over the neighbouring nations; and foreigners were eager to submit their works to Aldhelm for revision and approbation.—LINGARD, JOHN, 1844, *The History and Antiquities of the Anglo-Saxon Church, vol.* II, *p.* 169.

Aldhelm long enjoyed the highest reputation for learning; but his writings are chiefly remarkable for their elaborately unnatural and fantastic rhetoric. His Latin style bears some resemblance to the pedantic English, full of alliteration and all sorts of barbarous quaintness, that was fashionable among our theological writers in the reigns of Elizabeth and James the First.—CRAIK, GEORGE L., 1861, *A Compendious History of English Literature and of the English Language, vol.* I, *p.* 29.

We can understand how he came to imitate, in his Latin poems, certain peculiarities of the national versification, which, however, are oftentimes superfluous and disturbing elements. It is likewise conceivable that such a nature often bore itself with poor grace in the majestic garb of Latin prose.—TEN BRINK, BERNHARD, 1877-83, *History of English Literature (To Wiclif)*, *p.* 36.

In Aldhelm they had a Latin poet of much feeling and refinement.—SCHERER, WILHELM, 1883–86, *A History of German Literature, tr. Conybeare, vol.* I, *p.* 38.

Aldhelm is the first of the Anglo-Latin poets, and he was a classical scholar at a time when to be so was a great distinction. Both in prose and verse, his style has the faults which belong to an age of revived study. His love of learning, his keen appreciation of its beauty and its value, have tended to inflate his sentences with an appearance of display. His poetic diction is simpler than that of his prose; but here, too, he is habitually over-elevated, whence he becomes sometimes stilted, and oftentimes he drops below pitch with an inadequate and disappointing close. But we must honour him in the position which he holds. He is the leader of that noble series of English scholars who represent the first endeavoring stage of recovery after the great eclipse of European culture.—EARLE, JOHN, 1884, *Anglo-Saxon Literature, p.* 89.

Aldhelm, of whom the great King Alfred speaks admiringly; who not only knew his languages but could sing a song; a sort of early Saxon Sankey who beguiled wanderers into better ways by his homely rhythmic utterance. I think we may safely count this old Aldhelm, who had a strain of royal blood in him, as the first of English ballad-mongers.—MITCHELL, DONALD G., 1889, *English Lands, Letters and Kings, From Celt to Tudor, p.* 10.

Bede

The Venerable

C. 673–735

Born near Monkwearmouth, in Durham, about 673 A. D. He was educated there at the Benedictine Monastery of St. Peter's, and in that of St. Paul's at Jarrow, in which latter he remained until his death. Was diligent in observing the discipline of his order, as well as in the daily services of the church; successfully ordained deacon and priest; employed in reading, writing and teaching; besides Latin and Greek, classical as well as patristic literature, he studied Hebrew, medicine, astronomy, and prosody; he wrote homilies, lives of saints, hymns, epigrams, works on chronology and grammar, and commentaries on the Old and New Testament; died 26th May, 735; buried at Jarrow; in the 11th century his bones were removed to Durham. Principal work *Historia Ecclesiastica Gentis Anglorum;* frequently printed since 1473—as in 1838, 1846, 1869; a standard English edition of Bede's complete works is by Giles (12 vols. 1844).—MOULTON, CHARLES WELLS, 1900.

PERSONAL

Me, Bede, the servant of God, and priest of the monastery of the blessed apostles, Peter and Paul, which is at Wearmouth and Jarrow, who being born in the territory of that same monastery, was given, at seven years of age, to be educated by the most reverend Abbot Benedict, and afterwards by Ceolfrid; and spending all the remaining time of my life in that monastery, I wholly applied myself to the study of Scripture, and amidst the observance of regular discipline, and the daily care of singing in the church, I always took delight in learning, teaching, and writing. In the nineteenth year of my age, I received deacon's orders; in the thirtieth, those of the priesthood, both of them by the ministry of the most reverend Bishop John, and by order of the Abbot Ceolfrid. From which time, till the fifty-ninth year of my age, I have made it my business, for the use of me and mine, to compile out of the works of the venerable Fathers, and to interpret and explain according to their meaning.—BEDE, 731, *Ecclesiastical History, bk. v, ch.* xxiv, (*A. D.* 731), *ed. Giles, p.* 297.

One of the last things he did was the translating of the Gospel of St. John into English. When death seized on him, one of his devout scholars, whom he used for his secretary or amanuensis, complained, "My beloved master, there remains yet one sentence unwritten." "Write it, then, quickly," replied Bede, and, summoning all his spirits together, like the last blaze of a candle going out, he indited it, and expired. . . . Nor have I aught else to observe of Bede, save only this: A foreign ambassador, some two hundred years since, coming to Durham, addressed himself first to the high and sumptuous shrine of St. Cuthbert, "If thou beest a saint, pray for me;" then, coming to the plain, low, and little tomb of Bede, "Because," said he, "thou art a saint, good Bede, pray for me."—FULLER, THOMAS, 1655, *The Church History of Britain, ed. Nichols, bk.* ii, *sec.* iii, *par.* 18.

Never, perhaps, was name more appropriately conferred than was that of the child Bede. In Anglo-Saxon it means "prayer," and was thoroughly indicative of the spirit which guided its possessor.—DOUGHERTY, J. J., 1882, *A True Monk—The Venerable Bede, Catholic World vol.* 34, *p.* 559.

Of the well-known line inscribed to Bede's memory in Durham Cathedral, where his bones lay till, in the days of Henry VIII., their rich shrine was broken, and the bones themselves were scattered by the mob, there is a legend that might well be true if angels took part in the affairs of men. A pupil who had been chosen to write his master's epitaph laboured in vain to complete the hexameter line in which he was to record that "In this grave are the bones of Bede." He fell asleep over his toil at the unfinished line—

"Hac sunt in fossa, Bedæ ossa."

But an angel bent over the sleeping youth, and with a pencil of light supplied the missing word. The student awoke and read, "Hac sunt in fossa, Bedæ Venerabilis ossa." England has ratified the title, and to the end of time his countrymen will look back with affectionate honour to the sinless student-life of Venerable Bede.—MORLEY, HENRY, 1888, *English Writers, vol.* II, *p.* 157.

Such a man would not, of course, be a Chrysostom or an Ambrose, dealing with sinners in corrupt cities. His was rather the oratory which corresponds to that of an Oxford or Cambridge university-preacher, dealing with theological themes for the defence and confirmation of the faith. Forty-seven of his sermons are on the course of the ecclesiastical year, setting forth objective truths in the order of the calendar, in a scholarly and practical way. Twenty-two belong to the Lenten season, and forty-eight were delivered on days commemorating the saintly characters who have been eminent enough to be canonized in the good opinion of succeeding ages. Twenty more of a different character are manifestly intended for country congregations. It was in the darkest period of letters that this man became the embodiment of what learning survived the decay of Roman literature. And if as an orator he cannot be ranked with the great preachers of the fourth century, he certainly kept alive the spark of eloquence until better conditions for it appeared.—SEARS, LORENZO, 1895, *The History of Oratory, p.* 178.

Bede died on May 25, A. D. 735, on Wednesday evening before Ascension Day, "after the first Vespers of our LORD'S Ascension," whence he is said to have died on the Feast of Ascension, because our Saxon ancestors reckoned Festivals from the first Vespers. His remains were first deposited in the south Porch of the Church. Thence they were removed to a more honourable situation within the Church. Elfrid, a priest of Durham, who had been accustomed to offer up his prayers at Bede's tomb annually on the anniversary of his death, stole his remains, and carried them off to Durham. There he secreted them in the coffin of S. Cuthbert. Here they remained, the theft not being discovered, till A. D. 1104, when they were separated from S. Cuthbert's relics; and fifty years later Hugh Pudsey erected a most beautiful shrine of gold and silver, adorned with jewels, in which he enclosed them. This shrine was pillaged and demolished in King Henry VIII. time. A long inscription now alone remains in Durham Cathedral, concluding with the well-known rhyme,

"Hac sunt in fossâ,
Bede venerabilis Ossa."

—ADAMS, D. C. O., 1897, *The Saints and Missionaries of the Anglo-Saxon Era, First Series, p.* 456.

ECCLESIASTICAL HISTORY

The profoundest scholar in his age, for Latin, Greek, philosophy, history, divinity, mathematics, music, and what not? Homilies of his making were read in his lifetime, in the Christian churches; a dignity afforded to him alone. We are much beholding to his "Ecclesiastical History," written by him, and dedicated to Ceolwolfus, king of Northumberland. A worthy work, indeed; though, in some respect, we could heartily wish that his faith had been less, and his charity more. —FULLER, THOMAS, 1655, *The Church History of Britain, ed. Nichols, bk.* ii, *sec.* iii, *par.* 15.

Is his only work which is now read. He candidly cites the authorities, on which his narrative rests, and as these were sometimes oral, they might be fallacious; but no better could be found. The credulity of Bede is seen in the admission of idle tales into a history, which, in other respects, merits the highest praise. For my part, I should lament, had the historian of those times been guided, in the selection of his materials, by a more discriminating scepticism; for we should have wanted a just transcript of the age in which he lived; and might even have doubted the authenticity of the composition. As it is, we see what was at that period the superstitious character of our ancestors; and in the historian we behold a man, endowed with great talents, and possessed of extraordinary erudition, but in those habits of his mind—in which virtue was not concerned—not less weak nor credulous than his contemporaries. . . . The style of Bede is sufficiently perspicuous and flowing, but not always pure, and seldom elegant.—BERINGTON, JOSEPH, 1814, *A Literary History of the Middle Ages, p.* 144.

The author received secondary evidence with caution, for he distinguishes between the statements which he received from eye-witnesses, and those which reached him through a succession of informants. In the last of these instances, the channel of information is always pointed out with scrupulous exactness, whatever opinion we may entertain, as in the case of some visions and miracles, of the credibility of the facts themselves.—STEVENSON, JOSEPH, 1838, *ed. Bedæ Historia Ecclesiastica Gentis Anglorum, etc., Preface.*

The style of Bede, if not elegant Latin, is yet correct, sufficiently classical. It is a written style, such as was learnt in the cloister schools by the help of Donatus and the Rhetorica of Cicero, and matured by reading the Latin fathers, St. Augustine, and St. Ambrose. . . . Bede viewed the world only from the retirement of his cell. He knew events chiefly as they appeared in books. Even the history of his own time is drawn from what was communicated to him. So that, however correct it may be, it wants that truth of delineation which can only be given by one who has been himself an agent in the scenes he describes.—PATTISON, MARK, 1845, *Gregory of Tours, Christian Remembrancer; also Essays, vol.* I, *p.* 13.

Thus was the time of that excellent man employed in doing good to mankind, seldom or never moving beyond the limits of his own monastery, and yet in the dark cloister of it surveying the whole world, and dispensing to it the gifts entrusted to him; it seems not a little surprising, that one who had scarcely moved away from the place of his nativity, should so accurately describe those at a distance; and this quality in his writings, when considered with reference to the age in which he lived, is the more remarkable, as there is but one other recorded in history who possessed it in equal perfection,—the immortal Homer.—GILES, J. A., 1847, *ed. The Venerable Bede's Ecclesiastical History of England, Preface, p.* xv.

Pre-eminently a teacher, not a thinker. . . . He had high powers of arrangement and exposition. . . . His style is nervous and good, with scarcely any admixture of barbarisms; and his patience and love of truth leading him to collect knowledge from all quarters, have made his "Ecclesiastical History" of inestimable value. — PEARSON, CHARLES H., 1867, *History of England During the Early and Middle Ages, vol.* I, *p.* 302.

From the first the "Ecclesiastical History" of Bede has always been regarded as a work of the highest interest. After the lapse of several centuries it was still looked upon as the model of what a history ought to be, and after which other histories ought to be written. It was translated by the great king Alfred into the vernacular English of his own day, and it has been frequently translated since. No one, indeed, can be indifferent to such a remarkable record of the dawn of Christian civilization in this country, written so near the time itself by one of the most vigorous and many-sided intellects that England ever produced.—GAIRDNER, JAMES, 1879, *Early Chroniclers of Europe, England, p.* 28.

He lacks art, but not straightforwardness.—JUSSERAND, J. J., 1895, *A Literary History of the English People, p.* 67.

Of the "Ecclesiastical History," it is difficult to over-estimate the value. Perhaps those alone can fully appreciate its worth whose business it has been to investigate the original sources from which our knowledge of the early Church, and, it may be added, of the mediæval Church in England, is derived. A feeling of utter blank comes over them when Bede's "History" ends, and they are forced to have recourse to less trustworthy sources of information. It is not criticism, but sheer philistinism, to cavil at the simplicity—call it credulity, if you will—with which he records in perfect good faith the countless miracles attributed to his heroes; or at the prejudices which he shows against the British, and to a less extent against the Irish or Celtic, Church; or at the artless way in which he connects natural phenomena, such as comets and eclipses, with coming evil. It is quite easy, by the exercise of a little acumen, to disentangle the historical from the legendary, and to make due allowance for the natural prepossessions of a writer brought up in the school of Benedict Biscop. And when this is done, you have not only a most vivid and fascinating narrator, but a most honest and trustworthy guide.—OVERTON, JOHN HENRY, 1897, *The Church in England, vol.* I, *p.* 101.

GENERAL

This venerable man divided the life-giving bread of the Old and New Testament among the children of Christ, by his lucid commentaries, explaining in his works more than sixty mysterious subjects, and thus gained lasting honour, both in his own and foreign countries.—ORDERICUS VITALIS, 1141, *The Ecclesiastical History of England and Normandy, tr. Forester, vol.* II, *p.* 38.

A man whom it is easier to admire than worthily to extol: who, though born in a remote corner of the world, was able to dazzle the whole earth with the brilliancy of his learning. . . . Here my abilities fail, here my eloquence falls short: ignorant which to praise most, the number of his writings, or the gravity of his style. No doubt he had imbibed a large portion of heavenly wisdom, to be able to compose so many volumes within the limits of so short a life. . . . With this man was buried almost all knowledge of history down to our times, inasmuch as there has been no Englishman either emulous of his pursuits, or a follower of his graces, who could continue the thread of his discourse. — WILLIAM OF MALMESBURY, c. 1142, *Chronicle of the Kings of England, bk.* i, *ch.* iii, *tr. Sharpe, pp.* 54, 57, 60.

An account of his writings is an account of the English learning in that age, taken in its most advantageous view. . . . On the whole, though this father of the English learning seems to have been but a genius of the middle class, neither elevated nor subtile, and one who wrote in a low style, simple, but not elegant, yet, when we reflect upon the time in which he lived, the place in which he spent his whole life, within the walls of a monastery, in so remote and wild a country, it is impossible to refuse him the praise of an incredible industry and a generous thirst of knowledge.—BURKE, EDMUND, 1769?, *An Abridgment of English History, Works, vol.* VII, *pp.* 250, 253.

The style of Bede in all his works is plain and unaffected. Attentive only to his matter, he had little solicitude for the phrase in which he dressed it. But though seldom eloquent, and often homely, it is clear, precise, and useful.—TURNER, SHARON, 1799–1836, *The History of the Anglo-Saxons, vol.* III, *bk.* ix, *ch.* vi.

Shone like a single star, serene in a night of darkness.—SOUTHEY, ROBERT, 1821, *A Vision of Judgment,* ix.

The Venerable Bede, as he was afterwards styled, early in the eighth century, surpasses every other name of our ancient literary annals; and, though little more than a diligent compiler from older writers, may perhaps be reckoned superior to any man whom the world (so low had the East sunk like the West) then possessed.—HALLAM, HENRY, 1837–39, *Introduction to the Literature of Europe, pt.* i, *ch.* i, *par.* 7.

That primeval gossiper.—DISRAELI, ISAAC, 1841, *Cædmon and Milton, Amenities of Literature.*

The reputation of Beda survived and grew after his death. The Saxons were proud that their nation had produced so eminent a writer; the monks of Wearmouth and Jarrow were harassed with solicitations for copies of his works; and, at the distance of a hundred years, the prelates of the Franks, in the council of Aix-la-Chapelle, numbered him among the Fathers of the church, and styled him the venerable and admirable doctor. If the improvements of modern times have diminished the value of his writings, this circumstance ought no more to detract from his merit than it does from that of the philosophers of Greece and Rome. Beda was a great man for the age in which he lived; he would have been so had he lived in any other age.—LINGARD, JOHN, 1844, *The History and Antiquities of the Anglo-Saxon Church, vol.* II., *p.* 183.

Bede was the parent of theology in England. . . . The theology of Bede flowed directly from the fountain of Christian doctrine, the sacred writings. It consists in commentaries on the whole Bible. But his interpretation is that which now prevailed universally in the Church. By this the whole volume is represented as a great allegory. Bede probably did little more than select from the more popular Fathers, what appeared to him the most subtle and ingenious, and therefore most true and edifying exposition. Even the New Testament, the Gospels, and Acts, have their hidden and mysterious, as well as their historical signification. No word but enshrines a religious and typical sense.—MILMAN, HENRY HART, 1854, *History of Latin Christianity, vol.* II, *p.* 92.

Born at the end of the Christian world, and of a race which half a century before his birth was still plunged in the darkness of idolatry, at once reveals himself clothed in the fulness of all enlightenment known to his time. . . . He was for England what Cassiodorus was for Italy and St. Isidore for Spain. But he had, in addition, an influence and echo beyond his own country which has been surpassed by none: his influence upon Christendom was as rapid as it was extensive, and his works, which soon found a place in all the monastic libraries of the West, brought down his fame to the period of the Renaissance. He wrote at his pleasure in prose or verse, in Anglo-Saxon and in Latin; and many of his writings prove that he was acquainted with Greek. The greater part of his works were devoted to theology and its cognate studies. . . . Far from confining himself to theology, he wrote with success upon astronomy and meteorology, physics and music, philosophy and geography, arithmetic and rhetoric, grammar and versification, without omitting medicine, and without disdaining to descend even to orthography and numeration. His treatises have almost always the form of abridgments or catechisms adapted to the education of his monastic disciples. He thus penetrated, with a bold and unwearying step, into all the paths then open to the human intelligence, with a clearness and extent of vision truly surprising for the age and circumstances under which he lived. He thus won the name of Father of English learning, given to him by the greatest of modern Englishmen. — MONTALEMBERT, CHARLES FORBES, 1860–68, *The Monks of the West, vol.* V, *pp.* 58, 59, 60.

The first German who made the universal learning, derived from antiquity, his own, was an Anglo-Saxon, the Venerable Beda.—RANKE, LEOPOLD VON, 1875, *A History of England, vol.* I, *p.* 13.

First among English scholars, first among English theologians, first among English historians, it is in the monk of Jarrow that English literature strikes its roots. In the six hundred scholars who gathered round him for instruction he is the father of our national education. In his physical treatises he is the first figure to which our science looks back.—GREEN, JOHN RICHARD, 1877, *History of the English People, vol.* I, *bk.* i, *ch.* ii.

Bede has been my guide. His records are, indeed, often "rough," as rough as the crab-tree, but, at the same time, as fresh as its blossom. Their brief touches reveal all the passions of the Barbaric races; but the chief human affections, things far deeper than the passions, are yet more abundantly illustrated by them. It was a time when those affections were not frozen by conventionalities and forced to conceal themselves until they forgot to exist.—DE VERE, AUBREY, 1879, *Legends of the Saxon Saints, Preface, p.* xlvii.

The Venerable Bede is one of the most striking figures in the history of the English Church. It would be difficult to find a parallel to him in the history of any Church. A voluminous and learned Christian writer on many subjects, theological, historical, grammatical, and physical, he sprang from an immediate ancestry of unlettered pagans The first preacher of Christianity who visited his fathers arrived in the country only fifty years before Bede's birth. Forty years before his birth, the kings of the land were heathens.—BROWNE, REV. G. F., 1879, *The Venerable Bede, p.* 5.

Cynewulf

C. 8th Century?

Lived probably in the 8th century A. D. A Northumbrian (?) poet. He was a scôp or bard, but there is no evidence that he was a priest. He was the author of "Elene," "Juliana," "Crist," "Riddles," perhaps of "Phœnix," "Guthlac;" and the reputed author of the "Wanderer," etc. Even "Beowolf" has been credited to him.—SMITH, BENJAMIN E., *ed.* 1894–97, *The Century Cyclopedia of Names, p.* 299.

Cynewulf the poet was unknown until the runes were read by which he had worked his name into his poem of "Elene." Those runes were first read in the year 1840 by two independent workers—by Jacob Grimm in his edition of "Andreas" and "Elene," and by John Mitchell Kemble in his essay upon Anglo-Saxon Runes, published that year in the "Archæologia." Each discoverer of the names endeavored also to find who Cynewulf was, and when he lived. Grimm placed him in the eighth century. Kemble placed him in the end of the tenth century and the beginning of the eleventh, by suggesting that he was the Cynewulf who was Abbot of Peterborough between the years 992 and 1006, who succeeded Ælfeage as Bishop of Winchester in the year 1006.—MORLEY, HENRY, 1888, *English Writers, vol.* II, *p.* 206.

The poems of Cynewulf show us the artist with whom Christian ideas have become spontaneous, who is completely filled with the fervour of Christian feeling, and who, at the same time, disposes like a master of the rich legacy of epic diction and perception. His taste is not so cultivated as his faculty of imagination and his power of language. Sometimes his subject-matter is obnoxious to our sense; at other times our ardour is dampened by the ever-crowding outbreaks of the poet's enthusiasm. In the last instance the discord between the old form and the new matter prevents a quite complete enjoyment.—TEN BRINK, BERNHARD, 1877–83, *History of English Literature (To Wiclif), tr. Kennedy, p.* 59.

Perhaps the most genuinely poetical of all the early minstrels after Cædmon. —ALLEN, GRANT, 1881, *Anglo-Saxon Britain, p.* 214.

Here [Elene] more than in any other piece of Anglo-Saxon poetry we feel near the mediæval drama. Almost every canto is like a scene; and little adaptation would be required to put it upon the stage. The narrative at the beginning is like a prologue, and then after the close of the piece we have an epilogue, in which the author speaks about himself, and weaves his name with Runes into the verses.—EARLE, JOHN, 1884, *Anglo-Saxon Literature, p.* 238.

Of England's early poets, Cædmon's name is still the most familiar—perhaps because he was the first, and because his name and history were embalmed in the pages of the Venerable Bede and other writers. But a greater poet than Cædmon was to follow him a century later—and that greater was the poet Cynewulf.—ROBINSON, W. CLARKE, 1885, *Introduction to Our Early English Literature, p.* 59.

Constantine's vision of the cross, after having experienced the terrors of imminent danger, is the type of Helena's vision of the true cross, after braving the dangers of the deep, hostile peoples, and conspiring enemies. From one vision to another we are led without much clogging of dramatic action, save that due to the peculiarities of Old English style, in describing effects of events by corresponding states of mind, in adding predicate after predicate to personalities, etc. On the whole, however, little time is lost, few words wasted, in picturing fully Helena's journeyings, her pleadings, her stratagem, and her success. One cannot help feeling that the climax has been reached with the discovery of the cross. The historical account of Judas sounds like an author's postscript to tell the reader what became of a certain character; while Helena's anxiety about the nails may contribute to the perfection of her saintly character, but in nowise to the unity and harmony of the poem.—KENT, CHARLES W., 1889, *Elene, An Old English Poem, Introduction, p.* 7.

Shelley, who was himself an ancient Nature-worshipper born out of due time, a maker of Nature-myths, and as innocent as a young Aryan in doing so, is on that account very like Cynewulf when both are writing about natural phenomena. Both of them write as the people talked in old time about the Wind, and the Clouds, and the Sea; and in Cynewulf's case this is all the plainer when we compare his work with the riddles on the same subject which Ealdhelm and Eusebius put forth, which use the classical conventions, and which gave to Cynewulf nothing but the theme of his poem. . . . We possess then not only his name, but we can also realise him as a man; and he is not unlike some of our own poets, though so many centuries have passed away. He is, for instance, as personal as Cowper, and in much the same way. No other of the Anglo-Saxon poets has this fashion of talking about himself, and it is so unique, and the manner of it so distinct, that when I find it in a poem which is not signed by him—in the "Dream of the Rood"—it seems to me to be as good as his signature.—BROOKE, STOPFORD A., 1892, *The History of Early English Literature, pp.* 183, 371.

It seems almost certain then that the "Christ" is an Anglian poem, written before Northumbria ceased to be the great centre of poetical activity, *i. e.*, before the beginning of the ninth century, and critics are at one in placing the "floruit" of its poet during the second half of the eighth century.—GOLLANCZ, ISRAEL, 1892, *Cynewulf's Christ, Preface, p.* xxii.

One of the few poets of the Anglo-Saxon period known by name, and the greatest of all.—JUSSERAND, J. J., 1895, *A Literary History of the English People, p.* 2.

A great number of critics are even enthusiastic on behalf of Cynewulf, whom in point of sublimity they are ready to raise to a level with Cædmon. This is an estimate I must venture, with all deference, to question, and I am inclined to think that those who have formed it have been misled by the exuberance in Cynewulf of a poetical diction, which often continues after the genuine springs of inspiration have begun to fail.—COURTHOPE, W. J., 1895, *A History of English Poetry, vol.* I, *p.* 103.

That ancient bard is indeed a problematical character; he has roamed like a restless ghost through centuries far apart, appearing now in the latest, now in the earliest period of the literature. He has been identified as an abbot of the eleventh century, as a bishop of the eighth, and, finally, all ecclesiastical rank has been denied him. To increase our uncertainty, there has been a tendency to attribute to him almost all the floating, anonymous minor poems in the language; besides his Riddles, the Phœnix, and Elene—the Finding of the Cross,—Andreas, Crist,

Juliana, Guthlac, and the Wanderer have been fathered upon him. His case is a notable example of the difficulty that attends any attempt at a reliable interpretation of the development of the literature.—WHITE, GREENOUGH, 1895, *Outline of the Philosophy of English Literature, The Middle Ages, p.* 5.

Alcuin

C. 735–804

Alcuin (originally *Ealhwine*), or Albinus, the adviser of Charlemagne, was born at York in 735, and educated at the cloister-school, of which in 778 he became master. In 781, returning from Rome, he met Charlemagne at Parma, and on his invitation attached himself to the court at Aix-la-Chapelle. Here he devoted himself first to the education of the royal family itself, and through his influence the court became a school of culture for the hitherto almost barbarous Frankish empire. In 796 he settled at Tours as abbot; and the school here became one of the most important in the empire. Till his death here in 804, he still corresponded constantly with Charlemagne. His works comprise poems; works on grammar, rhetoric, and dialectics; theological and ethical treatises; lives of several saints; and over two hundred letters.—PATRICK AND GROOME, *eds.*, 1897, *Chambers's Biographical Dictionary, p.* 19.

But I, your Flaccus, am doing as you have urged and wished. To some who are beneath the roof of St. Martin I am striving to dispense the honey of Holy Scripture; others I am eager to intoxicate with the old wine of ancient learning; others again I am beginning to feed with the apples of grammatical refinement; and there are some whom I long to adorn with the knowledge of astronomy, as a stately house is adorned with a painted roof. I am made all things to all men that I may instruct many to the profit of God's Holy Church and to the lustre of your imperial reign. So shall the grace of Almighty God toward me be not in vain and the largess of your bounty be of no avail.—ALCUIN, 796, *To Charlemagne, Alcuini Epistolæ, Patrologia Latina, ed. Migne, vol. c., p.* 208, *tr. C. W. Colby, Sources of English History, p.* 17.

There was in England a remarkable teacher named Albinus (Alcuin), and he had great reputation. He taught many of the English in the sciences contained in books, as he well knew how, and afterwards went across the sea to the wise King Charles, who had great wisdom in divine and worldly matters, and lived wisely. Albinus the noble teacher came to him, and, there a foreigner, he dwelt under his rule, in St. Martin's monastery, and imparted to many the heavenly wisdom which the Saviour gave him.—ALFRIC, C 998, *Passiones Sanctorum, Introduction.*

Alcuin was, of all the Angles, of whom I have read, next to St. Aldhelm and Bede, certainly the most learned, and has given proof of his talents in a variety of compositions. He lies buried in France, at the church of St. Paul, of Cormaric, which monastery Charles the Great built at his suggestion: on which account, even at the present day, the subsistence of four monks is distributed in alms, for the soul of our Alcuin, in that church.—WILLIAM OF MALMESBURY, C 1142, *Chronicle of the Kings of England, bk.* i, *ch.* iii, *tr. Sharpe, p.* 63.

It being questionable, whether he were more famous for Venerable Bede, who was his master, or Charles the Great, who was his scholar; whilst it is out of doubt, that he is most honoured for his own learning and religion.—FULLER, THOMAS, 1655, *The Church History of Britain, ed. Nichols, bk.* ii, *sec.* iii, *par.* 40.

He is a theologian by profession, the atmosphere in which he lived, in which the public to whom he addresses himself lived, is essentially theological; and yet the theological spirit does not reign alone in him, his works and his thoughts also tend towards philosophy and ancient literature; it is that which he also delights in studying, teaching, and which he wished to revive. Saint Jerome and Saint Augustin are very familiar to him; but Pythagoras, Aristotle, Aristippus, Diogenes, Plato, Homer, Virgil, Seneca, Pliny, also occur to his memory. The greater part of his writings are theological; but mathematics, astronomy, logic, rhetoric, habitually occupy him. He is a monk, a deacon, the light of the contemporaneous church; but he is at the same time a scholar, a classical man of letters. In him, at length, commenced the alliance of these two elements of which the modern mind had so long borne the incoherent impress, antiquity and the church—the admiration, the taste, the regret, shall I call it, for pagan literature, and the sincerity of Christian faith, the zeal to sound its mysteries, and to defend its power.—GUIZOT, FRANCOIS PIERRE GUILLAUME, 1828–30, *History of Civilization, tr. Hazlitt, Lecture* xxii.

A man fully equal to Bede in ability, though not in erudition.—HALLAM, HENRY, 1837–39, *Introduction to the Literature of Europe, pt.* i, *ch.* i, *par.* 7.

Alcuin has, on the whole, more simplicity and less pretension in his poetry than his predecessor Aldhelm, and so far he is more pleasing; but, unfortunately, where the latter was turgid and bombastic, the former too often runs into the opposite extreme of being flat and spiritless. His style is seen to best advantage in his calm details of natural scenery.—WRIGHT, THOMAS, 1842, *Biographia Britannica Literaria, vol.* I, *p.* 46.

Alcuin's instructions were given rather in the form of conversation than of lectures. He taught the seven sciences which were distinguished as liberal, and were afterwards classified under the titles of *Trivium* and *Quadrivium*—the Trivium consisting of grammar, rhetoric, and dialectics; the Quadrivium comprising arithmetic, music, geometry, and astronomy; while above these two classes theology held a place by itself. Alcuin's writings on these subjects contain little of an original kind, and may be regarded as mere notebooks of his teaching. His other works are very various—commentaries on Scripture, liturgical treatises, tracts on the controversies of the age and on practical religion, poems, lives of saints, and a large collection of letters. They appear to be justly described as displaying more of labour than of genius, more of memory than of invention or taste; but in estimating the merit of the man we are bound to compare him with his contemporaries. His work was that of a reviver.—ROBERTSON, JAMES CRAIGIE, 1858-75, *History of the Christian Church, vol.* III, *bk.* iv, *ch.* vi, *p.* 118.

The brightest ornament of the court of Charlemagne, and the soundest thinker between John of Damascus and Anselm.—SHEDD, WILLIAM G. T., 1863, *A History of Christian Doctrine, vol.* I, *p.* 177.

Alcuin's "Letters" are of great importance from the illustration they afford of the relations between England and Frankland in the eighth and ninth centuries. His poetical history of the bishops and archbishops of York is also of considerable value as a record of events in connexion with the chief centre of English learning at this period.—MULLINGER, J. BASS, 1881, *English History for Students, Authorities, p.* 248.

His work was the highest that could have been committed to human hand. It was the civilization of a kingdom; it was to aid in the renaissance of learning for Christendom; and his was the noble achievement of connecting the intellect of Britain with that of Western Europe.—TOWNSEND, W. J., 1881, *The Great Schoolmen of the Middle Ages, p.* 26.

The first theologian, philosopher, and teacher of his age.—SCHERER, WILHELM, 1883-86, *A History of German Literature, tr. Conybeare, vol.* I, *p.* 47.

As a man he was remarkable for his singular modesty, piety, and good sense; as a scholar his learning was extensive and profound; but as a writer his style is often commonplace and redundant.—MURRAY, JOHN O'KANE, 1884, *Lessons in English Literature, p.* 42.

His relations to Charles were intimate, cordial, and confidential. One can hardly err in ascribing to him almost all the theological documents and writings interblended with the political growth and development of the Frankish empire in that reign; the theology of Charles; the theology, and probably much of the jurisprudence of the Capitularies; to his influence must be traced some of the enlightened views of Charles; the mercy, the lofty aims, and the ethical apothegms, so remarkable in the life and speech of that remarkable monarch.—MOMBERT, J. I., 1888, *A History of Charles the Great, p.* 242.

It belongs to the glory of England to say that it was an English scholar of York who exactly at the right time bore off to the Continent the whole of English learning, and out of English learning built up a new world. Had Alcuin remained in England, had learning been confined to our shores, it would have perished in a few years under the destroying flood of the Danish invasions.—BROOKE, STOPFORD A., 1892, *The History of Early English Literature, p.* 451.

In every way that lay in his power, Alcuin endeavored to put the fortunes of learning for the times that should succeed him in a position of advantage, safeguarded by an abundance of truthfully transcribed books, interpreted by teachers of his own training, sheltered within the Church and defended by the civil power.—WEST, ANDREW FLEMMING, 1893, *Alcuin and the Rise of the Christian Schools.*

Certain it is, however, that he did not forsake the study of the profane authors, until they had thoroughly permeated his style. Although an ecclesiastic he wrote Latin, both prose and verse, of which no Roman in the first century need have been ashamed. To pass from the continual barbarisms, obscurities, puerilities of Gregory of Tours, of Fredegarius, or even of the authors of the *Liber Pontificalis,* to the easily flowing prose, or hexameter verse of Alcuin is like going from the ill-spelt productions of a half-educated ploughman to the letters of Cowper or the poetry of Goldsmith.—HODGKIN, THOMAS, 1897, *Charles the Great, p.* 189.

John Scotus Erigena

Fl. 850

Born probably in Ireland between 800 and 815; died probably about 891. A noted scholar of the Carlovingian period. He came to the court of Charles the Bald before 847, and became director of the palatial school, during the incumbency of which office his chief literary work was done. He is said by William of Malmesbury and others to have been invited to England by Alfred the Great (about 883?), to have been appointed teacher at the school of Oxford and abbot of Malmesbury, and to have been killed by his own pupils. His chief work was the translation of Dionysius Areopagita, and the consequent introduction of Neoplatonism into Western Europe. The most notable of his original productions is "De Divisione Naturæ" (edited by Gale 1681, Schlüter 1838, and Floss 1853).—SMITH, BENJAMIN E., *ed.* 1894-97, *The Century Cyclopedia of Names, p.* 366.

A man of clear understanding and amazing eloquence. He had long since, from the continued tumult of war around him, retired into France to Charles the Bald, at whose request he translated the "Hierarchia" of Dionysius the Areopagite, word for word, out of the Greek into Latin. He composed a book also, which he entitled "περὶ φύσεων μερισμοῦ" or "Of the Division of Nature" extremely useful in solving the perplexity of certain indispensable inquiries, if he be pardoned for some things in which he deviated from the opinions of the Latins, through too close attention to the Greeks. In after time, allured by the munificence of Alfred, he came into England, and at our monastery, as report says, was pierced with iron styles of the boys whom he was instructing, and was even looked upon as a martyr.—WILLIAM OF MALMESBURY, c 1142, *Chronicle of the Kings of England, bk.* ii, *ch.* iv, *tr. Sharpe.*

Erigena was the forerunner of the Pantheism of the Middle Ages, and of the heresy of Berengarius on the Eucharist; and his writings indirectly led the way to false theories on the relation of faith to science, on the nature of evil, and on predestination. From what has been said, it will scarcely be a matter of surprise that his works were in subsequent years frequently condemned. But, in justice to Erigena, it must be said that his writings possess a certain elevation and grandeur, a freshness and originality, and a brilliancy that dazzle and please. He was an elegant Greek scholar; was perfectly familiar with the writings and systems of Greek philosophers, and with the works of the Fathers of the Church, both Greek and Latin; combined skill in method with a luminous exposition; and was frequently so full of his subject that he resorted to the form of soliloquy to give it adequate expression. He was also the forerunner of the mysticism of the Schoolmen, or the *union* of contemplative piety with scientific theology, and led off in the controversy on Universals.—ALZOG, JOHN, 1840-78, *Manual of Universal Church History, tr. Pabisch and Byrne, vol.* II, *sec.* 203, *p.* 302.

He was a strange mysterious man, of profound thought, and as much raised above the doctors of his age by the boldness of his ideas, as Charlemagne above the princes of his day by the force of his will.—D'AUBIGNE, J. H. MERLE, 1853, *History of the Reformation of the Sixteenth Century, tr. White, vol.* V, *bk.* xvii, *ch.* iv, *p.* 76.

In the ninth century Scotus Erigena, tne most acute mind of his time, in his speculations upon the mutual relations of the world and God, unfolded a system that is indisputably pantheistic.—SHEDD, WILLIAM G. T., 1863, *A History of Christian Doctrine, vol.* I, *p.* 226.

Erigena is undoubtedly the most prominent and interesting literary character of the early Middle Age. He was a man of unremitting industry; he amassed such large stores of information as made him the wonder of his contemporaries; and he had great acuteness of mind. He was the greatest intellectual force of the ninth century; but though he had a bold and adventurous mind, he did not manifest thorough originality in his thinking. He seems to have had a special aptitude for gathering knowledge from many sources, and then constructing systems and theories; but in many places the logical consistency of his theories is marred by his desire to remain within the limits of Church teaching, and by the occasional ascendency of the spiritual over the metaphysical in his nature. He rendered immense service to the cause of learning in his own and the following centuries; and especially he conferred a great blessing on the world in becoming the leader of a line of brilliant and powerful thinkers, who fought out to a successful issue the right of man's judgment and reason to pronounce upon matters of opinion and doctrine, in opposition to the absolute supremacy over reason and conscience claimed by the Church. Erigena was thus a Protestant born out of due time, and the forerunner of those who battled against spiritual assumption until the Reformation. He anticipated many of the metaphysical questions which have since agitated Europe, and which are being discussed now as earnestly as ever. His theories were framed and published when the world was not prepared to properly estimate or appreciate them, and therefore the heretical character of his philosophy was not fully recognized for some ages.—TOWNSEND, W. J., 1881, *The Great Schoolmen of the Middle Ages, p.* 56.

If he deserves the name given to him sometimes as the father of Western scholastic philosophy, he earns it, not for his dogmatism, but by the honour due to him of being the first who taught distinctively and effectively the certain truth that between true religion and a true philosophy there is and can be no antagonism, but that they are one and inseparable.—MORLEY, HENRY, 1888, *English Writers, vol.* II, *p.* 258.

His learning rises far beyond the scientific level of the Carlovingian epoch. Besides Latin, he knew Greek and perhaps also Arabic. In addition to his knowledge of the Greek Fathers and Neo-Platonism, he possessed wonderful powers of speculation and boldness of judgment. He stands out like a high volcano on a perfectly level plane.—WEBER, ALFRED, 1892–96, *History of Philosophy, tr. Thilly, p.* 204.

The system of Scotus was unique in its character. It is an episode in the theological records of his time, where his very existence almost seems an anachronism. . . . In the character of his mind, as well as the drift of his system, Scotus anticipates modern thinkers whose creed is an ideal Pantheism.—FISHER, GEORGE PARK, 1896, *History of Christian Doctrine, p.* 204.

In some respects he may be accounted the herald of the movement of the eleventh century, but in more he is the last prophet of a philosophy belonging to earlier ages. When, in the first years of the thirteenth century, his books "de Divisione Naturæ" won a passing popularity through the teaching of Amalric of Bène, their pantheistic tendency was at once detected, and the work suppressed by Honorius III in 1225. . . . It was not John's original writings, but his translations which exercised a notable influence on mediæval theology.—POOLE, R. L., 1897, *Dictionary of National Biography, vol.* LI, *p.* 119.

Alfred the Great

849-901

Alfred (al'fred), or Ælfred (alf'rād), surnamed "The Great." Born at Wantage, Berkshire, 849: died Oct. 28, 901. King of the West Saxons 871-901, fifth and youngest son of Æthelwulf, king of the West Saxons, and his wife Osburh (daughter of Oslac his cup-bearer), and brother of Æthelred whom he succeeded. He fought against the Danes in the defensive campaign of 871, serving under his brother Æthelred at Ashdown, Basing, and Merton, and commanded as king at Wilton. In 878 he receded before the Danes to Athelney, but later obtained a decisive victory over them at Ethandun. By the treaty of Wedmore, which followed, Guthrum consented to receive baptism and to retire north of Watling Street. Alfred fortified London in 886, and carried on a defensive war with the Danes 894-897, which ended in the withdrawal of the invaders, and in which, by the aid of ships of improved model, the English for the first time gained a decided naval advantage over the vikings. . . . His administration was also marked by judicial and educational reforms. He compiled a code of laws, rebuilt the schools and monasteries, and invited scholars to his court. He was himself a man of learning, and translated into Saxon the "Ecclesiastical History" of the Venerable Bede, the "Epitome of Universal History" of Paulus Orosius, and the "Consolations of Philosophy" by Boethius, and corrected a translation of the "Dialogues" of Gregory the Great.—SMITH, BENJAMIN E., *ed.* 1894-97, *The Century Cyclopedia of Names, p.* 38.

PERSONAL

He was loved by his father and mother, and even by all the people, above all his brothers, and was educated altogether at the court of the king. As he advanced through the years of infancy and youth, his form appeared more comely than that of his brothers; in look, in speech, and in manners he was more graceful than they. His noble nature implanted in him from his cradle a love of wisdom above all things; but, with shame be it spoken, by the unworthy neglect of his parents and nurses, he remained illiterate even till he was twelve years old or more; but he listened with serious attention to the Saxon poems which he often heard recited, and easily retained them in his docile memory. He was a zealous practiser of hunting in all its branches, and hunted with great assiduity and success. . . . Now the king was pierced with many nails of tribulation, though placed in the royal seat; for from the twentieth year of his age to the present year, which is his fortieth, he has been constantly afflicted with most severe attacks of an unknown complaint, so that he has not a moment's ease either from suffering the pain which it causes, or from the gloom which is thrown over him by the apprehension of its coming. . . . Besides the disease above mentioned, he was disturbed by the quarrels of his friends, who would voluntarily endure little or no toil, though it was for the common necessity of the kingdom; but he alone, sustained by the divine aid, like a skilful pilot, strove to steer his ship, laden with much wealth, into the safe and much desired harbour of his country, though almost all his crew were tired, and suffered them not to faint or hesitate, though sailing amid the manifold waves and eddies of this present life.—ASSER, 888, *Annals of the Reign of Alfred the Great, ed. Giles, pp.* 51, 77.

Lastly, in the same year [A. D. 900], king Alfred departed out of this world, that immoveable pillar of the Western Saxons, that man full of justice, bold in arms, learned in speech, and, above all other things, imbued with the divine instructions. For he had translated into his own language, out of Latin, unnumbered volumes, of so varied a nature, and so excellently, that the sorrowful book of Boethius seemed, not only to the learned, but even to those who heard it read, as it were, brought to life again. The monarch died on the seventh day before the solemnity of All Saints, and his body rests in peace in the city of Winton. Pray, O reader, to Christ our Redeemer, that he will save his soul!—ETHELWERD, FABIUS, c1090, *Chronicle, ed. Giles, p.* 37.

That renowned, warlike, and victorious king was the zealous guardian of the widows and fatherless, orphans, and the poor. He was a perfect master of Saxon

ALFRED THE GREAT

From Engraving by Hinchliff, from a Picture in the Bodleian Library.

poetry, fondly loved by his own subjects, most affable and generous to all the world, endowed with prudence, fortitude, justice, and temperance, he was a model of patience under his inveterate disease, acute and impartial in the administration of justice, and vigilant and devout in the service of God.—FLORENCE OF WORCESTER, c1118, *Chronicle, tr. Forester,* (*A. D.* 901), *p.* 85.

In the year of our Lord's incarnation 849, arose light out of darkness: Elfred, king of the English, was born in the royal vill, which is called Wanatinge by the English.—SIMEON OF DURHAM, 1129, *Annals.*

Innate nobility hath given thee honour,
Brave Alfred; and thy honour hath brought toil,
Thy toil hath given thee lasting reputation.
Joy mixed with grief was thine, hope blent with fear,
When victor, thou did'st fear to flight o' the morrow;
Beaten, wast ready for tomorrow's fight,
Thy robes dropp'd sweat, thy sword dropp'd blood, and shewed,
How heavy task it was to be a king.
Through all earth's climes none but thyself e'er lived,
With power to breathe 'neath such calamities.
Defeat ne'er struck the sword from his hand's grasp,
Nor could the sword cut short his thread of life.
But now his toils of life and rule are done,
And may Christ give him rest and rule for ever.

—HENRY OF HUNTINGDON, 1154, *History of England.*

Alfrede, the fourth Son to King Athelwolph, was born at Wantage, a Market-town in this* County; an excellent Scholar, though he was past *twelve years of age* before he knew *one letter in the Book.* And did not he *run fast,* who *starting* so *late* came *soon to the mark?* He was a curious Poet, excellent Musician, a valiant and successful Souldier, who fought seven Battles against the Danes in one year, and at last made them his subjects by conquest, and God's servants by Christianity. He gave the first Institution, or (as others will have it) the best Instauration, to the University of Oxford. A Prince who cannot be painted to the life without his losse, no *words* reaching his *worth.* . . . He left Learning, where he found Ignorance; Justice, where he found Oppression; Peace, where he found Distraction. And, having reigned about four and thirty years, he dyed, and was buryed at Winchester, anno 901. He loved Religion more than Superstition, favoured *learned men* more than *lasie Monks,* which (perchance) was the cause that his *memory* is not loaden with *Miracles,* and *he* not solemnly *Sainted* with other Saxon Kings who far less deserved it.—FULLER, THOMAS, 1662, *The Worthies of England, ed. Nichols, vol.* I, *p.* 94.

The merit of this prince, both in private and public life, may with advantage be set in opposition to that of any monarch or citizen which the annals of any age or any nation can present to us. He seems indeed to be the model of that perfect character, which, under the denomination of a sage or wise man, philosophers have been fond of delineating, rather as a fiction of their imagination, than in hopes of ever seeing it really existing: so happily were all his virtues tempered together; so justly were they blended; and so powerfully did each prevent the other from exceeding its proper boundaries. . . . Nature also, as if desirous that so bright a production of her skill should be set in the fairest light, had bestowed on him every bodily accomplishment, vigour of limbs, dignity of shape and air, with a pleasing, engaging, and open countenance. Fortune alone, by throwing him into that barbarous age, deprived him of historians worthy to transmit his fame to posterity; and we wish to see him delineated in more lively colours, and with more particular strokes, that we may at least perceive some of those small specks and blemishes, from which, as a man, it is impossible he could be entirely exempted.—HUME DAVID, 1762, *The History of England, vol.* I, *p.* 744.

But as the greatest minds display themselves in the most turbulent storms, on the call of necessity; so England has to boast among others her Alfred; a pattern for kings in a time of extremity, a bright star in the history of mankind. . . . Living a century after Charlemagne he was perhaps a greater man, in a circle happily more limited.—HERDER, JOHN GODFREY, 1784-91, *Philosophy of the History of Mankind, tr. Churchill, bk.* xviii, *ch.* iv.

If this is a character to make emulation despair, it is a character also to make

*Bark-shire.

despair itself patient, and to convert it into an invincible spirit.—HUNT, LEIGH, 1814-15, *The Feast of the Poets, notes, p.* 43.

One of the most august characters that any age has ever produced; and when I picture him after the toils of government and the dangers of battle, seated by a solitary lamp, translating the holy scriptures into the Saxon tongue,—when I reflect on his moderation in success, on his fortitude and perseverance in difficulty and defeat, and on the wisdom and extensive nature of his legislation, I am really at a loss which part of this great man's character most to admire. Yet above all, I see the grandeur, the freedom, the mildness, the domestic unity, the universal character of the middle ages, condensed into Alfred's glorious institution of the trial by jury.—COLERIDGE, SAMUEL TAYLOR, 1818, *The Middle Ages; Miscellanies, Æsthetic and Literary, p.* 94.

Lord of the harp and liberating spear;
Mirror of princes! Indigent Renown
Might range the starry ether for a crown
Equal to *his* deserts.

—WORDSWORTH, WILLIAM, 1821-22, *Ecclesiastical Sonnets, pt.* I, XXVI.

Greater and better earned glory has never been attached to the memory of any chieftain than that which encircles the name of Ælfred. What a phenomenon, when compared with the bigoted, dastardly and lawless kings, under whom the independence, prosperity and civilization of the Anglo-Saxons were destroyed! Even when we compare him with all those great princes, who in external circumstances and by the magnitude of their deeds may be likened to him—with the energetic and sagacious Ecgberht, with the lord of half and the wonder of the whole contemporary and after-world—the Frankish Charles,—with the Czar Peter, or the Great Frederick, yet to none of these wonderful men can we yield precedence over the great West Saxon king, whose lifecourse at once reminds us of all those great rulers, without being sullied by pernicious ambition and lust of conquest.—LAPPENBERG, JOHANN MARTIN, 1834-37, *A History of England under the Anglo-Saxon Kings, tr. Thorpe, vol.* II, *p.* 83.

Truth-teller was our England's Alfred named.—TENNYSON, ALFRED, 1852, *Ode on the Death of the Duke of Wellington.*

He was a German, and the influence of his descent was far stronger than that which ancient Rome exercised over him. Those powerful German songs which the boy had received as a lasting gift from his beloved mother, often rang in his ears during the vicissitudes of his chequered career. The youth passionately following the chase, rejoiced in the gigantic images of his traditionary ancestors, of whom poets sung in all lands from the Danube to the Rhine, from the Apennines to his own island; the king, in the most troubled hours of his sovereignty, strengthened and confirmed his anxious heart by the examples of patient endurance which this poetry revealed to him; and the father caused his own and his people's children to learn betimes those poetical treasures with which he constantly consoled himself.—PAULI, GEORG REINHOLD, 1851-53, *Life of Alfred the Great, p.* 166.

Under the great Alfred, all the best points of the English-Saxon character were first encouraged, and in him first shown. It has been the greatest character among the nations of the earth.—DICKENS, CHARLES, 1854, *A Child's History of England, ch.* iii.

It is no easy task for any one who has been studying his life and works to set reasonable bounds to their reverence, and enthusiasm, for the man.—HUGHES, THOMAS, 1869, *Alfred the Great, ch.* xxiv.

No other king ever showed forth so well in his own person the truth of the saying, "He that would be first among you, let him be the servant of all."—GARDINER, SAMUEL RAWSON, 1890, *A Student's History of England, p.* 62.

Alfred's name is almost the only one in the long roll of our national worthies which awakens no bitter, no jealous thought, which combines the honour of all; Alfred represents at once the ancient monarchy, the army, the navy, the law, the literature, the poetry, the art, the enterprise, the industry, the religion of our race. Neither Welshman, nor Scot, nor Irishman can feel that Alfred's memory has left the trace of a wound for his national pride. No difference of Church arises to separate any who would join to do Alfred honour. No saint in the Calendar was a more loyal and cherished member of the ancient faith; and yet no Protestant can imagine a purer and more simple follower of the Gospel. Alfred was a victorious warrior whose victories have left no curses behind them: a king whom no man ever charged with a harsh act: a scholar who never became a pedant: a saint who knew no superstition: a hero as bold as Launcelot—as spotless as Galahad.—HARRISON, FREDERIC, 1899, *Alfred the Great, ed. Bowker, p.* 65.

One who may rightly be regarded as one of the principal founders of the English nation and its language, a pioneer of improvement, liberty, learning and education, and who, though a thousand years have sped, still forms a mighty beacon of all the highest aims and the noblest aspirations that may dominate the hearts of men.—BOWKER, ALFRED, 1899, *Alfred the Great, Preface, p.* xii.

Some lights there be within the Heavenly Spheres
Yet unrevealed, the interspace so vast:
So through the distance of a thousand years
Alfred's full radiance shines on us at last.

. . . .

Of valour, virtue, letters, learning, law,
Pattern and prince, His name will now abide,
Long as of conscience Rulers live in awe,
And love of country is their only pride.

—AUSTIN, ALFRED, 1899, *Alfred the Great, ed. Bowker, p.* vii.

GENERAL

Alfred, king was translator (of) this book* and he (it) from book-latin into English turned as it now is done. Whiles he set word by word, whiles sense for sense just as he it the clearest and fullest of sense speak might for the distracting and manifold world business (which) him oft both in mind (and) in body busied. The businesses to us are very hard to count which in his days on those kingdoms came that he undertaken had, and yet when he this book had learned and from Latin into English speech turned (it) then wrought he it afterwards to (a) lay so as it now done is, and now prays and for God's name implores each (of) them that this book to read lists, that he for him pray and him not blame if he it rightlier understand than he might; for that each man should by his understanding measure and by his leisure speak that he speaketh, and do that he doeth.—ALFRED, KING, ? c 897, *De Consolatione Philosophiae, Preface.*

*"Consolation of Philosophy."

He himself was, probably, the most learned person of his kingdom, and he stands at the head of the list of royal authors.—CAMPBELL, JOHN, 1742-44, *Naval History of Great Britain, vol.* I.

Alfred's versification shows poorly indeed beside that of Cædmon. He seems to have had little more command over his rhythm, than some of our modern poets. The sectional pause (always a dangerous thing to meddle with) is often used by him, and seldom happily; and the management of his accents is such, as very rarely to assist his meaning. But Alfred was something greater than a poet. Who can read these lines without emotion, when he remembers that the writer—while discharging his kingly duties as no other man discharged them—was daily sinking under a painful disease, that ended only with his life?—GUEST, EDWIN, 1838, *A History of English Rhythms, vol.* II, *p.* 60.

To praise such a wonderful man is to gild the rainbow or to paint the lily!—to criticise his writings for any other purpose than to admire, would be unjust towards their author, who had no model to copy, no rules to follow, and who was forced, in the intellectual sterility of his age, not to imitate what had gone before, but to carve out models for those who should come after him. Viewed in this light, the works of King Alfred give us a magnificent idea of his superiority over the rest of the world: for he was the inventor, if we may use the expression, of a vernacular literature. His writings are not stored up in the obscurities of monkish Latin, of which it is hard to say whether the trouble of reading it or of writing it is the greater; but they were written in plain English, which the ploughboy, as he whistled his way to the furrow in the neighbourhood of Wantage, might have read with ease, and with profit. And what adds to the merit of these works is the ascertained fact, that the king of England was working alone at that time in pioneering and opening the road to a national literature. All besides himself were grinding in the heavy mill of the Fathers and the Schoolmen, putting forth to the world masses of literary rubbish, which, without doing one atom of good to mankind, swelled the libraries of the monasteries, entailing a load of mental tribulation on posterity for centuries to come.—GILES, J. A., 1852, *ed. Works of King Alfred, Jubilee ed., Preface, vol.* I, *p.* xi.

Although King Alfred professed to translate the work of Boethius, yet he inserted in various parts many of his own thoughts and feelings, and thus composed several moral essays, in which he has, in a manner, transmitted himself to posterity. The imperfection of King Alfred's early education will account for a few mistakes in names and historical facts. These, however, by no means lessen the value of the translation; and instead of wondering at their occurrence, one should rather feel surprised that they are not more numerous and more important, considering the disadvantages under which he laboured.—FOX, SAMUEL, 1864, *ed. Boethius by King Alfred, Preface, p.* v.

It is perhaps, after all, in his literary aspect that the distinctive beauty of Ælfred's character shines forth most clearly. The mere patronage of learning was common to him with many princes of his age. Both Charles the Great and several of his successors had set brilliant examples in this way. What distinguished Ælfred was his own personal appearance as an author. Now, as a rule, literary Kings have not been a class deserving of much honour. They have commonly stepped out of their natural sphere only to display the least honourable characteristics of another calling. But it was not so with the Emperor Marcus; it was not so with our Ælfred. In Ælfred there is no sign of literary pedantry, ostentation, or jealousy; nothing is done for his own glory; he writes, just as he fights and legislates, with a single eye to the good of his people. He shows no signs of original genius; he is simply an editor and translator, working honestly for the improvement of the subjects whom he loved. This is really a purer fame, and one more in harmony with the other features of Ælfred's character, than the highest achievements of the poet, the historian, or the philosopher.—FREEMAN, EDWARD A., 1867-69, *The History of the Norman Conquest of England, vol.* I, *p.* 51.

This very translation ["Boethius"] bears witness to the barbarism of his audience. He adapts the text in order to bring it down to their intelligence; the pretty verses of Boethius, somewhat pretentious, laboured, elegant, crowded with classical allusions of a refined and polished style worthy of Seneca, become an artless, long drawn out and yet abrupt prose, like a nurse's fairy tale, explaining everything, recommencing and breaking off its phrases, making ten turns about a single detail; so low was it necessary to stoop to the level of this new intelligence, which had never thought or known anything.—TAINE, H. A., 1871, *History of English Literature, tr. Van Laun, vol.* I, *p.* 50.

The Anglo-Saxon translations ascribed to Alfred are among the best specimens of Anglo-Saxon prose.—CORSON, HIRAM, 1871, *Hand-Book of Anglo-Saxon and Early English, p.* 510.

How many years had passed since the hour when an illuminated initial letter gave him his first taste for a book, before he could master even the elementary branches of knowledge! then he devoted his whole efforts to instil new life into the studies that had almost perished, and to give them a national character. He not merely translated a number of the later authors of antiquity, whose works had contributed most to the transmission of scientific culture; in the episodes which he interweaves in them he shows a desire for knowledge that reaches far beyond them; but especially we find in them a reflective and thoughtful mind, solid sense at peace with itself, a fresh way of viewing the world, a lively power of observation. This King introduced the German mind with its learning and reflection into the literature of the world; he stands at the head of the prose-writers and historians in a German tongue—the people's King of the most primeval kind, who is also the teacher of his people. We know his laws, in which extracts from the books of Moses are combined with restored legal usages of German origin; in him the traditions of antiquity are interpenetrated by the original tendencies of the German mind. We completely weaken the impression made on us by this great figure, so important in his first limited and arduous efforts, by comparing him with the brilliant names of antiquity. —RANKE, LEOPOLD VON, 1875, *A History of England, vol.* I, *p.* 19.

Wide however and various as was the King's temper, its range was less wonderful than its harmony. Of the narrowness, of the want of proportion, of the predominance of one quality over another which goes commonly with an intensity of moral purpose Ælfred showed not a trace. Scholar and soldier, artist and man of business, poet and saint, his character kept that perfect balance which charms us in no other Englishman save Shakspere. But full and harmonious as his temper was, it was the temper of a king. Every power was bent to the work of rule.—GREEN, JOHN RICHARD, 1877, *History of the English People, vol.* I, *bk.* i, *ch.* iii.

The preparation of a separate edition of Ælfred's Legal Code is due to the conviction that the nature of this work rendered desirable its consideration from a literary point of view. Philologically also its existence in one very old manuscript gives it among Anglo-Saxon Law-Books a peculiar value. But its chief claim to special consideration rests upon its author's great significance in Anglo-Saxon Literature. King Ælfred's literary tastes and occupations strongly colour this work; indeed in the Introduction the lawgiver is plainly supplanted by the man of letters, who, even in the actual laws, often presses close to the view.—TURK, MILTON HAIGHT, 1889, *The Legal Code of Ælfred the Great, Preface, p.* v.

Ælfred, whom men have called the "Great" and the "Truthteller;" whom the England of the Middle Ages named "England's Darling;" he who was the Warrior and the Hunter, the Deliverer and the Law-maker, the Singer and the Lover of his people,—"Lord of the harp and liberating spear"—was, above all, for the purposes of this book, the creator and then the father of English prose literature. The learning which had been lost in the North he regained for the South, and York, where the centre of literature had been, was now replaced by Winchester. There, Ælfred in his king's chamber, and filled with longing to educate his people, wrote and translated hour by hour into the English tongue the books he thought useful for that purpose. They are the origins of English prose.—BROOKE, STOPFORD A., 1898, *English Literature from the Beginning to the Norman Conquest, p.* 212.

The last, not the least, of his achievements is that to Alfred we owe the foundations of our literature: the most noble literature that the world has ever seen. He collected and preserved the poetry based on the traditions and legends brought from the German Forests. He himself delighted to hear and to repeat these legends and traditions: the deeds of the mighty warriors who fought with monsters, dragons, wild boars, and huge serpents. He made his children learn their songs: he had them sung in his Court. The tradition goes that he could himself sing them to the music of his own harp. This wild and spontaneous poetry which Alfred preserved is the beginning of our own noble choir of poets. In other words, the foundation of that stately Palace of Literature, built up by our poets and writers for the admiration and instruction and consolation of mankind, was laid by Alfred. Well, but he did more than collect the poetry, he began the prose. Before Alfred there was no Anglo-Saxon prose.—BESANT, WALTER, 1899, *Alfred the Great, ed. Bowker, Introduction, p.* 29.

Asser

-910?

Asser, a monk of Celtic extraction, belonging to the monastery of St. David's, who became bishop of Sherborne and died in the year 910, was the adviser and coadjutor of king Alfred in the latter's efforts to revive learning throughout the country. He is generaly believed to have been the author of an extant "Life" of Alfred, consisting of two parts: (1) a chronicle of events extending from 851 to 887; (2) personal events respecting Alfred himself, designed as a kind of Appendix.—MULLINGER, J. BASS, 1881, *English History for Students, Authorities, p.* 245.

It appears, in the first place, strange that the life of Alfred should have been written in his life time, when he was in the vigour of his age (in his forty-fifth year), and particularly by a man in the position of Asser. It is not easy to conceive for what purpose it was written, or to point out any parallel case; but it is still more difficult to imagine why (if Asser the biographer and Asser bishop of Sherborne be the same) its author, who lived nine years after Alfred's death, did not complete it. When we examine the book itself, we see at once that it does not support its own character; it has the appearance of an unskilful compilation of history and legend. Asser's life of Alfred consists of two very distinct parts; first, a chronicle of events, strictly historical, from 851 to 887; and, secondly, a few personal anecdotes of Alfred, which are engrafted upon the chronicle at the years 866 and 884, without any particular reference to those years, and at the conclusion. No person can compare the first, or strictly historical part of the work, with the Saxon Chronicle, without being convinced that it is a mere translation from the corresponding part of that document, which was most probably not in existence till long after Alfred's death. . . . If the suspicions of the authenticity of this biography be well founded, its historical value is considerably diminished, although it is not entirely destroyed. It contains interesting traditions relating to Alfred's life and character, many of which were without doubt true in substance; while our opinion of Alfred will be rather elevated, than lowered, by the right which is thus given us to separate the legendary matter from the truth. There is nothing remarkable in the style of the book attributed to Asser.—WRIGHT, THOMAS, 1842, *Biographia Britannica Literaria, vol* I, *pp.* 408-412.

Though most of the public events recorded in this book are to be found in the Saxon Chronicle, yet for many interesting circumstances in the life of our great Saxon king we are indebted to this biography alone. But, as if no part of history is ever to be free from suspicion, or from difficulty, a doubt has been raised concerning the authenticity of this work. . . . As the work has been edited by Petrie, so has it been here translated, and the reader, taking it upon its own merits, will find therein much of interest about our glorious king, concerning whom he will lament with me that all we know is so little, so unsatisfying.—GILES, J. A., 1848, *ed. Six Old English Chronicles, Preface, p.* vi.

Although Alfred lived at a time when our perception of his individuality is not obscured by the shadowy clouds of tradition, and in a country where the sober prose of reality had early taken the place of all the poetry of more southern lands, yet he was never fortunate enough to find a Cassiodorus or an Eginhard amongst those by whom he was surrounded. At the first glance, indeed, Asser might be compared with the latter; but, if the Gesta Alfredi is somewhat more closely observed, one doubt after another will arise, whether, in the form which is preserved to us, this can really be the work of that bishop who was so trusted by his king. Criticism has been frequently employed on this little book, but it has never decided the important question. For my own part, I shall not undertake to solve such a problem in its full extent; and I doubt much whether it is possible to determine the point with absolute certainty. I find, so far, that, with the single exception of Thomas Wright, in the "Biographia Literaria Britannica, I., 405-413," no one has thought of denying the authenticity of the book; the best English and German authors rather maintain that it was really written by Asser, and is our best authority for the life of this great king.—PAULI, GEORG REINHOLD, 1851-3, *Life of Alfred the Great, p.* 3.

Matthew of Westminster; Ingulphus, the author of the "Life of St. Neots;" Simon Dunel; William of Malmesbury; Roger of Wendover; Roger de Hoveden; Henry of Huntingdon; John Harding, or Capgrave, who wrote in the 14th or 15th century; Grafton; Fabian, or Rastul, who wrote 1529; and indeed numbers of those upon whom we are bound to depend for our notions of history, all are equally silent as to Asser and his history. It has even been questioned seriously whether there ever was an Asser, Bishop of Sherborne; but that is going too far. If we can credit any fact of that period, we can believe in the bishop; and we know just enough about him to make it probable that any forger knowing as much would deem him a proper person upon whose reputation to pin the history.—YEATMAN, JOHN PYM, 1874, *An Introduction to the Study of Early English History, p.* 306.

We pass over an interval of nearly two hundred years before we come to another historian of real graphic power. Nor have we even then a great historian, much less a man of anything like Bede's comprehensiveness and universality of mind. He is, in fact, not an historian at all, but only a biographer; his work is little more than a fragment, of which a very small portion is original, and the interest of it is mainly due to the genuine greatness of the man whom he describes to us. Nevertheless, Asser's "Life of Alfred" is by no means contemptible, even as a literary composition; and if it is seldom studied in the original, some part of its contents is known to all and related in other language to children in the nursery at this day.—GAIRDNER, JAMES, 1879, *Early Chroniclers of Europe, England, p.* 30.

In 1574 appeared Parker's edition of Asser's Life of Alfred, and we read in Strype that "of this edition of Asserius there had been great expectation among the learned." We can add, that of this edition the interest is not yet extinct. . . I venture to think that the internal evidence corresponds to the author's name, that it was written at the time of, and by such a person as, Alfred's Welsh bishop. The evident acquaintance with people and with localities, the bits of Welsh, the calling of the English uniformly "Saxons," all mark the Welshman who was at home in England. In the course of this biography, which seems to have been left in an unfinished state, there is a considerable extract from the Winchester Chronicles translated into Latin.—EARLE, JOHN, 1884, *Anglo-Saxon Literature, pp.* 43, 183.

We have little reason to doubt that the bulk of the book is by the man whose name it bears. Additions have probably been made to it, legends inserted, events coloured and heightened to glorify the King, but on the whole its record is historical, and contemporary with Ælfred. —BROOKE, STOPFORD A., 1898, *English Literature from the Beginning to the Norman Conquest, p.* 237, *note.*

Dunstan

925–988

Born at Glastonbury in 925 A. D. He was a man of extraordinary abilities, and gained renown by his ascetic piety. Of gentle birth and dauntless courage, he acquired the favor of Edred, who began to reign in 946 A. D., and he took a prominent part in the government during the reign. He was banished by Edwy in 955, but obtained the chief power under Edgar, who became king in 959 and appointed Dunstan Archbishop of Canterbury. Dunstan enriched and exalted the monks, in learning, religion, and morals, and deprived the married clergy of their class privileges. On the accession of Ethelred in 978 his political power was lost, but he kept the archbishopric. Died in Canterbury, May 19, 988.—JACKSON, SAMUEL MACAULEY, REV, 1897, *Johnson's Universal Cyclopædia, vol.* II., *p.* 858.

A strenuous bishop, zealous without dread of person, and for aught appears, the best of many ages, if he busied not himself too much in secular affairs.—MILTON, JOHN, 1670, *History of Britain, bk.* vi

Relatively to the times then, when the smallest ascent above the common level of gross ignorance, excited wonder, we may readily allow, that the archbishop was an accomplished man; and the marvellous tales, with which the histories of his life abound, are not necessary to convince us that, in other respects, he was great and good; however much certain parts of his public conduct, when he came into power, may by some have been deemed deserving of censure.—BERINGTON, JOSEPH, 1814, *A Literary History of the Middle Ages, p.* 200.

Urged by Ambition, who with subtlest skill
Changes her means, the Enthusiast as a dupe
Shall soar, and as a hypocrite can stoop,
And turn the instruments of good to ill,
Moulding the credulous people to his will.
Such DUNSTAN:—from its Benedictine coop
Issues the master Mind, at whose fell swoop
The chaste affections tremble to fulfil
Their purposes. Behold, pre-signified,
The Might of spiritual sway! his thoughts, his dreams,
Do in the supernatural world abide:
So vaunt a throng of Followers, filled with pride

In what they see of virtues pushed to extremes,
And sorceries of talent misapplied.
—WORDSWORTH, WILLIAM, 1821–22, *Ecclesiastical Sonnets, pt.* i, xxviii.

The spirit lives on in spite of self-destructive falsehood, and of metamorphoses supplanting one another, and the mind and works of Dunstan have outlived the Anglo-Saxon language and dynasty, and even catholicism itself in England; nor can their influence at the present day be denied by the Anglican church, nor by dissenters, even quakers, who, like Dunstan, are earnestly desirous for what to them appears the truest and the best.—LAPPENBERG, JOHANN MARTIN, 1834–37, *A History of England under the Anglo-Saxon Kings, tr. Thorpe, vol.* II, *p.* 148.

The whole tenour of Dunstan's life shows that his mind was distinguished more by its extraordinary activity, than by a tendency to solitude and contemplation; his leisure employments were chiefly works of the hand, the mechanical sciences and the fine arts. Yet he appears to have been a man of considerable learning, and not devoid of literary taste. Although he regarded the Scriptures, and the writings of the theologians, as the grand object of study to Christians, yet he taught that the writings of the poets and other ancient authors were not to be neglected, because they tended to polish the minds, and improve the style of those who read them. His favourite studies were arithmetic, with geometry, astronomy, and music, the quadrivium of the schools, the highest and most difficult class of scholastic accomplishments. He is said to have imbibed his taste from the Irish monks, who cultivated science with more zeal than literature. He also employed much time in his youth in writing and illuminating books, and in making ornaments of different kinds, for he excelled in drawing and sculpture. He appears to have possessed little taste for literary compositions, for we hear nothing of his skill in poetry, he attained no reputation for eloquence, and the writings which have been attributed to him, of little importance in their character, are such as would have originated in the necessity of the moment. But his influence on the literature of his country was great; the innumerable monasteries which grew up under his auspices became so many schools of learning, and the few writings of that period which now remain must be but a small portion of the numerous books which perished with the monasteries in which they were written, during the new series of Danish invasions which prevented their being recopied and multiplied.—WRIGHT, THOMAS, 1842, *Biographia Britannica Literaria, vol.* I, *p.* 457.

DUNSTAN (*alone*).
Kings shall bow down before thee, said my soul,
And it is even so. . . .
Cherished by His smile
My heart is glad within me, and to Him
Shall testify in works a strenuous joy.
Methinks that I could be myself that rock
Whereon the Church is founded,—wind and flood
Beating against me, boisterous in vain.
I thank you, gracious powers! supernal host!
I thank you that on one, though young in years,
To put the glorious charge to try with fire,
To winnow and to purge. I hear you call!
A radiance and a resonance from heaven
Surrounds me, and my soul is breaking forth
In strength, as did the new-created sun
When earth beheld it first on the fourth day.
God spake not then more plainly to that orb
Than to my spirit now. I hear the call
—TAYLOR, SIR HENRY, 1842, *Edwin the Fair.*

Since the Reformation, it has been a favourite occupation with many writers to tear from his grave the laurels planted upon it by the gratitude of his contemporaries. There is, however, something very suspicious in that sagacity which, at the distance of several hundred years, pretends to see more deeply and more clearly into the character of a man than was seen by those who lived at the same time, and who profited by his services; and that sagacity becomes still more suspicious, when the only proof which we have of its existence, is a determination to attribute to selfish or odious motives, actions of themselves the most harmless, often the most praiseworthy.—LINGARD, JOHN, 1844, *The History and Antiquities of the Anglo-Saxon Church, vol.* II, *p.* 244.

We may fully admit Dunstan's sincerity. Riches he utterly despised—when in his cell, he bestowed the whole of his ample patrimony, as well as the other great property which he acquired by bequests, upon the monastery. He had mortified his flesh, subdued his appetites and passions; and, from a deep sense of duty, however mistaken, he had abandoned that which was dearest to him in the world. But this painful process had left terrible effects behind; his heart was now seared against all those affections and feelings of humanity, which connect us with our fellow creatures, and afford the best means of testifying our love toward our common father. His mind was narrowed to the compass of his order; and the single object of his existence was, the establishment of the Benedictine rule and the extension of the Papal power.—PALGRAVE, FRANCIS, 1850, *A History of the Anglo-Saxons, p.* 200.

But in the year 988, when his life-work was finished, and the worn-out, weary servant was awaiting his summons, he was at Canterbury, a fine noble-looking old man, to be seen haunting the cathedral aisles, muttering his prayers as he passed, or musing dreamily of by-gone times at the tomb of his friend and predecessor, Odo the Good. His career had been a glorious one; he had been the companion and even the maker of kings; his life had been spent in the whirl of courts; in his hands he had held the reins of government; he had purged the Church of what he honestly thought a scandalous vice; he had quelled internal dissensions, had kept foreign depredators at bay, and now he had crept back to his church like a weary pilgrim, to lay down his bones at the altar of his Master, whom he had so long served, the fires of ambition all burnt out of him, and the soul longing to be free. The unseen messenger came. On the day of Ascension he preached his last sermon, and gave the people his last public blessing; his subject was the Incarnation; he told his auditors they would never hear him again; and as he was returning through the church, indicated the spot where he should be buried. . . . The greatest man of his age, greatest churchman, and greatest statesman. He stands out boldly on the page of history even now, though nearly a thousand years have crowded that page with a multitude of names and figures; still towering above the mass he is prominent as the earliest of a long list of great ecclesiastical statesmen, numbering such spirits as Hildebrand, Mazarin, Wolsey, and Richelieu, men who have impressed their characters upon their age, who with one hand upheld the Church, and with the other guided the State.—HILL, O'DELL TRAVERS, 1867, *English Monasticism, pp.* 168, 169.

St. Dunstan, patron saint of goldsmiths and jewellers. He was a smith, and worked up all sorts of metals in his cell near Glastonbury Church. It was in this cell that, according to legend, Satan had a gossip with the saint, and Dunstan caught his sable majesty by the nose with a pair of red-hot forceps.—BREWER, E. COBHAM, 1880, *The Reader's Handbook, p.* 280.

There are not many men who can boast on laying down their work that so much of it has been good.—WAKEMAN, HENRY OFFLEY, 1896, *An Introduction to the History of the Church of England, p.* 72.

Ælfric

955?–1025?

955 Birth, 972-987 Life at Winchester, 987-1004 Life at Cernel, 990-991 The Catholic Homilies I., 992 The De Temporibus, 994 The Catholic Homilies, II., 995 Grammar, 998 Lives of the Saints, 997-999 The Glossary, 998 Translations from the Old Testament, 998-1001 Pastoral Letter for Wulfsige, 995-1005 The Colloquium, 1005 Ælfric Abbot of Eynsham, 1005-1006 Tract composed for Wulfgeat, 1005 Excerpts from the De Consuetudine, 1006 Latin Life of Æthelwold, 1005-12 Treatise on the Old and New Testaments, 1007-1012 Sermon on Vigilate Ergo, 1014-1016 Pastoral Letter for Wulfstan, 1020 Second edition of the Catholic Homilies, 1020-1025 Death.—WHITE, CAROLINE LOUISA, 1898, *Ælfric, A New Study of his Life and Writings, p.* 11.

Ælfric, surnamed *Grammaticus*, the well-known writer, scholar, and theologian, must be carefully distinguished from three or four contemporaries who bore the same name. He must not be confounded with Ælfric, at first Bishop of Ramsbury, and afterwards Archbishop of Canterbury, who died before him (A. D. 1005). Nor may *Grammaticus* be identified either with Ælfric, Abbot of Malmesbury, or Ælfric, Abbot of Evesham; nor again with Ælfric, surnamed Puttoc, who became Archbishop of York in 1023, and died in 1051. Yet another Ælfric must be distinguished in the person of Ælfric Bata, the disciple of *Grammaticus.*—RAMSAY, SIR JAMES H., 1898, *The Foundations of England, vol.* I, *p.* 345.

I, Ælfric, monk and mass-priest, although more weakly than for such orders is fitting, was sent in King Æthelred's days to a certain minster which is called Cernel, at the request of Æthelmaer, the thegn, whose borth and goodness are everywhere known. Then it occurred to my mind, I trust through God's grace, that I would turn this book from Latin speech into English.—ÆLFRIC, 990, *Homilies, Preface.*

This Alfric was a very wise man, so that there was no sager man in England. —THE ANGLO-SAXON CHRONICLE, 995 *ed., Giles, p.* 391.

The learned energy of his earlier years has, indeed, rarely been surpassed; and although, like other Anglo-Saxons, he wrote but little quite original, yet, considering the time of his appearance, he has fully earned a foremost rank in the literature of England.—SOAMES, HENRY, 1835, *The Anglo-Saxon Church, p.* 189.

After the name of Alfred, that of Alfric stands first among the Anglo-Saxon vernacular writers, both for the number and the importance of his works. — WRIGHT, THOMAS, 1842, *Biographia Britannica Literaria, vol.* I, *p.* 61.

His sermons . . . equally exhibit what were the doctrines of the Anglo-Saxon church at the period in which they were compiled or translated, and are for the most part valuable in matter, and expressed in language which may be pronounced a pure specimen of our noble, old, Germanic mother tongue.—THORPE, BENJAMIN, 1844, *ed., The Homilies of the Anglo-Saxon Church, vol.* I, *Preface.*

So far as we can follow the busy career of Ælfric, he was always the same in his aims, his ideas, and the manner of bringing them into practice. His knowledge might increase, his arguments might gain depth and stringency, but the essence of his nature, as of his writings, remained the same. He appears to us from the beginning a finished, completely developed personality. Even his style is as lucid, fluent, and upon occasion as forcible, in the first collection of homilies as in his latest writings, although his command of language and of alliteration increased as time went on. In regard to his art, it was perhaps unfortunate that Ælfric yielded so early to the allurement of alliteration, which never lost its hold upon him. The writings of the second period, almost without exception, even including the rule of St. Basil and the introduction to the Old and New Testaments, appear with this adornment. The prose expression certainly did not gain precision by this.—TEN BRINK, BERNHARD, 1877-83, *History of English Literature (To Wiclif), tr. Kennedy, p.* 110.

Equally clear in his prose with Alfred and even more poetic and finished, he had to a less degree that masculine vigor that marked the king. Most of his prose is so alliterative as to mar its character and, yet, what he lacks in solidity he supplies in a more modern, lucid and facile expression.—HUNT, THEODORE W., 1887, *Representative English Prose and Prose Writers, p.* 18.

Ælfric is altogether the most important writer of the late West-Saxon period. . . . Ælfric's career is conspicuous in its relation to the reform of Dunstan and Æthelwold, and his writings mark a culmination in prose style. His language is always clear, and when not forced into an artificial alliterative mould, it is flexible and forcible.—BRIGHT, JAMES W., 1891, *An Anglo-Saxon Reader, pp.* 212, 213, *notes.*

The best of Ælfric's homilies are as good as the best of their kind anywhere. —KER, W. P., 1893, *English Prose, ed. Craik, Introduction, vol.* I, *p.* 6.

Ælfric's style exhibits decided advance over his predecessors in power of graceful transition. One paragraph leads to another, and there are varied devices of explicit reference.—LEWIS, EDWIN HERBERT, 1894, *The History of the English Paragraph, p.* 70.

What Bæda was to England in the eighth, Ælfric was to the eleventh century.

He had no creative power; nothing imaginative comes from his hand, but he had an affection for imaginative work. Some have traced in his work that he had read the poets, and he was always playing at poetry in his prose. Not original in thought, he had a gentle eagerness in writing; he had warmth and moral dignity. His charity, his affectionate friendship, his tact, his practiced skill in the affairs of men, appear in all his books and letters. He possessed the excellent power of putting into popular form the thoughts of other men, and of epitomising good books. He gathered together, absorbed, and well expressed the learning of his time; he had a strong sense of the duty of communicating it in English to the people, and he passed all the years of his manhood in teaching and writing. And as Ælfred was the creator of the elder, so Ælfric was of the younger Anglo-Saxon prose.—BROOKE, STOPFORD A., 1898, *English Literature from the Beginning to the Norman Conquest, p.* 279.

When judged fairly according to the conditions of his time, he stands forth an eminent man among the Old English. But his chief excellence is not to be sought in special learnedness, nor in the distinguished place assigned him in relation to traditional Catholicism. Rather it is to be found in the fidelity with which he devoted whatever learning his opportunities enabled him to acquire to the education of the people, adapting to their needs his whole thought and activity. . . . As an author, considered in the general sense of that term, we cannot rank him with those who have promoted the development of knowledge. He belonged to an age in which there was almost no struggle for the formulation of doctrine, and in which all learning languished. His aim was chiefly a practical one; his writings were to serve the church of his time, and were called forth by pressing needs. . . . The literary aspect of our author is attractive in its noble simplicity, clearness and vigor of expression. . . . He was the most efficient of the writers of his time; none before him had written such urgent, impressive reproofs to the shepherds of the people; none had attained to such dignity, fullness, and power of discourse. It was reserved for him to establish the reformatory movement among the English, and to gather its fruits. His fame is to be compared with that of an Aldhelm in an earlier time, and with that of a Wyclif in a later riper age.—WHITE, CAROLINE LOUISA, 1898, *Ælfric, A New Study of his Life and Writings, pp.* 71, 83, 84, 87.

Lanfranc

1005?-1089

Archbishop of Canterbury, was born at Pavia about 1005, and educated for the law. About 1039 he founded a school at Avranches, in 1041 became a Benedictine at Bec, and in 1046 was chosen prior. He contended against Berengarius in the controversy as to the real presence. He at first condemned the marriage of William of Normandy with his cousin, but in 1059 went to Rome to procure the papal dispensation; and in 1062 William made him prior of St. Stephen's Abbey at Caen, and in 1070 Archbishop of Canterbury. He died 24th May 1089. His chief writings are Commentaries on the Epistles of St. Paul, a Treatise against Berengar, and Sermons.—PATRICK AND GROOME, *eds.*, 1897, *Chambers's Biographical Dictionary, p.* 569.

A man of unbounded learning, master of the liberal arts, and of both sacred and secular literature, and of the greatest prudence in counsel and the administration of worldly affairs.—FLORENCE OF WORCESTER, c 1118, *Chronicle, tr. Forester*, (*A. D.* 1070), *p.* 175.

To understand the admirable genius and erudition of Lanfranc, one ought to be an Herodian in grammar, an Aristotle in dialectics, a Tully in rhetoric, an Augustine and Jerome, and other expositors of the law and grace, in the sacred scriptures. Athens itself, in its most flourishing state, renowned for the excellency of its teaching, would have honoured Lanfranc in every branch of eloquence and discipline, and would have desired to receive instruction from his wise maxims. —ORDERICUS VITALIS, 1141, *The Ecclesiastical History of England and Normandy, tr. Forester, vol.* II, *bk.* iv, *ch.* vii.

A man worthy to be compared to the ancients, in knowledge, and in religion: of whom it may be truly said, "Cato the third is descended from heaven;" so much had an heavenly savour tinctured his heart and tongue; so much was the whole Western world excited to the knowledge of the liberal arts, by his learning; and so earnestly did the monastic profession labour in the work of religion, either from his example, or authority.—WILLIAM OF MALMESBURY, c1142, *Chronicle of the Kings of England, bk.* III, *tr. Sharpe.*

A. D. 1089. Lanfranc, archbishop of Canterbury, died on the twenty-fourth of March, who had restored the large church in Canterbury, and all its offices. He procured many additional dignities for that church; he restored its manors, he established two receiving houses for strangers, by condemning heresies he confirmed the faith, . . . he restored the church at Rochester; he diligently corrected, by a comparison with the ancient copies, the books which the rude simplicity of the English had corrupted; in the confirmation of which the church delights to feel itself strengthened.—MATTHEW OF WESTMINSTER, c1307, *The Flowers of History, tr. Yonge, vol.* II, *ch.* ii.

His contemporaries, who extol the learning of Lanfranc in hyperbolical terms, do so in very indifferent Latin of their own; but it appears indeed more than doubtful, whether the earliest of them meant to praise him for this peculiar species of literature. The Benedictines of St. Maur cannot find much to say for him in this respect. They allege that he and Anselm wrote better than was then usual,—a very moderate compliment; yet they ascribe a great influence to their public lectures, and to the schools which were formed on the model of Bec: and perhaps we could not, without injustice, deprive Lanfranc of the credit he has obtained for the promotion of polite letters. There is at least sufficient evidence that they had begun to revive in France not long after his time.—HALLAM, HENRY, 1837-39, *Introduction to the Literature of Europe, pt.* i, *ch.* i, *par.* 79.

Though the name of Lanfranc has descended to us almost without reproach, we feel bound to say that his worldly wisdom seems to have been greatly in advance of his piety; and that the facts of his history, as a whole, force upon us the impression, that he could descend to artifice, not to say craft, to accomplish his purpose, and that his inordinate ambition is as little to be doubted as his knowledge and sagacity.—VAUGHAN, ROBERT, 1859-65, *Revolutions in English History, vol.* I, *p.* 381.

An Archbishop of Canterbury was something more than merely the first of English bishops. Setting aside his loftier ecclesiastical claims as the second Pontiff of a second world, he held within the realm of England itself a position which was wholly his own. . . . Lanfranc stood by the side of William, as Dunstan had stood by the side of Eadgar. In every gathering of the Church and of the people, in every synod, in every gemot, the Archbishop of Canterbury held a place which had no equal or second, a place which was shared by no other bishop or earl or ætheling. If we reckon the King as the head of the assembly, the Archbishop is its first member. If we reckon the King as a power outside the assembly, the Archbishop is himself its head. He is the personal counsellor of the King, the personal leader of the nation, in a way in which no other man in the realm could be said to be.—FREEMAN, EDWARD A., 1882, *The Reign of William Rufus and the Accession of Henry the First, vol.* I, *pp.* 357, 358.

His writings show less of the rudeness of the age in which he wrote, and more order, precision, and ease, than the other productions of the eleventh century. He displays a great knowledge of Holy Scripture, of tradition, and of canon law.—JENKINS, O. L., 1876, *The Student's Handbook of British and American Literature, p.* 53.

He is styled saint in the "Benedictine Martyrology," and there were pictures of him in the abbey churches of Caen and Bec; as, however, he had no commemorative office, he should perhaps be styled "Beatus" rather than "Sanctus." Although a large part of his life was spent in transacting ecclesiastical and civil affairs, he never lost the habits and tastes which he had acquired at Bec; he remained a devout man, constant in the discharge of his religious duties. Strenuous in all things, far-seeing and wise, resolute in purpose, stern towards those who persisted in opposing his policy, and not over-scrupulous as to the justice of the means which he employed in carrying it out, or the sufferings which it entailed on others, he was in many respects like his master and friend, William the Conqueror, and men looked on the king and the archbishop as well matched in strength of character (*Brevis Relatio*, p. 10). In Lanfranc there was, moreover, the subtlety of the Italian lawyer, and his power of drawing distinctions, the quickness of his perception, and the acuteness of his intellect must have rendered him vastly superior to the churchmen and nobles of the court. Combined with these traits were others more suited to his profession, for he was humble, munificent, and, when no question of policy was concerned, gentle and considerate towards all.—HUNT, REV. WILLIAM, 1892, *Dictionary of National Biography, vol.* XXXII, *p.* 88.

Anselm

1033–1109

Born in or near Aosta, in Piedmont, in 1033; 1060, pupil of Lanfranc, and an inmate of the abbey of Bec in Normandy; 1063, chosen prior; 1078, abbot; 1093, Archbishop of Canterbury; 1109, died April 21; buried next to Lanfranc at Canterbury. Wrote "Monologion," "Proslogion," "Cur Deus Homo." His "Meditations" and "Letters" have also come down to us.—MOULTON, CHARLES WELLS, 1900.

He was a second Augustin; superior to those of his age in the acuteness of his understanding and powers of logic; and equal to the most illustrious men of his day for virtue and piety.—TENNEMANN, WILHELM GOTTLIEB, 1812, *A Manual of the History of Philosophy, tr. Johnson, p.* 217.

The man who exerted the most important influence on the theological and philosophical turn of the twelfth century. . . . In Anselm, we see the different main directions of the spirit that actuated his times harmoniously combined; but the spiritual elements that were blended together in him became separated in the progress of the spiritual life of this period, and proceeded to antagonisms, which belong amongst the most significant appearances of the twelfth century.—NEANDER, AUGUSTUS, 1825-52, *General History of the Christian Religion and Church, tr. Torrey, vol.* VIII, *pp.* 10, 23.

Anselm was equal to Lanfranc in learning, and far exceeded him in piety. In his private life he was modest, humble, and sober in the extreme. He was obstinate only in defending the interests of the church of Rome, and, however we may judge the claims themselves, we must acknowledge that he supported them from conscientious motives. Reading and contemplation were the favourite occupations of his life, and even the time required for his meals, which were extremely frugal, he employed in discussing philosophical and theological questions. By his rare genius he did much towards bringing metaphysics into repute. He laid the foundation of a new school of theology, which was free from the servile character of the older writers, who did little more than collect together a heap of authorities on the subjects which they treated. The Monologium and the Proslogium are admirable specimens of abstract reasoning. His reading was extensive, and his style is clear and vigorous.—WRIGHT, THOMAS, 1846, *Biographia Britannica Literaria, vol.* II, *p.* 59.

Scholasticism, of which Anselm was the first representative, freed the church from the yoke of royalty, but only to chain it to the Papal chair.—D'AUBIGNE, J. H. MERLE, 1853, *History of the Reformation of the Sixteenth Century, tr. White, vol.* V, *bk.* xvii, *ch.* v.

In what lively colours does the prelate's last wish, his regret at being unable to finish a philosophical work, paint for us the active mind and firm will of the immortal philosopher! History offers no other example of a man sharing in such violent and multiplied contests, yet remaining throughout devoted to such metaphysical speculations as seem to require an undisturbed mind and a life of external calm. Amidst so much commotion and trouble, Anselm carried on side by side his theological and philosophical researches, and a correspondence of immense extent.

In such a man no doubt the uprightness and simplicity of his soul doubled the powers of his intellect. His range of thought was as wide as his courage was invincible. Care for the good of individual souls was as powerful with him as his ardent zeal for the interests of the universal Church. Amidst the deepest tribulations of all kinds, Anselm guided with most scrupulous attention the conduct of his sister, his brother-in-law, and of his nephew whom he had the happiness of drawing into the cloister. With that tenderness of heart which was a secret of his time, he was neither limited to the narrow sphere of family life nor the wider one of a special church. He governed the consciences of a vast number of pious women, monks, and foreigners.—MONTALEMBERT, CHARLES FORBES, 1860-68, *The Monks of the West, vol.* VII, *p.* 284.

It is no disparagement to the powerful *a priori* arguments that have characterized modern Protestant theology, to say, that the argument from the necessary nature of the Deity, is unfolded in these tracts of Anselm with a depth of reflection, and a subtlety of metaphysical acumen, that places them among the finest pieces of Christian speculation. . . . Anselm is the first instance in which the theologian plants himself upon the position of philosophy, and challenges for the doctrine of vicarious satisfaction, both a rational necessity, and a scientific rationality.—SHEDD, WILLIAM G. T., 1863, *A History of Christian Doctrine, vol.* I, *p.* 231, *vol.* II, *p.* 275.

Later centuries have cast down the whole structure that Anselm and the men of his day laboriously built up. But thought and nobleness of character are longer-lived than the causes which they consecrate; and it can hardly be fanciful to associate the peculiar virtues of the Anglican Church, sobriety of tone and independence of popular clamour, with the example of severe reason and fearless love of truth in the greatest of mediæval primates. . . . Anselm as a thinker may be placed by the side of Kant. . . . . The philosophy of Anselm is, in a certain sense, the key-note to all mediæval literature.—PEARSON, CHARLES H., 1867, *History of England During the Early and Middle Ages, vol.* I, *pp.* 463, 608, 609.

He died, leaving a name equally illustrious as a scholar and as a divine.—WILLIAMS, FOLKESTONE, 1868, *Lives of the English Cardinals, vol.* I, *p.* 61.

St. Anselm, one of the most remarkable men and most attractive characters, not only of the Middle Ages but of the whole Christian history. . . . Anselm's character, has joined his name at once with those who had stood for truth in the face of kings and multitudes, and with one who was the type of the teachers of children in the first steps of knowledge: the masters of thought and language in its highest uses and its humblest forms; with the seer whose parable rebuked King David; with the preacher who thundered against Antioch and Constantinople; with the once famous grammarian, St. Jerome's master, from whom the Middle Age schools learnt the elementary laws which govern human speech, and out of whose book of rudiments Anselm had doubtless taught his pupils at Bec:

"Nathan the seer, the metropolitan
John Chrysostom, Anselm, and he whose hands—
Donatus—deigned the primer's help to plan."

It is his right place:—in the noble company of the strong and meek, who have not been afraid of the mightiest, and have not disdained to work for and with the lowliest: capable of the highest things; content, as living before Him with whom there is neither high nor low, to minister in the humblest.—CHURCH, R. W., 1870, *Saint Anselm, pp.* 6, 303.

The moral of the life of Anselm is the immortality there is in thought. Anselm the monk would long since have been forgotten with the multitude of other monks who said their quiet prayers in a thousand monasteries during the eleventh century. Anselm the Archbishop and Statesman might have been remembered longer, but only by historians and students of the by-ways of history. But Anselm the Thinker, who succeeded in thinking out a new theological argument and a new form of Christian doctrine, will have a name forever among the leaders of human opinion. His theory of the Atonement, mutilated, indeed, and dilapidated, is, nevertheless, still preached in numerous pulpits by honest men who think they have found it in the Bible,—not knowing that it came to them from the brain of an Italian monk meditating by the Seine some centuries ago.—CLARKE, JAMES FREEMAN, 1881, *Events and Epochs in Religious History, p.* 156.

It was not only in the church which was one day to be his own, or among men of his own order only, that Anselm made friends in England. He made a kind of progress through the land, being welcomed everywhere, as well in the courts of nobles as in the houses of monks, nuns, and canons. Everywhere he scattered the good seed of his teaching, speaking to all according to their several callings, to men and women, married and unmarried, monks, clerks, laymen, making himself, as far as was lawful, all things to all men. Scholar and theologian as Anselm was, his teaching was specially popular; he did not affect the grand style, but dealt largely in parables and instances which were easy to be understood. The laity therefore flocked eagerly to hear him, and every man rejoiced who could win the privilege of personal speech with the new apostle.—FREEMAN, EDWARD A., 1882, *The Reign of William Rufus and the Accession of Henry the First, vol.* I, *p.* 378.

Writers with nothing else in common have been equally attracted by Anselm. To the student of ecclesiastical biography he is one of the most perfect examples of the piety of the cloister—a piety which retains a charm even for those who have rejected all the ideas that gave it birth. Hegel and Cousin found in Anselm a mediæval Descartes who spoke the first word of modern philosophy amid the litanies of the Middle Ages. The student of the constitutional history of England finds Anselm's career to be of the first importance; for during the reign of William Rufus, and during part of that of Henry Beauclerc, Anselm, like Laud in the reign of Charles I., is in reality, as well as in name, the second personage in the realm. To those who care for the honour of the Church of England the name of Anselm is, or ought to be, precious, for in him they have an archbishop who was never timorous either in thought or in action. With his name, if with no other, they can answer the taunt, "*Episcopi Anglicani semper pavidi.*"—GIBB, JOHN, 1883, *The Life and Times of St. Anselm, British Quarterly Review, vol.* 78, *p.* 265.

It was not till several centuries after his death, that his remarkable originality of genius was fully appreciated. He anticipated Descartes in his argument to prove the existence of God. He is generally regarded as the profoundest intellect among the early schoolmen, and the most original that appeared in the Church after Saint Augustine. He was not a popular preacher like Saint Bernard, but he taught theology with marvellous lucidity to the monks who sought the genial quiet of his convent. . . . He was a true scholar of the Platonic and Augustinian school; not a dialectician like Albertus Magnus and Abélard, but a man who went beyond words to things, and seized on realities rather than forms; not given to disputations and the sports of logical tournaments, but to solid inquiries after truth. The universities had not then arisen, but a hundred years later he would have been their ornament, like Thomas Aquinas and Bonaventura.—LORD, JOHN, 1884, *Beacon Lights of History, vol.* II, *pp.* 213, 214.

If his philosophical treatises exhibit the profundity, the daring originality, and masterly grasp of his intellect, his meditations and prayers reveal the spiritual side of his nature, the deep humility of his faith, and the fervour of his love towards God, while his letters show him in his more human aspect—his tender sympathy and affection, his courtesy and respectfulness, combined with firmness in maintaining what he believed to be right, and in reproving what he believed to be wrong. Thus his writings completely verify the statement of William of Malmesbury that he was thoroughly spiritual and industriously learned—"penitus sanctus, anxie doctus."—STEPHENS, W. R. W., 1885, *Dictionary of National Biography, vol.* II, *p.* 29.

In him the two elements—the speculative and logical tendency on the one hand, and the devout and contemplative on the other—are so evenly balanced and so thoroughly commingled that he fulfils the ideal of the scholastic theologian.—FISHER, GEORGE PARK, 1887, *History of the Christian Church, p.* 212.

Though Anselm was thus early invested with the aureole of the saint, the process preliminary to his canonisation, committed to the care of Becket by Alexander III. in

1163, was abandoned in consequence of the subsequent troubles; nor was it revived until 1494, and then, in the irony of fate, by Alexander VI. of evil memory. Whether it resulted in a decree does not appear; but Anselm belongs to the number of those Blessed Doctors whom the ancient and universal consent of the Church has canonised. His feast, 21 April, was raised from a semi-double to a double by Clement XI. in 1720.—RIGG, J. M., 1896, *St. Anselm of Canterbury, Appendix, p.* 284.

Eadmer

1060?-1124?

Eadmer (b. circa 1060, d. 1124) was a monk of Canterbury, and the confidential adviser of Anselm. He was elected Bishop of St. Andrews, but, owing to a misunderstanding, was never consecrated. He wrote several ecclesiastical biographies and theological tracts, besides a "Life of St. Anselm" (*Vita Anselmi*), and a "History of His own Times" (*Historia Novorum*), extending from 959 to 1122. Both these works rank very high as authorities for the reigns of William II. and Henry II., and the *Vita Anselmi* is one of the chief sources of information with regard to the archbishop. Eadmer's works were published at Paris, 1721.—LOW AND PULLING, *eds.* 1884, *Dictionary of English History, p.* 396.

Eadmer is a trustworthy historian.—DIBDIN, THOMAS FROGNALL, 1824, *The Library Companion, p.* 157.

As a writer, Eadmer appears under three characters, those of a historian, of a compiler of lives of saints, and of a theologian. His principal historical work, the "Historia Novorum," or history of his own times, in six books, is the most valuable work we possess relating to the events of the reign of William Rufus, and of the earlier part of that of Henry I. The life of Anselm, in two books, forms a necessary supplement to this history. The "Historia Novorum" was first printed by Selden: it appears to have been very popular in the twelfth century, and is spoken of in high terms of praise by William of Malmesbury. . . . Eadmer's theological and miscellaneous writings are brief, and without importance.—WRIGHT, THOMAS, 1846, *Biographia Britannica Literaria, vol.* II, *pp.* 81, 82.

One distinction belonging to Eadmer's narrative is the nearly entire absence of miracles. He probably considered it improper to introduce such high matter into a composition which did not profess to be of a sacred or spiritual nature. Much of his work, however, is occupied with ecclesiastical transactions, which indeed formed almost the entire home politics, and no small part of the foreign politics also, of that age. He has in particular entered largely into the great controversy between the crown and the pope about investiture; and one of the most curious parts of his history is a long and detailed account which he gives of his own appointment to the bishopric of St. Andrew's in Scotland, and his contest about his consecration with the stout Scottish king, Alexander I.—CRAIK, GEORGE L., 1861, *A Compendious History of English Literature and of the English Language, vol.* I, *p.* 102.

The work, ("Historia Novorum") is more of an ecclesiastical than a political history. Written with great clearness and elegance.—GAIRDNER, JAMES, 1879, *Early Chroniclers of Europe, England, p.*66.

It is in the writings of Eadmar, a Benedictine monk of Canterbury, that we find the first indications of original and independent thought and the first faint glimmer of a promise heralding the new national literature. The two most important works of Eadmar are his history of his own times, "Historia Novorum," and his "Biography of Archbishop Anselm," in which he gives a faithful and somewhat minute account of affairs in England from the time of the Conquest to the year 1112. These works are distinguished for their accuracy of statement and for the soundness of judgment displayed in their composition; and, in describing the struggles of Anselm with William Rufus in defense of the claims of the church against the despotic exactions of kingly authority, they occasionally rise to the dignity and value of genuine literature. They are the most trustworthy authorities that we have for the history of the period immediately succeeding the Conquest.—BALDWIN, JAMES, 1883, *English Literature and Literary Criticism, Prose, p.* 27.

William of Malmesbury

C. 1095–1143

Chronicler, became a monk in the monastery at Malmesbury, and in due time librarian and precentor. He took part in the council at Winchester against Stephen in 1141. His "Gesta Regum Anglorum" gives the history of the kings of England from the Saxon invasion to 1128; the "Historia Novella" brings down the narrative to 1142 (both ed. by Hardy, 1840; trans. by Sharpe, 1847*). The "Gesta Pontificum" gives an account of the bishops and chief monasteries of England to 1123 (ed. by Hamilton, 1870). Other works are an account of the church at Glastonbury and a Life of St. Dunstan.—PATRICK AND GROOME, *eds.*, 1897, *Chambers's Biographical Dictionary, p.* 624.

William, quitting his own name of Summerset, assumed that of Malmesbury, because there he had (if not born) his best Preferment. Indeed he was a Duallist in that Convent (and if a Pluralist no ingenious person would have envied him), being Canter of that Church, and Library-Keeper therein. Let me adde, and Library-Maker too, for so may we call his "History of the Saxon Kings and Bishops" before the Conquest, and after it untill his own time; an History to be honoured, both for the Truth and Method thereof. If any Fustiness be found in his Writings, it comes not from the Grape, but from the Cask. The smack of Superstition in his books is not to be imputed to his person, but to the Age wherein he lived and dyed, viz. anno Domini 1142, and was buried in Malmesbury.—FULLER, THOMAS, 1662, *The Worthies of England, ed. Nichols, vol.* II, *p.* 448.

William of Malmsbury must be acknowledged both for style and judgment, to be by far the best writer of them all.—MILTON, JOHN, 1670, *History of Britain, bk.* iv.

One of the best of the old English historians. . . . A judicious man.—HUME, DAVID, 1762, *History of England, ch.* i, *and ch.* vii, *note.*

Well entitled to stand at the head of our historians of the twelfth century.—HENRY, ROBERT, 1771-90, *The History of Great Britain, bk.* iii, *ch.* iv.

Of his acquirements as a scholar it is indeed difficult to speak in terms of sufficient commendation. That he had accurately studied nearly all the Roman authors, will be readily allowed by the classical reader of his works. From these he either quotes or inserts so appositely, as to show how thoroughly he had imbibed their sense and spirit. His adaptations are ever ready and appropriate; they incorporate with his narrative with such exactness that they appear only to occupy their legitimate place. His knowledge of Greek is not equally apparent; at least his references to the writers of Greece are not so frequent, and even these might probably be obtained from translations: from this, however, no conclusion can be drawn that he did not understand the language. With respect to writers subsequent to those deemed classics, his range was so extensive that it is no easy matter to point out many books which he had not seen, and certainly he had perused several which we do not now possess.—SHARPE, JOHN, 1815, *tr. William of Malmesbury's Chronicle of the Kings of England, Preface.*

The modest, faithful, and erudite historian of the twelfth century.—DIBDIN, THOMAS FROGNALL, 1824, *The Library Companion, p.* 147.

William of Malmesbury deserves to be considered as one of the most remarkable writers of the twelfth century. . . . The first English writer after the time of Bede who attempted successfully to raise history above the dry and undigested details of a chronicle. . . . Next to the Saxon Chronicle, he is the most valuable authority for Anglo-Saxon history. In his annals of the Norman period, and of his own time, he is judicious, and, as far as could be expected, unprejudiced.—WRIGHT, THOMAS, 1846, *Biographia Britannica Literaria, vol.* II, *pp.* 134, 137, 138.

*First published in 1815.

The classical reader will probably lament with me that our early historians should have used a style so cumbersome and uninviting. To this general censure Malmesbury is certainly no exception. His Latinity is rude and repulsive, and the true value of his writings arises from the fidelity with which he has recorded facts, which he had either himself witnessed or had obtained from eye-witnesses.—GILES, J. A., 1847, *ed. William of Malmesbury's Chronicle of the Kings of England, p.* x, *note.*

William of Malmesbury enjoys the reputation of being a more learned historian, and of endeavouring to invest the dry form of the Old Chronicle with a more attractive style; but his researches are often by no means correct, and his errors cannot be forgotten.—PAULI, GEORG REINHOLD, 1851–3, *Life of Alfred the Great, p.* 13.

William of Malmesbury, on Roman affairs no high authority.—MILMAN, HENRY HART, 1854, *History of Latin Christianity, vol.* II, *bk.* V, *ch.* XIV, *note.*

His Histories are throughout original works, and, in their degree, artistic compositions. He has evidently taken great pains with the manner as well as with the matter of them. But he also evinces throughout a love of truth as the first quality of historical writing, and far more of critical faculty in separating the probable from the improbable than any other of his monkish brethren of that age who have set up for historians, notwithstanding his fondness for prodigies and ecclesiastical miracles, in which of course he had the ready and all-digestive belief which was universal in his time.—CRAIK, GEORGE L., 1861, *A Compendious History of English Literature and of the English Language, vol.* I, *p.* 101.

We may see the tendency of English literature at the close of the Norman period in William of Malmesbury. In himself, as in his work, he marks the fusion of the conquerors and the conquered, for he was of both English and Norman parentage, and his sympathies were as divided as his blood. In the form and style of his writings he shows the influence of those classical studies which were now reviving throughout Christendom. Monk as he is, he discards the older ecclesiastical models and the analistic form. Events are grouped together with no strict reference to time, while the lively narrative flows rapidly and loosely along, with constant breaks of digression, over the general history of Europe and the Church.—GREEN, JOHN RICHARD, 1874, *A Short History of the English People, ch.* iii, *sc.* i.

In William of Malmesbury we cannot fail to see the familiarity of the true scholar with the books which he had really mastered.—FREEMAN, EDWARD A., 1876, *The History of the Norman Conquest of England, vol.* V, *p.* 578.

Though the single existing manuscript has reached us in a defective condition, some parts being altogether wanting, while the end is lost, the work is valuable from its graphic description of many of the incidents of the civil war, and the picture it supplies of the prevalent anarchy and suffering. — MULLINGER, J. BASS, 1881, *English History for Students, Authorities, p.* 261.

A man of great reading, unbounded industry, very forward scholarship, and of thoughtful research in many regions of learning.—STUBBS, WILLIAM, 1887, *ed. Gesta Regum, Preface, vol.* I, *p.* x.

He was a man of sound judgment and cultured taste, and in consequence shows great love for delineation of character. He has considerable power of tracing the tendencies of important events and the development of political institutions. He is wonderfully broadminded and free from party-feeling, in sympathy with Normans and English alike, while his work is made bright by humour and sharply pointed remarks.—HEATH, H. FRANK, 1894, *Social England, vol.* I, *p.* 352.

Sprung from a Norman father and an English mother, he represents the growing fusion of the two races; though his sympathies are manifestly on the Norman side. He is a good specimen of a Benedictine scholar. By general consent he takes the foremost place among the authorities for the Anglo-Norman period. He may be designated the English Herodotus; in the sense of being the Father of its History. His industry in collecting materials, and his skill and judgment in arranging them, were marvellous for that age; considering his opportunities and the means at his command.—AUBREY, W. H. S., 1895, *The Rise and Growth of the English Nation, vol.* I, *p.* 158.

Geoffrey of Monmouth

C. 1100–1154

Goeffrey of Monmouth, d. 1154, Archdeacon of Monmouth, was made Bishop of St. Asaph in 1152, but afterwards returned to the monastery of Abingdon, where he was abbot. He wrote a Latin version of the prophecies, &c. of Merlin, Chronicon sive Historia Britonum, (written about 1138?); and some other works are ascribed to him. His History became very popular, and there are few works of which so many MSS. are extant. Edits. in Latin, Paris, 1508, 4to. Aaron Thompson's trans. into English was pub. Lon. 1718, 8vo. New ed., by J. A. Giles, LL.D., 1842. 8vo.—ALLIBONE, S. AUSTIN, 1854–58, *A Critical Dictionary of English Literature and British and American Authors, p.* 659.

The manner in which the British History or Chronicle was published, was as follows:—At some period before the year 1147, Geoffrey of Monmouth became possessed of an ancient British Chronicle brought to him from Britany, which, if not the same as the Chronicle of Tysilio, preserved in Jesus College, appears to have been in all probability a varying copy of it. Walter Calenius, archdeacon of Oxford, by some supposed to be the same person as Walter de Mapes the poet, which is somewhat uncertain, brought it over. However, Geoffrey of Monmouth determined upon publishing it, and a copy of Merlin's Prophecies coming also into his hands, he published both. He took a most unwise course, we may be justified in saying, latinizing the names, making various additions and embellishments of his own, and uniting Merlin's Prophecy to his volume, which is to be regarded as having formed no part of the original. Having done this, and loaded the narrative already disguised by extravagant legends, with many additional fictions, he strongly protests its truth.—POSTE, BEALE, 1853, *Britannic Researches, p.* 197.

A certain writer has come up in our times to wipe out the blots on the Britons, weaving together ridiculous figments about them, and raising them with impudent vanity high above the virtue of the Macedonians and Romans. This man is named Geoffrey, and has the by-name of Arturus, because he cloaked with the honest name of history, coloured in Latin phrase, the fables about Arthur taken from the old tales of the Bretons, with increase of his own. . . . Moreover, in this book that he calls the History of the Britons, how saucily and how shamelessly he lies almost throughout, no one, unless ignorant of the old histories, when he falls upon that book, can doubt. . . . I omit how much of the acts of the Britons before Julius Caesar that man invented, or wrote from the invention of others as if authentic. — WILLIAM OF NEWBURY, c 1208, *Gulielini Neubrigensis Rerum Anglicarum in Proem.*

He is the Welsh Herodotus, the father of ancient history and fables; for, he who will have the first must have the latter. Polydore Virgil accuseth him of many falsehoods; (so hard it is to halt before a cripple!) who, notwithstanding, by others is defended, because but a translator, and not the original reporter.—FULLER, THOMAS, 1655, *The Church History of Britian, ed. Nichols, vol.* I, *bk.* iii, *sec.* ii, *par.* 51.

Camden disliked the British history of Geoffrey of Monmouth, and his authority drew others to treat it with absolute contempt. But, since his time, through the indefatigable labours of many industrious men, other ancient authors have been published, which plainly shew, that much true history is to be met with, even in that book, though embarrassed with fiction.—CAMPBELL, JOHN, 1742-44, *Lives of the British Admirals, vol.* I.

Notwithstanding this author has not been without his advocates, particularly the famous J. Leland, his history is now universally regarded in no other light than that of a romance.—PRIESTLEY, JOSEPH, 1788, *Lectures on History and General Policy, p.* 161.

We do not insert the "British History" in our series of Early English Records as a work containing an authentic narrative, nor do we wish to compare Geoffrey of Monmouth with Bede in point of veracity. But the fact of his having supplied our early poets so large a portion of their subjects, and the universal belief which at one time prevailed as to the authenticity of his history, make it in every respect a question whether he ought not to be preserved, whilst the ample allusions, and, if we may use the expression, the ground-work, on which many of the facts are based, enable us indubitably to introduce him into our series as an addition (though secondary in value) to materials which our readers will find not to be inexhaustible, respecting our early history.—GILES, J. A., 1842, *ed. The British History of Geoffrey of Monmouth, Introduction, p.* xvii.

One of the most remarkable writers of the twelfth century, both for the popular reputation which he has since continued to enjoy, and the influence he exercised over subsequent historians. . . . Geoffrey's "History" soon became extensively popular, and within no long time after its publication the celebrity which he had given to the legendary king Arthur obtained for him the title of *Galfridus Arturus.* It is impossible to consider Geoffrey of Monmouth's History of the British Kings in any other light than as a tissue of fables. Its author was either deceived by his materials, or he wished to deceive his readers. It is certain that, if he did not intentionally deceive, we must understand, by *translating* the Breton book, that he meant only working up the materials furnished by it into his history; for some parts of the latter work are mere compilations by himself from the old writers on British affairs then commonly referred to.—WRIGHT, THOMAS, 1846, *Biographia Britannica Literaria, vol.* II, *pp.* 143, 144.

The Livy of the monkish historians. . . . His style is clear and simple, his narrative told in an effective manner, while his authenticity has found such eminent supporters as Leland and Usher.—LAWRENCE, EUGENE, 1855, *The Lives of the British Historians, vol.* I, *p.* 26.

But Geoffrey's work sufficiently shows that he wrote, as he professed to write, from documents. He probably rationalized a little, tampered with genealogies, arranged dates, and in other ways did infinite mischief; but it would be monstrous to suppose that he invented the history he set forth. If he did, he ought to rank as one of the first artists in literature. But in fact nothing is more difficult than to invent a new story, let alone twenty; and the exploit becomes incredible, if we add the difficulty of palming the forgeries upon a nation as its own history. There can be no doubt that Geoffrey derived the bulk of his work from old traditions, and probably, as he himself states, from some old compilation.—PEARSON, CHARLES H., 1867, *History of England During the Early and Middle Ages, vol.* I, *p.* 621.

A monument of stupendous delusion; but in which he seems to have been the deceiver rather than the deceived. . . . If there were many scholars who saw through this tissue of lies, the great mass were carried away by it. Men believed the stories presented with so much gravity by a Benedictine and a bishop, and they certainly found their contents most fascinating. The sense of the marvellous and the mysterious was nourished not less than the sense of the chivalric and heroic, or the love for the glitter and splendour of a kingly life; and Geoffrey's rhetorical, even poetical, style brought to bear with their full force all these elements. The effect of the work was therefore tremendous. Geoffrey's influence grew through the entire course of the Middle Ages, and spreading in a thousand channels, reached far into modern times, down to Shakspere, nay to Tennyson.—TEN BRINK, BERNHARD, 1877-83, *History of English Literature (To Wiclif), tr. Kennedy, pp.* 134, 135.

One of the most extraordinary works of art that the Middle Ages ever succeeded in producing. Of mythical tales and curious legends there was certainly no lack in those days; but the fabrication of a long consecutive history, to fill up a gap or form a prelude to the authentic annals of a nation, was something altogether new. Yet the story was so wonderfully told, the invention was so admirable, and the marvels related appealed so strongly to the imagination, that the world for ages after seems to have been at a loss what to make of it. It was not easy, even at the first, for a man of any judgment to be a thorough believer; but it required some boldness, even after centuries had passed away, to dispute the authority of fictions which owed their vitality in the first instance to Geoffrey's imaginative pen.—GAIRDNER, JAMES, 1879, ***Early Chroniclers of Europe, England, p.*** **157.**

Dear old Geoffrey of Monmouth, the wonderful Munchausen who in his Latin pages embalmed all the legends, and fed half the romances.—WASHBURN, EMELYN W., 1884, *Studies in Early English Literature, p.* 30.

Monmouth's chronicle was the book that, above all others, brought King Arthur home again out of Brittany to Britian. . . . In the literature of its time the book was as the ugly duck of the farmyard where not a fowl could recognise the future swan.—MORLEY, HENRY, 1888, *English Writers, vol.* III, *pp.* 44, 48.

Geoffrey of Monmouth was at least fifty years of age when he was ordained priest in 1152. His literary career was already over, and its record is a brilliant one notwithstanding the charges made on one side that his Cymric scholarship was faulty, and on the other that his Latinity is of vulgar order. The metrical "Vita Merlini" has been considered too excellent a piece of composition for his pen, and therefore supposititious; but Mr. Ward gives good reason for believing it genuine. Indeed, the suggestion—however gratuitous—that Geoffrey was a Benedictine monk is almost a necessary one to account for the education evinced by his labours, not the most important part of them being the reduction of ancient British legends into respectable mediæval Latin history—a task accomplished with manifest literary skill and tact. His allusions to antecedent and contemporary writers are a proof that he was no mere monkish student eager to swallow wondrous stories, but a shrewd scholar equipped with all the learning of his age. "He was a man whose like could not be found for learning and knowledge," says the "Gwentian Brut," and had a charm of manner which made his society agreeable to men of high station.—TEDDER, H. R., 1890, *Dictionary of National Biography, vol.* XXI, *p.* 134.

The work must be regarded as an historical novel, in which the chief part is played by Arthur, whose deeds, however, form only the central chapters in a long account of struggles between the owners of the soil and foreign assailants: the interest is racial, rather than personal.—NEWELL, WILLIAM WELLS, 1898, *King Arthur and the Table Round, vol.* I, *p.* xv.

Saxon Chronicle

45–1154

The first history in any Germanic language. In the form of annals, it covers the history of England from the invasion of Britain by Julius Cæsar to the accession of Henry II. It was begun about the year 900 (some think by King Alfred), and was continued by numerous writers, usually churchmen. It is monastic in tone, favors church rather than state, but is trustworthy and the foundation of English history. Its language varies from purest Anglo-Saxon to early English.—EMERY, FRED PARKER, 1891, *Notes on English Literature, p.* 7.

Taking the chronicle as a whole, I know not where else to find a series of annals which is so barren of all human interest, and for all purposes of real history so worthless.—MARSH, GEORGE P., 1862, *The Origin and History of the English Language, etc., p.* 105.

The great mental activity which the Conquest created in England showed itself not only in poetry but in history. Chroniclers sprang up in great numbers. They were chiefly monks, and most of them wrote in Latin. "The Saxon Chronicle" indeed was still carried on in more than one of the monasteries. The annalists, full of despondency, set down many facts, but record with evident satisfaction omens which seemed to betoken evil to the oppressors of their nation. They tell how blood gushed out of the earth in Berkshire near the birth-place of Alfred, and how at Peterborough, then placed under a Norman abbot, horns were heard at dead of night, and spectral huntsmen were seen to ride through the woods. Meanwhile French words so press upon the writer's brain, and the old snytax becomes so mixed with the grammar of the invading speech, that the chronicler is obliged to cease, and ends his work abruptly in the first year of Henry II.—ANGUS, JOSEPH, 1865, *The Handbook of English Literature, p.* 27.

In summing up the evidence, we may safely conclude—That the Saxon Codes are only scraps of British or English laws, dishonestly selected and intermixed with errors and lies. That the Saxon charters and other documents are a mass of forgeries. That Saxon literature is represented alone by the Saxon Chronicle and Asser's "Life of Alfred," and that these works are shocking impositions; and that, indeed, the Saxons had neither laws nor literature. —YEATMAN, JOHN PYM, 1874, *An Introduction to the Study of Early English History, p.* 340.

But simple as was his aim, Ælfred created English literature. Before him, England possessed in her own tongue one great poem, that of Cædmon, and a train of ballads and battlesongs. Prose she had none. The mighty roll of the books that fill her libraries begins with the translations of Ælfred, and above all with the Chronicle of his reign. It seems likely that the King's rendering of Bæda's history gave the first impulse toward the compilation of what is known as the English or Anglo-Saxon Chronicle, which was certainly thrown into its present form during his reign. The meagre lists of the kings of Wessex and of the bishops of Winchester, which had been preserved from older times, were roughly expanded into a national history by insertions from Bæda; but it is when it reaches the reign of Ælfred that the Chronicle suddenly widens into the vigorous narrative, full of life and originality, that marks the gift of a new power to the English tongue. Varying as it does from age to age in historic value, it remains the first vernacular history of any Teutonic people, the earliest and the most venerable monument of Teutonic prose. The writer of English history may be pardoned if he lingers too fondly over the figure of the king in whose court, at whose impulse, it may be in whose very words, English history begins.—GREEN, JOHN RICHARD, 1874, *A Short History of the English People, ch.* i, *sc.* v.

The mere language of different manuscripts affords an interesting study to the philologist, the variations of the dialect in different parts bearing witness to different degrees of antiquity in the composition, and the existence of concurrent texts in several places show that it was transcribed and added to by different and independent writers. The existing manuscripts also come to an end at very different dates, and special circumstances contained in particular texts seem occasionally to indicate the monastery in which a particular edition was composed.—GAIRDNER, JAMES, 1879, *Early Chroniclers of Europe, England, p.* 50.

Is a work of superlative value.—ROSS, JOHN MERRY, 1884, *Scottish History and Literature, etc., ed. Brown, p.* 43.

Preserving amid drier annals some exceedingly interesting fragments of composition of the more original kind, both in prose and verse, manifesting an ability to manage the subject which was only much later shown in other vernacular languages, and bridging for us, with a thin but distinct streak of union, the gulf between the decadence or ruin of Anglo-Saxon even before the Conquest and the rise of English proper more than a century subsequent to it.—SAINTSBURY, GEORGE, 1898, *A Short History of English Literature, p.* 25.

Henry of Huntingdon

C. 1084–1155

Archdeacon, and historian, flourished in the middle of the twelfth century, and is best known by his "History of England to the Death of Stephen," founded to a large extent upon Bede and Geoffrey of Monmouth, and edited by Sir Henry Savile in 1596. It was translated in 1853 by Thomas Forrester. . . . Henry wrote on "The Contempt of the World" and other subjects, both in prose and verse.—ADAMS, W. DAVENPORT, 1877, *Dictionary of English Literature, p.* 330.

Henry of Huntingdon's poetry is superior to the general standard of mediæval Latin verse. It is somewhat miscellaneous, consisting of metrical treatises on herbs, gems, spices, etc., of hymns, of amatory poetry, and epigrams.—WRIGHT, THOMAS, 1846, *Biographia Britannica Literaria, vol.* II, *p.* 169.

Henry of Huntingdon has, unfortunately, never found an intelligent editor even in the Mon. Hist. Brit., though he merits one more than any other historian of the middle ages of England. The spirited manner in which he describes battles was, most probably, caused by his intimate acquaintance with the old songs of the people.—PAULI, GEORG REINHOLD, 1851-3, *Life of Alfred the Great*, p. 13.

Savile describes him as, in respect of historical merit, although separated by a long interval from Malmesbury, yet making as near an approach to him as any other writer of the time, and as deserving to be placed in the first rank of the most diligent explorers and most truthful expounders of the times preceding their own. He is, indeed, more of an antiquary than an historian. His work, in so far as it is a history of his own time, is of little importance.—CRAIK, GEORGE L., 1861, *A Compendious History of English Literature, and of the English Language*, *vol.* I, *p.* 107.

His easy, interesting, and fluent narrative, breaking out occasionally into poetry, differs certainly not a little in character, even from the lively pages of William of Malmesbury. Yet it is equally characteristic of the new era and of the revival of letters which began under Henry Beauclerc. For with all his warmth of colouring he is a true historian, who seems to have weighed authorities in his own mind, moralises upon events, and draws his own conclusions.—GAIRDNER, JAMES, 1879, *Early Chroniclers of Europe, England*, *p.* 99.

He had ambition, literary taste, and intellectual quickness, but little perseverance, and less accuracy or judgment. If he wanders less from the subject than his contemporaries, it is because the material he used was scanty, and there was less temptation to stray. It used to be thought that he made use of many Old English popular songs; for in his description of battles in the fifth and sixth centuries he always adds picturesque details to the accounts in the English Chronicles, but close investigation shows that he drew on his imagination for these. He found Old English of even the tenth century hard to translate, and makes astounding mistakes in rendering the Battle of Brunanburh. He is important in the development of historical writing as the last translator of the English Chronicles and the first to accept Welsh tradition and romance without question—a bad precedent. The epigrams occurring in the history are probably from his hand, and the eleventh and twelfth books are wholly poetical.—HEATH, H. FRANK, 1894, *Social England*, *vol.* I, *p.* 351.

John of Salisbury

1120?-1182?

John of Salisbury, Bishop of Chartres, in France, was born at Salisbury, in Wiltshire, in the beginning of the 12th century. He studied at Oxford, and afterwards under Abelard and other eminent teachers on the continent. After his return to England, he became the intimate friend and companion of Thomas à Becket, whom he had attended in his exile, and he is said to have been present when he was murdered in Canterbury Cathedral. He was one of the best classical scholars of his time, and an elegant Latin poet. He has a place too in the history of philosophy, the progress of which he promoted by his attacks on the scholastic logic. He left numerous works, among which are Lives of Archbishops Anselm and Becket, and a very curious book entitled "Polycraticon." Died, 1182.—CATES, WILLIAM L. R., *ed.*, 1867, *A Dictionary of General Biography*, *p.* 570.

Is perhaps the most celebrated writer of the reign of Henry II. . . . As a writer, John of Salisbury is estimable for his great erudition, and for the general correctness of his style. We learn from his own writings that his favourite pursuits were grammar and rhetoric, *i. e.*, the study of the ancient writers, and he quotes several who are no longer extant. His style is however sometimes confused. He seems to have had little taste for scientific studies; and he appears less as a philosopher himself than as a critic of the systems of the various sects of antiquity, as well as of those of the age in which he lived. He avows a strong leaning towards the doctrines of the Peripatetics.—WRIGHT, THOMAS, 1846, *Biographia Britannica Literaria*, *pp.* 230, 235.

The style of John of Salisbury, far from being equal to that of Augustin, Eutropius, and a few more of those early ages, does not appear to me by any means elegant. Sometimes he falls upon a good expression; but the general tone is not very classical.—HALLAM, HENRY, 1837-39, *Introduction to the Literature of Europe, pt.* i, *ch.* i, *pr.* 83.

He wrote Latin verses with extreme elegance.—CRAIK, GEORGE L., 1861, *A Compendious History of English Literature and of the English Language, vol.* I, *p.* 82.

In John of Salisbury, a disciple of Anselm, we have one of the most enthusiastic students of the great classic authors of antiquity, and he is placed by Eichhorn and Heeren at the head of his contemporaries.—ANGUS, JOSEPH, 1865, *The Handbook of English Literature, p.* 77.

Living in the twelfth century, a man of scholarly tastes, he devotes himself, by preference, to the study of so much as was then known of the classic literature of antiquity, Cicero being his favorite author. The influence of these studies on his own Latin style was such that he has received frequent and high praise for his elegant diction. An earnest churchman and sincere believer, he is yet, as a practical Englishman, more concerned with the external political relations of the church than with those subtle and, in his view, comparatively nugatory discussions regarding questions of doctrine, of faith and philosophy, which were going on in the church's schools.—MORRIS, GEORGE S., 1880, *British Thought and Thinkers, p.* 36.

He represents the humanist or literary spirit, so different from the subtle inquiries and logical refinements of the schoolmen of his time.—FISHER, GEORGE PARK, 1887, *History of the Christian Church, p.* 215.

Robert Wace

C. 1124–1184

Wace, or Eustace, who has been christened Robert on mistaken authority, was born at Jersey, probably about the year 1124, was taught at Caen, and was in after life resident in Normandy. For a long time he was at Caen, where he was a *clerc lisant,* reading clerk or teacher. He employed himself with writing in romance rhymes, for the people, of St. Nicolas and other saints and martyrs; afterwards King Henry II. gave him a prebend at Bayeux. . . . His translation of Geoffrey of Monmouth into French verse as "Li Romans de Brut" was completed in the year 1155, immediately after the accession of Henry II., and presented to Queen Eleanor His other great poem, the Romance of Rou or Rollo, giving the story of the Norman Conquest—the "Roman de Rou"—was produced by him some years later.—MORLEY, HENRY, 1888, *English Writers, vol.* III, *pp.* 55, 56.

Neither the poetical form adopted by Wace, ["Roman de Rou"] or the designation of *Roman,* given to his work, can be fairly held in any degree to invalidate the claims of this production to be looked upon as a true account of the events which it records. Wace wrote at the period when the desire for more accessible sources of information, than those afforded by the Monkish Chroniclers, began to be felt, but while the habit of listening to the Troubadour was still prevalent. His work is then to be considered as a remarkable monument;—marking as it does a period of *literary transition;*— produced by a Clerk or Churchman, but in the vulgar tongue, and, in reality, a tribute or concession to the growing spirit of inquiry of his age.—MALET, SIR ALEXANDER, 1860, *The Conquest of England, from Wace's Poem of the Roman de Rou, Introduction, p.* x.

The name of Wace I can never utter without thankfulness, as that of one who has preserved to us the most minute, and, as I fully believe, next to the contemporary stitchwork, the most trustworthy narrative of the central scene of my history.—FREEMAN, EDWARD A., 1876, *The History of the Norman Conquest of England, vol.* V, *p.* 581.

Wace's poem is indeed no more than a metrical expansión of the "History" of Geoffrey of Monmouth; but the touches which he has added, recording the institution by Arthur of the Round Table, and of feasts and tourneys, introduce into the growing myth the first glimpse of the spirit of chivalry. He is, however, far from yielding to the wild and romantic impulse of Celtic superstition, and, whether from the scepticism of the scholar, or from a certain Northern robustness of mind, he seeks to test the marvels reported to him by the experience of his senses.—COURTHOPE, W. J., 1895, *A History of English Poetry, vol.* I, *p.* 114.

Wace is no "romance-writer" in the modern sense. He indulges in no rhetorical embellishments; in the historical parts of his greatest work he refuses to set down anything for which he has not authority; and when his authorities differ, he frequently gives two alternative versions. He is less credulous than many of his contemporaries, and he is transparently honest. In intention, as well as in fact, he is always an historian first and a poet afterwards.—NORGATE, KATE, 1899, *Dictionary of National Biography, vol.* LVIII, *p.* 404.

Walter Map

C. 1140—1210?

Archdeacon and poet; born in England, probably in Herefordshire, about the middle of the twelfth century; studied in Paris; became a noted theologian; a favorite of Henry II., by whom he was sent on missions to the French and papal courts; was canon of St. Paul and of Salisbury, precentor of Lincoln, incumbent of Westbury, Gloucestershire, and Archdeacon of Oxford (1196). Died about 1210. He wrote many Norman-French and Latin poems on festive and romantic topics, as also in prose in both languages, but the authenticity of the poems now attributed to him has been seriously questioned. The "Latin Poems commonly attributed to Walter Mapes" were edited by Thomas Wright for the Camden Society in 1841, and the prose work "De Nugis Curialium," in 1850.—BEERS, HENRY A., *rev.* 1897, *Johnson's Universal Cyclopædia, vol.* V, *p.* 535.

The Anacreon of the eleventh century. —LYTTELTON, GEORGE LORD, 1768, *Notes to the Second Book of the Life of King Henry II, p.* 152.

Two writers, neither of them undistinguished, and one of them, if we may trust the impression made on his contemporaries, *the* man of his century—I mean Lawrence, Prior of Durham, and Walter Mapes, Archdeacon of Oxford—have left us numerous specimens of this "sibilant" versification. In their songs we find not only specimens of our psalm-staves, but also other specimens of mixed rhime fully as complicated, and apparently as anomalous, as any that was used by the Troubadour. The hymns of the poetical Prior are for the most part in MS. They are much inferior to the jovial songs and biting satires of the Archdeacon. The latter, indeed, manages both rhythm and rhime with admirable skill; his numbers seem almost to reel beneath his merriment and sarcasm.—GUEST, EDWIN, 1838, *A History of English Rhythms, vol.* II, *p.* 422.

He was evidently a man, not only of much learning and extensive reading, but of great taste for lighter literature. His mind appears to have been stored with legends and anecdotes, and he was universally admired for his ready wit and humour. He speaks of himself as enjoying the reputation of a poet, but he gives us no clue to the character of the compositions by which he had entitled himself to this name. His Latin is very unequal; but we are perhaps not entirely competent to pronounce judgment in this respect, as the text in the unique manuscript of his prose Latin work which has come down to us is extremely corrupt. His style is in general not pure; he often becomes wearisome by his attempts at embellishment, and his writings are too much interspersed with puns and jests. His knowledge of the world was evidently extensive, and his observations on men and politics are judicious and acute. He sometimes rises above the prejudices of his age.—WRIGHT, THOMAS, 1846, *Biographia Britannica Literaria, vol.* II, *p.* 298.

Who after all is not to be despised, for though no remarkable poet, he was a stout satirist, and the school of verse which he founded valuably illustrates the popular movements in England during the twelfth and thirteenth centuries.—BRISTED, C. A., 1851, *The "Walter Mapes"*

Poems, Knickerbocker Magazine, vol. 37, *p.* 292.

There is a want of artistic finish about Anglo-Norman poetry; but the main conception of the "Quest of the Sangréal," and the chief traits of the story, entitle its author, Walter de Mapes, to the rank of an epic poet. Had those romances ever been remodeled by a Dante, instead of a Malory, the world would have judged the middle ages more truly.—PEARSON, CHARLES H., 1867, *History of England During the Early and Middle Ages, vol.* I, *p.* 608.

Walter was one of two remarkable men who stand before us as the representatives of a sudden outburst of literary, social, and religious criticism which followed the growth of romance and the appearance of a freer historical tone in the court of the two Henries. . . . He only rose to his fullest strength when he turned from the fields of romance to that of Church reform, and embodied the ecclesiastical abuses of his day in the figure of his "Bishop Goliath."—GREEN, JOHN RICHARD, 1874, *A Short History of the English People, ch.* iii, *sc.* i.

Walter Map was no trivial jester, although the misreading of a piece of his most scathing satire has attached to him the cant name of "the jovial Archdeacon." Undoubtedly he had a lively wit, could make even an abbot blush, and send table companions out of doors to explode in laughter at his broad contemptuous jest against a blasphemous hypocrisy. He was a wit somewhat of Chaucer's pattern, ready against cowled hypocrites, and striking, as Chaucer often did, after the manner of his time, with a coarse jest out of the strength of a clean heart. It was the wit also of a true poet. Among the high dignitaries of the Roman Church he was an entirely orthodox divine, and looked down from the heights of theological scholarship upon what seemed to him the ignorant piety of the Waldenses. But the first Church reform concerned Church morals more nearly than theology, and in this sense, by his Latin verse and prose, Walter Map represents the chief of the Reformers before Wyclif. In French, then the vernacular tongue of English literature, he it was who gave a soul to the Arthurian romances, writing, most probably, the Latin original of Robert Borron's introductory romance of the Saint Graal, and certainly Lancelot of the Lake, the Quest of the Saint Graal, and the Mort Artus. Unassuming as Chaucer, and, before Chaucer, the man of highest genius in our literature, Map was a frank man of the world with ready sympathies, a winning courtesy, warm friendships, and well-planted hatreds.—MORLEY, HENRY, 1888, *English Writers, vol.* III, *p.* 120.

In the first place, he was an essayist; the "De Nugis Curialium" is not primarily an historical document, but a collection of the essays and miscellaneous papers. . . . The papers often consist of a mere paragraph containing an anecdote or squib, not what we should be justified in calling an essay; but it is the air of immediate contact with the reader which distinguishes the essayist, though it may take other matters to furnish forth the essay, and on the other hand many of Map's subjects are all that a Lamb or Leigh Hunt would require. The essay in Map's time had no precedents, and consequently no recognized literary form; but all the essential qualities of it are found in the "De Nugis Curialium," and Map will be better understood under this name and view of him than any other.—COLTON, ARTHUR W., 1893, *The First English Essayist: Walter Map, Poet-Lore, vol.* 5, *p.* 538.

Walter Map's undoubted literary remains are scarcely commensurate with the reputation which he has almost continuously enjoyed.—KINGSFORD, C. L., 1893, *Dictionary of National Biography, vol.* XXXVI, *p.* 110.

This Welshman has the vivacity of the Celts his compatriots; he was celebrated at the court of Henry II., and throughout England for his repartees and witticisms, so celebrated indeed that he himself came to agree to others' opinion, and thought them worth collecting. He thus formed a very bizarre book, without beginning or end, in which he noted, day by day, all the curious things he had heard—"ego verbum audivi"—and with greater abundance those he had said, including a great many puns. Thus it happens that certain chapters of his "De Nugis Curialium," a title that the work owes to the success of John of Salisbury's, are real novels, and have the smartness of such; others are real fabliaux, with all their coarseness; others are scenes of comedy, with dialogues, and indications of characters as in a play; others again are anecdotes of the East, "quoddam mirabile," told on their return by pilgrims or crusaders.—JUSSERAND, J. J., 1895, *A Literary History of the English People, p.* 190.

Roger de Hoveden

Fl., C. 1200

Lived in the last half of the 12th century naving probably been born in Howden in Yorkshire. His Latin Chronicle ends with the year 1201. He was a member of the royal household of Henry II. His Chronicle was first printed in 1596. It was edited by Stubbs for the Rolls Series (1868-71) and translated by Riley (1853).—MOULTON, CHARLES WELLS, 1900.

If we consider his diligence, his knowledge of antiquity, and his religious strictness of veracity, he may be considered as having surpassed not only the rude historians of the preceding ages, but even what could have been expected of himself. If to that fidelity, which is the first quality of a historian, he had joined a little more elegance of Latin style, he might have stood the first among the authors of that class.—LELAND, JOHN, 1542? *Works, Allibone's Dictionary, vol.* I, *p.* 898.

He is the chiefest (if not sole) Lay-Historian of his age; who, being neither Priest nor Monk, wrote a "Chronicle of England," beginning where Bede ended, and continuing the same until the fourth of King John. When King Edward the First layed claim to the Crown of Scotland, he caused the "Chronicles" of this Roger to be diligently searched, and carefully kept many authentical passages therein tending to his present advantage. —FULLER, THOMAS, 1662, *The Worthies of England, ed., Nichols, vol.* II, *p.* 513.

His most meritorious work was, his annals of England, from A. D. 731, when Bede's ecclesiastical history ends, to A. D. 1202. This work, which is one of the most voluminous of our ancient histories, is more valuable for the sincerity with which it is written and the great variety of facts which it contains, than for the beauty of its style, or the regularity of its arrangement.—HENRY, ROBERT, 1771-90, *The History of Great Britain, vol.* VI, *p.* 141.

On many accounts one of the most valuable historical writers of this age.—WRIGHT, THOMAS, 1846, *Biographia Britannica Literaria, vol.* II, *p.* 410.

Hoveden is of all our old chroniclers the most of a matter-of-fact man; he indulges occasionally in an epithet, rarely or never in a reflection, his one notion of writing history seems to be to pack as many particulars as possible into a given space, giving one the notion in perusing his close array of dates and items that he had felt continually pressed by the necessity of economizing his paper or parchment. It is true that he has no notion of the higher economy of discrimination and selection; but among the multitude of facts of all kinds that crowd his pages are many that are really curious and illustrative.—CRAIK, GEORGE L., 1861, *A Compendious History of English Literature and of the English Language, vol.* I, *p.* 109.

Roger of Hoveden's Chronicle was based first upon a compilation made probably at Durham between the years of 1148 and 1161, and known as the "Historia Saxonum vel Anglorum post obitum Bedæ." This chronicle was compiled from the histories of Simeon of Durham and Henry of Huntingdon. Roger of Hoveden added to this an account of the miracles of Edward the Confessor; an abstract of a charter of William the Conqueror, granting Heminburgh and Brackenholm to Durham; a copy of a charter by which Thomas I., archbishop of York, released Durham churches in his diocese from customary payments to the Archbishop; a list in French of warriors at the siege of Nice; and about eight other additions. The part of Hoveden's Chronicle which extends from 1148 to 1170 is not founded upon any written authority except the chronicle of Melrose. . . . The Melrose Chronicle was based upon Simeon of Durham until the year 1121, and was then continued until 1169 with contemporary record. Between 1163 and 1169 Roger of Hoveden draws largely from the lives of Becket in the record of his quarrel with the king. . . . From 1169 to the spring of 1192 Roger of Hoveden's Chronicle embodies, with occasional divergence, and addition of documents, chiefly northern, that of Benedict of Peterborough; and from 1192 to 1201, at which date the chronicle ends, the addition of documents especially relating to the north of England becomes a marked feature of the work. This is the part of the chronicle in which Roger of Hoveden is historian of his own time, and his work is of the highest value. The reputation of the chronicle was in its own time so good that Edward I. is said to have caused diligent search to be made for copies of it in the year 1291, in order that on its evidence he might adjust the disputes as to homage due to him from the Crown of Scotland.—MORLEY, HENRY, 1888, *English Writers, vol.* III, *pp.* 193, 194.

Layamon

Fl., C. 1200

Layamon: poet; a priest at Arley Regis on the Severn, Worcestershire, England; wrote about 1200 the "Brut," a rhyming chronicle of English history from the time of the fabulus Brutus of Troy to the death of King Cadwallader (689 A. D.). His work is an amplified translation of the "Brut d' Angleterre" of the Anglo-Norman poet Wace, the additions being derived chiefly from the writings of Bede and St. Augustine of Canterbury, while Wace's work is itself little more than a translation of Geoffrey of Monmouth's Latin "Historia Brittonum." The value of Layamon's chronicle is mainly philological. It contains 32,250 lines, some alliterative, but more imitating the imperfect rhyme of its Anglo-Norman original. The best edition is that of Sir Frederic Madden, with a literal translation, notes, and a grammatical glossary, published by the English Society of Antiquaries (3 vols., 1847).—BEERS, HENRY A., *rev.* 1897, *Johnson's Universal Cyclopædia, vol.* V, *p.* 144.

Layamon's versification also is no less remarkable than his language. Sometimes he seems anxious to imitate the rhymes, and to adopt the regular number of syllables which he had observed in his original; at other times he disregards both; either because he did not consider the laws of metre, or the consonance of final sounds, as essential to the gratification of his readers, or because he was unable to adopt them throughout so long a work, from the want of models in his native language on which to form his style. The latter is, perhaps, the most probable supposition; but, at all events, it is apparent that the recurrence of his rhymes is much too frequent to be the result of chance; so that, upon the whole, it seems reasonable to infer that Layamon's work was composed at or very near the period when the Saxons and Normans in this country began to unite into one nation, and to adopt a common language. —ELLIS, GEORGE, 1790-1845, *Specimens of the Early English Poets, vol.* I, *p.* 60.

No work shews more satisfactorily than his "Chronicle," the benefits which English poetry and literature have derived from the Anglo-Norman. In this composition we see a poem substantially Anglo-Saxon, but with none of that peculiar style of Anglo-Saxon mind and phrase which were its pervading characteristics; it is the simple style of the Anglo-Norman poetry transferred into the Anglo-Saxon: Hence, it presents to us the first state of our vernacular English poetry, divested of the inversions, transitions, obscurities, and metaphors of the Anglo-Saxon school, and approaching that form of easy and natural phrase which has been the nurse of our truest poetry and cultivated intellect.—TURNER, SHARON, 1814-23, *The History of England During the Middle Ages, vol.* V, *p.* 212.

It is a remarkable circumstance, that we find preserved in many passages of Layamon's poem the spirit and style of the earlier Anglo-Saxon writers. No one can read his descriptions of battles and scenes of strife, without being reminded of the Ode on Æthelstans victory at Brunanburh. The ancient mythological genders of the sun and moon are still unchanged; the memory of the *witenagemot* has not yet become extinct, and the neigh of the *hængest* still seems to resound in our ears. Very many phrases are purely Anglo-Saxon, and with slight change, might have been used in Cædmon or Ælfric. A foreign scholar and poet, versed both in Anglo-Saxon and Scandinavian literature, has declared, that tolerably well read as he is in the rhyming chronicles of his own country and of others, he has found Layamons beyond comparison the most lofty and animated in its style, at every moment reminding the reader of the splendid phraseology of Anglo-Saxon verse. It may also be added, that the colloquial character of much of the work renders it peculiarly valuable as a monument of language, since it serves to convey to us, in all probability, the current speech of the writers time as it passed from mouth to mouth.—MADDEN, SIR FREDERIC, 1847, *ed. Layamon's Brut, Preface, vol.* I, *p.* xxiii.

His poem has more spirit and fire, in the Scandinavian and Anglo-Saxon style than had been supposed. Upon the whole, Layamon must be reckoned far more of the older than the newer formation: he is an *eocene,* or at most a *miocene*; while his contemporaries, as they seem to be, belong philologically to a later period.—HALLAM, HENRY, 1847, *Introduction to the Literature of Europe, pt.* i, *ch.* i, *par.* 50, *note.*

Here is evidently a considerable amount of true poetic life in the conception, and also, as far as the apparent rudeness of the language will admit,—if we ought not perhaps rather to say as far as the imperfect knowledge of its laws now attainable enables us to form a judgment,—considerable care and aptness of expression.—CRAIK, GEORGE L., 1861, *A Compendious History of English Literature and of the English Language, vol.* I, *p.* 209.

He seldom conforms closely to the text of Wace, and his comparative elevation of diction, of thought, and of imagery, entitles his work to a higher rank than that of his original, and stamps it as a production of some literary merit. . .

His merits as a translator seem to be greater than his power as an original writer.—MARSH, GEORGE P., 1862, *The Origin and History of the English Language, etc., pp.* 155, 158.

Sometimes happens to rhyme, sometimes fails, altogether barbarous and childish, unable to develop a continuous idea, babbling in little confused and incomplete phrases, after the fashion of the ancient Saxon.—TAINE, H. A., 1871, *History of English Literature, tr. Van Laun, vol.* I, *p.* 76.

As one man from the banks of the Severn, born of a foreign father, living in a foreign land, writing in a foreign tongue, never lost his English heart, his love for England and her history, so it was another man by the banks of the Severn who first taught the English tongue to bear witness against itself, who degraded it to become the channel of those wretched fables which in the minds of so many Englishmen have displaced alike the true history and the worthier legends of our fathers. The opposite to Orderic of Ettingsham is Layamon of Ernley. He had read the English book of Bæda and the Latin book of Austin, but he turned from them to the book that a French clerk made that was hight Wace. Wace truly well could write; we blame not him for writing, nor do we blame the noble Eleanor, that was Henry's Queen the high King's, for hearkening to what he wrote. It was something that the Duchess of Aquitaine and the Canon of Bayeux should seek to know something of the past days of the conquered island; and, if ill luck threw the monstrous fables of Geoffrey in their way, the blame was his and not theirs. It was no crime in Wace to write a Brut in French; it was treason against the tongue and history of his race for Layamon to translate that Brut into English.—FREEMAN, EDWARD A., 1876, *The History of the Norman Conquest of England, vol.* V, *p.* 590.

Of all English poets after the Conquest, none approached the Old English epos so closely as he, and hardly any metrical chronicle of the Middle Ages can rival Layamon's "Brut" in poetical worth. The merits of his style appear most brilliantly in the portrayal of battle and strife, and of the combat with the surging sea. Though his diction has none of the copiousness of the ancient epic language, yet in comparison with later times, it must be termed rich, and most graphic and effective. It is highly imaginative, but contains few detailed similes. . . .

A most significant figure, Layamon stands upon the dividing line between two great periods, which he unites in a singular manner. He once more reproduces for us an age that is forever past. At the same time he is the first English poet to draw from French sources, the first to sing of King Arthur in English verse.—TEN BRINK, BERNHARD, 1877-83, *History of English Literature (To Wiclif), tr. Kennedy, pp.* 192, 193.

The "preost Layamon ihoten" makes no inconsiderable additions to the matter embodied by the authorities whom he professes to follow; and his additions are by far the ablest and most spirited portions of his work.—GILMORE, J. H., 1878, *The English Language and its Early Literature, p.* 94.

Layamon is filled full of illustrations of the shall-and-will idiom. There is hardly a score of lines in which the distinction is not made.—WHITE, RICHARD GRANT, 1880, *Every-Day English, p.* 354, *note.*

Layamon was a modest, pious English priest, who loved his country, and enjoyed traditions of its ancient time. Having the true fine natural spirit of a poet and a scholar, he was among the many in almost every part of Europe who had their imagination kindled by Geoffrey of Monmouth's patriotic fictions. He had discoursed much and pleasantly with his neighbours, for his mind was stored with the oral tradition only to be gathered in familiar social talk; and when he translated Wace's "Brut" he added not only fresh legends of his own gathering, but new touches to the old. . . . From his work, then, we have a right to infer that this earliest poet in our modern tongue was a devout, gentle, an affectionate parish priest, who loved his home and his country, and was friend as well as spiritual counsellor to the small flock of rustic parishioners, whose boys he taught and whose good will satisfied all but his intellectual wants. — MORLEY, HENRY, 1888, *English Writers, vol.* III, *p.* 229.

That monumental testimony to the self-sustaining vigour of our English tongue which, written nearly a century and a half after the Conquest, contains in thirty thousand lines but some fifty words of the Conqueror's language. — TRAIL, H. D., 1894, *Social England, Introduction, vol.* I, *p.* xxxviii.

Layamon, who was stirred thus deeply by the genius of the ancient Saxon poetry, naturally sought to mould his matter in the traditional forms of song. But his metrical style remains a striking monument of the inward changes wrought in the language since it had passed from the lips of the singer to the pen of the literary composer. It was not only that terminations had been assimilated, genders confused, inflections dropped, the weak ending of the preterite tense substituted for the internal change of the vowel: the whole character of the metrical sentence had been altered by the introduction of the article, by the frequent use of conjunctions, and by the constant association of the preposition "to" with the infinitive mood. The abrupt, energetic effects of the ancient recitation were modified to suit the literary style of the historian, and the rhythmical period was broken up by the insertion of numerous wedges, in the shape of small auxiliary words, which pointed the logic of the thought, while they destroyed the compactness of the syntax. In a measure distinctively Teutonic the influence of French verse is of course scarcely perceptible; Layamon's vocabulary contains scarcely more foreign elements than Ormin's. The laws of alliteration, however, are not strictly observed; in many verses the dominant letter is capriciously distributed; in others it is altogether absent; and the alliterative couplet is often replaced by a rhyming one. Compared with "Beowulf," the metrical structure of the "Brut" resembles those debased forms of architecture in which the leading external features are reproduced long after the reason for their invention has been forgotten.—COURTHOPE, W. J., 1895, *A History of English Poetry, vol.* I, *p.* 127.

His alliterative poem—in which now and then a stammer of rhyme is heard—belongs to the threshold of the thirteenth century, and stands at the head of English literature: its author has been called the English Ennius. A qualification is necessary, however; Layamon wrote in a dialect, in the speech of the south of England—one of the three dialects among which English writings are to be divided for the next hundred and fifty years. His language is difficult, no doubt; special preparation is required to understand it, and a glossary must be constantly consulted; but it is not like learning a foreign tongue,—two or three hours of study a day for three or four days would make one master of the grammatical difficulties that stand in the way of one's enjoyment of the poem.—WHITE, GREENOUGH, 1895, *Outline of the Philosophy of English Literature, The Middle Ages, p.* 24.

As Geoffrey fell into the hands of Wace, so did Wace fall into those of Layamon; but here the result is far more interesting, both for the history of the legend itself and for its connection with England. Not only did the priest of Ernley or Arley-on-Severn do the English tongue the inestimable service of introducing Arthur to it, not only did he write the most important book by far, both in size, in form, and in matter, that was written in English between the Conquest and the fourteenth century, but he added immensely to the actual legend.—SAINTSBURY, GEORGE, 1897, *The Flourishing of Romance and the Rise of Allegory, p.* 98.

Giraldus Cambrensis

Girald de Barry

C. 1147–1220

Ecclesiastic and author; of Norman descent on his father's side; born about 1147, at the castle of Manorbeer, near Pembroke, in South Wales. The last seventeen years of his life were spent in studious retirement. He spent about eight years in the University of Paris—four years from 1168 to 1172, and another four years from 1176 to 1180. He was made Archdeacon of Brecknock in 1172. He was a restless, ambitious ecclesiastic, refusing in 1190 the bishopric of Bangor and in 1191 the bishopric of Llandaff in the hope of being made Bishop of St. David's. Died in St. David's, after 1216, perhaps in 1220. He was a witty, brilliant, but egotistical writer. His most famous books, both written in Latin, are the "Topography of Ireland" (1188) and the "Itinerary through Wales" (1191). His complete works, edited by Brewer and Dimock, were published, under the direction of the master of the rolls, in seven volumes (London 1861-1877.)—JACKSON, SAMUEL MACAULEY, *rev.*, 1897, *Johnson's Universal Cyclopædia, vol.* III, *p.* 789.

That Girald of Wales was a man of uncommon activity, genius, and learning, is undeniable; but these and his other good qualities were much tarnished by his insufferable vanity, which must have been very offensive to his contemporaries, as it is highly disgusting to his readers.—HENRY, ROBERT, 1771-90, *The History of Great Britain, vol.* VI, *p.* 154.

Noble in his birth, and comely in his person; mild in his manners, and affable in his conversation; zealous, active, and undaunted in maintaining the rights and dignities of his church; moral in his character, and orthodox in his principles; charitable and disinterested, though ambitious; learned, though superstitious; such was Giraldus. And, in whatever point of view we examine the character of this extraordinary man, whether as a scholar, a patriot, or a divine, we may justly consider him as one of the brightest luminaries that adorned the annals of the twelfth century.—HOARE, SIR RICHARD COLT, 1806, *ed. The Itinerary of Archbishop Baldwin Through Wales.*

The works of Giraldus Cambrensis are numerous, and they are all interesting for the light they throw on the historical events and on the political and religious condition of the age in which he lived. They are not the meditations of the solitary student, or the controversial disquisitions of the theologian; but they reflect faithfully the thoughts and opinions of a man busy in all the intrigues and convulsions of the world around him, and are filled with minute and private anecdotes and stories of the people among whom he lived and with whom he acted. His style, though less ostentatiously learned than that of Peter of Blois, is that of a scholar and a man of extensive reading. His descriptions are generally marked by a clearness of narrative and a distinctness of conception which are not often found among the medieval writers; and, when he dwells on his own wrongs, or enters upon his own enmities, his style is distinguished by a warmth of eloquence which is peculiar to him.—WRIGHT, THOMAS, 1846, *Biographia Britannica Literaria, vol.* II, *p.* 389.

Tall, stalwart, bushy-browed Gerald the Welshman, called also Silvester (the Savage)—which was but an English word for Welshman in his day—represented in the twelfth century the church militant in Wales. A man ready at the worst season to cross Alps, or defy archbishops, if not kings, in the pursuit of his idea, he really lives in his writings. They are yet warm with his own natural heat. The strong flavour of his personality in all he writes, and his Welsh blood, give often to his manner an excess of boastfulness, and there is some Welsh pedantry, perhaps, but it is not the vanity of a weak self-contemplation that mingles with Gerald's flow of social anecdote and hearty comment on affairs of men, while jest and pun and practical home-thrusting humanise his use of his book-knowledge. He planned his narratives upon no model, good or bad, but spoke his mind with vivid earnestness, with strength and fearless truth that was the more genuine for its impetuosity. His sketches of his own career ("De Rebus a se Gestis") and his letters are alive with action and the soul of action in the mind and temper that beget the stir which they describe. His personal account of Ireland, to be found in Camden's "British Writers," is no dry antique itinerary, but a series of vigorous and graphic sketches both of men and things, unequalled in Gerald's own time for its spirit and truth; as a picture of Ireland, remaining without equal till the time of Spenser.—MORLEY, HENRY, 1888, *English Writers, vol.* III, *p.* 64.

Michael Scott

1180?-1235

The "wondrous wizard," was tutor and astrologer at Palermo to Frederick II., settled at Toledo 1209-20, and translated Arabic versions of Aristotle's works and Averrhoes' commentaries, returned to the Imperial Court at Palermo, and refused the proffered archbishopric of Cashel (1223.) His translation of Aristotle was seemingly used by Albertus Magnus, and was one of the two familiar to Dante. . . . Dempster (1627) may be right in maintaining that "Scotus" was the name of his nation, not of his family, in which case he would be probably an Irishman; but by Boece (1527) he was falsely identified with a Sir Michael Scott of Balwearie in Fife, who went on embassies to Norway in 1290 to 1310. Camden (1580) asserts that he was a Cistercian monk of Holme Cultram in Cumberland; and Satchells that in 1629 he had examined at Burgh-under-Bowness a huge tome held to be his *grimoire*.—PATRICK AND GROOME, *eds.* 1897, *Chambers's Biographical Dictionary, p.* 836.

That other one who is so spare about the loins, was Michael Scott, who verily knew the trick of the impostures of magic. —DANTE, ALIGHIERI, 1300-1318, *Inferno, Canto* XX.

"You must know then, my dear master," quoth he, "that there was lately a necromancer in this city called Mr. Michael Scotus, because he was a Scotchman, who had great honour shown him by many of the gentry, few of whom are now living; and he, being about to quit this place, at their request left it in charge with two of his disciples, that they should always be ready to serve those people who had honoured him."—BOCCACCIO, GIOVANNI, 1358, *Decameron, Eighth Day, Novel* ix.

In our endeavours to estimate the talents of a sage of the thirteenth century, we must beware of looking at his attainments through the medium of our own times. He must be compared with men of his own age; his powers must be determined by the state of science in the countries where he lived, and wrote, and became celebrated. Appealing to such a criterion, the Scottish Wizard is entitled to no ordinary rank amongst those who were then esteemed the philosophers and scholars of Europe. He was certainly the first who gave Aristotle in a Latin translation to the learned world of the West. He was eminent as a mathematician and an astronomer—learned in the languages of modern Europe—deeply skilled in Arabic, and in the sciences of the East; he had risen to high celebrity as a physician —and his knowledge of courts and kings, had recommended him to be employed in a diplomatic capacity by his own government. Nor has he been cheated of his fame. If we look to older authors, he lives in the pages of Roger Bacon, of Picus Mirandula, of Cornelius Agrippa. If we ask for his historical immortality, he is commemorated by Lesley and Buchanan,—if for his poetic honours, has not Dante snatched him from oblivion, and the last of the minstrels embalmed him in the imperishable substance of his first and most romantic poem?—nay, if he seeks for more popular and wider honour, even here he may not complain, whilst his miracles and incantations are yet recorded beside the cottage fire by many a grey-headed crone, and his fearful name still banishes the roses from the cheeks of the little audience that surround her. —TYTLER, PATRICK FRASER, 1831, *Lives of Scottish Worthies, vol.* I, *p.* 127.

The extant writings of Scot are universally admitted to give him no claim to remembrance, comparable in any degree with that which belongs to his contemporary, Roger Bacon.—SPALDING, WILLIAM, 1852-82, *A History of English Literature, p.* 92.

From Malcolm Ceannmor to Alexander III. not a solitary poet or scholar appears to break the monotonous sterility of two hundred years. Michael Scot, an apparent exception, is half a mystery and half a myth, but he was not a product of the Scottish Church, and the works that have been ascribed to him were written in foreign lands.—ROSS, JOHN MERRY, 1884, *Scottish History and Literature, etc., ed. Brown, p.* 42.

He may well therefore have died while on the borders of Scotland. This idea agrees curiously with the fact that Italy has no tradition of his burial-place, while on the other hand northern story points to his tomb in Melrose Abbey, Glenluce, Holme Coltrame, or some other of the great Cistercian foundations of that country. Satchells, who visited Burgh-under-Bowness in 1629, found a guide named Lancelot Scot, who took him to the parish church, where he saw the great scholar's tomb, and found it still the object of mysterious awe to the people there. The resting-place of Michael Scot will never now be accurately known, but there is every reason to suppose that it lies not far from that of his birth, in the sweet Borderland, amid the green hills and flowing streams of immemorial story.—BROWN, REV. J. WOOD, 1896, *An Enquiry into the Life and Legend of Michael Scot, p.* 176.

Richard Poor

?-1237

"Ancren Riwle"

Richard Poor, also Poore, Poure, and de Poor, bishop of Chichester, 1214, bishop of Salisbury, 1217, and bishop of Dunham, 1228, was born in twelfth century, and died 1237. He was a rich and influential churchman. Removed the See of Salisbury to New Sarum, and erected the present cathedral. Bishop Poor's position in English literature is given to him through his supposed authorship of the "Ancren Riwle." The work was printed for the Camden Society, in 1853.—MOULTON, CHARLES WELLS, 1900.

The title, "Ancren Riwle," means "Anchoresses' Rule,"—*Ancren* being the abbreviated form of the old genitive "Ancrena," and *Riwle* being the old spelling for "Rule." The "Ancren Riwle" is a treatise on the duties of the monastic life, written by an ecclesiastic, apparently one in high authority, for the direction of three ladies, to whom it is addressed, and who, with their domestic servants, or lay sisters, formed the entire community of a religious house.—HART, JOHN S., 1872, *A Manual of English Literature, p.* 30.

Wanley, who, in describing the four different copies of the work, attributes it to Simon of Ghent, had evidently some doubt upon the subject, for upon one occasion he speaks of it as merely supposed ("ut putatur"). No other person is anywhere mentioned as having written it; but there are circumstances which render it not improbable that Bishop Poor was the author, and wrote it for the use of the nuns at the time when he re-established or enlarged the monastery. He was born at Tarente, and evidently took great interest in the place. It was the scene of his exemplary death, and he chose to be buried there. His great learning, his active benevolence, the sanctity of his life, and his tender concern for the spiritual welfare of his friends and dependents, shewn in the pious exhortations which he repeatedly addressed to them immediately before his death, agree well with the lessons of piety and morality so earnestly and affectionately addressed, in this book, to the anchoresses of Tarente.—MORTON, JAMES, 1853, *ed. The Ancren Riwle.*

In a literary point of view, it has no such value as to entitle it to critical notice, and, bearing no stamp of English birth-right but its dialect, it is only for the value of its vocabulary and its syntax that I embrace it in my view of English philological history.—MARSH, GEORGE P., 1862, *The Origin and History of the English Language, etc., p.* 170.

Is one of the most perfect models of simple, natural, eloquent prose in our language; without it indeed, the history of English prose from the close of the Old English period down to the beginning of the seventeenth century would be little more than a dreary blank. As a picture of contemporary life, manners, and feeling it cannot be over-estimated. The passage in which Christ is described as a Norman Knight in homeliest English phrase is alone enough to give a vivid idea of that fusion of English and French traditions and sentiments which—in spite of "Ivanhoe"—was almost completely carried out by the beginning of the thirteenth century. The conclusion of the allegory of Christ's wooing of the soul is, on the other hand, thoroughly Old English in its combined picturesqueness and grandeur. Thoroughly English, too, though in a totally different way, is the humorous description of the troubles of the nun with her cow: how she curses when the cow is impounded, and yet has to pay the damages. Equally good is the description of the chattering nun, and the comparison of her to a cackling hen.—SWEET, HENRY, 1884, *First Middle English Primer, Preface, p.* vi.

After a long period barren of prose, we come to the "Ancren Riwle," 1220. Here we have an alert and cultivated style. The MSS. are divided systematically into books, and these into simple capital-paragraphs. The main fault of this style is the abrupt transition between these paragraphs.—LEWIS, EDWIN HERBERT, 1894, *The History of the English Paragraph, p.* 70.

The strictly devotional parts are animated by a mysticism which is of the kindly order likewise, and the illustrations, parables, and the like are frequently of considerable literary interest, while the style shows at least possibilities of splendour as well as an actual command of ease.—SAINTSBURY, GEORGE, 1898, *A Short History of English Literature, p.* 53.

The keynote of the work is the renunciation of self. Few productions of modern literature contain finer pictures of the Divine love and sympathy. Across the fierce storm clouds of theology, which continued to sweep the heavens for hundreds of years, the pages of the "Ancren Riwle" reflect the rainbow hues of the Galilean's compassion for laboring and heavy-laden humanity.—HALLECK, REUBEN POST, 1900, *History of English Literature, p.* 60.

Ormin

Fl., C. 1200–1240

"The Ormulum"

A series of Homilies, in an imperfect state, composed in metre without alliteration, and, except in very few cases, also without rhyme; the subject of the Homilies being supplied by those portions of the New Testament which were read in the daily service of the Church. Of the personal history of the author no record remains beyond the bare statement contained in the Dedication, in which he informs us that his baptismal name was Ormin, and that he was a Canon Regular of the Order of Saint Augustine. He adds, that at the request of his brother Walter, also an Augustinian Canon, he had composed these Homilies in English for the spiritual improvement of his countrymen.—WHITE, ROBERT MEADOWS, 1852, *ed. The Ormulum, Preface, p.* lxx.

Usually assigned to the same, or nearly the same, age with the Brut of Layamon. It exists only in a single manuscript, which there is some reason for believing to be the author's autograph, now preserved in the Bodleian Library among the books bequeathed by the great scholar Francis Junius, who appears to have purchased it at the Hague in 1659 at the sale of the books of his deceased friend Janus Ulitius, or Vlitius (van Vliet), also an eminent philologist and book-collector. It is a folio volume, consisting of ninety parchment leaves, besides twenty-nine others inserted, upon which the poetry is written in double columns, in a stiff but distinct hand, and without division into verses, so that the work had always been assumed to be in prose till its metrical character was pointed out by Tyrwhitt in his edition of Chaucer's "Canterbury Tales," 1775. Accordingly no mention is made of it by Warton, the first volume of whose History was published in 1774. But it had previously been referred to by Hickes and others; and it has attracted a large share of the attention of all recent investigators of the history of the language.—CRAIK, GEORGE L., 1861, *A Compendious History of English Literature and of the English Language, vol.* I, *p.* 211.

I consider it as the oldest, the purest, and by far the most valuable specimen of our Old English dialect, that time has left us. Layamon seems to have halted between two languages, the written and the spoken. Now he gives us what appears to be the Old English dialect of the West; and, a few sentences further, we find ourselves entangled in all the peculiarities of the Anglo-Saxon. But Ormin used the dialect of his day; and, when he wanted precision or uniformity, he followed out the principles on which that dialect rested. Were we thoroughly masters of his grammar and vocabulary, we might hope to explain many of the difficulties, in which blunders of transcription and a *transitional* state of language have involved the syntax and the prosody of Chaucer.—GUEST, EDWIN, 1838, *A History of English Rhythms, vol.* II, *p.* 186.

The most remarkable general characteristic of the syntax is its regularity, which, in spite of the temptations to licence, common to all modes of versification, is greater than is to be found in any other English composition, except those of modern date. . . . Considered as a poem, the Ormulum has no merit but that of smooth, fluent, and regular versification, and it exhibits none of the characteristic traits of English genius.—MARSH, GEORGE P., 1862, *The Origin and History of the English Language, etc., pp.* 179, 180.

Whatever we say of Layamon, we have no charge to bring against Ormin, who in Layamon's day kept up the succession of our sacred poets in honest English.—FREEMAN, EDWARD A., 1876, *The History of the Norman Conquest of England, vol.* V, *p.* 594.

Reflections, it may be, of a glory long set, serving too well to show that the sceptre has departed from the ancient speech.—METCALFE, FREDERICK, 1880, *The Englishman and the Scandinavian, p.* 195.

First English spelling reformer.—WHITE, RICHARD GRANT, 1880, *Every-Day English, p.* 152.

Of the literary merits of the Ormulum little can be said, for it has none whatever. The author was, in fact, a spelling-reformer and philologist who mistook his vocation. The Old English picturesqueness and power disappears entirely from his verse together with the traditional alliteration, and the only compensation is a dry, practical directness of style and metre which is anything but poetical.—SWEET, HENRY, 1884, *First Middle English Primer, Preface, p.* vii.

Alexander Hales

?-1245

Alexander of Halés or Alès,—hence called Alexander Alesius, from the name of his birthplace, near Glocester. Although early raised to an archdeaconry, he resolved to study at Paris, where he quickly became one of the most famous teachers at the most brilliant epoch of the scholastic philosophy. One of his pupils was St. Bonaventura, but it is not true that he had the honour of teaching St. Thomas and Duns Scotus. He died in Paris in 1245. His great work is "Summa Theologiæ." Aquinas reproduced many of his dicta. He was surnamed in the middle ages, "Infallible Doctor" and "Fountain of Light."—NICHOL, JOHN PRINGLE, 1866, *Imperial Dictionary of Universal Biography, vol.* I, *p.* 97.

As for this our Alexander, as he had the name of that great Conqueror of the World, so was he a grand Captain and Commander in his kind: for, as he did follow Peter Lombard, so he did lead Thomas Aquinas, and all the rest of the Schoole-men. He was the first that wrote a Comment on the Sentences, in a great Volumn, called "The Summe of Divinity," at the instance of Pope Innocent the Fourth, to whom he dedicated the same. For this, and other of his good services to the Church of Rome, he received the splendid Title of *Doctor Irrefragabilis.*—FULLER, THOMAS, 1662, *The Worthies of England, ed. Nichols, vol.* I, *p.* 383.

His life was pure and beautiful, his insight clear, and undimmed by passion. Of some of his works it was said by Gerson, two centuries later, that he had been reading them for thirty years, and yet had scarcely attained to a first taste of their sweets, which always presented to him something fresh and delightful whenever he recurred to them.—GAIRDNER, JAMES, 1879, *Early Chroniclers of Europe, England, p.* 226.

He introduced into the theology of Scholasticism the notion of Fate, which he defined to be the co-operation of all causes directed by a higher law. By this he did not intend to infringe upon the notion of free will, because he reckoned it to be one of the co-operating causes. By Fate, all causes free and natural work together in their proper relations, and the actions of free will are only controlled by the connection in which they stand to other causes. He thought that evil served to contribute to the general perfection of the universe, inasmuch as it displayed in fullest measure the essential excellence of goodness. He taught that man was originally created in a state purely human, and that the Divine likeness was afterwards added, being thus an accidental and not an essential portion of the man, and showing the distinction between a state of nature and a state of grace even in man primæval. Grace was not created in man, but was reserved until by reason he had become fit to receive it. On the subject of the sinner's justification, he taught that no certain knowledge was vouchsafed, because Divine grace did not come within the circle of knowledge, either as to its cause or mode, and a man could only judge of his salvation by the measure of light, peace, and joy he experienced inwardly. The uncertainty arising from this condition he considered would have a helpful effect upon the believer by leading him to greater watchfulness, and by supplying an urgent stimulus to constant progress. He strongly dissented from the view of Augustine and other Church teachers concerning the freedom of man and the operation of Divine grace on the soul, and taught that the measure of grace received by the soul was entirely conditioned by the willingness or otherwise of the soul to receive it.—TOWNSEND, W. J., 1881, *The Great Schoolmen of the Middle Ages, p.* 181.

Alexander's reputation secured for him the honourable titles of "Doctor Irrefragabilis," "Doctor doctorum," "Theologorum monarcha," and the like, but his operose work has only historic value. On no point of general interest does it furnish any hint that was fruitful for after-thinkers, nor was it of much effect as stimulating discussion even in its own age. Roger Bacon sarcastically remarks that the very Franciscans did not concern themselves with it, but allowed the huge manuscript to rot and corrupt.—ADAMSON, R., 1885, *Dictionary of National Biography, vol.* I, *p.* 271.

Robert Grosseteste

C. 1175–1253

Bishop of Lincoln, one of the greatest scholars and most energetic prelates of his age, was born probably about 1175. He studied with great distinction at the universities of Oxford and Paris, and became a teacher at the former. He obtained the patronage of Hugh de Wells, bishop of Lincoln, and after holding several subordinate church appointments, he became bishop of that diocese in 1235. During his episcopate he displayed great earnestness, decision, and courage in the discharge of his ecclesiastical and political duties, maintaining his authority and the liberties of the church alike against Pope and King.—CATES, WILLIAM L. R., *ed.*, 1867, *A Dictionary of General Biography, p.* 454.

The mere list of his own writings occupies three and twenty closely printed quarto pages.—MORLEY, HENRY, AND TYLER, MOSES COIT, 1879, *A Manual of English Literature, p.* 55.

Thus, therefore, departed from the exile of this world, which he had never liked, the holy Robert, the second, bishop of Lincoln, who died at his manor of Buckdon, in the night of St. Denis's day. During his life, he had openly rebuked the pope and the king; had corrected the prelates, and reformed the monks; in him the priests lost a director—clerks an instructor—scholars a supporter—and the people a preacher; he had shown himself a persecutor of the incontinent, a careful examiner of the different scriptures, and a bruiser and despiser of the Romans. He was hospitable and profuse; civil, cheerful, and affable at the table for partaking of bodily nourishment; and at the spiritual table, devout, mournful, and contrite. In the discharge of his pontificial duties, he was attentive, indefatigable, and worthy of veneration.—PARIS, MATTHEW, 1259, *English History, tr. Giles, vol.* III, *p.* 50.

Jehosophat, seeing four hundred Prophets of Baal together, and suspecting they were too many to be good, cast in that shrewd question; "Is there not here a Prophet of the Lord besides?" and thereupon Micaiah was mentioned unto him. Possibly the Reader, seeing such swarms of Popish Saints in England, will demand, "Is there not yet a Saint of the Lord besides?" And I conceive myself concerned to return a true answer, that there is Robert Grosseteste by name.—FULLER, THOMAS, 1662, *The Worthies of England, ed. Nichols, vol.* II, *p.* 328.

Were I to speak of such works of this prelate as I have seen, I should say that, though they, certainly, announce talents and reading, they are destitute of elegance, and evince no acquaintance with classical authorities. But still, when compared with those of Friar Bacon, who seems to have utterly disregarded all embellishments of style, they may be deemed entitled to some encomium in point of scholarship.—BERINGTON, JOSEPH, 1814, *Literary History of the Middle Ages, p.* 379.

He was a Churchman of the highest hierarchical notions. Becket himself did not assert the immunities and privileges of the Church with greater intrepidity: rebellion against the clergy was as the sin of witchcraft; but those immunities, those privileges, implied heavier responsibility; that authority, belonged justly only to a holy, exemplary, unworldly clergy. Everywhere he was encountered with sullen, stubborn, or open resistance. He was condemned as restless, harsh, passionate: he was the Ishmael of the hierarchy, with his hand against every man, every man's hand against him.—MILMAN, HENRY HART, 1855, *History of Latin Christianity, vol.* IV, *bk.* ix, *ch.* xv, *p.* 469.

Probably no one has had greater influence upon English thought and English literature for the two centuries which followed his age.—LUARD, HENRY RICHARD, 1861, *Roberti Grosseteste Epistolæ, (Rolls Series) Preface.*

In his episcopal office, Grossetête displayed an indefatigable activity, with an earnest and somewhat intolerant zeal for the reformation of his own flock and of the church at large. In him the new orders found a hearty patron; he employed them in his vast diocese, as instruments for reaching those classes which were neglected by the secular clergy; and in the university of Oxford, of which he was chancellor, his favour encouraged them as teachers. Yet the especial principle of these orders was not unreservedly approved by him; for we are told that, after having cried up mendicancy as the highest step of the ladder which leads to heaven, he added privately that there is one step yet higher—namely, to live by the labour of one's own hands. And it is said that in his last days he strongly reprobated the change by which the friars, instead of being censors of the great, had become their flatterers.—ROBERTSON, JAMES CRAIGIE, 1866–75, *History of the Christian Church, vol.* VI, *bk.* vii, *ch.* ii, *p.* 204.

There were few souls high enough fully to appreciate and love him; he was looked upon as an Ishmael, whose hand was against every man, and every man's hand was against him. Still, the beautiful legends told of what happened at his death, and the miracles said to have been performed at his shrine, show that the classes in which his friends the friars had most influence revered him as a saint.—PROTHERO, GEORGE WALTER, 1877, *The Life and Times of Simon de Montfort*, p. 143.

As Protestants, we have both a right and a duty to hold in honour the memory of a man like Grossetête. His creed, indeed, was not the pure confession of the Evangelical Churches; but his fear of God was so earnest and upright; his zeal for the glory of God was so glowing; his care for the salvation of his own soul and of the souls committed to him by virtue of his office was so conscientious; his faithfulness so approved; his will so energetic; his mind so free from man-fearing and man-pleasing; his bearing so inflexible and beyond the power of corruption,—that his whole character constrains as to the sincerest and deepest veneration.—LECHLER, GOTTHARD, 1878, *John Wiclif and his English Precursors, tr. Lorimer, vol.* I, *p.* 54.

We must remember that Grossetête held the highest hierarchical notions. Sacerdotalism was the very life of his soul. The clergy were with him God's vicegerents upon earth, invested with the tremendous prerogatives claimed by the Church of Rome for those who minister at her altars in every age. He was not a reformer in the sense of Luther or Cranmer, or Knox, or even as Reuchlin, Ersamus, or Colet. He adhered to the strictest orthodoxy of his time. His views of reformation embraced only the discipline and administration of the Church, and though he did not hesitate to speak of an individual Pope as Antichrist, he stoutly maintained that it was only through the Papacy all ecclesiastics could derive their commission and spiritual power.—COWAN, REV. W., 1897, *Pre-Reformation Worthies, p.* 10.

Matthew Paris

?–1259?

All we really know about him, is that he made his profession as a monk of St. Alban's on the 21st January, 1217, and that nineteen years afterwards, that is to say in 1236, he was appointed to succeed Wendover as chronographer to the abbey, in which capacity he must have been busily occupied till his death, or at least for about seventeen years, with one remarkable interruption. In 1248 he was sent by the Pope on a special mission to the monks of Holm, in Norway, but returned after an absence of eighteen months and resumed his duties in the abbey. His death must have occurred between the years 1253 and 1259.—GAIRDNER, JAMES, 1879, *Early Chroniclers of Europe, England, p.* 245.

His History is unpartially and judiciously written (save where he indulgeth too much to monkish Miracles and Visions); and no Writer so plainly discovereth the pride, avarice, and rapine of the Court of Rome, so that he seldome "kisseth the Pope's toe without biting it." Nor have the Papists any way to wave his true jeeres, but by suggesting, *hæc non ab ipso scripta, sed ab aliis falsò illi ascripta;* insinuating a suspicion of forgery in his last edition; understand then in what some 80 years since was set forth by Matthew Parker; whereas it was done with all integrity, according to the best and most ancient Manuscripts, wherein all those Anti-papal passages plainly appear, as since in a latter and exacter Edition, by the care and industry of Dr. William Watts. This Matthew left off living and writing at the same time, *viz.* anno 1259. I will only adde, that though he had sharp nailes, he had clean hands; strict in his own, as well as striking at the loose conversations of others; and, for his eminent austerity, was employed by Pope Innocent the Fourth, not only to visit the Monkes in the Diocess of Norwich, but also was sent by him into Norway, to reform the discipline in Holui, a fair Convent therein, but much corrupted. —FULLER, THOMAS, 1662, *The Worthies of England, ed. Nichols, vol.* I, *p.* 162.

A work wherein its author has condensed all that former writers had said about the times that preceded, and to which all succeeding writers must have recourse for the history of the period in which its author lived.—GILES, J. A., 1852, *Matthew Paris's English History, from the year* 1235 *to* 1273, *Preface.*

For sincerity of narration, truth of colouring, and extent of information, the "Historia Major" may be justly deemed as valuable a work, as this or any other age had produced. Though Matthew Paris were not the sole author, yet he made it his own; and as he is chargeable with its defects, he is entitled to the praise due to its excellence. If we except, perhaps, the two Williams of Malmesbury and Neuburg; the most Latin of our Latin historiographers is the monk of St. Alban's. His style, however, is unequal. It is sometimes remarkable for its spirit or its elegance; and at others for its inflation, or its insipidity; or in other words, it is ever in unison with the character of the age. What is most singular in him, redounds much to his praise. He was ever a warm advocate for justice and for truth; whilst abuses, of every description, and from whatever quarter they might proceed, provoked his inexorable enmity. His humour has been thought too severe and caustic: Trojan and Tyrian equally smart under his lash; and it is with strong approbation we see, that when monk, prelate, prince, emperor, or pope, has incurred his displeasure, that is, has deviated from what, in his apprehension, was the line of rectitude; he is unreserved in his censure, and his language is that of vigour and intrepidity. Those who have been too servilely devoted to the Roman court, have blamed this undaunted freedom of the English monk, whom they represent as ill-affected towards their bishop; and have seized with avidity every opportunity of aspersing his fame, vilifying his conduct, exposing his councils, and loading him with invective. "Take from the work," says the learned Baronius, "these fatal blemishes; and I will call it a golden volume, admirably compiled from authentic documents, and faithfully reporting their contents."—BERINGTON, JOSEPH, 1814, *Literary History of the Middle Ages, p.* 388.

Matthew Paris, however in some respects not an absolutely trustworthy authority for events which happened out of England, is the best unquestionably for the rumours and impressions prevalent in Christendom,—rumours, which as rumours, and showing the state of the public mind, are not to be disdained by history.—MILMAN, HENRY HART, 1854, *History of Latin Christianity, vol.* VI, *bk.* X, *ch.* V, *p.* 236, *note.*

Matthew Paris is the greatest, as he in reality is the last, of our monastic historians. The school of St. Alban's survived indeed till a far later time, but its writers dwindle into mere annalists whose view is bounded by the abbey precincts and whose work is as colourless as it is jejune. In Matthew the breadth and precision of the narrative, the copiousness of his information on topics whether national or European, the general fairness and justice of his comments, are only surpassed by the patriotic fire and enthusiasm of the whole.—GREEN, JOHN RICHARD, 1877, *History of the English People, vol.* I, *bk.* iii, *ch.* iii.

Matthew Paris is among the very best of mediæval historians. His style is vivid and picturesque, and his book gives us a series of brilliant criticisms on the men and events of his time. He is honest in purpose, a lover of truth, a keen observer, and, on the whole, just, though occasionally he gives vent to violent expressions when he feels ecclesiastical interests are at stake. He is practically the only authority for the years of Henry's reign between 1248 and 1253, and he shows much knowledge of contemporary affairs in the Empire, France, and Rome. He is, as a rule, quite trustworthy, far more so than the forerunners in his school. Where parallel authorities exist they bear out his truthfulness, and recent investigations have in every case confirmed it. He is even more fearless than Wendover in his outspoken blame of those who deserve it, no matter what their position in society. —HEATH, H. FRANK, 1894, *Social England, vol.* I, *p.* 446.

He writes clearly and correctly, with much force and picturesque power, and gives many details. . . . The freshness of his narrative is partly due to the frankness with which he wrote, and partly also to his habit of collecting information from eye-witnesses of the events that he relates. . . . His narrative may be accepted as thoroughly accurate, though in so large a work as his greater chronicle some slips of course occur.—HUNT, REV. WILLIAM, 1895, *Dictionary of National Biography, vol.* XLIII, *p.* 209.

He was a much more enthusiastic politician than any of the writers who preceded him; besides being more outspoken in criticism; though he says,—"The case of historical writers is hard. If they will tell the truth, they offend men; if they write what is false, they offend God." Intensely patriotic, he displays a strong bias against foreign favourites, and has little to say in praise of kings and popes, as a class. He lived in a period when his country was beginning to taste the sweets of liberty; the consummation of which was yet to be struggled for. As an Englishman, he groans under the humiliation and is indignant at the wrongs then endured; and he writes sharp and bitter things.—AUBREY, W. H. S., 1895, *The Rise and Growth of the English Nation, vol.* I, *p.* 161.

Nicholas of Guildford

Fl. 1250

"Owl and the Nightingale."

Nicholas de Guildford, (*fl.* 1250), poet, is the supposed author of an English poem, "The Owl and the Nightingale," which takes the form of a contest between the two birds as to their relative merits of voice and singing. Master Nicholas de Guildford is chosen as umpire, and we then learn that his home is at Porteshom (now Portisham) in Dorset. Master Nicholas has very commonly been supposed to be the author himself, but Professor Ten Brink argues that the manner in which his many virtues are dwelt on makes this improbable, and suggests that the author was a friend of Guildford's. . . . There are two manuscripts of "The Owl and the Nightingale;" (1) MS. Cotton Caligula A. ix., of the first half of the thirteenth century; (2) MS. Jesus Coll. Oxford, 29 (Coxe, *Cat. MSS. Coll. Oxon*), about fifty years later. Dr. Stratmann considers that the two copies are independent. The poem has been thrice edited: by Mr. Stevenson for the Roxburghe Club, 1838, by Mr. T. Wright for the Percy Society, 1842 (vol. xi.), and by Dr. F. H. Stratmann, Krefeld, 1868.—KINGSFORD, C. L., 1890, *Dictionary of National Biography, vol.* XXIII, *p.* 327.

Probably written not long after the year 1200. Its author, I have little doubt, was John of Guildford; for it follows (in the Oxford MS.) a poem, that was avowedly written by him; and the praises it bestows upon Nichol of Guildford, could only have proceeded from one, who was an intimate and friend. The two were probably fellow-townsmen.—GUEST, EDWIN, 1838, *A History of English Rhythms, vol.* II, *p.* 135.

The earliest known narrative poem, of a wholly imaginative character, conceived in the native tongue after the Saxon period.—MARSH, GEORGE P., 1862, *The Origin and History of the English Language, etc., p.* 205.

Although the poem is full of wisdom, the moral is not obtruded, as is the rule in mediæval work. The contending sides are balanced with wonderful skill, and the verse, which is the French short rimed couplet, is as smooth as any that Chaucer wrote.—HEATH, H. FRANK, 1894, *Social England, vol.* I, *p.* 448.

The earliest work in which we find the simple octosyllabic couplet used with any degree of artistic skill is the remarkable poem called "The Hule and the Nightingale," a composition which deserves attention for other than metrical reasons. . . . In "The Hule and the Nightingale," however, we make the acquaintance of a mind which has attempted to think for itself, and an invention capable of shaping discursive fancies and sentiments in a poetical mould. . . . But whatever the meaning of the writer may have been, he was certainly a poet capable of forming a clear conception of his subject, and of giving expression to it in a well-proportioned composition. The characters and arguments of the disputing birds are well distinguished, and the slight dramatic touches with which the narrative is enlivened are in excellent taste. Not only has the author shown real power of invention in adapting the allegorical spirit of the Bestiary to his own ends, but he has understood how to combine the clerical spirit of these manuals with the romance of the Breton lay. When he borrows for his argument an anecdote from Alexander of Neckham, he shows an appreciation of the improvements made in the story by the colours added in the version of Marie of France. The influence of French models is indeed very noticeable throughout the poem, not indeed in the vocabulary, which is singularly archaic, but in the syntax, where the words closely follow the order of the thought, and in the rhythm, which, both in the distribution of the accent and in the number of the syllables in each verse, shows a careful study of the style of Marie.—COURTHOPE, W. J., 1895, *A History of English Poetry, vol.* I, *pp.* 131, 132, 135.

On the whole, this is the best example of the octosyllabical couplet to be found before the fourteenth century. The poet (who, by the way, quotes "Alfred" repeatedly, and little else) occasionally commits the fault—specially unpleasing to modern English ears, but natural at his early date, and probably connected with the indifference of his French originals to identical rhymes,—of making the same rhyme do for two successive couplets; but this does not occur often enough to interfere seriously with harmony. His variations from eights to sevens are not more than the genius of the language specially allows. His style is easy and his poetical imagery and apparatus generally, though comparatively simple, well at command, and by no means of a rude or rudimentary order.—SAINTSBURY, GEORGE, 1898, *A Short History of English Literature, p.* 60.

Roger Bacon

1214–1292

An English philosopher, one of the greatest mediæval scholars. He was born of good family in Somersetshire, about 1214; died about 1294. He studied at Oxford, taking orders there 1233; proceeded to Paris, returned, and entered the Franciscan Order 1250. His discoveries in chemistry and physics brought upon him accusations of magic, and he was imprisoned at Paris, 1257. At the request of Pope Clement IV. in 1265 he drew up his "Opus Majus." He gained his liberty a little later, but suffered a further imprisonment of ten years under Nicholas II., and was not finally liberated till 1292, two years before his death. He was learned in several languages and wrote elegant Latin. His wide knowledge gained for him the name of Doctor Admirabilis. His chief work, the "Opus Majus," shows great learning and remarkably advanced thinking, considering the age in which he lived. He treats of the unity of the sciences, of the necessity of a true linguistic science for the understanding either of philosophy, science, or the Scriptures; he treats also of mathematics, as "the alphabet of philosophy," and of geography and astronomy as related thereto, of perspective, and of experimental science, foreshadowing the inductive method. The portion relating to geography was read by Columbus, who was strongly influenced by it.—WARNER, CHARLES DUDLEY, *ed.*, 1897, *Library of the World's Best Literature, Biographical Dictionary of Authors, vol.* XXIX, *p.* 34.

PERSONAL

BACON.—Men call me Bacon.

VANDERMAST. Lordly thou lookest, as if thou wert learnd;
Thy countenance, as if science held her seat
Betweene the circled arches of thy brow.

—GREENE, ROBERT, 1591, *Frier Bacon and Frier Bungay, v.* 1295–98.

Every ear is filled with the story of Friar Bacon, that made a brazen head to speak these words, *time is*. Which though there want not the like relations, is surely too literally received, and was but a mystical fable concerning the philosopher's great work, wherein he eminently laboured: implying no more by the copper head, than the vessel wherein it was wrought, and by the words it spake, than the opportunity to be watched, about the *tempus ortus*, or birth of the mystical child, or philosophical king of Lallius; the rising of the *terra foliata* of *Arnoldus*, when the earth, sufficiently impregnated with the water, ascendeth white and splendent.—BROWNE, SIR THOMAS, 1646, *Pseudodoxia Epidemica, ed. Wilkin, bk.* vii, *ch.* xvii, *p.* 275.

For mine own part, I behold the name of Bacon in Oxford, not as of an individual man, but corporation of men; no single cord, but a twisted cable of many together. And as all the acts of strong men of that nature are attributed to an Hercules; all the predictions of prophesying women to a Sibyl; so, I conceive, all the achievements of the Oxonian Bacons, in their liberal studies, are ascribed to one, as chief of the name. And this in effect is confessed by the most learned and ingenious orator of that university. Indeed, we find one Robert Bacon who died *anno* one thousand two hundred forty-eight, a learned doctor; and Trithemius styleth John Baconthorpe, plain Bacon, which addeth to the probability of the former assertion. However, this confounding so many Bacons in one hath caused antichronisms in many relations. For how could this Bacon ever be a Reader of Philosophy in Brasen-nose college, founded more than one hundred years after his death? so that his brasen head, so much spoken of, to speak, must make time past to be again, or else these inconsistencies will not be reconciled.—FULLER, THOMAS, 1655, *The Church History of Britain, ed. Nichols, vol.* I, *bk.* iii, *par.* 18.

Roger Bacon, friar ordinis (S.Francisci):—Memorandum, in Mr. Selden's learned verses before Hopton's *Concordance of yeares*, he speakes of friar Bacon, and sayes that he was a Dorsetshire gentleman. There are yet of that name in that countie, and some of pretty good estate. I find by . . . (which booke I have) that he understood the making of optique glasses; where he also gives a perfect account of the making of gunpowder, vide pag . . . ejusdem libri. —AUBREY, JOHN, 1669-96, *Brief Lives, ed. Clark, vol.* I, *p.* 84.

THE REV. DR. FOLLIOTT.—Oxford was a seat of learning in the days of Friar Bacon. But the Friar is gone, and his learning with him. Nothing of him is left but the immortal nose, which, when his brazen head had tumbled to pieces, crying "Time's Past," was the only palpable fragment among its minutely pulverised atoms, and which is still resplendent over the portals of its cognominal college. That nose, sir, is the only thing to which I shall take off my hat in all this Babylon of buried literature.—PEACOCK, THOMAS LOVE, 1831, *Crotchet Castle, ch.* ix.

It is impossible to avoid thinking, that if Roger, instead of becoming a Franciscan monk, had made the attempt to reach as *secularis* in the Paris University, his lot would have been more favourable, and he would have worked with better results and with greater contentment.—ERDMANN, JOHANN EDUARD, 1865-76, *A History of Philosophy, ed. Hough, vol.* I, *p.* 484.

Oh, could I once but touch, or faintly see,
Or clearly dream of things I feel must be,
The secret might be gained of Nature's mastery.
But in monastic walls of flesh confined,
Our sun hath burst not yet all buds of mind,
Which bloom in hope alone, not knowing what's designed.
I would be far—be first, in man's advance;
But when my hand was thrust beyond my trance,
Parhelion* smote to earth the fool of Thought's Romance.

—HORNE, R. H., 1882, *Soliloquium Fratris Rogeri Baconis, Fraser's Magazine,* N. S. *vol.* 26, *p.* 114.

That Bacon's imprisonment for twenty-four years, because he loved science, was really the act of the whole Church, is shown by the unwillingness of contemporary and later authors, for instance Dante, to mention his name, by the mutilated condition of his writings, said to have been nailed down to the shelves by his brother-monks, and by the failure to publish them until after the Reformation.—HOLLAND, FREDERIC MAY, 1884, *The Rise of Intellectual Liberty, p.* 183.

The "Old Hodge Bacon" of Hudibras, and the hero of "the honourable History of Frier Bacon and Frier Bongay," is the person who acquired his skill by promising himself to the devil when he died, whether he died in the church or out of it, and who at last cheated the devil cleverly by dying in a hole in the church-wall. Four centuries before the day of small philosophy, when such stories were credited, an anxious simple-minded man, in the grey habit of the lowliest of the religious orders—one who had spent a handsome patrimony for the love of knowledge, and who waited on the outcast leper for the love of God—walked barefoot in the streets of Oxford. His home was in no stately monastery, but in the poorhouse in the suburbs, in the parish of St. Ebbe's, which had been given to the Franciscans by a citizen. In the wretched chamber that was the appointed

*The Pope, or mock sun (Nicholas III.), who ordered Friar Bacon's imprisonment.

dwelling of a Minorite while still the doctrine of St. Francis was in force among his followers, Roger Bacon made lament sometimes for want of ink, and sometimes was by the Superior of his order confined as a prisoner on bread and water, because he had plunged rebelliously into the luxury of books, or made his knowledge known too freely to others. Beyond these punishments for breach of discipline it does not appear that Friar Roger Bacon suffered, as many accounts of him would have us to believe, chains and persecution from the Church. Neither did he occupy any such middle place between the Church and the world as might be represented by the hole in the church wall, wherein tradition tells us that he died. Within the church he lived and died, and all the labour of his life, in science and philosophy, as in the daily ministering to the sorrows of the poor, was worship.—MORLEY, HENRY, 1888, *English Writers, vol.* III, *p.* 315.

He was persecuted and imprisoned, not for the commonplace and natural reason that he frightened the Church, but merely because he was eccentric in his habits and knew too much.—LODGE, OLIVER, 1892, *Pioneers of Science, p.* 9.

If the account of his imprisonment be true (of which there is no contemporary evidence) our own celebrated English philosopher, Roger Bacon, is one of the earliest scientific authors whose works proved fatal to them.—DITCHFIELD, P. H., 1894, *Books Fatal to Their Authors, p.* 78.

GENERAL

Roger Bacon treated more especially of physics, but remained without influence. —HEGEL, GEORG WILHELM FRIEDRICH, 1816?, *Lectures on the History of Philosophy, tr. Haldane and Simson, vol.* III, *p.* 92.

The marvellous Friar. — SOUTHEY, ROBERT, 1821, *A Vision of Judgment*, IX.

One of the extraordinary men of the thirteenth century, who stood forth to resist the ruling authorities of their times, was the Englishman Roger Bacon, a man of a free spirit beyond all others, full of great ideas of reform; ideas that contained the germs of new creations, reaching farther in their consequences and results than he himself, firmly rooted as, with all his aspirations, he still was in the times in which he lived, either understood or intended.—NEANDER, AUGUSTUS, 1825-52, *General History of the Christian Religion and Church, tr. Torrey, vol.* VIII, *p.* 97.

Not a good writer. . . . Some have deemed him overrated by the nationality of the English; but, if we may have sometimes given him credit for discoveries to which he has only borne testimony, there can be no doubt of the originality of his genius.—HALLAM, HENRY, 1837-39, *Introduction to the Literature of Europe, pt.* i, *ch.* i, *par.* 87, *ch.* ii, *par.* 33.

That Bacon's fame was not evanescent, we have good proof in the numerous MS. copies of his works, or parts of them, which occupy places in the various university and national libraries at home and abroad, and from the careful way in which his correspondence with Pope Clement, and the holy Father's replies, are preserved in the Vatican library.—NEIL, SAMUEL, 1865, *Epoch Men, p.* 116.

The most remarkable man in the most remarkable century of the Middle Ages. —PLUMPTRE, E. H., 1866, *Roger Bacon, Contemporary Review, vol.* II, *p.* 364.

Roger Bacon, having been a monk, is frequently spoken of as a creature of Catholic teaching. But there never was a more striking instance of the force of a great genius in resisting the tendencies of his age. At a time when physical science was continually neglected, discouraged, or condemned, at a time when all the great prizes of the world were open to men who pursued a very different course, Bacon applied himself with transcendent genius to the study of nature. Fourteen years of his life were spent in prison, and when he died his name was blasted as a magician.—LECKY, WILLIAM EDWARD HARTPOLE, 1869, *History of European Morals, ch* iv.

The chief theoretical interest of Bacon lies in the knowledge of nature, in the discovery of her mechanical secrets, the consequent dispelling of the rude ignorance of which he complains as universal, and the improvement of man's present estate. . . . It is reported that it was a passage stolen from Roger Bacon by some author known to Columbus that, arresting the attention of the latter, led him to the formation of his world-discovering plans. By his appreciation of mathematics, and the solidity of his own scientific work (*e. g.* in optics), Roger Bacon certainly is superior to his successor, Francis Bacon, Lord Verulam.—MORRIS, GEORGE S., 1880, *British Thought and Thinkers, pp.* 40, 42.

Bacon's works possess much historical value, for his vigorous thinking and pronounced scientific inclinations are not to be regarded as abnormal and isolated phenomena. He represents one current of thought and work in the middle ages which must have run strongly though obscurely, and without a thorough comprehension of his position our conceptions of an important century are incomplete and erroneous.—ADAMSON, R., 1885, *Dictionary of National Biography, vol.* II, *p.* 378.

There was hardly any department of knowledge this great Franciscan had not investigated. He was learned in theology and philosophy, in grammar, language and music. His researches in mathematics and the natural sciences were aided by the writings of the Arabian philosophers. From these sources he enlarged his knowledge of geometry and astronomy. To these same observers he was possibly indebted for his profound acquaintance with optics, and the laws of refraction and perspective. In the extent of his chemical knowledge he had no equals in Europe, even if he did not surpass the most learned of the Arabian and Jewish philosophers. He anticipated many of the discoveries of after ages. His suggestions as to what might be accomplished in mechanics show a deep acquaintance with the forces of natural agents, whilst in experimental philosophy in general he foreshadowed, even if he did not directly suggest, the system of his great namesake, Francis Bacon. He was unfortunate in the days which succeeded those in which he lived. The torch he lighted was almost quenched in the times of confusion and darkness following on the death of Edward I. It was reserved to a later age, and to the father of inductive philosophy, to recall the memory of Roger Bacon, and to add to it fresh lustre.—DENTON, REV. W., 1888, *England in the Fifteenth Century, p.* 59.

Nor does he fail to reproduce some of the characteristic superstitions of the Middle Ages. He, too, has a faith in alchemy, he accepts the influence of the stars, he even anticipates the modern magic of mesmerism. He, too, will try to find the philosopher's stone and the secret of a life which exceeds the normal measure of man. What he had done in science seems but an earnest of what science can do; and there is at once scientific faith and childish credulity in his anticipations of the future.—COURTNEY, W. L., 1889, *Roger Bacon, Fortnightly Review,* N. S. *vol.* 46, *p.* 262.

Roger Bacon is more rarely than Francis led astray by verbal ambiguities, and his etymologies are generally more correct.—NICHOL, JOHN, 1889, *Francis Bacon, His Life and Philosophy, pt.* ii, *p.* 53.

He is worthy to be kept in mind as the Englishman who above all others living in that turbid thirteenth century, saw through the husks of things to their very core.—MITCHELL, DONALD G., 1889, *English Lands, Letters, and Kings, From Celt to Tudor, p.* 81.

His three works, *Opus majus, Opus minus, and Opus tertium,* the fruit of twenty years' investigation, to which he devoted his entire fortune, constitute the most remarkable scientific monument of the Middle Ages. Not only does he call attention to the barrenness of the scholastic *logomachies*, the necessity of observing nature and of studying the languages, but he recognizes, even more clearly than his namesake of the sixteenth century, the capital importance of mathematical deduction as an auxiliary to the experimental method. Nay, more than that; he enriches science, and especially optics, with new and fruitful theories.—WEBER, ALFRED, 1892-96, *History of Philosophy, tr. Thilly, p.* 258.

The coincidence that Roger Bacon bore, in a time before surnames had come into general use, the same surname that was to be carried to fame four centuries later by "the wisest, brightest, meanest of mankind," has cast into deeper eclipse the reputation of one of the most penetrating thinkers who have from time to time revolted against false teaching and unsound systems of science. Hardly for every hundred persons who have a general idea of the life and works of Francis Bacon of Verulam shall one be found who could give an outline of those of Roger Bacon the Franciscan. Yet with the fruit of four additional centuries of learning and civilisation at his command, the secret of the later Bacon's philosophy was none other than the earlier Bacon had imparted to ears that would not hear—that the road to knowledge lay, not through scholastic argument and self-confident routine, but by way of cautious induction and patient experiment.—MAXWELL, HERBERT, 1894, *Roger Bacon, Blackwood's Magazine, vol.* 156, *p.* 610.

Roger Bacon, it needs not be said, stands quite by himself—not by any means because he limited himself to the physical studies by which in modern times he is renowned, but because, having learned all that could be learned of the current philosophy, scholarship, science, and literature of his day, knowing Greek, Hebrew, and Arabic, and having advanced in some directions far beyond the limit of performance then deemed possible, he was able to judge the existing state of knowledge, and apportion its excellences and its defects from a point of view immeasurably more independent than any other man. He is not merely the original investigator and discoverer of physical truths, but the wisest critic of the learning of his age. — POOLE, R. L., 1894, *Social England, vol.* I, *p.* 438.

A man who saw the danger of reliance upon authority, and proclaimed the methods of criticism and observation, and pointed out the way in which investigation should go, and the use which should be made of the new materials which had been gained, in a spirit almost modern and with such a clearness of insight as should have led to the revival of learning as one of the immediate results of the thirteenth century. But he could get no one to hear him. The scholastic methods and the scholastic ideals had become so firmly seated in their empire over men, under the influence of the great minds of that century, that no others seemed possible. His works passed out of the world's knowledge with no discoverable trace of influence until the Renaissance was fully under way, and then only the very slightest.—ADAMS, GEORGE BURTON, 1894, *Civilization During the Middle Ages, p.* 369.

The greatest name in Oxford science. —WELLS, J., 1897, *Oxford and its Colleges, p.* 12.

Robert of Gloucester

Fl. 1260–1300

Beyond the fact that the name of the writer of a portion of the "Chronicle" was Robert, and that from the dialect in which he wrote he was probably a Gloucestershire monk, there is nothing whatever known about him.—WRIGHT, WILLIAM ALDIS, 1887, *ed. Metrical Chronicle of Robert of Gloucester, Parts* I *and* II.

I am very sensible that the obsoleteness of the language will deter many from reading this very useful historian; but to such as shall be pleased to make themselves acquainted with him, . . . he will appear very pleasant, entertaining and diverting, and they will value him the more as he comes out in his primitive dress.—HEARNE, THOMAS, 1724, *ed. Robert of Gloucester's Chronicle, vol.* I, *Preface,* lxxxv.

This rhyming chronicle is totally destitute of art or imagination. The author has clothed the fables of Geoffrey of Monmouth in rhyme, which have often a more poetical air in Geoffrey's prose.—WARTON, THOMAS, 1774-81, *History of English Poetry, sec.* ii.

Robert of Gloucester, though cold and prosaic, is not quite deficient in the valuable talent of arresting the attention; and the orations, with which he occasionally diversifies the thread of his story, are, in general, appropriate and dramatic, and not only prove his good sense, but exhibit no unfavourable specimens of his eloquence. In his description of the first crusade he seems to change his usual character, and becomes not only entertaining, but even animated; and the vision, in which a "holy man" is ordered to reproach the Christians with their departure from their duty, and, at the same time, to promise them the divine intervention, to extricate them from a situation in which the exertions of human valour were apparently fruitless, would not, perhaps, to contemporary readers appear less poetical, nor less sublime and impressive, than the introduction of the heathen mythology into the works of the early classics.—ELLIS, GEORGE, 1790-1845, *Specimens of the Early English Poets, vol.* I, *p.* 79.

After observing some traits of humour and sentiment, moderate as they may be, in compositions as old as the middle of the thirteenth century, we might naturally expect to find in Robert of Gloucester not indeed a decidedly poetical manner, but some approach to the animation of poetry. But the Chronicle of this *English Ennius*, as he has been called, whatever progress in the state of the language it may display, comes in reality nothing nearer the character of a work of imagination than Layamon's version of Wace, which preceded it by a hundred years. One would not imagine, from Robert of Gloucester's style, that he belonged to a period when a single effusion of sentiment, or a trait of humour and vivacity, had appeared in the language. On the contrary, he seems to take us back to the nonage of poetry, when verse is employed not to harmonize and beautify expression, but merely to assist the memory. . . . As a relater of events, he is tolerably succinct and perspicuous; and wherever the fact is of any importance, he shows a watchful attention to keep the reader's memory distinct with regard to chronology, by making the date of the year rhyme to something prominent in the narration of the fact.—CAMPBELL, THOMAS 1819, *An Essay on English Poetry.*

The MS. from which Hearne published his edition was, I suspect, a very corrupt copy of the original; but, with all its faults, it tells our national story with a simplicity, and occasionally with a dramatic power, that have been much undervalued. In sketching the character of our kings this chronicler is sometimes singularly happy.—GUEST, EDWIN, 1838, *A History of English Rhythms, vol.* II, *p.* 412.

The poems—for such we must call them if all rhymed compositions are poetry—of Robert of Gloucester, who flourished about the year 1300, are of considerable philological importance, and of some value as contributions to our knowledge of the history of England, though their literary merit is of a humble order.—MARSH, GEORGE P., 1862, *The Origin and History of the English Language, etc., p.* 231.

Robert as poet was much less gifted than Layamon, but had in him more of the scholar. Archæology, topography, ethnology, and topics of political economy aroused his interest. He was everywhere tempted to compare the past with the present. His erudition was not especially great, nor his field of vision broad, nor his insight very keen; but he was a man of warm feelings, and was clear-sighted within his sphere. He was fain to discern the finger of God in historical events; his moral standard of measurement was strict, but not illiberal. Although devoted to the interests of the church, he was a good Englishman. Party considerations and prejudices clouded his judgment less than they obscure that of many a prominent historian. It was always his aim to distribute praise or blame according to merit.—TEN BRINK, BERNHARD, 1877-83, *History of English Literature (To Wiclif), tr. Kennedy, p.* 275.

It was in long lines of seven accents, and occasionally six, and was the first complete history of his country, from the earliest times to his own day, written in popular rhymes by an Englishman. The language is very free from Norman admixture, and represents West Midland Transitional English of the end of the thirteenth century.—MORLEY AND TYLER, 1879, *A Manual of English Literature, p.* 64.

Robert of Gloucester wrote for "simple Englishmen," and his verse has all the interest of unadorned style, while the language in which he writes is a valuable illustration of the change through which our tongue was then passing. As a historian he is of considerable importance.—HUTTON, WILLIAM HOLDEN, 1888, *Simon of Montfort and His Cause, p.* 180.

Besides the industry he shows in consulting the best authorities, he takes a real interest in his subject on its moral side, and his reflections have often great significance, as showing the feelings of the native English towards the Norman conquerors.—COURTHOPE, W. J., 1895, *A History of English Poetry, vol.* I, *p.* 146.

Robert of Gloucester is a very interesting person, and a much better poet than it has been the fashion to represent him, though his first object was not poetry, and though, had it been so, he was but ill-equipped.—SAINTSBURY, GEORGE, 1898, *A Short History of English Literature, p.* 63.

Thomas of Erceldoune

Thomas the Rhymer

C. 1225–C. 1300

Thomas of Erceldoune, called also the Rhymer (c.1225–c.1300), occupies a prominent place as a poet and prophet in the mythical and legendary literature of Scotland. The historical person of that name figures in two charters of the 13th century, and from these it appears that he owned lands in Erceldoune (now Earlston), in Berwickshire, which were made over by his son and heir to the cloister of the Holy Trinity at Soltra, or Soutra, on the borders of the same county. He figures in the works of Barbour and Blind Harry as the sympathizing contemporary of their heroes, and Wyntoun tells how he prophesied a battle. In the folk-lore of Scotland his name is associated with numerous fragments of rhymed or alliterative verse of a more or less prophetic and oracular character; but the chief extant work with which his name is associated is the poem of "Sir Tristrem," edited from the Auchinleck MS. by Sir Walter Scott in 1804, and again in 1886 for the Scottish Text Society by Mr. G. P. M'Neill. In the latter edition the claim of Thomas to the authorship of this work (conceded by both editors) is fully discussed.—BAYNES, THOMAS S., *ed.*, 1888, *Encyclopaedia Britannica, vol.* XXIII, *p.* 308.

Y was at Ertheldoune:
With Tomas spak Y thare:
Ther herd Y rede in roune
Who Tristrem gat and bare,
Who was king with croun,
And who him forsterd yare,
And who was bold baroun,
As thair elders ware.
Bi yere
Tomas tells in toun
This auentours as thai ware.

—ERCELDOUNE, THOMAS OF, 1299?, *Sir Tristrem, Fytte First.*

Sir Tristrem
Over Gestes it has the 'steem
Over all that is, or was.

—BRUNNE, ROBERT DE, 1338?, *Annals, Prolog.*

The prophecies yet extant in Scottish *Rithmes*, whereupon he was commonly called Thomas the Rhymer, may justly be admired, having foretold, so many ages before, the union of England and Scotland, in the ninth degree of the Bruce's blood, with the succession of Bruce himself to the crown, being yet a child, and other diuers particulars which the event hath ratified and made good. . . . Whence or how he had this knowledge, can hardly be affirmed; but sure it is, that he did divine and answer truly of many things to come.—SPOTTISWOOD, JOHN, 1639? *History of the Church and State of Scotland, ed.* 1851, *vol.* I, *p.* 93.

For, let it be considered that the name of Thomas the Rhymer is not forgotten in Scotland, nor his authority altogether slighted, even at this day. Within the memory of man, his prophecies, and the prophecies of other Scotch soothsayers, have not only been reprinted, but have been consulted with a weak, if not criminal curiosity. I mention no particulars; for I behold it ungenerous to reproach men with weaknesses of which they themselves are ashamed. The same superstitious credulity might again spring up. I flatter myself that my attempts to eradicate it will not prove altogether vain.—HAILES, LORD, 1773, *Remarks on the History of Scotland.*

From Ercildoun's lone walls the prophet came,
A milk-white deer stood lovely by his side:—
Oh! long shall Scotland's sound with Rymour's name,
For in an unknown cave the seer shall bide,
Till through the realm gaunt kings and chiefs shall ride,
Wading through floods of carnage, bridle-deep:
The cries of terror and the wailing wide
Shall rouse the prophet from his tranced sleep;
His harp shall ring with wo, and all the land shall weep.

—FINLAY, JOHN, 1802, *Wallace; or the Vale of Ellerslie.*

"Sir Tristrem," even as it now exists, shows likewise that considerable art was resorted to in constructing the stanza, and has, from beginning to end, a concise, quaint, abstract turn of expression, more like the Saxon poetry than the simple, bald, and diffuse details of the French minstrel.—SCOTT, SIR WALTER, 1824, *Essay on Romance Works, vol.* VI, *p.* 207.

The romance ascribed to Thomas of Erceldoune is deservedly regarded as a precious relique of early British poetry; it is highly curious as a specimen of language, and not less curious as a specimen of composition. The verses are short, and the stanzas somewhat artificial in their structure; and amid the quaint simplicity of the author's style, we often distinguish a forcible brevity of expression. But his narrative, which has a certain air of originality, is sometimes so abrupt as to seem obscure, and even enigmatical.—IRVING, DAVID, 1861, *History of Scottish Poetry, ed. Carlyle, p.* 60.

He had the fame not only of an epic poet or bard, but of a prophet, occupying in his own country somewhat of the position held by Merlin in England, and afterwards by Nostradamus in France.—BURTON, JOHN HILL, 1867, *The History of Scotland, vol.* IV, *p.* 119.

We can see in him, as he lived, an obvious awakening to the powers of outward nature, the feeling of the spring-tide and the rejoicing birds, the love of lonely lingering among the hills, the sense of the unspeakable silence and solitude of the benty moorland, and the poetic yearning for some form of a mysterious life with which he might commune on the wild. Thomas of Erceldoune was the man of the time who felt these influences, and doubtless expressed them, more powerfully than any other. The mythical story of his intercourse and selection by the Queen of Faërie was the imaginative embodiment in a free, wild, and graceful form of the Rhymour as he appeared to the people around him—the theory of his somewhat mysterious life.—VEITCH, JOHN, 1878, *The History and Poetry of the Scottish Border, p.* 236.

Whether the earlier figure of Thomas of Erceldoune is more than a phantom may still be doubted, and there is no satisfactory evidence for believing him to be the author of the "Romance of Sir Tristrem" which Scott published in 1804. We are not even certain that this romance has any claim to be regarded as a product of Scottish literature; it exists only in a transcript executed in England, and it has no Scottish peculiarities.—ROSS, JOHN MERRY, 1884, *Scottish History and Literature, ed. Brown, p.* 107.

The arguments which assail the trustworthiness of these documents are suggested by somewhat hypercritical doubts, and the theories designed to supplant them are based upon conjectures wholly unsupported by evidence.—M'NEILL, G. P., 1886, *ed. Sir Tristrem (Scottish Text Society).*

The poem is written in an involved stanza in striking contrast to the simple style of the narrative and the obvious eagerness of the narrator to press on with his tale. The design of the composition, as in most old romances, is of the character best adapted for recitation—a series of adventures, each complete in itself, strung upon the lives of the lovers. At the same time there is a certain arrangement, a proportion and balance of parts around the central idea, which give to the story an artistic unity. The situations frequently possess strong dramatic point, as when Tristrem, having drunk the love-potion with Isonde, has to fulfil his mission and hand her over in marriage to the king. Most notable of all, the characters of the tale from first to last are firmly and even subtly drawn. Limned from the outside by their action and words, they stand distinct as if reproduced from life or from the most intimate tradition.—EYRE-TODD, GEORGE, 1891, *Early Scottish Poetry, p.* 17.

"Thomas the Rhymer" . . . is a brilliant example of a ballad in which the art of minstrelsy is employed to preserve, in a glorified form, the memory of a real man in whom the popular imagination is interested. From the beginning of the fourteenth century the fame of Thomas of Erceldoune, or Thomas Rymour, or True Thomas, for prophecy, was celebrated through Scotland; and the predictions attributed to him had so much consistency, that in 1603 they were collected into a volume with the Prophecies of Merlin. Thomas Rymour of Erceldoune is known to have been a real person, who is reported to have been alive in the closing years of the thirteenth century. . . . Not original enough to invent a story for himself, the minstrel who took Thomas as his hero sought his materials in existing romances, and by the middle of the fifteenth century a poem, which forms the groundwork of the ballads on the subject, was committed to writing. In its most essential features the story in the poem was taken from the romance of "Ogier le Danois," which relates how that hero was carried to Avalon by Morgan the Fay, and lived there for centuries without perceiving the lapse of time; moreover, the style of the narrative, particularly the length and detail of the descriptions, was in the approved manner of metrical romance. — COURTHOPE, W. J., 1895, *A History of English Poetry, vol.* I, *p.* 458.

Duns Scotus

1265?–1308?

Johannes Duns Scotus, was b. in 1260 or 1274, according to Matthæus Veglensis and Dempster, at Duns, in the southern part of Scotland; according to Leland and others, at Dunstane, in Northumberland; according to Wadding, in Ireland; d. at Cologne, 1308. He early became a Franciscan, and studied theology at Oxford, under William de Vuarra (Varro). When the latter went to Paris, Duns succeeded to his chair, and taught in Oxford with great success. He is said to have had three thousand pupils. It was especially his keenness and subtlety which impressed people; for which reason he received the title of *doctor subtilis.* While in Oxford he wrote a commentary upon the Sentences of the Lombard,—"Opus Oxoniense." About 1301 he went to Paris, and there he also lectured on the Sentences; which lectures afterwards were published under the title "Reportata Parisiensia." In 1305 he obtained the degree of a doctor. After the order of Clement V. he held a grand disputation with the Dominicans concerning the immaculate conception of Mary. He came out victorious. Even the marble statue of the Virgin, standing in the disputation hall, bowed to him when he descended from the cathedra; and it became a rule in the university, that he who obtained a degree there should take an oath to defend the doctrine of the immaculate conception. In 1308 Duns was sent to Cologne, by the general of his order, to contend with the Beghards, who were numerous in those regions, and with the Dominicans, who refused to accept the new dogma. He was received with great honors, but died in the same year from apoplexy. The best edition of his works is that by Wadding, Lyons, 1639, in 12 vols. fol.—DORNER, AUGUST, 1882, *Schaff-Herzog Religious Encyclopædia, vol.* I, *p.* 674.

Hitherto all School-men were (like the World before the building of Babel) "of one language, and of one speech;" agreeing together in their opinions, which hereafter were divided into two Regiments, or Armies rather, of Thomists and Scotists, under their several Generals opposing one another. Scotus was a great stickler against the Thomists for that "sinful opinion, that the Virgin Mary was conceived without sin;" which if so, how came she to rejoyce in God her Saviour? He read the Sentences thrice over in his solemn Lectures, once at Oxford, again at Paris, and last at Colen, where he died, or was kill'd rather, because, falling into a strong fit of an appoplexy, he was interred whilst yet alive, as afterwards did appear. Small amends were made for his hasty burial, with an handsome Monument erected over him, at the cost of his Order (otherwise, whether a Scot, Scholar, or Franciscan, he had little wealth of his own), in the Quire before the High Altar. On his Monument are inscribed the names of fifteen Franciscans, viz. three Popes, and two Cardinals on the top, and ten doctors (whereof six English) on the sides thereof; all his Contemporaries, as I conceive.—FULLER, THOMAS, 1662, *The Worthies of England, ed. Nichols, vol.* II, *p.* 194.

Less of a moralist than Saint Thomas,* he was a greater dialectician.—COUSIN, M. VICTOR, 1841, *History of Modern Philosophy, tr. Wight, vol.* II, *Lecture* ix.

Not that we have found that language so entirely rugged and uncouth as it is often represented to be. Aquinas is in many ways less difficult; all who desire to have their intellectual food cooked for them will resort to him. Those who like to prepare it, and even now and then to hunt it for themselves; will find their interest in accompanying Duns.—MAURICE, FREDERICK DENNISON, 1850–62, *Moral and Metaphysical Philosophy, vol.* I, *p.* 646.

Duns Scotus is an Aristotelian beyond Aristotle, a Platonist beyond Plato; at

*Aquinas.

the same time, the most sternly orthodox of Theologians. On the eternity of matter he transcends his master: he accepts the hardy saying of Avicembron, of the universality of matter. He carries matter not only higher than the intermediate world of Devils and Angels, but up into the very Sanctuary, into the Godhead itself. . . . God is still with him the high, remote Monad, above all things, though throughout all things. In him, and not without him, according to what is asserted to be Platonic doctrine, are the forms and ideas of things. With equal zeal, and with equal ingenuity with the Thomists, he attempts to maintain the free will of God, whom he seems to have bound in the chain of inexorable necessity. He saves it by a distinction which even his subtlety can hardly define. Yet, behind and without this nebulous circle, Duns Scotus, as a metaphysical and an ethical writer, is remarkable for his bold speculative views on the nature of our intelligence, on its communication with the outward world, by the senses, by its own innate powers, as well as by the influence of the superior Intelligence. He thinks with perfect freedom; and if he spins his spiderwebs, it is impossible not to be struck at once by their strength and coherence. Translate him, as some have attempted to translate him, into intelligible language, he is always suggestive, sometimes conclusive.—MILMAN, HENRY HART, 1855, *History of Latin Christianity, vol.* VI, *bk.* xiv, *ch.* iii, *pp.* 467, 468.

Between his Scholasticism and the Romanic Scholasticism of Thomas Aquinas, there is, indeed, this distinction: that in the former, clearer traces are discernable of the ethical tendency which characterizes the Germanic mind. Scotus presents to us the picture of a vigorous wrestling mind, in which a new principle travails unto birth, still struggling with the chains imposed upon it by the antagonistic principle which had held sway. Whereas, previously, the theoretical and physical, necessity and nature (essence), had held almost undisputed sway, he now puts forth the claims of free will, though his mode of doing so is marked by abruptness and exclusiveness.—DORNER, J. A., 1861, *History of the Doctrine of the Person of Christ, tr. Simon, vol.* I, *div.* ii, *p.* 346.

As an opponent of Thomism he founded the philosophical and theological school names after him. His strength lay rather in acute, negative criticism of the teachings of others, than in the positive elaboration of his own. Strict faith in reference to the theological teachings of the Church and the philosophical doctrines corresponding with their spirit, and far-reaching skepticism with reference to the arguments by which they are sustained, are the general characteristics of the Scotist doctrine. After having destroyed by his criticism their rational grounds, there remains to Scotus as the objective cause of the verities of faith only the unconditional will of God, and as the subjective ground of faith only the voluntary submission of the believer to the authority of the Church. Theology is for him a knowledge of an essentially practical character.—UEBERWEG, FREDERICH, 1862–71, *A History of Philosophy, tr, Morris, vol.* I, *p.* 452.

If the disputed question, as to whether Duns Scotus was an Englishman, a Scotchman, or an Irishman were to be decided by asking which land was the most devoted to the extension of his fame, he belongs unquestionably to Ireland.—ERDMANN, JOHANN EDUARD, 1865-76, *A History of Philosophy, ed. Hough, vol.* I, *p.* 485.

He was rightly named by the crowds that flocked round him in Paris and Cologne the Subtle Doctor; he made distinctions and definitions until he seemed to bewilder himself, but his erudition, his patience, his industry, and his dialectic skill, have not had a compeer altogether in European literature. The services he rendered to the cause of psychology and theology have never been fairly acknowledged; by giving extreme and undue prominence to one principle, which had been almost entirely overlooked by his predecessors, he banished others equally as important into the shade, and thus vitiated his whole system as a system, but he undoubtedly drew attention to some points which have never since lost their hold in philosophy or dogma, and which have tended to give increased richness and fulness to each of them. Had his genius been less critical and more philosophic, less merely microscopic and more comprehensive, he might have exercised an influence in no degree less mighty than his great Dominican rival.—TOWNSEND, W. J., 1881, *The Great Schoolmen of the Middle Ages, p.* 263.

His chief service is that by his unmatched logical faculty he was able to erect a battery of criticism against the dominant school of thought which saved it from the perils of absolutism. The controversies for the moment cleared the air and gave room for reflexion.—POOLE, R. L., 1894, *Social England, vol.* I, *p.* 439.

Scotus was appropriately named "doctor mirabilis." So far did he push the process of hair-splitting analysis that he was driven to invent many new terms. His style, compared with that of his Scholastic predecessors, is marked by its barbarous latinity. A sincere Christian believer, and standing in his own day within the lines of admissible orthodoxy, he yet lacks the religious depth of Aquinas. In philosophy, he did not stop with Aristotle, but was more Platonic in his Realism. In his theology, he was Semi-Pelagian. The effect of the teaching of Scotus was to begin the work of undermining the Scholasticism of which he was so famous a leader. This effect was produced, partly by his critical treatment of the arguments drawn from reason for the propositions of the creed. Very little space was conceded to possible demonstration.—FISHER, GEORGE PARK, 1896, *History of Christian Doctrine, p.* 232.

Robert Mannyng

Robert de Brunne

1260–1340

Robert De Brunne, the name by which Robert Manning, or Mannyng, is usually designated from his birthplace Bourn, in Lincolnshire, which is 6 miles from the Gilbertine monastery of Sempringham that he entered in 1288. He died about 1338. His chief work is his "Handlyng Synne" (1303), a free and amplified translation into English verse of William of Wadington's "Manuel des Pechiez," with such judicious omissions and excellent additions as made his version much more entertaining than the original. It is one of our best landmarks in the transition from early to later Middle English. He also made a new version in octosyllabic rhyme of Waces' "Brut d' Angleterre," and added to it a translation of the French rhyming chronicle of Peter Langtoft.—PATRICK AND GROOME *eds.*, 1897, *Chambers's Biographical Dictionary, p.* 144.

Has scarcely more poetry than Robert of Gloucester. . . . Yet it should be remembered, that even such a writer as Robert de Brunne, uncouth and unpleasing as he naturally seems, and chiefly employed in turning the theology of his age into rhyme, contributed to form a style, to teach expression, and to polish his native tongue. In the infancy of language and composition, nothing is wanted but writers: at that period even the most artless have their use.—WARTON, THOMAS, 1778-81, *History of English Poetry, sec.* ii.

The style of Robert de Brunne is less marked by Saxonisms than that of Robert of Gloucester; and though he can scarcely be said to come nearer the character of a true poet than his predecessor, he is certainly a smoother versifier, and evinces more facility in rhyming.—CAMPBELL, THOMAS, 1819, *An Essay on English Poetry.*

Ritson (Bibliographia Poetica, p. 33) is very wroth with Warton for describing De Brunne as having "scarcely more poetry than Robert of Gloucester;"—"which only proves," Ritson says, "his want of taste or judgment." It may be admitted that De Brunne's chronicle exhibits the language in a considerably more advanced state than that of Gloucester, and also that he appears to have more natural fluency than his predecessor; his work also possesses greater interest from his occasionally speaking in his own person, and from his more frequent expansion and improvement of his French original by new matter; but for poetry, it would probably require a "taste or judgment" equal to Ritson's own to detect much of it.—CRAIK, GEORGE L., 1861, *A Compendious History of English Literature and of the English Language, vol.* I, *p.* 239.

The style of de Brunne is superior to that of Robert of Gloucester in ease, though we can hardly say, grace of expression. His literary merits are slender.—MARSH, GEORGE P., 1862, *The Origin and History of the English Language, etc., p.* 235.

Robert was a pious ecclesiastic, yet any propensity to asceticism was far from him. He was ever ready to grant an innocent amusement to others as well as to himself, and especially to the poor. His was an unassuming, genial spirit, with a light touch of humour; he was a friend of music and good stories. He did not ascend to the higher regions of thought, and mystical contemplation was quite foreign to him; but his eye scanned the world around him with all the greater interest; and his view, if not particularly sharp, was very clear. Robert was curious and even inquisitive; but his curiosity had the background of a warm sympathy for the lot of his fellow-men. Like his namesake of Gloucester, he was the friend and advocate of the poor. High position and birth did not blind him to the faults and vices behind their glitter.—TEN BRINK, BERNHARD, 1877-83, *History of English Literature (To Wiclif), tr. Kennedy, p.* 298.

It was in 1303 that Robert of Brunne (known also as Robert Manning) began to compile the "Handlyng Synne," the work which, more clearly than any former one, foreshadowed the road that English literature was to tread from that time forward. . . . There are so many foreign words, that we should set the writer fifty years later than his true date had he not himself *written* it down. In this book we catch our first glimpse of many a word and idiom that were afterwards to live for ever in the English Bible and Prayer-book, works still in the womb of Time. . . . Robert of Brunne, the Patriarch of the New English, fairly well foreshadowed the proportion of outlandish gear that was to be the common rule in our land after his time. He has six French words out of fifty; a little later Mandeville and Chaucer were to have eight French words of fifty; this is the proportion in Shakespere's comic parts; and it is also the proportion in the every-day talk of our own time, as may be seen in the dialogues of Miss Yonge's and Mr. Trollope's works.—OLIPHANT, T. L. KINGTON, 1878, *The Old and Middle English, pp.* 447, 448, 588.

Manning is remarkable as being the first to use the modern English order of words.—EMERY, FRED PARKER, 1891, *Notes on English Literature, p.* 9.

Robert was doubtless one of the most important links in the chain immediately preceding Chaucer, but he cannot be called the "patriarch" of modern literary English with any more justice than Wycliffe, or the authors of "Havelok" and "King Horn," or the poets of the "Cædmon School."—HEATH, H. FRANK, 1894, *Social England, vol.* II, *p.* 541.

In the "Handlyng Synne" the reader may still breathe the same atmosphere that inspired the "Dialogues" of Gregory the Great; but he will also detect the presence of an element that prepares him for the transition to the style of Gower's "Confessio Amantis;" from which point he may travel by easy stages to the plots of the Elizabethan dramatists.—COURTHOPE, W. J., 1895, *A History of English Poetry, vol.* I, *p.* 142.

This is not, as might be supposed, a dry book. Mannyng dearly loved a tale, and the more bizarre it was, the better. He distributes his censures broadcast, but the worst offenders, from his point of view, are the women, who, he pleasantly observes, do no wrong except all day.—SNELL, F. J., 1899, *The Fourteenth Century, Periods of European Literature, p.* 390.

Richard de Bury

Richard Aungerville

1287–1345

Richard Aungerville (1281*-1345), churchman, is known as Richard de Bury, from his birthplace, Bury St. Edmunds. He studied at Oxford, became a Benedictine monk

*The "Dictionary of National Biography," following the "Encyclopaedia Britannica," and the "Biographia Britannica," says 1281, but this date rests upon an entirely mistaken reading of the final note in the Cottonian copy.—THOMAS, ERNEST C., 1888, *ed. Philobiblon, Introduction, p.* xii, *note.*

at Durham, and having been tutor to Edward III., was made successively Dean of Wells and Bishop of Durham, besides acting for a time as high chancellor, as ambassador to France and Germany, and as commissioner for a truce with Scotland. He had a passion for collecting manuscripts and books; and his principal work, "Philobiblon," intended to serve as a handbook to the library which he founded in connection with Durham College at Oxford (afterwards suppressed), describes the state of learning in England and France. See E. C. Thomas's edition of the "Philobiblon" (1888).—PATRICK AND GROOME, *eds.* 1897, *Chambers's Biographical Dictionary, p.* 52.

The end of the Philobiblon of Master Richard de Aungervile, surnamed de Bury, late Bishop of Durham. This treatise was finished in our manor-house of Auckland on the 24th day of January in the year of our Lord one thousand three hundred and forty-four, the fifty-eighth year of our age being exactly completed and the eleventh year of our pontificate drawing to an end; to the glory of God. Amen.—DE BURY, RICHARD, 1344, *Philobiblon, ed. and tr. Thomas, ch.* 29, *p.* 251.

He (Richard) saith of himselfe, "exstatico quodam librorum amore potenter se abreptum," that he was mightily carried away, and even beside himself, with immoderate love of bookes and desire of reading. He had alwaies in his house many chaplains, all great schollers. His manner was, at dinner and supper time, to haue some good booke read unto him, whereof he would discourse with his chaplaines a great part of the day following, if business interrupted not his course. He was very bountiful unto the poore.—GODWIN, FRANCIS, 1601, *Catalogue of the Bishops of England, p.* 524.

We will now, my dear Sir, begin "making out the catalogue" of victims to the BIBLIOMANIA! The first eminent character who appears to have been infected with this disease was Richard De Bury, one of the tutors of Edward III, and afterwards Bishop of Durham; a man, who has been uniformly praised for the variety of his erudition, and the intenseness of his ardor in book-collecting.—DIBDIN, THOMAS FROGNALL, 1809, *The Bibliomania; or Book-Madness, p.* 15.

His erudition appears crude and uncritical, his style indifferent, and his thoughts superficial. Yet I am not aware that he had any equal in England during this century.—HALLAM, HENRY, 1837-39, *Introduction to the Literature of Europe, pt.* i, *ch.* i, *par.* 88.

To solace his declining years, he wrote the "Philobiblon," in praise of books; a treatise which may now be perused with great pleasure, as it shows that the author had a most intimate acquaintance with the classics, and not only a passion for books exceeding that of any modern collector, but a rich vein of native humour, which must have made him a most delightful companion.—CAMPBELL, JOHN, LORD, 1845-56, *Lives of the Lord Chancellors and Keepers of the Great Seal of England, vol.* I, *p.* 194.

Widely varying judgments have been passed upon the intellectual position of De Bury. It was long the fashion to speak of him with Sir Henry Savile as the learnedest man of his age. More recent critics have regarded him as not a scholar himself, but a patron and encourager of scholarship. The truth lies perhaps midway between these different verdicts. . . . We must bear in mind that De Bury was essentially a man of affairs, and that his official preoccupations left him comparatively scanty intervals of time to devote to literature. The judgment of Petrarch may be sufficient to satisfy us as to the extent of his knowledge and the width of his literary interests. . . . The special interest to us of Richard De Bury is that he is, if not the prototype, at least the most conspicuous example of a class of men who have been more numerous in modern than in ancient or mediæval times. No man has ever carried to a higher pitch of enthusiasm the passion for collecting books. On this point, at least, De Bury and Petrarch were truly kindred spirits, and their community of feeling finds expression in a striking similarity of language. . . . There seems no sufficient reason to suppose that De Bury wrote any other book than the "Philobiblon."—THOMAS, ERNEST C., 1888, *ed. and tr. The Philobiblon of Richard de Bury, Introduction, pp.* xxxiv, xxxvii, xli.

William of Occam

1270–1347

Occam, or Ockham, William of, an English monk and scholastic philosopher of the 14th century, was a native of Ockham, in Surrey. He entered the Franciscan Order; was sent to study at Paris under the celebrated Duns Scotus; became a fellow of Merton College, Oxford, and a renowned teacher of the Scholastic philosophy. He was the greatest dialectician of his age, and obtained the name of "the Invincible Doctor." He asserted without reserve the rights of temporal sovereigns against the papal claims, and denied to the Pope any authority in secular affairs. He wrote against Pope John XXII., whom he treated as a heretic, and supported the anti-pope, Nicholas V., set up by the Emperor Louis of Bavaria. In the quarrel between the pope and the Franciscans, William of Ockham was the assertor of absolute poverty. His famous "Defence of Poverty" was condemned by the Pope, and he, with others, was arrested. But he escaped and took refuge at the Imperial Court. He was soon after excommunicated, and he died, at Munich, in 1347. . . . Among his most celebrated works are the "Disputatio super Potestate Ecclesiastica," the "Defence of Poverty," and the "Summa totius Logicæ." It is said that Luther had the works of Ockham at his fingers' ends, and that he was the only schoolman in his library whom he esteemed.—CATES, WILLIAM L. R., *ed.* 1867, *A Dictionary of General Biography*, *p.* 817.

Our Ockham, flushed with success against John Scotus, undertook another John, of higher Power and Place, even Pope John the three-and-twentieth, (?) and gave a mortal wound to his Temporal Power over Princes. He got a good Guardian, viz. Lewis of Bavaria the Emperor, whose Court was his Sanctuary, so that we may call him a School-man-Courtier. But he was excommunicated by the Pope, and the Masters of Paris condemned him for a Heretick, and burnt his Books. This, I conceive, was the cause why Luther was so vers'd in his Works, which he had at his fingers' ends, being the sole Schoolman in his Library whom he esteemed. However, at last the Pope took Wit in his Anger, finding it no policy to enrage so sharp a Pen; and though I find no Recantation or publick Submission of Ockham, yet he was restored to his state, and the repute of an acute School-man.—FULLER, THOMAS, 1662, *The Worthies of England, ed. Nichols, vol.* II, *p.* 362.

He did but sketch the principles of a philosophy afterwards completed; but his labours sufficed to withdraw the attention of his followers from the all-engrossing question of the principle of *Individuality*, and directed them rather to the acquirement of fresh knowledge.—TENNEMANN, WILLIAM GOTTLIEB, 1812–52, *A Manual of the History of Philosophy, tr. Johnson, ed. Morell, p.* 244.

Perhaps the hardest and severest intellectualist of all; a political fanatic, not like his visionary brethern, who brooded over the Apocalypse and their own prophets, but for the Imperial against the Papal Sovereignty. . . . In philosophy as intrepid and as revolutionary as in his political writings. He is a consummate schoolman in his mastery, as in his use of logic; a man who wears the armour of his age, engages in the spirit of his age, in the controversies of his age; but his philosophy is that of centuries later.—MILMAN, HENRY HART, 1855, *History of Latin Christianity, vol.* VI, *bk.* XIV, *ch.* III, *pp.* 451, 472.

That Occam has exercised a great influence on Philosophy in the large sense of that word, cannot, we think, be doubted. Though he never meddled with physical studies, as such, he did much to break those logical fetters by which Physics as much as Theology, were bound. His Nominalism was the assertion that a science exists purely for Names; it was therefore a step towards the separation of Real sciences from this. Occam perceived that Theology had a real *invisible* object, not to be enslaved by men's theories and conceptions. With a Roger Bacon at Oxford,—with all the new experience of Nature which the coming centuries were to bring forth,—how certain it was that in due time some method would be discovered of examining *visible* objects, as they are in themselves, not as we make them by the impressions of our senses, or the conclusions of our intellects.

Englishmen have a right to claim Occam as one of the instruments in this mighty scientific revolution, which it was the especial privilege of her sons to accomplish.—MAURICE, FREDERICK DENISON, 1862–73, *Moral and Metaphysical Philosophy, vol.* II, *p.* 16.

No Schoolman since Abelard had devoted himself to the study of logic with such fondness as William.—ERDMANN, JOHN EDUARD, 1865-76, *A History of Philosophy, ed. Hough, vol.* I, *p.* 503.

Refused to logic the exalted station which his master Duns Scotus had claimed for it. But by excluding from the field of discussion the chief dogmas of theology, as beyond the province of reason, and thus, with the English prudence and common sense which marks him as a forerunner of Bacon and Locke, avoiding the aërial heights of metaphysics, he was enabled to study logic more thoroughly at the lower level to which he had brought it.—TILLEY, ARTHUR, 1885, *The Literature of the French Renaissance, p.* 105.

Occam's influence was felt by Wyclif, and affected strongly the Gallican leaders in the reforming councils. It extended still later. His principles, and those of his disciples, were the maxims on which the resistance of Protestant princes to the authority of Rome was, to a considerable extent, based. Luther was a student of Occam, praises him as the most ingenious of the schoolmen, and derived from him his conception of the Lord's Supper—a conception suggested by Occam as a reasonable view, yet as one that furnishes an instance of the possible inconsistency of faith and reason. Notwithstanding the revolutionary influence that went forth from Occam, he was a conscientious and orthodox believer in the dogmas of the Church. His whole method of discussion is scholastic, and, in theology, he added a third school, that of the Occamists, to the previously existing parties, the Thomists and the Scotists.—FISHER, GEORGE PARK, 1887, *History of the Christian Church, p.* 271.

He was indeed strongest on the critical or negative side; and while he denied the "plenitudo potestatis" claimed for the papacy, he was not altogether disposed to place the emperor above the pope, nor was he happy in invoking, as was required by the controversy, the ultimate resort of a general council, even though formed alike of clergy and laymen, men and women. The infirmity of reason was with him the counterpart to the strength of the logician. He could criticise with freedom, but had scruples in reconstructing. He furnished invaluable weapons to those after him who opposed the authority of the pope, and even helped Luther in the elaboration of his doctrine concerning the sacrament; but his most enduring monument is found in the logical tradition which he established in the university of Paris.—POOLE, R. L., 1895, *Dictionary of National Biography, vol.* XLI, *p.* 361.

Richard Rolle of Hampole

C. 1290–1349

Richard Rolle (c.1290-1349), the "Hermit of Hampole," near Doncaster, was born at Thornton in Yorkshire, and was sent to Oxford, but from nineteen devoted himself to asceticism. He wrote religious books and rendered the Psalms into English prose. His great work is "The Pricke of Conscience" (*Stimulus Conscientiæ*), a poem written both in English and in Latin, on the instability of life, death, purgatory, doomsday, the pains of hell, and the joys of heaven (ed. by Morris, Philolog. Soc. 1863). Some of his prose pieces were edited by Perry in 1866; others Dr. Carl Horstmann in 1894-96.—PATRICK AND GROOME, *eds.*, 1897, *Chambers's Biographical Dictionary, p.* 458.

Richard Role, alias Hampole, had his first Name from his Father, the other from the place (three Miles from Doncaster) where living he was honoured, and dead was buried and sainted. He was an Heremite, led a strict life, and wrote many Books of Piety, which I prefer before his Propheticall Predictions, as but a degree above Almanack Prognostications. He threatened the Sins of the Nation with future Famine, Plague, Inundations, War, and such general Calamities, from which no Land is long free, but subject to them in some proportion. Besides, his Predictions, if *hitting*, were *heeded*: if *missing*, not *marked*. However, because it becomes me not ἁγιομαχεῖν, let him pass for a Saint. I will adde, that our Saviour's Dilemma to the Jews may partly be pressed on the Papists his Contemporaries. If Hampole's Doctrine was of Men, why was he generally reputed a Saint; if from God, why did they not obey him, seeing he spake much against the viciousness and covetousness of the Clergy of that Age?—FULLER, THOMAS, 1662, *The Worthies of England, ed. Nichols, vol.* II, *p.* 498.

His Latin theological tracts, both in prose and verse, are numerous; in which Leland justly thinks he has displayed more erudition than eloquence. His principal pieces of English rhyme are a Paraphrase of part of the book of Job, of the Lord's prayer, of the seven penitential psalms, and the "Pricke of Conscience." But our hermit's poetry, which indeed from these titles promises but little entertainment, has no tincture of sentiment, imagination, or elegance.—WARTON, THOMAS, 1778-81, *The History of English Poetry, sec.* vii.

The penitential psalms and theological tracts of a hermit were not likely to enrich or improve the style of our poetry; and they are accordingly confessed, by those who have read them, to be very dull. His name challenges notice, only from the paucity of contemporary writers.—CAMPBELL, THOMAS, 1819, *An Essay on English Poetry.*

Hampole commands a large vocabulary, from which he draws with lavish hand. He likes to mass synonyms, and does not hesitate to repeat words and turns of expression; nor does he in general proceed with pedantic uniformity, but occasionally looks forward and backward. Making no æsthetic claims, with only the desire to instruct and edify, striving only to make what is black, right black, and what is bright, very brilliant, he has, nevertheless, produced many very effective passages. His verses are flowing, but unlike most northern poets, he does not trouble himself at all about the number of syllables. The verses of his short couplets have always four accents, but often more than four unemphatic syllables. This, too, is characteristic of the man, who was indifferent to external symmetry. All in all, Hampole is the most notable English religious writer of the first half of the fourteenth century, and he had a corresponding influence upon later religious literature, especially that of the fifteenth century.—TEN BRINK, BERNHARD, 1877-83, *History of English Literature (To Wiclif), tr. Kennedy, p.* 296.

Noticeable for his English and Latin compositions, in prose and verse, and still more so by his character. He is the first on the list of those lay preachers, of whom England has produced a number, whom an inward crisis brought back to God, and who roamed about the country as volunteer apostles, converting the simple, edifying the wise, and, alas! affording cause for laughter to the wicked. They are taken by good folks for saints, and for madmen by sceptics: such was the fate of Richard Rolle, of George Fox, of Bunyan, and of Wesley. . . . Rolle of Hampole is, if we except the doubtful case of the "Ancren Riwle," the first English prose writer after the Conquest who can pretend to the title of original author. To find him we have had to come far into the fourteenth century. When he died, in 1349, Chaucer was about ten years of age and Wyclif thirty.—JUSSERAND, J. J., 1895, *A Literary History of the English People, pp.* 216, 218.

Richard Rolle was one of the most remarkable men of his time—yea, of history. It is a strange and not very creditable fact that one of the greatest of Englishmen has hitherto been doomed to oblivion. In other cases the human beast first crucifies and then glorifies or deifies the nobler minds who, swayed by the Spirit, do not live as others live, in quest of higher ideals by which to benefit the race. He, one of the noblest champions of humanity—a hero, a saint, a martyr in this cause—has never had his resurrection yet.—HORSTSMANN, CARL, 1896, *ed. Richard Rolle of Hampole, Introduction.*

Though not "the father of English literature," yet Richard Rolle may have influenced both prose and verse, as every skilled and popular writer must do. There is, however, nothing to show that he formed or modified it to any great extent. He was not a man of letters, like Spenser, striving to mould or polish a rugged speech. He used it as he found it. In his poetry it is improbable that he introduced any new measure or metre. To have done so would have frustrated his purpose. He wished to popularize sacred poetry, in order to banish profane love-songs.—BRIDGETT, T. E., 1897, *Richard Rolle, the Hermit, Dublin Review, vol.* 121, *p.* 292.

For the attribution to him of the revival of strictly alliterative verse there is little if any more warrant than for the ascription to him of the invention of the heroic. We can at the most (and also at the least) allow that this revival was a very reasonable consequence of the increased stimulus to literary composition in the North—always fonder of alliterative rhythm, and more rebel to strict metrical ways, than the South—of which he certainly was one of the lights and leaders.—SAINTSBURY, GEORGE, 1898, *A Short History of English Literature p.* 76.

Lawrence Minot

1300?-1352?

Poet (circa 1350), wrote a series of short poems on the victories of Edward III., beginning with the battle of Halidon Hill (1333), and ending with the siege of Guines Castle (1352). Among them is a lyric in celebration of the battle of Crecy (1346). An edition of his works was published by Ritson in 1795, and later in 1825.—ADAMS, W. DAVENPORT, 1877, *Dictionary of English Literature, p.* 438.

For want of a better poet, he may, by courtesy, be called the Tyrtæus of his age.—CAMPBELL, THOMAS, 1819, *An Essay on English Poetry.*

Ritson, the editor of Minot, praises his author for the ease, variety, and harmony of his versification, in which qualities he declares him to have no equals, previous to the sixteenth century, except Robert of Brunne and Tusser. As a poet Minot is certainly equal to these two writers, though perhaps not much superior. In one respect, however, he is entitled to some praise; he is the first English versifier who quits the beaten track of translation from chronicle, romance, and theology. As regards choice of subject he may be classed with his northern contemporary Barbour, though, in every other respect, he is far inferior to the Scottish Homer.—HIPPISLEY, J. H., 1837, *Chapters on Early English Literature, p.* 16.

He stands out clearly from the more ancient ballad-writers, in the subjective side of his poetry. We see Laurence Minot personally anxious for the welfare of England, personally praying for country and king; and the proud exultation over victories won that breaks forth in his songs, sounds from lips that speak in the name of the whole nation, but none the less in the name of this definite personality. The style and metrical form of Minot's songs are also individual, however they may conform to tradition, and regardless of the fact that all the elements into which exact analysis resolves them, were found already existing by the poet. His originality consists in the blending of the *technique* of the gleemen's song with that of the clerical lyric. . . . He has not, after all, given a vivid picture of the event that he sings. We obtain the parts of such a picture singly, like fragments that the waves of lyrical movement have borne to the shore. For with Minot the lyrical element is decidedly uppermost; it is unfortunately not powerful enough in itself to enchain our interest. Thus the impression we receive is very positive, but by no means unmixed; the impression made by a gifted man, who, half folk-poet and half art-poet, is neither entirely, and hence must rank beneath many less important writers.—TEN BRINK, BERNHARD, 1877-83, *History of English Literature (To Wiclif), tr. Kennedy, pp.* 322, 324.

His verses are sometimes spirited, but never especially significant.—GILMORE, J. H., 1880, *The English Language and its Early Literature, p.* 104.

No wonder that when the battles were fought by the people itself, and when the cost of the wars was to so large an extent defrayed by its self-imposed contributions, the Scottish and French campaigns should have called forth that national enthusiasm which found an echo in the songs of Lawrence Minot, as hearty war-poetry as has been composed in any age of our literature. They were put forth in 1352, and considering the unusual popularity they are said to have enjoyed, it is not impossible that they may have reached Chaucer's ears in his boyhood.—WARD, ADOLPHUS WILLIAM, 1880, *Chaucer, English Men of Letters, p.* 14.

Minot's verse is fluent; he can expatiate on an old current prophecy and follow the old military fashion of comparing men to beasts, but he has not the imagination or the insight of a poet, and is an artist only in the mechanism of his verse. —MORLEY, HENRY, 1888, *English Writers, vol,* IV, *p.* 262.

In the war-lyrics of our earliest national poet Laurence Minot,—who may be appropriately termed the laureate of Edward the Third's reign, as all his extant works celebrate the victories of that monarch,—we, for the first time in the history of our poetry, meet with original invention combined with vigorous expression.—FITZGIBBON, H. MACAULAY, 1888, *Early English and Scottish Poetry, Introduction, p.* xx.

Minot neither founded nor belonged to a school. In metrical form he presents, in various combinations, the accentual, alliterative verse of the west and north; and the syallabic, rhymed verse of the east and south; rhyme and some degree of alliteration being constant features. . . . While thus profuse in metrical ornament, Minot cannot, however, be said to show any further care for literary art. He writes in impetuous haste, but without true lyric inspiration; and his energy often confuses his narrative instead of driving it home. But while Minot has no great literary value, and gives almost no new information, he embodies in a most vivid way the militant England of his day. He has but one subject, the triumph of England and the English king over French and Scots. The class divisions among Englishmen are for him wholly merged in the unity of England; himself probably of Norman origin, his habitual language is the strongest and homeliest Saxon.—HERFORD, C. H., 1894, *Dictionary of National Biography, vol.* XXXVIII, *p.* 47.

He is given to expletives, he seldom or never succeeds in giving us a distinct visual picture; his very variety of metre, etc., looks more like the absence of any distinct grasp and command of one form than like a sense of general mastery. But, as has hardly been the case for three hundred years and more, he has a fairly settled tongue and a generally accepted prosody, with its peculiarities of lilt and swing all ready to his hands; and he manages to make very tolerably good use of them. Indeed, though it may seem rather ungracious, it is not impossible to say that his chief use in literature proper is that he *explains* Chaucer—shows how the tools were ready for the workman.—SAINTSBURY, GEORGE, 1898, *A Short History of English Literature, p.* 78.

It is in technical points that this writer displays his skill, and he half succeeds in elevating popular verse into a fine art. Minot is something of a court-minstrel, something of a ballad-singer, but he was not strong enough to do what Chaucer might have done in his place—transfigure this combination in the *rôle* of a great national poet.—SNELL, F. J., 1899, *The Fourteenth Century, Periods of European Literature, p.* 59.

Sir John Mandeville

1300?–1372?

Sir John Mandeville, *fl.* 1350 (?). The name under which the famous book of travels, composed about 1350, was written. The author is possibly identical with Jean de Bourgogne, who died at Liège, Nov. 1372. Earliest known MS. in French, 1371. First printed: in Dutch, 1470 (?); in German, 1475 (?); in French, 1480; in Italian, 1480; in Latin, 1485 (?); in English, 1499.—SHARP, R. FARQUHARSON, 1897, *A Dictionary of English Authors, p.* 185.

Besides the French, English, and Latin texts, there are others in Italian and Spanish, Dutch and Walloon, German, Bohemian, Danish, and Irish, and some three hundred manuscripts are said to have survived. In English Dr. Vogels enumerates thirty-four. In the British Museum are ten French, nine English, six Latin, three German, and two Irish manuscripts.—WARNER, G. F., 1893, *Dictionary of National Biography, vol.* XXXVI, *p.* 28.

I, John Maundevylle, Knyght, alle be it I be not worthi, that was born in Englond, in the Town of Seynt Albones, passed the See, in the Zeer of our Lord Jesu Crist MCCCXXII, in the Day of Seynt Michelle; and hidre to have ben longe tyme over the See, and have seyn and gon thorghe manye dyverse Londes, and many Provynces and Kingdomes and Iles, and have passed thorghe Tartarye, Percye, Ermonye the litylle and the grete; thorghe Lybye, Caldee, and a gret partie of Ethiope; thorghe Amazoyne, Inde the lasse and the more, a gret partie; and thorghe out many othere Iles, that ben abouten Inde; where dwellen many dyverse Folkes, and of dyverse Maneres and Lawes, and of dyverse Schappes of Men. . . . And zee schulle undirstonde, that I have put this Boke out of Latyn into Frensche, and translated it azen out of Frensche into Englyssche, that every Man of my Nacioun may undirstonde it.—MANDEVILLE, SIR JOHN, 1356? *Voiage and Travaile, The Prologue.*

A lytell Treatise or Booke, named John Mandevyll, Knyht, borne in Englande, in the towne of Saynt Abone, and speaketh of the wayes of the Holy Lande toward Jherusalem, and of the Marvyles of Ynde and other diverse Countries.—WORDE, WINKYN DE, 1499, *Mandeville, First ed. Title.*

John Mandevil Knight, borne in the Towne of S. Albans, was so well given to the study of Learning from his childhood, that he seemed to plant a good part of his felicitie in the same: for he supposed, that the honour of his Birth would nothing availe him, except he could render the same more honourable, by his knowledge in good letters. Having therefore well grounded himselfe in Religion, by reading the Scriptures, he applied his studies to the Art of Physicke, a Profession worthy a noble Wit: but amongst other things, he was ravished with a mightie desire to see the greater parts of the World, as Asia and Africa.—BALE, JOHN, 1549-57, *Scriptorum Illustrium Majoris Britanniæ, tr. Hakluyt.*

Captain Robert Pugh assures me that Sir John Mandeville, the famous traveller, lyes buryed at Liege in Germany, with which note amend lib. B[d], where I thought he had been buryed at St. Alban's abbey church as Mr. Thomas Gore told me. But I thinke I remember something writt of him there in a table on a pillar or wall: but he was there borne (as in his life).—AUBREY, JOHN, 1669-96, *Brief Lives, ed. Clark, vol.* II, *p.* 42.

There are no books, which I more delight in than in travels, especially those that describe remote countries, and give the writer an opportunity of showing his parts without incurring any danger of being examined or contradicted. Among all the authors of this kind, our renowned countryman, Sir John Mandeville, has distinguished himself, by the copiousness of his invention and greatness of his genius. The second to Sir John I take to have been Ferdinand Mendez Pinto, a person of infinite adventure, and unbounded imagination. One reads the voyages of these two great wits, with as much astonishment as the travels of Ulysses in Homer, or of the Red Cross Knight in Spenser. All is enchanted ground, and fairy-land.—ADDISON AND STEELE, 1710, *The Tatler, No.* 254, *Nov.* 23.

Mandeville has become proverbial for indulging in a traveler's exaggerations; yet his accounts of the countries which he visited have been found far more veracious than had been imagined. His descriptions of Cathay, and the wealthy province of Mangi, agreeing with those of Marco Pollo, had great authority with Columbus. —IRVING, WASHINGTON, 1828–55, *The Life and Voyages of Columbus, vol.* iii, *p.* 399, *Appendix*

I will undertake to say that, of no book, with the exception of the Scriptures, can more manuscripts be found of the end of the fourteenth and beginning of the fifteenth centuries.—HALLIWELL-PHILLIPS, JAMES ORCHARD, 1839, *ed. The Voiage and Travaile of Sir John Maundevile, kt., Introduction, p.* xii.

Mandeville was the Bruce of the fourteenth century, as often calumniated, and even ridiculed. The most ingenuous of voyagers has been condemned as an idle fabulist; the most cautious, as credulous to fatuity; and the volume of a genuine writer, which has been translated into every European language, has been formally ejected from the collection of authentic travels. His truest vindication will be found by comprehending him; and, to be acquainted with his character, we must seek for him in his own age. . . . Sir John Mandeville's probity remains unimpeached; for the accuracy of whatever he relates from his own personal observation has been confirmed by subsequent travellers.—DISRAELI, ISAAC, 1840, *Mandeville, Our First Traveller; Amenities of Literature.*

More credulous than the most bigotted monk.—WRIGHT, THOMAS, 1848, *Early Travels in Palestine, Introduction, p.* XXV.

Although the dialect of Mandeville exhibits the language, upon the whole, in a more developed phase than the works of any preceding author, there is otherwise nothing in his volume which marks him as an Englishman. It is purely a record of observations, and a detail of information gathered from other resources.—MARSH, GEORGE P., 1862, *The Origin and History of the English Language, etc., p.* 271.

His style is clear, simple, and natural. It is to a modern reader the easiest of all the English writings of the fourteenth century; and it is certainly the most entertaining.—CREASY, SIR EDWARD S., 1870, *History of England, vol.* II, *p.* 548.

Extraordinary legends and fables, every sort of credulity and ignorance, abound in his book.—TAINE, H. A., 1871, *History of English Literature, tr. Van Laun, vol.* I, *bk.* i, *ch.* ii, *p.* 85.

Gives us his gossipy, fugacious travels that stint at no marvels, and grant to myths as easy admittance as if the author were at a fairy tale. There are thus huddled together, fancies for the poet and a few facts for the historian; as first reapers, on the margin of a great field, may gather and bind in one sheaf, grass and flowers and scattered heads of grain. —BASCOM, JOHN, 1874, *Philosophy of English Literature, p.* 49.

One of the most remarkable features of this singular work is the evidence it affords of a great advance in geographical knowledge since the period of the first crusade. Mandeville devotes the whole of a highly-interesting chapter to an attempt to prove the earth a sphere, and the existence of antipodes not only possible but in the highest degree probable. From a scientific point of view this chapter is worth all the rest of the book put together, as it affords evidence that during his long sojourn at Cairo he had become indoctrinated with the systems of Arab geographers.—BECKER, BERNARD HENRY, 1878, *Adventurous Lives, vol.* II, *p.* 98.

An ingenuous voyager; the first example of the liberal and independent gentleman journeying over the world in pursuit of knowledge, honored wherever he went for his talents and personal acomplishments. If he was gossipy and credulous, it was because his age was so. The critic who thus comprehends him, will neither calumniate nor ridicule him. A journey over the globe at that distant day was scarcely less solemn than a departure to the realm of spirits; and, considering the circumstances under which he travelled and wrote, he must be conceded to have been a remarkable man. If he related fables, he did it honestly, while other accounts, long resting on his single and unsupported authority, have been confirmed by later discoveries,—as the burning of widows on the funeral pile of their husbands—the artificial egg-hatching in Egypt—the spheroidal form of the earth—the crocodile—the hippopotamus—the Chinese predilection for small feet—the trees which bear wool of which clothing is made.—WELSH, ALFRED H., 1882, *Development of English Literature and Language, vol.* I, *p.* 198.

That none of the forms of the English version can conceivably be from the same hand which wrote the original work is made patent to any critical reader by their glaring errors of translation, but the form now current asserts in the preface that it was made by Mandeville himself, and this assertion has been taken on trust by almost all modern historians of English literature. The words of the original "je eusse cest livret mis en latin. . . mais. . . je l'ay mis en romant" were mistranslated as if "je eusse" meant "I had" instead of "I should have," and then (whether of fraudulent intent or by the error of a copyist thinking to supply an accidental omission) the words were added "and translated it agen out of Frensche and Englyssche." Schönborn and Mätzner respectively seem to have been the first to show that the current Latin and English texts cannot possibly have been made by Mandeville himself. Dr. J. Vogels states the same of unprinted Latin versions which he has discovered in the British Museum, and he has proved it as regards the Italian version. The terseness, the simplicity, and the quaintness of the English version, together with the curiosity of the subject-matter, will always make it delightful reading; but the title "father of English prose," which in its stricter sense already belonged to King Alfred, must in its looser sense be now transferred to Wickliffe.—NICHOLSON, E. B., AND YULE, H., 1883, *Encyclopaedia Britannica, 9th ed., vol.* XV, *p.* 475.

SIR JOHN,—Wit you well that men holden you but light, and some clepen you a Liar. And they say that you never were born in Englond, in the town of Seynt Albones, nor have seen and gone through manye diverse Londes. And there goeth an old knight at arms, and one that connes Latyn, and hath been beyond the sea, and hath seen Prester John's country. And he hath been in an Yle that men clepen Burmah, and there bin women bearded. Now men call him Colonel Henry Yule, and he hath writ of thee in his great booke, Sir John, and he holds thee but lightly. For he saith that ye did pill your tales out of Odoric his book, and that ye never saw snails with shells as big as houses, nor never met no Devyls, but part of that ye say, ye took it out of William of Boldensele his book, yet ye took not his wisdom, withal, but put in thine own foolishness. Nevertheless, Sir John, for the frailty of Mankynde, ye are held a good fellow, and a merry; so now, come, I shall tell you of the new ways into Ynde.—LANG, ANDREW, 1886, *Letters to Dead Authors, p.* 110.

There seems to be no reason for questioning the authenticity of Maundeville's book, but very great reason for considering it to have been based partly upon actual experience, partly upon compilation from records of other men who had been about in the world. The object was to make a book of travels in which, for unity of plan, the Holy Places of Jerusalem should be approached from different directions, and the record of what was to be seen should be made full, lively, and interesting. Obviously, also, the information given would be received most easily and pleasantly if it were associated throughout with the movements of a single traveller. In all forms of instruction writers then incorporated the experiences and thoughts of their predecessors, and repeated thoughts or facts without much regard for the claims of the men by whom they were first uttered or discovered. What should we think now of a Dan Michel who issued an "Ayenbite of Inwit" as a book for the English people without mentioning that it was translated from the French? Remembering the difference of times, and that in a tale of travel there must be a traveller, who will excite most interest when he speaks in his own person, we need not reproach Sir John Maundeville—who is but a name—for eking out his own experience with the experiences of other men when he made a travel book for general instruction and delight.—MORLEY, HENRY, 1888, *English Writers, vol.* IV, *p.* 282.

What we may count for certain about the matter is this:—There does exist a very considerable budget of delightfully extravagant travellers' tales, bearing the Mandeville name, and written in an English which—with some mending of bygone words—is charming now: and which may be called the first fair and square book of the new English prose;—meaning by that—the first book of length and of popular currency which introduced a full measure—perhaps over-running measure—of those words of Romance or Latin origin, which afterward came to be incorporated in the English of the fifteenth century. The book has no English qualities—beyond its language; and might have been written by a Tartar, who could tell of Munchausen escapes and thank God in good current dialect of Britain.—MITCHELL, DONALD G., 1889, *English Lands, Letters, and Kings, From Celt to Tudor, p.* 60.

For a long time, and up to our day, the title and dignity of "Father of English prose" has been borne by Sir John Mandeville, of St. Albans, knight, who, "in the name of God glorious," left his country in the year of grace 1322, on Michaelmas Day, and returned to Europe after an absence of thirty-four years, twice as long as Robinson Crusoe remained in his desert island. This title belongs to him no longer. The good knight of St. Albans, who had seen and told so much, has dwindled before our eyes, has lost his substance and his outline, and has vanished like smoke in the air. His coat of mail, his deeds, his journeys, his name: all are smoke. He first lost his character as a truthful writer; then out of the three versions of his book, French, English, and Latin, two were withdrawn from him, leaving him only the first. Existence now has been taken from him, and he is left with nothing at all. Sir John Mandeville, knight, of St. Albans, who crossed the sea in 1322, is a myth, and never existed; he has joined, in the kingdom of the shades and the land of nowhere, his contemporary the famous "Friend of God of the Oberland," who some time ago also ceased to have existed. One thing however remains, and cannot be blotted out: namely, the book of travels bearing the name of Mandeville the translation of which is one of the best and oldest specimens of simple and flowing English prose.—JUSSERAND, J. J., 1895, *A Literary History of the English People, p.* 403.

Dauntless literary freebooter, dowered with an imagination so tremendous in its inventiveness as at times to make even the grasping credulity of the Middle Ages stand aghast. . . . But take Sir John with an open mind, and in the spirit of his age, and you will find his "Voiage and Travaile" one of the most entertaining and delightful of books.—GRANT, JOHN CAMERON, 1895, *ed. Mandeville, Preface.*

The more one examines the Mandeville problem the more bewildering does it appear. The only thing that seems at all certain is that the English book is based on a French original produced at Liège soon after the middle of the fourteenth century, by a physician of that city who had visited the court of a Mameluke Sultan some thirty years before. Whether he was a Belgian posing as an English knight, or an English knight disguised as a Belgian, will perhaps remain unknown to the end of time. . . . In short, if the interest of a problem were to be measured by its difficulty rather than by its importance, it must be allowed that this Mandeville question deserves a place by the side of the "Letters of Junius," or the "Man in the Iron Mask." The old notion of Mandeville, as the "father of English prose," may indeed be considered as abandoned. But whether the author of the original French book was a Belgian doctor or a knight of St. Albans will perhaps always remain an open question.—KEENE, H. G., 1896, *Sir John Mandeville, Westminster Review, vol.* 146, *pp.* 52, 54.

He uses many French words, while his English is as modern in the main as that of the Elizabethan age.—HUTSON, CHARLES WOODWARD, 1897, *The Story of Language, p.* 286.

The French version of Mandeville may be—very likely is—the oldest. It may have been—it very likely though by no means necessarily was—written by some one who was not an Englishman. But it is a book which, in the history of literature, has very little importance. French prose had been written currently on all subjects for two centuries before it; and there was nothing remarkable in its existence. No one has contended that the French author can for a moment vie with Villehardouin, or Joinville, of his own contemporary Froissart, as a prose writer. The book has had no influence on French literary history—no great French writer has been inspired by it, none of its "notes" in the least corresponds to any mark of French. The contrary of all these things is the case in regard to the English version. Even the infidels do not place that version much later than 1400, and it may be permitted to doubt whether it is not older; for though the prose shows an advance in ease and resource on Wyclif, a great one on Trevisa, it is not much, if at all, in front of Chaucer. It is quite an admirable thing in itself; it shows, if it be a translation, that some third person must be added to Malory and Berners to make a trinity of such English translators, as the world has rarely seen, in the fifteenth century. It expresses with remarkable fidelity the travelling mania of the English, and in the stories of the "Watching of the Falcon," the "Daughter of Hippocrates," and others, it has supplied romantic inspiration for generation after generation. As French it is little or nothing to Frenchmen or to France; as English it is a great thing to England and to Englishmen.—SAINTSBURY, GEORGE, 1898, *A Short History of English Literature, p.* 148.

JOHN KNOX

From Engraving by B. Holl, from

JOHN WYCLIF

From Engraving by Edward Finden,

John Wyclif

1324?-1384

Born, 1320(?). Educated at Oxford. Fellow, and afterwards Master of Balliol Coll. Rector of Fillingham, 1361-69; Rector of Ludgershall, 1369-74. D.D., Oxford, 1370. Rector of Lutterworth, 1374-84. Attended conference with Papal Legates at Bruges, 1375. Accused of heresy, 1377 and 1378. Forbidden to lecture at Oxford, 1381. Again accused of heresy, 1382. Engaged on English translation of Bible, from 1382. Died, at Lutterworth, 31 Dec. 1384. Buried there. *Works:* Wyclif's translation of the Bible was published complete, ed. by J. Forshall and Sir F. Madden (4 vols.), 1850; "Select English Works," ed. by T. Arnold (3 vols.), 1869-71; "English Works hitherto unprinted," ed. by F. D. Matthew, 1880.—SHARP, R. FARQUHARSON, 1897, *A Dictionary of English Authors, p.* 306.

PERSONAL

By the institution of many, if they are indeed worthy of belief, deploring it deeply, it has come to our ears that John de Wycliffe, rector of the church of Lutterworth, in the diocese of Lincoln, Professor of the Sacred Scriptures, (would that he were not also Master of Errors,) has fallen into such a detestable madness that he does not hesitate to dogmatize and publicly preach, or rather vomit forth from the recesses of his breast certain propositions and conclusions which are erroneous and false. He has cast himself also into the depravity of preaching heretical dogmas which strive to subvert and weaken the state of the whole church and even secular polity, some of which doctrines, in changed terms, it is true, seem to express the perverse opinions and unlearned learning of Marsilio of Padua of cursed memory, and of John of Jandun, whose book is extant, rejected and cursed by our predecessor, Pope John XXII, of happy memory This he has done in the kingdom of England, lately glorious in its power and in the abundance of its resources, but more glorious still in the glistening piety of its faith, and in the distinction of its sacred learning; producing also many men illustrious for their exact knowledge of the Holy Scriptures, mature in the gravity of their character, conspicuous in devotion, defenders of the Catholic church. He has polluted certain of the faithful of Christ by besprinkling them with these doctrines, and led them away from the right paths of the aforesaid faith to the brink of perdition. . . . Moreover, you are on our authority to arrest the said John, or cause him to be arrested and to send him under a trustworthy guard to our venerable brother, the Archbishop of Canterbury, and the Bishop of London, or to one of them. . . . Given at Rome, at Santa Maria Maggiore, on the 31st of May, the sixth year of our pontificate.—GREGORY XI, 1378, *Bull Against John Wycliffe, England in the Time of Wycliffe, ed. Cheyney, pp.* 11, 12.

In the ix zere of this king, John Wiclef, the organ of the devel, the enemy of the Cherch, the confusion of men, the ydol of heresie, the meroure of ypocrisie, the norischer of scisme, be the rithful dome of God, was smet with a horibil paralsie throw oute his body.—CAPGRAVE, JOHN, 1385, *A Chronicle of England.*

On the day of St. Thomas the Martyr, Archbishop of Canterbury, that organ of the Devil, that enemy of the Church, that confusion of the populace, that idol of heretics, that mirror of hypocrites, that instigator of schism, that sower of hatred, that fabricator of lies, John Wiclif,—when, on the same day, *as it is reported,* he would have vomited forth the blasphemies, which he had prepared in his sermon against St. Thomas,—being suddenly struck by the judgment of God, felt all his limbs invaded by the palsy. That mouth, which had spoken monstrous things against God and his Saints, or the holy Church, was then miserably distorted, exhibiting a frightful spectacle to the beholders. His tongue, now speechless, denied him even the power of confessing. His head shook, and thus plainly showed that the curse which God had thundered forth against Cain, was now fallen upon him. And, that none might doubt of his being consigned to the company of Cain, he showed by manifest outward signs, that he died in despair.—WALSINGHAM, THOMAS c 1400, *History, p.* 338.

Hitherto the corpse of John Wickliffe had quietly slept in his grave, about one-and-forty years after his death, till his body was reduced to bones, and his bones almost to dust. For though the earth in the chancel of Lutterworth in Leicestershire, where he was interred, hath not so quick a digestion with the earth of Aceldama, to consume flesh in twenty-four hours, yet such the appetite thereof, and all other English graves, to leave small reversions of a body after so many years. But now, such the spleen of the council of Constance, as they not only cursed his memory, as dying an obstinate heretic, but ordered that his bones (with this charitable caution, "if it may be discerned from the bodies of other faithful people,") to be taken out of the ground, and thrown far off from any Christian burial. In obedience hereunto, Richard Fleming, bishop of Lincoln, diocesan of Lutterworth, sent his officers (vultures with a quick sight scent at a dead carcase) to ungrave him accordingly. To Lutterworth they come, Sumner, Commissary, Official, Chancellor, Proctors, Doctors, and the servants (so that the remnant of the body would not hold out a bone, amongst so many hands) take what was left out of the grave, and burnt them to ashes, and cast them into Swift, a neighbouring brook running hard by. Thus this brook hath conveyed his ashes into Avon, Avon into Severn, Severn into the narrow seas, they into the main ocean. And thus the ashes of Wickliffe are the emblem of his doctrine, which now is dispersed all the world over.—FULLER, THOMAS, 1655, *The Church History of Britain, bk.* iv, *sec.* ii, *par.* 51–3.

I know no person of ecclesiastical eminence, whose life and character have cost me more thought and care, than Wickliff's. And after all, there is not much to record that deserves the peculiar attention of godly persons. I have consulted the best authorities, and in scrutinizing their contents have been mortified to find, that I could not conscientiously join with the popular cry in ranking this man among the highest worthies of the church. A political spirit, as we have seen, deeply infected his conduct.—It nevertheless remains true, that sincere Christians, and more particularly the protestants of all succeeding ages, are bound thankfully to acknowledge the divine goodness, for that there actually existed in the personal character of Wickliff "some good thing toward the Lord," that such a character was providentially raised up at the very time it was so much wanted, and, that from his labours considerable benefit accrued to the church of Christ, both in England and upon the continent.—MILNER, JOSEPH, 1794-1809, *History of the Church of Christ, ed. Haweis, Century* XIV, *ch.* iii, *p.* 597.

Once more the Church is seized with sudden fear,
And at her call is Wicliffe disinhumed:
Yea, his dry bones to ashes are consumed
And flung into the brook that travels near;
Forthwith, that ancient Voice which Streams can hear,
Thus speaks (that Voice which walks upon the wind,
Though seldom heard by busy human-kind)—
"As thou these ashes, little Brook! wilt bear
Into the Avon, Avon to the tide
Of Severn, Severn to the narrow seas,
Into main Ocean they, this deed accurst
An emblem yields to friends and enemies
How the bold Teacher's Doctrine, sanctified
By truth, shall spread, throughout the world dispersed."

—WORDSWORTH, WILLIAM, 1821–22, *Ecclesiastical Sonnets, pt.* ii, xvii.

We know not the number of sermons composed by Wycliffe, but that copies of nearly three hundred should have escaped the effort which was so long made to effect the destruction of whatever his pen had produced, is sufficient to assure us, that his labours as a preacher were abundant. His zeal was not of that spurious kind which assails the vast only, or which expatiates on the great and the future, at the cost of every nearer and more humble department of duty. Accordingly, to appreciate the character of the English reformer, it is necessary to view him, not only as advocating the claims of his sovereign before the delegates of the pontiff; as solving the questions which perplexed the English parliament; or as challenging the most intellectual of the age to discussions on the truth of his acknowledged doctrine. To all this he added the diligent performance of those less imposing duties which devolve on the parish priest. It was no novelty to see the venerable Wycliffe in a village pulpit, surrounded by his rustic auditory; or in the lowest hovel of the poor, fulfilling his office at the bedside of the sick and the dying, whether freeman or slave. It was over a sphere thus extended, that his genius and benevolence were diffused. —VAUGHAN, ROBERT, 1828–31, *The Life and Opinions of John de Wycliffe, vol.* II, *p.* 12.

To us he appears, for the most part, as a sort of unembodied agency. To delineate his *character*, in the fullest and most interesting sense of that word, would be to write romance, and not biography. During a portion of his life, indeed, he is more or less mixed up with public interests and transactions: but of these matters our notices are but poor and scanty; and, if they were more copious, they would, probably, do little towards supplying us with those nameless particulars to which biography owes its most powerful charm. . . . He stands before us in a sort of grand and mysterious loneliness. To group him, if we so may speak, with other living men, would require a very strong effort of the imagination.—LE BAS, CHARLES WEBB, 1832, *The Life of Wiclif, pp.* 266, 267.

After the lapse of four centuries and a half, his memory is as fresh as ever; the very children in our cottages are taught to love their native place the better, because it was once his home, and afforded him a grave, and the simple announcement that we desire to "thank God for that which he wrought," becomes a rallying cry for a whole neighborhood.—GURNEY, REV. J. HAMPDEN, 1837, *Sermon Preached on the Erection of a Monument to the Memory of Wycliffe.*

Lutterworth is a small market town in the neighbourhood of Leicester. There the church may still be seen, where this great and early reformer of the English Church preached the Gospel of Christ crucified in its entireness and its simplicity. The very pulpit is the same from which he held forth the word of life to his people, and in the vestry is preserved the old oak chair in which, according to the tradition of the place, the pastor of Lutterworth died; this with a solid table, which is also said to have been his, came out of the old Rectory, when it was pulled down some fifty years ago. The church tower is a sort of landmark to the country round, standing on the highest spot in the immediate neighborhood.—TAYLER, C. B., 1853, *Memorials of the English Martyrs, Lutterworth.*

The German Reformers of the sixteenth century never accorded to Wycliffe that frank, impartial acknowledgment which was due to him, owing probably to the lack of accurate historical information. Between him and the Reformers of the Swiss school there is however a specific resemblance. This is true with regard even to personal character: pure intellect without, mythic, contemplative, romantic elements, overruling imagination and feeling, combined with a stern temperament like that of Calvin.—BÖHRINGER, FRIEDRICH, 1856, *Life of Wycliffe, p.* 606.

In the pictures and representations that have come down to us, he appears as an old, thin, and slenderly formed man, while in some he is represented as having sunken features. He is dressed in the robe commonly worn by ecclesiastics at Oxford during that age, and carries a staff and book in his hands. In one portrait of him, which has only been recently discovered, his name has been carefully covered by the words, "Robert Langton;" and it is obvious that this must have been done by some friend and adherent, who wished by this device to save the picture during the period of persecution. From the testimony of all who came in contact with him, he must have possessed very remarkable powers of exhortation and persuasion; for, three and twenty years after his death, one of those who subsequently suffered martyrdom for adhering to his doctrines, declares that Wiclif was the first theologian of his age; while in the year 1406, the University of Oxford gave expression to its admiration of the man by declaring, that both in word and deed he was a true champion of the faith, untainted by the leaven of heresy; and that he stood foremost and without a rival among all who had either taught or written on logic or philosophy, or on ethical and speculative theology. His knowledge, his talents and his piety secured to him the esteem and devotion of all classes, whether high or low.—PAULI, REINHOLD, 1861, *Pictures of Old England, tr. Otté, p.* 289.

It would be difficult to find another character in English history whose individuality is so thoroughly lost in his deeds as in the case of John Wiclif, the Reformer. We know him as the indefatigable Oxford student, as the humble parish priest, as the controversial disputant, as the first complete English translator of the Scriptures, as a voice which made itself heard in a dark time, as a witness for the pure Gospel of Christ when that Gospel was hidden from men's eyes by the interpolation of many human errors and human vices; as the philosopher, the divine, the faithful Reformer of a corrupt Church, we know John Wiclif—but of the incidents of his life, of his origin, his childhood, his domestic being, we know nothing; and so great is the magnitude and so vitally important to the destinies of the country is the work which he accomplished, that the natural curiosity we have for prying into the interior life of great men is extinguished in the case of John Wiclif.—HILL, O'DELL TRAVERS, 1867, *English Monasticism; p.* 427.

The world lost in him one of the most sturdy heroes that the fruitful soil of England ever bore. The reformer of the fourteenth century does not belie his origin; we see it in that practical tendency which, with all his idealism, pulsates through his veins; in that measured boldness which marks all his doings. The great reformers of the sixteenth century throw his figure somewhat into the shade. Wyclif does not possess the genial vein of a Luther, nor the stern greatness of a Calvin. He does not rouse our enthusiasm like the former, nor impress us with fearful admiration like the latter. But he is, perhaps, better balanced than either, and unites many of their excellences, though he possesses these excellences in a less degree; the impression he produces is therefore weaker and less direct. On his contemporaries his personality exercised an irresistible fascination; but it is only, as it were, indirectly and by reflection that we can appreciate Wyclif to-day, while the names of Luther and Calvin arouse our imagination at once. In commendation of his character it is sufficient to say that he was one of the most moral, active, and courageous men that ever lived.—TEN BRINK, BERNHARD, 1892, *History of English Literature* (*Wyclif, Chaucer, Earliest Drama, Renaissance*), *tr. Robinson, p.* 29.

It is but a melancholy picture which is presented to us of these Richmondshire Wycliffes, poor in purse, proscribed in religion, proud of heart, gradually fading away amongst the more substantial Northern Catholics, sternly repudiating the one strong member of their race who ranks with the great Worthies of England, and owing much of their later misfortune to the obstinacy with which they cherished the discarded faith. The last of the Wycliffes was a poor gardener, who dined every Sunday at Thorpe Hall, as the guest of Sir Marmaduke Tunstall, on the strength of his reputed descent. But five hundred years ago the family was anything but inconsiderable; and a lord of Wycliffe who renounced his lordship in order to embrace ecclesiastical poverty would enjoy a high reputation for that reason alone, both at Oxford and at London. We are not without evidence that John Wyclif made such a renunciation.—SERGEANT, LEWIS, 1892, *The Birth and Parentage of Wyclif, The Athenæum, No.* 3359, *p.* 345.

TRANSLATION OF THE BIBLE

This Master John Wyclif translated into the Anglic—not Angelic—tongue, the Gospel that Christ gave to the clergy and the doctors of the Church, that they might minister it gently to laymen and weaker persons, according to the exigence of their time, their personal wants, and the hunger of their minds; whence it is made vulgar by him, and more open to the reading of laymen and women than it usually is to the knowledge of lettered and intelligent clergy; and thus the pearl of the Gospel is cast forth and trodden under feet of swine.—KNIGHTON, HENRY, 1395?, *Decem Scriptores* X, *ed. Twysden, col.* 2664.

It is a dangerous thing to translate the text of Holy Scripture out of one tongue into another. . . . We therefore decree and ordain, that no man henceforth by his own authority translate any text of the Scriptures into English or any other tongue by way of a book, pamphlet, or treatise; and that no man read any such book, pamphlet, or treatise, now lately composed in the time of Wyclif . . . upon pain of the greater excommunication, until the said translation be approved by the ordinary of the place, or, if the case so require, by the council provincial.—*Convocation of Oxford*, 1408.

There was another weapon which the rector of Lutterworth wielded with equal address and still greater efficacy. In proof of his doctrines he appealed to the scriptures, and thus made his disciples judges between him and the bishops. Several versions of the sacred writings were even then extant: but they were confined to libraries, or only in the hands of persons who aspired to superior sanctity. Wycliffe made a new translation, multiplied the copies with the aid of transcribers, and by his poor priests recommended it to the perusal of their hearers. In their hands it became an engine of wonderful power. Men were flattered by the appeal to their private judgment: the new doctrines insensibly acquired partisans and protectors in the higher classes, who alone were acquainted with the use of letters; a spirit of inquiry was generated; and the seeds were sown of that religious revolution which in little more than a century astonished and convulsed the nations of Europe.—LINGARD, JOHN, 1819-30, *A History of England, vol.* IV, *p.* 266.

One of the most important effects produced by the Wycliffite versions on the English language is . . . the establishment of what is called the sacred or religious dialect, which was first fixed in those versions, and has, with little variation, continued to be the language of devotion and of scriptural translation of the present day. . . . In fact, so much of the Wycliffite sacred dialect is retained in the standard version, that though a modern reader may occasionally be embarrassed by an obsolete word, idiom, or spelling, which occurs in Wycliffe's translation, yet if the great reformer himself were now to be restored to life, he would probably be able to read our common Bible from beginning to end, without having to ask the explanation of a single passage. —MARSH, GEORGE P., 1862, *The Origin and History of the English Language, etc., pp.* 365, 370.

The books which he wrote, so far as they were merely controversial books denouncing his opponents, may have some value for the ecclesiastical reader; but I should not care to notice them here; they would have left no stamp upon subsequent times, whatever they might have done for his own. But the book by which he really spoke to the hearts of the English tradesmen and farmers was his translation of the Bible. This was not an attack upon friars, but a living substitute for their legends and fictions. It was written in letters, but it came to the English citizens like a voice which was speaking to them rather than as something which was to be spelt out. It spoke to them as men busy in handicrafts, as men who had the earth to till and subdue. It spoke to them as husbands, fathers, citizens. It spoke to them as men, as having that in them which united them to the doctors and the nobles; to people in the times of old, to people in the farthest corners of the earth. As a mere translation, it is of only secondary value, for it is taken from the Latin. The worth of it lies in its English; it has fixed the language, it has become a ground of the literature. No other book could have been that—no book which did not address itself directly to the people, no book which did not come with an authority. I do not mean with an ecclesiastical or state authority—the ecclesiastics and the King forbade the reading of it—I mean with the authority which the people of Judæa felt when they stood about the mount, and One opened His mouth who spake to them, not as a scribe, but as a King.—MAURICE, FREDERICK DENISON, 1865-74, *The Friendship of Books and other Lectures, ed. Hughes, p.* 74.

Wyclif's translations of the Scriptures, as well as those of his time generally, were themselves made from a translation, the Vulgate of Jerome. Even if he had understood Greek,—he occasionally uses Greek words,—it is not likely that he could have found, in all England, a copy of the Greek Testament accessible, from which to make his translation. Copies of the New Testament manuscripts, and other manuscripts in Greek, were almost unknown in Western Europe until the capture of Constantinople by the Turks in 1543, and the consequent diffusion of Greek learning by the wide dispersion of Greek fugitives. The Hebrew of the Old Testament, too, was only known through the same Latin version. . . . Without doubt Wyclif used the text of the Vulgate current in his time, but, as we have reason to believe, in connection with it, he also collated such scanty Latin manuscript copies as were accessible. Considerable evidence has been adduced to show that he used a text which appeared to him after a comparison of old copies to be on the whole the most correct.—BISSELL, EDWIN CONE, 1873, *The Historic Origin of the Bible, pp.* 11, 12.

The two great authors of this time are Wycliffe and Chaucer; and their influence upon the language cannot well be overestimated. To the translation of the Scriptures, completed about 1380 by the former and his disciples, we owe that peculiar religious dialect, alike remarkable for simplicity, for beauty, and for force, which we still see preserved in the more modern versions of the Bible, and which renders the prose of that work distinct from every other existing form of English prose. It is only through this translation that Wycliffe can be said to have exerted a lasting influence upon our tongue.—LOUNSBURY, THOMAS R., 1879, *History of the English Language, p.* 57.

We drink many a refreshing draught without knowing what mountain's summit caught it from the heavens or what stream forwarded it to our cup. But that this man opened the Bible first to our English fathers we know; and our Christian days and institutions, and our noble literature are all saturated with the imperishable results of his toil. We cannot put it into words, we cannot even measure it in our thought. The Bible that we read to-day does not look to our eyes like the page of Wiclif; the men of the fourteenth century would have as great difficulty in reading it as we have in deciphering their rude and grotesque utterance. But his work underlies and supports the precious superstructure through which we walk as by still waters, or in which we lie down as in green pastures, even as the rough granite underlies all nature's quiet beauty or impressive sublimity. The work of this man underlies the lisping utterance of the infant scholar who repeats "The Lord is my shepherd" in our own dear English speech, as that granite makes possible the nodding daisy or the flower of grass. And that work too is, as I said, in all our literature. It did more than anything else to form and fix our English speech. Your newspaper to-morrow morning would not have been possible without it. It was the seed out of which our libraries have grown. It has made the common mind intelligent. It has made the peasant the peer of the priest. It was the quickening of that national thought which has blossomed and fruited in Bacon and Milton and Shakespeare, in Mrs. Browning and George Eliot, in Thackeray and Hawthorne. Better than all this, it was the liberation of Christian faith and hope. It unbound these twin sisters to go whereever there should be English homes, to brighten and bless them; wherever there should be English toil, to dignify it; wherever there should be English graves, to tell of the Resurrection and the Life. In one final word, Wiclif's translation of the Bible was, for the English-speaking race around the world, the second Resurrection. The day of its completion was the Easter day of the English language.—HERRICK, S. E., 1884, *Some Heretics of Yesterday, p.* 43.

Wiclif like many another man of genius, had not the minor gift of phrase-making; and the better English of his Bible was owing to his collaborators who possessed that gift. Wiclif with the rest of his knowledge, had self-knowledge; he knew his own defects and how to obviate them. —LEAKE, FREDERIC, 1896, *Historic Bubbles, p.* 213.

It is impossible to overestimate the gift of Wycliffe to English prose in placing the Bible at the command of every common reader. But the value of Wycliffe as an independent writer may easily be exaggerated. If we compare his New Testament with the work of Nicholas of Hereford, we may conjecture that Wycliffe had a certain conception of style undreamed of by his wooden disciple. But his own manner is exceedingly hard and wearisome, without suppleness of form.—GOSSE, EDMUND, 1897, *Short History of Modern English Literature, p.* 31.

GENERAL

Had it not bin the obstinat perversnes of our Prelats against the divine and admirable spirit of *Wicklef*, to suppresse him as a schismatic and *innovator*, perhaps neither the *Bohemian Husse* and *Jerom*, no nor the name of *Luther*, or of *Calvin* had bin ever known: the glory of reforming all our neighbours had bin compleatly ours.—MILTON, JOHN, 1644, *Areopagitica, Prose Works, Bohn ed., vol.* II, *p.* 91.

Dr. Caius had a mean opinion of John Wickliff, and therefore he thought the Oxonians ought not to be proud that John Wickliff was educated among them.—HEARNE, THOMAS, 1729, *Reliquiæ Hearnianæ, Sept.* 30, *vol.* III, *p.* 31.

Besides this defect of power in the church, which saved Wickliffe, that reformer himself, notwithstanding his enthusiasm, seems not to have been actuated by the spirit of martyrdom; and in all subsequent trials before the prelates, he so explained away his doctrine by tortured meanings, as to render it quite innocent and inoffensive.—HUME, DAVID, 1762, *The History of England, vol.* II, *ch.* xvii, *p.* 270.

To complete our idea of the importance of Wickliffe, it is only necessary to add, that as his writings made John Huss the reformer of Bohemia, so the writings of John Huss led Martin Luther to be the reformer of Germany; so extensive and so incalculable are the consequences which sometimes follow from human actions.—TURNER, SHARON, 1814-23, *The History of England During the Middle Ages, vol.* V, *p.* 200.

The merit of Wickliffe lay in seizing the favourable moment for disseminating his doctrine. In most of his principles he had been in a great measure anticipated, even by writers whose names are forgotten; but the profoundness of his learning, and greatness of his abilities, enabled him at once to take the lead, and thus gave to the sect the name of its champion.—BRODIE, GEORGE, 1822-65, *A Constitutional History of the British Empire, vol.* I, *p.* 35.

His philosophy and theology were closely interwoven: accordingly the antagonism of realism and nominalism entered deeply also into his theology. . . . We see in Wickliff the tendency of reform combined with an Augustinianism which went far beyond Augustin himself in its polemical hostility to everything that seemed verging on Pelagianism; to all worth or ability on the part of the creature; and which, in fact, amounted to the denial of free-will. A one-sided religious element in Wickliff here united itself with his stern speculative consistency: we meet with elements which in their logical evolution would have led to pantheism. Everything, according to his notions, enters as a part necessarily into the fulfilment of the decrees of predestination. This excludes all conditions. . . . It is plain that from Wickliff's doctrine follow unconditional necessity, and the denial of free-will and of contingency. . . . The true protestant principle comes forth in Wickliff when he ascribes the whole work of salvation to Christ alone.—NEANDER, AUGUSTUS, 1825-52, *General History of the Christian Religion and Church, tr. Torrey, vol.* IX, *pp.* 238, 240, 241, 242.

He was indeed a man of massy, voluminous, and subtle knowledge; one who, with the intellectual sinews and skill to win the unbloody crown of the athlete, chose rather the sweat and toil and peril of the militant soldier. He had all the learning and agility of mind required for the calm contentions of libraries and colleges, so fruitful at that period in power and worldly honour. But did he, like so many among his contemporaries, thus employ his talents? Where shall we find, in any age or country, amongst the lowest ranks of vulgar fanaticism, a man more zealous to encourage and animate the consciences of the poor and ignorant? Is it not admirable to see that he, the doctor and philosopher of the old schools, introduced into the church the practice of that diligent and, as it were, rustic preaching, so especially designed and fitted to enlighten the lowly mass of the people? Nor was this adaptation of his own great mind to the needs of the weakest a small sacrifice in Wycliffe. For it is clear from his writings that, if ever there was any one who delighted in long and difficult trains of reasoning for their own sake, as giving pleasurable exercise to his faculties,—who loved to busy himself in the building up and compacting of scientific knowledge,—he was the man. Yet through these fine and immense webs of reasoning, how lion-like does he constantly break forth with some bold, direct appeal to that moral sense, which is the great practical standard of truth!—STERLING, JOHN, 1829, *Shades of the Dead, Essays and Tales, ed. Hare, vol.* I, *p.* 39.

The first, and perhaps the greatest of the reformers.—MACAULAY, THOMAS BABINGTON, 1832, *Nares's Memoir of Burghley, Edinburgh Review, Critical and Miscellaneous Essays.*

In estimating his rank among the great intellects which have influenced the fortunes of mankind, we shall hardly, perhaps, be justified in assigning him a place with those who have been most distinguished for philosophic depth, or steadiness of judgment. . . . Admirable as he was, he seems to have been somewhat better fitted for the business of demolition than of building up. As the fearless assailant of abuse, nothing could well be more noble than his attitude and bearing. But, had he succeeded in shaking the established system to pieces, one can scarcely think, without some awful misgivings, of the fabric which, under his hand, might have risen out of the ruins. If the reformation of our Church had been conducted by Wiclif, his work, in all probability, would nearly have anticipated the labours of Calvin; and the Protestantism of England might have pretty closely resembled the Protestantism of Geneva. . . . It must plainly be confessed, that there is a marvellous resemblance between the Reformer, with his poor itinerant priests, and at least the better part of the Puritans, who troubled our Israel in the days of Elizabeth and her successors. The likeness is sufficiently striking, almost to mark him out as their prototype and progenitor: and therefore it is, that every faithful son of the Church of England must rejoice with trembling, that the work of her final deliverance was not consigned to him.—LE BAS, CHARLES WEBB, 1832, *The Life of Wiclif, pp.* 324, 325.

Seems to have been the representative of every false principle of philosophy and every erroneous doctrine of theology current during this age throughout the Church of the West.—ALZOG, JOHN, 1840-78, *Manual of Universal Church History, tr. by Pabisch and Byrne, vol.* III, *p.* 96.

It would be absurd to attribute this disaster * to Wycliffe, nor was there any desire to hold him responsible for it; but it is equally certain that the doctrines which he had taught were incompatible, at that particular time, with an effective repression of the spirit which had caused the explosion. It is equally certain that he had brought discredit on his nobler efforts by ambiguous language on a subject of the utmost difficulty, and had taught the wiser and better portion of the people to confound heterodoxy of opinion with sedition, anarchy, and disorder. So long as Wycliffe lived, his own lofty character was a guarantee for the conduct of his immediate disciples; and although his favour had far declined, a party in the state remained attached to him, with sufficient influence to prevent the adoption of extreme measures against the "poor priests." . . . With him departed all which was best and purest in the movement which he had commenced. The zeal of his followers was not extinguished, but the wisdom was extinguished which had directed it; and perhaps the being treated as the enemies of order had itself a tendency to make them what they were believed to be.—FROUDE, JAMES ANTHONY, 1856-70, *History of England, vol.* II, *pp.* 29, 31.

*Wat Tyler's Insurrection.

It is not by his translation of the Bible, remarkable as that work is, that Wyclif can be judged as a writer. It is in his original tracts that the exquisite pathos, the keen delicate irony, the manly passion of his short nervous sentences, fairly overmasters the weakness of the unformed language, and gives us English which cannot be read without a feeling of its beauty to this hour.—SHIRLEY, WALTER WADDINGTON, 1858, *ed. Fasciculi Zizaniorum, Introduction, p.* xlv.

John Wyclif may be justly accounted one of the greatest men that our country has produced. He is one of the very few, who have left the impress of their minds, not only on their own age, but on all time. He it was, who first, in the middle ages, gave to faith its subjective character. His first grand position was taken on the ground of faith. . . . His next step was, to maintain, that the only proof, by which we can establish a disputed proposition in revealed religion, must be deduced from the bible.—HOOK, WALTER FARQUHAR, 1860-76, *Lives of the Archbishops of Canterbury, vol.* III, *p.* 76.

When we consider the early period at which he appeared, and how strong a hold the doctrines which he assailed had universally obtained over the minds of men, Wycliffe must be ranked among the most remarkable of those who are entitled to the highest of all fame, that of being greatly in advance of their age.—BROUGHAM, HENRY, LORD, 1861, *History of England and France under the House of Lancaster, p.* 23.

Whose writings contributed more than those of any other writer to the Great Reformation of the Church of England, and its severance from the Church of Rome a century and a half later.—LONGMAN, WILLIAM, 1869, *The History of the Life and Times of Edward the Third, vol.* II, *p.* 281.

On the whole, we shall not misrepresent the position of Wickliffe, if we say that he began by being a comparatively moderate reformer in the Church to which he belonged; that his disapprobation of the doctrine, and practice of that Church, deepened as he advanced in years, and as different circumstances happened to place him in that attitude of hostility which is favourable to criticism; and that he ended by being, in all the most important particulars, a Protestant.—RANDS, WILLIAM BRIGHTY, (MATTHEW BROWNE), 1869, *Chaucer's England, vol.* II, *p.* 149.

The importance of what Wyclif did, and preached, and wrote, can hardly be exaggerated. His influence is felt not only among all the English race, but among all mankind, wherever the Bible is read, and spiritual liberty is valued. . . . It is easy to mark the faults in his character. They are obvious on the face of his own works. Wyclif's writings are often deformed by intemperate and violent expressions, though never exhibiting the coarse savagery, with which, a century and a half afterwards, Luther and his contemporaries carried on their literary warfare. He was also in his controversial treatises somewhat given to mystical and far-fetched Biblical expositions and metaphors; although he recognised and enforced on others the principle of adhering to the grammatical and historical sense of texts, and of extreme caution in imposing a meaning on Scripture, which the Holy Spirit does not clearly command. The "root and branch" spirit, with which he assails existing institutions, appears sometimes to show a love of destruction, rather than a wish for reform.—CREASY, SIR EDWARD S., 1870, *History of England, vol.* II, *pp.* 308, 329.

What shall we say in parting from Wiclif and his work? And first, with all due thankfulness to Almighty God that He raised up this witness for so much of truth, we, members of the Anglican Church, may be thankful too that the Reformation was not in his time, nor of his doing. From a Church reformed under the auspices of one who was properly the spiritual ancestor of our Puritans, the Catholic element would in good part, perhaps altogether, have disappeared. Overthrowing much, he built up very little. In that knowledge of Holy Scripture which by his translation he diffused among the English people, there were good foundations laid; but in the main we must see in him rather a clearer of the ground than a builder thereupon.—TRENCH, RICHARD CHENEVIX, 1877, *Lectures on Medieval Church History p.* 314.

The English church had up to the close of the fourteenth century been singularly free from heresy. . . . The first person against whom any severe measures were taken was John Wycliffe himself. He had risen to eminence as a philosophic teacher at Oxford. Although he was in the main a Realist, he had adopted some of the political tenets of the Franciscan Nominalists, and, hating the whole policy of the mendicant orders, had formed views on the temporal power of the papacy akin to those of Marsilius and Ockham, blending with them the ideal of apostolic poverty as the model of clerical life. As his opinions in the later years of his life developed rapidly, it is not surprising that he came to look on the sacramental system of the medieval church with suspicion and dislike, as the real basis on which papal and clerical authority rested. . . . His opinions regarding the wealth and power of the clergy were the occasion of the first attack upon him; the pretext of the second was his theory on the papacy; and he was not formally brought to trial for his views on the sacraments. Of the spiritual, the philosophical, and the political elements in Wycliffe's teaching, the last was far the most offensive to the clergy and the most attractive to the discontented laity. In Wycliffe himself there is no reason to doubt that all the three were matters of conviction; but neither is there any reason to doubt that the popular favour which attended on his teaching was caused mainly by the desire for social change. Both he and his adversaries recognised the fact that on the sacramental system the practical controversy must ultimately turn; the mob was attracted by the idea of confiscation.—STUBBS, WILLIAM, 1878, *The Constitutional History of England, vol.* III, *ch.* xix, *pp.* 365, 367.

It was in his pulpit, however, that Wyclif's light shone out most brightly.

Taking the lesson of the day, or some pointed verse of scripture, he would give short pithy explanations, attacking the old errors when they came in his way with keen homespun sentences, with many a sarcasm about Pope and priest as he went along, but trying most of all to bring out the practical lesson for the lives of his hearers. These little sermons, or lectures, were copied out and circulated among his followers far and wide, so that even at the present day there are no less than three hundred of Wyclif's "Postils," as they are called, still extant.—HERFORD, BROOKE, 1878, *The Story of Religion in England*, p. 135.

A character like that of Wycliffe is an appearance rare in the history of a nation. Luther was not more resolute in his demand for freedom of the conscience, though he came four generations after; and Wycliffe was far in advance of him in the clearness and depth of many of his views.—GEIKIE, JOHN CUNNINGHAM, 1878, *The English Reformation*, p. 48.

The importance of Wiclif, as seen from an age five hundred years later than his own time, is in no respect less imposing than it seemed to his contemporaries, in so far as they were not pre-occupied by party prejudice against him. But the judgment of the present time must needs differ from that of his own period, as to where the chief importance of his personality and work lay. To the men of his own age his greatness and his chief distinction lay in his intellectual pre-eminence. Not only his adherents, but even his opponents, looked upon him as having no living equal in learning and scientific ability—to all eyes he shone as a star of the first magnitude. But the reference in these judgments was entirely to *scholastic* learning in philosophy and theology; and along with scholasticism itself, Wiclif's mastery as a scholastic lost immensely in value in the eyes of later generations. But we frankly confess, notwithstanding, that to our thinking this depreciation has been carried too far, and that Wiclif's scientific importance is wont, for the most part, to be undervalued unduly.—LECHLER, GOTTHARD, 1878, *John Wiclif and his English Precursors, tr. Lorimer, vol.* II, *p.* 298.

One of Wyclif's most marked characteristics is his essential moderation. Even when his language is most vehement the thought and purpose beneath it are sane and reasonable. . . . But if we go down to the kernel of thought, we find no wildness. Whether the question in hand be one of doctrine or discipline, Wyclif has considered it carefully both in principle and in its practical bearings. It is this characteristic that entitles him to his eminence as the first of the Reformers. Long before his time there had been heated sectaries who had denounced the whole system of the Church, but Wyclif was the first to submit it to a searching proof, to examine the prevalent practices and ask how it was they bent away from the ideal at which they ought to aim. In his conclusions he forestalled in many points the judgments of the more moderate reformers of the sixteenth century.—MATTHEW, F. D., 1880, *ed., The English Works of Wyclif Hitherto Unprinted, Introduction, p.* xl.

To Wiclif we owe, more than to any one person who can be mentioned, our English language, our English Bible, and our reformed religion. How easily the words slip from the tongue! But is not this almost the very atmosphere we breathe? Expand that three-fold claim a little further. It means nothing less than this:—that in Wiclif we have the acknowledged "father of English prose," the first translator of the whole Bible into the language of the English people, the first disseminator of that Bible amongst all classes, the foremost intellect of his times brought to bear upon the religious questions of the day, the patient and courageous writer of innumerable tracts and books, not for one, but for all the different classes of society, the sagacious originator of that whole system of ecclesiastical reformation, which in its separate parts had been faintly shadowed forth by a genius here and there, but which acquired consistency in the hands of the master. By him and by those he had trained that Reformation was so firmly planted that it took deep root in the land, and after giving the impulse to similar and later movements on the continent, issued at last in the great system under which we live, one almost identical with that of the Rector of Lutterworth, who died a century and a half before his work had fulfilled its appointed results. Wiclif founded no colleges, for he had no means; no human fabric enshrines his ideas; no great institution bears his name. The country for which he lived and died is only beginning to wake up to a sense of the debt it owes his memory. And yet so vast is that debt, so overpowering the claim, even when thus briefly summarised, that it might be thought no very extravagant recognition if every town in England had a monument to his memory, and every university a college named in his honour. It is something to be thankful for that a private Theological Hall, bearing that illustrious name, has been recently built in our suburbs.—BURROWS, MONTAGU, 1881-4, *Wiclif's Place in History, p.* 8.

One whom this College*, and the University of Oxford, may justly regard as the greatest of her sons.—JOWETT, BENJAMIN, 1881, *Sermons, ed. Fremantle, p.* 18.

In relation to the religious movement connected with his name Wycliffe stands absolutely alone. What names of followers of his have lived down to the present day? Probably the only names known to the general reader are those of William Sawtrey, John Badby, and Sir John Oldcastle, the last being known because he took up arms for freedom of conscience, the two former because they suffered at the stake; but neither of them left any personal mark on the thought of the age. Wycliffe had no coadjutor or follower of any eminence in the world of letters. Perhaps the most learned of his disciples were Philip Repingdon and John Purvey, the reviser of Wycliffe's translation of the Bible; but both of these recanted under pressure.—RAMSAY, J. H., 1882, *Wycliffe's Place in History, The Academy, vol.* 21, *p.* 359.

The relation of Luther to these Reformers still remains extremely obscure. The Germans, it is true, repudiate any possible influence; but, when it is remembered that Germany was at the beginning of the sixteenth century honeycombed by Husite societies; that there is scarcely an idea or argument used by Luther, with the doubtful exception of the famous doctrine of salvation, which is not to be found in the works of Wiclif; that Wiclif's "Trialogus" and innumerable works of Hus, or concerning him, were published in the early days of the Reformation by the Reformers or their friends; and that there is in existence at Vienna a Wiclif MS. inscribed "Doctor Martinus Luther"—remembering these things, there are obviously facts sufficient to demand a critical and impartial investigation.—PEARSON, KARL, 1884, *Recent Wiclif Literature, Academy, vol.* 25, *p.* 177.

Persecutions in previous centuries Wycliffe nowhere seems to regret, nor does he give reason more than a subordinate place, but distinctly condemns those who claim a special inspiration enabling them to find a new and peculiar meaning in the Bible, as false disciples. He was no Mystic or rationalist, and his views of predestination resembled Luther's and Calvin's, but he did not hold their doctrine of justification by faith. His demand for liberty to read and expound the Bible, as well as his attacks on clerical endowments, the confessional, and the authority of bishops and popes gave powerful, though undesigned, aid to the cause of free thought; and his own special work for biblical authority was so well organized, as not to be interrupted by his death.—HOLLAND, FREDERIC MAY, 1884, *The Rise of Intellectual Liberty, p.* 248.

Above all, he had opened a new well of authority in his translation of the Scriptures into English; and by his strictness of life, his courage, his subtlety in wit and argument, he had set ablaze a fire in men's minds that could not be put out. This was the only bond of union among those who came after him—the claim of reason to assert a higher truth, which all good men felt, but which the Churchmen dared not allow.—WYLIE, JAMES HAMILTON, 1884, *History of England Under Henry the Fourth, vol.* I, *p.* 175.

Towards the end of the fifteenth century there arose a teacher in England, who, like many other heresiarchs, was a victim to foiled ambition, and who, under the specious guise of reform, sowed broadcast in Church and State the seeds of revolt.—DELPLACE, L., 1884, *Wycliffe and his Teaching Concerning the Primacy, Dublin Review, vol.* 94, *p.* 25.

In truth England may be proud of him, who at the same time was the founder of her later prose, a national politician, an unsparing assailant of abuses, a bold and

*Balliol.

indefatigable controversialist, the founder of a new religious order, the great Reformer who did not shrink from questioning the truth of the Roman dogma, who broke through the traditions of the past, and who, while bound in his whole teaching by the Word of God, became the great advocate of the freedom of religious thought.—BUDDENSIEG, RUDOLF, 1884, *John Wiclif, Patriot and Reformer, p.* 81.

The career of Wycliff, indeed, belongs to the University quite as much as to the Church. It was as the last of the Oxford schoolmen, and mostly from Oxford itself, that he put forth his series of books and pamphlets on the relations of Church and State, on the subjection of the clergy to civil rule, civil taxation and civil tribunals, on pardons, indulgences, the worship of saints, transubstantiation, the supremacy of Holy Scripture, and other like topics, besides those abstruse scholastic themes which have lost their interest for the present age. During his earlier struggles, the open patronage of John of Gaunt, with the occasional protection of the Court, stood him in good stead, and enabled him to brave not only episcopal censures but Papal anathemas. His real strength, however, consisted in the influence which he commanded in the University itself and, through it, in the English people. . . . The spirit which he had kindled continued to animate the University for many years after his death. In Merton College alone several eminent fellows were known as Wycliffites in the next generation, and after the condemnation of Lollardism by the Council of London in 1411, it was thought necessary to pass a stringent University statue to check the propagation of Lollard doctrines. By this statue, the penalty of the greater excommunication was imposed upon all who should disseminate Lollardism, candidates for degrees were required to abjure it, and heads of colleges or halls were enjoined to exclude from their societies any person even suspected of it.—BRODRICK, GEORGE C., 1886, *A History of the University of Oxford, pp.* 35, 36.

This man's works . . . have recently been reprinted; for there appears to be no ancient or modern heretic too absurd or too wild in his notions who may not obtain a band of noisy admirers amongst the shallow sentimentalists and fadmongers of the present day.—LEE, FREDERICK GEORGE, 1888, *The Life of Cardinal Pole, p.* 188, *note.*

The chief anarchist of his time.—EGAN, MAURICE FRANCIS, 1889, *Lectures on English Literature, p.* 26.

It may at least be said that he is the man who has left a broader mark on England and on Europe generally than any single man in the Middle Ages. Others have dominated the intellect of an age, or built up a wide-spreading system of government. Their work had long crumbled into dust; but Wiclif's services to the human race can only be compared to an abounding river, receiving in its ever-broadening course the minor streams, but yet retaining from beginning to end the original impulse and direction. As the contemporary of Chaucer, the Black Prince, and Wykeham, he owed much, no doubt, to the elevation of the age in which his lot was cast,—an age superior to the twelfth century, if fruit is to be preferred to blossom; but it is as the inheritor of all previous ages that he stands before us unequalled and sublime.—BURROWS, MONTAGU, 1892, *Commentaries on the History of England, p.* 179.

Wyclif was no mere forerunner of the Protestant Reformation, but the Reformer in chief. In the intellectual domain, in the field of ideas and of spiritual activity, he originated the movement which had its issue in the sixteenth century, when the Tudor monarchs rode but did not raise the storm. For one reason or another Wyclif was long excluded from his proper place in history; but the nineteenth century, bringing together for the first time all the main contemporary documents, has been able to take the true bearings of the epoch of religious reform.—SERGEANT, LEWIS, 1892, *John Wyclif, Last of the Schoolmen and First of the English Reformers, p.* 359.

He was a worthy successor, as a philosopher of bold originality of thought, of the great English schoolmen, Duns Scotus and Occam, and, in piety and purity of life, as well as in literary skill, he rivalled his predecessor Bradwardine. But Wyclif was no mere scholar, "schoolman," or dialectician. He was the hardest worker and the ablest statesman of the time. Tall and spare in form, of quick and restless temper, ready wit, and winning manners, the shrewd Yorkshireman, subtle in logic and eloquent in speech, was full of the energy and courage, the firmness of conviction, and the hatred of hypocrisy and wrong, that should be found in him whose life-work it is to attack abuses, to be foremost in controversy, to defy the world, if need be, in doing battle for moral, intellectual, and religious reform. The literary gifts of this illustrious man included a style now charged with persuasive power, and, in due season, keen in irony, and strong in the invective that pleases the popular taste. With all these resources he combined the worldly wisdom that enables the skilled politician and partisan to make every kind of man an instrument for his chosen work, and to refrain from playing into the hands of those who oppose him.—SANDERSON, EDGAR, 1893, *History of England and the British Empire, p.* 256.

Comparing Wycliffe's style with that of the book of travels to which the name of Mandeville is attached, we see at once that his English is that of a scholar who has lost much of what may be called the childishness of archaicism, and who is ready to enrich his language with words borrowed freely either from a French or a classical source. We recognise that we are in the hands of one who, though he has nothing that could fairly be called a formed style, yet uses the direct and forcible English of a master, and whose example could not fail to influence the future of English prose.—CRAIK, HENRY, 1893, *English Prose, vol.* I, *p.* 28

By a strange fate Wyclif's posterity continued to flourish out of the kingdom. Bohemia had just given a queen to England, and used to send students every year from its University of Prague to study at Paris and Oxford. In that country the Wyclifite tenets found a multitude of adepts; the Latin works of the thinker were transcribed by Czech students, and carried back to their own land; several writings of Wyclif exist only in Czech copies. His most illustrious disciple, John Hus, rector of the University of Prague, was burnt at the stake, by order of the Council of Constance, on the 6th of July, 1415. But the doctrine survived; it was adopted with modifications by the Taborites and the Moravian Brethern, and borrowed from them by the Waldenses; the same Moravian Brethern who, owing to equally singular vicissitudes, were to become an important factor in the English religious movement of the eighteenth century: the Wesleyan movement. In spite of differences in their doctrines, the Moravian Brethern and the Hussites stand as a connecting link between Wesley and Wyclif.—JUSSERAND, J. J., 1895, *A Literary History of the English People, p.* 438.

As regards his attitude toward the fine arts, Wyclif was no iconoclast: in his "Trialogus" an approved speaker points out that Christ did not condemn signs in themselves, but only abuse of them; the brazen serpent, the crucified Lord himself, were both signs. Nevertheless, in Wyclif's nature the moral element was developed to the sacrifice of the ideal: his intense seriousness, his fear lest symbols should become to the simple occasions of idolatry, made him suspicious of the use of the arts in the service of the sanctuary, while his deep sympathy with the poor made him intolerant of the diversion of wealth that would relieve their necessities to the production of works of art.—WHITE, GREENOUGH, 1895, *Outline of the Philosophy of English Literature, The Middle Ages, p.* 96.

In England it was said at the beginning of the fifteenth century that every third man was a Lollard; and the first Parliament of Henry V. was so swayed by Wycliffe's anti-clerical principles that the ecclesiastics trembled for their estates. But the renewal of the French wars drew the whole mind of the country in another direction; and the movement of Wycliffe, already compromised during his lifetime by its supposed connection with Wat Tyler's agrarian revolt, was finally discredited when its leader, Sir John Oldcastle, was provoked in 1417 to take arms against his King. But though Lollardry was crushed, the influence of Wycliffe was never extinguished. As many as a hundred and fifty copies of Wycliffe's Bible still remain; and there is no doubt that it was widely read by the common people, for whom it was written, throughout the fifteenth century. When, in 1510, a raid against heretics was made by Fitzjames, Bishop of London, so violent that Colet wrote to Erasmus that all the prisons were full of them, the articles in almost all cases stated that the accused possessed copies of Wycliffe's Bible or of some of his works; and Erasmus, in his account of his pilgrimage to the shrine of Becket, at Canterbury, when he tells how his companion (Colet) questioned the advantage of such an exhibition of relics, represents his interlocutor as saying: "Who was your friend? Some Wycliffite, I suppose." Thus the reformer of the fourteenth century joins hands with the reformer of the sixteenth.—FREMANTLE, REV. W. H., 1896, *John Wycliffe, Prophets of the Christian Faith, p.* 103.

The interest which attaches to Wycliffe has grown deeper in recent years, as his writings have been more clearly studied, and especially his unpublished manuscripts. A sense of the greatness of his personality has increased, of his representative character as a comprehensive mind in whom his age found its most ample reflection. He went deeper also than his contemporaries could follow; indeed, his principles seem to ally him with the modern socialistic conception of reform. He appears at times to be one-sided and extreme in his passionate opposition to great evils imbedded in corporate ecclesiastical institutions. He was claimed by the later Puritans as their forerunner and representative, because of his principle of the parity of the ministry, and for other reasons, but in reality he belonged to another cause, the sacredness of the state and its organic relation to the church—that doctrine which has been the mainspring of what is highest and most attractive in English history, which was reaffirmed with deeper emphasis at the Reformation, and which still survives in the English Church, as one source of its strength, as that which differentiates it to some extent in principle from the other Protestant churches. — ALLEN, ALEXANDER V. G., 1897, *Christian Institutions, p.* 264.

The general effect of his conduct was to defeat, or, at least, to postpone, the realisation of his hopes. The authorities were alarmed, and adopted vigorous measures for repressing the new heresy. —SNELL, F. J., 1899, *Periods of European Literature, The Fourteenth Century, p.* 413.

Wycliffe, in spite of some crudity of thought and utterance, was the only man of his age who saw deeply into the needs of the present and the possibilities of the future, and his life has had an incalculable effect on the religion of England, and through religion on politics and society. —TREVELYAN, GEORGE MACAULAY, 1899, *England in the Age of Wycliffe, p.* 169.

If ever man was, John Wicklif was in antagonism to his age, and he is certainly, in some respects, the most remarkable man of the century. From such a man, in character, in thought, in moral and spiritual feeling, John of Ghent was as far sundered as the poles. Yet, as often happens, they had some ideas in common, and events then, as in Reformation days, threw reformers and unscrupulous politicians into the same camp. John of Ghent was the aggressive enemy of an over-rich priesthood, an advocate of the encroachment by the State on the autonomy of the Church, and here the high-toned reformer and the crafty and ambitious man of the world were on the same plane. His connection with Wicklif was of long standing, and it is likely enough that he owed his nomination as one of the commissioners at Bruges to the duke's influence. It was unfortunate that the spiritually-minded Wicklif became the *protégé* of such a man, though it is most improbable that he sympathised with much of the duke's action. In the eye of the Church, at all events, he was identified with the interests of his patron, and that was enough for the duke's clerical opponents to strike at the reformer. Their hostility was inspired as much by political as by theological animosity. To be original, independent, assertive against the abuses by which a large class earned its living, and hugged tradition all the more firmly in consequence, was in such an age a deadly offence. To be in addition, as these resentful dignitaries believed him to be, the duke's tool, was the worst of all heresies. It is easy to see why they should single him out for uncompromising attack. It is likewise easy to understand how a man standing alone at bay before the enormous forces of convention and prejudice, would be only too glad to avail himself of such powerful protection as that of the virtual autocrat of the day.—MACKINNON, JAMES, 1900, *The History of Edward the Third, p.* 598.

John Barbour

1316?-1395

The father of Scottish poetry and history, was born about 1316; paid several visits to England and France; and was Archdeacon of Aberdeen from 1357, or earlier, till his death, on 13th March 1395. His national epic, "The Brus," first printed at Edinburgh in 1571, has been reprinted by Dr. Jamieson in 1820; by Cosmo Innes, for the Spalding Club, in 1856; and by Professor Skeat, for the Early English Text Society, in 1870-77, and the Scottish Text Society in 1893-94. Of the "Legends of the Saints," unearthed by Mr. Bradshaw in the Cambridge University Library, and doubtfully ascribed to him, there is a German edition by Horstmann (2 vols. Heilbronn, 1881-82), and one by Metcalfe for the Scottish Text Society (1887-89).—PATRICK AND GROOME, *eds.* 1897, *Chambers's Biographical Dictionary, p.* 67.

It is remarkable, that though Barbour was a Scotsman, his language is rather more intelligible to a modern English reader than that of any other poet of the fourteenth century, his great contemporary Chaucer himself not excepted.—HENRY, ROBERT, 1771-90, *The History of Great Britain, vol.* VIII, *bk.* iv, *ch.* v, *sec.* ii.

Adorned the English language by a strain of versification, expression, and poetical imagery far superior to his age. —WARTON, THOMAS, 1778-81, *History of English Poetry.*

Perhaps the editor may be accused of nationality, when he says that, taking the total merits of this work together, he prefers it to the early exertions of even the Italian muse, to the melancholy sublimity of Dante, and the amorous quaintness of Petrarca, as much as M. Le Grand does a *fabliau* to a Provenaçl ditty. Here indeed the reader will find few of the graces of fine poetry, little of the Attic dress of the muse: but here are life, and spirit, and ease, and plain sense, and pictures of real manners, and perpetual incident, and entertainment. The language is remarkably good for the time, and far superior, in neatness and elegance, even to that of Gawin Douglas, who wrote more than a century after. But when we consider that our author is not only the first poet, but the earliest historian of Scotland, who has entered into any detail, and from whom any view of the real state and manners of the country can be had; and that the hero, whose life he paints so minutely, was a monarch equal to the greatest of modern times; let the historical and poetical merits of his work be weighed together, and then opposed to those of any other early poet of the present nations in Europe.—PINKERTON, JOHN, 1790, *ed. The Bruce of John Barbour, Preface, p.* x.

Given his countrymen a fine example of the simple energetic style, which resembled Chaucer's best manner, and wanted little to make it the genuine language of poetry.—NOTT, GEORGE FREDERICK, 1815, *Dissertation on the State of English Poetry, in Surrey and Wyatt's Poems, p.* cxc.

We may consider John Barbour. . . as the father of regular Scotch history; although that history be known to the world as a metrical composition, under the name of "The Bruce."—DIBDIN, THOMAS FROGNALL, 1824, *The Library Companion, p.* 261.

When we compare such poetry with the contemporary productions of the bards of England under the reign of Edward III.—with Laurence Minot, for example, or Langland, the reputed author of the "Vision of Pierce Plowman"—the superiority of the Archdeacon completely justifies the encomium of Warton, whether we look to the poetical spirit of the author, to the taste and judgment in the pictures or reflections which he brings before us, or to the clear and forcible language in which he expresses himself.—TYTLER, PATRICK FRASER, 1838, *Lives of Scottish Worthies, vol.* II, *p.* 164.

If we were to compare it with the contemporary poetry of England, its place would be very high, Chaucer being set aside as unapproachable. Barbour must be pronounced much superior to Gower, and still more so to the anonymous writers of the very best of the metrical romances. —SPALDING, WILLIAM, 1852-82, *A History of English Literature, p.* 93.

Fortunate in the choice of a subject, he has unfolded a series of remarkable events, and has diffused over a very long narrative that lively interest which an ordinary writer is incapable of exciting.

Here we are not to expect the blandishments of modern poetry: the author stands conspicuous amid the ruins of time, and, like an undecayed Gothic tower, presents an aspect of majestic simplicity. The lively strain of his narrative, the air of sincerity which he always exhibits, his earnest participation in the success or sufferings of his favourite characters, as well as the splendid attributes of the characters themselves, cannot fail of arresting the attention of every reader familiarly acquainted with the language in which he writes.—IRVING, DAVID, 1861, *History of Scotish Poetry, ed. Carlyle, p.* 101.

Throughout his long work he shows, for his time, a very remarkable feeling of the *art* of poetry, both by the variety which he studies in the disposition and treatment of his subject, and by the rare temperance and self-restraint which prevents him from ever overdoing what he is about either by prosing or raving. Even his patriotism, warm and steady as it is, is wholly without any vulgar narrowness or ferocity: he paints the injuries of his country with distinctness and force, and celebrates the heroism of her champions and deliverers with all admiration and sympathy; but he never runs into either the gasconading exaggerations or the furious deprecatory invectives which would, it might be thought, have better pleased the generality of those for whom he wrote. His understanding was too enlightened, and his heart too large, for that. His poem stands in this respect in striking contrast to that of Harry, the blind minstrel, on the exploits of Wallace; . . . but each poet suited his hero,—Barbour, the magnanimous, considerate, and far-seeing king; Blind Harry, the indomitable popular champion, with his one passion and principle, hatred of the domination of England, occupying his whole soul and being.—CRAIK, GEORGE L., 1861, *A Compendious History of English Literature and of the English Language, vol.* I, *p.* 349.

Barbour's poem has always been admired for its strict accuracy of statement, to which Bower, Wynton, Hailes, Pinkerton, Jamieson, and Sir Walter Scott all bear testimony; for the picturesque force of its natural descriptions; for its insight into character, and the lifelike spirit of its individual sketches; for the martial vigour of its battle-pictures; for the enthusiasm which he feels, and makes his reader feel, for the valiant and wise, the sagacious and persevering, the bold, merciful, and religious character of its hero, and for the piety which pervades it, and proves that the author was not merely a churchman in profession, but a Christian at heart. Its defects of rude rhythm, irregular constructions, and obsolete phraseology, are those of its age; but its beauties, its unflagging interest, and its fine poetic spirit, are characteristic of the writer's own genius.—GILFILLAN, GEORGE, 1860, *Specimens With Memoirs of the Less-Known British Poets, vol.* I, *p.* 19.

Some of his battle-pieces have an animation that might almost be called Homeric.—FRISWELL, JAMES HAIN, 1869, *Essays on English Writers, p.* 51.

Barbour's "Brus," if not precisely a poem, has passages whose simple tenderness raises them to that level. That on Freedom is familiar. But its highest merit is the natural and unrestrained tone of manly courage in it, the easy and familiar way in which Barbour always takes chivalrous conduct as a matter of course, as if heroism were the least you could ask of any man. . . . The "Brus" is in many ways the best rhymed chronicle ever written. It is national in a high and generous way, but I confess I have little faith in that quality in literature which is commonly called nationality,—a kind of praise seldom given where there is anything better to be said. —LOWELL, JAMES RUSSELL, 1875–90, *Spenser, Prose Works, Riverside ed., vol.* IV, *pp.* 269, 270.

Believers in race will not fail to observe that Barbour was born in the north-east of Scotland, and that in the population of this district there was a large admixture of settlers from the opposite coasts of Norway and Denmark—men of the same race as the Norman founders of chivalry —so that the patriotic, warlike-minded churchman may have inherited from roving and reaving ancestors his passion for celebrating heroic achievements. At all events, race or no race, the passion was strong within him. He enters the battle with his hero, and lays about him with sturdy enthusiasm. The shock of Bruce's spear is irresistible; and when his spear is shivered and his good sword drawn, there is death in every sweep of his arm: heads are smitten off, helmets cleft, shoulder-plated arms shorn away like corn before the scythe. He does not hesitate to oppose the Bruce single-handed to two hundred men, and bring him off victorious after much slaughter; comparing this incomparable achievement with the defeat of fifty men by the hardy son of Tydeus. With what energy he recounts the discomfiture of the three gigantic Macindrossans, who attempted to take Robert alive! How thoroughly he enjoys the feat of the king in bringing the giant who has leapt on his horse behind him round from the crupper within reach of his deadly sword!—MINTO, WILLIAM, 1874-85, *Characteristics of English Poets, p.* 66.

In clearness and simplicity it must rank before either Gower or Chaucer. . . To this day "The Bruce"—the first epic in the English language—is a favourite work among the common people of Scotland, through the medium of a modern version.—WILSON, JAMES GRANT, 1876, *The Poets and Poetry of Scotland, vol.* I, *pp.* 4, 5.

He was gifted with good natural faculties; his imaginative and reproductive powers were considerable, and he showed practical insight and good judgment; his feelings and sentiments were keen and warm, and his opinions were very liberal for the age. His general fairness and moderation was characteristic, though in a few instances his love of freedom and his patriotism caused him to use harsh expressions. . . . The literary merits of Barbour's work, taking everything into account, were great. His language and style were, for the period, remarkably good. His style possessed the qualities of clearness, brevity, terseness, and point; his descriptions of scenes and positions, and delineations of historic characters, were generally vivid and interesting; while, in short, his poem was pervaded by a dignified simplicity and a directness of aim admirably calculated to attract and to sustain attention; its historical value has been long recognised by Scottish historians.—MACKINTOSH, JOHN, 1878-1892, *The History of Civilization in Scotland, vol.* I, *pp.* 452, 453.

Of John Barbour's life we know little besides the facts that he was Archdeacon of Aberdeen, and that he wrote a metrical account of the Scotch rulers beginning with Brutus called *The Brute*, and a poem on The Lives of the Northern Saints,—besides this poem of *The Bruce*. But when we read this last work we do not feel that we lack any further knowledge to make us acquainted with John Barbour. About a hundred and fifty years before Barbour a very fervent English poet named Orrmin called his poem "The Ormulum," or little Orrmin, as if it were a sort of miniature copy of himself; and so we might call Barbour's Romance the Barbulum. It shows him to us over again. We see clearly how simple, how lofty, how clean are all his thoughts; how fervent are his love and admiration of all manful deeds; how keen and intelligent are his ideas of the remarkable degree in which Robert Bruce added perseverance, prudence, ready wit in emergencies, wisdom in handling his resources, to his personal bravery and physical strength; how true is his passion for freedom; and how fine and large is his ideal of manhood as given in his account of James the Douglas.—LANIER, SIDNEY, 1881? *John Barbour's Bruce, Music and Poetry, p.* 213.

The father of the Anglic literature of Scotland.—ROSS, JOHN MERRY, 1884, *Scottish History and Literature, etc., ed. Brown, p.* 49.

Not only the first but the most famous of the poet-chroniclers of Scotland. But for his pen the passion of patriotism which gave Scotland a soul for four hundred years might have died with Douglas and Bruce, and but for him the living heroes of the Scottish wars of succession and independence might have come down to us little more than empty names.—EYRE-TODD, GEORGE, 1891, *Early Scottish Poetry, p.* 61.

The "Legends of the Saints" demand concessions from us much more frequently than "The Bruce," and, indeed, concessions of various kinds—to the spirit of the age in which the poem originated, to the power of tradition which even the most gifted poet cannot ignore, and to the various influences and conditions which compel him to accept all manner of things not adapted to poetry, even things that are insipid. It is saying a good deal that we are able to recognize in these religious epics the patriotic singer of the war of independence. It is not the inevitable defects attached to the poetry, but its great merits, that should excite our astonishment. Barbour, as a very old man, thus created a work which far surpassed almost everything of its kind that English literature had to show, and, indeed, he was not surpassed in this domain even at a later date. Huchown in his "Susannah" exhibits greater brilliancy of diction, Chaucer's "Cecilia" more completely captivates our ear by the pleasant sound of its strophes; but, as a whole, it will be found that Barbour's simple as well as vivid form of representation corresponds best with the character of the genus, and that it is the only form which can be carried out successfully, especially in poems of longer effort or in compilations. . . . English literature—and, indeed, Scottish literature—can show no more brilliant figure or richer nature than his.—TEN BRINK, BERNHARD, 1892, *History of English Literature, (Fourteenth Century to Surrey), tr. Schmitz, pp.* 60, 61.

During all last century, despite the various editions of Barbour, it was Blind Harry who was the favourite, and even if we admit that this was because he could be read in the modernized version by Hamilton of Gilbertfield, yet there must be some merit in a poem which could go through this process and yet live. The work it did during two generations in fostering Scottish patriotism and developing Scottish character is well known from the testimony of Burns. Barbour, on the other hand, was scarcely known, and this cannot have come altogether from the difference in language, but must have been also due to the difference in the good Archdeacon's idea of a national poem. With the critical study of Scottish history begins the above-mentioned confusion between the merits of a poem and the truth of its historical basis, and straightway Barbour begins to supplant Blind Harry in the favour of the critics. As no one will venture to quote the latter as an authority for anything, so writers on literature, whether English literature in general or Scottish in particular, dispose of their best epithets on Barbour, and apologetically give their remaining ones to blind Harry, if indeed they do not leave him only the disparaging ones.—CRAIGIE, W. A., 1893, *Barbour and Blind Harry as Literature, Scottish Review, vol.* 22, *p.* 175

Barbour's intention is to write a true history; he thus expects, he says, to give twofold pleasure: firstly because it is a history, secondly because it is a true one. But where passion has a hold it is rare that Truth reigns paramount, and Barbour's feeling for his country is nothing short of passionate love; so much so that, when a legend is to the credit of Scotland, his critical sense entirely disappears, and miracles become for him history. Thus with monotonous uniformity, throughout his poem a handful of Scotchmen rout the English multitudes; the highlanders perform prodigies, and the king still surpasses them in valour; everything succeeds with him as in a fairy tale.—JUSSERAND, J. J., 1895, *A Literary History of the English People, p.* 362.

Barbour is not a brilliant writer, and, in strange contradistinction to the Scotch poets who followed him, he is austerely bare of ornament. He tells a patriotic story very simply and fluently, with a constant appeal to chivalrous instincts, and with a remarkable absence of all mythological machinery.—GOSSE, EDMUND, 1897, *Short History of Modern English Literature, p.* 27.

William Langland

C. 1322–1400?

Langland, Langelande, or Longland, William: author; born probably at Cleobury Mortimer, Shropshire, England, about 1332; was educated at Oxford; became a fellow of Oriel College, and a tonsured clerk at Malvern. His "Vision of Piers Plowman," in alliterative verse, written about 1362, was a religious and moral allegory, containing much satire upon ecclesiastical corruption and the social abuses of the time. It was originally in eight divisions, or "passus," to which was added a continuation in three parts, *Vita Do Wel, Do Bet and Do Best.* About 1377 the whole was greatly enlarged by the author. The best edition is that of W. W. Skeat (four parts with glossary 1867-84; another edition in 2 vols., 1886). Langland died about 1400.—BEERS, HENRY A., *rev.* 1897, *Johnson's Universal Cyclopædia, vol.* v, *p.* 87.

VISION OF PIERS PLOWMAN

We may iustly cōiect therfore y[t] it was firste written about two hundred yeres paste, in the tyme of Kynge Edwarde the thyrde. In whose tyme it pleased God to open the eyes of many to se hys truth, geuing them boldenes of herte, to open their mouthes and crye oute agaynste the worckes of darckenes, as did Iohn wicklefe, who also in those dayes translated the holye Bible into the Englishe tonge, and this writer who in reportynge certaine visions and dreames, that he fayned him selfe to haue dreamed: doeth moste christianlye enstruct the weake, and sharply rebuke the obstinate blynde. There is no maner of vice, that reigneth in anye estate of men, whiche this wryter hath not godly, learnedlye, and wittilye, rebuked. He wrote altogyther in miter: but not after y[e] maner of our rimers that write nowe adayes (for his verses ende not alike) but the nature of hys miter is, to haue thre wordes at the leaste in euery verse whiche beginne with some one letter. . . . Loke not vpon this boke therfore, to talke of wonders paste or to come, but to amende thyne owne misse, which thou shalt fynd here moste charitably rebuked. The spirite of god gyue the grace to walke in the waye of truthe, to Gods glory, & thyne owne soules healthe. So be it.—CROWLEY, ROBERT, 1550, *ed. The Vision of Pierce Plowman, The Printer to the Reader.*

In hys dooinges is somewhat harshe and obscure, but indeede a very pithy wryter, and (to hys commendation I speake it) was the first that I have seene, that observed ye quantity of our verse without the curiosity of Ryme.—WEBBE, WILLIAM, 1586, *A Discourse of English Poetrie, Arber ed., p.* 32.

He that wrote the Satyr of Piers Ploughman, seemed to have bene a malcontent of that time, and therefore bent himselfe wholy to taxe the disorders of that age, and specially the pride of the Romane Clergy, of whose fall he seemeth to be a very true Prophet, his verse is but loose meetre, and his termes hard and obscure, so as in them is litle pleasure to be taken. —PUTTENHAM, GEORGE, 1589, *The Arte of English Poesie, Arber ed., p.* 76.

It is written in a kind of English meeter, which for discovery of the infecting corruptions of those times, I preferre before many of the more seemingly serious Invectives, as well for Invention as Judgement.—SELDEN, JOHN, 1613, *Notes and Illustrations on Drayton's Polyolbion, p.* 109.

Forgive me, Reader, though placing him (who lived one hundred and fifty years before) since the Reformation: for I conceive that the Morning-star belongs rather to the Day, than to the Night. On which account this Robert (regulated in our Book not according to the Age he was in, but Judgement he was of) may by Prolepsis be termed a Protestant. . . . It's observable that Pits (generally a perfect Plagiary out of Bale) passeth this Langland over in silence. And why? Because he wrote in oppositum to the Papal interest. Thus the most light-finger'd Thieves will let that alone, which is too hot for them.—FULLER, THOMAS, 1662, *The Worthies of England, ed. Nichols, vol.* II, *pp.* 261, 262.

The metre of Pierce Plowman's Visions has no kind of affinity with what is commonly called Blank Verse; yet has it a sort of harmony of its own, proceeding not so much from its alliteration, as from the artful disposal of its cadence, and the contrivance of its pause; so that when the ear is a little accustomed to it, it is by no means unpleasing; but claims all the merit of the French heroic numbers, only far less polished; being sweetened, instead of their final rhymes, with the internal recurrence of similar sounds.—PERCY, THOMAS, 1765, *Reliques of Ancient English Poetry, 2nd S., bk.* iii, *pt.* i.

This poem abounds with the boldest personifications, the keenest satire, the most expressive descriptions, and the most singular versification.—HENRY, ROBERT, 1771-90, *The History of Great Britain, vol.* VIII, *bk.* iv, *ch.* v, *sec.* ii.

Instead of availing himself of the rising and rapid improvements of the English language, Longland prefers and adopts the style of the Anglo-Saxon poets. Nor did he make these writers the models of his language only: he likewise imitates their alliterative versification, which consisted in using an aggregate of words beginning with the same letter. He has therefore rejected rhyme, in the place of which he thinks it sufficient to susbtitute a perpetual alliteration. But this imposed constraint of seeking identical initials, and the affectation of obsolete English, by demanding a constant and necessary departure from the natural and obvious forms of expression, while it circumscribed the powers of our author's genius, contributed also to render his manner extremely perplexed, and to disgust the reader with obscurities.—WARTON, THOMAS, 1778-1781, *The History of English Poetry.*

Langland's work, whatever may be thought of its poetical merit, cannot fail of being considered as an entertaining and useful commentary on the general histories of the fourteenth century, not only from its almost innumerable pictures of contemporary manners, but also from its connexion with the particular feelings and opinions of the time.—ELLIS, GEORGE, 1790-1845, *Specimens of the Early English Poets, vol.* I, *p.* 132.

Wherever born or bred, and by whatever name distinguished, the author of these Visions was an observer and a reflector of no common powers. I can conceive him (like his own visionary William) to have been sometimes occupied in contemplative wanderings on the Malvern Hills, and dozing away a summer's noon among the bushes, while his waking thoughts were distorted into all the misshapen forms created by a dreaming fancy. Sometimes I can descry him taking his staff, and roaming far and wide in search of manners and characters; mingling with men of every accessible rank, and storing his memory with hints for future use. I next pursue him to his study, sedate and thoughtful, yet wildly inventive, digesting the first rude drafts of his Visions, and in successive transcriptions, as judgment matured, or invention declined, or as his observations were more extended, expanding or contracting, improving and sometimes perhaps debasing his original text. The time of our author's death, and the place of his interment, are equally unknown, with almost every circumstance relating to him. His contemporaries, Chaucer and Gower, repose beneath magnificent tombs, but Langland (if such were really his name) has no other monument than that which, having framed for himself, he left to posterity to appropriate.—WHITAKER, THOMAS DUNHAM, 1813, *ed. Vision of William concerning Piers Ploughman, Introduction.*

His style, even making allowance for its antiquity, has a vulgar air, and seems to indicate a mind that would have been coarse, though strong, in any state of society. But, on the other hand, his work, with all its tiresome homilies, illustrations from school divinity, and uncouth phraseology, has some interesting features of originality. He employs no borrowed materials; he is the earliest of our writers in whom there is a tone of moral reflection; and his sentiments are those of bold and solid integrity. The zeal of truth was in him; and his vehement manner sometimes rises to eloquence, when he denounces hypocrisy and imposture. The mind is struck with his rude voice, proclaiming independent and popular sentiments, from an age of slavery and superstition, and thundering a prediction in the ear of papacy, which was doomed to be literally fulfilled at the distance of nearly two hundred years. His allusions to contemporary life afford some amusing glimpses of its manners. There is room to suspect that Spenser was acquainted with his works; and Milton, either from accident or design, has the appearance of having had one of Langlande's passages in his mind, when he wrote the sublime description of the lazar-house, in "Paradise Lost."—CAMPBELL, THOMAS, 1819, *An Essay on English Poetry.*

The work of Langland is also curious, as being the product of a rich and powerful mind, drawing upon its own stores, unaided (perhaps I might have said unfettered) by rule and precedent. When carefully examined, it will not be found wanting in the important quality of *unity*, the absence of which so much lessens our enjoyment of many contemporary poems; but the execution of the work is certainly superior to its conception, and shows indeed a wonderful versatility of genius. A high tone of feeling is united to the most searching knowledge of the world; sarcastic declamation is succeeded by outpourings of the most delicate poetry; and broad humour or homespun motherwit by flights, which neither Spenser nor

Milton have disdained to follow.—GUEST, EDWIN, 1838, *A History of English Rhythms, vol.* II, *p.* 163.

The "Visions of Piers Ploughman" will always offer studies for the poetical artist. This volume, and not Gower's nor Chaucer's, is a well of English undefiled. Spenser often beheld these Visions; Milton, in his sublime description of the Lazar House, was surely inspired by a reminiscence of Piers Ploughman. Even Dryden, whom we should not suspect to be much addicted to black-letter reading beyond his Chaucer, must have carefully conned our Piers Ploughman; for he has borrowed one very striking line from our poet, and possibly may have taken others. Byron, though he has thrown out a crude opinion of Chaucer, has declared that "the Ploughman" excels our ancient poets. And I am inclined to think that we owe to Piers Ploughman an allegorical work of the same wild invention, from that other creative mind, the author of the "Pilgrim's Progress." How can we think of the one, without being reminded of the other? Some distant relationship seems to exist between the Ploughman's *Dowell* and *Dobet*, and *Dobest*, Friar *Flatterer*, *Grace* the portress of the magnificent Tower of *Truth* viewed at a distance, and by its side the dungeon of *Care*, *Natural Understanding*, and his lean and stern wife *Study*, and all the rest of this numerous company, and the shadowy pilgrimage of the "Immortal Dreamer" to "the Celestial City." Yet I would mistrust my own feeling, when so many able critics, in their various researches after a prototype of that singular production, have hitherto not suggested what seems to me obvious.—DISRAELI, ISAAC, 1841, *Piers Ploughman, Amenities of Literature.*

The Poem of "Piers Ploughman" is peculiarly a national work. It is the most remarkable monument of the public spirit of our forefathers in the middle, or, as they are often termed, dark ages. It is a pure specimen of the English language at a period when it had sustained few of the corruptions which have disfigured it since we have had writers of "Grammars;" and in it we may study with advantage many of the difficulties of the language which these writers have misunderstood. It is, moreover, the finest example left of the kind of versification which was purely English, inasmuch as it had been the only one in use among our Anglo-Saxon progenitors, in common with the other people of the North.—WRIGHT, THOMAS, 1842, *ed. The Vision and Creed of Piers Ploughman, Introduction, p.* xxvii.

Genius was thrust onward to a new slope of the world. And soon, when simpler minstrels had sat there long enough to tune the ear of the time,—when Layamon and his successors had hummed long enough, like wild bees, upon the lips of our infant poetry predestined to eloquence,—then Robert Langlande, the monk, walking for cloister "by a wode's syde," on the Malvern Hills, took counsel with his holy "Plowman," and sang of other visions than their highest ridge can show. While we write, the woods upon those beautiful hills are obsolete, even as Langlande's verses; scarcely a shrub grows upon the hills! but it is well for the thinkers of England to remember reverently, while, taking thought of her poetry, they stand among the gorse,—that if we may boast now of more honoured localities, of Shakespeare's "rocky Avon," and Spenser's "soft-streaming Thames," and Wordsworth's "Rydal Mere," still our first holy poet-ground is there.—BROWNING, ELIZABETH BARRETT, 1842-63, *The Book of the Poets, p.* 109.

The Visionary is no disciple, no precursor of Wycliffe in his broader religious views; the Loller of Piers Ploughman is no Lollard—he applies the name as a term of reproach for a lazy, indolent vagrant. The Poet is no dreamy speculative theologian; he acquiesces seemingly with unquestioning faith in the creed and in the usages of the Church. . . . It is in his intense absorbing moral feeling that he is beyond his age: with him outward observances are but hollow shows, mockeries, hypocrisies without the inward power of religion. It is not so much in his keen cutting satire on all matters of the Church as his solemn installation of Reason and Conscience as the guides of the self-directed soul, that he is breaking the yoke of sacerdotal domination: in his constant appeal to the plainest, simplest Scriptural truths, as in themselves the whole of religion, he is a stern reformer.—MILMAN, HENRY HART, 1855, *History of Latin Christianity, vol.* VI, *bk.* xiv, *ch.* vii, *p.* 537.

It is hardly less important to the philologist that the Mercian dialect, which he seems to have preferred, and which is still heard in the speech of Salopian laborers, appears visibly changed in the successive MS. copies that were made during the lifetime of the author, and thus show how, within the limits of one generation, the language was improved and developed. —DeVere, M. Schele, 1853, *Outlines of Comparative Philology, p.* 168.

Though highly original, thoroughly genial, and fully imbued with the spirit of the age and of the commonwealth of which he was the first-born intellectual son, yet, in his versification, he was little better than a servile imitator. . . . The poem, if not altogether original in conception, is abundantly so in treatment. The spirit it breathes, its imagery, the turn of thought, the style of illustration and argument it employs, are as remote as possible from the tone of Anglo-Saxon poetry, but exhibit the characteristic moral and mental traits of the Englishman, as clearly and unequivocally as the most national portions of the works of Chaucer or of any other native writer.—Marsh, George P., 1862, *The Origin and History of the English Language, etc., pp.* 286, 303.

The poem—in all its shapes—abounds with passages which we could ill afford to lose; the vivid truthfulness of its delineations of the life and manners of our forefathers has been often praised, and it is difficult to praise it too highly. . . . The extreme earnestness of the author and the obvious truthfulness and blunt honesty of his character are in themselves attractive and lend a value to all he utters, even when he is evolving a theory or wanders into abstract questions of theological speculation. But we are the more pleased when we perceive, as we very soon do, that he is evidently of a *practical* turn of mind, and loves best to exercise his shrewd English commonsense upon topics of every day interest. —Skeat, Walter W., 1867, *ed. The Vision of William concerning Piers Plowman, Introduction, pp.* iv, v.

Langland's verse runs mostly like a brook, with a beguiling and well nigh slumberous prattle, but he, more often than any writer of his class, flashes into salient lines, gets inside our guard with the homethrust of a forthright word, and he gains if taken piecemeal. His imagery is naturally and vividly picturseque. . . "Piers Ploughman" is the best example I know of what is called popular poetry,—of compositions, that is, which contain all the simpler elements of poetry, but still in solution, not crystallized around any thread of artistic purpose. In it appears at her best the Anglo-Saxon Muse, a first cousin of Poor Richard, full of proverbial wisdom, who always brings her knitting in her pocket, and seems most at home in the chimney-corner. It is genial; it plants itself firmly on human nature with its rights and wrongs; it has a surly honesty, prefers the downright to the gracious, and conceives of speech as a tool rather than a musical instrument. If we should seek for a single word that would define it most precisely, we should not choose simplicity, but homeliness.—Lowell, James Russell, 1870–90, *Chaucer, Prose Works, Riverside ed., vol.* III, *pp.* 332, 334.

The strength of Langland's genius is shown in stern invective:—not vague declamation, but invective, which is prompted and guided by a true insight into the vanities and vices and negligences of mankind in their various stations of life.—Creasy, Sir Edward S., 1870, *History of England, vol.* II, *p.* 537.

His world is the world of the poor; he dwells on the poor man's life, on his hunger and toil, his rough revelry and his despair with the narrow intensity of a man who has no outlook beyond it. The narrowness, the misery, the monotony of the life he paints reflect themselves in his verse. It is only here and there that a love of nature or a grim earnestness of wrath quickens his rhyme into poetry; there is not a gleam of the bright human sympathy of Chaucer, of his fresh delight in the gayety, the tenderness, the daring of the world about him, of his picturesque sense of even its coarsest contrasts, of his delicate irony, of his courtly wit. The cumbrous allegory, the tedious platitudes, the rhymed texts from Scripture which form the staple of Longland's work, are only broken here and there by phrases of a shrewd common sense, by bitter outbursts, by pictures of a broad Hogarthian humor.—Green, John Richard, 1874, *A Short History of the English People, ch.* v, *sec.* v.

Before middle life, William, like Dante, had recognised that the world was out of joint. He too looked with longing for the deliverer who should set it right; he too, with all the powers of his soul, wrestled for the knowledge of salvation, for himself as for others; he too lifted up his voice in warning and menace, before the great and mighty of the earth, before princes and priests; he too held up a mirror to the world, in which it saw both its own image and the ideal to which it had grown faithless. But unlike the Italian poet, William did not attain a full and clear theory of life, and hence he failed to put together what he had lived and seen, in a symmetrical, distinctly-drawn picture, with the mighty personality of the poet for its centre. The "Vision concerning Piers Plowman" is a series of paintings whose mutual connection lies more in the intention than in actual execution, and each of them has, besides clearly illumined groups, others that seem enveloped in mist, whose outlines we may feel rather than perceive, and still others whose dim figures first receive colour and life from our fancy.—TEN BRINK, BERNHARD, 1877-83, *History of English Literature (To Wiclif), tr. Kennedy, p.* 353.

The writer who, before Chaucer's prime, and in so close proximity to him and to the influences which moulded him, had already succeeded in distancing all predecessors, and in leaving a lasting bequest to his posterity of English readers, and to ours. — ROSSETTI, WILLIAM MICHAEL, 1878, *Lives of Famous Poets, p.* 3.

The whole drift of the poem is to recommend practical Christianity. The kernel of its moral teaching is the pure Christian love of our neighbour—love especially to the poor and lowly; a love of our neighbour reaching its highest point in patient forbearance, and love towards enemies—a love inspired by the voluntary passion of Christ for us.—LECHLER, GOTTHARD, 1878, *John Wiclif and his English Precursors, tr. Lorimer, vol.* I, *p.* 103.

Nowhere had the English mind found so real an opportunity of poetic utterance in the days of Chaucer's own youth as in Langland's unique work, national in its allegorical form and in its alliterative metre; and nowhere had this utterance been more stern and severe. — WARD, ADOLPHUS WILLIAM, 1880, *Chaucer, (English Men of Letters), p.* 174.

Probably no rhythm was ever so thoroughly misunderstood as the gentle and incessant sing which winds along through these alliterative fixed-points as a running brook among its pebbles.—LANIER, SIDNEY, 1880, *The Science of English Verse, p.* 163.

"Piers Plowman's Vision" is one of the first declarations of the intrinsic holiness of honest industry.—HOLLAND, FREDERICK MAY, 1884, *The Rise of Intellectual Liberty, p.* 295.

So ends the Vision, with no victory attained. There is a world at war, and a renewed cry for the grace of God, a new yearning to find Christ and bring with Him the day when wrongs and hatreds are no more. . . . Fourteenth Century yielded no more fervent expression of the purest Christian labour to bring men to God. . . . Langland lays fast hold of all the words of Christ, and reads them into a Divine Law of Love and Duty. He is a Church Reformer in the truest sense, seeking to strengthen the hands of the clergy by amendment of the lives and characters of those who are untrue to their holy calling. The ideal of a Christian Life shines through his poem, while it paints with homely force the evils against which it is directed. On points of theology he never disputes; but an ill life for him is an ill life, whether in Pope or peasant.—MORLEY, HENRY, 1889, *English Writers, vol.* IV., *p.* 353.

It makes a little book—earliest, I think, of all books written in English—which you will be apt to find in a well-appointed private library of our day. I won't say that it is bought to read, so much as to stand upon the shelves (so many books are) as a good and sufficient type of old respectabilities. Yet, for all this, it is reasonably readable; with crabbed alliterative rhythm;—some Latin intermixed, as if the writer had been a priest (as some allege); and such knowledge of life and of current shortcomings among all sorts of people as showed him to be a wide-awake and fearless observer. . . . Langlande is a little mixed and raw oftentimes; but he is full of shrewdness and of touches of a rough and unwashed humor. There is little tenderness of poetic feeling in his verse; and scarcely ever does it rise to anything approaching stateliness; but it keeps a good dog-trot jog, as of one who knew what he was doing, and meant to do it. What he meant was—to whip the vices of the priests and to scourge the covetousness of the rich and of the men in power. It is English all over; English in the homeliness of its language; he makes even Norman words sound homely; English in spirit too; full of good, hearty, grumbling humor—a sort of predated and poetic kind of Protestantism. Plums might be picked out of it for the decoration of a good radical or agrarian speech of to-day. —MITCHELL, DONALD G., 1889, *English Lands Letters and Kings, From Celt to Tudor, pp.* 84, 85.

No doubt his peasant was idealised, as no one knew better than himself; but it was honesty of work in the place of dishonest idleness which he venerated. It was the glory of England to have produced such a thought far more than to have produced the men who, heavy with the plunder of unhappy peasants, stood boldly to their arms at Creçy and Poitiers.—GARDINER, SAMUEL RAWSON, 1890, *Student's History of England, p.* 259.

He seems to have had a hard life, for he speaks of himself as earning a scanty living by the performance of minor clerical duties, such as singing the *placebo, dirige*, and "the seven psalms," for the good of men's souls, and he often alludes to his extreme poverty. Being married, he was, of course, only in minor orders, and thus could never rise to any rank in the Church. His poverty made him bitter and proud, and he hated, he tells us, to bow to the gay lords and dames who rode, richly dressed in silver and miniver, adown Cheapside. But perhaps it was well for others that he was poor, for his world is the world of the poor; he tells of their life and labours, their toil and hunger, their rude merriment and their helpless despair, till the misery and even the narrow bitterness of their thought is reflected in his verse.—GIBBINS, H. DE B., 1892, *English Social Reformers, p.* 7.

Because Langland reveres virtue, many commentators have made a saint of him; because he condemns, as an abuse, the admission of peasants' sons to holy orders, they have it that he was born of good family; and because he speaks in a bitter and passionate way of the wrongs of his time, they have made him out a radical reformer, aiming at profound changes in the religious and social order of things. He was nothing of all this. The energy of his language, the eloquence and force of his words may have given rise to this delusion. In reality, he is, from the religious and social points of view, one of those rare thinkers who defend moderate ideas with vehemence, and employ all the resources of a fiery spirit in the defence of common sense.—JUSSERAND, J. J., 1894, *Piers Plowman, A Contribution to the History of English Mysticism, p.* 103.

The earliest poem of high value which we meet with in modern English literature is the thrilling and mysterious "Vision of Piers Plowman." According to the view which we choose to adopt, this brilliant satire may be taken as closing the mediæval fiction of England or as starting her modern popular poetry. . . . One of the greatest writers of the Middle Ages. . . . In the "Vision of Piers Plowman" the great alliterative school of West-Midland verse culminated in a masterpiece, the prestige of which preserves that school from being a mere curiosity for the learned. In spite of its relative difficulty, "Piers Plowman" will now always remain, with the "Canterbury Tales," one of the two great popular classics of the fourteenth century. . . . It is an epitome of the social and political life of England, and particularly of London, seen from within and from below, without regard to what might be thought above and outside the class of workers. It is the foundation of the democratic literature of England, and a repository of picturesque observations absolutely unique and invaluable.—GOSSE, EDMUND, 1897, *A Short History of Modern English Literature, pp.* 7, 8, 12.

Even Langland, a much more interesting and striking figure than Gower to us, could have been much better spared by his own generation than Gower himself. In literary form Langland had nothing to teach: he was in fact merely rowing off-stream, if not against it, up a backwater which led nowhither. In substance he was powerful rather than profitable, offering nothing but allegory, of which there was already only too much, and political-ecclesiastical discussion, a growth always nearer to the tares than to the wheat of literature. In other words, and to vary the metaphor, he gave the workmen in the new workshop of English letters no new or improved tools, he opened up to them no new sources of material. He was a genius, he was a seer, he was an artist; but he was neither master nor stock-provider in literature.—SAINTSBURY, GEORGE, 1898, *A Short History of English Literature, p.* 141.

It is one thing to reach the public, quite another to reach the people; and the more difficult achievement was Langland's. His grave verse went straight to the heart of the still Teutonic race, indifferent to the facile French lilts of Chaucer. Serfs and laborers, seemingly inaccessible to influences of culture, as they staggered along under their heavy loads, eagerly welcomed the Visions of Piers the Plowman, of Do Well, Do Better, and Do Best. They heard, pondered, and repeated, till they realized that their souls had found utterance at last. The central version of the great poem—for the author rewrote it three times—antedated by only two or three years the Peasants' Revolt under Wat Tyler and John Ball. This was the first largely significant prophecy in England of a distinct industrial movement. Its inspiration was no gentle Christian idealism, such as stirred the followers of St. Francis, but a spirit of fierce rebellion, flinging itself with awakened intelligence and destructive ardor against established law. The first note of the social revolution is heard in its confused echoes. No one can trace the thrilling story of its hope and passions, and fail to see how potent had been the poem of Langland in arousing and shaping its ideals. Phrases from the poem were used as watchwords in the uprising; more than this, the central personage, the intensely conceived Piers the Plowman, became a spiritual presence to the laboring classes of England. In those days before telegram or press, association was difficult; this poem, quietly passing from lip to lip, helped bind together the scattered and voiceless workingmen of the eastern counties with a new sense of fellowship. Langland was thus a direct power, as few poets have ever been, upon an awakening national life. . . . Art knows no classes; and the self-expression of a class, though that class be the very heart of the nation, cannot be immortal. This is the book of the people; and the people, even when thinking, feeling, seeing aright, is yet unable, except by occasional chance, to find the inevitable word. The burden of the popular heart remains forever undelivered. This book is like all others that seek to give it. Sharing the people's sorrows, it shares also their fate: it is forgotten.—SCUDDER, VIDA D., 1898, *Social Ideals in English Letters, pp.* 21, 24.

PIERS PLOWMAN CREED

1394?

"The Crede of Piers Ploughman," if not written by the author of the "Vision," is at least written by a scholar who fully emulates his master; and Pope was so deeply struck with this little poem, that he has very carefully analyzed the whole. —DISRAELI, ISAAC, 1841, *Piers Ploughman, Amenities of Literature.*

The mention of Wycliffe and of Walter Brute and other circumstances, fix the date of "Piers Ploughman's Creed" with tolerable certainty in the latter years of the reign of Richard II. It was probably written very soon after the year 1393, the date of the persecution of Walter Brute at Hereford; and from the particular allusion to that person we may perhaps suppose that like the Vision it was written on the Borders of Wales.—WRIGHT, THOMAS, 1842, *ed. The Vision of Piers Ploughman, Introduction, p.* xxiv, *note.*

This poem, consisting of 850 lines, was written in alliterative verse by a disciple of Wycliffe, whose name has not been ascertained. The title and form of it are both imitated from William Langland's more famous poem, known as "The Vision of William concerning Piers the Plowman." Though these two poems, the "Crede" and the "Vision," are, in fact, by different authors, and express different sentiments on some points, they are, to the disgrace of students of English literature, continually being confounded with each other. There is every reason to believe that the anonymous author of the "Crede" was also author of "The Plowman's Tale," a satirical poem which has often been wrongly ascribed to Chaucer. —SKEAT, WALTER W., 1871, *Specimens of English Literature,* 1394–1579, *p.* 1.

Geoffrey Chaucer

1340?–1400

Born in London(?), 1340(?). Page in household of Duke of Clarence, 1357. Took part in King's expedition into France, 1359; taken prisoner in Brittany. Was "Valettus" to the King in 1361. Pension of 20 marks granted him by King, June, 1367; Yoeman of King's Chamber at that time. Abroad again, 1369 and 1370. To Italy on Commission respecting commercial treaty, Dec. 1372 to autumn of 1373. Married, 1374(?). Grant of daily pitcher of wine (afterward commuted to second pension of 20 marks), 23 April, 1374. Comptroller of Customs, 8 June, 1374. Pension of £10 granted him by Duke of Lancaster, 13 June, 1374. Two custodianships, 1375. On secret service with Sir John Burley, 1376; with Sir Thomas Percy in Flanders, 1377; in France and Italy, 1378 and 1379. Second Comptrollership of Customs, 1382. Knight of the Shire for Kent, 1386. Deprived of Comptrollerships, 1386. "Canterbury Tales" probably written, 1387 to 1393. Financial difficulties; sold pensions, May, 1388. Appointed Clerk of King's Works, 1389; superseded, 1391. Probably Forester of North Petherton Park, Somersetshire, 1391-98. Grant of £20 a year for life from King Richard II., 1394; of 40 marks from King Henry IV., 1399. Took lease of house in Westminster, Christmas Eve, 1399. Died 25 Oct., 1400. Buried in Westminster Abbey. *Works:* "Assembly of Fowls," first printed, 1478; "Canterbury Tales," first printed by Caxton, 1478 (?), by Pynson, 1493(?), by Wynken de Worde, 1498; "Troilus and Cressida," first printed (anon.), 1482(?); "The House (or "Book") of Fame," first printed by Caxton, 1486(?); Chaucer's translation of Boethius' "De Consolatione Philosophiæ," first printed, 1490(?). *Collected Works:* earliest, 1532, 1542, etc.; latest (Kelmscott Press), 1896.—SHARP, R. FARQUHARSON, 1897, *A Dictionary of English Authors, p.* 53.

Of his collected works that of 1532 was edited by Thynne, 1561 by Stowe, 1598 by Speight, 1721 by Urry, and the most important that of Skeat 1894–97, 6 vols. The first important edition of the "Canterbury Tales" is Tyrwhitt. 1775-78. The first important biography, but unreliable, is by Godwin 1803–04.—MOULTON, CHARLES WELLS, 1900.

PERSONAL

Til that our hoste Iapen tho bigan,
And than at erst he loked up-on me,
And seyde thus, "what man artow?" quod he;
"Thou lokest as thou woldest finde an hare,
For ever up-on the ground I see thee stare.
Approche neer, and loke up merily.
Now war yow, sirs, and lat this man have place;
He in the waast is shape as wel as I;
This were a popet in an arm tenbrace
For any womman, smal and fair of face.
He semeth elvish by his contenaunce,
For un-to no wight dooth he daliaunce.
. . . . now shul we here
Som deyntee thing, me thinketh by his chere"

—CHAUCER, GEOFFREY, 1387-93? *Prologue to Sir Thopas.*

And grete well Chaucer, when ye mete,
As my disciple and my poete.
For in the floures of his youth,
In sondry wise, as he well couth,
Of dittees and of songes glade,
The which he for my sake made,
The lond fulfilled is over all,
Whereof to him in speciall
Above all other I am most holde.
Forthy now in his daies olde
Thou shalt him telle this message,
That he upon his later age
To sette an end of all his werke,
As he, which is min owne clerke,
Do make his testament of love,
As thou hast do thy shrifte above,
So that my court it may recorde.

—GOWER, JOHN, C. 1383, *Confessio Amantis, Liber Octavus, MS. Harl.*, 3490.

Al-thogh his lyf be queynt, the résemblaunce
Of him hath in me so fresh lyflinesse
That, to putte othere men in rémembraunce
Of his persone, I have heer* his lyknesse
Do makë, to this ende, in sothfastnesse,
That they, that have of him lest thought and minde,
By this peynturë may ageyn him finde.

—OCCLEVE, THOMAS, 1411-12, *Governal of Princes, or De Regimine Principum, ed. Wright, p.* 179, *MS. Harl*, 4866.

He was buried in the Abbey of Westminster, before the chapel of St. Bennet; by whose sepulchre is written on a tablet hanging on a pillar, his epitaph made by a poet laureate.—CAXTON, WILLIAM, c 1480, *ed. Chaucer's Translation of Boethius.*

*Accompaning the portrait of Chaucer.

GEOFFREY CHAUCER

From Engraving by H. Robinson.

M. S.
Qui fuit Anglorum vates ter maximus olim,
GALFRIDUS CHAUCERUS conditur hoc tumulo:
Annum si quæras Domini, si tempora vitæ
Ecce notæ subsunt, quæ tibi cuncta notant.
25 Octobris 1400.
Ærumnarum requies mors.
N. Brigham hos fecit musarum nomine sumptus
1556.

—BRIGHAM, NICHOLAS, 1556, *Inscription on Tomb in Westminster Abbey.*

His stature was not very tall;
Lean he was; his legs were small,
Hos'd within a stock of red;
A button'd bonnet on his head,
From under which did hang, I ween,
Silver hairs both bright and sheen;
His beard was white, trimmèd round;
His countenance blithe and merry found;
A sleveless jacket, large and wide,
With many plaits and skirts side,
Of water-camlet did he wear;
A whittle by his belt he bear;
His shoes were cornèd, broad before;
His ink-horn at his side he wore,
And in his hand he bore a book:—
Thus did this ancient poet look.

—GREENE, ROBERT, ? 1592 ? *Greene's Vision, Greene's Works ed. Dyce, p.* 320.

I dobte whether Chaucer were of the temple or noe, unless yt were towardes his latter tyme, for he was an olde manne, as appereth by Gower in Confessione Amantis in the XVI yere of R. 2: when Gower wroote that Booke. And yt is most certeyne to be gathered by cyrcumstances of Recordes, that the lawyers were not in the temple vntill towardes the latter parte of the reygne of kinge Edwarde the thirde; at w*hi*che tyme Chaucer was a grave manne, holden in greate credyt, and employed in embassye, so that me thinkethe he sholde not be of that howse; and yet, yf he then werė, I sholde iudge yt strange that he sholde violate the rules of peace and gravytye yn those yeares.—THYNNE, FRANCIS, 1598, *Animadversions upon Chaucer's Works, ed. Kingsley, Early English Text Society, vol.* IX, *p.* 16.

Dunnington Castle, neer Newbury, was his; a noble seate and strong castle, which was held by the King (Charles 1st) (who governour?) but since dismanteled. Memorandum:—neer this castle was an oake, under which Sir Jeofrey was wont to sitt, called *Chaucer's -oake,* which was cutt downe by . . . tempore Caroli I^mi^; and so it was, that . . . was called into the starre chamber, and was fined for it. . . . Judge Richardson harangued against him long, and like an orator, had topiques from the Druides, etc. This information I had from . . . an able attorney that was at the hearing. His picture is at his old howse at Woodstock (neer the parke-gate), a foot high, halfe way: has passed from proprietor to proprietor.—AUBREY, JOHN, 1669–96, *Brief Lives, ed. Clark, vol.* I, *p.* 170.

April 28. *Note out of Sir Fra. Kinnaston, of Oatly, in Salop, his Comments on Chaucer's Troilus and Cressida.* For Chaucer's personage, it appears by an excellent piece of him limmed, by the life, of Thomas Occlive, his schollar, and now remaining as a high-prized jewell in the hands of my honoured friend sir Thomas Cotton, kt. and bart. that Chaucer was a man of an even stature, neither too high nor too low, his complection sanguine, his face fleshie but pale, his forehead broad but comely, smooth and even. His eyes rather little than great, cast most part downward, with a grave aspect. His lipps plump and ruddy, and both of an equal thickness, the hair on the upper being thin and short, of a wheat colour; on his chin two thin forked tuffs. His cheeks of like colour, with the rest of his face being either shaved, or wanting hair. All which considered, together with his witt and education in the court, and his favour among great ladys, one of whose women he married, it was his modesty made him speaks of his unlikeliness to be a lover.—HEARNE, THOMAS, 1711, *Reliquiæ Hearnianæ, vol.* I, *p.* 219.

As to his temper he had a mixture of the gay, the modest and the grave. His reading was deep and extensive, his judgment sound and discerning; he was communicative of his knowledge, and ready to correct or pass over the faults of his contemporary writers. He knew how to judge of and excuse the slips of weaker capacities, and pitied rather than exposed the ignorance of that age. In one word, he was a great scholar, a pleasant wit, a candid critic, a sociable companion, a stedfast friend, a great philosopher, a temperate economist, and a pious Christian.—URRY, JOHN, ? 1721, *ed. Life and Works of Chaucer.*

Was buried before the Chapel of St. Bennet, where his stone of broad gray marble, as I take it, was not long since remaining: but was taken up when Mr. Dryden's monument was erected and sawn to mend the pavement.—DART, JOHN, 1723, *History and Antiquities of Westminster Abbey*, p. 85.

Geoffrey Chaucer, one of the greatest, as well as most ancient, of the English Poets, is said by some writers to have been a native of Berkshire, by others of Oxfordshire, but by others, with much greater probability, of London. He was descended from a good family, and born in the year 1328. His first studies were in the University of Cambridge, where he wrote his Court of Love. He removed from Cambridge to complete his studies at Oxford, where after a considerable stay, he became, says Leland, "an acute Logician, a smooth rhetorician, a pleasant poet, a grave philosopher, an ingenious mathematician, and a holy divine." He then travelled into France, Holland, and other countries, and on his return entered himself in the Inner Temple, where he studied the municipal Laws of England. But he had not long followed that study before his singular accomplishments were discovered at Court, whither he next made his approaches. He mixed in the political troubles of the times, during the latter part of the reign of Edward III. and in those of Richard II. and Henry IV. in the two former of which he enjoyed various confidential situations. He died at London, October 25th, 1400, in the 72d year of his age, and was interred in Westminster Abbey.—BIRCH, THOMAS, 1743, *The Heads of Illustrious Persons with their Lives and Character.*

It is in one of the royal MSS. of this poem* in the British Museum that Occleve has left a drawing of Chaucer: according to which, Chaucer's portraiture was made on his monument, in the chapel of Saint Blase in Westminster-abbey, by the benefaction of Nicholas Brigham, in the year 1556. And from this drawing, in 1598, John Speed procured the print of Chaucer prefixed to Speght's edition of his works; which has been since copied in a most finished engraving by Vertue. Yet it must be remembered, that the same drawing occurs in an Harleian MSS. written about Occleve's age, and in another of the Cottonian department. Occleve himself mentions this drawing in his "Consolatio Servilis." It exactly resembles the curious picture on board of our venerable bard, preserved in the Bodleian gallery at Oxford. I have a very old picture of Chaucer on board, much like Occleve's, formerly kept in Chaucer's house, a quadrangular stone-mansion, at Woodstock in Oxfordshire; which commanded a prospect of the ancient magnificent royal palace, and of many beautiful scenes in the adjacent park: and whose last remains, chiefly consisting of what was called Chaucer's bed-chamber, with an old carved oaken roof, evidently original, were demolished about fifteen years ago.—WARTON, THOMAS, 1778-81, *The History of English Poetry*, sec. xx.

Through all the works of Chaucer there reigns a cheerfulness, a manly hilarity, which makes it almost impossible to doubt a correspondent habit of feeling in the author himself.—COLERIDGE, SAMUEL TAYLOR, 1817, *Biographia Literaria*, ch. ii.

For the well-known portrait of Chaucer we are indebted to an old MS. of the Canterbury Tales, belonging to the fifteenth century, which is at present in the possession of the Marquis of Stafford. This MS., at the commencement of the tale of Melibœus, represents the poet riding on horseback, in a vest or gipoun of dark velvet, with a bonnet of the same colour, with gilt anelace, or dagger, black boots, and with the trappings of his horse partially gilt. In the part of the tale of Melibœus in which the poet pourtrays himself, he hints that he was rather corpulent, and was in the habit of looking down on the ground. He also gives a similar portrait of himself in the Prologue to the "Rime of Sire Thopas." But, notwithstanding this tendency to be corpulent, his appearance conveys the impression of great delicacy. He seems to have been short of stature. His countenance, calm and composed as it was, appears to have been expressive of a high degree of naïve humour. The character and temperament of Chaucer are clearly and beautifully set forth in his own works. He was cheerful, kind, open and serene to the last moments of his life, and gained the affections of all with whom he came in contact; his social habits were formed by the various circumstances

*De Regimie Principum.

and spheres in which he had lived and moved. He was naturally social, and even convivial, and, like many other poets, he paid little regard to his financial means; hence we find him involved in difficulties at times, when, considering his ample income, we should have least expected it. But, notwithstanding this carelessness about his own affairs, Chaucer was, in the highest degree, strict and punctual in the performance of all his official duties.—SCHMITZ, LEONHARD, 1841, *A Life of Chaucer, The Poems of Geoffrey Chaucer, p.* cxxxvi.

The figure, which is half-length, has a back-ground of green tapestry. He is represented with grey hair and beard, which is biforked; he wears a dark-coloured dress and hood; his right hand is extended, and in his left he holds a string of beads. From his vest a black case is suspended, which appears to contain a knife, or possibly a "penner," or pen-case. The expression of the countenance is intelligent; but the fire of the eye seems quenched, and evident marks of advance age appear on the countenance.—NICOLAS, SIR NICHOLAS HARRIS, 1845, *Life of Chaucer, Aldine ed. British Poets.*

Chaucer's face is to his writings the best preface and commentary; it is contented-looking, like one familiar with pleasant thoughts, shy and self-contained somewhat, as if he preferred his own company to the noisy and rude companionship of his fellows; and the outlines are bland, fleshy, voluptuous, as of one who had a keen relish for the pleasures that leave no bitter traces. Tears and mental trouble, and the agonies of doubt, you cannot think of in connexion with it; laughter is sheathed in it, the light of a smile is diffused over it.—SMITH, ALEXANDER, 1863, *Dreamthorp, p.* 212.

His visible figure, at all events, stands plainly before us—a large head, a little body, but with broad shoulders, and small extremities. His physical energy must have been enormous—in terms of physiology, he must have had large viscera—to support the incessant and varied labour of his life.—RANDS, WILLIAM BRIGHTY, (MATTHEW BROWNE), 1869, *Chaucer's England, vol.* I, *p.* 7.

The window is placed immediately over the tomb where Chaucer's dust reposes. It was designed by Waller, and executed by Baillie and Mayer, last year, in London. . . . At the base are pictures of the pilgrims setting out from London, and their arrival at Canterbury. Above are two medallions, representing Chaucer receiving his commission in 1372, from Edward III., to the Doge of Genoa, and his reception by the latter. At the apex is represented, allegorically, as two ladies, one in white, the other in green, "The Floure and the Leafe." "As they which honour the Flower, a thing fading with every blast, are such as look for beauty and worldly pleasure; but they that honour the Leaf, which abideth with the root, notwithstanding the winter storms, are they which follow virtue and during qualities, without regard to worldly respects." In the spandrels and traceries are heraldries, and portraits of Edward III., and Philippa, Gower, and John of Gaunt, Wycliffe and Strode—Chaucer's contemporaries. They are fringed with the arms of England, France, Hainault, Lancaster, Castile, and Leon. At the bottom is written "Geoffrey Chaucer, died A. D. 1400." . . . There is a still, religious light about the window, which may well denote the quiet beauty with which the sacred stream of thought flows ever through the ages, shining above the mouldering monuments of kings, luminous after their strifes and ambitions are forgotten. Little did King Edward III. dream that in the end he might be chiefly remembered as the monarch who recognized Chaucer!—CONWAY, MONCURE D., 1870, *South-Coast Saunterings in England, Harper's Magazine, vol.* 41, *p.* 343.

If character may be devined from works, he was a good man, genial, sincere, hearty, temperate of mind, more wise, perhaps, for this world than the next, but thoroughly humane, and friendly with God and men. I know not how to sum up what we feel about him better than by saying (what would have pleased most one who was indifferent to fame) that we love him more even than we admire.—LOWELL, JAMES RUSSELL, 1870-90, *Chaucer, Prose Works, Riverside ed., vol.* III, *p.* 365.

An old man in a lodge within a park;
  The chamber walls depicted all around
  With portraitures of huntsman, hawk, and
    hound,
And the hurt deer. He listeneth to the lark,

Whose song comes with the sunshine through
 the dark
Of painted glass in leaden lattice bound;
He listenth and he laugheth at the sound,
Then writeth in a book like any clerk
—LONGFELLOW, HENRY WADSWORTH, 1873, *A Book of Sonnets, Poems, Cambridge ed., p.* 315.

With this guide every reader can work out the succession of the Tales for himself, and mix them in proper order with the Minor Poems. . . . He will then see Chaucer, not only outwardly as he was in the flesh—page, soldier, squire, diplomatist, Custom-house officer, Member of Parliament, then a suppliant for protection and favour, a beggar for money; but inwardly as he was in the spirit—clear of all nonsense of Courts of Love, &c.—gentle and loving, early timid and in despair, sharing others' sorrow, and, by comforting them, losing part of his own; yet long dwelling on the sadness of forsaken love, seeking the "consolation of philosophy," watching the stars, praying to the "Mother of God;" studying books, and, more still, woman's nature; his eye open to all the beauties of the world around him, his ear to the "heavenly harmony" of birds' song; at length becoming the most gracious and tender spirit, the sweetest singer, the best pourtrayer, the most pathetic, and withal the most genial and humourful healthy-souled man that England had ever seen. Still, after 500 years, he is bright and fresh as the glad light green of the May he so much loved; he is still second only to Shakespeare in England, and fourth only to him and Dante and Homer in the world. When will our Victorian time love and honour him as it should? Surely, of all our poets he is the one to come *home* to us most. — FURNIVALL, FREDERICK JAMES, 1873, *Recent Work at Chaucer, Macmillan's Magazine, vol.* 27, *p.* 389

We must be careful about filling in details of his inner history from supposed autobiographical references in his poems. Chaucer's biographers too often take the poet literally, ignoring his ironic humour and his conventional artistic pretences. They argue from one or two jests at his wife's expense, of a kind that might be made by the most affectionate of husbands, provided there was no real ground for them, that his wife was a shrew and his married life far from happy. They accept as matter of fact to be gravely discussed the poet's statement in the opening of the "Book of the Duchess," which serves happily as part of the artistic setting of that poem, that he has been unable to sleep night or day for eight years. This confession of a long and hopeless love-passion is taken with such unhesitating faith, that it is set against and allowed to overbear otherwise plain documentary evidence of the date of Chaucer's marriage to one of the "damoiselles" of the Queen's Chamber. But why take such conventional artistic pretences literally? . . . There is every indication in his works that he was not an eager, excitable man; moody and uncertain. On the contrary, he would seem to have been tranquil and leisurely, with his wits in easy command; patient, not self-assertive, yet with sufficient backbone to defy Fortune when the worst came to the worst. Such, at least, he appears in his works, and such, from his diplomatic success, we may presume him to have been in actual business; though we should err greatly if in every case we concluded that the diplomatist with the pen has equanimity enough to be diplomatic with the tongue. In his works, at least, he displays the most artful and even-tempered courtesy. We see him with easy smile deferentially protesting ignorance of the flowers of rhetoric; throwing the blame of disagreeable things in his story on some author that he professes to follow; dismissing knotty inquisitions as too difficult for his humble wit; evading tedious or irrelevant narrations by referring the reader to Homer, or "Dares," or "Dyte."—MINTO, WILLIAM, 1874-85, *Characteristics of English Poets, pp.* 8, 9.

For the present at least Chaucer's married life is involved in obscurity. That it was not a success there are many indications; but the causes of its unhappiness have not hitherto been discovered —are, perhaps, undiscoverable.—HALES, JOHN W., 1888, *Folia Litteraria, p.* 113.

Geoffrey Chaucer is said to have lived not only at Woodstock but also at Donington Castle in Leicestershire, where there used to be an old oak, called Chaucer's Oak. But these traditions, so far as they have any foundation, probably should be referred to his son Thomas, born about the year 1367. Thomas Chaucer succeeded his father in the office of forester of North Petherton. . . . Thomas Chaucer married, early in life, a daughter of Sir John Burghersh, with whom he acquired large estates in Oxfordshire and other counties, including the manor of Ewelme in Oxfordshire. He received grants both from Richard II., to whom he was made chief butler, and from John of Gaunt; and he was advanced by Henry IV., from whose queen he received the manor of Woodstock, in February, 1411. He sat for Oxfordshire in several parliaments, and was chosen Speaker in 1407, and again in 1410, 1411, and 1414. He served in France at the battle of Agincourt, furnishing twelve men-at-arms and thirty-seven archers. He died very rich, at Ewelme, in November, 1434, leaving a daughter Alice, born about 1404, whose third husband, by whom only she had children, was William de la Pole, Earl of Suffolk. Their eldest son John married the sister of King Edward IV.; and the eldest son of that marriage, John de la Pole, created Earl of Lincoln, was declared by Richard III. heir-apparent in the event of the death of the Prince of Wales without issue. John de la Pole was killed at the battle of Stoke in 1487, and he died childless. Thus the last of Chaucer's race was the great-great-grandson of the poet, one who stood so near the throne that, through him, Chaucer might have been forefather to a line of English kings.—MORLEY, HENRY, 1890, *English Writers, vol.* V., *p.* 248, *note.*

The life of Chaucer is a field that blossoms luxuriantly with conjectures, and it is asking a good deal of him who enters it to abstain from plucking occasionally one of its flowers. . . . To read a life of Chaucer cannot by any possibility be so tedious as to write one; but it approaches dangerously near. . . . While he lived he was regarded by his contemporaries as the chief poet of Britain. Men admired him, men imitated him; they strove to reproduce in their own work the manner and spirit of the master they loved. They were never weary of celebrating his praises, and the tributes paid to his greatness are couched in language of warmest eulogy and sometimes of fairly affectionate devotion. The one thing they neglected to do entirely was to give an account of his life, and even of the most insignificant detail belonging to it or connected with it. No contemporary writer has preserved for us a single anecdote. No contemporary chronicle contains a single saying or reports a single fact. The appreciation which gladly recognized Chaucer as standing at the head of all living English poets never, to our knowledge, inspired a solitary disciple to place upon record the slightest particular in the story of his career. His superiority remained unchallenged during the century that followed his death. Yet no account of him on even the most insignificant scale was even attempted till after he had been in his grave almost a hundred and fifty years. Nothing could show more pointedly how alien was the spirit of the past to that of the present. . . . The biography of Chaucer is built upon doubts and thrives upon perplexities. Without these there would be exceedingly little to say. Uncertainty begins with the date of his birth, it hovers over most of his career, and adds to the length of the narrative as inevitably as it detracts from its interest. About some of the facts the evidence is conflicting; about others that cannot be questioned there is conflict of opinion as to their interpretation. In consequence, he who sets out to gain a knowledge of the poet's life enters at once into an arena of controversy, and of controversy that can usually never be carried to a satisfactory conclusion because of the absence of satisfactory data. For this very reason the discussion is apt to be as exciting to the disputant as it is dull to the reader.—LOUNSBURY, THOMAS R., 1891, *Studies in Chaucer, vol.* I, *pp.* XV, XVI, 8, 11.

Poet's Corner is the name given to the eastern angle of the South Transept, from the tombs and honorary monuments of Chaucer, Spenser, Shakespeare, and several of our greatest poets. Tomb of Geoffrey Chaucer, the father of English poetry (d. 1400); erected in 1555, by Nicholas Brigham, a scholar of Oxford, and himself a poet; Chaucer was originally buried in this spot, Brigham removing his bones to a more honourable tomb.

A portrait of Chaucer originally ornamented the back of the tomb. Its loss was in part supplied in the painted glass window above the tomb, erected in 1868, in which are medallions of Chaucer and Gower and scenes from Chaucer's poems. —WHEATLEY, HENRY B., 1891, *Westminster Abbey, London Past and Present, Based upon the Handbook of London by Peter Cunningham, vol.* III, *p.* 475.

Chaucer was thus, at various times of his life, a courtier, soldier, diplomatist, and man of business, and it was mainly by hard work done in these various capacities that he earned his living, though in his old age the fact that he was a great poet may have won for him rather more consideration than kings always show to their worn-out servants. Probably no other poet of equal rank has ever led so active and varied a life, and it is because we find Chaucer in his poems so shrewd a man of the world, so astonishingly observant, and so good a judge of character, that we take an interest in finding out how he obtained his experience. When we come to examine his writings we shall find that the double life he was obliged to lead had one bad effect: it caused him to leave many of his poems unfinished. If we may take a passage in his "Hous of Fame" (Bk. ii, ll. 139-152) quite literally, he must often have been in danger of over-work, though the absolutely healthy tone of his poems forbids us to think that he ever fell a victim to it.—POLLARD, ALFRED W., 1893, *Chaucer* (*Literature Primers*), *p.* 21.

As the exact date* still remains uncertain, I can only say that we must place it between 1330 and 1340. The reader can incline to whichever end of the decade best pleases him. I merely record my opinion, for what it is worth, that "shortly before 1340" fits in best with *all* the facts. . . . I believe his wife's death to have been a serious loss to him in one respect at least. Most of his early works are reasonably free from coarseness; whereas such Tales as those of the Miller, the Reeve, the Shipman, the Merchant, and the Prologue to the Wife's Tale, can hardly be defended. All these may confidently be dated after the year 1387.—SKEAT, WALTER W., 1894, *Complete Works of Geoffrey Chaucer, vol.* I, *pp.* xvi, liii.

Here** he† sat to Brown‡ for the head of Chaucer in the very large picture—now in the museum of Sydney, Australia—of *Chaucer reading to the Court of Edward* 3 *the Legend of Custance.* The head was painted in one night, 11 P.M. to 4 A.M., and was never afterwards touched upon. This is recognizably like Chaucer, and is also a very fair portrait of Rossetti.—ROSSETTI, WILLIAM MICHAEL, 1895, *Dante Gabriel Rossetti, His Family Letters, vol.* I, *p.* 170.

ROMAUNT OF THE ROSE
1360–65?

Thou art in Albion the god of worldly love; and into good English thou didst translate the book of the Rose.—DESCHAMPS, EUSTACHE, c 1370, *Ballade Addressed to Geoffrey Chaucer.*

For in pleyn text, hit nedeth nat to glose,
Thou hast translated the Romauns of the Rose.

—CHAUCER, GEOFFREY, 1384? *Legend of Good Women, Prologue, v.* 254–5.

This poem is esteemed by the French the most valuable piece of their old poetry. It is far beyond the rude efforts of all their preceding romancers; and they have nothing equal to it before the reign of Francis I., who died in the year 1547. —WARTON, THOMAS, 1778-81, *History of English Poetry, sec.* xiii.

His translation of the decidedly uninteresting allegory known as the "Romaunt of the Rose," is no doubt the production of his earlier years, as we infer from the language and from the mode of versification, which he copied from the original, and which was also adopted by Gower in his English poems. The translation, however, attracted some notice even on the Continent, for the somewhat common-place French poet, Eustace Deschamps, flattered by seeing his soft-sounding French translated into rough Saxon, felt himself called upon to laud "the great translator, the noble Geoffrey Chaucer," in a composition of many strophes. Happily the poet did not long continue to occupy himself with such subordinate labours.—PAULI, REINHOLD, 1861, *Pictures of Old England, p.* 227.

No verse so flowing and harmonious as this, no diction at once so clear, correct, and expressive, had, it is probable, adorned and brought out the capabilities of his native tongue when Chaucer began

*Of birth. **17 Newman Street. †Dante Gabriel Rossetti. ‡Madox Brown.

to write.—CRAIK, GEORGE L., 1861, *A Compendious History of English Literature and of the English Language, vol.* I, *p.* 301.

Chaucer knew his countrymen well, and did not care to give them more than 3629 out of the 17,930 verses of Jean de Meung. He omits the democracy as well as the seductive indecency of his original; and in both cases he doubtless followed the lead of his personal taste, as well as of his literary judgment. He had been brought up at court, and was by training in harmony with the loyal aristocratic feeling of his day; and he was, moreover, in all probability, a Lollard, or at least a sympathiser with the Lollards, having married the sister of John of Gaunt's second wife, and being, we may presume, no little influenced by the opinions of that staunch patron of the religious purists. But indeed his genius was cast in a different mould from that of Jean de Meung, who was natural philosopher first, and romancist afterwards. Chaucer, like Guillaume de Lorris, was before all a romancist; and it is therefore perfectly natural that he should have reproduced the latter's verses with the greatest zest and completeness.—VAN LAUN, HENRI, 1876, *History of French Literature, vol.* I, *p.* 184.

It has already been said that Chaucer translated the "Romaunt," and that a version has been current under his name for centuries. There is only one MS. of this translation, in the Hunterian Museum at Glasgow, so that we have no means of comparing texts, and thus settling the difficult questions that have been raised about it. As it stands, the poem contains various features which, in the opinion of the most advanced school of Chaucerian criticism, mark it out as being not Chaucer's; the principal difficulty being connected with the rhymes, some of which seem to be irreconcilable with Chaucer's principles of pronunciation. The question cannot be properly discussed here, but in deference to what seems to be the balance of opinion we quote the "Romaunt" under the head of "Poems attributed to Chaucer."—WARD, THOMAS HUMPHRY, 1880, *The English Poets, vol.* I, *p.* 82.

In spite of occasional variation in the character of the version, the work, as a whole, bears its own overwhelming testimony as to its having come but from one hand. To arrive at any other conclusion, one must fix his eyes so closely upon certain points of detail that he loses sight both of other details and of the general view. The arguments that have been adduced for a dual authorship are so far from convincing that they cannot even be called specious.—LOUNSBURY, THOMAS R., 1891, *Studies in Chaucer, vol.* II, *p.* 12.

We are compelled to admit the disagreeable fact that Chaucer's imitation of the famous French poem is lost to us. Of the numerous losses which we mourn in mediæval English literature, this is one of those which cause us the most pain. At the stage of development which the poet had attained at this time, he must have translated this peculiar work in a manner peculiarly his own. We may assume that he softened if not eliminated the incongruity in treatment and tone existing between the two parts; that he perhaps imparted to Guillaume de Lorris's poem some of the biting satire of his successor, and that he certainly condensed and poetically enriched the poem of Jean de Meung, and rendered it closer to the style of his predecessor.—TEN BRINK, BERNHARD, 1892, *History of English Literature (Wyclif, Chaucer, Earliest Drama, Renaissance), tr. Robinson, p.* 77.

The result of the discussion seems clear. The affirmative evidence brought forward by Mr. Lounsbury, when reduced to its lowest terms, we have found to be entirely consistent with the belief that the translation is not by Chaucer, but by an imitator. The negative evidence, on the other hand, from dialect, grammar, and metre, if it does not show conclusively that Chaucer and the translator were two persons, still creates the strongest kind of probability in favor of that supposition. We must therefore be allowed to prefer the theory that is in accordance with all the facts to the theory that is strongly opposed to the most significant of them, and to believe that the "Romaunt" is not Chaucer's with the possible exception of the first seventeen hundred lines.—KITTREDGE, GEORGE LYMAN, 1892, *Authorship of the Romaunt of the Rose, Harvard Studies and Notes in Philology and Literature, vol.* I, *p.* 65.

The supremacy of Chaucer is in nothing more clearly seen than in the fact that for more than a century after his death he was the sole source of inspiration for the poets. . . . It was Chaucer the student of the "Roman de la Rose," not Chaucer the poet of his fellow-men, nor even Chaucer the student of Italian literature, after whom the younger versifiers stumbled.—HEATH, H. FRANK, 1894, *Social England, vol.* II, *p.* 376.

Chaucer's translation of the "Romaunt of the Rose" is not remarkable only as making a landmark in the refinement of our versification. It marks with equal significance the rise of a new spirit in English poetry, the importation of thoughts and themes from the Continent, announcing the approach of the Renaissance.—COURTHOPE, W. J., 1895, *A History of English Poetry, vol.* I, *p.* 258.

Whoever wrote it, the translation is well worthy to take a place beside Chaucer's best work; and it is difficult to understand how this comes to be the only surviving work of a poet who was such a master of English verse and had such power of reproducing with added skilful touches of his own Jehan de Meung's "Roman de la Rose."—LIDDELL, MARK H., 1898, *The Works of Geoffrey Chaucer, Globe ed., Introduction, p.* lv.

BOOK OF THE DUTCHESS
1369–70?

The charm of this poem, notwithstanding all the artificialities with which it is overlaid, lies in its simplicity and truth to nature. A real human being is here brought before us instead of a vague abstraction; and the glow of life is on the page, though it has to tell of death and mourning. Chaucer is finding his strength by dipping into the true spring of poetic inspiration; and in his dreams he is awaking to the real capabilities of his genius. Though he is still uncertain of himself and dependent on others, it seems not too much to say that already in this "Book of the Duchess" he is in some measure an original poet.—WARD, ADOLPHUS WILLIAM, 1880, *Chaucer (English Men of Letters), p.* 72.

Artistically considered, the work, though not without beauty, is juvenile and crude. It is conventional in form, awkward in arrangement, inadequate in expression. There is scarcely anything specially Chaucerian in it.—HALES, JOHN W., 1887, *Dictionary of National Biography, vol.* X, *p.*160.

A multitude of ideas and images, which were very common in French literature since the "Romance of the Rose," appear here for the first time in an English dress—such as reminiscences from classical antiquity or even from the Old Testament, long spun-out allegories, witty and uncouth touches from the wisdom of the mediæval schoolmen. However much the mind may be distracted by all this learning, parenthetically introduced, we nevertheless frequently hear the voice of real passion from the strange figure, and in some passages of the knight's discourse—as in his invectives against Fortune, or in his complaints, given in antithetic form—the student of Shakspere is reminded of the great bard's earlier works, especially Romeo and Juliet.—TEN BRINK, BERNHARD, 1892, *History of English Literature, (Wyclif, Chaucer, Earliest Drama, Renaissance), tr. Robinson, p.* 42.

The poem has many of the faults of an early effort. Its many learned references, its long-spun allegories, its philosophical platitudes, all tend to destroy the effect aimed at. But a real power of characterisation, and the germs at least of the poet's later dramatic power, are evident. Though the speeches are too long and too full of digressions, the dialogue between the poet and the unknown knight is well conceived, but the retarded crisis intended to come as a surprise fails of its effect, because too long postponed.—HEATH, H. FRANK, 1894, *Social England, vol.* II, *p.* 209.

A distinguished English scholar has been moved to undertake Chaucer's defence against the strictures passed on this poem by a French critic; he finds it graceful and pathetic. I confess that it seems to me few readers, who judge the composition apart from Chaucer's prestige, are likely to share his opinion. The design . . . is singularly barren of genuine invention Simple as it is, the action is clumsily conducted, for the knight acquaints the reader from the first with his lady's death, thus spoiling what might have been a dramatic climax, if the fact had been withheld till after the recital of all her amiable qualities. Nor is the crudeness of the general conception relieved by any remarkable beauties of detail. The story serves to piece together a certain number of "purple patches," taken from various poems which the author has read and admired; but these do not seem to be in any way necessarily connected with the central thought. It would, in fact, be as exacting to look for pathos in a poem of this order, as in Spenser's "Astrophel," or in the pastoral elegies described in the 30th number of the "Guardian." The mourning is of that conventional kind which is prescribed for a conventional class of poetry, and, owing to a certain lack of skill, the composition fails to attain a high place even in that lowly sphere. —COURTHOPE, W. J., 1895, *A History of English Poetry, vol.* I, *p.* 267.

THE COMPLAINT OF MARS
1380?

Thus eondithe here this Complaynt, whiche some men sayne was made by* my lady of York, doughter to the kyng of Spaygne, and my lord Huntingdon, some tyme Duc of Excestre.—SHIRLEY, JOHN, 1458? *In the MS. at Trinity College, Cambridge.*

There is no firm ground of historical truth in a note that professes only to report what "some men say."—MORLEY, HENRY, 1890, *English Writers, vol.* V, *p.* 151.

According to the tradition established in the reign of Henry VI. by a disciple and copier of Chaucer, Mars represented John Holland, third son of Thomas, Earl of Kent, afterwards Earl of Huntingdon and Duke of Exeter; and the Venus of the poem was Isabella, Countess of Edmund, Earl of Cambridge, who was made Duke of York in 1386. John of Gaunt was doubly related to this Venus—Isabella, who is reported by a chronicler as being "*mulier mollis et delicata,*" and towards the close of her life "*satis pœnitens et conversa.*" She was the younger sister of his wife, Constance of Castile, and her husband Edmund was his own younger brother. Mars (Holland) also came after a time into family relationship with Chaucer's patron, by marrying Elizabeth, the divorced Countess of Pembroke, who was a daughter of Blanche and John of Gaunt. The whole atmosphere in this affair is not at all refreshing. John of Gaunt may have followed, with a malicious pleasure, the progress of the adulterous connection between John Holland and the Countess of Cambridge; and when at length a kind of catastrophe supervened, he shook with laughter, and Chaucer had to write out the story for him in flowing rhymes.—TEN BRINK, BERNHARD, 1892, *History of English Literature, (Wyclif, Chaucer, Earliest Drama, Renaissance), tr. Robinson, p.* 74.

Whatever one may think of the poem as a poem, it—perhaps more than the treatise on the Astrolabe itself—makes clear that even though Chaucer says of "retrograd," "combust" and "aspecte infortunat:" "theise ben obseruaunces of iudicial matiere & rytes of paiens, in which my spirit ne hath no feith, ne no knowyng of hir horoscopum," he is hardly open to the charge of ignorance, usually brought by astrologers against those who have no faith.—MANLY, JOHN MATTHEWS, 1896, *The Date and Interpretation of Chaucer's Complaint of Mars, Harvard Studies in Philology and Literature, vol.* V, *p.* 126.

TRANSLATION OF BOETHIUS
1380–83?

Chaucer did not English Boethius second-hand, through any early French version, as some have supposed, but made his translation with the Latin original before him—MORRIS, RICHARD, 1868 *ed., Chaucer's Translation of Boethius's "De Consolatione Philosophiæ," Introduction, p* xiii.

When we come to consider the style and manner in which Chaucer has executed his self-imposed task, we must first of all make some allowance for the difference between the scholarship of his age and of our own. One great difference is obvious, though constantly lost sight of, viz. that the teaching in those days was almost entirely oral, and that the student had to depend upon his memory to an extent which would now be regarded by many as extremely inconvenient. Suppose that, in reading Boethius, Chaucer comes across the phrase "ueluti quidam clauus atque gubernaculum" (Bk. iii. pr. 12, note to l. 55), and does not remember the sense of *clauus;* what is to be done? It is quite certain, though this again is frequently lost sight of, that he had no access to a convenient and well-arranged Latin Dictionary, but only to such imperfect glossaries as were then in use. Almost the only resource, unless he had at hand a friend more learned than

*With respect to.

himself, was to guess. He guesses accordingly; and, taking *clauus* to mean much the same thing as *clauis*, puts down in his translation: "and he is as a *keye* and a stere." Some mistakes of this character were almost inevitable; and it must not greatly surprise us to be told, that the "inaccuracy and infelicity" of Chaucer's translation "is not that of an inexperienced Latin scholar, but rather of one who was no Latin scholar at all," as Mr. Stewart says in his Essay, p. 226. It is useful to bear this in mind, because a similar lack of accuracy is characteristic of Chaucer's other works also; and we must not always infer that emendation is necessary, when we find in his text some curious error.—SKEAT, WALTER W., 1894, *ed. The Complete Works of Geoffrey Chaucer, Introduction to Boethius, vol.* ii, *p.* xxi.

Chaucer could not translate a work like Boethius' "Consolation" without being profoundly influenced by the thought, if indeed interest in the thought did not occasion the translation. The interest and influence are visible in two ways. First, in modifying Chaucer's conceptions of love—in substituting for the chivalrous notion expounded in his earlier works the more philosophic idea of love as a chain binding earth and sea, as a universal, all-pervading bond of union. Secondly, in inducing a sort of scepticism. How is it possible to reconcile the freedom of the human will with the fact of Divine providence? The problem is insoluble, and so Chaucer found it. —SNELL, F. J., 1899, *Periods of European Literature, The Fourteenth Century, p.* 298.

PARLIAMENT OF FOULES
1382?

Here foloweth the Assemble of foules veray pleasaunt and compendyous to rede or here compyled by the preclared and famous Clerke Geffray Chaucer.—WORDE, WYNKYN DE, 1530, *Assembly of Foules, Preface.*

Then forth issewed (great goddesse) great
Dame Nature
With goodly port and gracious Majesty, . . .
So hard it is for any living wight
All her array and vestiments to tell,
That old Dan Geffrey (in whose gentle spright
The pure well head of Poesie did dwell)
In his Foules Parley durst not with it mel,
But it transfered to Alane, who he thought
Had in his Plaint of Kinde describ'd it well:
Which who will read set forth so as it ought,
Go seek he out that Alane where he may be
sought.

—SPENSER, EDMUND, 1596, *Of Mutabilitie: Faerie Queene.*

The general conception had . . . about it nothing novel; but, as regards the main incident from which Chaucer's poem takes its name, no particular resemblance has ever yet been discovered between it and any other production which has been described. In this respect it was probably a pure creation of his own, and perhaps alluded, in a covert way, to some event of which we now know nothing. At the same time, "The Parlament of Foules" is, to a certain extent, penetrated with the atmosphere of the books with which the poet was familiar. Not only are direct references made to them, but numerous passages show the traces of remote suggestion, if not of actual imitation. But it was never an atmosphere of the kind that hid from the poet his insight into life, or dulled in the slightest his sympathy with nature. Chaucer read much in old books, as he often tells us; but he thoroughly assimilated what he read, and it became all his own. What he borrowed he gave again to the world in a new, and often in a more striking form.—LOUNSBURY, THOMAS R., 1877 *ed., The Parlament of Foules, Introduction, p.* 8.

There are no signs of an unripe intellect about the poem. It is full of the freshness and life which always remained such distinguishing characteristics of Chaucer. . . . This charming little poem may almost be taken as a type of the excellencies of Chaucer. It shows us his love of nature, his vivacity, his humour. Like all that he has written, it reflects faithfully the spirit of his age, and breathes the very atmosphere of chivalry.—CREIGHTON, LOUISE, 1877, *Life of Edward the Black Prince, pp.* 134, 135.

His early poetry scans far better than it reads. Proof abounds upon every page that he is bent rather upon making out his scheme of feet than delivering himself of his thought in a normal way. In the "Parlament of Foules" it is not easy to determine at sight where the emphasis belongs. There is dull, monotonic dispersion of stress, which comes from the meter and not the sense, and there are forced accents,—not less than three in the first stanza, and two of these upon rhyme words.—SHERMAN, L. A., 1893, *Analytics of Literature, p.* 45.

Though so many ideas are borrowed, they are worked into the texture of the poem with much skill; the allegory is extremely ingenious; and the descriptions of the birds and of their conversation are given with the vivacity of a fancy evidently delighted with the humours of the Bestiary.—COURTHOPE, W. J., 1895, *A History of English Poetry, vol.* I, *p.* 270.

TROILUS AND CRESSIDE

1380–83?

Go, litel book, go litel myn tregedie . . .
And kis the steppes, whereas thou seest pace
Vergile, Ovyde, Omer, Lucan and Stace.
And for ther is so greet diversitee
In English and in wryting of our tonge,
So preye I god that noon miswryte thee,
Ne thee mismetre for defaute of tonge.

—CHAUCER, GEOFFREY, 1380? *Troilus and Criseyde, bk.* v, *ss.* 256–7.

(Qd. Loue). I shall tell thee this lesson to learne: myne owne true seruaunt, the noble Phylosophicall Poete in English, whych euermore him busieth and trauaileth right sore my name to encrease, wherfore all that willen me good, owe to doe hym worship and reuerence both; truely his better ne his pere, in schoole of my rules cud I neuer find: He (qd. she) in a treatise that he made of my seruant Troylus, hath this matter touched, and at the full this question assoiled. Certainly his noble sayings can I not amend: in goodnesse of gentle manliche speech, wythout any manner of nicetie of stafieres imagination, in wit and in good reason of sentence, he passeth all other makers.—ANONYMOUS, 1387? *Testament of Love, Chaucer's Works, ed. Speght,* 1602, *p.* 301.

I mend the fyre, and beikit me about,
  Than tuik ane drink my spreitis to comfort,
And armit me weill fra the cauld thairout;
  To cut the winter nicht, and mak it schort,
  I tuik ane quair, and left all uther sport,
Written be worthie Chaucer glorious,
Of fair Cresseid and lusty Troylus

—HENRYSON, ROBERT, 1493, *Testament of Cresseid, s.* 6.

Chaucer, undoubtedly did excellently in hys "Troylus and Cresseid;" of whom, truly I know not, whether to mervaile more, either that he in that mistie time, could see so clearely, or that wee in this cleare age, walke so stumblingly after him.—SIDNEY, SIR PHILIP, 1595, *An Apologie for Poetrie.*

Read as fair England's Chaucer doth unfold,
Would tears exhale from eyes of iron mould.

—PEELE, GEORGE, 1604, *The Tale of Troy, v.* 286–7.

Chaucer, of all admired, the story gives;
There constant to eternity it lives.
. . . .
For, to say truth, it were an endless thing,
And too ambitious, to aspire to him,
Weak as we are, and almost breathless swim
In this deep water. Do but you hold out
Your helping hands, and we shall tack about
And something do to save us; you shall hear
Scenes, though below his art, may yet appear
Worth two hours' travail. To his bones sweet sleep!
Content to you!

—FLETCHER, JOHN AND SHAKESPEARE, WILLIAM?, 1616? *The Two Noble Kinsmen, Prologue.*

I'm glad, the stomach of the time's so good,
That it can relish, can digest strong food;
That learning's not absurd; and men dare know
How poets spake three hundred years ago.
Like travellers, we had been out so long,
Our native was become an unknown tongue,
And homebred Chaucer unto us was such,
As if he had been written in High Dutch:
Till thou the height didst level, and didst pierce
The depth of his inimitable verse.
Let others praise thy how, I admire thy what:
'Twas noble, the adventure to translate
A book not tractable to ev'ry hand,
And such as few presum'd to understand.
Those upstart verse-wrights, that first steal his wit,
And then pronounce him dull; or those that sit
In judgment of the language they ne'er view'd,
And, because they are lazy, Chaucer's rude;
Blush they at these fair dealings, which have shewn
Thy worth, and yet reserv'd to him his own?

—BARKER, WILLIAM, 1635, *Commendatory Verses Prefixed to Sir Francis Kynaston's Translation of Chaucer's Troilus and Cresseide.*

A great black-letter book of verses rare;
Wherein our Chaucer, years and years ago,
  Wove the sad tale of Cryseyde untrue,
    And Troylus yearning with a broken heart.

—GOSSE, EDMUND, 1873, *Fortunate Love,* xi, *On Viol and Flute, p.* 29.

Perhaps the most beautiful narrative poem of considerable length in the English language.—ROSSETTI, WILLIAM MICHAEL, 1873-83, *Chaucer's "Troylus and Cryseyde" compared with Boccaccio's "Filostrato," Prefatory Remarks, p.* viii.

Perhaps the most interesting and subtle of all Chaucer's portraits of women is the Cressida in the romance of "Troilus and Cressida." Womanly, attractive, well-meaning, she is the kind of woman we meet every day, and who every day makes shipwreck of men's lives. Not that Chaucer points any officious morals at her; he knows her worthlessness, but he feels her charm, as Troilus felt it, as we feel it. When in her fickleness and frailty she falls, he recognises that it lies in the nature of things, and leaves posterity to be her judge. Only we feel an implied reproach of Cressida in the respect and tenderness with which he treats the honest passion of Troilus. It is with Chaucer as with Thackeray, at least he believes in the entire good faith and unselfish passion of his hero. Troilus loves as Clive loved, as Harry Esmond loved, as Mr. Arthur Pendennis never loved after he left his teens. It is this thorough and delicate comprehension of this love of Troilus that makes Chaucer's romance one of the most natural and poignant, and—but that it ends badly—most delightful of love stories. And to write truthfully and sympathetically of love is to secure readers in all ages. "Yongë fresshë loveres, he and she," may if they care see their own faces in this quaint fourteenth-century "Love's Mirror," and find them very little altered.—MACCUNN, FLORENCE, 1893, *A Study of Chaucer's Women, Good Words, vol.* 34, *p.* 776.

Despite occasional prolixity and a few artistic flaws "Troilus and Cressida" is perhaps the most beautiful poem of its kind in the English language.—POLLARD, ALFRED W., 1893, *Chaucer,* (*Literature Primers,*) *p.* 85.

Chaucer wrote one romance which more than "The Canterbury Tales" contains the spirit of our modern novel. This is the "Troylus and Criseyde." . . . No work in character drawing superior to some of that in this poem was ever done by Chaucer. . . . This slowness in the development of English prose narrative is not altogether to be wondered at. Force of example is strong; and this is what made the "Troylus and Criseyde" a metrical romance—the last, as it was the best—rather than, as it might naturally have been, the first of English romances in prose. This was an accident in form. What is more remarkable is the fact that Chaucer had no immediate successor in the field of realistic art, in prose or poetry; that he marked not only the climax, but the culmination of this new movement in English literature.—SIMONDS, WILLIAM EDWARD, 1894, *An Introduction to the Study of English Fiction, pp.* 22, 23.

In "Troilus and Criseyde" we find another Chaucer, far more complete and powerful; he surpasses now even the Italians whom he had taken for his models, and writes the first great poem of renewed English literature. . . . In "Troilus and Criseyde" the Celt's ready wit, gift of repartee, and sense of the dramatic; the care for the form and ordering of a narrative, dear to the Latin races; the Norman's faculty of observation, are allied to the emotion and tenderness of the Saxon. This fusion had been brought about slowly, when however the time came, its realisation was complete all at once, almost sudden. Yesterday authors of English tongue could only lisp; to-day, no longer content to talk, they sing.—JUSSERAND, J. J., 1895, *A Literary History of the English People, pp.* 299, 300.

The dramatist's conception of Cressida's character necessarily limits the function of her uncle, and the Pandarus of Shakspere is of far less importance in the development of the plot than his namesake in Chaucer's poem. It is difficult to see why some critics should speak of the later Pandarus as a more finished type than the earlier. We find in him not a trace of the fascination, the high-bred polish, the stores of humour and worldly wisdom which distinguish Chaucer's masterly portrait. We see instead a cringing hanger-on of the court and of great houses, whose conversational stock-in-trade consists of honeyed, scented phrases, and gossip of the boudoir. Chaucer's Pandarus has a real affection for his friend, and takes care that his affairs of the heart shall be kept a secret from the world. But in the play he is simply a busybody, who revels in holding the threads of a fashionable intrigue, and who is at trouble, by sly looks and hints, to make it plain to outsiders that he knows more than he cares to speak of.—BOAS, FREDERICK S., 1896, *Shakspere and his Predecessors, p.* 376.

The poem in which medieval romance passes out of itself into the form of the modern novel. What Cervantes and what Fielding did was done first by Chaucer; and this was the invention of a kind of story in which life might be represented no longer in a conventional or abstract manner, or with sentiment and pathos instead of drama, but with characters adapting themselves to different circumstances, no longer obviously breathed upon by the master of the show to convey his own ideas, but moving freely and talking like men and women. The romance of the Middle Ages comes to an end, in one of the branches of the family tree, by the production of a romance that has all the freedom of epic, that comprehends all good and evil, and excludes nothing as common or unclean which can be made in any way to strengthen the impression of life and variety.—KER, W. P., 1897, *Epic and Romance, p.* 420.

THE HOUS OF FAME
1383–84

J. fynde nomore of this werke to fore sayd / For as fer as I can vnnderstōde / This noble man Gefferey Chaucer fynysshyd at the sayd conclusion of the metyng of lesying and sothsawe / where as yet they ben chekked and maye not departe / whyche werke as me semeth is craftyly made / and dygne to be wreton & knowen / For he towchyth in it ryght grete wysdom & subtyll vnderstondying / And so in alle hys werkys he excellyth in myn oppynyon alle other wryters in our Englyssh / For he wrytteth no voyde wordes / but alle hys mater is ful of hye and quycke sentence / to whom ought to be gyuen laude and preysyng for hys noble makyng and wrytyng / For of hym alle other haue borrowed syth and taken / in alle theyr wel sayeing and wrytyng / And I humbly beseche & praye yow / emonge your prayers to remembre hys soule / on whyche and on alle crysten soulis I beseche almyghty god to haue mercy Amen.—CAXTON, WILLIAM, 1486? *The Book of Fame, Epilogue.*

This poem contains great strokes of Gothic imagination, yet bordering often on the most ideal and capricious extravagance. . . . Pope has imitated this piece, with his usual elegance of diction and harmony of versification. But in the mean time, he has not only misrepresented the story, but marred the character of the poem. He has endeavoured to correct its extravagancies, by new refinements and additions of another cast: but he did not consider, that extravagancies are essential to a poem of such a structure, and even constitute its beauties. An attempt to unite order and exactness of imagery with a subject formed on principles so professedly romantic and anomalous, is like giving Corinthian pillars to a Gothic palace. When I read Pope's elegant imitation of this piece, I think I am walking among the modern monuments unsuitably placed in Westminster-abbey.—WARTON, THOMAS, 1778-81, *The History of English Poetry, sec.* xiv.

If Chaucer was indebted to any of the Italian poets for the idea of his "House of Fame," it was to Petrarca, who in his "Trionfo della Fama" has introduced many of the most eminent characters of ancient times. It must however be observed, that the poem of Petrarca is extremely simple and inartificial, and consists only in supposing that the most celebrated men of ancient Greece and Rome pass in review before him; whilst that of Chaucer is the work of a powerful imagination, abounding with beautiful and lively descriptions, and forming a connected and consistent whole. . . . Pope's "Temple of Fame" is one of the noblest, though earliest, productions of the author, displaying a fertile invention and an uncommon grandeur and facility of style. It is confessedly founded on Chaucer's "House of Fame;" but the design is greatly altered and improved, and many of the thoughts and descriptions are entirely his own; yet such is the coincidence and happy union of the work with its prototype, that it is almost impossible to distinguish those portions for which he is indebted to Chaucer from those of his own invention.—ROSCOE, WILLIAM, 1824, *ed. Works of Alexander Pope, vol.* II.

The "House of Fame," in homeliness of style, and lameness of versification, falls below almost all the poems of

Chaucer, while, in grandeur of scenes and images, it rises above them. In this latter respect, as in the unearthliness of the whole subject, it may be compared to the Commedia of Dante: and the bold and rough sketches which it contains are sometimes not much unlike those of the Italian poet. The "House of Fame" itself, placed on an almost inaccessible rock of ice, is an image of this nature, at once extravagant and sublime.—HIPPISLEY, J. H., 1837, *Chapters on Early English Literature, p.* 131.

The criticism of so strange a composition is hardly to be attempted. It shows a bold and free spirit of invention, and some great and poetical conceiving. The wilful, now just, now perverse, dispensing of fame, belongs to a mind that has meditated upon the human world. The poem is one of the smaller number, which seems hitherto to stand free from the suspicion of having been taken from other poets.—WILSON, JOHN, 1845, *North's Specimens of the British Critics, Blackwood's Magazine, vol.* 57, *p.* 621.

In none of his other poems has Chaucer displayed such an extent of knowledge, or drawn his images from such a variety of sources. The Arabic system of numeration, then lately introduced into Europe, the explosion of gunpowder, and the theory of sound, may be mentioned as examples of the topics of illustration and disquisition in which he abounds. His intimate acquaintance with classical authors is exhibited in the felicitous judgments he pronounces on their writings.—BELL, ROBERT, 1854-56, *Poetical Works of Geoffrey Chaucer, vol.* VI, *p.* 193.

"The Palice of Honour," for example, is far more densely crowded with historical imagery than "The House of Fame," but in vividness of representation it is not even distantly to be compared to Chaucer's poem. With quick, subtle strokes, Chaucer brings a scene or a character so distinctly before our imagination that it hardly ever fades from it, while Douglas's personages are almost all shadowy phantasms, *voces et praeterea nihil.*—ROSS, JOHN MERRY, 1884, *Scottish History and Literature, etc., ed. Brown, p.* 334.

No other of his poems has such a personal character as this one, which marks the climax of one species of art in middle English poetry. The allegory grows here so immediately out of the fundamental idea of the work that it remains perfectly transparent, notwithstanding the minutely detailed execution; for the inner truth of what is presented forces itself upon the reader, and never allows the impression of caprice to occur. How ingeniously soever the whole is designed and completed, we feel that there is here more than a mere play of wit; that a full and profound individuality has listened to its own promptings and spoken out its dominating sentiments and views, and was led by a sort of necessity in the choice of the form of expression.—TEN BRINK, BERNHARD, 1892, *History of English Literature, (Wyclif, Chaucer, Earliest Drama, Renaissance), tr. Robinson, p.* 107.

It is needless to say that this Poem is genuine, as Chaucer himself claims it twice over; once in his Prologue to the Legend of Good Women, I. 417, and again by the insertion in the poem itself of the name *Geffrey*. . . . The authorities for the text are few and poor; hence it is hardly possible to produce a thoroughly satisfactory text. There are three MSS. of the fifteenth century, viz. F. (Fairfax MS. 16, in the Bodleian Library); B. (MS. Bodley, 638, in the same); P. (MS. Pepys 2006, in Magdalene College, Cambridge). The last of these is imperfect, ending at l. 1843. There are two early printed editions of some value, viz. Cx. (Caxton's edition, undated); and Th. (Thynne's edition, 1532). None of the later editions are of much value, except the critical edition by Hans Willert (Berlin, 1883).—SKEAT, WALTER W., 1894 *ed., Complete Works of Geoffrey Chaucer, vol.* III, *pp.* vii, xiii.

The nature of Chaucer's debt is clear; it is in no sense literary copying, but is a more or less distinct recollection of an oral tale, heard perhaps in boyhood. When we consider the evident love for folk-lore which characterized Shakspere's youth, it seems inconceivable that Chaucer was not familiar as a boy with the multitudes of folk-tales rife in early days. Wherever an imaginative mind was free from monastic bonds, it must have met with great quantities of such material; Chaucer, as one of the first great authors thoroughly so emancipated, may well show traces of such knowledge, outgrown perhaps, but undestroyed.—GARRETT, A. C., 1896, *Studies in Chaucer's House of Fame, Harvard Studies and Notes in Philology and Literature, vol.* v, *p.* 175.

Manuscripts of this poem were, probably, even in our printer's time, difficult to obtain. The copy used by him was certainly very imperfect. Many lines are altogether omitted, and in the last page Caxton was evidently in a great strait, for his copy was deficient 66 lines, probably occupying one leaf in the original. We know from his own writings the great reverence in which our printer held the "noble poete," and we can imagine his consternation when the choice had to be made, either to follow his copy and print nonsense, from the break of idea caused by the deficient verses, or to step into Chaucer's shoes and supply the missing links from his own brain. He chose the latter course, and thus instead of the original 66 lines, we have two of the printer's own, which enable the reader to reach the end of the poem without a break-down.—BLADES, WILLIAM, 1897, *William Caxton, p.* 295.

The "House of Fame" is introspective. In it Chaucer reviews his life and his aims, and the work affords evidence of some discontent. Apart from books and dreams, the world is a dismal waste. From what is said later it is plain that, under this similitude, he alludes to the dry ciphering which occupied him in his official post. At the date of the composition of the poem he had just come back from a pilgrimage, from mingling with his kind; and, fresh from the delights of society, he seems to have asked himself, with reference to his wearisome toil and fine-spun ideal world, "What profit?" Chaucer, moreover, had not been happy in love, and it is for that reason that the walls of the Temple of Venus are glum with the story of Æneas, and more particularly with Dido's martyrdom. The poet needed distraction.—SNELL, F. J., 1899, *Periods of European Literature, The Fourteenth Century, p.* 303.

LEGENDE OF GOOD WOMEN

1384–85

This poete wrote, at the requeste of the quene,
A Legende of perfite holynesse,
Of good Women to fynd out nynetene
That did excell in bounte and fayrenes,
But for his labour and besinesse
Was importable his wittes to encombre
In all this world to fynd so grete a nombre.

—LYDGATE, JOHN, c 1430-31, *Fall of Princes, Prologue.*

When, in the chronicle of wasted time,
I see descriptions of the fairest wights,
And beauty making beautiful old rhime,
In praise of ladies dead, and lovely knights;
Then, in the blazon of sweet beauty's best,
Of hand, of foot, of lip, of eye, of brow,
I see their antique pen would have express'd
Even such a beauty as you master now.

—SHAKESPEARE, WILLIAM, 1609, *Sonnet* cvi.

I read, before my eyelids dropt their shade,
"The Legend of Good Women," long ago
Sung by the morning star of song, who made
His music heard below;
Dan Chaucer, the first warbler, whose sweet breath
Preluded those melodious bursts that fill
The spacious times of great Elizabeth
With sounds that echo still.

—TENNYSON, LORD, 1830, *A Dream of Fair Women.*

Part of the "Legende of Good Women" is of great excellence and value. The prologue is to be classed with Chaucer's best writings.—HALES, JOHN W., 1887, *Dictionary of National Biography, vol.* x., *p.* 164.

The "Legend of Good Women," besides the general interest of all Chaucer's verse, besides its own intrinsic attraction (for the "good women" are the most hapless and blameless of Ovid's *Heroides*), and the remembrance of its suggestion of what is perhaps, all things considered, the most perfect example of Tennyson's verse, has the additional charm of presenting to us Chaucer's first experiment in the heroic couplet, the main pillar, with blank verse, of later English poetry, and the medium of his own greatest work.—SAINTSBURY, GEORGE, 1898, *A Short History of English Literature, p.* 125

In the "Legende" it is the Prologue, in its two drafts, which gives him his opportunity. Of the nine stories of loving women which he had patience to complete, only the first three (those of Cleopatra, Thisbe, and Dido) are in any way worthy of him.—POLLARD, ALFRED W., 1898, *The Works of Geoffrey Chaucer, Globe ed., Introduction, p.* xxiv.

The chief significance of the poem lies in this—that, whilst its contents may be deemed in a certain sense reactionary, its outward form marks another stage in the direction of the "Canterbury Tales." The "Legende of Goode Women" is, in fact, the first example in English of a connected series of short versified tales in decasyllabic couplet.—SNELL, F. J., 1899, *Periods of European Literature, The Fourteenth Century, p.* 309.

For charming and not too prolix description, for a land where the beautiful creatures of one's dreams move in an ideal landscape, we find not the like of the prologue of the "Legende" until the "Faerie Queene." . . . The poem is a well-nigh perfect example of its artificial, if charming, class. Many will prefer its sweetness and quiet humor to the brilliancy and wit of "The Rape of the Lock." It is equally a classic of occasional poetry.—MATHER, JR., FRANK JEWETT, 1899, *The Riverside Literature Series, No.* 135, *Introduction, p.* xxvii.

A TREATISE ON THE ASTROLABE
1391

When I happenyd to look upon the conclusions of the "Astrolabie" compiled by Geffray Chaucer and founde the same corrupte and false in so many and sondrie places that I doubted whether the rudeness of the worke were not a greater sclander to the authour than trouble and offense to the readers, I dyd not a lytell mervell if a book should come oute of his handes so imperfect and indigest whose other workes weare not onely rekoned for the best that ever weare set forthe in oure english tonge, but also weare taken for a manifest argument of his singular witte and generalitie in all kindes of knowledge. However be it when I called to remembrance that in his prohem he promised to sette forthe this worke in five partes, whereof weare never extante but those two first partes onely, it made me to believe that either the work was never fynisshed of the authour, or els to have ben corrupted sens by some other meanes, or what other thynge might be the cause thereof, I wiste not.—STEVINS, WALTER, 1555? *MS. Conclusions of the Astrolabe, quoted by Brae, p.* 9.

In some respects, the most interesting of Chaucer's works — inasmuch as it brings us into familiar and almost domestic communion with his individual self, while he describes to his "lytel sonne," with delightful simplicity and in the most inartificial language, the sort of scientific knowledge which in those early days, even more than at present, was considered necessary to a gentleman's education. . . . When the period at which Chaucer wrote is taken into consideration, and that after all he was but an *amateur* astronomer, his general correctness is something admirable.—BRAE, ANDREW EDMUND, 1869, *ed. The Treatise on the Astrolabe of Geoffrey Chaucer, Introduction, pp.* 1, 12.

The existing MSS. of the "Astrolabe" are still numerous. I have been successful in finding no less than twenty-two. . . . It is remarkable that, although many printed editions of the treatise have appeared, no first-class MS. has ever hitherto come under the notice of any one of the various editors.—SKEAT, WALTER W., 1894, *ed. Complete Works of Geoffrey Chaucer, vol.* III, *p.* lvii.

Ripeness of scholarship, certainty of style, clearness of judgment; all these come out clearly in this later work. . . . There is little of that uncertainty which characterises the "Boece," and no infelicities of idiom or mistakes in construing the Latin. — LIDDELL, MARK H., 1898, *The Works of Geoffrey Chaucer, Globe ed., Introduction, p.* liii.

CANTERBURY TALES
1387?–1393?

O ye so noble and worthy Princes and Princesses, or estates or degrees, whatever ye be, that have disposition or pleasure to read or hear the stories of old times passed, to keep you from idleness and sloth, in eschewing other follies that might be cause of more harm following, vouchsafe, I beseech you, to find your occupation in the reading here of the Tales of Canterbury, which he compiled in this book following, first founded, imagined, and made, both for disport and learning of all those that be gentle of birth or of conditions, by the laureal and most famous poet that ever was before him in the embellishing of our rude mother's English tongue, called Chaucer a Gaufrede, of whose soul, God, for his mercy, have pity of his grace. Amen.—SHIRLEY, JOHN, 1458? *MS., Quoted by Furnivall, F. J.,* 1873, *Recent Work at Chaucer, Macmillan's Magazine, vol.* 27, *p.* 385.

Whiche book I have dylygently oversen, and duly examyned to the ende that it be made accordyng unto his owne makyng; for I fynde many of the sayd bookes, whiche wryters have abrydgyd it, and many thynges left out, and in some places have sette certayn versys that he never made ne sette in hys booke; of whyche bookes so incorrecte was one broughte to me vi. yere passyd, whiche I supposed had ben veray true and correcte, and accordyng to the same I dyde do emprynte a certayn nomber of them, whyche anon were solde to many and dyverse gentyl men, of whom one gentylman cam to me, and sayd that this book was not according in many places unto the book that Gefferey Chaucer had made. To whom I answered, that I had made it accordyng to my copye, and by me was nothyng added ne mynushyd. Thenne he sayd, he knewe a book whyche hys fader had and meche lovyd, that was very trewe, and accordyng unto his owen first book by hym made; and sayd more, yf I wold emprynte it agayn, he wold gete me the same book for a copye. How be it he wyst well that hys fader wold not gladly departe fro it. To whom I said, in caas that he coude gete me suche a book, trewe and correcte, yet I woid ones endevoyre me to emprynte it agayn, for to satisfy the auctour, where as tofore by ygnoraunce I erryd in the hurtyng and dyffamyng his book in dyverce places, in setting in somme thynges that he never sayd he made, and leving out many thynges that he made, whyche ben requysite to be sette in it. And thus we fyll at accord, and he full gentylly gate of hys fader the said book, and delyvered it to me, by whiche I have corrected my book, as heere after alle alonge by the ayde of almighty God shal folowe, whom I humbly beseche, &c.—CAXTON, WILLIAM, 1481, *The Canterbury Tales, Caxton's 2nd ed., Preface.*

And upon hys ymaginacyon
He made also the tales of Canterbury;
Some vertuous, and some glad and merry, . . .
And many other bokes, doubtles,
He dyd compyle, whose godly name
In printed bokes doth remayne in fame.
—HAWES, STEPHEN, 1506, *The Pastime of Pleasure, C.* 14.

The Canterbury tales were *Chaucers* owne invention as I suppose, and where he sheweth more the naturall of his pleasant wit, then in any other of his workes, his similitudes comparisons and all other descriptions are such as can not be amended. His meetre Heroicall of "Troilus" and "Cresseid" is very grave and stately, keeping the staffe of seven, and the verse of ten, his other verses of the Canterbury tales be but riding ryme, neverthelesse very well becomming the matter of that pleasaunt pilgrimage in which every mans part is playd with much decency.—PUTTENHAM, GEORGE, 1589, *The Arte of English Poesie, ed. Arber, p.* 75.

It is a blabb: but not every man's blabb, that casteth a sheepes-eye out of a Calves-head; but a blabb with judgement; but a blabb, that can make excrements blush, and teach Chawcer to retell a Canterbury Tale.—HARVEY, GABRIEL, 1593, *Pierces Supererogation, ed. Grosart, Harvey's Works, vol.* II, *p.* 228.

He must have been a man of a most wonderful comprehensive nature, because, as it has been truly observed of him, he has taken into the compass of his "Canterbury Tales" the various manners and humours (as we now call them) of the whole English nation, in his age. Not a single character has escaped him. All his pilgrims are severally distinguished from each other; and not only in their inclinations, but in their very physiognomies and persons. Baptista Porta could not have described their natures better, than by the marks which the poet gives them. The matter and manner of their tales, and of their telling, are so suited to their different educations, humours, and callings, that each of them would be improper in any other mouth. Even the grave and serious characters are distinguished by their several sorts of gravity: their discourses are such as belong to their age, their calling, and their breeding; such as are becoming of them, and of them only. —DRYDEN, JOHN, 1700, *Preface to the Fables, Works, ed. Scott and Saintsbury, vol.* XI, *p.* 229.

I hold Mr. Dryden to have been the first who put the merit of Chaucer into its full and true light by turning some of the Canterbury Tales into our language, as it is now refined, or rather as he himself refined it.—OGLE, GEORGE, 1739, *Preface to the Clerk of Oxford's Tale.*

The general plan of "The Canterbury Tales" may be learned in a great measure from the Prologue, which Chaucer himself has prefixed to them. He supposes there, that a company of Pilgrims going to Canterbury assemble at an Inn in Southwark, and agree, that, for their common amusement on the road, each of them shall tell at least one Tale in going to Canterbury, and another in coming back from thence; and that he, who shall tell the best Tales, shall be treated by the rest with a supper upon their return to the same Inn. This is shortly the *Fable.* The *Characters* of the Pilgrims are as various as, at that time, coud be found in the several departments of *middle* life; that is, in fact, as various as coud, with any probability, be brought together, so as to form one company; the highest and the lowest ranks of society being necessarily excluded. It appears, further, that the design of Chaucer was not barely to recite the Tales told by the Pilgrims, but also to describe their journey, *And all the remenant of* their *pilgrimage* (ver. 726); including, probably, their adventures at Canterbury as well as upon the road. If we add, that the Tales, besides being nicely adapted to the Characters of their respective Relaters, were intended to be connected together by suitable introductions; and interspersed with diverting episodes; and that the greatest part of them was to have been executed in Verse; we shall have a tolerable idea of the extent and difficulty of the whole undertaking: and admiring, as we must, the vigor of that genius, which in an advanced age coud begin so vast a work, we shall rather lament than be surprised that it has been been left imperfect.—TYRWHITT, THOMAS, 1775-78, *An Introductory Discourse to the Canterbury Tales.*

After the dramas of Shakespear, there is no production of man that displays more various and vigorous talent than the "Canterbury Tales." Splendour of narrative, richness of fancy, pathetic simplicity of incident and feeling, a powerful style in delineating character and manners, and an animated vein of comic humour, each takes its turn in this wonderful performance, and each in turn appears to be that in which the author was most qualified to excel.—GODWIN, WILLIAM, 1803, *Life of Geoffrey Chaucer, Preface, vol.* I, *p.* i.

The characters of Chaucer's Pilgrims are the characters which compose all ages and nations. As one age falls another rises, different to mortal sight, but to immortals only the same; for we see the same characters repeated again and again, in animals, vegetables and minerals, and in men. Nothing new occurs in identical existence; accident ever varies, substance can never suffer change or decay. Of Chaucer's characters, as described in his "Canterbury Tales," some of the names or titles are altered by time, but the characters themselves for ever remain unaltered; and, consequently, they are the physiognomies or lineaments of universal human life, beyond which nature never steps. Names alter, things never alter. I have known multitudes of those who would have been monks in the age of monkery, who in this deistical age are Deists. As Newton numbered the stars, and as Linnæus numbered the plants, so Chaucer numbered the classes of men. . . . It is necessary here to speak of Chaucer's own character, that I may set certain mistaken critics right in their conception of the humour and fun that occur on the journey. Chaucer is himself the great poetical observer of men, who in every age is born to record and eternise its acts. This he does as a master, as a father and superior, who looks down on their little follies, from the Emperor to the Miller, sometimes with severity, oftener with joke and sport. . . . Chaucer's characters live age after age. Every age is a Canterbury Pilgrimage; we all pass on, each sustaining one or other of these characters; nor can a child be born who is not one of these characters of Chaucer. . . . The reader will observe that Chaucer makes every one of his characters perfect in his kind; every one is an Antique Statue, the image of a class, and not of an imperfect individual. —BLAKE, WILLIAM, 1809, *Illustrated Catalogue of Pictures. Canterbury Poets, Blake, pp.* 244, 247, 250, 251.

What an intimate scene of English life in the fourteenth century do we enjoy in those tales, beyond what history displays by glimpses, through the stormy atmosphere of her scenes, or the antiquary can discover by the cold light of his researches! Our ancestors are restored to us, not as phantoms from the field of battle, or the scaffold, but in the full enjoyment of their social existence. After four hundred years have closed over the mirthful features which formed the living originals of the poet's descriptions, his pages impress the fancy with the momentary credence that they are still alive; as if Time had rebuilt his ruins, and were reacting the lost scenes of existence.—CAMPBELL, THOMAS, 1819, *Specimens of the British Poets.*

Among his more elevated compositions, the Knight's Tale is abundantly sufficient to immortalize Chaucer, since it would be difficult to find anywhere a story better conducted, or told with more animation and strength of fancy.—HALLAM, HENRY, 1818, *View of the State of Europe During the Middle Ages, ch.* ix, *pt.* ii.

The story of the Cock and the Fox, in the "Nun's Priest's Tale," is allowed by all judges to be the most admirable fable (in the narration) that ever was written. —CLARKE, CHARLES COWDEN, 1835, *The Riches of Chaucer, vol.* I, *p.* 46.

The metre of five accents, with couplet-rhyme, may have got its earliest name of "riding rhyme" from the *mounted* pilgrims of the Canterbury Tales. It was long used for light and trifling subjects; and by the critics of the sixteenth century was very unfavourably contrasted with the stately ballet-stave.—GUEST, EDWIN, 1838, *A History of English Rhythms, vol.* II, *p.* 238.

In Canterbury, also, the pilgrim's inn is said to have continued to the present time, no longer, indeed, existing as an inn, but divided into a number of private tenements in High-street. The old inn mentioned by Chaucer was called the Checkers. It stands in High-street, at the corner of the lane leading to the Cathedral, just below the parade, on the left-hand side going into Canterbury. Its situation was just that which was most convenient for the pilgrims to Thomas à Becket's tomb. It was a very large inn, as was necessary for the enormous resort of votaries to the shrine of this pugnacious saint. It is now divided into several houses, and has been modernized externally, having no longer a trace of having been an inn. The way to the court-yard is through a narrow doorway passage, and around the court you see the only evidences of its antiquity, remains of carved wood-work, now white-washed over.—HOWITT, WILLIAM, 1847, *Homes and Haunts of the most Eminent British Poets, vol.* I, *p.* 11.

The world has rightly considered the "Canterbury Tales" as the work by which Chaucer is to be judged. In truth, common renown forgets all the rest; and it is by the "Canterbury Tales" only that he can properly be said to be known to his countrymen. Here it is that he appears as possessing the versatility of poetical power which ranges from the sublime, through the romantic and the pathetic, to the rudest mirth—choosing subjects the most various, and treating all alike adequately. Here he discovers himself as the shrewd and curious observer, and close painter of manners. Here he writes as one surveying the world of man with enlarged and philosophical intuition, weighing good and evil in even scale. Here, more than in any other, he is master of his matter, disposing it at his discretion, and not carried away with or mastered by it. Here he is master, too, of his English, thriftily culling the fit word, not effusing a too exuberant stream of description. Here he has acquired his own art and his own style of versification, which is here to be studied accordingly.—WILSON, JOHN, 1845, *North's Specimens of the British Critics, Blackwood's Magazine, vol.* 57, *p.* 630.

The Harleian manuscript, No. 7334, is by far the best manuscript of Chaucer's "Canterbury Tales" that I have yet examined, in regard both to antiquity and correctness. The hand-writing is one which would at first sight be taken by an experienced scholar for that of the latter part of the fourteenth century, and it must have been written within a few years after 1400, and therefore soon after Chaucer's death and the publication of the "Canterbury Tales." Its language has very little, if any, appearance of local dialect; and the text is in general extremely good, the variations from Tyrwhitt being usually for the better. Tyrwhitt appears not to have made much use of this manuscript, and he has not even classed it among those to which most credit is due.—WRIGHT, THOMAS, 1847, *ed. The Canterbury Tales of Geoffrey Chaucer, vol.* I, *p.* XXXV.

His method of proceeding in "The Canterbury Tales" is the most effective that could be devised for transmitting to subsequent ages an accurate expression of the social and moral development of his own. He never generalizes—he never falls into disquisitions—he never draws conclusions. He avoids all modes of treatment that might afterwards become wearisome or unintelligible: and, descending into the common life of the day, he shows us, as it were, the spirit of transition in actual operation amongst the different classes of the people, modifying their customs and opinions, drawing out into full play the salient points of the national character, and colouring even individual peculiarities to the most trivial details, which, in this aspect, acquire a special historical value. The humanity he thus imparts to his subjects invests them with a permanent interest, which neither the lapse of time, nor the revolutions of language, can impair or render obsolete; and the instruction which, in another shape, would become dry and heavy, is here made to assume the most attractive forms.—BELL, ROBERT (JOHN M. JEPHSON), 1854, *ed. Poetical Works of Geoffrey Chaucer, Introduction, p.* 43.

The design of this poem is one of the happiest thoughts that ever housed itself in a poet's heart.—REED, HENRY, 1855, *Lectures on English Literature, From Chaucer to Tennyson, p.* 137.

These opening lines give the colour to Chaucer's whole work; it is in every sense the spring of English poetry; through every line we seem to feel the freshness and vigour of that early morning start—as the merry cavalcade winds its way over the hills and forests of Surrey or of Kent. Never was the scene and atmosphere of a poem more appropriate to its contents, more naturally sustained and felt through all its parts.—STANLEY, ARTHUR P., 1855, *Historical Memorials of Canterbury, p.* 212.

This is not only his greatest work, but it towers above all else that he has written, like some palace or cathedral ascending with its broad and lofty dimensions from among the common buildings of a city. His genius is another thing here altogether from what it is in his other writings. Elsewhere he seems at work only for the day that is passing over him; here, for all time. . . . Among ourselves at least, if we except Shakspeare, no other poet has yet arisen to rival the author of the "Canterbury Tales" in the entire assemblage of his various powers. Spenser's is a more aerial, Milton's a loftier, song; but neither possesses the wonderful combination of contrasted and almost opposite characteristics which we have in Chaucer:—the sportive fancy, painting and gilding everything, with the keen, observant, matter-of-fact spirit that looks through whatever it glances at; the soaring and creative imagination, with the homely sagacity, and healthy relish for all the realities of things; the unrivalled tenderness and pathos, with the quaintest humor and the most exuberant merriment; the wisdom at once and the wit; the all that is best, in short, both in poetry and in prose, at the same time.—CRAIK, GEORGE L., 1861, *A Compendious History of English Literature and of the English Language, vol.* I, *p.* 313.

In its own way, and within its own limits, it is the most wonderful thing in the language. The people we read about are as real as the people we brush clothes with in the street,—nay, much *more* real, for we not only see their faces, and the fashion and texture of their garments, we know also what they think, how they express themselves, and with what eyes they look out on the world. Chaucer's art in this prologue is simple perfection. He indulges in no irrelevant description; he airs no fine sentiments; he takes no special pains as to style or poetic ornament; but every careless touch tells,—every sly line reveals character; the description of each man's horse-furniture and array reads like a memoir. The nun's pretty oath bewrays her. We see the bold, well-favoured countenance of the Wife of Bath beneath her hat, as "broad as a buckler or a targe;" and the horse of the clerk, "as lean as is a rake," tells tales of his master's cheer. Our modern dress is worthless as an indication of the character, or even of the social rank, of the wearer; in the olden time it was significent of personal tastes and appetites, of profession, and condition of life generally. . . . Chaucer's range is wide as that of Shakspeare—if we omit that side of Shakspeare's mind which confronts the other world, and out of which Hamlet sprang—and his men and women are even more real, and more easily matched in the living and breathing world.—SMITH, ALEXANDER, 1863, *Dreamthorp, pp.* 225, 228.

Though the character of Griselda is not the original creation of Chaucer, he has filled up the outline with such a wealth of detail, and worked into it such beauty of colouring and expression—meekness, gentleness, tenderness, and piety—resignation, fortitude, and long-suffering—that he may well claim Griselda as his own. Whoever compares the heroine of Chaucer with that of Boccaccio in the original, notwithstanding all the beauty of the Italian narrative, will at once understand this.—WALLER, JOHN FRANCIS, 1870, *Pictures from English Literature, p.* 2.

I know of nothing that may be compared with the prologue to the "Canterbury Tales," and with that to the story of the "Chanon's Yeoman" before Chaucer. Characters and portraits from real life had never been drawn with such discrimination, or with such variety, never with such bold precision of outline, and with such a lively sense of the picturesque. His Parson is still unmatched, though Dryden and Goldsmith have both tried their hands in emulation of him. And the humor also in its suavity, its perpetual presence and its shy unobtrusiveness, is something wholly new in literature. For anything that deserves to be called like it in English we must wait for Henry Fielding.—LOWELL, JAMES RUSSELL, 1870–90, *Chaucer, Prose Works, Riverside ed., vol.* III, *p.* 364.

He is the poet of the dawn, who wrote
The Canterbury Tales, and his old age
Made beautiful with song; and as I read
I hear the crowing cock, I hear the note
Of lark and linnet, and from every page
Rise odors of ploughed field or flowery mead.

—LONGFELLOW, HENRY WADSWORTH, 1873, *A Book of Sonnets, Poems, Cambridge ed., p.* 315.

One of the most undeniable social features of the time, showing their half-barbaric cast, was that sensuality of language which is the cheap dye of vulgar wit. The taint of it is especially strong in Chaucer, frequently quite overpowering the poetic aroma. One wonders what evil beast has strayed among these flowers. I confess to a certain shame in speaking of Chaucer to the healthy and pure, so far is he from wholesome companionship. As mirrored in the "Canterbury Tales," English speech was at once gross and licentious. . . . Closely allied to this sportive vein of Chaucer is his vulgarity. He has the sensual vulgarity of grossness, up to, or very nearly up to, his times. Yet it is not the sin, the filth, but the fun of the thing that he is after; and so manifest is this, that we laugh away in part our irritation and shame. We feel that we have been caught, yet so fairly caught, that we are unwilling to be angry. . . . With Chaucer, vulgarity lay under the broad heavens, an offensive fact indeed, but one with which he had no more to do than another. He chose to laugh, others might run away and hide, if they pleased. So much perhaps may be fairly said in extenuation; yet these low, sensual features remain, a thing of bad significance. One needs to know the moral constitution of the recipient, or he may breathe pestilence in this atmosphere. If one goes to Chaucer for pleasure, he eats honey from the carcase of a lion; while he feeds one sense, he may have occasion to close others. Yet with all we acquit him of the lasciviousness of later periods.—BASCOM, JOHN, 1874, *Philosophy of English Literature, pp.* 43, 61, 62.

No poetry was ever more human than Chaucer's; none ever came more frankly and genially home to men than his "Canterbury Tales." . . . It is the first time in English poetry that we are brought face to face, not with characters or allegories or reminiscences of the past, but with living and breathing men, men distinct in temper and sentiment, as in face or costume or mode of speech; and with this distinctness of each maintained throughout the story by a thousand shades of expression and action. It is the first time, too, that we meet with the dramatic power which not only creates each character, but combines it with its fellows; which not only adjusts each tale or jest to the temper of the person who utters it, but fuses all into a poetic unity. It is life in its largeness, its variety, its complexity, which surrounds us in the "Canterbury Tales." In some of the stories, indeed, which were composed, no doubt, at an earlier time, there is the tedium of the old romance or the pedantry of the schoolman; but, taken as a whole, the poem is the work not of a man of letters, but of a man of action. Chaucer has received his training from war, courts, business, travel—a training not of books, but of life. And it is life that he loves—the delicacy of its sentiment, the breadth of its farce, its laughter and its tears, the tenderness of its Griseldas, or the Smollett-like adventures of the miller and the clerks. It is this largeness of heart, this wide tolerance, which enables him to reflect man for us as none but Shakespeare has ever reflected him, and to do this with a pathos, a shrewd sense, and kindly humor, a freshness and joyousness of feeling, that even Shakespeare has not surpassed.—GREEN, JOHN RICHARD, 1877, *History of the English People, vol.* I, *bk.* iv, *ch.* iv.

A charming freshness forms the atmosphere of all his work; he is perpetually new.—ROSSETTI, WILLIAM MICHAEL, 1878, *Lives of Famous Poets, p.* 14.

Has there been any man since St. John so lovable as "the Persoune"? or any sermon since that on the Mount so keenly analytical, so pathetic, so deep, so pitiful, so charitable, so brotherly, so pure, so manly, so faithful, so hopeful, so sprightly, so terrible, so childlike, so winning, so utterly loving, as "The Persoune's Tale."?—LANIER, SIDNEY, 1880?, *Paul H. Hayne's Poetry, Music and Poetry, p.* 200.

Can we not see Madame Eglantine as plain as if she stood before us in broad day, with her grey eyes, her little, soft, red mouth, her fair forehead, and her dainty ways when she sits at the table.—RICHARDSON, ABBY SAGE, 1881, *Familiar Talks on English Literature, p.* 73

In seeking to trace the origin and progress of the English novel as it is now written, we must record the first appearance of its special characteristics in the works of Chaucer. Here are first to be seen real human beings, endowed with human virtues and subject to human frailities; here fictitious characters are first represented amid the homely scenes of daily life; here they first become living realities whose nature and dispositions every one may understand, and with whose thoughts every one may sympathize.—TUCKERMAN, BAYARD, 1882, *A History of English Prose Fiction, p.* 43.

As writer of tales, as "narrative poet," Chaucer is without a peer in English Literature. His reticence, in that garrulous age, is sublime.—GUMMERE, FRANCIS B., 1885, *A Handbook of Poetics, p.* 21.

There is Chaucer's strength in the dramatic liveliness with which this story* is told within short compass; and the four persons of it, are vividly painted and characterised by master-touches. The first source of its plot is unknown. Doubtless it was a variation of one of the numberless rough jesting tales of his day, that sin greatly against our modern notions of propriety. The old husband, beguiled and betrayed by a young wife, is a time-honoured figure in story. Breaches of marriage duty, worse than that of the carpenter's wife and his lodger, are made in our day the theme of plays and tales in which the conventional proprieties are observed, though true morality is outraged, and sin is plated with false sentiment. The churl's tale of the Miller does nothing of this. There is no moral evil in the part of it which most shocks the modern notion of propriety. It only tells, with a bygone outspokeness, of coarse behaviour; and, be it observed, makes this proceed in such a way from Alison and the clerk Nicholas, who would be the triumphant hero and heroine of an immoral tale, that though the Miller, who tells the tale, must not play moralist, theirs is the conduct which excites disgust, and we feel that the discipline of the hot coulter is not more than Nicholas deserves. Young girls in our own day read stories and see plays at which they do not blush, as they should, and would, if the coarse mind of the fascinating heroine were made to declare itself as Alison's does in the Miller's tale, and if for the interesting hero there were an avenging Absalon at the end to strike at the root of lust with a hot coulter.—MORLEY, HENRY, 1890, *English Writers, vol.* V, *p.* 317.

The Knight's tale, in particular, naturally attracted the attention of the dramatists of the Elizabethan age, who were always on the lookout for suitable material. Upon it was founded an early play called "Palemon and Arcite" that has not come down. It was the work of Richard Edwards, and was produced in 1566 at Oxford University before Queen Elizabeth. A play with this title is also recorded by Henslowe under the year 1594 as having been acted four times. From the same tale also was avowedly taken the drama called "The Two Noble Kinsmen," which, when first printed in 1634,

* "The Miller's Tale."

had on its title-page as authors the names of Shakspeare and Fletcher. Whether either had anything to do with it is still a debated question; but the tribute paid to Chaucer in the prologue furnishes important evidence as to the estimation in which the early poet continued to be held.—LOUNSBURY, THOMAS R., 1891, *Studies in Chaucer, vol.* III, *p.* 68.

As the Wife of Bath herself unrolls her own picture with a flippant ease and a delightful mixture of ingenuousness and confidential impudence not without wit, and begins with the greatest indignation to quote the sayings of learned woman-haters, the comic effect of her story and descriptions is raised to the highest pitch, and the satire loses very much of its bitterness, but nothing whatever of its pungency. We can almost hear, and see bodily before us, the well-to-do middle class Englishwoman, in her heavy and somewhat gaudy garments, her scarlet stockings, her red cheeks, her saucy looks, her sensual mouth, her quick, energetic movements, her glib tongue and penetrating voice; and what she relates becomes to us as vivid as if we had ourselves beheld the individual incidents.—TEN BRINK, BERNHARD, 1892, *History of English Literature, (Wyclif, Chaucer, Earliest Drama, Renaissance), tr. Robinson, p.* 126.

If men should have suddenly to choose the one English poem which should survive, all others to be at once destroyed; a very large number of voices would doubtless be raised in favor of the "Canterbury Tales." And if the nineteenth-century reader can spare time but for one book of all written in English before the Elizabethan age, he may take the same immortal work, sure of finding himself better instructed than if he had read all the others and left that out.—KIRKLAND, ELIZABETH STANSBURY, 1892, *A Short History of English Literature, p.* 35.

Perhaps the best short narrative poem* in the language.—KITTREDGE, GEORGE LYMAN, 1893, *Chaucer's Pardoner, Atlantic Monthly, vol.* 72, *p.* 830.

The "Tale of Melibeus" makes one doubt whether the change between the tenth century and the fourteenth was not for the worse. There are curious inanities in old, popular, edifying books, like the Dialogues of Gregory. But the "Tale of Melibeus" is beyond rivalry for its enjoyment of the rankest commonplaces. There is glow and unction about its mediocrity; the intolerable arguments of Dame Prudence are a masterpiece, as though written in an orgy and enthusiasm of flatness and insipidity. Why it was selected by Chaucer for translation is mysterious enough. Yet the monstrous virtue of Dame Prudence has affinities with some of the untruths in the "Canterbury Tales"—with Griselda, with the point of honour in the "Franklin's Tale;" after all, it is only an exaggeration of what is well known in all medieval literature: it is not a new element. It is hard to forgive, especially when one thinks that it was to this the innocent Sir Thopas was sacrificed. In one sense, however, the "Tale of Melibeus" displays the foundation of all Chaucer's works. The peculiarity of Chaucer is that with all his progress in his art he kept close to the general sense of his age, and had always, in some corner of his being, the average mind of the fourteenth century. To that part of him belong all his prose works. The "Tale of Melibeus" is representative of the ideas and tastes of millions of good souls. Being representative, it could not be alien from Chaucer.—KER, W. P., 1893, *English Prose, ed. Craik, vol.*I *p.* 42.

Herein the wise, shrewd, and humorous author, with the forked beard, face of kindly cunning, portly frame, and genial ways—albeit silent and devoted to his books—displayed a power of insight into human character, and a knowledge of the human heart, which have been surpassed, in all our literature, by one man alone, and that the greatest writer of the world. The joyous freedom of his song is full as pleasant to the modern reader as it can have been to those who hailed it with delight five-hundred years ago.—SANDERSON, EDGAR, 1893, *History of England and the British Empire, p.* 273.

The number of words now obsolete in the *Prologue* to the "Canterbury Tales" is unusually high, and for this reason it should not be read the first among Chaucer's poems; nevertheless it usually is read first, and is so well known that little need here be said of it. For keen observation and vivid presentment this gallery of character-sketches has never been surpassed. The portraits, we

*"Pardoner's Tale."

should note, are all such as one traveller might draw of another. There is no attempt to show that the best of the pilgrims had their weak points, and the worst their good ones. For the best Chaucer has hearty admiration, for the worst a boundless tolerance, which yet only thinly cloaks the keenest satire. One and all he views from his holiday standpoint, building up his descriptions with such notes as he would naturally gather as he rode along with them on his pilgrimage—notes of dress, of speech and manner, of their talk about themselves and their doings—until we can see his fellow-pilgrims as clearly as if we, too, had mounted our rouncies and ridden along with them.—POLLARD, ALFRED W., 1893, *Chaucer, Literature Primers, p.* 115.

The unrivalled array of poetic qualities, both of feeling and expression, which it presents to us, the grace and gaiety of the poet, his humour and pathos, his dramatic force of portraiture, the catholicity of his sympathies, never to be again approached in literature till the coming of Shakespeare, his fine broad artistic treatment of the human figure, the dewy freshness of his landscape studies, and the clear sunny atmosphere through which he looks out alike upon Nature and upon man—it is these things which have raised the Father of English Poetry to the rank of one of the great poets of the world. It is in virtue of such things that that train of pilgrims which left Southwark for the shrine of St. Thomas of Canterbury, on a certain day of April in or about the year 1383, remains so real to us, that the student still labours to fix the precise date of its departure and the time and places of its halts. It is for such reasons that these shadows of the poet's fancy are shadows more enduring than their substance, and that knight and squire, clerk and franklin, reeve and miller, pardoner and sompnour, priorness and nun, and wife much widowed, move still, and will ever move, before us across the great imaginative panorama of the past, joyous and immortal as a Bacchic procession on a frieze of Phidias.—TRAIL, H. D., 1894, *Social England, Introduction, vol.* I, *p.* xxxix.

The idea of joining together a series of Tales by means of fitting them into a common frame-work is a very old one, and doubtless originated in the East. There is an English collection of this character known as "The Seven Sages," of which various versions have come down to us. The earliest of these, as published in the second volume of Weber's Metrical Romances, has been dated about 1320; and is, at any rate, older than any of Chaucer's poems. Another collection, of a similar character, and likewise of Eastern origin, is a Latin work by Petrus Alphonsus, a converted Spanish Jew, entitled De Clericali Disciplina. See Dunlop's History of Fiction, chap. vii. From one of these Chaucer may have taken the general idea of arranging his tales in a connected series; and we must not forget that his Legend of Good Women, which was the immediate forerunner of his greater work, is likewise, practically, a collection of Tales, though sadly lacking in variety, as he discovered for himself in the course of writing it. It is highly improbable that he was indebted for the idea to Boccaccio's Decamerone, as has been sometimes hastily suggested; since we might, in that case, have expected that he would also have drawn from that collection the plot of some one of his tales; which is not found to be the case. The Clerk's Tale occurs, indeed, in the Decamerone; but we know it to have been borrowed from Petrarch's Latin version of it. The Franklin's Tale has some resemblance to another tale in the same collection, but was evidently not taken from it directly, and the same is true in other cases; so that we are quite justified in supposing that Chaucer was wholly unacquainted, at first hand, with Boccaccio's work.—SKEAT, WALTER W., 1894, *ed. Complete Works of Geoffrey Chaucer, vol.* III, *p.* 371.

So the new England has its Froissart, who is going to tell feats of arms and love stories glowing with colour, and take us hither and thither, through highways and byways, giving ear to every tale, observing, noting, relating? This young country has Froissart and better than Froissart. The pictures are as vivid and as clear, but two great differences distinguish the ones from the others: humour and sympathy. Already we find humour well developed in Chaucer; his sly jests penetrate deeper than French jests; he does not go so far as to wound, but he does more than merely prick skin-deep; and in so doing, he laughs silently to himself. . . . Moreover, Chaucer sympathies; he has a quivering heart that tears move, and that all sufferings touch, those of the poor and those of princes. The rôle of the people, so marked in English literature, affirms itself here, from the first moment.—JUSSERAND, J. J., 1895, *A Literary History of the English People, pp.* 317, 318.

The "Knight's Tale" is a complete and perfect version of a medieval romance, worked out with all the resources of Chaucer's literary study and reflexion; tested and considered and corrected in every possible way.—KER, W. P., 1897, *Epic and Romance, p.* 417.

It was largely due to his wide relationship with, and his active participation in, civil and state affairs, as stimulating and determining agencies, that Chaucer's poetical genius gave us, in "The Canterbury Tales," and in the Prologue thereto, a better idea of what manner of people lived in England in the fourteenth century than do all the histories of that period which have been written. And he did this without in the least transgressing the legitimate limits of his art, and because he did not transgress them. With a poet's impressibility, and a poet's eye for the characteristic, the picturesque, and the essential, he delineated for all time the features of the society around him.—CORSON, HIRAM, 1897, *ed. Selections from Chaucer's Canterbury Tales, Introduction, p.* xvii.

Chaucer's "Canterbury Tales," *first edition,* (12). J. West (1773), £47, 15s.—George III. J. Ratcliffe (1776), £6. White Knights supplementary sale (1820), £31, 10s.—T. Payne, (imperfect); not recorded by Blades. The highest price recorded by Blades is £300, given by Mr. Huth at Lilly's sale, 1861. In 1896 two copies (both imperfect) were sold for over £1000; Mrs. Corbet's (Barlaston Hall), wanting nineteen leaves, £1020; R. E. Saunders (wanting only two leaves, a few wormed, lower margins in Melibeus mended), £1880. Earl of Ashburnham (1897), £720—Pickering & Chatto (imperfect, also some leaves from a shorter copy). — WHEATLEY, HENRY R., 1898, *Prices of Books, p.* 200.

REJECTED POEMS

It must suffice to say here that most of the later editions, since the publication of Tyrwhitt's remarks on the subject, reject many of these additional pieces, but still unadvisedly admit the poems entitled "The Court of Love," "The Complaint of the Black Knight," "Chaucer's Dream," "The Flower and the Leaf," and "The Cuckoo and the Nightingale." Of these, the "Complaint of the Black Knight" is now known to be by Lydgate; "The Flower and the Leaf" cannot be earlier than 1450, and was probably written, as it purports to be, by a lady; whilst "The Court of Love" can hardly be earlier than 1500, and "Chaucer's Dream" (so called) is of still later date. Nothing but a complete ignorance of the history of the English language can connect these fifteenth-century and sixteenth-century poems with Chaucer. The only poem, in the above set, which can possibly be as old as the fourteenth-century, is "The Cuckoo and the Nightingale." There is no evidence of any kind to connect it with Chaucer; and Professor Lounsbury decisively rejects it, on the internal evidence. It admits a few rimes such as Chaucer nowhere employs.—SKEAT, WALTER W., 1894, *ed. The Student's Chaucer, Introduction, p.* xv.

TESTAMENT OF LOVE
C. 1387

Chaucer seems to have been a right Wicklevian, or else there never was any; and that, all his works almost, if they be thoroughly advised, will testify (albeit it be done in mirth and covertly), and especially the latter end of his third book of the Testament of Love; for there purely he toucheth the highest matter, that is, the Communion; wherein, except a man be altogether blind, he may espy him at the full.—FOXE, JOHN, 1562, *Acts and Monuments of the Church.*

It is probable that the lapse of a single generation would have blotted out from the memory of his countrymen these censures upon the father of English poetry. Who now appears as his accuser? Chaucer: Chaucer only. We have no evidence but what we draw from this production, that he was ever concerned in the turmoils of the city, that he was an exile, a prisoner in the Tower, and that he was finally led by resentment or by terror to the dishonourable act of impeaching his confederates. Little did the poet think, when he sat down to write this laborious apology for his conduct, that he was hereby perpetuating an imputation, which without his interference Time was preparing to blot out for ever from the records of memory, while his poetical compositions were destined to render him dear to the lovers of the muse as long as the English language shall endure. How feeble and erroneous are the calculations of the wisest of mankind!—GODWIN, WILLIAM, 1803, *Life of Geoffrey Chaucer, vol.* IV, *p.* 55.

We are thankful that Chaucer's shoulders are finally discharged of that weary load, "The Testament of Love."—LOWELL, JAMES RUSSELL, 1870–90, *Chaucer, Prose Works, Riverside ed., vol.* III, *p.* 296.

The Testament of Love was greatly relied upon by Godwin and others. They thence inferred that Chaucer was mixed up with the dispute as to the appointment of John of Northampton to the mayoralty of London in 1382; that he was imprisoned; that he fled to Zealand; that he was in exile for two years; that, on his return, he was sent to the Tower for three years, and not released till 1389; with more rubbish of the same sort. However, it so happens that Chaucer did not write this piece.—SKEAT, WALTER W., 1894, *Complete Works of Geoffrey Chaucer, vol.* I, *p.* 53, *note.*

I have lately made a curious discovery as to the "Testament of Love." The first paragraph begins with a large capital M; the second with a large capital A; and so on. By putting together all the letters thus pointed out, we at once have an acrostic, forming a complete sentence. The sentence is—MARGARET OF VIRTW, HAVE MERCI ON TSKNVI. Of course the last word is expressed as an anagram, which I decipher as KITSVN, i. e. Kitsun, the author's name. The whole piece is clearly addressed to a lady named Margaret, and contains frequent reference to the virtues of pearls, which were supposed to possess healing powers. Even if "Kitsun" is not the right reading, we learn something; for it is quite clear that TSKNVI cannot possibly represent the name of Chaucer.—SKEAT, WALTER W., 1894, *The Complete Works of Geoffrey Chaucer, vol.* V, *p.* xii, *note.*

THE CUCKOO AND THE NIGHTINGALE

I cannot believe that it was written by Chaucer.—TYRWHITT, THOMAS, 1775-78, *An Account of the Works of Chaucer.*

THE FLOWER AND THE LEAF
C. 1450

The various picturesque occurrences, the romantick vein, throughout the poem, are surely in no respect unworthy the pen of Chaucer.—TODD, HENRY JOHN, 1810, *Illustrations of Gower and Chaucer, p.* 280.

O, for that pencil, erst profuse
Of chivalry's emblazoned hues,
That traced of old, in Woodstock bower,
The pageant of the Leaf and Flower,
And bodied forth the tourney high,
Held for the hand of Emily!
—SCOTT, SIR WALTER, 1813, *Rokeby, c.* yi, *s.* xxvi.

There is, in the whole scenery and objects of the poem, an air of wonder and sweetness; an easy and surprising transition that is truly magical.—CAMPBELL, THOMAS, 1819, *Specimens of the British Poets.*

One of the brightest dreams that poet ever fashioned out of shadowy imaginings, is the allegory, "The Flower and the Leaf," with its beautiful moral, and an exuberance of fancy seldom met with out of the region of early poetry.—REED, HENRY, 1855, *Lectures on English Literature, p.* 136.

It must be regarded as among the most truly original, as it certainly is one of the finest, of Chaucer productions.—MARSH, GEORGE P., 1862, *The Origin and History of the English Language, etc., p.* 414.

A beautifully-tinted dream. — SMITH, ALEXANDER, 1863, *Dreamthorp, p.* 221.

I hold, therefore, that Chaucer's authorship of "The Flower and the Leaf" cannot yet be regarded as a settled question. Each reader may incline as freely as he will to one opinion or the other. Let him be positive in his own mind, if he will, but he must not turn his positive opinion into a dogma, and call all men heretics whose opinions face another way.—MORLEY, HENRY, 1890, *English Writers, vol.* V, *p.* 253.

Although not equal to Chaucer's work in power, yet there is a tender refinement of feeling, a chivalrous note in this poem, which is less frequent in the great writer than one might wish.—PALGRAVE, FRANCIS T., 1897, *Landscape in Poetry, from Homer to Tennyson, p.* 122.

COURT OF LOVE
C. 1500

I am induced by the internal evidence to consider it as one of Chaucer's genuine productions.—TYRWHITT, THOMAS, 1775–78, *An Account of the Works of Chaucer, p.* 445.

At the age of eighteen, and while yet a student in the university of Cambridge, Chaucer produced a poem, entitled the "Court of Love," consisting, as it has come down to us, of 1443 lines, but which could not originally have consisted of fewer than two thousand. This poem was first committed to the press by John Stow, the well-known compiler of the Chronicle of England, in an edition he gave of the works of Chaucer in the year 1561. No manuscript of it is known to exist. It is impossible however to entertain a rational doubt of its authenticity. The manner in which it is written is precisely the manner of Chaucer, and it is conspicuously superior to the composition of any other English poet, from the dawn of our language to Sackville earl of Dorset, whose poetical career commenced from about the time when Stow's edition of Chaucer made its appearance.—GODWIN, WILLIAM, 1803, *Life of Geoffrey Chaucer, vol.* I, *p.* 328.

As an early production, it presents, as may be anticipated, little attraction with regard to plot, variety of incident, or vigour of description: upon these points, indeed, it is positively defective; but it otherwise lays claim to eminent merits, and these will be found in an agreeably humourous delineation of manners and peculiarities of custom.—CLARKE, CHARLES COWDEN, 1835, *The Riches of Chaucer, vol.* I, *p.* 3.

Now I am not particularly concerned to stand up for the "Court of Love" as Chaucer's, for the simple reason that my business is with his character as a poet; and it seems to me so thoroughly Chaucerian in spirit, that my impressions of the man would be the same whether it was written by him or not. In its curious mediæval doctrine on the subject of love, it is in complete harmony with the Prologue to the "Legend of Good Women," —Cupid's martyrology, the Lives of the Saints of Love. If not written by Chaucer, it must have been written by a very clever and observant imitator—one might even say, looking to small coincidences, a deliberate and dexterous forger. The great difficulty in the way of not assigning the "Court of Love" or the "Flower and the Leaf" to Chaucer is this, that between him and Surrey there is no English poem half so good, and that it is next to incredible that the name of any poet capable of such work should have perished. If Chaucer did not write it, who did? This, I take it, is the feeling of everybody who still thinks it possible that Chaucer may have been the author. That the grammatical differences, which are doubtless very striking, should have been introduced by a transcriber, seems to them more likely on the whole than that a nameless poet, in an age whose known poets never rise anywhere near such a level, should have produced works that have received enthusiastic admiration from such judges as Dryden and Mr. Swinburne.—MINTO, WILLIAM, 1874–85, *Characteristics of English Poets, p.* 15.

Apart from the natural influence of the literature read in its own time, the "Court of Love" is an original poem, into which its author put the breath of his own life. Its allegory is no servile copy of other men's inventions, and it stops short of the prolixity usual in the refinements of the school from which it came. The verse has its own music, joyous, firm, elastic. A smooth measure—marred for us now sometimes by bad copying, and often by bad reading—was the common property of all the rhyming of the fourteenth century. But here, as in Chaucer's undoubted verse, there is a rhythm of health in the beat of the music. The rhyming is unstrained, the clear stream of thought falls naturally into song, of which the cadences are not less felt to be an impulse of Heaven's gift ministering to man's health and pleasure, than the wind's tree-music, or the rush and rattle of the waves. Here, too, as in the "Canterbury Tales," there is a practical, good-humoured simplicity of thought, that is as the salt which seasons healthy sentiment and keeps the rot out.—MORLEY, HENRY, 1890, *English Writers, vol.* V, *p.* 132.

"The Court of Love" must be a composition considerably later in date than

"The Temple of Glass." A complete master of his metrical instrument, the author is also far superior to Lydgate in fancy and invention: he knows how to construct a poetical action, and how to make a proper use of the machinery of personification. He is, however, working on precisely the same conventional theme; and the peculiarly interesting feature in his poem is, that the advance in literary and allegorical skill is accompanied by a distinct decline in the delicacy of chivalrous manners.—COURTHOPE, W. J., 1895, *A History of English Poetry, vol.* I, *p.* 359.

In the present state of our knowledge of the history of the English language, any notion of attributing "The Court of Love" to Chaucer is worse than untenable; for it is wholly disgraceful. Everything points to a very late date, and tends to exclude it, not only from the fourteenth, but even from the fifteenth century. At the same time, it will readily be granted that the poem abounds with Chaucerian words and phrases to an extent that almost surpasses even the poems of Lydgate. The versification is smooth, and the poem, as a whole, is pleasing. I have nothing to say against it, when considered on its own merits.—SKEAT, WALTER W., 1897, *Chaucerian and Other Pieces, p.* lxxx.

GENERAL

O Socrates, full of philosophy, Seneca in morals, and English in practice, great Ovid in thy poetry, brief in speech, wise in eloquence, most lofty eagle, who by thy philosophy dost illumine the kingdom of Aeneas, the Island of the Giants (those Brutus slew), and who hast sown the flowers and planted the rose-bush for those who are ignorant of the tongue of Pandrasus, great translator, noble Geoffrey Chaucer.—DESCHAMPS, EUSTACHE, c 1370, *Ballade Addressed to Geoffrey Chaucer.*

O maister dere and fader reverent,
My maister Chaucer, flour of eloquence,
Mirour of fructuous entendement,
O universl fader in science,
Allas! that thou thyn excellent prudence
In thy bed mortel mightest not bequethe!
What eyled Deeth? Allas! why wolde he slee thee?
O Deeth! thou didest not harm singuler
In slaghtre of him, but al this londe it smerteth
But nathelees, yit hast thou no powèr
His name to slee; his hy vertu asterteth
Unslayn fro thee, which ay us lyfly herteth
Withe bokes of his ornat endyting,
That is to al this land enlumining. . .

—OCCLEVE, THOMAS, 1411-12, *Governail of Princes, or De Regimine Principum (ed. Wright, p.* 75.)

My maister Chaucer, with his fresh commedies,
Is deed, alas! chefe poete of Bretayne,
That sometime made full piteous tragedies,
The fall of princes, he did also complayne,
As he that was of makyng soverayne,
Whom all this lande of right ought preferre,
Sithe of our language he was the lode-sterre
By hym that was, yf I shall not fayne,
Floure of Poetes, thorugh out of all Bretayne,
Whiche sothly had moost of excellence
In Rethoryke and in eloquence.
Rede his makyng, who lyst the trouthe fynde
Whivh never shall appallen in my mynde,
But always freshe ben in my memorye,
To whom be yeve pryse, honour and glorye
Of well sayeing.

—LYDGATE, JOHN, c. 1420, *The Story of Thebes, Prologue.*

O reverend Chaucere, rose of rethoris all,
As in oure tong ane flour imperiall,
That raise in Britane evir, quho redis rycht,
Thou beris of makaris the tryumph riall;
Thy fresch anamalit termes celicall
This matir coud illumynit have full brycht:
Was thou noucht of oure Inglisch all the lycht,
Surmounting eviry tong terrestriall,
Alls fer as Mayes morow dois mydnycht.

—DUNBAR, WILLIAM, c 1508, *Golden Targe.*

The god of shepheards, Tityrus, is dead,
Who taught mee homely, as I can, to make;
Hee, whilst hee lived, was the soveraigne head
Of shepheards all that bene with love ytake:
Well couth hee waile his Woes, and lightly flake
The flames which love within his heart had bredd,
And tell us mery tales to keepe us wake,
The while our sheepe about us safely fedde.

—SPENSER, EDMUND, 1579, *Shepheards Calender, June, ed. Collier, p.* 75.

In Chauser I am sped,
His tales I haue red:
His mater is delectable,
Solacious, and commendable;
His Englysh well alowed,
So as it is enprowed,
For as it is enployd,
There is no Englysh voyd,
At those dayes moch commended,
And now men wold haue amended
His Englysh, whereat they barke,
And mar all they warke:
Chaucer, that famus clerke,

His termes were not darke,
But plesaunt, easy, and playne;
No worde he wrote in vayne.
—SKELTON, JOHN, 1508?, PHILLYP SPARROWE, v. 788–803, *ed. Dyce, vol.* I, *p.* 75.

Our Englyshe Homer.—ASCHAM, ROGER, 1544, *Toxophilus, bk. A.*

Sometimes he turned into the speech of his native land works composed carefully, ornately and eloquently in the French tongue. Sometimes he translated Latin verse into English, but with learning, with skill, with harmony. Sometimes he committed to writings destined to survive many original things which equalled the happiest success of the Latins. Sometimes he strove with all his power to instruct the reader, and again took pains as sedulously to give him pleasure. Nor did he cease from his labors until he had carried our language to that height of purity, of eloquence, of conciseness and beauty, that it can justly be reckoned among the thoroughly polished languages of the world.—LELAND, JOHN, 1545? *Itinerary.*

Diligence also must be used in keeping truly the order of time; and describing lively, both the site of places and nature of persons, not only for the outward shape of the body, but also for the inward disposition of the mind, as Thucydides doth in many places very trimly, and Homer every where, and that always most excellently, which observation is chiefly to be marked in him; and our Chaucer doth the same, very praiseworthily: mark him well and confer him with any other that writeth in our time in their proudest tongue whosoever list. —ASCHAM, ROGER, 1552, *A Report and Discourse of the Affaires and State of Germany, ed. Giles, vol.* III, *p.* 6.

Wittie *Chaucer* satte in a chaire of gold couered with roses, writying prose and risme, accompanied with the spirites of many kynges, knightes, and faire ladies, whom he pleasauntly besprinkeled with the sweete water of the welle, consecrated vnto the muses, ecleped Aganippe, and, as the heauenly spirite, commended his deare Brigham for the worthy entōbyng-ing of his bones, worthie of memorie, in the long slepyng chamber of moste famous kinges. Euen so in tragedie he bewailed the sodaine resurrection of many a noble man before their time, in spoilyng of epitaphes, wherby many haue loste their inheritaunce.—BULLEIN, WILLIAM, 1564 73? *A Dialogue Both Pleasaunt and Pietifull wherin is a Godlie Regiment against the Fever Pestilence, etc., Reliquiæ Hearnianæ, vol.* II, *p.* 118.

Our father Chaucer hath vsed the same libertie in feete and measures that the Latinists do vse: and who so euer do peruse and well consider his workes, he shall finde that although his lines are not alwayes of one selfe same number of Syllables, yet beyng redde by one that hath vnderstanding, the longest verse and that which hath most Syllables in it, will fall (to the eare) correspondent vnto that whiche hath fewest sillables in it: and like wise that whiche hath in it fewest syllables, shalbe founde yet to consist of woordes that haue suche naturall sounde, as may seeme equall in length to a verse which hath many moe sillables of lighter accentes.—GASCOIGNE, GEORGE, 1575, *Certayne notes of Instruction Concerning the Making of Verse or Ryme in English, ed. Arber, p.* 34.

Chawcer, who for that excellent fame which hee obtayned in his Poetry, was alwayes accounted the God of English Poets (such a tytle for honours sake hath beene giuen him) was next after, if not equall in time to *Gower*, and hath left many workes, both for delight and profitable knowledge, farre exceeding any other that as yet euer since hys time directed theyr studies that way. Though the manner of hys stile may seeme blunte and course to many fine English eares at these dayes, yet in trueth, if it be equally pondered, and with good iudgment aduised, and confirmed with the time wherein he wrote, a man shall perceiue thereby euen a true picture or perfect shape of a right Poet. He by his delightsome vayne, so gulled the eares of men with his deuises, that, although corruption bare such sway in most matters, that learning and truth might skant bee admitted to shewe it selfe, yet without controllment, myght hee gyrde at the vices and abuses of all states, and gawle with very sharpe and eger inuentions, which he did so learnedly and pleasantly, that none therefore would call him into question. For such was his bolde spyrit, that what enormities he saw in any, he would not spare to pay them home, eyther in playne words, or els in some prety and pleasant couert, that the simplest might espy him—.WEBBE, WILLIAM, 1586, *A Discourse of English Poetrie, ed. Arber, p.* 32.

But of them all particularly this is myne opinion, that *Chaucer* with *Gower, Lidgat,* and *Harding* for their antiquitie ought to haue the first place and *Chaucer* as the most renowmed of them all, for the much learming appeareth to be in him aboue any of the rest. And though many of his bookes be but bare translations out of the Latin and French, yet are they wel handled, as his bookes of "Troilus" and "Creffeid," and the Romant of the Rose, whereof he translated but one halfe, the deuice was *Iohn de Mehunes* a French Poet. —PUTTENHAM, GEORGE, 1589, *The Arte of English Poesie, ed. Arber, p.* 75.

That renowmed Poet . . .
Dan Chaucer, well of English undefyled,
On Fames eternall beadroll worthie to be fyled.

—SPENSER, EDMUND, 1590, *The Faerie Queene, bk.* iv, *c.* ii, s. 32.

Art, like yong grasse in the spring of *Chaucers* florishing, was glad to peepe vp through any slime of corruption, to be beholding to she car'd not whome for apparaile, trauailing in those colde countries.—NASHE, THOMAS, 1593, *Strange Newes, etc., ed. Grosart.*

According to Chawcers English, there can be little *adling,* without much *gabbing,* that is, small getting, without great lying, and cogging.—HARVEY, GABRIEL, 1593, *Pierces Supererogation, Harvey's Works, ed. Grosart. vol.* II, *p.* 311.

O, that I could old Gefferies Muse awake.
—DAVYS, SIR JOHN, 1596, *Orchestra.*

The God of English poets.—MERES, FRANCIS, 1597, *Palladis Tamia.*

You must be contented to gyve me leave in discharge of the duetye and love whiche I beare to Chaucer, (whome I suppose I have as great intereste to adorne withe my smale skyll as anye other hath, in regarde that the laborious care of my father made hym most acceptable to the worlde in correctinge and augmentinge his woorkes.)—THYNNE, FRANCIS, 1598, *Animaduersions uppon Chaucer's Workes, Early English Text Society, vol.* IX, *p.* 4.

Yet what a time hath he wrested from Time,
And wonne vpon the mighty waste of dayes,
Vnto th' immortale honour of our clime!
That by his meanes came first adorn'd with Bayes;
Vnto the sacred Relickes of whose rime,
We yet are bound in zeale to offer praise?
—DANIEL, SAMUEL, 1599?, *Musophilus, v.* 153–8, *ed. Grosart.*

For his verses, although, in divers places, they seem to us to stand of unequal measures, yet a skilful reader, who can scan them in their nature, shall find it otherwise. And if a verse, here and there, fall out a syllable shorter or longer than another, I rather aret* it to the negligence and rape† of Adam Scrivener, (that I may speake as Chaucer doth,) than to any unconning or oversight in the author.—SPEGHT, THOMAS, 1602‡, *Preface to Chaucer's Works.*

Some few ages after§ came Geoffrey Chaucer, who writing his poesies in English, is of some called the first illuminator of the English tongue: of their opinion I am not (though I reverence Chaucer as an excellent poet for his time). He was indeed a great mingler of English with French, unto which language, belike for that he was descended of French, or rather Walloon, race, he carried a great affection.—VERSTEGAN, RICHARD, 1605, *Restitution of Decayed Intelligence in Antiquities concerning the Most Noble and Renowned English Nation.*

Although the style for the antiquity may distaste you, yet as under a bitter and rough rind there lieth a delicate kernel of conceit and sweet invention.—PEACHAM, HENRY, 1622, *The Compleat Gentleman.*

That noble Chaucer in those former times
The first enriched our English with his rimes,
And was the first of ours that ever brake
Into the Muses' treasure, and first spake
In weighty numbers, delving in the mine
Of perfect knowledge, which he could refine
And coin for current; and as much as then
The English language could express to men
He made it do, and by his wondrous skill
Gave us much light from his abundant quill.
—DRAYTON, MICHAEL, c. 1627, *Of Poets and Poesie.*

So wise as our Chaucer is esteemed.—MILTON, JOHN, 1641, *Of Reformation in England, Prose Works, vol.* II, *p.* 396.

He was the prince of English poets. . . He was a great refiner and illuminer of our English tongue; and, if he left it so bad, how much worse did he find it!—FULLER, THOMAS, 1655, *The Church History of Britain, bk.* iv, *sec.* i, *par.* 47–48.

*Impute. †Haste. ‡Not in edition of 1598. §The Conquest.

Chaucer his sense can only boast;
The glory of his numbers lost!
Years have defaced his matchless strain;
And yet he did not sing in vain
—WALLER, EDMUND, c 1660, *Of English Verse.*

A Comment upon the Two Tales of our ancient, renowned, and ever-living poet, Sir Jeffray Chaucer, Knight, who for his rich fancy, pregnant invention, and present composure deserved the countenance of a prince and his laureat honor.—BRAITHWAITE, RICHARD, 1665, *Comment, Title-Page.*

Old Chaucer, like the morning star,
To us discovers day from far;
His light those mists and clouds dissolved,
Which our dark nation long involved;
But he descending to the shades,
Darkness again the age invades.
—DENHAM, SIR JOHN, c 1667, *On Mr. Abraham Cowley.*

The poet Chaucer set the worst example, who by bringing whole shoals of French words into our language, which was but too much adulterated before, through the effects of the Norman Conquest, deprived it almost wholly of its native grace and splendour, laying on paint over its pure complexion, and, for a beautiful face, substituted a downright mask. —SKINNER, STEPHEN, 1667-71?, *Etymological Dictionary.*

They who attempted verse in English down to Chaucer's time made an heavy pudder, and are always miserably put to it for a word to clink; which commonly falls so awkward and unexpectedly, as dropping from the clouds by some machine or miracle. Chaucer found an Herculean labour on his hands, and did perform to admiration. He seized all Provencal, French, or Latin that came in his way, gives them a new garb and livery, and mingles them amongst our English: turns out English gouty or superannuated, to place in their room the foreigners fit for service, trained and accustomed to poetical discipline. —RYMER, THOMAS, 1693, *A Short View of the Tragedy of the Last Age.*

Long had our dull forefathers slept supine,
Nor felt the raptures of the tuneful Nine;
Till Chaucer first, a merry bard, arose,
And many a story told in rhyme and prose.
But age has rusted what the poet writ,
Worn out his language and obscured his wit;
In vain he jests in his unpolish'd strain
And tries to make his readers laugh in vain.
—ADDISON, JOSEPH, 1694, *An Account of the greatest English Poets.*

As he is the father of English poetry, so I hold him in the same degree of veneration as the Grecians held Homer, or the Romans Virgil. He is a perpetual fountain of good sense; learned in all sciences; and, therefore, speaks properly on all subjects. As he knew what to say, so he knows also when to leave off; a continence which is practised by few writers, and scarcely by any of the ancients, excepting Virgil and Horace. . . . Chaucer followed nature everywhere, but was never so bold to go beyond her. . . . The verse of Chaucer, I confess, is not harmonious to us; but it is like the eloquence of one whom Tacitus commends, it was *auribus istius temporis accommodata.* They who lived with him, and some time after him, thought it musical; and it continues so, even in our judgment, if compared with the numbers of Lidgate and Gower, his contemporaries: —there is the rude sweetness of a Scotch tune in it, which is natural and pleasing, though not perfect. It is true, I cannot go so far as he* who published the last edition of him; for he would make us believe the faultis in our ears, and that there were really ten syllables in a verse where we find but nine: but this opinion is not worth confuting; it is so gross and obvious an error, that common sense (which is a rule in everything but matters of faith and revelation) must convince the reader, that equality of numbers, in every verse which we call heroic, was either not known, or not always practised, in Chaucer's age. It were an easy matter to produce some thousands of his verses, which are lame for want of half a foot, and sometimes a whole one, and which no pronunciation can make otherwise. We can only say, that he lived in the infancy of our poetry, and that nothing is brought to perfection at the first. . . . Chaucer, I confess, is a rough diamond, and must first be polished, ere he shines. I deny not likewise, that, living in our early days of poetry, he writes not always of a piece; but sometimes mingles trivial things with those of greater moment. Sometimes also, though not often, he runs riot, like Ovid, and knows not when he has said enough.—DRYDEN, JOHN, 1700, *Preface to the Fable, Works ed. Scott and Saintsbury, vol.* XI, *pp.* 223, 224, 233.

*Thomas Speght.

Cadence and sound which we so prize and use
Ill suit the majesty of Chaucer's muse:
His language only can his thoughts express;
Old honest Clytus scorns a Persian dress.
—HARRISON, WILLIAM, 1706, *Woodstock Park.*

Chaucer had all that beauty could inspire,
And Surrey's numbers glowed with warm desire:
Both now are prized by few, unknown to most,
Because the thoughts are in the numbers lost.
—FENTON, ELIJAH, 1711, *An Epistle to Mr. Southerne.*

Not Chaucer's beauties could survive the rage
Of wasting envy and devouring age:
One mingled heap of ruins now we see:
Thus Chaucer is, and Fenton thus shall be.
—HARTE, WALTER, 1727, *Poems on Several Occasions, p.* 98.

Laughing sage,
Chaucer, whose native manners-painting verse,
Well moralized, shines through the Gothic cloud
Of time and language o'er thy genius thrown.
—THOMSON, JAMES, 1727, *Summer.*

I read Chaucer still with as much pleasure as almost any of our poets. He is a master of manners, of description, and the first tale-teller in the true enlivened natural way.—POPE, ALEXANDER, 1728-30, *Spence's Anecdotes, ed. Singer, p.* 15.

Authors, like coins, grow dear as they grow old;
It is the rust we value, not the gold.
Chaucer's worst ribaldry is learned by rote,
And beastly Skelton heads of houses quote.
—POPE, ALEXANDER, 1733, *Imitations of Horace, bk.* ii, *ep.* I, *v.* 35.

I might now write to you in the language of Chaucer or Spenser, and assert that I wrote English, because it was English in their days; but I should be a most affected puppy if I did so, and you would not understand three words of my letter.—CHESTERFIELD, LORD, 1748, *Letters to his Son, O. S. Sept.* 27.

Not far from these, Dan Chaucer, ancient wight,
A lofty seat on Mount Parnassus held,
Who long had been the Muses' chief delight;
His reverend locks were silvered o'er with eld;
Grave was his visage and his habit plain;
And while he sung, fair nature he displayed,
In verse albeit uncouth and simple strain;
Ne mote he well be seen, so thick the shade
Which elms and aged oaks had all around him made.
—LLOYD, ROBERT, 1751, *The Progress of Envy.*

Chaucer is regarded rather as an old, than a good poet. We look upon his poems as venerable relics, not as beautiful compositions; as pieces better calculated to gratify the antiquarian than the critic. He abounds not only in strokes of humour, which is commonly supposed to be his sole talent, but of pathos, and sublimity, not unworthy a more refined age. His old manners, his romantic arguments, his wildness of painting, his simplicity and antiquity of expression, transport us into some fairy region, and are all highly pleasing to the imagination. It is true that his uncouth and unfamiliar language disgusts and deters many readers; but the principal reason of his being so little known, and so seldom taken in hand, is the convenient opportunity of reading him with pleasure and facility in modern imitations.—WARTON, THOMAS, 1754, *Observations on the Fairy Queen of Spenser, sec.* v.

The first of our versifiers who wrote poetically. He does not, however, appear to have deserved all the praise he has received, or all the censure he has suffered. Dryden, who, mistaking genius for learning, in confidence of his abilities, ventured to write of what he had not examined, ascribes to Chaucer the first refinement of our numbers, the first production of easy and natural rhymes, and the improvement of our language, by words borrowed from the more polished languages of the continent. Skinner contrarily blames him in harsh terms for having vitiated his native speech by whole cartloads of foreign words. But he that reads the works of Gower will find smooth numbers and easy rhymes, of which Chaucer is supposed to be the inventor, and the French words, whether good or bad, of which Chaucer is charged as the importer. Some innovations he might probably make, like others, in the infancy of our poetry, which the paucity of books does allow us to discover with particular exactness; but the works of Gower and Lydgate sufficiently evince that his diction was in general like that of his contemporaries; and some improvements he undoubtedly made by the various dispositions of the rhymes, and by the mixture of different numbers, in which he seems to have been happy and judicious.—JOHNSON, SAMUEL, 1755, *Dictionary of the English Language.*

Such was old Chaucer; such the placid mien
Of him who first with harmony inform'd
The language of our fathers. Here he dwelt
For many a cheerful day. These ancient walls
Have often heard him, while his legends blithe
He sang; of love, or knighthood, or the wiles
Of homely life: through each estate and age,
The fashions and the follies of the world
With cunning hand portraying. Though perchance
From Bleinheim's towers, O stranger, thou art come
Glowing with Churchill's trophies; yet in vain
Dost thou applaud them, if thy breast be cold
To him, this other hero; who, in times
Dark and untaught, began with charming verse
To tame the rudeness of his native land.

—AKENSIDE, MARK, 1758, *For a Statue of Chaucer at Woodstock.*

From what has been said I think we may fairly conclude, that the English language must have imbibed a strong tincture of the French, long before the age of Chaucer, and consequently that he ought not to be charged as the importer of words and phrases, which he only used after the example of his predecessors and in common with his contemporaries. This was the real fact, and is capable of being demonstrated to any one, who will take the trouble of comparing the writings of Chaucer with those of Robert of Gloucester and Robert of Brunne, who both lived before him, and with those of Sir John Mandeville and Wicliff, who lived at the same time with him. . . . The great number of verses, sounding complete even to our ears, which is to be found in all the least corrected copies of his works, authorises us to conclude, that he was not ignorant of the laws of metre. Upon this conclusion it is impossible not to ground a strong presumption, that he intended to observe the same laws in the many other verses which seem to us irregular; and if this was really his intention, what reason can be assigned sufficient to account for his having failed so grossly and repeatedly, as is generally supposed, in an operation, which every Balladmonger in our days, man, woman, or child, is known to perform with the most unerring exactness, and without any extraordinary fatigue?—TYRWHITT, THOMAS, 1775-78, *Essay on the Language and Versification of Chaucer, par.* viii, xii.

In elevation and elegance, in harmony and perspicuity of versification, he surpasses his predecessors in an infinite proportion: that his genius was universal, and adapted to themes of unbounded variety: that his merit was not less in painting familiar manners with humour and propriety, than in moving the passions, and in representing the beautiful or the grand objects of nature with grace and sublimity. In a word, that he appeared with all the lustre and dignity of a true poet, in an age which compelled him to struggle with a barbarous language, and a national want of taste; and when to write verses at all, was regarded as a singular qualification. . . . I consider Chaucer as a genial day in an English spring.—WARTON, THOMAS, 1778-81, *The History of English Poetry, sec*, xviii, xxi.

. . . old Chaucer's merry page.

—COWPER, WILLIAM, 1781, *Anti-Thelyphthora.*

I am, too, though a Goth, so modern a Goth that I hate the black letter, and I love Chaucer better in Dryden and Baskerville, than in his own language and dress.—WALPOLE, HORACE, 1781, *Letter to Rev. William Mason, Letters, ed. Cunningham, vol.* viii, *p.* 108.

See, on a party-colour'd steed of fire,
With Humour at his side, his trusty Squire,
Gay Chaucer leads—in form a Knight of old,
And his strong armour is of steel and gold;
But o'er it age a cruel rust has spread,
And made the brilliant metals dark as lead

—HAYLEY, WILLIAM, 1782, *An Essay on Epic Poetry, Ep.* III, *v.* 383.

Chaucer's versification, wherever his genuine text is preserved, was uniformly correct; although the harmony of his lines has in many instances been obliterated by the changes that have taken place in the mode of accenting our language.—ELLIS, GEORGE, 1790-1845, *Specimens of the Early English Poets, vol.* I, *p.* 167.

The venerable father of English poetry had in his time penned "many a song and many a lecherous lay," of which we have infinitely more reason to regret the loss, than he had in his old age to repent the composition.—RITSON, JOSEPH, 1790, *Dissertation on Ancient Songs and Music, Ancient Songs and Ballads.*

Chaucer, notwithstanding the praises bestowed on him, I think obscene and contemptible:—he owes his celebrity merely to his antiquity, which he does not deserve so well as Pierce Plowman, or Thomas of Erceldoune.—BYRON, LORD, 1807, *Detached Thoughts.*

For variety of power has no competitor except Shakspeare.—SOUTHEY, ROBERT, 1811, *Letter to Landor, Life and Correspondence, ch.* xvi.

In the passages where Chaucer dramatises the manners of his day, or carries the voice of nature to the heart, or exhibits his characters and incidents as if passing in living motion before us, he produces an interest which neither the little feebleness that even here intermingle themselves, nor their unpruned prolixity, can destroy; but beyond these, he, like Gower, is dull, unmeaning now, and unreadable. Few poets have written so much, which so few desire to peruse or attempt to disturb.—TURNER, SHARON, 1814-23, *The History of England During the Middle Ages, vol.* V, *p.* 331.

In the fourteenth century Chaucer's verse is not unlike our homely rhymesters of the sixteenth century in Germany.—SCHLEGEL, FREDERICK, 1815, *Lectures on the History of Literature, ed. Bohn, p.* 273.

My admiration for him is very ardent. His poetry seems to me so healthy, so vigorous, so much in the thought, and so little in the expression; his powers are so various, so pliable, ranging at will from the thrilling pathos of Griselda to the wild fancy of "Cambuscan bold."

Setting Milton and Shakspeare aside, I am not sure that I don't prefer him to almost any writer in the circle of English poetry. I speak, of course, of his best works, and not of his poems *en masse;* but two or three of his "Canterbury Tales," and some select passages from his other productions, are worth all that the age of Queen Anne, our Augustan age as it has been called, ever produced.—MITFORD, MARY RUSSELL, 1815, *Letters, —Life ed. L'Estrange, vol.* I, *p.* 239.

I cannot, in my own taste, go completely along with the eulogies that some have bestowed upon Chaucer, who seems to me to have wanted grandeur, where he is original, both in conception and in language. But in vivacity of imagination and ease of expression, he is above all poets of the middle time, and comparable perhaps to the greatest of those who have followed. He invented, or rather introduced from France, and employed with facility the regular iambic couplet; and though it was not to be expected that he should perceive the capacities latent in that measure, his versification, to which he accommodated a very licentious and arbitrary pronunciation, is uniform and harmonious.—HALLAM, HENRY, 1818, *View of the State of Europe During the Middle Ages, ch.* ix, *Part* II.

His poetry resembles the root just springing from the ground rather than the full-blown flower. His muse is no "babbling gossip of the air," fluent and redundant; but, like a stammerer, or a dumb person, that has just found the use of speech, crowds many things together with eager haste, with anxious pauses, and fond repetitions, to prevent mistake. His words point as an index to the objects, like the eye or finger. There were none of the common-places of poetic diction in our author's time, no reflected lights of fancy, no borrowed roseate tints; he was obliged to inspect things for himself, to look narrowly, and almost to handle the object, as in the obscurity of morning we partly see and partly grope our way; so that his descriptions have a sort of tangible character belonging to them, and produce the effect of sculpture on the mind. Chaucer had an equal eye for truth of nature and discrimination of character; and his interest in what he saw gave new distinctness and force to his power of observation. The picturesque and the dramatic are in him closely blended together, and hardly distinguishable; for he principally describes external appearances as indicating character, as symbols of internal sentiment. —HAZLITT, WILLIAM, 1818, *Lectures on the English Poets, Lecture* ii.

In what terms some speak of him! while I confess I find him unreadable.—MOORE, THOMAS, 1819, *Diary, Memoirs, ed. Russell, vol.* II, *p.* 290.

I would rather read Chaucer than Ariosto.—KEATS, JOHN, 1819, *Letters, ed. Colvin, p.* 333.

. . . loved Bard! whose spirit often dwelt
In the clear land of vision . . .
O great Precursor, genuine morning Star.
—WORDSWORTH, WILLIAM, 1821-22, *Ecclesiastical Sonnets, pt.* i, xxxi.

He is famed rather as the animated painter of character, and manners, and external nature, than the poet of love and sentiment; and yet no writer, Shakespeare always excepted, (and perhaps Spenser) contains so many beautiful and tender passages relating to, or inspired by, women.—JAMESON, ANNA BROWNELL, 1829, *The Loves of the Poets, vol.* I, *p.* 137.

It is idle at this day to say any thing of the moral influence of Chaucer: we might as well enlarge upon the absurdity of the Koran.—PEABODY, WILLIAM B. O., 1830, *Studies in Poetry, Literary Remains, p.* 10.

I take unceasing delight in Chaucer. His manly cheerfulness is especially delicious to me in my old age. How exquisitely tender he is, and yet how perfectly free from the least touch of sickly melancholy or morbid drooping! The sympathy of the poet with the subjects of his poetry is particularly remarkable in Shakspere and Chaucer; but what the first effects by a strong act of imagination and mental metamorphosis, the last does without any effort, merely by the inborn kindly joyousness of his nature. How well we seem to know Chaucer! How absolutely nothing do we know of Shakspere!—COLERIDGE, SAMUEL TAYLOR, 1834, *Table Talk, March* 15.

The line of English poets begins with him, as that of English kings with William the Conqueror; and if the change introduced by him was not so great, his title is better. Kings there were before the conquest, and of great and glorious memory too; but the poets before Chaucer are like the heroes before Agamemnon; even of those whose works have escaped oblivion, the names of most have perished. Father Chaucer, throwing off all trammels, simplified our verse. Nature had given him the ear and the eye and the imagination of a poet; and his diction was such as that of all great poets has ever been, and ever will be, in all countries,—neither cramped by pedantic rules, vitiated by prevailing fashions, nor raised on stilts, nor drooping for want of strength, but rising and falling with the subject, and always suited to it. —SOUTHEY, ROBERT, 1835, *Life of Cowper, Bohn ed., p.* 295.

The English language of Chaucer is far from possessing the polish of old French, which already attains some degree of perfection in this* minor species of literature. Nevertheless, the idiom of the Anglo-Saxon poet, a heterogeneous medley of various dialects, has become the stock of modern English.—DE CHATEAUBRIAND, FRANÇOIS RENÉ, VICOMTE, 1837, *Sketches of English Literature, vol.* I, *p.* 99.

That Chaucer was a *master* of English versification no one, that reads him with due care and attention, can well doubt. There are many passages in his works, which, from the agreement of MSS. and the absence of all those peculiarities of structure that leave matter for doubt, have, in all probability, come down to us as Chaucer wrote them—and in *these* the versification is as exquisite as the poetry. It needs not the somewhat suspicious apology of Dryden. I am not one of those who assert, that Chaucer has always "ten syllables in a verse, where we find but nine;" but I am as far from believing, that "he lived in the infancy of our poetry," because the scheme of his metre somewhat differs from our own. As far as we have the means of judging, it was not only *"auribus istius temporis accommodata,"* but fulfilled every requisite that modern criticism has laid down, as either essential to the science, or conducive to the beauty of a versification. — GUEST, EDWIN, 1838, *A History of English Rhythms, vol.* II, *p.* 237.

Chaucer excels in pathos, in humor, in satire, character, and description. His graphic faculty, and healthy sense of the material, strongly ally him to the painter; and perhaps a better idea could not be given of his universality than by saying that he was at once the Italian and the Flemish painter of his time, and exhibited the pure expression of Raphael, the devotional intensity of Domenechino, the color and corporeal fire of Titian, the manners of Hogarth, and the homely domesticities of Ostade and Teniers! His faults are coarseness, which was that of his age; and, in some of his poems, tediousness, which is to be attributed to the same cause.—HUNT, LEIGH, 1840, *Specimens of Chaucer, No. I., The Seer; or, Common-places Refreshed.*

The herculean labor of Chaucer was the creation of a new style. In this he was as fortunate as he was likewise unhappy.

*Ballads.

He mingled, with the native rudeness of our English, words of Provencal fancy, and some of French and of Latin growth. He banished the superannuated and the uncouth, and softened the churlish nature of our hard Anglo-Saxon; but the poet had nearly endangered the novel diction when his artificial pedantry assumed what he called "the ornate style" in "the Romaunt of the Rose" and in his "Troilus and Cressida." This "ornate style" introduced sesquipedalian Latinisms, words of immense dimensions, that could not hide their vacuity of thought. Chaucer seems deserted by his genius when "the ornate style" betrays his pangs and his anxiety. . . . Are the works of our great poet to be consigned to the literary dungeon of the antiquary's closet? I fear that there is more than one obstruction which intervenes between the poet's name, which will never die, and the poet's works, which will never be read.—DISRAELI, ISAAC, 1841, *Chaucer, Amenities of Literature.*

Now, what was the character of Chaucer's diction? A great delusion exists on that point. Some ninety or one hundred words that are now obsolete, certainly not many more, vein the whole surface of Chaucer; and thus a *primâ facie* impression is conveyed that Chaucer is difficult to understand, whereas a very slight practice familiarises his language.—DE QUINCEY, THOMAS, 1841, *Homer and the Homeridæ, Collected Writings, ed. Masson, vol.* VI, *p.* 70.

Had Chaucer's poems been written in Greek or Hebrew, they would have been a thousand times better known. . . . Our position is, that Chaucer was a most harmonious and melodious poet, and that he was a perfect master of the various forms of versification in which he wrote; that the principle on which his rhythm is founded fuses and subjects within itself all the minor details of metre; that this principle, though it has been understood only by the few, and never systematically explained, is, more or less, inseparable from the composition of an harmonious versification in the English language; and that he, the first man, if not unrivalled in the varied music of his verse, has scarcely been surpassed by any succeeding poet. . . . Of the occasional deficiencies or "lameness" in his verse, of which Chaucer has been accused, it is hoped that little need now be said. In the first place, we are to allow for his quantities, so far as we know them, or can feasibly conjecture what they were. In the second place, we are to give to a great poet who has accomplished so much harmony which *is* manifest, due credit for many instances where we are unable to perceive it, from our deficiency of knowledge. Thirdly, we are to allow for the errors of copyists, of whose ungodly pens Chaucer shows himself to be in much dread,—in his address to Adam Scrivener, his amanuensis, and on other occasions. It might be suggested, fifthly, that something should be allowed for the unsettled condition of the English language at his time, and that it was accounted an accomplishment for a man to be able even to write his own name. But this consideration I do not care to dwell upon in the case of one who shows such mastery.—HORNE, R. H., 1841, *The Poems of Geoffrey Chaucer Modernized, Introduction, pp.* v, xxxviii, lxxvi.

He was made for an early poet, and the metaphors of dawn and spring doubly become him. . . . He is a king and inherits the earth, and expands his great soul smilingly to embrace his great heritage. Nothing is too high for him to touch with a thought, nothing too low to dower with an affection. As a complete creature cognate of life and death, he cries upon God,—as a sympathetic creature he singles out a daisy from the universe ("si douce est la marguerite,") to lie down by half a summer's day and bless it for fellowship. His senses are open and delicate, like a young child's—his sensibilities capacious of supersensual relations, like an experienced thinker's. Child-like, too, his tears and smiles lie at the edge of his eyes, and he is one proof more among the many, that the deepest pathos and the quickest gayeties hide together in the same nature. He is too wakeful and curious to lose the stirring of a leaf, yet not too wide awake to see visions of green and white ladies between the branches; and a fair house of fame and a noble court of love are built and holden in the winking of his eyelash. . . . Not one of the "Queen Anne's men," measuring out tuneful breath upon their fingers, like ribbons for topnots, did know the art of versification as the old rude Chaucer knew it. Call him rude for the picturesqueness of the epithet; but his verse has, at least, as much regularity in the sense of true art, and more manifestly in proportion to our increasing acquaintance with his dialect and pronunciation, as can be discovered or dreamed in the French school.—BROWNING, ELIZABETH BARRETT, 1843-63, *The Book of the Poets, pp.* 111, 113.

And Chaucer, with his infantine
Familiar clasp of things divine;
That mark upon his lip is wine.

—BROWNING, ELIZABETH BARRETT, 1844, *A Vision of Poets, v.* 388-90.

To learn my lore on Chaucer's knee,
I left much prouder company.

—LANDOR, WALTER SAVAGE, 1846, *To Wordsworth.*

It may be safely asserted that very few poets in any modern language are more exquisitely and uniformly musical than Chaucer.—SHAW, THOMAS B., 1847, *Outlines of English Literature, p.* 37.

What strikes us most, however, and remains with us longest after reading his* poetry, is the natural and spirited tone that prevails over every other. In this he is like Chaucer, who wrote in the latter part of the same century. Indeed, the resemblance between the two poets is remarkable in some other particulars. Both often sought their materials in the Northern French poetry; both have that mixture of devotion and a licentious immorality, much of which belonged to their age, but some of it to their personal characters; and both show a wide knowledge of human nature, and a great happiness in sketching the details of individual manners. The original temper of each made him satirical and humorous; and each, in his own country, became the founder of some of the forms of its popular poetry, introducing new metres and combinations, and carrying them out in a versification which, though generally rude and irregular, is often flowing and nervous, and always natural. The Archpriest has not, indeed, the tenderness, the elevation, or the general power of Chaucer; but his genius has a compass, and his verse a skill and success, that show him to be more nearly akin to the great English master than will be believed, except by those who have carefully read the works of both.—TICKNOR, GEORGE, 1849-91, *History of Spanish Literature, vol.* I, *p.* 92.

*Archpriest of Hita.

The influence of Chaucer is conspicuous in all our early literature; and, more recently, not only Pope and Dryden have been beholden to him, but, in the whole society of English writers, a large unacknowledged debt is easily traced. One is charmed with the opulence which feeds so many pensioners. But Chaucer is a huge borrower. Chaucer, it seems, drew continually, through Lydgate and Caxton, from Guido di Colonna, whose Latin romance of the Trojan war was in turn a compilation from Dares Phrygius, Ovid and Statius. Then Petrarch, Boccaccio and the Provençal poets, are his benefactors: the Romaunt of the Rose is only judicious translation from William of Lorris and John of Meun: Troilus and Creseide, from Lollius of Urbino: The Cock and the Fox, from the *Lais* of Marie: The House of Fame, from the French or Italian: and poor Gower he uses as if he were only a brick-kiln or stone-quarry, out of which to build his house. He steals by this apology,—that what he takes has no worth where he finds it, and the greatest where he leaves it.—EMERSON, RALPH WALDO, 1850, *Shakespeare; or, the Poet, Representative Men.*

Grey with all honours of age! but fresh-featured and ruddy
As dawn when the drowsy farm-yard has thrice heard Chaunticlere.
Tender to tearfulness—childlike, and manly and motherly;
Here beats true English blood richest joyance on sweet English ground

—MEREDITH, GEORGE, 1851, *Poems, Works, vol.* xxxi.

Indeed I *do* admire him, or rather love him. In my opinion, he is fairly worth a score or two of Spensers. He had a knowledge of human nature, and not of doll-making and *fantoccini* dressing. . . . Pardon me if I say I would rather see Chaucer quite alone, in the dew of his sunny morning, than with twenty clever gentlefolks about him, arranging his shoestrings and buttoning his doublet. I like even his *language.* I will have no hand in breaking his dun but rich-painted glass, to put in (if clearer) much thinner panes.—LANDOR, WALTER SAVAGE, 1851, *Letter to R. H. Horne, Letters of Mrs. Browning, vol.* I, *p.* 78.

If any man or woman will not take the trifling trouble which is necessary to understand Chaucer's antique orthography, let them be ignorant. The last "Minerva" novel will prove metal more attractive to such painstaking "students of English Literature."—ALLIBONE, S. AUSTIN, 1854-58, *Dictionary of English Literature, vol.* I, *p.* 374.

. . . rich as Chaucer's speech.

—DOBELL, SYDNEY, 1855, *America, Sonnets on the War.*

Ah! Dan Chaucer!—art thou he,
Morning star of minstrelsy?
Eldest of the English choir,
Highest hill – touched first with fire.

—ARNOLD, SIR EDWIN, 1856, *Alla Mano Della Mia Donna.*

On every page and every line of his writings, a reminiscence of our trouvères betrays itself, sometimes veiled, sometimes apparent.—SANDRAS, E.-G., 1859, *Étude sur G. Chaucer considéré comme Imitateur des Trouvères.*

Compared with his productions, all that precedes is barbarism. But what is much more remarkable is that very little of what has followed in the space of nearly five centuries that has elapsed since he lived and wrote is worthy of being compared with what he has left us. He is in our English poetry almost what Homer is in that of Greece, and Dante in that of Italy,—at least in his own sphere still the greatest light.—CRAIK, GEORGE L., 1861, *A Compendious History of English Literature and of the English Language, vol.* I, *p.* 267.

From this Babylonish confusion of speech, the influence and example of Chaucer did more to rescue his native tongue than any other single cause; and if we compare his dialect with that of any writer of an earlier date, we shall find that in compass, flexibility, expressiveness, grace, and all the higher qualities of poetical diction, he gave it at once the utmost perfection which the materials at his hand would admit of. . . . In the hands of Chaucer, the English language advanced, at one bound, to that superiority over the French which it has ever since maintained, as a medium of the expression of poetical imagery and thought. . . . Chaucer, in fine, was a genuine product of the union of Saxon and Norman genius, and the first well-characterized specimen of the intellectual results of a combination, which has given to the world a literature so splendid, and a history so noble. . . . May fairly be said to be not only the earliest dramatic genius of modern Europe, but to have been a dramatist before that which is technically known as the existing drama was invented.—MARSH, GEORGE P., 1862, *The Origin and History of the English Language, etc., pp.* 381, 390, 401, 419.

Chaucer is admitted on all hands to be a great poet, but, by the general public at least, he is not frequently read. He is like a cardinal virtue, a good deal talked about, a good deal praised, honoured by a vast amount of distant admiration, but with little practical acquaintance. And for this there are many and obvious reasons. He is an ancient, and the rich old mahogany is neglected for the new and glittering veneer. He is occasionally gross; often tedious and obscure; he frequently leaves a couple of lovers to cite the opinions of Greek and Roman authors; and practice and patience are required to melt the frost of his orthography, and let his music flow freely. In the conduct of his stories he is garrulous, homely, and slow-paced. He wrote in a leisurely world, when there was plenty of time for writing and reading; long before the advent of the printer's devil or of Mr. Mudie. There is little of the lyrical element in him. He does not dazzle by sentences. He is not quotable. He does not shine in extracts so much as in entire poems. There is a pleasant equality about his writing: he advances through a story at an even pace, glancing round him on everything with curious, humorous eyes, and having his say about everything. He is the prince of story-tellers, and however much he may move others, he is not moved himself. His mood is so kindly that he seems always to have written after dinner, or after hearing good news—that he had received from the king another grant of wine, for instance—and he discourses of love and lovers' raptures, and the disappointments of life, half sportively, half sadly, like one who has passed through all, felt the sweetness and the bitterness of it, and been able to strike a balance. — SMITH, ALEXANDER, 1863, *Dreamthorp, p.* 211.

Chaucer is the genuine specimen of an English poet—a type of the best who were to come after him; with cordial affection for men and for nature; often tempted to coarseness, often yielding to his baser nature in his desire to enter into all the different experiences of men; apt through this desire, and through his hatred of what was insincere, to say many things of which he had need to repent, and of which he did repent; but never losing his loyalty to what was pure, his reverence for what was divine.—MAURICE, FREDERICK DENISON, 1865, *The Friendship of Books and Other Lectures, p.* 77.

The essential quality of Chaucer is the deep, penetrating, Dantean intensity of his single conceptions, which go right to the heart of the objects conceived, so that there is an absolute contact of thought and thing without any interval.—WHIPPLE, EDWIN P., 1866, *The English Mind, Character and Characteristic Men, p.* 193.

And if it hap that midst of thy defeat,
Fainting beneath thy follies' heavy load,
My Master, Geoffry Chaucer, thou do meet,
Then shalt thou win a space of rest full sweet. . . .
O Master, O thou great of heart and tongue.
. . . .
O Master, if thine heart could love us yet,
Spite of things left undone, and wrongly done,
Some place in loving hearts then should we get,
For thou, sweet-souled, didst never stand alone,
But knew'st the joy and woe of many an one.
—By lovers dead, who live through thee, we pray,
Help thou us singers of an empty day!

—MORRIS, WILLIAM, 1868, *The Earthly Paradise, L'Envoi.*

He is as superior to the ordinary historian as a troop of soldiers is to a regiment of wax-works.—FRISWELL, JAMES HAIN, 1869, *Essays on English Writers, p.* 45.

His verse is full of buoyancy; its very art is easy, the wind is not freer, it is a south-west air with a rhythm in it, and a masterly skill in the pauses. . . . His poetry is penetrated with the social spirit. He loves the haunts of men, the places where they dwell, the episodes of mutual need that bring and keep them together; meat and drink; industry and play; the uprisings and downsittings, the incomings and outgoings of men and women.—RAND, WILLIAM BRIGHTY, (MATTHEW BROWNE), 1869, *Chaucer's England, vol.* I, *pp.* 41, 47.

Chaucer's "well of English undefiled" is very pleasant and wholesome drinking; but pronouns, prepositions, conjunctions, and "auxiliary" verbs aside, it is a mixture in which Normanized, Gallicized Latin is mingled in large proportion with a base of degraded Anglo-Saxon.—WHITE, RICHARD GRANT, 1870–99, *Words and their Uses, Introduction, p.* 9.

Chaucer must be studied in order to be read; but when Chaucer has been studied so as to be easily followed, he confronts you with the dawn of a brilliant day—dewy, fresh, transparent, and invigorating. He gives you the Odyssey of the English poetry, and reveals the springtime of English life.—PORTER, NOAH, 1870, *Books and Reading, p.* 261.

There is a pervading wholesomeness in the writings of this man,—a vernal property that soothes and refreshes in a way of which no other has ever found the secret. . . . It is good to retreat now and then beyond earshot of the introspective confidences of modern literature, and to lose ourselves in the gracious worldliness of Chaucer. Here was a healthy and hearty man, so genuine that he need not ask whether he were genuine or no, so sincere as quite to forget his own sincerity, so truly pious that he could be happy in the best world that God chose to make, so humane that he loved even the foibles of his kind. . . . There is no touch of cynicism in all he wrote. . . . One of the world's three or four great story-tellers, he was also one of the best versifiers that ever made English trip and sing with a gayety that seems careless, but where every foot beats time to the tune of the thought. . . . He reconciled, in the harmony of his verse, the English bluntness with the dignity and elegance of the less homely Southern speech. . . . When I remember Chaucer's malediction upon his scrivener, and consider that by far the larger proportion of his verses (allowing always for change of pronunciation) are perfectly accordant with our present accentual system, I cannot believe that he ever wrote an imperfect line. . . . His best tales run on like one of our inland rivers, sometimes hastening a little and turning upon themselves in eddies that dimple without retarding the current; sometimes loitering smoothly, while here and there a quiet thought, a tender feeling, a pleasant image, a golden-hearted verse, opens quietly as a water-lily, to float on the surface without breaking it into ripple. . . . There is something in him of the disinterestedness that made the Greeks masters in art. His phrase is never importunate. His simplicity is that of elegance, not of poverty. The quiet unconcern with which he says his best things is peculiar to him among English poets, though Goldsmith, Addison, and Thackeray have approached it in prose. He prattles inadvertantly away, and all the while, like the princess in the story, lets fall a pearl at every other word.—LOWELL, JAMES RUSSELL, 1870-90, *Chaucer, Prose Works, Riverside ed., vol.* III, *pp.* 291, 293, 325, 336, 338, 355, 356.

There is no majesty, no stately march of numbers, in his poetry, still less is there of fire, rapidity, or conciseness.—BRYANT, WILLIAM CULLEN, 1870, *A New Library of Poetry and Song, Introduction, p.* 39.

He is like a precocious and poetical child, who mingles in his love-dreams quotations from his prayer-book and recollections of his alphabet. Even in the "Canterbury Tales" he repeats himself, unfolds artless developments, forgets to concentrate his passion or his idea. He begins a jest, and scarcely ends it. He dilutes a bright colouring in a monotonous stanza. His voice is like that of a boy breaking into manhood. At first a manly and firm accent is maintained, then a shrill sweet sound shows that his growth is not finished, and that his strength is subject to weakness.—TAINE, H. A., 1871, *History of English Literature, tr. Van Laun, vol.* I, *bk.* i, *ch.* iii, *p.* 131.

His range, is extremely limited, but within the limits his landscape is exquisitely fresh, natural, and true in spite of its being conventional. The fact is, though the elements of the scenery were ready made, the composition of them gave great scope to originality, and Chaucer being a man of unique individuality, could not adopt the landscape even of those poems which he translated without making alterations; and being an Englishman, could not write about the May morning without introducing its English peculiarities. Moreover, the delightful and simple familiarity of the poet with the meadows, brooks, and birds, and his love of them, has the effect of making every common aspect of nature new; the May morning is transfigured by his enjoyment of it; the grass of the field is seen as those in Paradise beheld it; the dew lies on our heart as we go forth with the poet in the dawning, and the wind blows past our ear like the music of an old song heard in the days of childhood. Half this power lies in the sweet simplicity of the words and in the pleasant flowing of the metre.—BROOKE, STOPFORD A., 1871, *The Descriptive Poetry of Chaucer, Macmillan's Magazine, vol.* 24, *p.* 269.

There can be no better testimony to the true greatness of the old poet than that half a thousand years after the age in which he wrote he is held in higher estimation than ever; that, whatever intermissions of his popularity there may have been in times that cared nothing for, as they knew little of, the great Romantic School to which he belonged, and that were wholly incapable of understanding the very language in which he expressed and transcribed his genius, he this day speaks with increasing force and power. Through all the obsoletenesses of his language, and all the lets and impediments to a full enjoyment of his melody caused by our ignorance of fourteenth-century English, through all the conventional and social differences which separate his time from ours, we yet recognize a profoundly human soul, with a marvellous power of speech. We are discovering that he is not only a great poet, but one of our greatest. It is not too much to say that the better acquaintance with Chaucer's transcendent merits is gradually establishing the conviction that not one among all poets deserves so well as he the second place.—HALES, JOHN W., 1873-84, *Notes and Essays on Shakespeare, p.* 57.

That tenderest, brightest, most humourful sweet soul, of all the great poets of the world, whom a thousand Englishmen out of every thousand and one are content to pass by with a shrug and a sneer: "How can one find time to read a man who makes 'poore' two syllables?

Life is not long enough for that."—FURNIVALL, FREDERICK JAMES, 1873, *Recent Work at Chaucer, Macmillan's Magazine, vol.* 27, *p.* 383.

In Spring, when the breast of the lime-grove gathers
Its roseate cloud; when the flushed streams sing,
And the mavis tricks her in gayer feathers;
Read Chaucer then; for Chaucer is spring!
On lonely evenings in dull Novembers
When rills run choked under skies of lead,
And on forest-hearths the year's last embers
Wind-heaped and glowing, lie, yellow and red,
Read Chaucer still! In his ivied beaker
With knights, and wood-gods, and saints embossed
Spring hides her head till the wintry breaker
Thunders no more on the far-off coast.

—DE VERE, AUBREY, 1874, *Chaucer, Alexander the Great and Other Poems, p.* 348.

It is not on Nature as a great whole, much less as an abstraction, that his thought usually dwells. It is the outer world in its most concrete forms and objects, with which he delights to interweave his poetry—the homely scenes of South England, the oaks and other forest trees, the green meadows, quiet fields, and comfortable farms, as well as the great castles where the nobles dwelt. One associates him with the green lanes and downs of Surrey and Kent, their natural copsewoods and undulating greenery. I know not that the habitual forms of English landscape, those which are most rural and most unchanged, have ever since found a truer poet, one who so brings before the mind the scene and the spirit of it uncolored by any intervention of his own thought or sentiment.—SHAIRP, JOHN CAMPBELL, 1877, *On Poetic Interpretation of Nature, p.* 171.

There died with that old century's death,
I wot, five hundred years ago,
One whose blithe heart, whose morning art,
Made England's Castaly to flow.
He in whose song that fount we know,
With every tale the sky-larks tell,
Had right, Saint Bennet's wall below
To slumber well.

—STEDMAN, EDMUND CLARENCE, 1879, "*Y^e Tombe of Y^e Poet Chaucer,*" *Poems Now First Collected, p.* 10.

It is unlikely that his personality will ever become more fully known than it is at present; nor is there anything in respect of which we seem to see so clearly into his inner nature as with regard to these twin predilections, to which he remains true in all his works and in all his moods. While the study of books was his chief passion, nature was his chief joy and solace; while his genius enabled him to transfuse what he read in the former, what came home to him in the latter was akin to that genius itself. . . . There is nothing that can fairly be called rugged in the verse of Chaucer. . . . Our first great English poet was also our first English love-poet, properly so called. . . . In his poetry there is *life*. . . . The legacy which Chaucer left to our literature was to fructify in the hands of a long succession of heirs; and it may be said, with little fear of contradiction, that at no time has his fame been fresher and his influence upon our poets—and upon our painters as well as our poets—more perceptible than at the present day. —WARD, ADOLPHUS WILLIAM, 1880, *Chaucer, (English Men of Letters), pp.* 162, 172, 175, 188, 189.

Chaucer is not one of the great classics. His poetry transcends and effaces, easily and without effort, all the romance-poetry of Catholic Christendom; it transcends and effaces all the English poetry contemporary with it, it transcends and effaces all the English poetry subsequent to it down to the age of Elizabeth. Of such avail is poetic truth of substance, in its natural and necessary union with poetic truth of style. And yet, I say, Chaucer is not one of the great classics. He has not their accent. . . . However we may account for its absence, something is wanting, then, to the poetry of Chaucer, which poetry must have before it can be placed in the glorious class of the best. And there is no doubt what that something is. It is the *σπουδαιότης*, the high and excellent seriousness, which Aristotle assigns as one of the grand virtues of poetry. The substance of Chaucer's poetry, his view of things and his criticism of life, has largeness, freedom, shrewdness, benignity; but it has not this high seriousness. Homer's criticism of life has it, Dante's has it, Shakespeare's has it. It is this chiefly which gives to our spirits what they can rest upon; and with the increasing demands of our modern ages upon poetry, this virtue of giving us what we can rest upon will be more and more highly esteemed. A voice from the slums of Paris, fifty or sixty years after Chaucer, the voice of poor Villon out of his life of riot and crime, has at its happy moments (as, for instance, in the last stanza of "La Belle Heaulmière") more of this important poetic virtue of seriousness than all the productions of Chaucer. But its apparition in Villon, and in men like Villon, is fitful; the greatness of the great poets, the power of their criticism of life, is that their virtue is sustained. To our praise, therefore, of Chaucer as a poet there must be this limitation; he lacks the high seriousness of the great classics, and therewith an important part of their virtue. Still, the main fact for us to bear in mind about Chaucer is his sterling value according to that real estimate which we firmly adopt for all poets. He has poetic truth of substance, though he has not high poetic seriousness, and corresponding to his truth of substance he has an exquisite virtue of style and manner. With him is born our real poetry. —ARNOLD, MATTHEW, 1880, *The English Poets, ed. Ward, General Introduction, vol.* I, *p.* xxxiv, *Essays in Criticism, Scond Series, p.* 31.

Let us Shakspere-worshippers not forget that Chaucer lived two centuries earlier than Shakspere, and had to deal with a crude poetic language which Shakspere found a magnificent song-instrument, all in tune and ready to his hand. Let us not forget that Shakspere is first poet and Chaucer second poet, and that these two repose alone, apart, far, far above any spot where later climbers have sunk to rest. And this adjuration is here made with a particular and unequivocal solemnity, because of the conviction that we expressed in the outset of this subject, that the estimate of these two poets which would have them like enough to be father and son, involves deeper matter than mere criticism.—LANIER, SIDNEY, 1880? *Paul H. Hayne's Poetry, Music and Poetry, p.* 201.

The two greatest English poets, Chaucer and Shakespeare. . . . Nobody who has read Chaucer through, or who has fairly read through only the Canterbury Tales, can look upon Chaucer as an animal poet. No man before Shakespeare dwelt as Chaucer dwelt upon the beauty of a perfect womanhood, the daisy was for him its emblem, with its supposed power to heal inward bruises, its modest beauty, its heart of gold, and its white crown of innocence. He is not less deeply because unaffectedly religious. His absolute kindliness made part of his perception of the highest truth, and it increased greatly the power of his teaching. —MORLEY, HENRY, 1881, *Of English Literature in the Reign of Victoria, p.* 14.

Chaucer imported so many "wagonfuls" of French words into our language, that he was nicknamed "The French Brewer." —MATHEWS, WILLIAM, 1881, *Literary Style, and other Essays, p.* 326.

He was the Father of English Versification as he was the Father of English Poetry. Five centuries have passed since he created it, and it remains to-day as he left it. Nothing has been taken from it, and nothing added to it, except the mighty line which Surrey was the first to use in English Verse. He gave us the seven-line stanza, so admirable for narrative purposes, and he gave us the heroic couplet. . . . A great poet by virtue of his natural gifts, he was the greatest of narrative poets by virtue of his knowledge of mankind. His range was large, and his sympathies quick. Idealist and realist, nothing was too high or too low for his pencil,—nothing too tragic or too comic. His art was conscious and profound. His details never degenerated into the catalogue manner of the metrical romances, for though abundant, they were always subordinated to the main effect. He attained Style. The general impression left by his poetry is, that it was sung when the world was fresher and fairer than it is now, when man was younger, and healthier, and happier, when the sun was brighter and the moon clearer, when the Spring was longer, the daisies thicker, and the lark sang endlessly at the gate of heaven,—a world of childhood, and innocence, and love,—the Golden Age.—STODDARD, RICHARD HENRY 1883, *English Verse, Chaucer to Burns, Introduction, pp.* xviii, xxi.

If he resembles Shakespeare in his cheerfulness, and power of describing character and telling a story, he resembles Wordsworth in his freedom from mere "poetic phraseology."—FARRAR, FREDERICK WILLIAM, 1883, *With The Poets, Preface, p.* v.

Our father, lord long since of lordly rhyme
. .
Each year that England clothes herself with May,
She takes thy likeness on her. Time hath spun
Fresh raiment all in vain and strange array
For earth and man's new spirit, fain to shun
Things past for dreams of better to be won,
Through many a century since thy funeral chime
Rang, and men deemed it death's most direful crime
To have spared not thee for very love or shame;
And yet, while mists round last year's memories climb,
Our father Chaucer, here we praise thy name . . .
the soul sublime
That sang for song's love more than lust of fame.

—SWINBURNE, ALGERNON CHARLES, 1884, *On a Country Road, A Midsummer Holiday, pp.* 9, 10.

Chaucer is a pre-Râphaelite. There is a particularity in every scene, and it was shrewdly guessed by Pope that each was a copy of some original. Each garden is one in which he has walked; each flower is a primrose or a columbine.—WASHBURN, EMELYN W., 1884, *Studies in Early English Literature, p.* 75.

There has been of late years a striking revival of popularity in the case of Barbour's great contemporary Chaucer. Let us hope that your countryman may have a similar fortune. But we cannot easily rank any one with Chaucer. For variety, for power of description, for touching, tender appeals to the feelings, for genuine though sometimes rather coarse fun, and for delineation of character, he occupies a place in the world of poetry such as few can aspire to.—NORTHCOTE, HENRY STAFFORD, EARL OF IDDESLEIGH, 1885, *Desultory Reading, p.* 51.

Is always of the fourteenth century; he understood man, individually, well enough, but when he tries to describe man collectively, man in some other age, he is still only mediæval. He has only got the mediæval standpoint.—GALTON, ARTHUR, 1885, *Urbana Scripta, p.* 11.

It is through no lack of love and reverence for the name of Chaucer that I must question his right, though the first narrative poet of England, to stand on that account beside her first dramatic, her first epic, or her first lyric poet. But, being certainly unprepared to admit his equality with Shakespeare, with Milton, and with Shelley, I would reduce Mr. Rossetti's mystic four to the old sacred number of three.—SWINBURNE, ALGERNON CHARLES, 1886, *Short Notes on English Poets, Miscellanies, p.* 2.

I have spoken of Chaucer's humor, and hinted at its occasional coarseness, referring briefly to the over-crowding of that age; to the absence of night-dresses; to the fact that, even in highly respectable houses, many grown-up people of different sexes occupied one sleeping room; and to the consequences, as reflected in ordinary sentiment and speech at this common familiarity with the baser functions of animal being. I merely suggest the apology. The question is not a nice one, and I do not care to pursue it. The best that can be said for Chaucer is that his coarseness is his worst offense; there is no *double entendre*, no nasty hint, no unclean innuendò. His liberties are like the unconscious exposure of an infant rolling on the carpet.—FRASER, JOHN, 1887, *Chaucer to Longfellow, p.* 111.

Chaucer might be styled, although living in a rude age, the poet of the affections,—few writers having ever excelled him for his animated portraits, as well as for beautiful passages relating to or inspired by woman.—SAUNDERS, FREDERICK, 1887, *The Story of Some Famous Books, p.* 21.

Æschylus flattered neither archon nor mob; Chaucer is almost as frank as Burns.—NICHOL, JOHN, 1888, *Francis Bacon, His Life and Philosophy, pt.* i, *p.* 25.

Great poet as he was, there is nothing of the prophet about him—the *mens divinior* is absent. With Dante and Petrarch he justly ranks in what has been called the triumvirate of the mediæval poets; but his work shows no sign whatever of their patriotic passion, none of their interest in statesmanship and politics: to take a phrase from the *Commedia*, he cannot discern even the tower of the heavenly City. Thus, although Chaucer heads magnificently the long list of our poets, and has never wanted some of the honour which was paid to Homer in his own land, yet I think he must be regarded as essentially retrospective; nay, in a certain sense, if I may venture on the word, superficial. In his brilliant criticism of the humours of his day, in his freshness and lucidity of style, in the movement of his narrative, he is modern. But in the choice of subjects, in the general matter of his tale, in the feelings with which he seems to look upon life, he scarcely rises above the showy court-atmosphere of Edward's reign. It is less the dawn of modern ways in thought and literature which we see in him, than the gorgeous sunset of chivalry:—his poetry reflects the earlier rays of the Italian Renaissance, but its massive substance is essentially mediæval. . . . He is among our greatest poets; but no other among them keeps so steadily to the mere average level—one might almost hint, the *bourgeois* level, of his time, as Chaucer; he is of his age, not above it.—PALGRAVE, FRANCIS TURNER, 1888, *Chaucer and the Italian Renaissance, The Nineteenth Century, vol.* XXIV, *pp.* 344, 355.

How did he manage in his old age to keep such perfect youth and heartiness? One never feels as if he were old. The heart springs up and sings in every line. His gayety is irrepressible. The world is always young to him. His humor is so sly and sharp; his pathos so tender and refined; his gladness so pulsing and contagious; his romance so chivalrous; his sympathies so large; that he carries one away with him at his "own sweet will." Yet I hear many persons say they cannot read him. His quaint spelling disturbs them, and they find his verses halting and unfinished. . . . I know no poet whose verse is to me more charming, more full of exquisite cadence and variety. He prided himself on the exactness of his feet and measure. One must know, to be sure, how to read and accent it—but that is learned with so little trouble; and when one has caught the inflections, the rhythm is beautiful. Besides, its very quaintness lends it a certain charm to me. How terribly he loses in Dryden's transcripts! all the soul and heart is gone.—STORY, WILLIAM WETMORE, 1890, *Conversations in a Studio, vol.* II, *p.* 402.

Editions of the poems of Chaucer, in whole or in part, are coming out constantly in England, in Germany, and in America. It is well within bounds to say that he has been more read and studied during the past twenty years than during the previous two hundred. If this indicated nothing else, it shows the existence of a large class to whom Chaucer is something more than a name. A generation which could scarcely be spoken of as knowing him at all has been supplanted by a generation with which he is becoming a familiar and favorite author. . . . I am not claiming for Chaucer that he is one of the few supremest poets of the race. His station is near them, but he is not of them. Yet, whatever may be the rank we accord him among the writers of the world's chief literatures, the position he holds in his own literature is one that can no longer be shaken by criticism or disturbed by denial. Time has set its final seal upon the verdict of his own age, and the refusal to acknowledge his greatness has now no effect upon the opinion we have of the poet himself, but upon our opinion of those who are unable to appreciate his poetry. To one alone among the writers of our own literature is he inferior. Nor even by him has he been surpassed in every way. There are characteristics in which he has no superior, and, it may be right to add, in which he has no equal. . . . There is one particular in which his merits in reference to the literature are simply transcendent. He overcame its natural tendencies to a dull seriousness which could sometimes be wrought into vigorous invective, but had little power to fuse the spiritual element of poetry with the purely intellectual. Into the stolid English nature, which may be earnest, but evinces an almost irresistable inclination toward heaviness, he brought a lightness, a grace, a delicacy of fancy, a refined sportiveness even upon the most unrefined themes, which had never been known before save on the most infinitesimal scale, and has not been known too much since. Nor is this the only distinctive characteristic in which Chaucer excels. There is no other English author so absolutely free, not merely from effort, but from the remotest suggestion of effort. Shakspeare mounts far higher; yet with him there are times when we seem to hear the flapping of the wings, to be vaguely conscious that he is lashing his imagination to put forth increased exertions. But in Chaucer no slightest trace of strain is to be detected.—LOUNSBURY, THOMAS R., 1891, *Studies in Chaucer, vol.* I, *p.* xi, *vol.* III, *pp.* 443, 444.

There has certainly never been an English poet so far in advance of his times, and whose loss to poetry was therefore so absolutely irreparable, as Chaucer.—TEN BRINK, BERNHARD, 1892, *History of English Literature, (Wyclif, Chaucer, Earliest Drama, Renaissance,) tr. Robinson, p.* 209.

Chaucer's verse to us is *now* as veritably dialect as to that old time it *was* the chastest English; and even then his materials were essentially dialect when his song was at best pitch.—RILEY, JAMES WHITCOMB, 1892, *Dialect in Literature, The Forum, vol.* 14, *p.* 465.

To-day Chaucer has more readers and more lovers than at any previous time. . . . As an artist, a master of his craft, Chaucer has no superior, not Shakspere himself. The wonderful music in which a great thought finds expression in inevitable words came to him but seldom; but for sustained beauty, for continuous charm, his verse has never been surpassed. Alone among English poets he possesses the art of narration in its perfection. Save in one or two early poems he is never for a moment dull, and he never cloys his readers with excess of sweetness. We feel that he is the most direct of story-tellers, and yet his narrative is never bald or thin; he has always ready at hand a touch of philosophy, a stroke of humour, or a vivid description, with which to keep up our interest and attention. The humour has never been surpassed for quaintness and subtlety. When can we be sure that we have exhausted it, or that beneath some seemingly simple phrase there is not waiting us a quiet jest? The vivid colour of his descriptions illumine Chaucer's pages with the brightness of a mediæval manuscript. But of this most human, most lovable of English poets, it is idle, indeed, to try to summarise the just meed of praise.—POLLARD, ALFRED W., 1893, *Chaucer, (Literature Primers), pp.* 2, 133.

It is hard to conceive a poet who had steeped his soul in the joy of the dawn, confining himself to the car of Phœbus or the rosy fingers of Aurora. Yet Chaucer does not describe such moments in the natural method, nor is he drawn to them. No; the early morning, when matters are settled, when we are sure of a number of hours of good, steady daylight, is the time he loves. Even when the idea of motion would seem to be inherent in the object described, he evades it. His delight in the fresh country is summed up in his love for his favorite "briddes." Allusions to them are constant in his poems; but for all that he gives of their airiness and lightness, these winged spirits of the breeze incarnate might just as well be little birds of wood. They sit on branches and converse politely; they do not fly, they simply change their position; one is sure that they would settle with a thud. Never once, so far as I know, does Chaucer note the characteristic flight of a bird. . . . The inevitable progression of years leaves no mark even on the outward man. Helen returns to the home she had left thirty years before, still calm in eternal beauty; Palamon and Arcite, an indefinite number of "years or tweye" having elapsed, fight for Emelye with all the ardor of youth. Neither is there any change of the inner nature. Circumstances may storm and rage and batter; extremes of fortune succeed each other with startling rapidity; death threatens, love encircles, power crowns,—yet the hero remains throughout passive and unmoved; as he was in the beginning, so he emerges at the end. Griselda the girl receives with meek brow and folded hands the summons to wed her feudal lord; with meek brow and folded hands Griselda the matron welcomes her husband's bride. Years have passed by, filled with strange and bitter experience; but they have not affected her,—she remains a constant quantity. — SCUDDER, VIDA D., 1895, *The Life of the Spirit in the Modern English Poets, pp.* 17, 23.

After all is said and done, we, with our average life of three-score years and ten, are the heirs of all the poetry of all the ages. We must do our best in our allotted time, and Chaucer is but one of the poets. He did not write for specialists in his own age, and his main value for succeeding ages resides, not in his vocabulary, nor in his inflections, nor in his indebtedness to foreign originals, nor in the metrical uniformities or anomalies that may be discovered in his poems; but in his *poetry*. Other things are accidenttal; his poetry is essential. Other interests—historical, philological, antiquarian—must be recognized; but the poetical, or (let us say) the spiritual, interest stands first and far ahead of all others.—QUILLER-COUCH, A. T., 1895, *Adventures in Criticism, p.* 6.

I may fairly class Chaucer among my passions, for I read him with that sort of personal attachment I had for Cervantes, who resembled him in a certain sweet and cheery humanity. But I do not allege this as the reason, for I had the same feeling for Pope, who was not like either of them. Kissing goes by favor, in literature as in life, and one cannot quite account for one's passions in either; what is certain is, I liked Chaucer and I did not like Spenser; possibly there was an affinity between reader and poet, but if there was I should be at a loss to name it, unless it was the liking for reality, and the sense of mother earth in human life. . . . Compared with the meaner poets the greater are the cleaner, and Chaucer was probably safer than any other English poet of his time, but I am not going to pretend that there are not things in Chaucer which one would be the better for not reading; and so far as these words of mine shall be taken for counsel, I am not willing that they should unqualifiedly praise him. . . . I loved my Chaucer too well, I hope, not to get some good from the best in him; and my reading of criticism had taught me how and where to look for the best, and to know it when I had found it.—HOWELLS, WILLIAM DEAN, 1895, *My Literary Passions, pp.* 108, 110, 111.

If Langland may be regarded in some respects as the Nævius of English poetry, Chaucer is certainly its Ennius. . . . Ennius taught his countrymen how to refine their native genius by the use of Greek forms; Chaucer succeeded in expanding the vigorous but limited range of the Anglo-Saxon imagination, by bringing it into touch with the life and art of continental Europe. In the poetical models which he imported from France, and in the poetical themes suggested to him by Italy, he found a medium for reflecting the English conception of the manners and fashions of chivalry. But by his instinctive sympathy with that deeper and more enduring movement, afterwards known as the Renaissance, he may also be said to have invented a national mode of thought, which imparted a character of its own to the whole course of English poetry. . . . It is certain that Chaucer was the first Englishman to *write* metrical stories for their own sake. . . . Looking back over this survey of Chaucer's poetical progress, we find scarcely one of his works in which we are not called upon to admire the presence of a powerful and penetrating genius. When the language came into his hands it was rude and inharmonious, inadequate to express either the complex ideas of philosophy or the finer shades of character; when he left it it had been endowed with a copious vocabulary, refined syntax, musical numbers; it was fitted to become the vehicle of a noble literature.—COURTHOPE, W. J., 1895, *A History of English Poetry, vol.* I, *pp.* 247, 286, 296.

In 1500 his popularity was at its height. During the latter part of the sixteenth century it began to decline. From that date till the end of William III.'s reign—in spite of the influence which he undoubtedly exercised over Spenser, and in spite of the respectful allusions to him in Sidney, Puttenham, Drayton, and Milton—his fame had become rather a tradition than a reality. In the following age the good-natured tolerance of Dryden was succeeded by the contempt of Addison and the supercilious patronage of Pope. Between 1700 and 1782 nothing seemed more probable than that the writings of the first of England's narrative poets would live chiefly in the memory of antiquarians. In little more than half a century afterwards we find him placed, with Shakspeare and Milton, on the highest pinnacle of poetic renown.—COLLINS, JOHN CHURTON, 1895, *Essays and Studies, p.* 107.

In many ways he was still in bondage to the mediæval, and wholly uncritical, tradition. One classic, we may almost say, was as good to him as another. He seems to have placed Ovid on a line with Virgil; and the company in his House of Fame is undeniably mixed. His judgments have the healthy instinct of the consummate artist. They do not show, as those of his master, Petrarch, unquestionably do, the discrimination and the tact of the born critic.—VAUGHAN, C.E., 1896, *English Literary Criticism, Introduction*, p. ix.

The sweetness, the wholesomeness, the kindliness, the sincerity, the humor, and the humanity of Chaucer can hardly be overpraised.—BATES, ARLO, 1897, *Talks on the Study of Literature*, p. 152.

It is known now that to all intents and purposes the heroic couplet had been brought to a high degree of perfection by Chaucer about 250 years before Waller had written a line.—TOVEY, DUNCAN C., 1897, *Reviews and Essays in English Literature*, p. 93.

Chaucer was to him* a kindred spirit, as a lover of nature and as a word-painter of character: and he enjoyed reading him aloud more than any poet except Shakespeare and Milton.—TENNYSON, HALLAM, 1897, *Alfred Lord Tennyson, A Memoir, vol.* II, *p.* 284.

Chaucer continues to be one of the great masters of verse in the literature, Dryden's monstrous chatter about the progress of English verse to the contrary notwithstanding. . . . In the use of the rhyming couplet, Chaucer surpasses immeasurably both Dryden and Pope. His thought is not so paddocked therein. In his hands, it is not the "rocking horse," as Keats characterizes it, which it is in the hands of Dryden and Pope. . . . His sensitiveness as to melody did not allow him to run into a mechanical uniformity.—CORSON, HIRAM, 1897, *ed. Selections from Chaucer's Canterbury Tales, Introduction, p.* lii.

The prosody of Chaucer's later and more elaborate works is not, as was so long supposed, an arbitrary or a loose one. Even Dryden knew no better than to discover in the verse of the "Canterbury Tales" "a rude sweetness of a Scotch tune"; it is obvious that he was quite unable to scan it. It was, on the contrary, not merely not "rude," but an artistic product of the utmost delicacy and niceness, a product which borrowed something from the old national measure, but was mainly an introduction into English of the fixed prosodies of the French and the Italians, the former for octosyllabic, the latter for decasyllabic verse. The rules of both, but especially the latter, are set, and of easy comprehension; to learn to read Chaucer with a fit appreciation of the liquid sweetness of his versification is as easy an accomplishment as to learn to scan classical French verse, or easier. But it must be remembered that, in its polished art, it was a skill fully known only to its founder, and that, with Chaucer's death, the power to read his verses as he wrote them seems immediately to have begun to disappear. Chaucer gave English poetry an admirable prosody, but it was too fine a gift to be appreciated by those for whom it was created.—GOSSE, EDMUND, 1897, *Short History of Modern English Literature, p.* 24.

The notion of Chaucer as having flooded the language with French words in contradistinction to the sound Saxon vocabulary of his contemporary Langland died hard, and perhaps simulates life even yet; but its obstinacy in surviving is merely Partridgean.—SAINTSBURY, GEORGE, 1898, *A Short History of English Literature, p.* 110.

Chaucer's philosophy is of a sane, practical mind. Nature is delightful, but it is the quiet, reposeful nature of southern England. That the sea or the storms or any exhibition of great force attracted or excited his imagination I can nowhere find. Men and women are entertaining. His idea of virtue is temperance, courage, fidelity to comrades. He hates a cheat or a coward. He has a great deal of tolerance for the faults of others, because men are so interesting to him that he can forgive a good deal of vulgarity for the sake of the unadulterated human nature it illustrates. He detests a hypocrite, especially one who trades in virtue or religion; but it seems to be with an artistic quite as much as an ethical hatred that he regards hypocrisy. He makes his villians physically repulsive, and dangerous only to dupes of little discernment. The profound selfishness and cruelty of Iago covered with an exterior of soldier-like frankness is beyond his horizon. He does not scrutinize moral phenomena very closely, nor does the misery of men condemned to a life of hopeless toil oppress his imagination.—JOHNSON, CHARLES F., 1898, *Elements of Literary Criticism, p.* 105.

*Alfred, Lord Tennyson.

John Gower

1325?–1408

Born about 1325: died in the priory of St. Mary Overies, Southwark, 1408. An English poet. Little is known of his early life, but he appears to have lived in Kent and to have been a man of wide reading. He was well known at court in his later years. His principal work, the "Confessio Amantis" (written in English, probably in 1386), was originally dedicated to Richard II., but in 1394 he changed the dedication to Henry of Lancaster (afterward Henry IV.). Caxton printed it in 1483. Among his other works are "Speculum Meditantis" (written in French, recently found) and "Vox Clamantis" (a poem written in Latin, begun in 1381). After the accession of Henry VI., Gower, then an old man, added a supplement, the "Tripartite Council." It treats of occurrences of the time, and the strength of its aspirations and teaching caused Chaucer to call him "the moral Gower." "Ballades" and other poems (mostly in French) were printed in 1818.—SMITH, BENJAMIN E., *ed.* 1894-97, *The Century Cyclopedia of Names p.* 451.

PERSONAL

Having written on the vanities of the world, I am about to leave the world. In my last verse I write that I am dying. Let him that comes after me write more discreetly than I have done, for now my hand and pen are silencing. I can do nothing of any value now with my hands. The labour of prayers is all that I can bear. I pray then with my tears, living, but blind. O God! protect the future reigns which thou hast established, and give me to share thy holy light.—GOWER, JOHN, 1400, *MS. Cot. Lib. Tib. A* 4.

Bale makes him *Equitem auratum & Poetam Laureatum*, proving both from his Ornaments on his Monumental Statue in Saint Mary Overies, Southwark. Yet he appeareth there neither laureated nor hederated Poet (except the leaves of the Bayes and Ivy be withered to nothing since the erection of the Tomb) but only rosated, having a Chaplet of four Roses about his head. Another Author* unknighteth him, allowing him only a plain Esquire, though in my apprehension the Colar of S.S.S. about his neck speak him to be more. Besides (with submission to better judgments) that Colar hath rather a Civil than Military relation, proper to persons in places of Judicature; which makes me guess this Gower some Judge in his old age, well consisting with his original education. — FULLER, THOMAS, 1662, *The Worthies of England, ed. Nichols, vol.* II, *p.* 513.

This tripartite work is represented by three volumes on Gower's curious tomb in the conventual church of Saint Mary Overee in Southwark, now remaining in its ancient state; and this circumstance furnishes me with an obvious opportunity of adding an anecdote relating to our poet's munificence and piety, which ought not to be omitted. Although a poet, he largely contributed to rebuild that church in its present elegant form, and to render it a beautiful pattern of the lighter Gothic architecture: at the same time he founded, at his tomb, a perpetual chantry. —WARTON, THOMAS, 1778-81, *History of English Poetry, sec.* xix.

In the life of this poet, almost the only certain incident seems to be his sepulchral monument: and even this it had been necessary to repair after the malignity of the iconoclasts; and, of the three sculptured volumes which support the poet's head, a single one only has been opened by the world; for the tomb has perpetuated what the press has not. —DISRAELI, ISAAC, 1841, *Gower, Amenities of Literature.*

CONFESSIO AMANTIS

1386?

And who so ever in redynge of this worke doth consider it well, shall fynde that it is plentifully stuffed and fournished with manifolde eloquent reasons, sharpe and quicke argumentes, and examples of great aucthoritie, perswadynge unto vertue, not only taken out of the poets, oratours, historie-writers, and philosophers, but also out of the holy scripture. There is to my dome no man but that he maie by readinge of this worke get righte great knowledge, as well for the understandynge of many and divers auctours, whose reasons, sayenges, and histories, are translated in to this worke, as for the pleintie of English words and vulgars,

*Stowe.

beside the furtherance of the life to vertue.—BERTHELETTE, THOMAS, 1532, *ed. Gower's Confessio Amantis, Dedication.*

As Gower wrote much in French, it is but natural, that there should be in his English a large proportion of Norman-French words; even in the spelling, in which he adheres, if we go back to the more ancient MSS, to the form used by the French writers of his day. Yet the Saxon ingredient in his language is as large as in the works of his great contemporary, and comprises a considerable number of words, which at present are either obsolete, or have altogether changed their meaning. There are very few examples of alliteration and other characteristics of pure Saxonism. . . . His sentences are often diffuse, and ungrammatical; and it was evidently no easy task for him to compose this long poem in English.—PAULI, REINHOLD, 1856, *ed. Confessio Amantis, Introductory Essay, vol.* I, *pp.* XXXV, XXXVI.

For the fashionable device of his poem Gower, infirm and elderly, cared little. To the best of his power he used it as a sort of earthwork from behind which he set himself the task of digging and springing a mine under each of the seven deadly sins.—MORLEY, HENRY, 1873, *First Sketch of English Literature, p.* 157.

The verse is smooth and fluent, but the reader feels it to be the product of literary skill. It wants what can be imparted only by an unconscious might back of the consciously active and trained powers.—CORSON, HIRAM, 1886, *An Introduction to the Study of Robert Browning's Poetry, p.* 6.

Old Classic, and Romance tales come into it, and are fearfully stretched out; and there are pedagogic Latin rubrics at the margin, and wearisome repititions, with now and then faint scent of prettinesses stolen from French *fabliaux*: but unless your patience is heroic, you will grow tired of him; and the monotonous, measured, metallic jingle of his best verse is provokingly like the "Caw-caw" of the prim, black raven. He had art, he had learning, he had good-will; but he could not weave words into the thrushlike melodies of Chaucer. Even the clear and beautiful type of the Bell & Daldy edition does not make him entertaining. You will tire before you are half through the Prologue, which is as long, and stiff as many a sermon. And if you skip to the stories, they will not win you to liveliness: Pauline's grace, and mishaps are dull; and the sharp, tragic twang about Gurmunde's skull, and the vengeance of Rosemunde (from the old legend which Paul the Deacon tells) does not wake one's blood.—MITCHELL, DONALD G., 1889, *English Lands Letters and Kings, From Celt to Tudor, p.* 128.

For if there be one indisputable fact in literary history, it is that Gower did not have the fame of Chaucer in his own age, and that he has never had it in any age that followed. Upon this matter enough has been said in the preceding pages to show that the reputation for good sense and good taste of the contemporaries of the two poets needs no defence upon this score. The same remark can be made of their immediate successors. Later times continue to bear testimony similar to that furnished by the earlier. The mere fact that no edition of the "Confessio Amantis" appeared form 1554 until 1857 disposes of itself of the fancy that Gower's popularity ever stood for a moment in rivalry with that of Chaucer. Caxton had, indeed, printed his poem. During the sixteenth century two other editions of it appeared. These were sufficient to supply the demand both for that time and for the three hundred years that followed.—LOUNSBURY, THOMAS R., 1891, *Studies in Chaucer, vol.* III, *p.* 70.

Clearly a work of this sort cannot be read through, and as "skipping" must be indulged in, the most sensible course is to peruse only the tales. These tales are introduced nominally as *exempla*, though, in many instances, Gower ignores the true moral and drags in an application which does not tally; but that is one more reason why the context should be neglected. . . . The "Confessio Amantis," however, is of considerable importance as the first collection of "novels" in English, and it is highly probable that its publication assisted, even more than the "Decameron," in determining the form of the "Canterbury Tales."—SNELL, F. J., 1899, *Periods of European Literature, The Fourteenth Century, pp.* 323, 324.

GENERAL

O moral Gower.

—CHAUCER, GEOFFREY, c 1380, *Troilus and Cresside*, v. 1856.

Vnto (the) impnis* of my maisteris dere,
Gowere and Chaucere, that on the steppis satt
Of rethorike quhill thai were lyvand here,
Superlatiue as poetis laureate,
In moralitee and eloquence ornate,
I recommend my buk in lynis sevin,
And eke thair saulis vn-to the blisse of hevin.

—JAMES I, 1423? *King's Quair*, s. 197.

Gower, that *first* garnisshed our Englisshe rude.—SKELTON, JOHN, c 1489, *Crowne of Laurell.*

O pensyfe herte, . . .
Remembre the of the trace and daunce
Of poetes olde wyth all the purveyaunce:
As morall Gower, whose sentencyous dewe
Adowne reflayreth with fayre golden bemes.

—HAWES, STEPHEN, 1506, *The Pastime of Pleasure, ed. Wright, cap.* xiv. *ss.* 3, 4.

And nere theim satte old morall Goore, with pleasaunte penne in hande, commendyng honeste love without luste, and pleasure without pride. Holinesse in the Cleargy without hypocrisie, no tyrannie in rulers, no falshode in Lawiers, no usurie in Marchauntes, no rebellion in the Commons and unitie emong kyngdomes. —BULLEIN, WILLIAM, 1564-73, *A Dialogue Both Pleasaunt and Pietifull, wherein is a Godlie Regiment against the Fever Pestilence, with a Consolation and Comforte against Death.*

The first of our English Poets that I haue heard of, was *Iohn Gower*, about the time of king *Rychard* the seconde, as it should seeme by certayne coniectures bothe a Knight, and questionlesse a singuler well learned man: whose workes I could wysh they were all whole and perfect among vs, for no doubt they contained very much deepe knowledge and delight: which may be gathered by his freend *Chawcer*, who speaketh of him oftentimes, in diuer(s) places of hys workes. —WEBBE, WILLIAM, 1586, *A Discourse of English Poetrie, ed. Arber, p.* 31.

Gower sauing for his good and graue moralities, had nothing in him highly to be commended, for his verse was homely and without good measure, his wordes strained much deale out of the French writers, his ryme wrested, and in his inuentions small subtillitie: the aplications of his moralities are the best in him, and yet those many times very grossely bestowed, neither doth the substance of his workes sufficiently aunswere the subtilitie of his titles.—PUTTENHAM, GEORGE, 1589, *The Arte of English Poesie, ed. Arber, p.* 76.

Enter Gower. *Before the Palace* of Antioch.

To sing a song of old was sung,
From ashes ancient Gower is come;
Assuming man's infirmities,
To glad your ear, and please your eyes.
It hath been sung at festivals,
On ember-eves, and holy ales;
And lords and ladies of their lives
Have read it for restoratives:
'Purpose to make men glorious;
Et quo antiquius, eo melius.
If you, born in these latter times,
When wit's more ripe, accept my rhymes,
And that to hear an old man sing,
May to your wishes pleasure bring,
I life would wish, and that I might
Waste it for you, like taper-light.

—SHAKESPEARE, WILLIAM?, 1609? *Pericles, Prologue.*

Gower being very gracious with King Henrie the fourth, in his time carried the name of the only poet; but his verses, to say truth, were poor and plaine, yet full of good and grave moralitie, but while he affected altogether the French phrase and words, made himself too obscure to his reader, beside his invention cometh far short of the promise of his titles.—PEACHAM, HENRY, 1622, *The Compleat Gentleman.*

That he was of all, the first polisher of his paternal tongue. For before his age the English language lay uncultivated, and almost entirely rude. Nor was there any one who had written any work in the vernacular tongue, worthy of an elegant reader. Therefore he thought it worth his while to apply a diligent culture, that thus the rude herbs being extirpated, the soft violet and the purple narcissus might grow instead of the thistle and thorns.—LELAND, JOHN, c 1550, *Commentarii de Scriptoribus Britannicis, p.* 415.

He was the first Refiner of our English Tongue, effecting much, but endeavouring more therein. Thus he who sees the Whelp of a Bear but half lickt, will commend it for a comely Creature, in comparison of what it was when first brought forth. Indeed Gower left our

*Hymns.

English Tongue *very bad*, but found it *very very bad*.—FULLER, THOMAS, 1662, *The Worthies of England, ed. Nichols, vol.* II, *p.* 513.

There is but little that is worth reading in Gower: he wants the spirit of poetry, and the descriptiveness, that are in Chaucer.—POPE, ALEXANDER, 1728-30, *Spence's Anecdotes, ed. Singer, p.* 16.

The first of our authours, who can be properly said to have written *English*, was Sir John Gower. —JOHNSON, SAMUEL, 1755, *Dictionary of the English Language.*

His education was liberal and uncircumscribed, his course of reading extensive, and he tempered his severer studies with a knowledge of life. By a critical cultivation of his native language, he laboured to reform its irregularities, and to establish an English style. In these respects he resembled his friend and cotemporary Chaucer: but he participated no considerable portion of Chaucer's spirit, imagination, and elegance. His language is tolerably perspicuous, and his versification often harmonious: but his poetry is of a grave and sententious turn. He has much good sense, solid reflection, and useful observation. But he is serious and didactic on all occasions: he preserves the tone of the scholar and the moralist on the most lively topics. For this reason he seems to have been characterised by Chaucer with the appellation of the Morall Gower. But his talent is not confined to English verse only. He wrote also in Latin; and copied Ovid's elegiacs with some degree of purity, and with fewer false quantities and corrupt phrases, than any of our countrymen had yet exhibited since the twelfth century. —WARTON, THOMAS, 1778-81, *The History of English Poetry, sec.* xix.

When in generous emulation of his contemporary, he felt impelled to write verses in his native tongue, he showed himself certainly not inferior in this new department of the poetic art, to what he had previously appeared in Latin and in French. He was not unworthy to be the fellow-labourer of Chaucer in the task of polishing our language; and there is a refinement of sentiment, and a gentle flow of expression in his English poetry, which sets him far above his successors of the fifteenth century.—GODWIN, WILLIAM, 1803, *Life of Geoffrey Chaucer, vol.* II, *p.* 12.

But Gower is not merely the moralist; he is also the genuine poet. Chaucer was his superior; but of all the authors who attempted narrative poetry in the fourteenth and fifteenth centuries, Gower may claim the seat nearest to his friend. . . Gower's mind had embraced the whole range of thought and study in that day. He had identified with his genius all the tales of the romances, as well as the knowledge of the academy; and he, and perhaps he only, could then combine so much ethical reasoning, so many interesting tales, such a power of riming, and such ability of narration. We must all feel, that in illustrating the use and effects of the virtues and vices of mankind by pleasing tales of life and fancy, instead of monstrous and enslaving legends, he contributed more to the improvement of society than any writer in England that had preceded him. He put English poetry into a better path than it had then visited; he gave it more imagery, feeling, dialogue, sentiment, and natural incident, than it had been connected with, until he wrote. He must therefore be allowed an honourable rank among the intellectual benefactors of his country, whether his actual writings be perused or forgotten. —TURNER, SHARON, 1814-23, *The History of England During the Middle Ages, vol.* V, *pp.* 259, 283.

His writings exhibit all the crude erudition and science of his age; a knowledge sufficient to have been the fuel of genius, if Gower had possessed its fire.— CAMPBELL, THOMAS, 1819, *Specimens of the British Poets.*

A vast interval must be made between Chaucer and any other English poet; yet Gower, his contemporary, though not, like him, a poet of Nature's growth, had some effect in rendering the language less rude, and exciting a taste for verse. If he never rises, he never sinks low: he is always sensible, polished, perspicuous, and not prosaic in the worst sense of the word.—HALLAM, HENRY, 1837-39, *Introduction to the Literature of Europe, pt.* i, *ch.* i, *par.* 51.

Side by side with Chaucer comes Gower, who is ungratefully disregarded too often, because side by side with Chaucer. He who rides in the king's chariot will miss the people's "hic est." Could Gower be considered apart, there might be found signs in him of an independent royalty, however his fate may seem to lie in waiting for ever in his brother's ante-chamber, like Napoleon's tame kings. To speak our mind, he has been much undervalued. He is nailed to a comparative degree; and everybody seems to make it a condition of speaking of him, that something be called inferior within him, and something superior out of him. He is laid down flat, as a dark background for "throwing out" Chaucer's lights; he is used as a *του στω* for leaping up into the empyrean of Chaucer's praise. This is not just nor worthy.—BROWNING, ELIZABETH BARRETT, 1842-63, *The Book of the Poets*, *p.* 115.

The reputation of Gower, which was, for a long time, above his merits, seems to be in some measure due to his connection with Chaucer, though he did not entertain the views of reform which Chaucer shared with the other great writers of that century whom we have just named. . . . Though not without power as a sentenious thinker, Gower gives little evidence of artistic skill, or of the possession of any of the higher attributes of the poet.—MARSH, GEORGE P., 1862, *The Origin and History of the English Language, etc.*, *pp.* 431, 438.

Gower has positively raised tediousness to the precision of science, he has made dullness an heirloom for the students of our literary history. As you slip to and fro on the frozen levels of his verse, which give no foothold to the mind, as your nervous ear awaits the inevitable recurrence of his rhyme, regularly pertinacious as the tick of an eight-day clock and reminding you of Wordsworth's

"Once more the ass did lengthen out
The hard, dry, seesaw of his horrible bray,"

you learn to dread, almost to respect, the powers of this indefatigable man. He is the undertaker of the fair mediæval legend, and his style has the hateful gloss, the seemingly unnatural length, of a coffin. Love, beauty, passion, nature, art, life, the natural and theological virtues,—there is nothing beyond his power to disenchant, nothing out of which the tremendous hydraulic press of his allegory (or whatever it is, for I am not sure if it be not something even worse) will not squeeze all feeling and freshness and leave it a juiceless pulp. It matters not where you try him, whether his story be Christian or pagan, borrowed from history or fable, you cannot escape him. Dip in at the middle or the end, dodge back to the beginning, the patient old man is there to take you by the button and go on with his imperturbable narrative.—LOWELL, JAMES RUSSELL, 1870-90, *Chaucer, Works, Riverside ed., vol.* III, *p.* 329.

Doubtless here and there he contains a remnant of brilliancy and grace. He is like an old secretary of a Court of Love, Andre le Chapelain or any other, who would pass the day in solemnly registering the sentences of ladies, and in the evening, partly asleep on his desk, would see in a half-dream their sweet smile and their beautiful eyes. The ingenious but exhausted vein of Charles of Orléans still flows in his French ballads. He has the same fine delicacy, almost a little finicky. The poor little poetics pring flows yet in thin transparent films under the smooth pebbles, and murmurs with a babble, pretty, but so weak that at times you cannot hear it. But dull is the rest!—TAINE, H. A., 1871, *History of English Literature, tr. Van Laun, vol.* I, *bk.* i, *ch.* iii, *p.* 136.

Gower is intrinsically a much less significant figure than Langland.—MINTO, WILLIAM, 1871-85, *Characteristics of English Poets, p.* 54.

Gower was prolix where Chaucer was garrulous, and where Chaucer merely nodded he was overcome with slumber. No one cares to awaken the moral Gower: he sleeps the sleep of the just.—STODDARD, RICHARD HENRY, 1883, *English Verse, Chaucer to Burns, Introduction, p.* xxiv.

He undoubtedly lacks the poet's inspiration, but he claims to be nothing more than a moralist, an enthusiastic student of classical and mediæval literature, keenly alive to the failings of his own age. His varied erudition, his employment in his writings of the English language, in spite of his facility in both French and Latin, his simplicity and directness as a story-teller who is no servile imitator of his authorities, give his "Confessio" an historical interest which the frozen levels' of its verse with "the clocklike tick of its rhymes" cannot destroy. In his French "balades" Gower reached a higher poetic standard. He shows much metrical skill, and portrays love's various phases with the poet's tenderness and sympathy. The literary quality of "Vox Clamantis" is not great. It is marred by false quantities and awkward constructions; but its high moral tone, and its notices of contemporary society, give it an important place in historical literature. —LEE, SIDNEY, 1890, *Dictionary of National Biography, vol.* XX, *p.* 304.

His poetic talents were rather tame; he had a particularly receptive nature, and a decided mastery in the arrangement and form of verse, but was inclined to devote his powers to subjects that had no relation whatever to poetry.—TEN BRINK, BERNHARD, 1892, *History of English Literature, (Wyclif, Chaucer, Earliest Drama, Renaissance), tr. Robinson, p.* 39.

He was wholly conservative, wholly mediæval. He was a man of great learning and with considerable sense of style, but he had no instinct for variety. His English verse is fluent and harmonious, his language lucid, and even forcible at times, but he has no touch of brilliancy, no play of fancy, still less any imagination. He is earnest, sententious, and grave; he is never profound.—HEATH, H. FRANK, 1894, *Social England, ed. Traill, vol.* II, *p.* 228.

And yet to this poor, prosy old poet was granted the supreme vision of that age: "One man, if he behave well, is worth more than planets and stars to Him who wields them all."—WHITE, GREENOUGH, 1895, *Outline of the Philosophy of English Literature, The Middle Ages, p.* 105.

An absence of critical judgment, at which it is needless to affect surprise, led the contemporaries and successors of Chaucer to mention almost upon equal terms with him his friend and elder John Gower. To modern criticism this comparison has seemed, what indeed it is, preposterous, and we have now gone a little too far in the opposite direction. Gower is accused of extreme insipidity by those who, perhaps, have not read much of the current poetry of his day. He is sinuous, dull, uniform, but he does not deserve to be swept away with scorn. Much of his work has great historical value, much of it is skilfully narrated, and its long-winded author persists in producing some vague claim to be considered a poet.—GOSSE, EDMUND, 1897, *Short History of Modern English Literature, p.* 24.

It would be a very great mistake to minimise or, like many, to pass by as negligible the contribution of Gower to English literature. Even in itself, if it has not the very highest qualities, it is far above contempt. Coleridge's rather pettish wish that Chalmers had given Lydgate instead, must have been caused either by very excusable ignorance of Lydgate's actual worth; or by a complete failure to recognise the formal superiority of Gower and the importance of his priority in time; or perhaps, and even probably, by that capriciousness which too often mars Coleridge's criticism. The contemporaries of Chaucer and Gower, and the immediate successors who entered into their labours, made no such mistake, though in the fifteenth century they sometimes, and not quite unjustly, promoted Lydgate himself to the actual company of his masters. That, historically and as a master, Gower had a real right to be ranked with Chaucer, is as unquestionable as that Gower is vastly Chaucer's inferior as a poet.—SAINTSBURY, GEORGE, 1898, *A Short History of English Literature, p.* 140.

Andrew Wyntoun

1395?-1420?

Born sometime in the reign of David II., he was chosen prior of the monastery of St. Serf's Inch in Loch Leven, before the close of the fourteenth century, for his name appears in the "Chartulary of St. Andrews," under the date 1395, as "Andreas de Wynton, prior insule lacus de Levin." He was also a canon regular of St. Andrews. The year of his death has not been ascertained, but it is probable he did not long survive the completion of his work, which was finished after the death of Albany and before the return of James I to Scotland, or between 1420 and 1424.—ROSS, JOHN MERRY, 1884, *Scottish History and Literature, etc., ed. Brown, p.* 104.

Of my defaute it is my name
Be baptisme, Andrewe of Wyntoune,
Of Sanct Andrew's a chanoune
Regulare; bot, noucht forthi
Of thaim all the elest worthy.
Bot of thair grace and thair favoure
I wes but meryt, made prioure
Of the Ynch withen Lochlevyne.

—WYNTOUN, ANDREW, 1420? *Cronykil of Scotland.*

His genius is certainly inferiour to that of his predecessor, Barbour; but, at least, his versification is easy, his language pure, and his style often animated. As an historian he is highly valuable.—ELLIS, GEORGE, 1790–1845, *Specimens of the Early English Poets, vol.* I, *p.* 201.

Though his work in general partakes little or nothing of the nature of poetry, unless ryme can be said to constitute poetry, yet he now and then throws in some touches of true poetic description, and paints the scenery of his battles with so exact a pencil, that a person, who is on the spot, may point out the various scenes of each particular action.—MACPHERSON, DAVID, 1795, *ed. Cronykil of Scotland, Preface, p.* xxix.

In enumerating the merits of Wynton, the first place ought undoubtedly to be given to his historical accuracy. . . . Next to his value as a historical authority, Wynton possesses great merit in the fresh and curious pictures which he has preserved to us of the manners and superstitions of the times.—TYTLER, PATRICK FRASER, 1838, *Lives of Scottish Worthies, vol.* II. *pp.* 180, 183

As Wynton wrote about the year 1420, Hugh may have flourished at the close of the fourteenth century. He is certainly the oldest English poet born north of Tweed, whose works have reached us. His stave is peculiar to him; and consists of an irregular number of verses, separated by a kind of wheel, or burthen.—GUEST, EDWIN, 1838, *A History of English Rhythms, vol.* II, *p.* 167.

His simple pages present to our view many curious prospects of society; and with a perseverance of industry which had numerous difficulties to encounter, he has collected and preserved many anecdotes that tend to illustrate the history of his native country. Rude and unadorned as his composition may appear, it is not altogether incapable of interesting a reader of the present age of refinement. Here we discover the rudiments of good sense and of literary excellence; but his good sense is often enveloped in the mist of ignorance and superstition; and those talents which in another age might have ranked their possessor with Robertson, Hume, or Ferguson, appear without that lustre which arises from a participation of the general refinement incident to more happy times.—IRVING, DAVID, 1861, *History of Scotish Poetry, ed. Carlyle, p.* 115.

The Cronykil is principally interesting in an historical point of view, and in that respect it is of considerable value and authority, for Wynton, besides his merits as a distinct narrator, had evidently taken great pains to obtain the best information within his reach with regard to the events both of his own and of preceding times. —CRAIK, GEORGE L., 1861, *A Compendious History of English Literature and of the English Language, vol.* I, *p.* 404.

From the view which he took of his task, he would probably have been as little grateful for compliments to his poetic power as any historian of later times is to those who call him flowery and imaginative.—BURTON, JOHN HILL, 1867, *The History of Scotland, vol.* IV, *p.* 124.

The reader will look through the "Cronykil of Scotland" almost in vain for the excitement of a dramatic situation, the contrast and climax of human emotion. Hardly at all will he find that focusing of objects to their most interesting point of view which distinguishes a picture from a map, the work of the artist from the work of the artizan. Nowhere, it may safely be said, will he taste the breath of that ethereal wine, strangely stirring the heart, which is the vintage of great poetic genius. . . . It is nearly five hundred years since Wyntoun laid down his pen. During that time, though never popular with the popularity of Barbour and Blind Harry, he has probably never been quite forgotten. His position as a national chronicler accounts to a large extent for this. But the reader who grows familiar with his pages to-day discovers what may perhaps be another reason. He finds himself making the acquaintance, not only of a teller of quaint historic tales, but of a gentle and pious soul.—EYRE-TODD, GEORGE, 1891, *Early Scottish Poetry, pp.* 132, 141.

James I. of Scotland

1394-1437

Born 1394. Captured by the English in time of peace 1405, and kept a prisoner in the Tower, in Nottingham Castle, at Croydon, and at Windsor, till 1424, when he was released. In that year he married Lady Jane Beaufort, daughter of the Earl of Somerset, and granddaughter of John of Gaunt. She was the heroine of his principal poem, "The King's Quair." In 1437, after reigning thirteen years in Scotland, the king was assassinated at Perth. Besides "The King's Quair," he is commonly supposed to have written one or two other poems, notably the humorous ballad "Christ's Kirk on the Green."—WARD, THOMAS HUMPHREY, 1880, *The English Poets, vol.* I, *p.* 129.

PERSONAL

Our James was, if we may trust the chroniclers, short of stature but robust and stout of body. . . . He was a man of the finest natural gifts, and of a very lofty spirit. He took, in all manly exercises, a foremost part: farther than any he could put the large stone or throw the heavy hammer; swift he was of foot; a well-skilled musician; as a singer second to none. With the harp like another Orpheus he surpassed the Irish or the Wild Scots who are in that art preeminent. It was in the time of his long captivity in France and England that he learned all these accomplishments.—MAJOR, JOHN, 1521, *History of Greater Britain.*

Yit be benevolence of King Hary, war chosin sa wise and expert praeceptouris to instruk him in virtew and science; that he was na les resolute in every science, then he had bene perpetually eccupyit bot in ane: for he wes weill leirnit to fecht with the swerd, to just, to turnay, to worsill, to sing and dance: and was ane expert medicinar: richt crafty in playing baith of lute and harp and sindry othir instrumentis of musik. He was expert in gramer oratry and poetry: and maid sa flowand and sententious versis that appeirit weill he was ane naturall borne poete. He was als ane cunning theolog. For he lernit all his science during the time of his captivite.—BOYES, HECTOR, 1526, *The History of Scotland, tr. Bellenden,* 1536.

Was of midway stature, brade schoudert, and the rest of his memberis equal with this forme. When Aeneas Sylvius wald expreme the conjunction of his memberis with the majestie of his persoune, he calls him squair; as he wald say, his memberis war of sik equalitie that Nature culde forme nathing mare decent to the decore of a king, ather mair perfyt til a Kingis majestie. . .

Althoch he obteynet throuch benifite of nature sum commend of thir vertues, yit speciallie throuch the discipline of the zeris quhen he was captive in Ingland, throuch the kingis favour and gud wil, he was sa weil instructed, and diligent kair of his maistir; and in all sciences was sa scientive and cunning that in quhat science he was cunningest culd na man tel. In al kynde of musik he was excellent, upon the cythar mervellous, in oratrie nane mare artificious: in poetrie that he usit nocht only throuch arte to compound verse, but naturallie in a maner to speik verses. This will testifie the dyverse kyndes quhilkes he maid in Scotis metre, sa cunninglie, sa artificiouslie, and sa prudentlie that he was thocht verilie equal in quiknes, gravitie, and prudencie to the alde poetes of antiquite. Appeiris wonduerful heir quhat we speik and sik diligence far to excel the diligence of kings in our aige and skairs possible to believe. But quhen it was verilie trew and confirmit be thame quha spak with him, war familiar with him and quha perfytlie knew him, suld be writne to his perpetual prayse.—LESLIE, JOHN, 1578, *The History of Scotland, tr. Dalrymple,* 1596, *Book* vii.

He was popular among the people, who appreciated the advantages and the effects of his Government. He struggled hard to redress the oppression and to reform the intolerable evils which Norman feudalism had generated in Scotland. He clearly understood and thoroughly realised in his mind that which all his predecessors had failed to see, namely, that Norman feudalism contained in itself the essence of anarchy and injustice. He had a true conception of the form of government which the people of Scotland needed; though, unhappily, his ideas were too far in advance of his time. No historian who has studied his legislation can fail to admire his grasp of the fundamental principles of effective government, and the efficient administration of justice. Still the historian may not justify all his proceedings, and it seems to me that James I. sometimes pushed his depression of the nobles beyond the limits of justice and political wisdom. — MACKINTOSH, JOHN, 1878-92, *The History of Civilisation in Scotland, vol.* I, *p.* 337.

Unable to rule it, he dreaded the inherited spirit of the Stuarts.

Lat wisedome ay to thy will be iunyt,

had been the timely warning given him by the Goddess Minerva. But James was not the master of his own will. He did not see his goal as it was, but he saw it surrounded with such a halo that he became blind to all dangers. No prince evinced more cruelty in his vengeance than the poet of the gold-lattered gillyflowers; it seems as if the hatreds of Rimini or Ferrara had been transplanted to northern climes.—JUSSERAND, J. J., 1896, *The Romance of a King's Life, p.* 42.

THE KING'S QUAIR
1423?

Go litill tretise, nakit of eloquence,
  Causing simplese and pouertee to wit;
And pray the reder to haue pacience
  Of thy defaute, and to supporten it,
  Of his gudnese thy brukilnese to knytt,
And his tong for to reule and to stere,
That thy defautis helit may bene here.

—JAMES I., 1423? *The Kingis Quair s.* 194.

The design, or theme, of this work is the royal poet's love for his beautiful mistress, Jane Beaufort, of whom he became enamoured whilst a prisoner at the castle of Windsor. The recollection of the misfortunes of his youth, his early and long captivity, the incident which gave rise to his love, its purity, constancy, and happy issue, are all set forth by way of allegorical vision, according to the reigning taste of the age, as we find in the poems of Chaucer, Gower, and Lydgate, his contemporaries.—TYTLER, WILLIAM, 1783, *Poetical Remains of James the First, p.* 47.

It would, perhaps, be difficult to select even from Chaucer's most finished works a long specimen of descriptive poetry so uniformly elegant as this: indeed some of the verses are so highly finished, that they would not disfigure the compositions of Dryden, Pope, or Gray. — ELLIS, GEORGE, 1790-1845, *Specimens of the Early English Poets, vol.* I, *p.* 251.

Amid the bards whom Scotia holds to fame,
She boasts, nor vainly boasts, her James's
  name;
And less, sweet bard! a crown thy glory
  shows,
Than the fair laurels that adorn thy brows.

—DYER, GEORGE, 1801, *The Balance Poems, p.* 230.

James had learnt to be a poet before he was a king: he was schooled in adversity, and reared in the company of his own thoughts. Monarchs have seldom time to parley with their hearts, or to meditate their minds into poetry; and had James been brought up amidst the adulation and gayety of a court, we should never, in all probability, have had such a poem as the Quair. . . . As an amatory poem, it is edifying in these days of coarser thinking, to notice the nature, refinement, and exquisite delicacy which pervade it; banishing every gross thought or immodest expression, and presenting female loveliness, clothed in all its chivalrous attributes of almost supernatural purity and grace.—IRVING, WASHINGTON, 1819–48, *A Royal Poet, The Sketch-Book.*

Though its subject and purpose did not give much room for much fertility of invention, it is full of delicacy, grace and feeling, smooth and artistic in versification, and, in general poetic merit, superior to any other English verse of the fifteenth or even the first half of the sixteenth century. — MARSH, GEORGE P., 1862, *The Origin and History of the English Language, etc., p.* 458.

Though he has no title to the rank of original poet, which some of his admirers claim for him, his "King's Quhair" (*Quire* or *Book*) is justly the most celebrated English poem of the fifteenth century. . . . It must be owned that, while the "King's Quhair" seems deficient in richness and delicacy of colouring when placed side by side with the work of the master, it reads remarkably well when removed from damaging comparison, and is infinitely the best composition produced in the school of Chaucer. There is real passion in it, and a real sense of beauty, though the expression fails to strike through and rise above the embarrassing self-criticism that cramps so many Scotch attempts at eloquence and poetry. The proportions are good, but the surface is dry and hard.—MINTO, WILLIAM, 1874-85, *Characteristics of English Poets, pp.* 94, 95.

It is most undoubtedly true that neither Chaucer nor any contemporary poet of either England or Scotland is characterized by that delicacy which distinguishes the productions of King James. Considering the rude age in which he wrote, and that Chaucer and Gower, with whose writings he was well acquainted, and whom indeed he acknowledges in one of his stanzas for his masters, were so distinguished, as well as Dunbar, for an opposite character, it is certainly one of the greatest phenomena in the annals of poetry. — WILSON, JAMES GRANT, 1876, *The Poets and Poetry of Scotland, vol.* I, *p.* 13.

Full of the fragrance of a most sweet, romantic, innocent, and at last, as we are glad for once to know, a happy and rewarded love. — PRESTON, HARRIET W., 1879, *The Latest Songs of Chivalry, Atlantic Monthly, vol.* 43, *p.* 14.

the nightingale through his prison wall
Taught him both lore and love.
For once, when the bird's song drew him close
To the opened window-pane,
In her bower beneath a lady stood,
A light of life to his sorrowful mood,
Like a lily amid the rain.
And for her sake, to the sweet bird's note,
He framed a sweeter Song,
More sweet than ever a poet's heart
Gave yet to the English tongue.

—ROSSETTI, DANTE GABRIEL, 1881, *The King's Tragedy, ss.* 8–10.

If rather deficient in originality—for it is impossible to believe that the "King's Quhair" would ever have been written if the works of Chaucer had not been already in existence—James I. had a fine poetical spirit, and were it not for the many difficulties of dialect which it presents, his poem would be much more generally read than it is.—NICOLL, HENRY J., 1882, *Landmarks of English Literature, p.* 38.

The "Kingis Quhair" marks a new epoch in the history of Scottish poetry. The plain, unadorned, semi-prosaic style of the metrical chronicles gave place to a delicacy and refinement of imaginative feeling, a richness and elegance of diction, and an artistic melody of verse hitherto unknown. The revolution in the national literature was as great as the revolution in the national policy, but it was more benign in its operation and more lasting in its effects. Henceforth Scotland has a share in the culture of western Christendom.—ROSS, JOHN MERRY, 1884, *Scottish History and Literature, ed. Brown, p.* 155.

Few poems deserving permanence in literature, yet almost unread, are better known by repute than that in which this captive king sang of his love in the year 1423. He sang according to the fashion of the day, and with so much honour to himself that the seven-lined Chaucer stanza which he followed—a familiar and favourite one with Lydgate, Occleve, and all other poets of the generation after Chaucer—was thenceforth, because enamoured majesty had used it, called rhyme royal. Such royal patronage might be left now to the buttermen. In Literature Chaucer was the king, and James his liegeman.—MORLEY, HENRY, 1890, *English Writers, vol.* VI, *p.* 166.

No poet has ever painted love-longing and the dawn of love more delicately or with subtler artistic touch; no poet has given a more exquisite impression of the sweet awe and loveliness of womanhood. As it stands, "The Kingis Quair" places James in the gallery of the world's immortal lovers. Beside Petrarch penning his sonnets to Laura, and the pale Dante gazing on his dead Beatrice, must remain the picture of the captive prince looking forth from his lattice in the tower of Windsor, while below in the garden alleys there lingers for a space, half-consciously, the maid of "beautee eneuch to mak a world to dote." — EYRE-TODD, GEORGE, 1892, *Mediæval Scottish Poetry, p.* 20.

The poem ends, as was customary, with an envoy, and a reference to the "superlative poets," Gower and Chaucer, whose soul its royal author commends to the bliss of heaven in a line that haunts the ear with a fine, far-off, aeolian melody such as distinguishes mediaeval poetry at its best; he who has never caught it has missed an exquisite satisfaction, a pure and humanizing pleasure.—WHITE, GREENOUGH, 1895, *Outline of the Philosophy of English Literature, The Middle Ages, p.* 131.

If we suppose our standpoint to be that of an editor coming now to weigh the evidence for the first time, is there anyone so bold as to assert that James would be named as the author? The Bodleian manuscript—half a century at least later than the reign of James—breaks dôwn altogether under fair and ordinary tests, its false ascriptions numbering at least one half of the whole. John Major—a sixteenth century historian, writing eighty-four years after the death of the king—is found in the very passage in which the "Kingis Quair" is attributed to James, to be indisputably untrustworthy about the other vernacular poems. But the historical evidence must also take account of Walter Bower, William Dunbar, and Sir David Lindsay. Bower, the sole contemporary, and for that reason, in a strict sense, the only competent witness, must be held to be against James. In the minutely particular description, he has attributed to the king more "virtues" than any one man ever possessed—many of them insignificant enough taken alone —yet, although taking care to preserve a specimen of Latin versification, he nowhere suggests that James wrote vernacular poetry. So too, Dunbar, in a deliberate survey of the whole field of Scottish poetry, omits all mention of the ancestor of his patron, James the Fourth: while Lindsay—who had lauded James V. as a poet—in a poem that certainly gave him the opportunity of naming James the First in company with the eight makars singled our for praise, is also silent. The plain inference surely is that Bower, Dunbar, and Lindsay were not aware that James the First had written vernacular poetry. They are to be regarded as witnesses—qualified to speak with authority—who in giving evidence have significantly testified against the king by omitting all mention of his name as a Scottish makar.—Brown, J. T. T., 1896, *The Authorship of the Kingis Quair*, *p.* 66.

In spite of this state of pupilage, and in spite of his employment of the old French machinery of a dream, allegorical personages and supernatural conventions, the poem of James I. is a delicious one. His use of metre was highly intelligent; he neither deviated back towards the older national prosody, like Lydgate, nor stumbled aimlessly on, like Occleve; he perceived what it was that Chaucer had been doing, and he persued it with great firmness, so that, in the fifty or sixty years which divided the latest of the "Canterbury Tales" from "The Flower and the Leaf," the "King's Quair" is really the only English poem in which a modern ear can take genuine pleasure.—Gosse, Edmund, 1897, *Short History of Modern English Literature*, *p.* 39.

CHRIST'S KIRK (?)

One likes no language but the Faiery Queen;
A Scot will fight for Christ's Kirk o' the Green.

—Pope, Alexander, 1733, *Imitations of Horace*, *bk.* ii, *ep.* I. *v.* 39–40.

For James the Muses tuned their sportive lays,
And bound the monarch's brow with Chaucer's bays:
Arch Humour smiled to hear his mimic strain,
And plausive Laughter thrill'd through every vein.

—Langhorne, John, 1763, *Genius and Valour*, *v.* 51–54.

A ludicrous poem, describing low manners with no less propriety than sprightliness.—Horne, Henry, 1774, *Sketches of the History of Man*, *vol.* I, *p.* 292.

Christis Kirk of the Grene, to whatever author it may be referred, must undoubtedly be regarded as an exquisite specimen of ancient humour.—Irving, David, 1861, *History of Scotish Poetry, ed. Carlyle*, *p.* 149.

"Peblis to the Play" and "Christis Kirk on the Green" are poems full of the very breath of rural life and the rude yet joyous meetings of the country folk at kirk and market, which with wonderfully little difference of sentiment and movement also inspired Burns. He must have had a mind full of variety and wide human sympathy almost Shakspearian, who could step from the musings of Windsor and the beautiful heroine, all romance and ethereal splendour, to the lasses in their gay kirtles, and Hob and Raaf with their rustic "daffing," as true to the life as the Ayrshire clowns of Burns, and all the clumsy yet genial gambols of the village festival. It is one of the most curious and least to be expected transformations of poetic versatility—for it is even amazing how he could know the life into which he thus plunged joyous, as if he had been familiar with it from his childhood.—Oliphant, Margaret, O. W., 1890, *Royal Edinburgh*, *p.* 64.

John Lydgate

1370?-1451?

One of the most prolific poets known to English literature, and esteemed the greatest of his age. Was born at Lydgate near Newmarket, about 1370. Was a monk of the Benedictine Abbey of Bury St. Edmund's, and became successively sub-deacon, deacon, and priest. Studied in Oxford and traveled in France and Italy. Upon his return established a school in his monastery. Received a pension in 1439. Died about 1451. *Works*, Ritson enumerates two-hundred-fifty-one, without finishing his catalogue. The most important are "Storie of Thebes;" "Fall of Princes;" "Troy Book," (first printed by Pynson in 1513); "The Life of Our Lady" (printed by Caxton in 1484); "The Dance of Death;" "The Temple of Glas," (printed by Caxton 1479?), ed. Schick (Early English Text Society, 1891). Halliwell edited a selection from the minor poems in 1840.—MOULTON, CHARLES WELLS, 1900.

The most dulcet sprynge of famous rhetoryke.—HAWES, STEPHEN, 1506, *The Pastime of Pleasure, ed. Wright, cap.* xiv, *s.* 12.

Also Johnn Lydgate
Wryteth after an hyer rate;
It is dyffuse to fynde
The sentence of his mynde,
Yet wryteth he in his kynd,
No man that can amend
Those maters that he hath pende;
Yet some men fynde a faute,
And say he wryteth to haute.

—SKELTON, JOHN, 1508? *Phillyp Sparrowe, v.* 804-812.

Lamentyng Lidgate, lurking emong the illie(s), with a bald skons, with a garlande of willowes abont his pate: booted he was after sainct Benets guise, and a blacke stamell robe, with a lothlie monsterous hoode hangyng backwarde, he stoopyng forwar, bewailyng every estate with the spirite of prouidence; forseyng the falles of wicked men, and the slipprie seates of Princes; the ebbyng and flowyng, the risyng and falling of men in auctoritie, and how vertue do advaunce the simple, and vice overthrow the most noble of the worlde.—BULLEIN, WILLIAM, 1564-73, *A Dialogue Both Pleasaunt and Pietifull, wherein is a Godlie Regiment against the Fever Pestilence, with a Consolation and Comforte against Death.*

Neere in time vnto him was *Lydgate* a Poet, surely for good proportion of his verse, and meetely currant style, as the time affoorded comparable with *Chawcer*, yet more occupyed in supersticious and odde matters, then was requesite in so good a wytte: which, though he handled them commendably, yet the matters themselues beeing not so commendable, hys estimation hath beene the lesse.—WEBBE, WILLIAM, 1586, *A Discourse of English Poetrie, ed. Arber, p.* 32.

Lydgat a translatour onely and no deuiser of that which he wrate, but one that wrate in good verse.—PUTTENHAM, GEORGE, 1589, *The Arte of English Poesie, ed. Arber, p.* 76.

He was another disciple and admirer of Chaucer, and it must be owned far excelled his master, in the article of versification. . . . His verses were so very smooth, and indeed to a modern ear they appear so, that it was said of him by his contemporaries, that his wit was framed and fashioned by the Muses themselves. — CIBBER, THEOPHILUS, 1753, *Lives of the Poets, vol.* I, *pp.* 23, 24.

I do not pretend to set him on a level with his master, Chaucer, but he certainly comes the nearest to him of any contemporary writer that I am acquainted with. His choice of expression, and the smoothness of his verse, far surpass both Gower and Occleve. He wanted not art in raising the more tender emotions of the mind, of which I might give several examples. . . . I stop here, not because there are not great beauties in the remainder of this epistle, but because Lydgate, in the three last stanzas of this extract, has touched the very heart-springs of compassion with so masterly a hand, as to merit a place among the greatest poets. —GRAY, THOMAS, 1761? *On the Poems of Lydgate, Essays, Works, vol.* I, *pp.* 397, 399.

Had the reputation of a person much accomplished by his travels into Italy, and France; and besides several things of his, of polite argument in prose, was much esteemed for what he wrote also in verse; as his Eglogues, Odes, Satyres, and other poems.—PHILLIPS, EDWARD, 1675, *Theatrum Poetarum Anglicanorum, ed. Brydges, p.* 21.

He is the first of our writers whose style is cloathed with that perspicuity in which the English phraseology appears at this day to an English reader. To enumerate Lydgate's pieces, would be to write the catalogue of a little library. No poet seems to have posesssed a greater versatility of talents. He moves with equal ease in every mode of composition. His hymns, and his ballads, have the same degree of merit: and whether his subject be the life of a hermit or a hero, of saint Austin or Guy earl of Warwick, ludicrous or legendary, religious or romantic, a history or an allegory, he writes with facility. His transitions were rapid from works of the most serious and laborious kind to sallies of levity and pieces of popular entertainment. His muse was of universal access; and he was not only a poet of his monastery, but of the world in general. If a disguising was intended by the company of goldsmiths, a mask before his majesty at Eltham, a maygame for the sheriffs and aldermen of London, a mumming before the lord mayor, a procession of pageants from the creation for the festival of Corpus Christi, or a carol for the coronation, Lydgate was then consulted and gave the poetry.—WARTON, THOMAS, 1778-81, *History of English Poetry, sec.* XXI.

"The Story of Thebes," which Speght has printed in his edition of Chaucer, and which was intended as a continuation of the Canterbury Tales, contains some poetical passages, which Mr. Warton has extracted. But Lydgate's style, though natural, and sometimes rich, does not possess that strength and conciseness which is observable in the works of his master. It is dangerous for a mere versifier to attempt the completion of a plan which has been begun by a poet. Lydgate's poem is not long; but it is possible to be tedious in a very small compass. —ELLIS, GEORGE, 1790-1845, *Specimens of the Early English Poets, vol.* I, *p.* 225.

Voluminous, prosaick, and driveling monk. . . . In truth, and fact, these stupid and fatigueing productions, which by no means deserve the name of poetry, and their stil more stupid and disgusting author, who disgraces the name and patronage of his master Chaucer, are neither worth collecting (unless it be as typographical curiositys, or on account of the beautyful illuminations in some of his presentation-copys), nor even worthy of preservation. . . . How little he profited by the correction, or instructions of his great patron is manifest in almost every part of his elaborate drawlings, in which there are scarcely three lines together of pure and accurate metre.—RITSON, JOSEPH, 1802, *Bibliographia Poetica, pp.* 87, 88.

Has been oftener abused than read. As voluminous as Don Lopez de Vega, and often as dull as the worst-natured critics have not been displeased to find him; yet he abounds with passages that are either curious for their relation of manners, or for their true poetical feeling, or for the vigour and harmony of their versification. In this latter quality he is superior to Chaucer, and sometimes approaches him in his higher merit. He has not Chaucer's felicity in selecting, nor his facility or spirit in describing, the characterising traits of the events which he exhibits; but he has sometimes a greater condensation of expression, if not of thought, and in general better rhythm in his versification.—TURNER, SHARON, 1814-23, *The History of England During the Middle Ages, vol.* V, *p.* 340.

Lydgate is rather food for the Antiquary than the general reader; and without wishing him a place on the *principal* shelf of the "Old Man's" library, I must rather insist upon his introduction into some obscurer corner of his Collection.—DIBDIN, THOMAS FROGNALL, 1824, *The Library Companion, p.* 677.

Lydgate, his* contemporary, was of a more sensitive cast. He even complained of critics, and his is the first mention of that race of men, so common in our day, as existing in England.—KNAPP, SAMUEL L., 1832, *Advice in the Pursuits of Literature, p.* 21.

An easy versifier, he served to make poetry familiar to the many, and may sometimes please the few. Gray, no light authority, speaks more favourably of Lydgate than either Warton or Ellis, or than the general complexion of his poetry would induce most readers to do. . . . Though probably a man of inferior powers of mind to Gower, has more of

*Occleve.

the minor qualities of a poet: his lines have sometimes more spirit, more humor, and he describes with more graphic minuteness. But his diffuseness becomes generally feeble and tedious; the attention fails in the schoolboy stories of Thebes and Troy; and he had not the judgment to select and compress the prose narratives from which he commonly derived his subject. It seems highly probable that Lydgate would have been a better poet in satire upon his own times, or delineation of their manners; themes which would have gratified us much more than the fate of princes. — HALLAM, HENRY, 1837-39, *Introduction to the Literature of Europe, pt.* i, *ch.* ii, *par.* 48.

The delectable catalogue of his writings, great and small, exceeds two hundred and fifty; and may not yet be complete, for they lie scattered in their manuscript state. A great multitude of writings, the incessant movements of a single mind, will at first convey to us a sense of magnitude; and in this magnitude, if we observe the greatest possible diversity of parts, and, if we may use the term, the flashings of the most changeable contrasts, we must place such a universal talent among the phenomena of literature. . . . Alas! apologies only leave irremediable faults as they were. The tediousness of Dan Lydgate remains as languid, his verse as halting, and "Thebes" and "Troy" as desolate, as we found them!—DISRAELI, ISAAC, 1841, *Lydgate, Amenities of Literature.*

An elegant poet—"poeta elegans"—was he called by the courteous Pits,—a questionable compliment in most cases, while the application in the particular one agrees not with that same. An improver of the language he is granted to be by all; and a voluminous writer of respectable faculties, in his position, could scarcely help being so: he has flashes of genius, but they are not prolonged to the point of warming the soul,—can strike a bold note, but fails to hold it on,—attains to moments of power and pathos, but wears, for working days, no habit of perfection. These are our thoughts of Lydgate; and yet when he ceased his singing, none sang better; there was silence in the land. — BROWNING, ELIZABETH BARRETT, 1842-63, *The Book of the Poets, p.* 120.

He accumulates, to wearisomeness, both thoughts and words. But he has an earnestness which often rises into enthusiasm, and which gives a very impressive air to the religious pieces that make up a majority of his minor poems. Although his originality of invention is small, he sometimes works up borrowed ideas into exceedingly striking combinations. His descriptions of scenery are often excellent.—SPALDING, WILLIAM, 1852-82, *A History of English Literature, p.* 87.

Lydgate is, so far as we know, the first British bard who wrote for hire. At the request of Whethamstede, the Abbot of St. Alban's, he translated a "Life of St. Alban" from Latin into English rhymes, and received for the whole work one hundred shillings. — GILFILLAN, GEORGE, 1860, *Specimens of the Less-Known British Poets, vol.* I, *p.* 47.

Indeed he seems to have followed the manufacture of rhymes as a sort of trade, furnishing any quantity to order whenever he was called upon. . . . Though excessively diffuse, and possessed of very little strength or originality of imagination, is a considerably livelier and more expert writer than Occleve. His memory was also abundantly stored with the learning of his age; he had travelled in France and Italy, and was intimately acquainted with the literature of both these countries; and his English makes perhaps a nearer approach to the modern form of the language than that of any preceding writer. — CRAIK, GEORGE L., 1861, *A Compendious History of English Literature and of the English Language, vol.* I, *p.* 403.

He had some talent, some imagination, especially in high-toned descriptions: it was the last flicker of a dying literature; gold received a golden coating, precious stones were placed upon diamonds, ornaments multiplied and made fantastic; as in their dress and buildings, so in their style. . . . When we can no more speak to the soul, we try to speak to the eyes. This is what Lydgate does, nothing more.—TAINE, H. A., 1871, *History of English Literature, tr. Van Laun, vol.* I, *bk.* i, *ch.* iii, *p.* 137.

He could write morality in the old court allegorical style; he could kneel at the foot of the Cross and offer to his God the sacrifice of a true outburst of such song as there was in him. John Lydgate was not a poet of great genius, but he was a man with music in his life. He was full of a harmony of something more than words, not more diffuse than his age liked him to be, and, therefore, with good reason, popular and honoured among English readers in the fifteenth century. —MORLEY, HENRY, 1873, *First Sketch of English Literature*, p. 179.

He was long accepted, and is even now occasionally accepted, at a valuation which was put upon him at a period when there was not a sufficient quantity of literature in the language to make men very discriminating about its quality. I am aware that he was spoken of respectfully by a man of genius such as was Gray, and was not disrespectfully spoken of by a woman of genius such as was Mrs. Browning. It only proves that, in spite of the dictum of Horace, there are middling verses which the immortals do not despise. There was apparently no topic upon which he was not ready to express himself at a moment's notice. He produced, in consequence, a good deal of matter which it presumably gratified him to write; though it seems inconceivable that there was ever a state of the human intellect in which gratification could have come to any one from its perusal. In his versification there is no harmony, no regular movement. In his expression, he had gained facility at the expense of felicity. He is one of those noted, or rather notorious, authors whose fame, such as it is, rests not upon their own achievements, but upon the kindness with which others have been induced to look upon their achievements. There is, accordingly, no necessity of reading his works resting upon any one save him who has to make a professional study of English literature. For this unfortunate being the dead past, so far from being able to bury its dead, is not even able to bury its bores.—LOUNSBURY, THOMAS R., 1892, *Studies in Chaucer, vol.* III, *pp.* 25, 27.

The more arid Occleve goes securely on his way, and we read his verses with a quiet pleasure; Lydgate, endowed by nature with a much more musical soul, appears to stumble every moment, so that in reading him we feel again and again as if thrown out of the saddle. . . . In his poems there is much that is good, and even excellent of its kind. He is, however, so very variable that he has scarcely produced any work of greater length, and only a few short ones, which leave a pure, uniform impression. He never acquired any original style, but rather a sort of mannerism, in which he at length appears to have taken a sort of pleasure, and in which at least he could express his thoughts as rapidly as water from a sponge.—TEN BRINK, BERNHARD, 1892, *History of English Literature, (Wyclif, Chaucer, Earliest Drama, Renaissance), tr. Robinson, pp.* 223, 224.

A worthy man, it seems, if ever there was one, and industrious, and prolific, above all prolific, writes according to established standards, tales, lays, fabliaux satires, romances of chivalry, poetical debates, ballads of former times, allegories, lives of the saints, love poems, fables; five thousand verses a year on an average, and being precocious as well as prolific, leaves behind him at his death a hundred and thirty thousand verses, merely counting his longer works. Virgil had only written fourteen thousand.—JUSSERAND, J. J., 1895, *A Literary History of the English People*, *p.* 498.

It is not probable that the entire works of Lydgate will ever be made accessible to readers, nor is it to be conceived that they would reward the labours of an editor. But although it must be repeated that Lydgate is an author of inferior value, excessively prosy and long-winded, and strangely neglectful both of structure and of melody, a selection could probably be made from his writings which would do him greater justice than he does to himself in his intolerable prolixity. He has a pleasant vein of human pity, a sympathy with suffering that leads him to say, in a sort of deprecating undertone, very gentle and gracious things. He is a storehouse of odd and valuable antiquarian notes.—GOSSE, EDMUND, 1897, *Short History of Modern English Literature, p.* 36.

Lydgate's most agreeable poems are certainly those in which he speaks about himself. In his "Testament" and his "London Lackpenny" he has given us some suggestive glimpses of his life and character; and he will sometimes rest in the midst of his translations, to relieve his weariness by a moment's gossip with the reader. These green oases are so welcome, in the midst of the desert of dulness surrounding them, that the traveller, refreshed by the little spring of garrulous doggerel, is inclined to celebrate it as a fountain of pure poetry. This however is mistaken gratitude.—COURTHOPE, W. J., 1895, *A History of English Poetry, vol.* I, *p.* 326.

Thomas Occleve

C. 1370–1454

Hoccleve, or Occleve, Thomas, poet, was born about 1368, was a clerk in the Exchequer, and was writing verse so late as 1448. His chief work is a free but tedious version of the "De Regimine Principum" of Ægidius Romanus, over five thousand lines in length, and written in Chaucer's seven-line stanza. In the prologue (about one-third of the whole) the author tells us a good deal about himself, and speaks out his grief for the death of his great master Chaucer. The poem was edited by T. Wright for the Roxburghe Club in 1860. Many other poems are ascribed to Hoccleve, some still unprinted, and some of them stories from the "Gesta Romanorum." His "Minor Poems" and "Compleint" were edited by Dr. Furnivall for the Early English Text Society in 1892, the first-fruits of a complete edition.—PATRICK AND GROOME, *eds.*, 1897, *Chambers's Biographical Dictionary, p.* 493.

We may suppose that he took his name from his birthplace, and was born in Bedfordshire, in the small parish of Hockliffe, about five miles from Dunstable. The only alternative would be Ockley, in Surrey. The old confusion with the aspirate has caused the name to be written both "Hoccleve" and "Occleve." But in a copy of "The Governail of Princes," which the poet wrote with his own hand, the name occurs in the text, and is written "Occleve." Another day he might have written "Hoccleve." . . . But the name is Occleve in the only place where we are sure, or nearly sure, that he himself has written it.—MORLEY, HENRY, 1890, *English Writers, vol.* VI, *p.* 122.

Well I wot, the man . . .
. . . did quench his thirst
Deeply as did ever one,
In the Muse's Helicon.

—BROWNE, WILLIAM, 1614-20, *The Shepherd's Pipe, Eclogue I.*

A very famous English poet in his time which was the reign of king Henry the fourth, and Henry the fifth; to which last he dedicated his "Government of a Prince," the chiefly remember'd of what he writ in poetry, and so much the more famous he is by being remembered to have been the disciple of the most famed Chaucer.—PHILLIPS, EDWARD, 1675, *Theatrum Poetarum Anglicanorum, ed. Brydges, p.* 19.

Occleve is a feeble writer, considered as a poet: and his chief merit seems to be, that his writings contributed to propagate and establish those improvements in our language which were now beginning to take place. . . . The titles of Occleve's pieces . . . indicate a coldness of genius.—WARTON, THOMAS, 1778–81, *History of English Poetry, sec.* XX.

It is not easy to select a tolerable extract from this writer.—ELLIS, GEORGE, 1790-1845, *Specimens of the Early English Poets, vol.* I, *p.* 213.

Has not had his just share of reputation, . . . whose compositions greatly assisted the growth and diffused the popularity of our infant poetry.—TURNER, SHARON, 1814–23, *History of England During the Middle Ages, vol.* V, *p.* 335.

Occleve speaks of himself as Chaucer's scholar. He has, at least, the merit of expressing the sincerest enthusiasm for his master. But it is difficult to controvert the character which has been generally assigned to him, that of a flat and feeble writer. Excepting the adoption of his story of Fortunatus, by William Browne, in his pastorals, and the modern republication of a few of his pieces, I know not of any public compliment which has ever been paid to his poetical memory. —CAMPBELL, THOMAS, 1819, *An Essay on English Poetry.*

The poetry of Hoccleve is wretchedly bad, abounding with pedantry, and destitute of all grace or spirit.—HALLAM, HENRY, 1837-39, *Introduction to the Literature of Europe, pt.* i, *ch.* ii, *par.* 48.

Was a shrewd observer of his own times. . . . To us he remains sufficiently uncouth.—DISRAELI, ISAAC, 1841, *Occleve, Amenities of Literature.*

On the whole, Occleve's verse must be judged rather by its quantity than its quality. His admission into the ranks of our English writers of note is owing to the circumstance of his writing in a barren age, when every versifier was a man of mark.—COLLIER, WILLIAM FRANCIS, 1861, *A History of English Literature*, p. 69.

The first important poetical writer of the fifteenth century, whose works have come down to us. . . . Most of his works exist only in manuscript, and those that have been printed are not of a character to inspire a very lively desire for the publication of the remainder.—MARSH, GEORGE P., 1862, *The Origin and History of the English Language, etc.*, p. 455.

As to deficiency in fire and spirit, he is on a level with Gower; but he is rather more interesting.—CREASY, SIR EDWARD S., 1870, *History of England, vol.* II, p. 543.

He is supposed to have been born in 1370, and he emerges at the Court of Richard II. in 1387. The luxurious extravagance of that Court found in him a congenial spirit. He could never pass the sign of Bacchus, with its invitation to thirsty passengers to moisten their clay, so long, at least, as he had anything in his purse; and he spent much money in the temples of a goddess of still more questionable character. He was a favourite among cooks and taverners, from the circumstance that he always paid them what they asked. Only two men of his acquaintance could equal him in drinking at night and lying in bed in the morning. The only thing that preserved his life from the brawls incident to such habits was an invincible cowardice: he never traduced men except in a whisper. All this we know from his own humorous confessions. He tells us also that his excesses exhausted his money, although he held a valuable office—and impaired his health, though nature had given him a strong constitution. — MINTO, WILLIAM, 1874-85, *Characteristics of English Poets*, p. 71.

When a man's only merit is a fond idolatry of his master, let him be forgotten.—WELSH, ALFRED H., 1882, *Development of English Literature and Language, vol.* I, p. 245.

A Chaucer "sans eyes, sans ears, sans teeth, sans everything." — WASHBURN, EMELYN W., 1884, *Studies in Early English Literature*, p. 91.

Occleve is a good, harmless fellow, who has read with advantage many books, has observed correctly all sorts of things within the circle of his experience, and has thought much. To this must be added the gift of easy poetic composition, and a decided talent for form, which he happily modeled on Chaucer's style. In the clearness of his diction, and occasionally in the excellent choice of his expressions in the construction of his verses and stanzas, he comes nearer to the great model than almost any of the poets of the fifteenth century. Everywhere we can trace the influence of the master, without being able to call it mere imitation. Direct reminiscences are very seldom used in a wrong place. Occleve has his own style; he does not attempt a rivalry with the style of his model, which is pithy, forcible, vivid, and significant in every line, but he knows how to ingratiate himself easily with his readers, both to their pleasure and profit. In the long run, indeed, the want of any strong colors in his broad descriptions becomes insipid.—TEN BRINK, BERNHARD, 1892, *History of English Literature (Wyclif, Chaucer, Earliest Drama, Renaissance), tr. Robinson*, p. 215.

Occleve was a frivolous, tame-spirited creature, tainted with insanity.—GOSSE, EDMUND, 1897, *Short History of Modern English Literature*, p. 35.

Reginald Pecock

1395?-1460?

Reginald Pecock, divine, born in Wales about 1395, was a fellow of Oriel, Oxford, and received priest's orders in 1422. His preferments were the mastership of Whittington College, London, together with the rectory of its church (1431); the bishopric of St. Asaph's (1444); and that of Chichester (1450). He plunged into the Lollard and other controversies of the day, and compiled many treatises, of which the "Donet" (c. 1440), on the main truths of Christianity, and his "Treatise on

Faith" (c. 1456), are still extant. The object of his "Repressor of Over Much Blaming of the Clergy" (c. 1455) was to promote the peace of the church by plain arguments against Lollardy. His philosophic breadth and independence of judgment brought upon him the suspicions of the church. In 1457 he was denounced for having written in English, and for making reason paramount to the authority of the old doctors. He was summoned before Archbishop Bourchier, condemned as a heretic, and given the alternative of abjuring his errors or being burned. He elected to abjure, gave up fourteen of his books to be burnt, and, concussed into resigning his bishopric, spent the rest of his days in the Abbey of Thorney in Cambridgeshire, dying about 1460.—PATRICK AND GROOME, *eds.*, 1897, *Chambers's Biographical Dictionary, p.* 726.

He shall have a secret closed chamber having a chimney, and convenience within the abbey, where he may have sight to some altar to hear mass; and that he pass not the said chamber. To have but one person that is sad (grave) and well-disposed to make his bed, and to make him fire, as it shall need. That he have no books to look on, but only a portuous (breviary), a mass-book, a psalter, a legend, and a Bible. That he have nothing to write with; no stuff to write upon. That he have competent fuel according to his age, and as his necessity shall require. That he be served daily of meat and drink as a brother of the abbey is served when he is excused from the freytour (*i. e.*, from dining in hall), and somewhat better after the first quarter, as his disposition and reasonable appetite shall desire, conveniently after the good discretion of the said abbot.—BOURCHIER, THOMAS, ARCHBISHOP OF CANTERBURY, 1459, *To William Ryall, Abbot of Thorney.*

For twenty years together he favoured the opinions of Wicliffe, and wrot many Books in defence thereof, untill, in a Synod held at Lambeth by Thomas Bourchier Arch-bishop of Canterbury 1457, he was made to recant at Paul's Cross (his Books being burnt before his eyes), confuted with seven solid arguments, thus reckoned up, *Authoritate, Vi, Arte, Fraude, Metu, Terrore & Tyrannide.* Charitable men behold this his Recantation as his suffering, and the act of his enemies: some account it rather a slip then a fall, others a fall, whence afterwards he did arise. It seems, his recanting was little satisfactory to his Adversaries, being never restored to his Bishoprick, but confined to a poor pension in a mean Monastery, where he died obscurely, though others say, he was privily made away in prison. He is omitted by Pitseus in his Catalogue of Writers; a presumption that he apprehended him finally dissenting from the Popish perswasion.—FULLER, THOMAS, 1662, *Worthies of England, ed. Nichols, vol.* II, *p.* 558.

It is a very memorable circumstance in the story of this extraordinary man, that his life was passed in a conflict with the errors of Wiclif, and yet that, after his death, his name was solemnly coupled with the name of the Reformer, and, in that company was, in due form, consigned to immortality. The foundation of King's College, Cambridge, took place about fourteen years before Pecock's conviction and imprisonment: and such was the zeal and orthodoxy of his Majesty, or his advisers, that a clause was added to the statues of the society, providing, that every scholar, on the expiration of his probationary years, should take an oath, that he would not favour the condemned opinions or heresies of John Wiclif, Reginald Pecock, or any other heretic, so long as he should live, on pain of perjury and expulsion, *ipso facto.*—LE BAS, CHARLES WEBB, 1832, *The Life of Wiclif, p.* 377.

Bishop Pecock's answer to the Lollards of his time contains passages well worthy of Hooker, both for weight of matter and dignity of style.—HALLAM, HENRY, 1848, *View of the State of Europe During the Middle Ages, vol.* II, *ch.* ix, *pt.* ii, *note.*

The earliest piece of good philosophical disquisition of which our English prose literature can boast.—BABINGTON, CHURCHILL, 1860, *ed. The Repressor.*

The works of Pecock afford a gratifying proof that the mantle of the reformer had fallen on worthy shoulders, though he who bore it was so little able to comprehend the scope and logical consequences of the principles on which he acted, that he knew not even in what direction he was marching. . . . While Pecock was grammatically behind his age, he was rhetorically far in advance of it.—MARSH, GEORGE P., 1862, *The Origin and History of the English Language, etc., pp.* 473, 487.

The work appeals to reason, but is not open to the charge of deism. In tone it may be compared to Locke's "Reasonableness of Christianity."—FARRAR, ADAM STOREY, 1862, *A Critical History of Free Thought.*

He is almost a solitary instance of anything like spiritual or intellectual enlightenment combining with heretical leanings to provoke the enmity or jealousy of the clergy.—STUBBS, WILLIAM, 1874-78, *Constitutional History of England, vol.* III, *ch.* xix, *p.* 376.

Few men have been so plainly in advance of their age, and seldom has the Church shown herself so decidedly hostile to liberty of thought. We may regret his cowardice, but we must thank England for being the first, not only to establish biblical authority, but to show how it could be struck down when it had served its end.—HOLLAND, FREDERIC MAY, 1884, *The Rise of Intellectual Liberty, p.* 301.

Pecock sympathised with ultramontane theories of Church government, and was one of those who wrote against Wyclif, but, at the same time, he was an ardent advocate of popular education. His views and arguments would lead us, indeed, to conclude that he would have been a vigorous supporter of the university extension movement of the present day.—MULLINGER, J. BASS, 1888, *History of the University of Cambridge, p.* 52.

The "Repressor" is one of the most valuable monuments of English theology, and one of the most important productions of English prose bequeathed to us by the fifteenth century. The method pursued by Pecock, of first letting his opponents thoroughly explain their own motives, and then driving them triumphantly from the field by their own arguments, affords us a most instructive glance into the religious views of those times. The rich intellectual resources, the logical energy, and the dialectic subtlety of the author, will be admitted even by those who take most offense at the sophistical application to which these talents are occassionally put. And although Pecock knew no Greek, and was even deceived as to the authorship of many of the works going under false names, we must nevertheless concede to him an amount of learning by no means despicable in that age, and, what is more, a clearness and boldness of critical perception far in advance of his times.—TEN BRINK, BERNHARD, 1892, *History of English Literature, (Wyclif, Chaucer, Earliest Drama, Renaissance), tr. Robinson, p.* 335.

His diction is archaic for his own age, and is even affected in its discarding of all those stores with which not Chaucer only, but even Wycliffe, had enriched our language. The strained archaicism—because we can call it nothing else—is all the more curious when taken in connection with the elaborate statement of arguments in the logical forms of the schools, with his accuracy of definition, and with his careful recapitulation of terms, which might remind us of the iteration of a legal document.—CRAIK, HENRY, 1893, *English Prose, vol.* I, *p.* 52.

The "Repressor" is a monument of fifteenth-century English, clear and even pointed in style, forcible in thought. The argument is logical and subtly critical, informed by wide, if not deep, learning. On the other hand, in the detailed application of his principles Pecock often fails to carry conviction, and his tendency to casuistry irritates the modern reader. He sets forth, however, the views of his opponents so clearly as to render his book an invaluable record of the theological opinions of his time.—COOKE, MISS A. M., 1895, *Dictionary of National Biography, vol.* XLIV, *p.* 200.

Had Pecock confined himself to the Latin language, he might have closed a splendid career at Canterbury, instead of expiring like a starved lamp under the extinguisher of his prison at Thorney.—GOSSE, EDMUND, 1897, *Short History of Modern English Literature, p.* 43.

Though this compound of forms that never took permanent place in the language, with archaisms on the one hand, and Latinisms on the other, makes Pecock's pages look very harsh and obscure, it is clear that his scheme was a possible one; that it actually did exercise English in form, and enrich it in matter, to no small degree; and that, though the classical reaction of the Renaissance prevented much of his vocabulary from receiving final letters of naturalisation, a good deal more than has actually been naturalised might have been admitted with no disadvantage.—SAINTSBURY, GEORGE, 1898, *A Short History of English Literature, p.* 207.

Juliana Berners

C. 1388, C. 1461

About 1481, Juliana Berners, a sister of Lord Berners, and Prioress of the Nunnery of Sopewell, composed what is regarded as the great literary curiosity of the time, a work, containing treatises on hawking, hunting, and heraldry, which, in 1486, was printed. A second edition has a treatise on angling, and a sort of lyrical epilogue to the treatise on hunting, which last is written in rhyme.—RYDER, ELIOT, 1881. *The Household Library of Catholic Poets, p.* 21.

From an abbess disposed to turn author, we might more reasonably have expected a manual of meditations for the closet, or select rules for making salves, or distilling strong waters. But the diversions of the field were not thought inconsistent with the character of a religious lady of this eminent rank, who resembled an abbot in respect of exercising an extensive manorial jurisdiction; and who hawked and hunted in common with other ladies of distinction. This work, however, is here mentioned, because the second of these treatises is written in rhyme. It is spoken in her own person; in which, being otherwise a woman of authority, she assumes the title of dame. I suspect the whole to be a translation from the French and Latin.—WARTON, THOMAS, 1778-81, *History of English Poetry, sec.* xxvii.

But the greatest literary curiosity of this reign* is the work of the Lady Juliana, sister to Richard Lord Berners, and prioress of the nunnery of Sopewell, which was written in 1481, and published soon after at the neighbouring monastery at St. Alban's. It contains treatises on hawking, hunting, and heraldry: in all of which the good lady seems to have rivalled the most eminent professors of those arts.—ELLIS, GEORGE, 1790–1845, *Specimens of the Early English Poets, vol.*I, *p.* 291.

This is not only the earliest, but by far the most curious essay upon angling which has ever appeared in the English, or perhaps any other language. In the most important features, Walton has closely followed this production. In piety and virtue,—in the inculcation of morality,—in an ardent love for their art, and still more, in that placid and Christian spirit for which the amiable Walton was so conspicuous, the early writer was scarcely inferior to his or her more celebrated successor.—LOWNDES, WILLIAM THOMAS, 1834, *The Bibliographer's Manual of English Literature, ed. Bohn, vol.* I, *p.* 118.

Leads the fair train in a manner singularly masculine and discordant, blowing a horn, instead of playing on a lute; for the reverend dame was a hunting parson in petticoats. She is the author of three tracts, well known to antiquaries, on Hawking, Hunting, and Armory (heraldry); and her verses, as might be expected, are more curious than bewitching.—HUNT, LEIGH, 1847, *Specimens of British Poetesses; Men, Women, and Books.*

The first British Poetess of whom we have any record. . . . Her style is excessively coarse and unfeminine, and wholly inconsistent with her sacred calling; but the barbarism of the times is a sufficient, if not a complete excuse for her.—ROWTON, FREDERIC, 1848, *The Female Poets of Great Britain, p.* 25.

So rare is this volume, that Dr. Dibdin estimates a perfect copy (of which Earl Spencer and the Earl of Pembroke each had one) to be worth £420; a very imperfect copy produced £147 at the sale of the Library of the Duke of Roxburghe; resold at the sale of the White Knight's (Duke of Marlborough's) Library for £84. The third book, on Heraldic Blazonry, is supposed to be an addendum to the two preceding, and a portion of a work by Nicholas Upton, written about 1441. Indeed Mr. Haslewood considers that the only portions of the book which can safely be attributed to Dame Berners are: 1. A small portion of the "Treatise on Hawking." 2. "The Treatise upon Hunting." 3. "A Short List of the Beasts of Chase;" and "Another Short one of Beasts and Fowls."—ALLIBONE, S. AUSTIN, 1854–58, *A Critical Dictionary of English Literature, vol.* I, *p.* 180.

What is really known of the dame is almost nothing, and may be summed up in the following few words. She probably lived at the beginning of the fifteenth century, and she possibly compiled from existing MSS. some rhymes on hunting.—BLADES, WILLIAM, 1881 *ed., The Boke of St. Albans in Facsimile, p.* 13.

*Edward IV.

The dame is said to have spent her youth probably at the court, and to have shared in the woodland sports then fashionable, thus acquiring a competent knowledge of hunting, hawking, and fishing. Having withdrawn from the world, and finding plenty of leisure in the cloister after being raised to the position of prioress, it is next believed that she committed to writing her experience of these sports. As for fishing, if she were an active prioress, the exigencies of fasting days would demand that she should busy herself in the supply of fish required for the sisterhood. Like all observant anglers, she would daily learn more of that craft as she grew older, and so she naturally treats of it more fully and in a clearer order than the other subjects of the "Boke" are handled. . . . Only three perfect copies of this first edition are known. One is in the Althorp Library, another in the Earl of Pembroke's collection, and the third is in the library of the Earl of Devon. The only copy which has appeared in an auction-room this century (with the exception of that in the Duke of Roxburghe's sale, which was very imperfect) was itself imperfect. It came from the library of Mr. F. L. Popham of Littlecote, and was sold in March 1882 for 600 guineas to Mr. Quaritch.—WATKINS, REV. M. G., 1885, *Dictionary of National Biography, vol.* IV, *pp.* 391, 392.

John Capgrave

1393–1464

Chronicler, theologian and provincial of the Augustine Friars in England, was born and died at Lynn, studied probably at Cambridge, and was ordained priest about 1418, having already entered his order at Lynn. His works include, in Latin, Bible commentaries; sermons; "Nova legenda Angliæ," printed by Wynkyn de Worde in 1516; "De illustribus Henricis," giving the lives of twenty-four emperors of Germany, kings of England, &c., all of the name of Henry; and "Vita Humfredi Ducis Glocestriæ." Among his English works are a life of St. Katherine in verse (ed. by Horstmann, Early English Text Society 1893), and "A Chronicle of England from the Creation to 1417." The last and the "De illustribus Henricis" were edited by F. C. Hingeston for the "Rolls Series" in 1858.—PATRICK AND GROOME, *eds.*, 1897, *Chambers's Biographical Dictionary, p.* 177.

Capgrave's biographers eulogise his character in the highest terms. The most learned of English Augustinians whom the soil of Britain ever produced, he was distinguished as a philosopher and theologian, practically rejecting in his writings the dreams of sophists, which lead only to strife and useless discussions.—THOMPSON, E. MAUNDE, 1887, *Dictionary of National Biography, vol.* IX, *p.* 21.

Brother John—as he generally calls himself—was a doctor of divinity, a learned gentleman, a good monk, a good prior, a very orthodox and zealous Catholic; also a warm patriot and a good man, bitter and unjust only when the subject touched Wyclif or Sir John Oldcastle. Capgrave possessed no such critical a brain as Reginald Pecock, and as little had he felt any breath of the awakening spirit of humanism, although it occurred to him at one time to change his honest English name into the wondrous Latin form of *De monumento pileato.* The world in which he lived and worked was thoroughly mediæval. He drew his chief mental nourishment from the Bible, the Fathers of the Church, and the Schoolmen, from Martyrologies, Lives of the Saints, and Chronicles. He occupied himself dilligently not only with the moral application of words and matters, but also with their allegorical significance, and with the mystic value of numbers. Where he quotes a verse from Vergil, or even merely from Geoffroy de Viterbo, he frequently makes bad blunders; his own Latin is not altogether exemplary, although in its way tolerable enough. If the Life of Duke Humphrey—which he is said to have written—had been preserved, our praise would probably have referred more to his good intentions than to his intellectual ability. Otherwise, Capgrave was a very shrewd man in his own sphere, of sound understanding, and a skillful compiler, who sometimes, it is true, makes arrant confusion of historical matter beyond his grasp, and also allows himself to be carried away by loyal zealousness; upon the whole, however, he leaves the impression of a clear-headed, sober-minded man, honest and, in many respects, a trustworthy and well-informed authority. With such advantages and such limitations in his character, he was the very man to make use of the variety of materials at his command for reproducing an exact picture of the vanishing era, and for collecting its characteristic features for future generations.—TEN BRINK, BERNHARD, 1892, *History of English Literature, (Fourteenth Century to Surrey) tr. Schmitz, p.* 17.

In point of style Capgrave is as inferior to his predecessors as he is to his successors. Incomparably inferior in point of vigour, grace, rhythm, and copiousness and choice of words to the composition of the chief contemporaries of Chaucer, his style as compared with that of Pecock seems almost a relapse into barbarism. Without vigour or colour, without grace or ornament, his style is singularly jejune and feeble. Here and there, indeed, a neatly turned sentence and a rhythmic paragraph indicate that the example of his more accomplished predecessors had not been without effect. Considering how much our language had been enriched by Chaucer and Lydgate in verse, and by Pecock and others in prose, it is surprising that Capgrave's vocabulary should be so limited; and limited it is in a remarkable degree. But the explanation of his literary deficiencies is no doubt partly to be found in the temper of the man himself, and partly in the fact that his life was passed, not at any of the centres of culture, but in a remote and obscure corner of the provinces. His temper is the temper of the pedant and the monk, neither curious nor intelligent when important matters are in question, but scrupulous about trifles, and delighting uncritically to record them; inordinately superstitious, narrow alike in sympathy and understanding, without grasp and without vigour.—COLLINS, CHURTON, J. 1893, *English Prose, ed. Craik, vol.* I, *p.* 90.

The fillip that Wyclif had given to the development of English prose is completely lost as far as John Capgrave is concerned. Living and dying at King's Lynn, remote from the centres of culture, he was untouched by the movements of his day, and his "Chronicle of England" is as devoid of literary interest as its author is of personal interest.—WYATT AND LOW, 1896, *English Literature to* 1580, *p.* 110.

John Harding

C. 1378–1465?

A rhyming chronicler, in 1390 entered the household of Harry Percy, "Hotspur," whom he saw fall on Shrewsbury Field in 1403. Pardoned for his treason, he became constable of Warkworth Castle, fought at Agincourt, and served the crown in confidential missions to Scotland. His chronicle, composed in limping stanzas, and treating the history of England from the earliest times down to Henry VI.'s flight into Scotland, he rewrote and presented to Edward IV. just after his accession. It is poor history and poorer poetry, but the account of the Agincourt campaign has the interest of the eye-witness. Richard Grafton continuued it down to Henry VIII. See edition by Sir Henry Ellis (1812.)—PATRICK AND GROOME, *eds.* 1897, *Chambers's Biographical Dictionary, p.* 462.

Harding a Poet Epick or Historicall, handled himselfe well according to the time and maner of his subiect.—PUTTENHAM, GEORGE, 1589, *The Arte of English Poesie, ed. Arber, p.* 76.

In my Judgement, he had drank as hearty a draught of Helicon as any in his age.—FULLER, THOMAS, 1662, *Worthies of England, ed. Nichols, vol.* II, *p.* 514.

He seems to me to be totally destitute of poetry, both from the wretchedness of his lines, and the unhappiness of his subject.—CIBBER, THEOPHILUS, 1753, *Lives of the Poets, vol.* I, *p.* 26.

Almost beneath criticism, and fit only for the attention of an antiquary. Harding may be pronounced to be the most impotent of our metrical historians, especially when we recollect the great improvements which English poetry had now received. I will not even except Robert of Gloucester, who lived in the infancy of taste and versification. The chronicle of this authentic and laborious annalist has hardly those more modest graces, which could properly recommend and adorn a detail of the British story in prose.—WARTON, THOMAS, 1778-81, *The History of English Poetry, sec.* XXV.

JOHN Harding, whose "chronicle" is beneath criticism in point of composition, and can only be an object of curiosity to the antiquary.—ELLIS, GEORGE, 1790-1845, *Specimens of the Early English Poets, vol.* I, *p.* 291.

He left a "Chronicle of the History of England," which possesses an incidental interest from his having been himself a witness to some of the scenes which he records; for he lived in the family of the Percys, and fought under the banners of Hotspur; but from the style of his versified "Chronicle," his head would appear to have been much better furnished for sustaining the blows of the battle, than for contriving its poetical celebration.—CAMPBELL, THOMAS, 1819, *Essay on English Poetry.*

Hardyng's "Chronicle" occupied his leisure for very many years. His relations with the Percy family and with persons of influence in the first half of the fifteenth century give much value to his later chapters, although his information is usually meagre. The earlier chapters which begin with Brute are useless. The "Chronicle" is in English verse which is hardly better than doggerel; each stanza consists of seven lines rhyming *a b a b b c c.* Although his name is often mentioned in early lists of English poets, his work has no literary merit. The extant manuscripts of the "Chronicle" differ in important respects, and show that Hardyng was constantly rewriting it to adapt it to new patrons.—LEE, SIDNEY, 1890, *Dictionary of National Biography, vol.* XXIV, *p.* 363.

Sir John Fortescue

1394?-1476?

Sir John Fortescue, (died after 1476), was descended from an old Devonshire family, and in 1442 was made Chief Justice of the King's Bench. He was a strong partisan of the Lancastrian cause, and in the first Parliament of Edward IV. was attainted of high treason. He fled to Scotland, and afterwards to France, where he became the tutor of the young Prince Edward, for whose instruction he wrote his famous work, "De Laudibus Legum Angliæ." He was present at the battle of Tewkesbury, and in 1473 obtained a reversal of his attainder by retracting what he had written against Edward IV.'s title to the crown. The date of his death is uncertain. His book is of much interest, from its picture of a constitutional ideal that had almost been realised in the preceding generation.—LOW AND PULLING, 1884, *The Dictionary of English History, p.* 470.

All good men, and lovers of the English constitution, speak of him with honour, and that he still lives in the opinions of all true Englishmen, in as high esteem and reputation, as any judge that ever sat in Westminster Hall. He was a man acquainted with all sorts of learning, besides his knowledge in the law, in which he was exceeded by none; as will appear by the many judgments he gave, when on the bench, in the year-book of Henry VI. His character, in history, is that of pious, loyal, and learned; and he had the honour to be called the chief counsellor of the King. He was a great courtier, and yet a great lover of his country. — ALAND, JOHN FORTESCUE, 1714, *ed. The Difference between an Absolute and Limited Monarchy.*

One of the first important prose-writers in the language.—SHAW, THOMAS B., 1847, *Outlines of English Literature, p.* 30.

The works of his three predecessors, Glanville, Bracton, and Hengham, were no doubt more useful to the legal student and forensic practitioner; but that of Fortescue offered greater attractions to general readers by its popular form and its historical details; and the consequence is that while the former have become almost obsolete, the latter is still read with interest by the curious and philosophical enquirer.—FOSS, EDWARD, 1851, *Judges of England, vol.* IV, *p.* 308.

The great value of the book* consists in the emphatic testimony which it bears to the free principles of our Constitution as

* "Monarchy."

then fully recognised; but it has also considerable literary merit. It is forcibly and clearly written, without prolixity or repetition. The English is very easy. Indeed, as we read it in the printed editions, it seems so much more like common English than any other book of the century is, that it makes us suspect that the book has been to some extent modernised by its printers and publishers. —CREASY, SIR EDWARD S., 1870, *History of England, vol.* II, *p.* 553.

The spirit is the spirit of Alfred of old, and he writes as a man who was looking forward more than two centuries when English liberties were to be fully established at the revolution of 1688, under William.—HUNT, THEODORE W., 1887, *Representative English Prose and Prose Writers, p.* 34.

In his works Fortescue proves himself an Englishman whose expressions of patriotism at times surpass the bounds of absurdity, a warm friend of his nation, a man clear in thought and humane in feeling, a zealous advocate of freedom as well as of political order, a learned lawyer and devoted to his profession. And although of a strictly ecclesiastical turn of mind—in other words, with a leaning towards ultramontanism—he was a man of upright and sincere piety, as is evident from his beautiful "Dialogue between Understanding and Faith," which discusses, from the point of view of a faithful and devout Christian, the difficult problem of the sovereignty of a merciful and just Providence amid the perplexed and often most sorrowful form assumed by our life here on earth. . . . While he is clear and convincing in the development of his thoughts—which are not, indeed, presented altogether methodically, yet in synoptical order—and happy in the selection of his explanatory illustrations and detail, he is further distinguished by the choice of his expressions, by the formation and combination of his sentences in their simple appropriateness and definiteness. Besides this, he manages to produce increased effect, within modest limits, by gradation, repetition, and antithesis; at times also he brings his periods to a full-sounding close by making use of a greater flow of language. The Renaissance did not quite reach him, and yet his earnest inquiry into the actualities of his own domain, gives him an attitude in some measure connected with the Renaissance.—TEN BRINK, BERNHARD, 1892, *History of English Literature, (Fourteenth Century to Surrey) tr. Schmitz, pp.* 31, 32.

As a writer of English prose, Fortescue's chief merit lies in the fact that he was the first to adapt it to the discussion of political and constitutional problems. His phraseology is, of course, somewhat antiquated: he preserves the *en* termination of the infinitive and of the plural of verbs, together with a few other archaisms which have disappeared by the reign of Henry VIII. His style, moreover, being necessarily experimental, lacks elegance and harmony; but it is never undignified, it always exhibits the vigour, lucidity, and method of the practised lawyer, and occasionally kindles with the glow of patriotism or professional pride.—REICHEL, H. R., 1893, *English Prose, ed. Craik, vol.* I, *p.* 80.

He deserves the praise of being our earliest political historian. Fortescue is one of our greatest Latin authorities on constitutional law, and as a writer on definitely national themes in a purely colloquial English he is an innovator among those who wrote, if not in Latin or French, in a style obviously translated from one of those tongue. His sentences are short, but abrupt and inelegant; he performs his task, and we acknowledge his courage, but we cannot pretend to enjoy the manner of delivery.—GOSSE, EDMUND, 1897, *Short History of Modern English Literature, p.* 52.

Fortescue's fame has rested almost entirely on the dialogue "De Laudibus." Coke, speaking with the exaggeration which he used in referring to Fortescue's contemporary, Littleton, described it as worthy, "si vel gravitatem vel excellentiam spectemus," of being written in letters of gold (Pref. to 8th Rep.), and Sir W. Jones following him, called it "aureolum hunc dialogum." . . . The editor of his less known treatise, "On the Governance of England," however, has good reason for his opinion that the historical interest of the latter is far higher. It is less loaded with barren speculations, and it shows a real insight into the failure of the Lancastrian experiment of government; while it is invaluable as the earliest of English constitutional treatises.—MACDONELL, G. P., 1889, *Dictionary of National Biography, vol.* XX, *p.* 44.

Sir Thomas Littleton

1402–1481

Littleton, or Lyttleton, Sir Thomas: jurist; born at Frankley, Worcestershire, England, in 1402. He was the eldest son of Thomas Westcote, but was baptized in the name of his mother's family, she being sole heir of Thomas de Littleton, lord of the manor of Frankley. He was a member of the Inner Temple, and was in practice as a pleader in 1445, and in 1453 was called to the degree of sergeant-at-law. He held several public offices, among which were the shrievalty of Worcestershire and the recordership of Coventry. In 1455 he was made king's sergeant and acted as justice of assize in the northern circuit, and before the death of Henry VI. he was appointed steward of the Marshalsea court and justice of the county palatine of Lancaster. He appears to have been involved in the political troubles of the times, and on the accession of Edward IV. obtained a general pardon under the great seal, and was soon in favor with the new king, by whom he was made a justice of the court of common pleas (Apr. 27, 1466), and created a Knight of the Bath (Apr. 18, 1475). He died at Frankley, Aug. 23, 1481, and was buried in the nave of the Worcester Cathedral under a marble alter-tomb erected by himself, upon which was an effigy of himself in brass, which, however, was removed during the civil wars. Littleton's fame rests chiefly upon his treatise on tenures, which was a short work written in law (Norman) French.—ALLEN, F. STURGES, 1897, *Johnson's Universal Cyclopædia, vol.* V, *p.* 301.

Thomas Littleton, alias Westcote, the famous lawyer, to whose Treatise of Tenures the students of the Common Law are no less beholden than the Civilian to Justinian's Institutes.—CAMDEN, WILLIAM, 1586-1789, *Britannia, ed. Gough.*

It is a desperate and dangerous matter for Civilians and Canonists (I speak what I know, and not without just cause) to write either of the Common Laws of England, which they profess not, or against them, which they know not. And for Littleton's Tenures I affirm, and will maintain against all opposites whatever, that it is a work of absolute perfection in its kind, and as free from error as any book that I have known to be written of human learning. — COKE, SIR EDWARD, 1628, *Institutes of the Laws of England.*

The very adepts in the law are not ashamed frequently to read it. I knew a Lord-Keeper that read it every Christmas, as long as he lived.—NORTH, ROGER, 1733?-1824, *A Discourse on the Study of the Laws.*

The reputation of Littleton's "Treatise on Tenures" is too well established to require any mention of the praises which the most respectable writers of our country have bestowed on it. No work on our laws has been more warmly or generally applauded by them.—BUTLER, CHARLES, 1789, *Preface to* 14*th ed., Coke on Littleton.*

Littleton's fame rests upon a short treatise on "Tenures" written primarily for the instruction of his son Richard, to whom it is addressed, but which early attained the rank of a work of authority. Though preceded by, and to some extent based upon, a meagre tract of uncertain date known as "Olde Tenures," Littleton's work was substantially original, and presented in an easy, and, notwithstanding it is written in law-French, agreeable style, and within moderate compass, a full and clear account of the several estates and tenures then known to English law with their peculiar incidents. Probably no legal treatise ever combined so much of the substance with so little of the show of learning, or so happily avoided pedantic formalism without forfeiting precision of statement. The date at which it came to be recognised as an authority cannot be exactly fixed; it is, however, cited by Fitz Herbert in his "Novel Natura Brevium," published in 1534 (see the chapter on *Formedon*). Coke's elaborate commentary upon it testifies to the position which it held in his day. He himself evidently regarded it with a reverence bordering on superstition. "The most perfect and absolute work," he calls it, "that ever was written in any huamn science," and extravagance of eulogy provoked and excused by the absurd and ignorant censure of the civilian, Francis Hotman (see Coke, *Inst.* pt. I, Pref., and *Rep.* pt. x. Pref.) Littleton's text with Coke's comment long remained the principal authority on English real property law.—RIGG, J. M., 1893, *Dictionary of National Biography, vol.* XXXIII, *p.* 374.

William Caxton

1422?–1492

Was born in the Weald of Kent, about 1422. The particulars of the life of this great benefactor of his country are scanty. He was apprenticed in 1439 to Robert Large, a wealthy London mercer. At the death of the latter in 1441, he went to Bruges, where in 1462 or 1463 he seems to have been governor of a chartered association of English adventurers trading to foreign parts. In 1471, Caxton entered the service of Margaret, the duchess of Burgundy, formerly an English princess; and apparently towards the end of 1476 he set up his wooden printing-press at the sign of the red pale in the almonry at Westminster. The art of printing he had acquired during his sojourn in Bruges, doubtless from Colard Mansion, a well-known printer of that city; and in 1474 he put through the press the first book printed in the English tongue, the "Recuyell of the Historyes of Troye," a translation of Raoul le Fevre's work. The "Game and Playe of the Chesse" was another of Caxton's earliest publications; but the "Dictes and Notable Wise Sayings of the Philosophers," published in 1477, is the first book which can with certainty be maintained to have been printed in England. All the eight founts of type from which Caxton printed may be called black letter. . . . In 1877, the printer and his work were fittingly commemorated by a typographical exhibition in London.—PECK, HARRY THURSTON, *ed.* 1898, *The International Cyclopœdia, vol.* III, *p.* 583.

PERSONAL

To the Memory
of
William Caxton,
Who first introduced into Great Britain
The Art of Printing,
And who, A. D. 1477, or earlier,
Exercised that Art
In the Abbey of Westminster,
THIS TABLET
In remembrance of One
To whom
The Literature of this Country
Is so largely indebted,
Was raised
Anno Domini MDCCCXX.
By the Roxburghe Club.
Earl Spencer, K. G., President.

—*Inscription on Tomb, St. Margaret's, Westminster*, 1830.

If it plese ony man spirituel or temporel to bye ony pyes of two and thre comemoracious of Salisburi use enpryntid after the forme of this preset lettre whiche ben wel and truly coreect—late hym come to westmonester in to the almonesrye at the reed pale and he shal haue them good chepe.

Supplico stet cedula.

—CAXTON, WILLIAM, 1477–78? *Advertisement.*

Mr. Caxton appears to have been a very humble, modest, and virtuous man. He often styles himself a rude and simple person, confesses his ignorance, and humbly beseeches the pardon of his readers, and the patience to correct his works; and expresses himself in other terms so submissive and self-abasing as are very uncommon, and more easily admired than imitated. . . . He was a man of no more learning than, as he ingeniously confessed, he had by his knowledge of the English and French languages, in which he modestly acknowledged, he remembered himself of his rudeness and unperfitness. By the account which he has given of his printed books, it sufficiently appears in how great favour and request he was with the princes and great men of his own time.—LEWIS, JOHN, 1737, *Life of Mayster Wyllyam Caxton.*

That the end of Caxton was a good end we have little doubt. We have a testimony . . . that he *worked* to the end. He worked upon a book of pious instruction to the last day of his life. He was not slumbering when his call came. He was still labouring at the work for which he was born.—KNIGHT, CHARLES, 1844, *William Caxton, the First English Printer*, p. 195.

As we write the name of CAXTON, a grave and beardless face, with an expression somewhat akin to sadness, rises from the past, looking calmly out from the descending lappets of the hood, which was the fashionable head-dress of his day. All honour to the memory of the Father of the English Press! . . . He united in himself nearly all the occupations connected with the production and sale of books; for in the infancy of printing there was no division of labour. Author, inkmaker, compositor, pressman, corrector, binder, publisher, bookseller,—Caxton was all these.—COLLIER, WILLIAM FRANCIS, 1861, *A History of English Literature, pp.* 72, 74.

There is no extant portrait of England's first printer. That accepted as his by Lord Orford is based on the small defaced vignette in the manuscript of "The Dictes and Sayings" at Lambeth Palace. King Edward the Fourth is represented on his throne, with the young Prince of Wales—to whom Lord Rivers was tutor—standing by his side; there are two kneeling figures, one of which, Lord Rivers, is presenting to the king a copy of his own translation. The other, assumed by Lord Orford to be Caxton, is the portrait of an ecclesiastic, with evident tonsure, and probably represents Haywarde the scribe, who certainly engrossed the copy, and perhaps executed both the illumination and its accompanying rhythmical dedication. The portrait commonly assigned to Caxton, which first appeared in his life by the Rev. Mr. Lewis, of Margate, is like a large percentage of historical portraits—a picture of somebody else, if of anybody in particular. A portrait of Burchiello, an Italian poet, from a small octavo edition of his work on Tuscan poetry, of the date of 1554—wherein it is introduced merely as an illustration of a Florentine with the "capuchin" and "becca," the turban cap with a streamer—was copied by Faithhorn for Sir Hans Sloane as the portrait of Caxton; one more proof that a demand will generally create a supply. Lewis improved upon his predecessor by adding a thick beard to Burchiello's chin, and otherwise altering his character, and in this form the Italian poet made his appearance upon copper as Caxton.—BECKER, BERNARD HENRY, 1878, *Adventurous Lives, vol.* I, *p.* 286.

GENERAL

William Caxton . . . was a menial servant, for thirty years together, to Margaret Duchess of Burgundy, sister to our King Edward IV. in Flanders. He afterwards returned into England; where finding, as he says, an imperfect history, begun by one of the monks of St. Albans, says John Pits very unadvisedly, he continued it in English, giving it only the Latin title of Fructus Temporum. How small a portion of this work is owing to this author, has been observed before; but he now usually bears the name of the whole, which begins with the first inhabiting of this island, and ends (the last year of Edward IV.) A.D. 1483. The opportunities he had of being acquainted with the court transactions of his own time, would encourage his readers to hope for great matters from him; but his fancy seems to have led him into an undertaking above his strength.—NICOLSON, WILLIAM, 1696–1714, *English Historical Library, pt.* i.

Whoever turns over Caxton's printed works must contract a respect for him, and be convinced that he preserved the same character through life, of an honest, modest man: greatly industrious to do good to his country, to the best of his abilities, by spreading among the people such books as he thought useful to religion and good manners, which were chiefly translated from the French.—MIDDLETON, CONYERS, 1735, *A Dissertation Concerning the Origin of Printing in England.*

In the choice of his authors, that liberal and industrious artist was reduced to comply with the vicious taste of his readers; to gratify the nobles with treatises on heraldry, hawking, and the game of chess, and to amuse the popular credulity with romances of fabulous knights, and legends of more fabulous saints. The father of printing expresses a laudable desire to elucidate the history of his country; but instead of publishing the Latin chronicle of Radulphus Higden, he could only venture on the English version by John de Trevisa; and his complaint of the difficulty of finding materials for his own continuation of that work, sufficiently attests that even the writers, which we now possess, of the fourteenth and fifteenth centuries, had not yet emerged from the darkness of the cloister. His successors, with less skill and ability, were content to tread in the footsteps of Caxton; almost a century elapsed without producing one original edition of any old English historian.—GIBBON, EDWARD, 1794, *An Address, Miscellaneous Works ed. Sheffield, p.* 836.

Exclusively of the labours attached to the working of his press as a new art, our typographer contrived, though well stricken in years, to translate not fewer than five thousand closely printed folio pages. As a translator, therefore, he ranks among the most laborious, and, I would hope, not the least successful, of his tribe. The foregoing conclusion is the result of a careful enumeration of all the books translated as well as printed by him; which, (the translated books,) if published in the modern fashion, would extend to nearly twenty-five octavo volumes! — DIBDIN, THOMAS FROGNALL, 1810–20, *Typographical Antiquities of Great Britain.*

Venerable shade of Caxton! the award of the tribunal of posterity is a severe decision, but an imprescriptible law. Men who appear at certain eras of society, however they be lauded for what they have done, are still liable to be censured for not doing what they ought to have done. Patriarch of the printing press, who to thy last and dying day withdrew not thy hand from thy work! it is hard that thou shouldst be amenable to a law which thy faculties were not adequate to comprehend: surely thou mayst triumph, thou simple man! amid the echoes of thy "Caxtonians" rejoicing over thy Gothic leaves; but the historian of the human mind is not the historian of typography. —DISRAELI, ISAAC, 1841, *The First English Printer, Amenities of Literature.*

As a linguist, Caxton undoubtedly excelled. In his native tongue, notwithstanding his self-depreciation, he seems to have been a master. His writings, and the style of his translations, will bear comparison with Lydgate, with Gower, with Earl Rivers, the Earl of Worcester, and other contemporaneous writers. Many of his readers, indeed, thought him too "ornate" and "over curious" in his diction, and desired him to use more homely terms; but, since others found fault with him for not using polished and courtly phrases, we may fairly presume that he attained the happy medium, "ne over rude, ne over curious," at which he aimed. When excited by a favourite subject, as the "Order of Chivalry," he waxed quite eloquent; and the appeal of Caxton to the knighthood of England has been often quoted as a remarkable specimen of fifteenth-century declamation. With the French tongue he was thoroughly conversant, although he had never been in France; but Bruges was almost French, and in the Court of Burgundy, as well as in that of England, French was the chief medium of conversation. With Flemish he was also well acquainted. as shown by his translation of "Reynart;" indeed, this language, after so long a residence in Bruges, must have become almost his mother-tongue. Caxton's knowledge of Latin has often been denied or underrated; but as governor of the English nation in Bruges, and as ambassador, he must have been able to read the treaties he assisted to conclude, and the correspondence with the king's council. Moreover, he printed books entirely in the Latin tongue, some of which were full of contractions, and could only have been undertaken by one well acquainted with that language. . . . As translator, editor, and author, Caxton has not received his due meed of praise The works which he undertook at the suggestion of his patrons, as well as those selected by himself, are honestly translated, and, considering the age in which he lived, are well chosen. . . . As to Caxton's industry, it was marvellous; at an age when most men begin to take life easily, he not only embarked in an entirely new trade, but added to the duties of its general supervision and management, which could never have been light, the task of supplying his workmen with copy from his own pen.—BLADES, WILLIAM, 1861-97, *The Biography and Typography of William Caxton, pp.* 88, 89, 90.

His own style is full of Gallicisms in vocabulary and phrase.—MARSH, GEORGE P., 1862, *The Origin and History of the English Language, etc., p.* 483.

Thy prayer was "Light—more Light—while Time shall last!"
Thou sawest a glory growing on the night,
But not the shadows which that light would cast,
Till shadows vanish in the Light of Light.

—TENNYSON, ALFRED LORD, 1885, *Epitaph on Caxton, in St. Margaret's, Westminster.*

Caxton cannot be said to have creative power or literary invention of his own. But it is a mistake to conceive of him as only a diligent and humble translator, content to spread abroad the work of others, and without discernment or judgment of his own. His own translations, if we may give the name to his free paraphrase of French books of romance and chivalry, and to his compilations from the tales then floating about Europe, are unambitious and of no great interest in matter. They are filled with the usual tedious moralisings, and show no great power of selection or force of narrative. But they have the essential element of literary power in a style of admirable clearness, in a certain easy and polished grace of language, and in a bold adoption of words of foreign origin which were fitted to enrich the storehouse of English, and to give to our tongue the most valuable quality of facility and variety of expression. It is for this that Caxton deserves not only the praise due to a pioneer in his craft, but also that due to a weighty contributor to the development of our literary style.—CRAIK, HENRY, 1893, *English Prose, vol.* I, *p.* 97.

The work he did was of great importance in his age; he was its representative man of letters.—WHITE, GREENOUGH, 1895, *Outline of the Philosophy of English Literature, The Middle Ages, p.* 175.

Caxton, without any very great genius for writing, was at least vivid and amusing. When he excuses himself for scribbling, unauthorised, an epilogue to Lord Rivers's "Dictes," saying that "peradventure the wind had blown over the leaf," Caxton introduces a playfulness, a lightness of touch that had been hitherto unknown in English prose. He was a man, not of genius, but of industry and taste, born at a fruitful moment.—GOSSE, EDMUND, 1897, *Short History of Modern English Literature, p.* 53.

Take him with Pecock, who was probably not twenty years his senior, and we see that his form, if not quite so interesting to the historian, is far more adapted for general literature; take him with Malory, who was probably of his own age, and we find from a different point of comparison the same result. It is clear that Caxton was in at least two senses a man of letters, that he had the secret of literary craftsmanship.—SAINTSBURY, GEORGE, 1898, *A Short History of English Literature, p.* 209.

In 1496 the church wardens of St. Margaret, Westminster, were possessed of fifteen copies of "The Golden Legend," bequeathed by Caxton. Ten of these took five years to sell. In 1496 one copy was sold for 6s. 8d., and in 1500 the price had gone down to 5s. In 1510 R. Johnson, M. D., bought five Caxtons ("Godefroy of Boleyn," "Eneydos," "Faytes of Arms," "Chastising," and "Book of Fame") for a total expenditure of 6s. 8d. These are now in the University Library, Cambridge. In the sale of 1678, to which the name of Voetius is attached, three Caxtons sold for 7s. 10d. At the sale of Secondary Richard Smith's library (1682) eleven Caxtons realised £3, 4s. 2d.; at Dr. Francis Bernard's sale (1697), ten for £1, 15s. 4d. There were a considerable number of Caxtons in the Harleian Library, and several of these were duplicates. They do not appear to have sold very readily, and they occur in several of Osborne's catalogues at a fairly uniform price of one guinea for the folios and 15s. for the quartos. At the Hon. Bryan Fairfax's sale (1756) nine Caxtons sold for £33, 4s. At James West's sale (1773) the price had considerably advanced, and thirty-four Caxtons realised £361, 4s. 6d. John Ratcliffe's forty-eight Caxtons brought £236, 5s. 6d. At Dr. Richard Farmer's sale (1798) five sold for £19, 11s. 6d. An astonishing advance in price is found at the Duke of Roxburghe's sale (1812), where fourteen fine Caxtons brought £3002, 1s. At the sale of Stanesby Alchorne's library in 1813 nine fetched £666, 15s. Ralph Willett's seven brought in 1813 £1319, 16s. John Towneley's nine sold in 1814 for £1127. The Marquis of Blandford's (White Knights) eighteen Caxtons brought in 1819 £1316, 12s. 6d. At Watson Taylor's sale in 1823 nine brought £319, 14s. 6d.; John Inglis (1826), thirteen for £431, 15s. 6d.; John Dent (1827), four for £162, 16s. 6d.; George Hibbert (1829), five for £339, 13s. 6d.; P. A. Hanrott (1833), six for £180, 16s.; R. Heber (1834), six for £219, 16s.; Thomas Jolley (1843-51), six for £325, 15s.; E. V. Utterson (1852), three for £116; J. D. Gardner (1854), seven for £739. It will be seen from these totals that the present high prices did not rule at the sales in the middle of the present century. In 1897 the total for the ten Caxtons in the first portion of the Ashburnham library reached £5622, and the six in the second portion fetched £4264.—WHEATLEY, HENRY B., 1898, *Prices of Books, p.* 193.

Henry the Minstrel

(Blind Harry)

Fl. 1460–1492

A Scottish minstrel, blind from his birth, who lived by telling tales, and in 1490-92 was at the court of James IV., receiving occasional small gratuities. His poem on Wallace exists in a MS. of 1488, copied by John Ramsay. This MS. does not ascribe the work to Blind Harry, nor is his name given to it in the earlier printed editions. The poem, which contains 11,861 lines, is written in rhyming couplets. The language is frequently obscure, but the work is written with vigour, and kindles sometimes into poetry. The author seems to have been familiar with the metrical romances, and represents himself as indebted to the Latin Life of Wallace by Master John Blair, Wallace's chaplain, and to another by Sir Thomas Gray, parson of Liberton. The poem was at one time regarded as a work of fiction, but authentic documents have shown that, in spite of many mistakes or misrepresentations, it is on the whole a valuable narrative. It is believed to have been printed in Edinburgh in 1520, but no perfect copy is known of any earlier edition than that of 1570. "The Actis and Deidis of the Maist Illuster and Vailyeand Campioun Schir William Wallace, Knicht of Ellerslie." Good editions are by Jamieson (1820) and by Moir for the Scottish Text Society (1885-89). The work was for 200 years one of the most popular in Scotland, but as its language ceased to be understood, its place was supplied by a modernised version by Hamilton of Gilbertfield (1722).—PATRICK AND GROOME, *eds.*, 1897, *Chambers's Biographical Dictionary, p.* 466.

During my infancy, Henry, a man blind from his birth, composed a separate work on the exploits of Sir William Wallace; collecting such accounts as were then preserved by popular tradition, he exhibited them, in popular rhyme, which he had cultivated with success; but writings of this kind I only credit in part: the author was a person who, by the recitation of stories before men of the highest rank, earned his food and raiment, of which he was worthy.—MAIR, JOHN, 1521, *Major De Gestis Scotorum, f.* lxxiiii.

The story of Wallace poured a Scottish prejudice in my veins, which will boil along there till the flood-gates of life shut in eternal rest.—BURNS, ROBERT, 1787, *Letter to Dr. Moore.*

That a man *born* blind should excel in any science is sufficiently extraordinary, though by no means without example; but that he should become an excellent poet is almost miraculous; because the soul of poetry is description. Perhaps, therefore, it may be easily assumed, that Henry was not inferior in point of genius either to Barbour or Chaucer, nor indeed to any poet of any age or country; but it is our present business to estimate the merits of the work rather than the genius of the author. The similarity of the subject will naturally induce every reader to compare the life of Wallace with Barbour's life of Bruce; and on such a comparison, it will probably be found that Henry excels his competitor in correctness of versification, and, perhaps, in perspicuity of language (for both of which he was indebted to the gradual improvements which had taken place during near a century); but that in every other particular he is greatly inferior to his predecessor.—ELLIS, GEORGE, 1790–1845, *Specimens of the Early English Poets, vol.* I, *p.* 284.

I must express a doubt whether, as a biography, it deserves the unmeasured neglect or contempt with which it has been treated. Of this neglect I plead guilty, amongst the rest of my brethren, for I have scrupulously avoided consulting him as an historical authority; but some late researches, and an attentive perusal of his poem, comparing it as I went along with contemporary documents, have placed the "Life of Wallace" in a different light. I am persuaded that it is the work of an ignorant man, who was yet in possession of valuable and authentic materials. . . . The work cannot be treated as an entire romance—still less is it to be regarded as a uniformly veracious chronicle: but it exhibits the anomalous and contradictory appearance of a poem full of much confusion, error, and absurdity, yet through which there occasionally runs a valuable vein of historic truth.—TYTLER, PATRICK FRASER, 1833, *Lives of Scottish Worthies, vol.* III, *pp.* 299, 300.

In general poetical capacity the Scottish minstrel is incomparably inferior to Homer; but it was owing doubtless to the entireness and intensity of his patriotic devotion to Scotland and to Wallace, that his book was for centuries "the Bible of the Scottish people," and that it profoundly affected the boyish imaginations of Robert Burns, of Walter Scott, and of Hugh Miller. The fiery patriotism of this book inspired those national songs of Burns, and those magical tones occurring at intervals in all his poems, which will thrill readers to their inmost hearts so long as love of country endures. Its effect on Hugh Miller was to make him a Scottish patriot to the finger-tips. Affection for his country was from that time a ruling passion in his breast, and his ideal of a great man was a great Scotchman. . . . He who, as a boy, is indifferent to his own country, will, as a man, be indifferent to all countries. Hugh Miller, we need not doubt, owed much of that home-bred vigor, that genial strength, racy picturesqueness and idiomatic pith, which characterize his writings, to the early influence of Blind Harry.—BAYNE, PETER, 1871, *The Life and Letters of Hugh Miller, vol.* I, *pp.* 39, 40.

One does not like to say severe things about a poor old wandering minstrel. Like many other bygones that were interesting to bygones, he and his heroic verse, once an acceptable arrival at many a lively feast and proud residence, would be considered a terrible visitation in modern society. Blind Harry has not the elements of perennial interest. Only strong patriotism could have composed, and only strong patriotism could have listened to, his strains. Till very recently, however, he was popular among the Scottish peasantry, circulating no longer in oral recitation, but in printed copies, often boardless and well-thumbed. Of late he has been superseded by Miss Porter's "Scottish Chiefs."—MINTO, WILLIAM, 1874–85, *Characteristics of English Poets, p.* 69.

It is difficult from our point of view to approach Blind Harry's poem seriously; but it would certainly be a mistake to consider it a mere fabricated romance of a peasant minstrel. It is much more than that. It is the garner into which has been gathered all that harvest of popular legend about Wallace which had been ripening for nearly two centuries. We do not suppose that the author was at all scrupulous in his treatment of traditions, or that he shrank from contributing his quota to the general sum of patriotic fiction. Everywhere in the work there is evidence of more than poetical license; but we are convinced that in the main it recites and re-echoes the "Gests" that had enraptured and amazed successive generations of his countrymen.—ROSS, JOHN MERRY, 1884, *Scottish History and Literature, etc., ed. Brown, p.* 76.

About the poetic merits of the poem opinions have widely differed, some critics placing it above Barbour's "Bruce," and others treating it as chiefly valuable for the ardent love of liberty it displays. If Blind Harry had not high poetical gifts he had a modest and simple style, and a natural eloquence more telling because never overstrained. Like Barbour, who in this he probably followed, his poem is an early example of rhymed heroic metre, and is singularly free from alliteration. The effect of its popularity can scarcely be over-estimated. Next to the deeds of their heroes the poems of Barbour and Blind Harry created Scottish nationality, and spread through all classes the spirit of independence.—MACKAY, ÆNEAS, 1891, *Dictionary of National Biography, vol.* XXVI, *p.* 121.

Where does our whole idea of Wallace in the first instance come from except from the pages of Blind Harry himself, or rather Hamilton's version of him? But for this poem, Wallace would never have occupied a prominent place in the popular imagination, for the simple reason that so little would have appeared about him in history, to say nothing of the impossibility of writing such books as the "Scottish Chiefs" and other more or less inspiring works, whereby Wallace's fame has been spread.—CRAIGIE, W. A., 1893, *Barbour and Blind Harry as Literature, Scottish Review, vol.* 22, *p.* 196.

The presence of indignation and the absence of information combine in him to make an exceedingly spirited romance, which was naturally and deservedly popular in Scotland from the very first, but which, of course, has the slightest—if the slightest—pretence to historical importance. The ghostly apparition of

Fawdone, in the finest passage of all, is not more a thing of the imagination than the still more famous fishing story with which the poem opens, or the stock incident (very freshly and excellently told) of the visit of the Queen of England to Wallace, and her mediation with her no less cowardly than ferocious husband. But it was all perfectly right and proper, according to the laws of the class of composition to which Blind Harry's work belongs; and it is a compensation for the extreme lateness and comparative scantiness of Scottish literature that it was thus able to produce the latest, and very far indeed from the worst, example of the national folk-epic which blends traditions of all sorts, adds commonplaces from the general stock of fiction, and makes the whole thick and slab with original sauce, in order to exalt and consecrate the deeds of a popular hero.—SAINTSBURY, GEORGE, 1898, *A Short History of English Literature*, p. 174.

Sir Thomas Malory

1430?-1496?

No details of his life are known. Probably born about 1430 in Wales. His "Le Morte Arthur" was printed by Caxton in 1485 (only two copies known); reprinted by Wynkyn de Worde in 1498 (only one copy known) and 1529 (only one copy known). A great many modern editions hav been published in America and Great Britain.—MOULTON, CHARLES WELLS, 1900.

Here is the end of the booke of kyng Arthur and of his noble knyghtes of the Rounde Table, that whan they were hole togyders there was ever an C and xl. And here is the ende of the deth of Arthur. I praye you, all jentyl men and jentyl wymmen that redeth this book of Arthur and his knyghtes from the begynnyng to the endyng, praye for me whyle I am on lyve that God sende me good delyveraunce, and whan I am deed, I praye you all praye for my soule; for this book was ended the ix yere of the reynge of kyng Edward the Fourth by Syr Thomas Maleore, knyght, as Jhesu helpe hym for hys grete myght, as he is the servaunt of Jhesu bothe day and nyght.—MALORY, SIR THOMAS, 1485? *Le Morte Darthur, bk.* xxi, *ch.* xiii.

¶Thus endeth thys noble and Ioyous book entytled le morte Darthur / Notwithstondyng it treateth of the byrth / lyf / and actes of the sayd kynge Arthur / of his noble knyghtes of the rounde table / theyr meruayllous enquestes and aduentures / thachyeuyng of the sangreal / & in thende the dolourous deth & departyng out of thys world of them al / Whiche book was reduced in to englysshe by syr Thomas Malory knyght as afore is sayd / and by me deuyded in to xxi bookes chapytred and enprynted / and fynysshed in thabbey westmestre the last day of Iuyl the yere of our Lord M / CCCC / lxxx / V / ¶Caxton me fieri fecit.—CAXTON, WILLIAM, 1485, *Colophon to First ed. Le Morte Darthur.*

In our forefathers tyme, whan Papistrie, as a standyng poole, couered and ouerflowed all England, fewe bookes were read in our tong, sauyng certaine bookes Cheualrie, as they sayd, for pastime and pleasure, which, as some say, were made in Monasteries, by idle Monkes, or wanton Chanons: as one for example, *Morte Arthure:* the whole pleasure of which booke standeth in two speciall poyntes, in open mans slaughter, and bold bawdrye: In which booke those be counted the noblest Knightes that do kill most men without any quarrell, and commit fowlest adoulter(i)es by sutlest shiftes: as Sir *Launcelot* with the wife of king *Arthure* his master: Syr *Tristram* with the wife of king Marke his vncle: Syr *Lamerocke* with the wife of king *Lote*, that was his owne aunte. This is good stuffe, for wise men to laugh at, or honest men to take pleasure at. Yet I know, when Gods Bible was banished the Court, and *Morte Arthure* receiued into the Princes chamber. What toyes, the dayly reading of such a booke, may worke in the will of a yong ientleman or a yong mayde, that liueth welthily and idelie, wise men can iudge, and honest men do pitie. And yet ten *Morte Arthures* do not the tenth part so much harme, as one of these books, made in *Italie* and translated in England.—ASCHAM, ROGER, 1570, *The Schoolmaster, ed. Arber*, p. 80.

A Book that is, in our Days, often sold by the Ballad-singers with the like

Authentick Records of *Guy of Warwick* and *Bevis of Southampton.* — NICOLSON, WILLIAM, 1696, *The English Historical Library, vol.* I, *p.* 98.

Indisputably the best Prose Romance the language can boast.—SCOTT, SIR WALTER, 1824, *Essay on Romance, p.* 267.

It is as if the book were the production of no one mind, nor even of a score of successive minds, nor even of any one place or time, but were a rolling body of British-Norman legend, a representative bequest into the British air and the air overhanging the English Channel, from the collective brain and imagination that had tenanted that region through a definite range of vanished centuries.—MASSON, DAVID, 1859, *British Novelists and their Styles, p.* 51.

Hardly any book in our language deserves the epithet of dull so little as the work of Sir Thomas Malory.—CREASY, SIR EDWARD S., 1870, *History of England, vol.* II, *p.* 555.

Sir Thomas Malory's "Morte d'Arthur" is a condensation of an extensive literature—the prose romances on the subject of Arthur and the Knights of the Round Table. Its humble prose is all that we have to show as a national epic. It is compiled and abridged from French prose romances written during the thirteenth, fourteenth, and fifteenth centuries, and contains the most famous exploits fabled of our national heroes. Its chief pretense to unity is that it begins with the birth of Arthur and ends with his death. It is, further, consistent in recognising throughout the invincible superiority of Lancelot of the Lake. Otherwise, its variety is somewhat bewildering, in spite of the obliging printer's division into twenty-one books. It is a book to choose when restricted to one book, and only one, as the companion of solitude; there might then be some hope of gaining a clear mastery over its intricacies, a vivid conception of each several adventure of Gawain and his brothers, of Pelinore, Lancelot, Pelleas, Tristram, Palamides, Lamorak, Percival, Galahad, and their interminable friends, foes, and fair ladies.—MINTO, WILLIAM, 1874–85, *Characteristics of English Poets, p.* 81.

In nothing has the revival of sound critical taste done better service than in recalling us to the Arthurian Cycle, the dayspring of our glorious literature. The closing books of Malory's Arthur certainly rank, both in conception and in form, with the best poetry of Europe; in quiet pathos and reserved strength they hold their own with the epics of any age. Beside this simple, manly type of the mediæval hero the figures in the Idylls of the King look like the dainty Perseus of Canova placed beside the heroic Theseus of Pheidias.—HARRISON, FREDERIC, 1879-86, *The Choice of Books and Other Literary Pieces, p.* 45, *note.*

Nor must I omit to mention Sir T. Malory's "Morte d'Arthur," though I confess I do so mainly in deference to the judgment of others.—LUBBOCK, SIR JOHN, 1887, *The Choice of Books, The Pleasures of Life, p.* 78.

I say in this new day of printing a certain Sir Thomas Mallory, who lived at the same time with Caxton, the first English printer, did, at the instance, I think, of that printer—put all these legends we speak of into rather stiff, homely English prose—copying, Caxton tells us, from a French original: but no such full French original has been found; and the presumption is that Mallory borrowed (as so many book-makers did and do) up and down, from a world of manuscripts. And he wrought so well that his work had great vogue, and has come to frequent issue in modern times, under the hands of such editors as Southey, Wright, Strachey and Lanier.—MITCHELL, DONALD G., 1889, *English Lands Letters and Kings, From Celt to Tudor, p.* 45.

The very soul of mediæval Christianity breathes out of the story of the Quest of the Graal as told with simple directness by Sir Thomas Malory. The great popularity of the romance of Tristram and King Mark's wife, the fair Isolde, made it impossible that Malory should have thought of omitting that. But in some sense Tristram is to Isolde as Lancelot to Guinevere. The romance of Tristran was an early offshoot from the sequence planned by Walter Map, and a reader of Sir Thomas Malory's "History of Arthur" might get a better impression of the sequence of adventures, as Map had arranged them, by omitting from the first reading those chapters which interweave the tale of Tristram and Isolde. They were inseparable from the Arthur Legend of Sir Thomas Malory's time, but they break the harmony of the first arrangement by burdening one part of it with variations on its motive.—MORLEY, HENRY, 1890, *English Writers, vol.* VI, *p.* 330.

The most remarkable prose romance that had yet been written in the English language. . . . Its appearance marks an epoch in the history of English romance literature.—JUSSERAND, J. J., 1890, *The English Novel in the Time of Shakespeare, p.* 54.

The "Morte d'Arthur"—by which title the work is generally known—can in no way divest itself of the character of being a compilation: repetitions, contradictions, and other irregularities are by no means of rare occurrence. At the same time, it is, upon the whole, arranged with a certain degree of skill, for in spite of the abundance of episode, Malory has succeeded in producing a kind of unity, and even though some monotony in the variety was unavoidable, still the plan and style of the narrative do not allow our interest to sleep, or, if asleep, it is aroused at definite points. Above all, the terse style of the narrative, in simple, but by no means colourless language, produces a good effect; and it was this alone which made it possible to compress the mass of material within a space readily surveyable.—TEN BRINK, BERNHARD, 1892, *History of English Literature, (Fourteenth Century to Surrey,) tr. Schmitz, p.* 46.

Speaking generally of the Arthur of Welsh literature, one may characterise him in few words:—His first appearance is found to conform itself with the rôle of a *Comes Britanniæ,* on whom it devolved to help the inhabitants of what was once Roman Britain against invasion and insult, whether at the hands of Angles and Saxons or of Picts and Scots: so we read of him acting for the kings of the Brythons as their *dux bellorum.* We next find his fame re-echoed by the topography of the country once under his protection, and his name gathering round it the legends of heroes and divinities of a past of indefinite extent. In other words, he and his men, especially Kei and Bedwyr, are represented undertaking perilous expeditions to realms of mythic obscurity, bringing home treasures, fighting with hags and witches, despatching giants, and destroying monsters. How greatly this rude delineation of the triumph of man over violence and brute force differs from the more finished picture of the Arthur of Malory's painting, it would be needless to try to shew to anyone bent on the pleasure of perusing the Morte Darthur. Such a reader may be trusted to pursue the comparison unassisted, in the fascinating pages of this incomparable book.—RHYS, JOHN, 1893, *ed. King Arthur, Preface, p.* XXXV.

Malory's prose, and not Chaucer's, is the prose analogue of Chaucer's poetry; summing up as it does some of the great attainments of the earlier Middle Ages, and presenting them in colours more brilliant, with a more conscious style, than they had possessed in their first rendering. . . . He is an author and an artist, and his style is his own.—KER, W. P., 1893, *English Prose, ed. Craik, Introduction, vol.* I, *pp.* 14, 15.

Above all, Malory's language and style exactly suit his subject. In no work is there a perfecter harmony—a more sympathetic marriage—of this kind. This chronicler of knighthood is himself a knight. His heart is devoted to the chivalry he portrays, and his tongue is the faithful spokesmen of his heart.—HALES, JOHN W., 1893, *English Prose, ed. Craik, vol.* I, *p.* 62.

Malory's style is characterised by the simplicity and perspicuity of his French originals, and although latinised words are not uncommon, and he connects his sentences with particles like "and," "then," and "so," his best effects are produced by the use of monosyllables. No effort in English prose on so large a scale had been made before him, and he did much to encourage a fluent and pliant English prose style in the century that succeeded him. In the nineteenth century, interest in his work was revived after a long interval. Tennyson's "Idylls of the King," Mr. William Morris's "Defence of Guinevere," Mr. Swinburne's 'Tristram of Lyoness," and Mr. Matthew Arnold's "Death of Tristram," were all suggested by Malory's book.—LEE, SIDNEY, 1893, *Dictionary of National Biography, vol.* XXXV, *p.* 440.

His simple forthright narrative is admirably lucid and effective, and makes amends for an inevitably rambling structure, while his flashes of chivalrous feeling illuminate the plains through which his story wanders. He is a master in the telling use of the Saxon speech, although he translates from the French.—RALEIGH, WALTER, 1894, *The English Novel, p.* 15.

Whatever may have influenced Malory, he produced a book which cannot safely be neglected by the student of mediæval life and manners, to say nothing of the reader who is interested in the "Morte Darthur" on purely literary grounds. One can hardly understand the spirit of the Middle Ages without giving much attention to the romances, and one can find no romance in English to compare with the "Morte Darthur." Even though the life there depicted is neither English nor French, and though the narrative has little or no basis in reality, the picture which the romance presents has just enough resemblance to the real society to be highly suggestive. Of course the picture needs interpretation and modification, yet it presents in a vivid light the ideals of what we somewhat vaguely call chivalry, and is steeped in the spirit of the great feudal society. This spirit it was, we may well believe, that made the book popular in its own time, and this will doubtless win for it favor in centuries to come.—MEAD, WILLIAM EDWARD, 1897, *ed. Selections from Sir Thomas Malory's Morte Darthur, Introduction, p.* xxviii.

The French romance reciting the death of Arthur, together with the English poem already mentioned, came into the hands of Thomas Malory, and contributed to the narrative which in 1485 was printed under the title of Le Morte Darthur. In addition, Malory used the Queste, and romances relating to Merlin and Tristan, together with other prose compositions in which the poetic spirit of the cycle had been buried by rambling adventures. Out of such a conglomerate it was impossible to produce an interesting whole. The attraction of Malory's work is chiefly owing to the language; only in the conclusion, where he borrowed from the English poem, has his account unquestioned merit. In spite of these inevitable difficulties, and of the consequent want of clearness and sequence, the history continues to be read and frequently printed; apart from the matter, the purity of style, as well as the enthusiasm of the compiler, will probably maintain its place as an English classic.—NEWELL, WILLIAM WELLS, 1897, *King Arthur and the Table Round, vol.* I, *p.* liv

The characters in Mallory's recasting of the Arthurian legends are to some extent individualized, but they are romantic. They do not speak the natural language of men, nor are they concerned about the ordinary activities of life. The poem is far from being a transcript of life or even an interpretation of life, since the artificial motives of chivalry and mystical religion are predominant in the personages represented. They are not from life, but from a three-century dream of life, though the tragedy of Launcelot's and Guinevere's love is conceived truthfully and profoundly.—JOHNSON, CHARLES F., 1898, *Elements of Literary Criticism, p.* 64.

Robert Fabyan

C. 1456–1512

Fabyan, or Fabian, Robert (died 1512), was an English chronicler of the fifteenth century. He was a prosperous London citizen, and became sheriff in 1493. His book "A Concordance of Histories," begins, as usual, with Brutus, and is a commonplace compilation up to his own time, when it becomes moderately useful as contemporary, if uncritical, evidence, and is especially full on London history. The first edition was printed in 1516.—LOW AND PULLING, 1884, *The Dictionary of English History, p.* 447.

The first post in the sixteenth century is due to Robert Fabian, an eminent merchant, and sometime sheriff of London. . . . Both Bale and Pitts subdivide his historical writings into a great many several treatises: but, I presume, what they call his Historiarum Concordantiæ is the sum of all. . . . He is very particular in the affairs of London, many good things being noted by him, which concern the government of that great city, hardly to be had elsewhere.—NICHOLSON, WILLIAM, 1696–1714, *English Historical Library, pt.* i.

A modern Master Wit, in the contest betwixt the Poets of our age for the

Laurel maketh Apollo to adjudge it to an Alderman of London, "because to have most wealth was a sign of most wit." But, had the scene of this competition been laid seven-score years since, and the same remitted to the umpirage of Apollo, in sober sadness he would have given the Laurel to this our Alderman.—FULLER, THOMAS, 1662, *Worthies of England, ed. Nichols, vol.* II, *p.* 79.

Is generally better known as an historian, than as a poet. He was esteemed, not only the most facetious, but the most learned, of all the mercers, sheriffs, and aldermen, of his time: and no layman of that age is said to have been better skilled in the Latin language. . . . Our author's transitions from prose to verse, in the course of a prolix narrative, seem to be made with much ease; and, when he begins to versify, the historian disappears only by the addition of rhyme and stanza. . . . As an historian, our author is the dullest of compilers. He is equally attentive to the succession of the mayors of London, and of the monarchs of England: and seems to have thought the dinners at Guildhall, and the pageantries of the city companies, more interesting transactions, than our victories in France, and our struggles for public liberty at home.—WARTON, THOMAS, 1778–81, *History of English Poetry, sec.* xxvii.

Fabyan's "New Chronicles" are worthy of mention as the massive and dull writings of a contemporaneous London alderman. His musty pages give much information in regard to the city, and a little in regard to the country as a whole. His partialities for the Lancasterian House were very strong.—ADAMS, CHARLES KENDALL, 1881, *A Manual of Historical Literature, p.* 512.

The day had now arrived, in the progress of society, when chronicles were written by laymen. The first in our vernacular prose was the labor of a citizen and alderman, and sometime sheriff of London, — Robert Fabyan; and was designed for "the unlettered who understand no Latin." In the accustomed mode, he fixes the historic periods by dates from Adam or from Brut, and composing in the spirit of the day, mentions the revolutions of government with the same brevity as he speaks of the price of wheat and poultry; passes unnoticed his friend Caxton, to speak of "a new weathercock placed on the cross of St. Paul's steeple;" tells us that of the French monarch's dress "*I might make a long rehearsal;*" finds the level of his faculties in recording "flying dragons in the air," or describing the two castles in space, whence issued two armies black and white, combating in the skies till the white vanished.—WELSH, ALFRED H., 1882, *Development of English Literature and Language, vol.* I, *p.* 254.

It is important as showing the first attempt, earnest although uncritical, to weigh authorities against one another. . . . His respect for preceding authorities, however fabulous their tales, was tempered only by the fact that they did not all agree. —CRAIK, HENRY, 1893, *English Prose, vol.* I, *p.* 109.

Fabyan's "Chronicles (Pynson, 1516), first edition. Dr. F. Bernard (1698), 4s. 8d. Roberts (1815), £84—North. John North (1819), £92. (Perfect). Samuel Lysons (1820), £35 — Lord Aylesford. Lord Aylesford (1888), £250—Christie Miller. (Completed by leaves from another edition.)—WHEATLEY, HENRY B., 1898, *Prices of Books, p.* 218.

Robert Henryson

1430?–1506?

A Scottish poet. He wrote "Schoolmaster of Dunfermline," "Testament of Cresseid" (a sort of sequel to Chaucer's "Troilus and Cressida"), "Robene and Makyne" (said to be the earliest English pastoral poem), "Fables of Esop" (probably written between 1470 and 1480), etc. The fables include "The Taill of the Uponlandis Mous and the Burges Mous" ("The Country Mouse and the City Mouse"). His collected works were edited by D. Laing (1865).—SMITH, BENJAMIN E., *ed.*, 1894–97, *The Century Cyclopedia of Names, p.* 495.

In Dunfermelyne he has done rovne
With gud Maister Robert Henrisoun;
Schir Iohne the Ros enbrast hes he;
Timor Mortis conturbat me.

—DUNBAR, WILLIAM, c 1530, *Lament for the Makaris.*

For the author of this supplement called the Testament of Creseid, which may passe for the sixt and last booke of this story, I have very sufficiently bin informed by Lr. Tho. Ereskin, late earle of Kelly, and divers aged schollers of the Scottish nation, that it was made and written by one Mr. Robert Henderson, sometimes chiefe schoole-master in Dumfermling, much about the time that Chaucer was first printed and dedicated to King Henry the 8th by Mr. Thiane, which was neere the end of his raigne. This Mr. Henderson wittily observing that Chaucer in his 5th booke had related the death of Troilus, but made no mention what became of Creseid, he learnedly takes upon him in a fine poeticall way to expres the punishment and end due to a false unconstant whore, which commonly terminates in extreme misery.—KYNASTON, SIR FRANCIS, 1635, *Loves of Troilus and Creseide translated into Latin, Commentary*, xxx.

Henryson perceived what there was defective in the close of the story of "Troilus and Creseide" as Chaucer has left it. . . . The Scottish was incapable of rising to the refinements, or conceiving the delicacies of the English poet: though it must be admitted that in the single instance of the state of mind, the half-recognition, half-ignorance, attributed to Troilus in his last encounter with Creseide, there is a felicity of conception impossible to be surpassed. In some respects the younger poet has clearly the advantage over the more ancient. There is in his piece abundance of incident, of imagery and of painting without tediousness, with scarcely one of those lagging, impertinent and unmeaning lines with which the production of Chaucer is so frequently degraded.—GODWIN, WILLIAM, 1803, *Life of Geoffrey Chaucer, vol.* I, *pp.* 487, 493.

The most beautiful of Henryson's productions is "Robene and Makyne," the earliest specimen of pastoral poetry in the Scotish language. I consider it as superior in many respects to the similar attempts of Spenser and Browne: it is free from the glaring improprieties which sometimes appear in the pastorals of those distinguished writers, and it exhibits many genuine strokes of poetical delineation. The Shepherd's indifference is indeed too suddenly converted into love; but this is almost the only instance in which the operations of nature are not faithfully represented. The story is skilfully conducted, the sentiments and manners are truly pastoral, and the diction possesses wonderful terseness and suavity. —IRVING, DAVID, 1861, *History of Scotish Poetry, ed. Carlyle, p.* 224.

As a poet who wrote in the language of the people, Henryson held a high place. His style was easy and flowing; and, though he did not show great inventive genius or passion, he had a fine perception of the beauties of external nature, and handled the objects around him with remarkable skill, and often presented vivid and touching descriptions.—MACKINTOSH, JOHN, 1878–92, *The History of Civilisation in Scotland, vol.* I, *p.* 462.

His verse is usually well-minted and of full weight. Weak lines are rare in him; he had the instinct of the refrain, and was fond of doing feats in rhythm and rhyme; he is close, compact, and energetic. Again, he does not often let his learning or his imagination run away with him and divert him from his main issue. He subordinates himself to the matter he has in hand; he keeps himself to the point, and never seeks to develop for development's sake; and so, as it appears to me, he approves himself a true artist. It follows that, as a storyteller, he is seen to great advantage. He narrates with a gaiety, an ease, a rapidity, not to be surpassed in English literature between Chaucer and Burns. That, moreover, he was a born dramatist, there is scarce one of his fables but will prove. It is to be noted that he uses dialogue as a good playwright would use it; it is a means with him not only of explaining a personage but of painting a situation, not only of introducing a moral but of advancing an intrigue. He had withal an abundance of wit, humor, and good sense; he had considered life and his fellow men, nature and religion, the fashions and abuses of his epoch, with the grave, observant amiability of a true poet.

. . His fables are perhaps the best in the language, and are worthy of consideration and regard even after La Fontaine himself.—HENLEY, WILLIAM ERNEST, 1880, *The English Poets, ed. Ward, vol.* I, *pp.* 137, 138.

Robert Henryson is the brightest light among the stars that circled in the train of Chaucer. . . . Henryson was a true poet, and he possessed what we call to-day a feeling for his art in a high degree. His narrative is gay, easy, rapid; his touch light and vivid, and his dramatic power, both in dialogue and construction, is not surpassed by Chaucer. His verse is musical and well weighed; he liked to try his hand at new refrains, strange metres, and unexpected rhymes. His dialect, to the modern eye and ear, is almost incomprehensible, but long study and great love will show him who cares to search that Henryson used it as the old composers used the harpsichord. It is an instrument of narrow compass, yet capable of exquisite harmonies under the hand of a master.—EGAN, MAURICE FRANCIS, 1880, *Chaucer and his Circle, Catholic World, vol.* 31, *p.* 708, *Lectures on English Literature, p.* 37.

All Henryson's writings are designed as lessons in good life, but he joins in his verse the finish of a scholar to kindly wisdom, twinkling with some sparks of humour in a simple homeliness of speech. He follows his time when he is somewhat over-curious of detail in working out his Fables into moral allegories, but in telling them he is not more prolix than a man should be who speaks to the ear, not to the eye, and seeks to recommend old home truths to the body of the people. If as poet he is schoolmaster, we do not tire over his lessons.—MORLEY, HENRY, 1890, *English Writers, vol.* VI, *p.* 254.

It is easy to trace the influence that this quiet retired life had upon his poetry, to which it has given a peculiar character that we do not find in any of the other early Scottish poets. There is a chastened, contemplative mood, much akin to the quality which it pleased Fletcher and Milton to call melancholy, which runs through most of Henryson's compositions—the serious, philosophical calm of a member of a quiet community who minded their own simple affairs, and meddled little with the outside world. His humour, of which there is an abundant store in his "Moral Fables," is of a quiet, cultivated type, dwelling on homely incidents of country life, but with the enjoyment of the scholar who sits apart and watches the play with a kindly but slightly superior amusement, instead of plunging into the thick of the fun as James I. or Dunbar would have done.—OLIPHANT, F. R., 1890, *Robert Henryson, Blackwood's Magazine, vol.* 148, *p.* 498.

Henryson is abreast of the culture of his time. . . . He is the first pure lyrist among Scottish poets. His ingenious rhymes and his mastery of pause and cadence, as seen, e.g., in the quatrain of the "Garmond" and the octave of the "Abbey Walk" and "Robene and Makyne," betoken a correct and disciplined ear. Besides giving special direction to the ballad, Henryson introduced into the language the moral fable and the pastoral. —BAYNE, THOMAS, 1891, *Dictionary of National Biography, vol.* XXVI, *p.* 131.

First of the greater Scottish makars whose life and work bore no direct relation to the political history of the country, the Dunfermline poet struck on the national lyre certain sweet and quaint new keys which ring yet with an undiminished charm, and preserve for him a unique place among the master-singers of the north.—EYRE-TODD, GEORGE, 1892, *Mediæval Scottish Poetry, p.* 79.

He was the first writer of pastoral poetry in these islands. It is no small praise to his "Robene and Makyne" to say that it anticipates "Duncan Gray"—which tells the same tale with the *rôles* of the lovers reversed—by something like four centuries and a half (?). Not that no pastoral poems of this description were written between the two referred to—not that Henryson's poem can compare with Burns's for either melody or dramatic condensation—but there is a freedom and originality of handling in both poems at the same time that the pastoral spirit is maintained, which justifies one in saying that with Henryson, as with Burns, the pastoral lyric was an independent and indigenous growth, rather than the often sickly and always artificial importation which obtained south of the Tweed. . . It is only because he wrote so comparatively little that was wholly original that he cannot be ranked along with

Dunbar; though even when he imitated others he always added something of his own.—HEATH, H. FRANK, 1894, *Social England, ed. Traill, vol.* II, *pp.* 516, 518.

Besides his fondness for classical themes and his tendency to regard all subjects from a moral point of view, Henryson gives signs of the approach of the Renaissance in his *pictorial* treatment of allegory. The descriptions of his abstract personages are highly generalised in the manner of the Latin poets, and at the same time show that attention to the effects of pageantry which is so marked a feature in the poetry of Spenser.—COURTHOPE, W. J., 1895, *A History of English Poetry, vol.* I, *p.* 369.

John Colet

1466–1519

Dean of St. Paul's, and founder of St. Paul's School (1512); born at London, 1466; died there Sept. 16, 1519, and was buried in St. Paul's Cathedral. He was one of the "Reformers before the Reformation." He took his M. A. at Oxford (1490), and went abroad (1493) to study Greek and Latin. On his return, in 1497, he publicly expounded Paul's Epistles at Oxford, and there became acquainted with Erasmus, with whom he maintained an intimate friendship. He was promoted to various positions,—made D. D. 1504, and Dean of St. Paul's 1505. His great reform was to introduce expository preaching, and a perpetual divinity-lecture on three days in each week, in St. Paul's Church. By his well-known disapproval of auricular confession, celibacy of the clergy, and other Roman practices, he was considered by the faithful little short of a heretic: hence he was subject to a variety of persecutions. He wrote "Absolutissimus de octo orationis partium constructione Libellus," London, 1530; "Rudimenta Grammatices," London, 1510 (a book designed for use in St. Paul's School, and dedicated to its first master, the famous George Lilly); "Daily Devotions, or the Christian's Morning and Evening Sacrifice" (Darling mentions only the edition of 1693).—SCHAFF-HERZOG, *eds.* 1882, *A Religious Encyclopædia, vol.* I, *p.* 508.

Let every man have his own doctor, and every one follow his liking; but this is the doctor for me.—HENRY VIII, 1513, *Quoted by Erasmus in Life of Colet, p.* 46.

It was but a very small portion of this religious spirit that he owed to nature. For he was gifted with a temper singularly high and impatient of affront; he was, as he himself confessed to me, naturally prone to incontinence, luxuriousness, and indulgence in sleep; overmuch disposed to jests and raillery; and he was besides not wholly exempt from the taint of covetousness. But these tendencies he combated so successfully by philosophy and sacred studies, by watching, fasting, and prayer, that he led the whole course of his life free from the pollutions of the world. As far as I could gather from my intimate acquaintance and conversations with him, he kept the flower of chastity even unto death. His fortune he spent on charitable uses. Against his high temper he contended with the help of reason, so as to brook admonition even from a servant. Incontinence, love of sleep, and luxuriousness, he vanquished by an uniform abstinence from supper, by constant sobriety, by unwearied exertions in study, and by religious conversation. Yet if an occasion had ever presented itself, either of conversing with ladies, or being a guest at sumptuous repasts, you might have seen some traces of the old nature in him. And on that account he kept away, as a rule, from laymen's society, and especially from banquets. If forced at times to attend them, he would take me or some similar companion with him; in order, by talking Latin, to avoid wordly conversation. Meanwhile he would partake sparingly of one dish only, and be satisfied with a single draught or two of ale. He was abstemious in respect of wine; appreciating it, if choice, but most temperate in the use of it. Thus, keeping a constant watch upon himself, he carefully avoided everything by which he might cause anyone to stumble; not forgetting that the eyes of all were upon him. I never saw a more highly-gifted intellect. But though he felt a peculiar pleasure, on this account, in kindred intellects, he liked better to bend his mind to such things as fitted it for the immortality of the life to come. If at times he sought relaxation in sprightlier talk, he would still philosophize on every topic. He took a delight in the purity and simplicity of nature that is in children; a nature that Christ bids His disciples imitate; and he was wont to compare them to angels.—ERASMUS, DESIDERIUS, 1519, *Letter to Justus Jonas, tr. Lupton, p.* 30.

For generations we have not had amongst us any one man more learned or holy.—MORE, SIR THOMAS, 1519, *Epistolâe aliquot Eruditorum, p.* 122.

He should have bin burnt if God had not turned the King's heart to the contrarie.—LATIMER, HUGH, 1535, *Sermons.*

This Colet had travelled through France and Italy, and upon his return he settled for some time at Oxford, where he read divinity lectures, without any obligation or reward for it. His readings brought him all the learned and studious persons in the University. He read not according to the custom that prevailed universally at that time, of commenting on Thomas Aquinas, or on Scotus; but his readings were upon St. Paul's Epistles.—BURNET, GILBERT, 1679–1715, *The History of the Reformation of the Church of England, ed. Nares, vol.* III, *pt.* iii, *bk.* i, *p.* 41.

So exquisitely Learned, that all Tully's Works were as familiar to him, as his Epistles. He was also no Stranger to Plato and Plotinus, whom he not only read, but conferred and paralelled, perusing the one, as a Commentary on the other. And as for the Mathematicks, there was scarce any part thereof wherein he was not seen above his years.—WOOD, ANTHONY, 1691–1721, *Athanæ Oxonienses, vol.* I, *p.* 11.

We see a full reformation of moral and religious truth serenely and quietly accomplished in the mind of Dr. Colet, before the name of Luther had passed beyond his own threshold.—TURNER, SHARON, 1829, *History of the Reigns of Edward the Sixth, Mary, and Elizabeth, p.* 141.

The very boldness of the lecturer and the novelty of the subject were enough to draw an audience at once. Doctors and abbots, men of all ranks and titles, flocked with the students into the lecture hall, led by curiosity doubtless at first, or it may be, like the Pharisees of old, bent upon finding somewhat whereof they might accuse the man whom they wished to silence. But since they came again and again, as the term went by, *bringing their notebooks with them,* it soon became clear that they continued to come with some better purpose. . . . They were in almost every particular in direct contrast with those of the dominant school. They were not *textarian.* They did not consist of a series of wiredrawn dissertations upon isolated texts. They were no "thread of nine days long drawn from an antitheme of half an inch." Colet began at the beginning of the Epistle to the Romans, and went through with it to the end, in a course of lectures, treating it as a whole, and not as an armoury of detached texts. Nor were they on the model of the *Catena aurea,* formed by linking together the recorded comments of the great Church authorities. There is hardly a quotation from the Fathers or Schoolmen throughout the exposition of the Epistle to the Romans. Instead of following the current fashion of the day, and displaying analytical skill in dividing the many senses of the sacred text, Colet, it is clear, had but one object in view, and that object was to bring out the direct practical meaning which the apostle meant to convey to those to whom his epistles were addressed. To him they were the earnest words of a living man addressed to living men, and suited to their actual needs. He loved those words because he had learned to love the apostle—the *man* —who had written them, and had caught somewhat of his spirit. He loved to trace in the epistles the marks of St. Paul's own character.—SEEBOHM, FREDERIC, 1867–69, *The Oxford Reformers, pp.* 32, 33.

He was a man of some eccentricity, over-confident in argument, and not so deeply learned in theology as some writers have taken for granted. But of his truthfulness and earnest desire to promote holy living there can be no doubt; and his testimony to the need of reformation in the Church of England is that of a witness whose character makes it worth while to give his words in some detail.—BLUNT, JOHN HENRY, 1869, *The Reformation of the Church of England, p.* 10.

By the new method of interpretation of scripture, and the new style of preaching which he initiated, he was a benefactor to his own age; by the school which he founded he has been a benefactor to all succeeding ages. But although his love of learning was great, his love of Christ was greater.—STEPHENS, W. R. W., 1878, *John Colet, Dean of St. Paul's, Good Words, vol.* 19, *p.* 409.

Some Catholics have denounced Colet as a "heretic," and Anglican writers assert that he was "a hidden Protestant." He was neither, but rather an austere man, who wished to see churchmen living according to the discipline of primitive Christianity.—BURKE, S. HUBERT, 1882, *John Fisher, Bishop of Rochester, Catholic World, vol.* 34, *p.* 590.

The great name of John Colet deserves something more than the mere passing notice which I can give it here. He deserves honor, especially in these times of ours, as having fought, amid circumstances immeasurably more trying and oppressive, the same battle which is now being waged under obloquy, against the vicious principles and methods of scholasticism.—HERRICK, S. E., 1884, *Some Heretics of Yesterday, p.* 103.

Colet's achievements seem slight compared with his posthumous fame. On education alone, where he diminished the ecclesiastical control at the same time that he increased the religious tone, did he exert a practical influence. He printed very few of his books, and their effect must have been consequently small. "As for John Colet," wrote Harding to Jewell, "he hath never a word to show, for he wrote no workes." His knowledge of Greek—the chief source of the New Learning—was slight. Hearne contended on slender grounds that he knew nothing of it till he was fifty. His Latin style is neither elegant nor correct; his English is not distinctive. His scriptural exegesis often takes refuge in mystical subtleties. His practical efforts of church reform were confined to the reissue of old rules of discipline to prevent the clergy from neglecting their duties. He was, however, among the first not only to recognise the necessity of making the scriptures intelligible to the masses in vernacular translations, but to criticise their subject-matter with any approach to scholarly method. Yet his chief strength lay in the overwhelming force of his personal conviction that the church had lost its primitive purity, and that the schoolmen had contributed less to the advantage of piety or of human intelligence than the early fathers or the classics, a conviction which impressed itself on all with whom he came into close contact, stirring active antagonism in the slow-witted or self-interested, but stimulating men of Erasmus's or More's intelligence into effective thought and action.—LEE, SIDNEY, 1887, *Dictionary of National Biography, vol.* XI, *p.* 326.

In what sense was Colet a reformer? It cannot be said that Colet distinctly repudiated any of the dogmas of the Church of his time. He simply shelved them in favor of the simple declarations of the Bible and the Apostles' Creed. A standpoint so liberal and yet intensely Christian makes Colet a kind of standard bearer for all, a man around whom the Churches may rally in this age of Christian union. His latest biographer and successor in St. Paul's School, London, which he founded, calls attention to this aspect of Colet. Even if we cannot trace the great Reformation movement to him, an instinctive feeling remains that in Colet we have a strong connecting link between the old and the new. In his many-sided character there is something in which all may claim a share. The Roman Catholic must honor one of whom More declares that "none more learned or more holy had lived among them for many ages past." The High Churchman will probably find but little in his extant writings from which he would feel bound to dissent.—HURST, JOHN FLETCHER, 1900, *History of the Christian Church, vol.* II, *p.* 373

Gawin Douglas

1474?-1522

A Scotch divine and poet of some eminence, was the son of Archibald, fifth Earl of Angus, and was born at Brechin in 1474. After receiving a liberal education he entered the church, was made provost of St. Giles's, and eventually obtained the abbacy of Aberbrothick and the bishopric of Dunkeld. Political dissensions induced him to seek refuge in England, where he was liberally treated by Henry VIII., but he fell a victim to the plague at London, in 1522. He wrote "The Palace of Honour" and other works; but his chief performance is a translation of Virgil's Æneid, noteworthy as the first translation of a Roman classic into English. It was completed in 1513, but not published till 1553.—CATES, WILLIAM L. R., *ed.*, 1867, *A Dictionary of General Biography, p.* 305.

He died at London, having proceeded so far on his journey to Rome, to the great regret of all those good men who admired his virtues. To splendour of birth, and a handsome and dignified person, he united a mind richly stored with the learning of the age, such as it then existed. His temperance and moderation were very remarkable; and living in turbulent times, and surrounded by factions at bitter enmity with each other, such was the general opinion of his honesty and uprightness of mind, that he possessed a high influence with all parties. He left behind him various monuments of his genius and learning of no common merit, written in his native tongue.—BUCHANAN, GEORGE, 1581, *History of Scotland, b.* 14, *c.* 13.

A man learned, wise, and given to all virtue and goodness.—SPOTISWOOD, JOHN, 1639? *History of the Church and State of Scotland, p.* 101.

In his prologues before every book,* where he hath his liberty, he showeth a natural and ample vein of poesy, so pure, pleasant, and judicious, that I believe there is none that hath written before or since, but cometh short of him. And in my opinion, there is not such a piece to be found as his prologue to the eighth book, beginning *Of drevilling and Dreams*, etc., at least in our language.—HUME, DAVID, 1644, *History of the Houses of Douglas and Angus, p.* 220.

Was so far from seeking popularity from English readers, that, in his excuses for his defects of style, he only laments the impossibility of making it purely and exclusively Scotish. — ELLIS, GEORGE, 1790–1845, *Specimens of the Early English Poets, vol.* I, *p.* 320.

Dunkeld, no more the heaven-directed chaunt
Within thy sainted walls may sound again,
But thou, as once the muse's favourite haunt,
Shalt live in Douglas' pure Virgilian strain,
While time devours the castle's crumbling wall,
And roofless abbeys pine, low-tottering to their fall.

—DYER, GEORGE, 1801, *Poems, p.* 89.

A bishop by the altar stood,
A noble lord of Douglas blood,
With mitre sheen and rochet white.
Yet showed his meek and thoughtful eye
But little pride of prelacy;
More pleased that in a barbarous age
He gave rude Scotland Virgil's page,
Than that beneath his rule he held
The bishopric of fair Dunkeld.

—SCOTT, SIR WALTER, 1808, *Marmion, c.* vi, *s.* xi.

In his political conduct Douglas supported a party which had been called into existence by the precipitate and imprudent marriage of the queen, and was animated by the selfish and often treacherous policy of the Earl of Angus. In his individual conduct he was pacific, temperate, and forgiving; but his secret correspondence with Henry VIII. and his ministers, instead of commanding the reverence, was probably the great cause of the animosity with which he was treated by his countrymen; nor can he be very consistently held up as a model of primeval purity, whom we find in the next sentence to have been the father of a natural daughter, from whom the house of Foulewood is descended. His genius and learning are unquestionable; his temper was mild and affectionate; and we may hope that his munificence rests on a more certain evidence than his patriotic feelings or political integrity. — TYTLER, PATRICK FRASER, 1833, *Lives of Scottish Worthies, vol.* III, *p.* 187.

The character of Douglas's original poetry seems to be that of the middle ages in general, — prolix, though sometimes animated, description of sensible objects.—HALLAM, HENRY, 1837–39, *Introduction to the Literature of Europe, pt.* i., *ch.* iv, *par.* 33.

Douglas's "Prologue," whether we look to its subject, or to its present waning popularity, may well take for its text "all is vanity." Its merit is not easy to estimate under the disadvantages of an obsolete dialect, bygone idioms, and a reference to a state of life and manners so unlike our own. Many strokes of satire, which at the time may have had a direct

*Of Virgil.

and personal application, are now sunk into vapid generalities, or lost from our ignorance of local circumstances. Still enough remains to excuse, if not to justify, the praises that were once lavished on this favourite poem. The crowd of images, and the grotesque combinations, produce almost the same effect on the mind as the noise, and hubbub, and confusion of another vanity-fair upon the ear of Bunyan's pilgrim. The broken and sketchy style, and the curious idiomatic turns, must, even at the time, have given the work a character of quaintness and oddity; and may have recommended it to many, who otherwise were little likely to pay attention to the lesson it reads them. —GUEST, EDWIN, 1838, *A History of English Rhythms, vol.* II, *p.* 172.

The fire in Douglas' original verses is occasionally lost in smoke, and the meaning buried in flowery verbiage. —GILFILLAN, GEORGE, 1860, *Specimens of the Less-Known British Poets, vol.* I, *p.* 72.

Nor were his talents less conspicuous than his learning. In all his writings he evinces an excursive fancy, with much of the fervour of genius. His allegorical sketches are efforts of no common ingenuity; but what chiefly renders his works interesting, is the frequent occurrence of those picturesque and characteristic touches which can only be produced by a man capable of accurate observation and original thinking. He exhibits perpetual vestiges of a prolific and even exuberant imagination, and his very faults are those of super-abundance rather than deficiency. In his descriptions, which are often admirable, he occasionally distracts the attention by a multiplicity of objects, nor is he sufficiently careful to represent each new circumstance in a definite and appropriate manner. His style is copious and impetuous, but it cannot be commended for its purity.—IRVING, DAVID, 1861, *History of Scotish Poetry, ed. Carlyle, p.* 266.

A little later came Gawain Douglas, whose translation of the Æneid is linguistically valuable, and whose introductions to the seventh and twelfth books —the one describing winter and the other May—have been safely praised, they are so hard to read. There is certainly some poetic feeling in them, and the welcome to the sun comes as near enthusiasm as is possible for a ploughman, with a good steady yoke of oxen, who lays over one furrow of verse, and then turns about to lay the next as cleverly alongside it as he can. But it is a wrong done to good taste to hold up this *item* kind of description any longer as deserving any other credit than that of a good memory. It is a mere bill of parcels, a *post-mortem* inventory of nature, where imagination is not merely not called for, but would be out of place. Why, a recipe in the cookery-book is as much like a good dinner as this kind of stuff is like true word-painting.—LOWELL, JAMES RUSSELL, 1875–90, *Spenser, Prose Works, Riverside ed., vol.* IV, *p.* 271.

To each book of the "Æneid" he wrote a prologue of his own. And it is chiefly by these that he takes rank among the Scottish poets. Three of them are descriptions of the country in May, in autumn, and in winter. The scenery is altogether Scotch, and the few Chaucerisms that appear seem absurdly out of place in a picture of nature which is as close as if it had been done by Keats in his early time. The colour is superb, the landscape is described with an excessive detail, but it is not composed by any art into a whole. Still it astonishes the reader, and it is only by bringing in the Celtic element of love of nature that we can account for the vast distance between work like this and contemporary work in England such as Skelton's. —BROOKE, STOPFORD, 1876, *English Literature, (Primer), p.* 55.

The work by which Douglas lives, and deserves to live, is his translation of the "Aeneid." It is a singular fruit of a barren and unlearned time, and, as a romantic rendering of the "Aeneid," may still be read with pleasure. The two poets whom Douglas most admired of all the motley crowd who pass through "The Palice of Honour" were Virgil and Chaucer. Each of these masters he calls an *a per se.* He imitated the latter in the manner of his allegorical verse, and he translated the former with complete success. We must not ask the impossible from Douglas,—we must not expect exquisite philological accuracy; but he had the "root of the matter," an intense delight in Virgil's music and in Virgil's narrative, a perfect sympathy with "sweet Dido," and that keen sense of the human life of Greek, Trojan, and Latin, which enabled him in turn to make them live in Scottish rhyme. If he talks of "the nuns of Bacchus," and if his Sibyl admonishes Aeneas to "tell his beads," Douglas is merely using what he thinks the legitimate freedom of the translator. —LANG, ANDREW, 1880, *English Poets, ed. Ward, vol.* I, *p.* 161

As the effort of a youth of twenty-six, "The Palice of Honour" is in some respects a remarkable performance. Its literary execution is of a high order. Douglas already shows himself a master of the art of versification. He has a fine sense of melody and an exhaustless wealth of words. Images rise freely at the summons of his brilliant fancy, but he sees nothing which has not been seen before, or, to put it more exactly, he designs with the same kind of figures and paints with the same kind of colours as his predecessors of the allegorical school. What is chiefly distinctive about the work is not its poetry, but its scholarship. He is the first Scottish poet whose verse breathes the odour of the Renaissance.—ROSS, JOHN MERRY, 1884, *Scottish History and Literature, ed. Brown, p.* 331.

He wears the stiff plate armor of the time.—WASHRURN, EMELYN W., 1884, *Studies in Early English Literature, p.* 93.

Of Douglas's ability, extensive and accurate learning, and strong and vigorous literary gift, there cannot be the shadow of a doubt. When we consider that his first considerable poem—marked by rich fancy, and compassing a lofty ideal—was produced when he was about the age at which Keats issued his last volume, and that all his literary work was done when he was still under forty, we cannot but reflect how much more he might have achieved but for the harassing conditions that shaped his career.—BAYNE, THOMAS, 1888, *Dictionary of National Biography, vol.* XV, *p.* 294.

He was a *dilettante* rather than a genuine poet. — EGAN, MAURICE FRANCIS, 1889, *Lectures on English Literature, p.* 39.

He was a man of a firm yet frank nature, not without ambition, and—to his misfortune—was involved in the party-feuds of the Scottish nobility, but full of genuine kindliness of feeling; as an ecclesiastic and prelate, a man of sound religious principles, opposed to scholastic cavilling, and faithfully attached to the fundamental doctrines of the Christian faith; above all, a devoted servant of the Muses and a zealous promoter of high culture. As a poet he is not one of the first rank; but, among those occupying the second stage, he was one of the most influential. As the translator of Vergil, the sublime painter of nature, the keen observer, the earnest and skilful delineator of life and of the human heart, Douglas will be remembered as long as Scottish literature is able to attract sympathetic admirers. — TEN BRINK, BERNHARD, 1892, *History of English Literature, (Fourteenth Century to Surrey) tr. Schmitz, p.* 92.

"King Hart," though in the same conventional vein of allegory, exhibits riper powers than Douglas's earlier work. So vivid, indeed, sometimes become the circumstances and characters that the reader forgets the allegory, and catches fire at the story itself. The narrative is full of action, the personifications are natural and real as life, and the plot has strong human interest, while the allegory is original, consistent throughout, and forcible. In all respects this must be reckoned a greater performance than its more famous sister piece. As the study of the growth and decline of an emotion it will, behind its archaic method, bear comparison with some of the best analytical novel-writing of the present day.—EYRE-TODD, GEORGE, 1892, *Mediæval Scottish Poetry, p.* 232.

Gavin Douglas anticipates Spenser, not only in his metrical style, but also in his use of allegory as a method of interpreting nature. As the expectation of the approaching end of the visible world, which had for so many centuries haunted the imagination of men, waned, the desire to realise the nature of the unseen universe also began to dissappear, leaving, however, behind it, in minds of a religious temper, a profound sense of the vanity of mortal things. This feeling, blended with the growing habit of moral reflection and the quickened perception of beauty, was fostered by the love which the pioneers of the Renaissance entertained for Virgil, an author whose depth of religious sentiment was only equalled by his profound knowledge of the resources of his art. No poet, not even Dante himself, ever drank more deeply of the spirit of Virgil than Gavin Douglas. Deeply versed in Catholic doctrine, he read into his theological studies the gravity, the melancholy, the sweetness, of his master in poetry. He showed his love for him by turning the "Æneid" for the first time into English ten-syllable rhyming couplets, and even more by the sentiment and style of the original Prologues which he prefixed to each book of his translation. Particularly notable are the Prologues to the sixth and seventh books.—COURTHOPE, W. J., 1895, *A History of English Poetry, vol.* I, *p.* 378.

Went beyond any other poet of the age in his power of rendering a true landscape, in regard to wealth of detail, varied imagery, and singularly spirited execution. This early art, however, has not yet always mastered the sense of proportion or of wholeness: the details of a May scene in the country are here catalogued in words rather than arranged or selected. Hence, and even more from the extreme rudeness or obscurity of the dialect employed, it is difficult to give a fair notion of the poet's great merit.—PALGRAVE, FRANCIS T., 1896, *Landscape in Poetry, p.* 127.

Critics of weight have held up Douglas, on the strength of this "Virgil," as representing, or at any rate anticipating, the new movement in poetry, that which incorporates the classical and modern tradition, and so as occupying a position at least historically more important than that of his more intensely and poetically gifted contemporary Dunbar. With all due deference, this may well be deemed a mistake. Even in the selection of Ovid and Virgil, Douglas, though he may have been slightly further affected by the classical influence "in the air," did not go very much further than Chaucer a century and more before him. And in the manner of his work, both original and translated, he is not modern at all. He is with Hawes, even with Lydgate; not with Wyatt and Surrey.—SAINTSBURY, GEORGE, 1898, *A Short History of English Literature, p.* 189.

While he altogether lacks the soaring sublimity of Dunbar, and the artistic finish of Kennedy, he surpasses both in his amatory warmth and his love of his fellows. He is dainty rather than strong, and more quaint and versatile than profound.—SMEATON, OLIPHANT, 1898, *William Dunbar, Famous Scots Series, p.* 21.

Stephen Hawes

1476?–1523?

Probably born in Suffolk. Educated at Oxford. Groom of Chamber to Henry VII. Died, about 1523 (?). *Works:* "The Passetyme of Pleasure," 1506; "The Conversyon of Swerers," 1509; "A Joyfull Medytacyon" (1509); "A Compendyous story . . . called the Example of Vertu" (1512?); "The Comfort of Lovers," *n. d.*—SHARP, R. FARQUHARSON, 1897, *A Dictionary of English Authors, p.* 127.

Very little is known of Stephen Hawes, and that little does not include the date either of his birth or of his death. He is said to have been a gentleman of birth, an Oxford man, a pretty considerable traveller, a master of modern languages, a man of great memory (seeing he could repeat by heart the works of Lydgate), and the possessor of a critical faculty somewhat smaller, inasmuch as he made that voluminous person equal in some respects with Geoffrey Chaucer. It is said with probability that he was Groom of the Chamber to Henry VII.; he certainly wrote verses to congratulate Henry VIII. on his accession; and it seems likely that he died in Suffolk in early middle age, certainly before 1530, and probably about 1523.—SAINTSBURY, GEORGE, 1898, *A Short History of English Literature, p.* 163.

Go, little boke! I praye God the save
From misse metryng by wrong impression;
And who that ever list the for to have,
That he perceyve well thyne intencion,
For to be grounded without presumption,
As for to eschue the synne of ydlenes;
To make suche bokes I apply my busines.
—HAWES, STEPHEN, 1506, *The Excusation of the Author, The Pastime of Pleasure.*

Such is the Fate of Poetry, that this Book, which in the Time of Henry 7 and 8, was taken into the Hands of all ingenious men, is now thought but worthy of a Ballad-monger's Stall!—WOOD, ANTHONY, 1691–1721, *Athenæ Oxonienses, vol.* I, *p.* 5.

If the poems of Rowlie are not genuine, the "Pastime of Pleasure" is almost the only effort of imagination and invention which had yet appeared in our poetry since Chaucer. This poem contains no common touches of romantic and allegoric fiction. The personifications are often happily sustained, and indicate the writer's familiarity with the Provencal school. The model of his versification and phraseology is that improved harmony of numbers, and facility of diction, with which his predecessor Lydgate adorned our octavo stanza. But Hawes has added new graces to Lydgate's manner.—WARTON, THOMAS, 1778–81, *History of English Poetry, sec.* xxviii.

Graund Amour (true Gallantry), the hero of the piece, falls asleep and sees a vision. He receives from *Fame* the first account of *La Belle Pucelle* (perfect Beauty), and is by her referred for farther particulars to the *Tower of Doctrine.* Here, certainly, is a beginning very much in the spirit of the times; but the subsequent conduct of the poem is not very well calculated to gratify the impatience of any reader who shall have taken a lively interest in the success of *Graund Amour's* passion. An accurate knowledge of the seven sciences, viz. grammar, logic, rhetoric, arithmetic, music, geometry, and astronomy, does not seem to be indispensably requisite to the success of a love adventure. These sciences, it is true, are all ladies; but many of them are dreadfully prolix in their instructions.—ELLIS, GEORGE, 1790–1845, *Specimens of the Early English Poets, vol.* I, *p.* 331.

In this work the personified characters have all the capriciousness and vague moral meaning of the old French allegorical romance; but the puerility of the school remains, while the zest of its novelty is gone. There is also in his foolish personage of Godfrey Gobelive, something of the burlesque of the worst taste of Italian poetry. It is certainly very tiresome to follow Hawes's hero, Grandamour, through all his adventures, studying grammar, rhetoric, and arithmetic, in the tower of Doctrine; afterwards slaughtering giants, who have each two or three emblematic heads; sacrificing to heathen gods; then marrying according to the Catholic rites; and, finally, relating his own death and burial, to which he is so obliging as to add his epitaph. Yet, as the story seems to be of Hawes's invention, it ranks him above the mere chroniclers and translators of the age.—CAMPBELL, THOMAS, 1819, *Essay on English Poetry.*

The popularity of Hawes, whatever it might have been during his own time, must now depend on a perusal of the analysis of his "Pastime of Pleasure" by Warton. The whole of this piece of criticism is the masterly effort of an ingenious and eloquent advocate. The sentence of Mr. Campbell, less favourable to the reputation of the poet, appears to be more consistent with the canons of just criticism.—DIBDIN, THOMAS FROGNALL, 1824, *The Library Companion, p.* 681.

Skelton, a contemporary with Hawes, falls below him, as well in style and diction, as in taste and invention.—HIPPISLEY, J. H., 1837, *Chapters on Early English Literature, p.* 219.

Those who require the ardent words or the harmonious grace of poetical diction will not frequently be content with Hawes. Unlike many of our older versifiers, he would be judged more unfavorably by extracts than by a general view of his long work. He is rude, obscure, full of pedantic Latinisms, and probably has been disfigured in the press; but learned and philosophical, reminding us frequently of the school of James I. The best, though probably an unexpected parallel for Hawes, is John Bunyan: their inventions are of the same class, various and novel, though with no remarkable pertinence to the leading subject, or naturally consecutive order; their characters, though abstract in name, have a personal truth about them, in which Phineas Fletcher, a century after Hawes, fell much below him; they render the general allegory subservient to inculcating a system, the one of philosophy, the other of religion. I do not mean that the "Pastime of Pleasure" is equal in merit, as it certainly has not been in success, to the "Pilgrim's Progress." Bunyan is powerful and picturesque from his concise simplicity; Hawes has the common failings of our old writers, a tedious and languid diffuseness, an expatiating on themes of pedantry in which the reader takes no interest, a weakening of every picture and every reflection by ignorance of the touches that give effect. But, if we consider the "Historie of Graunde Amour" less as a poem to be read than as a measure of the author's mental power, we shall not look down upon so long and well-sustained an allegory. — HALLAM, HENRY, 1837–39, *Introduction to the Literature of Europe, pt.* i, *ch.* iv, *par.* 73.

"The Pastime of Pleasure," which Warton characterises as his "capital work," is one of those allegorical writings which were popular with our forefathers, but which can now only be looked upon as monuments of the bad taste of a bad age. It is however a monument; and being one of the most remarkable productions between the age of Lydgate and that of Wyatt and Surrey, it deserves to be reprinted as one of the links in the history of English poetry, without which that history would be incomplete. The old editions of this poem are very rare.—WRIGHT, THOMAS, 1845, *ed. The Pastime of Pleasure, Preface, p.* v.

His model and master was, as he is constantly reiterating, Lydgate, though he was well acquainted with the works of Chaucer, whose comic vein he occasionally affects, with the verses of Gower, and with the narrative poetry of France and Italy. His poem is elaborately allegorical, though the allegory is not always easy to follow in detail, and is obviously much impeded with extraneous matter. The style has little of the fluency of Lydgate, and none of his vigour; the picturesqueness and brilliance which are characteristic of Chaucer are not less characteristic of Chaucer's Scotch disciples who were Hawes' contemporaries. The narrative, though by no means lacking incident, and by no means unenlivened with beauties both of sentiment and expression, too often stagnates in prolix discussions, and wants as a rule life and variety. The composition is often loose and feeble, the vocabulary is singularly limited, and bad taste is conspicuous in every canto. But Hawes, with all his faults, is a true poet. He has a sweet simplicity, a pensive gentle air, a subdued cheerfulness about him which have a strange charm at this distance of dissimilar time. Though the hand of the artist is not firm, and the colouring sometimes too sober, his pictures are very graphic.—COLLINS, J. CHURTON, 1880, *The English Poets, ed. Ward, vol.* I, *p.* 175.

Has certainly one of the most misleading titles to be found in English literature. The trivial and the careless, least of all, need delude themselves with the fancy that it was for them the work was designed. It provides just the sort of pastime and furnishes just the degree of pleasure that might be expected from one who looked upon Lydgate as his master and took him for his model.—LOUNSBURY, THOMAS R., 1891, *Studies in Chaucer, vol.* III, *p.* 32.

Other parts of a true poet, in the care spent mainly on essentials of life, in choice and treatment of his fable, Stephen Hawes had; but if he wrote his lines as they are printed, he was not skilled in the mechanism of his art. He was held by the ears when he was dipped in Helicon. —MORLEY, HENRY, 1891, *English Writers, vol.* VII, *p.* 73.

Hawes is very far from being able to compete with Lydgate in poetic productivity, yet he excels him, perhaps, in the art of invention and in working out allegorical motives. The style of art exhibited here is certainly of questionable value, but we must not overlook the fact that even Hawes forms a step in the ladder that leads up to Spenser. . . . His language is tolerably fluent, but little accurate and to the point; smooth, it is true, but bare and unsatisfactory. He shows undoubted talent for versification, yet, like other poets of his day, he was troubled by the struggle between the rigidity of scholastic tradition, and the progressive development of the language; it may also be that the type-setter has, at times, spoiled his verse. . . . Of the spirit of humanism, Hawes shows about as much as his master, Lydgate—that is, very little.—TEN BRINK, BERNHARD, 1892, *History of English Literature, (Fourteenth Century to Surrey) tr. Schmitz, pp.* 97, 98.

Here we have the unmistakable sign-manual of the literary dilettante, of one who would establish an esoteric cult in poetry by reversing the popular, the vulgar estimate, who seeks distinction by an amiable eccentricity of judgment, an affectation of special insight. Hawes was in fact the representative man of letters of the reign, the exponent of its culture; he was its product, for he was yet young when towards its close he composed his principal work. He was an ornament of the court, being in great request for his talents in composition, conversation and recitation from the elder poets—for he had a capacious memory. The king made him his Groom of the Chamber.—WHITE, GREENOUGH, 1895, *Outline of the Philosophy of English Literature, The Middle Ages, p.* 200.

The style of the composition is as languid and prolix as might be expected from its motive, and the versification gives no sign of the approach of Surrey. One beautiful image has survived the insipidities of which the poem is mainly composed, and has secured a place in the national memory:—

For though the dayës be nevir so long,
At last the bellës ringeth to evensong.

But as a whole the intellectual atmosphere we breathe makes us feel that life has been crushed out of feudalism by the Wars of the Roses; that Henry VII. is king; and that the brilliant, if fantastic, ideal of the knight has been replaced by the hollow artifices of the courtier.—COURTHOPE, W. J., 1895, *A History of English Poetry, vol.* I, *p.* 382.

There is both learning and philosophy in Hawes, but his style is pedantic and obscure.—HUTSON, CHARLES WOODWARD, 1897, *The Story of Language, p.* 295.

John Skelton

C. 1460–1529?

Born about 1460: died probably in 1529. An English scholar and poet. He was a proétgé of Henry VII., a noted scholar, and the tutor of Henry VIII. He took holy orders in 1498, and for 25 years was rector of Diss in Norfolk: he was suspended from this office for marrying, but was not deprived. He wrote "The Bowge of Court," "The Boke of Phyllyp Sparrow," "Magnificence," "The Tunning of Elinor Rummyng," "The Garland of Laurel," "Colin Clout," a satire on the clergy, and "Why come ye not to Court?" a satire on Wolsey, etc. His rough wit and eccentric character made him the hero of a book of "merye" tales.—SMITH, BENJAMIN E., *ed*, 1894–97, *The Century Cyclopedia of Names, p.* 937.

With face so bold, and teeth so sharp,
Of viper's venome, why dost carp?
Why are my verses by thee weigh'd
In a false scale? may truth be said?
Whilst thou to get the more esteem
A learned Poet fain wouldst seem,
Skelton, thou art, let all men know it,
Neither learned, nor a Poet.

—LILY, WILLIAM, c 1500, *Lilii Hendecasyllabi in Scheltonum ejus carmina calumniantem, tr. Fuller.*

I praye Mayster John Skelton, late created Poete laureate in the Unyversite of oxenforde, to oversee and correcte thys sayd booke. And taddresse and expowne where as shalle be founde faulte to theym that shall require it. For hym I knowe for suffycyent to expowne and englysshe every dyffyculte that is therein. For he hath late translated the epystles of Tullye and the book of dyodorus syculus, and diverse other workes out of latyn in englysshe, not in rude and olde langage, but in polysshed and ornate termes craftely, as he that hath redde vyrgyle, ouyde, tullye, and all the other noble poets and oratours, to me unknowen: And also he hath redde the ix muses and understande theyr musicalle scyences, and to whom of theym eche scyence is appropred. I suppose he hath dronken of Elycon's well.—CAXTON, WILLIAM, 1490, *Book of Eneydos, Preface.*

Holde me excused, for why my will is good,
Men to induce vnto vertue and goodnes;
I write no ieste ne tale of Robin Hood,
Nor sowe no sparkles ne sede of viciousnes;
Wise men loue vertue, wilde people wantonnes;
It longeth not to my science nor cunning,
For Philip the Sparow the Dirige to singe.

—BARCLAY, ALEXANDER, 1509, *The Ship of Fooles.*

Skelton satte in the corner of a piller, with a frostie bitten face, frowning, and is scante yet cleane cooled of the hotte burnyng cholour kindeled against the cankered Cardinall Wolsey, writing many a sharpe disticon with bloudie penne againste hym; and sente them by the infernall rivers Styx, Flegiton and Acheron, by the Feriman of helle, called Charon, to the said Cardinall.—BULLEIN, WILLIAM, 1564–73, *A Dialogue Both Pleasaunt and*

Pietifull, wherein is a Godlie Regiment against the Fever Pestilence, with a Consolation and Comforte against Death.

By what means could Skelton, that laureat poet, have uttered his mind so well at large, as thorowe his cloke of mery conceytes, as in his "Speake Parrot, Ware the Hawke, The Tunning of Elinor Rumming, Why come ye not to the Court, &c." Yet what greater sense or better matter can be, than is in this ragged rhyme contayned? Or who would have hearde his fault so playnely told him, if not in such gibyng sorte?—GRANGE, JOHN, 1577, *The Golden Aphroditis.*

I wyth good ryght yeelde him the title of a Poet: hee was doubtles a pleasant conceyted fellowe, and of a very sharpe wytte, exceeding bolde, and would nyppe to the very quicke where he once sette holde.—WEBBE, WILLIAM, 1586, *A Discourse of English Poesie, ed. Arber, p.* 33.

Being in deede but a rude rayling rimer and all his doings ridiculous: he vsed both short distaunces and short measures, pleasing onely the popular eare.—PUTTENHAM, GEORGE, 1589, *Arte of English Poesie, ed. Arber, p.* 97.

Skelton, the Malancholy foole.—HARVEY, GABRIEL, 1593, *Pierces Supererogation, Works, ed. Grosart vol.* II, *p.* 132.

Angry Skelton's breathlesse rhymes. —HALL, JOSEPH, 1597–8, *Virgidemiarum, lib.* iv.

John Skelton, a jolly English rimer, and I warrant ye accounted a notable poet, as poetry went in those days, namely King Edward the fourth's reign, when doubtless good poets were scarce, for however he had the good fortune to be chosen poet laureat, methinks he hath a miserable loose rambling style.—PHILLIPS, EDWARD, 1675, *Theatrum Poetarum Anglicanorum, ed. Brydges, p.* 41.

Skelton's poems are all low, and bad: there's nothing in them that's worth reading.—POPE, ALEXANDER, 1734–36, *Spence's Anecdotes, ed. Singer, p.* 130.

It is in vain to apologise for the coarseness, obscenity, and scurrility of Skelton, by saying that his poetry is tinctured with the manners of his age. Skelton would have been a writer without decorum at any period. . . . Skelton's characteristic vein of humour is capricious and grotesque. If his whimsical extravagancies ever move our laughter, at the same time they shock our sensibility. His festive levities are not only vulgar and indelicate, but frequently want truth and propriety. His subjects are often as ridiculous as his metre: but he sometimes debases his matter by his versification. On the whole, his genius seems better suited to low burlesque than to liberal and manly satire. It is supposed by Caxton, that he improved our language; but he sometimes affects obscurity, and sometimes adopts the most familiar phraseology of the common people.—WARTON, THOMAS, 1778–81, *History of English Poetry, sec.* xxxiii.

Jonson was evidently fond of Skelton, and frequently imitates his short titupping style, which is not his best. I know Skelton only by the modern edition of his works, dated 1736. But from this stupid publication I can easily discover that he was no ordinary man. Why Warton and the writers of his school rail at him so vehemently, I know not, he was perhaps the best scholar of his day, and displays, on many occasions, strong powers of description, and a vein of poetry that shines through all the rubbish which ignorance has spread over it. He flew at high game, and therefore occasionally called in the aid of vulgar ribaldry to mask the direct attack of his satire. This was seen centuries ago, and yet we are not instituting a process against him for rudeness and indelicacy!—GIFFORD, WILLIAM, 1816, *The Works of Ben Jonson, vol.* VIII, *p.* 74, *note.*

Erasmus must have been a bad judge of English poetry, or must have alluded only to the learning of Skelton, when in one of his letters he pronounces him "Britannicarum literarum lumen et decus." There is certainly a vehemence and vivacity in Skelton, which was worthy of being guided by a better taste; and the objects of his satire bespeak some degree of public spirit. But his eccentricity in attempts at humour is at once vulgar and flippant; and his style is almost a texture of slang phrases, patched with shreds of French and Latin.—CAMPBELL, THOMAS, 1819, *Essay on English Poetry.*

Coarse and capricious as is Skelton, there is yet an abundance of genuine English humour in his metrical (rather than poetical) effusions. He is the "dear darling" of the thorough-bred black letter Collector; who never rests satisfied without the earlier impressions of his versification by *Pynson*, *Faques*, or *Kele:* but the sober reader and general collector will have reason to be contented with the correct and elegant impression of his works put forth (by an unknown editor) in 1736.—DIBDIN, THOMAS FROGNALL, 1824, *The Library Companion, p.* 677.

The power, the strangeness, the volubility of his language, the audacity of his satire, and the perfect originality of his manner, render Skelton one of the most extraordinary writers of any age or country.—SOUTHEY, ROBERT, 1814, *Chalmers's English Poets, Quarterly Review, vol.* 11, *p.* 485.

Skelton is certainly not a poet, unless some degree of comic humor, and a torrent-like volubility of words in doggerel rhyme, can make one; but this uncommon fertility, in a language so little copious as ours was at that time, bespeaks a mind of some original vigor. Few English writers come nearer, in this respect, to Rabelais, whom Skelton preceded. His attempts in serious poetry are utterly contemptible; but the satirical lines on Cardinal Wolsey were probably not ineffective.—HALLAM, HENRY, 1837–39, *Introduction to the Literature of Europe, pt.* i, *ch.* iv, *par.* 76

At a period when satire had not yet assumed any legitimate form, a singular genius appeared in Skelton. His satire is peculiar; but it is stamped by vigorous originality. The fertility of his conceptions in his satirical or his humorous vein is thrown out in a style created by himself. The Skeltonical short verse, contracted into five or six and even four syllables, is wild and airy. In the quick-returning rhymes the playfulness of the diction, and the pungency of new words, usually ludicrous, often expressive, and sometimes felicitous, there is a stirring spirit which will be best felt in an audible reading. The velocity of his verse has a carol of its own. The chimes ring in the ear, and the thoughts are flung about like coruscations. But the magic of the poet is confined to his spell: at his first step out of it, he falls to the earth, never to recover himself. Skelton is a great creator only when he writes what baffles imitation; for it is his fate, when touching more solemn strains, to betray no quality of a poet,—inert in imagination, and naked in diction. Whenever his Muse plunges into the long measure of heroic verse, she is drowned in no Heliconian stream. . . . He is a poet who has left his name to his own verse,—a verse airy, but pungent; so admirably adapted for the popular ear, that it has been frequently copied, and has led some eminent critics into singular misconceptions. The minstrel tune of the Skeltonical rhyme is easily caught; but the invention of style and "the pith" mock these imitators.—DISRAELI, ISAAC, 1841, *Skelton, Amenities of Literature.*

Skelton is to be regarded as one of the fathers of the English drama. His "Enterlude of Vertue" and his "Comedy callyd Achademios" have perished; so perhaps has his "Nigramansir;" but his "Magnyfycence" is still extant. To those who carry their acquaintance with our early play-wrights no farther back than the period of Peele, Greene, and Marlowe, this "goodly interlude" by Skelton will doubtless appear heavy and inartificial; its superiority, however, to the similar efforts of his contemporaries, is, I apprehend, unquestionable.—DYCE, ALEXANDER, 1843, *ed. Poetical Works of John Skelton, vol.* I, *p.* 1.

There is much of the old jollity and rude humor of England about Skelton—of that mixture of strength and fun which made our ancestors relish strong ale, and bull-baiting, and cudgel-play, and horse-laughter. There is the crackle of northern pine-logs in the fire he roasts people at—a kind of humour more old Roman than Attic, as native English humour certainly is. He faithfully represents the national tendency to despise a *novus homo* which is to be traced right through our satires, and was particularly indignant at the nobility for courting a butcher's son.—HANNAY, JAMES, 1856–61, *English Political Satires, Essays from "The Quarterly Review," p.* 83.

How dark must have been the night in which such a Will-o'-wisp was mistaken for a star! He has wit, indeed, and satirical observation; but his wit is wilder than it is strong, and his satire is dashed with personality and obscenity.—GILFILLAN, GEORGE, 1860, *Specimens of the Less-Known British Poets, vol.* I, *p.* 78.

It is little to the credit of modern taste and refinement, that so gross and repulsive an author as Skelton should be better known to students of old English literature, than the graceful and elegant Surrey and Wyatt. Puttenham well characterizes Skelton as a "rude rayling rimer," and it is not too much to say of him, that while he has all the coarseness of Swift, he does not atone for it by a spark of the genius of Chaucer. . . . It is more to his classical scholarship than to his poetical works that he owed his original literary reputation, and though his translations of some ancient authors, which are still preserved in manuscript, would be a valuable contribution to English philology, the loss of his rhymes would be but a trifling injury to English literature. His learning certainly did little for the improvement of his English style, and we may say of his diction in general, that all that is not vulgar is pedantic. —MARSH, GEORGE P., 1862, *Origin and History of the English Language, etc., p.* 511.

The last eminent person who received the shelter of the Sanctuary fled thither from the violence, not of Princes, but of Ecclesiastics. Skelton, the earliest known Poet Laureate, from under the wing of Abbot Islip, poured forth against Cardinal Wolsey those furious invectives, which must have doomed him to destruction but for the Sanctuary, impregnable even by all the power of the Cardinal at the height of his grandeur. No stronger proof can be found of the sacredness of the spot, or of the independence of the institution. He remained here till his death, and, like Le Sueur in the Chartreuse at Paris, rewarded his protectors by writing the doggerel epitaphs which were hung over the royal tombs, and which are preserved in most of the older antiquarian works on the Abbey.—STANLEY, ARTHUR PENRHYN, 1867–8, *Historical Memorials of Westminster Abbey, p.* 352.

A virulent pamphleteer, who, jumbling together French, English, Latin phrases, with slang, and fashionable words, invented words, intermingled with short rhymes, fabricates a sort of literary mud, with which he bespatters Wolsey and the bishops. Style, metre, rhyme, language, art of every kind, is at an end; beneath the vain parade of official style there is only a heap of rubbish.—TAINE, H. A., 1871, *History of English Literature, tr. Van Laun, vol.* I, *bk.* i, *ch.* iii, *p.* 139.

This is a fresh, audacious, boisterous, wayward pupil of Chaucer's, very different from the tame decorous Lydgate. He plays wanton freaks with the time-honoured copy-books of the school: writes a few lines in sober imitation, and then dashes off into all sorts of madly capricious irregularities. He is, indeed, so independent of models that he should have a chapter to himself, were it not that this would exaggerate him out of all proportion to his poetic importance. It wants some leniency in the definition of poetry to allow him the title of poet at all; he was not much more of a poet than Swift.—MINTO, WILLIAM, 1874–85, *Characteristics of English Poets, p.* 85.

One genuine English poet illustrated the early years of the sixteenth century, —John Skelton. He had vivacity, fancy, humor, and originality. Gleams of the truest poetical sensibility alternate in him with an almost brutal coarseness. He was truly Rabelaisian before Rabelais. But there is a freedom and hilarity in much of his writing that gives it a singular attraction. A breath of cheerfulness runs along the slender stream of his verse, under which it seems to ripple and crinkle, catching and casting back the sunshine like a stream blown on by clear western winds. But Skelton was an exceptional blossom of autumn. A long and dreary winter follows. —LOWELL, JAMES RUSSELL, 1875–90, *Spenser, Prose Works, Riverside ed., vol.* IV, *p.* 273.

Skelton, especially in his gay and frolicsome mood, is, no doubt, occasionally indelicate, but with none of that deep-seated licentiousness which taints some periods of our literature; and the laureate of those days may fairly be allowed some indulgence for the manners of his time, when, to judge from the letters of Henry VIII. to Anne Boleyn, there was no very fine sense of propriety even amongst the highest of the land. And as to the gross epithet which Pope has associated with his name, he deserves it far less than Pope's own bosom friend. There is more "beastliness" in a page of Swift than in these two volumes of Skelton.—HAMILTON, WALTER, 1879, *The Poets Laureate of England, p.* 28.

Skelton's claims to notice lie not so much in the intrinsic excellence of his work as in the complete originality of his stlye, in the variety of his powers, in the peculiar character of his satire, and in the ductility of his expression when ductility of expression was unique. . . . In "The Tunnyng of Elinore Rummynge" his powers of pure description and his skill in the lower walks of comedy are seen in their highest perfection. In this sordid and disgusting delineation of humble life he may fairly challenge the supremacy of Swift and Hogarth. But Skelton is, with all his faults, one of the most versatile and one of the most essentially original of all our poets. He touches Swift on one side, and he touches Sackville on the other. — COLLINS, J. CHURTON, 1880, *The English Poets, ed. Ward, vol.* I, *pp.* 184, 185.

Insufferably coarse, and deserving of more attention as a humorist than as a poet. Skelton's position and acquirements made him well known in his lifetime. From him the future king, Henry VIII., received his education, and that he was deeply learned is proved by the high praise bestowed on him by Erasmus. How far Skelton's buffoonery influenced the youthful prince can only be guessed at. His faults were common to the age, but the ability he possessed was as uncommon then as it is now, and it is impossible to believe it was wholly used for good. His writings, popular in his own day, are dead to the modern reader, and no republication can revive their fame. —DENNIS, JOHN, 1883, *Heroes of Literature, p.* 6.

Whatever may be thought of the merits of his verse it cannot be denied that it has a vigour and plainness which is peculiarly Saxon. — MURRAY, J. ROSS, 1886, *The Influence of Italian upon English Literature, p.* 10.

In Skelton there is a morning gale; we feel the breath of a new day. But Skelton was reckless, and asserted his individuality too extravagantly. He is a little Rabelais, full of *verve*, learned, free-spoken; capable at times of a certain frank and delicate charm. The palace of Art was not to be taken by violence, and the disorderly rabble of Skeltonical rhymes, laughing as they advance, presently fall back defeated from its outer wall.—DOWDEN, EDWARD, 1887, *Transcripts and Studies, p.* 274.

He is capricious, homely, never weak, often coarse, always quaint.—MITCHELL, DONALD G., 1889, *English Lands Letters and Kings, From Celt to Tudor, p.* 139.

Skelton was certainly not worse than most of his colleagues, and probably better than many of them. He had, however, peculiar ideas about many things, a peculiar temperament, which was but little fitted for the life of an ecclesiastic, and he was not the man to put any control upon himself, or to keep his views always under cover. Skelton was not without religious feelings, or without faith as a Christian; but his faith was mixed with a goodly amount of scepticism, his interests were mainly directed to secular concerns, and if he possessed reverence for the saints, it often took a peculiar form of expression. Above all, Skelton was one of the humanists, full of enthusiasm for classical culture, full of reverence for the sovereign importance of learning, and fully conscious of being a richly endowed and eminently learned son of the Muses. Self-denial, a secluded life, and asceticism, were foreign to his nature; he was fond of giving free play to his thoughts in poetry, and somewhat in his actions as well. The discordance between his inner nature and his position in life, between his Humanity and his Christianity, must often have forced itself upon him; his humour must have helped him over his difficulty, but his humour is often but little pleasant and much too negative in colouring. His conception of the world and of life seems, at times, pretty much that of the prelate, according to whom everything is a mere farce. Skelton was, at all events, inclined to play his part in the "farce" with all possible vivacity. His views of life are both those of a satirist and of a jester, and for both points of view, he had at his command a sprightly wit, a host of learned reminiscences, and a rich abundance of ideas and forms of expression which never failed him.—TEN BRINK, BERNHARD, 1892, *History of English Literature, (Fourteenth Century to Surrey) tr. Schmitz, p.* 110.

Skelton's verse is in general coarse and scurrilous, but vivacious and nimble.—HUTSON, CHARLES WOODWARD, 1897, *The Story of Language, p.* 295.

William Dunbar

1465-1530

William Dunbar was born about 1465, and educated at the University of St. Andrews. He entered the Franciscan order of Grey Friars, and travelled in the garb of the order in Scotland, England, and France. In 1500 he received a pension from the king, James IV. of Scotland. He is known to have survived the year 1517, and must have died about 1520, or later. His chief poems are "The Golden Terge" (Targe, or Shield), "The Thistle and the Rose," and the "Dance of the Seven Deadly Sins." . . . The only complete edition of Dunbar's works is that entitled, "The Poems of William Dunbar, now first collected, with Notes, and a Memoir of his Life, by David Laing;" 2 vols. 8vo., Edinburgh, 1834. "The Thistle and the Rose" is found in the Bannatyne MS. in the Advocate's Library at Edinburgh.—SKEAT, WALTER W., 1871, *Specimens of English Literature*, 1394-1579.

Yet still some pleasing monuments remain,
Some marks of genius in each later reign.
In nervous strains Dunbar's bold music flows,
And Time yet spares the Thistle and the Rose.

—LANGHORNE, JOHN, 1763, *Genius and Valour*, v. 61-64.

The imagination of Dunbar is not less suited to satirical than to sublime allegory: and that he is the first poet who has appeared with any degree of spirit in this way of writing since Pierce Plowman.—WARTON, THOMAS, 1778-81, *History of English Poetry, sec.* XXX.

The greatest poet that Scotland has produced.—ELLIS, GEORGE, 1790-1845, *Specimens of the Early English Poets, vol.* I, *p.* 304.

Where now Dunbar? The bard has run his race;
But glitters still the Golden Terge on high,
Nor shall the thunder storm that sweeps the sky,
Nor lightning's flash, the glorious orb deface.

—DYER, GEORGE, 1801, *Ode* xvi. *Poems, p.* 89.

In the poetry of Dunbar, we recognise the emanations of a mind adequate to splendid and varied exertion—a mind equally capable of soaring into the higher regions of fiction, and of descending into the humble walk of the familiar and ludicrous. He was endowed with a vigorous and well-regulated imagination, and to it was superadded that conformation of the intellectual faculties which constitutes the quality of good sense. In his allegorical poems we discover originality and even sublimity of invention, while those of a satirical kind present us with striking images of real life and manners. As a descriptive poet he has received superlative praise. In the mechanism of poetry he evinces a wonderful degree of skill. He has employed a great variety of metres; and his versification, when opposed to that of his most eminent contemporaries, will appear highly ornamental and poetical.—IRVING, DAVID, 1804, *Lives of the Scottish Poets.*

A poet of a rich and lively fancy, and possessing great natural command of language.—NOTT, GEORGE FREDERICK, 1815, *Dissertation on the State of English Poetry, Surrey and Wyatt's Poems, p.* cxci.

It is evident that a union of talents of this wide range must necessarily be of rare occurrence; nor can we wonder that a century should elapse before a poet in any high degree approaching the genius of Chaucer made his appearance in our island. Not indeed until Dunbar arose in the sister kingdom, had we another instance of the combination of first-rate abilities for humour and comic painting, with an equally powerful command over the higher regions of fiction and imagination.—DRAKE, NATHAN, 1828, *Mornings in Spring, vol.* II, *p.* 4.

This great genius, who has enriched the poetry of his country with a strain of versification superior in power, originality, and sweetness to any of his predecessors, we have to repeat, alas! the same story of unavailing regret, that little is known; and that little, founded on very imperfect evidence.—TYTLER, PATRICK FRASER, 1833, *Lives of Scottish Worthies, vol.* III, *p.* 89.

A poet, whose tales may be safely put in the same class with those of Chaucer and Prior, whose odes and songs are not unworthy to stand beside those of Horace, and whose burlesque is as glorious as that of Aristophanes himself.—WRIGHT, THOMAS, 1846, *Essays on the Middle Ages, vol.* II, *p.* 292.

We venture to call him the Dante of Scotland; nay, we question if any English poet has surpassed "The Dance of the Seven Deadly Sins through Hell" in its peculiarly Dantesque qualities of severe and purged grandeur, of deep sincerity, and in that air of moral disappointment and sorrow, approaching despair, which distinguished the sad-hearted lover of Beatrice, who might almost have exclaimed, with one yet mightier than he in his misery and more miserable in his might,

"Where'er I am is Hell—myself am Hell."

—GILFILLAN, GEORGE, 1860, *Specimens of the Less-Known British Poets, vol.* I, *p.* 59.

May justly be styled the Chaucer of Scotland, whether we look to the wide range of his genius, or to his eminence in every style over all the poets of his country who preceded and all who for ages came after him. That of Burns is certainly the only name among the Scottish poets that can yet be placed on the same line with that of Dunbar; and even the inspired ploughman, though the equal of Dunbar in comic power, and his superior in depth of passion, is not to be compared with the elder poet either in strength or in general fertility of imagination.—CRAIK, GEORGE L., 1861, *A Compendious History of English Literature and of the English Language, vol.* I, *p.* 456.

He is a name, and little more. He exists in a region to which rumour and conjecture have never penetrated. He was long neglected by his countrymen, and was brought to light as if by accident. He is the Pompeii of British poetry. We have his works, but they are like the circumvallations of a Roman camp on the Scottish hillside. We see lines stretching hither and thither, but we cannot make out the plan, or divine what purposes were served. We only know that every crumbled rampart was once a defence; that every half-obliterated fosse once swarmed with men; that it was once a station and abiding-place of human life, although for centuries now remitted to silence and blank summer sunshine.—SMITH, ALEXANDER, 1863, *Dreamthorp, p.* 92.

The very existence of the works of William Dunbar has been hailed as a signal proof of "the immortality of real merit;" for we know not at what precise time he was born, nor when he died, and his very name is not, with one solitary exception, to be met with in the whole compass of our Literature for two hundred years; nor was it till after the lapse of three centuries that his poems were collected and published—to secure him the reputation, among his own countrymen, of being one of the greatest of Scotland's poets.—JACOX, FRANCIS, 1872, *The Literary Life, or Aspects of Authorship.*

This jolly quick-witted friar and courtier is sometimes called the Scottish Chaucer. The two have, indeed, a good many points of resemblance. Both were men of the world and favourites at Court; companionable men, witty and good-humoured: both showed sufficient address and business dexterity to be employed on embassies of state. But if we wish to give the title of "Scottish Chaucer" its full significance, we must place considerable emphasis on the adjective. Dunbar and Chaucer belong to the same class of easy self-contained men, whose balance is seldom deranged by restless straining and soaring; but within that happy pleasure-loving circle they occupy distinct habitations: and one way of bringing out their difference of spirit is to lay stress upon their nationality. Dunbar is unmistakably Scotch. He is altogether of stronger and harder—perhaps of harsher—nerve than Chaucer; more forcible and less diffuse of speech; his laugh is rougher; he is boldly sarcastic and derisive to persons; his ludicrous conceptions rise to more daring heights of extravagance; and, finally, he has a more decided turn for preaching—for offering good advice. Not that he is always strong-headed, extravagantly humorous, or gravely moral; there are green places in his heart, and his fancies are sometimes sweet and graceful; but the strength of head, the extravagance of humour, and the gravity of good counsel are, upon the whole, predominant in his composition.—MINTO, WILLIAM, 1874–85, *Characteristics of English Poets, p.* 99.

His "Dance of the Seven Deadly Sins," over which the excellent Lord Hailes went into raptures, is wanting in everything but coarseness; and if his invention dance at all, it is like a galley-slave in chains under the lash. It would be well for us if the sins themselves were indeed such wretched bugaboos as he has painted for us. What he means for humor is but the dullest vulgarity; his satire would be Billingsgate if it could, and, failing, becomes a mere offence in the nostrils, for it takes a great deal of salt to keep scurrility sweet. Mr. Sibbald, in his "Chronicle of Scottish Poetry," has admiringly preserved more than enough of it, and seems to find a sort of national savor therein, such as delights his countrymen in a *haggis*, or the German in his *sauerkraut*. The uninitiated foreigner puts his handkerchief to his nose, wonders, and gets out of the way as soon as he civilly can. . . . Dunbar's works were disinterred and edited some thirty years ago by Mr. Laing, and whoso is national enough to like thistles may browse there to his heart's content. I am inclined for other pasture, having long ago satisfied myself by a good deal of dogged reading that every generation is sure of its own share of bores without borrowing from the past.—LOWELL, JAMES RUSSELL, 1875, *Spenser, Prose Works, Riverside ed., vol.* IV, *pp.* 269, 271.

The special characteristics of Dunbar's genius are variety and force. His volume is a medley in which tenderness and vindictiveness, blistering satire and exuberant fancy meet. His writings are only in a minor degree bound up with the politics of his age, and though they reflect its fashions, they for the most part appeal to wider human sympathies. He has not wearied us with any very long poem. His inspiration and his personal animus find vent within moderate bounds, but they are constantly springing up at different points and assuming various attitudes. At one time he is a quiet moralist praising the golden mean, at another he is as fierce as Juvenal. Devoid of the subtlety and the dramatic power of Chaucer, his attacks, often coarse, are always direct and sincere. His drawing, like that of the "Ballads," is in the foreground: there is no chiaroscuro in his pages, no more than in those of his countrymen from Barbour to Burns.—NICHOL, JOHN, 1880, *English Poets, ed. Ward, vol.* I, *p.* 149.

Has been called the Scotch Chaucer, a designation which recalls Coleridge's remark on hearing Klopstock styled the German Milton, "A very *German* Milton indeed."—NICOLL, HENRY J., 1882, *Landmarks of English Literature, p.* 38.

Indeed, with the exception of the Ayrshire Ploughman at his best, Dunbar is, perhaps, the greatest poet that Scotland has ever produced. No English poet from Chaucer to Spenser approaches him, and in some respects I would rank him above the latter. Wyat and Surrey are not to be spoken of in the same breath with this "darling of the Scottish muse," as Scott termed him.—FITZGIBBON, H. MACAULAY, 1888, *Early English and Scottish Poetry, Introduction, p.* lix.

In range and variety of interest and subject, in swiftness and force of attack, and in vividness and permanence of effect, Dunbar is equally remarkable. His allegories are more than merely ingenious exercises in the art of mystical deliverance, as such things had been prone to become after Chaucer's time; his lyrics are charged with direct and steadfast purpose, and while they are all melodious, the best of them are resonant and tuneful; and the humorous satires are manifestly the productions of a man of original and penetrating observation, gifted above most with a sense of the hollowness and weakness of evil, and with the ability to render it ridiculous.—BAYNE, THOMAS, 1888, *Dictionary of National Biography, vol.* XVI, *p.* 155.

He was the last great representative of Chaucer's School in Scotland; he stands on the boundary between the world of the Middle Ages and the world of the Renaissance. Like the rich and lovely architecture of his time, Dunbar's poetry is the fine flower of expiring Mediaevalism. —PALGRAVE, FRANCIS T., 1889, *The Treasury of Sacred Song, Notes, p.* 331.

The poet himself was not so dignified or harmonious as his verse. He possessed the large open-air relish of life, the broad humour, sometimes verging on coarseness, which from the time of James I. to that of Burns has been so singularly characteristic of Scots poetry: and found no scene of contemporary life too humble or too ludicrous for his genius—thus his more familiar poems are better for our purpose than his loftier productions, and show us the life and fashion of his town and time better than anything else can do.—OLIPHANT, MARGARET O. W., 1890, *Royal Edinburgh, p.* 188.

In "The Golden Terge" there is playful grace of the poet, who is the first since Chaucer in whom we recognise again a Master in his art. Dunbar was a man of genius, born poet, with wide range of powers, cultivated mind, and perfect training in the mechanism of verse.—MORLEY, HENRY, 1891, *English Writers, vol.* VII, *p.* 121.

No early poet has attempted so great a variety, either in subject, in style, or in form of verse, as Dunbar. In varying temper and on varying occasion he has essayed nearly every rôle of poetry, and to each he has given the supreme touch of the master-hand. Allegory, satire, and moral musing, invective, comic narrative, and natural description, personal pleading, courtly compliment, and the wild riot of Rabelaisian farce, all are here, treading each inimitably its appropriate measure. Smock and gay doublet, blackthorn cudgel and friar's hood, flashing rapier and dazzling pageant dress, each is assumed as occasion asks, and none is laid down till its part has been played to perfection. . . . Brilliant beyond any of the poet company he sang, Dunbar still lacked one thing to set him in the ranks of the greatest of the immortals. That place is reserved for those alone who, supreme in other gifts, possess also the key to the fountain of tears. Humour the wildest, wit the keenest, imagination the richest and most glowing, illumine his page; but nowhere, except lightly in "The Lament for the Makaris," and in one little love poem perhaps, does he stir the deeper currents of the heart. —EYRE-TODD, GEORGE, 1892, *Mediæval Scottish Poetry, pp.* 149, 157.

Dunbar's poetry does not possess altogether the directness of Chaucer's, it demands a greater amount of reflective power. The Scottish poet is a Master who shows himself in his limitation, and although he frequently does not limit himself in his descriptions, this is not done with the intention of becoming discursive, but because he takes artistic pleasure in his own charming delineations. His style is always clear, precise, and pregnant; and there are few poets who can command such a far-reaching scale of tones as he, where we have, at the same time, to admire so much gracefulness, so much intelligence, so much vigour and intrepidity; few poets have at their disposal so much sublime and lovely imagery, so much grotesque humour, and so much elegance in the expression of discrete worldly wisdom. As a writer of "occasional poems," in the narrowest, as well as in the widest sense, Dunbar raised lyrics on to a higher stage, in fact, was the first writer actually to create classic lyrics of an artistic kind, in English or the Scottish language.—TEN BRINK, BERNHARD, 1892, *History of English Literature (Fourteenth Century to Surrey) tr. Schmitz, p.* 78.

There is nothing which strikes one so much in reading the poems of Dunbar as the immense power of the writer—a power which, if it had ever found its fullest expression, might have raised him to equality with any poet of either kingdom, —the extraordinary command of language and the overflowing facility which enables him as readily to adorn the most delicate and scholarly conception with an exuberance of graces such as Spenser could hardly have surpassed, as to picture a scene of the coarsest merriment in such colours as even Hogarth would not have ventured to put upon canvas.—OLIPHANT, F. R., 1893, *William Dunbar, Blackwood's Magazine, vol.* 154, *p.* 416.

Warton was generous in his appreciation of Dunbar's merits. Scott, in the next generation, proclaimed him to be the greatest of Scottish poets. Campbell compared him with Chaucer. His poems, collected in 1834 by David Laing, allow us to form a cooler estimate of his genius, and show us that Dunbar, while possessing a rich, vigorous, and versatile imagination, wanted the qualities which entitle a man to the front rank in the history of national poetry. Essentially a poet of the court, his talents were always employed in satisfying the momentary tastes of his patrons, so that though his works are of great importance to the antiquary, he rarely touches those notes of human interest which are the passport to the sympathy of the general reader. . . . As a poet he may be described as a jongleur transformed to meet the requirements of a literary age. His poems show a shrewd knowledge of men and manners, and remarkable skill in presenting, under a variety of novel aspects, the somewhat narrow range of themes acceptable to a court. His favourite poetical device was to carry a single burden or refrain through a number of stanzas, each containing a different turn of thought; but he frequently amused the king and queen with personal satires on the courtiers, or with rapid sketches of scenes in actual life, which have all the character of improvisations.—COURTHOPE, W. J., 1895, *A History of English Poetry, vol.* I, *pp.* 370, 371.

Endowed with an ever-ready mind and an unfailing power of invention, Dunbar, following his natural tastes, and wishing, at the same time, to imitate Chaucer, decks his pictures with glaring colours, and "out-Chaucers Chaucer." His flowers are too flowery, his odours too fragrant; by moments it is no longer a delight, but almost a pain. It is not sufficient that his birds should sing, they must sing among perfumes, and these perfumes are coloured.—JUSSERAND, J. J., 1895, *A Literary History of the English People, p.* 511.

We gather, indeed, that Dunbar was recognised at once as the first poet of the age, and we may console ourselves by believing that in the ninety or a hundred poems of his which we are fortunate enough to possess, we hold the fine flower of Scotch Renaissance poetry. Dunbar, let it be plainly said, is the largest figure in English literature between Chaucer and Spenser, to each of whom, indeed, he seems to hold forth a hand. . . . In reaching Dunbar we find that we have escaped from the dead air of the late Middle Ages. The poetry of this writer is defective in taste—rhetorical, over-ornate; he delights to excess in such terms as "crystalline," "redolent," "aureate," and "enamelling." He never escapes—and it is this which finally leads us to refuse the first rank to his gorgeous talent—from the artificial in language. He does not display any considerable intellectual power. But when all this is admitted, the activity and versatility of Dunbar, his splendid use of melody and colour, his remarkable skill in the invention of varied and often intensely lyrical metres, his fund of animal spirits, combine to make his figure not merely an exceedingly attractive one in itself, but as refreshing as a well of water after the dry desert of the fifteenth century in England. . . . The analogy of Dunbar with Burns is very striking, and has often been pointed out; but the difference is at least that between a jewel and a flower, the metallic hardness of Dunbar being a characteristic of his style which is utterly out of harmony with the living sensitiveness of his greater successor. This metal surface, however, is sometimes burnished to a splendour that few poets have ever excelled. — GOSSE, EDMUND, 1897, *Short History of Modern English Literature, pp.* 48, 50, 51.

A short, rather rotund figure, a face ruddy and stamped with evidences of the love of good cheer; eyes small, beady, and dark, twinkling at times with an ever-present sense of the humorous side of life, then anon blazing with a fierce, contemptuous scorn of meanness, hypocrisy, and injustice; a tongue as mellifluous in speech as his to whom was given the title "Golden Mouth," yet betimes capable of a sardonic sarcasm that burned like an acid where it lighted,—such is the portrait that has come down to us from various sources of that mighty genius, who, though, alas! all too little known among us of these latter days, has yet been adjudged by many of our most competent English critics to be the peer, if not in a few qualities the superior, of Chaucer and Spenser. — SMEATON, OLIPHANT, 1898, *William Dunbar, Famous Scots Series, p.* 9.

Lord Berners

(John Bourchier)

1467–1533

John Bourchier was born about 1467, and succeeded to the title* in 1474. Even as a child he seems to have lived at the Court, and was knighted in 1477; but, according to the growing custom of the day which no longer countenanced the complete separation of arms from letters, he was sent to Oxford, where, according to Anthony Wood, he belonged to Balliol College. After his stay at the University he travelled

*Lord Berners.

abroad, returning to England when the Earl of Richmond became Henry VII., with the Bourchier family amongst his chief supporters. It was a member of that family, Cardinal Bourchier, Archbishop of Canterbury, who placed the crown on Henry's head. In the following years Lord Berners distinguished himself in military service, and he continued as high in favour with Henry VIII. as with his father. He served under Lord Surrey in Scotland, and was employed on embassies of high importance. About 1520 he seems to have been appointed Governor of Calais, and there he spent his last years, employed at Henry's command, upon the translation of Froissart's "Chronicles" from the French. He died in 1532.—CRAIK, HENRY, 1893, *English Prose, vol.* I, *p.* 121.

FROISSART'S CHRONICLES

In imitating the style of his original, Lord Berners's translation becomes peculiarly valuable to an English reader. His version is faithful, but not servile; and he imitates the spirit and simplicity of the original, without allowing us to discover, from any deficiency in either of these particulars, that his own work is a translation.—UTTERSON, E. V., 1812, *ed. Berners's Froissart's Chronicles*

A soldier, a statesman, and a scholar, this nobleman was singularly well adapted for the task which he undertook. Indeed, considering the period of its completion, it was a sort of literary miracle.—DIBDIN, THOMAS FROGNALL, 1824, *The Library Companion, p.* 164.

The most important English work of the first quarter of the sixteenth century, whether as a philological monument, or as a production which could not have failed to exert an influence on the tone of English literature. . . . The first really important work printed in the English language, relating to modern history. . . . The extraordinary literary merit and the popular character of the work eminently fitted it, both to initiate Englishmen into a knowledge of some of the principal epochs of their own national life, and to promote a taste for historical reading and composition. It must, therefore, independently of its philological worth, be considered as a work of great importance in English literary history, because it undoubtedly contributed essentially to give direction to literary pursuits in England, and thus to lay the foundation of an entire and very prominent branch of native literature. . . The translation is executed with great skill; for while it is faithful to the text, it adheres so closely to the English idiom that it has altogether the air of an original work, and, with the exception of here and there a single phrase, it would not be easy to find a passage which exhibits decisive internal evidence of having been first composed in a foreign tongue.—MARSH, GEORGE P., 1862, *The Origin and History of the English Language, etc., pp.* 495, 497, 498.

It is one of the best translations ever made.—BACKUS, TRUMAN J., 1875, *Shaw's New History of English Literature. p.* 57.

It is the best contemporary picture of feudalism and feudal manners in existence, and Lord Berners's translation retains, after the lapse of nearly four centuries, all its original interest and value. The quaintness of the English employed by the translator preserves to the reader of our own time the pleasing impression of the old-fashioned French in which the book was first written.—BALDWIN, JAMES, 1883, *English Literature and Literary Criticism, Prose, p.* 527.

Although Col. Johnes's translation of Froissart (1803-5) has now very generally superseded that of Berners, the later version is wanting in the literary flavour which still gives Berners's book an important place in English literature.—LEE, SIDNEY, 1886, *Dictionary of National Biography, vol.* VI, *p.* 13.

Though a translation, was a masterpiece of idiomatic English prose. Lord Berners was inspired, no doubt, by the liveliness of his original in style and matter, but he so translated as to give his Froissart a lasting place among the classics of the English language.—MORLEY, HENRY, 1891, *English Writers, vol.* VII, *p.* 281.

Berners was an industrious reader, and his chivalrous temperament was mainly attracted by historical works, whether true or fictitious, by accounts of great men, descriptions of battles, heroic deeds, and remarkable adventures. His acquaintance with the French language, together, perhaps, with some knowledge of Spanish, opened up to him many literary sources which were sealed to the majority of his countrymen, and it was his wish to make at least some of these works accessible to the English barons and knights. That his choice should have first fallen upon Froissart, whose vivacious account centres finally upon the differences between England and France, was natural enough in a Governor of Calais. In translating the old Chronicler, Berners was at the same time complying with the wishes —nay, with the commands—of the King, whose policy had meanwhile taken a direction antagonistic to France. Froissart's work was well adapted to stir up in the English people the old feelings of rivalry with France; and, by reminding them of their lost possessions there, and the glorious deeds of the Black Prince and other national heroes, aroused the English love of warfare.—TEN BRINK, BERNHARD, 1892, *History of English Literature, (Fourteenth Century to Surrey) tr. Schmitz, p.* 187.

John Fisher

1459?-1535

Born in Beverley, 1459; instructed by a priest; entered of Michael House, Cambridge; almoner and confessor to the Countess of Richmond, 1502; First Margaret's Professor 1503; Chancellor of Cambridge University, bishop of Rochester, 1504; superintends the foundation of Christ's College, 1505; opens John's College, 1516; appears as counsel for Queen Catharine, 1529; his life attacked by poison; and by shot, 1530; approves King's supremacy in Convocation, 1531; adjudged guilty of misprison of treason, refuses the oath, April 26 is committed to the tower, 1534; May 21, created Cardinal; June 22, executed, 1535. A collected edition of his works was published in Wurtzburg in 1595.—MOULTON, CHARLES WELLS, 1900.

John Fisher, you shall be led to the place from whence you came, and from thence again shall be drawn through the city to the place of execution at Tyburn, where your body shall be hanged by the neck; half alive you shall be cut down and thrown to the ground, your bowels to be taken out of your body before you, being still alive, your head to be smitten off, and your body to be divided into four quarters, and afterwards your head and quarters to be set up wheresoever the king shall appoint. And God have mercy upon your soul!—AUDLEY, SIR THOMAS, 1535, *State Trials of Reign of Henry* VIII.

In this realm no one man in wisdom, learning, and long approved vertue together, mete to be matched and compared with him.—MORE, SIR THOMAS, 1535? *English Works, p.* 1437.

Such a man for all purposes that the King of England had not the like of him in his realm; neither was he to be matched throughout Christendom.—CHARLES V. OF FRANCE, 1535, *Sir Thomas Eliot's Dispatches to Lord Cromwell.*

If an ambassador had to be sent from earth to heaven there could not among all the bishops and clergy be found so fit a man as John Fisher; for what other man have you at present, nor for many years past, who can be compared with him in sanctity, in learning, in zeal and careful diligence in the office and various duties of a bishop? Above all other nations we may justly rejoice in having such a man; and if all the parts of Christendom were searched there could not be found one man that in all things did accomplish the parts and the degrees of a bishop equal to John Fisher.—POLE, REGINALD, 1536, *Pro Ecclesiasticæ Unitatis Defensione.*

In stature Dr. Fisher was tall and comely, exceeding the middle sort of men; for he was to the quantity of six feet in height; and being very slender and lean, was nevertheless upright and well formed, straight-backed, big jaws, and strongly sinewed; his hair by nature black, though in his latter days, through age and imprisonment, turned to white; his eyes large and round, neither full black nor full gray, but of a mixt color between both; his forehead smooth and large; his nose of a good and even proportion; somewhat wide mouth and big-jawed, as one ordained by nature to utter much speech, wherein was, notwithstanding, a certain comeliness; his skin somewhat tawny, mixed with many blue veins; his face, hands, etc., all his body, so bare of flesh as is almost incredible, which came by the great abstinence and penance he used upon himself for many years, even from his youth. In speech he was mild, temperate, and kindly.—HALL, RICHARD (THOMAS BAYLY), 1604?-1653, *Life and Death of John Fisher, Bishop of Rochester.*

He was a prelate remarkable for his private virtues, for his learning, and for a zealous discharge of the duties of his pastoral function. At a time when the lower order of the clergy were distinguished by their ignorance and debauchery, and the higher by a more refined luxury, and a turn for political intrigue, this bishop's conduct displayed the pure simplicity of a primitive Christian, and rigid morality of a Roman Stoic; plain, patient, and sincere, humble but courageous, mild though determined, his character has defied that oblivion, which commonly obscures the favourers of an exploded cause, and in the midst of our proud veneration for the Protestant Martyrs of the 16th century, we regret that he suffered for the contrary doctrine, and feel that the name of this good Catholic would have been a valuable addition to the glorious catalogue.—LODGE, EDMUND, 1792-1800, *Imitations of Original Drawings by Hans Holbein with Biographical Tracts.*

Fisher was a worthy, but not a strong-minded man, and his literary works are of small value, and are now never, by any accident, consulted.—TURNER, SHARON, 1826, *The History of the Reign of Henry the Eighth, vol.* II, *p.* 394.

He neither flung away his life madly, nor preserved it basely. He was a martyr, if not to the truth that is recorded in the authentic book of Heaven, yet to that copy of it which he thought authentic, which was written on his heart in the antique characters of authoritative age. Those who think him right, justly hold him a martyr to the Faith; and we who think him mistaken, must still allow him to have been the martyr of Honesty.—COLERIDGE, HARTLEY, 1833, *Biographia Borealis, p.* 395.

A Yorkshire lad, born in the town of Beverley, though he went to Cambridge early, had not lost his northern grit and twang. His tones were rough, his phrases curt. What other men hardly dared to hint, Fisher would throw into the simplest words. He called a lie a lie, a knave a knave, not caring who might take offence. This roughness of his speech, combined with his repute for piety and learning, took the world by storm. A thorough scholar, armed at every point, he feared no combat, and his nature was unyielding as a rock.—DIXON, WILLIAM HEPWORTH, 1873-4, *History of Two Queens, bk.* xiii, *ch.* ii.

If *bonus textuarius* is indeed *bonus theologus*, Bishop Fisher may rank high among divines. He is at home in every part of scripture, no less than among the fathers. If the matter of his teaching is now for the most part trite, the form is always individual and life-like. Much of it is in the best sense catholic, and might be illustrated by parallel passages from Luther and our own reformers.—MAYOR, JOHN E. B., 1876, *Preface to Fisher's English Works, p.* xxii.

Dr. Fisher was not what the world might call a "great personage," but he was that which no sectarian prejudice, no sentiment that acknowledges virtue can deny—a good and holy Christian and a just man. He had very few equals on the long roll of English prelates; he used no weapons to enforce his convictions but those supplied from the armory of prayer and kindly counsel.—BURKE, S. HUBERT, 1882, *John Fisher, Bishop of Rochester Catholic World, vol.* 34, *p.* 769.

Fisher shared with the composers of the English liturgy a peculiarity which greatly contributed to the richness and variety of their diction—that coupling of the Saxon word with its classical synonym, which has become familiar to our ears through the Prayer Book. Fisher's prose style may, indeed, be considered as a corner-stone in the foundation of the best type of English pulpit eloquence—simple almost to an extreme, but yet instinct with earnestness and feeling, and at the same time with the balance that comes from careful scholarship and fastidious taste.—CRAIK, HENRY, 1893, *English Prose, vol.* I, *p.* 142.

He has already discovered, and deliberately experiments for, rhetorical effect with the peculiar resources provided by the double dictionary—Teutonic and Romance—of English, as well as by the more general devices of cadence, parallelism, and the usual figures of speech.—SAINTSBURY, GEORGE, 1898, *A Short History of English Literature, p.* 210.

Sir Thomas More

1478–1535

Born, in London, 7 Feb. 1478. Early education at a school in London. Entered household of Archbishop of Canterbury, 1491. At Canterbury Hall, Oxford, 1492-94. Student of Law at New Inn, 1494; removed to Lincoln's Inn, 1496; called to Bar, 1501; Reader in Law, Furnivall's Inn, 1501. Friendship with Erasmus begun, 1497. . . .

Member of Parliament, 1504. Married (i) Jane Colet, 1505; lived in Bucklersbury. Travelled on Continent, 1508. Wife died, 1511 (?); he married (ii) Mrs. Alice Middleton within a month afterwards. Bencher of Lincoln's Inn, 1509; "Reader," 1511 and 1516. Under-Sheriff of London, 1510-19. On Embassy to Flanders, May to Nov. 1515. On Commission of Peace for Hampshire, 1515 and 1528. On Embassy to Calais, autumn of 1516. Master of Requests, and Privy Councillor, 1518. With King at "Field of Cloth of Gold," June 1520. Knighted, and appointed Sub-Treasurer to King, 1521. With Wolsey on Embassy to Calais and Bruges, 1521. Removed to Chelsea, 1523. M. P. (for Middlesex?), 1523. Speaker of House of Commons, April 1523. High Steward of Oxford University, 1524; of Cambridge University, 1525. Chancellor of Duchy of Lancaster, July 1525. On Embassy to Amiens, Aug. 1527; to Cambrai, July 1528. Lord High Chancellor, Oct. 1529 to May 1532. Lived in retirement, 1532-34. Imprisoned in Tower for refusing oath to Act of Succession, 17 April 1534. Indicted of High Treason, 1 July 1535. Beheaded, 6 July 1535. Buried in Church of St.-Peter-in-the-Tower. . . . *Works:* "Utopia" (1516), (earliest English, tr. by R. Robinson, 1551); "Epigrammata," 1518; "Epistola ad Germanū Brixiū," 1520; "Eruditissimi viri G. Rossei (pseud.) opus . . . quo refellet . . . Lutheri calumnias," 1523; "A Dyaloge . . . of the Veneration and worshyp of Ymages, etc.," 1529; "Supplycacyon of Soulys" (1529?); "The Cõfutacyon of Tyndale's Answere" (to More's "Dyaloge"), 1532; "The Second parte of the Cõfutacyon," 1533; "The Apologye of Syr Thomas More," 1533; "The Debellacyon of Salem and Bizance," 1533; "A Letter impugnynge the erronyouse wrytyng of John Fryth against the blessed Sacrament," 1533; "The Answere to the fyrste parte of . . . The Souper of the Lorde," 1534; "The Boke of the fayre Gentylwoman," *n. d.* (only one copy known). *Posthumous:* "A Dyaloge of Comfort against Tribulation," 1553; "Workes . . . wrytten . . . in the Englysh tonge," 1557; "Omnia Latina Opera," 1565; "Epistola in qua . . . respondet literis Joannis Pomerani," 1568; "Dissertatio Epistolica de aliquot . . . Theologastrorum ineptiis," 1625; "Epistola . . . ad Academiam Oxon.," 1633. He *translated:* Lucian's "Dialogues" (with Erasmus), 1506; F. Pico's "Lyfe of John Picus, Earl of Mirandola" (1510). *Collected Works:* 1629.—SHARP, R. FARQUHARSON, 1897, *A Dictionary of English Authors*, p. 203.

PERSONAL

Whiles I doo dayelie bestowe my time aboute law matters: some to pleade, some to heare, some as an arbitratoure with myne awarde to determine, some as an umpier or a Judge, with my sentence finallye to discusse. Whiles I go one waye to see and visite my frende: an other waye about myne owne privat affaires. Whiles I spende almost al the day abrode emonges other, and the residue at home among mine owne; I leave to my self, I meane to my booke no time. For when I am come home, I muste commen with my wife, chatte with my children, and talke wyth my servauntes. All the whiche thinges I recken and accompte amonge businesse, forasmuche as they muste of necessitie be done: and done muste they nedes be, onelesse a man wyll be straunger in his owne house. And in any wyse a man muste so fashyon and order hys conditions, and so appoint and dispose him selfe, that he be merie, jocunde, and pleasaunt amonge them, whom eyther nature hathe provided, or chaunce hath made, or he hym selfe hath chosen to be the felowes, and companyons of hys life: so that with to muche gentle behavioure and familiaritie, he do not marre them, and by to muche sufferaunce of his servauntes, make them his maysters. Emonge these thynges now rehearsed, stealeth awaye the daye, the moneth, the yeare. When do I write then? And all this while have I spoken no worde of slepe, neyther

SIR THOMAS MORE

From Engraving by Freeman,
Painting by Holbein.

yet of meate, which emong a great number doth wast no lesse tyme, then doeth slepe, wherein almoste halfe the life tyme of man crepeth awaye. I therefore do wynne and get onelye that tyme, whiche I steale from slepe and meate. Whiche tyme because it is very litle, and yet somwhat it is, therfore have I ones at the laste, thoughe it be longe first, finished "Utopia;" and have sent it to you, frende Peter, to reade and peruse: to the intente that yf anye thynge have escaped me, you might put me in remembraunce of it.—MORE, SIR THOMAS, 1516, *Letter to Peter Giles, ed. Arber, p.* 22

Here I will remark that no one ever lived who did not first ascertain the meaning of words, and from them gather the meaning of the sentences which they compose—no one, I say, with one single exception, and that is our own Thomas More. For he is wont to gather the force of the words from the sentences in which they occur, especially in his study and translation of Greek. This is not contrary to grammar, but above it, and an instinct of genius. Indeed, his genius is more than human, and his learning not only eminent, but so various, that there is nothing of which he seems to be ignorant. His eloquence is incomparable and twofold, for he speaks with the same facility in Latin as in his own language. His sense of fun is joined with perfect refinement—you may call humour his father and wit his mother. When the matter requires it, he can imitate a good cook, and serve up the meat in sharp sauce.—PACE, RICHARD, 1517, *De Fructu qui ex Doctrina Percipitur, p.* 82.

In stature he is not tall, though not remarkably short. His limbs are formed with such perfect symmetry as to leave nothing to be desired. His complexion is white, his face fair rather than pale, and though by no means ruddy, a faint flush of pink appears beneath the whiteness of his skin. His hair is dark brown, or brownish black. The eyes are grayish blue, with some spots, a kind which betokens singular talent, and among the English is considered attractive, whereas Germans generally prefer black. It is said that none are so free from vice. His countenance is in harmony with his character, being always expressive of an amiable joyousness, and even an incipient laughter, and, to speak candidly, it is better framed for gladness than for gravity and dignity, though without any approach to folly or buffoonery. The right shoulder is a little higher than the left, especially when he walks. This is not a defect of birth, but the result of habit, such as we often contract. In the rest of his person there is nothing to offend. His hands are the least refined part of his body. . . His voice is neither loud nor very weak, but penetrating; not resounding or soft, but that of a clear speaker. Though he delights in every kind of music he has no vocal talents. He speaks with great clearness and perfect articulation, without rapidity or hesitation. He likes a simple dress, using neither silk nor purple nor gold chain, except when it may not be omitted. It is wonderful how negligent he is as regards all the ceremonious forms in which most men make politeness to consist. . . He seems born and framed for friendship, and is a most faithful and enduring friend. He is easy of access to all; but if he chances to get familiar with one whose vices admit no correction, he manages to loosen and let go the intimacy rather than to break it off suddenly. When he finds any sincere and according to his heart, he so delights in their society and conversation as to place in it the principal charm of life. He abhors games of tennis, dice, cards, and the like, by which most gentlemen kill time. Though he is rather too negligent of his own interests, no one is more diligent in those of his friends. In a word, if you want a perfect model of friendship, you will find it in no one better than in More. —ERASMUS, DESIDERIUS, 1519, *Letter to Ulrich von Hutten.*

The chancellor's seal has remained in the hands of the Duke of Norfolk till this morning, when it was transferred to Sir Thomas More. Everyone is delighted at his promotion, because he is an upright and learned man, and a good-servant of the Queen. —CHAPUYS, EUSTACE, 1529, *Letter to Charles V.*

The king's majesty hath raised to the most high dignity of Chancellorship Sir Thomas More, a man for his extraordinary worth and sufficiency well known to himself and the whole realm, for no other cause or earthly respect, but for that he hath plainly perceived all the gifts of nature and grace to be heaped upon him, which either the people could desire or himself wish for, for the discharge of so great an office. For the admirable wisdom, integrity, and innocence, joined with most pleasant facility of wit, that this man is endowed withal, have been sufficiently known to all Englishmen from their youth, and for these many years to the king's majesty himself. . . . He hath perceived no man in his realm to be more wise in deliberating, more sincere in opening to him what he thought, or more eloquent in expressing what he uttered.—NORFOLK, DUKE OF, 1529, *Speech at the Installation of More as Chancellor, Oct. 20th; Life of More by Cresacre More, pp.* 166, 168.

This we will say, that if he had been ours we should sooner have lost the best city in our dominions than so worthy a councillor.—CHARLES V., 1530, *Memoirs of Charles V.; Despatches of Sir Thomas Smythe.*

He was not able* for the maintenance of himself and such as necessarily belonged to him, sufficiently to find meat, drink, fuel, apparel and such other necessary things; but was enforced and compelled, for lack of other fuel, every night before he went to bed, to cause a great burden of ferns to be brought into his own chamber, and with the blaze thereof to warm himself, his wife and his children; and so, without any other fire, to go to their beds.—HARPSFIELD, NICHOLAS, c 1583, *Life of More, Lambeth MS. No.* 827.

CROM. Sir Thomas More is chosen
Lord Chancellor in your place.
WOLS. That's somewhat sudden;
But he's a learned man. May he continue
Long in his highness's favour, and do justice
For truth's sake, and his conscience.

—SHAKESPEARE, WILLIAM, 1613? *King Henry VIII, act.* iii, *sc.* ii.

He was of a middle stature, well proportioned, of a pale complexion; his hair of chestnut colour, his eyes grey, his countenance mild and cheerful; his voice not very musical, but clear and distinct; his constitution, which was good originally, was never impaired by his way of living, otherwise than by toc much study. His diet was simple and abstemious, never drinking any wine but when he pledged those who drank to him; and rather mortifying than indulging his appetite in what he ate.—MORE, CRESACRE, 1627? *Life of Sir Thomas More.*

*In 1532.

He was for some time much in the king's favour, and, had his temper been mercenary and ambitious, might have made his fortune to what degree he had pleased. But he was altogether above the consideration of money: his conscience was not flexible enough for this purpose: and thus he lost his life, and left his family but slenderly provided.—COLLIER, JEREMY, 1708–14, *An Ecclesiastical History of Great Britain, ed. Barham, vol.* IV, *p.* 281.

He maintained the same cheerfulness of heart upon the scaffold, which he used to show at his table; and, upon laying his head on the block, gave instances of that good humour with which he had always entertained his friends in the most ordinary occurrences. His death was of a piece with his life. There was nothing in it new, forced, or affected. He did not look upon the severing his head from his body as a circumstance that ought to produce any change in the disposition of his mind; and as he died under a fixed and settled hope of immortality, he thought any unusual degree of sorrow and concern improper on such an occasion, as had nothing in it which could deject or terrify him.—ADDISON, JOSEPH, 1712, *The Spectator, April* 10*th*.

A person of the greatest virtue this kingdom ever produced. — SWIFT, JONATHAN, 1736, *Concerning that Universal Hatred which prevails against the Clergy, Works, ed. Scott, vol.* VIII, *p.* 240.

A man who, besides the ornaments of an elegant literature, possessed the highest virtue, integrity, and capacity. — HUME, DAVID, 1759, *History of England, vol.* III, *ch.* XXX.

The only art which he employed to obtain success in his profession, or the favour of his prince, was the strenuous discharge of his duty; yet such a reputation did he acquire, that he was loaded with professional business amidst an extensive competition, and compelled by his sovereign to accept of the most coveted public employments. As a pleader, his exertions were never unapplauded; as a judge, his decisions were never controverted; as a statesman, his counsels were never suspected. In one unfortunate conjuncture, we find the prejudices of education, and the violence of theological dissensions, confounding his better judgment, and hurrying him into acts which neither justice nor humanity can pass uncensured; yet, even then, he acted from mistaken principle.—MACDIARMID, JOHN, 1807–20, *Lives of British Statesmen, vol.* I, *p.* 153.

More is the first person in our history distinguished by the faculty of public speaking. . . . Of all men nearly perfect, Sir Thomas More had, perhaps, the clearest marks of individual character. His peculiarities, though distinguishing him from all others, were yet withheld from growing into moral faults. It is not enough to say of him that he was unaffected, that he was natural, that he was simple; so the larger part of truly great men have been. But there is something homespun in More which is common to him with scarcely any other, and which gives to all his faculties and qualities the appearance of being the native growth of the soil. The homeliness of his pleasantry purifies it from show. He walks on the scaffold clad only in his household goodness. The unrefined benignity with which he ruled his patriarchal dwelling at Chelsea enabled him to look on the axe without being disturbed by feeling hatred for the tyrant. This quality bound together his genius and learning, his eloquence and fame, with his homely and daily duties,—bestowing a genuineness on all his good qualities, a dignity on the most ordinary offices of life, and an accessible familiarity on the virtues of a hero and a martyr, which silences every suspicion that his excellencies were magnified. He thus simply performed great acts, and uttered great thoughts, because they were familiar to his great soul. The charm of this inborn and homebread character seems as if it would have been taken off by polish. — MACKINTOSH, SIR JAMES, 1807, *Life of More, Miscellaneous Essays.*

More, who counteracted, if he did not curtail his own "Utopia," and whose other writings degrade him for their feebleness, their bigotry, their scurrility, and their persecuting tendency, below the educated men of his day, would have sunk into oblivion, except as a punster, as a worthy pattern of the domestic virtues, and as one who had been fond of literature, and had been famed for it, but who, in its most important department, was also its unsparing persecutor; if the oppressive violence of his death had not imparted that sympathy and sanctity to his memory, which the human heart liberally bestows on the victims of power, who unite firmness of principle with moral rectitude and intellectual cultivation.—TURNER, SHARON, 1826, *The History of the Reign of Henry the Eighth, vol.* II, *p.* 395.

Whose name can ask no epithet.—HALLAM, HENRY, 1827–46, *The Constitutional History of England, vol.* I, *ch.* i.

More's bigotry exceeds that of most men. It is perhaps the most remarkable instance of the prostration of great faculties by superstition. One of his principal charges against Luther is his being an enemy of crusades against the Turks. His answer to Tindale is unrivalled in weakness and in zeal. — BROUGHAM, HENRY, LORD, 1861, *History of England and France under the House of Lancaster, p.* 361, *note.*

Wolsey had chastised them (the innovators) with whips; Sir Thomas More* would chastise them with scorpions, and the philosopher of the "Utopia," the friend of Erasmus, whose life was of blameless beauty, whose genius was cultivated to the highest attainable perfection, was to prove to the world that the spirit of persecution is no peculiar attribute of the pedant, the bigot, or the fanatic, but may coexist with the fairest graces of the human character. The lives of remarkable men usually illustrate some emphatic truth. Sir Thomas More may be said to have lived to illustrate the necessary tendencies of Romanism, in an honest mind convinced of the truth, to show that the test of sincerity in a man who professes to regard orthodoxy as an essential of salvation is not the readiness to endure persecution, but the courage that will venture to inflict it.—FROUDE, JAMES ANTHONY, 1856–70, *History of England, vol.* ii, *ch.* vi.

The most amiable and religious, the most witty, learned, and accomplished Englishman of his time; almost of any time.—STEPHENS, W. R. W., 1878, *John Colet, Dean of St. Paul's, Good Words, vol.* 19, *p.* 405.

*In 1529.

In the old parish church near the river, More's monument still stands. The church is an interesting building of the most mixed character; so far, happily, not very much hurt by restorers. More made a chapel for his family tomb at the east end of the south aisle, and put up a black slab to record the fact. It has been twice "improved," and is said to have originally contained a reference to his persecution of heresy, for which a blank is now left in the renewed inscription, just the kind of evasion one can imagine the straightforward chancellor would himself have particularly disliked. The architectural ornaments of the monument are in what was then the new Italian style. It is uncertain where More is buried; some say here; some say in the Tower chapel.—LOFTIE, WILLIAM JOHN, 1883, *The Western Suburbs, A History of London, vol.* II, *p.* 263.

It has been asked, why was he, as Lord Chancellor, a cruel persecutor of the Lutherans? The charge of cruelty rests upon accusations that began with calumnies to which, even at this day, public men are exposed when they are strong on either side in a great controversy that has stirred the passions of the people. John Foxe was a good man, though he did not need much evidence to convict a Roman Catholic of any wrong-doing with which he might be charged. Bias directed judgment. Thirty years after More's death, Foxe charged him with the examination and torture of John Tewkesbury, who had retracted several months before More was Chancellor; with the death of John Frith, which was a year after More had resigned his office; he told also another story that, like the tale of Tewkesbury, worked up the old popular fable about a whipping-tree in More's garden at Chelsea, called Jesus' Tree, or the Tree of Truth. More in his lifetime explicitly contradicted accusations of this kind. No man, while More was Chancellor, was put to death by him for heresy. Among the passionate accusations, blindly hurled from one side to the other in More's time, that story of the Tree of Truth was current. More contradicted it when it was most easy, if he did not speak truth, to confute him. His whippings, he said, had been only two—one of a child in service of his house who sought to corrupt another child, and one a public whipping of a lunatic who brawled in churches, and was thereby restrained from continuance in that form of disorder.—MORLEY, HENRY, 1891, *English Writers, vol.* VII, *p.* 232.

UTOPIA

I toke upon me to tourne, and translate oute of Latine into oure Englishe tonge the frutefull, and profitable boke, which sir Thomas more knight compiled, and made of the new yle "Utopia," conteining and setting forth ye best state, and fourme of a publique weale: A worke (as it appeareth) written almost fourtie yeres ago by the said sir Thomas More ye authour thereof. . . . Is a work not only for ye matter yat it conteineth fruteful and profitable, but also for ye writers eloquent latine stiele pleasaunt and delectable. Which he yat readeth in latine, as ye authour himself wrote it, perfectly understanding ye same; doubtles he shal take great pleasure, and delite both in ye sweete eloquence of ye writer, and also in ye witte invencion, and fine conveiaunce, or disposition of ye matter: but most of all in the good, and holsome lessons, which be there in great plenty, and aboundaunce.—ROBINSON, RALPH, 1551, *tr. "Utopia," The Epistle.*

Among his Latin Books his "Utopia" beareth the bell, containing the *idea* of a compleat Common-wealth in an imaginary Island (but pretended to be lately discovered in America); and that so lively counterfeited, that many, at the reading thereof, mistook it for a real truth; insomuch that many great learned men, as Budeus, and Johannes Paludanus, upon a fervent zeal, wished that some excellent Divines might be sent thither to preach Christ's Gospel; yea, there were here amongst us at home sundry good men and learned Divines very desirous to undertake the Voyage, to bring the people to the faith of Christ, whose manners they did so well like.—FULLER, THOMAS, 1662, *Worthies of England, ed. Nichols, vol.* II, *p.* 69.

His "Utopia," though not written in verse, yet in regard of the great fancy, and invention thereof, may well pass for a poem.—PHILLIPS, EDWARD, 1675, *Theatrum Poetraum Anglicanorum, ed. Brydges, p.* 52.

A masterpiece of wit and fancy.—CAYLEY, ARTHUR, 1808, *Memoirs of Sir Thomas More.*

Perhaps we scarcely appreciate highly enough the spirit and originality of this fiction, which ought to be considered with regard to the barbarism of the times, and the meagreness of preceding inventions. The Republic of Plato, no doubt, furnished More with the germ of his perfect society: but it would be unreasonable to deny him the merit of having struck out the fiction of its real existence from his own fertile imagination; and it is manifest, that some of his most distinguished successors in the same walk of romance, especially Swift, were largely indebted to his reasoning as well as inventive talents. Those who read the "Utopia" in Burnet's translation may believe that they are in Brobdignag; so similar is the vein of satirical humor and easy language. If false and impracticable theories are found in the "Utopia" (and perhaps he knew them to be such), this is in a much greater degree true of the Platonic Republic; and they are more than compensated by the sense of justice and humanity that pervades it, and his bold censures on the vices of power. These are remarkable in a courtier of Henry VIII. . . . . We may acknowledge, after all, that the "Utopia" gives us the impression of its having proceeded rather from a very ingenious than a profound mind; and this, apparently, is what we ought to think of Sir Thomas More. —HALLAM, HENRY, 1837–39, *Introduction to the Literature of Europe, pt.* i, *ch.* iv, *sec.* 34, 35.

More's controversial writings, on which he bestowed most pains and counted most confidently for future fame, have long fallen into utter oblivion, the very titles of most of them having perished. But the composition to which he attached no importance, which, as a *jeu-d'esprit*, occupied a few of his idle hours when retired from the bar,—and which he was with great difficulty prevailed upon to publish, —would of itself have made his name immortal. Since the time of Plato, there had been no composition given to the world which, for imagination, for philosophical discrimination, for a familiarity with the principles of government, for a knowledge of the springs of human action, for a keen observation of men and manners, and for felicity of expression, could be compared to the "Utopia."—CAMPBELL, JOHN, LORD, 1845–56, *Life of Sir Thomas More; Lives of the Lord Chancellors, etc., vol.* II, *p.* 72.

By a strange fate, not a single copy of this work, in any language whatsoever, was printed in England in More's lifetime: or indeed prior to these English versions of Ralph Robinson. Yet—despite its original Latin garb—the work is essentially English, and will ever reckon among the treasures of our literature.—ARBER, EDWARD, 1869, *ed. More's Utopia, English Reprints, Introduction, p.* 3.

One trustworthy record we have, one which has ever been appealed to as authentic, as giving us an unbiassed statement of the miseries which were endured by the poor, and of the pomp and wastefulness of the rich. I refer to the "Utopia."—COWPER, J. M., 1871, *ed. Starkey's England in the Reign of King Henry the Eighth, Preface, p.* ciii.

The wit and humour of More is that of the thoughtful observant Englishman, not breaking out into peals of laughter, but so quiet, sedate, and serious as to demand on the part of the reader something of the same habit of quiet thought and observation, to be fully perceived and enjoyed. More hovers so perpetually on the confines of jest and earnest, passes so naturally from one to the other, that the reader is in constant suspense whether his jest be serious, or his seriousness a jest. The book is wonderfully Englishlike; wonderfully like that balancing habit of mind which trembles on the verge of right and wrong, sometimes struggling on in happier times to clearer vision, sometimes, like More, shutting its eyes and relapsing into older impressions unable to endure suspense any longer. —BREWER, JOHN SHERREN, 1884, *The Reign of Henry VIII, ed. Gairdner, vol.* I, *p.* 288.

We find beneath the idealism of the dreamer, not only a statement of all the grave social, religious, and political questions involved in the life about him, but also a series of philosophical speculations as to their solution, far in advance of the age in which the writer lived. In nothing is this prescience more manifest than in his premature announcement of the principle of religious toleration, embodied in the statement that in Utopia every man could hold whatsoever religious opinion he would, and propagate the same by argument, but without offence to the religion of others. It was, however, to the cause of the laboring poor—bowed down like beasts of burden under a system of social tyranny whose evils had been intensified by a scheme of erroneous legislation which extended from the earlier Statues of Laborers to the statue (6 Hen. VIII. c.3) by which parliament had last attempted to fix the rate of wages—that the sensitive mind of More addressed itself with the greatest zeal and sympathy.—TAYLOR, HANNIS, 1889, *Origin and Growth of the English Constitution, vol.* II, *p.* 46.

At the time of the Renaissance, Sir Thomas More, the wittiest Englishman of his day, whose English style was admirable and who moreover loved the language of his native land, wishing to publish a romance of social satire, the "Utopia," wrote it in Latin. It is one of the oldest examples in modern literature of that species of book which includes at a later date the story of Gargantua and Pantagruel, Bacon's "New Atlantis," Cyrano de Bergerac's "Etats et empires de la lune et du soleil," Fenelon's "Telémaque," "Gulliver's Travels," Voltaire's tales, &c. More's use of Latin is to be the more regretted since his romance exhibits infinite resources of spirit and animation; of all his writings it is the one that best justifies his great reputation for wit and enlightenment. His characters are living men and their conversation undoubtedly resembles that which delighted him in the society of his friend Erasmus. —JUSSERAND, J. J., 1890, *The English Novel in the Time of Shakespeare, p.* 50.

Without doubt "Utopia" is the most brilliant achievement which English humanism of that period has to show. The choice Latin which carries on the narrative so smoothly is but one of its lesser merits, for the treatise as a whole makes the impression of a work of art, and also contains a fund of deep thoughts and striking observations.—TEN BRINK, BERNHARD, 1892, *History of English Literature, (Fourteenth Century to Surrey,) tr. Schmitz, p.* 164.

Long before Professor Drummond had elucidated the important evolutionary truth that the ascent of man has been marked by the triumph of altruistic over egoistic sentiment, Sir Thomas More's keen insight and intellectual penetration enabled him to see that the highway upon which humanity must pass in order to secure progress, felicity and true civilization, must be other than the savage struggle for self alone which controlled man in the past when the animal overmastered the spiritual in governmental as well as individual life. The central idea of "Utopia" is the triumph of altruism over egoism.—FLOWER, B. O., 1896, *The Century of Sir Thomas More, p.* 211.

In some ways doubtless it loses, from the social point of view, if compared with the "Vision of Piers the Plowman." The "Vision" speaks from the people; the "Utopia" speaks for them. Langland has the impassioned sympathy of a comrade of the poor; More has the disinterested thoughtfulness of the scholar statesman. He has lived at the desk, not at the furrow; he moves among abstractions, and we infer rather than see the laborer in his work. But in compensation we know the author of the later book as we cannot know Langland. Through More's speculations shines a personality full of sweetness and light: humorous and worldly wise, yet pure and tender, swift in stern wrath, yet habitually suave. Langland's enormous book is the monument of an entire civilization, the symphonic expression of a mighty social class. More's short and compact work is the record of individual thought, to be accepted, criticised, discussed, on the same basis as the work of Matthew Arnold or William Morris. It is to all practical intents the book of a modern man. The "Utopia" is the first original story by a known English author. That this earliest English novel should deal with the romance, not of a private life, but of society at large, is curious enough; it is even more curious that this first coherent conception of an ideal social state in our literature should be the outcome of the new individualism of the Renaiscence.—SCUDDER, VIDA D., 1898, *Social Ideals in English Letters, p.* 49.

EPIGRAMMATA

More's "Epigrammata," though much admired in their day, not only in England, but all over Europe, are now only inspected by the curious, who wish to know how the Latin language was cultivated in the reign of Henry VII. The collection in its present form was printed at Basle from a manuscript supplied by Erasmus, consisting of detached copies made by various friends, without his authority or sanction. His own opinion of their merits is thus given in one of his epistles to Erasmus: "I was never much delighted with my Epigrams, as you are well aware; and if they had not pleased yourself and certain others better than they pleased me, the volume would never have been published." —CAMPBELL, JOHN, LORD, 1845–56, *Life of Sir Thomas More; Lives of the Lord Chancellors, etc., vol.* II, *p.* 70.

His English poems are of value only as proving that his bent lay in a different direction. The "Epigrammata" show that he was more at home in Latin elegiacs than in English Skeltonics or rhyme royal. They are rather *vers d'occasion* than epigrams in the modern sense, and often possess the same autobiographical interest which attaches to Swift's occasional pieces. The Latin elegiac couplet, in fact, was as much the proper vehicle for this kind of writing in the first quarter of the sixteenth century as the English heroic couplet afterwards became under Queen Anne. It is here sufficient to notice that More enjoyed in this respect a European reputation second only to that of Erasmus, and that Doctor Johnson even assigns to him the superiority. —REICHEL, H. R., 1893, *English Prose, ed. Craik, vol.* I, *p.* 156.

They are neither much better nor much worse than similar compositions of More's contemporaries. Their merit consists in the easy adaptation to poetic uses of the colloquial Latin of the time, not in style or accuracy of scholarship—for More was by no means always careful of the rules of prosody and metrical composition. They are in fact compositions remarkable neither in their own age nor in ours.—HUTTON, WILLIAM HOLDEN, 1895, *Sir Thomas More, p.* 98.

CONTROVERSIAL WRITINGS

His own controversial writings are inflamed by a passion which destroyed his mastery over self, and betrayed him, not only into hasty and violent expression, but into a confusion of thought which is remarkable in a man otherwise so clear-headed. More became a madman the moment he approached the question of religious reform.—MARSH, GEORGE P., 1862, *The Origin and History of the English Language, etc., p.* 502.

It* is replete with keen irony and powerful reasoning, as well as earnest and touching exhortation. That it is a pleasant book to read I do not contend, nor that it is free from language that is rude and nasty. But whether the language deserves the name of ribaldry depends on the question whether, when Shakespeare's Ajax boxes the ears of Thersites and calls him a "whoreson cur," he thereby places himself on a level with Thersites, pouring out his foul venom on Agamemnon, Achilles, and all the princes of the army. Sir Thomas More complains that he could not clean the mouth of Luther without befouling his own fingers.—BRIDGETT, T. E., 1891, *Blessed Thomas More, p.* 209.

The "Apology," although not a work of art, will always have a personal interest to More's admirers. The literary historian, however, would very gladly draw a veil over his polemical treatises on religious subjects. They certainly give us the opportunity of admiring More's enormous capacity for work, the fluency of his pen, his great learning and command of the English language; but one cannot help wishing that his capacity for work and his learning had been utilized for other purposes, and his good English applied to other subjects. . . . Everywhere traces of abundant talent are observable; but the occasion, More's own frame of mind, and the fatal diffuseness to which his ability and haste have misled him, do not allow of any æsthetic impression being made. Something of the old More is met with at times, inasmuch as in fundamental and general matters he manifests a certain large-heartedness and moderation; but this fundamental large-heartedness does not exclude much narrow-heartedness in his judgment of special cases. His moderation in general cases is coupled with great personal bitterness against his adversaries. More was unquestionably far superior to Tindale in intellect and learning, and yet in his dispute with Tindale he plays a miserable figure. . . . Few things are more adapted to make us realize the weakness of human nature, and the immense gulf that lies between mere theoretical speculation and the proof we have to offer of the sincerity of our ideas, than this melancholy episode in More's life, when it is compared with the glorious days of his

* "Work against Luther."

earlier years. Rarely has fate allowed herself to indulge in such trenchant irony as in the metamorphosis by which the author of "Utopia" became the author of the "Confutacyon of Tindale."—TEN BRINK, BERNHARD, 1892, *History of English Literature, (Fourteenth Century to Surrey,) tr. Schmitz, pp.* 183, 184

LIFE OF RICHARD III.

All the passages whereof are so elegantly related by Sir Thomas More, that a man shall get little who comes with a fork, where Sir Thomas hath gone with a rake before him, and by his judicious industry collected all remarkables.—FULLER, THOMAS, 1655, *The Church History of Britain, ed. Nichols, bk.* IV, *sec.* iv, *par.* i, *vol.* I, *p.* 525.

As if it had been the lot of More to open all the paths through the wilds of our old English speech, he is to be considered also as our earliest prose writer, and as the first Englishman who wrote the history of his country in its present language. The historical fragment commands belief by simplicity, and by abstinence from too confident affirmation. It betrays some negligence about minute particulars, which is not displeasing as a symptom of the absence of eagerness to enforce a narrative. The composition has an ease and a rotundity (which gratify the ear without awakening the suspicion of art) of which there was no model in any preceding writer of English prose. In comparing the prose of More with the modern style, we must distinguish the words from the composition. A very small part of his vocabulary has been superannuated; the number of terms which require any explanation is inconsiderable: and in that respect the stability of the language is remarkable. He is, indeed, in his words, more English than the great writers of a century after him, who loaded their native tongue with expressions of Greek or Latin derivation.—MACKINTOSH, SIR JAMES, 1807, *Life of More, Miscellaneous Essays.*

Our first prose composition worthy of the title of history.—MINTO, WILLIAM, 1872-80, *Manual of English Prose Literature, p.* 188.

Sir Thomas More's "History of Richard III.," though not precisely an original authority, set a seal upon the name of that monarch which no subsequent investigation has been able to break.—ADAMS, CHARLES KENDALL, 1881, *A Manual of Historical Literature, p.* 512.

It is certainly the first good historical English prose. This must be largely attributed to the union in More of two qualifications which had hitherto not been found together. He was at once a finished Latin scholar and the most racy English conversationalist of his day. Thus he has succeeded in investing his narrative with a certain classical shapeliness and dignity without impairing the freshness and vigour of the native vein; the former never becomes stilted, the latter never passes into the broad mannerisms which disfigure most Elizabethan and much Jacobean prose. In fact, what Chaucer had done for English vocabulary, More did for English style; to the two together we owe the fixing of the true proportion in which the Teutonic and Latin elements of the language are most effectively blended. Chaucer is the father of English verse; More has almost an equal claim to be called the father of English prose. Their genius, indeed, is not dissimilar though exercised in different domains; above all, they resemble each other in that subtle humour and perfect sanity of judgment, springing from a just balance of the faculties, which have stamped their literary innovations with classic permanence.—REICHEL, H. R., 1893, *English Prose, ed. Craik, vol.* I, *p.* 157.

A work left imperfect by the author, but full of graphic description and vigorous writing. The portrait drawn of Richard by Sir Thomas, though true in the main, is highly coloured.—GAIRDNER, JAMES, 1898, *History of the Life and Reign of Richard the Third, p.* 33.

Incomplete as it is, it is a work of the highest value; and this not only as an authority, for in stlye and method it far surpasses any previous history written in English. . . . Of the literary merit of the history there cannot be the shadow of a dcubt. The story is unfolded with admirable clearness, and the progress of events is followed by the reader with intense interest. The characters are drawn with remarkable precision and power, and the speeches are not the rhetorical offspring of the historian's imagination, but might well be the direct utterances of the historical characters themselves. The facts tell their own tale untrammelled by tedious moral commentary. The result is that an extraordinarily vivid picture is presented, the leading features of which are impressed upon the mind with striking and peculiar force. . . . It was he unquestionably who did most to originate the historical sympathy for the Tudor dynasty which has been so striking a feature of English literature. . . . More gave to English history an indelible portrait of Richard Crookback, and in giving it, his clear and incisive style taught a new school of historians to write so that all might read. With More history passed from the monastery into the market-place, and where he began, Holinshed, Cavendish, and Stow followed; and Bacon on his lines gave his masterly portrait of Henry VII.—HUTTON, WILLIAM HOLDEN, 1895, *Sir Thomas More, pp.* 107, 109, 110.

The eulogies of critics like Hallam were probably determined by the fact that it is an early and not unhappy example of the rather colourless "classical" prose, of which a little later we shall find the chief exponents to be Ascham and his friends at Cambridge. It is, of course, a good deal better than Capgrave, and it is free from Pecock's harshness and crudity of phrase. But as it cannot on the one hand compare for richness, colour, and representative effect with the style of Berners, one of the two best writers of prose nearly contemporary with More, so it is not to be mentioned with that of Fisher, the other, for nice rhetorical artifice and intelligent employment of craftsman-like methods of work. But it is much more "eighteenth century" than either, and this commended it to Hallam; while More's pleasant wit and great intellectual ability naturally set it above the work of mere translators or compilers. Sir Thomas has a secure place in English history, and no mean one in that very interesting history of works of distinction composed in Latin, since the arrival of the vernaculars at years of discretion, which has yet to be written. But his place in the strict History of English literature is very small, and not extraordinarily high. —SAINTSBURY, GEORGE, 1898, *A Short History of English Literature, p.* 212.

GENERAL

More was the special orator of the bishops, to feign lies for their purpose.—TYNDALE, WILLIAM, 1531, *Answer to More, p.*168.

Sir Tho. More is always wrangling and jangling, harping and carping, about No and Nay, Yea and Yes; this word and that word; an Elder, and an Elder stick: and as Rachell mourned for her children, because she had them not, so Sir Thomas More might mourn for more divinity, because he had it not.—DRANT, THOMAS, 1569-70, *Sermons.*

A great ornament to this land, and a Rymer.—DANIEL, SAMUEL, 1603, *A Defence of Ryme, Works, ed. Grosart, vol.* IV, *p.* 49.

More was no divine at all; and it is plain to any that reads his writings that he knew nothing of antiquity, beyond the quotations he found in the canon law and in the master of the sentences (only he had read some of St. Austin's treatises). —BURNET, GILBERT, 1679–1715, *The History of the Reformation of the Church of England, ed. Nares, vol.* I, *pt.* i, *bk.* iii.

The massive folio of Sir Thomas More's "English Works" remains a monument of our language at a period of its pristine vigor. Viewed in active as well as in contemplative life, at the bar or on the bench, as ambassador or chancellor, and not to less advantage, where, "a good distance from his house at Chelsea, he builded the new building, wherein was a chapel, a library, and a gallery," the character, the events, and the writings of this illustrious man may ever interest us. . . . More, however skilful as a Latin scholar, to promulgate his opinions aimed at popularity, and cultivated our vernacular idiom, till the English language seems to have enlarged the compass of its expression under the free and copious vein of the writer. It is only by the infecility of the subjects which constitute the greater portion of this mighty volume, that its author has missed the immortality which his genius had else secured.—DISRAELI, ISAAC, 1841, *The Psychological Character of Sir Thomas More, Amenities of Literature.*

It* was written by an Englishman, a very honest, brave, learned, and graceful Englishman. It was the work of a lawyer, one of the best of English lawyers; though it was written about a place that never existed, it laid bare corruptions that did exist, corruptions that were passing under Sir Thomas More's eyes, in his own country. Like a good man, he spoke most of the evils of his own profession,

*Utopia.

those which he knew best and had most to do with—the bribery, and denials of justice, from which his own hands were quite pure. But he also exposed the evils which he saw in the Church of his days; he spoke plainly and severely of its need of reformation. Nevertheless, when the Reformation came in his age, Sir Thomas More did not like it. He would have heartily supported one which had been managed by scholars and accomplished men; he did not sympathise with one which appealed directly to the sympathies of common men, suffering from the miseries of the world, and of their own sins. The brave Sir Thomas More would have checked such a Reformation as that by any means; he rather died on the scaffold than in any way sanction it. I should be ashamed not to feel a great reverence for him. It is strongest when I think him most wrong.—MAURICE, FREDERICK DENISON, 1865, *On Books, The Friendship of Books and Other Lectures.*

More is altogether before his time, so far as anyone can be said to occupy such a position, both in his thoughts and in his methods of expressing them. For nearly a hundred years afterwards we do not meet with such a vigorous, perspicuous, and above all such an evidently thoughtful style. He was perhaps one of the few men of the 16th century who had any command over their pens, who wrote as they thought; and his thoughts must have been always clear as they were always noble.—FLETCHER, C. R. L., 1881, *The Development of English Prose Style, p.* 7.

One among the Catholics was no doubt capable, if he had chosen, of borrowing not perhaps the unsavoury though pungent pen of Murner, but the finer Attic weapon of Erasmus and Hutten. But devoted as he was to the church, and prodigally as he spent his skill and learning in its cause, the huge volume that contains his best arguments for Catholicism could in no way rival one small but golden book in which he had embodied the more than half pagan inspiration of his early manhood. For the rest, this volume—a dialogue against Tyndale's book on the Mass—has pleasing qualities; but it belongs essentially to the less vivacious Ciceronian type. Every circumstance which could provoke any scintillation of dramatic liveliness and seduce the attention from the flow of cogent reasons, is carefully refined away.—HERFORD, CHARLES H., 1886, *Studies in the Literary Relations of England and Germany in the Sixteenth Century, p.* 47.

He was a Greek of the very Greeks, in both character and attainment.—MITCHELL, DONALD G., 1889, *English Lands Letters and Kings, From Celt to Tudor, p.* 175.

It is to be regretted that Sir Thomas More, the greatest humanist, perhaps the greatest intellect of his time, gave so much to Europe that was meant for England.—GOSSE, EDMUND, 1897, *Short History of Modern English Literature, p.* 62.

Hector Boece

1465?-1536

Wrote a history of the Bishops of Aberdeen, under the title of "Vitæ Episcoporum Murthlasensium et Aberdonensium," published in 1522. He also composed, in Latin, a History of Scotland, beginning with remote antiquity, and ending with the death of James I., which was published under the title of "Scotorum Historia ab illius Gentis Origine," in 1526. A translation of this work, executed at the command of James V., by John Bellenden, Archdeacon of Moray, and printed in 1536, forms the first existing specimen of Scottish literary prose, and was reprinted in 1821. Another version, by the English chronicler, Holinshed, was the source from which Shakespeare drew the materials for his tragedy of "Macbeth."—ADAMS, W. DAVENPORT, 1877, *Dictionary of English Literature, p.* 95.

In the six first books of his history there are great many particulars not to be had in Fordon, or any other writers now extant: and, unless the authors which he pretends to have seen, be hereafter discovered, he will continue to be shrewdly suspected for the contriver of almost as many tales as our Jeoffrey of Monmouth.—NICOLSON, WILLIAM, 1696–1714, *Scottish Historical Library.*

May be justly reverenced as one of the revivers of elegant learning. . . . The style of Boethius, though, perhaps, not always rigorously pure, is formed with great diligence upon ancient models, and wholly uninfected with monastic barbarity. His history is written with elegance and vigour, but his fabulousness and credulity are justly blamed. His fabulousness, if he was the author of fictions, is a fault for which no apology can be made; but his credulity may be excused in an age when all men were credulous. — JOHNSON, SAMUEL, 1775, *A Journey to the Western Isles of Scotland, Aberdeen.*

As a specimen of Latinity, the student of antiquity now remembers it only as a receptacle for the wildest of the fables which used to be authoritatively current in the earliest sections of our national annals.—SPALDING, WILLIAM, 1852–82, *A History of English Literature, p.* 192.

He seems to have been rather a good Latinist than a scholar imbued with the riches of classical study. That he was of the reforming party of the day—the *humanists*, as they were called in the continental schools—we learn from his own expressions, from his friends and associates, and especially from his profound admiration for Erasmus, with whom he had even the honour of corresponding. As a historian, he was at first admired and followed, and latterly condemned, in both cases much beyond reason. His object was to give a classical dress to his rude native chronicles. One must doubt whether he really meant his grave readers to credit his stories of "Veremund" and "Cornelius Campbell," and the records from Iona. He found, over a large period of his history, bare lists of kings, and he took the pains of dressing them in what he thought suitable characters and actions. Quite unembarrassed by facts, he proposed to treat his subject like an artist, with the proper balancing of light and shadow, and studied to administer among the persons of his drama some sort of poetical justice. Leslie compares him to Livy, and his most fabulous portions are perhaps not more romantic than Livy's first decade. The difference lies in the genius of the writers.—INNES, C., 1861, *Sketches of Early Scotch History, p.* 267.

Through his History—two editions of which were printed in Paris—the wondrous tale of the annals of Scotland got a hold on the European mind. It is noticeable that Hector Boece's narrative, wild as it would now be counted, was skilfully adjusted to the conditions of belief in his own time. In whatever savours of the supernatural, he deals with far more caution and reserve than Geoffrey of Monmouth, the chronicler of the Anglo-British heroics, or Geoffrey Keating, the historian of Ireland. It is easy, indeed, on a comparison, to imagine a time when these would be dealt with as wild romances, while Boece's work might be accepted as sober history.—BURTON, JOHN HILL, 1867, *The History of Scotland, vol.* IV, *p.* 125.

No doubt his method is that of a romancer. We cannot trust him whenever a point is in dispute. But he did not write to settle points. He wrote to celebrate in heroic fashion the far-descended fame of the Scottish kingdom, and his picturesque touches and full-blown fictions probably seemed to him only the appropriate decorations of his splendid theme. Something may be due to personal credulity and national vanity, but in the main we do think that these were the chief causes of the peculiar features of his work; and while we frankly admit that he has no claim to a place among trustworthy historians, we repudiate the idea that he is an imposter and a cheat. His aim was epic, though his genius and his taste were insufficient for his ambition.—ROSS, JOHN MERRY, 1884, *Scottish History and Literature, ed. Brown, p.* 226.

Prior to this no history of Scotland had been printed except the compendium of Major. . . . Lord Hailes declared that his countrymen were reformed from popery, but not from Boece, but now that the latter reformation has been accomplished we may do justice to his real merits as we do to those of the mediæval church. His learning and zeal co-operated with the liberality of Elphinstone in laying the foundation of the university which has diffused culture in the northern districts of Britain. A love of historical studies dating from his time has continued to mark the Aberdonian scholars, who have contributed more to Scottish history than the inhabitants of any other part of Scotland.—MACKAY, ÆNEAS, 1886, *Dictionary of National Biography, vol.* V, *pp.* 299, 300.

William Tyndale

C. 1484-1536

Born, in Gloucestershire, about 1484. Educated at Magdalen Hall, Oxford (possibly also at Cambridge). B. A., Oxford, 1512; M. A., 1515. Tutor in household of Sir John Welch, at Little Sodbury, 1521-23; in household of Humphrey Monmouth, in London, 1523-24. To Germany, 1524; occupied himself with his translation of New Testament into English. In consequence of this was arrested as a heretic, 1535; imprisoned in Vilvorde Castle; executed there, 6 Oct., 1536. *Works:* "The New Testament translated into English," 1525; "A Treatyse of Justificacyon by Faith only," 1528; "The Obediēce of a Christen Man," 1528; "The Parable of the Wycked Mammon," 1528; "Exposition on I Cor. vii." (anon.), 1529; "Translation of the Book of Moses called Genesis," 1530; "An Answere unto Sir T. More's Dialoge" (1530); "The Practice of Prelates," 1530; "The prophetic Jonas" (under initials W. T.), (1531?); "The Exposition of the fyrste Epistle of seynt Jhon" (under initials W. T.), 1531; "The Supper of the Lorde" (anon.), 1533; "The Pentateuch, newly corrected and amended," 1534; "An Exposicion upon the v., vi., vii., chapters of Matthew," 1548; "A Briefe Declaration of the Sacraments" (1550?). *Posthumous:* "A fruitefull Exposition. . . . upon the Epistle of Saint Paul to the Romans," 1642. *Collected Works:* in 2 vols., 1572-73.—SHARP, R. FARQUHARSON, 1897, *A Dictionary of English Authors, p.* 286.

PERSONAL

So skilled in seven languages, Hebrew, Greek, Latin, Italian, Spanish, English, French, that whichever he spoke you would suppose it his native tongue.—BUSCHIUS, HERMAN, 1526, *Schelhorn's Amœnitates Literariæ, vol.* IV, *p.* 431.

Upon four years and a half past and more, I heard the foresaid Sir William preach two or three sermons at St. Dunstan's-in-the-West, in London; and after that I chanced to meet with him, and with communication I examined what living he had. He said, "he had none at all; but he trusted to be with my Lord of London, in his service." And therefore I had the better phantasy to him. Afterward he went to my lord and spake to him, as he told me, and my lord answered him. "That he had chaplains enough"; and he said to him, "That he would have no more at that time." And so the priest came to me again, and besought me to help him, and so I took him into my house half a year; and there he lived like a good priest, as methought. He studied most part of the day and of the night at his book; and he would eat but sodden meat by his goodwill, nor drink but small single beer. I never saw him wear linen about him, in the space he was with me. I did promise him ten pounds sterling, to pray for my father and mother, their souls, and all Christian souls. I did pay it him, when he made his exchange to Hamborough, and thither I sent it him by one Hans Collenbeke. And since I have never sent him the value of one penny, nor never will.—MONMOUTH, HUMPHREY, 1528, *Petition to Wolsey, Harleian MSS., p.* 425, *Strype Memorials.*

He was a man without any spot or blemish of rancour or malice, full of mercy and compassion, so that no man living was able to reprove him of any sin or crime; although his righteousness and justification depended not thereupon before God; but only upon the blood of Christ and his faith upon the same. In this faith he died, with constancy, at Vilvorde, and now resteth with the glorious company of Christ's martyrs, blessedly in the Lord.—And thus much of the life and story of the true servant and martyr of God, William Tyndale, who for his notable pains and travail, may well be called the Apostle of England, in this our latter age.—FOXE, JOHN, 1562, *Acts and Monuments of the Church.*

To those who have never before been aware of the fact, it must appear extraordinary, that the *Martyrdom* of Tyndale, the first translator of our Bible into English, should stand so emphatically by itself. There was *no other*, with which the Councils of England, and of a Continental kingdom, were both concerned; *no other*, in the guilt of which, both our own country, and a foreign power, were alike involved. The eyes of Henry the Eighth, and those of his Ministers, were wide open, when the martyr fell under a

WILLIAM TYNDALE

From the Painting at Hertford College, Oxford.

decree of the Emperor Charles V. Considered as an event, amidst all the widespread and long-continued violence of the times, his martyrdom rises up to view, and appears like a conspicuous solitary column. If there be any memento inscribed, it is a *double* one—German on one side, but English on the other. . . . He had engaged attention not only abroad, but especially at home, and that of public men, both dead and still alive. But then, besides, he was not merely the only conspicuous Englishman thus slain, with the full cognition of this country and the Continent; but the *only translator of the Sacred Volume* in Europe, *so* put to death. The moral crime attached itself, at once, to home and foreign authorities.—ANDERSON, CHRISTOPHER, 1845–49, *The Annals of the English Bible, ed. Prime, p.* 223.

Tyndale indulged in his pleasant dreams no longer. He saw that he was on the point of being arrested, condemned, and interrupted in his great work. He must seek a retreat where he can discharge in peace the task God has allotted him. "You cannot save me from the hands of the priests," said he to Sir John, "and God knows to what troubles you would expose yourself by keeping me in your family. Permit me to leave you." Having said this, he gathered up his papers, took his Testament, pressed the hands of his benefactors, kissed the children, and then descending the hill, bade farewell to the smiling banks of the Severn, and departed alone, alone with his faith. What shall he do? What will become of him? Where shall he go? He went forth like Abraham, one thing alone engrossing his mind: the Scriptures shall be translated into the vulgar tongue, and he will deposit the oracles of God in the midst of his countrymen.—D'AUBIGNÉ, J. H. MERLE, 1853, *History of the Reformation of the Sixteenth Century, tr. White, vol.* V, *bk.* xviii, *ch.* iv.

In character, Tyndale was one of those fearless, simple-minded men whose heroism would be bound to show itself in times of peril. There was little of the worldly element in his nature; he lived for higher aims. To curry favour with the great, or to whittle down his opinions merely to please the higher powers in the State, was utterly repugnant to him. Morally, he was a high type of man; there is nothing to extenuate, and nothing to apologise for, as regards his personal character; for even his chief prosecutor, the Procureur-General, described him as "a learned, good, and godly man."—SMITH, GEORGE BARNETT, 1896, *William Tyndale and the Translation of the English Bible, p.* 159.

Gulielmus Tyndalus, Martyr
Olim ex Aul: Magd:
This canvas represents (which is all that Art can do)
The likeness of William Tyndale, formerly student and pride of this Hall;
Who after reaping here the happy first-fruits of a purer faith,
Devoted his energy at Antwerp to the translation
Of the New Testament and Pentateuch into the native language:
A work so beneficial to his English countrymen, that he is
Not undeservedly called the Apostle of England.
He received the crown of martyrdom at Vilvorde, near Brussels, 1536.
A man (if we may believe his opponent, the Procurator-General
Of the Emperor) very learned, pious, and good.

—INSCRIPTION ON PORTRAIT IN HERTFORD COLLEGE, OXFORD, *Demaus' Tyndale, p.* 33.

BIBLE

Them that are learned christenly, I beseche for as moche as I am sure and my concience beareth me recorde, that of a pure entent, singilly and faythfully, I have interpreted itt as farre forth as god gave me the gyfte of knowledge and understandynge: that the rudeness off this worke nowe at the fyrst tyme offende them not: but that they consyder howe that I had no man to counterfeit, nether was holpe with englysshe of eny that had interpreted the same or soche lyke thinge in scripture before tyme.—TYNDALE, WILLIAM, 1525, *New Testament, Epistle to Reader.*

Yet none will deny, but that many faults, needing amendment, are found in his translation; which is no wonder to those who consider: First. Such an undertaking was not the task for a *man*, but *men*. Secondly. No great design is invented and perfected at once. Thirdly. Tyndal, being an exile, wanted many necessary accomodations. Fourthly. His skill in Hebrew was not considerable; yea, generally, learning in languages was then but in the infancy thereof. Fifthly. Our English tongue was not improved to that expressiveness whereat at this day it is arrived. However, what he undertook was to be admired as glorious; what he performed, to be commended as profitable; wherein he failed, is to be excused as pardonable, and to be scored on the account rather of that age, than of the author himself. Yea, Tyndal's pains were useful, had his translation done no other good than to help toward the making of a better; our last translators having in express charge, for king James, to consult the translation of Tyndal.—FULLER, THOMAS, 1655, *The Church History of Britain, bk.* v, *sec.* iv, *par.* 39.

The book that had the greatest authority and influence, was Tindal's translation of the New Testament, of which the bishops made great complaints, and said, it was full of errors. But Tonstal, then Bishop of London, being a man of invincible moderation, would do nobody hurt, yet endeavoured as he could to get their books into his hands: so being at Antwerp in the year 1529, as he returned from his embassy at the treaty of Cambray, he sent for one Packington, an English merchant there, and desired him to see how many New Testaments of Tindal's translation he might have for money. Packington, who was a secret favourer of Tindal, told him what the Bishop proposed. Tindal was very glad of it; for, being convinced of some faults in his work, he was designing a new and more correct edition; but he was poor, and the former impression not being sold off, he could not go about it; so he gave Packington all the copies that lay in his hands, for which the Bishop paid the price, and brought them over, and burnt them publicly in Cheapside. This had such an hateful appearance in it, being generally called a burning of the word of God, that people from thence concluded there must be a visible contrariety, between that book and the doctrines of those who so handled it; by which both their prejudice against the clergy, and their desire of reading the New Testament was increased.—BURNET, GILBERT, 1679-1715, *The History of the Reformation of the Church of England, ed. Nares, vol.* I, *pt.* i, *bk.* ii.

Though it is far from a perfect translation, yet few first translations will be found preferable to it. It is astonishing how little obsolete the language of it is, even at this day; and in point of perspicuity and noble simplicity, propriety of idiom, and purity of style, no English version has yet approached it.—GEDDES, ALEXANDER, 1788, *Prospectus for a New Translation of the Holy Bible, p.* 88.

While the voices of antiquarians and critics unite in the highest eulogiums on the version itself, it is not to be disguised that, as to its mechanical part, every page is enstamped with marks of haste. The harrassed life of its unfortunate author is made present to our thought; and fancy paints, without effort, the bloodhounds of a merciless church tracking his footsteps. Broken in upon in the midst of the drudgery of the press in one city, he gathers up his fragments in what condition he may, and flees to another to complete his interrupted labors. With this in full remembrance, the orthography so curiously varying, even in the same paragraph or sentence, the confounding of distinct words through a single misplaced letter, the withholding or bestowment of capitals *ad libitum* as it were, the unsightly exchange of the leading vowels as initial letters,—as "o" for "a," &c.,—the seeming disdain of rule throughout, all find a prompt solution.—DABNEY, J. P., 1837, *An Edition of the New Testament by William Tyndale, the Martyr, Memoir, p.* 5.

Tyndale's translation of the New Testament is the most important philological monument of the first half of the sixteenth century, perhaps I should say of the whole period between Chaucer and Shakespeare, both as a historical relic, and as having more than any thing else contributed to shape and fix the sacred dialect, and establish the form which the Bible must permanently assume in an English dress.—MARSH, GEORGE P., 1860, *Lectures on the English Language, Lecture* v, *p.* 113.

The peculiar genius—if such a word may be permitted—which breathes through it—the mingled tenderness and majesty—the Saxon simplicity—the preternatural grandeur—unequalled, unapproached, in the attempted improvements of modern scholars—all are here, and bear the impress of the mind of one man—William Tyndal.—FROUDE, JAMES ANTHONY, 1856–70, *History of England, vol.* III, *ch.* xii.

This patience of laborious emendation completes the picture of the great translator. In the conception and style of his renderings, he had nothing to modify or amend. Throughout all his revisions he preserved intact the characteristics of his own great work. Before he began, he had prepared himself for a task of which he could comprehend the full difficulty. He had rightly measured the momentous issues of a vernacular version of the Holy Scriptures, and determined once for all the principles on which it must be made. His later efforts were directed simply to the nearer attainment of his ideal. To gain this end he availed himself of the best help which lay within his reach; but he used it as a master, not as a disciple. In this work alone, he felt that substantial independence was essential to success. In exposition or exhortation he might borrow freely the language or the thought which seemed suited to his purpose, but in rendering the sacred text he remained throughout faithful to the instincts of a scholar. From first to last, his style and his interpretation are his own; and in the originality of Tyndale is included, in a great measure, the originality of our English version.—WESTCOTT, BROOKE FOSS, 1868, *A History of the English Bible, p.* 209.

I have before me one of these old square folios, in black letter, in which the pages, worn by horny fingers, have been patched together, in which an old engraving figures forth to the poor folk the deeds and menaces of the God of Israel, in which the preface and table of contents point out to simple people the moral which is to be drawn from each tragic history, and the application which is to be made of each venerable precept. Hence have sprung much of the English language, and half of the English manners; to this day the country is biblical; it was these big books which had transformed Shakspeare's England. To understand this great change, try to picture these yeomen, these shopkeepers, who in the evening placed this Bible on their table, and bareheaded, with veneration, heard or read one of its chapters. Think that they have no other books, that theirs was a virgin mind, that every impression would make a furrow, that the monotony of mechanical existence rendered them entirely open to new emotions, that they opened this book not for amusement, but to discover in it their doom of life and death; in brief, that the sombre and impassioned imagination of the race raised them to the level of the grandeurs and terrors which were to pass before their eyes.—TAINE, H. A., 1871, *History of English Literature, tr. Van Laun, vol.* I, *bk.* iv, *ch.* v, *p.* 367.

Had the ravages of time alone been directed against the book, no doubt not a few might still be found safe in the shelter of our older libraries; but the New Testaments were for many years rigorously prohibited, they were eagerly sought for by the officers of the Church, and publicly burned whenever they were discovered. Thus it has happened that of the three thousand *quarto* New Testaments, only a single copy remains, and that in a most imperfect state: and of the *octavo* only two are known to exist; one, incomplete, in the library of St. Paul's Cathedral, and the other wanting only the title-page, in the Baptist College at Bristol. . . . The history of the one perfect copy of the *octavo* Testament of Worms can be traced back for upwards of a century. Somewhere about the year 1740, the Earl of Oxford, the collector of the famous Harleian Library, secured it through one of his numerous agents, whom he rewarded for the discovery with a payment of ten pounds, and an annuity of twenty. At the death of Lord Oxford his library was purchased by Osborne, the famous London bookseller, who, in complete ignorance of the value of the work, sold it to the great bibliographer, Joseph Ames, for fifteen shillings. After passing through the hands of another bookseller, it came into the possession of the Rev. Dr. Gifford, one of the Assistant Librarians of the British Museum, who gave twenty guineas for it. Dying in 1784, he bequeathed the precious treasure, with the rest of his valuable collection of Bibles and rare books, to the Baptist College in his native city of Bristol; and there the volume rests in a fire-proof safe, secure, it is to be hoped, against all further vicissitudes of time.—DEMAUS, ROBERT, 1871, *William Tyndale, A Biography, pp.* 123, 126.

That Tyndale's English is decidedly superior to the writings of his time which have come down to us, cannot be disputed; it is a noble translation, the basis of every subsequent English version (the Rhemish is not English), and on several accounts better than all subsequent versions; it has an individuality as pronounced as Luther's, its Saxon is racy and strong, sometimes majestic, and above all things, it is hearty and true, the reader feels that the translator felt what he wrote, that his heart was in his work, and that he strove in prayer to reproduce in his own mother-tongue to the very best of his ability what he believed to be the true sense of the word of God, as he understood it.—MOMBERT, J. ISIDOR, 1883, *English Versions of the Bible*, p. 93.

GENERAL

Now when Tyndale calleth his heresies by the name of faith, and maketh men to serve the devil while they wene to serve God, what abominable idolatry is this! If it be idolatry to put trust in the devil, and serve the devil with faith, it is worse than idolatry to make men wene they serve God with faith, whilst they despite him with a false belief. And if it be very infidelity to do as the Turks do,—bid men believe in Mahomet's Alchoran, it is more infidelity to do as Tyndale hath done,—purposely mistranslate Christ's holy gospel to set forth heresies as evil as the Alchoran. . . . These pestilent infidelities, and these abominable kinds of idolatries, far exceed and pass and incomparably more offend the majesty of our Lord God, than all the setting up of Bel, and Baal and Beelzebub and all the devils in hell.—MORE, SIR THOMAS, 1532-3, *Confution of Tyndale's Answer*.

It has been much the custom to speak of Sir Thomas More as the first great master of English prose-writing. Sir James Mackintosh, by some strange forgetfulness, even goes so far as to call him "the first writer of a prose which is still intelligible." More's "History of Richard III." was written some years before Tyndale began to write; but neither this, nor any other of his works, can be compared with those of Tyndale in excellence of style. The choice of words and the arrangement of sentences are less according to modern usage; and in place of the concise point and eloquent earnestness of Tyndale's pages, there is a heavy diffuseness, an inelegant strength, pervading those of the chancellor. But Tyndale's liberality of sentiment has prevented even the style of his works from being generally appreciated in England.—NORTON, CHARLES ELIOT, 1848, *The Life of William Tyndale, North American Review, vol.* 67, *p.* 342, *note.*

His principal works were the "Practice of Prelates," the "Obedience of a Christian Man," the "Parable of the Wicked Mammon," a book on the Sacraments, and his prologues, or prefaces, to the several books of the Pentateuch, the prophet Jonah, and the books of the New Testament. These works all show the marks of a keen and clever, but extremely self-sufficient man, with enough knowledge of languages to make such a man suppose himself learned, but without any real depth of learning, and with enough facility of expression to lead him to argue, but without any argumentative power. He was also of a very cankered and bitter temper, which led him to fill his pages with abusive language, even when writing of the most sacred subjects. His language respecting the latter was often so shocking, and at the same time so utterly illogical, that it led Sir Thomas More to stigmatize him as a "blasphemous fool." It is certainly a strong evidence of the extent to which party feeling will lead that Tyndale should ever have been respected as a theological writer.—BLUNT, JOHN HENRY, 1869, *The Reformation of the Church of England*, p. 547.

Tyndale, whose monument is the Reformation.—GEIKIE, JOHN CUNNINGHAM, 1878, *The English Reformation*, p. 190.

The medium between the fifteenth century and all after time. In him the best powers of the ripened language are harvested, recapitulated, and transmitted in a consecrated vessel to all posterity.—EARLE, JOHN, 1890, *English Prose*, p. 426.

In judging of Tindale as an author he must not be compared with Luther. The concise brevity, the striking logic, the genial flashes of intellect, which characterize the writings of the German Reformer, will be looked for in vain in the Englishman. The breadth of Tindale's presentation, his various digressions, render it difficult for the reader to concentrate his attention upon the subject;

whereas in Luther one argument follows the other in the simplest manner; each succeeding one strengthening the last, and placing it in a new light; all is unexpected, surprising, and, taken as a whole, a powerfully riveted chain which holds the reader's attention and keeps him to the subject. Tindale does not lay hold of his reader like Luther, time and inclination are needed to enjoy him. But, on the other hand, the reader is powerfully affected by the depth of his convictions, the fullness of his arguments, the force of his descriptions, and many good ideas—and, above all, affected by the sincerity of the man. —TEN BRINK, BERNHARD, 1892, *History of English Literature, (Fourteenth Century to Surrey) tr. Schmitz, p.* 179.

As an original author he is distinguished for the humble yet not too ordinary virtues of clearness and directness. He had a complete command of the language for the purposes of theological argument and controversy. His meaning is always plain, and if his treatises are not now popular, that comes from loss of general interest in his matter, and not from any deterrent or wearisome qualities in his style. Lofty and eloquent passages are hardly to be found in him, but his views are stated concisely and effectively. His phrases are generally short and free from encumbrance. There is little colour or imagination in his discourse, but it is not laboured or clumsy.—KER, W. P., 1893, *English Prose, ed. Craik, vol.* I, *p.* 181.

Though not perhaps the foremost figure of the English reformation, Tyndale was one of the most remarkable of its leaders. He left his country an unknown exile; he lived abroad in poverty, obscurity, and danger; and yet before his death he had made his name a household word in England. His original writings bear the impress of sound scholarship and of the highest literary power. They are unquestionably the ablest expositions of the views of the more advanced English reformers who triumphed under Edward VI, and developed into the Puritan party under Elizabeth. —CARLYLE, E. IRVING, 1899, *Dictionary of National Biography, vol.* LVII, *p.* 428.

Sir Thomas Wyatt

1503–1542

Born, at Allington Castle, Kent, 1503. Matriculate St. John's College, Cambirdge, 1515; B. A., 1518; M. A., 1520. Married Hon. Elizabeth Brooke, 1520 (?). In favour at Court of Henry VIII. Clerk of King's Jewels, Oct. 1524 to May 1531. On embassy to France, 1526. Marshal of Calais Castle, 1529-30. Commissioner of Peace for Essex, 1532. Imprisoned in Tower at time of Anne Boleyn's trial, spring of 1536; released soon afterwards. Knighted, 1537 (?). Ambassador in Spain, June 1537 to June 1539. On embassy in France and Holland, Nov. 1539 to May 1540. Imprisoned in Tower on charge of high treason, 1541; tried and acquitted, June 1541. Grant of land from King, July 1541. High Steward of Manor of Maidstone, 1542. Died, at Sherborne, 11 Oct. 1542. Buried in Sherborne Church. *Works:* Poems in the Earl of Surrey's "Songs and Sonnets," 1567; "Poetical Works," ed. by R. Bell, 1854; ed. by G. Gilfillan, 1858.—SHARP, R. FARQUHARSON, 1897, *A Dictionary of English Authors, p.* 305.

PERSONAL

A visage stern, and mild; where both did grow
Vice to contemn, in virtue to rejoice:
Amid great storms, whom grace assured so,
To live upright, and smile at fortune's choice.
A hand, that taught what might be said in rhyme;
That reft Chaucer the glory of his wit.
A mark, the which (unperfected for time)
Some may approach, but never none shall hit.
A tongue that served in foreign realms his king;
Whose courteous talk to virtue did inflame
Each noble heart; a worthy guide to bring
Our English youth by travail unto fame.
An eye, whose judgment none effect could blind.
Friends to allure and foes to reconcile;
Whose piercing look did represent a mind
With virtue fraught, reposed, void of guile.
A heart, where dread was never so imprest
To hide the thought that might the truth advance!
In neither fortune loft, nor yet represt,
To swell in wealth, or yield unto mischance.
A valiant corpse, where force and beauty met:
Happy, alas! too happy, but for foes,
Lived, and ran the race that nature set;
Of manhood's shape, where she the mould did lose.

—SURREY, EARL OF, 1542, *On the Death of Sir Thomas Wyatt.*

Of worthy memory for wit, learning, and experience.—ASCHAM, ROGER, 1552, *A Report and Discourse of the Affaires and State of Germany, ed. Giles, vol.* III, *p.* 9.

He possessed almost all the qualifications which go to constitute a consummate courtier. He had a noble appearance, a form where, according to Surrey, "force and beauty met," a face of perfect symmetry, eyes of dazzling lustre, a mouth of singular sweetness, and a carriage distinguished alike by dignity and ease—the dignity of the oak and the yielding grace of the willow. His accomplishments, too, were extensive, and yet hung elegantly about him, waving to his outline freely like the toga—not sternly girded around him like the tunic. He spoke French, Italian, and Spanish, like English, besides being thoroughly acquainted with the classical languages.—GILFILLAN, GEORGE, 1858, *ed., The Poetical Works of Sir Thomas Wyatt, p.* vii.

Wyatt was considered the greatest wit of his time, yet, in an age of gross indelicacy, was never known to utter an improper jest or word. He had a horror of joking on serious subjects. . . . As he advanced to middle life, as a man after thirty was in those days considered to be, he respectfully declined entering into the amusements in which the court was necessarily engaged. On being urged by Henry to join in a midnight mask, he refused: the King asked his reason. "Sir," he said, "he who would be thought a wise man in the daytime, must not play the fool at night." . . . But whilst naturally gay, full of spirits, and fond of society, Wyatt had a holy, heavenly frame of mind, combined with purity and elevation of thought.—THOMSON, KATHERINE, 1861, *Celebrated Friendships, vol.* I, *pp.* 80, 81.

Few men ever possessed a more unblemished reputation, or died more sincerely regretted and esteemed than Sir Thomas Wyatt. His talents and accomplishments, great as they undoubtedly were, yielded even to the higher qualities of frankness, integrity, and honour, in obtaining him the approbation and love of his contemporaries; and to judge from the numerous elegies by which minds of kindred excellence sought to commemorate his worth, Wyatt possessed the advantage of being appreciated by those whose praise is fame. His poems sufficiently attest the variety and scope of his abilities; and, like those of his friend Surrey, they are free from the slightest impurity of thought or expression. He spoke several languages, and was so richly stored with classical literature, that the erudite Camden says he was "splendide doctus." His prose is forcible and clear, and occasionally animated and eloquent. He excelled on the lute, and was eminent for his conversational powers; but all these merits were exceeded by the agreeable qualities of his private character. In person Wyatt was eminently handsome; tall, and of a commanding presence, elegantly formed, and gifted with a countenance of manly beauty.—YEOWELL, JAMES, 1894, *ed. The Poetical Works of Sir Thomas Wyatt, Memoir, p.* xlix.

GENERAL

In the latter end of the same kings raigne sprong vp a new company of courtly makers, of whom Sir *Thomas Wyat* th' elder and *Henry* Earle of Surrey were the two chieftaines, who hauing trauailed into Italie, and there tasted the sweete and stately measures and stile of the Italian Poesie as nouices newly crept out of the schooles of *Dante Arioste* and *Petrarch*, they greatly pollished our rude and homely maner of vulgar Poesie, from that it had bene before, and for that cause may iustly be sayd the first reformers of our English meetre and stile. . . . *Henry* Earle of Surrey and Sir *Thomas Wyat*, betweene whom I finde very litle difference, I repute them (as before) for the two chief lanternes of light to all others that haue since employed their pennes vpon English Poesie, their conceits were loftie, their stiles stately, their conueyance cleanely, their termes proper, their meetre sweete and well proportioned, in all imitating very naturally and studiously their Maister *Francis Petrarcha.*—PUTTENHAM, GEORGE, 1589, *The Arte of English Poesie, ed. Arber, pp.* 74, 76.

He does not appear to have much imagination, neither are his verses so musical and well polished as lord Surry's. Those of gallantry in particular seem to be too artificial and laboured for a lover, without that artless simplicity which is the genuine mark of feeling; and too stiff, and negligent of harmony for a poet.—CIBBER, THEOPHILUS, 1753, *Lives of the Poets, vol.* I, *p.* 54.

Although sufficiently distinguished from the common versifiers of his age, is confessedly inferior to Surrey in harmony of numbers, perspicuity of expression, and facility of phraseology. Nor is he equal to Surrey in elegance of sentiment, in nature and sensibility. His feelings are disguised by affectation, and obscured by conceit. His declarations of passion are embarrassed by wit and fancy; and his style is not intelligible, in proportion as it is careless and unadorned. His compliments, like the modes of behaviour in that age, are ceremonious and strained. He has too much art as a lover, and too little as a poet. His gallantries are laboured, and his versification negligent. The truth is, his genius was of the moral and didactic species: and his poems abound more in good sense, satire, and observations on life, than in pathos or imagination.—WARTON, THOMAS, 1778-81, *History of English Poetry, sec.* xxxviii.

One of the principal ornaments of an age unable to discern his merits, or unwilling to record them.—LODGE, EDMUND, 1792-1800, *Imitations of Original Drawings by Hans Holbein, with Biographical Tracts.*

Wyatt had a deeper and more accurate penetration into the characters of men than Surrey had; hence arises the difference in their satires. Surrey, in his satire against the citizens of London, deals only in reproach; Wyatt, in his, abounds with irony, and those nice touches of ridicule which make us ashamed of our faults, and therefore often silently effect amendment. Surrey's observation of nature was minute; but he directed it towards the works of nature in general, and the movements of the passions, rather than to the foibles and characters of men; hence it is that he excels in the description of rural objects, and is always tender and pathetic. In Wyatt's "Complaint" we hear a strain of manly grief which commands attention, and we listen to it with respect for the sake of him that suffers. Surrey's distress is painted in such natural terms that we make it our own, and recognize in his sorrows emotions which we are conscious of having felt ourselves. In point of taste and perception of propiety in composition, Surrey is more accurate and just than Wyatt: he therefore seldom either offends with conceits or wearies with repetition, and when he imitates other poets he is original as well as pleasing. In his numerous translations from Petrarch he is seldom inferior to his master, and he seldom improves upon him. Wyatt is almost always below the Italian, and frequently degrades a good thought by expressing it so that it is hardly recognizable. Had Wyatt attempted a translation of Virgil, as Surrey did, he would have exposed himself to unavoidable failure. —NOTT, GEORGE FREDERICK, 1815-16, *ed. Surrey and Wyatt's Poems, vol.* II, *p.* 156.

The genius of Sir Thomas Wyat was refined and elevated like that of his noble friend and contemporary; but his poetry is more sententious and sombrous, and in his lyrical effusions he studied terseness rather than suavity.—CAMPBELL, THOMAS, 1819, *Essay on English Poetry.*

Wyatt is an abundant writer; but he has wrought his later versification with great variety, though he has not always smoothed his workmanship with his nail. For many years, Wyatt had smothered his native talent by translation from Spanish and Italian poets, and in his rusty rhythmical measures. He lived to feel the truth of nature, and to practice happier art. Of his amatory poems, many are graceful, most ingenious.—DISRAELI, ISAAC, 1841, *The Earl of Surrey and Sir Thomas Wyatt, Amenities of Literature.*

In his Satires we find what we may call a mellowed souredness of spirit, like the taste of the plum or sloe when touched by the first frosts. There is no fury, no rancour, and but little bitterness. You have simply a good and great man, who has left the public arena early and without stain, giving the results of his experience, and deliberately preferring the life of rural simplicity and peace to that of courtly etiquette and diplomatic falsehood. How different from the savage and almost fiendish eye of retrospect such men as Swift and Byron cast upon a world which they have spurned, and which, with quite as much justice, has spurned them! Wyatt and the world, on the other hand, part fair foes, and shake hands ere they diverge from each other's paths for ever.—GILFILLAN, GEORGE, 1858, *ed. The Poetical Works of Sir Thomas Wyatt, p.* xvi.

Wyatt and Surrey are said to have been the introducers of the sonnet into English literature, but this credit is due especially to Wyatt, not only as the elder man and earlier writer, but as the one of the two who alone gave accurate models of the structure of that form of poem. . . . Although Surrey's sonnets are in fourteen lines, and closely imitate Petrarch's forms of thought, yet as to their mechanism they are all at fault. Wyatt studied the form of the verse before he imitated, and the true sonnet was introduced into our literature by him alone.—MORLEY, HENRY, 1873, *First Sketch of English Literature, pp.* 293, 294.

Wyatt and Surrey are usually classed together—*par nobile fratrum*—the Dioscuri of the Dawn. They inaugurated that important period in our literature known as the Era of Italian Influence, or that of the Company of Courtly Makers—the period which immediately preceded and ushered in the age of Spenser and Shakespeare. . . . In Surrey we find the first germ of the Bucolic Eclogue. In Wyatt we have our first classical satirist. Of our lyrical poetry they were the founders. . . . It is unfortunately not possible to decide how far these two poets acted and re-acted on each other. We are however inclined to think that Wyatt was the master-spirit, and that Surrey has been enabled to throw him so completely and so unfairly into the shade, mainly because he had his friend's patterns to work upon. . . . The dignity and gravity which characterise the structure of some of his lyric periods appear to have been caught from the poets of Castile. His general tone is sombre, sententious and serious, and he is too often reflecting when he ought to be feeling. The greater part of his poetry is wasted in describing with weary minuteness transports of slighted and requited affection, but his true place is among observant men of the world, scholars and moralists. His versification is often harsh and uncouth, except in some of his lyrics, which are occasionally very musical, and in his Satires, which are uniformly terse and smooth. He is inferior to Surrey in diction, in taste, in originality, and in poetical feeling; but it may be doubted whether the more delicate genius of the younger poet would have been able to achieve so complete a triumph over the mechanism of expression had he not been preceded by his robuster brother.—COLLINS, J. CHURTON, 1880, *The English Poets, ed. Ward, pp.* 248, 249, 250.

His love-sonnets and songs have none of that lightness and gaiety which we are apt to associate with such verses, but they contain much subtle thought, and bear the appearance of expressing a genuine passion.—NICOLL, HENRY J., 1882, *Landmarks of English Literature, p.* 51.

Now there is every reason to believe, if we study the biographies of Wyatt and Surrey, that Wyatt, and not Surrey as is so commonly stated, led the way in the work which is associated with their names—that Wyatt, and not Surrey, was the first to attempt the improvement of our metres by Italian example and precedent. As early as 1526, when Surrey was certainly not more than ten years old, perhaps only eight, Leland had "honoured" Wyatt, then twenty-three, as the most accomplished poet of his time. . . . *Tulit alter honores.* But surely it is time Wyatt had a more general recognition as the first, in time at least, of those "courtly makers." . . . Surely it is time he should more generally have some credit for having introduced the sonnet into our literature. Yet, in his otherwise admirable remarks on the sonnet in the recently published edition of Milton's Sonnets, Mr. Mark Pattison, a singularly accomplished scholar, and a most excellent writer and critic, as all the world knows, does not even mention poor Sir Thomas. *Sic vos non vobis.*—HALES, JOHN W., 1883–93, *Folia Litteraria, pp.* 152, 154.

So stumbling and knock-kneed is his verse that any one who remembers the admirable versification of Chaucer may now and then be inclined to think that Wyatt had much better have left his innovations alone.—SAINTSBURY, GEORGE, 1887, *History of Elizabethan Literature, p.* 5.

Wyatt gave abundant promise of the broad daylight of poetry that was to follow hard upon these crepuscular rays.—SCHELLING, FELIX E., 1891, *Poetic and Verse Criticism of the Reign of Elizabeth, p.* 5.

Wyatt is not one of the great masterminds, but certainly occupied one of the most distinguished positions in the history of his own nation. Owing to the soundness and complete harmony of his nature, he exercised an enduring influence upon English poetry at a period when its culture was specially in need of inward consistency.—TEN BRINK, BERNHARD, 1892, *History of English Literature, (Fourteenth Century to Surrey) tr. Schmitz, p.* 236.

Rank undoubtedly placed Surrey's name on the Title page; but Sir T. Wyatt is the most important of all the Contributors, both as to priority in time, as to literary influence, and as to the number of poems contributed.—ARBER, EDWARD, 1895, *ed. Tottel's Miscellany, Introduction, p.* xvi.

Two very marked and contrary features distinguish Wyatt's poetry, the individual energy of his thought, and his persistent imitation of foreign models. . . . His actual poetical achievements are of very unequal merit; he often aims at objects which he ought to have avoided, or at effects to which his resources are unequal; he is most successful when his fiery genius can find out a way for itself untrammelled by the precedents of art. . . . Wyatt's best poems are written in simple metrical forms, which enable him to pour himself forth with a strength and energy rarely equalled in English poetry. . . . Wyatt is a noble figure in English poetry. His strength, his ardour, his manliness, his complete freedom from affectation, make him a type of what is finest in the national character. —COURTHOPE, W. J., 1897, *A History of English Poetry, vol.* II, *pp.* 49, 55, 66.

Wyatt's poetic efforts often lack grace, his versification is at times curiously uncouth, his sonnets are strained and artificial in style as well as in sentiment; but he knew the value of metrical rules and musical rhythm, as the "Address to his Lute" amply attests. Despite his persistent imitation of foreign models, too, he displays at all points an individual energy of thought, which his disciple Surrey never attained. As a whole his work evinces a robuster taste and intellect than Surrey's.—LEE, SIDNEY, 1900, *Dictionary of National Biography, vol.* LXIII, *p.* 186.

Sir Thomas Elyot

1490?—1546

Sir Thomas Elyot: author and diplomatist; born in Wiltshire, England, about 1490. The place of his education is not known, but the extent of his learning seems to prove him a university graduate. He held the office of clerk to the western assize from about 1511 to 1519, when he exchanged it for that of clerk of the king's council, a position which he held for six years and a half, as he complained, without compensation and without thanks. In 1532 he was sent on embassies to the pope and to the emperor, and while on the latter mission received instructions to cause the arrest of the Reformer Tyndale, but failed in the attempt. Though highly honored by his contemporaries for his learning, Elyot received but slight pecuniary rewards from his patrons for either his literary or official labors, and spent his life in straitened circumstances. Died at Carlton, Cambridgeshire, 1546. Of his works the most noted is "The Boke named the Gouernour" (London, 1531), which is a moral treatise on the way to fit a man for the duties of governing. Among his twelve other books are "Of the Knowledge that maketh a Wise Man" (1533); "Bibliotheca" (1538), the first Latin-English dictionary; "The Image of Governance" (1540); "Preservative against Death" (1545); "Defense for Good Women" (1545).—COLBY, F. M., 1897, *Johnson's Universal Cyclopædia, vol.* III, *p.* 79.

He wrote also an excellent Dictionary of Latine and English, if not the first, the best of that kind in that age; and England then abounding with so many learned Clergy-men, I know not which more to wonder at, that they mist, or he hit on so necessary a subject. Let me adde, Bishop Cooper grafted his Dictionary on the stocke of Sir Thomas Eliot.—FULLER, THOMAS, 1662, *The Worthies of England, ed. Nichols, vol.* I, *p.* 177.

Sir Thomas Elyot's "Governor" was designed to instruct men, especially great men, in good morals, and to reprove their vices.—STRYPE, JOHN, 1721, *Ecclesiastical Memorials.*

"The Governor" is one of those treatises, which, at an early period of civilization, when general education is imperfect, becomes useful to mould the manners and to inculcate the morals which should distinguish the courtier and the statesman. Elyot takes his future "Governor" in the arms of his nurse, and places the ideal being amid all the scenes which may exercise the virtues, or the studies which he develops. The work is dedicated to Henry the Eighth. The design, the imaginary personage, the author, and the patron are equally dignified. The style is grave; and it would not be candid in a modern critic to observe, that, in the progress of time, the good sense has become too obvious, and the perpetual illustrations from ancient history too familiar. The erudition in philology of that day has become a school-boy's learning. They had then no other volumes to recur to, of any authority, but what the ancients had left. . . . "The Boke of the Governor" must now be condemned to the solitary imprisonment of the antiquary's cell, who will pick up many curious circumstances relative to the manners of the age, — always an amusing subject of speculation, when we contemplate on the gradations of social life.—DISRAELI, ISAAC, 1841, *The Difficulties Experienced by a Primitive Author, Amenities of Literature.*

Sir Thomas Elyot stands as a character altogether typical of the period, and is one of the pleasantest figures of the time; as an able lawyer and man of business, a clever diplomatist with a grand capacity for work, and an ornament to English knighthood because of his extensive knowledge, a man strictly honourable in nature, and of genuine piety. The unselfish Renaissance-zeal for culture, the impulse to learn and to teach, live vigorously in him, and his entire literary activity testifies to the fact. In addition to this we have in him that naïve, joyous hopefulness, lost for the greater part to our age, the faith in the power of aiding the enlightenment and improvement of men by means of popular moralizing writings.—TEN BRINK, BERNHARD, 1892, *History of English Literature, (Fourteenth Century to Surrey) tr. Schmitz, p.* 194.

Sir Thomas Elyot's place in English prose seems to fall, in other respects than mere chronological order, between Sir Thomas More and Roger Ascham. In the English that he wrote, he is somewhat less archaic than the former, and less modern than the latter. If Elyot is less cumbrous than More, he never attains the vivacity of Ascham. Charm of style was hardly as yet a gift to which English prose had attained. Elyot has many virtues—clearness and precision among them—but if he seldom falls below a certain level, he as seldom rises above it.—AINGER, ALFRED, 1893, *English Prose, ed. Craik, vol.* I, *p.* 191.

It might be difficult to give any reason except the fact that it has been twice reprinted in the present century for the position held by "The Boke named the Governour," still more difficult to account for the reprinting itself. . . . In the history of prose style Elyot is commendable rather than distinguished; free from obvious and glaring defects rather than possessed of distinct merits. He is rather too much given to long sentences; he has little or nothing of Fisher's rhetorical devices, and while the romantic grace of his not much older contemporary Berners is far from him, so also is the deliberate classical plainness of his not very much younger contemporary Ascham. He is principally valuable as an example of the kind of prose which a cultivated man of ordinary gifts would be likely to write before the definite attempts of Ascham and his school.—SAINTSBURY, GEORGE, 1898, *A Short History of English Literature, pp.* 234, 235.

Elyot's literary work, although it exhibits no striking originality, illustrates the wide culture and erudition of Henry VIII's Court. Political philosophy and the theory of education chiefly interested him. His views were borrowed from the foreign writers of the Renaissance. Erasmus's influence is plainly discernable. Pico della Mirandola, Francesco Patrizi the elder, and other less-known Italian authors were familiar to him. His intimate friends included Sir Thomas More and Roger Ascham. As a Greek scholar who first translated part of Isocrates into English, and as an early student of both Greek and Latin patristic literature, he well deserves to be remembered. That he should have written all his books in his native language gives him a high place among the pioneers of English prose literature. His style is clear, although its literary flavour is thin. His fame as a translator lived through Elizabeth's reign.—LEE, SIDNEY, 1889, *Dictionary of National Biography, vol.* XVII, *p.* 348.

Earl of Surrey

Henry Howard

1516?—1547

Born about 1517: beheaded on Tower Hill, London, Jan. 21, 1547. . . . He received an unusually good education, and from 1530-32 lived at Windsor with the young Duke of Richmond, the natural son of Henry VIII., accompanying the king to France in 1532. He remained at the French court for about a year. In 1541 he was installed Knight of the Garter, and in 1543 joined the English forces at Landrecies with special recommendations from Henry VIII. to Charles V., and a little later was appointed cupbearer to the king. He was present at the surrender of Boulogne, of which he was made governor in 1545, but was recalled to England the next year. Henry VIII. was ill, and, when his death was near, Surrey's father, the Duke of Norfolk, who was premier duke, was suspected of aiming at the throne. A month before the king's death both were arrested, and the Duke of Norfolk, as peer of the realm, was tried by his peers. The Earl of Surrey, however, who had only a courtesy title, was tried by a jury picked for the occasion, who found that he "falsely, maliciously, and treacherously set up and bore the arms of Edward the Confessor, then used by the Prince of Wales, mixed up and joined with his own proper arms." He had borne these arms without question in the presence of the king, as the Howards before him had done since their grant by Richard II. He was tried for high treason and beheaded. His poems were first printed as "Songs and Sonetes" in "Tottel's Miscellany" in 1557, with those of Sir Thomas Wyatt. He was the first English writer of blank verse, translating the second and fourth books of the Æneid into this form, and with Wyatt he introduced the sonnet into English literature.—SMITH, BENJAMIN E., *ed.* 1894–97, *The Century Cyclopedia of Names*, p. 515.

PERSONAL

The gentle Surrey loved his lyre—
Who has not heard of Surrey's fame?
His was the hero's soul of fire,
And his the bard's immortal name

—SCOTT, SIR WALTER, 1806, *The Lay of the Last Minstrel, Canto* vi, *s.* xiii.

Thou, all-accomplished Surrey . . .
The flower of Knighthood, nipt as soon as blown!
Melting all hearts but Geraldine's alone!

—ROGERS, SAMUEL, 1819, *Human Life.*

As for the fair-haired, blue-eyed Geraldine, the mistress of his fancy and affections, and the subject of his verse, her identity long lay *entombed*, as it were, in a poetical name; but Surrey had loved her, had maintained her beauty at the point of his lance—had made her "famous by his pen, and glorious by his sword." This was more than enough to excite the interest and the inquiries of posterity, and lo! antiquaries and commentators fell to work, archives were searched, genealogies were traced, and at length the substance of this beautiful poetical shadow was detected: she was proved to have been the Lady Elizabeth Fitzgerald, afterwards the wife of a certain Earl of Lincoln, of whom little is known—but that he married the woman Surrey had loved. —JAMESON, ANNA BROWNELL, 1829, *The Loves of the Poets, vol.* I, *p.* 187.

To his father's hereditary sentiments Lord Surrey added a more than heriditary scorn of the "new men" whom the change of times was bringing like the scum to the surface of the state, and an ambition which no portion of his father's prudence taught him to restrain. With brilliant genius, with reckless courage, with a pride which would brook no superior, he united a careless extravagance which had crippled him with debt, and a looseness of habit which had brought him unfavourably under the notice of the government.—FROUDE, JAMES ANTHONY, 1856–70, *History of England, vol.* IV, *p.* 466.

In his purification of English verse, he did good service by casting out those clumsy Latin words, with which the lines of even Dunbar are heavily clogged. The poems of Petrarch ring the changes in exquisite music on his love for Laura. So the love-verses of Surrey are filled with the praises of the fair Geraldine, whom Horace Walpole has tried to identify with Lady Elizabeth Fitzgerald, a daughter of the Earl of Kildare. If this be so, Geraldine was only a girl of thirteen when the poet, already married to Frances Vere for six years, sang of her beauty and her virtue. It is no unlikely thing that Surrey, an instinctive lover of the beautiful, was smitten with a deep admiration of the fresh, young, girlish face of one—

"Standing with reluctant feet,
Where the brook and river meet,
Womanhood and childhood fleet."

Such a feeling could exist—it often has existed—in the poet's breast, free from all mingling of sin, and casting no shadow of reproach upon a husband's loyalty. —COLLIER, WILLIAM FRANCIS, 1861, *History of English Literature, p.* 92.

At the "barge procession" from Greenwich to the Tower, on the occasion of Anne Boleyn's coronation, a pale, sad, abstracted-looking gentleman sat beside the Duke of Norfolk in one of the royal barges. The sickly countenance of this young man presented a peculiar contrast with a rich crimson velvet dress, trimmed with miniver, and cap of the same colour, surmounted with a small white feather, and surrounded by a bandeau of rubies. He had small dark eyes, insignificant when bent upon the ground, but brilliant and piercing when raised to encounter the gaze of others; thin compressed lips; a sharp and beardless chin, and a delicate, almost languid appearance. Such was the poet Surrey, as he appeared at the coronation procession of his unfortunate cousin Anne Boleyn.—BURKE, S. HUBERT, 1882, *Historical Portraits of the Tudor Dynasty and the Reformation Period, vol.* iii, *p.* 125.

THE ÆNEID

Before in age, if not also in noble, courtly, and lustrous English, is that of the Songes and Sonnettes of Henry Howard earl of Surrey, . . . written chiefly by him, and by sir Thomas Wiat, not the dangerous commotioner, but his worthy father. Nevertheless, they who commend those poems and exercises of honourable wit, if they have seen that incomparable earl of Surrey his English translation of Virgil's Eneids, which, for a book or two, he admirably rendreth, almost line for line, will bear me witness that those other were foils and sportives. —BOLTON, EDMUND, 1624 *Hypercritica.*

We meet with so many expressions which Surrey has evidently borrowed, with so many lines adopted with hardly any other alteration than that which the difference of the dialect and of the measure made necessary, and so many taken without any alteration at all, that all doubt ceases. It becomes a matter of certainty that Surrey must have read and studied the Scottish translation before he began his own.—NOTT, GEORGE FREDERICK, 1815–16, *Dissertation on the State of English Poetry, in Surrey and Wyatt's Poems, p.* cciv.

The unrhimed metre of five accents, or as it is generally termed *blank verse*, we certainly owe to Surrey. English verse without rhime was no novelty; and the "cadence" of Chaucer comes full as near to the blank verse of five accents, as the loose rhythms of some of our dramatists; but I have seen no specimen of any definite unrhimed metre of five accents, which can date earlier than Surrey's translation of the fourth Eneid. His verse was certainly considered, at the time, as something new, for the second edition of his translation is entitled, "The fourth boke of Virgill, &c. translated into English, and drawn into a *straunge metre* by Henry, Earle of Surrey." As Surrey was well acquainted with Italy and its literature, and as the Italians were already making efforts to banish rhyme from their poetry, it is possible he may have taken the hint from them; but, in fact, the subject of unrhymed verse had for some time fixed the attention of *scholars*, very generally, throughout Europe.—GUEST, EDWIN, 1838, *A History of English Rhythms, vol.* II, *p.* 239.

There are passages of excellence in the work, and very rarely does a verse quite fail. But, as might be expected, it is somewhat stiff, and, as it were, stunted in sound; partly from the fact that the lines are too much divided, where *distinction* would have been sufficient. It would have been strange, indeed, if he had at once made a free use of a rhythm which every boy-poet now thinks he can do what he pleases with, but of which only a few ever learn the real scope and capabilities. Besides, the difficulty was increased by the fact that the nearest approach to it in measure was the heroic couplet, so well known in our language, although scarce one who has used it has come up to the variousness of its modelling in the hands of Chaucer, with whose writings Surrey was of course familiar.—MACDONALD, GEORGE, 1864–83, *The Imagination, and Other Essays, pp.* 94, 96.

GENERAL

In the Earle of Surries "Liricks," many things tasting of a noble birth, and worthy of a noble minde.—SIDNEY, SIR PHILIP, 1595, *An Apologie for Poetry, ed. Arber, p.* 62.

The particular fame of learning, wit, and poetic fancy, which he was thought once to have sufficiently made appear in his published poems, which nevertheless are now so utterly forgotten, as though they had never been extant; so antiquated at present, and as it were out of fashion, is the style and way of poetry of that age. —PHILLIPS, EDWARD, 1675, *Theatrum Poetarum Anglicanorum, ed. Brydges, p.* 43.

Here noble Surrey felt the sacred rage,
Surrey, the Granville of a former age:
Matchless his pen, victorious was his lance,
Bold in the lists, graceful in the dance:
In the same shades the Cupids tuned his lyre,
To the same notes of love, and soft desire:
Fair Geraldine, bright object of his vow,
Then filled the groves, as heavenly Mira now.
—POPE, ALEXANDER, 1704–13, *Windsor Forest, v.* 291–298.

Surrey, for his justness of thought, correctness of style, and purity of expression, may justly be pronounced the first English classical poet. He unquestionably is the first polite writer of love-verses in our language.—WARTON, THOMAS, 1778–81, *History of English Poetry, sec.* xxxvii.

One of the best and earliest attempts in England to naturalise the sonnet, is to be found in the pages of the gallant Surrey, whose compositions in this department, making due allowance for the imperfect state of the language in which he wrote, have a simplicity and chastity in their style and thought, which merit every encomium.—DRAKE, NATHAN, 1798, *Literary Hours, vol.* I, *no.* vi.

At length we reach the illustrious names of Surrey and Wyatt; whose productions, during a period devoted to dull allegory, duller romance, and the dullest of all possible didactic and moral poetry, strike us as a green and refreshing *oasis* in a dreary desert. At the mention of *their* names—the heart of Hortensius feels an increased glow of inspiration: and the last and most learned Editor of their works finds himself naturally, as it were, discoursing with many of the most illustrious characters of the reign of Henry VIII. But the bibliomaniac secretly rejoices in the possession of the earlier, rarer, and more precious editions of the "Songes and Sonnettes," as among the *keimelia* of his Collection.—DIBDIN, THOMAS FROGNALL, 1824, *The Library Companion, p.* 682.

His poetry makes the ear lean to it, it is so sweet and low; the English he made it of, being ready to be sweet, and falling ripe in sweetness into other hands than his.—BROWNING, ELIZABETH BARRETT, 1842–63, *The Book of the Poets, p.* 129.

With all his taste and real feeling; his verse is a hollow artificial mockery to the living voice of Spenser's.—CRAIK, GEORGE L., 1845, *Spenser and his Poetry, vol.* I, *p.* 93.

His language is often happy, and never superfluous. There is a studious air in his lines which takes off something from the fresh flavour of the thought, presenting it rather in its prepared than in its natural form. Hence we have much sweetness, and even tenderness; but no spontaneous bursts of passion forcing their way through the restraints of art. He is amongst the earliest of our love poets, and will always be read with interest for the sake of his purity and refinement; but he is inferior in earnestness and depth of emotion to some who succeeded him, especially the poets of the age of Elizabeth.—BELL, ROBERT, 1854, *ed. Poetical Works of Surrey and Minor Contemporaneous Poets, p.* 35.

His poetry, with fine lines, and here and there passages of considerable power, would not, apart from his rank, his story, and his poetic *position*, preserve his name. It is full of crude conceits and unintelligible tortuosities of thought and rhyme. Much as he sings of love, he is, on the whole, a frigid writer, and has preserved purity at the expense of nature and fervour of passion. He was a star in the poetic horizon when stars were few, and owes it to darkness and to distance rather than to merit that his light still glimmers—it can hardly be said to shine—upon us; and we accept it not as poetry itself, but merely as containing in it the hope and promise of future and far superior song,—GILFILLAN, GEORGE, 1856, *ed. Poetical Works of the Earl of Surrey, p.* 227.

The true merit of Surrey is, that, proceeding upon the same system of versification which had been introduced by Chaucer, and which, indeed, had in principle been followed by all the writers after Chaucer, however rudely or imperfectly some of them may have succeeded in the practice of it, he restored to our poetry a correctness, polish, and general spirit of refinement such as it had not known since Chaucer's time, and of which, therefore, in the language as now spoken, there was no previous example whatever. To this it may be added that he appears to have been the first, at least in this age, who sought to modulate his strains after that elder poetry of Italy, which thenceforward became one of the chief fountain-heads of inspiration to that of England throughout the whole space of time over which is shed the golden light of the names of Spenser, of Shakspeare, and of Milton. Surrey's own imagination was neither rich nor soaring; and the highest qualities of his poetry, in addition to the facility and general mechanical perfection of the versification, are delicacy and tenderness. It is altogether a very light and bland Favonian breeze.—CRAIK, GEORGE L., 1861, *A Compendious History of English Literature, and of the English Language, vol.* I, *p.* 458.

Surrey's translation of Virgil is as bald and repulsive a version as can well be. Of his famous love poems in honor of Geraldine, nine are written in a metre so absurd (alternate twelve and fourteen syllable lines) that it would spoil the effect of far better matter; and the unchanging querulous whine which characterizes the whole series renders it tedious reading. In truth, notwithstanding the senseless encomiums which Dr. Nott lavished on his favorite author, the gems in Surrey are but few, and may be counted on one's fingers. The sonnets beginning "Give place, ye lovers," "The sote season," and "Set me whereas," nearly exhaust the list.—ARNOLD, THOMAS, 1862–87, *A Manual of English Literature, American ed., p.* 52.

An English Petrarch: no juster title could be given to Surrey, for it expresses his talent as well as his disposition. In fact, like Petrarch, the oldest of the humanists, and the earliest exact writer of the modern tongue, Surrey introduces a new style, a manly style, which marks a great transformation of the mind. . . . He looks forward to the last line whilst writing the first. He keeps the strongest word for the last, and shows the symmetry of ideas by the symmetry of phrases. Sometimes he guides the intelligence by a continuous series of contrasts to the final image; a kind of sparkling casket, in which he means to deposit the idea which he carries, and to which he directs our attention from the first. Sometimes he leads his reader to the close of a long flowery description, and then suddenly checks him with a sorrowful phrase. He arranges his process, and knows how to produce effects; he uses classical expressions, in which two substantives, each supported by its adjective, are balanced on either side of the verb. He collects his phrases in harmonious periods, and does not neglect the delight of the ears any more than of the mind. By his inversions he adds force to his ideas, and weight to his argument. He selects elegant or noble terms, rejects idle words and redundant phrases. Every epithet contains an idea, every metaphor a sentiment. There is eloquence in the regular development of his thought; music in the sustained accent of his verse. . . . We do not find in him a bold genius, an impassioned writer capable of wide expansion, but a courtier, a lover of elegance, who, penetrated by the beauties of two complete literatures, imitates Horace and the chosen masters of Italy, corrects and polishes little morsels, aims at speaking perfectly a fine language. Amongst semi-barbarians he wears a dress-coat becomingly. Yet he does not wear it completely at his ease: he keeps his eyes too exclusively on his models, and does not venture to permit himself frank and free gestures.—TAINE, H. A., 1871, *History of English Literature, tr. Van Laun, vol.* I, *bk.* ii, *ch.* i, *pp.* 160, 161.

Surrey has not the deep and subtle feelings of Wyat; but he has a captivating sweetness, a direct eloquence, a generous impetuosity, that make him a much more universal favourite. . . . Surrey's originality was not of the fastidious kind that rejects thoughts and images simply because they have occurred to a predecessor. His imagery is not strikingly new. In his irresistible energetic way he made free use of whatever suggested itself in the moment of composition, no matter where it might have come from. He borrowed many phrases, many images, and many hints of phrases and images, from his friend Wyat. What he borrowed, however, he passed through his own mint. . . . Compared with Wyat, Surrey strikes one as having much greater affluence of words—the language is more plastic in his hands. When his mind is full of an idea, he pours it forth with soft voluble eloquence; he commands such abundance of words that he preserves with ease a uniform measure. Uniformity, indeed, is almost indispensable to such abundance: we read him with the feeling that in a "tumbling metre" his fluency would run away with him. . . . Surrey goes beyond Wyat in the enthusiasm of nature, in the worship of bud and bloom. In the depths of his amorous despair, the beauty of the tender green, and the careless happiness of the brute creation, arrest his eye, and detain him for certain moments from his own sorrow. —MINTO, WILLIAM, 1874-85, *Characteristics of English Poets, pp.* 123, 124, 125.

He had the sentiment of nature and unhackneyed feeling, but he has no mastery of verse, nor any elegance of diction.—LOWELL, JAMES RUSSELL, 1875-90, *Spenser Prose Works, Riverside ed., vol.* IV, *p.* 274.

The distinctive feature of Surrey's genius is its ductility; its characteristic qualities are grace, vivacity, pathos, picturesqueness. He had the temperament of a true poet, refinement, sensibility, a keen eye for the beauties of nature, a quick and lively imagination, great natural powers of expression. His tone is pure and lofty, and his whole writings breathe that chivalrous spirit which still lingered among the satellites of the eighth Henry. His diction is chaste and perspicuous, and though it bears all the marks of careful elaboration it has no trace of stiffness or pedantry. His verse is so smooth, and at times so delicately musical, that Warton questioned whether in these qualities at least our versification has advanced since Surrey tuned it for the first time. Without the learning of Wyatt, his literary skill is far greater.—COLLINS, J. CHURTON, 1880, *The English Poets, ed. Ward, p.* 255.

Surrey has even no small mastery of what may be called the architecture of verse, the valuing of cadence in successive lines so as to produce a concerted piece and not a mere reduplication of the notes. —SAINTSBURY, GEORGE, 1887, *History of Elizabethan Literature, p.* 6.

The work of Surrey in the reform of English poetry was of a kind altogether different from that of Wyatt. His poems have none of the vehement individuality and character which distinguish the style of his predecessor and contemporary. He is essentially the representative of a class. . . . He follows Wyatt in the imitation of foreign models, but he succeeds where Wyatt failed, in naturalising the ideas he borrows by the beauty of his style. Style is, in fact, Surrey's predominant poetical virtue; and, appearing as he did when art was the one thing needful for the development of the language, it is to his style that he owes his great position in the History of English Poetry.—COURTHOPE, W. J., 1897, *A History of English Poetry, vol.* II, *p.* 68.

Edward Hall

1499?—1547

Was born in Shropshire at the end of the fifteenth century. He was in 1514 scholar of King's College, Cambridge, but removed to Oxford; about 1518, he entered at Gray's Inn, was called to the bar, became common sergeant and under-sheriff, and in 1540 one of the judges of the sheriff's court. His career belonged entirely to the reign of Henry VIII., and he died in 1547. His history of "The Union of the Two Noble and Illustre Families of Lancastre and Yorke," commonly called Hall's "Chronicle," ended with the year 1532. It was first published in 1548, after its author's death, by Richard Grafton.—MORLEY AND TYLER, 1879, *A Manual of English Literature, p.* 148.

This is to be noted that the author thereof, though not to all men, yet to many very well known, was a man in the later time of his life not so painful and studious as before he had been.—GRAFTON, RICHARD, 1550? *ed. Hall's Chronicles, Preface.*

He wrote a large account of the forementioned wars, which, in a very flattering epistle, he dedicates to Henry VIII. If the reader desires to know what sort of cloaths were worn in each king's reign, and how the fashions altered, this is an historian for his purpose; but in other matters his information is not very valuable.—NICHOLSON, WILLIAM, 1596–1714, *English Historical Library.*

All the copies I have yet seen or heard of are dedicated to Edw. VI., and the dedication is far from being flattering. The informations, too, are all along so very good, abating that the chronology is here and there wrong, that they have been, and will always be, highly valued by the most curious men. He declines giving any account of cloaths and fashion, excepting upon some solemn occasion in King Henry the Eighth's reign, and contents himself with what is truly momentous.—HEARNE, THOMAS, 1723, *Hemingi Chartularium Ecclesiae Wigormensis, Appendix, vol.* II, 673.

A good writer for his time, and a competent scholar.—PEGGE, SAMUEL, 1809, *Anonymiana, p.* 1.

Opinions differ as to Hall's value as an historian, so far as regards the important points of care and accuracy. It is a great misfortune, especially so far as regards the earlier part of his works, that he does not quote by name the authorities from whom he drew his materials. He frequently mentions the conflict of preceding writers, but does not specify who they were, or whether they were contemporaneous with the events which they recorded. He strives hard to rise above the meagre creeping gait of the old chroniclers, and the effects of a classical education are continually visible in his work.—CREASY, SIR EDWARD, 1850–75, *Memoirs of Eminent Etonians, p.* 47.

Is often coupled with Fabyan as one of the two beginners of English prose history. . . . There is no particular reason for coupling him with Fabyan. More comes between them as a historian with his "Edward V." Hall was a man of better education than Fabyan. . . . His style is not equal to More's, and better than Fabyan's.—MINTO, WILLIAM, 1872–80, *A Manual of English Prose Literature, p.* 190.

It was certainly, in its day, a wonderful example of what might be done in English prose; nor can we refuse to accord it a certain meed of admiration even now. There has certainly been much pompous English since Hall's day without half so much weight of matter.—GAIRDNER, JAMES, 1879, *Early Chroniclers of Europe, England, p.* 304.

It is for the early years of Henry VIII that he becomes an authority of the greatest value, not so much for the facts which he relates as for the light which he throws upon the social life and opinions of his times. He expresses the profound loyalty of the middle class, and represents the conditions which rendered possible the policy of the king. His descriptions of the festivities of the court are full and vivid; he shows us the discontent awakened by Wolsey, and gives many instructive accounts of London life, and of the growing spirit of independence among Englishmen. His literary merits are of high order, especially in his accounts of the opposition which Wolsey's masterful proceedings aroused; his power of describing the action of a mob is admirable. Hall has scarcely yet met with due recognition. His chronicle was one of the books prohibited by Mary in 1555, and in consequence became rare. The later chronicles of Grafton, Holinshed, and Stow borrowed a good deal from Hall, and became more popular, so that Hall's chronicle was not reprinted till 1809 by Ellis, and the only English historian who has seen its full value is Brewer in his "History of the Reign of Henry VIII."—CREIGHTON, MANDELL, 1890, *Dictionary of National Biography, vol.* XXIV, *p.* 64.

He does not bury little matter under many words.—MORLEY, HENRY, 1891, *English Writers, vol.* VII, *p.* 270.

Hall's historical account, owing to the limitation of its subject, acquires a kind of dramatic interest, and this is sometimes effectively heightened by his naïve and vivid representation. The historical value of the work consists in its containing various independent communications, and, above all, its full information concerning the state of civilization in the days of Henry VIII. The history of literature, too, is indebted to him for important notices relating to the first fruits of the secular drama.—TEN BRINK, BERNHARD, 1892, *History of English Literature,* (*Fourteenth Century to Surrey*) *tr. Schmitz, p.* 209.

Hall, who begins to tell a story better than Fabian, often loses the point of it in some silly detail.—GOSSE, EDMUND, 1897, *Short History of Modern English Literature, p.* 61.

Thomas Sternhold

C. 1500-1549

Was born (according to Wood) in Hampshire, or as Holinshed says, at Southampton; but Atkins ("Hist. of Gloucestershire") affirms that he was born at Awre, twelve miles from Gloucester. He studied at Oxford, but not long enough to take any degree. The office of groom of the robes to Henry VIII was secured to him, and he was continued in the same office by Edward VI. He died in 1549. He versified fifty-one of the Psalms, which were first printed by Edward Whitchurch, 1549, with the title "All such Psalms as Thomas Sternehold, late Groom of the Kinges Majestyes Robes, did in his Lyfetyme Drawe into English Metre." He was succeeded in the translation by John Hopkins (fifty-eight psalms), William Whittingham (five psalms), Thomas Norton (twenty-seven psalms), Robert Wisdome (Psa. xxv) and others. The complete version was entitled "The Whole Book of Psalms, Collected into English Metre by T. Sternhold, J. Hopkins, and others, etc." (printed in 1562, by John Day). "Certain Chapters of the Proverbs, etc.," is ascribed to him, but the authenticity is doubted.—M'CLINTOCK AND STRONG, *eds.* 1880, *Cyclopædia of Biblical, Theological and Ecclesiastical Literature, vol.* IX, *p.* 1017.

Who first translated into English certaine Psalmes of Dauid.—PUTTENHAM, GEORGE, 1589, *The Arte of English Poesie, ed. Arber, p.* 74.

About this time, David's Psalms were translated into English metre, and (if not publicly commanded) generally permitted to be sung in all churches. The work was performed by Thomas Sternhold, (an Hampshire-man, esquire, and of the Privy Chamber to king Edward VI. who for his part translated thirty-seven selected Psalms,) John Hopkins, Robert Wisedome, &c., men whose piety was better than their poetry; and they had drank more of Jordan than of Helicon. These Psalms were therefore translated, to make them more portable in people's memories, (verses being twice as light as the self-same bulk in prose,) as also to raise men's affections, the better to enable them to practise the apostle's precept: "Is any merry? let him sing psalms," James v. 13. Yet this work met afterwards with some frowns in the faces of great clergy-men, who were rather contented, than well pleased, with the singing of them in churches: I will not say, because they misliked so much liberty should be allowed the laity (Rome only can be guilty of so great envy) as to sing in churches: rather, because they conceived these singing-psalms erected in cor-rivality and opposition to the reading-psalms, which were formerly sung in cathedral churches; or else, the child was disliked for the mother's sake; because such translators, though branched hither, had their root in Geneva.—FULLER, THOMAS, 1655, *The Church History of Britain, vol.* II, *bk.* vii, *sec.* i, *par.* 31.

Thomas Sternhold, an associate with John Hopkins, in one of the worst of many bad Translations of the psalms of David: yet in regard, as first made choice of, they have hitherto obtained to be the only psalms sung in all parochial churches, (it hath long heartily been wished a better choice were made) he hath therefore perhaps been thought worthy to be mentioned among the poets that flourished in Q. Mary's, and the beginning of Q. Elizabeth's reign.—PHILLIPS, EDWARD, 1675, *Theatrum Poetarum Anglicanorum, ed. Brydges, p.* 59.

But being a most zealous Reformer, and a very strict liver, he became so scandaliz'd at the amorous and obscene Songs used in the Court, that he forsooth turn'd into English Metre 51 of David's

Psalms, and caused Musical Notes to be set to them, thinking thereby that the Courtiers would sing them instead of their Sonnets, but did not, only some few excepted. However, the Poetry and Music being admirable, and the best that was made and composed in those times, they were thought fit afterwards to be sung in all Parochial Churches, as they do yet continue.—WOOD, ANTHONY, 1691–1721, *Athenæ Oxonienses, vol.* I, *f.* 76.

The pious Thomas Sternhold and John Hopkins are the only immortal translators of David's Psalms.—WARTON, THOMAS, 1778–81, *History of English Poetry, sec.* xxxviii.

It certainly is not easy to discover the grand features of Hebrew poetry through the muddy medium of this translation; but it is a curious repertory, and highly characteristic of the time in which it was written. Metre was the universal vehicle of devotion. Our poets were inspired with a real and fervent enthusiasm; and though the tameness and insipidity of the language in which they vented this inspiration may surprise and disgust a modern reader, it was probably once thought to derive grandeur and sanctity from its subject.—ELLIS, GEORGE, 1790–1845, *Specimens of the Early English Poets, vol.* II, *p.* 99.

With the best intentions and the worst taste, degraded the spirit of Hebrew psalmody by flat and homely phraseology; and mistaking vulgarity for simplicity, turned into bathos what they found sublime.—CAMPBELL, THOMAS, 1819, *Essay on English Poetry.*

Though not good, it was better than the feeble modern rhymes by which it has been superseded.—SPALDING, WILLIAM, 1852–82, *A History of English Literature, p.* 181.

Sternhold is solely remembered as the originator of the first metrical version of the Psalms which obtained general currency alike in England and Scotland. . . . The only one of his psalms which remains current is the simple rendering of Psalm XXIII ("My Shepherd is the Living Lord").—BENNETT, LEIGH, 1898, *Dictionary of National Biography, vol.* LIV, *p.* 224.

John Leland

1506?—1552

Born in London, about the end of Henry the Seventh's reign; was educated at St. Paul's School, Christ's College, Cambridge, and All Souls, Oxford; and was made chaplain and librarian to Henry VIII., who also in 1533 appointed him his antiquary, with a commission to examine all the libraries of the cathedrals, abbeys, and colleges in the kingdom. He spent six years in travelling to collect materials for the history and antiquities of England and Wales, and retired to his house in London to arrange and methodize the stores of information which he had collected; but, after about two years, he died insane in 1552, without having completed his undertaking. We owe to his researches a large part of the valuable manuscripts in the Old Royal Collection, which was presented by George II., in 1757, to the British Museum. The great bulk of his collections, after passing through various hands, was placed in the Bodleian Library, in an unfinished state. Hearne published his "Itinerary" and "Collectanea," and Hall edited his "Commentarii de Scriptoribus Britannicis," 2 vols.—CATES, WILLIAM L. R., *ed.* 1867, *A Dictionary of General Biography, p.* 637.

The ordre of Leylandes worke into. iiii. bokes deuyded, begynnynge at the Druides, and endyng in the lattre yeares of Kynge Henry the. viii. as he hath herein vttered, is very commendable. Sumwhat more is it than a yeare past, sens I put fourth a worke of the same argument, entytled *de scriptoribus Britannicis*, conteynynge. v. bokes wyth serten addycyons whych I gathered togyther beynge out of the realme. Sens I returned agayne therunto, by the serche of dyuerse most ruynouslye spoyled, broaken vp, and dyspersed lybrayes, I haue collected by no small labour and dylygence, so muche as wyll make so many bokes more, besydes the necessarye recognycyon and frutefull augmentacyon of the seyd first worke. Thys lattre worke intende I to set fourth also, to the commodyte of my contrey, as it is ones fynyshed, yf pouerty withstande me not, as it is my most doubt. Yet wolde I haue no man to iudge my rude labours, to Leylandes fyne workemanshyp in any poynt equal but at all tymes to geue place vnto it.—BALE, JOHN, 1549, *ed. Leland's New Year's Gift to King Henry* VIII., *ed. Copinger, p.* 54.

Leland is the industrious bee, working all; Bate* is the angry wasp, stinging all; Pits is the idle drone, stealing all.—WARD, REV. JOHN, 1648–78, *Diary, ed. Severn, p.* 112.

The precious and voluminous MSS. of Leland were doomed to suffer a fate scarcely less pitiable than that of their owner. After being pilfered by some, and garbled by others, they served to replenish the pages of Stow, Lambard, Camden, Burton, Dugdale, and many other antiquaries and historians. DIBDIN, THOMAS FROGNALL, 1809, *The Bibliomania, or, Book-Madness, p.* 23, *note.*

The ruins of Leland's mind were viewed in his library; volumes on volumes stupendously heaped together, and masses of notes scattered here and there; all the vestiges of his genius, and its distraction. His collections were seized on by honest and dishonest hands; many were treasured, but some were stolen. Hearne zealously arranged a series of volumes from the fragments; but the "Britannia" of Camden, the "London" of Stowe, and the "Chronicles" of Holinshed, are only a few of those public works whose waters silently welled from the spring of Leland's genius; and that nothing might be wanting to preserve some relic of that fine imagination which was always working in his poetic soul, his own description of his learned journey over the kingdom was a spark, which, falling into the inflammable mind of a poet, produced the singular and patriotic poem of the "Polyolbion" of Drayton. Thus the genius of Leland has come to us diffused through a variety of other men's; and what he intended to produce it has required many to perform. —DISRAELI, ISAAC, 1812–13, *Literary Disappointments, Calamities of Authors.*

He became chaplain to Henry VIII., who gave him the rectory of Popeling in the marches of Calais, and in 1533 dignified him with the title of his antiquary. By this commission his majesty laid his commands on him to make search after "England's antiquities, and peruse the libraries of all cathedrals, abbies, priories, colleges, &c., and places where records, writings, and secrets of antiquity were reposited." Never did the enraptured heir of broad acres and well-filled coffers peruse a loving father's last testament with more delight than swelled the heart of our erudite Dominie Sampson as he gloated over this ravishing parchment: so, grasping his oaken staff, girding his loins, and binding tightly his sandal-shoon, the happy Oldbuck of a former generation went on his way rejoicing. Gruff old Harry, who, in spite of his odd habit of plundering monasteries and chopping off his wives' heads after breakfast, knew how to enjoy a quiet joke, no doubt gave a sly wink to some of the attendant courtiers (delighted with his honest enthusiasm) as he grasped the antiquary's hand at parting, charged him not to leave a parchment unturned nor a Roman hypocaust unexplored, and dismissed him with his benedictions and applause. Six years did the zealous Leland travel from library to scriptorium, from tumulus to tower, from castle to monastery. In 1542, he returned to give an account of his explorations to his royal master.—ALLIBONE, S. AUSTIN, 1854–8, *A Critical Dictionary of English Literature, vol.* I, *p.* 1082.

Leland is the earliest of modern English antiquaries. His industry in accumulating facts was remarkable, and as a traveller he was a close observer. His "Itinerary" carefully notes the miles distant between the places that he visited, the best way of approaching each city, and most of the objects of interest likely to interest an historian. But manuscripts attracted him more than acrhitecture, and he rarely rises in his descriptions of buildings above his designation of the abbey of Malmesbury as "a right magnificent thing." On very rare occasions he notices local customs or popular botany. In his "Collectanea" he shows himself to be a conscientious genealogist, but he was not an historical scholar. He defends with unnecessary zeal the truth of the Arthurian legends, and condemns the scepticism of Polydore Vergil. His English style is rough and disjointed, and both his "Itinerary" and "Collectanea" read like masses of undigested notes. As a Latin poet he is deserving of high regard. . . . He is said by Polydore

*Bale?

Vergil and Thomas Caius to have been personally vain and self-conceited, but his extant writings hardly corroborate this verdict. He had none of the virulence characteristic of the early professors of protestantism, and did not disdain social intercourse in his travels with abbots or friars. Pits's suggestion that his mental failure was due to his remorse at having abandoned Rome rests on no foundation. —LEE, SIDNEY, 1893, *Dictionary of National Biography, vol.* XXXIII, *p.* 15.

Leland's Latin style is fluent and copious, but not elegant. Of his English there is little to be said, except that it is clear and straightforward.—DODDS, JAMES MILLER, 1893, *English Prose, ed. Craik, vol.* I, *p.* 236.

John Leland continues for us the useful, and at this time really important, function of the "literary hodmen," as they have been contemptuously and ungratefully termed. . . . His phrase is sometimes quaint in itself, and always has the pleasant archaism of his time; but it possesses no individual savour, and is once more only the literary vehicle of a man who sets down what he wishes to set down clearly and without any decided solecisms, so far as the standard of correctness of his own time is fixed, but who neither has been taught any kind of "rhetoric" in the vernacular nor cares to elaborate one for himself.—SAINTSBURY, GEORGE, 1898, *A Short History of English Literature, pp.* 235, 236.

Alexander Barclay

1475?—1552

Born about 1475; died in Croydon, June 1552. The best authorities call him a Scotchman, and suppose him to have been educated at either Cambridge or Oxford, or possibly at both those universities. He traveled extensively, spoke many languages, and was long a priest in the college of Ottery St. Mary in Devonshire. Afterward he was a priest and monk of Ely, and joined the Franciscans at Canterbury. His "Eclogues," undated but written at Ely, are the first in the English language. Of more value is his translation (1509) of Sebastian Brandt's "Ship of Fools," which had appeared in Basel in 1494. It had great influence on English literature.—WARNER, CHARLES DUDLEY, *ed.* 1897, *Library of the World's Best Literature, vol.* XXIX, *Biographical Dictionary of Authors, p.* 42.

Then Bartlet, with an hoopyng russet long coate, with a pretie hoode in his necke, and five knottes upon his girdle, after Francis tricks. He was borne beyonde the cold river of Twede. He lodged upon a swete bed Chamomill, under the Sinamum tree: about hym many Shepherdes and shepe, with pleasaunte pipes; greatly abhorring the life of Courtiers, Citizens, Usurers and Banckruptes &c. whose olde daies are miserable. And the estate of Shepherdes and countrie people he accoumpted moste happie and sure.—BULLEIN, WILLIAM, 1564–73, *A Dialogue Both Pleasaunt and Pietifull, wherein is a Godlie Regiment against the Fever Pestilence, with a Consolation and Comforte against Death.*

An Author of great Eminence, and Merit; tho' not so much as mention'd in any Undertaking of this Nature before.—COOPER, ELIZABETH, 1737, *The Muses Library, p.* 33.

Our author's stanza is verbose, prosaic, and tedious: and for many pages together, his poetry is little better than a trite homily in verse. The title promises much character and pleasantry: but we shall be disappointed, if we expect to find the foibles of the crew of our ship touched by the hand of the author of the "Canterbury Tales," or exposed in the rough yet strong satire of Pierce Plowman. . . . Nor must it be denied, that his language is more cultivated than that of many of his cotemporaries, and that he contributed his share to the improvement of the English phraseology. . . . Our author's "Egloges," I believe, are the first that appeared in the English language.—WARTON, THOMAS, 1778–81, *History of English Poetry, sec.* xxix.

His poetical merit seems to have been a good deal overrated.—ELLIS, GEORGE, 1790–1845, *Specimens of the Early English Poets, vol.* I, *p.* 329.

His "Ship of Fools" has been as often quoted as most obsolete English poems; but if it were not obsolete it would not be quoted. He also wrote Eclogues, which are curious as the earliest pieces of that kind in our language. . . . Barklay, indeed, though he has some stanzas which might be quoted for their strength of thought and felicity of expression, is, upon the whole, the least ambitious of all writers to adorn his conceptions of familiar life with either dignity or beauty.—CAMPBELL, THOMAS, 1819, *An Essay on English Poetry.*

Barclay has a natural construction of style still retaining a vernacular vigor. He is noticed by Warton for having contributed his share in the improvement of English phraseology; and, indeed, we are often surprised to discover many felicities of our native idiom; and the work, though it should be repulsive to some for its black-letter, is perfectly intelligible to a modern reader. The verse, being prosaic, preserves its colloquial ease, though with more gravity than suits sportive subjects: we sometimes feel the tediousness of the good sense of the priest of St. Mary Ottery.—DISRAELI, ISAAC, 1841, *The Ship of Fools, Amenities of Literature.*

Barclay wrote at a period when the standard of English poetry was extremely low; and, as excellence is always comparative, this circumstance may partly enable us to account for the high reputation which he enjoyed among his contemporaries. If not entitled to the name of a poet, he is at least a copious versifier.—IRVING, DAVID, 1861, *History of Scotish Poetry, ed. Carlyle, p.* 327.

Is regarded as one of the improvers of the English tongue, and to him it is chiefly owing that a true Emblem-book was made popular in England.—GREEN, HENRY, 1870, *Shakespeare and the Emblem Writers, p.* 65.

Barclay applies the cudgel as vigorously to the priest's pate as to the Lollard's back. But he disliked modern innovation as much as ancient abuses, in this also faithfully reflecting the mind of the people.—JAMIESON, T. H., 1874, *ed. Barclay's Ship of Fools.*

His literary fame rests on his "Ship of Fools," and in a less degree on his "Eclogues." The former of these works remains essentially a translation, though Barclay truly states himself to have added and given an English colouring to his work. It is in any case the most noteworthy translation into a living tongue of a production of very high literary significance. . . . The English "Ship of Fools" exercised an important direct influence upon our literature, pre-eminently helping to bury mediæval allegory in the grave which had long yawned before it, and to direct English authorship into the drama, essay, and novel of character.—WARD, A. W., 1885, *Dictionary of National Biography, vol.* III, *p.* 160.

His merit rests chiefly upon the fact that he brought several important works of his day, and one from a not far-distant past, within reach of his countrymen, by correctly understanding what they specially required.—TEN BRINK, BERNHARD, 1892, *History of English Literature, (Fourteenth Century to Surrey) tr. Schmitz, p.* 99.

Barclay was a dull and clumsy versifier.—GOSSE, EDMUND, 1897, *Short History of Modern English Literature, p.* 57.

Barclay seems really to deserve the place of first Eclogue-writer in English, if any one cares for this fortuitous and rather futile variety of eminence. His Eclogues, moreover, are not merely more original, but, so far as they are accessible, seem to be less jejune than the "Ship." This latter owes its fame partly to its rarity before the reprint of five and twenty years ago, partly to the famous and really admirable woodcuts which it contains. The first "fole"—the possessor of unprofitable books—has a certain savour of promise which is unluckily but seldom fulfilled afterwards. Still, mainly thanks to the illustrations and to the general sympathy with Puck in seeing and saying, "Lord, what fools these mortals be!" it is possible to make one's way through the long catalogue which fills from two thousand to two thousand five hundred stanzas of rhyme-royal. The individual line is rather an interesting one, showing a sort of intermediate stage between the would-be rigid decasyllable of Lydgate and Occleve and the long rambling twelves or fourteeners of the mid-sixteenth century poets. Sometimes Barclay permits himself a full Alexandrine; oftener (in fact, in the majority of cases) he lengthens out his line with trisyllabic feet, so arranged as sometimes to take very little keep of the iambic basis.—SAINTSBURY, GEORGE, 1898, *A Short History of English Literature, p.* 167.

Nicholas Ridley

1500?–1555

Nicholas Ridley, was born in the county of Northumberland, near the Scottish border, early in the sixteenth century, but the exact date has not been preserved. He was educated at Newcastle-on-Tyne and Pembroke College, Cambridge, of which he was elected Fellow in 1524, went to Paris and studied at the Sorbonne in 1527, returned to England in 1530, was chaplain to the University, and public orator in 1534, chaplain to Archbishop Cranmer in 1537, Master of Pembroke, D. D. and chaplain to Henry VIII. in 1540, Prebendary of Canterbury in 1541, and of Westminster in 1545, Bishop of Rochester in 1547, and was translated to London in 1550. He was nominated for the bishopric of Durham in 1553, but soon after the accession of Mary was committed to the Tower, and was sent to Oxford, where he held numerous disputations, and one in particular of which a record remains, Tuesday, April 16, 1555. He was condemned as a heretic Tuesday, Oct. 1, 1555, degraded Tuesday, Oct. 15, and suffered at the stake with Bishop Latimer, Wednesday, Oct. 16.—TOWNSEND, GEORGE H., 1870, *The Every-Day Book of Modern Literature, vol.* II, *p.* 62.

He was a man right comely and well proportioned in all points, both in complexion and lineaments of the body. He took all things in good part, bearing no malice nor rancour from his heart, but straightways forgetting all injuries and offences done against him. He was very kind and affectionate to his kinsfolk, and yet not bearing with them anything otherwise than right would require, giving them always for a general rule, yea, to his own brother and sister, that they doing evil should seek or look for nothing at his hand, but should be as strangers and aliens to him; and that they were his brother and sister, who lived honestly, and a godly life. Using all kinds of ways to mortify himself, he was given to much prayer and contemplation.—FOXE, JOHN, 1562, *Book of Martyrs, ed. Kennedy, bk.* viii, *p.* 574.

Rome thundered death; but Ridley's dauntless eye
Stared in Death's face, and scorned Death standing bye.
In spite of Rome, for England's faith he stood;
And in the flames he sealed it with his blood.
—QUARLES, FRANCIS, 1644? *Poems.*

Bonner had made an ill retribution to Ridley, for the kindness he had shewed his friends when he was in possession at London: for he had made Bonner's mother always dine with him, when he lived in his country-house of Fulham, and treated her as if she had been his own mother; besides his kindness to his other friends. Heath, then bishop of Worcester, had been kept prisoner a year and a half in Ridley's house, where he lived as if he had been at his own; and Heath used always to call him the best learned of all the party: yet he so far forgot gratitude and humanity, that though he went through Oxford when he was a prisoner there, he came not to see him.—BURNET, GILBERT, 1681, *The History of the Reformation of the Church of England, ed. Nares, vol.* II, *pt.* ii, *bk.* ii, *p.* 497.

How fast the Marian death-list is unrolled!
See Latimer and Ridley in the might
Of Faith stand coupled for a common flight!
One (like those prophets whom God sent of old)
Transfigured, from this kindling hath foretold
A torch of inextinguishable light;
The Other gains a confidence as bold;
And thus they foil their enemy's despite.
The penal instruments, the shows of crime,
Are glorified while this once-mitred pair
Of saintly Friends the "murtherer's chain partake,
Corded, and burning at the social stake:"
Earth never witnessed object more sublime
In constancy, in fellowship more fair!
—WORDSWORTH, WILLIAM, 1821–22, *Ecclesiastical Sonnets, Part* ii, *s.* xxxiv.

In every relation of life, the power of his intellect, the integrity of his principles, and the piety of his heart were conspicuous.—HOOK, WALTER FARQUHAR, 1852, *Ecclesiastical Biography, vol.* VIII, *p.* 215.

The few tracts of Ridley's that remain are less eloquent than learned.—CRAIK, GEORGE L., 1861, *A Compendious History of English Literature and of the English Language, vol.* I, *p.* 438.

Ridley always knew what he meant, and had the moral courage to say it, and to act upon it, but he would have been a most dangerous man in Cranmer's position; the National Church would probably have become a sect, like the many which arose and flourished on the Continent.—OVERTON, JOHN HENRY, 1897, *The Church in England, vol.* I, *p.* 426.

Hugh Latimer

1485?-1555

Born at Thurcaston, Leicestershire, England—it is generally said in 1491, but Demaus thinks the date should be 1484 or 1485. He was educated at Clare Hall, Cambridge, where he was chosen a fellow 1509; passed a bachelor 1510, and a master 1514; was cross-bearer to the university, and in 1516 became Greek professor; was ordained a priest at Lincoln; became interested in the principles of the Reformation through the labors of Bilney; was dismissed from the university as a heretic by Wolsey 1527; became chaplain to Henry VIII. 1530; became rector of West Kingston, Wilts, 1531; was excommunicated, but absolved on his submission, 1532; was chaplain to Anne Boleyn 1534; became Bishop of Worcester 1535; resigned his office 1539, not being able to accept the Six Articles (31 Hen. VIII., c. 14,) and was imprisoned in the keeping of the Bishop of Chichester; was afterwards silenced by authority and shut up in the Tower 1546-47; declined his former bishopric 1548; was preacher to Edward VI. 1549-50; was imprisoned in the Tower by proclamation of Queen Mary 1553; transferred to the Bocardo of Oxford, with Ridley, 1554; tried and condemned by order of Cardinal Pole 1555; and burned at the stake with Ridley in the ditch near Baliol College, Oct. 16, 1555. Latimer was one of the most influential and fearless of the English Reformers, and his admirable "Sermons" (4 vols., London, 1845) are models of forcible and witty speech.—PERRY, W. S., *rev.*, 1897, *Johnson's Universal Cyclopaedia, vol.* v, *p.* 117.

PERSONAL

Did there ever any one (I say not in England only, but among other nations) flourish since the time of the Apostles, who preached the gospel more sincerely, purely, and honestly, than Hugh Latimer, Bishop of Worcester?—MORISON, SIR RICHARD, 1537, *Apomaxis Calumniarum . . . quibus Joannes Cocleus, etc., p.* 78.

The 7. of March, being Wednesday was a pulpit set up in the kings prime garden at Westminster, and there in doctor *Latimer* preached before the king, where he mought be heard of more than foure times so manie people as could have stod in the kings chappel: and this was the first sermon preached there.—STOWE, JOHN, 1548, *Chronicles.*

Moses, Ieremyas, Helias, did neuer declare ye true message of god vnto their rulers and people, wyth a more syncere spirite, faythful mynde and godly zeale, then godlye Latymer doth now in oure daies vnto our most noble kyng and vnto the whole realme.—SOME, THOMAS, 1549, *Dedication to Seven Sermons Before Edward* VI., *Arber Reprint, p.* 20.

First cometh to my remembrance a man worthy to be loved and reverenced of all true-hearted Christian men, not only for the pureness of his life, which hath always before the world been innocent and blameless, but also for the sincerity and godliness of his evangelic doctrine, which since the beginning of his preaching hath in all points been so comfortable to the teaching of Christ and his apostles, that the very adversaries of God's truth, with all their menacing words and cruel imprisonments could not withdraw him from it, but whatsoever he had once preached, he valiently defended the same before the world without fear of any mortal creature, although of never so great power and high authority, wishing and minding rather to suffer not only loss of worldly possessions, but also of life, than the glory of God, and the truth of Christ's gospel should in any point be obscured or defaced through him.—BECON, THOMAS, 1570? *Jewel of Joy, Works, Parker Society ed., vol.* II, *p.* 424.

I cannot here omit old father Latimer's habit at this his appearing before the commissioners, which was also his habit while he remained a prisoner in Oxford. He held his hat in his hand; he had a kerchief on his head, and upon it a night-cap or two, and a great cap such as townsmen used, with two broad flaps, to button under his chin: an old threadbare Bristow freez gown, girded to his body with a penny leather girdle, at which hanged, by a long string of leather, his testament, and his spectacles, without case, hanging about his neck upon his breast.—STRYPE, JOHN, 1694, *Memorials of Archbishop Cranmer, Oxford ed., vol.* III, *p.* 110.

Latimer, more than any other man, promoted the Reformation by his preaching. The straightforward honesty of his remarks, the liveliness of his illustrations, his homely wit, his racy manner, his manly freedom, the playfulness of his temper, the simplicity of his heart, the sincerity of his understanding, gave life and vigour to his sermons when they were delivered, and render them now the most amusing productions of that age, and to us, perhaps, the most valuable.—GILPIN, WILLIAM, 1755–1809, *Lives of the Reformers.*

Few men have deserved better of their fellows, in life and word, than he. He was a genuine Englishman, conscientious, courageous, a man of common sense and good upright practice, sprung from the labouring and independent class, with whom were the heart and thews of the nation. . . . Sick, liable to racking headaches, stomachaches, pleurisy, stone, he wrought a vast work, travelling, writing, preaching, delivering at the age of sixty-seven two sermons every Sunday, and generally rising at two in the morning, winter and summer, to study. Nothing can be simpler or more effective than his eloquence; and the reason is, that he never speaks for the sake of speaking, but of doing work.—TAINE, H. A., 1871, *History of English Literature, tr. Van Laun, vol.* I, *pp.* 372, 373.

Perhaps no preacher has ever lived, not even excepting St. Paul, who has united in a more remarkable degree than Hugh Latimer the qualities of fearlessness and modesty, courage and gentleness, hardihood and tenderness, boldness and meekness, inflexible sincerity of conviction and tolerance rising to the pitch of magnanimity. Nor have there been any who were more uncompromising in the delivery of the message committed to them, or less respecters of persons when sin was to be exposed and wickedness rebuked. His audacity was sublime, and was without any trace of arrogance; his piety was fervent, but simple and free from extravagance; his courage was finely tempered by his humility; and his insight of the character of men and of the spirit of the times in which he lived was marvellously acute.—DESHLER, CHARLES D., 1878, *Hugh Latimer, Harper's Magazine, vol.* 57, *p.* 88.

Hugh Latimer, another of the same destructive gang, equally heretical, bitterly persecuting and much more violent in his words and predictions, because of his "seditious demeanour," often so ostentatiously and abundantly made manifest, was very properly sent to the same place.*—LEE, FREDERICK GEORGE, 1888, *The Life of Cardinal Pole, p.* 62.

GENERAL

Hugh Latymer is said by some to have very much assisted archbp. Cranmer in compiling the Homilies, which I veryly believe to be true, considering the learning and simplicity of the man, who however in this work used nothing ludicrous, as he thought proper to do sometimes in his sermons, as the occasion required, the better to expose vice and to please his auditors.—HEARNE, THOMAS, 1729, *Reliquiæ Hearnianæ, ed. Bliss, vol.* III, *p.* 35.

I never read any sermons so much like Whitefield's manner of preaching as Latimer's. You see a simple mind uttering all its feelings, and putting forth everything as it comes, without reference to books or men, with a *naïveté* seldom equalled.—CECIL, RICHARD, 1811, *Remains, ed. Pratt.*

It is, however, impossible not to feel, and to acknowledge, in the Sermons of Latimer, a familiarity, and yet force of style, upon which Swift, if not Sterne, in after days, but with occasionally greater coarseness of expression, might have formed their own. There is, throughout Latimer, a purity, ease, and perfection of English idiom—to say nothing of the curious personal and historical anecdotes with which they are mixed up, and which render his discourses invaluable to the lexicographer and philologist. At the same time there is, frequently, a good deal of what may be called *gossipping*—in the sermons of this worthy old Bishop: for he not only seems to have spoken, more than any other divine with whom I am acquainted, from the impulses excited by the evidence of the outward senses, but he also seems to have always spoken the truth, even in its most unpalateable form,—although the Court, with the King at its head, were frequently his auditors.—DIBDIN, THOMAS FROGNALL, 1824, *The Library Companion, p.* 72, *note.*

Brave, sincere, honest, inflexible, not distinguished as a writer or a scholar, but exercising his power over men's minds by a fervid eloquence flowing from the deep

*The Tower.

conviction which animated his plain, pithy, and free-spoken sermons.—MACKINTOSH, SIR JAMES, 1831, *History of England, vol.* II, *p.* 291.

No English treatise on a theological subject, published before the end of 1550, seems to deserve notice in the general literature of Europe, though some may be reckoned interesting in the history of our Reformation. The sermons of Latimer, however, published in 1548, are read for their honest zeal and lively delineation of manners. They are probably the best specimens of a style then prevalent in the pulpit, and which is still not lost in Italy, nor among some of our own sectaries; a style that came at once home tc the vulgar; animated and affective, picturesque and intelligible, but too unsparing both of ludicrous associations and commonplace invective. — HALLAM, HENRY, 1837–39, *Introduction to the Literature of Europe, pt.* i, *ch.* vi, *par.* 31.

Latimer, by his *naïveté* and simplicity, his wit, honesty, and piety, has, more than the other Reformers, retained his popularity. He will furnish many hints for useful addresses to the people. . . . His sermons are fine specimens of godly intrepidity, simplicity, and piety.—BICKERSTETH, EDWARD, 1844, *The Christian Student.*

He was the Cobbett of the Reformation, with more honesty than Cobbett, and more courage; but very like him in the character of his understanding.—MACAULAY, THOMAS BABINGTON, 1856–58, *Life and Letters, ed. Trevelyan, ch.* xiv.

Latimer's discourses are rather quaint and curious than either learned or eloquent in any lofty sense of that term. Latimer is stated to have been one of the first English students of the Greek language; but this could hardly be guessed from his Sermons, which, except a few scraps of Latin, show scarcely a trace of scholarship or literature of any kind. In addressing the people from the pulpit, this honest, simple-minded bishop, feeling no exaltation either from his position or his subject, expounded the most sublime doctrines of religion in the same familiar and homely language in which the humblest or most rustic of his hearers were accustomed to chaffer with one another in the marketplace about the price of a yard of cloth or a pair of shoes. Nor, indeed, was he more fastidious as to matter than as to manner: all the preachers of that age were accustomed to take a wide range over things in general; but Latimer went beyond everybody else in the miscellaneous assortment of topics he used to bring together from every region of heaven and earth,—of the affairs of the world that now is as well as of that which is to come.—CRAIK, GEORGE L., 1861, *A Compendious History of English Literature and of the English Language, vol.* I, *p.* 438.

His discourses have not come down to us, but we may be sure they showed the same fearless honesty as made the Londoners cheer him in after years, and struggle to touch his gown, as he walked down the Strand to preach at Whitehall. Instinct with the fire of genius, and yet simple, the plain talk of a plain man, who sprang from the body of the people; who sympathized strongly with their wants and feelings, and uttered their opinions with an earnestness that knew no fear, they spread far and wide a contagious enthusiasm for opinions thus nobly advanced.—GEIKIE, JOHN CUNNINGHAM, 1878, *The English Reformation, p.* 199.

Latimer was no sour ascetic: he loved a racy anecdote or a humorous saying, and was ready to make use of them even when dealing with the most serious subject. A true Englishman, somewhat of the "John Bull" type, frank, manly, honest, courageous, he exerted a wonderful influence over the minds of his contemporaries, and his sermons, though their diction is occasionally rather startling, are still well worth reading as the utterances of a brave, thoroughly sincere man.—NICOLL, HENRY J., 1882, *Landmarks of English Literature, p.* 47.

Speaking from his pulpit — "The Shrouds at Paul's Church," or elsewhere —he has often the aspect of some primitive dramatist on his cart, acting his own tragedy. The character that Latimer represents is his own; and, as was to be expected in that city and nation and time, along with the tragedy there is a good deal of comedy intermingled. It is his own life and experience that he puts before his audience; not elevated and elaborated with classical rhetoric, but he declared frankly in his natural language.—KER, W. P., 1893, *English Prose, ed. Craik, vol.* I, *p.* 223.

Holds a very important and somewhat peculiar position, ranking with Bunyan, Cobbett, and in a lesser degree Defoe, as the chief practitioner of a perfectly homely and vernacular style. Such a style naturally connects itself with an intense egotism; and Latimer is as egotistic, though not as arrogant, as Cobbett himself. He was a thoroughly honest and a thoroughly practical man, no partisan in the bad sense (that is to say, in the way of winking at practices by friends which he would have stormed against in foes), with all the taste of the common people for vivid homely illustration, and sometimes, as in the universally known description of the paternal household, capable of extraordinarily graphic presentment of fact. Beyond the range of personal description and shrewd, unadorned argument or denunciation his literary gifts would probably not have extended in any case very far. But as a popular sermon-writer in his own days, or as a popular journalist in these, he had in the one case, and could have had in the other, but very few rivals and no superiors.—SAINTSBURY, GEORGE, 1898, *A Short History of English Literature*, p. 212.

Thomas Cranmer

1489–1555

Born at Aslacton, Nottinghamshire, July 2, 1489: died at Oxford, March 21, 1556. Archbishop of Canterbury. He was educated at Cambridge, where he took the degree of B. A. in 1512 and that of M. A. in 1515. In 1529 he obtained the favor of Henry VIII. by proposing that, in order to avoid the necessity of an appeal to Rome, the question of the king's marriage with Catharine of Aragon should be referred to the universities. He was appointed chaplain to the king, and in 1530 accompanied the Earl of Wiltshire on a mission to the Pope in reference to the divorce. In 1532 he was sent on a mission to the emperor in Germany, and in the same year infringed the rule of the Roman Catholic Church by marrying a niece of Osiander. He was appointed archbishop of Canterbury in 1533, and in the same year pronounced the marriage of Henry with Catharine of Aragon invalid. He abjured his allegiance to Rome in 1535, and became a member of the regency for Edward VI. in 1547, and in 1548 was head of the commission which composed the first English prayer-book. He invited a number of distinguished foreign Protestants to settle in England, including Peter Martyr, Ochino, Bucer, and Alasco the Pole. He was induced by Edward VI. in 1553 to sign the patent which settled the crown on Lady Jane Grey to the exclusion of Mary and Elizabeth, and was in consequence committed to the Tower for treason on the accession of Mary. He was subsequently tried for heresy, and in spite of numerous recantations (which he repudiated at his execution) was sentenced to the stake.—SMITH, BENJAMIN E., *ed.* 1894–97, *The Century Cyclopedia of Names*, p. 288.

PERSONAL

He never placed the function of a bishop in the administration of secular things, but in a most faithful dispensation of God's Word. In the midst of wicked Babylon he always performed the part of a good guide of Israel. And among papists, that tyrannised against the truth of Christ, he governed the people of God with an admirable prudence. No man ever so happily and steadily persisted, with Christ himself, in the defence of the truth, in the midst of falsely learned men, in such imminent hazard of his life, and yet without receiving any harm. No man did more prudently bear with some false apostles for a time, although, with St. Paul, he knew what most pestilent men they were, that so they might not be provoked to run into greater rage and madness.—BALE, JOHN, 1549–59, *Scriptorum Illustrium Majoris Britanniæ*, p. 690.

He feared not to ride the roughest horse that came into his stable, which he would do very comely; as otherwise at all times there was none that would become his horse better. And when time served for recreation after study, he would both hawk and hunt, the game being prepared for him beforehand, and would sometime shoot in the long-bow, but many times kill his deer with the cross bow; and yet his sight was not perfect, for he was purblind. — MAURICE, RALPH, 1555? *A Declaration Concerning Archbishop Cranmer.*

THOMAS CRANMER

NICHOLAS RIDLEY

Who that considered their preferments in time past, the places of honour that they some time occupied in this commonwealth, the favour they were in with their princes, and the opinion of learning they had, could refrain from sorrow with tears, to see so great dignity, honour, and estimation, so many godly virtues, the study of so many years, such excellent learning, put into the fire, and consumed in one moment.—FOXE, JOHN, 1562, *Book of Martyrs, ed. Kennedy.*

He was a man raised of God for great services; and well fitted for them. He was naturally of a mild and gentle temper, not soon heated, nor apt to give his opinion rashly of things, or persons: and yet his gentleness, though it oft exposed him to his enemies, who took advantages from it to use him ill, knowing he would readily forgive them, did not lead him into such a weakness of spirit, as to consent to everything that was uppermost. . . . His meekness was really a virtue in him, and not a pusillanimity in his temper. He was a man of great candour; he never dissembled his opinion, nor disowned his friend: two rare qualities in that age, in which there was a continued course of dissimulation, almost in the whole English clergy and nation, they going backward and forward, as the court turned. . . . He had a good judgment, but no great quickness of apprehension, nor closeness of style, which was diffused and unconnected: therefore, when anything was to be penned that required more nerves, he made use of Ridley. He laid out all his wealth on the poor, and pious uses: he had hospitals and surgeons in his house for the king's seamen; he gave pensions to many of those that fled out of Germany into England; and kept up that which is hospitality indeed at his table, where great numbers of the honest and poor neighbours were always invited. . . . He was so humble and affable, that he carried himself in all conditions at the same rate. His last fall was the only blemish of his life; but he expiated it, with a sincere repentance, and a patient martyrdom. . . . Those who compared modern and ancient times, found in him so many and excellent qualities, that they did not doubt to compare him to the greatest of the primitive bishops; not only to the Chrysostoms, Ambroses, and Austins, but to the fathers of the first rate that immediately followed the apostles, to the Ignatiuses, Polycarps, and Cyprians. — BURNET, GILBERT, 1681, *The History of the Reformation of the Church of England, ed. Nares, vol.* II, *pt.* ii, *bk.* ii, *pp.* 521, 522, 523.

The name of the most reverend prelate deserves to stand upon eternal record; having been the first protestant archbishop of this kingdom, and the greatest instrument, under God, of the happy Reformation of this Church of England: in whose piety, learning, wisdom, conduct, and blood, the foundation of it was laid. And therefore it will be no unworthy work to revive his memory now, though after an hundred and thirty years and upwards.—STRYPE, JOHN, 1694, *Memorials of Archbishop Cranmer, Oxford ed., p.* 3.

Bearing the palm of martyrdom, Cranmer was there in his meekness,
Holy-name, to be ever revered!

—SOUTHEY, ROBERT, 1821, *A Vision of Judgment,* ix.

Outstretching flameward his upbraided hand
(O God of mercy, may no earthly Seat
Of judgment such presumptuous doom repeat!)
Amid the shuddering throng doth Cranmer stand;
Firm as the stake to which with iron band
His frame is tied; firm from the naked feet
To the bare head. The victory is complete;
The shrouded Body to the Soul's command
Answers with more than Indian fortitude,
Through all her nerves with finer sense endued,
Till breath departs in blissful aspiration:
Then, 'mid the ghastly ruins of the fire,
Behold the unalterable heart entire,
Emblem of faith untouched, miraculous attestation!

—WORDSWORTH, WILLIAM, 1821–22, *Ecclesiastical Sonnets, pt.* ii, xxxv.

Cranmer rose into favour by serving Henry in a disgraceful affair of his first divorce. He promoted the marriage of Anne Boleyn with the king. On a frivolous pretence, he pronounced it null and void. On a pretence, if possible, still more frivolous, he dissolved the ties which bound the shameless tyrant to Anne of Cleves. He attached himself to Cromwell, while the fortunes of Cromwell flourished. He voted for cutting off his head without a trial, when the tide of royal favour turned. He conformed backwards and forwards as the king changed his mind. While Henry lived, he assisted in condemning to the flames those who denied the doctrine of transubstantiation. When Henry died, he found out that the doctrine was false. He was, however, not at a loss for people to burn. . . . Equally false to political and to religious obligations, he was the first tool of Somerset, and then the tool of Northumberland. When the former wished to put his own brother to death, without even the form of a trial, he found a ready instrument in Cranmer. In spite of the canon law, which forbade a churchman to take any part in matters of blood, the archbishop signed the warrant for the atrocious sentence. . . . If he had shown half as much firmness when Edward requested him to commit treason, as he had before shown when Edward requested him not to commit murder, he might have saved the country from one of the greatest misfortunes that it ever underwent. . . . We do not mean, however, to represent him as a monster of wickedness. He was not wantonly cruel or treacherous. He was merely a supple, timid, interested courtier, in times of frequent and violent change. That which has always been represented as his distinguishing virtue, the facility with which he forgave his enemies, belongs to the character.—MACAULAY, THOMAS BABINGTON, 1827, *Hallam's Constitutional History, Edinburgh Review, and Essays.*

Lingard speaks of *seven* recantations signed with his name. Yet the whole of this transaction was in the space of two days. We may suppose him under a degree of mental alienation, brought on by want of firmness and resolution. Or, we may conclude with the Catholics, that the recantation was occasioned by the fear of an agonizing death. To us it matters little. It was extorted from him by that kind of force, which induces a victim to lay his head voluntarily upon the block, when brought to the place of execution. —LEE, H. F., 1840, *The Life and Times of Thomas Cranmer, p.* 266.

The incidents of Cranmer's death were but too conformable to those of his consecration, and his general public career. As long as he had a hope of life, he made but little difficulty in subscribing to any confession of faith, however different from that of either the Calvinists or the Lutherans. He made no fewer than six recantations; and acknowledged at the stake that they were all insincere; all made "to save his life if it might be."—FLANAGAN, THOMAS, 1857, *A History of the Church in England, vol.* II, *p.* 126.

Both by his character and by his ability Cranmer was eminently fitted to become a useful tool in the hands of Henry and Cromwell. He was now* a man of forty-three, rather learned, of ready wit, a good controversialist, and withal elegant, graceful, and insinuating. An admirable deceiver, he possessed the talent of representing the most infamous deeds in the finest words. — FRIEDMANN, PAUL, 1884, *Anne Boleyn, vol.* I, *p.* 176.

Men will continue to judge him very variously, according as they agree with his opinions or disagree; but it may be hoped that from henceforth one fault will not be so frequently laid to his charge—a fault which was wholly foreign to his character. Whatever else he was, Cranmer was no crafty dissembler. He was as artless as a child. Even those actions of his which have brought upon him the accusation of double dealing—the reservation with which he took the oath at his consecration, the acknowledgment that he should not have withdrawn his recantation if he had been allowed to live—are instances of his naïve simplicity. He may sometimes have deceived himself; he never had any intention to deceive another. Trustful towards others, even to a fault, he had little confidence in himself. His humility amounted almost to a vice. His judgment was too easily swayed by those who surrounded him—especially by those in authority. . . . He was indefatigable in his industry. His placid character knew no ambition. In an age of rapine, the friend of Henry remained unenriched. So courteous and amiable in his manners that his enemies found fault with him on that account, he was unstinted in his hospitality, especially toward scholars, and lavish in his gifts. Unless marriage is a sin, no breath ever assailed the purity of his life.—MASON, ARTHUR JAMES, 1898, *Thomas Cranmer, (Leaders of Religion), pp.* 199, 201.

GENERAL

Cranmer was more remarkable for his patronage of theological learning, than

*1532.

for the merit possessed by any writings of his own.—SPALDING, WILLIAM, 1852–82, *A History of English Literature, p.* 165.

Cranmer's extant original works are very many, and possess considerable merit; but his literary reputation will always rest mainly on the fact that he was what we may call editor-in-chief of those three great works of the English Reformation already noticed,—the Book of Common Prayer, the Twelve Homilies and the Great Bible.—COLLIER, WILLIAM FRANCIS, 1861, *History of English Literature, p.* 89.

Cranmer was the greatest writer among the founders of the English Reformation. —CRAIK, GEORGE L., 1861, *A Compendious History of English Literature and of the English Language, vol.* I, *p.* 438.

He holds the highest rank as a writer among the Reformers, and was influential in establishing the present polity of the Church of England. —GILMAN, ARTHUR, 1870, *First Steps in English Literature, p.* 62.

Cicero himself had not a nicer and more exquisite ear for rhythm, for the rhythm of prose as distinguished from the rhythm of poetry. Cranmer's sentences are not like those of Hooker and the Elizabethan rhetoricians framed on the Latin model, and his music is not the music of the Ciceronian period. But as Cicero modified the harmony of Isocrates to suit the genius of the Latin language, so Cranmer modified the harmony of Ciceronian rhetoric to suit the genius of our vernacular. He adjusted with exquisite tact and skill the Saxon and Latin elements in our language both in the service of rhythm and in the service of expression. He saw that the power of the first lay in terseness and sweetness, the power of the second in massiveness and dignity, and that he who could succeed in tempering artfully and with propriety the one by the other, would be in the possession of an instrument which Isocrates and Cicero might envy. He saw too the immense advantage which the co-existence of these elements afforded for rhetorical emphasis. And this accounts for one of the distinctive features of the diction of our liturgy, the habitual association of Saxon words with their Latin synonyms for purposes of rhetorical emphasis. —COLLINS, J. CHURTON, 1893, *English Prose, ed. Craik, vol.* I, *p.* 212.

Cranmer was, of all men of his time, most powerful in hastening the English reformation. —HURST, JOHN FLETCHER, 1893, *Short History of the Christian Church, p.* 249.

Sir David Lyndsay

1490?-1555

Sir David Lyndesay (generally surnamed "of the Mount," from the name of an estate in Fifeshire, in the parish of Monimail) was born about 1490, and educated at the university of St. Andrew's. He was the companion of the young Scottish prince, afterwards James V., whose course he watched from his earliest days till his death in 1542. He was knighted by James, and made Lord Lyon King-at-Arms in 1530. . . . Lyndesay retired in his latter days to the Mount, where he died about 1557. His principal works are "The Dreme," written about 1528; "The Complaynt," 1529; "The Complaynt of the Kingis Papyngo" (Parrot), 1530; "Ane Satyre of the Thrie Estaits," 1535; "The Historie of William Meldrum, Squyer," before 1550; and "The Monarche" (i. e. Monarchie or Monarchy), 1552.—SKEAT, WALTER W., 1871, *Specimens of English Literature*, 1394–1579, *p.* 248.

Sir David Lindesay of Mont shall first be named, a man honorably descended, and greatly favored by King James the Fifth. Besides his knowledge and deep judgment in heraldry (whereof he was the chief) and in other publick affairs, he was most religiously inclined, but much hated by the clergy, for the liberty he used in condemning the superstition of the time, and rebuking their loose and dissolute lives. Nottheless he went unchallenged, and was not brought in question; which showed the good account wherein he was held.—SPOTISWOOD, JOHN, 1639? *History of the Church and State of Scotland, p.* 97.

In the works of Sir David Lindsay we do not often find either the splendid diction of Dunbar, or the prolific imagination of Gawin Douglas. Perhaps, indeed, "The Dream" is his only composition which can be cited as uniformly poetical: but his various learning, his good sense, his perfect knowledge of courts and of the world, the facility of his versification, and, above all, his peculiar talent of adapting himself to readers of all denomi nations, will continue to secure to him a considerable share of that popularity, for which he was originally indebted to the opinions he professed, no less than to his poetical merit.—ELLIS, GEORGE, 1790–1845, *Specimens of the Early English Poets, vol.* II, *p.* 17.

About this time, he published the most pleasing of all his poems, "The Historie and Testament of Squyer Meldrum." He, on this occasion, tries to amuse as well as to reform; but he shows his own coarseness by addressing his "trifling jests and fulsom ribaldry" to "companies unlettered, rude, and shallow."—CHALMERS, GEORGE, 1806, *ed. Poetical Works of Sir David Lyndsay, Life, vol.* I, *p.* 36.

. . . in the glances of his eye,
A penetrating, keen, and sly
Expression found its home;
The flash of that satiric rage
Which, bursting on the early stage,
Bradned the vices of the age,
And broke the keys of Rome . . .
Still is thy name in high account,
And still thy verse has charms,
Sir David Lindesay, of the Mount,
Lord Lion King-at-arms!

—SCOTT, SIR WALTER, 1808, *Marmion, canto* iv, *s.* vii.

He was esteemed one of the first poets of the age, and his writings had contributed greatly to the advancement of the Reformation. Notwithstanding the indelicacy which disfigures several of his poetical productions, the personal deportment of Lindsay was grave, his morals were correct, and his writings discover a strong desire to reform the manners of the age, as well as ample proofs of true poetical genius, extensive learning, and wit the most keen and penetrating.—M'CRIE, THOMAS, 1811–31, *Life of John Knox, p.* 45.

Inferior in high poetical genius to Dunbar or Douglas, he yet pleases by the truth and natural colouring of his descriptions, his vein of native humour, his strong good sense, and the easy flow of his versification. For the age in which he lived, and considering the court-like occupations in which his time was spent, his learning was various and respectable; and were he only known as a man whose writings contributed essentially to the introduction of the Reformation, this circumstance alone were sufficient to make him an object of no common interest.—TYTLER, PATRICK FRASER, 1833, *Lives of Scottish Worthies, vol.* III, *p.* 191

Though inferior to Dunbar in vividness of imagination and in elegance of language, he shows a more reflecting and philosophical mind; and certainly his satire upon James V. and his court is more poignant than the other's panegyric upon the Thistle. But, in the ordinary style of his versification, he seems not to rise much above the prosaic and tedious rhymers of the fifteenth century. His descriptions are as circumstantial without selection as theirs; and his language, partaking of a ruder dialect, is still more removed from our own.—HALLAM, HENRY, 1837–39, *Introduction to the Literature of Europe, vol.* I, *pt.* i, *ch.* viii, *par.* 17.

A warm-hearted, truth-loving gentleman, who took up Satire half as an amateur, but produced an effect with it that makes us honor his memory long after the Mount has vanished from his kindred; in days when the brave and beautiful symbols on his armorial coat look dim and old-fashioned, and when even his gentile name of Lindsay must owe its chief honor to the merits of those who bear it.—HANNAY, JAMES, 1854, *Satire and Satirists, p.* 92.

Whose productions are not indeed characterized by any high imaginative power, but yet display infinite wit, spirit, and variety in all the forms of the more familiar poetry. . . . If Dunbar is to be compared to Burns, Lyndsay may be said to have his best representative among the more recent Scottish poets in Allan Ramsay, who does not, however, come so near to Lyndsay by a long way as Burns does to Dunbar.—CRAIK, GEORGE L., 1861, *A Compendious History of English Literature and of the English Language, vol.* I, *p.* 457.

His works indeed exhibit considerable inequalities; but where they are not distinguished by any superior force of imagination, they are often entertaining by their strokes of humour, or instructive by their views of life and manners. He was evidently a man of sense and observation, with serious impressions of virtue and piety; nor was he destitute of those higher powers of mind which enable a writer to communicate his ideas with due effect. He frequently displays no mean vivacity of fancy; and the extensive and continued popularity to which he attained, must have rested on some solid foundation. . . . Lindsay's versification is generally distinguished by its ease and fluency. His style often rises to a considerable degree of elegance, but on some occasions is overloaded with extraneous terms.—IRVING, DAVID, 1861, *History of Scotish Poetry, ed. Carlyle, pp.* 340, 341.

There are some satirists in this group of poets—among these Sir David Lindsay stood unrivalled. . . . Old Davy Lindsay was transcendently popular. We see the marks of his influence on the history of the times, and can understand how it was so, when we read his potent attacks on the abuses of the day. He was a consummate artist. His riotous wit seems to drive him before it; but when his sarcasm is sharpened for a hit it never misses its aim, but strikes the victim right in the face. We have seen in the history of the Reformation some traces of his handiwork. —BURTON, JOHN HILL, 1867, *The History of Scotland, vol.* IV, *p.* 133.

In estimating the literary character of Lyndsay, we cannot claim for him the name of a Great Poet. Without either "the language at large," which he assigns to Dunbar, or his inventive genius, our Author is nevertheless entitled to no ordinary place among our ancient Makaris. He exhibits (without the least scruple in altering words to suit the rhyme) a great command of versification, a fine feeling for the beauties of external nature, and a fund of what may be called, low genuine humour and keen satire; while for a vivid conception and delineation of individual character, even in his impersonations of abstract Virtues and Vices, he displays great Dramatic power, and in this respect he far surpasses any one of the early Scottish Poets.—LAING, DAVID, 1871, *ed., The Poetical Works of Sir David Lyndsay, Memoir, p.* l.

Before the voice of Dunbar was silent, Lindsay took up the strain and was free Scotland, canny, humorous, sincere, with a direct earnestness that brings out notes of the deeper poetry of life; the voice for Scotland of that spirit of reformation which had grown up, as we have seen, among true men of all theological creeds during the fifteenth century, and had been strengthened by all influences of the time. —MORLEY, HENRY, 1873, *First Sketch of English Literature, p.* 256.

His works are specially remarkable as having exerted great influence in helping forward the cause of the Reformation.—LOUNSBURY, THOMAS R., 1879, *History of the English Language, p.* 107.

Lyndesay was rather a man of action bent on popularising his keen convictions than a professional writer. The bias of his mind and the temper of his time were alike unfavourable to finished works of art. His superabundant energy and ready humour made him a power, but he had no inclination to philosophise in solitude or to refine at leisure. His life was spent amid stormy politics, and we need not wonder that a pressure of affairs similar to that which for a space held even the genius of Milton in abeyance, should have marred the literary productions of a man who had more talent than genius, and who wrote "currente calamo" on such various themes with an almost fatal fluency.—NICHOL, JOHN, 1880, *The English Poets, ed. Ward, vol.* I, *p.* 194.

It is a characteristic of Lyndsay, as of Swift, Defoe, and some other writers, that he does not produce a striking result by brilliant flashes of fancy, but by a series of minute, cunning touches. His strength lies for the most part in details; his imagination can work only in prosaic channels; his satiric humour is raciest in petty familiarities. It is only where hatred of priestly hypocrisy impassions his speech that he rises into eloquence; and even then the elevation of his style comes from the Mount of Sinai and not from the heights of Parnassus.—ROSS, JOHN MERRY, 1884, *Scottish History and Literature, ed. Brown, p.* 410.

Lyndsay was a satirist, powerful in invective, fluent in style, and abounding in proverbial philosophy. But his poems were of local, and to a large extent of temporary interest. Yet these very limitations gave them an immediate fame and more extensive currency than the works of any other early Scottish poet, and render them invaluable to students of the time of James V. It passed into a proverb for what was not worth knowing, "You will not find that in David Lyndsay," and his writings were at one time in the library of every castle and the shelves of many cottages of Scotland.—MACKAY, ÆNEAS, 1893, *Dictionary of National Biography, vol.* XXXIII, *p.* 294.

No elaborate summing-up of Lindsay's work and position is necessary: he has spoken for himself. He was not a great poet; although in a few passages, such as the prologue to "The Dreme" and the prologue to "The Monarchie," he shows the marks of a poetic mind, imagination was not his strongest faculty. His own words, "I did never sleip on Pernasso," had perhaps a deeper truth than he realised. His work is inartistic, harsh in versification, formless in style, marred by a coarseness which it would be difficult to parallel, impossible to outdo. All attempts to palliate his defects are vain. The appeal to the coarseness of the age is but a partial excuse, and any other is out of the question. The Kirk was not without excuse in putting sternly down exhibitions which admitted of ribaldry and licentiousness such as we find in "The Satyre of the Thrie Estaitis." And yet, the more Lindsay is read, the firmer will be the conviction that all this is external to his work. Despite his faults he still retains a true claim to greatness, namely, that of being the literary leader in the Reformation of the life and faith of his time.—WALKER, HUGH, 1893, *Three Centuries of Scottish Literature, vol.* I, *p.* 38.

A vigorous and voluble writer of verse rather than a poet. . . . Robust, often coarse, humor, a large share of vigorous common-sense, and a strong power and constant habit of speaking his mind without needing or caring to pick his words, are the chief characteristics of Lindsay's verse. —ROBERTSON, J. LOGIE, 1894, *A History of English Literature, p.* 66.

For the best dramatic relic of the day* —the best morality, perhaps, ever written in Britain—we have to cross once more the Scottish border.—WHITE, GREENOUGH, 1895, *Outline of the Philosophy of English Literature, The Middle Ages, p.* 240.

Is not so good a poet as Douglas, but is no less interesting as a writer. He had great political insight, a considerable power of putting things pithily, and no small gift of wit, but, like Lydgate, his poetical ambition exceeded his capacity. Lyndsay, indeed, drew his inspiration from Dunbar as Lydgate did from Chaucer, but directly he leaves politics or the life of the times his work becomes bad.—HEATH, FRANK H., 1895, *Social England, ed. Traill, vol.* III, *p.* 111.

Lyndesay's interests and instincts were not artistic, and it is plain that he wrote in verse mainly because it was the only convenient weapon to his hand.—GOSSE, EDMUND, 1897, *Short History of Modern English Literature, p.* 60.

*"Three Estates."

Thomas, Lord Vaux

1510–1557

Thomas, Lord Vaux: poet; born at Harrowden, England, about 1516; educated at Cambridge; attended Cardinal Wolsey in his embassy to Charles V. 1527; succeeded to the title, and took his seat in the House of 1530; accompanied Henry VIII. to Calais and Boulogne 1532; became a Knight of the Bath and governor of the island of Jersey 1533. He was the author of a number of admired poems in the collection called "The Paradise of Daynty Devises" (1576), of which the best are entitled "The Assault of Cupid" and "The Aged Lover renounceth Love," first published in Tottel's "Miscellany of Songs and Sonnets" (1557). Died in Oct. 1556.—BEERS, H. A., *rev.*, 1897, *Johnson's Universal Cyclopœdia, vol.* VIII, *p.* 451.

A man of much facilitie in vulgar makings. . . . His commendation lyeth chiefly in the facilitie of his meetre, and the aptnesse of his descriptions such as he taketh vpon him to make, namely in sundry of his Songs, wherein he sheweth the counterfait action very liuely and pleasantly.—PUTTENHAM, GEORGE, 1589, *The Arte of English Poesie, ed. Arber, pp.* 74, 76.

The lord Vaulx, whom I have supposed, and on surer proof, to be another contributor to this miscellany, could not be the Nicholas lord Vaux, whose gown of purple velvet, plated with gold, eclipsed all the company present at the marriage of prince Arthur; who shines as a statesman and a soldier with uncommon lustre in the history of Henry VII., and continued to adorn the earlier annals of his successor, and who died in the year 1523. Lord Vaux the poet, was probably Thomas lord Vaux, the son of Nicholas, and who was summoned to parliament in 1531, and seems to have lived till the latter end of the reign of queen Mary. . . . Great numbers of Vaux's poems are extant in the "Paradise of Dainty Devises;" and, instead of the rudeness of Skelton, they have a smoothness and facility of manner, which does not belong to poetry written before the year 1523, in which lord Nicholas Vaux died an old man.—WARTON, THOMAS, 1778–81, *History of English Poetry, sec.* xxxix.

The compositions of Lord Vaux are uniformly of a moral and pensive cast, and breathe a spirit of religion and resignation often truly touching, and sometimes bordering on the sublime.—DRAKE, NATHAN, 1817, *Shakspeare and his Times, vol.* I. *p.* 713

Vaux belonged to the cultured circle of the courts of Henry VIII and Edward VI, and emulated the poetic efforts of Sir Thomas Wyatt the elder and the Earl of Surrey. Such of his work as survives and has been identified consists of short lyrics. Most of it breathes an affected tone of melancholy which is unredeemed by genuine poetic feeling; but some of Vaux's poems show metrical facility and a gentle vein of commonplace reflection which caught the popular ear. —LEE, SIDNEY, 1899, *Dictionary of National Biography, vol.* LVIII, *p.* 195.

Sir John Cheke

1514–1557

Was born in 1514 at Cambridge, and in 1529 obtained a fellowship of St. John's College, where he embraced the Reformed doctrines. He laboured earnestly to advance Greek studies, and in 1540 was appointed first regius professor of Greek. His new mode of pronouncing Greek, assailed by Bishop Gardiner in vain, resembled that still in vogue in England. In 1544 he became tutor to the Prince, afterwards Edward VI., whose accession secured Cheke a seat in parliament (1547), the provostship of King's College (1548), and knighthood (1552). He was stripped of everything at Mary's accession, and went abroad, but in 1556 was treacherously seized in Belgium, and brought to the Tower. Fear of the stake induced him to abjure Protestantism, but his recantation preyed on his mind, and he died 13th September, 1557.—PATRICK AND GROOME, *eds.*, 1897, *Chambers's Biographical Dictionary, p.* 209.

The Exchequer of Eloquence; Sir Ihon Cheeke, a man of men, supernaturally traded in all tongues.—NASH, THOMAS, 1589, *To the Gentlemen Students of Both Vnieursities, Nash's Works, ed. Grosart, vol.* I, *p.* xxviii.

Sir John Cheekes stile was the honybee of Plato. —HARVEY, GABRIEL, 1593, *A New Letter of Notable Contents, Works, ed. Grosart, vol.* I, *p.* 266.

Thy age like ours, O soul of Sir John Cheek,
Hated not learning worse than toad or asp,
When thou taughtest Cambridge and King
Edward Greek.
—MILTON, JOHN, 1645–6, *Sonnets.*

There had been in King Henry's time a great contest raised concerning the pronunciation of the Greek vowels. That tongue was but lately come to any perfection in England, and so no wonder the Greek was pronounced like English, with the same sound and apertures of the mouth: to this, Mr. Cheek, then reader of that tongue in Cambridge, opposed himself, and taught other rules of pronunciation. Gardiner was, it seems, so afraid of every innovation, though ever so much in the right, that he contended stiffly to have the old pronunciation retained: and Cheek, persisting in his opinion, was either put from the chair, or willingly left it, to avoid the indignation of so great and so spiteful a man as Gardiner was, who was then chancellor of the university. Cheek wrote a book in vindication of his way of pronouncing Greek; of which this must be said, that it is very strange to see how he could write with so much learning and judgment on so bare a subject. Redmayn, Poinet, and other learned men, were of his side, yet more covertly: but Sir Thomas Smith, now secretary of state, writ three books on the same argument, and did so evidently confirm Cheek's opinion, that the dispute was now laid aside, and the true way of pronouncing the Greek took place; the rather, because Gardiner was in disgrace, and Cheek and Smith were in such power and authority: so great an influence had the interests of men in supporting the most speculative and indifferent things.—BURNET, GILBERT, 1681, *The History of the Reformation of the Church of England, ed. Nares, vol.* II, *pt.* ii, *bk.* i, *p.* 192.

He happens, indeed, to be the very person who has the credit of amending the English style of writing, as well as the language; and that he contributed to the amendment of both is beyond dispute, though some of his improvements were never generally adopted.—NARES, EDWARD, 1828, *Memoirs of Lord Burghley, vol.* I, *p.* 251, *note.*

A refined critic of our language then was the learned Sir John Cheke, who at this early period considered that the English language was capable of preserving the utmost purity of style, and he was jealously awake to its slightest violations. —DISRAELI, ISAAC, 1841, *Vicissitudes of the English Language, Amenities of Literature.*

Is perhaps the first Englishman in whose prose style the influence of a familiarity with classical literature is fully and clearly manifested.—MARSH, GEORGE P., 1862, *The Origin and History of the English Language, etc., p.* 521.

Cheke was unquestionably one of the most learned men of his age. He was a felicitous translator and a judicious imitator of the ancient classical authors. . . . He failed in his attempt to introduce a phonetic method of spelling English. He is described as beneficent, charitable, and communicative. It has been said that he was a libertine, but there seems to be no ground for the imputation. —COOPER, THOMPSON, 1887, *Dictionary of National Biography, vol.* X, *p.* 181.

Nicholas Udall

C. 1506–C. 1557

Author of the earliest English comedy, born in Hampshire, was admitted a scholar of Corpus, Oxford, took his B. A. in 1524, and became the stern master of Eton and of Westminster, and canon of Windsor. His translations from Erasmus and Peter Martyr, his "Flovres for Latin Spekynge" (from Terence), or his Latin plays ("De Papatu, Ezekias") would never have preserved his name without his "Ralph Roister Doister," a merry comedy in the manner of Plautus, licensed in 1566. Editions are by Durant Cooper (1847) and Arber (1869).—PATRICK AND GROOME, *eds.*, 1897, *Chambers's Biographical Dictionary, p.* 931.

PERSONAL

From Powles I went, to Aeton sent,
To learne straight wayes, the Latin phraise,
Where fiftie three stripes giuen to mee,
  at once I had:
For faut but small, or none at all,
It came to passe, thus beat I was,
See Udall see, the mercy of thee,
  to mee poore lad.

—TUSSER, THOMAS, 1573, *Fiue Hundreth Points of Good Husbandrie, The Author's Life*

RALPH ROISTER DOISTER

"Ralph Roister Doister" has fortunately come down to us in a printed shape, although it is now not possible to settle from whose press it issued. In 1566, Thomas Hacket had a licence to print "a play, intitled "Rauf Ruyster Duster," and a copy, perhaps from his press, but without a title-page, (so that the printer's name cannot be ascertained,) was discovered in 1818, and after a limited reprint had been made of it by the Rev. Mr. Briggs, the original was deposited in the library of Eton College. That such a piece once had existence has been long known, and the allusions to it in later authors afford evidence of its popularity. . . . The scene of this comedy is laid in London, so that in no slight degree it is a representation of the manners of more polished society, exhibiting some of the peculiarities of thinking and acting in the metropolis at the period when it was written: in this respect it has a decided advantage over "Gammer Gurton's Needle," which only pretends to depict the habits of coarse, rustic life. "Ralph Roister Doister" is divided into acts and scenes, and is one of the earliest productions for the stage which has reached us in a printed shape, with these distinctions: the characters are thirteen, nine male and four female, and the performance

REGINALD POLE

From Painting by Titian.

could not have been concluded in less time than about two hours and a half, while few of the Morals we have examined would require more than about an hour for their representation. . . . The plot of "Ralph Roister Doister" is amusing and well constructed, with an agreeable intermixture of serious and comic dialogue, and a variety of character, to which no other piece of a similar date can make any pretension. When we recollect, that it was perhaps written in the reign of Henry VIII., we ought to look upon it as a masterly production. —COLLIER, JOHN PAYNE, 1831, *History of English Dramatic Poetry, vol.* II, *pp.* 448, 450, 460.

It is unquestionably superior to "Gorboduc" both in subject and language, and is not without merit, and possesses some life in the movement and action; but, as to progressive development of plot, the organic evolution of several elements out of the unity of a single leading idea—wherein consists the secret of dramatic form—of this it exhibits little more than the very first germ.—ULRICI, HERMANN, 1839, *Shakspeare's Dramatic Art, p.* 18.

The father of English Comedy.—COOPER, WILLIAM DURRANT, 1847, *Ralph Roister Doister, Introductory Memoirs, p.* xi.

It is impossible to say what may have been the single influence of "Roister Doister" on English comedy: the probability is that its influence was inconsiderable. It was not printed till 1566, and by that time the more powerful influences of early Italian comedy were beginning to operate. Besides, with all its cleverness and delicate humour, the spirit of "Roister Doister" is essentially boyish: it was written to be acted by boys, and its extravagant incidents are of a kind to draw shouts of delight from boys. There are shrewd touches of worldly wisdom in it; but, as a whole, it has not the robustness of comedy framed for the enjoyment of full-grown men and women.—MINTO, WILLIAM, 1874–85, *Characteristics of English Poets, p.* 141.

The composition of a scholar, who has studied Terence and Plautus to good purpose. . . . The conduct of the piece is spirited and easy. The author's art, though refined by scholarship, is homely. Between "Ralph Roister Doister" and "The Merry Wives of Windsor" there is, in point of construction and conception, no immeasurable distance, although the one play is the work of mediocrity, the other of genius.—SYMONDS, JOHN ADDINGTON, 1884, *Shakspere's Predecessors in the English Drama, pp.* 203, 204.

Is amusing and not offensive.—SAINTSBURY, GEORGE, 1895, *Social England, ed. Traill, vol.* III, *p.* 339.

It is written in sufficiently brisk lines of no great regularity; and there are much duller plays. Ralph's courtship of Dame Christian Custance, who will have none of him, is lively. On the whole, the play leaves the impression that Udall was more than a mere imitator of Plautus, but it is only the school exercise of a clever man.—HANNAY, DAVID, 1898, *The Later Renaissance, p.* 231.

"Ralph Roister Doister" enjoys the distinction of being the earliest English comedy known, and, in the capacity of its author, Udall is universally recognised as one of the most notable pioneers in the history of English dramatic literature.—LEE, SIDNEY, 1899, *Dictionary of National Biography, vol.* LVIII, *p.* 9.

Reginald Pole

1500–1558

Born at Stourton Castle, Staffordshire, England, March 3, 1500: died at London, Nov. 18, 1558. An English Roman Catholic prelate. He was the son of Sir Richard Pole and Margaret, countess of Salisbury, niece of Edward IV. He entered Magdalen College, Oxford, and at the age of 19 went to Padua to complete his education, returning in 1525. In 1532 he went again to Italy, and was created cardinal Dec. 22, 1536. He quarreled with Henry VIII., who caused a bill of attainder to be passed against him and set a price on his head. His mother was thrown into the Tower and beheaded. In 1545 he was a legate-president of the Council of Trent. On the death of Edward VI. he was sent to England to assist Queen Mary. Pole, who was only in deacon's orders, desired to marry the queen, and she for a time favored the project, but it was finally abandoned. After the burning of Cranmer, Pole was ordained priest, and on March 22, 1556, was consecrated archbishop of Canterbury. His legation as papal ambassador to England was canceled by Paul IV. His death occurred on the day after that of the queen. He was largely responsible for the persecution of Protestants during her reign.—SMITH, BENJAMIN E., *ed.*, 1894–97, *The Century Cyclopedia of Names, p.* 815.

PERSONAL

Such a one as, for his wisdom, joined with learning, virtue, and godliness, all the world seeketh and adoreth. In whom it is to be thought that God hath chosen a special place of habitation. Such is his conversation adorned with infinite godly qualities, above the ordinary sort of men. And whosoever within the realm liketh him worst, I would he might have with him the talk of one half-hour. It were a right stony heart that in a small time he could not soften.—MASON, SIR JOHN, 1554? *Letter to Queen Mary, MS.*

He still lives an overthrower of evangelical truth and a most impious betrayer of his country, advising the Emperor that his first care should be to bring all England into his power. May our omnipotent Lord God confound him with all his shaven and anointed ones. Amen.—BALE, JOHN, 1557, *Scriptorum Illustrium Majoris Britanniæ.*

The same daye Reygnold Poole, Cardinall, and not long before made Archbishop of Canterbury, departed this life, doubtfull whether by naturall disease, or by violence of griefe, or by some other strange inforcement. . . . Hee was learned and eloquent, of noe comely presence, but of good grace in delivering his speach: herewith haughty, ambitious, and vehement in the pursuite of his purposes. Whereupon, as he had been formerly impatient for not atteyning to the full degrees of his desires and hopes, so now, most of all, in fore-seeing the abatement of his honour, and the alteratione of the relligeone which hee did professe; for establishment whereof, in former times, he had practised so farr that he had reasone to conceive he could not be indured in the change.—HAYWARD, SIR JOHN, 1612?, *Annals of the First Four Years of the Reign of Queen Elizabeth, ed. Bruce, p.* 3.

The Cardinal was not a man made to raise a fortune, being, by the greatness of his birth and his excellent virtues, carried far above such mean designs. He was a learned, modest, humble, and good-natured man; and had indeed such qualities, and such a temper, that, if he could have brought the other bishops to follow his measures, or the Pope and Queen to approve of them, he might have probably done much to have reduced this nation to popery again. But God designed better things for it: so he gave up the Queen to the bloody counsels of Gardiner, and the rest of the clergy. It was the only thing in which she was not led by the Cardinal. But she imputed his opinion in that particular, rather to the sweetness of his temper, than to his wisdom and experience: and he, seeing he could do nothing of what he projected in England, fell into a languishing, first of his mind, that brought after it a decay of his health, of which he died.—BURNET, GILBERT, 1681, *The History of the Reformation of the Church of England, ed. Nares, vol.* II, *pt.* ii, *bk.* ii, *p.* 575.

He was a man of great learning and of great humanity, very modest and obliging, and very well qualified for publick employ. He was of a midling stature, fresh-colour'd, and had eyes very lively and sparkling, and a cheerful look. . . . He was buried fourty Days after his Death in a Leaden Coffin on the North-side of *Becket's* Crown, where is a Table-Monument of Brick Plaister'd over and Painted, and against the Wall a Painting of the Resurrection, a Sepulchre, twelve Angels, our God in Hebrew written, and Angels supporting the Cardinal's Arms.—DART, JOHN, 1726, *History and Antiquities of the Cathedral Church of Canterbury, pp.* 169, 171.

The benign character of this prelate, the modesty and humanity of his deportment, made him be universally beloved; insomuch that in a nation where the most furious persecution was carried on, and where the most violent religious factions prevailed, entire justice, even by most of the reformers, has been done to his merit. —HUME, DAVID, 1762, *The History of England, vol.* III, *ch.* xxxvii.

He was of middle stature, and of a healthy rather than robust constitution; though he was sometimes subject to a defluxion which fell on his arm and caused an inflamation in his right eye. His complexion was fair, mixed with an agreeable vermillion, and his beard and hair in his youth, of a light colour, his countenance was open and serene, enlivened with a cheerful and pleasant eye, the index of his mind, which was unsuspecting, honest, and benevolent.—PHILLIPS, THOMAS, 1764–67, *The History of the Life of Reginald Pole.*

The cardinal was a man of letters, polished in manners and virtuous in mind, generous, humane, and to a certain extent liberal in feeling. Yet religion made him a traitor to his sovereign and benefactor, a scurrilous libeller, and a persecutor even unto death of those who dissented from his creed. For though it may be true that he did not urge on the persecution, he always assented to it; and not a week before his death, five persons, the last of the victims whom his own certificate had given over to the secular arm, were burnt in his diocese.—KEIGHTLEY, THOMAS, 1837–59, *The History of England, vol.* I, *p.* 456.

To a natural kindness of temper he united an urbanity and a refinement of manners, derived from familiar intercourse with the most polished society of Europe. His royal descent entitled him to mix on terms of equality with persons of the highest rank, and made him feel as much at ease in the court as in the cloister. His long exile had opened to him an acquaintance with man as he is found in various climes, while as a native-born Englishman, he perfectly understood the prejudices and peculiar temper of his own countrymen. "Cardinal Pole," says the Venetian minister, "is a man of unblemished nobility, and so strict in his integrity, that he grants nothing to the importunity of friends. He is so much beloved, both by prince and people, that he may well be styled the king where all is done by his authority."—PRESCOTT, WILLIAM H., 1855, *History of the Reign of Philip the Second of Spain, vol.* I, *p.* 131.

The cultured and gentle Reginald Pole. —WELLS, J., 1897, *Oxford and Its Colleges, p.* 167.

GENERAL

As concerning the king's cause, master Raynolde Poole hath written a book much contrary to the king's purpose, with such wit, that it appeareth that he might be for his wisdom of the council to the king's grace; and of such eloquence, that if it were set forth and known to the common people, I suppose it were not possible to persuade them to the contrary. The Principal intent whereof is, that the king's grace should be content to commit his great cause to the judgment of the pope; wherein meseemeth he lacketh much judgment. But he (per)suadeth that with such goodly eloquence, both the words and sentence, that he were like to persuade many: but me he persuadeth in that point nothing at all. But in many other things he satisfieth me very well.—CRANMER, THOMAS, 1531? *Letter to Thomas Boleyn, Strype's Memorials of Cranmer, Appendix* i.

This Pasquil is an Author eminent on many accounts. First, for his self-concealment, being *noscens omnia, & notus nemini.* Secondly, for his intelligence, who can display the deeds of midnight at high noon, as if he hid himself in the holes of their bed-staves, knowing who were Cardinals' Children better than they knew their Fathers. Thirdly, for his unpartial boldness. He was made all of tongue and teeth, biting whate'er he touch'd, and it bled whate'er he bit; yea, as if a General Council and Pasquil were only above the Pope, he would not stick to tell where he trod his holy sandals awry. Fourthly, for his longevity, having lived (or rather lasted) in Rome some hundreds of years, whereby he appears no particular person, but a successive Corporation of Satyrists. Lastly, for his impunity, escaping the Inquisition; whereof some assign this reason, because hereby the Court of Rome comes to know her faults, or rather to know that their faults are known; which makes Pasquil's Converts (if not more honest) more wary in their behaviour. . . . Yet afterwards he became Alterious Orbis Papa, when made Arch-bishop of Canterbury by Queen Mary. He was a person free from passion, whom none could anger out of his ordinary temper. His youthful Books were full of the Flowers of Rhetorick; whilst the withered stalkes are only found in the writings of his old Age, so dry their style, and dull their conceit. —FULLER, THOMAS, 1662, *The Worthies of England, ed. Nichols, vol.* II, *p.* 305.

His learning and eloquence were remarkable, while his perfect knowledge of the Latin language was unique. If certain critics have regarded his style as somewhat diffuse; others, again admit that, even when he was wrong, it was so perfect and graceful alike in its simplicity and force, that it scarcely seemed capable of improvement. The long list of his works, which stands at the close of this chapter —many of them exceedingly rare—proves that both in dogmatic and moral theology, in history, biography, politics, and law, he was a very master in the Church Universal. Few prelates of his day did more to undermine error and establish and settle his readers in the Faith. His great and chief treatise, "On the Unity of the Church," a very masterpiece of reasoning, is full of divine wisdom, carefully set forth with perfect truth, much skill, and the greatest prudence.—LEE, FREDERICK GEORGE, 1888, *The Life of Cardinal Pole, p.* 249.

Another fatal book which belongs to this period is "Pro unitate ecclesiæ ad Henricum VIII.," written by Reginald Pole in the secure retreat of Padua, in which the author compares Henry to Nebuchadnezzar, and prays the Emperor of Germany to direct his arms against so heretical a Christian, rather than against the Turks. Secure in his retreat at the Papal Court, Pole did not himself suffer on account of his book, but the vengeance of Henry fell heavily upon his relations in England.—DITCHFIELD, P. H., 1894, *Books Fatal to Their Authors, p.* 122.

As a writer Pole's style is verbose, but he never cared for literary fame. None of his writings were penned with a mere literary aim, except his early anonymous life of Longolius.—GAIRDNER, JAMES, 1896, *Dictionary of National Biography, vol.* XLVI, *p.* 45.

George Cavendish

1500-1561?

George Cavendish, the biographer of Wolsey, was born about 1500, and became Wolsey's gentleman-usher at least as early as 1527. In attendance upon his great master till the end (November 28, 1530, he afterwards retired to his house at Glemsford, in Suffolk, where he lived quietly with his wife, a niece of Sir Thomas More, till the close of his own life in 1561 or 1562. The best edition of his "Life of Cardinal Wolsey" is Singer's (1815), reprinted with a good introduction in Morley's "Universal Library" (1886).—PATRICK AND GROOME, *eds.*, 1897, *Chambers's Biographical Dictionary, p.* 192.

LIFE OF WOLSEY

The reason of this multiplication of copies by the laborious process of transcription, seems to have been this: the work was composed in the days of Queen Mary by a zealous catholic, but not committed to the press, during her short reign. It contained a very favourable representation of the conduct of a man who was held in but little esteem in the days of her successor, and whom it was then almost treason to praise. The conduct of several persons was reflected on who were flourishing themselves, or in their immediate posterity, in the court of Queen Elizabeth: and it contained also the freest censures of the Reformation, and very strong remarks upon the conduct and character of Anne Boleyn, the Cardinal's great enemy. It is probable that no printer could be found who had so little fear of the Star-Chamber before his eyes as to venture the publication of a work so obnoxious; while such was the gratification which all persons of taste and reading would find in it, from its fidelity, its curious minuteness, its lively details, and above all, from that unaffected air of sweet natural eloquence in which it is composed, that many among them must have been desirous of possessing it.—HUNTER, REV. JOSEPH, 1814, *Who wrote Cavendish's Life of Wolsey? ed. Singer, vol.* II, *p.* xxvii.

Though Cavendish was a friendly witness, he yet evidently recorded with fidelity and accuracy what he actually saw and heard. His memoirs of Wolsey, for that is the real character of the work, are of great value, therefore, to the historian, as containing authentic information on many important points connected with that reign. The work, moreover, is written in a sort of gossiping, conversational style, that makes it pleasant reading. Another circumstance gives special value to this work. His account of Henry and Wolsey was the one followed by Shakespeare, in the play of Henry VIII., many of the passages in Shakespeare being Cavendish's prose turned into verse.—HART, JOHN S., 1872, *A Manual of English Literature, p.* 57.

For a long time there was some uncertainty about the authorship, whether it was the work of George Cavendish or of his better known brother William. The question was settled in 1814, by Rev. Joseph Hunter of Bath, in a pamphlet, "Who wrote Cavendish's Life of Wolsey?" which is reprinted in vol. ii, of Singer's edition. Hunter proved satisfactorily by internal evidence that George, not William, Cavendish was Wolsey's usher, and consequently author of the book. . . . It is the production of a refined, pious, and gentle nature, which looks back over many years of quiet melancholy upon a period when he too had borne a part in great affairs. The view of Wolsey taken by Cavendish is substantially the same as that of Shakespeare, and it is by no means improbable that Shakespeare had read Cavendish in manuscript. Cavendish writes with the fullest admiration for Wolsey and sympathy with his aims; but reflection has taught him the pathetic side of all worldly aims. . . . The refinement, the simplicity, the genuine goodness of the writer is present at every page. The fulness of portraiture, the clearness of personal details, the graceful description, the reserve shown in drawing from memories of a time long past and outlived, give the book a distinction of its own, and place it high among English biographies.—CREIGHTON, MANDELL, 1887, *Dictionary of National Biography, vol.* IX, *pp.* 346, 347.

George Cavendish, in the writing of this book, which is one of the most interesting pieces of biography in English literature, was looking back upon what he had known thirty years before, with the reflection of ripe years to soften all; and he made of it one harmonious picture of the vanity of that ambition through which, perhaps, he had himself partly learnt the blessedness of being little. Old memories of love and duty temper the religious spirit in which Wolsey's faithful servant, grey with years that had slipped by since his master's death, shaped what he had known into a picture of life so single and so true that the direct suggestion to Shakespeare of his play of "King Henry VIII." may have come from the reading of George Cavendish's "Life of Wolsey."—MORLEY, HENRY, 1892, *English Writers, vol.* VIII, *p.* 252.

Nicholas Grimoald

1519—1562.

Born in Huntingdonshire (at "Brownshold," according to his own statement), 1519; died about 1562. An English writer, the contributor of 40 poems to the first edition of "Tottel's Miscellany" (of which he was, perhaps, the editor), many of which were omitted from the second edition. He also published a translation of Cicero's "De Officiis." He was probably of Italian parentage (son of a certain Gianbatista Grimaldi), studied at Cambridge and Oxford, and was chaplain to Bishop Ridley.—SMITH, BENJAMIN E., *ed.*, 1894–97, *The Century Cyclopedia of Names, p.* 461.

I have taken more pains to introduce this Nicholas Grimoald to the reader's acquaintance, because he is the second English poet after lord Surrey, who wrote in blank-verse. Nor is it his only praise, that he was the first who followed in this new path of versification. To the style of blank-verse exhibited by Surrey he added new strength, elegance, and modulation. In the disposition and conduct of his cadencies, he often approaches to the legitimate structure of the improved blank-verse: but we cannot suppose, that he is entirely free from those dissonancies and asperities, which still adhered to the general character and state of our diction. . . . Grimoald, as a writer of verses in rhyme, yields to none of his contemporaries, for a masterly choice of chaste expression, and the concise elegancies of didactic versification. Some of the couplets, in his poem, "In Praise of Moderation," have all the smartness which marks the modern style of sententious poetry, and would have done honour to Pope's ethic epistles.—WARTON, THOMAS, 1778–81, *History of English Poetry, sec.* xl.

His principal claim to a place amongst English poets rests upon the distinction to which he is fairly entitled as the second writer who attempted blank verse in our language. The two pieces of this kind he has given us are, "The Death of Zoroas," and "Marcus Tullius Cicero's Death," which Warton seems to treat as original compositions, but which are really translations, — the former from the "Alexandried" of Philip Gaultier, and the latter from Beza. The versification, however, is his own; and certainly contrasts favourably with that of Surrey, upon which it presents a marked improvement in art and power. He is seldom so sweet as Surrey, but his modulations are more varied and skilful, and in vigour and elevation he far surpasses him. The structure of the lines in these pieces is so dexterous, and the diction so effective, that it is not easy to believe they were written in the very infancy of this form of verse.—BELL, ROBERT, 1854, *ed., Poetical Works of Surrey, p.* 208.

Nicholas Grimald is chiefly remembered as the author of a considerable quantity of verse, preserved in "Tottel's Miscellany" with that of Wyatt and Surrey, and not altogether unworthy of the companionship. He is entitled however to an equally distinguished position in the history of the English drama, as the author of the first extant tragedy. For such, beyond question, though it has scarcely been recognised, in his "Archipropheta, sive Johannes Baptista," printed at Köln in 1548, probably performed at Oxford in the previous year.—HERFORD, CHARLES H., 1886, *Studies in the Literary Relations of England and Germany in the Sixteenth Century, p.* 113.

Nicholas Grimoald's blank-verse . . . is superior to Surrey's. There is more spontaneity, more *go* in it; and it does not show so much metre consciousness as is always present in Surrey's.—CORSON, HIRAM, 1892, *A Primer of English Verse, p.* 188.

Arthur Brooke

D. 1563

Arthur Broke or Brooke, (died 1563), translator, was the author of "The Tragicall Historye of Romeus and Iulieit written first in Italian by Bandell, and nowe in English by Ar. Br. In ædibus Richard Tottelli." The colophon runs: "Imprinted at London in Flete Strete within Tremble barre at the signe of the hand and starre of Richard Tottill, the xix day of Nouember An. do. 1562." The book was entered in the Stationers' Register late in 1562 as "The Tragicall History of the Romeus and Juliett with sonettes." The volume is mainly of interest as the source whence Shakespeare drew the plot of his tragedy of "Romeo and Juliet." It is written throughout in rhymed verse to alternate lines of twelve and fourteen syllables. Broke did not (as the title-page states) translate directly from the Italian of Bandello, but from the "Histoires Tragiques extraictes des'Œuvres de Bandel" (Paris, 1559), by Pierre Boaistuan surnamed Launay and Francois de Belle-Forest. Broke does not adhere very closely to his French original: he develops the character of the Nurse and alters the concluding scene in many important points, in all of which he is followed by Shakespeare.—LEE, SIDNEY, 1886, *Dictionary of National Biography, vol.* VI, *p.* 385.

ROMEUS AND JULIET

For there he shewde his cunning passing well,
When he the tale to English did translate.

—TUBERVILLE, GEORGE, 1567, *Epitaphs, Epigrams, Songs, and Sonnets.*

Those who have hitherto spoken of Brooke's poem, have not spoken of it as it deserves. . . . In general the tale is told with much simplicity, and the descriptions are sometimes elaborately minute, and afford very striking and graceful pictures. —COLLIER, JOHN PAYNE, 1843, *Shakespeare's Library, Introduction to Romeus and Juliet, vol.* II, *p.* iii.

Brooke declares that he had seen the same argument lately set forth on the stage, and there would thus appear to have been some early dramatic version of the theme which has not come down to us, though it may have been known to Shakspere, and used by him. In any case, Brooke's own poem must have furnished the basis for Shakspere's crowning treatment of the story. It was Brooke who first gave prominence to the character of the Nurse, and put into her mouth speeches which the dramatist followed in parts with curious fidelity. It was Brooke also who invented the scene of Romeo's despair in the Friar's cell after the murder of Tybalt, and it was he who called Friar Lawrence's messenger John instead of Anselm. Nor was "Romeus and Juliet" an unworthy model. It was a well-proportioned narrative, in long flowing couplets, consisting of an Alexandrine followed by a Septenar. This metre, which Surrey had made fashionable, was skillfully handled by Brooke, and in spite of overdone antithesis, and of occasional luxuriance of sensuous description, balanced by a vein of sententious moralizing, the poem was warmed with true pathos, and showed an eye for dramatic types and situations. But dominating every other personality is that of Fortune, who sports with her victims as she pleases, lifting them to a height only afterwards to cast them down in her rage. The same conception of Fortune was inspiring at almost the same date "The Mirror for Magistrates," and it should certainly be borne in mind in the consideration of the play. —BOAS, FREDERICK S., 1896, *Shakspere and his Predecessors, p.* 200.

This poem is composed in rhymed iambic verses of twelve and fourteen syllables alternately, whose rhythm indeed jogs somewhat heavily along, but is not unpleasant and not too monotonous. The method of narration is very artless, loquacious, and diffuse; it resembles the narrative style of a clever child, who describes with minute exactitude and circumstantiality, going into every detail, and placing them all upon the same plane. —BRANDES, GEORGE, 1898, *William Shakespeare, A Critical Study, vol.* I, *p.* 87.

John Bale

1495–1563

An English theologian and dramatist; born at Cove, Suffolk, Nov. 21, 1495; died at Canterbury, November 1563. Originally a Catholic, he became Protestant bishop of Ossory, Ireland (1552). Besides numerous controversial works, he wrote in Latin a "Catalogue of the Illustrious Writers of Great Britain" (1548–49), the first history of English literature, and a number of interludes and moralities (i. e., religious plays) in the interest of Protestantism, the most important of these being the historical drama "King John." On account of his bad temper he was known as "Bilious Bale." Select works, Cambridge, 1849.—WARNER, CHARLES DUDLEY, *ed.* 1897, *Library of the World's Best Literature, vol.* XXIX, *p.* 38.

KING JOHN

This early application of historical events of itself is a singular circumstance, but it is the more remarkable when we recollect that we have no drama in our language of that date in which personages connected with, and engaged in, public affairs are introduced. . . . Bale's play, therefore, occupies an intermediate place between moralities and historical plays. . . . On this account, if on no other, "Kynge Johan" deserves the special attention of literary and poetical antiquaries.—COLLIER, JOHN PAYNE, 1838, *ed. Kynge Johan, Preface, pp.* viii, ix

The "Kynge Johan" is the most original of Bale's works. It is easy however to trace this and that element in it to foreign suggestion. The famous "Satire of the Three Estates," for instance, which became known in England soon after its performance in 1539, at the earliest, and must have dazzled many others beside Bale with its polish and wealth of language,—evidently supplied the hint of the corresponding three classes of John's subjects. The spiritual and temporal lords and the burgesses, and the suffering John Common-weale who pleads his wrongs before them, are the principal objects in Lyndsay's satire; with Bale they are less important, but their resemblance is unmistakable. Lyndsay wrote as a high-minded layman, Bale as before all things an ardent churchman. To Lyndsay the worst of ecclesiastical abuses was the legalised oppression of the poor; to Bale this was but an incident of the appalling "Babylonian captivity" from which the true Church, as he thought, had just broken free. Of more importance, in my view, was another influence. It appears to me clear that the "Kynge Johan" owes much of its peculiar construction to a deliberate imitation of the "Pammachius," and that it was this imitation which finally emancipated Bale from his clumsy efforts to build a Protestant drama on the ruins of the Catholic mystery.—HERFORD, CHARLES H., 1886, *Studies in the Literary Relations of England and Germany in the Sixteenth Century, p.* 135.

Its right to be regarded as the first of our historical dramas has even been denied, on the plea that it is only a didactic interlude with a historical subject. This seems a little hard, for Bale is surely entitled to the credit of seeing that the didactic interlude—that is to say, the play in the only state it had then reached—was capable of being applied to historical subjects, and so becoming the historic play in time. His object here, as in all his other literary work, was no doubt polemical—to advance the cause of the Reformation by exhibiting the patriotic objection to the power of the Pope; and his play does not exhibit much dramatic grasp. But he had already written Protestant mysteries, and evidently had a pretty clear inkling of the popularity and possibilities of the drama.—SAINTSBURY, GEORGE, 1898, *A Short History of English Literature, p.* 227.

GENERAL

Good aged Bale, that with thy hoary heares
Dost yet persyste to turne the paynefull Booke,
O happye man! that hast obtaynde suche yeares,
And leavst not yet on papers pale to looke:
Gyve over now to beate thy weryed braine,
And rest thy pen that long hath laboured sore.
For aged men unfyt, sure, is suche paine,
And the(e) beseems to laboure now no more;
But thou, I thynke, Don Platoes part will playe,
With Booke in hand to have thy dyeng daye.
—GOOGE, BARNABE, 1563, *Eglogs Epytaphes and Sonettes.*

Probably he was a person more learned than discreet, fitter to write than to govern, as unable to command his own passion; and *biliosus Balæus* passeth for his true Character.—FULLER, THOMAS, 1662, *The Worthies of England, ed. Nichols, vol.* II, *p.* 332.

Lying Bale.—HEARNE, THOMAS, 1729, *Reliquiæ Hearnianæ, ed. Bliss, vol.* III, *p.* 31.

The fashion of acting mysteries appears to have expired with this writer. . . . A low vein of abusive burlesque, which had more virulence than humour, seems to have been one of Bale's talents. . . . Next to exposing the impostures of popery, literary history was his favorite pursuit: and his most celebrated performance is his account of the British writers. But this work, perhaps originally undertaken by Bale as a vehicle of his sentiments in religion, is not only full of misrepresentations and partialities, arising from his religious prejudices, but of general inaccuracies, proceeding from negligence or misinformation. Even those more ancient Lives which he transcribes from Leland's commentary on the same subject, are often interpolated with false facts, and impertinently marked with a misapplied zeal for reformation. He is angry with many authors, who flourished before the thirteenth century, for being catholics.—WARTON, THOMAS, 1778–81, *History of English Poetry, sec.* xli.

A foul-mouth'd railer against, and bitter enemy to the papists.—RITSON, JOSEPH, 1802, *Bibliographia Poetica, p.* 123.

Obliged to fly from England on the fall of his first patron Cromwell, he employed some part of the leisure forced on him by his exile, in the composition of several Miracle-Plays, all of which were intended for instructing the people in the errors and abuses of Popery and in the distinctive tenets of the Reformation. Their chief merit consists in their being almost entirely free from the levities which degrade other works of the kind: and they scarcely seem, now, to possess a literary excellence justifying the satisfaction they gave to their venerable author, who has carefully enumerated them in his own list of his works.—SPALDING, WILLIAM, 1852–82, *A History of English Literature, p.* 184.

A foul-mouthed ruffian.—FROUDE, JAMES ANTHONY, 1856–70, *History of England, vol.* VII, *ch.* ii, *p.* 179.

His industry and energy seem never to have flagged; and although much indebted to Leland for the groundwork of his bibliographical collections, yet these were enlarged and improved by his own extensive researches. He was the first also to point out the value of the early English historians, and to urge in the most strenuous language their publication.—MADDEN, SIR FREDERICK, 1866, *Matthæi Parisiensis Historia Anglorum, Preface, p.* 23.

John Bale was indeed a railer, and not a very modest or clean one. The license of his day in the matter of expression was great, but he exceeded it. He smote with the readiest and most trenchant weapons he could find, and he did not stop to consider whether they were fashioned in the correctest taste.—PERRY, GEORGE G., 1869, *John Bale, Contemporary Review, vol.* 10, *p.* 96

Occasionally, however, the dreary waste is relieved by a sparkling interval. There are two songs in "Lusty Juventus" which step out of their lifeless surroundings, and challenge comparison with the new poetry of the period. They appeal to us as things of native growth against the imports of the Italian school. They are genuinely English, and have something of the quality of the snatches of song interspersed through the mature Elizabethan drama. —MINTO, WILLIAM, 1874–85, *Characteristics of English Poets, p.* 134.

Bale was a man of great theological and historical learning, and of an active mind. But he was a coarse and bitter controversialist and awakened equal bitterness amongst his opponents. None of the writers of the reformation time in England equalled Bale in acerbity. He was known as "Bilious Bale." His controversial spirit was a hindrance to his learning, as he was led away by his prejudices into frequent misstatements. The most important work of Bale was a history of English literature, which first appeared in 1548 under the title "Illustrium Majoris Britanniæ Scriptorum Summarium in quinque centurias divisum." It is a valuable catalogue of the writings of the authors of Great Britain chronologically arranged. . . . The plays of Bale are doggerel, and are totally wanting in decorum.—CREIGHTON, MANDELL, 1885, *Dictionary of National Biography, vol.* III, *p.* 42.

Richard Edwards

1523?–1566

Richard Edwards, 1523–1566? an early dramatic writer, educated at Corpus Christi College, and Christ Church, Oxford, is best known as the designer and principal contributor to "The Paradyse of Daynty Deuises," and as the author of "Damon and Pythias," certainly one of the first English dramas upon a classical subject. This tragedy—published London, 1570, '71, '82, 4to—was acted before Queen Elizabeth in 1566. Her majesty also witnessed the performance of Edwards's "Comedy of Palæmon and Arcyte" in Christ Church Hall, 1566.—ALLIBONE, S. AUSTIN, 1854–58, *Dictionary of English Literature, vol.* I, *p.* 547.

Devyne Camenes, that with your sacred food
Have fed and fosterde up from tender yeares
A happye man, that in your favour stoode,
Edwardes, in Courte that can not fynde his feares,
Your names be blest, that in the present age
So fyne a head by Arte have framed out,
Whom some hereafter, healpt by Poets rage,
Perchaunce may matche, but none shall passe (I doubt).
O Plautus! yf thou wert alyve agayne,
That Comedies so fynely dydste endyte;
Or Terence thou, that with thy pleasaunt brayne
The hearers mynde on stage dydst much delyght,
What would you say, syrs, if you should beholde,
As I have done, the doyngs of this man?
No worde at all, to sweare I durst be bolde,
But burne with teares that which with myrth began;
I meane your bookes, by which you gate your name
To be forgot, you wolde commit to flame.
Alas! I wolde, Edwards, more tell thy prayse,
But at thy name my muse amased stayes.
—GOOGE, BARNABE, 1563, *Eglogs, Epytaphes, and Sonettes.*

In the beginning of Queen Elizabeth, he was made one of the Gentlemen of her Chapel, and Master of the Children there, being then esteemed not only an excellent Musician, but an exact Poet, as many of his compositions in Music (for he was not only skill'd in the practical but theoretical part) and Poetry do shew, for which he was highly valued by those that knew him, especially his associates in Lincolns Inn (of which he was a member, and in some respects an Ornament) and much lamented by them, and all ingenious Men of his time, when he died. — WOOD, ANTHONY, 1691–1721, *Athenæ Oxonensis, vol.* I, *f.* 151.

Edwards, besides that he was a writer of regular dramas, appears to have been a contriver of masques, and a composer of poetry for pageants. In a word, he united all those arts and accomplishments which minister to popular pleasantry: he was the first fiddle, the most fashionable sonnetteer, the readiest rhymer, and the most facetious mimic, of the court. . .

If I should be thought to have been disproportionately prolix in speaking of Edwards, I would be understood to have partly intended a tribute of respect to the memory of a poet, who is one of the earliest of our dramatic writers after the reformation of the British stage.—WARTON, THOMAS, 1778–81, *History of English Poetry, sec.* lii.

His popularity seems to have altogether arisen from those pleasing talents, of which no specimens could be transmitted to posterity; and which prejudiced his partial cotemporaries in favour of his poetry.—BRYDGES, SIR SAMUEL EDGERTON, 1800, *ed. Phillips' Theatrum Poetarum Anglicanorum, p.* 84.

It was nearly new, at the date when this piece was written, to bring stories from profane history upon the stage: "Damon and Pythias" was one of the earliest attempts of the kind; and at any other period, and without the Queen's extraordinary commendations, it may at least be doubted whether Edwards would have acquired an equal degree of notoriety. —COLLIER, JOHN PAYNE, 1831, *History of English Dramatic Poetry, vol.* iii, *p.* 6.

In the general estimation of his contemporaries, seems to have been accounted the greatest dramatic genius of his day, at least in the comic style. His "Damon and Pytheas" does not justify their laudation to a modern taste; it is a mixture of comedy and tragedy, between which it would be hard to decide whether the grave writing or the gay is the rudest and dullest. The play is in rhyme, but some variety is produced by the measure or length of the line being occasionally changed. . . . Edwards, however, besides his plays, wrote many other things in verse, some of which have an ease, and even an elegance that neither Surrey himself nor any other writer of that age has excelled. —CRAIK, GEORGE L., 1861, *A Compendious History of English Literature and of the English Language, vol.* I, *p.* 484.

Roger Ascham

1515—1568.

Roger Ascham, a celebrated English scholar and teacher, who flourished during the reigns of Henry VIII., Mary, and Elizabeth, was born in 1515, and died in 1568. He graduated at St. John's College, Oxford, in 1537, became a college tutor, and was appointed to read Greek in the public schools. In 1545, he published "Toxophilus," or the "School of Shooting," in which, as Dr. Johnson says, "he designed not only to teach the art of shooting, but to give an example of diction more natural and more truly English than was used by the common writers of that age." In 1548, he was appointed teacher of the learned languages to the lady Elizabeth, afterwards Queen, and continued to perform that service for two years. In 1553, he was appointed Latin secretary to Queen Mary, and was continued in the same office by Elizabeth, besides acting as her tutor in Latin and Greek. His most noted work is "The Scholemaster, or a Plain and Perfite Way of teaching Children to understand, read, and write the Latin Tonge," published by his widow in 1571.—KIDDLE AND SCHEM, *eds.*, 1877, *The Cyclopædia of Education, p.* 54.

PERSONAL

I had rather have thrown ten thousand pounds into the sea than have lost my Ascham.—QUEEN ELIZABETH, 1568.

O'er Ascham, withering in his narrow urn,
The Muses—English, Grecian, Roman—mourn;
Though poor, to greatness dear, to friendship just;
No scandal's self can taint his hallowed dust.

—BUCHANAN, GEORGE, 1582? *tr. Wrangham, Epitaph on Ascham, Cooper's Athenæ Cantabrigiensis.*

Ascham never had a robust or vigorous body, and his excuse for so many hours of diversion was his inability to endure a long continuance of sedentary thought. In the latter part of his life he found it necessary to forbear any intense application of the mind from dinner to bedtime, and rose to read and write early in the morning. He was for some years hectically feverish; and, though he found some alleviation of his distemper, never obtained a perfect recovery of his health. The immediate cause of his last sickness was too close application to the composition of a poem, which he purposed to present to the Queen on the day of her accession. To finish this, he forbore to sleep at his accustomed hours, till in December 1568 he fell sick of a kind of lingering disease, which Graunt has not named, nor accurately described. The most afflictive symptom was want of sleep, which he endeavoured to obtain by the motion of a cradle. Growing every day weaker, he found it vain to contend with his distemper, and prepared to die with the resignation and piety of a true Christian.—JOHNSON, SAMUEL, 1763, *Preface to Ascham's Works.*

There was a primitive honesty, a kindly innocence, about this good old scholar, which give a personal interest to the homeliest details of his life. He had the rare felicity of passing through the worst of times without persecution and without dishonour. He lived with princes and princesses, prelates and diplomatists, without offence and without ambition. Though he enjoyed the smiles of royalty, his heart was none the worse, and his fortune little the better. He had that disposition which, above all things, qualifies the conscientious and successful teacher; for he delighted rather to discover and call forth the talents of others than to make a display of his own.—COLERIDGE, HARTLEY, 1833? *Biographia Borealis, p.* 293.

There are too many complaints of poverty in Ascham's letters to allow of our looking upon him as a man of exalted mind. Great men either bear privations bravely, or, engrossed in their own elevated pursuits, are not aware of their existence. It is much to be feared that the real truth of Ascham's character has still to be discovered. There are contradictions and inconsistencies in most men that it is not easy to reconcile or to account for.—GILES, REV. J. A., 1865, *ed., The Whole Works of Roger Ascham, vol.* I, *pt.* i, *p.* xcix.

He must have studied the art of keeping silence as well as the arts of speech. . . . He was full of American pluck, aptness, and industry; was known specially for his large gifts in language; a superb penman too, which was no little accomplishment in that day; withal, he excelled in athletics, and showed a skill with the long-bow which made credible the traditions about Robin Hood. They said he wasted time at this exercise; whereupon he wrote a defense of Archery, which under the name of "Toxophilus" has come down to our day—a model even now of good, homely, vigorous English.—MITCHELL, DONALD G., 1889, *English Lands Letters and Kings, From Celt to Tudor, p.* 198.

TOXOPHILUS
1545

He designed not only to teach the art of shooting, but to give an example of diction more natural and more truly English than was used by the common writers of that age, whom he censures for mingling exotic terms with their native language, and of whom he complains that they were made authors, not by skill or education, but by arrogance and temerity. He has not failed in either of his purposes.—JOHNSON, SAMUEL, 1763, *Preface to Ascham's Works.*

It affords some consolation to authors, who often suffer from neglect, to observe the triumph of an excellent book. Its first appearance procured him a pension from Henry the Eighth, which enabled him to set off on his travels. Subsequently, in the reign of Mary, when that eventful change happened in religion and in politics, adverse to Ascham, our author was cast into despair, and hastened to hide himself in safe obscurity. It was then that this excellent book (and a better at that time did not exist in the language) once more recommended its author: for Gardiner, the papal Bishop of Winchester, detected no heresy in the volume; and by his means, the Lords of the Council approving of it, the author was fully reinstated in royal favor. Thus Ascham twice owed his good fortune to his good book.—DISRAELI, ISAAC, 1841, *Roger Ascham, Amenities of Literature.*

SCHOLEMASTER

1570

The Scholemaster, or plaine and perfite way of teachyng children, to understand, write, and speake, the Latin tong, but specially purposed for the private brynging up of youth in Jentlemen and Noble mens houses, and commodious also for all such as have forgot the Latin tonge, and would, by themselves, without a Scholemaster, in short tyme, and with small paines, recover a sufficient habilitie to understand, write, and speake Latin. At London, printed by John Daye, dwelling over Aldersgate.—ASCHAM, ROGER, 1570, *The Scholemaster, ed. Giles, Title page.*

But although there was a great stir in education throughout this century, and several English books were published about it, we come to 1570 before we find anything that has lived till now. We then have Roger Ascham's "Scholemaster," a posthumous work brought out by Ascham's widow, and republished in 1571 and 1589. The book was then lost sight of, but reappeared, with James Upton as editor, in 1711, and has been regarded as an educational classic ever since.—QUICK, ROBERT HERBERT, 1868–90, *Essays on Educational Reformers, p.* 81.

After the lapse of more than three centuries his views are mainly in accordance with those of the best scholars of our day—UNDERWOOD, FRANCIS H., 1871, *A Hand-book of English Literature, British Authors, p.* 4.

Ascham's rhythm in the sentence and the paragraph is monotonous. He has plenty of balanced Euphuistic sentences, that help his coherence, but the balance is monotonous. And where else in the language but in the "Scholemaster" can be found an author who will write you *seven* consecutive paragraphs of exactly twenty-five sentences each, the group being followed by three paragraphs of just fifty sentences each? I half suspect that Ascham (or the printer) told those groups off on his fingers.—LEWIS, EDWIN HERBERT, 1894, *The History of the English Paragraph, p.* 80.

Although his method failed to gain currency, Ascham's "Scholemaster" at once took its permanent place as an English classic. The whole work abounds with choice anecdotes, admirable reflexions, pregnant sentiments from pagan authors scholarly criticisms; and exhibits throughout, moreover, a deep yet kindly estimate of the boy nature, which makes it one of the most suggestive and fascinating books in the English language, and justly entitles the author to the praise bestowed upon him by Gabriel Harvey, of being "a flowing spring of humanity."—MULLINGER, J. BASS, 1895, *Social England, ed. Traill, vol.* III, *p.* 97.

GENERAL

He had a facile and fluent Latine-style not like those who, counting obscurity to be elegancy, weed out all the hard words they meet in Authors): witness his "Epistles," which some say are the only Latine-ones extant of any Englishman, and if so, the more the pity. . . . In a word, his "Toxophilus" is accounted a good Book for *young men*, his "Schoolmaster" for *old men*, his "Epistles" for *all men.*—FULLER, THOMAS, 1662, *The Worthies of England, ed. Nichols, vol.* II. *p.* 516.

A man born and bred for that Age, which was to refine the *Greek* and *Latin* to a Politeness, and raise them to an Eloquence.—BOHUN, EDMUND, 1693, *The Character of Queen Elizabeth, p.* 4.

It must be owned that Ascham contributed very much to refine and improve the language, and, as he was an eminent scholar, to bring the practice of writing in it into repute.—HURD, RT. REV. RICHARD, 1808? *Commonplace Book, ed. Kilvert, p.* 307.

One of those men of genius born to create a new era in the history of their nation. The first English author who may be regarded as the founder of our *prose style* was Roger Ascham, the venerable parent of our *native literature*. . . . His pristine English is still forcible without pedantry, and still beautiful without ornament.—DISRAELI, ISAAC, 1812–13, *The Case of Authors Stated, Calamities and Quarrels of Authors.*

Ascham is a thorough bred philologist, and of the purest water. . . . I have unhesitatingly ranked Ascham among my more illustrious Bibliomaniacs—DIBDIN, THOMAS FROGNALL, 1824, *The Library Companion, note, p.* 587.

Old Ascham is one of the freshest, truest spirits I have met with; a scholar and writer, yet a genuine man—CARLYLE, THOMAS, 1830, *Letter, Correspondence of Macvey Napier, p.* 77

Ascham is plain and strong in his style, but without grace or warmth: his sentences have no harmony of structure. He stands, however, as far as I have seen, above all other writers in the first half of the Queen's reign.—HALLAM, HENRY, 1837–39, *Introduction to the Literature of Europe, pt.* ii, *ch.* vii, *par.* 9.

The writings of the learned and judicious Ascham possess, both in style and in matter, a value which must not be measured by their inconsiderable bulk. Their language is pure, idiomatic, vigorous English: they exhibit great variety of knowledge, remarkable sagacity, and sound common-sense.—SPALDING, WILLIAM, 1852–82, *A History of English Literature p.* 172.

A scholar possessed of a far greater familiarity with the classics than with either his own or with other modern literatures. Moreover, Ascham, although unusually liberal for his age, was not without his prejudices, and one of the strongest was his prejudice against Italy, which extended, in some degree, to her authors.—SCHELLING, FELIX E., 1891, *Poetic and Verse Criticism of the Reign of Elizabeth, p.* 11.

It is impossible to call Ascham an agreeable writer, and pure pedantry to insist upon his mastery of English. His efforts were all in an academic direction, and his suspicion of ornament was in diametric opposition to the instinct of the nation, as to be presently and in the great age abundantly revealed.—GOSSE, EDMUND, 1897, *Short History of Modern English Literature, p.* 79.

Ascham's is, in short, the first accomplished plain style in English—the first, that is to say, that, while deliberately aiming at a certain amount of rhetorical effect, rigidly eschews the production of that effect by any such means as elaborate, highly coloured, or quaint vocabulary, by unusual and invented tricks of arrangement, or by anything that can come under the phrases (often loosely used, but intelligible) of ornate, poetical, or impassioned prose.—SAINTSBURY, GEORGE, 1898, *A Short History of English Literature, p.* 240.

As a result of his humanistic training, became not only the first English man of letters, but also the first English classicist.—SPINGARN, JOEL ELIAS, 1899, *A History of Literary Criticism in the Renaissance, p.* 255.

Miles Coverdale

1488–1568

English bishop and Reformer; born probably at Cover-dale, in Yorkshire, in 1488; was educated at Cambridge, and became an Augustine monk in 1514. He was one of the first Englishmen who adopted the doctrines of the Reformed Church of England (1526). He left the convent and became an evangelist, and then went to the Continent. In 1535 he published an English translation of the Bible, which was reissued in 1537 with the royal sanction. The version of the Psalms is that of the present Prayer-book. This was the first entire Bible ever published in English. It is not a direct translation from the original text, but only a rendering from the German and Latin versions. It has, nevertheless, great merits, and its influence on the Authorized Version, especially in rhythm and style, is easily recognized. He edited the "Great Bible," or Cranmer's Bible (1540). In 1551 he was appointed Bishop of Exeter. On the accession of Mary in 1553 he was deprived of his office and imprisoned for a year. He was then permitted to take refuge on the Continent, whence he returned in 1558. He died in London and was buried Feb. 19, 1568. He also translated from the works of Luther, Calvin, Bullinger, and other Reformers. See his "Writings and Translations," edited for the Parker Society (2 vols., Cambridge, 1844-46).—ADAMS, CHARLES KENDALL, *ed.*, 1897, *Johnson's Universal Cyclopædia, vol.* II, *p.* 557.

I myself, and so did many hundreds beside me, hear the reverend father, M. Doctor Coverdale, of holy and learned memory, in a sermon at Paul's Cross, upon occasion of some slanderous reports that then were raised against his translation, declare his faithful purpose in doing the same; which after it was finished, and presented to King Henry VIII, of famous memory, and by him committed to divers bishops of that time to peruse, of which (as I remember) Stephen Gardiner was one; after they had kept it long in their hands, and the king was divers times sued unto for the publication thereof, at the last being called for by the king himself, they redelivered the book, and being demanded by the king what was their judgment of the translation, they answered that there were many faults therein. "Well," said the king, "but are there any heresies maintained thereby?" They answered, There were no heresies that they could find maintained thereby. "If there be no heresies," said the king, "then in God's name let it go abroad among our people." According to this judgment of the king, and the bishops, M. Coverdale defended his translation, confessing that he did now himself espy some faults, which if he might review it once over again, as he had done twice before, he doubted not but to amend, but for any heresy, he was sure there was none maintained by his translation. —FULKE, WILLIAM, 1580–9, *Defence of the Translation of the Bible, Parker Society ed, p.* 98.

A fair estimate of Coverdale's character is hardly possible on account of its striking contrast with that of Tyndale. He fell far behind the latter with respect to originality, boldness, knowledge of the original tongues of Scripture, and in the apparent motives leading to the work of translation. His intimate connection with a government, ordinarily so hostile to the Reformation, seems almost like truckling, compared with Tyndale's independence, and not infrequent defiance. But, undoubtedly, the two men were differently constituted by nature, and the conception of the reform to be accomplished was, in the one case, wholly seized and operative at once; in the other, a slow product of discipline and growth. Coverdale was nearly sixty years of age before he reached Tyndale's standard of ecclesiastical independence, and then no honors or emoluments of office could tempt him from the path of conscientious duty. . . . The influence of Coverdale's labors upon the translation of 1611, as it would be natural to expect, was but slight. His translation stands outside of the lineal history of the latter. The most that it did was to furnish a few ecclesiastical words, some of which might perhaps have been better omitted altogether.—BISSELL, EDWIN CONE, 1873, *The Historic Origin of the Bible, pp.* 41, 43.

Bishop Coverdale occupies among the English Reformers a somewhat analogous position to that of Coleridge among the English romantic poets. Each took a leading part in a movement mainly of German origin: each was conspicuous for the extent of his German culture and his personal sensitiveness to German influence. If Coleridge was a fragmentary Schelling, Coverdale, the translator of the Bible and singer of "Spiritual Songs," may be said to have groped along the path of Luther. He was one of the first English translators of the German theologians; Bulliger, Osiander, Jan of Campen, Wermüller, Luther himself, all owed something to his industry. As he worked at his translation of the Bible, the Zürich Bible lay open before him, and counted for more, as Dr. Ginsburg has shown, than either Vulgate, Septuagint, or Hebrew. . . . Coverdale was the one English lyric poet of his century who drew what may be called by courtesy his inspiration, neither from Italy nor from France, but from the equally great and varied stores of the songs of Germany; and, however completely he may have failed, he deserves on this account a moment's notice.—HERFORD, CHARLES H., 1884, *Coverdale's "Spiritual Songs" and the German "Kirchenlied," The Academy, May* 31, *vol.* XXV, *p.* 385.

The name of Coverdale will always be revered as that of a man who first made a complete translation of the Bible into English, but he was not a figure of marked historical interest. He was somewhat weak and timorous, and all through his life leaned on a more powerful nature. Barnes, Cromwell, Cranmer, and Grindal were successively his patrons. In the hour of trouble he was content to remain in obscurity, and left the crown of martyrdom to be earned by men of tougher fibre. But he was pious, conscientious, laborious, generous, and a thoroughly honest and good man. He knew German and Latin well, some Greek and Hebrew, and a little French. He did little original literary work. As a translator he was faithful and harmonious. He was fairly read in theology, and became more inclined to puritan ideas as his life wore on. All accounts agree in his remarkable popularity as a preacher. He was a leading figure during the progress of the reformed opinions, and had a considerable share in the introduction of German spiritual culture to English readers in the second quarter of the sixteenth century.—TEDDER, H. R., 1887, *Dictionary of National Biography, vol.* XII, *p.*369.

It is curious to note that Coverdale's style is less harmonious in his original writings than in his translations: his disposition was of the generous sort that delights in the embellishment of other men's work.—DODDS, JAMES MILLER, 1893, *English Prose, ed. Craik, vol.* I, *p.* 204.

John Jewell

1522–1571

Bishop of Salisbury in the reign of Queen Elizabeth, and a great polemical writer against Popery. He was born in 1522 at the village of Buden, near Ilfracombe, Devonshire; studied at Oxford; and in 1546 openly professed the tenets of the Reformers. Having obtained the living of Sunningwell, Berks, he distinguished himself by his zeal and assiduity as a parish priest; but, at the accession of Queen Mary to avoid prosecution as a heretic, he made his escape to the continent, and became vice-master of a college at Strasburg. On the death of Mary he returned to England, was received with great favour by her successor, and in 1560 he was raised to the bishopric of Salisbury. His principle work is entitled "An Apology for the Church of England," originally written in elegant Latin, but translated into every European language; and which, it is said, had more effect in promoting the Reformation than any other book ever published. He died in 1571.—CATES, WILLIAM L. R., *ed.* 1867, *A Dictionary of General Biography, p.* 566.

This Apology cometh to me in good season, as your Grace shall see by a letter received out of France this morning from our ambassador, which when you have read I beseech your grace to return. You may see how he would mingle policy and religion together. Surely he is wise and a good servant in this time. This book is negligently printed, and the margin would (sic) have had the common places marked. I mean to send five or six into France, and as many into Scotland.—CECIL, SIR WILLIAM, 1561, *Letter to Archbishop Parker, Correspondence of Matthew Parker, ed. Bruce and Perowne, p.* 161.

Was the worthiest divine that Christendom hath bred for some hundreds of years. —HOOKER, RICHARD, 1600? *Ecclesiastical Polity.*

A Jewel (sometimes taken for a single precious stone) is properly a collective of many, orderly set together to their best advantage. So several eminencies met in this worthy man; naturals, artificials, (amongst which I recount his studied memory, deserving, as well as Theodectes the sophister, the surname of *Mnemonicus,*) morals, but principally spirituals: so devout in the pew where he prayed, diligent in the pulpit where he preached, grave on the bench where he assisted, mild in the consistory where he judged, pleasant at the table where he fed, patient in the bed where he died, that well it were if, in relation to him, *secundum usum Sarum,* were made precedential to all posterity.—FULLER, THOMAS, 1655, *The Church History of Britain, bk.* ix, *sec.* iii, *par.* 2.

One of the greatest lights that the reformed Church of England hath produced. —WOOD, ANTHONY, 1691–1721, *Athenæ Oxonienses.*

Jewel's "Apology" is an account of the grounds of our separation from the Church of Rome, as maintained after the separation had finally taken place. It was publicly received and allowed, and has also a claim to the attention of the reader, both for its clearness of argument and elegance of language. —RANDOLPH, JOHN, 1792, *Enchiridion Theologicum.*

Methinks that I could trip o'er heaviest soil,
Light as a buoyant bark from wave to wave,
Were mine the trusty staff that JEWELL gave
To youthful HOOKER, in familiar style
The gift exalting, and with playful smile:
For thus equipped, and bearing on his head
The Donor's farewell blessing, can he dread
Tempest, or length of way, or weight of toil?
—WORDSWORTH, WILLIAM, 1821–22, *Ecclesiastical Sonnets, pt.* ii, xxxix.

This short book is written with spirit; the style is terse, the arguments pointed, the authorities much to the purpose, so that its effects are not surprising. This treatise is written in Latin; his "Defence of the Apology," a much more diffuse work, in English. Upon the merits of the controversy of Jewell with the Jesuit Harding, which this defence embraces, I am not competent to give any opinion: in length and learning, it far surpasses our earlier polemical literature.—HALLAM, HENRY, 1837-39, *Introduction to the Literature of Europe, pt.* ii. *ch.* ii, *par.* 35.

The contemporary of Archbishop Parker, Bishop Jewell, Bishop of Salisbury, with equal learning, united a more glowing style and richer eloquence. Jewell was indeed the most accomplished scholar who had yet appeared in the reformed Church of England.—CATTERMOLE, RICHARD, 1844, *The Literature of the Church of England.*

Jewell is eminent for his extensive learning, his sound views, and his Christian eloquence. All his works are valuable. . . . The finest Christian eloquence, deep learning, sound wisdom, and evangelical piety, mark the writings of this Reformer.—BICKERSTETH, EDWARD, 1844, *The Christian Student.*

Jewel's "Apology" is the most perfect expression of the peculiar position of the English Church. It is divided into six parts, and refutes the charges of heresy, godlessness, libertinism, apostasy from the Church, etc. In the doctrinal treatment he shows the influence of Calvin and Peter Martyr; and in the articles on the Person of Christ, the Power of the Keys, and the Sacraments, he is in perfect agreement with them. On the other hand, the doctrine of predestination is wanting; and in regard to justification, he says that our salvation depends entirely upon Christ, and not upon works. He makes no distinction between the visible and invisible Church. He teaches that there are three orders, but defines their functions in a Calvinistic sense, and grants to laymen the exercise of ministerial duties in cases of necessity. The statement is repeated again and again, that the English Reformation was only a return to the old true Catholic Church of the first centuries; and the charge of innovation he repels by affirming it of the Roman-Catholic Church, which had forsaken Christ and the Apostles and Fathers. The Scriptures are the ultimate rule of faith; and the Fathers are not our spiritual "lords, but our leaders."—SIGWART, CHRISTIAN, 1883? *Schaff-Herzog's Religious Encyclopaedia, vol.* II, *p.* 1178.

The "Apologia" is the first methodical statement of the position of the church of England against the church of Rome, and forms the groundwork of all subsequent controversy. In it Jewel sketched the doctrines and practice of the English church, defended them against the charges of heresy and disorder, justified the deviations from Roman belief and usage, explained the grounds on which the papal supremacy was not *de fide*, pointed out the long-felt need of a reformation, and claimed that, as it was impossible to proceed with it by means of a general council, national churches were at liberty to act through provincial synods. . . . The great interest attaching to Jewel's writings is the insight which they give into the process by which the anglican system was established on a logical basis. Jewel began his episcopate with decided leanings to Calvinism, and hoped that the Elizabethan church would develope in a Calvinistic direction. But he soon saw that the first necessity was to make good its position against the discontented adherents of the Marian church, and in arguing against them he discovered the strength of the Elizabethan system. When the puritan party began to press for further changes, and demanded the abolition of the surplice, Jewel vigorously opposed them in the interests of peace and order. He had unconsciously shifted his position, and was somewhat inconsistent.—PETERBOROUGH, BISHOP OF, 1892, *Dictionary of National Biography, vol.* XXIX, *p.* 380.

It is recorded of him that in his Oxford days his practice was to rise at four of the clock, and to continue his studies with but little intermission till ten at night. His culture was wide in its extent. . . . Jewel was certainly the most learned theologian who had yet appeared in the reformed Church of England; and from his copious stores later controversialists have freely drawn. It would be wearisome to quote the numerous testimonies to his commanding powers.—DOWDEN, JOHN, 1897, *Outlines of the History of the Theological Literature of the Church of England, pp.* 20, 28.

John Knox

1505–1572

Born, at Haddington, 1505. Educated at Haddington School. To Glasgow University, 25 Oct. 1522. Practiced as a notary in Haddington. Probably ordained Deacon. Private tutor, 1544 (?) –47. Received "call" as preacher at St. Andrews, 1547; preached Reformed doctrine. Prisoner in French galleys, July 1547 to Feb. 1549. Returned to England, 1549. Preached at Berwick, 1549–51. Prosecuted by Catholics, 1550; but prosecution abandoned. Preached at Newcastle, 1550–51. Chaplain to King, 1551–53. Preached in Buckinghamshire and Kent, June to Oct. 1553. Married Marjory Bowes, July (?) 1553. To Newcastle, Dec. 1553. At Dieppe, Jan. to Feb., 1554. Travelled in France and Switzerland, March to Nov. 1554. Intimacy with Calvin begun. English pastor at Frankfort-on-Maine, Nov. 1554 to March 1555. At Geneva, March to Aug. 1555. Returned to Berwick, Aug. 1555. Returned to Geneva, July 1556. Received Freedom of City of Geneva, 1559. Left Geneva, Jan. 1559. Returned to Scotland, April 1559. His preaching at Perth resulted in insurrection. Formal establishment of Reformed Church in Scotland, Aug. 1560. Active in spread of Reformation doctrine. Prosecuted for treason, and acquitted, Dec. 1563. Visit to England, Dec. 1566 to June 1567. Died, in Edinburgh, 24 Nov. 1572. Buried in St. Giles's Churchyard. *Works:* Tract on the Sacrament (1549 ?); "A Declaration what true Prayer is," 1554; "A Confession and Declaration of Prayer," 1554; "An Exposition of the Sixth Psalm," 1554; "A Godly Letter," 1554; "A Faythfull Admonition," 1554; "The Order of Geneva" (liturgy; compiled by Knox, Whittingham, and others), 1556; Letter to the Queen Dowager, 1556 (enlarged edn., 1558); "Apology for the Protestants in Prison in Paris," 1557; "The First Blast of the Trumpet" (anon.), 1558; "The Appellation of John Knox . . . from the cruell Sentence pronounced by the Bishops and Clergy," 1558; "A Letter addressed to the Commonalty of Scotland," 1558; "The First Book of Discipline" (compiled by Knox and others), 1560; "An Answer to a great number of Blasphemous Cavillations written by an . . . Adversarie to God's Eternal Predestination," 1560; "The Ordoure and Doctrine of the General Faste" (compiled by Knox and John Craig), 1560; "A Sermon preached . . . in the Publique audience, etc.," 1566. *Posthumous:* "A Fort for the Afflicted," 1580; "History of the Reformation," bks. i.-iii., 1584; bks. iv., v., 1644. *Collected Works:* ed. by D. Laing (6 vols.), 1846–64.—SHARP, R. FARQUHARSON, 1897, *A Dictionary of English Authors, p.* 160.

PERSONAL

Of all others, Knoxces name, if it be not Goodman's, is most odiouse here, and therefore I wish no mention of hym hither. —CECIL, WILLIAM, LORD BURGHLEY, 1559, *Letter to Sir R. Saddler and Sir Jas. Croft, Oct.* 31*st.*

On this manner departed this man of God, the light of Scotland, the comfort of the Kirk within the same, the mirror of godliness, and patron and example to all true ministers in purity of life, soundness in doctrine, and in boldness of reproving of wickedness; and one that cared not the favor of men, how great soever they were, to reprove their abuses and sins. In him was such a mighty spirit of judgment and wisdom, that the trouble never came to the Kirk sin his entering on pulpit-preaching but he foresaw the end thereof, so that he had ever ready a new counsel and a faithful to teach men that would be taught to take the best and leave the worst; so that he that followed his counsel, in the end had ever occasion never to repent him; and contrarie, such as have rejected the same have casten themselves in most shameful wickedness, and have come in a part, and daily more and more are like to come and fall to a most miserable ruin, both of soul and bodie—whilk undoubtedly shall come upon them if repentance prevent not God's judgments—as may be well verified this day in the Hamiltons, the Laird of Grange, and William Maitland, whose end behauld when it comes. —BANNATYNE, RICHARD, 1572, *Memorials, p.* 289.

The opening of his mouth, was drawn out to such a length of deformity, that his face resembled that of a dog, as his voice also did the barking of that animal. The voice failed from that tongue, which had been the cause of so much mischief, and his death, most grateful to his country, soon followed. In his last sickness, he was occupied not so much in meditating upon death, as in thinking upon civil and worldly affairs. —HAMILTON, ARCHIBALD, 1577, *De Confusione Calvin, Sectæ apud Scotos, fol.* 66, 67.

I heard him preach the prophecies of Daniel. . I had my pen and my little buik and took away sic things as I could comprehend. In the opening of the text he was moderate the space of half an hour; but when he enterit to application he made me so to grew and tremble that I could not hold a pen to write. . . . He was very weak. I saw him every day of his doctrine go hulie and fear with a furring of marticks about his neck, a staff in the ane hand, and gude godly Richard Ballandene, his servant, holding up the other oxter, from the Abbey to the Parish Kirk, and by the said Richard and another servant lifted up to the pulpit, whare he behoved to lean at his first entrie, but ere he had done with his sermon he was sae active and vigorous that he was like to ding the pulpit in blads and flie out of it. —MELVILLE, JAMES, 1601, *Diary.*

Zeal, intrepidity, disinterestedness, were virtues which he possessed in an eminent degree. He was acquainted too with the learning cultivated among divines in that age; and excelled in that species of eloquence which is calculated to rouse and to inflame. His maxims, however, were often too severe, and the impetuosity of his temper excessive. Rigid and uncomplying himself, he showed no indulgence to the infirmities of others. Regardless of the distinctions of rank and character, he uttered his admonitions with an acrimony and vehemence, more apt to irritate than to reclaim. This often betrayed him into indecent and undutiful expressions with respect to the queen's person and conduct. Those very qualities, however, which now render his character less amiable, fitted him to be the instrument of providence for advancing the reformation among a fierce people, and enabled him to face dangers, and to surmount opposition, from which a person of a more gentle spirit would have been apt to shrink back. By an unwearied application to study and to business, as well as by the frequency and fervour of his public discourses, he had worn out a constitution naturally robust. During a lingering illness he discovered the utmost fortitude; and met the approaches of death with a magnanimity inseparable from his character. —ROBERTSON, WILLIAM, 1758–59, *History of Scotland, vol.* II, *bk.* vi.

The ringleader in all these insults on majesty was John Knox; who possessed an uncontrolled authority in the church, and even in the civil affairs of the nation, and who triumphed in the contumelious usage of his sovereign. His usual appellation for the queen was Jezebel; and though she endeavoured, by the most gracious condescension, to win his favour, all her insinuations could gain nothing on his obdurate heart. . . . The political principles of the man, which he communicated to his brethern, were as full of sedition as his theological were of rage and bigotry.—HUME, DAVID, 1759, *The History of England, vol.* III, *ch.* xxxviii

A fanatical incendiary, a holy savage, the son of violence and barbarism, the religious sachem of religious Mohawks.—WHITAKER, JOHN, 1787, *Mary Queen of Scots Vindicated.*

With his brethren in the ministry he lived in the utmost cordiality. We never read of the slightest variance between him and any of his colleagues. . . . In private life he was beloved and revered by his friends and domestics. He was subject to the illapses of melancholy and depression of spirits, arising partly from natural constitution, and partly from the maladies which had long preyed upon his health; which made him (to use his own expression) churlish, and less capable of pleasing and gratifying his friends than he was otherwise disposed to be. This he confessed, and requested them to excuse; but his friendship was sincere, affectionate, and steady. When free from this morose affection, he relished the pleasures of society, and, among his acquaintances, was accustomed to unbend his mind, by indulging in innocent recreation, and in the sallies of wit and humour, to which he had a strong propensity, notwithstanding the graveness of his general deportment. . . . Most of his faults may be traced to his natural temperament, and to the character of the age and country in which he lived. His passions were strong; he felt with the utmost keenness on every subject which interested him; and as he felt he expressed himself, without disguise and without affectation. The warmth of his zeal was apt to betray him into intemperate language; his inflexible adherence to his opinions inclined to obstinacy; and his independence of mind occasionally assumed the appearance of haughtiness and disdain. . . . He was austere, not unfeeling; stern, not savage; vehement, not vindictive.—M'CRIE, THOMAS, 1811–31, *Life of John Knox, pp.* 351, 352.

A man of stern unbending nature, actuated by principle alone, far above all sordid selfish considerations, but narrow in mind and only moderately learned, had adopted in their utmost extent the rigid principles of Calvin, the apostle of Geneva. Gospel truth (in his own sense of the term) he held to be paramount to all considerations, and all the laws of society should yield before it. — KEIGHTLEY, THOMAS, 1837–59, *The History of England, vol.* I, *p.* 466.

Our primary characteristic of a Hero, that he is sincere, applies emphatically to Knox. . . An honest-hearted, brotherly man; brother to the high, brother also to the low; sincere in his sympathy with both. He had his pipe of Bordeaux too, we find, in that old Edinburgh house of his; a cheery social man, with faces that loved him! They go far wrong who think this Knox was a gloomy, spasmodic, shrieking fanatic. Not at all: he is one of the solidest of men. Practical, cautious-hopeful, patient; a most shrewd, observing, quietly discerning man. In fact, he has very much the type of character we assign to the Scotch at present: a certain sardonic taciturnity is in him; insight enough; and a stouter heart than he himself knows of. . . . This Prophet of the Scotch is to me no hateful man!—He had a sore fight of an existence; wrestling with Popes and Principalities; in defeat, contention, life-long struggle; rowing as a galley-slave, wandering as an exile. A sore fight, but he won it. "Have you hope?" they asked him in his last moment, when he could no longer speak. He lifted his finger, "pointed upwards with his finger," and so died. Honour to him! His works have not died. The letter of his work dies, as of all men's; but the spirit of it never.—CARLYLE, THOMAS, 1840, *Heroes and Hero-Worship.*

To say that he was fearless and incorruptible, that he advocated with unflinching zeal what he believed to be the truth, and that he devoted himself with untiring energy to what he deemed the highest of all objects, is only to render common justice to the many noble attributes which he undoubtedly possessed. But, on the other hand, he was stern, unrelenting, and frequently brutal; he was not only callous to human suffering, but he could turn it into a jest, and employ on it the resources of his coarse, though exhuberant, humour; and he loved power so inordinately, that, unable to brook the slightest opposition, he trampled on all who crossed his path, or stood even for a moment in the way of his ulterior designs. — BUCKLE, HENRY THOMAS, 1861, *History of Civilization in England, vol.* III, *ch.* ii.

The rigid Sabbatarianism of modern times received no sanction either from his practice or his teaching. He supped with Randolph on one Sunday evening, and visited Calvin during a game of bowls on another. The austere theology of Andrew Melville was tempered by an interest in classical and academical literature, the very reverse of a hard and narrow Puritanism.—STANLEY, ARTHUR PENRHYN, 1872, *Lectures on the History of the Church of Scotland, p.* 113.

Women, he has said in his "First Blast," are "weak, frail, impatient, feeble, and foolish;" and yet it does not appear that he was himself any less dependent than other men upon the sympathy and affection of these weak, frail, impatient, feeble, and foolish creatures; it seems even as if he had been rather more dependent than most. . . Here was this great-voiced, bearded man of God, who might be seen beating the solid pulpit every Sunday, and casting abroad his clamorous denunciations to the terror of all, and who on the Monday would sit in their parlours by the hour, and weep with them over their manifold trials and temptations. — STEVENSON, ROBERT LOUIS, 1882, *John Knox and his Relations to Women, Familiar Studies of Men and Books, pp.* 299, 323

His special vocation was that of the preacher rather than of the author. The pulpit was the throne of his peculiar and pre-eminent power. Other men might equal or surpass him elsewhere, but *there* he was supreme. Different excellencies might come out in himself on different occasions; but in the pulpit all his abilities were conspicuous, and they were always at their best. It was the glass which focussed all his powers into a point, and quickened their exercise into a burning intensity which kindled everything it touched. It brightened his intellect, enlivened his imagination, clarified his judgment, inflamed his courage, and gave fiery energy to his utterance. He was never elsewhere so great in any one of these particulars, as he was, when in the pulpit, in them all; for there, over and above the "*præfervidum ingenium*," which he had in common with so many of his countrymen, and the glow of animation which fills the soul of the orator when he looks upon an audience, he had the feeling that he was called of God to be faithful, and that made him almost like another Paul. Behind him was the cross of his Lord; before him was the throne at which he was to be accountable, and between these two he stood "watching for souls as one that must give account."—TAYLOR, WILLIAM M., 1885, *John Knox, p.* 204.

On the singular figure of Knox himself—the undoubted leader of the religious movement in Scotland—men will continue to look, as his contemporaries looked, with mingled feelings of admiration and aversion. In the case of so unique a personality, the temptation to burn or to adore becomes wellnigh irresistible. The flaws in a character of exceptional force and masterfulness are of course accentuated by its virility; and in Knox especially, it cannot be denied, there was much that was not admirable. Such words as charity, chivalry, magnanimity, were not to be found in his dictionary, and the ideas which they represented he would have laughed to scorn. The coarse strain in his nature is most noticeable, perhaps, in his estimate of, and in his intercourse with, women: there are allusions to his first wife in his letters which no man of natural delicacy could have committed to paper. Marjory Bowes died when he was almost an old man, and then he married the daughter of Lord Ochiltree, a girl in her teens. . . . It is needless to repeat that Knox was intensely superstitious. The changes of wind and weather were spiritual portents which the Almighty permitted him to interpret. His disciples believed, indeed, that the gift of prophecy had been given to their master, as it had been given to Isaiah and Ezekiel.—SKELTON, JOHN, 1888, *Maitland of Lethington, vol.* II, *pp.* 74, 75.

He lies, it is thought, if not within the walls of St. Giles's under the flags between the Cathedral and the Parliament House, with all the busy life of modern Edinburgh, the feet of generations of men treading out the hours and years over his head; a more appropriate bed for him than green mound or marble monument. That stony square is consecrated ground blessed near a thousand years ago by ancient priests who cared little more for Rome than do their modern successors now. But little heeded Knox for priestly blessing or consecrated soil. "The earth is the Lord's and the fulness thereof" was the only consecration of which he thought.—OLIPHANT, MRS. MARGARET, O. W., 1890, *Royal Edinburgh, p.* 372.

Between John Wyclif and John Knox there is a curious and striking resemblance, in more points than one—such a resemblance as occurs not infrequently between two historical characters who from similar beginnings have pursued a somewhat similar course in life. No one who has made himself familiar with the various portraits and engravings which preserve for us at any rate the traditional features of Wyclif can fail to be arrested when he sees the face of Knox, as Wilkie has reproduced it from earlier pictures. It is not so much that the exact lineaments correspond in such a way as to catch the attention of a casual observer, though even in this sense the parallel is sufficiently remarkable. The type and character of the two heads are the same; you cannot look at one without thinking of the other. The keen intelligent eyes, the drawn features with their ascetic cast, the resolute lips which bespeak an absolutely fearless heart, are present in all the pictures; and a grizzled patriarchal beard serves to deepen the similarity.—SERGEANT, LEWIS, 1893, *John Wyclif, Last of the Schoolmen and First of the English Reformers, p.* 3.

The strong, crafty, unmerciful shrewd, victorious Reformer.—STODDART, ANNA M., 1895, *John Stuart Blackie, vol.* II, *p.* 83.

FIRST BLAST OF THE TRUMPET
1558

He was too proud either to recant the tenets of this book, or even to apologize for them; and his conduct showed, that he thought no more civility than loyalty due to any of the female sex.—HUME, DAVID, 1759, *The History of England, vol.* III, *ch.* xxxviii.

Whatever opinion may be taken on the main question, however,—and the very existence of the Salic law in some states still proves that there *are* two sides to it, there can be no doubt that Knox's treatment of it at all, not to speak of the sort of treatment which he gave it, was at this time impolitic and imprudent.—TAYLOR, WILLIAM M., 1885, *John Knox, p.* 109.

Has the force which never failed its author, and a degree of polish which in subsequent more distracted days he was seldom able to give to his writings. Its boldness, its dramatic fitness for the time (or unfitness as it might with equal truth be phrased), arrested and held the attention of men. It is now by far the best known of its author's works.—WALKER, HUGH, 1893, *Three Centuries of Scottish Literature, vol.* I, *p.* 111.

The "First Blast" was published in the spring of 1558, and in the following autumn Mary Tudor died, and Elizabeth, the hope and the mainstay of the Protestants, ascended the English throne. This fact is the completest and the most ironical comment upon Knox's arguments against the "Regiment of Women." The echoes of that ill-timed "Blast" were to ring in his ears all his life.—MACCUNN, FLORENCE A., 1895, *John Knox* (*Leaders of Religion*), *p.* 56.

HISTORY OF THE REFORMATION

It is a racy, vigorous narrative, crowded with pictures in rich and powerful colouring—like a gallery of historical paintings by Rubens. What chiefly, however, fascinates the reader, is the unrivalled potency of its vituperative rhetoric. His scolding is sublime and awful. But throughout there is a sort of noble fairness in it. Of course, all who withstood him and called forth his wrath were in some form or other knaves and ruffians. How could it be otherwise with those who had set themselves against him, the Deity's representative on earth—the head of the theocracy! But he was not given to the practice so common in his day of assassinating reputations by those vile imputations, the touch of which leaves a taint which all the perfumes of Arabia are insufficient to sweeten out. The tenor of his wrath was ever for a fair stand-up fight; and in his wordy battles he was a champion few would care to join issue with.—BURTON, JOHN HILL, 1864, *The Scot Abroad, vol.* II, *p.* 72.

John Knox, the Reformer, was a glorious egotist. In his chronicle he speaks of himself always in the third person, as if he were writing the biography of some great man whose deeds he had had the good fortune to witness. John Knox's figure is ever the conspicuous figure in John Knox's book.—MATHEWS, WILLIAM, 1881, *Literary Style, and other Essays, p.* 95.

His "History" is written throughout in the spirit of a censor. The other side is not allowed to possess a shred of honesty. Its supporters are "perfect hypocrites," "bloody worms," or worse. There is something ignoble in the sense of almost personal triumph which he exhibits in recounting the death of Cardinal Beaton, or the last days of Mary of Guise. One may doubt if, in the whole range of literature, there are to be found more dramatic illustrations of the gulf which difference of character and training can create between two human minds than the celebrated dialogues with Mary Queen of Scots, which fill the most picturesque pages in the "History."—DODDS, JAMES MILLER, 1893, *English Prose, ed. Craik, vol.* I, *p.* 298.

Knox's first intention was to tell of the work of Reformation from the year 1558 to the coming of Queen Mary from France, in August, 1561. But he prefixed afterwards, as a general introduction, what is now the First Book, chiefly written in 1566, with a sketch of events concerning Church Reformation from the burning of Patrick Hamilton in 1527 to 1558, and some preceding detail of articles set forth in 1494 by reformers who were known as the Lollards of Kyle. This he took from the records of Glasgow. Knox was led also, in 1566, to continue his narrative in a Fourth Book, as far as the year 1564. The Third Book had been followed by a full copy of the Reformer's "Buke of Discipline," inserted, says Knox, "to the end that the Posterities to come may juge alsweill quhat the warldlingis refused, as quhat Policie the godlie Ministeris requyred." Knox wrote the whole of his Fourth Book in 1566. There was added afterwards, by another writer, a Fifth Book, of which no manuscript is known, and which was first published in 1644 by David Buchanan, added in a folio to the authentic four. David Buchanan said that all was "gathered out of Knox's Papers and Manuscripts." Probably the Fifth Book does contain gatherings from Knox, but it was put together after Knox's death; and for what part of it we are indebted to Knox, for what part to David Buchanan or some unknown writer, it is not possible to say. It continues Knox's narrative from September, 1564, to August, 1567, when the Earl of Moray became regent.—MORLEY, HENRY, 1892, *English Writers, vol.* VIII, *p.* 337.

Written in his busiest years, and often uncouth in style and disjointed from want of revision, it yet displays qualities far higher and more varied than anything else that ever came from his pen. Its position among histories is remarkable, in truth not much short of unique. An original authority written with the fullest knowledge by a man of genius and incomparable force, who himself made the history he narrates, is clearly a precious possession—at once the richest storehouse of facts and the most vivid picture of the age. . . . "The History of the Reformation" professedly leaves out of account many of the elements in the life of the nation. It is the work of a contemporary, subject to the errors inseparable from nearness to the events narrated. It is the work also of a partisan deeply committed to a particular view of the central controversy, and incapable of sympathy with the other side. Nevertheless it is incomparably the best account of the time. The limitation to matters of religion is less cramping than it might seem; for in that age above all others the question of religion included everything; and the undoubted prejudice of the writer is balanced by his transparent truthfulness, and the courage and intense conviction which disdains, or rather never dreams of concealment. The history is therefore a trustworthy record of the knowledge of the man who knew most about the most important questions of his time. How far it towers above all other annals of the age can only be seen by comparison.—WALKER, HUGH, 1893, *Three Centuries of Scottish Literature, vol.* I, *p.* 114.

GENERAL

God is my witness, whom I have served in the spirit in the gospel of his Son, that I have taught nothing but the true and solid doctrine of the gospel of the Son of God, and have had it for my only object to instruct the ignorant, to confirm the faithful, to comfort the weak, the fearful, and the distressed, by the promises of grace, and to fight against the proud and rebellious by the Divine threatenings. I know that many have frequently complained, and do still complain, of my too great severity; but God knows that my mind was always void of hatred to the persons of those against whom I thundered the severest judgments.—KNOX, JOHN, c 1572, *Preface to Sermons.*

If ever God shall vouchsafe the Church so greate a benefite; when his infinite letters, and sundry other treatises shall be gathered together, it shall appear what an excellent man he was, and what a wonderful losse that Church of Scotland susteined when that worthie man was taken from them. If, by yourselfe or others, you can procure any other his writings or letters here at home, or abroad in Scotland, be a meane that we may receive them. It were great pittie that any the least of his writinges should be lost; for he ever more wrote both godly and diligently, in questions of divinitie, and also of church policie; and his letters being had togeather, would togeather set out an whole historie of the churches where he lived.—FIELD, JOHN, 1587? *ed., Exposition of the Temptation of Christ.*

The firebrand of his country.—PERSONS, ROBERT, 1604, *Three Conversions of England, vol.* II, *p.* 220.

Nay, which is more lamentable, if the work of any deceased author, though never so famous in his lifetime, and even to this day, comes to their hands for licence to be printed, or reprinted, if there be found in his book one sentence of a venturous edge, uttered in the height of zeal, (and who knows whether it might not be the dictate of a divine spirit?) yet, not suiting with every low decrepit humour of their own, though it were Knox himself, the Reformer of a kingdom, that spake it, they will not pardon him their dash. —MILTON, JOHN, 1644, *Areopagitica.*

About this time Mr. John Knox came from Geneva, and was chosen by the congregation of Frankfort for their constant minister. Let none account it incongruous, that, among so many able and eminent English divines, a Scotchman should be made pastor of the English church, seeing Mr. Knox's reputed merit did naturalize him (though a foreigner) for any protestant congregation. —FULLER, THOMAS, 1655, *The Church History of Britain, bk.* viii, *sec.* iii, *par.* 1.

Of him it may be said, that if Shakespeare was the most giant-like man, and the highest of poets, John Knox seems, if one knew him rightly, to have been as entirely destitute of immorality as Shakespeare was of prose. I cannot, however, think that he is to be compared with Luther, as some of the Germans in these days have done, who have set him even above Luther; struck with the great veracity of Knox. Luther would have been a great man in other things besides the Reformation; a great, substantial, happy man, who must have excelled in whatever matter he undertook. Knox had not that faculty, but simply this, of standing entirely upon truth; it is not that his sincerity is known to him to be sincerity, but it arises from a sense of the impossibility of any other procedure.—CARLYLE, THOMAS, 1838, *Lectures on the History of Literature, ed. Greene, p.* 160.

The *secret history of toleration* among certain parties has been disclosed to us by a curious document, from that religious Machiavel, the fierce ascetic republican John Knox, a calvinistical Pope. . . . Knox the reformer possessed an extraordinary portion of this awful prophetic confidence: he appears to have predicted several remarkable events, and the fates of some persons. We are told, that, condemned to a galley at Rochelle, he predicted that "within two or three years he should preach the gospel at Saint Giles's in Edinburgh;" an improbable event, which happened. Of Mary and Darnley, he pronounced, that "as the king, for the queen's pleasure, had gone to mass, the Lord, in his justice, would make her the instrument of his overthrow." Other striking predictions of the deaths of Thomas Maitland, and of Kirkaldy of Grange, and the warning he solemnly gave to the Regent Murray not to go to Linlithgow, where he was assassinated, occasioned a barbarous people to imagine that the prophet Knox had received an immediate communication from Heaven. . . . Knox exercised that deep sagacity which took in the most enlarged views of the future, as appears by his Machiavelian foresight on the barbarous destruction of the monasteries and the cathedrals.—DISRAELI, ISAAC, 1841, *Toleration, Prediction, Curiosities of Literature.*

Morton spoke only of what he knew: the full measure of Knox's greatness neither he nor any man could then estimate. It is as we look back over that stormy time, and weigh the actors in it one against the other, that he stands out in his full proportions. No grander figure can be found, in the entire history of the Reformation in this island, than that of Knox. Cromwell and Burghley rank beside him for the work which they effected, but, as politicians and statesmen, they had to labour with instruments which they soiled their hands in touching. In purity, in uprightness, in courage, truth, and stainless honour, the Regent Murray and our English Latimer were perhaps his equals; but Murray was intellectually far below him, and the sphere of Latimer's influence was on a smaller scale. The time has come when English history may do justice to one but for whom the Reformation would have been overthrown among ourselves; for the spirit which Knox created saved Scotland; and if Scotland had been Catholic again, neither the wisdom of Elizabeth's Ministers, nor the teaching of her Bishops, nor her own chicaneries, would have preserved England from revolution. His was the voice which taught the peasant of the Lothians that he was a free man, the equal in the sight of God with the proudest peer or prelate that had trampled on his forefathers. He was the one antagonist whom Mary Stuart could not soften nor Maitland deceive; he it was that raised the poor Commons of his country into a stern and rugged people, who might be hard, narrow, superstitious, and fanatical, but who, nevertheless, were men whom neither king, noble, nor priest could force again to submit to tyranny. And his reward has been the ingratitude of those who should most have done honour to his memory.—FROUDE, JAMES ANTHONY, 1867, *History of England, vol.* X, *ch.* xxiii, *p.* 457.

The inner character of the man, as made up of the motives on which he acted, has been so torn between contending zealots, that to set it apart in peaceful composure, and contemplate it with perfect candour, is such a task as it would be hopeless to perform with satisfaction. In fact it is out of that great contest which has for centuries raged around his name that his great fame has grown. In his day he was an all-important man in Scotland, and of some consequence in England on account of his influence in his own country. But he was little known elsewhere. While the name of his quiet neighbour Buchanan spread over all literature, and was repeated in every university and cluster of learned men, the contemporary notices of Knox are extremely scanty, and, from uncertainty in spelling, not easily identified. When contemporary foreign writers name him, it is generally to commend his services in a branch of that contest in which Calvin and Beza were the commanders. Nor was this an entirely false appreciation of his place, for he did implicitly the work which they had planned. He was no deviser of creeds and organisations; he had nothing original about him but his individuality of character and his power over his native tongue. —BURTON, JOHN HILL, 1870, *The History of Scotland, vol.* V, *p.* 322.

Is often wordy, sometimes tedious, now and then narrow as a village gossip, always supremely and absolutely dogmatic, seeing no way but his own and acknowledging no possibility of error; and the extreme and perpetual movement of his ever-active mind, his high-blooded intolerance, the restless force about him which never pauses to take breath, is the chief impression produced upon the reader by his own unfolding of himself in his wonderful history. Though he is too great and important to be called a busybody, we still feel sympathetically something of the suppressed irritation and sense of hindrance and interruption with which the lords must have regarded this companion with his "devout imaginations," whom they dared not neglect, and who was sure to get the better in every argument, generally by reason, but at all events by the innate force of his persistence and daring. —OLIPHANT, MRS. MARGARET O. W., 1890, *Royal Edinburgh, p.* 296.

No man in England or Scotland who values liberty, national, civil, or religious, can speak of Knox without reverence and gratitude.—STIRLING-MAXWELL, SIR WILLIAM, 1891, *Miscellaneous Essays and Addresses, p.* 298.

It cannot be said that his writings have contributed much to his fame. . . . Such distinction as his writings possess is due to the sincerity and force of the writer, and not to the conscious exercise of literary art. . . . His gift of language, and especially of denunciation, was immense and, backed by a fearless temperament, was never known to fail him. He does not attract by the humane breadth of wisdom and simple-hearted gaiety which make of Luther such a typical Christian. An unpleasant vein of bitterness crosses most of his writings. But it is proper to remember that this man's spiritual father, Wishart, was burnt alive; that he served a hard apprenticeship amid the horrors of the French galleys; that many of his best years were spent in exile; that he suffered much from ill-health; and that at least part of his vehement temper belongs to his time and to his country rather than to himself. —DODDS, JAMES MILLER, 1893, *English Prose, ed. Craik, vol.* I, *pp.* 295, 296, 297.

Knox, uncompromising and dictatorial, was a Pope in Scotland.—CHURCH, SAMUEL HARDEN, 1894, *Oliver Cromwell, p.* 81.

In the case of all men who have distinguished themselves beyond their fellows, the definitive judgment must rest with the people from whom they spring, and to whom the heritage of their labours is a permanent and vital question of the balance of good or ill. In this final court of appeal the judgment is undeniably for Knox and against all his cavillers. For the mass of his countrymen — those who have shaped the nation's destinies in the past as they must shape them in the future —Knox is the greatest person their country has produced, and the man to whom in all that makes a people great they owe the deepest and most abiding debt. — BROWN, P. HUME, 1895, *John Knox, A Biography, vol.* II, *p.* 297.

The greatest public man whom Scotland has known. . . . Knox's public life was not the whole of his work: in bulk, it was a small part of it. When he became minister of Edinburgh in 1560 there was only one church there; St. Cuthberts and Canongate were country parishes outside. It was some years before he got a colleague; and, as sole minister of Edinburgh, he preached twice every Sunday *and three times during the week* to audiences which sometimes were numbered by thousands. Once a week he attended a Kirk Session; once a week he was a member of the assembly or meeting of the neighbouring elders for their "prophesying" or "exercise on Scripture." Often he was sent away to different districts of the country on preaching visitations under the orders of the Church. But when Knox was at home, his preparations for the pulpit, which were regular and careful, and his other pastoral work, challenged his whole time. And this work was carried on in two places chiefly; in St. Giles, which now became the High Church of Edinburgh, and in his house or lodging, which was always in or near the Netherbow, a few hundred yards farther down the High Street.—INNES, A. TAYLOR, *John Knox (Famous Scots Series), p.* 144:

The great truth which he grasped with satisfying clearness was that the call of God comes to every man direct, without any intervention except the open word. This was the glory of his message—a message which quickened all Scotland and started it on its career of intellectual and spiritual achievement. Nor did Knox claim any special inspiration above other believers, or to be in any miraculous sense a prophet of God. He was not a prophet by unique revelation, but he was a witness-bearer of unique consecration.—HURST, JOHN FLETCHER, 1900, *History of the Christian Church, vol.* II, *p.* 455.

Matthew Parker

1504–1575

Born at Norwich, England, Aug. 6, 1504: died at London, May 17, 1575. Archbishop of Canterbury. He graduated at Cambridge (Corpus Christi College) in 1525, and was appointed chaplain to Anne Boleyn. He was selected to preach at Paul's Cross by Thomas Cromwell. In 1545 he was appointed vice-chancellor of Cambridge. On the accession of Mary Tudor he resigned, and lost all his preferments. He was consecrated archbishop of Canterbury Dec. 17, 1559. As primate he devoted himself to the organization and discipline of the English Church, and was a firm opponent of puritanism.—SMITH, BENJAMIN E., *ed.*, 1894–97, *The Century Cyclopedia of Names, p.* 782.

Wrote a treatise "De Antiquitate Britannicæ Ecclesiæ et Priviligiis Ecclesiæ Cantuariensis, cum Archiepiscopis ejusdem 70" (1572), superintended the production of the "Bishop's Bible" (1568), and edited the works of Matthew of Paris and other writers.—ADAMS, W. DAVENPORT, 1877, *Dictionary of English Literature, p.* 504.

He was a Parker indeed,—careful to keep the fences, and shut the gates of discipline against all such night-stealers as would invade the same. No wonder, then, if the tongues and pens of many were whetted against him, whose complaints are beheld, by discreet men, like the exclamations of truantly scholars against their master's severity, correcting them for their faults —FULLER, THOMAS, 1655, *The Church History of Britain, bk.* ix, *sec.* iii, *par.* 17.

His apostolical virtues were not incompatible with the love of learning, and while he exercised the arduous office, not of governing, but of founding the Church of England, he strenously applied himself to revive the study of the Saxon tongue, and of English antiquities.—GIBBON, EDWARD, 1794, *An Address, Miscellaneous Works, ed. Sheffield.*

A name, never to be pronounced without emotions of pious respect.—DIBDIN, THOMAS FROGNALL, 1824, *The Library Companion, p.* 107

On the accession of Queen Mary, Matthew Parker shared the fate of all the married clergymen who would not part with their wives. He was stripped of his preferments, and lived, poor and content, under the shelter of a friend's house in Norfolk, with his wife and their two little sons. He was sometimes looked for; and once, in escaping, had a fall from a horse, of which the hurt remained for life. When Parker, in his day of trouble under

Mary, turned the Psalms into English verse, he did so for comfort to himself like that of David, for whom, he says in his metrical preface to this work,

"With golden stringes such harmonie
His harpe so sweete did wrest
That he relieved his phrenesie
When wicked sprites possest."

This version of the Psalter—the first in which all the Psalms were fashioned by one person into English metre—finished in 1557, was printed about 1560 by John Day.—MORLEY, HENRY, 1892, *English Writers, vol.* VIII, *p.* 196.

Parker kept a staff of scribes and painters in miniature, and had his own press and fount of type. He published many scarce tracts to save them from oblivion. Others he ordered to be copied in manuscript, and these and all his ancient books he caused to be "trimly covered;" so that we may say with Dibdin, "a more determined book-fancier existed not in Great Britain." He gave some of his books to "his nurse Corpus Christi" at Cambridge, and some to the public library; and his gift to the College was compared to "the sun of our English antiquity," eclipsed only by the shadow of Cotton's palace of learning.—ELTON, CHARLES ISAAC AND MARY AUGUSTA, 1893, *The Great Book-Collectors, p.* 113.

His position gave him exceptional opportunities for securing and preserving literary treasures, and he turned them to the best account. . . . Though highly esteemed by Elizabeth, he was but an indifferent courtier. He shunned all occasions of pomp and parade, his natural bashfulness having been increased, according to his own statement (Correspondence p. 199), "with passing those hard years of Mary's reign in obscurity." He avoided the society of the great, and especially that of foreigners; and at the council-board he sat diffident and mostly silent. His modesty however, conciliated those who disapproved his policy, and by the great majority of his contemporaries to whom the fame and prosperity of England were dear he was honoured and esteemed. In the exercise of hospitality he was materially aided by his wife, whose tact and genial disposition signally fitted her for such duties; and Elizabeth herself, touched by the grace and courtesy of her reception when on a visit to Lambeth Palace, but unable altogether to suppress her dislike of clerical matrimony, took leave of her hostess with the oft-quoted words; "Madam I may not call you; mistress I am ashamed to call you; but yet I thank you."—MULLINGER, J. BASS, 1895, *Dictionary of National Biography, vol.* XLIII, *pp.* 260, 261.

John Heywood

1497?-1575?

John Heywood was born, in 1497, perhaps at North Mims, in Hertfordshire, where afterwards he certainly had a home. He was opposed to Lutheranism; and his friendship for Sir Thomas More having brought him into the king's favour, he retained it by his wit. His name first appeared in the King's Book of Payments in 1515, when he had eight-pence a day for wages. In 1519 he was called a singer. In 1521 he had an annuity of ten marks as the king's servant. In 1526 he was entered as "player of the king's virginals," and he held that office to the end of Henry VIII.'s reign. He was much liked by the Princess Mary, and in March, 1538, received forty shillings for playing an interlude with his children before her. It is to be inferred, therefore, that he directed a small company of interlude players. He remained at Court when Edward VI. was king, and under Queen Mary, for whom, when a young princess, he had shown a particular respect. He had composed, when she was eighteen, a poem in her praise. But on the accession of Elizabeth he went abroad, and died at Mechlin in 1575, in which year he wrote of himself to Burleigh as an old man of seventy-eight. Besides his interludes, John Heywood wrote six hundred epigrams.—MORLEY, HENRY, 1892, *English Writers, vol.* VIII, *p.* 79.

Works: "A Mery Play between the Pardoner and the Frere," 1533 (anon.; only one copy known); "A Mery Play between Johan the Husband, Tyb the Wife, and Sir Jhan the Priest," 1533 (anon.; only one copy known); "The Play of the Wether," 1533; "The Play of Love," (1533); "Of Gentylnes and Nobylyte" (anon.; attrib. to

Heywood) (1535); "The Four P. P." (1545?); "A dialogue conteining the number in effect of all the proverbes in the Englishe tongue" (1549); "The Spider and the Flie," 1556. *Posthumous:* "A Dialogue on Wit and Folly," ed. F. W. Fairholt, 1846.—SHARP, R. FARQUHARSON, 1897, *A Dictionary of English Authors, p.* 132.

THE SPIDER AND THE FLY

Lucian and Apuleius wrote of an Asse, Themison in praise of the herbe Plantaine, Homere in commendation of Wine, Ephren in dispraise of Laughing, Orpheus and Hesiodus of Fumigations or Perſumes, Chrysippus of Colewortes, Phanias of Nettles, Messala made of everie severall letter of the A, B, C, a severall booke, Virgil of a Gnat, Ovid of a Nut, and Erasmus of the praise of follie, and Heywood, yet later, of the Spider and the Flie.—FLEMING, ABRAHAM, 1579, *A Paradoxe.*

He dealeth so profoundly, and beyond all measure of skill, that neither he himself that made it, neither anyone that readeth it, can reach unto the meaning thereof.—HARRISON, WILLIAM, 1592? *Historical Description of the Island of Britain.*

It is a very long poem in the octavo stanza, containing 98 chapters. Perhaps there never was so dull, so tedious, and trifling an apologue: without fancy, meaning, or moral. A long tale of fictitious manners will always be tiresome, unless the design be burlesque: and then the ridiculous, arising from the contrast between the solemn and the light, must be ingeniously supported. Our author seems to have intended a fable on the burlesque construction: but we know not when he would be serious and when witty, whether he means to make the reader laugh, or to give him advice.—WARTON, THOMAS, 1778–81, *History of English Poetry, sec.* xlii.

GENERAL

Iohn Hoywood the Epigrammatist who for the myrth and quicknesse of his conceits more then for any good learning was in him came to be well benefited by the king. —PUTTENHAM, GEORGE, 1589, *The Arte of English Poesie, ed. Arber, p.* 74.

Haywood, that did in Epigrams excell,
Is now put downe since my light Muse arose,
As Buckets are put downe into a Well,
Or as a schoole boy putteth downe his hose.

—DAVYS, SIR JOHN, 1593, *Epigrams.*

Heywood for his Proverbs and Epigrams is not yet put downe by any of our countrey, though *one* doth indeed come neare him, that graces him the more in saying he puts him downe.—HARRINGTON, SIR JOHN, 1596, *"Metamorphosis" of Ajax.*

His comedies, most of which appeared before the year 1534, are destitute of plot, humour, or character, and give us no very high opinion of the festivity of this agreeable companion. They consist of low incident, and the language of ribaldry. But perfection must not be expected before its time. He is called our first writer of comedies. But those who say this, speak without determinate ideas, and confound comedies with moralities and interludes. We will allow, that he is among the first of our dramatists who drove the Bible from the stage, and introduced representations of familiar life and popular manners. —WARTON, THOMAS, 1778–81, *History of English Poetry, sec.* xlii.

His pieces, which may in some sense be compared to the mimes of Sophron, were but a succession of scenes, for the most part comic, but destitute of every thing like complication of plot, yet boldly sketched, lively, and teeming with popular wit, directed to matters of public or domestic interest, or existing characters, manners, and opinions.—ULRICI, HERMANN, 1839, *Shakspeare's Dramatic Art, p.* 13.

Warton and his followers have obscured a true genius for exuberant humor, keen irony, and exquisite ridicule, such as Rabelais and Swift would not have disdained, and have not always surpassed.—DISRAELI, ISAAC, 1841, *The Romanist John Heywood, Amenities of Literature.*

It is clear, also, that Warton had never seen one of Heywood's most humorous pieces; and he does not give him the credit he deserves as the inventor of a new species of theatrical entertainment, which, in the middle of the reign of Henry VIII., superseded both Miracle-plays and Moralities, and directly led the way to the introduction of genuine comedy. —COLLIER, JOHN PAYNE, 1865, *A Bibliographical and Critical Account of the Rarest Books in the English Language, vol.* I, *p.* 370.

Though he was a professional jester, gaining his livelihood and taking his position in society as a recognised mirthmaker, he allowed no considerations of personal profit to cloud his conscience. He remained an Englishman to the backbone, loyal to his party and his religious convictions, outspoken in his condemnation of the superstitions which disgraced the Church of his adoption. This manliness of attitude, this freedom from time-service, this fearless exposure of the weak points in a creed to which he sacrificed his worldly interests, give a dignity to Heywood's character, and prepossess us strongly in favour of his writings. Their tone, like that of the man, is homely, masculine, downright, and English, in the shrewdness of the wit, the soundness of the sense, and the jovial mirth which pervades each scene. . . . The "Four P's," which I propose to examine more closely, is an excellent comic dialogue. More than this it cannot claim to be; for it has no intrigue, and aims at the exhibition of characters by contrast and collocation, not by action. Its motive is a witty situation, and its *dénouement* is a single humorous saying. Thus this Interlude has not the proportions of a play, although its dialogue exhibits far more life, variety, and spirit than many later and more elaborate creations of the English stage. It is written in pure vernacular, terse and racy if rude, and undefiled by classical pedantry or Italianising affectation. Heywood, here as elsewhere, reminds us of Chaucer without his singing robes. As Charles Lamb called his namesake Thomas Heywood a prose Shakspere, so might we style John Heywood a prose Chaucer. The humour which enchants us in the "Canterbury Tales," and which we claim as specifically English, emerges in Heywood's dialogue, less concentrated and blent with neither pathos nor poetic fancy, yet still indubitably of the genuine sort.—SYMONDS, JOHN ADDINGTON, 1884, *Shakspere's Predecessors in the English Drama, pp.* 187, 188.

John Heywood still represented for England, as Hans Sachs did for mediaeval Germany, the mediaeval disputation of abstractions, though, if it is rightly assigned to him, he also produced a more characteristic piece of genuine human conversation in the "Gentylnes and Nobility," where a Merchant, a Knight and a Plowman dispute "Who is a very gentleman?" —HERFORD, CHARLES H., 1886, *Studies in the Literary Relations of England and Germany in the Sixteenth Century, p.* 32.

His works may be said to mark an epoch in the history of the drama. Inclination and a knowledge of his own powers wisely determined him to limit himself, to concentrate his faculties. The era in which he lived had gropingly attempted to produce dramas of various kinds; and Heywood, by taking up such as were best suited to his ability, and by developing them after his own fashion, threw new life into forms of mediæval dramatic poetry that had almost become extinct. . . . Heywood did not actually create English comedy, but certainly many of its essential elements. He prepared the way for it much in the same way as the *commedia dell'arte* served as the first stage to Molière's art. Successful delineation of character (even though not carried to any great depth), an inexhaustible fund of whimsical ideas, dramatic animation, the development of an effective though drastic species of comicality,—these are the qualities we specially value in Heywood's works. . . . The earlier blossoms of English Comedy cannot compete with his modest one-act plays in freshness of life and vigour. In their own period, and in their own way, they stand unrivalled. —TEN BRINK, BERNHARD, 1892, *History of English Literature, (Fourteenth Century to Surrey) tr. Schmitz, pp.* 135, 140.

"The Four P's," is the last typical utterance on the stage of the Pre-Renaissance spirit in this country. It shows absolutely no trace of foreign influence, and is English to the core alike in its excellences and its faults. Its dialogue is pungent and nervous in a high degree; its sketches of character are firm and effective; its mixture of good sense, humour, and piety is singularly pleasing. But it lacks the distinctive mark of the higher drama, for in spite of the neatness of the *denouement*, there is nothing that can seriously be called a plot. Many of the features that go to make a first-rate comedy are present, but we miss one that is essential—the constructive faculty. This was a gift almost entirely withheld from the mediaeval playwrights, and in his lack of it Heywood proves himself a late-born son of the era which produced the "Miracle" and the "Morality."—BOAS, FREDERICK S., 1896, *Shakspere and his Predecessors, p.* 17.

George Gascoigne

1530–1577

Born, at Cardington, Beds., 1530 (?). Educated, probably in Westmoreland, and at Trinity College, Cambridge. Took no degree. Entered at Middle Temple, 1547 (?). Student of Gray's Inn, 1555. M. P. for Bedford, 1557–59. Married Mrs. Elizabeth Breton, 1566 (?). Lived at Walthamstow from about 1566 till death. M. P. for Midhurst, 1572. Unseated on petition. To Holland, March 1572. Served for short time under Prince of Orange. Returned to England, 1575. Devoted himself to literature. Died, at Stamford, Lincolnshire, 7 Oct. 1577. *Works:* "A Hundred Sundrie Flowres," unauthorized publication, 1572; authorized version, called "The Posies of George Gascoigne," 1575; "The Glasse of Government," 1575; "The Princelye Pleasures at the Courte of Kenelworthe," 1576; "The Steele Glas," 1576; "The Droomme of Doomesday," 1576; "A Delicate Diet," 1576; "The Spoyle of Antwerp" (anon.; attrib. to Gascoigne), (1577?). He *edited:* Sir H. Gilbert's "Discourse of a new Passage, etc.," 1576; and contrib. commendatory verses to: Holiband's "French Littleton," 1566; "The Noble Art of Venerie," 1575; "Cardanus Comfort," 1576. *Collected Works:* ed. by A. Jeffes, 1587; ed. by W. C. Hazlitt (2 vols.), 1868–70.—SHARP, R. FARQUHARSON, 1897, *A Dictionary of English Authors, p.* 109.

To write my censure of this booke,
This "Glasse of Steele" unpartially doth shewe,
Abuses all, to such as in it looke,
From prince to poore; from high estate to lowe.
As for the verse, who list like trade to trye,
I feare me much, shall hardly reache so high.
—RALEIGH, SIR WALTER, 1576, *Upon Gascoign's Poem, "The Steele Glasse."*

For Gaskoygnes death, leave to mone or morne
You are deceived, alive the man is stil:
Alive? O yea, and laugheth death to scorne,
In that, that he, his fleshly lyfe did kil.
For by such death, two lyves he gaines for one,
His soule in heaven dooth live in endles joye
His woorthy woorkes, such fame in earth have sowne
As sack nor wrack, his name can there destroy.
—WHETSTONE, GEORGE, 1577, *A Remembraunce of the wel imployed life, and godly end of George Gascoigne Esquire.*

Philomele, the Nightingale: whome the Poetes faine once to haue bene a Ladye of great beauty, till ravished by hir sisters husbande, she desired to be turned into a byrde of hir name, whose complaintes be very wel set forth of Ma. George Gaskin, a wittie gentleman, and the verie chefe of our late rymers, who, and if some parts of learning wanted not (albee it is well knowen he altogyther wanted not learning) no doubt would have attayned to the excellencye of those famous Poets. For gifts of wit and naturall promptnesse appeare in hym aboundantly. —KIRK, EDWARD? 1579, *Spenser's The Shepherd's Calendar, Glosse to November, ed. Collier, vol.* I, *p.* 133.

As painefull a Souldier in the affayres of hys Prince and Country, as he was a wytty Poet in his wryting.—WEBBE, WILLIAM, 1586, *A Discourse of English Poetrie, ed. Arber, p.* 33.

Who euer my priuate opinion condemneth as faultie, Master *Gascoigne* is not to bee abridged of his deserued esteeme, who first beate the path to that perfection which our best Poets haue aspired too since his departure; whereto he did ascend by comparing the Italian with the English, as *Tullie* did *Græca cum Latinis.* —NASHE, THOMAS, 1589, *Letter to the Gentlemen Students of both Universities.*

Gascon for a good meeter and for a plentifull vayne.—PUTTENHAM, GEORGE, 1589, *The Arte of English Poesie, ed. Arber, p.* 77.

Among the lesser late poets, George Gascoigne's works *may be endured.*—BOLTON, EDMUND, 1624, *Hypercritica.*

Gascoigne and Churchyard after them again,
In the beginning of Eliza's reign,
Accompted were great meterers many a day,
But not inspired with brave fire: had they
Lived but a little longer, they had seen
Their works before them to have buried been.
—DRAYTON, MICHAEL, c. 1627, *Of Poets and Poesie.*

In his smaller poems he is certainly too diffuse, and full of conceit. —ELLIS, GEORGE, 1790–1845, *Specimens of the Early English Poets, vol.* II, *p.* 147.

Has much exceeded all the poets of his age, in smoothness and harmony of versification. —WARTON, THOMAS, 1754, *Observations on the Faerie Queen of Spenser, vol.* II, *p.* 168, *note.*

A writer, whose mind, though it exhibits its few marks of strength, is not destitute of delicacy; he is smooth, sentimental, and harmonious.—HEADLEY, HENRY, 1787, *Select Beauties of Ancient English Poetry.*

The works of this early English Poet now sell for a most enormous price. Collectors in general are not aware, that there exists in the British Museum an unpublished Poem by Gascoigne. Great as the research is, and extravagant as the price which is given, for the printed publications of Gascoigne, I question whether it would not be a very hazardous experiment to print this Poem.—BELOE, WILLIAM, 1807, *Anecdotes of Literature and Scarce Books, vol.* II, *p.* 294.

Gascoyne's long poem, called the "Fruits of War," is in the doggerel style of his age; and the general commendations of Chalmers on this poet seem rather hyperbolical. But his minor poems, especially one called "The Arraignment of a Lover," have much spirit and gayety; and we may leave him a respectable place among the Elizabethan versifiers. — HALLAM, HENRY, 1837–39, *Introduction to the Literature of Europe, pt.* ii, *ch.* v, *par.* 60.

In his writings we do not meet with the chivalric fervour and impassioned sentiment of Surrey and Wyatt, or with the polish and melody of the Spenserian stanza; but Gascoigne, nevertheless, exhibits and represents a large advance both in copiousness and propriety of language, and in his command over, and compliance with, metrical canons, upon those poets who had gone before, excepting, may be, one or two foremost men. Compare him, again, with his contemporaries, with Churchyard, Tubervile, Grimoald, Googe, Whetstone, and observe his unmistakable superiority — his master-hand in what he does. Gascoigne's works are indisputably valuable, by reason of their personal and autobiographical allusions, their picturesque, vivid and delicate delineations of incidents and feelings, and of their contributions to our philological stores. He stood, as it were, midway between the school of Surrey and the school of Spenser, but nearer to the former; and he deserves to be regarded as one of the earliest of our strictly *vernacular* writers. He has left to us the second blank-verse Tragedy, the earliest regular Satire, and the earliest dissertation on English rhythms, which our language and literature possess.—HAZLITT, WILLIAM CAREW, 1869, *ed. Complete Poems of George Gascoigne, Preface, vol.* I, *p.* xxvii.

His lyrics are occasionally characterised by a certain lightness and grace, which give and will give them a permanent life. Singing of all a lover's moods and experiences — how he passions, laments, complains, recants, is refused, is encouraged —he is never a mere mimic of his Italian masters, or, though somewhat monotonous, wanting in vigour and sincerity. His style is clear and unaffected. The crude taste of his age is often enough apparent; and in this respect his "poor rude lines," if we "compare them with the bettering of the tiems," may sometimes make but no great show; but here too he rises above his fellows, who are often simply grotesque when they mean to be fervent, and are dull when they are not grotesque. He writes in various metres with various facility and skill. Of blank verse his mastery is imperfect; he is like a child learning to walk, whose progress is from chair to chair; he lacks freedom and fluency. — HALES, JOHN W., 1880, *English Poets, ed. Ward, vol.* I, *p.* 264.

With Gascoigne properly closes the discussion not only of the Latin drama, but of the entire *genre* of *theological belles-lettres* of which it was the most conspicuous class, and which the Reformation, comparatively barren elsewhere, produced with prolific energy in the country of its birth. Still in the vigour of manhood when Marlowe and Decker were at school, Calvinist "by grace," but a true "Elizabethan" by nature, Gascoigne is as it were the meeting-point of the literature represented by the "Acolastus" and the "Pammachius," and that other, not less vast or original, which is represented by "Faustus" and "Fortunatus," by tales of magicians and witches, of fools and rogues, of Grobians and Owlglasses; a literature not, like the former, essentially composed of Christian materials, and called to life under a Christian inspiration, but a genuine and characteristic creation of the Teutonic genius,—a heap of fantastic and uncouth shapes, permeated and tinged no doubt at every point by Christian emotion, but in fundamental structure disclosing, unalloyed, the very native stuff of genial, lawless, untameable human nature. —HERFORD, CHARLES H., 1886, *Studies in the Literary Relations of England and Germany in the Sixteenth Century, p.* 163.

A character of interest inferior only to the men of the very first rank in English letters, as Chaucer, Spenser, and Shakespeare. Gascoigne fitly introduced his great successors of the later Elizabethan period. —SOUTHWORTH, GEORGE C. S., 1888, *Introduction to the Study of English Literature, p.* 49.

Gascoigne died when he had only reached the age of forty, but he had lived long enough for his fame. He was the strongest of the English poets of his generation, and he did not, like Churchyard, live to see how greater poets rose and his light paled in their brightness,—how little wits grew dainty-mouthed, and lisped and trilled, and smiled at Gascoigne's plain song as old-fashioned. He was "old Gascoigne" to the generation of men who were boys in 1579. —MORLEY, HENRY, 1892, *English Writers, vol.* VIII, *p.* 283.

The style of Gascoigne whether in verse or prose is singularly direct and free from the involutions and inversions which mark his latinized contemporaries. He is generally clear, and simple, except where intentionally allegorical or "mystical" as he calls it; remarkably consecutive, though easily diverted from his main purpose. His prose often exhibits greater elegance and grace than his verse, from the fact that the latter is apt to ramble and lose the sense of form and proportion in a profusion of detail. Gascoigne's verse, however, is far from devoid of the quality of music, and displays a general smoothness and evenness of flow from his close regard for the number of syllables, from the correspondence of word and logical or rhetorical accent with the accentual scheme of his verse, from the regularity of his phrasing and from his constant employment of alliteration and its resulting ease of utterance. Gascoigne's diction often rises to dignity and real eloquence, and his figures are frequently original and well chosen. As is to be expected from the prevailing looseness of his structure of sentence, Gascoigne prefers set and fully expounded simile to the flash and inspiration of metaphor, although it cannot be denied that he is often peculiarly happy in the use of the latter.—SCHELLING, FELIX E., 1894, *The Life and Writings of George Gascoigne, p.* 30.

It is no mean feat, indeed, to rank in history as George Gascoigne ranks, with fair documentary evidence to prove his title, as the actual first practitioner in English of comedy in prose, satire in regular verse, short prose tales, translated tragedy, and literary animadversion. But the above-mentioned student of literature as a whole, or as nearly as may be in its wholeness, would be rather surprised if he found a clever, enterprising, industrious innovator of this kind rising at once to mastery in his innovations. The most brilliant pioneers and leaders of cavalry raids are not generally the generals who win epoch-making battles, or hold down the country they have scoured. And in this particular Gascoigne, who is, perhaps, the most notable and characteristic figure of our earlier period, of which his manhood covers the greater part, is no exception. . . . The blank verse, of which Gascoigne was but the fourth or fifth practitioner in English, is not without merit; his prose is spirited and vigorous, if not elegant; and in his lyrics there is not seldom a touch of that unforced and childlike pathos which is the best point of these earlier Elizabethans, and which, in the later and greater school, is rather hushed by higher notes, except in the case of some of the lesser men, such as Gascoigne's step-son, Nicholas Breton. On the other hand, his metres are still alternately limp and wooden; his style is still stiffened with the old clumsy alliteration; there is no fire or splendour in his poetry; his prose has neither continuity nor gorgeousness. He is merely a clever man living an active life in times of both material and mental activity, but with nothing very particular to say and no very exquisite manner of saying it. —SAINTSBURY, GEORGE, 1895, *Social England, ed. Traill, vol.* III, *pp.* 343, 344.

Without being a great poet Gascoigne is a representative English writer. He originated no fresh movement in metrical composition, but his active and robust intelligence enabled him to express clearly in verse the thoughts and feelings that were interesting his age. He called himself "Chaucer's boy and Petrarch's journeyman," but he was himself a master of the English language; and his metrical style is singularly free from those learned affectations and conceits to the fascinations of which many of his contemporaries fell easy victims.—COURTHOPE, W. J., 1897, *A History of English Poetry, vol.* II, *p.* 177.

Thomas Tusser

1524?-1580

Successively a musician, schoolmaster, serving man, husbandman, grazier, and poet; born at Rivenhall, Essex, England, about 1515; educated at Eton and at Cambridge. Died in London about Apr., 1580. He was the author of "Five Hundred Points of Good Husbandry, united to as many of Good Housewifery, etc." (1573), in verse, with a metrical autobiography. His book is chiefly valuable for its picture of the manners and domestic life of English farmers.—BEERS, HENRY A., *rev.* 1897, *Johnson's Universal Cyclopædia, vol.* VIII, *p,* 319.

GOOD HUSBANDRY
1573

Whether he bought or sold, he lost; and, when a renter, impoverished himself and never enriched his landlord. Yet hath he laid down excellent rules in his "Book of Husbandry and Houswifery," (so that the observer thereof must be rich) in his own defence.—FULLER, THOMAS, 1662, *The Worthies of England, ed. Nichols, vol.* I, *p.* 354

It must be acknowledged, that this old English georgic has much more of the simplicity of Hesiod, than of the elegance of Virgil: and a modern reader would suspect, that many of its salutary maxims originally decorated the margins, and illustrated the calendars, of an ancient almanac. It is without invocations, digressions, and descriptions: no pleasing pictures of rural imagery are drawn from meadows covered with flocks, and fields waving with corn, nor are Pan and Ceres once named. Yet it is valuable, as a genuine picture of the agriculture, the rural arts, and the domestic economy and customs, of our industrious ancestors.—WARTON, THOMAS, 1778-81, *History of English Poetry, sec.* liii.

There is nowhere to be found excepting perhaps in Swift's "Directions to Servants," evidence of such rigid and minute attention to every department of domestic economy. . . . Although neither beauty of description nor elegance of diction was Tusser's object, he has frequently attained, what better indeed suited his purpose, a sort of homely, pointed and quaint expression, like that of the old English proverb, which the rhyme and the alliteration tend to fix on the memory of the reader.—SCOTT, SIR WALTER, 1810, *ed. Five Hundred Points of Good Husbandry, Somers Tracts, vol,* III.

The great merit of Tusser's book, independent of the utility of its agricultural precepts, consists in the faithful picture which it delineates of the manners, customs, and domestic life of the English farmer, and in the morality, piety, and benevolent simplicity which pervade the whole. In a poetical light its pretensions are not great.—DRAKE, NATHAN, 1817, *Shakspeare and his Times, vol.* I, *p.* 657.

Such was the ancient farmer's year, which Tusser has described with wonderful spirit, even to the minutest detail, and such were the operations of husbandry that the boy Shakspere would have beheld with interest amidst his native corn-fields and pastures.—KNIGHT, CHARLES, 1842, *William Shakspere: A Biography.*

Tusser's versification, however, is curiously elaborate for the time when he wrote. Warton has pointed this out. His rhythm also seems to be always good, and his language free from inversions; two merits that have probably gone far in insuring his permanent popularity among the class for which he wrote.—CREASY, SIR EDWARD, 1850-75, *Memoirs of Eminent Etonians, p.* 69.

Good, honest, homely, useful old rhymer. —SOUTHEY, ROBERT, 1843?-1851, *Commonplace Book.*

The precepts of Tusser are excellent, and show very much cool collected sense. —DONALDSON, JOHN, 1854, *Agricultural Biography.*

Tusser's strength may have been in high farming, it was not in high poetry.

Nevertheless, there is a musical sententiousness in his terse rhymes, and an air of business about them; his Pegasus tugged over the clods with his shoulder well up to the collar, and the maxims were in a form likely to ensure for them wide currency among the people. —MORLEY, HENRY, 1873, *First Sketch of English Literature, p.* 349.

He is our only, or almost our only, English Georgic poet, and his poetry frankly acquiesces in doggerel. —SAINTSBURY, GEORGE, 1898, *A Short History of English Literature, p.* 253.

Raphael Holinshed

D. 1580

Raphael Holinshed, or Holingshed, an English chronicler of the Elizabethan age. He is said to have been descended from a respectable family in Cheshire; and from his own will it appears, that in the latter part of his life he was steward to Thomas Burdet, Esq., of Bromcote, Warwickshire. The "Chronicles of Holinshed" were first published in 1577; and prefixed to them is one of the most curious and interesting memorials existing of the manners and domestic history of the English, in the 16th century. Died about 1580.—CATES, WILLIAM L. R., *ed.* 1867, *A Dictionary of General Biography, p.* 520.

CHRONICLE

They have reprinted at London the castrated sheets of Holinshead's "Chronicle," but done so as there is a great quarrell between some of the London booksellers on this score, some of them having one impression, and some another; so that there are two new impressions of these sheets, in one impression of which Fletcher Gyles, a bookseller, is concerned, and he was urgent with me to correct them, but I declined it, being sensible that the reprinting them might disoblige some gentlemen, who had given great prices for their books, as it seems it hath done. But, however, the booksellers are not like to be very great gainers by this work, the castrated Hollingsheads being now like to be dearer than those that are perfect.—HEARNE, THOMAS, 1723, *Reliquiæ Hearnianæ, ed. Bliss, vol.* II, *p.* 167.

Are by far the most popular and important of our historical records, in print, during the time of Queen Elizabeth; and from which, indeed, all modern historians have freely and largely borrowed. —DIBDIN, THOMAS FROGNALL, 1824, *The Library Companion, p.* 185, *note.*

The pages of Holinshed more truly reflect the living language of Queen Elizabeth's time than the stanzas of Spenser. —MARSH, GEORGE P., 1859, *Lectures on the English Language, p.* 112.

The total absence of the critical spirit in his work seems to show that he could not have belonged to the general literary fraternity of Europe.—ARNOLD, THOMAS, 1862-87, *A Manual of English Literature, American ed. p.* 125.

A homely, honest, simple-hearted chronicler (somewhat thievish, as all the old chroniclers were) but whose name is specially worth keeping in mind, because he—in all probability—supplied Shakespeare's principal historic reading, and furnished the crude material, afterward beaten out into those plaques of gold, which we call Shakespeare's Historic Plays. Therefore, we must always, I think, treat Holinshed with respect.—MITCHELL, DONALD G., 1889, *English Lands Letters and Kings, From Celt to Tudor, p.* 212.

The "Chronicles" form a very valuable repertory of historical information. The enormous number of authorities cited attests Holinshed's and his successors' industry. The style is clear, although never elevated, and the chronicler fully justified his claim "to have had an especial eye unto the truth of things," although his protestant bias is very marked throughout and his treatment of early times is very uncritical. The patriotic tone of the book led Holinshed's assistants to insist so strenuously on the rights of the English sovereigns to exact homage from the Scottish rulers, that Sir Thomas Craig was moved to write a reply, entitled "De Hominio," in 1605. The Elizabethan dramatists drew many of their plots from Holinshed's pages, and nearly all Shakespeare's historical plays (as well as

"Macbeth," "King Lear," and part of "Cymbeline") are based on Holinshed's "Chronicles." At times (as in the two parts of "Henry IV") Shakespeare adopted not only Holinshed's facts, but some of his phrases.—LEE, SIDNEY, 1891, *Dictionary of National Biography, vol.* XXVII, *p.* 132.

Holinshed was an Elizabethan among the Elizabethans. His style, cumbrous with reflection, spangled with wise saws and modern instances, and curious with grammatical inversions, is of a vivid picturesqueness. If he does not criticise his materials, if he is prone to the marvellous, and unable to resist a telling story, he is capable none the less of the boldest plain-speaking in defence of his convictions, and tells the truth to the Queen and Privy Council. His conception of accuracy is different from ours: he is at little pains to establish the exact conditions of a given fact, but he bestows endless patience in revealing that state of mind in the actor which made the fact a possibility. Every detail of history is food for his psychology; and his "Chronicles" are an epitome of the work of conscience in the human soul, and a record of the marvellous ways of God to Man. The very fashion of his wisdom is different from ours; it is often trite if always judicial, it is less original than profound; it is constantly preoccupied with the moral root of the matter. There is little irony in it, for his abuse of analysis never soured in Holinshed the milk of human kindness, and his liberal humanity is backed up by an unshakable religion. Such as he is, large and slow and solid, he is so sure a guide in the desperate places of the human conscience, that the dramatists of his time, and especially Shakespeare, conveyed from his chronicles whole characters, entire scenes, with scarce an alteration. — DARMESTETER, MARY, 1893, *English Prose, ed. Craik, vol.* I, *p.* 317.

Sir Thomas Wilson

1525?-1581

One of the earliest English philologists, was educated at Eton and at King's College, Cambridge, and afterwards became tutor to the two sons of Charles Brandon, Duke of Suffolk; lived abroad during the reign of Mary, and was imprisoned by the Inquisitor at Rome on account of the heresy alleged to be contained in his treatises on Logic and Rhetoric; after torture, which failed to shake his constancy, he escaped in consequence of a fire which caused the populace to release the prisoners from their incarceration; on the accession of Elizabeth returned to England, and became a Master of Requests, Master of St. Katherine's Hospital near the Tower, and Private Secretary to the Queen; Envoy to the Low Countries, 1576: Secretary of State, 1577; Dean of Durham, 1579; died 1581.—ALLIBONE, S. AUSTIN, 1871, *Dictionary of English Literature, vol.* III, *p.* 2783.

And so is now our witty Wilson, who, for learning and extemporal wit in this faculty, is without compare or compeer; as to his great and eternal commendations, he manifested in his challenge at the Swan, on the Bank Side.—MERES, FRANCIS, 1598, *Palladis Tamia.*

It* may therefore be justly considered as the first book or system of criticism in our language.—WARTON, THOMAS, 1778–81, *History of English Poetry, sec.* lv.

The "Treatises" of Wilson powerfully assisted the cause which Ascham had been advocating; it displays much sagacity and good sense, and greatly contributed to clear the language from the affectation consequent on the introduction of foreign words and idioms. — DRAKE, NATHAN, 1817, *Shakspeare and his Times, vol.* I, *p.* 440.

*Art of Rhetoric.

Sir Thomas Wilson is worthy of the phalanx of Knights in which he is here embodied; and will be long remembered as a philologist, rather than as a statesman or divine. His slender little volume, entitled "Epistola de vita et obitu duorum fratrum Suffolciensium, Henrici et Caroli Brandon," 1552, 4to. is a volume to rack the most desperate with torture, as to the hopelessness of its acquisition. The Bodleian Library possesses it; so does the British Museum; and so does Earl Spencer. Another copy is not known to me. —DIBDIN, THOMAS FROGNALL, 1824, *The Library Companion, p.* 588, *note.*

Warton says that it is the first system of criticism in our language. But, in the common use of the word, it is no criticism at all, any more than the treatise of Cicero de Oratore. . . . Wilson was a man of considerable learning, and his "Art of Rhetorique" is by no means without merit. —HALLAM, HENRY, 1837–39, *Introduction to the Literature of Europe, pt.* ii, *ch.* vii, *par.* 32.

Our English Aristarchus. —DISRAELI, ISAAC, 1841, *Origin of the Vernacular Languages of Europe, Amenities of Literature.*

Thomas Wilson belongs to that earlier academic school of Tudor prose writers, whose chief characteristic is a direct and nervous simplicity and purity of diction, due partly to a growing native pride in the English tongue, partly to the revived study of Greek. He has not the sweetness and Herodotean ease of More, who, though a forerunner of the group, represents its style as a historian. He has not the homely poignancy of Latimer, its preacher, nor the graceful learning of Ascham, its teacher, with whom indeed Wilson has most in common. Versed in travel, in trade, in the region of practical politics, he may, however, be taken to stand in that group for its man of affairs.—TRENCH, F. H., 1893, *English Prose, ed. Craik, vol.* I, *p.* 285.

Wilson has more merit than that of merely protesting against affectation: he not only lays down sensible laws for English writing, but to a certain extent exemplifies them. He has more command over the language than Ascham, and his style is not so repellantly wooden.—WYATT AND LOW, 1896, *English Literature to* 1580, *p.* 181, *note.*

Wilson, however, did good service by his denunciation of pedantry, "strange inkhorn terms," and the use of French and "Italianated" idiom, which "counterfeited the kinges Englishe." In this way Wilson may have stimulated the development of English prose, and it has been maintained that Shakespeare himself owes something, including hints for Dogberry's character, to a study of Wilson's book.—POLLARD, A. F., 1900, *Dictionary of National Biography, vol.* LXII, *p.* 132.

George Buchanan

1506–1582

Born at Killearn, Stirlingshire, Feb. 1506. Educated at Parish School. In Paris, studying Latin, 1520-22. Served with French troops in Scotland under Albany, 1523. To St. Andrews 1524; B. A., 3 Oct. 1825. To Paris, 1526. B. A., Scottish College, Paris, 10 Oct. 1527; M. A., Mar. 1528. Elected "Procurator of German nation," 3 June 1529; taught in Coll. of St. Barbe, 1529-32. Tutor to Gilbert, Earl of Cassilis, 1532-36. Returned to Scotland. Tutor to a natural son of King James, 1537-38. Arrested on charge of Lutheranism, Jan. 1539; escaped from prison and fled to London, and thence to Paris and Bordeaux. Taught Latin in College of Guienne, 1539-42. Returned to Paris; taught in College of Cardinal Le Moine, 1544-47. To Portugal; to Coll. at Comibra, 1547. Returned to England, 1552; to Paris 1553, taught in Coll. of Boncourt. Tutor to son of Count de Brissac, 1555-60 Returned to Scotland; classical tutor to Queen. Joined Reformed Church; sat in assemblies of 1563-67; Moderator, 1567; Principal of St. Andrews, 1566. To England as secretary to Commission respecting Queen Mary, 1568. Returned to St. Andrews, Jan. 1569. Tutor to King James, Aug. 1569 to May 1578. Director of Chancery 1570; Keeper of Privy Seal, 1570-78. Died, at Edinburgh, 29 Sept. 1582. Buried there, in churchyard of Grey Friars. *Works:* "Jephthes," 1554; "De Caleto nuper ab Henrico II. . . . recepta Carmen," 1558; "Franciscanus," 1566; "Psalmorum Davidis paraphrasis poetica," 1566; "Elegiæ, Silvæ, Hendecasyllabi," 1567; De Maria Scotorum Regina totaque ejus contra Regem conjuratione" (anon.), 1571; "An Admonition direct to the Trew Lordis Mantenairs of the Kingis graces authoritie" (under initials: M. G. B.), 1571; "Baptistes," 1578; "De Jure Regni apud Scotos Dialogus," 1579; "Rerum Scoticarum Historia," 1582. *Posthumous:* "De Sphæra, Libri V.," 1587; "Satyra in Cardinalem Lotharingum," 1590; "De Prosodia libellus," 1596; "Tragœdiæ Sacræ & exteræ," 1597; "Vita ab ipso scripta," 1608; "Poemata

Omnia," 1615; "The Chameleon," 1710; "Letters," 1711. He *translated:* Linacre's "Rudimenta Grammatices," 1533; Euripide's "Alcestis," 1557; "Medea and Alcestis," 1567. *Collected Works:* edited by T. Ruddiman (2 vols.) 1715.—SHARP, R. FARQUHARSON, 1897, *A Dictionary of English Authors, p.* 36.

PERSONAL

When we cam to his chalmer we fand him sitting in chaire, teatching his young man that servit him in his chalmer to spell a, b, ab; e, b, eb; etc. Efter salutation Mr. Andre sayes, "I sie, sir, yie are nocht ydle." "Better this," quoth he, "nor stelling sheipe, or sytting ydle, quhilk is als ill." Thereafter he schew ws the Epistle Dedicatorie, quhilk, when Mr. Andre had read, he tauld him that it was obscure in sum places, and wanted certean words to perfyt the sentence. Sayes he "I may do no mair for thinking on another matter." "What is that?" says Mr. Andre. "To die," quoth he; "bot I leave that and manie ma things for yow to helpe."—MELVILLE, JAMES, 1601, *Diary.*

Roughhewn, slovenly, and rude, in his person, behaviour, and fashion; seldom caring for a better outside than a rugge-gown girt close about him: yet his inside and conceipt in poesie was most rich, and his sweetness and facilitie in verse most excellent.—PEACHAM, HENRY, 1622, *The Compleat Gentleman.*

Cheery, impressible George Buchanan; a Presbyterian, austere but half way through, with a face like a Scotch Socrates, although more apt than Socrates to take offence, familiar with Latin as with his native tongue, full of anecdote and good talk, familiar also with languages and people round about, and liking Scotland all the better for experience in other lands.—MORLEY, HENRY, 1873, *First Sketch of English Literature, p.* 404.

While his title to learning is thus beyond dispute, the rest of his character has been the subject of vehement controversy. Nor is it a character easy to read. Some points will be generally allowed. With him the love of education was not merely a virtue but a passion, early conceived and never abandoned. But he was not only a professor but a man of the world. The world in which he lived was distracted by the deepest and widest controversy in modern history; between tradition and the new learning, between absolute and constitutional government, between the romanist and the reformed doctrines and discipline. In this controversy, not only in the field of literature, but of action, Buchanan took a prominent part on the side of the reformers. He is still deemed a traitor, a slanderer, and an atheist by some, while to others he is a champion of the cause of liberty and religion, and one of its most honoured names. His character may perhaps be more justly represented as combined of strange contradictions; he was at the same time humane and vindictive, mirthful and morose, cultured and coarse, fond of truth, but full of prejudices. It is these contradictions and his great learning and literary power which make him so striking a figure in the history of Scotland and of literature.—MACKAY, ÆNEAS, 1886, *Dictionary of National Biography, vol.* VII, *p.* 193.

DE JURE REGNI
1579

There is a singular spirit of freedom in this tract, especially for the time when it was written, and it gives me a high idea of the honesty or boldness of this writer, that he presumed to address a discourse of this sort to his pupil, King James the Sixth. This strong love of liberty, to which his warm temper and elevated genius naturally inclined him, was catched or at least much confirmed in him by his familiarity with the classical story of the Greeks and Romans, the great doctors of civil liberty to all countries and ages. The whole was written with a view to the late dealings about the Queen of Scots. The dialogue, as to its manner, is very masterly, except that there seems a little affectation in conducting it according to the Socratic method.—HURD, RICHARD, 1808? *Commonplace Book, ed. Kilvert, p.* 225.

The dialogue of our illustrious countryman Buchanan, "De Jure Regni apud Scotus," though occasionally disfigured by the keen and indignant temper of the writer, and by a predilection (pardonable in a scholar warm from the schools of ancient Greece and Rome) for forms of policy unsuitable to the circumstances of modern Europe, bears nevertheless, in its general spirit, a closer resemblance to the political philosophy of the eighteenth century, than any composition which had previously appeared.—STEWART, DUGALD, 1815–21, *First Preliminary Dissertation, Encyclopædia Britannica.*

The opinions which Knox embodied chiefly in fierce declamations, and which he advocated mainly with a view to religious interests, were soon after systematised and at the same time secularised by Buchanan in a short dialogue entitled, "De Jure Regni apud Scotos," which was published in 1579, and which bears in many respects a striking resemblance to some of the writings that afterwards issued from the Jesuits. In Buchanan, however, we find none of those countless subtleties and qualifications to which the Catholic theologians commonly resorted in order to evade the decisions of the Fathers or the schoolmen, nor do we find anything about the deposing power of the Pope. The principles that were enunciated were perfectly clear and decisive: they were derived exclusively from reason, and they were directed equally against every form of tyranny.—LECKY, WILLIAM EDWARD HARTPOLE, 1865, *Spirit of Rationalism in Europe, vol.* II, *p.* 175.

For Buchanan's politics were too advanced for his age. Not only Catholic Scotsmen, like Blackwood, Winzet, and Ninian, but Protestants like Sir Thomas Craig and Sir John Wemyss, could not stomach the "De Jure Regni." They may have had some reason on their side. In the then anarchic state of Scotland, organization and unity under a common head may have been more important than the assertion of popular rights. Be that as it may, in 1584, only two years after his death, the Scots parliament condemned his Dialogue and History as untrue, and commanded all possessors of copies to deliver them up, that they might be purged of "the offensive and extraordinary matters" which they contained. The "De Jure Regni" was again prohibited in Scotland, in 1664, even in manuscript; and in 1683, the whole of Buchanan's political works had the honour of being burned by the University of Oxford, in company with those of Milton, Languet, and others, as "pernicious books, and damnable doctrines, destructive to the sacred persons of Princes, their state and government, and of all human society." And thus the seed which Buchanan had sown, and Milton had watered (for the allegation that Milton borrowed from Buchanan is probably true, and equally honourable to both), lay trampled into the earth, and seemingly lifeless, till it tillered out, and blossomed, and bore fruit to a good purpose, in the Revolution of 1688.—KINGSLEY, CHARLES, 1868, *George Buchanan, Scholar; Good Words, vol.* 9, *p.* 735.

The political views for which Buchanan contended appear in the present day sufficiently commonplace; but that they are commonplace and out of date is due in great measure to the successful efforts of writers like Buchanan himself.—RITCHIE, DAVID G., 1890, *George Buchanan; The Westminster Review, vol.* 134, *p.* 522.

HISTORY OF SCOTLAND
1582

In his old age he applied himself to write the Scots' History, which he renewed with such judgment and eloquence, as no country can show a better.—SPOTISWOOD, JOHN, 1639? *History of the Church and State of Scotland.*

His style is so natural and nervous, and his reflections on things are so solid, . . . that he is justly reckoned the greatest and best of our modern authors. — BURNET, GILBERT, 1679–1715, *History of the Reformation of the Church of England, ed. Nares, pt.* i, *bk.* iii.

The last twelve or thirteen years of his life were spent in writing the History of his country, in which he has united the brevity and force of Sallust, with the elegance and perspicuity of Livy. — BIRCH, THOMAS, 1743–52, *Heads of Illustrious Persons with their Lives and Character.*

If his accuracy and impartiality had been, in any degree, equal to the elegance of his taste, and to the purity and vigour of his style, his history might be placed on a level with the most admired compositions of the ancients. But, instead of rejecting the improbable tales of chronicle writers, he was at the utmost pains to adorn them; and hath clothed, with all the beauties and graces of fiction, those legends which formerly had only its wildness and extravagance.—ROBERTSON, WILLIAM, 1758–59, *History of Scotland, vol.* I, *bk.* i.

Though the early portion of it is unmistakably fabulous, it is written throughout with great animation and force. For the part of it which relates to the history of the sixteenth century, he is an original and contemporary authority, and from his official position it may reasonably be assumed that he had access to the most trustworthy sources of information for the later portion of his history. Though an ardent party man, he had a strong sense of justice, a good judgment, and a love of truth. His narrative is enriched with wise and just political reflections, and his sentiments are almost always liberal, and for the time even radical. This feature of his History drew down upon it the vengeance of all who were attached to Romanism, all the enemies of freedom and all the lovers of despotism; even at this day, there are some who utterly detest the political principles of George Buchanan. —MACKINTOSH, JOHN, 1878–92, *The History of Civilisation in Scotland, vol.* II, *p.* 367

POEMS

Buchanan's paraphrase continues to be read in the principal schools of Scotland, and perhaps in those of some other countries. Lauder's attempt to supersede it by that of Johnston proved unsuccessful. During the lifetime of Buchanan, it had begun to be introduced into the schools of Germany; and its various measures had been accommodated to appropriate melodies, for the purpose of being chanted by academics. Pope Urban VII., himself a poet of no mean talent, is said to have averred that it was a pity it was written by so great a heretic, for otherwise it should have been sung in all churches under his authority.—IRVING, DAVID, 1807, *Memoirs of the Life and Writings of Buchanan, p.* 130

The most distinguished among the Latin poets of Europe in this age was George Buchanan, of whom Joseph Scaliger and several other critics have spoken in such unqualified terms, that they seem to place him even above the Italians at the beginning of the sixteenth century. If such were their meaning, I should crave the liberty of hesitating. The best poem of Buchanan, in my judgment, is that on the Sphere, than which few philosophical subjects could afford better opportunities for ornamental digression. He is not, perhaps, in hexameters inferior to Vida, and certainly far superior to Palearius. In this poem, Buchanan descants on the absurdity of the Pythagorean system, which supposes the motion of the earth. Many good passages occur in his elegies, though we may not reckon him equal in this metre to several of the Italians. His celebrated translation of the Psalms I must also presume to think overpraised: it is difficult, perhaps, to find one, except the 137th, with which he has taken particular pains, that can be called truly elegant or classical Latin poetry. Buchanan is now and then incorrect in the quantity of syllables, as indeed is common with his contemporaries. —HALLAM, HENRY, 1837–39, *Introduction to the Literature of Europe, pt.* ii, *ch.* v, *par.* 97.

Buchanan in his Latin was a poet-scholar, not a scholar who wrote verse. He shows himself in these poems generous in friendship although quick in scorn, graceful in compliment, and concerned chiefly with affairs of men, though he knew how to write a May-Day poem that was a joy even to Wordsworth. Ascham agreed with the learned throughout Europe in regarding George Buchanan as the best Latin poet of his time. Probably he was, as many thought him, the best of Latin poets since the days when Latin was their mother tongue. —MORLEY, HENRY, 1892, *English Writers, vol.* VIII, *p.* 349.

GENERAL

That notable man, Mr. George Bucquhanane—remains alyve to this day, in the yeir of God 1566 years, to the glory of God, to the gret honour of this natioun, and to the comfort of thame that delyte in letters and vertew. That singulare wark of David's Psalmes, in Latin meetre and poesie, besyd mony uther, can witness the rare gracies of God gevin to that man. —KNOX, JOHN, 1566, *History of the Reformation.*

I meane not of such infamous inuectiues, as Buchanans or Knoxs Chronicles: and if any one of these infamous libels remaine vntill your daies, vse the law vpon the keepers thereof.—JAMES VI. OF SCOTLAND, 1616, *Basilikon Doron, ed. Morley, Universal Library, p.* 143.

A serpent—a daring caluminator—leviathan of slander—the second of all human forgers, and the first of all human slanderers. —WHITAKER, JOHN, 1787, *Mary Queen of Scots Vindicated.*

In a conversation concerning the literary merits of the two countries, in which

Buchanan was introduced, a Scotchman, imagining that on this ground he should have an undoubted triumph over him, exclaimed, "Ah, Doctor Johnson, what would you have said of Buchanan, had he been an Englishman?"—"Why, sir," said Johnson after a little pause, "I should *not* have said of Buchanan, had he been an *Englishman*, what I will now say of him as a *Scotchman*,—that he was the only man of genius his country ever produced."—BOSWELL, JAMES, 1790, *Life of Dr. Samuel Johnson, ch.* li.

George Buchanan is justly considered one of the brightest ornaments of his country, both as a poet and an historian.—DIBDIN, THOMAS FROGNALL, 1824, *The Library Companion, p.* 264.

A man justly entitled to the epithet great, if the true criteria of such a character are originality of genius, and the impression left by it upon his age. His intellect, naturally fearless and inquisitive, caught an early and eager hold of the principles of the Reformation; and having gone abroad, and fallen into the toils of the inquisition, persecution completed what nature had begun.—TYTLER, PATRICK FRASER, 1843-64, *The History of Scotland, vol.* IV, *p.* 53.

His Satire is of the contemptuous order. He was one of those satirists who do not profess to tickle, nor pretend to that happy temperament which makes a man, with a smiling good-natured face and a perfectly-balanced system, smile while he strikes, and wound without an imputation on his good-nature. . . . I fancy Buchanan was, for the most part, very impassioned and serious in the satirical work he took in hand. Waving the question of art, which would of course deal with productions on a different principle, I confess I would rather have as a friend, and specially as an ally, the man who on the surface looks the more ferocious and bloodthirsty of the two. Of Erasmus's good nature and general friendliness I have the highest opinion; but I think it likely that Buchanan had the deeper heart, and generally the deeper moral nature.—HANNAY, JAMES, 1854, *Satire and Satirists, p.* 91.

There could be no better type of the man of letters of his time, in whom the liberality of the cosmopolitan was united with the exclusiveness of the member of a very strait and limited caste. He had his correspondents in all the cities of the Continent, and at home his closest associates were among the highest in his own land. Yet he was the son of a very poor man, born almost a peasant and dying nearly as poor as he was born. From wandering scholar and pedagogue he became the preceptor of a King and the associate of princes; but he was not less independent, and he was scarcely more rich in the one position than the other. His pride was not in the high consultations he shared or the national movements in which he had his part, but in his fine Latinity and the elegant turn of those classical lines which all his learned compeers admired and applauded. The part that he played in history has been made to look odious by skilled critics; and the great book in which he recorded the deeds of his contemporaries and predecessors has been assailed violently and bitterly as prejudiced, partial, and untrue. But nobody has been able to attack his Latin or impair the renown of his scholarship; and perhaps had he himself chosen the foundation on which to build his fame, this is what he would have preferred above all. History may come and politics go, and the principles of both may change with the generations, but Latin verse goes on for ever: no false ingenuity of criticism can pick holes in the deathless structure of an art with which living principles have had nothing to do for a thousand years and more.—OLIPHANT, MARGARET O. W., 1890, *Royal Edinburgh, p.* 378

Comparatively few have an intelligent notion of the nature and scope of his works; and the stereotyped criticisms which have passed current from generation to generation are sufficient evidence that some of those few have talked about them rather than read them. His only works which are popularly known by name are the "History of Scotland" and the paraphrase of the Psalms, regarding the latter of which his biographer Irving wrote in the early part of the present century that it was read in many schools as a text-book of the Latin language. In the present day many of the class of readers to whom Irving refers, and not a few of their teachers, would be unable to say in what language the famous paraphrase was composed.—WALKER, HUGH, 1893, *Three Centuries of Scottish Literature, vol.* I, *p.* 51.

Thomas Norton

1532–1584

Born at London, 1532: died at Sharpenhoe, Bedfordshire, 1584. An English lawyer, translator, and author. He wrote (with Sackville) the first English tragedy, "Gorboduc, or Ferrex and Porrex." He published a "Translation of Calvin's Institutes" (1561), and translated many of the psalms in the Psalter of Sternhold and Hopkins (1561), etc.—SMITH, BENJAMIN E., ed. 1894–97, *The Century Cyclopedia of Names, p.* 745.

As to Norton's assistance in this play, it is said on better authority than that of Anthony Wood, who supposes "Gordobuc" to have been in old English rhyme, that the three first acts were written by Thomas Norton, and the two last by Sackville. But the force of internal evidence often prevails over the authority of assertion, a testimony which is diminished by time, and may be rendered suspicious from a variety of other circumstances. Throughout the whole piece, there is an invariable uniformity of diction and versification. Sackville has two poems of considerable length in the "Mirrour of Magistrates," which fortunately furnish us with the means of comparison: and every scene of "Gordobuc" is visibly marked with his characteristical manner, which consists in a perspicuity of style, and a command of numbers, superior to the tone of his times. Thomas Norton's poetry is of a very different and a subordinate cast: and if we may judge from his share in our metrical psalmody, he seems to have been much more properly qualified to shine in the miserable mediocrity of Sternhold's stanza, and to write spiritual rhymes for the solace of his illuminated brethren, than to reach the bold and impassioned elevations of tragedy.—WARTON, THOMAS, 1778-81, *History of English Poetry, sec.* lvii.

The style of this old play is stiff and cumbersome, like the dresses of its times. There may be flesh and blood underneath, but we cannot get at it. Sir Philip Sidney has praised it for its morality. One of its authors might easily furnish that. Norton was an associate to Hopkins, Sternhold, and Robert Wisdom, in the singing psalms. I am willing to believe that Lord Buckhurst supplied the more vital parts. —LAMB, CHARLES, 1827, *Notes on the Garrick Plays, Essays.*

On the title-page of the first edition, printed in 1565, which, however, was surreptitious, it is stated that the three first acts were written by Norton, and the two last by Sackville; and, although this announcement was afterwards withdrawn, it was never expressly contradicted, and it is not improbable that it may have a general foundation of truth. It must be confessed, however, that no change of style gives any indication which it is easy to detect of a succession of hands; and that, judging by this criterion, we should rather be led to infer that, in whatever way the two writers contrived to combine their labors, whether by the one retouching and improving what the other had rough-sketched, or by the one taking the quieter and humbler, the other the more impassioned, scenes or portions of the dialogue, they pursued the same method throughout the piece. —CRAIK, GEORGE L., 1861, *A Compendious History of English Literature and of the English Language, vol.* I, *p.* 478.

Norton owes his place in literature to his joint authorship with Sackville of the earliest tragedy in English and in blank verse. Sackville's admirers have on no intelligible ground contested Norton's claim to be the author of the greater part of the piece. Of "The Tragedie of Gorboduc," three acts (according to the published title-page) "were written by Thomas Nortone, and the two last by Thomas Sackuyle," and it was first performed "by the Gentlemen of Thynner Temple" in their hall on Twelfth Night, 1560–1. The plot is drawn from Geoffrey of Monmouth's "History of Britain," book ii, chap. xvi., and relates the efforts of Gorboduc, king of Britain, to divide his dominions between his sons Ferrex and Porrex; a fierce quarrel ensues between the princes, which ends in their deaths and in the death of their father, and leaves the land a prey to civil war. The moral of the piece "that a state knit in unity doth continue strong against all force, but being divided is easily destroyed," commended it to political circles, where great anxiety prevailed at the date of its representation respecting the succession to the throne. Norton had himself called attention to the dangers of leaving the question unsettled in the House of Commons. The play follows the model of Seneca, and the tragic deeds in which the story abounds are mainly related in the speeches of messengers. Each act is preceded by a dumb show portraying the action that is to follow, and a chorus concludes the first four acts. Blank verse had first been introduced into English literature by Henry Howard, earl of Surrey, Nicholas Grimoald, who, like Norton, contributed to Turner's "Prerogative," and was doubtless personally known to him, had practiced it later. But Norton and Sackville were the first to employ it in the drama. They produced it with mechanical and monotonous regularity, and showed little sense of its adaptability to great artistic purposes.—LEE, SIDNEY, 1895, *Dictionary of National Biography, vol.* XLI, *p.* 224.

Alexander Scott

1525?–1584?

Born about 1525, is supposed to have been the son of Alexander Scott, prebendary of the Chapel Royal of Stirling, whose two sons, John and Alexander, were legitimated 21 November 1549 (*Privy Council Register*, xxiii 50). There is no evidence of his having followed any profession, but all allusions in his poems establish the fact that much of his time was spent in or near Edinburgh. In a sonnet by Alexander Montgomerie (1556?-1610?), written apparently about 1584, he is spoken of as "Old Scot," and as then living; he probably died in that year or soon after. He was married, but his wife eloped with a "wantoun man." Scott's extant work consists of thirty-six short pieces, the longest numbering a little over two hundred lines. They are preserved only in the Bannatyne manuscript compiled in 1568 (now in the Advocates' Library, Edinburgh). The earliest poem by Scott to which a date can be assigned is "The Lament of the Maister of Erskyn," written in 1547. The two most important poems are "A New Yeir Gift to Quene Mary," which throws much light on the social life and lamentable condition of the people in 1562; and "The Justing at the Drum," a clever imitation of "Chrystis Kirk on the Grene," in which the practice of the tournament is ridiculed. The rest of the poems, written in a great variety of measures, are for the most part amatory. A few, in a satirical vein, are very coarse. All are marked by felicity of diction and directness of expression. Scott is called by Pinkerton "the Anacreon of old Scotish poetry." But among the ancient minor poets of Scotland his place should be below Montgomerie.—CRANSTOUN, JAMES, 1897, *Dictionary of National Biography, vol.* LI, *p.* 10.

The productions of Scott may be classed with the most elegant Scotish poems of the sixteenth century. They are generally founded on subjects of an amatory kind, and discover no inconsiderable degree of fancy and harmony. His lyric measures are skilfully chosen; and his language, when compared with that of contemporary poets, will be found to possess an uncommon share of terseness and precision.—IRVING, DAVID, 1861, *History of Scotish Poetry, ed. Carlyle, p.* 418.

Scott wrote several short satires, and some miscellaneous poems, the prevailing amatory character of which has caused him to be called the *Scottish Anacreon*, though there are many points wanting to complete his resemblance to the Teian bard.—CARRUTHERS, ROBERT, 1876, *Chambers's Cyclopaedia of English Literature, Third Period*

With the exception of the burlesque poem, "The Justing betwixt Adamson and Sym," at the Drum, near Dalkeith, and his "Address to Queen Mary," his original poems are all amatory. The "Justing," which is in the measure of "Christ's Kirk on the Green," though wanting the rude but natural vigour and simple freshness of that racy sketch of rustic recreation, is not devoid of humour, and, in common with all Scott's poems, exhibits that skill in the art of poesy which is his most distinguishing characteristic; indeed, so great is their artistic perfection, that they convey an impression of elegant insincerity, such as we attach to the character of a gay gallant, or an accomplished man of the world.—ROSS, J., 1884, *The Book of Scottish Poems*, p. 312.

Is one of the very best lyrists we possess previous to the Elizabethan period.—FITZGIBBON, H. MACAULAY, 1888, *Early English and Scottish Poetry, Introduction*, p. lxvi.

Sir Philip Sidney

1554–1586

Born at Penshurst, Kent, 30 November 1554. Lay Rector of Whitford, Flintshire, May 1564. Educated at Shrewsbury School, Novemebr 1564 to 1568. Matriculated Christ College, Oxford, 1568. Probably took no degree. Member of Gray's Inn., 1568. To Paris, in suite of Earl of Lincoln, May 1572. Appointed Gentleman of Bedchamber to Charles IX., with title of Baron, August 1572. Studying in Lorraine, and at Strasburg, Heidelberg, Frankfort, and Vienna, September 1572 to autumn 1573; in Italy, October 1573 to July 1574; at Vienna, July 1574 to February 1575; visited Prague and Dresden; returned to London, May 1575. Attached to Court of Queen Elizabeth. On Embassy to Germany, February to June, 1577. His masque, "The Lady of May," performed before the Queen at Wanstead, May 1578. Friendship with Spenser begun, 1578. President of "The Areopagus," 1578. Being temporarily out of favor at Court, spent some months in retirement at Wilton (seat of his sister, Countess of Pembroke) in 1580; returned to Court, October 1580. Steward to Bishopric of Winchester, 1580. M. P. for Kent, January 1581 to September 1585. With Duke of Anjou in Antwerp, February to March 1582. Knighted, 8 January 1583. General of the Horse, 1583. Grant of land in colony of Vrignia, 1583. Married Frances Walsingham, 20 September 1583. Joint Master of Ordnance with Earl of Warwick, July 1585. Governor of Flushing and Rammekins, November 1585. Died at Arnhem, 17 October, 1586. Buried, in St. Paul's Cathedral, 16 February, 1587. *Works:* "The Countesse of Pembroke's Arcadia," 1590 (later edns., "with sundry new additions of the same author," 1598, etc.); "Syr P. S., his Astrophel and Stella," 1591; "An Apologie for Poetry," 1595. *Posthumous:* "Correspondence of Sir Philip Sidney and H. Languet," ed. by S. A. Pears, 1845. *Collected Poems:* ed. by A. B. Grosart (2 vols.), 1873.—SHARP, R. FARQUHARSON, 1897, *A Dictionary of English Authors*, p. 257.

PERSONAL

To the Noble and Vertuous Gentleman, most worthy of all titles both of Learning and Chevalrie.—SPENSER, EDMUND, 1579, *Title Page of the Shepheardes Calender*.

To the right noble Gentleman, Master Philip Sidney Esquier, Stephan Gosson wisheth health of body, wealth of minde, rewarde of vertue, aduauncement of honour and goood successe in godly affaires.—GOSSON, STEPHAN, 1579, *The Schoole of Abuse, Dedication*.

The return of the young gentleman, your sonne, whose message verie sufficientlie performed, and the relatinge thereof, is no less gratefully received and well liked of Her Majestie, than the honourable opinion he hath left behinde him with all the princes with whomme he had to negotiate, hathe left a most sweet savor and grateful remembraunce of his name in those parts. . . . There hath not been any gentleman, I am sure, these many yeres, that hathe gon through so honourable a charge with as great commendacions as he.—WALSINGHAM, SIR FRANCIS, 1586, *Letter to Sir Henry Sidney*.

Silence augmenteth griefe, writing encreaseth rage,
Staid are my thoughts, which loved and lost, the wonder of our age,
Yet quickened now with fire, though dead with frost ere now,
Enraged I write I know not what: dead, quick, I know not how.
Hard hearted mindes relent, and Rigor's tears abound,
And Envy strangely rues his end, in whom no fault she found.;
Knowledge his light hath lost, Valor hath slaine her knight:
Sidney is dead, dead is my friend, dead is the world's delight.

. . . .

A spotless friend, a matchless man, whose vertue ever shined.

. . . .

He onely like himselfe, was second unto none.

. . . .

Death slue not him, but he made death his ladder to the skies.

—GREVILLE, FULKE (LORD BROOKE), 1586, *On Sir Philip Sidney*.

SIR PHILIP SIDNEY

From the Miniature by Isaac Oliver,
at Winsor Castle.

A king gave thee thy name; a kingly mind,—
That God thee gave,—who found it now too dear
For this base world, and hath resumed it near
To sit in skies, and sort with powers divine.
. . . .
What hath he lost that such great grace hath won?
Young years for endless years, and hepe unsure
Of fortune's gifts for wealth that still shall dure:
O happy race, with so great praises run!
England doth hold thy limbs, that bred the same;
Flanders thy valour, where it last was tried;
The camp thy sorrow, where thy body died;
Thy friends thy want; the world thy virtue's fame;
Nations thy wit; our minds lay up thy love;
Letters thy learning; thy loss years long to come;
In worthy hearts sorrow hath made thy tomb;
Thy soul and spright enrich the heavens above.
Thy liberal heart embalmed in grateful tears,
Young sighs, sweet sighs, sage sighs, bewail thy fall;
Envy her sting; and spite hath left her gall;
Malice herself a mourning garment wears.
That day their Hannibal died, our Scipio fell,—
Scipio, Cicero, and Petrarch of our time;
Whose virtues, wounded by my worthless rhyme,
Let angels speak, and heaven thy praises tell.

—RALEIGH, SIR WALTER? 1586, *An Epitaph upon the Right Honourable Sir Philip Sidney.*

All haile, therefore, O worthie Phillip immortall!
The flowre of Sydneyes race, the honour of thy name!
Whose worthie praise to sing my Muses not aspire,
But sorrowfull and sad these teares to let thee fall;
Yet wish their verses might so farre and wide thy fame
Extend, that envies rage, nor time, might end the same.

—BRYSKETT, LODOWICK, 1587, *The Mourning Muse of Thestylis, Spenser's Works, ed. Collier, vol.* V, *p.* 88.

Gentle *Sir Philip Sidney,* thou knewest what belonged to a Scholler, thou knewest what paines, what toile, what travell, conduct to perfection: wel couldst thou give every Vertue his encouragement, every Art his due, every writer his desert: cause none more vertuous, witty, or learned than thy selfe.—NASHE, THOMAS, 1592, *Pierce Penilesse.*

Within these woods of Arcadie
He chiefe delight and pleasure tooke;
And on the mountaine Parthenie,
Upon the chrystall liquid brooke,
The Muses met him ev'ry day,
That taught him sing, to write, and say.
. . . .
A sweet attractive kinde of grace,
A full assurance given by lookes,
Continuall comfort in a face,
The lineaments of Gospell bookes,
I trowe, that countenance cannot lie
Whose thoughts are legible in the eie.

—ROYDON, MATTHEW, 1593, *An Elegie, or Friends Passion for his Astrophill, Spenser's Works, ed. Collier, vol.* V, *p.* 99.

Sidney, the Syren of this latter Age;
Sidney, the Blazing star of England's glory;
Sidney, the Wonder of the wise and sage;
Sidney, the Subject of true Virtue's story;
This Syren, Star, this Wonder, and this Subject,
Is dumb, dim, gone, and marr'd by Fortune's Object.

—BARNFIELD, RICHARD, 1594, *The Affectionate Shepherd.*

Still living Sidney, Cæsar of our land,
Whose never daunted valure, princely minde,
Imbellished with art and conquests hand,
Did expleiten his high aspiring kinde
(An eagles hart in crowes we cannot finde)
If thou couldst live and purchase Orpheus quill,
Our Monarches merits would exceed thy skill.

—HARBERT, SIR WILLIAM, 1604, *A Prophesie of Cadwallader, etc.*

Immortall *Sidney*, glory of the field
And glory of the Muses, and their pen
(Who equall bare the *Caduce* and the *Shield*).

—DANIEL, SAMUEL, 1606, *A Funerall Poeme upon the Earle of Devonshire, Works, ed. Grosart, vol.* I, *p.* 176.

O! but Gentry now degenerates! Nobilitie is now come to be *nuda relatio,* a meere bare relation and nothing else. How manie Players haue I seene vpon a stage, fit indeede to be Noblemen! how many that be Noblemen, fit onely to represent them.—Why, this can Fortune do, who makes some companions of her Chariot, who for desert should be lackies to her Ladiship. . . . Rise, Sidney, rise! thou England's eternall honour!

Reuiue and lead the reuolting spirits of thy countreymen, against the basest foe, Ignorance. But what talke I of thee? Heauen hath not left earth thy equall: neither do I thinke that *ab orbe condito*, since Nature first was, any man hath beene in whom *Genus* and *Genius* met so right. Thou Atlas to all vertues! Thou Hercules to the Muses! Thou patron to the poor! Thou de3ervst a Quire of ancient *Bardi* to sing thy praises, who with their musickes melody might expresse thy soules harmonie. Were the transmigration of soules certaine—I would thy soule had flitted into my bodie or wold thou wert aliue again, that we might lead an indiuiduall life together! Thou wast not more admired at home then famous abroad; thy penne and thy sword being the Heraldes of thy Heroicke deedes.—STAFFORD, ANTHONY, 1611, *Niobe, p.* 112.

Th' admired mirrour, glory of our Isle,
Thou far-far-more than mortall man, whose stile
Strucke more men dumbe to hearken to thy song,
Then Orpheus Harpe, or Tuilies golden tongue.
To him (as right) for wits deepe quintessence,
For honour, valour, virtue, excellence,
Be all the Garlands, crowne his toombe with Bay,

Who spake as much as eer our tongue can say.

—BROWNE, WILLIAM, 1613, *Britannia's Pastorals, ed. Hazlitt, vol.* I, *bk.* ii, *Song* ii.

Of whose Youth I will report no other wonder, but thus: That though I lived with him, and knew him from a child, yet I never knew him other than a man: with such staiedness of mind, lovely, and familiar gravity, as carried grace, and reverence above greater years. His talk ever of knowledge, and his very play tending to enrich his mind; So as even his teachers found something in him to observe, and learn, above that which they had usually read, or taught. Which eminence, by nature, and industry made his worthy Father stile Sir *Philip* in my hearing (though I unseen) *Lumen familiæ suæ*.—GREVILLE, FULKE (*Lord Brooke*), 1628 ?–52, *Life of Sir Philip Sidney, p.* 7.

For his education, it was such as travell, and the University could afford, or his Tutours infuse; for after an incredible proficiency in all the species of Learning; he left the Academicall life, for that of the Court, whither he came by his Uncles invitation, famed afore-hand by a noble report of his accomplishments, which together with the state of his person, framed by a naturall propension to Armes, he soon attracted the good opinion of all men, and was so highly prized in the good opinion of the Queen, that she thought the Court deficient without him: And whereas (through the fame of his deserts) he was in the election for the Kingdom of *Pole*, she refused to further his advancement, not out of emulation, but out of fear to lose the jewell of her times. —NAUNTON, SIR ROBERT, 1630? *Fragmenta Regalia, ed. Arber, p.* 34.

Sir Philip Sydney, knight, was the most accomplished cavalier of his time. . . . He was not only of an excellent witt, but extremely beautifull; he much resembled his sister, but his haire was not red, but a little inclining, viz. a darke amber colour. If I were to find a fault in it, methinkes 'tis not masculine enough; yett he was a person of great courage.—AUBREY, JOHN, 1669–96, *Brief Lives, ed. Clark, vol.* II, *p.* 247

No man seems to me so astonishing an object of temporary admiration as the celebrated friend of the lord Brooke, the famous Sir Philip Sidney. The learned of Europe dedicated their works to him; the republic of Poland thought him at least worthy to be in the nomination for their crown. All the muses of England wept his death. When we, at this distance of time, inquire what prodigious merits excited such admiration, what do we find? Great valour. — But it was an age of heroes.—In full of all other talents, we have a tedious, lamentable, pedantic, pastoral romance, which the patience of a young virgin in love cannot now wade through; and some absurd attempts to fetter English verse in Roman chains; a proof that this applauded author understood little of the genius of his own language. The few of his letters extant are poor matters; one to a steward of his father, an instance of unwarrantable violence. By far the best presumption of his abilities (to us who can judge only by what we see) is a pamphlet published amongst the Sidney papers, being an answer to the famous libel called "Leicester's Commonwealth." It defends his uncle with great spirit. What had been said in derogation to their blood seems to have touched sir Philip most. He died with the rashness of a volunteer, having lived to write with the *sang-froid* and prolixity of mademoiselle Scuderi.—WALPOLE, HORACE, 1758, *A Catalogue of the Royal and Noble Authors of England, Scotland, and Ireland, ed. Park, vol.* II, *p.* 230.

Sidney here was born;
Sidney, than whom no gentler, braver man
His own delightful genius ever feigned,
Illustrating the vales of Arcady
With courteous courage and with loyal loves.
Upon his natal day, an acorn here
Was planted: it grew up a stately oak,
And in the beauty of its strength it stood
And flourished, when his perishable part
Had mouldered, dust to dust. That stately oak
Itself hath mouldered now, but Sidney's fame
Endureth in his own immortal works.

—SOUTHEY, ROBERT, 1799, *For a Tablet at Penshurst.*

The life of Sir Philip Sydney was poetry put into action.—CAMPBELL, THOMAS, 1819, *Essay on English Poetry.*

. . . Sidney, as he fought
And as he fell and as he lived and loved
Sublimely mild, a Spirit without spot.

—SHELLEY, PERCY BYSSHE, 1821, *Adonais,* xlv.

The noble images, passions, sentiments, and poetical delicacies of character, scattered all over the "Arcadia" (spite of some stiffness and encumberment), justify to me the character which his contemporaries have left us of the writer. I cannot think with the Critic, that Sir Philip Sydney was that *opprobrious thing* which a foolish nobleman in his insolent hostility chose to term him. I call to mind the epitaph made on him, to guide me to juster thoughts of him.—LAMB, CHARLES, 1823, *Some Sonnets of Sir Philip Sydney, London Magazine, Sept., Essays.*

Was the idol of his time, and perhaps no figure reflects the age more fully and more beautifully. Fair as he was brave, quick of wit as of affection, noble and generous in temper, dear to Elizabeth as to Spenser, the darling of the Court and of the camp, his learning and his genius made him the centre of the literary world which was springing into birth on English soil. He had traveled in France and Italy, he was master alike of the older learning and of the new discoveries of astronomy. Bruno dedicated to him as to a friend his metaphysical speculations; he was familiar with the drama of Spain, the poems of Ronsard, the sonnets of Italy. He combined the wisdom of a grave councilor with the romantic chivalry of a knight-errant.—GREEN, JOHN RICHARD, 1874, *A Short History of the English People, ch.* vii.

Sidney was prompt and rapid in mental movement; he formed opinions and translated them into action with great alacrity. In the very typical case of his quarrel with Lord Oxford we find him keeping his head when most men would have lost it from sheer rage; but it was all that the Queen and the Privy Council could do to prevent him from having the Earl's blood. Unquestionably he looked mild; he had a girlish face of pink and white; and Oxford, no doubt, did not know his man when he dared to bully him. But there was wiry fibre in Sidney's mind and body, and we may be sure that, in those fighting days, no mere carpet-knight would have impressed himself on the popular mind as a hero. His extraordinary ability in all the diplomatic arts is quite beyond dispute. To be a diplomatist, a man must possess sympathy, and have a rare judgment in the use of it. The ideal diplomatist, like the ideal poet, is a man in whom the masculine and feminine qualities of the intellect balance one another with absolute harmony, each supplying the wants of the other side of the character. What is related of Sidney tends to prove that he possessed this equilibrium to a very extraordinary degree, and I take it to have been the secret of his charm and of his power.—GOSSE EDMUND, 1886, *Sir Philip Sidney, Contemporary Review, vol.* 50, *p.* 638.

The real difficulty of painting an adequate portrait of Sidney at the present time is that his renown transcends his actual achievement. Neither his poetry nor his prose, nor what is known about his action, quite explains the singular celebrity which he enjoyed in his own life, and the fame which has attended his memory with almost undimmed lustre through three centuries. . . . Few spirits so blameless, few so thoroughly prepared to enter upon new spheres of activity and discipline, have left this earth. The multitudes who knew him personally, those who might have been jealous of him, and those who owed him gratitude, swelled one chorus in praise of his natural goodness, his intellectual strength and moral beauty. We who study his biography, and dwell upon their testimony to his charm, derive from Sidney the noblest lesson bequeathed by Elizabethan to Victorian England.—SYMONDS, JOHN ADDINGTON, 1886, *Sir Philip Sidney, (English Men of Letters), pp.* 1, 199.

Englishmen, everywhere, are proud of this fine gentleman, Sidney, who can talk in so many languages, who can turn a sonnet to a lady's eyebrow, who can fence with the best swordsmen of any court, who can play upon six instruments of music, who can outdance even his Grace of Anjou.—MITCHELL, DONALD G., 1889, *English Lands Letters and Kings, From Celt to Tudor, p.* 239.

ARCADIA

Read the Countesse of Pembrookes Arcadia, a gallant Legendary, full of pleasurable accidents, and profitable discourses; for three thinges especially, very notable; for amorous Courting, (he was young in yeeres;) for sage counselling, (he was ripe in iudgement;) and for valorous fighting, (his soueraine profession was Armes:) and delightfull pastime by way of Pastorall exercises, may passe for the fourth. He that will Looue, let him learn to looue of him, that will teach him to Liue; & furnish him with many pithy, and effectuall instructions, delectably interlaced by way of proper descriptions of excellent Personages, and common narrations of other notable occurrences. . .

Liue ever sweete Booke; the siluer Image of his gentle witt, and the golden Pillar of his noble courage: and euer notify vnto the worlde, that thy Writer, was the Secretary of Eloquence; the breath of the Muses; the hooneybee of the dayntiest flowers of Witt, and Arte; the Pith of morall, & intellectuall Vertues; the arme of Bellona in the field; the toung of Suada in the chãber; the spirite of Practise in esse; and the Paragon of Excellency in Print.—HARVEY, GABRIEL, 1593, *Pierces Supererogation, Works, ed. Grosart, vol.* II, *pp.* 100, 101.

Sir Philip Sidney writ his immortal poem, The Countess of Pembroke's "Arcadia" in prose, and yet our rarest poet.—MERES, FRANCIS, 1598, *Palladis Tamia, p.* 96.

Besides its excellent language, rare contrivances, and delectable stories, hath in it all the strains of poesy, comprehendeth the universal art of speaking, and, to them who can discern and will observe, affordeth notable rules for demeanour both private and public.—HEYLIN, PETER, 1622, *Description of Arcadia in Greece.*

Merely the desire of understanding so rare a book caused me to go to England, where I remained for two years in order to gain a knowledge of it.—BAUDOIN, J., 1624, *L'Arcadie de la Comtesse de Pembrok, mise en nostre langue.*

Those that knew him well will truly confess it to be, both in form and matter, much inferior to that unbounded spirit of his, as the industry and images of other men's works are many times raised above the writers' capacities; and besides acknowledge that however he could not choose but give them aspersions of spirit and learning from the father, yet that they were scribbled rather as pamphlets for the entertainment of time and friends than any account of himself to the world; because, if his purpose had been to leave his memory in books, I am confident, in the right use of logic, philosophy, history and poesie, nay, even in the most ingenious and mechanical arts, he would have showed such tracts of a searching and judicious spirit as the professors of every faculty would have striven no less for him than the seven cities did to have Homer of their sept; but the truth is, his end was not writing, even while he wrote, nor his knowledge moulded for tables and schools,—but both his wit and understanding bent upon his heart, to make himself and others, not in words or opinion, but in life and action, good and great.—GREVILLE, FULKE (*Lord Brooke*), 1628?-52, *Life of Sir Philip Sidney.*

Sidney, warbler of poetic prose.

COWPER, WILLIAM, 1785, *The Task, bk.* iv.

It would be an easier, though a less moral, task, to praise, than to read, four hundred and eighty-six, close printed, folio pages of such mawkish writing as this. It is singular that so gallant and distinguished a personage as sir Philip Sidney, should have written a work of these dimensions, so near to the being utterly void of all genuine passion and manly spirit. To read this performance, one would think that our ancestors who admired it, had a blood that crept more feebly in their veins than we have, and that they were as yet but half awaked from the stupidity of the savage state, or, what has been called, the state of nature.—GODWIN, WILLIAM, 1797, *Of English Style, The Enquirer.*

What can be more unpromising at first sight, than the idea of a young man disguising himself in woman's attire, and passing himself off for a woman among women; and that for a long space of time? Yet Sir Philip has preserved so matchless a decorum, that neither does Pyrocles' manhood suffer any stain for the effeminacy of Zelmane, nor is the respect due to the princesses at all diminished when the deception comes to be known. In the sweetly constituted mind of Sir Philip Sidney, it seems as if no ugly thought or unhandsome meditation could find a harbour. He turned all that he touched into images of honour and virtue.—LAMB, CHARLES, 1808, *Specimens of Dramatic Poets, Essays.*

There are passages in this work exquisitely beautiful,—useful observations on life and manners, a variety and accurate discrimination of characters, fine sentiments, expressed in strong and adequate terms, animated descriptions, equal to any that occur in the ancient or modern poets, sage lessons of morality, and judicious reflections on government and policy. A reader who takes up the volume may be compared to a traveller who has a long and dreary road to pass. The objects that successively meet his eye may not in general be very pleasing, but occasionally he is charmed with a more beautiful prospect, with the verdure of a rich valley, with a meadow enamelled with flowers, with a murmur of a rivulet, the swelling grove, the hanging rock, the splendid villa. These charming objects abundantly compensate for the joyless regions he has traversed. They fill him with delight, exhilarate his drooping spirits, and, at the decline of day, he reposes with complacency and satisfaction.—ZOUCH, THOMAS, 1808, *Memoirs of the Life and Writings of Sir Philip Sidney.*

Extremely tiresome, and its chief interest consists in the stately dignity, and often graceful beauty, of the language.—DUNLOP, JOHN, 1814–45, *The History of Fiction, p.* 342.

Sir Philip Sydney's "Arcadia," the immortality of which was so fondly predicted by his admirers, and which, in truth, is full of noble thoughts, delicate images, and graceful turns of language, is now scarcely ever mentioned.—IRVING, WASHINGTON, 1819-48, *The Mutability of Literature, Sketch Book,*

Sir Philip Sidney is a writer for whom I cannot acquire a taste. As Mr. Burke said, "he could not love the French Republic"—so I may say, that I cannot love the "Countess of Pembroke's Arcadia," with all my good-will to it. . . . It is to me one of the greatest monuments of the abuse of intellectual power upon record. It puts one in mind of the court dresses and preposterous fashions of the time, which are grown obsolete and disgusting. It is not romantic, but scholastic; not poetry, but casuistry; not nature, but art, and the worst sort of art, which thinks it can do better than nature. Of the number of fine things that are constantly passing through the author's mind, there is hardly one that he has not contrived to spoil, and to spoil purposely and maliciously in order to aggrandise our idea of himself. . . . Every page is "with centric and eccentric scribbled o'er;" his muse is tattooed and tricked out like an Indian goddess. He writes a court-hand, with flourishes like a schoolmaster; his figures are wrought in chain-stitch. All his thoughts are forced and painful births, and may be said to be delivered by the Cæsarean operation. At last, they become distorted and rickety in themselves; and before they have been cramped and twisted and swaddled into lifelessness and deformity. . . . Is spun with great labour out of the author's brains, and hangs like a huge cobweb over the face of Nature!—HAZLITT, WILLIAM, 1820, *Lectures on the Literature of the Age of Elizabeth, Lecture* vii.

Enjoying for above a century a popularity which may well be compared with that of the "Diana" of Montemayor, if indeed, it did not equal it.—TICKNOR, GEORGE, 1849–91, *History of Spanish Literature, vol.* III, *p.* 106.

It would be mere pretence to say that the romance could be read through now by any one not absolutely Sidney-smitten in his tastes, or that, compared with the books which we do read through, it is not intolerably languid. It is even deficient in those passages of clear incisive thought which we find in the author's "Essay on Poetry." No competent person, however, can read any considerable portion of it without finding it full of fine enthusiasm and courtesy, of high sentiment, of the breath of a gentle and heroic spirit. There are sweet descriptions in it, pictures of ideal love and friendship, dialogues of stately moral rhetoric. In style there is a finish, an attention to artifice, a musical arrangement of cadence, and occasionally a richness of phrase, for which English Prose at that time might well have been grateful. Seeing, too, that the complaints of wearisomeness which we bring against the book now, were not so likely to be made at the time of its publication, when readers had not been taught impatience by a surfeit of works of the same class—seeing, in fact, that the book was so popular as to go through ten editions in the course of fifty years—I am disposed to believe that this last merit was not the least important.—MASSON, DAVID, 1859, *British Novelists and Their Styles, p.* 65.

The form of the "Arcadia," it must be confessed, is somewhat fantastic, and the story tedious; but the work is still so sound at the core, so pure, strong, and vital in the soul that animates it, and so much inward freshness and beauty are revealed the moment we pierce its outward crust of affectation, that no changes in the fashions of literature have ever been able to dislodge it from its eminence of place. —WHIPPLE, EDWIN P., 1859–69, *The Literature of the Age of Elizabeth, p.* 258.

This kind of books shows only the externals, the current elegance and politeness, the jargon of the world of culture, —in short, that which should be spoken before ladies; and yet we perceive from it the bent of the general spirit.—TAINE, H. A., 1871, *History of English Literature, tr. Van Laun, vol.* I. *p.* 164.

It was not a studied work, but as the story came he wrote it down on loose sheets of paper, most of it whilst his sister was beside him, and some of it as he rode or hunted over Salisbury Plain. Many of the descriptions of rural scenery he took from scenes he saw before him at Wilton. He did not finish it at Wilton, but took it up again at different times, and sent off the sheets as soon as written to his sister. The want of plan makes the story long and unartistic; perhaps Sidney was aware of this, as he never wished it to be published; but after his death, his sister thought it too rare to be lost to the world, and for some time it was a very popular book, many persons finding great delight in the complicated adventures of the various characters.—BUCKLAND, ANNA, 1882, *The Story of English Literature, p.* 113.

The student of English fiction would fain linger long over the pages which describe the loves of Pamela and Philoclea. For when these pages are laid aside, it is long before he may again meet with the poetry, the manly and womanly sentiment, and the pure yet stirring passion which adorn the romance of Elizabeth's Philip. Three centuries have passed away since the "Arcadia" was written, and we who live at the end of this period not unjustly congratulate ourselves on our superior civilization and refinement. And yet in all this time we have arrived of no higher conception of feminine virtue or chivalrous manhood than is to be found in this sixteenth-century romance, and during one-half of these three hundred years there was to be seen so little trace of such a conception, whether in life or in literature, that the word love seemed to have lost its nobler meaning and to stand for no more than animal desire. There is not in English fiction a more charming picture of feminine modesty than that of Pamela hiding her love for Musidorus.—TUCKERMAN, BAYARD, 1882, *A History of English Prose Fiction, p.* 98.

Sidney has, among several others, created one character which, forgotten as it is now, would be enough to give a permanent interest to this too much neglected romance; it is the Queen Gynecia, who is consumed by a guilty love, and who is the worthy contemporary of the strongly passionate heroes of Marlowe's plays. With her, and for the first time, the dramatic power of English genius leaves the stage and comes to light in the novel; it was destined to pass into it entirely.—JUSSERAND, J. J., 1890, *The English Novel in the Time of Shakespeare, p.* 247.

"The Countess of Pembroke's Arcadia" resembles a beautiful and elaborate headgear such as Sidney's sister might have worn at Court while witnessing his prowess at the barriers—a product of nature interspersed with a hundred quaint artifices of wreaths and bugles and ouches and rings.—WARD, ADOLPHUS WILLIAM, 1893, *English Prose, ed. Craik, vol.* I, *p.* 407.

The "Arcadia," in fact, is in some sort a halfway house between the older romances of chivalry and the long-winded "heroic" romances of the seventeenth century. Action and adventure are already giving way to the description of sentiment, or are remaining merely as a frame on which the diverse-coloured flowers of sentiment may be broidered.—RALEIGH, WALTER, 1894, *The English Novel, p.* 60.

ASTROPHEL AND STELLA

Sir Philip Sidney's "Astrophel and Stella" consists of a number of sonnets, which have been unaccountably passed over by Dr. Drake, and all our other critics who have written on this subject. Many of them are eminently beautiful.—WHITE, HENRY KIRKE, 1806? *Melancholy Hours, Remains, ed. Southey, vol.* II, *p.* 247.

Sidney's sonnets—I speak of the best of them—are among the very best of their sort. They fall below the plain moral dignity, the sanctity, and high yet modest spirit of self-approval, of Milton in his compositions of a similar structure. . . . They are struck full of amorous fancies—far-fetched conceits, befitting his occupation; for True Love thinks no labour to send out Thoughts upon the vast, and more than Indian voyages, to bring home rich pearls, outlandish wealth, gums, jewels, spicery, to sacrifice in self-depreciating similitudes, as shadows of true amiabilities in the Beloved. . . . I confess I can see nothing of the "jejune" or "frigid" in them; much less of the "stiff" and "cumbrous"—which I have sometimes heard objected to the "Arcadia." The verse runs off swiftly and gallantly. It might have been tuned to the trumpet; or tempered (as himself expresses it) to "trampling horses' feet."—LAMB, CHARLES, 1823, *Some Sonnets of Sir Philip Sydney, London Magazine, Sept.*

The Stella of Sydney's poetry, and the Philoclea of his "Arcadia," was the Lady Penelope Devereux, the elder sister of the favourite Essex. While yet in her childhood, she was the destined bride of Sidney, and for several years they were considered as almost engaged to each other: it was natural, therefore, at this time, that he should be accustomed to regard her with tenderness and unreproved admiration, and should gratify both by making her the object of his poetical raptures. She was also less openly, but even more ardently, loved by young Charles Blount, afterwards Lord Mountjoy, who seems to have disputed with Sidney the first place in her heart. She is described as a woman of exquisite beauty, on a grand and splendid scale; dark sparkling eyes; pale brown hair; a rich vivid complexion; a regal brow and a noble figure. . . . A dark shade steals, like a mildew, over this bright picture of beauty, poetry, and love, even while we gaze upon it. The projected union between Sydney and Lady Penelope was finally broken off by their respective families, for reasons which do not appear. Sir Charles Blount offered himself, and was refused, though evidently agreeable to the lady; and she was married by her guardians to Lord Rich, a man of talents and integrity, but most disagreeable in person and manners, and her declared aversion.—JAMESON, ANNA BROWNELL, 1829, *The Loves of the Poets, v.* I, *pp.* 251, 255.

It is rather a singular circumstance, that, in her own and her husband's lifetime, this ardent courtship of a married woman should have been deemed fit for publication. Sidney's passion seems indeed to have been unsuccessful, but far enough from being Platonic. "Astrophel and Stella" is too much disfigured by conceits, but it is in some places very beautiful.—HALLAM, HENRY, 1837-39, *Introduction to the Literature of Europe, pt.* ii, *ch.* v, *par.* 66.

In a certain depth and chivalry of feeling—in the rare and noble quality of disinterestedness (to put it in one word),—he has no superior, hardly perhaps an equal, amongst our Poets; and after or beside Shakespeare's "Sonnets," his "Astrophel and Stella". . . offers the most intense and powerful picture of the passion of love in the whole range of our poetry.—PALGRAVE, FRANCIS TURNER, 1861-92, *Golden Treasury of English Lyrics, p.* 351, *note.*

Penelope Devereux, daughter to his old friend the late Earl of Essex, had once been talked of as his own possible wife.

Her father said that he would have been proud of Philip Sidney for a son-in-law. And if so why had the match not taken place? If Sidney had been really devoted to the lady he could have married her. He did not marry her because he did not wish to do so, and in his own day no reasonable being ever supposed that he paid suit to her, except in the way of verse. . . . Philip Sidney was an old friend of her father's, and he gave her the place of honour in his sonnet-writing, wherein she was to be Stella ("the Star"), he Astrophel ("the Lover of the Star"); and certainly, as all the court knew, and as the forms of such ingenious love-poetry implied, so far as love in the material sense was concerned, with as much distance between them as if she had shone upon him from above the clouds. Sidney's "Astrophel and Stella" sonnets were being written at the time when he was about to marry Fanny Walsingham; and in those earnest Elizabethan days, at the fitfully strict court of Elizabeth, since the character of such poetical love-passions was then understood, they brought upon Sidney's credit not a breath of censure. As for Lady Rich, she gave herself to Sir Christopher Blount, who became Lord Mountjoy in 1600, and after divorce from her husband she married him. But that was a real passion, and what each felt in it was not told for the amusement of the public.—MORLEY, HENRY, 1873, *First Sketch of English Literature, pp.* 421, 422.

Now if you don't like these love-songs, you either have never been in love, or you don't know good writing from bad, (and likely enough both the negatives, I'm sorry to say, in modern England).—RUSKIN, JOHN, 1873, *Fors Clavigera, Letter,* XXXV.

"Stella" has "for all time" taken her place in the heaven of Literature beside not merely the Geraldine of Surrey earlier, or the Mary of Robert Burns later, but with the Laura of Petrarch, and Beatrice of Dante, and Rosalind and Elizabeth of Spenser, and Celia of Carew, and Castara of Habington, and Leonora of Milton, and Sacharissa of Waller.—GROSART, ALEXANDER B., 1877, *ed. Complete Poems of Sir Philip Sidney, Memorial-Introduction, vol.* I, *p.* lxi.

As a series of sonnets the "Astrophel and Stella" poems are second only to Shakespeare's; as a series of love-poems they are perhaps unsurpassed. Other writers are sweeter, more sonorous; no other love-poet of the time is so real. The poems to Stella are steeped throughout in a certain keen and pungent individuality which leaves a haunting impression behind it. They represent, not a mere isolated mood, whether half-real like Daniel's passion for Delia, or wholly artificial like the mood of Thomas Watson's "Passions," but a whole passage in a genuine life. . . . Not that "Astrophel and Stella" is without its make-believes. It has its "conceits," its pieces of pure word-play, in the common Elizabethan manner. No writer in the full tide of literary fashion like Sidney could afford to neglect these. But it would be scarcely fanciful to say that even in the most clearly marked of what one may call his conceited sonnets, the true Sidneian note to a reader who has learnt to catch it is almost always discernible, a note of youth and eagerness easily felt but hard to be described.—WARD, MARY A., 1880, *English Poets, ed. Ward, vol.* I, *p.* 344.

The lover of Penelope Rich certainly did not find his "heart's desires" in wedlock. He chose to find his high ideal of a woman in his married sister Mary, Countess of Pembroke, and gave his romantic imagination free scope in writing her "Arcadia." When he had been two years married, and just before he became a father, he was burning to visit the ends of the earth with Drake. Then he passed over to the Continent, and perished, the high-souled victim of his own rash enterprise—Argalus, but without a Parthenia. Dame Frances Sidney, strangely enough, married again, Robert, second Earl of Essex, the brother in arms and affection of her late husband. Their son Robert was the famous general of the Parliament, first husband of the aristocratic adulteress and murderess, Frances Howard.—HALL, HUBERT, 1886, *Society in the Elizabethan Age, p.* 91.

It is of the smallest possible importance or interest to a rational man to discover what was the occasion of Sidney's writing these charming poems—the important point is their charm. And in this respect (giving heed to his date and his opportunities of imitation) I should put Sidney third to Shakespere and Spenser.—SAINTSBURY, GEORGE, 1887, *History of Elizabethan Literature, p.* 101.

AN APOLOGY FOR POETRIE

The stormie Winter (deere Chyldren of the Muses) which hath so long held backe the glorious Sunshine of diuine Poesie, is heere by the sacred pen-breathing words of diuine Sir *Philip Sidney,* not onely chased from our fame-inuiting Clyme, but vtterly for euer banisht eternitie: then graciously regreet the perpetuall spring of euer-growing inuention, and like kinde Babes, either enabled by wit or power, help to support me poore Midwife, whose daring aduenture, hath deliuered from Obliuions wombe, this euer-to-be admired wits miracle. Those great ones, who in themselues haue interr'd this blessed innocent, wil with *Aejculapius* condemne me as a detractor from their Deities: those who Prophet-like haue but heard presage of his coming, wil (if they wil doe wel) not onely defend, but praise mee, as the first publique bewrayer of Poesies *Messias.* Those who neither haue seene, thereby to interre, nor heard, by which they might be inflamed with desire to see, let them (of duty) plead to be my Champions, sith both theyr sight and hearing, by mine incurring blame is seasoned. Excellent Poesie, (so created by this Apologie,) be thou my Defendresse; and if any wound mee, let thy beautie (my soules Adamant) recure mee: if anie commend mine endeuored hardiment, to them commend thy most diuinest fury as a winged incouragement; so shalt thou have deuoted to thee, and to them obliged.—OLNEY, HENRY, 1595, *Publisher to the Reader, An Apology for Poetrie, ed. Arber, p.* 16.

I have been blamed for not mentioning sir Philip's "Defence of Poetry," which some think his best work. I had indeed forgot it when I wrote this article; a proof that I at least did not think it sufficient foundation for so high a character as he acquired. This was all my criticism pretended to say, that I could not conceive how a man, who in some respects written dully and weakly, and who, at most, was far inferior to our best authors, had obtained such immense reputation. Let his merits and his fame be weighed together, and then let it be determined whether the world has overvalued, or I undervalued, sir Philip Sidney.—WALPOLE, HORACE, 1759, *A Catalogue of Royal and Noble Authors of England, Scotland, and Ireland, ed. Park, 2d ed., vol.* II, *p.* 232, *note.*

Sir Philip Sidney is said to have miscarried in his essays; but his miscarriage was no more than that of failing in an attempt to introduce a new fashion. The failure was not owing to any defect or imperfection in the scheme, but to the want of taste, to the irresolution and ignorance of the public.—GOLDSMITH, OLIVER, 1773, *Essays,* xviii.

The "Defense of Poesy" has already been reckoned among the polite writings of the Elizabethan age, to which class it rather belongs than to that of criticism; for Sidney rarely comes to any literary censure, and is still farther removed from any profound philosophy. His sense is good, but not ingenious, and the declamatory tone weakens its effect.—HALLAM, HENRY, 1837-39, *Literary History of Europe, pt.* ii, *ch.* vii, *par.* 35.

The book on which Sidney's reputation as an English classic writer rests.—COLLIER, WILLIAM FRANCIS, 1861, *History of English Literature, p.* 117.

It is not only an earnest and persuasive argument, but was, in style and diction, the best secular prose yet written in England, and indeed the earliest specimen of real critical talent in the literature.—MARSH, GEORGE P., 1862, *The Origin and History of the English Language, etc., p.* 547.

Is worthy of a writer who had a poet's phantasy and a critic's delicacy of discrimination.—PORTER, NOAH, 1870, *Books and Reading, p.* 293.

The elegant and too-little known treatise. . . . The only pages of his "Apologie for Poetrie" generally quoted, are those in which he laughs at the playwrights of his time for violating the unities of time and place. The drawback to this isolated quotation is that it gives the perfectly false notion of Sir Philip Sidney that he was a narrow-minded pedant, whereas, in reality, there was nowhere to be found a more liberal and delicately cultured mind than his. His criticism was founded upon the noblest philosophy of art, and amongst the numerous treatises on poetry, which form an entire and very curious branch of literature in the sixteenth century, that of Sir Philip Sidney is in every respect the most remarkable. In addition to the learning of a Scaliger, and the enthusiasm of a

Ronsard, he possessed a quality that both these men were lacking in, which, for want of a better word, I must call an *atticism*, or, more strictly speaking, an *urbanity*, taking care to retain the especial meaning of a graceful and witty raillery, which is contained in the Latin word but not to the same degree in the Greek.—STAPFER, PAUL, 1880, *Shakespeare and Classical Antiquity, tr. Carey, p.* 41.

Sidney's flawless "Defense of Poesie."—STEDMAN, EDMUND CLARENCE, 1892, *The Nature and Elements of Poetry, p.* 23.

From its historical position Sidney's "Defense of Poesy" is an important work in the development of English criticism. It is one of those inquiries into the nature of poetry that have appealed to philosophical curiosity from classical times down to our own, and that are interesting and suggestive, even if not of the most valuable order. Sidney's work is especially noteworthy as a landmark in the evolution of English prose, and as an indication of the classical spirit of the circle to which he belonged. For he writes more as a student than as an alert contemporary of the men of 1580; he was scholastically blind to the signs of the times. Fortunately Marlowe and Shakspere did not take the essay as a literary guide. Yet for a professed classicist, Sidney is not narrow, as his love for English ballads indicates, and his pure and ideal spirit is shown in the serious ethical conception of poetry that marks his entire work.—McLAUGHLIN, EDWARD T., 1893, *Literary Criticism for Students, p.* 1.

The monument of the noblest phase of perhaps the noblest movement of English thought. Filled with a longing for perfection, but a perfection beyond the thought of any but a poet, Sidney gives us the poetry rather than the art or the theory of criticism.—WYLIE, LAURA JOHNSON, 1894, *Evolution of English Criticism, p.* 12.

His "Defence of Poesy" is a veritable epitome of the literary criticism of the Italian Renaissance; and so thoroughly is it imbued with this spirit, that no other work, Italian, French, or English, can be said to give so complete and so noble a conception of the temper and the principles of Renaissance criticism.—SPINGARN, JOEL ELIAS, 1899, *A History of Literary Criticism in the Renaissance, p.* 268.

GENERAL

Our English Petrarch.—HARRINGTON, SIR JOHN, 1591, *Translation of Ariosto, Notes on Book* xvi, *p.* 126.

Liberal Sidney, famous for the love
He bare to learning and to chivalry.

—PEELE, GEORGE, 1593, *The Honour of the Garter, Ad Mæcenatem Prologus.*

. . . he could pipe, and daunce, and caroll sweet,
Emongst the shepheards in their shearing feast;
As Somers larke that with her song doth greet
The dawning day forth comming from the East:
And layes of love he also could compose:
Thrise happie she, whom he to praise did chose!

—SPENSER, EDMUND, 1595, *Astrophel, Works, ed. Collier, vol.* v, *p.* 69.

Oh, for some excellent pen-man to deplore their state: but he which would lively, naturally, or indeed poetically, delyneate or enumerate these occurrents, shall either lead you thereunto by a poeticall spirit, as could well, if well he might, the dead-living, life-giving Sydney, Prince of Poesie.—SMITHES, SIR THOMAS, 1605, *Voiage and Entertainment in Rushia.*

That poets are far rarer births than kings,
Your noblest father proved; like whom, before,
Or then, or since, about our Muses' springs,
Came not that soul exhausted so their store.

—JONSON, BEN., 1616, *To Elizabeth, Countess of Rutland, Epigrams,* lxxix.

The King said Sir P. Sidney was no poet.—DRUMMOND, WILLIAM, 1619, *Notes of Ben Jonson's Conversations, ed. Laing, p.* 26.

The noble Sidney . . .
That hero for numbers, and for prose,
That thoroughly pac'd our language, as to show
The plenteous English hand in hand might go
With Greek and Latin, and did first reduce
Our tongue from Lilly's writing then in use.

—DRAYTON, MICHAEL, *c.* 1627, *Poets and Poesy.*

The true spirit or vein of ancient poetry in this kind seems to shine most in Sir Philip Sidney, whom I esteem both the greatest poet and the noblest genius of any that have left writings behind them, and published in ours or any other modern language; a person born capable not only of forming the greatest ideas, but of leaving the noblest examples, if the length of his life had been equal to the excellence of his wit and virtues.—TEMPLE, SIR WILLIAM, 1628–98, *Of Poetry, Works, vol.* III, *p.* 412.

Love's foe profess'd! why dost thou falsely feign
Thyself a Sidney? from which noble strain
He sprung, that could so far exalt the name
Of Love, and warm a nation with his flame;
That all we can of love or high desire
Seems but the smoke of amorous Sidney's fire.
—WALLER, EDMUND, c 1636, *At Penshurst.*

Philip and *Alexander* both in one;
Heir to the Muses, the Son of *Mars* in Truth,
Learning, Valour, Wisdome, all in virtuous youth,
His praise is much, this shall suffice my pen,
That *Sidney* dy'd 'mong most renown'd of men.
—BRADSTREET, ANNE, 1638, *Elegy upon Sir Philip Sidney, Works, ed. Ellis, p.* 351.

Sidneian showers
Of sweet discourse, whose powers
Can crown old winter's head with flowers.
—CRASHAW, RICHARD, 1646–48, *Wishes to his Supposed Mistress, The Delights of the Muses.*

Nor can the Muse the gallant Sidney pass,
The plume of war! with early laurels crown'd,
The lover's myrtle and the poet's bay.
—THOMSON, JAMES, 1727, *The Seasons, Summer.*

Sidney's verse halts ill on Roman feet.
—POPE, ALEXANDER, 1733, *Imitations of Horace, Book* ii, *Epistle* I, *v.* 98.

Had Sir Philip paid an exclusive attention to the poetical art, there is every reason to suppose that he would have occupied a master's place in this department; as it is, his poetry, though too often vitiated by an intermixture of antithesis and false wit, and by an attempt to introduce the classic metres, is still rich with frequent proofs of vigour, elegance, and harmony.—DRAKE, NATHAN, 1817, *Shakspeare and His Times, vol.* I, *p.* 652.

Though we cannot admit for a moment that the poetry of Sidney is debased by the vile alloy of licentiousness and pruriency, we are not blind to many other vices with which it may most justly be charged. Our author was styled, by Raleigh, the English Petrarch; and without doubt he derived many of his faults as well as excellencies from the bard of Arezzo, whom he frequently imitated both in his manner and in his exaggerated turn of expression. It was from this foreign prototype that he was probably smitten with the love of antithesis and conceit, and the other fashionable absurdities in which our best writers of sonnets then abounded.—GRAY, WILLIAM, 1829, *Life of Sidney, Boston ed., p.* 36.

Penshurst, when I first saw it (in 1791), was the holiest ground I had ever visited. Forty years have not abated my love and veneration for Sydney. I do not remember any character more nearly without reproach. His prose is full of poetry; and there are very fine passages among his poems,—distinguishing them from his metres, in which there is scarcely even a redeeming line, thought, or expression.—SOUTHEY, ROBERT, 1830, *Letter to Sir Egerton Brydges, Brydge's Autobiography, vol.* II, *p.* 267.

The truth is, that the life of Sidney is more poetical than his works; the whole tenor of his conduct is romance brought into action; and we insensibly transfer the admiration we feel for his warm humanity and his nobleness of soul, to works, which, except as they are tinged with the poetry of his character, possess little literary value.—HIPPISLEY, J. H., 1837, *Chapters on Early English Literature, p.* 250.

The silver speech
Of Sidney's self, the starry paladin,
Turn intense as a trumpet sounding in
The knights to tilt,—wert thou to hear!
—BROWNING, ROBERT, 1840, *Sordello, bk.* i, *v.* 68–71.

There is hardly a character in history upon which the imagination can dwell with more unalloyed delight. Not in romantic fiction was there ever created a more attractive incarnation of martial valour, poetic genius, and purity of heart. —MOTLEY, JOHN LOTHROP, 1860, *History of the United Netherlands, vol.* I, *p.* 357.

In the world of letters, then, Sir Philip Sidney took, for his years, rank singularly high. But we must never forget that literature was his only amusement. He knew that he had statesmanly and martial powers, which he was eager to be using. He longed, with the wild earnestness of a caged bird, for room to take his part in the great battle of freedom which was going on around him. For such work he was best fitted, and it is for the glorious beginning made by him herein that we owe him largest honour. But, knowing this we can only the more marvel that the songs with which he lightened his captivity were so eloquent, and that the truths which his youth enforced in idle moments came out of the depths of so mature a mind.—BOURNE, H. R. FOX, 1862, *A Memoir of Sir Philip Sidney, p.* 419.

His prose, as prose, is not equal to his friend Raleigh's, being less condensed and stately. It is too full of fancy in thought and freak in rhetoric to find now-a-days more than a very limited number of readers; and a good deal of the verse that is set in it, is obscure and uninteresting, partly from some false notions of poetic composition which he and his friend Spenser entertained when young; but there is often an exquisite art in his other poems.—MACDONALD, GEORGE, 1868, *England's Antiphon, p.* 77.

Sir Philip Sidney, born the year after him,* with a keener critical instinct, and a taste earlier emancipated than his own, would have been, had he lived longer, perhaps even more directly influential in educating the taste and refining the vocabulary of his contemporaries and immediate successors. The better of his pastoral poems in the "Arcadia" are, in my judgment, more simple, natural, and, above all, more pathetic than those of Spenser, who sometimes strains the shepherd's pipe with a blast that would better suit the trumpet. Sidney had the good sense to feel that it was unsophisticated sentiment rather than rusticity of phrase that befitted such themes. He recognized the distinction between simplicity and vulgarity, which Wordsworth was so long in finding out, and seems to have divined the fact that there is but one kind of English that is always appropriate and never obsolete, namely, the very best. With the single exception of Thomas Campion, his experiments in adapting classical metres to English verse are more successful than those of his contemporaries. Some of his elegiacs are not ungrateful to the ear, and it can hardly be doubted that Coleridge borrowed from his eclogue of Strephon and Klaius the pleasing movement of his own *Catullian Hendecasyllabics.*—LOWELL, JAMES RUSSELL, 1875–90, *Spenser, Prose Works, Riverside ed., vol.* IV, *p.* 276.

Sidney, the radiant "Hesper-Phosphor" of the time of Elizabeth, fades in the brightness of that great morning, yet no radiance that follows is quite so clear and keen. He charmed by a sweet youthful gravity underlying a sweet youthful joyousness of nature. . . . He belonged heartily to the Renaissance, introducing into our prose literature the chivalric-pastoral romance, and engaging eagerly in the reform of versification and in the criticism of poetry.—DOWDEN, EDWARD, 1887, *Transcripts and Studies, pp.* 282, 283.

*Spenser.

Subtle, delicate, refined, with a keen and curious wit, a rare faculty of verse, a singular capacity of expression, an active but not always a true sense of form, he wrote for the few, and (it may be) the few will always love him. But his intellectual life, intense though it were, was lived among shadows and abstractions. He thought deeply, but he neither looked widely nor listened intently, and when all is said he remains no more than a brilliant amorist, too super-subtle for complete sincerity, whose fluency and sweetness have not improved with years.—HENLEY, WILLIAM ERNEST, 1890, *Views and Reviews, p.* 105.

Music bright as the soul of light, for wings an eagle, for notes a dove,
Leaps and shines from the lustrous lines where through thy soul from afar above
Shone and sang till the darkness rang with light whose fire is the fount of love.
Love that led thee alive, and fed thy soul with sorrows and joys and fears,
Love that sped thee, alive and dead, to fame's fair goal with thy peerless peers,
Feeds the fame of they quenchless name with light that lightens the rayless years.

—SWINBURNE, ALGERNON CHARLES, 1894, *Astrophel,* ii.

The sharper lyrical cry, the strenuous utterance of brief but deep emotion, first comes from Sidney, as in the sonnet beginning:

Leave me, O Love, which reachest but to dust.

After this the way is open to all comers, and the full choir of song is heard in the land.—CARPENTER, FREDERIC IVES, 1897, *English Lyric Poetry,* 1500–1700, *Introduction, p.* xliii.

Sidney is the most *dramatic* of sonneteers. In this capacity Shakespeare and he change places.—TOVEY, DUNCAN C., 1897, *Reviews and Essays in English Literature, p.* 178.

Sir Richard Maitland

1496-1586

Sir Richard Maitland, a poet, lawyer, and statesman, was born in 1496. He was the son of William Maitland of Lethington, and Martha, daughter of George, lord Seaton. Having received the usual university education at the college of St. Andrews, he went to France to study law. On his return to Scotland he was employed in various public offices by James V., and afterwards by the Regent Arran and Mary of Guise. In the year 1551 he was appointed Lord of Session, and soon after he was knighted. In his sixty-fourth year he had the misfortune to lose his sight, but his blindness did not incapacitate him for business. In 1562 he was made lord privy-seal and a member of the privy-council. He continued a Lord of Session during the reign of Queen Mary and the minority of her son James VI. In July, 1584, his great age compelled him to resign his seat on the bench, previous to which time he had relinquished the office of lord privy-seal to his second son John, afterwards Lord Thirlestane, Lord High-chancellor of Scotland. Sir Richard died March 20, 1586.—WILSON, JAMES GRANT, 1876, *The Poets and Poetry of Scotland, vol.* I, *p.* 38.

The verses of Maitland do not aim at any high degree of poetical excellence; but as they contain the thoughts, serious and gay, of an amiable old man extensively acquainted with the world, they cannot be considered as destitute of interest.—IRVING, DAVID, 1861, *History of Scotish Poetry, ed. Carlyle, p.* 409.

Sir Richard Maitland was himself a poet, but, what was more fortunate as regards posterity, he preferred the indulging of his poetic faculty in collecting the poems of others, to adding to the number of his own. —ROSS, J., 1884, *ed. The Book of Scottish Poems, p.* 332.

A great calamity overtook Sir Richard at a period of his life which cannot now be precisely fixed. We know, however, that before Mary returned to Scotland he was *blind*. The loss of sight to a man of his tastes must have been a severe privation; but he bore the affliction with characteristic calmness and cheerfulness. Fortunately it did not incapacitate him for active life, —he continued to occupy his seat on the bench, which he did not definitely resign, as we have seen, till within a year or two of his death. . . . Sir Richard's own verses—not as poetry indeed, but as records of the time—are interesting and valuable. They confirm the agreeable impression of his character which we otherwise obtain. The writer was not a man of any exceptional insight or brilliancy; but his sincerity, his shrewdness, his fine sense, his good feeling, his homely honesty and rectitude, are disclosed on every page. The passion of the Reformation does not appear to have touched him.—SKELTON, JOHN, 1887, *Maitland of Lethington, vol.* I, *pp.* 19, 20.

No portrait of him is known. Maitland's chief claim to remembrance is his collection of early Scottish poems, second only in importance to the Bannatyne collection. It is included with other manuscripts in two volumes, which were presented by the Duke of Lauderdale to Samuel Pepys, and are preserved in the Pepysian Library at Magdalene College, Cambridge. Among the amanuenses he employed was his daughter, Margaret Maitland. The collection has never yet been published in altogether complete form; but a large selection from it, including Maitland's own poems, was published by John Pinkerton, in two vols. 1786, under the title "Ancient Scottish Poems never before in Print," &c. Maitland's own poems were reprinted in Sibbald's "Chronicle of Scottish Poetry," 1807, vol. iii., and by the Maitland Club in 1830, an appendix being added of selections from the poems of his sons, Sir John Maitland of Thirlestane and Thomas Maitland, from the Drummond MS. in the university of Edinburgh. The poems of Sir Richard Maitland are of special interest from their bearing on the events, customs, and peculiarities of his time. Although manifesting small poetic ardour, they are characterised by grace, force, and picturesqueness of expression, by shrewd knowledge of the world, and by a gentle cynicism. Among the best known is his "Satire on Town Ladies," in which the "newfangledness of geir" is amusingly exposed.—HENDERSON, T. F., 1893, *Dictionary of National Biography, vol.* XXXV, *p.* 369.

George Whetstone

1544?–1587?

Dramatist and miscellaneous writer (temp. Elizabeth), produced "The Rocke of Regard" (1576); "'The right excellent and famous Historye of Promos and Cassandra" (1578); "An Heptameron of Civill Discourses" (1582); "A Mirur for Magestrates of Cyties" (1584); "An Addition or, Touchstone of the Time" (1584); "The Honourable Reputation of a Souldier" (1586); "The English Myrror" (1586); "The Enemie to Unthriftyness" (1586); "Amelia" (1593); and "Remembrances" of the lives of several worthies, including Sir Philip Sidney, Sir Nicholas Bacon, and George Gascoigne.—ADAMS, W. DAVENPORT, 1877, *Dictionary of English Literature, p.* 751.

One Gentleman notwithstanding among them may I not ouerslyppe, so farre reacheth his fame, and so worthy is he, if hee haue not already, to weare the Lawrell wreathe, Master *George Whetstone*, a man singularly well skyld in this faculty of Poetrie.—WEBBE, WILLIAM, 1586, *A Discourse of English Poetrie, ed. Arber, p.* 35.

A more enduring interest attaches, in the history of our dramatic literature, to the next play founded on a subject from Italian story. George Whetstone's "Promos and Cassandra," from which Shakspere took the story of his "Measure for Measure," was printed in 1578; and its subject is a novel of Giraldi Cinthio's, which Whetstone himself translated in his "Heptameron of Civil Discourses" (1582). Cinthio himself dramatised the story in a work of earlier date. The author of this play, in his Dedication, exhibits a very critical spirit, and for various reasons condemns the dramatic tastes of the principal literary nations of Europe, his own among the number. But though he takes lofty ground with reference to both diction and construction, it cannot be said that he was in practice highly successful in either respect. Consideration of "Decorum" preventing him from "convaying" his whole story in a single play of five acts, he has distributed it over two—but very unequally as to the serious interest of the argument, which is wholly absorbed by the first part. And to "work kindly" the action of his characters, he has made his low comedy very low, and his grosser characters very gross. . . . It was something different from mere condensation which converted "Promos and Cassandra" into "Measure for Measure."—WARD, ADOLPHUS WILLIAM, 1875, *A History of English Dramatic Literature, vol.* I, *pp.* 118, 119.

Whetstone's service is to have pointed out the way in which others more richly gifted than himself were hereafter to walk.—BOAS, FREDERICK S., 1896, *Shakspere and his Predecessors, p.* 28.

Whetstone's works are crude productions, and are interesting only to the historian of literature and the bibliographer. He achieved some reputation in his day.—LEE, SIDNEY, 1899, *Dictionary of National Biography, vol.* LX, *p.* 452.

John Foxe

1516–1587

The martyrologist, born at Boston in Lincolnshire, at sixteen entered Brasenose College, Oxford, and was fellow of Magdalen 1538–45. When tutor with Lucy of Charlecote he married (1547), and afterwards was tutor to the son of the Earl of Surrey, executed in 1547. During the reign of Mary he retired to the Continent, where he met Knox, Grindal, and Whittingham. On Elizabeth's accession he was pensioned by his old pupil, now Duke of Norfolk, and received a prebend of Salisbury (1563). He lived chiefly in London, and often preached. For a year he held a stall at Durham, but was debarred from further preferment by objection to the surplice. Foxe published numerous controversial treatises and sermons, besides an apocalyptic Latin mystery play, called "Christus Triumphans" (1556). But the work that has immortalised his name is his "History of the Acts and Monuments of the Church," popularly known as "Foxe's Book of Martyrs," the first part of which was published in Latin at Strasburg in 1554 (reprinted at Basel in 1559). The first English edition appeared in 1563, in folio. Sanctioned by the bishops, it went through four editions in Foxe's lifetime. It is a noble monument of English; and Foxe's story is doubtless substantially true, although disfigured by credulity and bitter prejudice. The biography of Foxe, attributed to his son Samuel, and published in the 1641 edition of the "Acts," is apocryphal. The best edition of Foxe is that in the "Reformation" series, edited by Mendham and Pratt (8 vols. 1853 *et seq.*).—PATRICK AND GROOME, *eds.*, 1897, *Chambers's Biographical Dictionary*, *p.* 376.

ACTS AND MONUMENTS OF THE CHURCH

That worthie Booke of Martyrs, made by that famous Father and excellent Instrument in God his Church, Maister John Fox, so little to be accepted, and all other good books little or nothing to be reverenced; whilst other toyes, fantasies, and bableries, whereof the world is ful, are suffered to be printed.—STUBBES, PHILIP, 1583, *The Anatomie of Abuses.*

The story is sufficiently known of the two Servants, whereof the one told his Master, "he would do every thing;" the other (which was even Esop himself) said, "he could do nothing;" rendering this reason, "because his former fellow servant would leave him nothing to do." But in good earnest, as to the particular subject of our English Martyrs, Mr. Fox "hath done every thing" (leaving posterity nothing to work upon); and to those who say "he hath overdone something," we have returned our answer before.—FULLER, THOMAS, 1662, *The Worthies of England, ed. Nichols, vol.* II, *p.* 22.

Having compared his "Acts and Monuments" with the records, I have never been able to discover any errors or prevarications in them, but the utmost fidelity and exactness.—BURNET, GILBERT, 1679-1715, *The History of the Reformation of the Church of England, ed. Nares, Preface.*

While he was here* employed by Oporinus, at spare hours he began his "History of the Acts of the Church," in Latin: which he drew out more briefly at first; and, before his return home into England, well near finished. Having here completed the copy, which was but the first part of what he intended, but making a just volume in folio, he sent this work to Basil to be printed: and so it was in the year 155–(9). It remained many years after in those parts in great request, and was read by foreign nations; although hardly known at all by our own. Being now in peace and safety at home, Foxe reviewed this his work, and, in the year 1566, first published it in English very voluminous, because of those many relations of the persecutions in queen Mary's days, that came to his hands. All this work he did himself, without the help of any amanuensis, nor had he any servant to do his necessary domestic business; being fain to be often diverted by his own private occasions from his work. He afterwards enlarged these his labours into three large volumes, which have since undergone many editions.—STRYPE, JOHN, 1694, *Memorials of Archbishop Cranmer, Oxford ed., vol.* III, *p.* 174.

*In Basel.

These writings have not proved, and it never will be proved, that John Foxe is not one of the most faithful and authentic of all historians. We know too much of the strength of Foxe's book, and of the weakness of those of his adversaries, to be further moved by such censures than to charge them with falsehood. All the many researches and discoveries of later times, in regard to historical documents, have only contributed to place the general fidelity and truth of Foxe's melancholy narrative, on a rock which cannot be shaken. — WORDSWORTH, CHRISTOPHER, 1810, *Ecclesiastical Biography, Preface.*

"The Acts and Monuments of the Martyrs" have long been, they still remain, and will always continue, substantial pillars of the Protestant Church; of more force than many volumes of bare arguments, to withstand the tide of popery; and, like a Pharos, should be lighted up in every age, as a warning to all posterity. —BROOK, BENJAMIN, 1813, *Lives of the Puritans.*

His "Book of Martyrs"—as it is called —was, and yet is, one of the most extraordinary and popular church histories in the world. The private history of this elaborate work might be worth knowing, but it is hopeless to enquire after it:— who were the author's chief authorities, and what artists he obtained to make the designs and engravings, are now, I believe, points upon which no correct information is likely to be obtained. Fox lived to see *four* editions of his labours, himself dying in 1587. These editions were succeeded by *five* more, of which the latest was published almost within a century after the death of the author. The *first* edition, in 1563, is of very rare occurrence in a perfect state; and has also some particulars which are omitted in the subsequent editions. . . . Fox was a sort of Luther in his way. His style is equally bold, and his enmity to the church of Rome equally bitter, with that of the great German reformer. His "Acts" are, indeed, an invaluable historical repertory, but, in some particulars, he seems to have gathered information too hastily, and to have detailed it too loosely.—DIBDIN, THOMAS FROGNALL, 1824, *The Library Companion, pp.* 105, 106, *note.*

John Foxe, the author upon whose printed words so many persons rely for their history of this complex period, is not to be depended on for his fiery and lurid descriptions, which are uniformly either false, romance-like, misleading, or greatly exaggerated.—LEE, FREDERICK GEORGE, 1888, *The Life of Cardinal Pole, p.* 189.

To a right student the value of such a book is rather increased than lessened by the inevitable bias of a writer who recorded incidents that had for him a deep, real, present interest, and who had his own part in the passion of the controversy he describes. The work is wonderfully rich in authentic papers, many of which would have been lost if Foxe had not preserved them. It vividly represents one aspect of the strong life of the sixteenth century. . . . Though written in the temper of a partisan, the book has withstood every attack upon its honesty. Foxe gave true transcripts of the documents on which he built his case; he referred honestly to records he had seen and used, when all the secrets of the prison houses were open to him. If we divest the book of its accidental character of feud between the churches, it yet stands, in the first years of Elizabeth's reign, a monument that marks the growing strength of the demand for spiritual freedom, defiance of those powers of the flesh that seek to stifle conscience and fetter thought. The day, however, was not come when they who claim such freedom grant it fully to their adversaries.—MORLEY, HENRY, 1892, *English Writers, vol.* VIII, *pp.* 203, 204.

When we recollect that until the appearance of the "Pilgrim's Progress," in the next century, the common people had almost no reading matter except the Bible and Foxe's "Book of Martyrs," we can understand the deep impression that this book produced, and how it served to mold the national character. Those who could read found there the full details of all atrocities committed on the Protestant Reformers: the illiterate could see the rude illustrations of the various instruments of torture, the rack, the gridiron, the boiling oil, and then the holy martyrs breathing out their souls amid the flames. Take now a people just awakening to a new intellectual and religious life; let several generations of them, from childhood to old age, pore over such a book as this, and its stories become traditions, as indelible and almost as potent as songs and customs on a nation's life. All the fiendish acts there narrated were the work of the Church of Rome, for no hint was given of any other side to the story. No wonder that among the masses, aside from any religious sentiment or conviction, there grew up a horror and detestation of the pope and the Romish Church which have not entirely lost their force after three centuries of Protestant domination.—CAMPBELL, DOUGLAS, 1892, *The Puritan in Holland, England, and America, vol.* I, *p.* 442.

After the Bible itself, no work so profoundly influenced early Protestant sentiment in England as the "Book of Martyrs." Even in our own time it is still a living force: some of its descriptions are burned into the memories of us all, and its spirit is perpetuated in the "Pilgrim's Progress" and in other religious classics, as well as in the tradition of countless houesholds. . . . The book is far more than a bare record of persecution. It is an arsenal of controversy, and a storehouse of romance, as well as a source of edification. Protestantism is traced to its origins in England, Bohemia, and Germany, and the corruptions which had crept into the Church of Rome are exposed at enormous length and with unsparing denunciation. The same method is continued in treating of the English Reformation, and Foxe thus avoids an error which makes so many Lives of the Saints mere catalogues of painful perfections. He plunges, indeed, into the opposite extreme. He accumulates details like Defoe; he is as garrulous as Dogberry. All is grist that comes to his mill. Citations, rejoinders, lengthy dialogues, eye-witnesses' narratives, judgments and sentences—whole piles of documents (with pithy commentaries on each) are heaped one upon the other till we almost hear the parchments crackling.—DODDS, JAMES MILLER, 1893, *English Prose, ed. Craik, vol.* I, *pp.* 327, 328.

The "Book of Martyrs" is the common property of all Protestants, and it would be an absurd pretension to claim it exclusively for the Puritans. At the same time it seems to belong in an especial manner to that party, and they perhaps valued it the most highly. By its authorship they certainly had the prior claim, and during the persecutions of Elizabeth they might compare their own sufferings with those of their heroic predecessors, and this the more fortunate Anglicans, safe within the pale of their Church, could hardly do.—HINDS, ALLEN B., 1895, *The Making of the England of Elizabeth, p.* 43.

Foxe's "Acts and Monuments" (John Daye, 1562–63), first edition, complete. Earl of Ashburnham (1897), £150.—WHEATLEY, HENRY B., 1898, *Prices of Books, p.* 218.

Thomas Watson

1557?–1592

Born in London, England, about 1557; educated at Oxford University; studied law in London; spent some time in Paris with members of the Walsingham family; settled in London, and acquired a high reputation by his pastoral and amatory poems, which rivaled in popularity those of his friends Spenser and Sidney. Died in 1592. He was the author of a translation of Sophocle's "Antigone" in Latin (1581); "Ekatompathia, or Passionate Centurie of Love," (1582); "Melibœus, sive Eclogain in Obitum Domini Francisci Walsinghami," (1590); "The Tears of Fancie, or Love Disdained" (1593); and many other poetical works, some of which have perished. The three last named were carefully edited by Edward Arber in his "English Reprints" (1870). Watson's love sonnets, many of which were imitations of Ferrabosco, Ronsard, and other foreign poets, were artificial and frigid.—BEERS, HENRY A., *rev.*, 1897, *Johnson's Universal Cyclopædia, vol.* VIII, *p.* 662.

. . . worthy many epitaphs
For his sweet poesy, for Amyntas' tears
And joys so well set down.
—PEELE, GEORGE, 1593, *The Honour of the Garter, Ad Mæcenatem Prologus.*

And thou, my sweete Amyntas, vertuous minde,
Should I forget thy learning and thy love,
Well might I be accounted but unkinde,
Whose pure affection I so oft did prove:
Might my poore plaints hard stones to pitty move,
His losse should be lamented of each creature,
So great his name, so gentle was his nature.
—BARNFIELD, RICHARD, 1594, *The Affectionate Shepherd.*

Amyntas, floure of shepheards pride forlorne,
He whilest he liued was the noblest swaine,
That euer piped in an oaten quill:
Both did he other, which could pipe, maintaine,
And eke could pipe himselfe with passing skill.
—SPENSER, EDMUND, 1595, *Colin Clouts Come Home Againe, v.* 439–43.

A man he was that I dearely lou'd and honor'd, and for all things hath left few his equalls in England.—NASHE, THOMAS, 1596, *Haue with you to Saffron-Walden, Works, ed. Grosart, vol.* III, *p.* 187.

Tom Watson . . . wrote
Able to make Apollo's self to dote
Upon his Muse.
—HEYWOOD, THOMAS, 1635, *The Hierarchy of the Blessed Angels,* iv.

Has he painted the natural emotions of the mind or the heart? Has he given
"a local habitation and a name"
to those airy nothings which more or less haunt every fancy? Or has he not sat down rather to exercise the subtlety of his wit than to discharge the fulness of his bosom.—BRYDGES, SAMUEL EDGERTON, *British Bibliographer,* 1811, *No.* 12, *p.* 4.

Of the sonnets of Watson, which were published about 1581, we . . . shall merely add here, that neither in their structure, nor in their diction or imagery, could they be, or were they, models for our author; and are indeed greatly inferior, not only to the sonnets of Shakspeare, but to those of almost every other poet of his day.—DRAKE, NATHAN, 1817, *Shakspeare and his Times, vol.* II, *p.* 54.

In the "Hecatompathia," to which we now turn, Watson's genius appears often weighted down by his own learning. He has, as will be seen, prefixed to each poem a sort of preface, which must be assigned to his own authorship; and when we read these and the poems themselves, we feel strongly how new a thing in England was then the whole range of classical and "polite" literature; the peculiar air of the Renaissance hangs about the book; it is like a gay and genial school-boy exulting in his studies; it breathes a kind of innocent and attractive pedantry. . . . What place shall we give to our newly regained poet in this noble army? Below Sidney, but above Spenser, and the rest of that day, as an Amourist, was that which we proposed at the outset of our notice; Shakespeare being excepted from the survey.—PALGRAVE, FRANCIS TURNER, 1872, *Thomas Watson the Poet, North American Review, vol.* 114, *pp.* 91, 109.

The "Passionate Century" is worth reading as a repertory of commonplace lover's hyperboles. There never was so sweet a lady, never so fond nor so distraught a lover. Hand, foot, lip, eye, brow, and golden locks are all incomparable. The ages never have produced, and never will produce, such another; Apelles could not have painted her, Praxiteles could not have sculptured her, Virgil and Homer could not have expressed her, and Tully would not have ventured to repeat the number of her gifts. She is superior to all the mythological paramours of Jove. The various goddesses have contributed their best endowments, mental and physical, to make her perfect.—MINTO, WILLIAM, 1874–85, *Characteristics of English Poets, p.* 203.

Watson, in fact, was a purely literary poet. At Oxford, says Antony Wood, he spent his time "not in logic and philosophy, as he ought to have done, but in the smooth and pleasant studies of poetry and romance." To these studies, however, his devotion was serious; for he mastered four languages, so that he writes as familiarly of Sophocles and Apollonius Rhodius as of Ovid, of Petrarch and Ariosto as of Ronsard. He translated the "Antigone" into Latin, and it was one of his Latin poems that gave him the fancy name of Amyntas, under which the poets of the time ranked him with Colin Clout and with Astrophel. But the literature that he affected most was the love-poetry of the Italians—of Petrarch and his followers, of Seraphine and Fiorenzuola, and many others that are quite forgotten now. Sometimes translating, sometimes paraphrasing, sometimes combining them, he tells the story of his imaginary love, its doubts and fears and hopes, its torments and disappointments and final death, in that melodius Elizabethan English which not even monotony and make-believe can wholly deprive of charm. But still, Watson and his kindred poets have little more than an historical interest. They are but the posthumous children of the Courts of Love; their occupation is to use the scholarship and the ingenuity of the Renascence to dress up the sentiment of the Middle Age—a sentiment no more real to them than it is to ourselves. They make no appeal to us; their note has nothing of the note of passion and of truth that rings in the verse of Sidney and of Shakespeare.—WARD, THOMAS HUMPHRY, 1880, *The English Poets, vol.* I, *p.* 389.

It may be surmised that others besides his contemporaries have overestimated Watson.—SCHELLING, FELIX E., 1895, *A Book of Elizabethan Lyrics, p.* 224.

More important than Dyer, and much more important than Fraunce, was Thomas Watson, a rather short-lived bard who died in 1592 at the age of thirty-five, but who, save for a certain frigidity, would take a high place, and who perhaps, considering his earliness, deserves no low one as it is. —SAINTSBURY, GEORGE, 1898, *A Short History of English Literature, p.* 273.

Watson's verse lacks passion, but is the accomplished work of a cultivated and well-read scholar. As a Latinist he stands first among contemporaries. It is as a sonneteer that he left his chief mark on English literature. He was the first English writer of sonnets after Surrey and Wyatt. Most of his sonnets were published before those of Sir Philip Sidney, and the popularity attending Watson's sonneteering efforts was a chief cause of the extended vogue of the sonnet in England among poets and their patrons in the last decade of the sixteenth century. Watson's sonnets were closely studied by Shakespeare and other contemporaries, and, despite their frigidity and imitative quality, actively influenced the form and topic of the later sonnets of the century. All manner of praise was bestowed on Watson at his death by his fellow poets and men of letters, who reckoned him the compeer of Spenser and Sidney.—LEE, SIDNEY, 1899, *Dictionary of National Biography, vol.* LX, *p.* 37.

Robert Greene

1560–1592

Novelist and dramatist (born 1560, died 1592). A full catalogue of this writer's Works may be found in Lowndes' "Bibliographer's Manual." The following are the most important:—*Romances*—"Pandosto, the Triumph of Time: or, the History of Doraustus and Faunia" (1588), "The Historie of Arbasto, King of Denmark" (1617); "A Pair of Turtle Doves; or, the Tragicall History of Bellora and Fidelio" (1606); "Menaphon" (1587).—*Autobiography*—"Greene's Never too Late" (1590); "Greene's Groats-worth of Wit, bought with a Million of Repentance" (1592); "Greene's Vision" (1592); "The Repentance of Robert Greene" (1592); "Farewell to Folly" (1591). *Plays*—"The Honorable Historie of Frier Bacon and Frier Bongay" (1594); "The Historie of Orlando Furioso" (1594); "The Comical Historie of Alphonsus, King of Arragon"; "A Looking-Glass for London and England" (with Lodge); "The Scottish Historie of James IV." (1598); "Mammilia" (1593). *Miscellaneous*—"The Myrour of Modestie" (1584); "Morando" (1584); "Euphues, his Censure to Philatus" (1587); "Perimedes the Blacksmith" (1588); "Alcida" (1588); "The Spanish Masquerado (1589); and numerous pamphlets exposing the sins and follies of town life.—ADAMS, W. DAVENPORT, 1877, *Dictionary of English Literature, p.* 286.

With him was the fifth, a man of indifferent yeares, of face amible, of body well proportioned, his attire after the habite of a scholler-like gentleman, onely his haire was somewhat long, whome I supposed to be Robert Greene, Maister of Artes.—CHETTLE, HENRY, 1592, *Kind-Harts' Dreame, sig. B.* 3.

I was altogether vnacquainted with the man, & neuer once saluted him by name: but who in London hath not heard of his dissolute, and licentious liuing; his fonde disguisinge of a Master of Arte with ruffianly haire, vnseemely apparell, and more vnseemelye Company; his vaineglorious and Thrasonicall brauinge: his piperly Extemporizing, and Tarletonizing; his apishe counterfeiting of euery ridiculous, and absurd toy: his fine coosening of Iuglers, and finer iugling with cooseners: hys villainous cogging and foisting; his monstrous swearinge, and horrible forswearing; his impious profaning of sacred Textes: his other scandalous, and blas phemous ravinge: his riotous and out ragious surfeitinge; his continuall shifting of lodginges: his plausible musteringe, and banquetinge of roysterly acquaintaunce at his first comminge; his beggarly departing in euery hostisses debt; his infamous resorting to the Banckside, Shorditch, Southwarke, and other filthy hauntes: his obscure lurkinge in basest corners: his pawning of his sword, cloake, and what not, when money came short; his impudent pamphletting, phantasticall interluding, and desperate libelling, when other coosening shifts failed.—HARVEY, GABRIEL, 1592, *Four Letters, Works, ed. Grosart, vol.* I, *p.* 168.

Hee inherited more vertues than vices: a jolly long red peake, like the spire of a steeple, hee cherisht continually without cutting, whereat a man might hang a Jewell, it was so sharpe and pendant. Why should art answer for the infirmities of manners? Hee had his faultes, and thou thy follyes. Debt and deadly sinne, who is not subject to? With any notorious crime I never knew him tainted.—NASHE, THOMAS, 1592, *Strange Newes of the Intercepting certaine Letters.*

As Achilles tortured the dead body of Hector; and as Antonius and his wife Fulvia tormented the lifeless corpse of Cicero; so Gabriel Harvey hath showed the same inhumanity to Greene, that lies full low in his grave. . . . As

Archesilaus Prytanœus perished by wine at a drunken feast, as Hermippus testifieth in Diogenes: so Robert Greene died by a surfeit taken of pickled herrings and Rhenish wine; as witnesseth Thomas Nash, who was at the fatal banquet.—MERES FRANCIS, 1598, *Palladis Tamia, p.* 103.

The shamelessness of the man is a sufficient guarantee for the truth of his personal revelations. Vain, and desirous of keeping his name before the public, but without a character to lose, he made a cynical exposure of his vices. These confessions, moreover, are stamped with indubitable signs of earnestness. The accent of remorse is too sincere and strongly marked in them to justify a suspicion of deliberate fiction. . . . Greene deserves almost unmitigated reprobation. He was not only profligate, but bad-hearted, and, as we shall see, he indulged a rancorous animosity upon his death-bed. Yet we may believe that had his youth escaped the contamination of Italian vices, had his abilities been recognised by society, or had a place among men of education and good manners been open to his choice, he might perhaps have prospered.—SYMONDS, JOHN ADDINGTON, 1884, *Shakspere's Predecessors in the English Drama, pp.* 544, 545.

I am myself by no means sure that Greene's supposed debauchery is not, to a great extent, "copy." — SAINTSBURY, GEORGE, 1887, *History of Elizabethan Literature, p.* 65.

Early in August 1592 Greene fell ill after a dinner, at which Nashe was present, of pickled herrings and Rhenish wine. The account of his last illness and death given by his malignant enemy, Gabriel Harvey, may be exaggerated in some particulars, but appears to be substantially true. Harvey called on Greene's hostess, and professes to record the information that she supplied. If his account be true, Greene was deserted by all his friends, Nashe among the number, and died in the most abject poverty. He lodged with a poor shoemaker and his wife, who attended him as best they could, and his only visitors were two women, one of them a former mistress (sister to the rogue known as "Cutting Ball," who had been hanged at Tyburn), the mother of his base-born son, Fortunatus Greene, who died in 1593. Having given a bond for ten pounds to his host, he wrote on the day before his death these lines to the wife whom he had not seen for six years: "Doll, I charge thee by the loue of our youth and by my sovles rest that thou wilte see this man paide for if hee and his wife had not succoured me I had died in the streetes. Robert Greene." He died 3 Sept. 1592, and his devoted hostess, obeying a wish that he had expressed, crowned his dead body with a garland of bays. On the following day he was buried in the New Churchyard, near Bethlehem Hospital.—BULLEN, A. H., 1890, *Dictionary of National Biography, vol.* XXIII, *p.* 67.

There were two separate selves in him, and they proved incompatible. One was full of reasonable, sensible, and somewhat *bourgeois* tendencies, highly appreciating honour, respectability, decorum, civic and patriotic virtues; of women liking only those that were pure, of men those that were honest, religious and good citizens. Greene's other self was not, properly speaking, the counterpart of the first, and had no taste for vices as vices, nor for disorder as disorder, but was wholly and solely bent upon *enjoyment*, immediate enjoyment whatever be the sort, the cost, or the consequence. Hence the glaring discrepancies in Greene's life, his faults, not to say his crimes, his sudden short-lived repentances, his supplications to his friends not to imitate his example, his incapacity to follow steadily one course or the other. His better self kept his writings free from vice, but was powerless to control his conduct.—JUSSERAND, J. J., 1890, *The English Novel in the Time of Shakespeare, p.* 151.

It is easy to condemn the man, impossible not to love him, important to understand him, for his is a typical figure. He may be taken as the very epitome of many writers of the time, wild, profligate Bohemians in their lives, and in their writings earnest and often terrible moralists. Yet it surely is not necessary, with M. Jusserand, to assign to Greene "two separate selves" in order to understand this. Rather, the man who should preach repentance without having felt, as Greene did, all the anguish of self-reproach and self-abasement, all the bitterness of the fruits of his misdoing, is in need of two selves, one for the pulpit, another for the complacent regulation of his private affairs. Greene had but one self, full of impulse, readily kindled to generosity, or carried by sympathy or ridicule into vice, and above all filled with that artistic instinct which compelled him to give expression in poetic or literary form to what he felt and knew.—RALEIGH, WALTER, 1894, *The English Novel, p.* 66.

ROMANCES

Robert Greene was a man who possessed all the advantages of education: he was a graduate of both Universities—he was skilled in ancient learning and in modern languages—he had, besides, a prolific imagination, a lively and elegant fancy, and a grace of expression rarely exceeded; yet let any person well acquainted with "The Winter's Tale" read the novel of "Pandosto," upon which it was founded, and he will be struck at once with the vast pre-eminence of Shakespeare, and with the admirable manner in which he has converted materials supplied by another to his own use. The bare outline of the story (with the exception of Shakespeare's miraculous conclusion) is nearly the same in both; but this is all they have in common, and Shakespeare may be said to have scarcely adopted a single hint for his descriptions, or a line for his dialogue; while in point of passion and sentiment Greene is cold, formal, and artificial: the very opposite of everything in Shakespeare.—COLLIER, JOHN PAYNE, 1843, *Shakespeare's Library, Introduction to Greene's Pandosto, vol.* I, *p.* i.

As a writer he was one amongst the most popular of his day. His little romances of some fifty pages each were the delight of readers for amusement, for half a century. They were the companions of the courtly and the humble,—eagerly perused by the scholar of the University and the apprentice of the City. They reached the extreme range of popularity. In Anthony Wood's time they were "mostly sold on ballad-monger's stalls;" and Sir Thomas Overbury describes his Chambermaid as reading "Greene's works over and over." Some of these tales are full of genius, ill-regulated no doubt, but so pregnant with invention, that Shakspere in the height of his fame did not disdain to avail himself of the stories of his early contemporary.—KNIGHT, CHARLES, 1849, *Studies of Shakspere, bk.* i, *ch.* v.

For his keen perception of character and the relations of social life, the playfulness of his fancy, and the liveliness of his style exerted an influence on his contemporaries, which was equalled by that of none but Marlowe and Peele. No figure better paints the group of young playwrights. . . . Wild as was the life of Greene, his pen was pure. He is steadily on virtue's side in the love pamphlets and novelettes he poured out in endless succession, and whose plots were dramatized by the school which gathered round him. —GREEN, JOHN RICHARD, 1874-87, *A Short History of the English People, ch.* vii.

Greene's tales had immense popularity. Some of them ran through several editions, and even held their ground until the modern English novel had fairly come in to supersede them.—MURRAY, J. ROSS, 1885, *The Influence of Italian upon English Literature, p.* 24.

"Menaphon," although equipped with a sub-title fathering this book also upon "Euphues," was in truth a direct challenge to the popularity of Sidney's "Arcadia," published about a year earlier. Although not his first, it proved Greene's most sustained and successful attempt to clothe chivalrous sentiment in the fashionable shepherd's weeds, trimmed with the inevitable Euphuistic garniture.—WARD, ADOLPHUS WILLIAM, 1893, *English Prose, ed. Craik, vol.* I, *p.* 553.

DRAMAS

If, as a dramatist, Greene fails to exhibit character with force and discrimination, if he has much both of the fustian and the meanness which are found more or less in all the plays of the period, and if his blank-verse is so monotonous as to pall upon the ear; it must be allowed, on the other hand, that he not unfrequently writes with elegance and spirit, and that in some scenes he makes a near approach to simplicity and nature.—DYCE, ALEXANDER, 1831-61, *ed. Dramatic and Poetical Works of Robert Greene, p.* 34.

Greene succeeds pretty well in that florid and gay style, a little redundant in images, which Shakspeare frequently gives to his princes and courtiers, and which renders some unimpassioned scenes in his historic plays effective and brilliant. —HALLAM, HENRY, 1837-39, *Introduction to the Literature of Europe, pt.* ii, *ch.* vi, *par.* 32.

Greene was a prolific and versatile author. Besides dramas, he was a writer of novels and poetical pieces, especially of instructive or moral works, which were occasionally in a semi-poetic and romantic form, and of several pamphlets of a satirical character. In all he displayed no common powers of mind—great sensibility and tenderness of feeling, a quick and lively fancy, a graceful vein of humour and raillery, but without profundity of genius, or deep and solid feelings, without fixed opinions in religion and morals, and above all, without that energy of character which is required to hold with a firm hand the reins of poesy not less than of life. . . . His dramas possess, indeed, form and proportion; they are not without keeping and light nimble movement; but this external regularity of form, this outward advance of the plot, does not compensate for the want of inward unity and organic necessity of the several parts. In perfect agreement with all this, his dramatic characters are, it is true, correctly drawn, and are also lively and graceful, but yet devoid of an inner motive of development provided and existing from the beginning; they are not full and well-finished figures, but, for the most part, as it were, sculptured in half-relief, or like ancient illuminations, in which the figures do not at all stand out from the brilliant ground of gold on which they are emblazoned. They are deficient in intrinsic massiveness and solidity of mind; like Greene himself, their life does not pass outwards from within, but conversely, and consequently their inmost and real personality is never laid bare, but reality and appearance float alike before us in a broad, loose, and vague indeterminateness. The language is pure, clear, and graceful, but without ebb and flow; proceeding in one broad unbroken line, and not so much the language of mind, feeling, and passion, as of conversation and narrative.—ULRICI, DR. HERMANN, 1839, *Shakspeare's Dramatic Art, pp.* 39, 40.

Greene was too cynical to have command of language for a character of sustained pride; he could pump up expression for a good many emotions, but his nature was dry in that region. He is, indeed, a standing refutation of the plausible idea that rant belongs to the infancy of the drama. Rant goes rather with the nature of the individual; and Greene, with all his roughness and recklessness, was fitted to be the pupil of Lyly more than of Marlowe. —MINTO, WILLIAM, 1874–85, *Characteristics of English Poets, p.* 243.

In style, again, Greene is father of Shakespere—as far, at least, as an ordinary man may be said to be father of a giant. When matured, their plays have none of the "thundering eloquence" or unrelieved passion of Marlowe's best work, nor of the delicate sweetness of Peele's. They have the irregular strength, the granite of Teutonic art. The gloom of gathering passion in them does not break in shower of tears and sorrow alone, but with lightning of laughter. They have as strong guiding intellects as they have emotions, and their emotions are therefore anything but one-sided. In the midst of some great passion, the thought turns upon itself, and a passing smile saves it from turgidity or paroxysm. Their humour ever dashes in, and makes softer as well as grander the storm of their tragedy. Contrast, relief, marks off their dramatic style; little touches of pathos breathe across their comedies; humorous passages chequer their serious plays as gratefully as clouds the midsummer sunlight. That humour of theirs, too, is, more frequently than other dramatists', of that wise, refreshing sort, which has the fear of fate before its eyes. The rollicking, reckless kinds—farce, burlesque, wit—have their place, but it is a subordinate one.—BROWN, J. M., 1877, *An Early Rival of Shakespere, New Zealand Magazine, April, p.* 101.

Certainly the title of "a vulgar writer" suits no one so well as Greene; for in the works of no other dramatist of his day shall we find so many scenes taken bodily, so to speak, out of English real life, and put into so pure and popular a language, free from all euphuistic admixture and florid classical figurativeness. Exactly half of those plays of Greene's which we still possess are devoted to the representation of the life of the people. For Chettle, who knew all Greene's plays, affirms that the percentage of the popular was considerably greater. Even in Greene's earlier dramatic attempts,—in which he imitated Marlowe's gorgeous manner and Lylly's euphuistic style,—we shall always find two or three scenes of popular life, which are so witty, lively and fresh, that they leave nothing to be desired. But another circumstance contributed not a little to Greene's popularity as a dramatist. His plays, with their fantastical characters and their numerous unexpected adventures, reminded the public of their favourite novels, tales of chivalry, and wonderful romances.—STOROJENKO, NICHOLAS, 1878, *Robert Greene; His Life and Works; A Critical Investigation, tr. Hodgetts, ed. Grosart, p.* 223.

In Greene's plays we can always trace the hand of the novelist. He did not aim at unity of plot, or at firm definition of character. Yet he manages to sustain attention by his power of telling a story, inventing an inexhaustible variety of motives, combining several threads of interest with facility, and so arranging his incongruous materials as to produce a pleasing general effect. He has the merit of simplicity in details, and avoids the pompous circumlocution in vogue among contemporary authors. His main stylistic defect is the employment of cheap Latin mythology in and out of season. But his scenes abound in vivid incidents, which divert criticism from the threadbare thinness of the main conception, and offer opportunities to clever actors.—SYMONDS, JOHN ADDINGTON, 1884, *Shakspere's Predecessors in the English Drama, p.* 557.

With a few touches from the master's hand, Margaret, the fair maid of Fressingfield, might serve as handmaid to Shakespere's women, and is certainly by far the most human heroine produced by any of Greene's own group. — SAINTSBURY, GEORGE, 1887, *History of Elizabethan Literature, p.* 73.

It was Greene who first brought Comedy into contact with the blithe bright life of Elizabethan England, into contact with poetry, into contact with romance. He took it out into the woods and the fields, and gave it all the charm of the idyll; he filled it with incident and adventure, and gave it all the interest of the novel. A freshness as of the morning pervades these delightful medleys. Turn where we will—to the loves of Lacy and Margaret at merry Fressingfield, to the wizard friar and the marvels of his magic cell at Oxford, to the patriot Pinner and his boisterous triumphs, to Oberon with his fairies and antics revelling round him, to the waggeries of Slipper and Miles—everywhere we find the same light and happy touch, the same free joyous spontaneity. His serious scenes are often admirable. We really know nothing more touching than the reconciliation of James and Dorothea at the conclusion of "James IV.," and nothing more eloquent with the simple eloquence of the heart than Margaret's vindication of Lacy in "Friar Bacon." The scene again in the second act of "James IV.," where Eustace first meets Ida, would in our opinion alone suffice to place Greene in the front rank of idyllic poets. Greene's plots are too loosely constructed, his characters too sketchy, his grasp and range too limited, to entitle him to a high place among dramatists, and yet as we read these medleys we cannot but feel how closely we are standing to the Romantic Comedies of Shakspeare.—COLLINS, JOHN CHURTON, 1895, *Essays and Studies, p.* 173.

His best plays breathe a thoroughly national spirit, and they are instinct with love of English traditions, English virtues, and English familiar scenes. "Friar Bacon and Friar Bungay" and "George-a-Greene" set before us pictures of country life as natural and attractive as any in "Love's Labour's Lost" or "The Merry Wives of Windsor." A pure and fragrant air ripples through their pages, blowing from over homestead, and meadow, and stream. Here too we meet with members of every social class, prince and peasant, earl and shoemaker, philosopher and clown, all mixing in easy familiarity. So it is in the world of Shakspere, where rank is never the measure of merit, and where the ideal ruler wandering in disguise among his soldiers declares to them that the King is but a man as other men, with like senses and conditions. But Greene in his popular sympathies goes further than Shakspere, who can never be strictly called democratic, and of whose heroes and heroines not one is taken from humble life. The portrait gallery of the greater dramatist, wide and varied as it is, contains no such figures as Margaret of Fresingfield or the Pinner of Wakefield. The village maid, who is really what she seems, not, like Perdita, a princess in disguise, and who yet may be worthy of an Earl's love; the yeoman, with the sturdy independence of his class united to genuine loyalty and ardour of heart—these are not types over which Shakspere lingers lovingly. For them we are indebted to Greene, who thus takes his place on the long list of our writers headed by Langland, and numbering Burns, Crabbe, and Wordsworth among its foremost names, who have found their truest inspiration in the joys and sorrows of the poor.—BOAS, FREDERICK S., 1896, *Shakspere and his Predecessors, p.* 87.

In Greene, the new spirit of Renaissance sensuousness, so unbridled in Marlowe, is found to be restrained by those cool and exquisite moral motives, the elaboration of which is the crowning glory of Shakespeare. Faint and pale as Greene's historical plays must be confessed to be, they are the first specimens of native dramatic literature in which we see fore-shadowed the genius of the romantic English stage.—GOSSE, EDMUND, 1897, *Short History of Modern English Literature, p.* 98.

GENERAL

Other newes I am advertised of, that a scald triviall lying Pamphlet, called "Greens Groats worth of Wit" is given out to be of my doing. God never have care of my soule, but utterly renounce me, if the least word or syllable in it proceeded from my penne, or if I were any way privie to the writing or printing of it.—NASHE, THOMAS, 1592, *Pierce Penilesse his Supplication to the Divell.*

Be not dismaied (my good freends) that a deade man shoulde acquaint you with newes; for it is I, I *per se* I, Robert Greene, *in Artibus Magister*, he that was wont to solicite your mindes with many pleasant conceits, and to fit your fancies, at the least every quarter of the yere, with strange and quaint devises, best beseeming the season, and most answerable to your pleasures.—RICH, BARNABE ? 1593, *Greenes Newes both from Heaven and Hell.*

He was . . . a pastoral sonnet-maker and author of several things which were pleasing to men and women of his time. They made much sport and were valued among scholars; but since they have been mostly sold on ballad-mongers stalls.—WOOD, ANTHONY, 1691-1721, *Fasti Oxonienses, vol.* I, *p.* 136.

He had great vivacity of intellect, a very inventive imagination, extensive reading, and his works abound with frequent and successful allusions to the Classics. It is surprising to see how polished and how finished some of his pieces are, when it is considered that he wrote most of them to supply his immediate necessities, and in quick succession one to another.—BELOE, WILLIAM, 1807, *Anecdotes of Literature and Scarce Books, vol.* II, *p.* 190.

It must be confessed that many of the prose tracts of Greene are licentious and indecent; but there are many also whose object is useful and whose moral is pure. They are written with great vivacity, several are remarkable for the most poignant raillery, all exhibit a glowing warmth of imagination, and many are interspersed with beautiful and highly-polished specimens of his poetical powers. On those which are employed in exposing the machinations of his infamous associates, he seems to place a high value, justly considering their detection as an essential service done to his country; and he fervently thanks his God for enabling him so successfully to lay open the "most horrible Coosenages of the common Conny-Catchers, Cooseners, and Crosse Biters," names which in those days designated the perpetrators of every species of deception and knavery. . . . Though most of the productions of Greene were written to supply the wants of the passing hour, yet the poetical effusions scattered through his works betray few marks of haste or slovenliness, and many of them, indeed, may be classed among the most polished and elegant of their day. To much warmth and fertility of fancy they add a noble strain of feeling and enthusiasm, together with many exquisite touches of the pathetic, and so many impressive lessons of morality, as, in a great measure, to atone for the licentiousness of several of his prose tracts.—DRAKE, NATHAN, 1817, *Shakspeare and his Times, vol.* I, *pp.* 494, 627.

Greene's style is in truth most whimsical and grotesque. He lived before there was a good model of familiar prose; and his wit, like a stream that is too weak to force a channel for itself, is lost in rhapsody and diffuseness.—CAMPBELL, THOMAS, 1819, *Specimens of the British Poets.*

A pretty little instructive bibliographical volume might be put forth, respecting the works—with choice morsels of quotations therefrom—of the above not very *harmonious* quartetto. Let Robert Greene play the first fiddle.—DIBDIN, THOMAS FROGNALL, 1824, *The Library Companion, p.* 591, *note.*

A pleasing wit, rich, graceful, who gave himself up to all pleasures, publicly with tears confessing his vices, and the next moment plunging into them again. . . . You see the poor man is candid, not sparing himself; he is natural; passionate in everything, repentance or otherwise; eminently inconstant; made for self-contradiction, not self-correction.—TAINE, H. A., 1871, *History of English Literature, tr. Van Laun, vol.* I, *bk.* ii, *ch.* ii, *p.* 236.

There was an absolute chasm between the foulness of his life and the serenity of his intellect, and, at least until he became a repentant character, no literary theme interested him very much, unless it was interpenetrated with sentimental beauty. This element inspired what little was glowing and eloquent in his plays; it tinctured the whole of his pastoral romances with a rosy Euphuism, and it turned the best of his lyrics to the pure fire and air of poetry. From his long sojourn in Italy and Spain he brought back a strong sense of the physical beauty of men and women, of fruits, flowers, and trees, of the coloured atmosphere and radiant compass of a southern heaven. All these things passed into his prose and into his verse, so that in many of the softer graces and innocent voluptuous indiscretions of the Elizabethan age he is as much a forerunner as Marlowe is in audacity of thought and the thunders of a massive line.—GOSSE, EDMUND, 1880, *English Poets, ed. Ward, vol.* I, *p.* 402.

I must take this fresh opportunity of recalling that, as the converse of Herrick's famous (or infamous) pleading that if his verse was impure his life was chaste, Greene's writings are exceptionally clean. Nor must he be refused the benefit of this in any judicial estimate of him. It is equally harsh and uncritical to say that this confessedly dissolute-living man wrote purely because it paid to do so. It did no such thing. It would have paid, and did pay, to write impurely, and as ministering to the insatiate appetite of readers for garbage. To his undying honour, Robert Greene, equally with James Thomson, left scarce a line that dying he need have wished "to blot." I can't understand the nature of any one who can think hardly of Greene in the light of his ultimate penitence and absolute confession. It is (if the comparison be not over-bold) as though one had taunted David with his sin after the fifty-first Psalm.—GROSART, ALEXANDER B., 1881–86, *ed. Life and Complete Works of Robert Greene, Editor's Introduction, vol.* I, *p.* xix.

Crowded with similes taken for the most part from the ancient classics, and appositely applied, his poetry is at once polished and elegant. Nor, strange to say, does he betray any of those signs of slovenliness which we should expect to find in the writings of the first English poet who is said to have written for bread. Occasionally, more especially in his prose, he becomes indecent; but we must remember the manners of the times, before false modesty and hypocritical Grundyism had been born. His lessons of morality are both impressive and virtuous, so that, in his own day, he became noted alike for his good advice and bad example.—UNDERHILL, GEORGE F., 1887, *Literary Epochs, p.* 84.

The coherence of Greene's paragraphs is fairly good. The movement is light and sometimes rapid, and the Euphuistic parallelism does not retard the general progress. Proportion, however, is wholly missing. Greene was guilty of numerous clause-heaps, and of unnecessary single-sentence sections. The general loose structure of his sentence does not save him from the bane of his day—the excessive use of intermediate punctuation.—LEWIS, EDWIN HERBERT, 1894, *The History of the English Paragraph, p.* 88.

We have read and re-read his poems, his novels, and his plays, and at each perusal, their pure and wholesome spirit, their liveliness, their freshness, their wealth of fancy and imagination, their humour, their tenderness, their many graces of style, have gained on us more and more. — COLLINS, JOHN CHURTON, 1895, *Essays and Studies, p.* 167.

The richer note of Greene, full of English feeling, strangely heightened with pastoral and Renaissance fancies, varied in rhythm, but somewhat languorous and overwrought.—CARPENTER, FREDERIC IVES, 1897, *English Lyric Poetry,* 1500–1700, *Introduction, p.* xliii.

Christopher Marlowe

1564–1593

Christopher Marlowe, 1564–1593. Born, at Canterbury, Feb. (?) 1564; baptized, 26 Feb. Educated at King's School, Canterbury. Matric. Corpus Christi College, Cambridge, 17 March 1581; B. A., 1583; M A., 1587. Probably settled in London soon afterwards. Warrant for his arrest, on ground of heretical views expressed in his writings, issued 18 May 1593. Killed, in a tavern quarrel at Deptford, 1 June 1593. *Works:* "Tamburlaine the Great" (anon.), 1590. *Posthumous:* "Edward II.," Cassel, 1594 (only one copy known; another edn., London, 1598); "The Tragedy of Dido" (with T. Nash), 1594; "Hero and Leander," 1598; "The Tragical History of . . . Dr. Faustus," 1601 (?), (earliest copy extant, 1604); "The Massacre at Paris" (1600); "The Famous Tragedy of the Rich Jew of Malta," 1633; "Lust's Dominion," 1657; "A Most Excellent Ditty of the Lover's promises to his beloved" (1650?). He *translated:* Ovid's "Amores," 1590 (?) and 1598 (?); "Lucan's First Booke," 1600. *Collected Works:* ed. by G. Robinson, 3 vols., 1826; ed. by A. Dyce, 3 vols., 1850; ed. by A. H. Bullen, 3 vols., 1885.—SHARP, R. FARQUHARSON, 1897, *A Dictionary of English Authors, p.* 186.

Christopher Marlow, slain by ffrancis Archer, the 1 of June 1593.—BURIAL-REGISTER, *Parish Church of St. Nicholas, Deptford*, 1593.

By practice a play-maker and a poet of scurrilitie, who, by giuing too large a swing to his owne wit, and suffering his lust to haue the full reines, . . . denied God and his sonne Christ, and not onely in word blasphemed the Trinitie, but also (as it is credibly reported) wrote bookes against it, affirming our Sauiour to be but a deceiuer, and Moses to be but a coniurer and seducer of the people, and the Holy Bible to bee but vaine and idle stories, and all religion but a deuice of policie. But see what a hooke the Lord put in the nostrils of this barking dogge! So it fell out, that, as he purposed to stab one whom he ought a grudge vnto, with his dagger, the other party perceiuing so auoyded the stroke, that withall catching hold of his wrist, hee stabbed his owne dagger into his owne head, in such sort that, notwithstanding all the meanes of surgerie that could bee wrought, hee shortly after died thereof; the manner of his death being so terrible . . . that it was not only a manifeste signe of God's judgement, but also an horrible and fearefull terror to all that beheld him. But herein did the justice of God most noteably appeare, in that hee compelled his owne hand, which had written these blasphemies, to bee the instrument to punish him, and that in his braine which had deuised the same.—BEARD, THOMAS, 1597, *Theatre of God's Judgments*

As Jodelle, a French tragical poet, being an epicure and an atheist, made a pitiful end: so our tragical poet Marlow, for his Epicurism and Atheism, had a tragical death; as you may read of this Marlow more at large, in the Theatre of God's judgments, in the 25th chapter, entreating of Epicures and Atheists. As the poet Lycophron was shot to death by a certain rival of his: so Christopher Marlow was stabbed to death by a baudy Servingman, a rival of his, in his lewd love.—MERES, FRANCIS, 1598, *Palladis Tamia.*

Not inferior to these was one Christopher Marlow, by profession a playmaker, who as it was reported, about fourteen years ago wrote a book against the Trinitie. But see the effects of God's justice! It so hapned that at Detford, a little village about three miles distant from London, as he meant to stab with his poniard one named Ingram, that had invited him thither to a feast, and was then playing at tables, hee quickly perceiving it, so avoyded the thrust, that with all drawing out his dagger for his defence, hee stabd this Marlowe into the eye, in such sort, his braynes comming out, at the daggers point, hee shortly after dyed. Thus did God, the true executioner of divine justice, work the end of impious atheists.—VAUGHAN, SIR WILLIAM, 1600, *Golden Grove.*

Marlowe was happy in his buskin ('d) Muse—
Alas, unhappy in his life and end!
Pitty it is that wit so ill should dwell,
Wit lent from heaven, but vices sent from hell.
Our theater hath lost, Pluto hath got
A tragick penman for a driery plot.

—ANON., 1606, *The Return from Pernassus.*

We read of one Marlow a Cambridge scholler, who was a poet and a filthy play-maker; this wretche accounted that meeke servant of God, Moses, to be but a conjurer, and our sweete Saviour but a seducer and deceiver of the people. But harken, ye brain-sicke and prophane poets and players, that bewitch idle eares with foolish vanities, what fell upon this prophane wretch:—having a quarrell against one whom he met in a streete in London, and would have stab'd him; but the partie perceiving his villany prevented him with catching his hand and turning his owne dagger into his braines, and so blaspheming and cursing he yeelded up his stinking breath. Marke this, ye players, that live by making fooles laugh at sinne and wickedness.—RUDIERDE, EDMOND, 1618, *The Thunderbolt of God's Wrath against Hard-hearted and Stiffe-necked Sinners.*

Marlow, renown'd for his rare art and wit,
Could ne'er attain beyond the name of *Kit;*
Although his "Hero and Leander" did
Merit addition rather.

—HEYWOOD, THOMAS, 1635, *Hierarchie of the Blessed Angels.*

But whatever our opinions may be as to the attending circumstances, the parish register leaves us in no doubt as to the main fact by recording the burial of "Christopher Marlow, slaine by ffrancis Archer, the 1 of June, 1593." The old church of St. Nicholas at Deptford, has been enlarged and rebuilt, and restored and re-restored, till nothing of the original except the old grey tower remains, and it is vain even to guess at the spot in which the body of the young poet was laid. He died we may well suppose in the worst inn's worst room, and his grave was dug we may be certain in the obscurest corner of the churchyard; but even had it been otherwise, all knowledge of the locality would have passed away during the dark hundred years in which Christopher Marlowe became a name unknown. —CUNNINGHAM, L'Col. FRANCIS, 1870, *ed. Works of Christopher Marlowe, Introduction, p,* xix.

The death of Marlowe was seized upon with avidity by the Puritans, and he was held up as an awful example of the judgment of God. He was a free-thinker, an atheist, a blasphemer; there was no known crime that was not imputed to him. As no one man could have been guilty of all the wickedness he was charged with, and as one of his accusers was afterwards hanged at Tyburn, let us charitably render the Scotch verdict—"Not proven." The Devil himself is not as black as he is painted by the theologians.—STODDARD, RICHARD HENRY, 1884, *ed. Selections from the Poetical Works of A. C. Swinburne, Introduction, p.* vii.

The accounts of his death are doubtful and confused, but the most probable account is that he was poniarded in self-defence by a certain Francis Archer, a serving-man (not by any means necessarily, as Charles Kingsley has it, a footman), while drinking at Deptford, and that the cause of the quarrel was a woman of light character. He has also been accused of gross vices not to be particularised, and of atheism. Fortunately or unfortunately, there is absolutely no valid testimony to support this latter charge, the expressions respecting it being for the most part quite vague and traceable on the one side to the Puritan hatred of plays, on the other to the unquestionably loose life of Marlowe and his set; while the one specified accusation existing is due to a scoundrel called Bame, who was afterwards hanged at Tyburn. That Marlowe was a Bohemian in the fullest sense is certain: that he was anything worse there is no evidence whatever.—SAINTSBURY, GEORGE, 1887, *History of Elizabethan Literature, p.* 76.

It is certain he had friends among the finest-natured men of his time. Walsingham was his patron; there seems a touch of tenderness in Shakespeare's apostrophe of the "dead shepherd" in "As you Like It;" Nash, who had sometimes been a jealous rival wrote an elegy "on Marlowe's untimely death" which has not survived; an anonymous writer in 1600 speaks lovingly of "kynde Kit Marloe;" Edward Blunt, Marlowe's friend and publisher, writes, in words that have a genuine ring, of "the impression of the man that hath been dear unto us, living an after-life in our memory;" Drayton's well-inspired lines are familiar. . . . There is no alloy of blame in the words of these men, Drayton and Chapman, and they were among the gravest as well as the best-loved of their time. One lingers over the faintest traces of this personality which must have been so fascinating, for we have no further trustworthy indications of the manner of man that he was in the eyes of those who knew him.—ELLIS, HAVELOCK, 1887, *ed. Marlowe, (Mermaid Series), p.* xlv.

The passionate, defiant youth, surcharged with genius, was fair game for the bigots and Pharisees, who found it only too easy to besmirch his memory.—BRANDES, GEORGE, 1898, *William Shakespeare, A Critical Study, vol.* I, *p.* 36.

TAMBURLAINE
1590

Tamburlaine the Great. Who, from a Scythian Shephearde by his rare and woonderfull Conquests, became a most puissant and mightye Monarque. And, (for his tyranny, and terrour in Warre) was tearmed, The Scourge of God. Deuided into two Tragicall Discourses, as they were sundrie times shewed vpon Stages in the Citie of London. By the right honourable the Lord Admyrall, his seruauntes. Now first, and newlie published. London. Printed by Richard Ihones: at the signe of the Rose and Crowne neere Holborne Bridge, 1590.—TITLE PAGE TO FIRST EDITION, 4*to.*

Idiote art-masters that intrude thẽselues to our eares as the alcumists of eloquence; who (mouted on the stage of arrogance) think to outbraue better pens with the swelling bumbast of a bragging blank verse. Indeed it may be the ingrafted ouerflow of some kilcow conceipt, that ouercloieth their imagination with a more than drunken resolution, beeing not extemporall in the inuention of anie other meanes to vent their manhood, commits the digestion of their cholerick incumbrances to the spacious volubilitie of a drumming decasillabon.—NASHE, THOMAS, 1587, *To the Gentlemen Students of both Universities, ed. Grosart, p.* xx.

I keep my old course, to palter vp some thing in Prose, vsing mine old poesie still, *Omne tulit punctum,* although latelye two Gentlemen Poets, made two mad men of Rome beate out of their paper bucklers: & had it in derision, for that I could not make my verses ilt vpon the stage in tragicall buskins, euerie worde filling the mouth like the faburden of Bo-Bell, daring God out of heauen with that Atheist Tamburlan, or blaspheming with the mad preest of the sonne.—GREENE, ROBERT, 1588, *Perimedes The Blacke Smith, To the Reader.*

From jigging veins of rhyming mother wits
And such conceits as clownage keeps in pay,
We'll lead you to the stately tent of war,
Where you shall hear the Scythian Tamburlaine:
Threatening the world with high astounding terms,
And scourging kingdoms with his conquering sword.
View but his picture in this tragic glass,
And then applaud his fortune as you please.

—MARLOWE, CHRISTOPHER, 1590, *Tamburlaine the Great, Part the First, The Prologue.*

The true artificer will not run away from Nature as he were afraid of her; or depart from life, and the likeness of truth; but speak to the capacity of his hearers. And though his language differs from the vulgar somewhat it will not fly from all humanity, with the Tamer-lanes and Tamer-chams of the late age, which had nothing in them but the scenical strutting, and furious vociferation, to warrant them to the ignorant gapers.—JONSON, BEN, 1630–7, *Timber, or, Discoveries,* lxxii.

It hath been told me there is a Cock-pit play going under the name of "The Scythian Shepherd, or Tamberlain the Great," which how good it is any one may judge by its obscurity, being a thing not a bookseller in London, or scarce the players themselves who acted it formerly, cow'd call to remembrance.—SAUNDERS, CHARLES, 1681, *Preface to Tamerlane.*

Marlow could not have selected for his purpose a better subject than the life and conquests of Tamburlaine, who rose from the lowest grade of life to the loftiest honours of a throne: instead of the "conceits which clownage kept in pay," he carried the spectators "to the stately tent of war," and took ample room for striking effects and novel situations. He seems, however, to have apprehended that he could not accomplish his great change instantly; and in order, to a certain extent, to gratify the appetite of the mob, he introduced into his performance scenes of low humour and buffoonery, which are omitted in the printed copies, the publisher informing the reader that he considered them derogatory "to so honourable and stately a history." The reason for their insertion was the same as for the employment of "high astounding terms"—not that they were good, but that they would be applauded; and Marlow himself no more approved of the one than of the other. . . . It is by no means fair, therefore, to examine "Tamburlaine the Great" without bearing this fact in memory:—that it was the first attempt of the kind, and that Marlow made great sacrifices, as a poet, to promote its success. It will at once account for all the fustian and hyperbole by which the production unquestionably is disfigured, but which is sometimes of such a striking character, that we must pronounce even its absurdities the work of a man of fervid and exalted genius.—COLLIER, JOHN PAYNE, 1831, *History of English Dramatic Poetry, vol.* III, *pp.* 119, 121.

"Tamburlaine" was ridiculed on account of its inflated style. The bombast, however, which is not so excessive as has been alleged, was thought appropriate to such oriental tyrants. This play has more spirit and poetry than any which, upon clear grounds, can be shown to have preceded it. We find also more action on the stage, a shorter and more dramatic dialogue, a more figurative style, with a far more varied and skilful versification.—HALLAM, HENRY, 1837–39, *Introduction to the Literature of Europe, pt.* ii, *ch.* vi, *par.* 28.

A strange compound of inspiration and desperation, has the mark of power equally on its absurdities and its sublimities.—WHIPPLE, EDWIN P., 1859–68, *The Literature of the Age of Elizabeth, p.* 26.

Laugh as we will, in this first of Marlowe's plays there is that incommunicable gift which means almost everything, *style*; a manner perfectly individual, and yet, at its best, free from eccentricity. The "mighty line" of which Jonson spoke, and a pleasure, equal to Milton's, in resounding proper names, meet us in the very first scene; and in not a few passages passion, instead of vociferating, finds its natural expression, and we hear the fully-formed style, which in Marlowe's best writing is, to use his own words,

"Like his desire, lift upward and divine."

"Lift upward" Marlowe's style was at first, and so it remained. It degenerates into violence, but never into softness. If it falters, the cause is not doubt or langour, but haste and want of care.—BRADLEY, ANDREW CECIL, 1880, *English Poets, ed. Ward, vol.* I, *p.* 413.

It is difficult to over-estimate the importance of "Tamburlaine" in the history of the English Drama. To appreciate how immensely Marlowe outdistances at one bound all his predecessors, the reader must summon courage to make himself acquainted with such productions as "Gorboduc," "The Misfortunes of Arthur," and "Sir Clyomon" and "Sir Clamydes." He will then perceive how real is Marlowe's claim to be regarded as the father of the English drama. That the play is stuffed with bombast, that exaggeration is carried sometimes to the verge of burlesque, no sensible critic will venture to deny. But the characters, with all their stiffness, have life and movement. The Scythian conqueror, "threatening the world in high astounding terms," is an impressive figure. There is nothing mean or trivial in the invention. The young poet threw into his work all the energy of his passionate nature. He did not pause to polish his lines, to correct and curtail; but was borne swiftly onward by the wings of his imagination. The absence of chastening restraint is felt throughout; and, indeed, the beauty of some of the most majestic passages is seriously marred by the introduction of a weak or ill-timed verse.—BULLEN, A. H., 1884, *ed. Works of Christopher Marlowe, Introduction, vol.* I, *p.* xviii.

EDWARD II
1594

The troublesome raigne and lamentable death of Edward the second, King of England: with the tragicall fall of proud Mortimer. As it was sundrie times publiquely acted in the honourable citie of London, by the right honourable the Earl of Pembroke his servants. Written by Chri. Marlow Gent. Imprinted at London for William Jones, dwelling neare Holborne conduit at the Signe of the Gunne, 1594.—TITLE PAGE TO FIRST EDITION, 4*to.*

In a very different style from mighty "Tamburlaine" is the tragedy of "Edward the Second." The reluctant pangs of abdicating royalty in Edward furnished hints, which Shakespeare scarcely improved in his "Richard the Second"; and the death-scene of Marlowe's king moves pity and terror beyond any scene ancient or modern with which I am acquainted.—LAMB, CHARLES, 1808, *Specimens of Dramatic Poets.*

He has handled the history of "Edward the Second" in a very artless manner it is true, but with a certain truth and simplicity, so that many scenes do not fail to produce a pathetic effect. His verses are flowing, but without energy; how Ben Jonson could come to use the expression, *Marlow's mighty line*, is more than I can conceive.—SCHLEGEL, AUGUSTUS WILLIAM, 1809, *Dramatic Art and Literature, tr. Black, Lecture XIII.*

"Edward II." is, according to the modern standard of composition, Marlowe's best play. It is written with few offences against the common rules, and in a succession of smooth and flowing lines. The poet, however, succeeds less in the voluptuous and effeminate descriptions which he here attempts, than in the more dreadful and violent bursts of passion. "Edward II." is drawn with historic truth, but without much dramatic effect.—HAZLITT, WILLIAM, 1820, *Lectures on the Literature of the Age of Elizabeth, Lecture II.*

Qualified, however, as must always be the praise assigned to the "Jew of Malta," the critics combine in a chorus of approbation when they come to speak of "Edward the Second," which is recognised by common consent as, after Shakspeare's, the finest specimen of the English historical drama; while, as regards its only superiors, it possesses the important advantage of being anterior to them all in the date of its production. The conclusion, in particular, has called forth the admiration of the highest judges.—CUNNINGHAM, Lt.Col. FRANCIS, 1870, *ed. Works of Christopher Marlowe, Introduction, p.* xv.

Of the murder of the king Charles Lamb has written that it "moves pity and terror beyond any scene, ancient or modern, with which I am acquainted." These may seem strong words when we think of Prometheus chained to the mountain top, or of Lear storm-tossed on the heath, but they are memorable as coming from so clear-eyed a critic. In any case there can be no doubt that the fifth act of Marlowe's tragedy far surpasses the corresponding portion of Shakspere's "Richard II." This is partly due to a characteristic difference between the dramatists in the handling of their allied themes. Shakspere's aim is to show how Richard's weakness and sentimentality bring about his downfall. The purpose of the play would have been defeated had he awakened a reaction in the unhappy king's favour by a vivid picture of his prison sufferings and death. This, on the contrary, is what Marlowe has done, and so persuasive is his art that our recollection of Edward's sins is almost effaced in the contemplation of his long-drawn agony. Here, as always, Shakspere's moral point of view is loftier than his forerunner's, and "Richard II" moreover breathes a spirit of fervent patriotism absent in the earlier work. But in the variety of its situations, and in closely sustained dramatic interest, "Edward II" has without question the advantage over Shakspere's play.—BOAS, FREDERICK S., 1896, *Shakspere and his Predecessors, p.* 57.

Mention is made of "Edward II." in Henslowe's "Diary," and the title-page of the last Quarto (1622) speaks of it as "acted by the Queenes Maiesties Seruants," *i. e.* Queen Anne's Company of actors, to whom had passed the rights of the original performers, Pembroke's Company. Otherwise, nothing, it would seem, is known with regard to its stage-history, and it thus presents a striking contrast to "Faustus" and "The Jew of Malta," the great popularity of which is attested by contemporary allusions and references, and the comments of later critics like Edward Phillips (in "Theatrum Poetarum," 1675) and Langbaine (in "Dramatick Poets," 1691). The fact that most of the prominent characters in "Edward II." excite little sympathy must, one would think, have told somewhat against it. To the student, however, it is a play of surpassing interest, for its intrinsic merits, its just claim to be the first specimen in our language of true historical drama, and its relation to "Richard II." — VERITY, A. W., 1896, *ed. Marlowe's Edward the Second, Preface, p.* ix.

FAUSTUS
1601

Of all that he hath written to the stage his "Dr. Faustus" hath made the greatest noise with its Devils, and such like tragical sport.—PHILLIPS, EDWARD, 1675, *Theatrum Poetarum Anglicanorum, ed. Brydges, p.* 113.

Marlowe is said to have been tainted with atheistical positions, to have denied God and the Trinity. To such a genius the history of Faustus must have been delectable food: to wander in fields where curiosity is forbidden to go, to approach the dark gulf near enough to look in, to be busied in speculations which are the rottenest part of the core of the fruit that fell from the tree of knowledge. Barabas the Jew, and Faustus the conjurer, are offsprings of a mind which at least delighted to dally with interdicted subjects. They both talk a language which a believer would have been tender of putting into the mouth of a character though but in fiction.—LAMB, CHARLES, 1808, *Specimens of Dramatic Poets.*

Though an imperfect and unequal performance, is his greatest work. Faustus himself is a rude sketch, but it is a gigantic one. This character may be considered as a personification of the pride of will and eagerness of curiosity, sublimed beyond the reach of fear and remorse.—HAZLITT, WILLIAM, 1820, *Lectures on the Literature of the Age of Elizabeth, Lecture II.*

It is full of poetical beauties; but an intermixture of buffoonery weakens the effect, and leaves it, on the whole, rather a sketch by a great genius than a finished performance. There is an awful melancholy about Marlowe's Mephistopheles, perhaps more impressive than the malignant mirth of that fiend in the renowned work of Goethe. But the fair form of Margaret is wanting; and Marlowe has hardly earned the credit of having breathed a few casual inspirations into a greater mind than his own.—HALLAM, HENRY, 1837–39, *Introduction to the Literature of Europe, pt.* ii, *ch.* vi, *par.* 29.

"Doctor Faustus" has many magnificent passages, such as Marlowe of the "mighty line" could not fail to write; but on the whole it is wearisome, vulgar, and ill-conceived. The lowest buffoonery, destitute of wit, fills a large portion of the scenes; and the serious parts want dramatic evolution. There is no character well drawn. The melancholy figure of Mephistopholis has a certain grandeur, but he is not the Tempter, according to the common conception, creeping to his purpose with the cunning of the serpent; nor is he the cold, ironical "spirit that denies;" he is more like the Satan of Byron, with a touch of piety and much repentance. The language he addresses to Faustus is such as would rather frighten than seduce him.—LEWES, GEORGE HENRY, 1855, *Life and Works of Goethe, p.* 469.

With regard to the buffoonery of which Hallam so justly complains, I have no hesitation in saying that it must be attributed to any hand rather than Marlowe's own. The edition of 1604 has been separately reprinted, with the view of showing that this debasing matter was of gradual introduction, the dose being made stronger and stronger to satisfy the taste of the groundlings, a proceeding which can hardly be complained of in a generation which appears to relish few things so much as the beastly grimaces, hurdy-gurdy tunes, and stupid threadbare jokes of pack after pack of buffoons smeared all over with filthy lampblack. If by any chance the original MS. of the "Tragical History of Dr. Faustus" is ever recovered, it is almost safe to predicate that Marlowe's share would be found to consist solely and entirely of those grand, daring, and affecting scenes which will last as long as the English language.—CUNNINGHAM, Lt Col. FRANCIS, 1870, *ed. Works of Christopher Marlowe, Introduction, p.* xiv.

"His raptures were all air and fire." In nothing has he shown himself so much a child of the Renaissance as in this repugnance to touch images of physical ugliness. Perondinus insists on Tamburlaine's lameness, of which Marlowe says no word; the "Volksbuch" is crammed with details concerning the medieval Hell; Malrowe's conception of Hell is loftier than Dante's or Milton's.—ELLIS, HAVELOCK, 1887, *ed. Marlowe,* (*Mermaid Series*), *p.* xxxix.

This is unquestionably Marlowe's greatest play; it is indeed one of the greatest plays that the world possesses; for in it the poet has been compelled, by the nature of his story and his own profound imagination, to pass beyond the limits of Machiavellism, and to sound the depths of the human heart, in an exhibition of that conflict between Will and Conscience which was embodied in outline in the old Moralities, and found its highest development in the dramas of Shakespeare. In this tragedy accordingly there are more distinct traces of the primitive traditions of the English theatre than in any other of Marlowe's works.—COURTHOPE, W. J., 1897, *A History of English Poetry, vol.* II, *p.* 410.

Although it is among the most chaotic, there can be little doubt that "Doctor Faustus" is the best of Marlowe's plays. For the chaos here is not quite out of keeping with the wild theme; and that theme itself, in every other respect, is absolutely suited to Marlowe's genius. The whole spirit of the Faust story comports with—nay, positively requires—not so much a regular dramatic action as a phantasmagoria; and its separate scenes are, most of them, well suited to stimulate the towering imagination, the passionate fancy, the tameless and restless energy of this wonderfully though partially endowed poet. That the Helen passage and the death scene contain, with the single exception—if with that—of the great purple patch of "Tamburlaine," as to "the pens that poets held," the most exquisite outbursts of sheer poetry in Marlowe is no more than we should expect from the coincidence of inspiring quality in the subject and formal competence in the worker.—SAINTSBURY, GEORGE, 1898, *A Short History of English Literature*, p. 292.

JEW OF MALTA

The author seems to have relied on the horror inspired by the subject, and the national disgust excited against the principal character, to rouse the feelings of the audience: for the rest, it is a tissue of gratuitous, unprovoked and incredible atrocities, which are committed, one upon the back of the other, by the parties concerned, without motive, passion, or object.—HAZLITT, WILLIAM, 1820, *Lectures on the Literature of the Age of Elizabeth, Lecture II.*

The first two acts of the "Jew of Malta" are more vigorously conceived, both as to character and circumstance, than any other Elizabethan play, except those of Shakspeare.—HALLAM, HENRY, 1837–39, *Introduction to the Literature of Europe, pt.* ii, *ch.* vi, *par.* 29.

Whatever may be thought of the extraordinary accumulation of villanies perpetrated by the hero, the construction of the plot is extremely ingenious, and, notwithstanding its elaborateness, singularly clear and intelligible. Though the action rises from startling to more startling effects, a climax is reserved to the last. And in form the play deserves high praise; for the vigour and ease of its versification are alike remarkable.—WARD, ADOLPHUS WILLIAM, 1875, *A History of English Dramatic Literature, vol.* I, *p.* 185.

The masterful grasp that marks the opening scene was a new thing in English tragedy. Language so strong, so terse, so dramatic, had never been heard before on the English stage. In the two first acts there is not a trace of juvenility; all is conceived largely and worked out in firm, bold strokes. Hardly Shakespeare's touch is more absolutely true and unfaltering; nor is it too much to say that, had the character been developed throughout on the same scale as in the first two acts, Barrabas would have been worthy to stand alongside of Shylock. But in the last three acts vigorous drawing is exchanged for caricature; for a sinister life-like figure we have a grotesque stage-villain, another Aaron. How this extraordinary transformation was affected, why the poet, who started with such clear-eyed vision and stern resolution, swerved so blindly and helplessly from the path, is a question that may well perplex critics.—BULLEN, A. H., 1884, *ed. Works of Christopher Marlowe, Introduction, vol.* I, *p.* xl.

DIDO

While following closely the story of the early books of the "Aeneid," and even putting into the mouths of the leading characters several Virgilian lines, the drama is thoroughly original and merits more attention than it usually receives, especially as it contains Marlowe's most elaborate picture of a woman.—BOAS, FREDERICK S., 1896, *Shakspere and his Predecessors, p.* 58.

HERO AND LEANDER
1598

Sir,—We think not ourselves discharged of the duty we owe to our friend when we have brought the breathless body to the earth; for albeit the eye there taketh his ever-farewell of that beloved object, yet the impression of the man that hath been dear unto us, living an after-life in our memory, there putteth us in mind of farther obsequies due unto the deceased; and namely of the performance of whatsoever we may judge, shall make to his living credit and to the effecting of his determinations prevented by the stroke of death. By these meditations (as by an intellectual will) I suppose myself executor to the unhappily deceased author of this poem; upon whom knowing that in his lifetime you bestowed many kind favours, entertaining the parts of reckoning and worth which you found in him with good countenance and liberal affection, I cannot but see so far into the will of him dead, that whatsoever issue of his brain should chance to come abroad, that the first breath it should take might be the gentle air of your liking; for since his self had been accustomed thereunto, it would prove more agreeable and thriving to his right children that any other foster-countenance whatsoever.—BLUNT, EDWARD, 1598, *Dedication of Hero and Leander to Sir Thomas Walsingham.*

Liue still in heauen thy soule, thy fame on earth!
Thou dead, of Marlos Hero findes a dearth.
Weepe, aged Tellus! all on earth complaine!
Thy chiefe-borne faire hath lost her faire againe:
Her faire in this is lost, that Marlo's want
Inforceth Hero's faire be wonderous scant.
Oh, had that king of poets breathed longer,
Then had faire beautie's fort been much more stronger!
His goulden pen had clos'd her so about,
No bastard æglet's quill, the world throughout,
Had been of force to marre what he had made;
For why they were not expert in that trade.
What mortall soule with Marlo might contend,
That could 'gainst reason force him stoope or bënd?
Whose siluer-charming toung mou'd such delight,
That men would shun their sleepe in still darke night
To meditate vpon his goulden lynes,
His rare conceyts, and sweet-according rimes.

—PETOWE, HENRY, 1598, *The Second Part of the Loves of Hero and Leander, To the Quick-Sighted Reader.*

Then, now, most strangely intellectual fire
That, proper to my soul, hast power to inspire
Her burning faculties, and with the wings
Of thy unspherèd flame, visits't the springs
Of spirits immortal. Now, as swift as Time
Doth follow motion, find th' eternal clime
Of his free soul, whose living subject stood
Up to the chin in the Pierian flood,
And drunk to me half this Musæan story,
Inscribing it to deathless memory:
Confer with it, and make my pledge as deep
That neither's draught be consecrate to sleep:
Tell it how much his late desires I tender
(If yet it know not), and to light surrender
My soul's dark offspring.

—CHAPMAN, GEORGE, 1600, *Hero and Leander, bk.* iii.

A kind of second Shakesphear (whose contemporary he was) not only because like him he rose from an actor to be a maker of plays, though inferior both in fame, and merit; but also because in his begun poem of "Hero and Leander," he seems to have a resemblance of that clean and unsophisticated Wit, which is natural to that incomparable poet.—PHILLIPS, EDWARD, 1675, *Theatrum Poetarum Anglicanorum, ed. Brydges, p.* 113.

The fragment of "Hero and Leander" is incomparably the finest product of Marlowe's genius: it is one of the chief treasures of the language. The poet is fairly intoxicated with the beauty of his subject: he has thought about the two lovers, and dreamed about them, and filled his imagination with their charms; he writes with ecstasy as if obeying an impulse that he can resist no longer, and in every other line expressions escape him that have all the warmth of involuntary bursts of admiration. He dashes into the subject with passionate eagerness, outlining the situation with a few impatient strokes.—MINTO, WILLIAM, 1874–85, *Characteristics of English Poets, p.* 239.

Written in the so-called heroic verse, it bears no resemblance to any other poem in that metre composed before, nor, perhaps, is there any written since which decidedly recalls it, unless it be "Endymion." "Pagan" it is in a sense, with the Paganism of the Renascence: the more pagan the better, considering the subject. Nothing of the deeper thought of the time, no "looking before and after," no worship of a Gloriana or hostility to an Acrasia, interferes with its frank acceptance of sensuous beauty and joy.—BRADLEY, ANDREW CECIL, 1880, *English Poets, ed. Ward, vol.* I, *p.* 415.

No poem in our language is more classical, in the sense at least in which Politian and Sanazzaro would have understood the term, and assuredly no poem in our language is more sensuously lovely, than "Hero and Leander." It reminds us in some respects of the best episodes in the "Metamorphoses," and it reminds us still more frequently of Keats's narratives, not, indeed, of "Isabella" or of "The Eve of Saint Agnes," but indirectly of "Endymion," and directly of "Lamia."—COLLINS, JOHN CHURTON, 1895, *Essays and Studies, p.* 161.

GENERAL

Marley, the Muses' darling . . .
Fit to write passions for the souls below,
If any wretched souls in passion speak.
—PEELE, GEORGE, 1593, *The Honour of the Garter, Ad Mœcenaatem Prologus.*

Marlow's mighty line.—JONSON, BEN, 1623, *To the Memory of my Beloved Master William Shakespeare, and what he hath left us.*

Neat Marlowe, bathed in the Thespian springs,
Had in him those brave translunary things
That the first poets had; his raptures were
All air, and fire, which made his verses clear;
For that fine madness still he did retain,
Which rightly should possess a poet's brain.
—DRAYTON, MICHAEL, c 1627, *Of Poets and Poesie.*

That smooth song* which was made by Kit Marlow, now at least fifty years ago: and . . . an answer to it which was made by Sir Walter Raleigh in his younger days. They were old-fashioned poetry, but choicely good.—WALTON, ISAAC, 1653, *The Complete Angler.*

His tragedies manifest traces of a just dramatic conception; but they abound with tedious and uninteresting scenes, or with such extravagancies as proceeded from a want of judgment, and those barbarous ideas of the times, over which it was the peculiar gift of Shakespeare's genius alone to triumph and to predominate.—WARTON, THOMAS, 1778–81, *History of English Poetry, sec.* lix.

Had he lived longer to profit by the example of Shakspeare, it is not straining conjecture to suppose, that the strong misguided energy of Marlowe would have been kindled and refined to excellence by the rivalship.—CAMPBELL, THOMAS, 1819, *Specimens of the British Poets.*

Christopher Marlow, whose name will live as long as tender sentiment, clothed in language the most felicitous, shall be understood and felt, is known rather as a dramatist than a professed poet.—DIBDIN, THOMAS FROGNALL, 1824, *The Library Companion, p.* 699, *note.*

Marlowe was in all essential points the direct opposite of Greene; while the latter delighted in a cheerful grace, and agreeableness of style, Marlowe aimed solely and exclusively at the forcible, extraordinary, and sublime. He possessed, in fact a vigorous, and—not to lay too much stress upon the term—a great mind; but his heart was waste and rude, and it is from the heart that every truly great thought proceeds. Accordingly, under his hand, the forcible becomes the forced, the uncommon the unnatural, while the great and sublime sinks into the grotesque and monstrous. . . . To such a height does he frequently accumulate terrific and monstrous events, deeds of violence, enormities and crimes, that no corresponding catastrophe nor adequate punishment, can be devised for them; and the close of the piece consequently appears as a low and narrow outlet through which the mass of the action seeks in vain to force its way. Accordingly, the last moments of his heroes, however they may distress and agitate, never exalt or elevate the feelings. His notion of tragedy comprehends in it nothing of solace and atonement. Nevertheless, his mental vigour alone has enabled him to do that which was wholly beyond the power of Greene; his poetical matter is well connected and condensed; his dramas have for their basis a vital concrete idea, a fully defined view of life and the world, out of which the whole composition appears to have grown naturally, and organically to have perfected itself.—ULRICI, HERMANN, 1839, *Shakspeare's Dramatic Art, p.* 45.

He is intense, but narrow. The central principle of his mind was self-will, and this is the bond which binds together his strangely huddled faculties. Of all English poets, he most reminds us of Byron; ruder, it may be, but at the same time more colossal in his proportions. He is a glorious old heathen, "large in heart and brain,"—a fiery and fickle Goth, on whose rough and savage energies a classical culture has been piled, tossed among the taverns, and theatres, and swelling spirits of London, to gratify the demands of his senses in some other way than by acts of brilliant pillage. In his lustiness, his absence of all weak emotions, his fierce delight in the mere feeling of self, in the heedlessness with which he heaps together rubbish and diamonds, and in the frequent "starts and strange far-flights of his imagination," he is the model of irregular genius. His mind, in its imperiousness, disregarded by instinct the natural relations of things, forced objects

*"The Passionate Shepard."

into the form of his individual passions, and lifted his vices into a kind of Satanic dignity, by exaggerating them into shapes colossal. His imagination, hot, swift, impatient of control, pervaded by the fiery essence of his blood, and giving wings to the most reckless desires, riots in the maddest visions of strength and pride. Of all writers, he seems to feel the heartiest joy in the mere exercise of power, regardless of all the restraints which make power beneficent.—WHIPPLE, EDWIN P., 1846, *North American Review, Essays and Reviews, vol.* II, *p.* 19.

Æschylus of the English stage, like his great Athenian prototype, seems to have impressed his contemporaries with a most exalted respect for his sublime and irregular genius.—SHAW, THOMAS B., 1847, *Outlines of English Literature, p.* 104.

The essential character of his mind was that of a lofty extravagance, shaping itself into words that may be likened to the trumpet in music, and the scarlet in painting—perpetual trumpet, perpetual scarlet. . . . Through five thousand lines have we the same pompous monotony, the same splendid exaggeration, the same want of truthful simplicity. But the man was in earnest. His poetical power had nothing in it of affectation and pretence. —KNIGHT, CHARLES, 1849, *Studies of Shakspere, p.* 32.

Marlowe had a rare imagination, a delicacy of sense that made him the teacher of Shakespeare and Milton in versification, and was, perhaps, as purely a poet as any that England has produced; but his mind had no balance-wheel.—LOWELL, JAMES RUSSELL, 1858–64–90, *Library of Old Authors, Prose Works, Riverside ed., vol.* I, *p.* 277.

Although we cannot say much for the dramatic *art* of Marlowe, he has far surpassed every one that went before him in dramatic *poetry*. The passages that might worthily be quoted from Marlowe's writings for the sake of their poetry are innumerable, notwithstanding that there are many others which occupy a border land between poetry and bombast, and are such that it is to us impossible to say to which class they rather belong. . . . His verse is, for dramatic purposes, far inferior to Shakspere's.—MACDONALD, GEORGE, 1864–83, *The Imagination and other Essays, pp.* 100, 101.

For thou, if ever godlike foot there trod
These fields of ours, wert surely like a god.
Who knows what splendour of strange dreams was shed
With sacred shadow and glimmer of gold and red
From hallowed windows, over stone and sod,
On thine unbowed, bright, insubmissive head?
The shadow stayed not but the splendour stays,
Our brother, till the last of English days.
No day nor night on English earth shall be
Forever, spring nor summer, Junes nor Mays,
But somewhat as a sound or gleam of thee
Shall come on us like morning from the sea.

—SWINBURNE, ALGERNON CHARLES, 1866, *In the Bay, Poems and Ballads, ss.* xviii, xix.

Marlowe was an ill-regulated, dissolute, outrageously vehement and audacious spirit, but grand and sombre, with the genuine poetic frenzy; pagan moreover, and rebellious in manners and creed. . . . Marlowe is to Shakspeare what Perugino was to Raphael.—TAINE, H. A., 1871, *History of English Literature, tr. Van Laun, vol.* I, *bk.* ii, *ch.* ii, *pp.* 237, 244.

His was a wild, volcanic nature, storming through life with the licence of genius. . . . The glowing imagination of this poet delighted in portraying the terrific struggle between the most violent passions, but he was never able to keep within the bounds of beauty; the conciliatory and elevating element is wanting in his tragedies; his delineation of character generally degenerates into monstrosity, and his energetic diction into an inflated and bombastic style. The boldness of his genius led him to choose subjects of historical significance or such as allowed in revelling in demoniacal emotions.—SCHERR, J., 1874, *A History of English Literature, p.* 59.

Marlowe has been styled, and not unjustly styled, the father of English dramatic poetry. When we reflect on the conditions of the stage before he produced "Tamburlaine," and consider the state in which he left it after the appearance of "Edward II.," we shall be able to estimate his true right to this title. . . . Out of confusion he brought order, following the clew of his own genius through a labyrinth of dim unmastered possibilities. Like all great craftsmen, he worked by selection and exclusion on the whole mass of material ready to his hand; and his instinct in this double process is the proof of his originality. — SYMONDS, JOHN ADDINGTON, 1884, *Shakspere's Predecessors in the English Drama, pp.* 585, 586.

Mr. J. A. Symonds has defined the leading motive of Marlowe's work as *L'Amour de l'Impossible*—"the love or lust of unattainable things." Never was a poet fired with a more intense aspiration for ideal beauty and ideal power. As some adventurous Greek of old might have sailed away, with warning voices in his ears, past the pillars of Hercules in quest of fabled islands beyond the sun, so Marlowe started on his lonely course, careless of tradition and restraint, resolved to seek and find "some world far from ours" where the secret springs of Knowledge should be opened and he should touch the lips of Beauty.—BULLEN, A. H., 1884, *ed. Works of Christopher Marlowe, Introduction, vol.* I, *p.* lxxii.

The career of Marlowe was more illustrious, it seems to me, than that of any other English poet; for no other English poet, so far as I remember, ever surpassed all his contemporaries at so early an age as he, or ever achieved so much distinction by his first work. Other poets, the most eminent, served their apprenticeship in the divine art: from the beginning, Marlowe was a master. That his success was resented, as we are told it was, by Greene and Nash, was natural; for, not to insist upon the jealousy and envy with which the poetic temperament has always been credited, and of which they had, no doubt, their full share, it touched them in that vital part,—the pocket. They had the market to themselves before this young interloper from Cambridge set up a stall of his own, and had his wares preferred to theirs. It was monstrous, sirs, monstrous. — STODDARD, RICHARD HENRY, 1884, *ed. Selections from the Poetical Works of A. C. Swinburne, Introduction, p.* v.

He is the undoubted author of some of the masterpieces of English verse; the hardly to be doubted author of others not much inferior. Except the very greatest names — Shakespere, Milton, Spenser, Dryden, Shelley—no author can be named who has produced, when the proper historical estimate is applied to him, such work as is to be found in "Tamburlaine," "Doctor Faustus," "The Jew of Malta," 'Edward the Second," in one department; "Hero and Leander" and the "Passionate Shepherd" in another. I have but very little doubt that the powerful, if formless, play of "Lust's Dominion" is Marlowe's, though it may have been rewritten, and the translations of Lucan and Ovid and the minor work which is, more or less probably attributed to him, swell his tale. Prose he did not write, perhaps could not have written. . . . Shakespere himself has not surpassed, which is equivalent to saying that no other writer has equalled, the famous and wonderful passages in "Tamburlaine" and "Faustus," which are familiar to every student of English literature as examples of the *ne plus ultra* of the poetic powers, not of the language but of language. The tragic imagination in its wildest flights has never summoned up images of pity and terror more imposing, more moving, than those excited by "The Jew of Malta." The riot of passion and of delight in the beauty of colour and form which characterises his version of "Hero and Leander" has never been approached by any writer. . . . It is impossible to call Marlowe a great dramatist, and the attempts that have been made to make him out to be such remind one of the attempts that have been made to call Molière a great poet. Marlowe was one of the greatest poets of the world whose work was cast by accident and caprice into an imperfect mould of drama; Molière was one of the greatest dramatists of the world who was obliged by fashion to use a previously perfected form of verse. The state of Molière was undoubtedly the more gracious; but the splendour of Marlowe's uncut diamonds of poetry is the more wonderful.—SAINTSBURY, GEORGE, 1887, *History of Elizabethan Literature, pp.* 76, 77, 78.

He had the freshness and splendour of Heosphoros, the bearer of light, the kindler of morning; as the dawn-star of our drama, he ascended the heavens, in the auroral flush of youth, to announce the approaching majesty of Shakespeare. But his early death, and the unexampled character of the genius who superseded him, have for centuries obscured the name of Marlowe, which scintillated half-extinguished in the blaze of "Hamlet" and "Othello." His reputation has, however, increased during the last generation with greater rapidity than that of any other of our elder poets, and a time may yet come when we shall have popularly isolated him from Shakespeare to such a degree as to enforce a recognition of his individual greatness. — GOSSE, EDMUND, 1889–93, *What is a Great Poet? Questions at Issue, p.* 108.

It may be said that Marlowe did more in the way of *indicating* the dramatic capabilities of blank verse, by freeing it from some of the fetters in which it had been bound, than of realizing those capabilities on the higher planes of expression to which Shakespeare carried them. He certainly did not do all that John Addington Symonds credits him with, in his "Shakespeare's Predecessors in the English Drama." There is not, generally, in his plays, that sanity of mind and heart, that well-balanced and well-toned thought and genuine passion, to have brought out the higher capabilities of the verse.—CORSON, HIRAM, 1892, *A Primer of English Verse, p.* 189.

As the real founder, though not precisely the initiator, both of English tragedy and English blank verse—as being thus in a certain sense the father of our poetry more truly than even Chaucer, for Chaucer's direct influence upon Shakespeare and Milton is not great, while Marlowe's unquestionably is—the immense importance of his position can scarcely be overstated. And it is not merely a relative or historical importance either. Judged upon their absolute merits as poetry, such passages as those in which Faustus addresses the apparition of Helen, disclose by their magnificence of hyperbole a power of style belonging to the great poets alone. His imagination is of wide sweep, with an adventurous, intrepid, and untamable wing. Violent, sinister, rebellious, unblest, he has something of the grandeur of a fallen angel about him, and in the dayspring of our drama he is Lucifer, son of the morning.—WATSON, WILLIAM, 1893, *Excursions in Criticism, p.* 5.

With wine and blood and wit and deviltry,
He sped the heroic flame of English verse:
Bethink ye, rhymers, what your claim may be,
Who in smug suburbs put the Muse to nurse?
—RHYS, ERNEST, 1894, *A London Rose and other Rhymes, p.* 91.

In reading Marlowe one is brought face to face, not only with tragic situations, but with the elemental tragedy,—the tragedy which has its rise in the conflict between the infinite desires of the soul and the rigid restrictions of its activity. The master of "the mighty line" never learned that lesson of self-mastery which Shakespeare studied so faithfully; he was always wasting his immense force on the impossible, and matching his powerful genius against those immutable conditions imposed upon men, not to dwarf but to develop them.—MABIE, HAMILTON WRIGHT, 1894, *My Study Fire, Second Series, p.* 138.

To no single man does our drama owe more than to this ill-starred genius. It was he who determined the form which tragedy and history were permanently to assume. It was he who first clothed both in that noble and splendid garb which was ever afterwards to distinguish them. It was he who gave the death-blow to the old rhymed plays on the one hand, and to the frigid and cumbersome unrhymed classical plays on the other. . . . He cast in clay what Shakspeare recast in marble. . . . It is more than probable that without the tragedies of Marlowe we should never have had, in the form at least in which they now stand, the tragedies of Shakspeare. Of the History in the proper sense of the title, Marlowe was the creator. In his "Edward I." Peele had, it is true, made some advance on the old Chronicles. But the difference between Peele's "Edward I." and Marlowe's "Edward II." is the difference between a work of art and mere botch-work.—COLLINS, JOHN CHURTON, 1895, *Essays and Studies, pp.* 149, 150.

Christopher Marlowe is one of the most fascinating figures in our own, or indeed in any, literature. In the temple of poetic fame the highest places are sacred to genius that has mounted securely to its meridian splendour, to Homer, Dante, Shakspere. But seats only lower than these, and hallowed with perhaps richer offerings of human sympathy and love, are granted to genius dead ere its time, cut down in the freshness of its morning radiance. It is here that Marlowe is to be sought, side by side with Collins and Shelley and Keats. What the world has lost by the untimely close of his career we cannot know; but we do know that, even had he lived, he could never have been "another Shakspere." For nature, so lavish to him in other ways, had entirely withheld from him the priceless gift of humour, and the faculty of interpreting commonplace human experience. He never learnt the secrets of a woman's heart, and he knew of no love lifted above the level of sense. Between him and his mighty successor there is, and there must always have been, an impassable gulf. Marlowe is the rapturous lyrist of limitless desire, Shakspere the majestic spokesman of inexorable moral law.—BOAS, FREDERICK S., 1896, *Shakspere and his Predecessors, p.* 61.

For a moment, and from time to time, he shoots up to the utmost height of poetry, but only in a beam of light, which lasts for a very brief space and then sinks out of view.—HANNAY, DAVID, 1898, *The Later Renaissance, p.* 243.

We often hear of "Marlowe's mighty line," but we seldom read it. This may be due to the fact that Shakespeare's sprightly line is so much more attractive, yet Marlowe occupies a commanding position among pre-Shakespearean dramatists, and is worthy of study both because of his intrinsic value as a poet and because of his relation to Shakespeare. In splendor of imagination, richness and stateliness of verse, strength and warmth of passion, he is at times almost the equal of Shakespeare.—GEORGE, ANDREW J., 1898, *From Chaucer to Arnold, Types of Literary Art, p.* 629.

Thomas Kyd

1557?-1595?

Dramatist, probably born in London, about 1557, and educated at Merchant Taylors' School, was most likely brought up as a scrivener under his father. His bloody and bombastic tragedies early brought him reputation, specially the two plays having for their hero Jeronimo, marshal of Spain. The first was not published till 1605; the second was licensed in 1592 as "The Spanish Tragedy." Kyd translated from the French (1594) a tedious tragedy on Pompey's daughter Cornelia, almost certainly produced "The Rare Triumphs of Love and Fortune" (1582) and "Solyman and Perseda" (1592), and has been credited with a share in other plays. He is supposed to have died in poverty in 1595. His name survives in Jonson's "sporting Kyd and Marlowe's mighty line."—PATRICK AND GROOME, *eds.*, 1897, *Chambers's Biographical Dictionary, p.* 561.

THE SPANISH TRAGEDY
1594

These scenes (of Hieronimo's madness), which are the very salt of the play (which without them is but a caput mortuum, such another piece of flatness as Locrine), Hawkins, in his re-publication of this tragedy, has thrust out of the text into the notes; as omitted in the second Edition, "printed for Ed Allde, amended of such gross blunders as passed in the first;" and thinks them to have been *foisted in by the players.*—A late discovery at Dulwich College has ascertained that two sundry payments were made to Ben Jonson by the theatre for furnishing additions to Hieronimo. There is nothing in the undoubted plays of Jonson which would authorize us to suppose that he could have supplied the scenes in question. I should suspect the agency of some "more potent spirit." Webster might have furnished them. They are full of that wild solemn preternatural cast of grief which bewilders us in the "Duchess of Malfy."—LAMB, CHARLES, 1827, *Notes on the Garrick Plays.*

Possesses merits and a character of his own. In direct and vivid energy of language, in powerful antithesis of character, and in skilful and effective construction of plot, in the chief qualities that make a good acting play, "The Spanish Tragedy" will bear comparison with the best work of any of Shakespeare's predecessors. That it passed through more editions than perhaps any play of the Elizabethan age is not at all surprising; it offered many points for ridicule to the wits of the time, but its unflagging interest and strong emotions of pity and suspense went straight to the popular heart.—MINTO, WILLIAM, 1874-85, *Characteristics of English Poets, p.* 251.

He lacked Marlowe's sensitive ear, his joy in the roll of golden periods. But his dialogue, at its best, has the quality of passionate directness and simplicity essential to the highest dramatic achievement. The love-scenes, short as they are, between Belimperia and Horatio touch a responsive chord in our hearts, and the mingled agony and rage of Hieronimo are rendered with masterly power. In this complex delineation of character Kyd made a notable step forward, and he may justly claim to be the pioneer of introspective tragedy in England. Yet the moral basis of the play is crude in the extreme. A wild insatiable fury of revenge is the sole animating impulse of all the chief personages, and suffices to condone every atrocity, even the murder of the innocent Duke of Castile. But, in spite of defects, "The Spanish Tragedy" is an organic creation, and fully deserved its widespread influence. It holds a unique place in dramatic literature, reaching back to "Gorboduc," and forward to Shakspere's early plays, probably even to "Hamlet" and "King Lear."—BOAS, FREDERICK S., 1896, *Shakspere and his Predecessors, p.* 65.

Kyd is a sort of English Lazare de Baïf, the *choragus* who directed the new dramatists and led them off. His early plays have disappeared, and Kyd's archaic "Spanish Tragedy," acted in 1587, shows him still in the trammels of pseudo-classicism. This fierce play, nevertheless, is pervaded by a wild wind of romantic frenzy which marks an epoch in English drama.—GOSSE, EDMUND, 1897, *Short History of Modern English Literature, p.* 97.

Kyd's style in the "Spanish Tragedy" is indeed made up of the more vulgar elements in Seneca's and Marlowe's plays, without the intellectual quality that distinguishes either. From Seneca he borrows ghosts and "sentences"; Marlowe provides him with precedents of rant and bloodshed. By the help of these hints, Kyd managed to put together a tragedy utterly devoid of any true tragic motive, but not wanting in striking scenes and melodramatic effects, and acceptable accordingly to that public taste which is always caught by loud noise and glaring colours. The "Spanish Tragedy" is, I think, plainly written in emulation of Marlowe's "Jew of Malta." Like that tragedy it represents an action of cold-blooded murder followed by a sanguinary revenge. But whereas Marlowe gives a certain intellectual interest to his play, by making the Jew the victim of injustice in a situation contrived with great force and probability, Kyd is utterly unable to produce such a complication among his *dramatis personæ* as shall prepare the way for the *denouement* he has imagined.—COURTHOPE, W. J., 1897, *A History of English Poetry, vol.* II, *p.* 424.

GENERAL

Sporting Kyd.—JONSON, BEN, 1623, *To the Memory of my Beloved Master William Shakespeare, and what he hath left us.*

A writer that seems to have been of pretty good esteem for versifying in former times, being quoted amongst some of the more fam'd poets, as Spenser, Drayton, Daniel, Lodge, &c. with whom he was either cotemporary or not much later. There is particularly remembered his tragedy "Cornelia."—PHILLIPS, EDWARD, 1675, *Theatrum Poetarum Anglicanorum, ed. Brydges, p.* 205.

His Tragedies with those of *Rotrou, Serre,* and others of that time, are of a mean Character. 'Tis evident to any that have read his Tragedies, which are Nine in Number, that he propos'd *Seneca* for his Model, and he was thought in those days to have happily succeeded in his Design. This Translation is writ in blank Verse, only here and there, at the close of a Paragraph (if I may so speak) the Reader is presented with a Couplet. The *Chorus's* are writ in several Measures of Verse, and are very sententious.—LANGBAINE, GERARD, 1691, *An Account of the English Dramatick Poets, p.* 316.

Kyd's bombast was proverbial in his own day. With him the genius of tragedy might be said to have run mad.—CAMPBELL, THOMAS, 1819, *An Essay on English Poetry.*

Kyd was a poet of very considerable mind, and deserves, in some respects, to be ranked above more notorious contemporaries: his thoughts are often both new and natural; and if in his plays he dealt largely in blood and death, he only partook of the habit of the time, in which good sense and discretion were often outraged for the purpose of gratifying the crowd. In taste he is inferior to Peele, but in force and character he is his superior; and if Kyd's blank-verse be not quite so smooth, it has decidedly more spirit, vigour, and variety. As a writer of blank-verse, I am inclined, among the predecessors of Shakespeare, to give Kyd the next place to Marlow.—COLLIER, JOHN PAYNE, 1831, *History of English Dramatic Poetry, vol.* III, *p.* 207.

Kyd was a dramatist of high capabilities in both construction and expression. Not that he is evenly excellent in either; but he is able to exhibit the operation of incidents upon character, and to depict with real force the workings of passion deeply moved. Herein lies the vast difference between him and the authors of "Gorboduc."—WARD, ADOLPHUS WILLIAM, 1875, *A History of English Dramatic Literature, vol.* I, *p.* 172.

Kyd is the merest *nominis umbra* of English letters; we hardly know anything of the author of "The Spanish Tragedy," perhaps of *Jeronimo* itself, and of *Cornelia*, except that he existed and was sportively called "sporting."—SAINTSBURY, GEORGE, 1887, *History of Elizabethan Literature, p.* 64.

Kyd's services to English tragedy were, we think, more important than is commonly supposed. He stands midway between two great schools; between the literary and academic school on the one hand, and the domestic and realistic school on the other. Regarded superficially, he might perhaps be confounded with a mere copyist of Italian models. . . . And yet, with all this, the impression which his plays make on us is very different from the impression made on us by the Italian tragedies. Nor is it difficult to explain the reason. The canvas of Kyd is more crowded; his touch is broader and bolder, his colour fuller and deeper; his action is infinitely more diversified, animated, and rapid; his characters are more human; he has more passion, he has more pathos. If he aims too much at sensational effects, he is sometimes simple and natural.—COLLINS, JOHN CHURTON, 1895, *Essays and Studies, p.* 180.

Thomas Kyd a satellite of Shakspere. A few years ago the world was startled by the splendid discovery that the mightiest of the planets had a fifth satellite. Four of them had been well known for centuries and had had a glorious place in the history of the stars and light; but the one vassal nearest to his king had been so outshone by the grand luminary that, down to our own day, it had been eclipsed to the eyes of man. Very similar is the case of the nearest vassal of another Jupiter, the Jupiter Tonitruans of the world's drama. Of his satellites, too, some four had been well known for as many centuries: one especially had, by his own brilliancy and fiery appearance, attracted the general eye; but in this case, too, the satellite nearest to the great luminary had hardly been taken notice of. And if we knew of his bare existence, we knew little or nothing of his orbit, of his history, of his magnitude, of the quality of his light—in short, nothing of all the details we care to know of poet or brilliant star.—SCHICK, J., 1898, *ed. The Spanish Tragedy, Preface, p.* vi.

Robert Southwell

1561?–1595

Robert Southwell, poet and martyr; was born at Horsham, St. Faith's, Norfolk, about 1562; and hanged at Tyburn, Feb. 22, 1595. He was educated at Paris, Douay, Tournay, and Rome; received into the Society of Jesus, Oct. 17, 1578, when not yet seventeen; ordained, 1584, and made prefect of the English college at Rome; sent as a missionary to England, 1586; chaplain to the Countess of Arundel; betrayed to the government, 1592, imprisoned for three years in the Tower, found guilty of "constructive treason," and executed. According to Cecil, he, though "thirteen times most cruelly tortured, cannot be induced to confess any thing, not even the color of the horse whereon, on a certain day, he rode, lest" thereby his friends might fall into the same trouble. His poems were published shortly after his death, and a complete edition appeared 1856, edited by W. B. Turnbull. Some of them, since then widely copied, are of a very high order, and no less philosophic than Christian.—BIRD, F. M., 1884, *Schaff-Herzog Encyclopædia of Religious Knowledge, vol.* III, *p.* 2219.

PERSONAL

Excelling in the art of helping and gaining souls, being at once prudent, pious, meek, and exceedingly winning.—GERARD, FATHER, 1585, *The Condition of Catholics under James I., Father Gerard's Narrative.*

Robert Southwel was born in this County*, as Pitseus affirmeth, who, although often mistaken in his locality, may be believed herein, as professing himself familiarly acquainted with him at Rome. But the matter is not much where he was born; seeing, though cried up by men of his own profession for his many Books in Verse and Prose, he was reputed a dangerous enemy by the State, for which he was imprisoned, and executed, March the 3d, 1595.—FULLER, THOMAS, 1662, *The Worthies of England, ed. Nichols, vol.* II, *p.* 344.

Southwell appears to have been a man of a most gentle disposition, and his poetry was long held in high esteem among his co-religionists, associated as it was with the memory of a man to murder whom at Tyburn was as horrible as it would have been to have treated Cowper, or Kirke White, or Robert Burns after the same manner, because they happened to be Protestants. The execution of Southwell was, besides this, a political blunder. He was no conspirator against the State, and consequently was made a martyr to his faith.—BELLEW, J. C. M., 1868, *Poets' Corner, p.* 92.

ST. PETER'S COMPLAINT

Never must be forgotten "St. Peter's Complaint" and those other serious poems, said to be father Southwell's; the English whereof, as it is most proper, so the sharpness and light of wit is very rare in them.—BOLTON, EDMUND, 1624, *Hypercritica.*

Southwell's poetry wears a deep tinge of gloom, which seems to presage a catastrophe too usual to have been unexpected.—HALLAM, HENRY, 1837–39, *Introduction to the Literature of Europe, pt.* ii, *ch.* v, *par.* 65.

His longest poem is "Saint Peter's Complaint," and is strongly religious, though often its strength is at the expense of its verse. It is generally harsh in its construction, and lacks the sweet flow and the noble ring which frequently marks the efforts of contemporary poets. It is direct; full of a fierce energy which is out of keeping with the character of the Apostle whose complaint it professes to be. It is finely exaggerated, and deals in hyperbole to an extraordinary extent. Perhaps the occasion justifies this.—LANGFORD, JOHN ALFRED, 1861, *Prison Books and their Authors, p.* 142.

Perhaps its chief fault is that the pauses are so measured with the lines as to make every line almost a sentence, the effect of which is a considerable degree of monotony.—MACDONALD, GEORGE, 1868, *England's Antiphon, p.* 97.

His poems show a true poetic power. They show a rich and fertile fancy, with an abundant store of effective expression at its service. He inclines to sententiousness; but his sentences are no mere prose edicts, as is so often the case with writers of that sort; they are bright and coloured with the light and the hues of a vivid imagination. In imagery, indeed, he is singularly opulent. In this respect "St. Peter's Complaint" reminds one curiously of the almost exactly contemporary poem, Shakespeare's "Lucrece." There is a like inexhaustibleness of illustrative resource. He delights to heap up metaphor on metaphor. . . . It is undoubtedly the work of a mind of no ordinary copiousness and force, often embarrassed by its own riches, and so expending them with a prodigal carelessness. Thus Southwell's defects spring not from poverty, but from imperfectly managed wealth; or, to use a different image, the flowers are overcrowded in his garden, and the blaze of colour is excessive. Still, flowers they are. Like many another Elizabethan, he was wanting in art; his genius ran riot.—HALES, JOHN W., 1880, *English Poets, ed. Ward, vol.* I, *pp.* 480, 481.

GENERAL

That Southwell was hanged; yet so he had written that piece of his, the "Burning Babe," he would have been content to destroy many of his.—DRUMMOND, WILLIAM, 1619, *Notes on Ben Jonson's Conversations, ed. Laing, p.* 13.

Both the poetry and the prose of Southwell possess the most decided merit; the former, which is almost entirely restricted to moral and religious subjects, flows in a vein of great harmony, perspicuity, and elegance, and breathes a fascination

*Suffolk.

resulting from the subject and the pathetic mode of treating it which fixes and deeply interests the reader.—DRAKE, NATHAN, 1817, *Shakspeare and his Times, vol.* I, *p.* 645.

His verses are ingenious, simpler in style than was common in his time—distinguished here by homely picturesqueness, and there by solemn moralising. A shade of deep but serene and unrepining sadness, connected partly with his position and partly with his foreseen destiny, (his larger works were written in prison,) rests on the most of his poems.—GILFILLAN, GEORGE, 1860, *Specimens with Memoirs of the Less-Known British Poets, vol.* I, *p.* 118.

Southwell, it seems, was the founder of the modern English style of religious poetry; his influence and example are evident in the work of Crashaw, or of Donne, or of Herbert, or Waller, or any of those whose devout lyrics were admired in later times.—ARNOLD, THOMAS, 1862-87, *A Manual of English Literature, American ed., p.* 84.

He shows in his poetry great simplicity and elegance of thought, and still greater purity of language. He has been compared in some of his pieces to Goldsmith, and the comparison seems not unjust. There is in both the same naturalness of sentiment, the same propriety of expression, and the same ease and harmony of versification; while there is a force and compactness of thought, with occasional quaintness not often found in the more modern poet.—ANGUS, JOSEPH, 1865, *Handbook of English Literature, p.* 155.

He paraphrases David, putting into his mouth such punning conceits as "fears are my feres," and in his "Saint Peter's Complaint" makes that rashest and shortest-spoken of the Apostles drawl through thirty pages of maudlin repentance, in which the distinctions between the north and northeast sides of a sentimentality are worthy of Duns Scotus. It does not follow, that, because a man is hanged for his faith, he is able to write good verses. We would almost match the fortitude that quails not at the good Jesuit's poems with his own which carried him serenely to the fatal tree. The stuff of which poets are made, whether finer or not, is of a very different fibre from that which is used in the tough fabric of martyrs.—LOWELL, JAMES RUSSELL, 1858-64-90, *Library of Old Authors, Prose Works, Riverside ed., vol.* I, *p.* 253.

The hastiest reader will come on "thinking" and "feeling" that are as musical as Apollo's lute, and as fresh as a spring budding spray; and the wording of all (excepting over-alliteration and inversion occasionally) is throughout of the "pure well of English undefiled." When you take some of the Myrtæ and Mæoniæ pieces, and read and re-read them, you are struck with their condensation, their concinnity, their polish, their *élan* their memorableness. Holiness is in them not as scent on love-locks, but as fragrance in the great Gardener's flowers of fragrance. His tears are pure and white as the "dew of the morning." His smiles—for he has humor, even wit, that must have lurked in the burdened eyes and corners o' mouth—are sunny as sunshine. As a whole, his poetry is healthy and strong, and, I think, has been more potential in our literature than appears on the surface. I do not think it would be hard to show that others of whom more is heard drew light from him, as well early as more recent, from Burns to Thomas Hood. —GROSART, ALEXANDER B., 1872, *ed. The Complete Poems of Robert Southwell, Fuller Worthies' Library.*

To the readers of poetry for its merely sensuous qualities of flowing measure, attractive imagery, and brilliant description, the poems of Southwell possess but few attractions. Their subjects are all religious, or, at least, serious; and, in reading him, we must totally forget the traditional pagan poet pictured to us as crowned with flowers, and holding in hand an overflowing anacreontic cup. Serious, indeed, his poems might well be, for they were all composed during the intervals of thirteen bodily rackings in a gloomy prison that opened only upon the scaffold. And yet we look in vain among them for expressions of the reproaches or repining such a fate might well engender, and we search with but scant result for record or trace of his own sufferings in the lines traced with fingers yet bent and smarting with the rack. The vanity of all earthly things, the trials of life, the folly and wickedness of the world, the uncertainty of life, and the consolations and glories of religion, are the constantly returning subjects of his productions, and, however treated, they always reflect the benignity and elevation of the poet's character.—MILINE, J. G, 1873, *Poet and Martyr, Catholic World, vol.* 17, *p.* 53.

They are marked by quaint figures, much beauty of language, and purity of sentiment; and as they were chiefly composed in prison, they breathe a tone of quiet, lofty resignation.—MURRAY, JOHN O'KANE, 1884, *Lessons in English Literature, p.* 142.

Southwell did not think much of poetry as an art; but this fault was not uncommon among the Elizabethan poets. His richness of expression is unbounded, unhusbanded. Nature, as nature, had no message for him. Nature was God's footstool; of the myriad voices, of the myriad phases in earth and heaven, he took no note for themselves. The rose and the lily were for him in their best place before the tabernacle, and the breath of the new-mown fields was less sweet to him than the incense that wreathed the pillars of a church. Rhythm and rhyme were fetters to his thought rather than helps to it. Verse in his hands was the nearest earthly approach to that divine expression which the seraphs have; it was powerless to hold the fervor of a heart that burned with desire for union with our Lord.—EGAN, MAURICE FRANCIS, 1880, *Three Catholic Poets, Catholic World, vol.* 32, *p.* 124, *Lectures on English Literature, p.* 62.

The first really fine child-poem in our literature is Southwell's "Burning Babe." Its exquisitely pure feeling, and the mystic light and heat of the language, render the poem so impressive that it can be learnt off by heart in two or three readings. Occurring so early in the present collection, the "Burning Babe" really shows us the point from which both the literature and the art of modern times had to start, in their treatment of the child—the glorification of young Jesus.—ROBERTSON, ERIC S., 1886, *The Children of the Poets, Introduction, p.* xxviii.

Whose vivid and emotional canzonets and hymns had introduced a new element into English literature, an element not to be taken up again until nearly twenty years after his death at Tyburn, but from that time onward to be carried on and up till it culminated in the raptures of Crashaw.—GOSSE, EDMUND, 1894, *The Jacobean Poets, p.* 6.

By modern critics Southwell's poetry has been rarely underrated. James Russell Lowell stands almost alone in pronouncing "St. Peter's Complaint" to be a drawl of thirty pages of maudlin repentance. A genuinely poetic vein is latent beneath all the religious sentimentalism which at times obscures the literary merit of Southwell's verse. As in his prose, his exuberant fancy, too, finds frequent expression in extravagant conceits, which suggest the influence of Marino and other Italian writers of pietistic verse. But many poems, like the "Burning Babe," which won Ben Jonson's admiration, are as notable for the simplicity of their language as for the sincerity of their sentiment, and take rank with the most touching examples of sacred poetry.—LEE, SIDNEY, 1898, *Dictionary of National Biography, vol.* LIII, *p.* 299.

George Peele

1558?–1597?

Born, in London, 1558 (?). At Christ's Hospital, 1565–70 (?). Matriculated, Broadgates Hall, Oxford, March 1571; removed to Christ Church, 1574; Student, 1574–79; B. A., 12 June 1577; M. A., 6 July 1579. Married, 1580 (?). Became actor and dramatist. Notorious for dissipated life. Died, 1597 (?). *Works:* "The Araygnement of Paris" (anon.), 1584; "The Device of the Pageant borne before Woolston Dixie, Mayor" (anon.), 1585; "A Farewell . . . to Sir John Norris & Syr Francis Drake," 1589; "An Eclogue Gratulatory," 1589; "Polyhymnia," 1590; "Descensus Astreæ," 1591; "The Famous Chronicle of King Edward the first," 1593; "The Honour of the Garter" (1593); "The Battell of Alcazar" (anon.), 1594; "The Old Wives' Tale" (under initials: G. P.), 1595. *Posthumous:* "The Love of King David and Fair Bethsabe," 1599; "Anglorum Feriæ" (priv. pdt.), 1830. *Collected Works:* ed. by A. Dyce (3 vols.), 1829–39; ed. by A. H. Bullen (2 vols.), 1888.—SHARP, R. FARQUHARSON, 1897, *A Dictionary of English Authors, p.* 225.

PERSONAL

And thou no lesse deseruing then the other two, in some things rarer, in nothing inferiour, driuen as myselfe, to extreame shifts, a little haue I to say to thee; and, were it not an idolatrous oath, I would sweare by sweet S. George thou art vnworthy better hap, sith thou dependest on so meane a stay. Base-minded men all three of you, if by my misery yee bee not warned; for vnto none of you, like me, sought those burs to cleaue; those puppits, I meane, that speake from our mouths, those anticks garnisht in our colours. Is it not strange that I to whome they all haue bin beholding, is it not like that you to whome they all haue bin beholding, shall, were yee in that case that I am now, be both of them at once forsaken?—GREENE, ROBERT, 1593, *Groatsworth of Wit.*

As Anacreon died by the pot: so George Peele, by the pox.—MERES, FRANCIS, 1598, *Palladis Tamia.*

A sad death for one who had sung "The Praise of Chastity." Had Peele been faithful to his honest wife and borne in mind the words of his Œnone—

"They that do change old love for new,
Pray God they change for worse!"

the end might have been different. But he died a long time ago, and possibly Meres was misinformed. He lives as the author of a charming pastoral and some dainty lyrics.—BULLEN, A. H., 1888, *ed. The Works of George Peele, Introduction, vol.* I, *p.* xliii.

ARRAIGNMENT OF PARIS
1584

The Araygnement of Paris A Pastorall. Presented before the Queenes Maiestie, by the Children of her Chappell. Imprinted at London by Henrie Marsh. Anno. 1584. —TITLE PAGE TO FIRST EDITION, 4*to.*

I dare commend him to all that know him, as the chiefe supporter of pleasance nowe liuing, the *Atlas* of Poetrie, & *primus verborum Artifex;* whose first encrease, the "Arraignement of Paris," might plead to your opinions, his pregnant dexteritie of wit, and manifold varietie of inuention; wherein (*me iudice*) hee goeth a step beyond all that write.—NASHE, THOMAS, 1587, *To the Gentlemen Students of both Universities, ed. Grosart, vol.* I, *p,* xxxvi.

Written in Lyly's manner, it is, nevertheless, far superior to the best pieces of that author: for Peele possessed all the excellencies of Lyly, in an equal, if not a higher degree, without his faults. Thomas Nash, who flourished about 1588, calls him, with good reason, "*primus verborum artifex.*" An elegant diction, graceful expression, and an harmonious and flowing versification, are, in fact, his principal merits. On the other hand, in force and depth of thought, in vigour of language and finish of composition, he did not come up to his model, the famous Marlowe. —ULRICI, HERMANN, 1839, *Shakspeare's Dramatic Art, p.* 37.

Peele's best work, "The Arraignment of Paris." . . . The "Arraignment" is indeed a choice piece of work, quaint and fanciful as some old curiously-knotted garden pranked in all its summer-bravery. It should be read when one is in the mood for appreciating it. If we are seeking in poetry a "criticism of life" it would be idle to turn to the "Arraignment;" but at times when we would fain forget life's perplexities, we shall find the pretty cadences of Peele's pastoral as grateful as the plashing of fountains in the dog-days. A variety of metres is employed in the "Arraignment." Rhymed lines of fourteen syllables (a pleasant measure, when properly handled, for pastoral subjects) and rhymed lines of ten syllables predominate; but there are passages, notably Paris' oration before the Council of the Gods, which show that Peele wrote a more musical blank verse than had yet been written by any English poet.—BULLEN, A. H., 1888, *ed. Works of George Peele, Introduction, vol.* I, *p.* xxvi.

EDWARD I.
1593

The Famous Chronicle of king Edward the first, sirnamed Edward Longshankes, with his returne from the holy land. Also the life of Llevellen rebell in Wales. Lastly, the sinking of Queene Elinor, who sunck at Charingcrosse, and rose againe at Pottershith, now named Queenehith. London Printed by Abell Jeffes, and are to be solde by William Barley, at his shop in Gratious streete. 1593.—TITLE PAGE TO FIRST EDITION, 4*to.*

The only part of "Edward the First" that has a fair claim to the epithet good is its opening, which relates to the arrival of the king from Palestine, and the reception of him by the queen mother. There is a degree of royalty and splendour about the air of this scene which leads us to expect more from the conclusion.—COLLIER, JOHN PAYNE, 1831, *History of English Dramatic Poetry, vol.* III, *p.* 199.

This play, commonly known as "Longshanks," was popular; and, after allowance for unusual mangling of the text under all the disadvantages of careless printing from a rough copy that, however obtained, was confused and inaccurate, we cannot think the play into a form that would have any artistic unity.—MORLEY, HENRY, 1893, *English Writers, vol.* X, *p.* 79.

DAVID AND BETHSABE
1598

The Love of King David and Fair Bethsabe. With the Tragedie of Absalon. As it hath ben diuers plaied on the stage. Written by George Peele. London, Printed by Adam Islip. 1599.—TITLE PAGE TO FIRST EDITION, *4to.*

The play here presented to the reader, and founded on Scriptural History, abounds with the most masterly strokes of a fine genius; and a genuine spirit of poetry runs through the whole.—HAWKINS, THOMAS, 1773, *The Origin of the English Drama, vol.* II, *p.* 125.

His "David and Bethsabe" is the earliest fountain of pathos and harmony that can be traced in our dramatic poetry. His fancy is rich and his feeling tender, and his conceptions of dramatic character have no inconsiderable mixture of solid veracity and ideal beauty. There is no such sweetness of versification and imagery to be found in our blank verse anterior to Shakspeare. David's character—the traits both of his guilt and sensibility—his passion for Bethsabe—his art in inflaming the military ambition of Urias, and his grief for Absalom, are delineated with no vulgar skill.—CAMPBELL, THOMAS, 1819, *An Essay on English Poetry.*

Bethsabe, with her maid, bathing. She sings: and David sits above viewing her. There is more of the same stuff, but I suppose the reader has a surfeit; especially as this Canticle of David has never been suspected to contain any pious sense couched underneath it, whatever his son's may. The kingly bower "seated in hearing of a hundred streams," is the best of it.—LAMB, CHARLES, 1827, *Notes on the Garrick Plays.*

As for "David and Bethsabe," it is crammed with beauties, and Lamb's curiously faint praise of it has always been a puzzle to me. As Marlowe's are the mightiest, so are Peele's the softest lines in the drama before Shakespere; while the spirit and humour, which the author also had in plenty, save his work from the merely cloying sweetness of some contemporary writers.—SAINTSBURY, GEORGE, 1887, *History of Elizabethan Literature, p.* 72.

It has been highly praised by critics of distinction, but I confess that I do not care two straws for it. . . . The play is exasperatingly insipid,—a mess of cloying sugar-plums. As being the only Elizabethan play extant that deals with a purely scriptural subject, it has a certain interest of its own; but judged on its literary merits it is surely a failure.—BULLEN, A. H., 1888, *ed. The Works of George Peele, Introduction, vol.* I, *p.* xli.

Peele's best play is undoubtedly "David and Bethsabe," but it is best only in the sense of containing his finest writing. As a drama it is neither better nor worse than the others—that is to say, it is perfectly worthless. . . . If that noble measure, which is to poetry what the organ is to music, owed its trumpet-stop to Marlowe, it may, we think, with equal truth be said to owe its flute-stop to Peele. The opening scene of "David and Bethsabe" is in mere mellifluousness equal to anything which has been produced in blank verse since. —COLLINS, JOHN CHURTON, 1895, *Essays and Studies, p.* 176.

GENERAL

(?) There eke is Palin worthie of great praise,
Albe he envie at my rustick quill.
—SPENSER, EDMUND, 1595, *Colin Clouts Come Home againe, Spenser's Works, Collier ed., vol.* V, *p.* 45.

His comedies and tragedies, were often acted with great applause, and did endure reading with due commendation many years after their author's death.—WOOD, ANTHONY, 1691–1721, *Athenæ Oxonienses, vol.* I, *p.* 300.

We are told that his works not only succeeded very greatly in his life but that they were read with great pleasure after his death. He is said in particular to have been a good pastoral poet. . . . He seems to have derived his reputation more from having been the object of patronage to a nobleman, than to the muses, for his merry pranks . . . lifted him into a degree of public opinion, which his works do not by any means appear to bear out. In short his profligate manners and irregular life but little qualified him for a knowledge of that novelty indispensably necessary in the composition of real dramatic entertainment; and it is, therefore, though one of his plays has been ignorantly attributed to Shakespeare, that the licentious George Peele, like his imitators, Rochester and Killigrew, is little known but by his jests, "which," an author says, "in literature may be compared to the tricks of a sharper in society, for they are false, specious and imposing."—DIBDIN, CHARLES, 1795, *A Complete History of the Stage, vol.* II, *p.* 336.

From the specimens which we possess of his dramatic genius, the opinion of Greene will not readily meet with a modern assent; the pastoral and descriptive parts of his plays are the best, which are often clothed in sweet and flowing verse; but, as dramas, they are nerveless, passionless, and therefore ineffective in point of character.—DRAKE, NATHAN, 1817, *Shakspeare and his Times, vol.* II. *p.* 240.

His genius was not bold and original, and he was wanting in the higher qualities of invention; but he had an elegance of fancy, a gracefulness of expression, and a melody of versification, which, in the earlier part of his career, was scarcely approached.—COLLIER, JOHN PAYNE, 1831, *History of English Dramatic Poetry, vol.* III, *p.* 191.

The versification of Peele is much inferior to that of Marlowe; and, though sometimes poetical, he seems rarely dramatic.—HALLAM, HENRY, 1837-39, *Introduction to the Literature of Europe, pt.* ii, *ch.* vi, *par.* 31.

Those of Peele's dramatic works which have come down to us afford evidence that he possessed great flexibility and rhetorical power, without much invention, with very little discrimination of character, and with that tendency to extravagance in the management of his incidents which exhibits small acquaintance with the higher principles of the dramatic art.—KNIGHT, CHARLES, 1849, *Studies of Shakspere, bk.* i, *ch.* vi, *p.* 28.

The reader must not imagine that I consider Peele on a par with Marlowe as an improver of the English drama. I cannot but be aware that Marlowe had a far more powerful intellect than Peele, and a far deeper insight into the human heart: yet, though Peele was quite unequal to the production of dramas so full of terror and pity as "Faustus" and "Edward the Second," it may not be too much to assert that his "David and Bethsabe" vies in tenderness and poetic beauty with any of the plays of his sublime associate.—The superiority of Peele to Greene is, I conceive, on the whole, unquestionable.—DYCE, ALEXANDER, 1861, *ed. The Works of George Peele, Life, p.* 346.

I will, however, notice here the opinion generally received, that Marlowe's talents were very far superior to those of either Greene or Peele—a judgment to which I cannot entirely assent, as far as Peele is concerned. Peele's plays, it is true, lack some of Marlowe's fire and fury; but they are also without much of his fustian. Peele's characters are less strongly marked than Marlowe's; but they are also less absurd and extravagant, and, in my opinion they are equally well discriminated, though that is little praise.—WHITE, RICHARD GRANT, 1865, *ed. The Works of William Shakespeare, Rise and Progress of the English Drama, vol.* I, *p.* clxxix.

Peele's want of native refinement kept him from rising high; but many of his verses are tuneful, and some of his thoughts pure and chaste.—LAWRENCE, EUGENE, 1878, *English Literature Primers, Romance Period, p.* 88.

Peele, from whose hand the sweet white locks of age
Took the mild chaplet woven of honoured hours.

—SWINBURNE, ALGERNON CHARLES, 1882, *The Many.*

The truth is that Peele exercised far less influence over the development of our Drama than either Lyly or Greene, not to mention Marlowe. . . . Peele's "Old Wives' Tale" deserves to be remembered because of its resemblance to "Comus." If Milton borrowed the conception of his Masque from this rustic comedy, he undoubtedly performed the proverbial miracle of making a silk purse out of a sow's ear.—SYMOND, JOHN ADDINGTON, 1884, *Shakspere's Predecessors in the English Drama, pp.* 564, 566.

His miscellaneous poems show a man by no means given to low company or low thoughts, and one gifted with the truest poetic vein; while his dramas, besides exhibiting a greater command over blank verse than any of his predecessors and than any except Marlowe of his contemporaries can claim, are full of charming passages. . . . "Edward I." and "The Battle of Alcazar," but especially the latter, contain abundance of the hectoring rant which has been marked as one of the characteristics of the school, and which is half-excused by the sparks of valour which often break from its smoke and clatter. But Peele would undoubtedly stand higher, though he might not be so interesting a literary figure, if we had nothing of his save "The Arraignment of Paris and David and Bethsabe." . . . As Marlowe's are the mightiest, so are Peele's the softest, lines in the drama before Shakspere. —SAINTSBURY, GEORGE, 1887, *History of Elizabethan Literature, pp.* 71, 72.

There were few poets of the Elizabethan age who could write blank verse, for non-dramatic purposes, with Peele's fluency. —BULLEN, A. H., 1888, *ed. The Works of George Peele, Introduction, vol.* I, *p.* XXXV.

The merits of Peele have been greatly over-rated. They were ridiculously over-rated by his contemporaries. They have been inexplicably over-rated by modern critics. Gifford classes him with Marlowe. Dyce ranks him above Greene. Campbell, in an often-quoted passage, pronounces his "David and Bethsabe" to be the "earliest fountain of pathos and harmony that can be traced in our dramatic literature," and goes on to speak of the "solid veracity" and "ideal beauty" of his characters. The tradition, originating from Isaac Reed, that Milton borrowed the plot of "Comus" from "The Old Wives' Tale," has, we suspect, greatly contributed to this factitious reputation. The truth is that of Peele's six plays there is not one which can be said to be meritorious as a drama, or to have contributed any new elements to dramatic composition.—COLLINS, JOHN CHURTON, 1895, *Essays and Studies, p.* 175.

Peele is one of the most prominent figures among those of Shakespeare's "predecessors" and earlier contemporaries. In his manipulation of his own language for metrical purposes he was skilful, and now and then wonderfully successful. His blank verse, usually fluent though monotonous, rises here and there to grandeur and force; and scattered through his plays and pastorals are more than one lyric of imperishable charm. His text is so largely corrupt as to make generalisations unsafe, but he seems hardly to have mastered the management of rhyme. . . . The growth of his powers had been stimulated by a university training, and his works abound in classical allusions; but he was not often markedly felicitous in his employment of them. He had, for better or worse, imbibed something, too, of the spirit of his Italian sources.—WARD, ADOLPHUS WILLIAM, 1895, *Dictionary of National Biography, vol.* XLIV, *p.* 229.

He can scarcely be said to show the instinct of a true master, whether in plot, portraiture, or versification. But his versatility, his urbane and graceful treatment of his themes, his command of imagery and language, his freedom from the sensuous taint—all these combine to give him an honourable place among the lieutenants, not the leaders, of Elizabethan drama.—BOAS, FREDERICK S., 1896, *Shakspere and his Predecessors, p.* 76.

Peele's few lyrics, golden in cadence, that go on murmuring in the memory.—CARPENTER, FREDERIC IVES, 1897, *English Lyric Poetry,* 1500–1700, *Introduction, p.* xliii.

A man less interesting in his life and character than Greene, but with a finer range of imagination, which gave an impulse of its own to the development of the drama. . . . His genius was the product of the love of pageantry and masquerade, a legacy of the allegorical tradition of the Middle Ages, which was deeply rooted in the taste of the English people under Elizabeth. He was a master of whatever was pictorial and external in theatrical art. As a dramatic rhetorician he was hardly, if at all, inferior to Marlowe; in wealth of poetic diction, warmth of fancy, and richness of invention, he perhaps excelled all his contemporaries whose names are usually coupled with his own. But in the higher creative powers he was deficient. His plays contain no character that rouses the affection; no imaginative situation that awakens the interest; no universal sentiment that touches the heart.—COURTHOPE, W. J., 1897, *A History of English Poetry, vol* II, *pp.* 396, 401.

Edmund Spenser

1552–1599

Born, in London, 1552 (?). Early education at Merchant Taylor's School. To Pembroke Hall, Cambridge, as Sizar, 20 May 1569; B. A., 16 Jan. 1573; M. A., 26 June 1576. Settled in London, 1578. Secretary to Lord-Lieut. of Ireland, 1580. Received grant of land in co. Cork, 1586. Clerk of Council of Munster, 1588. Visited by Sir Walter Raleigh, 1589; to England with him, to be presented at Court. Lived in Ireland, 1591–95. Married (Elizabeth Boyle?), 1595. Sheriff of co. Cork, 1598. Died, in London, 16 Jan. 1599. Buried in Westminster Abbey. *Works:* "The Shepheardes Calendar," 1579; "Three Proper, and Wittie, Familiar Letters: lately passed between Two Universitie Men" (anon.), 1580; "The Faerie Queene," bks. i–iii., 1590; bks. iv–vi., 1596; "Muiopotmos," 1590; "Complaints," 1591; "Prosopopoia," 1591; "Teares of the Muses," 1591; "Daphnaida," 1591; "Amoretti and Epithalamion," 1595; "Colin Clout's Come Home Againe," 1595; "Prothalamion," 1596; "Foure Hymnes, etc.," 1596; "A View of the State of Ireland," 1596. *Collected Works:* ed. by J. Aikin (5 vols.), 1842; ed. by A. B. Grosart (9 vols.), 1882–84.—SHARP, R. FARQUHARSON, 1897, *A Dictionary of English Authors, p.* 265.

PERSONAL

If I should now forget or not remember thee,
Thou, Spencer, might'st a foul rebuke and shame impute to me;
For I, to open show, did love thee passing well,
And thou wert he at parture whom I loathed to bid farewell;
And, as I went thy friend, so I continue still;
No better proof thou canst than this desire of true good will.
I do remember well, when needs I should away,
And that the post would license us no longer time to stay,
Thou wrung'st me by the fist, and, holding fast my hand,
Did'st crave of me to send thee news, and how I liked the land.

(?)—TURBERVILLE, GEORGE, 1569–87? *Tragical Tales.*

Lady Cope is dead, and Spenser the Poet, who lately came from Ireland, died at Westminster last Saturday.—CHAMBERLAIN, JOHN, 1599, *Letter to Sir Dudley Carleton, Jan.* 17, *Morley, English Writers, vol.* IX, *p.* 450.

The thrice three Muses mourning for the death
Of Learning, late deceased in beggary.

(?)—SHAKESPEARE, WILLIAM, 1600, *Midsummer Night's Dream, Act.* v., *Sc.* 1.

When hir Majestie had giuen order that Spenser should haue a reward for his poems, but Spenser could haue nothing, he presented hir with these verses:

It pleased your Grace vpon a tyme
To graunt me reason for my ryme,
But from that tyme vntill this season
I heard of neither ryme nor reason. (Touse.)

—MANNINGHAM, JOHN, 1602–3, *Diary, ed. Bruce, p.* 43.

Edmund Spencer, of London, far the first of the English Poets of our age, as his poems prove, written under the smile of the Muses, and with a genius destined to live. He died prematurely in the year of salvation 1598, and is buried near Geoffrey Chaucer, who was the first most happily to set forth poetry in English writing: and on him were written these epitaphs:—

Here nigh to Chaucer Spenser lies; to whom
In genius next he was, as now in tomb.

Here nigh to Chaucer, Spenser, stands thy hearse,
Still nearer standst thou to him in thy verse.
Whilst thou didst live, lived English poetry;
Now thou art dead, it fears that it shall die.

—CAMDEN, WILLIAM, 1606, *Reges Reginæ, Nobiles, et alij in Ecclesia Collegiata B. Petri Westmonasterii Sepulti usque ad annum,* 1606.

That the Irish having rob'd Spenser's goods, and burnt his house and a little child new born, he and his wyfe escaped; and after, he died for lake of bread in King Street, and refused 20 pieces sent to him by my Lord of Essex, and said, He was sorrie he had no time to spend them. That in that paper S. W. Raughly had of the Allegories of his Fayrie Queen, by the Blating Beast the Puritans were understood, by the false Duessa the Q. of Scots. —DRUMMOND, WILLIAM, 1619, *Notes of Ben Jonson's Conversations, ed. Laing, p.* 12.

How they from my deere Spenser stood alooff
When verbale drones, of vertuous merit scant,
Suffred that gentle poet *die of want!*
One onlie, knoeinge generositie,

EDMUND SPENSER.

From Engraving by W. H. Worthington.

And finding he n'oold crave for modestie.
Him sent in greatest sicknes crownes good store:
So Robert Essex did, honor's decore.
Nathles, of pininge griefe and wante's decaie,
Hee much thoncke that stowt Earle, that thus gau saie,
The medcine comes too late to the patient:
Tho died.

—LANE, JOHN, 1620, *Triton's Trumpet.*

Edmund Spenser, a Londoner by birth, and a scholar also of the University of Cambridge, born under so favourable an aspect of the Muses that he surpassed all the English Poets of former times, not excepting Chaucer himself, his fellow-citizen. But by a fate which still follows Poets, he always wrestled with poverty, though he had been secretary to the Lord Grey, Lord Deputy of Ireland. For scarce had he there settled himself into a retired privacy and got leisure to write, when he was by the rebels thrown out of his dwelling, plundered of his goods, and returned into England a poor man, where he shortly after died and was interred at Westminster, near to Chaucer, at the charge of the Earl of Essex, his hearse being attended by poets, and mournful elegies and poems with the pens that wrote them thrown into his tomb.—CAMDEN, WILLIAM, 1628, *Annales rerum Anglicarum et Hibernicarum regnante Elizabetha, ed. Hearne, Obituary, year* 1598–9, *vol.* III, *p.* 783.

How far these collections may conduce to the knowledge of the antiquities and state of this land, let the fit reader judge: yet something I may not passe by touching Mr. Edmund Spenser and the worke it selfe, lest I should seeme to offer injury to his worth, by others so much celebrated. Hee was borne in London of an ancient and noble family, and brought up in the Universitie of Cambridge, where (as the fruites of his after labours doe manifest) he mispent not his time. After this he became secretary to Arthur Lord Grey of Wilton, Lord Deputy of Ireland, a valiant and worthy governour, and shortly after, for his services to the Crowne, he had bestowed upon him by Queene Elizabeth, 3,000 acres of land in the countie of Corke. There he finished the latter part of that excellent poem of his "Faery Queene," which was soone after unfortunately lost by the disorder and abuse of his servant, whom he had sent before him into England, being then a *rebellibus* (as Camden's words are) *è laribus ejectus et bonis spoliatus.* He deceased at Westminster in the year 1599 (others have it wrongly 1598), soon after his return into England, and was buried according to his own desire in the collegiat church there, neere unto Chaucer whom he worthily imitated.—WARE, SIR JAMES, 1633, *ed. A View of the State of Ireland.*

Witnesse our Colin; whom though all the Graces,
And all the Muses nurst; whose well-taught song
Parnassus' self, and Glorian embraces,
And all the learn'd, and all the shepherds' throng;
Yet all his hopes were crosst, all suits deni'd;
Discourag'd, scorn'd, his writings vilifi'd.
Poorly—poore man—he liv'd; poorly—poore man—he di'd.

—FLETCHER, PHINEAS, 1633, *The Purple Island, ed. Grosart, vol.* IV, *s.* 19.

Grandson of Edmund Spenser, from whom an estate of lands in the barony of Fermoy, in the county of Cork, descended on him; . . . that the said estate hath been lately given out to the soldiers, in satisfaction of their arrears; . . . that his grandfather was *that Spenser who, by his writings touching the reduction of the Irish to civility, brought on him the odium of that nation;* and for those works and his other good services, Queen Elizabeth conferred on him that estate which the said William Spenser now claims. We have also been informed that the gentleman is of a civil conversation, and that the extremity his wants have brought him unto have not prevailed over him to put him upon indiscreet or evil practices for a livelihood. If, upon inquiry, you shall find his case to be such; we judge it just and reasonable, and do therefore desire and authorize you, that he be forthwith restored to his estate; and that reprisal lands be given to the soldiers elsewhere; in the doing whereof our satisfaction will be greater by the continuation of that estate to the issue of his grandfather, for whose eminent deserts and services to the Commonwealth that estate was first given him.—CROMWELL, OLIVER, c 1656, *Letters from the Lord Protector, Cromwellian Settlement of Ireland, pp.* 44, 45.

There passeth a story commonly told and believed, that Spenser presenting his poems to queen Elizabeth, she, highly affected therewith, commanded the Lord Cecil, her Treasurer, to give him an hundred pound; and when the Treasurer (a good Steward of the Queen's money) alledged that sum was too much; "Then give him," quoth the Queen, "What is reason;" to which the Lord consented; but was so busied, belike, about matters of higher concernment, that Spenser received no reward; whereupon he presented this petition in a small piece of paper to the Queen in her Progress:

"I was promis'd on a time,
To have reason for my ryme:
From that time unto this season,
I receiv'd nor rhyme nor reason."

Hereupon the Queen gave strict order (not without some check to her Treasurer), for the present payment of the hundred pounds she first intended unto him. He afterwards went over into Ireland, Secretary to the Lord Gray, Lord Deputy thereof; and though that his office under his Lord was lucrative, yet got he no estate; but, saith my Author "peculiari Poetis fato, semper cum paupertate conflictatus est." So that it fared little better with him than with William Xilander the German (a most excellent Linguist, Antiquary, Philosopher and Mathematician), who was so poor, that (as Thuauns saith), he was thought "fami non fame scribere." Returning into England, he was robb'd by the Rebels of that little he had; and, dying for grief in great want, anno 1598, was honourably buried nigh Chaucer in Westminster.—FULLER, THOMAS, 1662, *The Worthies of England, ed. Nichols, vol.* II, *p.* 80.

Mr. Beeston sayes he was a little man, wore short haire, little band and little cuffs.—AUBREY, JOHN, 1669–96, *Brief Lives, ed. Clark, vol.* II, *p.* 233.

From a MS. paper shew'd me by the rev. Mr. John Ball, who is now printing Spenser's Pastoral Kalendar in English and Latin. "From a MS. of Nicholas Stone, esq., master mason to their majesties king James y[e] first, and afterwards to king Charles the first. I also mad a monement for M[er] Spencer the pooett, and set it up at Wesmester, for which the contes of Dorsett payed me 40 lb." It is to be remark'd, that this monument was erected about 1619, as it appears in this book of Mr. Stone's handwriting. Also, that the date of 1510, when Spenser was born, is erroneous. It ought to be 1550.—HEARNE, THOMAS, 1731, *Reliquiæ Hearnianæ, vol.* III, *p.* 71.

Two miles north-west of Doneraile is Kilcoleman, a ruined castle of the Earls of Desmond, but more celebrated for being the residence of the immortal Spenser, when he composed his divine poem "The Faerie Queene." The castle is now almost level with the ground, and was situated on the north side of a fine lake, in the midst of a vast plain, terminated to the east by the county of Waterford mountains; Ballyhowra hills to the north, or, as Spenser terms them, the mountains of Mole, Nagle mountains to the south, and the mountains of Kerry to the west. It commanded a view of above half the breadth of Ireland; and must have been, when the adjacent uplands were wooded, a most pleasant and romantic situation; from whence, no doubt, Spenser drew several parts of the scenery of his poem.—SMITH, CHARLES, 1750, *The Ancient and Present State of the County and City of Cork, vol.* I, *bk.* i, *c.* i, *pp.* 58, 63.

There are in Pembroke Hall two pictures of Spenser; yet he is almost forgotten there as an *alumnus.*—CHALMERS, GEORGE, 1799, *Supplemental Apology for the Believers of the Shakspeare Papers, p.* 23.

The tender heart and luxuriant fancy of Spenser have thrown round his attachments all the strong interest of reality and all the charm of romance and poetry; and since we know that the first development of his genius was owing to female influence, his Rosalind ought to have been deified for what her beauty achieved, had she possessed sufficient soul to appreciate the lustre of her conquest. Immediately on leaving college, Spenser retired to the north of England, where he first became enamoured of the fair being to whom, according to the fashion of the day, he gave the fanciful appellation of Rosalind. We are told that the letters which form this word being "well ordered," (that is, *transposed*) comprehend her real name; but it has hitherto escaped the penetration of his biographers. Two of his friends were entrusted with the secret, and they, with a discretion more to be regretted than blamed, have kept it. One of these, who speaks from personal knowledge, tells us, in a note on the Eclogues, that she was the daughter of a widow; that she was a gentlewoman, and one "that for her rare and singular gifts of person and mind, Spenser need not have been ashamed to love."—JAMESON, ANNA BROWNELL, 1829, *The Loves of the Poets, vol.* I, *p.* 219.

So many living details of that golden bondage into which our poet was thrown, from his earliest to his latter days, discover the real source of his "secret sorrows,"—his unceasing and vain solicitation at court, the suitor of so many patrons: the *res angusta domi* perpetually pressed on the morbid imagination of the fortuneless man. I know of no satire aimed at Spenser; a singular fate for a great poet: even "satyric Nash" revered the character of the author of the "Faery Queen." I have often thought, that, among the numerous critics of Spenser, the truest was his keen and witty contemporary.—DISRAELI, ISAAC, 1841, *Spenser, Amenities of Literature.*

The "Faërie Queene," "Colin Clout," and his two cantos on "Mutabilitie," abound with allegorical or actual descriptions of his Irish life, and of the scenery, and especially the rivers, about his estate here. . . . The remains of the castle, which consist only of part of the tower, at the southernmost corner, stand on a green mound of considerable extent, overlooking the lake, or rather a winding sort of pond, overgrown with potamogeton . . . Here he spent twelve years, and, from every thing that we can learn from his poetry, to his own great satisfaction. . . . Here he accomplished and saw given to the world half his great work. . . . Here, too, he married the woman of his heart, chosen on the principle of his poetry, not for her lands, but for her beauty and her goodness. . . . Here, too, he enjoyed the memorable visit of Sir Walter Raleigh which he commemorates in "Colin Clout." . . . When we hear Kilcolman described by Spenser's biographers as "romantic and delightful," it is evident that they judged of it from mere fancy; and when all writers about him talk of the Mulla "flowing through his grounds," and "past his castle," they give the reader a most erroneous idea. The castle, it must be remembered, is on a wide plain; the hills are at a couple of miles or more distant; and the Mulla is two miles off. We see nothing at the castle but the wide boggy plain, the distant naked hills, and the weedy pond under the castle walls. Such is Kilcolman.—HOWITT, WILLIAM, 1847, *Homes and Haunts of the Most Eminent British Poets, pp.* 28, 34, 36, 38, 40, 41.

"Rosalinde" reads, anagrammatically, into Rose Daniel; for, according to Camden, "a letter may be doubled, or rejected, or contrariwise, if the sense fall aptly;" we thus get rid of the redundant *e*, and have a perfect anagram. Now Spenser had an intimate and beloved friend and brother-poet, named Samuel Daniel. . . . The supposition that Rose Daniel was Rosalinde satisfies every requisite, and presents a solution of the mystery; the anagram is perfect; the poet's acquaintance with the brother naturally threw him into contact with the sister; while the circumstance of her marriage with another justifies the complaint of infidelity, and accounts for the "insurmountable barrier," that is, a living husband.—HALPINE, C. G., 1858, *Atlantic Monthly, vol.* 2, *p.* 677.

He succeeded, with the remaining portion of his family, in escaping to London, where, in a common inn, overcome by his misfortunes, and broken in heart and brain, on the 16th of January, 1599, he died. The saddest thing of all remains to be recorded. Soon after his death—such is the curt statement—"his widow married one Roger Seckerstone." Did Edmund Spenser, then, after all, appear to his wife Elizabeth as he appeared to Mr. Beeston, —simply as "a little man, who wore short hair, little band, and little cuffs"? One would suppose that the memory of so much genius and glory and calamity would have been better than the presence of "one Roger Seckerstone"! Among the thousands of millions of men born on the planet, it was her fortune to be the companion of Edmund Spenser, and "soon after his death she married one Roger Seckerstone"! It required two years of assiduous courtship, illustrated by sonnets which have made her name immortal, before the adoring poet could hymn, in a transport of gratitude, her acceptance of his hand; but fortunate Mr. Seckerstone did not have to wait! She saw her husband laid in Westminster Abbey, mourned by all that was noble in rank or high in genius, and then, as in the case of another too-celebrated marriage,

"The funeral baked meats
Did coldly furnish forth the marriage tables!"

—WHIPPLE, EDWIN P., 1859–68, *The Literature of the Age of Elizabeth, p.* 203.

Without Sidney's help the author of "The Faerie Queene" would have trudged but lamely through the world.—BOURNE, H. R. FOX, 1862, *A Memoir of Sir Philip Sidney, p.* 413.

The differences between Chaucer and Spenser are seen at a glance in their portraits. Chaucer's face is round, good-humoured, constitutionally pensive, and thoughtful. You see in it that he has often been amused, and that he may easily be amused again. Spenser's is of sharper and keener feature, disdainful, and breathing that severity which appertains to so many of the Elizabethan men. A fourteenth-century child, with delicate prescience, would have asked Chaucer to assist her in a strait, and would not have been disappointed. A sixteenth-century child in like circumstances would have shrunk from drawing on herself the regards of the sterner-looking man. We can trace the descent of the Chaucerian face and genius in Shakspeare and Scott, of the Spenserian in Milton and Wordsworth. In our own day, Mr. Browning takes after Chaucer, Mr. Tennyson takes after Spenser.—SMITH, ALEXANDER, 1863, *Dreamthorp, p.* 214.

Among the memories of the street are its having contained the abodes of the poets Spenser, Sackville, Lord Buckhurst, the Earl of Dorset, and Carew the courtier. In an obscure lodging here, Spenser died "for lack of bread."—TIMBS, JOHN, 1865, *The Last Days of Downing Street, Walks and Talks about London, p.* 13.

We know but little of Spenser's history: if we might know all, I do not fear that we should find anything to destroy the impression made by his verse—that he was a Christian gentleman, a noble and pure-minded man, of highest purposes and aims. —MACDONALD, GEORGE, 1868, *England's Antiphon, p.* 63.

It was distinctly in his poetical character that he received the honours of a funeral from Devereux, Earl of Essex. His hearse was attended by poets, and mournful elegies and poems, with the pens that wrote them, were thrown into his tomb. What a funeral was that at which Beaumont, Fletcher, Jonson, and, in all probability, Shakspeare attended!—what a grave in which the pen of Shakspeare may be mouldering away! In the original inscription, long ago effaced, the vicinity to Chaucer is expressly stated as the reason for the selection of the spot. . . . The inscription, in pathos and simplicity, is worthy of the author of the "Faery Queen," but curious as implying the unconsciousness of any greater than he, at that very time, to claim the title then given him of "the Prince of Poets."—STANLEY, ARTHUR PENRHYN, 1867–96, *Westminster Abbey, ch.* iv.

Kilcolman had been recovered by the poet's widow after the suppression of Tyrone's rebellion, and had been wrongfully carried by her, as it seems, to her second husband; at least for a while. It had been a second time devastated, in the rebellion of 1641. It now returned to the Spensers by the justice of the Protector. Other lands near Kilcolman had passed from the poet's son and heir, Sylvanus, to his younger brother Peregrine. From Charles the Second, William Spenser obtained new lands in the counties of Galway and Roscommon. From William the Third, he obtained a grant of the forfeited estate of his cousin Ugolin Spenser, son of Peregrine. For the same man thus to have benefited by the grants of Cromwell, of Charles, and of William, is probably a circumstance almost unique, even in the eventful history of Tenures in Ireland. Such a fact certainly indicates qualities somewhat different from those of his great ancestor. But, eventually, as the Irish estates of Ralegh had passed to the Earls of Cork, so those of Spenser (or what had remained of them after previous alienations by piecemeal) passed to the Earls of Clancarty. At an early period of the last century, no heir of either Ralegh or Spenser possessed an acre of land in Ireland. It will be long, however, before the memory of either shall be wholly severed from its association with the many natural charms of Lismore and of Kilcolman.—EDWARDS, EDWARD, 1868, *The Life of Sir Walter Ralegh, vol.* I, *p.* 129.

Our external sources of information are, then, extremely scanty. Fortunately our internal sources are somewhat less meagre. No poet ever more emphatically lived in his poetry than did Spenser. The Muses were, so to speak, his own bosom friends, to whom he opened all his heart. With them he conversed perpetually on the various events of his life; into their ears he poured forth constantly the tale of his joys and his sorrows, of his hopes, his fears, his distresses. He was not one of those poets who can put off themselves in their works, who can forego their own interests and passions, and live for the time an extraneous life. There is an intense personality about all his writings, as in those of Milton and of Wordsworth. In reading them you can never forget the poet in the poem. They directly and fully reflect the poet's own nature and his circumstances. They are, as it were, fine spiritual diaries, refined self-portraitures. . . . Of him it is eminently true that we may know him from his works. His poems are his best biography.—HALES, JOHN W., 1869–96, *Spenser, Globe edition, Memoir, p.* xv.

Short curling hair, a full moustache, cut after the pattern of Lord Leicester's, close-clipped beard, heavy eyebrows, and under them thoughtful brown eyes, whose upper eyelids weigh them dreamily down; a long and straight nose, strongly developed, answering to a long and somewhat spare face, with a well-formed sensible-looking forehead; a mouth almost obscured by the moustache, but still showing rather full lips, denoting feeling, well set together, so that the warmth of feeling shall not run riot, with a touch of sadness in them—such is the look of Spenser as his portrait hands it down to us.—KITCHIN, G. W., 1867–9, *The Faery Queene, Clarendon Press ed., Introduction.*

Expectations and rebuffs, many sorrows and many dreams, some few joys, and a sudden and frightful calamity, a small fortune and a premature end; this indeed was a poet's life. But the heart within was the true poet—from it all proceeded; circumstances furnished the subject only; he transformed them more than they him; he received less than he gave. Philosophy and landscapes, ceremonies and ornaments, splendours of the country and the court, on all which he painted or thought, he impressed his inward nobleness. Before all, his was a soul captivated by sublime and chaste beauty, eminently platonic; one of these lofty and refined souls most charming of all, who, born in the lap of nature, draw thence their mother's milk, but soar above, enter the regions of mysticism, and mount instinctively in order to open at the confines of another world. —TAINE, H. A., 1871, *History of English Literature, tr. Van Laun, vol.* I, *bk.* ii, *ch.* i, *p.* 181.

Spenser was not without a full share of the poet's alleged peculiar failings, vanity and irritability. Like Sir Walter Scott, our other great poet of chivalrous heroism, he loved to dwell on his ancestry: he somewhat ostentatiously claimed kindred with the noble house of Spencer. Over his natural pride in the exercise of his great gift, he spread but a thin disguise: his transparent compliments to himself are almost unique. He wrote, or procured or allowed a mysterious friend to write, under the initials E. K., an introduction and explanatory notes to his "Shepherd's Calendar," comparing this trial of his wings with similar essays by Theocritus and Virgil, and announcing him as "one that in time shall be able to keep wing with the best." Among the shepherds he represents himself under the names of Colin Clout and young Cuddy, and makes other shepherds speak of these sweet players on the oaten pipe with boundless admiration as the joy of their fellows and the rivals of Calliope herself. As for the poet's irritability, that appears in the covert bitterness of his attacks on Roman Catholics and other subjects of his dislike, but most unmistakably in his "View of the State of Ireland." His temper was too thin for the asperities of public life. These, however, are the unfavourable aspects of the poet's amiable nature. More favourable aspects of the same reserved meditative disposition appear in his warm gratitude to benefactors, his passion for temperance and purity, and his deep religious earnestness. — MINTO, WILLIAM, 1874–85, *Characteristics of English Poets, p.* 167.

He died poor, but not in want. On the whole, his life may be reckoned a happy one, as in the main the lives of the great poets must have commonly been. . . . We should measure what Spenser says of his worldly disappointments by the bitterness of the unavailing tears he shed for Rosalinde. A careful analysis of these leaves no perceptible residuum of salt, and we are tempted to believe that the passion itself was not much more real than the pastoral accessories of pipe and crook. I very much doubt whether Spenser ever felt more than one profound passion in his life, and that luckily was for his "Faery Queen." He was fortunate in the friendship of the best men and women of his time, in the seclusion which made him free of the still better society of the past, in the loving recognition of his countrymen. All that we know of him is amiable and of good report. He was faithful to the friendships of his youth, pure in his loves, unspotted in his life. Above all, the ideal with him was not a thing apart and unattainable, but the sweetener and ennobler of the street and the fireside.—LOWELL, JAMES RUSSELL, 1875–90, *Spenser, Prose Works, Riverside ed., vol.* IV, *pp.* 297, 298.

There are two very diverse portraits extant, each of which has been said to represent Edmund Spenser. One, which is generally recognized as genuine, shows a long face, with a well-sized straight nose, brown eyes, short curling hair, a full moustache, and close-clipped beard; a thoughtful and rather saddened face, corresponding to what we understand his nature to have been—reserved and gentle. The other portrait cannot certainly have been taken from the same original: it is a physiognomy altogether keener—more active, bustling, and mundane.—ROSSETTI, WILLIAM MICHAEL, 1878, *Lives of Famous Poets, p.* 30.

HEARE LYES (EXPECTING THE SECOND COMMINGE OF OUR SAVIOUR JESUS) THE BODY OF EDMOND SPENSER, THE PRINCE OF POETS IN HIS TYME, WHOSE DIVINE SPIRIT NEEDS NOE OTHIR WITNESSE THEN THE WORKS WHICH HE LEFT BEHINDE HIM. HE WAS BORNE IN LONDON IN THE YEAR 1553, AND DIED IN THE YEARE 1598.—*Original Inscription on Tomb, Westminster Abbey.*

THE SHEPHERDS CALENDAR
1579

Loe! I have made a Calender for every yeare,
That steele in strength, and time in durance, shall outweare;
And, if I marked well the starres revolution,
It shall continewe till the worlds dissolution,
To teach the ruder shepheard how to feede his sheepe,
And from the falsers fraude his folded flocke to keepe.
Goe, lyttle Calender! thou hast a free passeporte;
Goe but a lowly gate emongste the meaner sorte:
Dare not to match thy pype with Tityrus his style,
Nor with the Pilgrim that the Ploughman playde awhyle;
But followe them farre off, and their high steppes adore;
The better please, the worse despise; I aske no more.

—SPENSER, EDMUND, 1579, *The Shepheards Calender, Epilogue.*

Now, as touching the generall dryft and purpose of his Æglogues, I mind not to say much, him selfe labouring to conceale it. Onely this appeareth, that his unstayed yougth had long wandred in the common Labyrinth of Love, in which time to mitigate and allay the heate of his passion, or els to warne (as he sayth) the young shepheards, s. his equalls and companions, of his unfortunate folly, he compiled these xij Æglogues, which, for that they be proportioned to the state of the xij monethes, he termeth the "Shepheards Calendar," applying an olde name to a new worke.—KIRKE, EDWARD? 1579, *Spenser's Shepheards Calender, Epistle to Gabriell Harvey.*

Our late famous English Poet, who wrote the "Sheepheards Calender," where lamenting the decay of Poetry, at these dayes, saith most sweetely to the same.

Then make thee winges of thine aspyring wytt,
And whence thou camest flye back to heauen apace, etc.

Whose fine poeticall witt, and most exquisite learning, as he shewed aboundantly in that peece of worke, in my iudgment inferiour to the workes neither of *Theocritus* in Greeke, nor *Virgill* in Latine, whom hee narrowly immitateth: so I nothing doubt, but if his other workes were common abroade, which are as I thinke in ye close custodie of certaine his freends, we should haue of our owne Poets, whom wee might matche in all respects with the best. And among all other his workes whatsoeuer, I would wysh to haue the sight of hys *English Poet*, which his freend E. K. did once promise to publishe, which whether he performed or not, I knowe not, if he did, my happe hath not beene so good as yet to see it. . . . This place haue I purposely reserued for one, who if not only, yet in my iudgment principally deserueth the tytle of the rightest English Poet, that euer I read: that is, the Author of the "Sheepeheardes Kalender," intituled to the woorthy Gentleman Master *Philip Sydney*, whether is was Master *Sp.* or what rare Scholler in Pembrooke Hall soeuer, because himself and his freendes, for what respect I knowe not, would not reeuale it.—WEBBE, WILLIAM, 1586, *A Discourse of English Poetrie, ed. Arber, pp.* 23, 35.

The last "Sheppards Calender" the reputed worke of S. Phil. Sydney—a worke of deepe learning, judgement and witte, disguised in Shep. Rules.—WHETSTONE, GEORGE, 1587, *Sir Philip Sidney, his honourable Life, his valiant Death, and true Virtues, note.*

Hath much Poetrie in his Eglogues: indeede worthy of the reading, if I be not deceiued. That same framing of his style to an old rustick language, I dare not alowe, sith neyther Theocritus in Greeke, Virgill in Latine, nor Sanazar in Italian, did affect it.—SIDNEY, SIR PHILIP, 1595, *An Apologie for Poetrie, ed. Arber, pp.* 62, 63.

As Theocritus is famoused for his "Idyllia" in Greeke, and Virgil for his "Eclogues" in Latin; so Spenser their imitatour in his "Shepheardes Calender," is renowned for the like argument, and honoured for fine poetical invention and most exquisit wit.—MERES, FRANCIS, 1598, *Palladis Tamia.*

Master Edmund Spenser had done enough for the immortality of his name had he only given us his "Shepherd's Kalendar;" a master-piece, if any.—DRAYTON, MICHAEL, 1605? *Poems Lyrick and Pastorall, Preface.*

The "Shepherd's Kalendar" of Spenser is not to be matched in any modern language, not even by Tasso's "Aminta," which infinitely transcends Guarini's "Pastor Fido," as having more of nature in it, and being almost wholly clear from the wretched affectation of learning. . . . Spenser, being master of our northern dialect, and skilled in Chaucer's English, has so exactly imitated the Doric of Theocritus, that his love is a perfect image of that passion which God infused into both sexes, before it was corrupted with the knowledge of arts, and the ceremonies of what we call good manners. — DRYDEN, JOHN, 1697, *Works of Virgil, Pastorals, Dedication, Works, ed. Scott and Saintsbury, vol.* XIII, *pp.* 324, 325.

His Eclogues are somewhat too long, if we compare them with the ancients. He is sometimes too allegorical, and treats of matters of religion in a pastoral style, as the Mantuan had done before him. He has employed the lyric measure, which is contrary to the practice of the old poets. His stanza is not still the same, nor always well chosen. . . . The addition he has made of a calendar to his Eclogues, is very beautiful; since by this, besides the general moral of innocence and simplicity, which is common to other authors of pastoral, he has one peculiar to himself; he compares human life to the several seasons, and at once exposes to his readers a view of the great and little worlds, in their various changes and aspects.—POPE, ALEXANDER, 1704, *A Discourse on Pastorals, Works, ed. Croker and Elwin, vol.* I, *pp.* 262, 263.

There seems to be the same difference between the "Faerie Queen" and the "Shepherd's Calendar," as between a royal palace and a little country-seat.—HUGHES, JOHN, 1715, *ed. Spenser's Works, with Life.*

Neither the "Shepherd's Calendar" of Spenser, nor the "Pastorals" of Gay, possess that native simplicity and close adherence to the manners and language of country life, which ought to form the basis of this kind of composition. — ROSCOE, WILLIAM, 1795, *Life of Lorenzo de Medici, notes.*

A few days since I had the pleasure of conversing with F. Schlegel, one of the first living poets, and a great Æsthetiker; he is the brother of the translator of Shakespeare. He seemed much pleased with one or two pieces by Wordsworth. We talked of our English poets. He holds Spenser to be the greatest in respect to the melody of verse. "When I read him," says he, "I can hardly think it is a Northern language, much less English." He holds his "Pastorals" to be his best work, and yet this is a book of which neither you nor I have read a word. I am resolved to leave my favorite authors and study those I have through mistaken notions or absurd prejudices neglected.—ROBINSON, HENRY CRABB, 1802, *Letter to T. R., Diary, Reminiscences, and Correspondence, vol.* I, *p.* 79.

Some have been led to assign the name of Edward Kerke to the old scholiast. Some also have not failed to suppose that King might be the name.—TODD, HENRY JOHN, 1805, *ed. Spenser's Works, vol.* I, *p.* xxi, *note.*

Yet two great defects have contributed deeply to injure the popularity of his Calender; the adoption of a language much too old and obsolete for the age in which it was written, and the too copious introduction of satire on ecclesiastical affairs. The consequence of this latter defect, this incongruous mixture of church polemics, has been, that the aeglogues for May, July, and September, are any thing but pastorals. Simplicity of diction is of the very essence of perfection in pastoral poetry; but vulgar, rugged, and obscure terms, can only be productive of disgust; a result which was felt and complained of by the contemporaries of the poet, and which not all the ingenuity of his old commentator, E. K., can successfully palliate or defend. The pieces which have been least injured by this "ragged and rustical rudeness," as the scholiast aptly terms it, are the pastorals for January, June, October and December, which are indeed very beautiful, and the genuine offspring of the rural reed.—DRAKE, NATHAN, 1817, *Shakspeare and his Times, vol.* I, *p.* 646.

To our minds the irredeemable sin of the "Shepherd's Calendar"—we wish we could use gentler words, but cannot find them—is the cold, uncomfortable, and unhappy air that hangs in it over almost the whole of rural life. We are always wishing for the sun, but no sun shews his face. Nature is starved, and life hungry —and sleep seems but the relief from labour. There is nowhere Joy.—WILSON, JOHN, 1833, *Spenser, Blackwood's Magazine, vol.* 34, *p.* 832.

The dialect of Theocritus is musical to our ears, and free from vulgarity; praise which we cannot bestow on the uncouth provincial rusticity of Spenser.—HALLAM, HENRY, 1837–39, *Introduction to the Literature of Europe, pt.* ii, *ch.* v. *par.* 61.

Compare the "Shepherd's Calendar" with any poetry produced by the best of Spenser's immediate predecessors, and we shall feel that he alone was all a poet, that they were only poets as it were by assuming and acting the character. . . . They* were poets on occasion, and by dint of tasking their faculties; he was all and always a poet. And, although this first published work, his "Shepherd's Calendar," was far from evidencing the full strength or extent of Spenser's poetic genius, still it was something which may be described as not only superior in excellence but unlike in kind to whatever had previously been produced in the existing form of the language—something as different from what had hitherto been the most approved modern English poetry as the dawn is from the brightest moonlight. It is not only our first English pastoral, but our earliest poetical work of any description, written since the language has been substantially the same that it now is, which can be called a classical work. It forms the commencement of our classical modern English literature.—CRAIK, GEORGE L., 1845, *Spenser and his Poetry, vol.* I, *p.* 93.

*Surrey and Buckhurst.

No descriptions of external nature since Chaucer's had equalled those in the "Shepherd's Calendar" in the combination of various excellences, though the excellences were still second-rate, exhibiting the beautiful genius of the author struggling with the pedantries and affectations of his time, and the pedantries and affectations which overlaid his own mind. Even in his prime, it was difficult for him to grasp a thing in itself, after the manner of the greatest poets, and flash its form and spirit upon the mind in a few vivid words, vital with suggestive meaning. In the "Shepherd's Calendar" this defect is especially prominent, his imagination playing round objects, illustrating and adorning them, rather than penetrating at once to their essence. Even in those portions where, as Colin Clout, he celebrates the beauty and bewails the coldness of Rosalind, we have a conventional discourse about love, rather than the direct utterance of the passion.—WHIPPLE, EDWIN P., 1859–68, *The Literature of the Age of Elizabeth, p.* 195.

Had it been required in 1579, as it was shortly afterwards, that a book licensed at Stationers' Hall should have first received the sanction of the Archbishop of Canterbury, the Bishop of London, or of some of the special persons appointed to that duty, it is just possible that "The Shepheardes Calender" might never have seen the light. Some of the eclogues are decidedly of a political and religious aspect; and though the dialogue is distributed among clowns and shepherds, their remarks are often so severe, personal, and objurgatory, that not a few public men might be disposed to take offence at them. Indeed, it is known that Lord Burghley was highly displeased by the applause bestowed upon Archbishop Grindal; and as a young man, who had his fortune to make, Spenser may have been unwilling to put his name to the publication. Edward Kirke subjoined only his initials to the epistle to Harvey, and afforded no clue to the discovery of the author: the words "unstayed youth," and the "labyrinth of love" in which that "unstayed youth" had involved himself, were much too general to lead even to an inference; while the anticipation of the manner in which the "new poet" would be admired thereafter, and "his worthiness founded by the tromp of fame," might only be looked upon as the expression of the somewhat extravagant opinion of enthusiastic friendship. —COLLIER, JOHN PAYNE, 1862, *ed. Works of Spenser, Life, vol.* I, *p.* xxxiv.

His "Shepherd's Calendar" is a pensive and tender pastoral, full of delicate loves, noble sorrows, lofty ideas, where no voice is heard but of thinkers and poets.—TAINE, H. A., 1871, *History of English Literature, tr. Van Laun, vol.* I, *bk.* ii, *ch.* i, *p.* 184.

I look upon the "Shepherd's Calendar" as being no less a conscious and deliberate attempt at reform than Thomson's "Seasons" were in the topics, and Wordsworth's "Lyrical Ballads" in the language of poetry. But the great merit of these pastorals was not so much in their matter as their manner. They show a sense of style in its larger meaning hitherto displayed by no English poet since Chaucer. Surrey had brought back from Italy a certain inkling of it, so far as it is contained in decorum. But here was a new language, a choice and arrangement of words, a variety, elasticity, and harmony of verse most grateful to the ears of men. If not passion, there was fervor, which was perhaps as near it as the somewhat stately movement of Spenser's mind would allow him to come. . . . The "Shepherd's Calendar" contains perhaps the most picturesquely imaginative verse which Spenser has written. —LOWELL, JAMES RUSSELL, 1875–90, *Spenser, Prose Works, Riverside ed., vol.* IV, *pp.* 301, 303.

The identity of "E. K." with Edmund Spenser is nowhere in contradiction with the form and the contents of the commentary. . . . It no longer excites surprise that the merits of G. Harvey, not to mention others, are so much expounded in the Epistle and in the notes. If "E. K." were not Spenser himself, he would have carefully avoided darkening the poet by praising others at his expense, but Spenser doing it himself simply expressed his gratitude to his best friend Harvey. Thus we now know that "E. K." means Edmund Spenser, and this result enables us to say that all allusions to the life and works of Spenser contained in the "Glosse" are genuine and valuable material for the completion of his biography, whereas the letters between him and Harvey have to be used with great care. But it still continues an open question why Spenser took these letters, or what is meant by them. Most probably this will remain an enigma, like the mysterious "W. H." of the dedication to Shakspere's Sonnets.—SOMMER, H. OSKAR, 1890, *ed., The Shepheardes Calender, Introduction, pp.* 24, 25.

When "The Shepheard's Calender" was born, the breath of genius inspired the old forms with a Chaucerian freshness and a new melody. And from this moment the popularity of the pastoral was assured. It became the normal mode alike for panegyric and erotic verse. . . . It was Spenser, then, who first made the pastoral a thing of significance for English writers; but he was by no means the creator of it as a literary species.—CHAMBERS, EDMUND K., 1895, *English Pastorals, p.* xix.

A long silence and two generations of effort preceded the renaissance of English poetry, which may conveniently, though perhaps somewhat arbitrarily, be said to date from the publication of the "Shepherd's Calendar" in 1579.—HANNAY, DAVID, 1898, *The Later Renaissance, p.* 185.

THE FAERY QUEEN
1590–96

The generall end therefore of all the booke is to fashion a gentleman or noble person in vertuous and gentle discipline: Which for that I conceived shoulde be most plausible and pleasing, being coloured with an historicall fiction, the which the most part of men delight to read, rather for variety of matter then for profite of the ensample, I chose the historye of King Arthure, as most fitte for the excellency of his person, being made famous by many mens former workes, and also furthest from the daunger of envy, and suspition of present time.—SPENSER, EDMUND, 1590, *Letter to Sir Walter Raleigh, The Faerie Queene, bk.* i.

Me thought I saw the grave where Laura lay,
Within that Temple where the vestall flame
Was wont to burne; and passing by that way
To see that buried dust of living fame,
Whose tumbe fair love, and fairer vertue kept,
All suddeinly I saw the Faery Queene:
At whose approch the soule of Petrarke wept,
And from thenceforth those graces were not seene;
For they this Queene attended: in whose steed
Oblivion laid him downe on Lauras herse.
Hereat the hardest stones were seene to bleed,
And grones of buried ghostes the hevens did perse:
Where Homers sprite did tremble all for griefe,
And curst th' accesse of that celestiall theife.

—RALEIGH, SIR WALTER, 1590, *A Vision upon this conceipt of the Faery Queene.*

Let others sing of Knights and Palladines
In aged accents, and untimely words;
Paint shadowes in imaginary lines,
Which well the reach of their high wit records.

—DANIEL, SAMUEL, 1592, *Delia.*

Immortall *Spencer*, no frailtie hath thy fame, but the imputation of this Idiots friendship: upon an unspotted *Pegasus* should thy gorgeous attired "Fayrie Queene" ride triumphant through all reports dominions, but that this mud-born bubble,* this bile on the browe of the Universitie, this bladder of pride newe blowne, challengeth some interest in her prosperitie.—NASHE, THOMAS, 1593, *Harvey-Greene Tractates, ed. Grosart, vol.* II, *p.* 213.

In thy sweete song so blessed may'st thou bee!
For learned Colin laies his pipes to gage,
And is to Fayrie gone a pilgrimage;
The more our mone.

—DRAYTON, MICHAEL, 1593, *Idea, The Shepheards Garland.*

I know not what more excellent or exquisite poem may be written.—MERES, FRANCIS, 1598, *Palladis Tamia.*

*Gabriel Harvey.

Graue Spencer was no sooner entred in to this chapell of Apollo, but these elder fathers of the diuine furie gaue him a lawrer, and sung his welcome: Chaucer call'de him his sonne, and plac'de him at his right hand. All of them (at a signe giuen by the whole of the muses that brought him thither) closing vp their lippes in silence, and turning their eares for attention, to heare him sing out the rest of his fayrie queenes praises.—DEKKER, THOMAS, 1606, *Newes from Hell, Non-Dramatic Works, ed. Grosart, vol.* V, *p.* xxi.

Live Spenser ever, in thy Fairy Queene,
Whose like (for deepe conceit) was never seene:
Crownd mayst thou be, unto thy more renowne,
(As King of Poets) with a Lawrell Crowne.

—BARNFIELD, RICHARD, 1605, *Remembrance of some English Poets.*

Shew now faire *Muse* what afterward became
Of great *Achilles Mother*; She whose name
The *Mermaids* sing, and tell the weeping strang
A brauer Lady neuer tript on land,
Except the euer-living *Fayerie Queene*,
Whose vertues by her *Swaine* so written beene,
That time shall call her high enhanced story
In his rare song, *The Muses chiefest glory.*

—BROWNE, WILLIAM, 1616, *Britannia's Pastorals, ed. Hazlitt, vol.* I, *bk.* ii, *Song* i, *p.* 190.

I remember when I began to read, and to take some Pleasure in it, there was wont to lye in my Mother's Parlour (I know not by what accident, for she herself never in her life read any Book but of Devotion) but there was wont to lye *Spencer's* works; this I happen'd to fall upon, and was infinitely delighted with the Stories of the Knights, and Giants, and Monsters, and brave Houses, which I found every where there: (Though my Understanding had little to do with all this) and by degrees with the Tinkling of the Rhyme and Dance of the Numbers, so that I think I had read him all over before I was twelve years old, and was thus made a Poet as irremediably as a Child is made an Eunuch.—COWLEY, ABRAHAM, 1667? *On Myself, Essays,* xi.

There is no uniformity in the design of Spenser: he aims at the accomplishment of no one action; he raises up a hero for every one of his adventures; and endows each of them with some particular moral virtue, which renders them all equal, without subordination, or preference. Every one is most valiant in his own legend: only we must do him that justice to observe, that magnanimity, which is the character of Prince Arthur, shines throughout the whole poem; and succours the rest, when they are in distress. The original of every knight was then living in the court of Queen Elizabeth; and he attributed to each of them that virtue, which he thought was most conspicuous in them; an ingenious piece of flattery, though it turned not much to his account. Had he lived to finish his poem, in the six remaining legends, it had certainly been more of a piece; but could not have been perfect, because the model was not true. But Prince Arthur, or his chief patron Sir Philip Sidney, whom he intended to make happy by the marriage of his Gloriana, dying before him, deprived the poet both of means and spirit to accomplish his design. For the rest, his obsolete language, and the ill choice of his stanza, are faults but of the second magnitude; for, notwithstanding the first, he is still intelligible, at least after a little practice; and for the last, he is the more to be admired, that, labouring under such a dfficulty, his verses are so numerous, so various, and so harmonious, that only Virgil, whom he professedly imitated, has surpassed him among the Romans; and only Mr. Waller among the English.—DRYDEN, JOHN, 1692, *Essay on Satire, Works, ed. Scott and Saintsbury vol.* XIII, *p.* 17.

Old Spenser next, warm'd with poetic rage,
In ancient tales amused a barbarous age;
An age that yet uncultivate and rude,
Where'er the poet's fancy led, pursued
Through pathless fields and unfrequented floods,
To dens of dragons and enchanted woods.
But now the mystic tale that pleased of yore,
Can charm an understanding age no more;
The long-spun allegories fulsome grow,
While the dull moral lies too plain below
We view well-pleased at distance all the sights
Of arms and palfreys, battles, fields, and fights,
And damsels in distress, and courteous knights.
But, when we look too near, the shades decay,
And all the pleasing landscape fades away.

—ADDISON, JOSEPH, 1694, *An Account of the greatest English Poets.*

When bright Eliza ruled Britannia's state,
Widely distributing her high commands,
And boldly wise, and fortunately great,
Freed the glad nations from tyrannic bands;
An equal genius was in Spenser found;
To the high theme he match'd his noble lays;
He travell'd England o'er on fairy ground,
In mystic notes to sing his monarch's praise:
Reciting wondrous truths in pleasing dreams,
He deck'd Eliza's head with Gloriana's beams.

—PRIOR, MATTHEW, 1706, *An Ode, Humbly Inscribed to the Queen, s.* ii

Spencer's general plan is the representation of six virtues, holiness, temperance, chastity, friendship, justice, and courtesy, in six legends, by six persons. The six personages are supposed, under proper allegories suitable to their respective characters, to do all that is necessary for the full manifestation of the respective virtues which they are to exert. These one might undertake to show, under the several heads are admirably drawn; no images improper, and most surprisingly beautiful. The Redcross Knight runs through the whole steps of the Christian life; Guyon does all that temperance can possibly require; Britomartis (a woman) observes the true rules of unaffected chastity; Arthegal is in every respect of life strictly and wisely just; Calidore is rightly courteous. In short, in fairyland, where knights-errant have a full scope to range, and to do even what Ariostos or Orlandos could not do in the world without breaking into credibility, Spencer's knights have, under those six heads, given a full and truly poetical system of Christian, public, and low life. His legend of friendship is more diffuse, and yet even there the allegory is finely drawn, only the heads various; one knight could not there support all the parts. To do honour to his country, Prince Arthur is an universal hero; in holiness, temperance, chastity, and justice, superexcellent. For the same reason, and to compliment Queen Elizabeth, Gloriana, queen of fairies, whose court was the asylum of the oppressed, represents that glorious queen. —STEELE, RICHARD, 1712, *The Spectator, No.* 540, *Nov.* 19.

If we consider the first book as an entire work of itself, we shall find it to be no irregular contrivance. There is one principal action, which is completed in the twelfth canto, and the several incidents are proper, as they tend either to obstruct or promote it. —HUGHES, JOHN, 1715, *ed. Spenser's Works, with Life, vol.* I.

Nor shall my verse that elder bard forget,
The gentle Spenser, Fancy's pleasing son;
Who, like a copious river, pour'd his song
O'er all the mazes of enchanted ground.

—THOMSON, JAMES, 1727, *Summer, Sea sons, v.* 1572–5.

After reading a canto of Spenser two or three days ago to an old lady, between seventy and eighty years of age, she said that I had been showing her a gallery of pictures.—I don't know how it is, but she said very right: there is something in Spenser that pleases one as strongly in one's old age, as it did in one's youth. I read the "Faerie Queene" when I was about twelve, with infinite delight; and I think it gave me as much, when I read it over about a year or two ago.—POPE, ALEXANDER, 1743–4, *Spence's Anecdotes, ed. Singer, p.* 224.

To imitate the fictions and sentiments of Spenser can incur no reproach; for allegory is perhaps one of the most pleasing vehicles of instruction. But I am very far from extending the same respect to his diction or his stanza. His style was in his own time allowed to be vicious, so darkened with old words and peculiarities of phrase, and so remote from common use, that Jonson boldly pronounces him to have written no language. His stanza is at once difficult and unpleasing; tiresome to the ear by its uniformity, and to the attention by its length. It was at first formed in imitation of the Italian poets, without due regard to the genius of our language. —JOHNSON, SAMUEL, 1751, *The Rambler, No.* 121, *May* 15.

The chief merit of this poem, no doubt, consists in that surprising vein of fabulous invention, which runs through it, and enriches it every where with imagery and descriptions, more than we meet with in any other modern poem. The author seems to be possessed of a kind of poetical magic, and the figures he calls up to our view rise so thick upon us, that we are at once pleased and distracted with the exhaustless variety of them; so that his faults may in a manner be imputed to his excellencies. His abundance betrays him into excess, and his judgment is overborn by the torrent of his imagination. That which seems the most liable to exception in this work is the model of it, and the choice the author has made of so romantic a story.—CIBBER, THEOPHILUS, 1753, *Lives of the Poets, vol.* I, *p.* 105.

Although Spenser formed his "Faerie Queene" upon the fanciful plan of Ariosto, yet it must be confessed, that the adventures of his knights are a more exact and immediate copy of those which we meet with in old romances, or books of chivalry, than of those which form the Orlando Furioso. Ariosto's knights exhibit surprising examples of their prowess, and achieve many heroic actions. But our author's knights are more professedly engaged in revenging injuries, and doing justice to the distressed; which was the proper business, and ultimate end of the ancient knight-errantry. And thus, though many of Spenser's incidents are to be found in Ariosto, such as that of blowing a horn, at the sound of which the gates of a castle fly open, of the vanishing of an enchanted palace or garden, after some knight has destroyed the enchanter, and the like; yet these are not more peculiarly the property of Ariosto, than they are common to all ancient romances in general.—WARTON, THOMAS, 1754, *Observations on the Fairy Queen of Spenser, vol.* I, *p.* 25.

This poet contains great beauties, a sweet and harmonious versification, easy elocution, a fine imagination. Yet does the perusal of his work become so tedious, that one never finishes it from the mere pleasure which it affords: it soon becomes a kind of task-reading; and it requires some effort and resolution to carry us on to the end of his long performance. . . . The tediousness of continued allegory, and that too seldom striking or ingenious, has also contributed to render the "Fairy Queen" peculiarly tiresome; not to mention the too great frequency of its descriptions, and the languor of its stanza. Upon the whole, Spenser maintains his place upon the shelves, among our English classics; but he is seldom seen on the table; and there is scarcely any one, if he dares to be ingenious, but will confess, that, notwithstanding all the merit of the poet, he affords an entertainment with which the palate is soon satiated. Several writers of late have amused themselves in copying the style of Spenser; and no imitation has been so indifferent as not to bear a great resemblance to the original: his manner is so peculiar, that it is almost impossible not to transfer some of it into the copy.—HUME, DAVID, 1759, *The History of England, vol.* IV, *Appendix* III.

Sage Spenser waked his lofty lay
To grace Eliza's golden sway:
O'er the proud theme new lustre to diffuse,
He chose the gorgeous allegoric muse,
And call'd to life old Uther's elfin tale,
And rov'd thro' many a necromantic vale,
Portraying chiefs that knew to tame
The goblin's ire, the dragon's flame,
To pierce the dark enchanted hall,
Where virtue sate in lonely thrall.
From fabling Fancy's inmost store
A rich romantic robe he bore;
A veil with visionary trappings hung,
And o'er his virgin-queen the fairy texture flung.

—WARTON, THOMAS, 1787, *Ode to the King.*

It is scarcely possible to accompany Spenser's allegorical heroes to the end of their excursions. They want flesh and blood; a want for which nothing can compensate. The personification of abstract ideas furnishes the most brilliant images for poetry; but these meteor forms, which startle and delight us when our senses are flurried by passion, must not be submitted to our cool and deliberate examination. — ELLIS, GEORGE, 1790-1845, *Specimens of Early English Poets, vol.* II, *p.* 200.

The nobility of the Spencers has been illustrated and enriched by the trophies of Marlborough; but I exhort them to consider "The Faerie Queene" as the most precious jewel of their coronet.—GIBBON, EDWARD, 1794, *Memoirs, p.* 3.

No author, perhaps, ever possessed and combined, in so a brilliant a degree, the requisite qualities of a poet. Learned, according to the learning of his times, his erudition never appears to load or encumber his powers of imagination; but even the fictions of the classics, worn out as they are by the use of every pedant, become fresh and captivating themes, when adopted by his fancy, and accommodated to his plan. If that plan has now become to the reader of riper years somewhat tedious and involved, it must be allowed, on the other hand, that from Cowley downwards, every youth of imagination has been enchanted with the splendid legends of the "Faery Queen."—SCOTT, SIR WALTER, 1805, *Todd's Edition of Spenser, Edinburgh Review, vol.* 7, *p.* 203.

I have finished the "Faerie Queene." I never parted from a long poem with so much regret. He is a poet of a most musical ear—of a tender heart—of a peculiarly soft, rich, fertile, and flowery fancy. His verse always flows, with ease and nature, most abundantly and sweetly; his diffusion is not only pardonable, but agreeable. Grandeur and energy are not his characteristic qualities. He seems to me a most genuine poet, and to be justly placed after Shakspeare and Milton, and above all other English poets.—MACKINTOSH, SIR JAMES, 1812, *Diary, Memoirs, ed. Mackintosh, vol.* II, *p.* 242.

Your abhorrence of Spenser is a strange heresy. I admit that he is inferior to Chaucer (who for variety of power has no competitor except Shakespeare), but he is the great master of English versification, incomparably the greatest master in our language. Without being insensible to the defects of the "Fairy Queen," I am never weary of reading it.—SOUTHEY, ROBERT, 1811, *Letter to Landor, Life and Correspondence.*

But some people will say that all this may be very fine, but that they cannot understand it on account of the allegory. They are afraid of the allegory, as if they thought it would bite them: they look at it as a child looks at a painted dragon, and think it will strangle them in its shining folds. This is very idle. If they do not meddle with the allegory, the allegory will not meddle with them. Without minding it at all, the whole is as plain as a pike-staff. It might as well be pretended that we cannot see Poussin's pictures for the allegory, as that the allegory prevents us from understandinng Spenser. . . . The language of Spenser is full and copious to overflowing; it is less pure and idiomatic than Chaucer's, and is enriched and adorned with phrases borrowed from the different languages of Europe, both ancient and modern. . .

His versification is at once the most smooth and the most sounding in the language. . . . Spenser is the most harmonious of our stanza-writers, as Dryden is the most sounding and varied of our rhymists. — HAZLITT, WILLIAM, 1818, *Lectures on the English Poets, Lects. II and III.*

A silver trumpet Spenser blows,
And, as its martial notes to silence flee,
From a virgin chorus flows,
A hymn in praise of spotless Chastity.
'Tis still! Wild warblings from the Æolian lyre
Enchantment softly breathe, and tremblingly expire.

—KEATS, JOHN, 1821? *Ode to Apollo, s.* 6.

Nay, even Spenser himself, though assuredly one of the greatest poets that ever lived, could not succeed in the attempt to make allegory interesting. It was in vain that he lavished the riches of his mind on the House of Pride and the House of Temperance. One unpardonable fault, the fault of tediousness, pervades the whole of the "Faerie Queen." We become sick of Cardinal Virtues and Deadly Sins, and long for the society of plain men and women. Of the persons who read the first Canto, not one in ten reaches the end of the First Book, and not one in a hundred perseveres to the end of the poem. Very few and very weary are those who are in at the death of the Blatant Beast. If the last six books, which are said to have been destroyed in Ireland, had been preserved, we doubt whether any heart less stout than that of a commentator would have held out to the end.—MACAULAY, THOMAS BABINGTON, 1830, *Southey's Edition of Pilgrim's Progress, Edinburgh Review, Critical and Miscellaneous Essays.*

The noblest allegorical poem in our own language,—indeed, the noblest allegorical poem in the world.—MONTGOMERY, JAMES, 1833, *Lectures on General Literature, Poetry, etc., p.* 146.

The poetry of Spenser is remarkable for brilliant imagination, fertile invention, and flowing rhythm; yet with all these recommendations, it is cold and tedious. To the English reader the "Faerie Queene" presents the charm of antiquated style, which never fails to please us in our own language, but which we cannot appreciate in a foreign tongue.—DE CHATEAUBRIAND, FRANCOIS RENÉ, VICOMTE, 1837, *Sketches of English Literature, vol.* I, *p.* 226.

The first book of the "Faery Queen" is a complete poem, and, far from requiring any continuation, is rather injured by the useless re-appearance of its hero in the second. It is generally admitted to be the finest of the six. In no other is the allegory so clearly conceived by the poet, or so steadily preserved, yet with a disguise so delicate, that no one is offended by that servile setting-forth of a moral meaning we frequently meet with in allegorical poems; and the reader has the gratification which good writing in works of fiction always produces,—that of exercising his own ingenuity without perplexing it. . . . Every canto of this book teems with the choicest beauties of imagination: he came to it in the freshness of his genius, which shines throughout with an uniformity it does not always afterwards maintain, unsullied as yet by flattery, unobstructed by pedantry, and unquenched by languor. . . . The inferiority of the last three books to the former is surely very manifest. His muse gives gradual signs of weariness, the imagery becomes less vivid, the vein of poetical description less rich, the digressions more frequent and verbose. It is true that the fourth book is full of beautiful inventions, and contains much admirable poetry; yet, even here, we perceive a comparative deficiency in the quantity of excelling passages, which becomes far more apparent as we proceed; and the last book falls very short of the interest which the earlier part of the "Faery Queen" had excited. —HALLAM, HENRY, 1837–39, *Introduction to the Literature of Europe, vol.* II, *pt.* ii, *ch.* v, *par.* 80, 86.

The noble stanza which we owe to Spenser, is formed by adding an alexandrine to the ballet-stave of eight—such alexandrine rhiming with the last verse of the ballet-stave. By this *banding* of the rhime, Spenser's stanza has all that connexion of parts which science demands, and which is so seldom to be met with in our later combinations. The sweeping length of the alexandrine furnishes also an imposing compass of sound, that to many ears is singularly delightful, and must, I think, convey to everyone an impression of grandeur and of dignity. When to these advantages of structure are added the associations, which Spenser's genius conferred upon it, we may understand the enthusiasm, that sees so many excellencies in Spenser's stanza, and pronounces it to be the most beautiful, as well as the most perfect of English combinations. Warton's notice of this stanza is almost the only exception to the eulogies of our critics.—GUEST, EDWIN, 1838, *A History of English Rhythms, vol.* II, *p.* 389.

Of his great poem we may say, that we miss no humanity in it, because we make a new humanity out of it and are satisfied in our human hearts—a new humanity vivified by the poet's life, moving in happy measure to the chanting of his thoughts and upon ground supernaturally beautified by his sense of the beautiful.—BROWNING, ELIZABETH BARRETT, 1842–63, *The Book of the Poets, p.* 138.

The advantage of the plan lies in what it gets rid of. To one who is not accustomed to it, Spenser's abundance is often oppressive: it is like wading among unmown grass. . . . It is not a poem like the Iliad, fiery, passionate, dramatic as life itself; it is all more like to a dream than to waking life. Its descriptions and pictures, it must be confessed, more resemble visions in the clouds than anything to be seen on the earth. And this, we apprehend, is what Coleridge must be understood to mean when he says that Spenser's descriptions are not, in the true sense of the word, picturesque; but then no more are Claude's landscapes picturesque. . . . He is surely one of the very greatest of painters in words; diffuse and florid, no doubt, rather than energetic and expressive; but of what affluence and prodigality of power and resources in his own style, of what inexhaustible ingenuity and invention, of what flowing freedom of movement, of how deep and exquisite a sense of beauty! He is, indeed, distinctively and pre-eminently the Poet of the Beautiful. . . . Spenser's verse is the most abundantly musical in English poetry. Even Milton's, more scientific and elaborate, and also rising at times to more volume and grandeur of tone, has not so rich a natural sweetness and variety, or so deep a pathos.—CRAIK, GEORGE L., 1845, *Spenser and his Poetry, vol.* III, *pp.* 123, 124, 125, 126.

We have thus a poet ungifted with the smiting directness of power, the soaring and darting imagination, of the very highest order of minds; a man sensitive, tender, grateful, dependent; reverential to the unseen realities of the spiritual world, defferential to the crowned and coroneted celebrites of the world of fact; but we still have not yet touched the peculiarities of his special genius. If we pass into the inner world of the poet's spirit, where he really lived and brooded, we forget criticism in the loving wonder and admiration evoked by the sight of that "paradise of devices," both "dainty" and divine. We are in communion with a nature in which the most delicate, the most voluptuous, sense of beauty is in exquisite harmony with the austerest recognition of the paramount obligations of goodness and rectitude. The beauty of material objects never obscures to him the transcendent beauty of holiness. In his Bowers of Bliss and his Houses of Pride he surprises even voluptuaries by the luxuriousness of his descriptions, and dazzles even the arrogant by the towering bravery of his style; but his Bowers of Bliss repose on caverns of bale, and the glories of his House of Pride are built over human carcasses.—WHIPPLE, EDWIN P., 1859–68, *The Literature of the Age of Elizabeth, p.* 211.

In Spenser's labyrinthine rhymes
I throw my arms o'erhead at times,
Opening sonorous mouth as wide
As oystershells at ebb of tide.
Mistake me not: I honour him
Whose magic made the Muses dream
Of things they never knew before,
And scenes they never wandered o'er.
I dare not follow, nor again
Be wafted with the wizard train.
No bodyless and soulless elves
I seek, but creatures like ourselves.
If any poet now runs after
The Faeries, they will split with laughter,
Leaving him in the desert, where
Dry grass is emblematic fare.

—LANDOR, WALTER SAVAGE, 1863, *Heroic Idyls, with Additional Poems, Works, vol.* VIII, *p.* 318.

His is the Germanic picture, but how beautiful are the colours with which it glows! What richness of that poetic sentiment with which English genius by reason of its depth and truth can animate nature! What beauty of language, what admirable propriety of epithet, what harmony of verse! . . . Spenser is one of the brightest glories of modern literature; and England may well be proud of him, for his genius was emphatically English.—BYRNE, REV. JAMES, 1863, *The Influence of National Character on English Literature, Dublin Afternoon Lectures on English Literature, vol.* I, *p.* 22.

If I spoke to you at all of him, I should soon weary your patience, for I could not speak briefly; I have so much regard and affection for him. I only mention him as one of the most remarkable instances that great poems are composed not in easy, lazy times, but when there is most work doing, and when there are the most strong and energetic men to do it. Spenser was fond of allegory. If he had lived in a leisurely age he might only have been an inventor of conceits and allegories. But he was a patriot; he visited Ireland and saw its miseries; he loved his queen; he dreamed of a more glorious queen than she had ever been. So, whether his book is called an allegory or not, it tells of real and not sham fights, fights in which you and I are engaged. When we read him, we need not trouble ourselves much about Fairy-land. Here, in this land, amidst our own hills and valleys, in the streets of that city where Spenser was born and died, in the streets of every English town, we shall find plenty of evil enchanters, and also divine helpers who can overcome them for us all.—MAURICE, FREDERICK DENISON, 1865, *The Friendship of Books and Other Lectures, p.* 84.

Beautiful vision! creature of the poet's soul! "heavenly Una with thy milk-white lamb!" let us, ere thou fadest away, look on thy brightness; that we may take thy picture into our hearts—even as the sunlight transfers the features of those we love into the darkened chamber, and fixes them for ever. Pure and holy and tender—and, above all, true. True when solitary and unprotected—true when assailed by falsehood. Strong and steadfast under trials unmerited, when the manhood of thy knight gave way, because he was frail and faulty. Type of all that woman should be: without a thought to mar thine innocence, or a speck to cloud thy purity!—WALLER, JOHN FRANCIS, 1870, *Pictures from English Literature, p.* 20.

In fact, among all these poems there is one truly divine, so divine that the reasoners of succeeding ages have found it wearisome, that even now but few understand it—Spenser's "Faërie Queene." Spenser's characteristic is the vastness and the overflow of picturesque invention. Like Rubens, he creates whole scenes, beyond the region of all traditions, to express distinct ideas. As with Rubens, his allegory swells its proportions beyond all rule, and withdraws fancy from all law, except in so far as it is necessary to harmonise forms and colours. For, if ordinary spirits receive from allegory a certain oppression, lofty imaginations receive wings which carry them aloft. Rescued by it from the common conditions of life, they can dare all things, beyond imitation, apart from probability, with no other guide but their inborn energy and their shadowy instincts.—TAINE, H. A., 1871, *History of English Literature, tr. Van Laun, vol.* I, *bk.* ii, *ch.* i, *pp.* 179, 195.

Profoundly earnest, and the work of a pure mind, the "Faerie Queene" is yet bitter at core. It is the work of a great poet, who felt and expressed both the essence and the accidents of the great struggle in which he was himself a combatant. Through all its delicious melody it breathes a stern defiance of whatever cause was not, in the eyes of a true-hearted Elizabethan Puritan, the cause of God. The deeper allegory that expresses abstract truth holds on throughout the "Faerie Queene" its steady course, but it is conveyed through many references, in their own time not in the least obscure, to affairs of England, Ireland, France, Spain, Belgium.—MORLEY, HENRY, 1873, *First Sketch of English Literature, p.* 456.

The appearance of the "Faerie Queen" is the one critical event in the annals of English poetry; it settled, in fact, the question whether there was to be such a thing as English poetry or not. . . . The new English verse has been true to the source from which it sprang, and Spenser has always been "the poet's poet." But in his own day he was the poet of England at large. The "Faerie Queen" was received with a burst of general welcome. It became "the delight of every accomplished gentleman, the model of every poet, the solace of every soldier." The poem expressed, indeed, the very life of the time. . . . The gorgeous colouring, the profuse and often complex imagery which Spenser's imagination lavishes, leave no sense of confusion in the reader's mind. Every figure, strange as it may be, is seen clearly and distinctly as it passes by. It is in this calmness, this serenity, this spiritual elevation of the "Faerie Queen," that we feel the new life of the coming age moulding into ordered and harmonious form the life of the Renascence. . . . He is habitually serious, and the seriousness of his poetic tone reflects the seriousness of his poetic purpose.—GREEN, JOHN RICHARD, 1874, *A Short History of the English People, ch.* vii.

That, when the personal allusions have lost their meaning and the allegory has become a burden, the book should continue to be read with delight, is proof enough, were any wanting, how full of life and light and the other-worldliness of poetry it must be. As a narrative it has, I think, every fault of which that kind of writing is capable. . . . His natural tendency is to shun whatever is sharp and abrupt. He loves to prolong emotion, and lingers in his honeyed sensations like a bee in the translucent cup of a lily. So entirely are beauty and delight in it the native element of Spenser, that, whenever in the "Faery Queen" you come suddenly on the moral, it gives you a shock of unpleasant surprise, a kind of grit, as when one's teeth close on a bit of gravel in a dish of strawberries and cream. He is the most fluent of our poets. Sensation passing through emotion into revery is a prime quality of his manner. And to read him puts one in the condition of revery, a state of mind in which our thoughts and feelings float motionless, as one sees fish do in a gentle stream, with just enough vibration of their fins to keep themselves from going down with the current, while their bodies yield indolently to all its soothing curves. He chooses his language for its rich canorousness rather than for intensity of meaning. To characterize his style in a single word, I should call it *costly*. None but the daintiest and nicest phrases will serve him, and he allures us from one to the other with such cunning baits of alliteration, and such sweet lapses of verse, that never any word seems more eminent than the rest, nor detains the feeling to eddy around it, but you must go on to the end before you have time to stop and muse over the wealth that has been lavished on you.—LOWELL, JAMES RUSSELL, 1875–90, *Spenser, Prose Works, Riverside ed.. vol.* IV, *pp.* 320, 334.

"The Faerie Queen" is the noblest monument of the fine cultivation of Elizabeth's age.—CREIGHTON, MANDELL, 1876, *The Age of Elizabeth, p.* 210.

An embattled cloudland lit by the most transfiguring tints of the rising and the setting sun.—ROSSETTI, WILLIAM MICHAEL, 1878, *Lives of Famous Poets, p.* 31.

So multifarious is the poem, full of all that he thought, or observed, or felt; a receptacle, without much care to avoid repetition, or to prune, correct, and condense, for all the abundance of his ideas, as they welled forth in his mind day by day. It is really a collection of separate tales and allegories, as much as the "Arabian Nights," or as its counterpart and rival of our own century, the "Idylls of the King." As a whole, it is confusing; but we need not treat it as a whole. Its continued interest soon breaks down. But it is probably best that Spenser gave his mind the vague freedom which suited it, and that he did not make efforts to tie himself down to his pre-arranged but too ambitious plan. We can hardly lose our way in it, for there is no way to lose. It is a wilderness in which we are left to wander. But there may be interest and pleasure in a wilderness, if we are prepared for the wandering.—CHURCH, RICHARD WILLIAM, 1879, *Spenser (English Men of Letters), p.* 128.

The pleasure derived from that poem to most minds is, I am convinced, analogous to that already spoken of as being imparted by a foreign author: namely, the satisfaction at finding it—in places—intelligible. For the few who possess the poetic faculty it has great beauties, but I observe, from the extracts that appear in Poetic Selections and the like, that the most tedious and even the most monstrous passages are those which are generally offered for admiration. The case of Spenser in this respect—which does not stand alone in ancient English literature—has a curious parallel in art, where people are positively found to go into ecstasies over a distorted limb or a ludicrous inversion of perspective, simply because it is the work of an old master, who knew no better, or followed the fashion of his time.—PAYN, JAMES, 1881, *Some Private Views, p.* 47.

I would sooner read through the whole poem than twenty pages of commentary. There is no mystery in its ground plan.—WASHBURN, EMELYN W., 1884, *Studies in Early English Literature, p.* 99.

It is not to the existence of allegory in Spenser that all save his fanatical admirers object; it is to the fact that this allegory, like Mrs. Malaprop's "on the banks of the Nile," is a rapacious and insatiable impostor who attracts and devours all living likenesses of men and women within reach. There is allegory also in Homer and in Dante; but prayers in Homer and qualities in Dante become vital and actual forms of living and breathing creatures. In Spenser the figure of a just man melts away into the quality of justice, the likeness of a chaste woman is dissolved into the abstraction of chastity. Nothing can be more alien from the Latin genius, with its love of clearness and definite limitation, than this indefinite and inevitable cloudiness of depiction rather than conception, which reduces the most tangible things to impalpable properties, resolves the solidest realities into smoke of perfumed metaphor from the crucible of symbolic fancy, and suffuses with Cimmerian mist the hard Italian sunlight. Add to this the cloying sweetness of the Spenserian metre, with all "its treasures of fluidity and sweet ease" (as Mr. Arnold, with his usual studious felicity of exquisite phrase, has so perfectly described it), which leaves at least some readers, after a dose of a few pages, overgorged with a sense that they have been eating a whole hive's harvest of thick pressed honey by great spoonfuls, without one halfpennyworth of bread to this intolerable deal of sweet-stuff; and it is easy to determine why the attraction of this noble poet, for all his luminous colour and lovely melody, the raiment of high thinking, and fine feeling, is perhaps less potent than it should be over minds first nurtured on the stronger fare of Greek or Latin or Italian song.—SWINBURNE, ALGERNON CHARLES, 1886, *Short Notes on English Poets, Miscellanies, p.* 7.

We need go no farther than the first book of the "Faery Queen" for a proof that Spenser could illustrate human nature as well as allegorise the Passions; for its heroine, Una, is one of the noblest contributions which poetry, whether of ancient or modern times, has made to its great picture gallery of character.—DE VERE, AUBREY, 1887, *Essays Chiefly on Poetry, vol.* I, *p.* 7.

The dullest portions of Spenser's poem are those in which he works with most self-consciousness, piecing together definite meanings to definite symbols; where his love of beauty slumbers and his spirit of ingenuity awakes; where his ideas do not play and part and gather themselves together and deploy themselves abroad, like the shifting and shredding of clouds blown by soft upper airs, but are rather cut out with hard edges by some process of mechanism. . . . . Two qualities of Spenser's genius have made the "Faerie Queene" a poem, and saved it from becoming a frigid moral allegory or a mere masque of the fancy: one was his delight in sensuous beauty; the other his delight in lovely and heroic human character.—DOWDEN, EDWARD, 1887, *Transcripts and Studies, pp.* 287, 308.

I will not ask if you have read the "Faery Queen": I fear that a great many dishonest speeches are made on that score; I am afraid that I equivocated myself in youngish days; but now I will be honest in saying—I never read it through continuously and of set purpose; I have tried it—on winter nights, and gone to sleep in my chair: I have tried it, under trees in summer, and have gone to sleep on the turf: I have tried it, in the first blush of a spring morning, and have gone—to breakfast. Yet there are many who enjoy it intensely and continuously: Mr. Saintsbury says, courageously, that it is the only long poem he honestly wishes were longer. It is certainly full of idealism; it is full of sweet fancies; it is rich in dragonly horrors; it is crammed with exquisite harmonies. But—its tenderer heroines are so shadowy, you cannot bind them to your heart; nay, you can scarce follow them with your eyes: Now, you catch a strain which seems to carry a sweet womanly image of flesh and blood—of heartiness and warmth. But—at the turning of a page—his wealth of words so enwraps her in glowing epithets, that she fades on your vision to a mere iridescence and a creature of Cloud-land.—MITCHELL, DONALD G., 1889, *English Lands Letters and Kings, From Celt to Tudor, p.* 222.

To tune the sensibilities to the subtlest elements of poetic form, one need not go outside of the wide domain of the "Faerie Queene."—CORSON, HIRAM, 1892, *A Primer of English Verse, p.* 106.

The "Faerie Queene" came, and in it the second, if not the first, great poem in English. It is not necessary to call or think Spenser a greater poet than Chaucer in order to give the "Faerie Queene," as a great poem, the precedence over the "Canterbury Tales." In some qualities, at least, of the poet, the master had the advantage over the scholar. But in others, the scholar's greatest production has by an even greater interval the precedence over any single work of the master's. It has more unity, a deeper-ingrained and more individual colour, a subtler if less primitive charm, and, above all, it has the attraction of an individual and original and, to some fancies at any rate, an absolutely unequalled metrical medium. . . . Such a melodious burst had never sounded in the English tongue before. The wonderful web of imagination, woven so silently and cunningly in its pages, the splendid creations—not merely of poetic fancy but of actual character drawing and ethical construction—which it displays, the consummate skill in language and metre (the former, it may be, like the latter, a little mannered and artificial, but with such an exquisite manner, such a consummate art), the learning, the grasp, the evident reserve of sustained capacity behind—these were things which had never, or but once, been seen before among us.—SAINTSBURY, GEORGE, 1895, *Social England, ed. Traill, vol.* III, *pp.* 514, 515.

Assuredly, when all that cavillers can say or do is said and done, "The Faerie Queene" is deservedly called one of the greatest poems of English literature. From the high place it took, and took with acclamation, when it first appeared, it has, in fact, never been deposed. It has many defects and imperfections, such as the crudest and most commonplace critic can discover, and has discovered with much self-complacency; but it has beauties and perfections that such critics very often fail to see; and, so far as the status of "The Faerie Queene" is concerned, it is enough for the ordinary reader to grasp the significant fact that Spenser has won specially for himself the famous title of "the poets' poet." Ever since his star appeared above the horizon, wise men from all parts have come to worship it; and amongst these devotees fellow-poets have thronged with a wonderful enthusiasm. . . . The lights in his temple, so to speak, have never been extinguished—never have there been wanting offers of incense and of praise; and, to repeat in other words what has already been said, as it is what we wish to specially emphasise, amidst this faithful congregation have been many who already had or were some day to have temples of their own.—HALES, JOHN W., 1897, *Stories from the Faerie Queene, ed. MacLeod, Introduction, p.* viii.

Taken without relation to its time, it is a miracle of sustained and extended beauty; but considered historically, it is nothing less than a portent. . . . The greatest of all English poems of romantic adventure is steeped in the peculiar enchantment of the Celts. It often seems little more or less than a *mabinogi* extended and embroidered, a Celtic dream tempered with moral allegory and political allusion. Not in vain had Spenser for so many years inhabited that "most beautiful and sweet country," the Island of Dreams and melancholy fantasy. Cradled in the richness of Italy, trained in the mistiness of Ireland, the genius of Spenser was enabled to give to English poetry exactly the qualities it most required. Into fields made stony and dusty with systematic pedantry it poured a warm and fertilising rain of romance. — GOSSE, EDMUND, 1897, *Short History of Modern English Literature, p.* 84.

The "Faerie Queene" is the typical work of the English renaissance; there hamadryads, satyrs, and river gods mingle unblushingly with knights, dragons, sorcerers, hermits, and personified vices and virtues.—BEERS, HENRY A., 1898, *A History of English Romanticism in the Eighteenth Century, p.* 37.

Spenser is the only Renaissance poet who entered with simple seriousness into the spirit of the chivalric romance, neither dallying with it nor ridiculing it, but inspired by its elements of beauty and greatness. His wonderfully vivid imaginative power enabled him to bring together mediæval knights and ladies, Olympian gods and goddesses, and all the woodland troop of satyrs and nymphs, mingling, without the least discord or incongruity, with his allegorical personages and working out his scheme of Christian morality. — FIELD, LILIAN F., 1898, *An Introduction to the Study of the Renaissance p.* 119.

AMORETTI

1595

To our tongue the sonnet is mortal, and the parent of insipidity. The imitation in some degree of it was extremely noxious to a true poet, our Spenser; and he was the more injudicious by lengthening his stanza in a language so barren of rhymes as ours, and in which several words whose terminations are of similar sounds are so rugged, uncouth, and unmusical. The consequence was, that many lines which he forced into the service to complete the quota of his stanza are unmeaning, or silly, or tending to weaken the thought he would express.—WALPOLE, HORACE, 1795, *Letter to William Roscoe, Letters of Horace Walpole, vol.* IX, *p.* 454.

Spenser wrote all the sonnets which he finally published when he was forty years of age, under the title of "Amoretti,"—Little Loves. The title is good; but compared with what was to be expected of them, these Little Loves—not to speak it irreverently — are rather a set of dull, middle-aged gentlemen, images of the author's time of life, and of the commonplace sufferings which he appears to have undergone from a young and imperious mistress.—HUNT, LEIGH, 1859?-1867, *An Essay on the Sonnet, ed. Lee, vol.* I, *p.* 73.

Spenser's own love-story forms the subject of the "Amoretti" (1595). Amid so much fruitless sonnet-wooing as was then in vogue, one welcomes the advent of a poet who to many higher merits adds the very rare one of having prosecuted a successful suit; though it is not in the "Amoretti," but in the glorious nuptial ode published with them, the "Epithalamion," that Spenser celebrates his triumph most divinely. Notwithstanding the exceptional feature referred to, however, and the oft-recurring signature of his genius throughout, unprejudiced readers must acknowledge that these sonnets are disappointing.—MAIN, DAVID M., 1879, *A Treasury of English Sonnets, p.* 240, *notes.*

The "Amoretti" written in this metre, and undoubtedly representing some, at least, of Spenser's latest written work, rank with the best of Sidney's, and hardly below the best of Shakespere's while both of them and in the earlier sonnets the note of regret mingled with delight—the special Renaissance note — sounds as it rarely does in any other English verse.—SAINTSBURY, GEORGE, 1887, *History of Elizabethan Literature, p.* 87.

He has not Shakespere's supreme greatness, he is not a mountain oak in strength and grasp, but he is like the graceful poplar that shoots high its slender spire of boughs by some quiet stream. Spenser's love-sonnets, his Amoretti, as he calls them, have the same *spirituelle* sensuousness, the same winsome grace and refined simplicity which so charm us in the "Faerie Queen." In them we find the *naïveté* not of the rustic, but of the gentleman.—STANLEY, HIRAM M., 1897, *Essays on Literary Art, p.* 4.

EPITHALAMION

1595

Sweet Spenser, sweetest Bard; yet not more sweet
Than pure was he, and not more pure than wise;
High Priest of all the Muses' mysteries.
I called to mind that mighty Master's song,
When he brought home his beautifulest bride,
And Mulla murmured her sweet undersong,
And Mole with all his mountain-woods replied;
Never to mortal lips a strain was given,
More rich with love, more redolent of Heaven.
His cup of joy was mantling to the brim,
Yet solemn thoughts enhanced his deep delight;
A holy feeling filled his marriage-hymn,
And Love aspired with Faith a heavenward flight.

—SOUTHEY, ROBERT, 1816, *Carmen Nuptiale, ss.* 18-20.

Spenser married his Elizabeth, about the year 1593, and he has crowned his amatory effusions with a most impassioned and triumphant epithalamion on his own nuptials, which he concludes with a prophecy, that it shall stand a perpetual monument of his happiness, and thus it has been. The passage in which he describes his youthful bride, is perhaps one of the most beautiful and vivid *pictures* in the whole compass of English poetry.—JAMESON, ANNA BROWNELL, 1829, *The Loves of the Poets, vol.* I, *p.* 231.

No poet that ever lived had a more exquisite sense of the Beautiful than Spenser. Of profounder passion many poets have been blest or cursed with the power. His were indeed "thoughts that breathe," but not "words that burn." His words have a lambent light. Reading him is like gazing on the starry skies—or on the skies without a star—except perhaps one—the evening star—and all the rest of heaven in still possession of the moon. His love of woman's life is spiritual—yet voluptuous; and desire itself is hallowed, kindling at sight of beauty "emparadised in such sweet flesh." Nothing meretricious in the Lady of his Lays. Chaste as Dian the Creature of his bridal, his nuptial Hymn. —WILSON, JOHN, 1833, *Spenser, Blackwood's Magazine, vol.* 34, *p.* 852.

It is a strain redolent of a bridegroom's joy, and of a poet's fancy. The English language seems to expand itself with a copiousness unknown before, while he pours forth the varied imagery of this splendid little poem. I do not know any other nuptial song, ancient or modern, of equal beauty. It is an intoxication of ecstasy, ardent, noble and pure.—HALLAM, HENRY, 1837–39, *Introduction to the Literature of Europe, pt.* ii, *ch.* v, *par.* 67.

I know no poem that realises so directly and vividly the idea of winged words: no poem whose verses soar and precipitate themselves with such a vehemence of impetuous ardour and exultation. —MINTO, WILLIAM, 1874–85, *Characteristics of English Poets p.* 169.

The whole "Epithalamion" is very noble, with an organ-like roll and majesty of numbers, while it is instinct with the same joyousness which must have been the familiar mood of Spenser. It is no superficial and tiresome merriment, but a profound delight in the beauty of the universe and in that delicately surfaced nature of his which was its mirror and counterpart. —LOWELL, JAMES RUSSELL, 1875–90, *Spenser, Prose Works, Riverside ed., vol.* IV, *p.* 338.

The finest composition of its kind, probably, in any language: so impetuous and unflagging, so orderly and yet so rapid in the onward march of its stately and varied stanzas; so passionate, so flashing with imaginative wealth, yet so refined and self-restrained.—CHURCH, RICHARD WILLIAM, 1879, *Spenser, (English Men of Letters), p.* 167.

I have heard Wordsworth remark, more than once, that in its long and exquisitely balanced stanzas there was a swanlike movement and a subtle metrical sweetness, the secret of which he could never wholly discover; and the like of which he found nowhere else except in Milton's "Lycidas." —DE VERE, AUBREY, 1887, *Essays Chiefly on Poetry, vol.* I, *p.* 46.

To my mind the gracious humanity—the exquisite naturalness of this is worth an ocean of cloying prettinesses about *Gloriana* and *Britomart.* —MITCHELL, DONALD G., 1889, *English Lands Letters and Kings, From Celt to Tudor, p.* 229.

COLIN CLOUTS COME HOME AGAIN

1595

Nature, it is true, contains one secret by no means easily discovered when it has once been obscured; but the poets throw over that secret an almost impenetrable covering of words, figures, and symbols, making the task of discovery infinitely more difficult than Nature left it; not, indeed, the best of the poets, whose representations are so completely artistic, that the sense is never perverted to positively mischievous ends, though the reader may miss the true sense. In the poem we have had under examination the true sense may be missed by many; but it is an offence only against taste—we mean literary taste. It is merely a sort of childish mistake to imagine that "Colin Clouts" was designed in any manner to refer to Queen Elizabeth, and does no visible injury in the world. —HITCHCOCK, E. A., 1865, *Colin Clouts Explained, p.* 109.

In "Colin Clout," as a piece from real life the ablest and most interesting poem which Spenser has left us, the place of landscape is filled in high allegorical style by a record of the Loves of the Rivers around his Irish home. But when he has to describe his voyage to England, all the poet awakes, and we have a picture of the sea, and of a vast royal ship of the day, which has never been surpassed in English literature.—PALGRAVE, FRANCIS TURNER, 1896, *Landscape in Poetry, p.* 136.

HYMNS OF LOVE AND BEAUTY

1596

In verse there are Edmund Spenser's "Hymnes." I cannot advise the allowance of other his poems as for practick English, no more than I can Jeffrey Chaucer, Lydgate, Pierce Plowman, or Laureate Skelton. —BOLTON, EDMUND, 1624, *Hypercritica.*

Nowhere does his genius soar and sing with such continuous aspiration, nowhere is his phrase so decorously stately, though rising to an enthusiasm which reaches intensity while it stops short of vehemence, as in his "Hymns to Love and Beauty," especially the latter. There is an exulting spurn of earth in it, as of a soul just loosed from its cage. —LOWELL, JAMES RUSSELL, 1875–90, *Spenser, Prose Works, Riverside ed., vol.* IV, *p.* 316.

Spenser's two Hymns to Love and Beauty were the poetical fruits of his University education. These contain little that is original, but show a remarkable power of rendering the current philosophical ideas into clear and flowing verse. Visible things, the poet taught, following the main axiom of his master, are patterns of things invisible. . . . Beauty is not only an image of the Divine Mind, but an informing power in the soul.—COURTHOPE, W. J., 1897, *A History of English Poetry, vol.* II, *p.* 241.

He has an adoration for beauty worthy of Dante and Plotinus. And this, because he never considers it a mere harmony of colour and form, but an emanation of unique, heavenly, imperishable beauty, which no mortal eye can see, and which is the prime work of the great Author of the worlds.—TAINE, H. A., 1871, *History of English Literature, tr. Van Laun, vol.* I, *bk.* ii, *ch.* i, *p.* 181.

The claim of Spenser to be considered as a sacred poet does by no means rest upon his hymns alone. . . . But whoever will attentively consider the "Fairy Queen" itself will find that it is, almost throughout, such as might have been expected from the author of those truly sacred hymns. It is a continual, deliberate endeavour to enlist the restless intellect and chivalrous feeling, of an inquiring and romantic age, on the side of goodness and faith, of purity and justice. . . . Spenser then was essentially a *sacred* poet; but the delicacy and insinuating gentleness of his disposition were better fitted to the veiled than the direct mode of instruction. . . . To Spenser therefore, upon the whole, the English reader must revert as being preeminently the sacred poet of his country. —KEBLE, JOHN, 1825, *Sacred Poetry, London Quarterly Review, vol.* 32, *pp.* 225, 228, 231.

MOTHER HUBBARD'S TALE

In this Poem we have a specimen of Spenser's genius in Satire, a talent he very seldom exercised. This Fable is after the old manner of Chaucer, of whom it is an excellent imitation; and perhaps the antiquated style has no ill effect in improving the humour of the story: the morality of it is admirable. Every one will observe that keeness of wit, with which he has represented the arts of ill courtiers. In the description of a good courtier, which is so finely set off by the contrary characters, it is believed the author had in his view Sir Philip Sidney, of whom this seems to be a very just as well as beautiful picture. —HUGHES, JOHN, 1715, *ed. Spenser's Works, with Life.*

It is throughout an admirable imitatior of Chaucer in his quieter or more familiar manner; there is indeed nothing else nearly so truly Chaucerian in our later English poetry.—CRAIK, GEORGE L., 1845, *Spenser and his Poetry, vol.* III, *p.* 151.

This is almost an open satire, and shows that if Spenser's genius had not found a less mongrel style to disport itself in, not merely would Donne, and Lodge, and Hall, and Marston have had to abandon their dispute for the post of first English satirist, but the attainment of really great satire in English might have been hastened by a hundred years, and "Absalom and Achitophel" have been but a second. —SAINTSBURY, GEORGE, 1887, *History of Elizabethan Literature, p.* 87.

He who reads, in particular, "Mother Hubbard's Tale" will gain a fair conception of the way in which Chaucer sounded to men of the sixteenth century. There are lines in this piece that lack the proper number of syllables. There are lines that are remarkable for nothing so much as for their lack of harmony. There are entire passages that are throughout written in what would strike us as a lame and halting metre. In a writer whose natural melody is almost cloying in its smoothness and sweetness, such a deviation from his usual practice could not be due to accident. It was the result of design. It was adopted for no other reason than that Chaucer was believed to have furnished the example of this sort of ruggedness in the measure.—LOUNSBURY, THOMAS R., 1891, *Studies in Chaucer, vol.* III, *p.* 56.

A VIEW OF THE STATE OF IRELAND
1596

In a country-house once belonging to the Desmonds on the banks of the Mulla, near Doneraile, the first three books of the "Faery Queen" were written; and here too the poet awoke to the sad realities of life, and has left us, in his "Account of the State of Ireland," the most full and authentic document that illustrates its condition. This treatise abounds with judicious observations; but we regret the disposition to recommend an extreme severity in dealing with the native Irish, which ill becomes the sweetness of his muse.—HALLAM, HENRY, 1827, *The Constitutional History of England, vol.* II, *ch.* xviii, *par.* 3.

Spenser is the author of a sort of essay on the manners and antiquities of Ireland, which I prefer to his "Faerie Queene."—DE CHATEAUBRIAND, FRANÇOIS RENÉ, VICOMTE, 1837, *Sketches of English Literature, vol.* I, *p.* 227.

This state memorial still makes us regret that our poet only wrote verse: there is a charm in his sweet and voluble prose, a virgin grace which we have long lost in the artificial splendor of English diction. Here is no affectation of Chaucerian words: the gold is not spotted with rust. The vivid pictures of the poet, the curiosity of the antiquary, and, above all, a new model of policy of the practical politician, combine in this inestimable tract. —DISRAELI, ISAAC, 1841, *Spenser, Amenities of Literature.*

Spenser shows in this work the temper of a statesmanly official, with breadth of mind for embracing the subject generally, and an active mastery and ready manipulation of ways and means: there is nothing in it of the unpractical dreamer, or the vaguely discursive smatterer. — ROSSETTI, WILLIAM MICHAEL, 1878, *Lives of Famous Poets, p.* 29.

The author of "The Faery Queen" writes an excellent prose style. It is unaffected, clear, vigorous, straightforward. It exactly suits and serves its purpose. It does not play with words, or cultivate any verbal artifices. It is perfectly simple, and by its very simplicity impressive and forcible. Spenser "only speaks right on." He is too much in earnest to be decorative or florid. He wishes to definitely instruct, and to move in a special direction those whom he addresses, not merely to entertain and please them. But being a great master of expression he accomplishes this latter end also, though it is not his prime object. His well-formed sentences and his trenchant phrases continually remind us that we are listening to an artist born and bred.—HALES, JOHN W., 1893, *English Prose, ed. Craik, vol.* I, *p.* 455.

MISCELLANEOUS WORKS

Collins gone home, the glorie of his clime,
The Muses Mirrour, and the Shepheard's
Saint.
Spencer is ruined, of our later time
The fairest ruine, Faeries foulest want:
Then his *Time ruines* did our ruine show,
Which by his ruine we untimely know:
Spencer therfore thy *Ruines* were cal'd in,
Too soone to sorrow least we should begin.
—WEEVER, JOHN, 1599, *Epigrammes in the Oldest Cut and Newest Fashion.*

One* of the most finished and beautiful elegies in the English language.—TYTLER, PATRICK FRASER, 1833, *Life of Sir Walter Raleigh, p.* 121.

Out of the magic circle of the "Faerie Queen," there is nothing so beautiful in Spenser as "Muiopotmos." He is indeed the most poetical of entomologists. That winged Impersonation of Youth and Joy, holding in fee earth, middle-air, and heaven, seems a vision sent to reveal to us the secret of happiness lying among flowers spread far and wide over the domains of Innocence. There may we feast at will — so we dream—without sin and without surfeit—as upon dewey air from blossom-beds in purity exhaled. But till Death himself die, no breath is drawn apart from danger. Boy, sea-bold!—girl, starbright! Look—look—look there—Death at your arm and into your breast, crawling like a spider.—WILSON, JOHN, 1833, *Spenser, Blackwood's Magazine, vol.* 34, *p.* 843.

He first shows his mature hand in the "Muiopotmos," the most airily fanciful of his poems, a marvel for delicate conception and treatment, whose breezy verse seems to float between a blue sky and golden earth in imperishable sunshine. No other English poet has found the variety and compass which enlivened the octave stanza under his sensitive touch.—LOWELL, JAMES RUSSELL, 1875-90, *Spenser, Prose Works, Riverside ed., vol.* IV, *p.* 310.

*"Astrophel."

Closely connected both with Gabriel Harvey and with Philip Sidney, he made certain experiments in applying the principle of syllabic "quantity" to English verse, of which it need only be said that they were not less uncouth and barbarous than those of his master at Cambridge.—COURTHOPE, W. J., 1897, *A History of English Poetry, vol.* II, *p.* 252.

BRITAIN'S IDA

Extremely like Keats with a mixture of the Shakspearian play on words.—BEDDOES, THOMAS LOVELL, 1824–95, *Letters, p.* 5.

We are unwilling to exclude anything that has ever been imputed to Spenser; and although we are convinced, with T. Warton, that Spenser was not the author of "Brittain's Ida," as it is short, and possesses considerable merit of its own, we insert it. The reader will thus be able to form his own opinion. T. Walkley, who first printed it in 12mo. in 1628, only tells us that he was "certainly assured" that "it must be a work of Spenser's;" but he furnishes no evidence beyond what is merely internal, unless we also take into account the assertion of the writer of the not ungraceful preliminary verses, "'tis learned Spenser's Muse." It has a much more modern air than anything else Spenser has left behind him, and we do not believe that it was produced, at the earliest, until near the close of the reign of James I: in St. xi of Canto iii. the author speaks of his "new-born quill." The poem is not even an imitation of Spenser, nor, as far as we can judge, was it intended to be so.—COLLIER, JOHN PAYNE, 1862, *ed. Works of Spenser, vol.* V, *p.* 273, *note.*

GENERAL

Sorry I am that I cannot find none other with whom I might couple him in this *Catologue*, in his rare gyft of Poetry: although one there is, though nowe long since seriously occupied ine grauer studies, (Master Gabriell Haruey) yet, as he was once his most special friende and fellow Poet, so because he hath taken such paynes, not onely in his Latin Poetry . . . but also to reforme our English verse . . . therefore wyll I aduenture to sette them together, as two of the rarest witts and learnedest masters of Poetrie in England.—WEBBE, WILLIAM, 1586, *A Discourse of English Poetrie, ed. Arber, pp.* 35, 36.

Yet lest my homespun verse obscure hir worth,
Sweet Spencer let me leave this task to thee,
Whose neverstooping quill can best set forth
Such things of state, as passe my Muse and me.
Thou, Spencer, art the alderliefest swaine,
Or haply if that word be all to base,
Thou art Apollo, whose sweet hunnie vaine
Amongst the Muses hath a chiefest place.

—WATSON, THOMAS, 1590, *An Eglogue upon the Death of the Right Honorable Sir Francis Walsingham.*

Great Hobbinol on whom our shepherds gaze.—PEELE, GEORGE, 1593, *The Honor of the Garter, Ad Mæcenatem Prologus.*

Goe, weeping Truce-men, in your sighing weedes;
Under a great Mecænas I have p(l)ast you:
If so you come where learned Colin feedes
His lovely flocke, packe thence, and quickly haste you:
You are but mistes before so bright a sunne,
Who hath the palme for deepe invention wunne.

—LODGE, THOMAS, 1593, *Phillis.*

Dear Collin, let my Muse excused be,
Which rudely thus presumes to sing by thee,
Although her straines be harsh untun'd and ill,
Nor can attayne to thy divinest skill.

—DRAYTON, MICHAEL, 1594, *Endimion and Phœbe.*

Colin, I know that in thy loftie wit
Thou wilt but laugh at these my youthfull lines:
Content I am they should in silence sit,
Obscurd from light to sing their sad designes;
But that it pleased thy grave shepheardhood
The Patron of my maiden verse to bee,
When I in doubt of raging Envie stood,
And now I waigh not who shall Chloris see:
For fruit before it comes to full perfection
But blossome is, as every man doth know:
So these being bloomes, and under thy protection,
In time, I hope, to ripenes more will grow.
And so I leave thee to thy woorthy muse,
Desiring thee all faults heere to excuse.

—SMITH, WILLIAM, 1596, *Chloris, or the Complaint of the Passionate Despised Shepheard.*

At Colins feet I throw my yeelding reed;
But let the rest win homage by their deed.

—HALL, JOSEPH, 1597–8, *Virgidemiarum.*

Spenser to me, whose deep Conceit is such,
As passing all conceit needs no defence.

—BARNFIELD, RICHARD, (?) 1598, *To his Friend, Master R. I., in Praise of Music and Poetry.*

Maister Spenser, following the counsel of Tully in "De Oratore" for reviving of ancient words, hath adorned his own style with that beauty and gravity which Tully speaks of, and his much frequenting of Chaucer's ancient speeches causeth many to allow far better of him than otherwise they would.—BEAUMONT, FRANCIS, 1598–1602, *Epistle prefixed to Speght's Chaucer.*

Spenser, to me, whose deep conceit is such,
As, passing all conceit, needs no defence.
—SHAKESPEARE, WILLIAM, ? 1599, *The Passionate Pilgrim, s.* VI.

Fairy Queen show fairest Queen
How her fair in the is seen;
Shepherd's Calender set down
How to figure best a clown.
As for *Mother Hubberts Tale,*
Crack the nut and leave the shale;
And for other works of worth
(All too good to wander forth),
Grieve that ever you were wrote,
And your author be forgot.
—BRETON, NICHOLAS, 1600, *An Epitaph upon Spenser.*

Iud. A sweeter Swan than ever song in Po,
A shriller Nightingale then ever blest
The prouder groves of selfe admiring Rome.
Blith was each vally, and each sheapeard proud,
While he did chaunt his rurall minstralsie.
Attentive was full many a dainty eare.
Nay, hearers hong upon his melting tong,
While sweetly of his Faiery Queene he song,
While to the waters fall he tun'd (her) fame,
And in each barke engrav'd Elizaes name.
And yet for all this, unregarding soile
Unlac't the line of his desired life,
Denying mayntenance for his deare releife,
Carelesse (ere) to prevent his exequy,
Scarce deigning to shut up his dying eye.
Ing. Pity it is that gentler witts should breed,
Where thick skin chuffes laugh at a schollers need.
But softly may our (Homer's) ashes rest,
That lie by mery *Chaucers* noble chest.
—*Anon. The Return from Parnassus: or the Scourge of Simony,* 1606, *Act.* I, *sc.* 2.

Famous aliue, and dead, here is the ods,
Then God of Poets, nowe Poet of the Gods.
—MANNINGHAM, JOHN, 1602–3, *Diary, ed. Bruce, p.* 2.

Albions Mœonian Homer, natures pride,
Spenser, the Muses sonne and sole delight,
If thou couldst through Dianas kingdome glide,
Passing the Palace of infernall night,
(The sentinels that keepe thee from the light)
Yet couldst thou not his retchlesse worth comprise,
Whose minde containes a thousand purities.
—HARBERT, SIR WILLIAM, 1604, *A Prophesie of Cadwallader, etc.*

. . . *Colin Clout* began to tune his quill
With such deepe Art, that euery one was giuen
To think *Apollo* (newly slid from heau'n)
Had tane a human shape to win his loue,
Or with the *Westerne Swaines* for glory stroue.
He sung th'heroicke Knights of *Faiery* land
In lines so elegant, of such command,
That had the *Thracian* plaid but halfe so well,
He had not left *Eurydice* in hell.
. . . .
Diuinest *Spencer* heau'n-bred, happy Muse!
Would any power into my braine infuse
Thy worth, or all that *Poets* had before,
I could not praise till thou deseru'st no more.
—BROWNE, WILLIAM, 1616, *Britannia's Pastorals, Book* ii, *Song* i, *Works, ed. Hazlitt, vol.* I, *p.* 193.

Spenser's stanzaes pleased him not, nor his matter; the meaning of which Allegorie he had delivered in papers to Sir Walter Raughlie.—DRUMMOND, WILLIAM, 1619, *Notes of Ben Jonson's Conversations, ed. Laing, p.* 2.

Grave moral Spenser after these came on,
Than whom I am persuaded there was none,
Since the blind bard his Iliads up did make,
Fitter a task like that to undertake;
To set down boldly, bravely to invent,
In all high knowledge surely excellent.
—DRAYTON, MICHAEL, c 1627, *Of Poets and Poesie.*

Our sage and serious Poet *Spenser,* whom I dare be known to think a better teacher than *Scotus* or *Aquinas.*—MILTON, JOHN, 1644, *Areopagitica.*

An excellent scholar; but especially most happy in English Poetry, as his works do declare; in which the many *Chaucerisms* used (for I will not say *affected* by him) are thought by the ignorant to be *blemishes,* known by the Learned to be *beauties* to his book; which notwithstanding had been more saleable, if more conformed to our modern language.—FULLER, THOMAS, 1662, *The Worthies of England, ed. Nichols, vol.* II, *p.* 80.

Whose purple blush the day foreshows.
—DENHAM, SIR JOHN, c 1667, *On Mr. Abraham Cowley.*

The religion of the Gentiles had been woven into the contexture of all the ancient poetry with a very agreeable mixture, which made moderns affect to give that of Christianity a place also in their poems. But the true religion was not found to become fictition so well as a false had done, and all their attempts of this kind seemed rather to debase religion than to heighten poetry. Spenser endeavoured to supply this with morality, and to make instruction, instead of story, the subject of an epic poem. His execution was excellent, and his flights of fancy very noble and high, but his design was poor, and his moral lay so bare, that it lost the effect; it is true, the pill was gilded, but so thin that the colour and the taste were too easily discovered.—TEMPLE, SIR WILLIAM, 1689–90, *Essay on Poetry: Miscellanea.*

Spenser may be reckoned the first of our heroic poets. He had a large spirit, a sharp judgment, and a genius for heroic poetry, perhaps above any that ever wrote since Virgil, but our misfortune is, he wanted a true idea, and lost himself by following an unfaithful guide. Tho' besides Homer and Virgil, he had read Tasso, yet he rather suffered himself to be misled by Ariosto, with whom blindly rambling on marvels and adventures, he makes no conscience of probability; all is fanciful and chimerical, without any uniformity, or without any foundation in truth; in a word his poem is perfect Fairy-Land. —RYMER, THOMAS, 1693, *A Short View of the Tragedy of the Last Age.*

Milton has acknowledged to me that Spenser was his original.—DRYDEN, JOHN, 1700, *Fables, Preface.*

Spenser himself affects the Obsolete.

—POPE, ALEXANDER, 1733, *Imitations of Horace, Book* ii, *Epistle* i, *l.* 97.

A Writer in so endearing, and amiable a Vein, that, if I may judge of Others by my self, 'tis impossible to read his Works, without being in Love with the Author; without the greatest Curiosity to inquire into the Circumstances of his Life; or feeling the whole Soul interested in his good or evil Fortune. . . . No Writer ever found so near a Way to the Heart as He, and there is scarce a Beauty in his Verses, that has not the peculiar Happiness of recommending the Author to our Friendship, as well as our Admiration. For my own Part, when I read Him, I fancy myself conversing with the *Graces*, and am led away as irresistibly, as if enchanted by his own *Merlin*.—COOPER, ELIZABETH, 1737, *The Muses' Library, pp.* 253, 255.

No writer ever found a nearer way to the heart than he, and his verses have a peculiar happiness of recommending the author to our friendship as well as raising our admiration; one cannot read him without fancying oneself transported into Fairy Land, and there conversing with the Graces, in that enchanted region: In elegance of thinking and fertility of imagination, few of our English authors have approached him, and no writers have such power as he to awake the spirit of poetry in others. Cowley owns that he derived inspiration from him; and I have heard the celebrated Mr. James Thomson, the author of the Seasons, and justly esteemed one of our best descriptive poets, say, that he formed himself upon Spenser. —CIBBER, THEOPHILUS, 1753, *Lives of the Poets, vol* I, *p.* 99.

With all his faults, no poet enlarges the imagination more than Spenser. Cowley was formed into poetry by reading him; and many of our modern writers, such as Gray, Akenside, and others, seemed to have studied his manner with the utmost attention; from him their compounded epithets, and solemn flow of numbers, seem evidently borrowed; and the verses of Spenser may, perhaps, one day be considered the standard of English poetry.—GOLDSMITH, OLIVER, 1759, *Works, ed. Cunningham.*

Is this the land, where, on our Spenser's tongue,
Enamour'd of his voice, Description hung?

—CHURCHILL, CHARLES, 1764, *The Author, v.* 57–8.

Spenser was learned in Latin and Greek, as well as in Italian. But either the fashion of the times, or some deficiency in his own taste, inclined him to prefer the modern to the ancient models. His genius was comprehensive and sublime, his style copious, his sense of harmony delicate: and nothing seems to have been wanting to make him a poet of the highest rank, but a more intimate acquaintance with the classic authors.—BEATTIE, JAMES, 1769, *On the usefulness of Classical Learning, Essays, p.* 492.

John Bunyan in rhyme.—WALPOLE, HORACE, 1782, *Letter to Rev. William Mason, Letters, vol.* VIII, *p.* 235.

. . . that gentle Bard,
Chosen by the Muses for their Page of State—
Sweet Spenser, moving through his clouded heaven
With the moon's beauty and the moon's soft pace,
I called him Brother, Englishman, and Friend!

—WORDSWORTH, WILLIAM, 1799–1805, *The Prelude, Book* iii.

The prince of English poets. —RITSON, JOSEPH, 1802, *Bibliographia Poetica, p.* 343.

. . . my Spenser, who so well could sing
The passions all, their bearings and their ties;
Who could in view those shadowy beings bring,
And with bold hand remove each dark disguise,
Wherein love, hatred, scorn, or anger lies.

—CRABBE, GEORGE, 1807–34, *The Birth of Flattery, v.* 1–5.

But Spenser I could have read forever. Too young to trouble myself about the allegory, I considered all the knights and ladies and dragons and giants in their outward and exoteric sense; and God only knows how delighted I was to find myself in such society. As I had always a wonderful facility in retaining in my memory whatever verses pleased me, the quantity of Spenser's stanzas which I could repeat was really marvellous.—SCOTT, SIR WALTER, 1808, *Autobiography, Ashestiel MS., Lockhart's Life of Scott, ch.* i.

When I began "Childe Harold," I had never tried Spenser's measure, and now I cannot scribble in any other.—BYRON, LORD, 1812, *To Lord Holland, Letters.*

Spenser is rich and picturesque; his lyrics breathe an idyllic tenderness, and his muse is altogether redolent of the old Troubadours. Not his poetic treatment alone, his very language bears striking resemblance to the old German chivalric and love-song.—SCHLEGEL, FREDERICK, 1815, *Lectures on the History of Literature.*

To one who had by Mulla's stream
Fondled the maidens with the breasts of cream;
Who had beheld Belphœbe in a brook,
And lovely Una in a leafy nook,
And Archimago leaning o'er his book:
Who had of all that's sweet tasted, and seen
From silvery ripple, up to beauty's queen;
From the sequester'd haunts of gay Titania,
To the blue dwelling of divine Urania.

—KEATS, JOHN, 1816, *An Epistle to Charles Cowden Clarke.*

In Spenser, indeed, we trace a mind constitutionally tender, delicate, and, in comparison with his three great compeers, I had almost said effeminate; and this additionally saddened by the unjust persecution of Burleigh, and the severe calamities, which overwhelmed his latter days. These causes have diffused over all his compositions "a melancholy grace," and have drawn forth occasional strains the more pathetic from their gentleness. But nowhere do we find the least trace of irritability, and still less of quarrelsome or affected contempt of his censurers.—COLERIDGE, SAMUEL TAYLOR, 1817, *Biographia Literaria.*

His command of imagery is wide, easy, and luxuriant. He threw the soul of harmony into our verse, and made it more warmly, tenderly, and magnificently descriptive than it ever was before, or, with a few exceptions, than it has ever been since. It must certainly be owned that in description he exhibits nothing of the brief strokes and robust power which characterize the very greatest poets; but we shall nowhere find more airy and expansive images of visionary things, a sweeter tone of sentiment, or a finer flush in the colours of language, than in this Rubens of English poetry. His fancy teems exuberantly in minuteness of circumstances, like a fertile soil sending bloom and verdure through the utmost extremities of the foliage which it nourishes. —CAMPBELL, THOMAS, 1819, *An Essay on English Poetry.*

I was and am villainously ignorant of him; but I have bought him in folio and intend to read him piece-meal.—BEDDOES, THOMAS LOVELL, 1824–94, *Letters, p.* 4.

Spenser's great characteristic is poetic luxury. If you go to him for a story, you will be disappointed; if for a style, classical or concise, the point against him is conceded; if for pathos, you must weep for personages half-real and too beautiful; if for mirth, you must laugh out of good breeding, and because it pleaseth the great, sequestered man to be facetious. But if you love poetry well enough to enjoy it for its own sake, let no evil reports of his "allegory" deter you from his acquaintance, for great will be your loss. . . . Any true lover of poetry, when he comes to know him, would as soon quarrel with repose on the summer grass.

. . . Spenser is the farthest removed from the ordinary cares and haunts of the world of all the poets that ever wrote, except perhaps Ovid. . . . He is not so great a poet as Shakspeare or Dante;—he has less imagination, though more fancy, than Milton. . . . His remoteness from everyday life is the reason perhaps why Somers and Chatham admired him; and his possession of every kind of imaginary wealth completes his charm with his brother poets. Take him in short for what he is, whether great or less than his fellows, the poetical faculty is so abundantly and beautifully predominant in him above every other, though he had passion, and thought, and plenty of ethics, and was as learned a man as Ben Jonson, perhaps as Milton himself, that he has always been felt by his countrymen to be what Charles Lamb called him, the "Poet's Poet." He has had more idolatry and imitation from his brethren than all the rest put together. The old undramatic poets, Drayton, Browne, Drummond, Giles and Phineas Fletcher, were as full of him as the dramatic were of Shakspeare. Milton studied and used him, calling him the "sage and serious Spenser;" and adding, that he "dared be known to think him a better teacher than Scotus or Aquinas." Cowley said that he became a poet by reading him. Dryden claimed him for a master. Pope said he read him with as much pleasure when he was old, as young, Collins and Gray loved him; Thomson, Shenstone, and a host of inferior writers, expressly imitated him; Burns, Byron, Shelley, and Keats made use of his stanza; Coleridge eulogized him; and he is as dear to the best living poets as he was to their predecessors. Spenser has stood all the changes in critical opinion; all the logical and formal conclusions of the understanding, as opposed to imagination and lasting sympathy.—HUNT, LEIGH, 1844, *Imagination and Fancy, pp.* 63, 64, 65.

Lakes where the sunsheen is mystic with
 splendour and softness;
Vales where sweet life is all Summer with
 golden romance;
Forests that glimmer with twilight round
 revel-bright palaces;
Here in our May-blood we wander, careering
 'mongst ladies and knights.

—MEREDITH, GEORGE, 1851, *Poems, Works, vol.* XXXI, *p.* 139.

Lord Chatham, according to Mrs. A. Pitt, was always reading Spencer. . . . She told Mr. Grattan that he had never read but one book,—"The Faëry Queene." . . . "He who knows Spencer," says Burke, "has a good hold on the English tongue." (Fox) liked a book of Spenser exceedingly, before something else.—ROGERS, SAMUEL, 1859, *Recollections, ed. Sharpe.*

But if Spenser's imagination was not comprehensive, precise, and bold, it was fertile, rich, and various. If he was destitute of profound passion and warm sympathy with his kind, he manifests a natural gentleness, a noble sentiment, and an exquisite moral purity, which thoroughly engage our interest and our esteem. The most characteristic quality of his mind is undoubtedly sensibility to beauty. This may account for whatever want of originality there may seem to be in his compositions, and for his dealing so little with real human concerns. Such a susceptibility would lead him to repose, rather than to action; to accept readily traditions of all sorts; to stand aloof from the harsh and vulgar facts of actual life; to linger among the mellow scenes of the past and in the twilight realms of fancy; to dream over the ruins of time, obsolete institutions, and creeds outworn. Most peculiar is the modification which this faculty, combined with moral purity, gives to his love of woman. Voluptuous though this be, it is ever controlled and chastened by a predominant feeling of the beauty of holiness. Spenser's most extraordinary power is that of language, the power of conveying impressions by sounds. It is through the ear more than the eye that he achieves his triumphs, and he makes up by his mastery over this art for many other deficiencies. The pathos of his verse affects us when his sentiments do not. In him more than in any other of our poets do music and sweet poetry agree; one of the arts is complementary to the other, and he produces some of the effects of both. No instrument known before his time was capable of expressing his deep and complex harmonies, and he invented one which many a genius has since touched skilfully, but none with the hand of the master, who, through nearly four thousand stanzas, adapted it to a great variety of subjects and proved it equal to all.—

CHILD, FRANCIS J., 1859, *ed. Poetical Works of Spenser, Memoir, vol.* I, *p.* lv.

Spenser's verse is fluid and rapid, no doubt, but there are more ways than one of being fluid and rapid, and Homer is fluid and rapid in quite another way than Spenser. Spenser's manner is no more Homeric than is the manner of the one modern inheritor of Spenser's beautiful gift; the poet, who evidently caught from Spenser his sweet and easy-slipping movement, and who has exquisitely employed it; a Spenserian genius, nay, a genius by natural endowment richer probably than even Spenser; that light which shines so unexpected and without fellow in our century, an Elizabethan born too late, the early lost and admirably gifted Keats.—ARNOLD, MATTHEW, 1861, *On Translating Homer, Lecture* iii.

Spenser was reproached in his own time with an excess of archaisms; but the real fault of his diction lies rather in the use of forms and expressions which had become obsolete because they deserved to perish, for which no good authority could be cited, and which were, probably, unauthorized coinages of the inferior poets from whom Spenser took them, or in many cases perhaps licenses of his own. In the employment of words of these classes, he is often far from happy, but in the mastery of the true English of his time, in acute sensibility of ear and exquisite skill in the musical arrangement of words, he has no superior in the whole compass of English literature. . . . The most striking peculiarity of Spenser's diction is analogous to that which I have before mentioned as one of Chaucer's greatest merits—a rare felicity in verbal combinations—and in Spenser it chiefly consists in a very nice sense of congruity in the choice and application of epithets. His adjectives not only qualify the noun, but they are so adapted to it, that they heighten or intensify its appropriate meaning; and they are often used with a reference to the radical sense of the noun, which shows that Spenser knew how to press even etymology into use as a means of the embellishment of poetical diction. The "Faery Queene" is at present more studied, I believe, than it was a century since; but the "Shepherd's Calendar," which is less familiarly known, is full of most exquisite poetry, and the minor works of Spenser are scarcely less interesting to the reader of taste, and to the philologist, than his great allegorical epic.—MARSH, GEORGE P., 1862, *The Origin and History of the English Language, etc., p.* 548.

Spenser's chaste soul.—HOLMES, OLIVER WENDELL, 1864, *Shakespeare, Tercentennial Celebration.*

He is always imaging; it is his specialty. He has but to close his eyes, and apparitions arise; they abound in him, crowd, overflow; in vain he pours them forth; they continually float up, more copious and more dense. Many times, following the inexhaustible stream, I have thought of the vapours which rise incessantly from the sea, ascend, sparkle, commingle their gold and snowy scrolls, while beneath them new mists arise, and others again beneath, and the splendid procession never grows dim or ceases. . . . He is epic, that is, a narrator, and not a singer like an ode-writer, nor a mimic like a playwriter. No modern is more like Homer. Like Homer and the great epic-writers, he presents consecutive and noble, almost classical images, so nearly ideas, that the mind seizes them unaided and unawares. Like Homer, he is always simple and clear: he makes no leap, he omits no argument, he robs no word of its primitive and ordinary sense, he preserves the natural sequence of ideas. Like Homer again, he is redundant, ingenuous, even childish. He says everything, he puts down reflections which we have made beforehand; he repeats without limit his ornamental epithets. We can see that he beholds objects in a beautiful uniform light, with infinite detail; that he wishes to show all this detail, never fearing to see his happy dream change or disappear; that he traces its outline with a regular movement, never hurrying or slackening. He is even a little prolix, too unmindful of the public, too ready to lose himself and fall into a dream. His thought expands in vast repeated comparisons, like those of the old Ionic poet.—TAINE, H. A., 1871, *History of English Literature, tr. Van Laun, vol.* I, *bk.* ii, *ch.* i, *p.* 183.

There is much in Spenser that is contemporary and evanescent; but the substance of him is durable, and his work was the deliberate result of intelligent purpose and ample culture. . . . The cold obstruction of two centuries thaws, and the stream of speech once more let loose, seeks out its old windings, or overflows musically in unpractised channels. The service which Spenser did to our literature by this exquisite sense of harmony is incalculable. His fine ear, abhorrent of barbarous dissonance, his dainty tongue that loves to prolong the relish of a musical phrase, made possible the transition from the cast-iron stiffness of "Ferrex and Porrex" to the Damascus pliancy of Fletcher and Shakespeare. . . . The language and verse of Spenser at his best have an ideal lift in them, and there is scarce any of our poets who can so hardly help being poetical. . . . Spenser was an epicure in language. He loved "seld-seen costly" words perhaps too well, and did not always distinguish between mere strangeness and that novelty which is so agreeable as to cheat us with some charm of seeming association. He had not the concentrated power which can sometimes pack infinite riches in the little room of a single epithet, for his genius is rather for dilation than compression. But he was, with the exception of Milton and possibly Gray, the most learned of our poets. His familiarity with ancient and modern literature was easy and intimate, and as he perfected himself in his art, he caught the grand manner and highbred ways of the society he frequented. But even to the last he did not quite shake off the blunt rusticity of phrase that was habitual with the generation that preceded him. —LOWELL, JAMES RUSSELL, 1875–90, *Spenser, Prose Works, Riverside ed., vol.* IV, *pp.* 299, 303, 308.

With all one's allegiance to Spenser, it is trying to feel, much more to think, one's way through the tropically thorny luxuriance of his language. —GROSART, ALEXANDER B., 1876, *Memorial Introduction to Giles Fletcher's Poems, p.* 50.

Spenser's poetry is indeed the precise antipodes of Pope's, and its tender romance aimed against all those canons of common sense in which Johnson was the sturdiest of believers. For that reason his fairyland was a delightful retreat for poets weary with the prevailing rigidity of form and coldness of sentiment. Steele had tried to bring Spenser into notice in the "Tatler" and "Spectator." Thomson's charming "Castle of Indolence" and Shenstone's "Schoolmistress" were popular echoes of Spenser's style; Beattie makes his "Minstrel" confute Hume in Spenserian stanzas; William Thompson, Gilbert West, the defender of the Resurrection, Lloyd, the friend of Colman, Wilkie, of the "Epigoniad," Mickle, the translator of Camoens, and Cambridge, best known by the "Scribleriad," all wrote imitations of more or less elaborate kind; Collins loved Spenser, and Gray paid him a more discriminating homage than that of sheer imitation, for he never wrote a line himself without attuning his mind by first reading Spenser for a considerable time. Pope himself, it may be noticed, was a lover of Spenser in his boyhood, though a coarse burlesque seems to imply that he regarded him with no particular reverence. In fact, the poets of the eighteenth century, with one or two exceptions, show a disposition to edge away from the types which they professed to admit as ideally correct.—STEPHEN, LESLIE, 1876, *History of English Thought in the Eighteenth Century, vol.* II, *p.* 359.

Spenser's perception of beauty of all kinds was singularly and characteristically quick and sympathetic. It was one of his great gifts; perhaps the most special and unstinted. Except Shakespere, who had it with other and greater gifts, no one in that time approached to Spenser, in feeling the presence of that commanding and mysterious idea, compounded of so many things, yet of which the true secret escapes us still, to which we give the name of beauty. A beautiful scene, a beautiful person, a beautiful poem, a mind and character with that combination of charms, which, for want of another word, we call by that half-spiritual, half-material word "beautiful," at once set his imagination at work to respond to it and reflect it. His means of reflecting it were as abundant as his sense of it was keen. They were only too abundant. They often betrayed him by their affluence and wonderful readiness to meet his call.—CHURCH, RICHARD WILLIAM, 1879, *Spenser, (English Men of Letters), p.* 143.

In readiness of descriptive power, in brightness and variety of imagery, and in flow of diction, Chaucer remained unequalled by any English poet, till he was surpassed—it seems not too much to say, in all three respects—by Spenser.—WARD, ADOLPHUS WILLIAM, 1880, *Chaucer*, (*English Men of Letters*), *p.* 168.

No man ever set thought to sweeter music, and there are some who are content with a mere enjoyment of the outward charm of Spenser's manner, as if that were all. But Spenser was the Elizabethan Milton, Puritan like Milton with no narrow zeal against the innocent delights of life, but with grand yearning for the victory of man over all that opposed his maintenance of a pure soul obedient to God in a pure body obedient to the laws of Nature. Shakespeare was universal poet. He saw through the accidents of life to its essentials. But the accidents of his time are never out of Spenser's verse. He is a combatant poet.—MORLEY, HENRY, 1881, *Of English Literature in the Reign of Victoria, p.* 31.

To Chaucer a beautiful woman is a beautiful creature of this good earth, and is often nothing more; her beauty suddenly slays the tender heart of her lover, or she makes glad the spirit of man as though with some light, bright wine. She is more blissful to look on than "the new perjonette tree," and softer than the wether's wool; her mouth is sweet as "apples laid in hay or heath;" her body is gent and small as any weasel. For Spenser behind each woman, made to worship or to love, rises a sacred presence—womanhood itself. Her beauty of face and limb is but a manifestation of the invisible beauty, and this is of one kin with the Divine Wisdom and the Divine Love. In the poet of Edward's reign a gay and familiar side of chivalry is presented, which existed in life and in art and literature along with that chivalry which was the mysticism of human passion. The more modern poet retains of chivalry only what is exalted, serious, and tender.—DOWDEN, EDWARD, 1887, *Transcripts and Studies, p.* 305.

He is one of those few who can challenge the title of "greatest English poet," and the reader may almost of right demand the opinion on this point of any one who writes about him. For my part I have no intention of shirking the difficulty. It seems to me that putting Shakespere aside as *hors concours*, not merely in degree but in kind, only two English poets can challenge Spenser for the primacy. These are Milton and Shelley. The poet of "The Faërie Queene" is generally inferior to Milton in the faculty of concentration, and in the minting of those monumental phrases, impressive of themselves and quite apart from the context, which often count highest in the estimation of poetry. His vocabulary and general style, if not more remote from the vernacular, have sometimes a touch of deliberate estrangement from that vernacular which is no doubt of itself a fault. His conception of a great work is looser, more excursive, less dramatic. As compared with Shelley he lacks not merely the modern touches which appeal to a particular age, but the lyrical ability in which Shelley has no equal among English poets. But in each case he redeems these defects with, as it seems to me, far more than counterbalancing merits. He is never prosaic as Milton, like his great successor Wordsworth constantly is, and his very faults are the faults of a poet. He never (as Shelley does constantly) dissolves away into a flux of words which simply bids good-bye to sense or meaning, and wanders on at large, unguided, without an end, without an aim.—SAINTSBURY, GEORGE, 1887, *History of Elizabethan Literature, p.* 93.

And thus the first poet of the new era was yet more emphatically the last poet of the old—at once the morning star of England's later, and the evening star of her earlier literature. . . . Where Spenser is himself, the greatness of his ideal hangs around his poetry like the halo round the head of a saint. His poetry has that gift without which all others, including even that of imagination itself, leaves it but a maimed and truncated thing—a torso without a head. It has a soul. In this respect Spenser was as like Tasso as he was unlike Ariosto, whom he too often imitated, but from whom he derived little save harm. . .

I cannot but believe that those stains on the surface of Spenser's poetry which, though seldom snares to moral principle, are serious insults to moral taste, and need to be stepped over like bad spots on a road, came to him from the coarseness of the age in which he lived, and to which the great Elizabethan drama, excepting in the main Shakespeare, bears so deplorable a witness.—DE VERE, AUBREY, 1887, *Essays Chiefly on Poetry, vol.* I, *pp.* 3, 4, 21.

O master, it was not on oaten reeds
Thou madest music for the world's delight,
Nor yet on Pan's shrill pipe didst thou e'er
flute;
To sing of courtly grace and lordly deeds,
Of lovely Una and the Redcross Knight,
Behold! thou hadst Apollo's silver lute.
—KENYON, JAMES B., 1892, *At the Gate of Dreams, p.* 326.

No English poets have surpassed Spenser, in a melodious marshalling of words. —CORSON, HIRAM, 1892, *A Primer of English Verse, p.* 87.

Spenser stands alone, the one supremely great undramatic poet of a play-writing time. In his youth he had, indeed, composed nine comedies, now lost, but the quality of his genius was apart from the dramatic temper of his greatest poetical contemporaries. With a wonderful richness and fluency of poetic utterance, with the painter's feeling for color, and the musician's ear for melody, Spenser lacked the sense of humor, the firm grasp of actual life, indispensable to the successful dramatist.—PANCOAST, HENRY S., 1893, *Representative English Literature, p.* 80.

Of all the nobly endowed men of his time he was the most spiritual. One feels in him that marvelous identification of the saint and the artist which gives the work of Fra Angelico a kind of spiritual radiance.—MABIE, HAMILTON WRIGHT, 1893, *Short Studies in Literature, p.* 126.

The opulence of Spenser's muse will always be the despair of the anthologist. —QUILLER-COUCH, A. T., 1894, *The Golden Pomp, p.* 334, *note.*

Heaven pardon me! I do not care much for Spenser.—LOCKER-LAMPSON, FREDERICK, 1895, *My Confidences, p.* 177.

Great poet as Spenser was, yet his landscape dissappoints us. It seems to form an exception—we might perhaps call it a reaction—from the general quality of the English Nature-poetry we have been surveying. — PALGRAVE, FRANCIS TURNER, 1896, *Landscape in Poetry, p.* 133.

Generally speaking, during the first half of the seventeenth century the genius of the author of the "Faerie Queene" is a far more potent influence in English literature than that of the author of "Hamlet." —MULLINGER, J. BASS, 1897, *The Age of Milton, by Masterman, Introduction, p.* xv.

The place of Spenser in the History of Poetry is a very peculiar one. He cannot be ranked with the great poets whose universal ideas, applicable to human nature in all times and places, raised them to the empyrean of imagination—with Homer and Dante and Shakespeare. He cannot be ranked with that great, though secondary, order of inventors whose penetrating insight pierces through the outward shows surrounding them in their own age to the ideal truth of things — with Chaucer, Ariosto, and Cervantes. In most respects his position in the world of imagination is analogous to the position of Sidney in the world of action. Both were inspired by ideals springing out of a decaying order of society; and the same environment of circumstance which prevented Sidney from putting his theories of knighthood into practice gave an appearance of unreality to Spenser's epical conceptions. . . . Whatever virtue there is in the subject-matter of Spenser's poetry, proceeds not from the ideas themselves so much as from the mind of the poet.—COURTHOPE, W. J., 1897, *A History of English Poetry, vol.* II, *p.* 283.

It is neither possible nor wise to attempt here a catalogue of books especially adapted to children. I should myself put Spenser high in the list.—BATES, ARLO, 1897, *Talks on the Study of Literature, p.* 197.

Lyrics in these forms reach their chief perfection, perhaps, in the more literary poets, such as Spenser, Daniel, Drayton, Browne, Drummond, and Milton. In Spenser's "Epithalamion" and the "Four Hymns," especially, is exemplified what has been called the Greater Lyric, the long-breathed lyric of elaborate involutions in subject-matter and in metrical form, which in the seventeenth and eighteenth centuries is represented principally by the formal ode, Pindaric and otherwise. No one in English has managed this difficult form of art with such constancy of poetic inspiration, and such unfailing harmony of the parts and of the whole, as has Spenser.—CARPENTER, FREDERIC IVES, 1897, *English Lyric Poetry*, 1500–1700, *Introduction, p.* xxxvii.

Spenser's poetry is the very mirror of the times at their best. Its bright and chivalric spirit scorns money as much as it cherishes what money brings. — SCUDDER, VIDA D., 1898, *Social Ideas in English Letters, p.* 83.

George Puttenham

1530?-1600?

Born about 1530: died about 1600. An English author. He was educated at Oxford, and had traveled. The "Art of English Poesie" (1589) has been attributed to him, but there is a dispute as to his authorship. He wrote a number of other works, of which 14 or 15 are extant.—SMITH, BENJAMIN E., *ed.*, 1894–97, *The Century Cyclopedia of Names, p.* 832.

For though the poore gentleman laboreth greatly to proue, or rather to make Poetrie an art, and reciteth as you may see in the plural number, some pluralities of patterns, and parcels of his owne Poetrie, with diuers pieces of Partheniads and hymnes in praise of the most praisworthy; yet whatsoever he would proue by all these, sure in my poore opinion he doth proue nothing more plainly, then that which M. *Sidney* and all the learneder sort that haue written of it, do pronounce, namely that it is a gift and not an art, I say he proueth it, because making himselfe and so manie others so cunning in the art, yet he sheweth himselfe so slender a gift in it.—HARRINGTON, SIR JOHN, 1591, *Orlando Furioso, Preface.*

Of the dignity of Poetry much hath beene said by the worthy Sir *Philipp Sidney*, and by the gentleman which proved that Poets were the first *Politicians*, the first *Philisophers*, the first Historiographers.—CAMDEN, WILLIAM, 1605, *Remaines of Greater Works concerning Britaine, etc.*

Queen Elizabeth's verses, those which I have seen and read, some extant in the elegant, witty and artificial Book of the "Art of English Poetrie," the work as the fame is of one of her gentlemen-pensioners, *Puttenham*, are Princely, as her prose.—BOLTON, EDMUND, 1624, *Hypercritica.*

It contains many pretty observations, examples, characters, and fragments of poetry for those times, now nowhere else to be met with.—OLDYS, WILLIAM, 1738, *Life of Sir Walter Raleigh.*

Puttenham was a candid but sententious critic. What his observations want in argument is made up for by the soundness of his judgment; and his conclusions, notwithstanding their brevity, are just and pertinent.—HASELEWOOD, JOSEPH, 1811, *The Arte of English Poetry, Preface, Ancient Critical Essays, vol.* I, *p.* xi.

By far the most valuable work which was published in the province of criticism, during the life-time of Shakspeare, was written by *George Puttenham.*—DRAKE, NATHAN, 1817, *Shakspeare and his Times, vol.* I, *p.* 465.

Puttenham is perhaps the first who wrote a well-measured prose: in his "Art of English Poesie," published in 1589, he is elaborate, studious of elevated and chosen expression, and rather diffuse, in the manner of the Italians of the sixteenth century, who affected that fulness of style, and whom he probably meant to imitate. . . . In some passages of Puttenham, we find an approach to the higher province of philosophical criticism. — HALLAM, HENRY, 1837–39, *Introduction to the Literature of Europe, vol.* II, *pt.* ii, *ch.* vii, *par.* 9, 34.

Was this critic qualified by nature and art to arbitrate on the destines of the Muses? Were his taste and sensibility commensurate with that learning which dictated with authority, and that ingenuity which reared into a system the diversified materials of his critical fabric? We hesitate to allow the claims of a critic whose trivial taste values "the courtly trifles," which he calls "pretty devices," among the inventions of poesy; we are startled by his elaborate exhibition of "geometrical figures in verse;" his delight in egg or oval poems, tapering at the ends, and round in the middle; and his columnar verse, whose pillars, shaft, and capital can be equally read upwards and downwards. This critic, too, has betrayed his utter penury of invention in "parcels of his own poetry," obscure conceits in barbarous rhymes; by his intolerable "triumphals," poetical speeches for recitation; and a series of what he calls "partheniades, or new-year's gifts,"—bloated eruptions of those hyperbolical adulations which the maiden queen could endure, but which bear the traces of the poetaster holding some appointment at court. When the verse flowed beyond the mechanism of his rule of scanning, and the true touch of nature beyond the sympathy of his own emotions, the rhetorician showed the ear of Midas.—DISRAELI, ISAAC, 1841, *The Arte of English Poesie, Amenities of Literature.*

The most valuable part of this work is that which treats of the formal requisites of poetry, and especially of versification, because it throws a good deal of light on the pronunciation of that age—a subject respecting which we are far from being well informed. When, however, we compare these chapters of Puttenham with what had long before been accomplished in the Romance languages in the same branch of criticism — for example, with the Provencal Flors del Gay Saber, estier dichas Las Leys d'Amors, of the fourteenth century, published by Gatien Arnoult—we must admit that the technicalities of the poetic art, if instinctively practised, had been as yet but imperfectly discussed in England. — MARSH, GEORGE P., 1862, *Origin and History of the English Language, etc., p.* 552.

It must ever be remembered that this Ladies' book was first published anonymously; that the printer was or feigned to be in ignorance of its Author; that similarly Sir John Harington, in 1591, only refers to him as "that unknowne Godfather, that this last yeare saue on, viz. 1589, set forth a booke called the 'Arte of English Poesie,'" and again as that "same *Ignoto;*" and lastly, that the authorship of the work was never openly claimed by any of Elizabeth's contemporaries. — ARBER, EDWARD, 1869, *Puttenham, English Reprints, p.* 3.

Has given us the most complete and elaborate Elizabethan treatise of its kind. He upholds the dignity and universality of poetry, and affirms, with entire confidence, the possibility of an art of English poetry, as complete and as perfect as that of either Greece or Rome. While drawing many of his illustrations, both historical and other, from the classic and foreign authors, he does not hesitate to give his judgment of the previous English poets, although in this, as we have seen above, greatly limited, as to his contemporaries, by his courtly vision. In Puttenham's second book we have an intelligent and systematic presentation of the subject of the art of versifying, in which not a few of the real principles underlying the subject are clearly set forth. If the chatty old critic does go off into a needlessly particular examination of the *carmina figurata* anagram and other curiosities, we can pardon him for the humor and good sense which form the two pervading traits of this engaging book.—SCHELLING, FELIX E., 1891, *Poetic and Verse Criticism of the Reign of Elizabeth, p.* 94.

The writer shows wide knowledge of classical and Italian literature; in his sections on rhetoric and prosody he quotes freely from Quintilian and other Classical writers, and bestows commendation on English poets that is often discriminating. He may fairly be regarded as the first English writer who attempted philosophical criticism of literature or claimed for the literary profession a high position in social economy. Compared with it, Webbe's "Discourse of English Poetry" (1586) and Sidney's "Apologie for English Poesie," first published in 1595, are very slight performances. The "Arte" at once acquired a reputation. — LEE, SIDNEY, 1896, *Dictionary of National Biography, vol.* XLVII, *p.* 64.

Puttenham, who quotes his own verse freely and seems to have written it fairly in the stiffer manner of the first half of the reign, is rather a formalist, but his judgment, when he can get it out of stays, is not contemptible. The book is very full, learned, and careful, the work of a scholar and a gentleman, and far exceeding in detail and scope anything of the kind that was written for ages afterwards. —SAINTSBURY, GEORGE, 1898, *A Short History of English Literature, p.* 306.

Richard Hooker

1553-1600.

Born, at Heavitree, Exeter, March 1554 (?). Educated at Exeter Grammar School. To Corpus Christi Coll., Oxford, as Clerk, 1567; Scholar, 24 Dec. 1573; B. A., 14 Jan. 1574; M. A., 29 March, 1577; Fellow of C. C. C., 1577-81; Deputy to Prof. of Hebrew, July 1579. Rusticated, Oct. to Nov., 1579. Ordained, 1581 (?). Married Joan Churchman, 1581. Rector of Drayton-Beauchamp, Bucks, Dec. 1584 to March 1585.

Master of the Temple, 17 March 1585 to 1591. Rector of Boscombe, Wilts, 1591-95. Sub-dean and Canon of Salisbury, 1591. Rector of Bishopsbourne, Canterbury, July 1595, till his death. Died, at Bishopsbourne, 2 Nov. 1600. Buried in Bishopsbourne church. *Works:* "Of the Lawes of Ecclesiastical Politie," Bks. i.-iv. (1594?); Bk. v., 1597. *Posthumous* (the first six of the following edited by H. Jackson): "Answer to the Supplication that Mr. Travers made to the Council," 1612; "A Learned Discourse of Justification," 1612; "A Learned Sermon of the Nature of Pride," 1612; "A Remedie against Sorrow and Fear," 1612; "A Learned and Comfortable Sermon of the Certainty . . . of Faith," 1612; "Two Sermons upon part of St. Jude's Epistles," 1614; "Of the Lawes of Ecclesiastical Politie," Bks. vi., viii., 1648; Bk. vii. (previously reported lost), in 1662 edn. of Hooker's "Works." *Collected Works:* ed. by Gauden, 1662; ed. by Keble, 7th edn. ed. by Dean Church and Canon Paget, 1888.—SHARP, R. FARQUHARSON, 1897, *A Dictionary of English Authors, p.* 137.

PERSONAL

SUNT MELIORA MIHI.

RICHARDUS HOOKER EXONIENSIS SCHOLARIS SOCIUSQ: COLLEGII CORP. XTII OXON. DEINDE LONDINIIS TEMPLI INTERIORIS IN SACRIS MAGISTER RECTORQ: HUJUS ECCLÆSCRIPSIT VIII LIBROS POLIITIÆ ECCLESIASTICÆ ANGLICANÆ, QUORUM TRES DESIDERANTUR. OBIIT AN$_o$. DOM. MDC. AETATIS SUÆ L.

POSUIT HOC PIISSIMO VIRO MONUMENTUM AN°. DOM. MDCXXXIII. GULIELMUS COWPER ARMIGER IN CHRISTO JESU QUEM GENUIT PER EVANGELIUM. 1 COR. IV. 15.—*Inscription on Monument.*

One of a solid judgment and great reading. Yea, such the depth of his learning, that his pen was a better bucket than his tongue to draw it out; a great defender both by preaching and writing of the discipline of the church of England, yet never got (nor cared to get) any eminent dignity therein; conscience, not covetousness, engaging him in the controversy. Spotless was his conversation; and, though some dirt was cast, none could stick on his reputation. . . . Mr. Hooker's voice was low, stature little, gesture none at all, standing stone-still in the pulpit, as if the posture of his body were the emblem of his mind, unmovable in his opinions. Where his eye was left fixed at the beginning, it was found fixed at the end of his sermon. In a word, the doctrine he delivered had nothing but itself to garnish it. His style was long and pithy, driving on a whole flock of several clauses before he came to the close of a sentence. So that when the copiousness of his style met not with proportionable capacity in his auditors, it was unjustly censured for perplexed, tedious, and obscure. His sermons followed the inclination of his studies, and were for the most part on controversies, and deep points of school-divinity.—FULLER, THOMAS, 1655, *The Church History of Britain, bk..* IX, *sec.* vii, *par.* 50, 53.

By this marriage the good man was drawn from the tranquility of his College; from that garden of piety, of pleasure, of peace, and a sweet conversation, into the thorny wilderness of a busy world; into those corroding cares that attend a married Priest, and a country Parsonage. . . And in this condition he continued about a year; in which time his two pupils, Edwin Sandys and George Cranmer, took a journey to see their tutor; where they found him with a book in his hand, — it was the Odes of Horace, — he being then like humble and innocent Abel, tending his small allotment of sheep in a common field; which he told his pupils he was forced to do then, for that his servant was gone home to dine, and assist his wife to do some necessary household business. But when his servant returned and released him, then his two pupils attended him unto his house, where their best entertainment was his quiet company, which was presently denied them; for Richard was called to rock the cradle; and the rest of their welcome was so like this, that they staid but till next morning, which was time enough to discover and pity their tutor's condition; and they having in that time rejoiced in the remembrance, and then paraphrased on many of the innocent recreations of their younger days, and other like diversions, and thereby given him as much present comfort as they were able, they were forced to leave him to the company of his wife Joan, and seek themselves a quieter lodging for next night. But at their parting from him, Mr. Cranmer said, "Good tutor, I am sorry your lot is fallen in no better ground, as to your parsonage; and more sorry that your wife proves not a more comfortable companion, after you have wearied yourself in your restless studies." To whom the good man replied, "My dear George, if Saints have usually a double share in the miseries of this life, I, that am none, ought not to repine at what my wise Creator hath appointed for me: but labour — as indeed I do daily — to submit mine to his will, and possess my soul in patience and peace." — WALTON, ISAAC, 1665, *The Life of Mr. Richard Hooker.*

Hooker's nature was essentially an intellectual one; and the wonder of his mental biography is the celerity and certainty with which he transmuted knowledge and experience into intelligence. It may be a fancy, but we think it can be detected in an occasional uncharacteristic tartness of expression, that he had carried up even Mrs. Hooker into the region of his intellect, and dissolved her termagant tongue into a fine spiritual essence of gentle sarcasm. Not only did his vast learning pass, as successively acquired, from memory into faculty, but the daily beauty of his life left its finest and last result in his brain. His patience, humility, disinterestedness, self-denial, his pious and humane sentiments, every resistance to temptation, every benevolent act, every holy prayer, were by some subtle chemistry turned into thought, and gave his intellect an upward lift, — increasing the range of its vision, and bringing it into closer proximity with great ideas. We cannot read a page of his writings, without feeling the presence of this spiritual power in conception, statement, and argument. And this moral excellence, which has thus become moral intelligence, this holiness which is in perfect union with reason, this spirit of love which can not only feel but see, gives a softness, richness, sweetness, and warmth to his thinking, quite as peculiar to it as its dignity, amplitude, and elevation. — WHIPPLE, EDWIN P., 1859–68, *The Literature of the Age of Elizabeth, p.* 351.

Go back yet a few years further, to the beginning of that century, carry back your thoughts to the month of November in the year 1600, when in this very church of Bishopsbourne, from the simple mansion close by, was borne to his last resting-place, beside the altar and the pulpit where he had ministered during his later years, Richard Hooker. For him, too, was raised a living likeness, yet more living than either of the other two, the only likeness of him that exists, as he appeared in his college-cap, small and frail in stature and form, with his quick, deep-set eyes, his broad, high forehead, his freckled face, and his closed lips. The grave in Bishopsbourne Church is, I grant, far from equal in fame to the other two. It has but a British, and not a world-wide glory. The genius of the "Ecclesiastical Polity" is not the genius of the "Novum Organum," or of "Hamlet" and "Othello." But still it may be said, without fear of contradiction, that if Bacon is the first of English philosophers, and Shakespeare the greatest of English poets, Hooker is the first and greatest of English theologians; and farther, that, even in that fruitful age, there is no other English writer to be placed on a level with these three. — STANLEY, ARTHUR PENRHYN, 1873, *Richard Hooker, Good Words, vol.* 14, *p.* 27.

Hooker was then nineteen, and his pupil —afterwards Sir Edwin Sandys, author of the "Speculum Europæ"—not very much younger; but the bishop wisely sought for his boy a tutor and friend who, as he said, "shall teach him learning by instruction and virtue by example: and my greatest care shall be of the last." George Cranmer (nephew's son to the archbishop) and other pupils soon joined Sandys, and found in Hooker a tutor with a rare power of communicating what he knew, and a life unostentatiously devout that stirred their affections. His health was not vigorous, and weakened by a sedentary life of study. He was short, stooping, very short-sighted, and subject to pimples: so shy and gentle that any pupil could look him out of countenance. He could look no man hard in the face, but had the habitual down look that Chaucer's host in the "Canterbury Tales" is made to ascribe to the poet. When Hooker was a rector, he and his clerk never talked but with both their hats off together. He was never known to be angry, never heard to repine, could be witty without the use of an ill word, and by his presence restrained what was unfit, without abating what was innocent, in the mirth of others. — MORLEY, HENRY, 1892, *English Writers, vol.* IX, *p.* 418.

GENERAL

All things written in this booke I humbly and meekly submit to the censure of the grave and reverend Prelates within this land, to the judgment of learned men, and the sober consideration of all others. Wherein I may happely erre as others before me have done, but an heretike by the help of Almighty God I will never be.—HOOKER, RICHARD, 1599, *MS. Note on the Title Leaf of the "Christian Letter."*

His Book of "Ecclesiastical Politie" is prized by all generally, save such who out of ignorance cannot, or envy will not understand it. But there is a kind of people who have a pike at him, and therefore read his Book with a prejudice; that, as Jephtha vowed to sacrifice the first living thing which met him, these are resolved to quarrel with the first word which occureth therein. Hereupon it is, that they take exception at the very Title thereof, "Ecclesiastical Politie," as if unequally yoked; Church with some mixture of Citynesse; that the Discipline, *jure divino*, may bowe to Humane Inventions. But be it reported to the judicious, whether, when all is done, a reserve must not be left for prudential supplies in Church Government. True it is, his Book in our late Times was beheld as an Old-Almanack grown out of date; but, blessed be God, there is now a Revolution, which may bring his Works again into reputation.—FULLER, THOMAS, 1662, *The Worthies of England, ed. Nichols, vol.* I, *p.* 290.

The English language hath been much cultivated during the last two hundred years.—But whatever other improvements it may have received, it hath made no advances in grammatical accuracy. *Hooker* is one of the earliest writers of considerable note within the period abovementioned: let his writings be compared with the best of those of more modern date; and, I believe, it will be found, that in correctness, propriety, and purity of English style, he hath hardly been surpassed, or even equaled, by any of his successors.—LOWTH, ROBERT, 1763, *Short Introduction to English Grammar, with Critical Notes, Preface.*

Such a sentence now sounds harsh in our ears. Yet some advantages certainly attended this sort of style; and whether we have gained or lost, upon the whole, by departing from it, may bear a question. By the freedom of arrangement which it permitted, it rendered the language susceptible of more strength, of more variety of collocation, and more harmony of period. But however this be, such a style is now obsolete; and no modern writer could adopt it without the censure of harshness and affectation. The present form which the language has assumed, has, in some measure, sacrificed the study of strength to that of perspicuity and ease. Our arrangement of words has become less forcible, perhaps, but more plain and natural: and this is now understood to be the genius of our language.—BLAIR, HUGH, 1783, *Lectures on Rhetoric and Belles Letters*, xviii.

Come, Hooker, with thee let me dwell on a phrase
Uncorrupted by wit, unambitious of praise:
Thy language is chaste, without aims or prétence;
'Tis a sweetness of breath from a soundness of sense.

—WEBB, DANIEL, 1787, *Literary Amusements.*

Hooker was undoubtedly a writer of superior merit. Whoever shall bestow upon him a diligent perusal, will find himself well rewarded by the venerable simplicity of his character, the profoundness of his thoughts, and the manliness of his eloquence. Those persons however have been, to say the least, very indiscreet friends to the fame of Hooker, who have held him up as a model of English style.—GODWIN, WILLIAM, 1797, *Of English Style, The Enquirer, p.* 383.

Far superior to Sir Philip Sidney in every requisite for good composition, the venerable HOOKER claims the highest station among the writers of Elizabeth's reign. If his language abound too much in inversions, it yet possesses a dignity and force, and in general an attention to grammatical accuracy, hitherto unknown to our literature. Even in the present day it may be read and admired. . . . The style of Hooker, however, is not without some striking defects; though the words for the most part are well chosen and pure, the arrangement of them into sentences is intricate and harsh, and formed almost exclusively on the idiom and construction of the Latin. Much strength and vigour are derived from this adoption; but perspicuity, sweetness, and ease are too generally sacrificed. — DRAKE, NATHAN, 1804, *Essays Illustrative of the Tatler, Spectator, and Guardian, vol.* II, *pp.* 9, 10.

Of the illustrious Hooker — whose memory is embalmed in the beautiful biography of him by Isaac Walton—it is sufficient to say, that his "Ecclesiastical Polity" is, of all works of that description, one of the most masterly and convincing. Never was logic more successfully employed to combat error and establish truth; and the vein of common sense, as well as of spiritual comfort, which pervades the pages of that Work, will render it, to the latest posterity, a popular as well as instructive performance.—DIBDIN, THOMAS FROGNALL, 1825, *The Library Companion, p.* 55.

Doubtless, Hooker was a theological Talus, with a club of iron against opponents with pasteboard helmets, and armed only with crab-sticks! But yet, I too, too often find occasion to complain of him as abusing his superior strength. . . . I begin to fear that Hooker is not suited to my nature. I can not bear roundabouts for the purpose of evading the short cut straight before my eyes.—COLERIDGE, SAMUEL TAYLOR, 1826, *Notes on Hooker, Literary Remains.*

The finest, as well as the most philosophical, writer of the Elizabethan period is Hooker. The first book of the "Ecclesiastical Polity" is at this day one of the masterpieces of English eloquence. His periods, indeed, are generally much too long and too intricate, but portions of them are often beautifully rhythmical; his language is rich in English idiom without vulgarity, and in words of a Latin source without pedantry; he is more uniformly solemn than the usage of later times permits, or even than writers of that time, such as Bacon, conversant with mankind as well as books, would have reckoned necessary: but the example of ancient orators and philosophers upon themes so grave as those which he discusses may justify the serious dignity from which he does not depart. Hooker is perhaps the first of such, in England, who adorned his prose with the images of poetry: but this he has done more judiciously and with more moderation than others of great name; and we must be bigots in Attic severity before we can object to some of his grand figures of speech. — HALLAM, HENRY, 1837–39, *Introduction to the Literature of Europe, vol.* II, *pt.* ii, *ch.* vii, *par.* 16.

He was an able champion for the ecclesiastical hierarchy. His work displays immense learning, reflection, and eloquence, and is still referred to as a great authority upon the whole range of moral and political principles. . . . The "Ecclesiastical Polity" has furnished, for nearly 200 years, an invaluable defence of the clergy to studious men. . . . Hooker is universally distinguished for long-drawn melody and mellifluence of language, and his works must find a place in every well-chosen clerical library. His eloquence has been deservedly praised; but the justice of the epithet "Judicious," which his admirers have attached to his name, is rather more questionable. Certainly there never was a more thoroughgoing advocate of things established than he has shown himself in the whole Fifth Book, forming more than a third part of the entire "Ecclesiastical Polity." — LOWNDES, WILLIAM THOMAS, 1839, *British Librarian, pp.* 380, 599.

The results of his publications were great and presently perceptible; a school of writers immediately sprung up, who by express reference, or style, or tone of thought, betray their admiration of Hooker; Covel, Edwin Sandys, Field, Raleigh, and others; and what was infinitely more important, Hooker had his full share in training up for the next generation, Laud, Hammond, Sanderson, and a multitude more such divines; to which succession and series, humanely speaking, we owe it, that the Anglican church continues at such a distance from that of Geneva, and so near to primitive truth and apostolical order. There have been and are those, who resort, or would be thought to resort, to the Books of "Ecclesiastical Polity," for conclusions and maxims very different from these. King James II., it is well known, ascribed to Hooker, more than to any other writer, his own ill-starred conversion to Romanism: against which, nevertheless, if he had thought a little more impartially, he might have perceived that Hooker's works every where inculcate that which is the only sufficient antidote, respect for the true Church of the Fathers, as subsidiary to Scripture and a witness of its true meaning. And the rationalists on the contrary side, and the liberals of the school of Locke and Hoadly, are never weary of claiming Hooker as the first distinct enunciator of their principles. Whereas, even in respect of civil government, though he might allow their theory of its origin, he pointedly deprecates their conclusion in favour of resistance. And in respect of sacramental grace, and the consequent nature and importance of Church communion, themselves have never dared to claim sanction from him.—KEBLE, JOHN, 1841, *ed. Works of Hooker, Preface, vol.* I, *p.* li.

What was transitory or what was partial in this great work may be subtracted without injury to its excellence or its value. Hooker has written what posterity reads. The spirit of a later age, progressive in ameliorating the imperfect condition of all human institutions, must often return to pause over the first book of "Ecclesiastical Polity," where the master-genius has laid the foundations and searched into the nature of all laws whatever. Hooker is the first vernacular writer whose classical pen harmonized a numerous prose. While his earnest eloquence, freed from all scholastic pedantry, assumed a style stately in its structure, his gentle spirit sometimes flows into natural humor, lovely in the freshness of its simplicity.—DISRAELI, ISAAC, 1841, *Hooker, Amenities of Literature.*

His works manifest great vigour of thought, eloquence of expression, soundness of judgment, and decidedly evangelical sentiment; his "Ecclesiastical Polity" is one of the bulwarks of the Established Church of England. — BICKERSTETH, EDWARD, 1844, *The Christian Student.*

However favourable the quiet of Corpus may have been to the meditation of such a work, the sheep, the cradle, and the wife Joan, may have had greater influence in the formation of its author's character, may have imparted to it less of a scholastic, more of an English, conservatism. For assuredly it is the work which, more perhaps than any in our language, embodies *that* conservatism, and distinguishes it from that other form of it which was conspicuous in "Nundinio" and the Ptolemaists whom Bruno ridicules. Hooker's sympathies would, no doubt, have been with them. If he and Bruno had met, they would not have had the slightest appreciation of each other's gifts or purposes. Now that he has become one of our classics, the reasons of our admiration are probably as little intelligible to accomplished foreigners—Frenchmen, Italians, Germans—as he himself would have been to a traveller of his own age. They would smile and shrug their shoulders if we presumed to call him a philosopher; they would find a ready, and by no means a wholly unfair solution of the influence he has acquired over us, in our preference of the actual to the ideal. Yet we are fully persuaded that the English judgment of two centuries and a-half, however affected by considerations specially belonging to ourselves, is a right one; that Hooker's principles have influenced the countries which care least for him, and that any sketch of moral or metaphysical inquiries would be grossly defective in which he was omitted.—MAURICE, FREDERICK DENISON, 1862, *Moral and Metaphysical Philosophy, vol.* II, *p.* 189.

Hooker's style is almost without a rival for its sustained dignity of march; but that which makes it most remarkable is its union of all this learned gravity and correctness with a flow of genuine, racy English, almost as little tinctured with pedantry as the most familiar popular writing. The effect, also, of its evenness of movement is the very reverse of tameness or languor; the full river of the argument dashes over no precipices, but yet rolls along without pause, and with great force and buoyancy. — CRAIK, GEORGE L., 1861, *A Compendious History of English Literature, and of the English Language, vol.* I, *p.* 612.

The diction of theology, perhaps I should say of English prose, reached its highest point of excellence in the works of Hooker. . . . The style of Hooker is sometimes unnecessarily involved and obscure, and he is fond of Latinisms, both in words and in the arrangements of his periods. . . . Hooker's periods are sometimes cumbrous and involved, partly from the influence of his devotion to Latin theological literature, and partly from his desire to accompany his general propositions with the conditions, qualifications, and limitations belonging to them; but he has many passages of the most admirable rhetorical beauty, and of a musical flow not less melodious than that of the periods of Milton. — MARSH, GEORGE P., 1862, *Origin and History of the English Language, etc., pp.* 559, 560.

Hooker — not indeed the greatest but perhaps the most majestic of English writers — was not more distinguished for his splendid eloquence than for his tendency to elevate the principles of natural right, and for his desire to make the Church independent of the State.—LECKY, WILLIAM EDWARD HARTPOLE, 1865, *Spirit of Rationalism in Europe, vol.* II, *p.* 183.

The learned and excellent Hooker, one of the sweetest and most conciliatory men, the most solid and persuasive of logicians, a comprehensive mind, who in every question remote from the principles introduces into controversy general conceptions, and the knowledge of human nature; beyond this, a methodical writer, correct and always ample, worthy of being regarded not only as one of the fathers of the English Church, but as one of the founders of English prose.—TAINE, H. A., 1871, *History of English Literature, tr. Van Laun, vol.* I, *bk.* ii, *ch.* v, *p.* 380.

Hooker's diction is not so modern as Sidney's. A glossary to Hooker would be at least ten times as large as a glossary to an equal amount of writing by Sidney. In great measure, of course, this is due to the difference of subject. By Swift he is coupled with Parsons the Jesuit as writing a purer style than other theologians of his time. He did not coin words like Jeremy Taylor, nor employ them in meanings warranted by derivation but not by usage—very common errors among his more pedantic contemporaries.—MINTO, WILLIAM, 1872–80, *Manual of English Prose Literature, p.* 215.

If the Church of England had never produced any other writer of the same stamp, it might have boasted in Hooker one of the noblest and most rational intellects which ever enriched Christian literature, or adorned a great cause. In combination of speculative, literary, imaginative, and spiritual qualities the 'Laws of Ecclesiastical Polity'' stands as a polemical treatise unrivalled. . . . Nowhere in the Literature of philosophy has ethical and political speculation essayed a profounder and more comprehensive task, or sought to take a broader sweep; and never has the harmony of the moral universe, and the interdependence and unity of man's spiritual and civil life, in their multiplied relations, been more finely conceived or more impressively expounded.—TULLOCH, JOHN, 1872, *Rational Theology and Christian Philosophy in England in the Seventeenth Century, vol.* I, *p.* 52.

The philosophical system of Hooker may be fairly accepted as akin to that of Lord Bacon; only it was far more explicit and comprehensive in its statements and more systematic in its form and completeness. It could not fail to exert a powerful influence on all subsequent discussions in metaphysical, ethical and political philosophy, anticipating as it does many of these discussions by providing the principles for their adjudication. — UEBERWEG, FREDERICH, 1873, *History of Philosophy, tr. Morris, vol.* II, *p.* 352.

Hooker, the first great prose writer of the Elizabethan age, shows the best results of the theological habit of mind. Sound, searching and liberal in thought, he presents a style massive, semi-fluent, pushing and formidable; yet from time to time breaking into a more easy and animated flow. By universal consent, he takes rank among great English writers. A tendency which could thus early ripen an author of so much power and skill, could get to itself such a head, vindicates easily and at once its claims to large literary influence. — BASCOM, JOHN, 1874, *Philosophy of English Literature, p.* 85.

It is a defence of the Church of England against dissenters. The author shows himself a bitter enemy of Catholics, whose doctrines he perverts, is full of inconsistencies and contradictions, and cannot disguise the Puritanical views which it was the purpose of this book to combat. His style is rich, dignified, elaborate, but marred by the length and intricacy of the sentences.—JENKINS, O. L., 1876, *The Students Handbook of British and American Literature, p.* 145.

To accede without explanation to the claim put forth for the "Ecclesiastical Polity" of Hooker, that it marks an epoch in English prose literature and English thought, would both be to do some injustice to writers previous to him, and, if not to overestimate his influence, to misinterpret its character. By no means can his excursions in English prose be regarded as chiefly those of a pioneer; and not only is his intellectual position inferior to that of Shakespeare, Spenser, and Bacon, who alone can be properly reckoned as the master spirits of the age, but in reality what effect he may have had upon the thought of his contemporaries was soon disregarded and swept out of sight in the hand-to-hand struggle with Puritanism, and his influence, so far from being immediate and confined to one particular era, has since the reaction against Puritanism been slowly and imperceptibly permeating and colouring English thought down to the present time. His work is, however, the earliest in English prose with enough of the preserving salt of excellence to adapt it to the mental palate of modern readers.—HENDERSON, T. F., 1881, *Encyclopædia Britannica, Ninth ed. vol.* XII, *p.* 151.

The contents are rather more philosophical than theological, and the work more valuable for its broad and fundamental principles than for the exactness of definition, or clearness of argument. It is in effect an answer to Puritanism, which had been bitterly attacking the episcopal system through a generation. Conceived in an admirable temper, and free from the heat and vituperation which characterized the controversial writings of the period, it makes no attempt to discredit the Presbyterian system. Its object is to assert the right of a broad liberty on the basis of Scripture *and reason*. . . . Hooker has been claimed as a champion of the High-Anglican doctrine of episcopacy, and, hardly less confidently, by the other side as the advocate of the view that church government is a matter of expediency. Isolated expressions can be found in favor of both, as even Keble qualifiedly admits. But neither view is true. Hooker holds a position intermediate between the school of the English Reformers, Archbishop Grindal and most of Elizabeth's bishops, and the school which grew up in the contest with Puritanism, and had its extreme representative in Archbishop Laud. Had he been more exact in his definitions, it might be possible to place him more confidently on the one side or on the other. As it is, he stands as the representative of toleration in the sphere of ecclesiastical polity and the advocate of the claims of reason against that narrow scripturalism which assumes to tolerate nothing which the Scriptures do not *expressly* command. —SCHAFF, D. S., 1883, *Schaff-Herzog, A Religious Encyclopædia, vol.* II, *p.* 1018.

The great type of the English Church. . . . He represents that stately, massive, harmonious mind which upbuilded it. The work of "Ecclesiastical Polity" remains to this day like the Pyramids, alone amidst the barren sands of church polemics. — WASHBURN, EMELYN W., 1884, *Studies in Early English Literature, p.* 174.

These, as we judge, are Hooker's two great characteristic merits as a prose writer — the philosophic and the logical cast. They carry a great deal with them which cannot be fully stated. They embody more than they express, and on the negative side prevent the presence and power of minor errors. They promise the reader something worth the reading, and are so presented as to be intelligible and impressive. There is an utter absence of the puerile and the frivolous. Everything is solid and germane to the subject, while through it all there is a moral sobriety of tone that is most healthful and uplifting. These are qualities somewhat Elizabethan and English, and for which there is yet room in modern prose. The later periods have improved on the earlier in vocabulary, diction, sentence and artistic finish, but not in mental and moral undertone. Each class of qualities is right in its place and time. Had their order been reversed, English Prose would not have been as stable and substantial as it is. — HUNT, THEODORE W., 1887, *Representative English Prose and Prose Writers, p.* 238.

I don't know if any of our parish will care to read the "Ecclesiastical Polity;" but if you have courage thereto, you will find in this old master of sound and cumbrous English prose, passages of rare eloquence, and many turns of expression, which for their winning grace, their aptitude, their quality of fastening themselves upon the mind, are not overmatched by those of any Elizabethan writer. —MITCHELL, DONALD G., 1889, *English Lands Letters and Kings, From Celt to Tudor, p.* 216.

If ever there was a writer who might challenge universal recognition, it was Hooker. — EARLE, JOHN, 1890, *English Prose, p.* 443.

It may at once be said of Hooker's work that his quality, his accomplishment (though of a high order in rhetoric, in composition governed by certain stately and scholastic laws), cannot rank him among the great creative writers of the world. As a man of thought, and as a man who set serious value by his thought: as a man who perpended every paragraph, and who carefully elaborated every parenthesis: as a man whose conscientious labour must ever be among the influences that drive the frivolous to despair, his superior or even his rival would not be easy to find. His workmanship, too, is very cunningly equipoised. He had an ear for the balance of parts, and for sonorousness of diction. He is never irresponsible, never gay, never passionate, never free from his own personal control. But for the artificial quality of his art he takes an exceptional eminence. There is something peculiarly satisfactory about all his writing; it is thorough.—BLACKBURN, VERNON, 1893, *English Prose, ed. Craik, vol.* I, *p.* 467.

The learning and research, the pure, rich style, the close reasoning, the admirable tone and spirit, displayed in this treatise, make it one of the masterpieces of all English literature.—SANDERSON, EDGAR, 1893, *History of England and the British Empire, p.* 484.

The greatest master of English prose whom the great age of Elizabeth produced. . . . He is the first master of English prose whose style is not only characteristic of his own age, but expressive of the purest genious of the English tongue. The rich and dignified vocabulary, the stately and majestic periods, which mark his best passages, are instinct with the power and the enthusiasm which made the greatness of Elizabeth's England. He does not scorn any of the arts of the rhetorician: he does not even avoid an intentional quaintness of expression which might seem at times out of keeping with the solemnity of his theme. As in thought so in utterance, he aims at comprehensiveness rather than clarity. There are passages of his which, it is not bold to say, will live as models so long as the English language is written or read. Hooker was the greatest of his school: but he had many imitators.—HUTTON, WILLIAM, HOLDEN, 1895, *Social England, ed. Traill, vol.* III, *pp.* 447, 449.

The book has remained ever since a standard work. It is as much moral and political as theological. Its style is grave, clear, and often musical. He adorned it with the figures of poetry, but he used them with temperance, and the grand and rolling rhetoric with which he often concludes an argument is kept for its right place. On the whole, it is the first monument of splendid literary prose that we possess.—BROOKE, STOPFORD A., 1896, *English Literature, p.* 109.

Hooker is the first important philosophical and religious English writer. He is the earliest to perceive the importance of evolution, the propriety of preparing and conducting to a conclusion a great, consistent scheme. He sees things clearly and cooly in an age when controversial passion and political turmoil turned all other men's blood to fever. . . . The style of Hooker is distinguished by a sober and sustained eloquence. Certain of his contemporaries might equal him in purple passages, but not one of them approached his even flight. He was Latinised, not as his lumbering predecessors had been, but in the true humanistic spirit; and he had studied Aristotle and Plato with constant advantage to his expression. Hooker is, indeed, one of the earliest of our authors, in prose or verse, to show the influence of pure Hellenic culture. The limpidity and elegance of his periods are extraordinary. When all England was in bondage, Hooker alone freed himself from the clogged concatenation of phrases which makes early English prose so unwieldy; yet he gained his liberty at no such cost of grace and fulness as Bacon did in the snip-snap of his "Essays." Hooker discovered, by the help of the ancients and the Bible, a middle way between long-drawn lusciousness and curt formality. He does not strive after effect; but when he is moved, his style is instinct with music. He never abuses quotations; he never forgets that he has an argument to conduct, and that life is short. In other words, he is the first great writer of practical English prose, and for a long time there is none other like unto him.—GOSSE, EDMUND, 1897, *Short History of Modern English Literature, pp.* 124, 125.

He is known beyond the circle of students of theology. His English style has given him a high place in general literature. The stately dignity of its movement, the depth and richness of its musical diapason, its variety and flexibility, its rhythmical grace, and its occasional flights of lofty eloquence have secured him a place of permanent honour among the greatest masters of the English tongue. And style, let us remember, is the outcome of the man. It is no artificial bedizenment of thought. It is thought making for itself a body fitted to its needs. It is a vital and intimate union of the immaterial and the material. And apart from the apt conveyance of thought and emotion, it is precious because it reveals to us the thinker himself. Who can rise from the study of Hooker without a sense of a greatness that lies beyond and above such qualities as acuteness of perception, or intellectual force, or imaginative fertility, or learning, or argumentative power? All these are there; but there is something more. We are conscious of a moral majesty that humbles us. We feel the quickened beat of the writer's heart as he treats of the revelation of the wisdom and goodness of the Eternal Giver of life and law. We are sensible of the wide, capacious, all-encircling atmosphere of awe and wonder in which the great thinker lives and moves; and our admiration passes into reverence.—DOWDEN, JOHN, 1897, *Outlines of the History of the Theological Literature of the Church of England*, p. 54.

Richard Hooker was dead; he had published in 1597 his fifth book of the immortal "Ecclesiastical Polity," and dedicated it to the Primate. What did Whitgift care for such as he? Hooker had been hunted out of the Mastership of the Temple, and sent to rock the cradle and watch his sheep at Bishopbourne, a short walk from Canterbury. There Saravia seems to have been his only friend. Some few bewailed him, and in their hearts cried "Shame"; but they held their peace when it was the time for silence. Donne read and absorbed Hooker's great work, especially the first book,—utilised it, made it his own, and reproduced it in his "Biathanatos,"—but he never so much as mentioned Hooker's name.—JESSOPP, AUGUSTUS, 1897, *John Donne, Sometime Dean of St. Paul's*, p. 54.

Hooker's style has the faults of its class—a classicism now timid, now unduly audacious; an unnecessary fear of vivid and vernacular expressions. But its author handles the methods and means which he has received with original genius, attaining to a really exquisite balance of sentence, to a harmony sometimes quite ineffable, adjusting his longer and shorter constructions with almost infallible art, and affording a specimen never surpassed, and hardly ever equalled since, of argument maintained on abstract and scholastic points without the slightest dulness, of ornament which is never daubed or stuck on, but arises from the proportion of the phrase, and the careful selection of the vocabulary. Had it been possible to have all prose written by Hookers, nobody need have wished to seek much further experiment.—SAINTSBURY, GEORGE, 1898, *A Short History of English Literature*, p. 300.

Thomas Nashe

1567–1600?

Born at Lowestoft (?), 1567; baptized, Nov. 1567. Matric., St. John's Coll., Camb., as Sizar, Oct. 1582; B. A., 1586. Settled in London, 1588; adopted literary career. Took active part in "Martin Mar-Prelate" controversy, under pseud. of "Pasquil." Play, "The Terrors of the Night," produced, 1593; "Summer's Last Will and Testament," privately performed, 1593; "The Isle of Dogs," performed by the Lord Admiral's Company, June 1597. In Fleet Prison, autumn of 1597. Died, 1601. *Works:* "The Anatomie of Absurditie," 1589; "A Countercuffe given to Martin Junior" (under pseud.: "Pasquil"), 1589; "The Returne of the Renowned Cavalier Pasquil of England" (anon.), 1589; "Martin's Month's Minde" (under pseud.: "Marphoreus"), 1589; "The First Parte of Pasquil's Apologie" (anon.), 1590; "A Wonderful. . . . Astrologicall Prognostication" (under pseud.: "Thomas Scarlet"), 1591; "Pierce Pennilesse his Supplication to the Devill," 1592 (another edn. same year); "Strange Newes of the Intercepting certaine Letters," 1592; "Christ's Teares over Jerusalem," 1593; "The Terrors of the Night," 1594; "The Unfortunate Traveller," 1594; "The

Tragedie of Dido" (with Marlowe), 1594; "Have with you to Saffron Walden," 1596; "Nashe's Lenten Stuffe," 1599; "A Pleasant Comedie called Summer's Last Will and Testament," 1600. He *translated:* Evenkellius "Γυμνασιαρχον" 1648; and *edited:* Sir Philip Sidney's "Astrophel and Stella," 1591. *Collected Works:* ed. by Grosart (6 vols.), 1883-85.—SHARP, R. FARQUHARSON, 1897 *A Dictionary of English Authors, p.* 210.

PERSONAL

A hundred unfortunate farewels, to fantasticall satirisme. In those vaines heretofore I misspent my spirit and prodigally conspired against good houres. Nothing is there now so much in my vowes as to be at peace with all men and make submissive amends where I have most displeased.—NASHE, THOMAS, 1593, *Christes Teares over Jerusalem, Dedication.*

As Eupolis of Athens used great liberty in taxing the vices of men: so doth Thomas Nash. Witness the brood of the Harveys! As Actæon was worried of his own hounds: so is Tom Nash of his Isle of Dogs. Dogs were the death of Euripides; but be not disconsolate, gallant young Juvenal! Linus, the son of Apollo died the same death. Yet God forbid that so brave a wit should so basely perish! Thine are but paper dogs, neither is thy banishment like Ovid's eternally to converse with the barbarous Getæ. Therefore comfort thyself, sweet Tom! with Cicero's glorious return to Rome; and with the Counsel Æneas gives to his seabeaten soldiers, Lib I, Æneid.

Pluck up thine heart! and drive from thence
both fear and care away!
To think on this, may pleasure be perhaps
another day.
Durato, et temet rebus servato secundis.

—MERES, FRANCIS, 1598, *Palladis Tamia.*

Or if in bitternes thou raile, like Nash:
Forgive me, honest Soule, that tearme thy
phrase
Rayling, for in thy workes thou wert not rash,
Nor didst affect in youth thy private praise.
Thou hadst a strife with that Trigemini;
Thou hurtst not them, till they had injurde thee.
. . . .
Thou wast, indeed, too slothfull to thy selfe,
Hiding thy better tallent in thy Spleene:
True spirits are not covetous of pelfe;
Youth's wit is ever ready, quick and keene.
Thou didst not live thy ripened Autumne day,
But wert cut off in thy best blooming May.
Else hadst thou left, as thou indeed hast left,
Sufficient test, though now in others Chests,
T' improve the basenes of that humorous theft
Which seemes to flow from selfe-conceving
Brests.
Thy name they burie, having buried thee:
Drones eat thy Honnie, thou wert the true Bee.

—MIDDLETON, THOMAS, 1604, *The Ant and the Nightingale.*

Marlow, Greene, and Peele had got vnder the shades of a large vyne, laughing to see Nash (that was but newly come to their colledge) still haunted with the sharpe and satyricall spirit that followed him heere vpon earthe: for Nash inueyed bitterly (as he had wont to do) against dryfisted patrons, accusing them of his vntimely death, because if they had giuen his muse that cherishment which she most worthily deserued, hee had fed to his dying day on fat capons, burnt sack and sugar, and not so desperately haue venturde his life, and shortned his dayes by keeping company with pickle herrings. —DECKER, THOMAS, 1606, *A Knights Conjuring, Non-dramatic Works, ed. Grosart, vol.* V, *p.* xxi.

Nash, a fanciful satirist, who abused his talent, and conspired like a prodigal against good fortune.—TAINE, H. A., 1871, *History of English Literature, tr. Van Laun, vol.* I, *bk.* ii, *ch.* ii, *p.* 236.

It is to be lamented that nothing whatever has been transmitted to enable us to know when exactly or where or under what circumstances he died, or where he found a grave. I was saddened in the knowledge that his father survived him until 1603 not to find him interred among his kin at Lowestoft. He had only reached his thirty-third year. It is to be feared that physically and every way life's candle was lit at both ends and flamed consumingly. The tragedy may not have been so absolute as that of Greene's death; but it must have been tragical enough.—GROSART, ALEXANDER B., 1883–84, *ed. Complete Works of Thomas Nashe, Memorial-Introduction, vol.* I, *p.* lxv.

GENERAL

With thee I ioyne young Iuuenall, that byting Satyrist, that lastlie with mee together writ a Comedie. Sweete boy, might I aduise thee, be aduised, and get not many enemies by bitter words: inueigh against vaine men, for thou canst do it, no man better, no man so wel; thou hast a libertie to reprooue all, and none more; for one being spoken to, all are offended, none being blamed, no man is iniuried. Stop shallow water still running, it will rage, tread on a worme, and it will turne; then blame not schollers vexed with sharpe lines, if they reproove thy too much libertie of reproofe.—GREENE, ROBERT, 1593, *Groatsworth of Wit, Works, ed. Grosart, vol.* xii, *p.* 143.

True English Aretine.—LODGE, THOMAS, 1596, *Wit's Miserie and the World's Madness.*

Let all his faultes sleepe with his mournfull chest,
And (there) for ever with his ashes rest.
His style was wittie, though (it) had some gal (l),
Something(s) he might have mended, so may all.
Yet this I say, that for a mother witt,
Few men have ever seene the like of it.
—ANON, 1606, *The Return from Pernassus,* 1606, *Act* i, *sc.* 2.

And thou, into whose soule (if ever there were a Pithagorean Metempsuchosis) the raptures of that fierce and inconfineable Italian spirit were bounteously and boundlesly infused; thou sometime Secretary to Pierce Pennylesse, and Master of his Requests, ingenious and ingenuous, fluent, facetious, T. Nash, from whose abundant pen hony flowed to thy friends, and mortall Aconite to thy enemies; thou that madest the Doctor* a flat dunce, and beatst him at two tall sundry weapons, Poetrie and Oratorie; sharpest Satyre, luculent Poet, elegant Orator, get leave for thy ghost to come from her abiding, and to dwell with me a while, till she hath carows'd to me in his owne wonted ful measures of wit, that my plump braynes may swell, and burst into bitter invectives against the Lieftenant of Limbo, if he cashiere Pierce Pennylesse with dead pay. —DEKKER, THOMAS, 1607, *Newes from Hell.*

And surely Nash, though he a proser were,
A branch of laurel yet deserves to bear;
Sharply satiric was he, and that way
He went, that since his being to this day
Few have attempted; and I surely think
Those words shall hardly be set down with ink
Should scorch and blast so as his could where he
Would inflict vengeance.
—DRAYTON, MICHAEL, C. 1627, *Of Poets, and Poesie.*

Besides this boldness of their becoming gods, so far as to set limits to his mercies; there was not only one *Martin Mar-Prelate,* but other venomous books daily printed and dispersed; books that were so absurd and scurrilous, that the graver divines disdained them an answer. And yet these were grown into high esteem with the common people, till Tom Nash appeared against them all; who was a man of a sharp wit, and the master of a scoffing satirical merry pen, which he employed to discover the absurdities of those blind, malicious, senseless pamphlets, and sermons as senseless as they; Nash his answers being like his books, which bore these titles, "An Almond for a Parrot," "A Fig for my Godson," "Come crack me this Nut," and the like; so that his merry wit made some sport, and such a discovery of their absurdities, as (which is strange) he put a greater stop to these malicious pamphlets than a much wiser man had been able.—WALTON, ISAAC, 1665, *The Life of Mr. Richard Hooker.*

*Harvey.

Noted and restless buffoon.—WOOD, ANTHONY, 1691-1721, *Athenæ Oxonienses.*

His Works are various, both in Verse and Prose; tho' all Biting, and Satirical, —By some he is call'd the *English Aretine;* By others, a Buffoon in Print.—COOPER, ELIZABETH, 1737, *The Muses' Library, p.* 182.

The most exquisite banterer of that age of genius.—DISRAELI, ISAAC, 1812-13, *Literary Ridicule, Calamities and Quarrels of Authors.*

But, besides these peculiar and especial claims to the attention of all who are interested in whatever relates to Shakespeare and his productions, "Pierce Penniless" is a very singular, highly finished, and, in many respects, amusing picture of the manners of the times when it was written. Some of the descriptions of persons and habits of different grades of society have remarkable force, and obvious fidelity, and carry with them the conviction, that little is to be allowed even for the exaggerations of a poet. Nash was a young man who had mixed in most of the scenes he paints; and his style is unusually pure and free from those inflations and bombastic expressions, which, as we read, induce a doubt as to the truth and accuracy of the representations of which they form a part. His eloquence is natural and flowing; and although now and then we meet with what may be looked upon as a trifling affectation of scholastic learning, yet compared with many, if not most, of his scribbling contemporaries, he is very free from this defect: his writings are generally to be regarded as models of choice, nervous, and idiomatic English. If not the best, he was certainly one of the best prose authors of the period in which he flourished. As a vigorous, pungent, and bitterly satirical writer, it may be doubted whether he ever had his equal in our language.—COLLIER, JOHN PAYNE, 1842, *ed. Pierce Penniless's Supplication to the Devil, Introduction, p.* vii.

There never perhaps was poured forth such a rushing and roaring torrent of wit, ridicule, and invective, as in the rapid succession of pamphlets which he published in the course of the year 1589 against the Puritans and their famous champion (or rather knot of champions) taking the name of Martin Mar-Prelate; unless in those in which he began two years after to assail poor Gabriel Harvey, his persecution of and controversy with whom lasted a much longer time—till indeed the Archbishop of Canterbury (Whitgift), interfered in 1597 to restore the peace of the realm by an order that all Harvey's and Nash's books should be taken wherever they might be found, "and that none of the said books be ever printed hereafter."—CRAIK, GEORGE L., 1861, *A Compendious History of English Literature, etc., vol.* I, *p.* 500.

His "Life of Jack Wilton" is well known to have originated one of the most long-lived fables in English literary biography. Altogether he was a most versatile proficient in literary composition; it was said of him that he "compiled a learned treatise in the praise of a red herring;" and in truth, with such a writer, the subject is of secondary importance; the style is the man.—WARD, ADOLPHUS WILLIAM, 1875, *A History of English Dramatic Literature, vol.* I, *p.* 232.

Has far better claims than Swift to be called the English Rabelais.—LOWELL, JAMES RUSSELL, 1875–90, *Spenser, Prose Works, Riverside ed., vol.* IV, *p.* 278, *note.*

Was famous no less for his acuteness, his knowledge, and his ready pen, than for his envious, spiteful, and abusive nature; personal polemics, the coarser the better, were the subjects he specially delighted in.—ELZE, KARL, 1876–88, *William Shakespeare, tr. Schmitz, p.* 141.

Whose English tongue
Is racy of the soil and strong—whose wit
Sarcastic, edg'd, now fooled men and now stung:
Ribald, perchance, with Harvey for his foe.
Of Sidney, Spenser, Greene, with reverence fit
He spoke, of "poore Kit Marlowe," soft and low.

—GROSART, ALEXANDER B., 1883–84, *ed. Complete Works of Thomas Nashe, Dedication.*

Thomas Nash claims a place of no little importance in the history of English prose. His pamphlets, modelled upon those in vogue among Italian writers of the school of Aretine, display a trenchant wit and a directness in the use of language, which were rare in that age. He was a born satirist, hitting hard, abstaining from rhetorical parades of erudition, sketching a caricature with firm and broad touches, and coining pithy epigrams which stung like poisoned arrows. No writer before Nash, and few since his death, have used the English language as an instrument of pure invective with more complete mastery and originality of manner.—SYMONDS, JOHN ADDINGTON, 1884, *Shakspere's Predecessors in the English Drama, p.* 573.

Diffuseness and want of keeping to the point too frequently mar Nash's work; but when he shakes himself free from them, and goes straight for his enemy or his subject, he is a singularly forcible writer. In his case more than in any of the others, the journalist born out of due time is perceptible. He had perhaps not much original message for the world. But he had eminently the trick both of damaging controversial argument made light to catch the popular taste, and of easy discussion or narrative. The chief defects of his work would probably have disappeared of themselves if he had had to write not pamphlets, but articles. He did, however, what he could; and he is worthy of a place in the history of literature if only for the sake of "Have with you to Saffron Walden"—the best example of its own kind to be found before the end of the seventeenth century, if not the beginning of the eighteenth.—SAINTSBURY, GEORGE, 1887, *History of Elizabethan Literature, p.* 234.

With all his fondness for merry authors, Nash can discern true poetry, and he adores it. If by chance, in the midst of an angry satirical disquisition, the word poetry comes to his pen, he is suddenly transformed, he smiles, he melts; nothing is left in him but human sympathies. . . . His vocabulary is very rich; he has always a variety of words at his disposal and uses often two or three the better to impress our minds with the idea in his own. He coins at need new words or fetches them from classical or foreign languages. He does not do this in an off-hand way, but on purpose and wilfully; he possessed much of that curious care for and delight in words which is one of the characteristics of the men of the Renaissance. To deal with words was in itself a pleasure for them; they liked to mould, to adopt, to combine, to invent them. Word painting delighted them; Nash has an extreme fondness for it, and satirical and comical as he is, he often astonishes us by the poetic gracefulness of his combinations of words. In this as in many other particulars he imitates, *longe sequens*, the master he seems to have admired above others, Rabelais, who, in the tempestuous rolls of his diverse waters, sometimes washes up on to the sand pearls fit to adorn the crown of any lyrical poet. . . . Had a particular literary hatred for mere empty bombast.—JUSSERAND, J. J., 1890, *The English Novel in the Time of Shakespeare*, *pp.* 299, 303.

Had there been no inkshed between Nash and Harvey, we should remember Harvey as he was, Nash as he was. Becuase they vilified each other, many have taken Gabriel Harvey for a ridiculous pedant upon the authority of Thomas Nash, and Thomas Nash for a railer, strong in personal attack, upon the authority of Gabriel Harvey—and of Nash himself in his writing against Harvey. Nash is the chief sufferer, because as an English Writer he had most to lose. He was a young man, with scholarship enough and wit abounding. His invectives against Harvey were in some degree half-playful exercises in pen-duel. They were for the amusement of the public after the manner of the "flytings" of the time of Dunbar and Kennedy, Skelton and Garnische. But they meant mischief, as those flytings did not. They were born of personal offence, and carried on with a real bitterness of feeling. If we could strike out of our literature all the tedious quarrel between Nash and Harvey, where the wit of the younger man and the rhetoric of the elder are much wasted upon matter trivial and low, how would the two stand? We should know Gabriel Harvey only as a respectable friend of some of the best writers of the day, who loved good literature without adding to it; as an affectionate brother who showed sense in discouragement of superstitious notions about earthquakes and conjunctions of the planets; and as chief advocate of an experiment in writing English hexameters, which has its own place and meaning in our literary history. We should have known Thomas Nash as a young wit and poet who cared for good literature and added to it; as one who wrote prose satire that looked mainly to the higher aims of life, a young Juvenal who struck heavily at the greater vices and more lightly at the follies of his age, without personal attack on any man, except so much as was incident to the general bad taste of the Marprelate controversy. All his other offence of that kind is against the Harveys.—MORLEY, HENRY, 1893, *English Writers, vol.* X, *p.* 191.

The redoubtable "English Aretine," with the swagger of a bully in almost all his prose, yet leaving us but too few of the purest and saddest of lyrics.—SCHELLING, FELIX E., 1895, *A Book of Elizabethan Lyrics*, *p.* xxix.

As a prose satirist he had neither equal nor second among his contemporaries.—COLLINS, JOHN CHURTON, 1895, *Essays and Studies*, *p.* 177.

An early English example of the picaresque is Nash's "Jack Wilton," which, clumsy as it is, and naively childish to modern taste, does nevertheless explain De Foe on the one hand and the penny-dreadful on the other.—BURTON, RICHARD, 1898, *Literary Likings*, *p.* 72.

Thomas Nash was himself perhaps intrinsically the most able, and certainly not the least typical, member of a whole class of Elizabethan men of letters. . . . Nash had ideas of style which sometimes led him into involved pomposity, but which also supplied him with an effective, though blackguard, controversial manner. Nobody was a greater master of loud-mouthed bragging, of the fashion of telling an opponent over pages of repetition of the dreadful things you are going to do with him.—HANNAY, DAVID, 1898, *The Later Renaissance*, *pp.* 274-5.

Thomas Cartwright

1535?-1603

Thomas Cartwright (1535–1603), "the incarnation of Presbyterianism," and for some time a thorn in the side of Whitgift, was born in Hertfordshire. He encountered Whitgift at Cambridge, and was worsted, being deprived of the Lady Margaret Professorship and of his fellowship in Trinity, and thus driven from the University in 1572. After spending some years as English Chaplain at Antwerp, he returned, got into trouble with the Church, and was imprisoned. In his later years he seems to have been conciliated by Whitgift, and to have made a less violent opposition. His works are—"An Admonition to Parliament," 1572; "An Admonition to the People of England," 1589; "A Brief Apology," 1596; also "A Directory of Church Government," and "A Body of Divinity," published after his death. Cartwright was a very popular preacher. He writes with great fervour, but his style is much more involved and antiquated than Whitgift's, and he has much less argumentative force.—MINTO, WILLIAM, 1872–80, *Manual of English Prose Literature, p.* 229.

For a polished, and garnished stile, fewe go-beyonde Cartwright.—HARVEY, GABRIEL, 1593, *Pierces Supererogation, ed. Grosart, p.* 290.

Early in life a disappointed man, the progress was easy to a disaffected subject. At a Philosophy Act, in the University of Cambridge, in the royal presence, the queen preferred and rewarded his opponent for the slighter and more attractive elegancies in which the learned Cartwright was deficient. He felt the wound rankle in his ambitious spirit. He began, as Sir George Paul, in his "Life of Archbishop Whitgift," expresses it, "to kick against her Ecclesiastical Government." He expatriated himself several years, and returned fierce with the republican spirit he had caught among the Calvinists at Geneva, which aimed at the extirpation of the bishops. It was once more his fate to be poised against another rival, Whitgift, the Queen's Prefessor of Divinity. . .
Cartwright was now to be confuted by other means. The University refused him his degree of D. D.; condemned the lecturer to silence; and at length performed that last feeble act of power, expulsion. In a heart already alienated from the established authorities, this could only envenom a bitter spirit. Already he had felt a personal dislike to royalty, and now he had received insult from the University: these were motives which, though concealed, could not fail to work in a courageous mind, whose new forms of religion accorded with his political feelings. The "Degrees" of the University, which he now declared to be "unlawful," were to be considered "as limbs of Antichrist." The whole hierarchy was to be exterminated for a republic of Presbyters; till, through the church, the republican, as we shall see, discovered a secret passage to the Cabinet of his Sovereign, where he had many protectors. . . . Cartwright, chilled by an imprisonment, and witnessing some of his party condemned, and some executed, after having long sustained the most elevated and rigid tone, suddenly let his alp of ice dissolve away in the gentlest thaw that ever occurred in political life. Ambitious he was, but not of martyrdom!—DISRAELI, ISAAC, 1814, *Martin Mar-Prelate, Quarrels of Authors.*

The ostensible founder of this new school (though probably its tenets were by no means new to many of the sect) was Thomas Cartwright, the Lady Margaret's professor of divinity at Cambridge. He began about 1570 to inculcate the unlawfulness of any form of church-government, except what the apostles had instituted, namely, the presbyterian. A deserved reputation for virtue, learning, and acuteness, an ardent zeal, an inflexible self-confidence, a vigorous, rude, and arrogant style, marked him as the formidable leader of a religious faction. In 1572 he published his celebrated Admonition to the Parliament, calling on that assembly to reform the various abuses subsisting in the church. In this treatise such a hardy spirit of innovation was displayed, and schemes of ecclesiastical policy so novel and extraordinary were developed, that it made a most important epoch in the contest, and rendered its termination far more improbable. — HALLAM, HENRY, 1827–46, *The Constitutional History of England, vol.* I, *ch.* iv.

No leader of a religious party ever deserved less of after sympathy than Cartwright. He was unquestionably learned and devout, but his bigotry was that of a mediæval inquisitor. The relics of the old ritual, the cross in baptism, the surplice, the giving of a ring in marriage, were to him not merely distasteful, as they were to the Puritans at large—they were idolatrous and the mark of the beast. . . . With the despotism of a Hildebrand, Cartwright combined the cruelty of a Torquemada.—GREEN, JOHN RICHARD, 1874, *A Short History of the English People, ch.* viii.

In August 1564, the queen's interest in the university was further indicated by a visit extending over five days, and characterised by a series of quaint ceremonies and not a few amusing incidents. In one of the "acts" or disputations performed in the royal presence, a disputant took part who was destined to exercise no small influence over the subsequent history of the university. This was Thomas Cartwright, afterwards Lady Margaret professor, to whom the distinction may fairly be conceded of having been the founder of the Puritan party in England.—MULLINGER, J. BASS, 1888, *History of the University of Cambridge, p.* 118.

That exhaustive controversy between the ablest advocate of the Puritan view of Church discipline, and one of the chief supporters of Queen Elizabeth's Church policy—both men of high character, much learning, and fervent zeal—gave the whole case on each side. The causes of the separation that broke the dream of unity in the Reformed Church of England are to be found in our literature, so fully stated in these volumes that whoever studies them can be as well informed as any Englishman then living. We have in them the never-ending action and reaction of the two opposing forms of thought. Whitgift's bias was Conservative, and Cartwright's that of the Reformer. The end of their controversy is not yet, though many now think they can tell what it will be. — MORLEY, HENRY, 1892, *English Writers, vol.* VIII, *p.* 330.

Thomas Churchyard

1520?-1604

Born at Shrewsbury, England, about 1520: died April 1604. An English poet and miscellaneous writer, and soldier. He was the author of numerous tracts and broad sides, "The Worthines of Wales," a poem (1587), "The Legend of Shore's Wife" (in the 1563 edition of Baldwin's "Mirror for Magistrates"), his best-known poem, "Churchyard's Challenge," a collection of prose and verse (1593), etc. As a soldier he served in Scotland, Ireland, the Low Countries, France, and elsewhere. — SMITH, BENJAMIN E., *ed.*, 1894–97, *The Century Cyclopedia of Names, p.* 251.

And there is old Palemon free from spight,
Whose carefull pipe may make the hearer rew;
Yet he himselfe may rewed be more right,
That sung so long untill quite hoarse he grew.

—SPENSER, EDMUND, 1595, *Colin Clouts Come Home Again, v.* 396–9.

Hath not *Shor's* wife, although a light-skirts she,
Given him a chast long lasting memory?

—ANON., 1606, *The Return from Pernassus; Act* i, *sc.* 2.

Though some conceive him to be as much beneath a *Poet*, as above a *Rhimer;* in my opinion, his Verses may go abreast with any of that age, writing in the beginning of Queen Elizabeth. It seems, by this his Epitaph in Mr. Camden's "Remains," that he died not guilty of much wealth:

"Come, *Alecto*, lend me thy Torch,
To find a *Church-yard* in a *Church-porch:*
Poverty and *Poetry* his Tomb doth enclose;
Wherefore, good nighbours, be merry in Prose."

—FULLER, THOMAS, 1662, *The Worthies of England, ed. Nichols, vol.* II, *p.* 262.

By the men of those times he was accounted a good poet, by others a poor court-poet; but since, as much beneath a poet as a rhimer.—WOOD, ANTHONY, 1691–1721, *Athenæ Oxonienses, vol.* I, *p.* 318.

An excellent soldier, and a man of honest principles.—STRYPE, JOHN, 1710, *Life of Edmund Grindal.*

By his writings, he appears a man of sense, and sometimes a poet, tho' he does not seem to possess any degree of invention. His language is generally pure, and his numbers not wholly inharmonious.—CIBBER, THEOPHILUS, 1753, *Lives of the Poets, vol.* I, *p.* 64.

One of those unfortunate men who have written poetry all their days, and lived a long life to complete the misfortune. His muse was so fertile, that his works pass all enumeration. He courted numerous patrons, who valued the poetry, while they left the poet to his own miserable contemplations. . . . Well might Churchyard write his own sad life under the title of "The Tragicall Discourse of the Haplesse Man's Life."—DISRAELI, ISAAC, 1812–13, *A Mendicant Author, Calamities of Authors.*

What is to be said of the strange and oft-times incomprehensible fecundity of the *first* of these poets, Churchyard? The very titles of his works, (all of which I will not venture to enumerate) are perfect reflexes of the motley imagery of his mind. We have his "Chips," his "Choice," his "Charge," "Chance," "Charity," "Challenge," and I know not what! An historian, a controversialist, a translator, and an original poet—we are alternately bewildered by the variety of his performances, and astounded at the enormous prices which the greater part of them produce. It is in vain you depreciate, ridicule, and run down, the black letter slim quartos—in which the poetry of Churchyard is usually cased—to collectors of the olden school of poetry. Speak till you are hoarse, and declaim till language fails you—with Licius—he will be only "subridens" all the time; and, pointing to his *yew*-ornamented Churchyards, will exclaim, "I am eclipsed only by Atticus." Let us therefore leave Atticus and Licius *at rest;* smiling, in their slumbers, at all the "Chips" by which they are surrounded.—DIBDIN, THOMAS FROGNALL, 1824, *The Library Companion, p.* 686.

Churchyard is not a poet who possessed any imagination, nor are his thoughts novel or striking: his language is often below his subject, but his versification is usually flowing, and his reflections frequently just and natural.—COLLIER, JOHN PAYNE, 1865, *A Bibliographical and Critical Account of the Rarest Books in the English Language, vol.* I, *p.* 136.

Much tamer in every way than Gascoigne was this other soldier and poet, yet he is an interesting man, if for no other reason than that he saw the wonderful growth of the Elizabethan literature from its beginnings to its maturity. . . . Though his poetry is of small account, his life was eventful and interesting. . . . In these works he appears as a garrulous, gossiping old fellow, fond of reciting his own exploits, and overflowing with good advice and general goodwill—on easy confidential terms with the public. So far as his works afford indications, he was tolerably happy in his old age. . . . He kept on writing with great activity till the very last, publishing no less than thirty-five works during the last twenty-five years of his long life. Such was the Nestor of the Elizabethan heroes.—MINTO, WILLIAM, 1874–85, *Characteristics of English Poets, pp.* 158, 159.

Thomas Churchyard was an inferior sort of Gascoigne, who led a much longer if less eventful life. He was about the Court for the greater part of the century, and had a habit of calling his little books, which were numerous, and written both in verse and prose, by alliterative titles playing on his own name, such as "Churchyard's Chips," "Churchyard's Choice," and so forth. He was a person of no great literary power, and chiefly noteworthy because of his long life after contributing to Tottel's *Miscellany,* which makes him a link between the old literature and the new.—SAINTSBURY, GEORGE, 1887, *History of Elizabethan Literature, p.* 18.

Churchyard was a minor poet who dealt with realities, bringing—as many a man then did—his sense of poetry into the work of life, and finding in the work of life the motive to his song. This union of thought with action into a true music of life was one source of the greatness of England under Elizabeth. In the second half of her reign, through which Churchyard lived, the intellectual life rose so high, that few men cared for the old poet who had ploughed his furlong at the foot of the great upward slope.—MORLEY, HENRY, 1892, *English Writers, vol.* VIII, *p.* 254.

His poetical resources were, indeed, but slender. He never advanced beyond the point he reached in "Jane Shore," which, considering the date at which it was composed, is remarkable for the smoothness of its versification.—COURTHOPE, W. J., 1897, *A History of English Poetry, vol.* II. *p.* 166.

John Stowe

1525? 1605

Was a tailor in Cornhill, but about his fortieth year devoted himself to antiquarian pursuits. His principal works are his "Summary of English Chronicles" (1561); "Annals, or a General Chronicle of England" (1580); and, most important of all, the "Survey of London and Westminster" (1598), an account of their history, antiquities, and government for six centuries. Stow also assisted in the continuation of Holinshed's Chronicle, Speght's Chaucer, &c.—PATRICK AND GROOME, *eds.*, 1897, *Chambers's Biographical Dictionary, p.* 886.

The memories of superstitious foundations, fables, and lies, foolishly STOWED together. — GRAFTON, RICHARD, 1570, *Chronicles, Dedication.*

I confess, I have heard him often accused, that (as learned Guicciardine is charged for telling *magnarum rerum minutias*) he reporteth *res in se minutas, toys* and *trifles*, being such a *Smell-feast*, that he cannot pass by *Guild-hall*, but his pen must tast of the good chear therein. However, this must be indulged to his education; so hard it is for a Citizen to write an History, but that the *fur* of his gown will be felt therein. Sure I am, our most elegant Historians who have wrote since his time (Sir Francis Bacon, Master Camden, &c.) though throwing away the basket, have taken the fruit; though not mentioning his name, making use of his endeavors. Let me adde of John Stow, that (however he kept *tune*) he kept *time* very well, no Author being more accurate in the notation thereof. Besides his "Chronicle of England," he hath a large "Survey of London;" and I believe no City in Christendome, Rome alone excepted, hath so great a volume extant thereof.—FULLER, THOMAS, 1662, *The Worthies of England, ed. Nichols, vol.* II, *p.* 81.

The honest historian Stowe. — HUME, DAVID, 1762, *The History of England, vol.* IV, *Appendix, note* LLL.

He well deserves to be remembered with honour. . . . He always protested, and we may take his honest word for it, that he never was swayed by favour or fear in any of his writings; but that he had impartially, to the best of his knowledge, delivered the truth. This good opinion the greatest of our later historians seem to have of him.—NICHOLSON, WILLIAM, 1696–1714, *English Historical Library.*

He felt through life the enthusiasm of study; and seated in his monkish library, living with the dead more than with the living, he was still a student of taste: for Spenser the poet visited the library of Stowe; and the first good edition of Chaucer was made so chiefly by the labours of our author. Late in life, worn out with study and the cares of poverty, neglected by that proud metropolis of which he had been the historian, his good-humour did not desert him; for being afflicted with sharp pains in his aged feet, he observed that "his affliction lay in that part which formerly he had made so much use of." Many a mile had he wandered and much had he expended, for those treasures of antiquities which had exhausted his fortune, and with which he had formed works of great public utility. It was in his eightieth year that Stowe at length received a public acknowledgment of his services, which will appear to us of a very extraordinary nature. He was so reduced in his circumstances that he petitioned James I. for a *licence to collect alms* for himself! "as a recompense for his labours and travel of *forty-five years*, in setting forth the *Chronicles of England*, and *eight years* taken up in the *Survey of the Cities of London and Westminster*, towards his relief now in his old age; having left his former means of living, and only employing himself for the service and good of his country." Letters-patent under the great seal were granted. After no penurious commendations of Stowe's labours, he is permitted "to gather the benevolence of well-disposed people within this realm of England; to ask, gather, and take the alms of all our loving subjects." These letters-patent were to be published by the clergy from their pulpits; they produced so little, that they were renewed for another twelvemonth: one entire parish in the city contributed seven shillings and sixpence! Such, then, was the patronage received by Stowe, to be a licensed beggar throughout the kingdom for one twelvemonth! Such was the public remuneration of a man who had been useful to his nation, but not to himself! —DISRAELI, ISAAC, 1812–13, *A Mendicant Author, Calamities of Authors.*

As we come to the conclusion of the sixteenth century, and commence with the seventeenth, we are immediately struck with the venerable name of Stow, a laborious and honest man; content to state simple facts, without any enlarged views, and in a style the most unpretending imaginable. But there are those who rank him even above Holinshed and the contemporaneous Chroniclers. That he was a diligent and careful collector of facts, and far better acquainted with ms. authorities (even with some, of which all traces are now lost) than any writer of his day, may be unequivocally allowed. —DIBDIN, THOMAS FROGNALL, 1824, *The Library Companion, p.* 187.

Stow and Grafton are said to have been jealous of each other's credit; there can, however, be no doubt of the former's superiority.—ALLEN, JOHN, 1831, *Lingard's History of England, Edinburgh Review, vol.* 53, *p.* 5.

England is indebted to him for the most elaborate coeval picture of the brilliant era of Elizabeth, and London for the traces of her growth during six centuries. He is the faithful chronicler of gaieties and gravities,—of whatever he conceived would interest his contemporaries and posterity. —CORNEY, BOLTON, 1838, *New Curiosities of Literature.*

A man surrounded with old books, who loved the past and studied it incessantly, exposed himself to criticism of the crowd who, as Chaucer observed, "demen gladly to the badder end." Two or three years after John Stow had begun to give his whole life to his chosen work, he was reported to Queen Elizabeth's Council as "a suspicious person with many dangerous and superstitious books in his possession." Edmund Grindal was then Bishop of London, by himself and through his chaplain one of the official licensers of books. They were days also of active search for "redusants," who remained Roman Catholics outside the English Church as it had been by law established. Grindal ordered his chaplain and two others to make search in John Stow's study and report on what they found there. John Strype tells us what the chaplain reported about Stow. "He had great collections of his own for the English chronicles, wherein he seemed to have bestowed much travail. They found also a great sort of old books printed; some fabulous, as of Sir Degorie, Triamour, &c., and a great parcel of old MS. chronicles, both in parchment and paper. And that besides he had miscellaneous tracts touching physic, surgery, and herbs; and also others, written in old English, in parchment. But another sort of books he had, more modern, of which the said searchers thought fit to take an inventory, as likely most to touch him; and they were books lately set forth in the realm or beyond sea in defence of Papistry, which books, as the chaplain said, declared him a great fautor of that religion." —MORLEY, HENRY, 1892, *English Writers, vol.* VIII, *p.* 361.

When he set to work upon his Survey of London, in which the stores of knowledge he had accumulated for his Chronicles and Annals enabled him to place the history of the city in relation to the history of England, he produced a book which was beyond competition. —ORDISH, T. FAIRMAN, 1897, *Shakespeare's London, p.* 22.

John Lyly

1554?–1606

John Lyly, 1554–1606. Born, in Kent, 1554. Student of Magdalen Hall, Oxford, 1569; matric., 8 Oct. 1571; B. A., 27 April 1573; M. A., 1 June 1575. Incorp. M. A., Cambridge, 1579. Settled in London, and engaged in literary work. Wrote plays for Children of the Revels. M. P. for Hindon, Feb. to March 1589; for Aylesbury, Feb. to April 1593; for Appleby, Sept. 1597 to Feb. 1598; for Aylesbury, Oct. to Dec. 1601. Married, 1595 (?). Died, in London, Nov. 1606; buried in Church of St. Bartholomew-the-Less, 30 Nov. *Works:* "Euphues," pt. i., 1579 (2nd edn. same year); pt. ii., 1580 (2nd. edn. same year); "Alexander and Campaspe," 1584 (another edn., called "Campaspe," same year); "Sapho and Phao "(anon.), 1584; "Pappe with a Hatchet" (anon.), [1589]; "Endimion," 1591; "Gallathea" (anon.), 1592; "Midas" (anon.), 1592; "Mother Bombie" (anon.), 1594; "The Woman in the Moone," 1597; "Love's Metamorphosis," 1601. *Collected Works:* "Six Court Comedies," 1632; "Dramatic Works," ed. by F. W. Fairholt (2 vols.), 1858.—SHARP, R. FARQUHARSON, 1897, *A Dictionary of English Authors, p.* 176.

EUPHUES

A manifest example thereof, may bee the great good grace and sweete vayne, which Eloquence hath attained in our speeche, because it hath had the helpe of such rare and singuler wits, as from time to time myght still adde some amendment to the same. Among whom I thinke there is none that will gainsay, but Master *Iohn Lilly* hath deserued moste high commendations, as he hath stept one steppe further therein than any either before or since he first began the wyttie discourse of his "Euphues." Whose workes, surely in respecte of his singuler eloquence and braue composition of apt words and sentences, let the learned examine and make tryall thereof thorough all the partes of Rethoricke, in fitte phrases, in pithy sentences, in gallant tropes, in flowing speeche, in plaine sence, and surely in my iudgment, I think he wyll yeelde him that verdict, which *Quintilian* giueth of bothe the best Orators *Demosthenes* and *Tully*, that from the one, nothing may be taken away, to the other, nothing may be added. But a more neerer example to prooue my former assertion true, (I meane ye meetnesse of our speeche to receiue the best forme of Poetry). — WEBBE, WILLIAM, 1586, *A Discourse of English Poetrie, ed. Arber, p.* 46.

A neat, spruce, affecting courtier, one that wears clothes well and in fashion: practiseth by his glass how to salute; speaks good remnants, notwithstanding the base viol and tobacco: swears tersely, and with variety; cares not what lady's favour he belies, or great man's familiarity: a good property to perfume the boot of a coach. He will borrow another man's horse to praise, and backs him as his own. Or, for a need, on foot can post himself into credit with his merchant, only with the gingle of his spur, and the jerk of his wand. — JONSON, BEN, 1599, *Every Man out of His Humour, Preface.*

"Euphues" is the title of a romance, wrote by one Lilly, that was in the highest vogue at this time. The court ladies had all the phrases by heart. The language is extremely affected; and . . . consists chiefly of antithesis in the thought and expression.—WHALLEY, PETER, 1756, *ed. Ben Jonson's Works, vol.* I, *p.* 286.

Lillye was a man of great reading, good memory, ready faculty of application and uncommon eloquence; but he ran into a vast excess of allusion: in sentence and conformity of style he seldom speaks directly to the purpose; but is continually carried away by one odd allusion or similie or other (out of natural history,—that yet is fabulous and not true in nature) and that still overborne by more, thick upon the back of one another, and thro' an eternal affectation of sententiousness keeps to such a formal measure of his periods as soon grows tiresome, and so by confining himself to shape, his sense so frequently into one artificial cadence, however ingenious or harmonious, abridges that variety which the style should be admired for. — OLDYS, WILLIAM, c 1761, *MS., note to Langbaine's Account of the English Dramatick Poets, p.* 328.

This romance, which Blount, the editor of the six plays, says introduced a new language, especially among the ladies, is in fact a most contemptible piece of affectation and nonsense: nevertheless it seems very certain, that it was in high estimation by the women of fashion of those times, who, we are told by Whalley the editor of Ben Jonson's works, had all the phrases by heart. As to Lilly's dramatic pieces, I have not seen any of them; but from the style of this romance, I have no doubt but they are wretched performances. — BERKENHOUT, JOHN, 1777, *Biographia Literaria, vol.* I, *p.* 377, *note.*

In the romance of "Euphues" there are chiefly three faults, which indeed pervade all the novels of the same school. 1. A constant antithesis, not merely in the ideas, but words, as one more given to *theft* than to *threft.* 2. An absurd affectation of learning, by constant reference to history and mythology. 3. A ridiculous superabundance of similitudes.—DUNLOP, JOHN, 1814–45, *The History of Fiction, p.* 403.

This production is a tissue of antithesis and alliteration, and therefore justly entitled to the appellation of *affected;* but we cannot with Berkenhout consider it as a most *contemptible piece of nonsense.* The moral is uniformly good; the vices and follies of the day are attacked with much force and keenness; there is in it much display of the manners of the times, and though, as a composition, it is very meretricious, and sometimes absurd in point of ornament, yet the construction of its sentences is frequently turned with peculiar neatness and spirit, though with much monotony of cadence.—DRAKE, NATHAN, 1817, *Shakspeare and his Times, vol.* I, *p.* 441.

These notable productions were full of pedantic and affected phraseology, (as Whalley truly says), and of high-strained antitheses of thought and expression. Unfortunately they were well received at court, where they did incalculable mischief, by vitiating the taste, corrupting the language, and introducing a spurious and unnatural mode of conversation and action, which all the ridicule in this and the following drama (Ben Jonson's "Cynthia's Revels," acted in 1600) could not put out of countenance.—GIFFORD, WILLIAM, 1816, *ed. The Works of Ben Jonson, vol.* II.

Notwithstanding all exaggeration, Lylly was really a man of wit and imagination, though both were deformed by the most unnatural affectation that ever disgraced a printed page.—SCOTT, SIR WALTER, 1820, *The Monastery, vol.* II, *p.* 44.

He it was that took hold of the somewhat battered and clipped but sterling coin of our old language, and, minting it afresh, with a very sufficient quantity of alloy, produced a sparkling currency, the very counters of court compliment.—KNIGHT, CHARLES, 1849, *Studies of Shakspere, bk.* i, *ch.* vi, *p.* 33.

In spite of occasional tediousness and pedantry, as brave, righteous, and pious a book as man need look into.—KINGSLEY, CHARLES, 1855, *Westward Ho.*

The success of "Euphues" was very great. The work was long a vade-mecum with the fashionable world, and considered a model of elegance in writing and the highest of authorities in all matters of courtly and polished speech. It contains, with all its affectations, a great multitude of acute observations, and just and even profound thoughts; and it was these striking qualities, not less than the tinsel of its style, which commended it to the practical good sense of contemporary England. —MARSH, GEORGE P., 1862, *Origin and History of the English Language, etc., p.* 546.

John Lyly, distinguished both as a dramatist and a poet, laid aside the very tradition of English style for a style modeled on the decadence of Italian prose. Euphuism, as the new fashion has been styled from the prose romance of "Euphues" in which Lyly originated it, is best known to modern readers by the pitiless caricature with which Shakspeare quizzed its pedantry, its affectation, the meaningless monotony of its far-fetched phrase, the absurdity of its extravagant conceits. Its representative, Armado, in "Love's Labor's Lost," is "a man of fire-new words, fashion's own knight," "that hath a mint of phrases in his brain; one whom the music of his own vain tongue doth ravish like enchanting harmony." But its very extravagance sprang from the general burst of delight in the new resources of thought and language which literature felt to be at its disposal; and the new sense of literary beauty which its affectation, its love of a "mint of phrases" and the "music of its own vain tongue" disclose—the new sense of pleasure in delicacy or grandeur of phrase, in the structure and arrangement of sentences, in what has been termed the atmosphere of words—was a sense out of which style was itself to spring.—GREEN, JOHN RICHARD, 1874, *A Short History of the Englsih People, ch.* vii, *sec.* v.

The story lacks definite outline and strong colouring, but it was of a kind which won acceptance in that age. The popularity of Greene's novels and Sidney's "Arcadia" is not less inexplicable to a modern reader than the fascination exercised by "Euphues." The thought—except, perhaps, in one tractate upon education, entitled "Euphues and his Ephœbus"—is rarely pregnant or profound. Yet Lyly's facile handling of grave topics, his casuistry of motives and criticism of life, exactly suited the audience he had in view. . . . "Euphues" entranced society in the sixteenth century, because our literature, in common with that of Italy and Spain and France, was passing through a phase of affectation, for which Euphuism was the national expression. It corresponded to something in the manners and the modes of thinking which prevailed in Europe at that period. It was the English type of an all but universal disease. There would have been Euphuism, in some form or other, without "Euphues;" just as the so-called æsthetic movement of to-day might have dispensed with its Bunthorne, and yet have flourished. Lyly had the fortune to become the hero of his epoch's follies, to fix the form of fashionable affectation, and to find the phrases he had coined in his study, current on the lips of gentlemen and ladies.—SYMONDS, JOHN ADDINGTON, 1884, *Shakspere's Predecessors in the English Drama, pp.* 502, 505.

Made his fame by a book, which grew out of suggestions (not only of name but largely of intent and purpose) in the "Schoolmaster" of Roger Ascham; and thus it happens over and over in the fields of literature, that a plodding man will drop from his store a nugget, over which some fellow of lively parts will stumble into renown. . . . Yet there was a certain good in this massing of epithets, and in this tesselated cumulation of nice bits of language, from which the more wary and skilful of writers could choose —as from a great vocabulary—what words were cleanest and clearest. Nor do I wish to give the impression that there were no evidences of thoughtfulness or of good purpose, under Lyly's tintinnabulation of words. Hazlitt thought excellently well of him; and Charles Kingsley, in these later times, has pronounced extravagant eulogy of him. Indeed he had high moral likings, though his inspirations are many of them from Plato or Boethius; it is questionable also if he did not pilfer from Plutarch; certainly he sugar-coats with his language a great many heathen pills. —MITCHELL, DONALD G., 1889, *English Lands Letters and Kings, From Celt to Tudor, pp.* 245, 247.

Euphuism is no singular or arbitrary phenomenon; it is a natural and recurrent feature in the development of great literatures. Moreover, it is not exactly the "euphuism" of "Euphues" that fatigues us; it is the poverty and pettiness and pretentiousness of his euphuism. We owe Lyly a debt on acconut of the smart and bold title which he has furnished for expressing the occasional outbreak of æstheticism in literary diction. When a genius has seized the passing wave-crest of such a modish enthusiasm, he has left to all time a conspicuous work of art. This I take to be the true account of that distinction which marks the styles of two great Roman historians, Sallust and Tacitus. We have ourselves had other exhibitions of this kind, which have been more genuinely "euphuistic" than that Elizabethan display which set the name. For Lyly's euphuism was only so far a genuine example as it testified to the preparedness of the soil. The manner itself seems to have been borrowed from Spanish literature, especially from the poet Gongora, after whom Spanish euphuism was called Gongorism. But the quaintness of the seventeenth century was also a euphuism, and *that* was a true home product; so was the euphuism of Johnsonese, which perhaps we may consider the last fully developed display of the kind, although there was at one time an appearance as if Carlylese would engender a nineteenth century euphuism.—EARLE, JOHN, 1890, *English Prose, p.* 437.

There is no possibility of error; with Lyly commences in England the literature of the drawing-room, that of which we speak at morning calls, productions which, in spite of vast and many changes, still occupy a favourite place on the little boudoir tables. We must also notice what pains Lyly gives himself to make his innovation a success, and so please his patronesses, and how he ornaments his thoughts and engarlands his speeches, how cunningly he imbues himself with the knowledge of the ancients and of foreigners, and what trouble he gives himself to improve upon the most learned and the most florid of them. His care was not thrown away. He was spoiled, petted, and caressed by the ladies; with an impartial heart they extended to the author the same favour they granted to the book, and to their little dogs. He was proclaimed king of letters by his admirers, and became, in fact, king of the *précieux.* He created a school, and the name of his hero served to baptize a whole literature. This particular form of bad style was called *euphuism.* — JUSSERAND, J. J., 1890, *The English Novel in the Time of Shakespeare, p.* 105.

There is, perhaps, no single book the reading of which is more necessary to anyone who is thoroughly to understand the age of Elizabeth from the literary side than "Euphues;" but there are not many more difficult to read. The merely literary characteristics of it, though they have often been strangely misunderstood, are not hard to sum up. —SAINTSBURY, GEORGE, 1895, *Social England, ed. Traill, vol.* III, *p.* 335.

The honor of being the first Englishman to raise fiction above the level of a mere tale must undoubtedly be assigned to Lyly, although the term novel can hardly be applied to his "Euphues." It is too plainly a hand-book of etiquette, made a little more palatable to the public by the employment of a hero and by a few indications of the trend of the hero's affections, to be treated under any other head than that of didactic fiction. . . Lyly was too much concerned with the ways of polite society, and too little with his plot or characters to be openly admitted to the sacred pale of novelists. Yet he very likely paved the way for more ambitious successors. —WARREN, F. M., 1895, *A History of the Novel Previous to the Seventeenth Century, p.* 336.

Looking broadly at the early prose of Elizabeth's reign, it is surely impossible not to recognise that a new element of richness, of ornament, of harmony, an element by no means wholly admirable, but extremely noticeable, was introduced by Lyly; that, in short, the publication of "Euphues" burnishes and suddenly animates—with false lights and glisterings, if you will, but still animates—the humdrum aspect of English prose as Ascham and Wilson had left it. Splendour was to be one of the principal attributes of the Elizabethan age, and "Euphues" is the earliest prose book which shows any desire to be splendid. —GOSSE, EDMUND, 1897, *Short History of Modern English Literature, p.* 80.

DRAMAS

The spring is at hand, and therefore I present you a Lilly growing in a Groue of Lawrels. For this Poet sat at the *Sunnes* Table. *Apollo* gaue him a wreath of his own *Bayes*, without snatching. The *Lyre* he played on, had no borrowed strings. . . . Our Nation are in his debt, for a new English, which hee taught them. *Euphues* and his England began first, that language: All our Ladies were then his Schollers; And that Beautie in Court, which could not Parley, *Euphueisme* was as little regarded; as she which now there, speaks not French. —BLOUNT, EDWARD, 1632, *ed. Lyly's Six Court Comedies.*

John Lilly, a writer of several old-fashioned Comedies and Tragedies, which have been printed together in a volume, and might perhaps when time was, be in very good request. —PHILLIPS, EDWARD, 1675, *Theatrum Poetarum Anglicanorum, ed. Brydges, p.* 199.

His comedy in prose, "Campaspe," is a warning example of the impossibility of ever constructing, from ancedotes and epigrammatic sallies, any thing like a dramatic whole. The author was a learned witling, but in no respect a poet. —SCHLEGEL, AUGUSTUS WILLIAM, 1809, *Dramatic Art and Literature, tr. Black, Lecture* xiii.

Worthy of their names ["Midas" and "Endymion,"] and of the subject. The story in both is classical, and the execution is for the most part elegant and simple. There is often something that reminds one of the graceful communicativeness of Lucian or of Apuleius, from whom one of the stories is borrowed. Lyly made a more attractive picture of Grecian manners at second-hand than of English characters from his own observation. —HAZLITT, WILLIAM, 1820, *Lectures on the Literature of the Age of Elizabeth, Lecture II.*

Whose dramas are distinguished by an exquisite grace and Grecian purity of construction, and whose songs in particular are models of airness and music. —SHAW, THOMAS B., 1847, *Outlines of English Literature, p.* 103.

The general character of Lilly's prose, in his dramas, consists only in a superabundance of poetic and witty language, in far-fetched similes and curious images on every occasion, however unsuitable; at the same time his prose, like that of all other conceit-writers, acquires by continual antitheses and epigrammatic allusions, somewhat of a sharpness, piquancy, and logical perspicuity, the worth of which, as regards the development of the language, was acknowledged with praise by such contemporaries as Webster. From no other of his predecessors has Shakespeare, therefore, especially as regards the dexterous play of words in the merry parts of his comedies and dramas, learned and obtained so much as from Lilly. The witty conversation, the comic demonstrations, the abundance of similes and startling repartees, are here prefigured; his *quibs*, which Lilly himself defines as the short expressions of a sharp wit, with a bitter sense lying in a sweet word, were a school to Shakespeare.—GERVINUS, G. G., 1849–62, *Shakespeare Commentaries, tr. Bunnett, p.* 76.

Of the dramatic works of Marston and Lilly it is enough to say that they are truly *works* to the reader, but in no sense dramatic, nor, as literature, worth the paper they blot. They seem to have been deemed worthy of republication because they were the contemporaries of true poets; and if all the Tuppers of the nineteenth century will buy their plays on the same principle, the sale will be a remunerative one.—LOWELL, JAMES RUSSELL, 1858-64-90, *Library of Old Authors, Prose Works, Riverside ed., vol.* I, *p.* 254.

Lilly is known in dramatic literature as the author of eight comedies written to be performed at the court of Elizabeth. They are in all respects opposed to the genius of the English drama. They do not even pretend to be representations of human life and human character, but are pure fantasy pieces, in which the personages are a heterogeneous medley of Grecian gods and goddesses, and impossible, colorless creatures with sublunary names, all thinking with one brain, and speaking with one tongue—the conceitful, crotchety brain and the dainty, well-trained tongue of clever, witty John Lilly. They are all in prose, but contain some pretty, fanciful verses called songs, which are as unlyrical in spirit as the plays in which they appear are undramatic. From these plays Shakespeare borrowed a few thoughts; but they exercised no modifying influence upon his genius, nor did they at all conform to that of the English drama, upon which they are a mere grotesque excrescence.—WHITE, RICHARD GRANT, 1865, *ed. The Works of William Shakespeare, Rise and Progress of the English Drama, vol.* I, *p.* clxxviii.

The classicism of Lyly was indeed neither profound in its depth nor extensive in its range; and though he was ever drawing bucket after bucket from the stream for his literary needs, he had never bathed in its waters and imbued himself with their influence. . . . Neither industry, nor ingenuity, nor wit, can be denied to him; in addition to which he possessed a lyric gift of no common kind, though he unfortunately only very rarely availed himself of it. For most of his lyrical passages are trivial both in subject and in execution, and in fact mere perfunctory transitions in the action of the play. His real service to the progress of the drama, which has not perhaps generally received sufficient attention, is to be sought neither in his choice of subjects nor in his imagery—though to his fondness for fairy-lore and the whole phantasmagoria of legend, classical as well as romantic, his contemporaries, and Shakspere in particular, were indebted for a stimulative precedent. It lies in his adoption of Gascoigne's innovation of writing plays in prose; and in his having, though under the fetters of an affected and vicious style, given the first example of brisk and vivacious dialogue.—WARD, ADOLPHUS WILLIAM, 1875, *A History of English Dramatic Literature, vol.* I, *pp.* 156, 159.

Lyly brought to the composition of his plays the same qualities which he had displayed in his romance—learning, fancy, and wit. All that characterises the style and diction of "Euphues" characterises the style and diction of these dramas: the same excess of smoothness, sententiousness, and epigram, of alliteration and assonance, the same studied antithesis, not merely in the arrangement of the words and clauses, but in the ideas and sentiments, the same accumulation of superfluous similes and illustrations, drawn sometimes from the facts but more frequently from the fictions of natural history, the same affectation of continuous references to ancient mythology and history pedantically piled up for the sake of learned display, the same plethora of wit as distinguished from humour, and of fancy as distinguished from imagination. —COLLINS, JOHN CHURTON, 1895, *Essays and Studies, p.* 186.

The great dramatist shows traces of his predecessor's influence in the remarkable frequency of the allusions to animals—sometimes of a fabulous nature—which occur in the early plays and poems, as well as in the later works like "Lear" and

"Coriolanus." Moreover, though Shakspere mocked at the artifices of Euphuism, he must have appreciated its incisive force, its lucidity and refinement. These are the qualities which specially distinguish his own colloquial prose, and when we listen to the brilliant sallies of Falstaff or Benedick, Beatrice or Rosalind, we should remember that they have their prelude in the witty dialogue of "Campaspe" or "Endimion." Lyly too set the fashion which Shakspere followed of introducing lyrics, as a musical relief; and his imaginative type of comedy, with its supernatural framework and allegorical design, pointed the way to "A Midsummer Night's Dream" and "The Tempest."—BOAS, FREDERICK S., 1896, *Shakspere and his Predecessors*, p. 73.

Lyly's plays, like his person, stand quite apart from those of the rest of the group, with which they have nothing in common except the strong classicism, the presence of "University wit," the striking breach with the old tradition of horseplay interlude or wooden tragedy, the exquisite lyric which sometimes diversifies them, and their influence on the greatest dramatist of the next or any age. Written not for the public stage but as court amusements (or "abridgments," as Thesus would say), they have a good deal in common with the Masque. The very marked, not to say conceited, style and the strong, almost bitter, satirical spirit which appear in "Euphues" are also visible. But their most interesting historical characteristic is the way in which, uncertainly and tentatively, they strike out the way of Romantic Comedy, the most arduous and least frequently trodden of all dramatic ways, but when trodden successfully the way to the rarest and choicest of dramatic paradises.—SAINTSBURY, GEORGE, 1898, *A Short History of English Literature*, p. 283.

GENERAL

He is but a little fellow, but he hath one of the best wits in England.—NASHE, THOMAS, 1592, *Pierce Pennilesse*.

Diuine wits, for many things as sufficient as all antiquity (I speake it not on slight surmise, but considerate iudgement). . . . *Lilly*, the famous for facility in discourse. —LODGE, THOMAS, 1596, *Wits Miserie, and the Worlds Madness*, p. 57.

Always averse to the crabbed studies of logic and philosophy. For so it was that his genie being naturally bent to the pleasant paths of poetry, (as if Apollo had given to him a wreath of his own bays, without snatching or struggling,) did in a manner neglect academical studies, yet not so much but that he took the degrees in arts, that of master being compleated 1575. At which time, as he was esteemed in the university a noted wit so afterwards was he in the court of Q. Elizabeth, where he was also reputed a rare poet, witty, comical, and facetious.—WOOD, ANTHONY, 1691–1721, *Athenæ Oxonenses*, vol. I, p. 295.

Sackville has strutted into obscurity; and even Lyly, though his writings were once the delight of a court, and apparently perpetuated by a proverb, is now scarcely known even by name.—IRVING, WASHINGTON, 1819–48, *The Mutability of Literature, Sketch-Book*.

John Lyly was an ingenious scholar, with some fancy; but if poetry be the heightened expression of natural sentiments and impressions, he has little title to the rank of a poet. His thoughts and his language are usually equally artificial, the results of labour and study; and in scarcely a single instance does he seem to have yielded to the impulses of genuine feeling.—COLLIER, JOHN PAYNE, 1831, *History of English Dramatic Poetry*, vol. III, p. 172.

On the whole, Lyly was a learned, elegant, and witty writer, a *bel esprit* in the manner of the sixteenth century, but no poet. Accordingly, his pieces can by no means be called popular. Nevertheless, his style of writing exercised so great an influence on the language of the age, that whatever in Shakspeare's diction appears far-fetched and affected,—his sharp-shooting, for instance, with antithesis and sententious pomp of phrase, his play of words, and occasionally artificial wit,—are to be laid to Lyly's account, and to be regarded as the echo of the prevailing tone of his day. That Shakspeare studied Lyly's pieces is clear, both from certain maxims and witticisms, which he must have borrowed from him, and from certain passages in which he has closely imitated him. Such passages, however, are only occasional, and therefore while Tieck is right in maintaining that the commentators of Shakspeare have much to learn from Lyly, the assertion of Schlegel is equally true, that

Shakspeare himself can have learned little if any thing from him.—ULRICI, HERMANN, 1839, *Shakspeare's Dramatic Art*, p. 36.

Lyly himself, so fantastic that he seems to write purposely in defiance of common sense, is at times a genuine poet, a singer, a man capable of rapture, akin to Spenser and Shakspeare.—TAINE, H. A., 1871, *History of English Literature, tr. Van Laun*, vol. I, bk. ii, ch. i, p. 163.

The airy mirthful plays and pretty little songs of the "witty, comical, facetiously quick and unparalleled John Lyly," as his publisher described him, are a standing refutation of M. Taine's picture of England in the Elizabethan age as a sort of den of wild beasts. No Frenchman in any age was ever more light and gay than Queen Elizabeth's favourite writer of comedies, and the inventor or perfecter of a fashionable style of sentimental speech among her courtiers. The epithet "unparalleled" applied to Lyly was more exact than puffs generally are. Though he is said to have set a fashion of talk among the ladies of the Court and their admirers, he found no imitator in letters; his peculiar style perished from literature with himself.—MINTO, WILLIAM, 1880, *English Poets, ed. Ward*, vol. I, p. 394.

It is his quickness of wit that is his strength. He knows the utmost that can be done with his resources, and he is satisfied with nothing short of the utmost. It is this unfailing certainty about his own faculties and his aims that preserves, even now, a certain grace in Lyly's moral story, though its day is so long passed over. In his comedy his aim was more distinct, his faculty less encumbered. His songs have a value not comparable with anything in his prose.—KER, W. P., 1893, *English Prose, ed. Craik*, vol. I, p. 378.

Exhausts the animal and vegetable kingdom to enhance a truism.—TOVEY, DUNCAN C., 1897, *Reviews and Essays in English Literature*, p. 39.

Lyly had made a discovery which was of permanent value, and for which he ought to receive full credit. While the language of philosophy and criticism was still in a fluid state, he had perceived the advantage of clearness, correctness, and precision, in the arrangement of words. It was not altogether his fault if his age was more favourable to the development of language than to the expression of thought. He at least showed the nation the possibilities of balance and harmony in English prose composition; and the form which he established in the structure of the English sentence has never been entirely lost sight of by his successors. Addison and Steele, while they aimed at something much beyond the "fit phrases, pithy sentences, and gallant tropes," which gratified the taste of Webbe, learned from Lyly how to present genuine thoughts in an artistic form; and Burke, Johnson, and Macaulay, avoiding the petty particularity of his contrasted words, followed his example in working up sentences and periods to the climax required for the just and forcible presentation of the argument. —COURTHOPE, W. J., 1897, *A History of English Poetry*, vol. II, p. 201.

In his grave and poetic moments there is a prim charm about Lyly, and a frosty moonlight glitter which is attractive. His snatches of song are among the best in an age of lyric poetry.—HANNAY, DAVID, 1898, *The Later Renaissance*, p. 237.

Sir Edward Dyer

1540?–1607.

Born in the reign of Henry VIII. Dyer lived till some years after King James's accession to the English throne. He was a friend of Sir Philip Sidney, who, in his verses, celebrates their intimacy. Dyer was educated at Oxford, and was employed in several foreign embassies by Elizabeth. He studied chemistry, and was thought to be a Rosicrucian. . . . The popular poem, "My Mind to Me a Kingdom Is," with additions, is credited in some collections to William Byrd (1543-1623), an eminent composer of sacred music, and who published in 1588 a volume of "Psalms, Sonnets," etc. Both Byrd and Joshua Sylvester seem to have laid claim to the best parts of Dyer's poem. A collection of Dyer's writings was printed as late as 1872.—SARGENT, EPES, 1881, *Harper's Cyclopædia of British and American Poetry*, p. 8.

His friendship is like a gem added to my treasures. —LANGUET, HUBERT, 1586? *Letter to Philip Sidney, Epistolae, p.* 215.

Maister *Edward Dyar*, for Elegie most sweete, solempne and of high conceit.—PUTTENHAM, GEORGE, 1589, *The Arte of English Poesie, ed. Arber, p.* 77.

Thou virgin knight, that dost thy selfe obscure
From world's unequal eyes.

—DAVIES, JOHN, OF HEREFORD, 1603, *Microcosmos, Preface.*

Sir Edward Dyer, of Somersetshire (Sharpham Parke, etc.), was a great witt, poet, and acquaintance of Mary, countesse of Pembroke, and Sir Philip Sydney. He is mentioned in the preface of the "Arcadia." He had four thousand pounds per annum, and was left fourscore thousand pounds in money; he wasted it almost all. This I had from captaine Dyer, his great grandsonne, or brother's great grandson. I thought he had been the sonne of the Lord Chiefe Justice Dyer, as I have inserted in one of these papers, but that was a mistake. The judge was of the same family, the captain tells me.—AUBREY, JOHN, 1669–96, *Brief Lives, ed. Clark, vol.* I, *p.* 243.

Sir Edward Dier, a person of good account in Queen Elizabeth's reign, poetically addicted, several of whose pastoral Odes and Madrigals are extant, in a printed Collection of certain choice pieces of some of the most eminent poets of that time.—PHILLIPS, EDWARD, 1675, *Theatrum Poetarum Anglicanorum, ed. Brydges, p.* 144.

A poet whose lot has been rather singular. His name is generally coupled with that of Sir Philip Sidney, and of the most fashionable writers of the age; and yet Bolton, who was almost a contemporary critic, professes "not to have seen much of his poetry." Though a knight, in a reign when knighthood was nobility, the time of his birth is unknown. . . . The letters M. D. in the "Paradise of Dainty Devices" are presumed (says Mr. Ritson in his "Bibliographia") to denote this Master Dyer. Of six pieces, preserved in "England's Helicon," only half of one appeared worth transcribing, as a specimen of his style.—ELLIS, GEORGE, 1790–1845, *Specimens of Early English Poets, vol.* II, *p.* 157.

Dyer is now remembered by one poem only, the well-known "My mind to me a Kingdom is," which though fluent and spirited verse, probably owes most of its reputation to the happiness of its opening. The little poem "To Phillis the Fair Shepherdess" is in the lighter, less hackneyed Elizabethan vein, and makes a welcome interlude among the "woeful ballads" which immediately surround it in "England's Helicon," where it first appeared. Still, when all is said, Dyer, a man of action and affairs rather than of letters, is chiefly interesting for his connection with Sidney and Greville; and that stiff pathetic engraving of Sidney's funeral, which represents him as pall-bearer side by side with Lord Brooke, throws a light upon his memory that none of his poems have power to shed.—WARD, MARY A., 1880, *English Poets, ed. Ward, vol.* I, *p.* 376.

Dyer gained considerable fame as a poet in the last quarter of the sixteenth century. Puttenham in 1589 pronounced him to be "for elegy most sweet, solemn, and of high conceit;" and Meres in "Wit's Treasury," 1598, mentions him as "famous for elegy." But his verse was never collected. During his lifetime, and early in the next century, critics were at a loss to know on what work his fame rested. Edmund Bolton in "Hypercritica" says that he "had not seen much of Sir Edward Dyer's poetry;" and William Drummond, coupling his name with Raleigh's, observes: "Their works are so few that have come to my hands, I cannot well say anything of them."—BULLEN, A. H., 1888, *Dictionary of National Biography, vol.* XVI, *p.* 284.

The number of poems which can be confidently ascribed to Dyer is small, but some of them have real merit, and not only justify the reputation which he enjoyed in his day, but are interesting as mirrors of his character and feelings. Oldys says of him that "he would not stoop to fawn;" and this may well be believed of the writer of the famous lines "My mind to me a kingdom is."—COURTHOPE, W. J., 1897, *A History of English Poetry, vol.* II, *p.* 307.

He had a very great reputation in his time as a poet, but his remains are small, and only one of them, the famous and excellent, but not superexcellent,

My mind to me a kingdom is,

has obtained much place in the general memory.—SAINTSBURY, GEORGE, 1898, *A Short History of English Literature, p.* 272.

Henry Chettle

1540?-1607?

Produced "A Doleful Ditty, or Sorrowful Sonet, of the Lord Darly" (1567); "Kinde Harts Dreame" (1593); "Piers Plainnes, Seven Yeres Prentiship" (1595); "The Pope's Pittiful Lamentation for the Death of his Deere Darling, Don Joan of Austria: and Death's Answer to the Same;" "England's Mourning Garment, worn here by Plain Shepherds in Memory of Elizabeth" (1603); and "The Tragedy of Hoffman: or, a revenge for a Father" (1631). He is said to have been concerned, with others, in the production of over two hundred dramatic pieces.—ADAMS, W. DAVENPORT, 1877, *Dictionary of English Literature, p.* 146.

This is the Jew, alyed uery near
Vnto the broker, for they both do beare
Vndoubted testimonies of their kinne;
A brace of rascals in a league of sinne:
Two filthy curres, that will on no man fawne,
Before they taste the sweetnesse of the pawne.
And then the slaues will be as kind forsooth,
Not as *Kind-heart*, in drawing out a tooth;
For he doth ease the patient of his paine,
But they disease the borrower of his gaine.
—ROWLANDS, SAMUEL, 1600, *The Letting of Humours Blood in the Head Vaine.*

In comes Chettle sweating and blowing, by reason of his fatnes; to welcome whom, because hee was of olde acquaintance, all rose vp, and fell presentlie on their knees, to drinck a health to all the louers of Hellicon.—DEKKER, THOMAS, 1606, *A Knight's Conjuring, non-Dramatic Works, ed. Grosart.*

Was very much superior to Munday. He seems to have been originally a printer or stationer (he subscribes himself "stationer" in a note of acknowledgment to Henslowe in 1598), and probably took to writing plays about the same time as Marlowe. . . . Chettle, like so many other of the Elizabethan poets, no matter how inflated he is in expressing vehement passions of rage, hatred, and revenge, displays considerable felicity in the expression of the tender feelings.—MINTO, WILLIAM, 1874-85, *Characteristics of English Poets, pp.* 253, 254.

. . . Chettle, in whose fresh funereal verse
Weeps Marian yet on Robin's wildwood hearse.
—SWINBURNE, ALGERNON CHARLES, 1882, *The Many.*

John Still

1543?-1608

Born at Grantham about 1543: died Feb. 26, 1607. An English prelate. He was a student at Christ's College, Cambridge; afterward dean of Bocking, canon of Westminster, master of St. Johns and of Trinity, vice-chancellor of Cambridge, and bishop of Bath and Wells (1593-1607.) In 1570 he was Lady Margaret's professor of divinity. He was probably the author of the comedy "Gammer Gurton's Needle." He made a large fortune in lead-mines discovered in the Mendip Hills.—SMITH, BENJAMIN E., *ed.,* 1894-97, *The Century Cyclopedia of Names, p.* 958.

PERSONAL

Some helpes, more hopes, all encouragements in my best studies; to whom I never came but I grew more religious; from whom I never went, but I parted better instructed. . . . His breeding was from his childhood in good literature and partly in musique. . . . I hold him a rare man for preaching, for arguing, for learning, for lyving; I could only wish that in all theise he would make lesse use of logique and more of rhetoricke.—HARINGTON, SIR JOHN, 1612?, *Nugæ Antiquæ, ed. Park, vol.* II, *pp.* 157, 158, 165.

He was one of a venerable presence, no lesse famous for a Preacher then a Disputant. Finding his own strength, he did not stick to warn such as he disputed with in their own arguments, to take heed to their answers, like a perfect Fencer, that will tell aforehand in what button he will give his Venew.—FULLER, THOMAS, 1662, *The Worthies of England, ed. Nichols, vol.* II, *p.* 12.

His effigy may still be seen beneath its canopy in Wells Cathedral. A grim Puritan divine, with pointed beard and long stiff painted robes, lies face-upward on the monument. This is the author of the first elaborately executed farce in our language. —SYMONDS, JOHN ADDINGTON, 1884, *Shakspere's Predecessors in the English Drama, p.* 205.

GAMMER GURTON'S NEEDLE

The writer has a degree of jocularity which sometimes rises above buffoonery, but is often disgraced by lowness of incident. Yet in a more polished age he would have chosen, nor would he perhaps have disgraced, a better subject.—WARTON, THOMAS, 1778-81, *History of English Poetry, sec.* xlvii.

The humour of this curious old drama. . . . is broad, familiar, and grotesque; the characters are sketched with a strong though coarse outline, and are to the last consistently supported.—DRAKE, NATHAN, 1817, *Shakspeare and his Times, vol.* II, *p.* 233.

"Gammer Gurton's Needle" has this peculiarity belonging to it, that it is, I believe, the first existing English play acted at either University; and it is a singular coincidence, (which is farther illustrated in "The Annals of the Stage,") that the author of the comedy so represented should be the very person who many years afterwards, when he had become Vice Chancellor of Cambridge, was called upon to remonstrate with the ministers of Queen Elizabeth against having an English play performed before her at that University, as unbefitting its learning, dignity, and character. —COLLIER, JOHN PAYNE, 1831, *History of English Dramatic Poetry, vol.* II, *p.* 463.

It is impossible for any thing to be meaner in subject and characters than this strange farce; but the author had some vein of humor, and writing neither for fame nor money, but to make light-hearted boys laugh, and to laugh with them, and that with as little grossness as the story would admit, is not to be judged with severe criticism.—HALLAM, HENRY, 1837-39, *Introduction to the Literature of Europe, pt.* ii, *ch.* vi, *par.* 23.

For the simple dry humour which prevails in it, as well as for the sustained tone and colouring, which are in perfect keeping with the subject, and the sphere of life in which its scene is laid, is not unworthy of its place in the history of the English drama.—ULRICI, HERMANN, 1839, *Shakspeare's Dramatic Art, p.* 18.

This ancient comedy is the work of a truly comic genius, who knew not how to choose his subject, and indulged a taste repulsive to those who only admit of delicate and not familiar humor. Its grossness, however, did not necessarily result from the prevalent grossness of the times; since a recent discovery, with which Warton was unacquainted, has shown the world that an English comedy, which preceded the hitherto supposed first comedy in our language, is remarkable for its chasteness, the propriety of its great variety of characters, the truth of the manners in a wide circle of society, and the uninterrupted gayety pervading the whole airy composition.—DISRAELI, ISAAC, 1841, *First Tragedy and First Comedy, Amenities of Literature.*

It may be coarse, earthy, but in reading it one feels that he is at least a man among men, and not a humbug among humbugs. —LOWELL, JAMES RUSSELL, 1875-90, *Spenser, Prose Works, Riverside ed., vol.* IV, *p.* 300.

"Gammer Gurton's Needle" is not such a play as a Bishop would have written, for its fun is associated with some coarseness of jesting common to the good old time, from which "Ralph Roister Doister" was free only because it was written by a schoolmaster for public acting by his boys. John Still wrote as a young man with high spirits, to amuse his comrades. Fun is abundant in this comedy of rustic life, and its jesting—at the rudest—only sins against later convention, the play being in no thought or word immoral. It is indelicate, but not indecent. —MORLEY, HENRY, 1892, *English Writers, vol.* VIII, *p.* 383.

The serious-minded Still has been generally claimed as the author of the boisterously merry comedy "Gammer Gurton's Needle," but the evidence in his favour proves on examination to be inconclusive. While Still was in residence at Christ's College the books of the bursar show that a play was performed there in 1566, when 20s. was paid "the carpenters for setting up the scaffold." It may be inferred (although there is no positive proof) that the play was identical with the one published in 1575 under the title of "A Ryght Pythy, Pleasaunt, and Merie Comedie: Intytuld Gammer Gurton's Needle: Played on Stage not long ago in Christes

Colledge in Cambridge. Made by Mr. S. Master of Art'' (London, 4to, by Thomas Colwell). It has been argued that the piece was written at an earlier date than 1566, on the ground that a play called "Dyccon of Bedlam'' (not now extant) was, according to the "Stationers' Register,'' licensed for publication to Thomas Colwell, the publisher of "Gammer Gurton's Needle,'' in 1563; and that "Diccon the Bedlam'' (a half-witted itinerant beggar) is a leading character in the extant comedy. But the sobriquet was at the period not uncommonly applied to any half-imbecile mendicant, and in itself offers no proof of the two plays' identity. "Mr. S. Master of Art,'' the author of "Gammer Gurton's Needle," was first identified with Still by Isaac Reed in 1782 in his edition of Baker's "Biographia Dramatica.'' Reed's main argument was that Still was the only M. A. of Christ's College whose name began with S. in 1566, when "Gammer Gurton's Needle'' may be assumed to have been first performed. This statement is not accurate, for William Sanderson graduated M. A. from Christ's College in 1555, and was living more than thirty years later, and twelve other masters of arts of the college, all of whose names began with S, proceeded to the degree in or before 1566, and were alive in 1575, when "Mr. S. Master of Art'' was put forth as the author of "Gammer Gurton's Needle'' on the title-page of the first edition. In his lifetime the comedy was not assigned to Still, who is not known to have manifested any interest in the English drama. The only contemporary references to the question of authorship are indeterminate, but they do not point in Still's direction. . . . A study of the play itself gives no assistance as to its authorship, which must be left undetermined.—LEE, SIDNEY, 1898, *Dictionary of National Biography, vol.* LIV, *p.* 372.

Thomas Sackville

Earl of Dorset

1536–1608

Born, at Buckhurst, Sussex, 1536. Probably educated at Sullington Grammar School. Incumbent of the Chantry at Sullington Church, 1546. Called to Bar at Inner Temple. Married Cicely Baker, 1554. M. P. for Westmoreland, 1558; for East Grinstead, 1559; for Aylesbury, 1563. Tragedy "Gorboduc'' (written with Norton), performed in Inner Temple Hall, 1561. Grand Master of Freemasons, 1561–67. Travelled on Continent, 1563–66. Knighted, and created Baron Buckhurst, 8 June 1567. Privy Councillor. Lord Lieutenant of Sussex, 1569. On political missions to France, 1568 and 1571. To Holland, 1587 and 1589; to France, 1591 and 1598. Created M. A., Cambridge, Aug. 1571. Commissioner for Ecclesiastical Causes, 1588. K. G., 24 April 1589. Chancellor of Oxford University, Dec. 1591; incorporated M. A., 6 Jan. 1592. Commissioner of Writs, 1592 (?). Lord Treasurer, 1599. Lord High Steward, 1601. Created Earl of Dorset, 13 March 1604. Died suddenly, at Whitehall, 19 April 1608. Buried in Westminster Abbey. *Works:* Contribution to "A Myrroure for Magistrates,'' 1559–63; "The Tragedy of Gorboduc'' (with Norton), 1565; Verses contributed to Sir T. Hoby's "Courtier,'' 1561; and possibly to "A Paradise of Dainty Devices,'' 1576. *Collected Works:* ed. by Rev. R. W. Sackville West, 1859. SHARP, R. FARQUHARSON, 1897, *A Dictionary of English Authors, p.* 245.

PERSONAL

He kept house for forty and two years in an honourable proportion. For thirty years of those his family consisted of little less, in one place or another, than two hundred persons. But for more than twenty years, besides workmen and other hired, his number at the least hath been two hundred and twenty daily, as appear on check-role. A very rare example in this present age of ours, when housekeeping is so decayed. — ABBOT, GEORGE, ARCHBISHOP OF CANTERBURY, 1608, *Sermon preached at Westminster, May* 26.

He was a very fine Gentleman of person and endowments both of art and nature; but without measure magnificent, till on the turn of his humor, and the allay that his yeares and good counsels had wrought upon those immoderate courses of his youth, and that height of spirit inherent to his House. And then did the Queen, as a most judicious and indulgent Prince, when she saw the man grow stayed and setled, give him her assistance, and advanced him to the Treasurership, where he made amends to his House for his misspent time, both in the increasement of Estate and Honour, which the Queen conferred on him, together with the opportunity to remake himself, and thereby to shew that this was a Childe, that should have a share in her grace, and a taste of her bounty. They much commend his Elocution, but more the excellency of his Pen, for he was a Schollar, and a person of a quick dispatch, (Faculties that yet run in the bloud.) And they say of him, that his Secretaries did little for him by the way of Inditement, wherein they could seldome please him, he was so facete and choice in his phrase and stile. —NAUNTON, SIR ROBERT, 1630? *Fragmenta Regalia, ed. Arber, p.* 55.

It is grievous to think that this splendid genius, who lived to a great age, and was created Earl of Dorset by King James I., afterwards sunk the poet in the coarser character of statesman. — BRYDGES, SIR SAMUEL EGERTON, 1834, *Autobiography, vol.* I, *p.* 279.

I might conclude this brief Memoir with the testimony of others to the character and genius of him who is the subject of it, and thus show, as Lord Orford remarks, that "few ministers have left behind them so unblemished a character;" but since the actions and words of a great man are the best biographical comment that can be offered, although it may be found that I have but faintly and imperfectly traced and set forth the former, with confidence as to the result I now place the latter in the hands of the reader. — SACKVILLE-WEST, REGINALD W., 1859, *ed. Sackville's Works, p.* xxvi.

Rich, cultivated, sagacious, and favoured by the queen, he possessed all the qualifications for playing a prominent part in politics, diplomacy, and court society. . . . Dorset is credited by Naunton with strong judgment and self-confidence, but in domestic politics he showed little independence. His main object was to stand well with his sovereign, and in that he succeeded. He was a good speaker, and the numerous letters and state papers extant in his handwriting exhibit an unusual perspicuity. In private life he was considerate to his tenants. . . . There are portraits of the Earl of Dorset at Knole and Buckhurst (by Marcus Gheeraerst the younger); while in the picture gallery at Oxford there is a painting of him in the robes of chancellor, with the blue ribbon, George, and treasurer's staff. This was presented by Lionel, duke of Dorset, in 1735. There are engravings by George Vertue, E. Scriven, and W. J. Alais.—LEE, SIDNEY, 1897, *Dictionary of National Biography, vol.* L, *pp.* 98, 100.

MIRROR FOR MAGISTRATES
1559-63

Then have we the "Mirrour of Magistrates" lately augmented by my friend mayster John Higgins, and penned by the choysest learned wittes, which for the stately-proportioned uaine of the heroick style, and good meetly proportion of uerse may challenge the best of Lydgate, and all our late rhymers.—HAKE, EDWARD, 1588, *Touch-Stone of Wittes.*

I account the "Mirrour of Magistrates," meetely furnished of beautiful parts.— SIDNEY, SIR PHILIP, 1595, *An Apologie for Poetrie, ed. Arber, p.* 62.

The Reader, in this Performance, will see that *Allegory* was brought to great Perfection, before *Spencer* appear'd, and that, if Mr. *Sackville* did not surpass him, 'twas because he had the Disadvantage of Writing first.—COOPER, ELIZABETH, 1737, *The Muses' Library, p.* 89.

Though the induction to the "Mirror for Magistrates" displays some potent sketches, it bears the complexion of a saturnine genius, and resembles a bold and gloomy landscape on which the sun never shines.—CAMPBELL, THOMAS, 1819, *Specimens of the British Poets.*

It was designed to form a series of dramatic soliloquies united in one interlude. Sackville, who seems to have planned the scheme, wrote an "Induction," or prologue, and also one of the stories, that of the first Duke of Buckingham. The "Induction" displays best his poetical genius: it is, like much earlier poetry, a representation of allegorical personages, but with a fertility of imagination, vividness of description, and strength of language, which not only leave his predecessors far behind, but may fairly be compared with some of the most poetical passages in Spenser. Sackville's "Induction" forms a link which unites the school of Chaucer and Lydgate to the "Faery Queen." It would certainly be vain to look in Chaucer, wherever Chaucer is original, for the grand creations of Sackville's fancy; yet we should never find any one who would rate Sackville above Chaucer. The strength of an eagle is not to be measured only by the height of his place, but by the time that he continues on the wing. Sackville's "Induction" consists of a few hundred lines; and even in these there is a monotony of gloom and sorrow which prevents us from wishing it to be longer. — HALLAM, HENRY, 1837–39, *Introduction to the Literature of Europe, pt.* ii, *ch.* v, *par.* 59.

The Induction to the "Mirror of Magistrates" is a *look in* at the infernal regions, and is like a portal to the allegorical part of the "Fairy Queen," or rather to the sadder portion of that part; for it has none of the voluptuousness, and but little imitation of the beauty; nor is the style anything nearly so rich. Perhaps a better comparison would be that of the quaint figures of the earliest Italian painters, compared with those of Raphael. Or it is a bit of a minor Dante. But the poetry is masterly of its kind, — full of passion and imagination, — true, and caring for nothing but truth. — HUNT, LEIGH, 1847, *Men, Women, and Books, vol.* I, *p.* 254.

A greater work than "Gorboduc" adorns the memory of Sackville. During the last years of Mary, which might well be called gloomy, were it not for the fiery glare that tinges them red as if with martyrs' blood, he sketched out the design of a great poem, which was to be entitled "The Mirrour of Magistrates," and was to embrace poetic histories of all the great Englishmen who had suffered remarkable disasters. . . . The "Induction" is a grand pictured allegory, which describes "within the porch and jaws of hell" Remorse, Dread, Revenge, and other terrible things, that are ever gnawing away at the root of our human life. It contains only a few hundred lines, and yet these are enough to place Sackville high on the list of British poets. — COLLIER, WILLIAM FRANCIS, 1861, *History of English Literature, p.* 133.

He infused into it a new and higher spirit. His coadjutors would have been content to drone on with scattered legends on the old plan, but Sackville aspired to emulate Dante with a connected epic. His language, also, as well as his conception, is fresh and powerful: his singing-robes are new and rich, and throw a double dinginess on the verses of his associates, which are covered with mean and incongruous patches.—MINTO, WILLIAM, 1874–85, *Characteristics of English Poets, p.* 145.

His contributions to "The Mirror for Magistrates" contain the best poetry written in the English language between Chaucer and Spenser, and are most certainly the originals or at least the models of some of Spenser's finest work. . . . But the poetical value of the whole is extraordinary. The two constituents of that value, the formal and the material, are represented with a singular equality of development. . . . He has not indeed the manifold music of Spenser — it would be unreasonable to expect that he should have it. But his stanzas, are of remarkable melody, and they have about them a command, a completeness of accomplishment within the writer's intentions, which is very noteworthy in so young a man. The extraordinary richness and stateliness of the measure has escaped no critic. There is indeed a certain one-sidedness about it, and a devil's advocate might urge that a long poem couched in verse (let alone the subject) of such unbroken gloom would be intolerable. But Sackville did not write a long poem, and his complete command within his limits of the effect at which he evidently aimed is most remarkable. The second thing to note about the poem is the extraordinary freshness and truth of its imagery.—SAINTSBURY, GEORGE, 1887, *History of Elizabethan Literature, pp.* 11, 12, 14.

GORBODUC
Or Ferrex and Porrex
1565

"Gorboduc" is a fable, doubtless better turned for tragedy than any on this side the Alps in his time; and might have been a better direction to Shakespeare and Ben Jonson than any guide they have had the luck to follow.—RYMER, THOMAS, 1693, *A Short View of Tragedy of the Last Age, p.* 84.

Yet it must be granted that the language of "Gordobuc" has great purity and perspicuity; and that it is entirely free from that tumid phraseology which does not seem to have taken place till play-writing had become a trade, and our poets found it their interest to captivate the multitude by the false sublime, and by those exaggerated imageries and pedantic metaphors, which are the chief blemishes of the scenes of Shakespeare, and which are at this day mistaken for his capital beauties by too many readers. Here also we perceive another and a strong reason why this play was never popular.—WARTON, THOMAS, 1778–81, *History of English Poetry, sec.* lvi.

Nothing can be more spiritless and inanimate, nor more drawling and monotonous in the tone of the language and in the versification, than this "Ferrex and Porrex;" and although the unities of place and time are in no manner observed, and a number of events are crowded into it, yet the scene is wholly destitute of movement: all that happens is previously announced in endless consultations, and afterwards stated in equally endless narratives.—SCHLEGEL, AUGUSTUS WILLIAM, 1809, *Dramatic Art and Literature, tr. Black, Lecture XIII.*

As a work of genius, it may be set down as nothing, for it contains hardly a memorable line or passage; as a work of art, and the first of its kind attempted in the language, it may be considered as a monument of the taste and skill of the authors. Its merit is confined to the regularity of the plot and metre, to its general good sense, and strict attention to common decorum. If the poet has not stamped the peculiar genius of his age upon this first attempt, it is no inconsiderable proof of strength of mind and conception sustained by its own sense of propriety alone, to have so far anticipated the taste of succeeding times as to have avoided any glaring offence against rules and models, which had no existence in his day.—HAZLITT, WILLIAM, 1820, *Lectures on the Literature of the Age of Elizabeth, Lecture* II.

The style of this old play is stiff and cumbersome, like the dresses of its times. There may be flesh and blood underneath, but we cannot get at it. Sir Philip Sidney has praised it for its morality. One of its authors might easily furnish that. Norton was an associate to Hopkins, Sternhold, and Robert Wisdom, in the singing psalms. I am willing to believe that Lord Buckhurst supplied the more vital parts.—LAMB, CHARLES, 1827, *Notes on the Garrick Plays.*

He was at least a poet, if he was not a dramatist. His style possesses all the gloomy grandeur of Spenser in his sombre mood; it is funereal indeed, but it represents the majesty of woe. . . . With all his deep pathos, and all his sublimity of imagination, Sackville wanted that animation which is essential to a dramatist. He excelled in narrative, but in dialogue he failed. Hence "Gorboduc" is more like an epic broken up into acts and scenes, than a work originally cast in a dramatic mould. — HOUSTON, ARTHUR, 1863, *The English Drama, Dublin Afternoon Lectures on English Literature, vol.* I, *p.* 147.

It shares the qualities, both good and bad, that belong to all the plays of the same kind: it is well written but it is tiresome, the speeches are eloquent but long and sententious, the characters talk too much and do too little, and the high-sounding maxims they pour forth have nothing to do with the plot of the play. There is nothing living or individual in its characters. But if it is devoid of passion this is due to no lack of murders, slaughter, and massacres, for the author, while not allowing himself to shed one drop of blood upon the stage, conscientiously performs his duty as a tragic poet and kills off all his characters one after another. —STAPFER, PAUL, 1880, *Shakespeare and Classical Antiquity, tr. Carey, p.* 34.

Instead of individual nature and real passion, it deals only in vague and labored declamations which never entered any head but the author's. Nothing is intricate, nothing unravelled, and little pathetic. It has the form of dialogue without the spirit. Singularly frigid and unimaginative, it is not without justness, weight, and fertility of thought. Its diction is transparent. It is celebrated, moreover, as being our first tragedy in blank verse. But the measure, though the embryon of Shakespeare's, conveys no notion of that elasticity and variety which it was destined shortly to attain.—WELSH, ALFRED H., 1882, *Development of English Literature and Language, vol.* I, *p.* 309.

"Gorboduc" is Senecan to the core, and judged from this standard it has very real merits. Its theme is serious, and of tragic significance; the treatment is dignified and, from the special point of view, adequate; there is no lack (to use Sidney's words) of "stately speeches and well-sounding phrases, climbing to the height of Seneca his style." As a fact, it is in the language rather than in the matter that the main interest of the play lies. . . . The verse of "Gorboduc," though not without vigour in parts, is monotonous and stiff, but it had in it, far beyond the conception of those who first used it, infinite possibilities. They had thought of it as a pale replica of classical measures: it was really destined to an existence in the world of art as independent, as glorious, as immortal as theirs. To have discovered the fitness of blank verse for high dramatic purposes is the distinctive achievement of the English classical playwrights. —BOAS, FREDERICK S., 1896, *Shakspere and his Predecessors, pp.* 24, 25.

GENERAL

In vain I thinke, right honourable Lord,
By this rude rime to memorize thy name,
Whose learned Muse hath writ her owne record
In golden verse, worthy immortal fame:
—SPENSER, EDMUND, 1590, *Sonnets Addressed to Various Noblemen, &c., The Faerie Queene, bk.* i.

The best of these times, if "Albion's England" be not preferred, for our business, is the "Mirrour of Magistrates," and in that "Mirrour," Sackvil's "Induction," the work of Thomas, afterward earl of Dorset and lord treasurer of England: whose also the famous Tragedy of "Gordobuc," was the best of that time, even in sir Philip Sidney's judgement; and all skilful Englishmen cannot but ascribe as much thereto, for his phrase and eloquence therein.—BOLTON, EDMUND, 1624, *Hypercritica.*

Lord Buckhurst is beyond all doubt the immediate father in verse of Spenser; he was by far the greatest, and (which is not always, nor even often a necessary result) the most influential poet of his generation.—SOUTHEY, ROBERT, 1830, *Letter to Sir Egerton Brydges, Brydge's Autobiography, vol.* II, *p.* 266.

It is probable that Sackville ceased to cultivate poetry because he failed to reap its internal rewards. His genius had no joy in it, and its exercise probably gave him little poetic delight. With great force of imagination, his was still a somewhat dogged force. He could discern clearly, and shape truly, but no sudden ecstasy of emotion gave a "precious seeing" to his eye or unexpected felicity to his hand. There is something bleak in his noblest verse.—WHIPPLE, EDWIN P., 1859-68, *The Literature of the Age of Elizabeth, p.* 192.

There is a greater restraint and severity than had yet been seen in the choice of language and ornament, though stiffness and awkwardness of phrase, and the still imperfect sense of poetical fitness and grace, show that the writer could not yet reach in execution what he aimed at in idea. And there is visible both in the structure of the seven-line stanzas, and in the flow of the verses themselves, a feeling for rhythmic stateliness and majesty corresponding to his solemn theme. In their cadences, as well as in the allegorical figures and pathetic moralising of Sackville's verses, we see a faint anticipation of Spenser.—CHURCH, R. W., 1880, *English Poets, ed. Ward, vol.* I, *p.* 270.

The defect of Sackville, as a dramatist, is that, with all his great intellectual power, he failed to perceive that the principle of tragic action had altered its sphere. His mind was essentially political. Deeply impressed with the evils and horrors of the Civil Wars, which yet lingered in men's memories, he sought, in "Ferrex and Porrex," as in his "Induction," to draw from the history of Britain examples to warn his countrymen against conduct likely to occasion the recurrence of these calamities. His imagination therefore naturally dwelt on the Greek stories of hereditary Nemesis. He did not see that the evils he dreaded belonged to a past stage of society, and that what was henceforth to make the greatness of the English stage was the representation of the conflict between Good and Evil *in the soul of Man.*—COURTHOPE, W. J., 1897, *A History of English Poetry, vol.* II, *p.* 372.

One musician, indeed, there was who produced for a very short time a harmony which was both powerful and novel. The solitary poet of a high order between Dunbar and Spenser is Thomas Sackville, afterwards Lord Buckhurst and Earl of Dorset. . . . Sackville's poetical life, therefore, closed at about the same age as Keats's did; he is among "the inheritors of unfulfilled renown." His withdrawal from the practice of his art probably delayed the development of English literature by a quarter of a century, since of Sackville's potentiality of genius there can be no question. What he has left to us has a sombre magnificence, a stately fullness, absolutely without parallel in his own age. The poetlings around him were timid, crude, experimental, but Sackville writes like a young and inexperienced master perhaps, yet always like a master. He shows little or not at all the influence of Wyatt and Surrey, but with one hand he takes hold of the easy richness of Chaucer and with the other of the majesty of Dante, to whose "Inferno" the plan of his "Induction" is deeply indebted. In his turn, Sackville exercised no slight fascination over the richer, more elaborate and florid, but radically cognate fancy of Spenser; and even Shakespeare must have read and admired the sinister fragments of the Lord High Treasurer. Scarce an adjective here and there survives to show Sackville faintly touched by the tasteless heresies of his age. His poetry is not read, partly because of its monotony, partly because the subject-matter of it offers no present entertainment; but in the history of the evolution of style in our literature the place of Sackville must always be a prominent one.—GOSSE, EDMUND, 1897, *Short History of Modern English Literature, pp.* 77, 78.

William Warner

1558?-1609

William Warner, born 1558, died 1609, was a native of Oxfordshire, an attorney of the Common Pleas, and the author of "Albion's England." This poem, published in 1586, is a history of England from the Deluge to the reign of James I. It supplanted in popular favour the "Mirror for Magistrates."—BEETON, S. O., 1870, *Great Book of Poetry.*

Master William Warner, a man of good yeares and of honest reputation; by his profession an Atturnye of the Common Pleas; author of Albions England, diynge suddenly in the night in his bedde, without any former complaynt or sicknesse, on thursday night beeinge the 9th daye of March; was buried the satturday following, and lyeth in the church at the corner under the stone of Walter Ffader.—PARISH REGISTER OF AMWELL, 1609.

In his absolute "Albion's England," hath most admirably penned the history of his own country from Noah to his time, that is, to the reign of Queen Elizabeth. I have heard him termed of the best wits of both our Universities, our English Homer. As Euripides is the most sententious among the Greek poets: so is Warner among our English poets.—MERES, FRANCIS, 1598, *Palladis Tamia.*

Then Warner, though his lines were not so
trimm'd,
Nor yet his poem so exactly limb'd
And neatly jointed but the critic may
Easily reprove him, yet thus let me say
For my old friend: some passages there be
In him, which, I protest, have taken me
With almost wonder; so fine, clear, and new,
As yet they have been equalled by few.

—DRAYTON, MICHAEL, c1627, *Of Poets and Poesie.*

A good honest plain writer of moral rules and precepts, in that old-fashioned kind of seven-footed verse, which yet sometimes is in use, though in different manner, that is to say, divided into two—PHILLIPS, EDWARD, 1675, *Theatrum Poetarum Anglicanorum, ed. Brydges, p.* 215.

An Author only unhappy in the Choice of his Subject, and Measure of his Verse. —COOPER, ELIZABETH, 1737, *The Muses' Library, p.* 157.

To his merit nothing can be objected, unless perhaps an affected quaintness in some of his expressions, and an indelicacy in some of his pastoral images. . . . Warner rather resembled Ovid, whose Metamorphosis he seems to have taken for his model, having deduced a perpetual poem from the deluge down to the era of Elizabeth, full of lively digression and entertaining episodes. And though he is sometimes harsh, affected, and obscure, he often displays a most charming and pathetic simplicity.—PERCY, THOMAS, 1765, *Reliques of Ancient English Poetry, p.* 254.

There is in Warner occasionally a pathetic simplicity that never fails of engaging the heart. His tales, though often tedious, and not unfrequently indelicate, abound with all the unaffected incident and artless ease of the best old ballads, without their cant and puerility. The pastoral pieces that occur are superior to all the eclogues in our language, those of Collins only excepted. —HEADLEY, HENRY, 1787, *Select Beauties of Ancient English Poetry.*

The astonishing popularity of this poem, which by Warner's contemporaries was even preferred to their favourite "Mirror for Magistrates," is a proof that he possessed the most valuable talent of a poet, that of amusing and interesting his readers. This he affected partly by means of numerous episodes, which are always lively though not always to the purpose, and partly by means of a style which, at the time, was thought highly elegant, and which certainly possesses the merit of uncommon ease and simplicity. —ELLIS, GEORGE, 1790-1845, *Specimens of the Early English Poets, vol.* II, *p.* 260.

Of the singular production of Warner, there is, I believe, no modern edition, yet few among our elder poets more deserve the attention of the lover of nature and rural simplicity.—DRAKE, NATHAN, 1798, *Literary Hours, vol.* I, *p.* 255.

His contemporaries compared him to Virgil, whom he certainly did not make his model. Dr. Percy thinks he rather resembled Ovid, to whom he is, if possible, still more unlike. His poem is, in fact, an enormous ballad on the history, or rather on the fables appendant to the history of England; heterogeneous, indeed, like the Metamorphoses, but written with an almost doggrel simplicity. Headley has rashly preferred his works to our ancient ballads; but with the best of these they will bear no comparison. Argentile and Curan has indeed some beautiful touches, yet that episode requires to be weeded of many lines to be read with unqualified pleasure; and through the rest of his stories we shall search in vain for the familiar magic of such ballads as Chevy Chase or Gill Morrice. —CAMPBELL, THOMAS, 1819, *Specimens of the British Poets.*

Has at least the equivocal merit of great length. It is rather legendary than historical: some passages are pleasing; but it is not a work of genius, and the style, though natural, seldom rises above that of prose.—HALLAM, HENRY, 1837-39, *Introduction to the Literature of Europe, vol.* II, *ch.* V, *par.* 66.

Its most obvious fault is the awkwardness with which it oscillates between the rude simplicity of the ballad, and the regularity of the sustained narrative poem: but it contains some very pleasing passages in a quiet strain.—SPALDING, WILLIAM, 1852-82, *A History of English Literature, p.* 278.

After having conscientiously waded through immense masses of uninteresting rhyme, as we have been compelled to do in the preparation of these notices, we confess, with a not unmalicious exultation, that we know Warner's poem only by description and extracts. Albion is an ancient name for Great Britain; and Albion's England is a metrical history—"not barren," in the author's own words, "of inventive intermixtures"—of the southern portion of the island, beginning at the deluge, and ending with the reign of James I. As James might have said, "After me the deluge," Warner's poem may be considered as ending in some such catastrophe as that with which it begins. The merit of Warner is that of a story-teller, and he reached classes of readers to whom Spenser was hardly known by name. The work is a strange mixture of comic and tragic fact and fable, exceedingly gross in parts, with little power of imagination or grace of language, but possessing the great popular excellence of describing persons and incidents in the fewest and simplest words. The best story is that of Argentile and Curan, and it is told as briefly as though it were intended for transmission by telegraph at the cost of a dollar a word. Warner has some occasional touches of nature and pathos which almost rival the old ballads for directness and intensity of feeling.—WHIPPLE, EDWIN P., 1859-68, *The Literature of the Age of Elizabeth, p.* 228.

Albion's England is undoubtedly a work of very remarkable talent of its kind. . . . It is one of the liveliest and most amusing poems ever written. Every striking event or legend that the old chronicles afford is seized hold of, and related always clearly, often with very considerable spirit and animation. But it is far from being a mere compilation; several of the narratives are not to be found anywhere else, and a large proportion of the matter is Warner's own, in every sense of the word. In this, as well as in other respects, it has greatly the advantage over the "Mirror for Magistrates," as a rival to which work it was perhaps originally produced, and with the popularity of which it could scarcely fail considerably to interfere. . . . For fluency, combined with precision and economy of diction, Warner is probably unrivalled among the writers of English verse. . . . His command of the vulgar tongue, in particular, is wonderful. This indeed is perhaps his most remarkable poetical characteristic; and the tone which was thus given to his poem (being no doubt that of his own mind) may be conjectured to have been in great part the source both of its immense popularity for a time, and of the neglect and oblivion into which it was afterwards allowed to drop. That Warner's poetry and that of Spenser could have ever come in one another's way is impossible. "Albion's England" must from the first have been a book rather for the many than the few,—for the kitchen rather than the hall; its spirit is not, what it has been sometimes called, merely naïve, but essentially coarse and vulgar. We do not allude so much to any particular abundance of warm description, or freedom of language, as to the low note on which the general strain of the composition is pitched. With all its force and vivacity, and even no want of fancy, at times, and graphic descriptive power, it is poetry with as little of high imagination in it as any that was ever written.—CRAIK, GEORGE L., 1861, *A Compendious History of English Literature and of the English Language, vol.* I, *pp.* 548, 549.

His poem was of Albion's England, because it did not, like Albion, include Scotland. It was an easy, lively, homely history of England, from the Deluge down to Warner's own time, homely in use of simple idiomatic English, full of incidents and stories, often rudely told, and often with a force or delicacy of touch that came of the terse directness with which natural feeling was expressed. Warner's poem had for a time great popularity. He was not a great poet, but the times were stirring, and they drew ten thousand lines of lively verse upon his country, even out of an attorney.—MORLEY, HENRY, 1873, *First Sketch of English Literature, p.* 428.

The first of the so-called historians, William Warner, belongs in point of poetical style to the pre-Spenserian period, and like its other exponents employs the fourteener; while, unlike some of them, he semes quite free from any Italian influence in phraseology or poetical manner. Nevertheless "Albion's England" is not merely in bulk but in merit far ahead of the average work of our first period, and quite incommensurable with such verse as that of Grove or even of Turberville.—SAINTSBURY, GEORGE, 1887, *History of Elizabethan Literature, p.* 132.

He does not always escape the tendency of his metre to drop into a jog-trot, yet in the main he canters briskly along with a very fair proportion of spirited lines.—HANNAY, DAVID, 1898, *The Later Renaissance, p.* 212.

George Turberville

1540?–1610?

Born at Whitchurch, in Dorsetshire, educated at Winchester and New College, Oxford, became secretary to Sir Thomas Randolph, ambassador at the Court of Russia, and lived into the latter part of Elizabeth's reign. He published in 1567 two translations—one of "The Heroical Epistles of Ovid," six of them translated into blank verse, and the others into four-lined stanzas; the other of the Latin "Eclogues of Mantuan," an Italian poet, who had died in 1516. In 1570 there appeared a volume of his own poems, as "Epitaphes, Epigrams, Songs, and Sonets; with a Discourse of the friendly Affections of Tymetes to Pindara his Ladie." Turbervile takes a pleasant place among the elder Elizabethan poets. He wrote also books of Falconrie and Hunting, and made versions from the Italian, notably ten "Tragical Tales translated by Turbervile, in Time of his Troubles, out of sundrie Italians, with the Argument and L'Envoye to each Tale," published in 1576.—MORLEY, HENRY, 1892, *English Writers, vol.* VIII, *p.* 286.

Broken the ice for our quainter poets that now write. —TOFTE, ROBERT, 1615, *tr. Varchi's "Blazon of Jealousie."*

Occasional felicity of diction, a display of classical allusion, and imagery taken from the amusements and customs of the age, are not wanting; but the warmth, the energy, and the enthusiasm of poetry are sought for in vain.—DRAKE, NATHAN, 1817, *Shakspeare and his Times, vol.* I. *p.* 656.

Certainly the best poet of the time (always excepting Sackville) next to Gascoigne, and perhaps Gascoigne's equal.—SAINTSBURY, GEORGE, 1898, *A Short History of English Literature, p.* 253.

He himself writes with becoming diffidence of his poetical pretensions in the epilogue to his "Epitaphs and Sonets," where he describes himself as paddling along the banks of the stream of Helicon, like a sculler against the tide, for fear of the deep stream and the "mighty hulkes" that adventured out so far. His fondness for the octave stanza would probably recommend him to the majority of modern readers, and there is something decidedly enlivening (if not seldom crude and incongruous) in the blithe and ballad-like lilt of his verse. He did good service to our literature in familiarising the employment of Italian models, he himself showing a wide knowledge of the literature of the Latin speech, and of the Greek Anthology; and also as a pioneer in the use of blank verse and in the record of impressions of travel. —SECCOMBE, THOMAS, 1899, *Dictionary of National Biography, vol.* LVII, *p.* 323.

Barnabe Barnes

1569–1609

Wrote "The Praise of Musike "(1586); "Parthenophil and Parthenophe" (1593); "A Divine Centurie of Spirituall Sonnets" (1595); "Four Books of Offices: Enabling private persons for the Speciall service of all good Princes and Policies" (1606); "The Devil's Charter" (1607); "The Battle of Hexham," an unprinted play; and some verses prefixed to Harvey's "Pierce's Supererogation" (1593), Florio's "Worlde of Wordes" (1598), and Ford's "Fame's Memoriall" (1606).—ADAMS, W. DAVENPORT, 1877, *Dictionary of English Literature, p.* 67.

Barneus' verse, unless I do him wrong,
Is like a cuppe of sacke, heady and strong.
—BASTARD, THOMAS, 1598, *Chrestoleros.*

In the main, however, the poetry of Barnes moves in a world of imagination, into which the virtue of any real incidents has entered invisibly through the solvent of beauty; it is a land of clear colours, and smooth air; a "region of shadowless hours;" mighty Pan presides over it; the lovely Virgin Mary is a shepherdess who may be gained by the promise of a firstling of the flock to further lovers; Apollo is a saint of the religion of joy. But it is not only the Renaissance with its rehabilitation of the senses which we find in these poems; there is in them also the Renaissance with its ingenuity, its fantasticality, its passion for conceits, and wit, and clever caprices, and playing upon words. With this it is harder and perhaps not wholesome to attempt to enter into sympathy. The sympathy of the most favourably disposed modern reader would be somewhat stringently tested by a poem of many lines in which the marks of punctuation, comma, and colon, and period, are constrained to become the emblems and exponents of passion. —DOWDEN, EDWARD, 1876, *Parthenophil and Parthenophe, Academy, vol.* X, *p.* 231.

Now that Barnes's secular poems are removed from the category of unattainable things, and a study of them becomes practicable, Dr. Grosart having recently (1875) reprinted and edited, from the unique exemplar in the possession of the Duke of Devonshire at Chatsworth, the long-hidden and all but unheard-of "Parthenophil and Parthenophe" (1593), there can be little doubt that this fine old singer, hitherto so strangely neglected, and known only to the few by his later "Divine Centurie" (also reprinted by Dr. Grosart) as a minor but sweet and fervid voice in England's antiphon, is at length on the eve of having justice rendered him. It may be predicted with some confidence that it is on the recovered treasure that Barnes's fame will henceforth mainly rest. The Sonnets, of which it largely consists, are of special importance in a study of the development of that species of composition in our literature. Apart from their essential poetical qualities, which, though considerable and undoubted, are surpassed by those of the Odes and Madrigals, with their passionate adoration of beauty, their sensuous delight, their glories of pure and lovely colour, and fragrance of choice flowers, they entitle Barnes to rank as one of the most artistic sonneteers of Elizabeth's reign; for while on every side the sonnet-form was deteriorating, we find this poet habitually, though not invariably, employing in the service of his Parthenophe a stanza as obedient to technical prescription—the inevitable riming couplet of the period always excepted—as those in which Laura's name is laid up for ever, or those Mr. Rossetti has given us towards "The House of Life." —MAIN, DAVID M., 1880, *A Treasury of English Sonnets, p.* 303, *note* cviii, *on Barnabe Barnes.*

As a sonnetteer and lyrist Barnes takes high rank among the minor Elizabethans. His sonnets, fervent, and richly coloured, suffer from over-elaboration and conceit; but these were the faults of the age. His imagery is not of the cheap, commonplace character affected by Watson, but testifies to rare imaginative power joined to the gift of true poetic expression. The madrigals, fine and free (but unfortunately too few), prove him to have been a born singer.—BULLEN, A. H., 1885, *Dictionary of National Biography, vol.* III, *p.* 248.

His poetical worth, though there are fine passages in "The Devil's Charter" and in the "Divine Centurie," must rest on "Parthenophil." . . . The style, both verbal and poetical, needs chastising in places, and Barnes's expression in particular is sometimes obscure. He is sometimes comic when he wishes to be passionate, and frequently verbose when he wishes to be expressive. But the fire, the full-bloodedness, the poetical virility, of the poems is extraordinary. A kind of intoxication of the eternal-feminine seems to have seized the poet to an extent not otherwise to be paralleled in the group, except in Sidney; while Sidney's courtly sense of measure and taste did not permit him Barnes's forcible extravagances.—SAINTSBURY, GEORGE, 1887, *History of Elizabethan Literature, pp.* 108, 109.

That isolated Ronsardist among our London poets, published no lyrics after 1595. His plays, perhaps, were Jacobean, but we possess only one of them, "The Devil's Charter," not printed till 1607, which seems to belong to the school of Marlowe. —GOSSE, EDMUND, 1894, *The Jacobean Poets, p.* 9.

Sir John Harrington

1561–1612

Born at Kelston near bath, from Eton passed in 1578 to Christ's College, Cambridge, and thence to the court of his god-mother, Queen Elizabeth. His wit brought him into much favour, which he endangered by the freedom of his satires. In 1599 he served under Essex in Ireland, and was knighted by him on the field, much to the queen's displeasure. To fortify his amazing application to King James for the office of chancellor and archbishop of Ireland he composed in 1605 "A Short View of the State of Ireland," an interesting and singularly modern essay (ed. by Macray, 1880). He is remembered as the metrical translater of Ariosto's "Orlando Furioso" (1591); his other writings include Rabelaisian pamphlets, epigrams, and a "Tract on the Succession to the Crown" (ed. by Clements Markham, with Memoir, Roxb. Club, 1880). —PATRICK AND GROOME, *eds.*, 1897, *Chambers's Biographical Dictionary, p.* 464.

Well-letter'd and discreet,
That hath so purely naturalized
Strange words and made them all free denizens.

—PEELE, GEORGE, 1593, *The Honour of the Garter, Ad Mæcenatem Prologus.*

That (Sir) John Harington's Ariosto, under all translations, was the worst. That when Sir John Harrington desyred him to tell the truth of his Epigrames, he answered him, that he loved not the truth, for they were Narrations, and not Epigrames. —DRUMMOND, WILLIAM, 1619, *Notes on Ben Jonson's Conversations, ed. Laing, p.* 3.

Sir John Harrington, no less noted for his book of witty epigrams, than his judicious translation of Ariosto's "Orlando Furioso." —PHILLIPS, EDWARD, 1675, *Theatrum Poetarum Anglicanorum, ed. Brydges, p.* 189.

Sir *John* appears to be a gentleman of great Pleasantry, and Humour; his Fortune was easy, the Court his Element, and Wit not his Business, but Diversion.—'Tis not to be doubted, but his Translation of *Ariosto*, was publish'd after *Spencer's Fairy Queen;* and yet, both in Language, and Numbers, is greatly Inferior.—Indeed, if I may be forgiven, for daring to meddle with Studies so much beyond me, the whole Poem of *Orlando* is a tedious Medley of unnatural Characters, and improbable Events; and the Author's Patron, Cardinal *Hippolito De Este*, had some Reason for that severe Question, — *Where the Devil, Signor* Ludovico, *did you pick up all these damn'd Lies?*—COOPER, ELIZABETH, 1737, *The Muses' Library, p.* 297.

'Tis not to be doubted, but his translation of Ariosto was published after Spenser's Fairy Queen, and yet both in language and numbers it is much inferior, as much as it is reasonable to suppose the genius of Harrington was below that of Spenser. —CIBBER, THEOPHILUS, 1753, *Lives of the Poets, vol.* I, *p.* 151.

Exhibited an English version of Ariosto's "Orlando Furioso:" which, although executed without spirit or accuracy, unanimated and incorrect, enriched our poetry by a communication of new stores of fiction and imagination, both of the romantic and comic species, of Gothic machinery and familiar manners. — WARTON, THOMAS, 1778–81, *History of English Poetry, sec.* lx.

If the poem here selected be rightly attributed to him by the Harington papers, he cannot be denied the singular merit of having united an elegance of taste with an artifice of style which far exceeded his contemporaries. — ELLIS, GEORGE, 1790–1845, *Specimens of the Early English Poets, vol.* II, *p.* 139.

Sir John Harington's translation of the "Orlando Furioso" first appeared in 1591, when the author was in his thirtieth year. It does not convey all the glow and poetry of Ariosto; but it is, nevertheless, a performance of great ingenuity and talent.—CRAIK, GEORGE L., 1861, *A Compendious History of English Literature, and of the English Language, vol.* I, *p.* 575.

Harington's letters owe their value to the character of their author, which strongly resembles that of an Italian humorist attached to a court. Harington considered himself a privileged person who might jest at will. He had a quick power of observation, and was entirely destitute of restraint. Though desirous of pushing his fortunes, he had none of the qualities necessary for success; Elizabeth spoke of him as "that saucy poet, my godson," and he was generally regarded as an amusing gossip. He wrote easily, and certainly was not a hero to himself. The most intimate facts of his domestic life afforded him materials for an epigram, and his frankness was entire. Hence he gives a living picture of life and society in his times, and abounds in incidental stories which throw great light upon many prominent persons. A detailed life of Harington would present an interesting sketch of Elizabethan times. As a poet he has received scanty justice from posterity. His translation of the "Orlando Furioso" has been superseded, and his epigrams, disfigured by coarseness, are forgotten.—CREIGHTON, MANDELL, 1890, *Dictionary of National Biography, vol.* XXIV, *p.* 388.

Without being a great poet, Harington rhymed easily, and had a ready pen. His version of "Orlando" attempts no subtleties of skill in the exact rendering of lines and stanzas; but as a reproduction of the whole poem for English readers it was, and is, a very pleasant book. It pleased Elizabeth.—MORLEY, HENRY, 1893, *English Writers, vol.* X, *p.* 456.

Sir Thomas Overbury

1581–1613

Statesman and author; born at Ilmington, Warrickshire, England, in 1581; educated at Queen's College, Oxford, and graduated 1598; traveled on the Continent; became a resident of Edinburgh 1601, where he was an intimate friend of Robert Carr, afterwards Viscount Rochester and Earl of Somerset; was knighted 1608; traveled on the Continent 1609; wrote "Observations upon the State of the Seventeen United Provinces;" incurred the enmity of his former friend, Lord Rochester, and of the Countess of Essex, by his opposition to their criminal intrigues; refused a foreign mission offered him as a means of removing him from the kingdom, and was thereupon thrown into the Tower, where he was cruelly treated, and died Sept. 15, 1613. In 1619 Lord Rochester, then Earl of Somerset, and his countess were convicted of having poisoned Overbury. His popular volume of "Characters" was published posthumously in 1614.—BEERS, HENRY A., *Rev.*, 1897, *Johnson's Universal Cyclopædia, vol.* VI, *p.* 371.

Overbury was first his friend, then turn'd his mortall enimie. — DRUMMOND, WILLIAM, 1619, *Notes on Ben Jonson's Conversations, ed. Laing, p.* 12.

And as the Hebrews in an obscure pit
Their holy Fire hid, not extinguish'd it,
And after time, that broke their bondage chaine,
Found it, to fire their sacrifice againe:
So lay thy Worth some while, but being found,
The Muses' altars plentifully crown'd
With sweet perfumes by it new kindled be,
And offer all to thy dear Memorie.
Nor haue we lost thee long: thou art not gone,
Nor canst descend into Obliuion.
But twice the Sunne went round since thy soule fled,
And onely that time men shall terme thee dead.
Hereafter (rais'd to life) thou still shalt haue
An antidote against the silent Graue.

—BROWNE, WILLIAM, 1615? *An Elegy on Sir Thomas Overbury, ed. Hazlitt, vol.* II, *p.* 318.

The noble Overbury's Quill has left
A better Wife, than he could ever find. . . .
. . . Strange power of womankind,
To raise, and ruin; for all he will claim
Is from that Sex: his Birth, his Death, his Fame.

—DANIEL, GEORGE, 1647, *A Vindication of Poesy.*

Bred in Oxford, and attained to be a most accomplished Gentleman, which the happiness of his Pen, both in Poetry and Prose, doth declare. In the latter he was the first writer of Characters of our Nation, so far as I have observed. But, if the great parts of this Gentleman were guilty of insolency and petulancy, which some since have charged on his memory; we may charitably presume that his reduced age would have corrected such juvenile extravagancies. It is questionable, whether Robert Carre, Earl of Somerset, were more in the favour of King James, or this Sir Thomas Overbury in the favour of the Earl of Somerset, until he lost it by disswading that Lord from keeping company with a Lady (the Wife of another Person of Honour), as neither for his credit here, or comfort hereafter.—FULLER, THOMAS, 1662, *The Worthies of England, ed. Nichols, vol.* I, *p.* 385.

Sir Thomas was about 32 years old when he was murthered, and is said to have possessed an accuteness, and strength of parts that was astonishing; and some have related that he was proud of his abilities, and over-bearing in company; but as there is no good authority for the assertion, it is more agreeable to candour to believe him the amiable knight Winstanley draws him; as it seldom happens that a soul formed for the noble quality of friendship is haughty and insolent. There is a tragedy of Sir Thomas Overbury wrote by the late Richard Savage, son of earl Rivers, which was acted in 1723, (by what was then usually called The Summer Company) with success. — CIBBER, THEOPHILUS, 1753, *Lives of the Poets, vol.* I, *p.* 119.

Few poems have been more popular than Overbury's "Wife;" owing partly to the good sense with which it abounds, and partly to the interesting and tragic circumstances which accompanied the author's fate. It was speedily and frequently imitated.—DRAKE, NATHAN, 1817, *Shakspeare and His Times, vol.* I, *p.* 694, *note.*

His "Characters, or Witty Descriptions of the Properities of Sundry Persons," is a work of considerable merit; but unfortunately his prose, as well as his verse, has a dryness and quaintness that seem to oppress the natural movement of his thoughts. As a poet, he has few imposing attractions: his beauties must be fetched by repeated perusal. They are those of solid reflection, predominating over, but not extinguishing, sensibility; and there is danger of the reader neglecting, under the coldness and ruggedness of his manner, the manly but unostentatious moral feeling that is conveyed in his maxims, which are sterling and liberal, if we can only pardon a few obsolete ideas on female education. — CAMPBELL, THOMAS, 1819, *Specimens of the British Poets.*

As a poet, he was perhaps not remarkable for any particular graces of expression, or smoothness of versification; yet his poem of "The Wife"—no small favourite in its day — contains some pretty passages, and a host of precepts which even the most fastidious will hardly dispute. It is upon his "Characters" that Overbury's fame must chiefly rest; and here he displays the fertile and observant powers of his mind, great ingenuity of conceit, and a force of expression rarely equalled by any of the numerous followers of Theophrastus.—RIMBAULT, EDWARD F., 1856, *ed. Miscellaneous Works of Sir Thomas Overbury, Introduction, p.* ix.

Sir Thomas Overbury's "Characters" are interesting illustrations of contemporary manners, and a mine of foot-notes to the works of better men, — but, with the exception of "The Fair and Happy Milkmaid," they are dull enough to have pleased James the First; his "Wife" is a *cento* of far-fetched conceits, — here a tomtit, and there a hen mistaken for a pheasant, like the contents of a cockney's game-bag, and his chief interest for us lies in his having been mixed up with an inexplicable tragedy and poisoned in the Tower, not without suspicion of royal complicity. —LOWELL, JAMES RUSSELL, 1858–64–90, *Library of Old Authors, Prose Works, Riverside, ed., vol.* I, *p.* 252.

In Overbury's "Characters" we not only meet with the Englishman of the day, the milkmaid, tinker, soldier, yeoman, or franklin, and the clown, or plain countryman, but we see the lines laid down whereon Dickens and Thackeray, who may never have seen the book, build their descriptive characters. Above all, when the student meets with these books he may be certain that he holds in his hands sound honest thought, not very acute, not very high, but thought; not mere words spun into never-ending, bombastic sentences. — FRISWELL, JAMES HAIN, 1869, *Essays on English Writers, p.* 103.

Overbury was widely popular in his day. His spirit kindled kindred spirits. His originality of tone and treatment; his graphic delineation; the Dutch-like pictures, the neat sentences pointed to an apophthegm, or rounded with a witticism, found the truest test that admiration can take, that of imitation. But in after years the tide of popularity quite turned. Even those authors who delight in the quaint beauty and the picturesque prose of our old writers, seem to have no knowledge of him. Johnson preserves an ominous silence when we mention the author of "the unmatcht Poeme, the Wife." Of all the lovers of character and the sweet old prose, Charles Lamb, who was charmed with Kit Marlowe's luscious smoothness, "beds of roses, buckles of gold" style, knows not our author by name; and among De Quincey's curious essays, and more curious footnotes, we have in vain searched for evidence that he knew of him. Even Macaulay does not make mention of his name or his writings. Others are acquainted with Overbury only to depreciate him; stately Hallam pats the knight with a mild reference, and dismisses his characters with a Gerard Dow comparison. He appears to us to deserve a better fate, and his "characters" live before us in a very real manner. Country and domestic life, courtier life, the duns, the whims and fashions of contemporary manners, are etched in his pages with poetic imagery, a rare if sometimes coarse skill, and a graphic veracity which make them still worthy of notice, and may reward the reader who loves characteristic bits of old manners set in quaintly vivid phraseology. — PURVES, JAMES, 1880, *Overbury's Characters, Fraser's Magazine, vol.* 22, *p.* 376.

Sir Thomas Overbury's "Characters," written in the Baconian age, are found delightful by some; but for my own part, though I have striven to follow the critic's golden rule, to have preferences but no exclusions, Overbury has for me no savour. —MORLEY, JOHN, 1887–90, *Aphorisms, Studies in Literature, p.* 72.

The social prominence and mysterious murder of Sir Thomas Overbury gave an exaggerated interest to his brief posthumous exercise in verse, "A Wife," 1614, and to his version of Ovid's "Remedy of Love," 1620.—GOSSE, EDMUND, 1894, *The Jacobean Poets, p.* 115.

Overbury's chief work, "A Wife now the Widdow of Sir T. Overburye," a sensible little poem on marriage, of slender poetic merit, was first published in London in 1614. It was licensed for the press on 13 Dec. 1613, and became exceptionally popular, five editions appearing in 1614. One of the last lines—

He comes too near who comes to be denied,—

obtained currency as a proverb. Contemporary imitations abounded. . . . The latest and fullest edition of his works was edited by Edward F. Rimbault in 1856, in Russell Smith's Library of Old Authors. —LEE, SIDNEY, 1895, *Dictionary of National Biography, vol.* XLII, *p.* 381.

Henry Constable

1562–1613

Born at Newark, England, 1562: died at Liège, Belgium, Oct. 9, 1613. An English poet, son of Sir Robert Constable of Newark. He was graduated at Cambridge (St. John's College) in 1580; became a Roman Catholic; and for the greater part of his later life resided in Paris occupied with political affairs, and especially with schemes for promoting the interests of Catholicism. In 1603 he came to London, and was for a short time confined in the Tower. He published in 1592 a collection of 23 sonnets entitled "Diana: the Praises of his Mistress in certaine sweete Sonnets by H. C."—SMITH, BENJAMIN E., *ed.*, 1894–97, *The Century Cyclopedia of Names*, p. 274.

Sweate *Constable* doth take the wond'ring eare
And layes it up in willing prisonment.

—ANON, 1606, *The Return from Pernassus.*

Noble Henry Constable was a great master in English tongue, nor had any gentleman of our nation a more pure, quick, or higher delivery of conceit, witness among all other that Sonnet of his before his Majesty's Lepanto. — BOLTON, EDMUND, 1624, *Hypercritica.*

Constable's ambrosiac muse
Made Dian not his notes refuse.

—JONSON, BEN, 1637? *An Ode, Underwoods*, xlv.

He was highly praised by Edmond Bolton, Ben Jonson, and others, and Mr. Warton mentions him as "a noted sonnet writer;" yet the following, though as notable sonnets as his "Diana" could furnish, can hardly entitle him to be denominated "the first sonneteer of his time."—ELLIS, GEORGE, 1790–1845, *Specimens of the Early English Poets, vol.* II, *p.* 267.

Few men of his day enjoyed a higher reputation, especially as a sonnet-writer, than Henry Constable; yet, as far as is known, it was built upon a very narrow foundation.—COLLIER, JOHN PAYNE, 1865, *A Bibliographical and Critical Account of the Rarest Books in the English Language, vol.* I, *p.* 151.

The slight but graceful genius of Constable is best defined by some of the epithets which his contemporary critics employed. They spoke of his "pure, quick, and high delivery of conceit." Ben Jonson alludes to his "ambrosiac muse." His secular poems are "Certaine sweete sonnets in the praise of his mistress, Diana," conceived in the style of Ronsard and the Italians. The verses of his later days, when he had learned, as he says, "to live alone with God," are also sonnets in honour of the saints, and chiefly of Mary Magdalene. They are ingenious, and sometimes too cleverly confuse the passions of divine and earthly love. . . . Constable was neither more nor less than a fair example of a poet who followed rather than set the fashion. His sonnets were charged and overladen with ingenious conceits, but the freshness, the music, of his more free and flowing lyrics remain, and keep their charm.—LANG, ANDREW, 1880, *The English Poets, ed. Ward, vol.* I, *p.* 381.

Like Daniel, Constable does not attempt the delineation of stormy passions, yet his deepest vein is quite different from Daniel's. He has a more ardent soul than Daniel; his imagination is more warmly and richly coloured: he has more of flame and less of moisture in him. Daniel's words flow most abundantly and with happiest impulse when his eye is dim with tears; Constable's when his whole being is aglow with the rapture of beauty.—MINTO, WILLIAM, 1874–85, *Characteristics of English Poets, p.* 195.

Henry Constable, whose "Diana" reached a second edition in 1594, was highly commended as a sonneteer by his contemporaries; but the specimens of his handwork which have come down to us in the collections do not justify their commendations.—STODDARD, RICHARD HENRY, 1881, *The Sonnet in English Poetry, Scribner's Monthly, vol.* 22, *p.* 910.

He was a close friend of Sidney, many of whose sonnets were published with his, and his work has much of the Sidneian colour, but with fewer flights of happily expressed fancy.—SAINTSBURY, GEORGE, 1887, *History of Elizabethan Literature, p.* 113.

Whether "Diana," the reputed inspirer of Constable's verse, is more than a poet's fiction or an ideal personage—the outcome of many experiences—is very doubtful. Critics have pointed to Constable's cousin, Mary, countess of Shrewsbury (her husband was Constable's second cousin on his mother's side), as the lady whom the poet addressed; one or two sonnets, on the other hand, confirm the theory that Penelope, lady Rich, Sir Philip Sidney's "Stella," is the subject of the verse, but the difficulty of determining the authorship of any particular sonnet renders these suggestions of little service to Constable's biographer. . . . Constable's sonnets are too full of quaint conceits to be read nowadays with much pleasure, but his vocabulary and imagery often indicate real passion and poetic feeling. The "Spirituall Sonnettes" breathe genuine religious fervour. His pastoral lyrics are less laboured, and their fresh melody has the true Elizabethan ring.—LEE, SIDNEY, 1887, *Dictionary of National Biography, vol.* XII, *p.* 35.

Like all the Petrarchists, his aim was to discover some new metaphysical idea about love, to embody it in a sensible image, and to wind up the sonnet with an epigram. It is needless to say that, as the "metaphysics" of the subject had been long since exhausted, all that he was really in quest of was images and epigrams.—COURTHOPE, W. J., 1897, *A History of English Poetry, vol.* II, *p.* 302.

Richard Hakluyt

1552?-1616

Richard Hakluyt, 1552 (?)-1616. Born, in Herefordshire, 1552 (?). Educated at Westminster School. To Ch. Ch., Oxford, as Student, 1570; B. A., 19 Feb. 1574; M. A., 27 Jan. 1577. Ordained, 1575 (?). To France, with Sir Edward Stafford, as Chaplain, 1583. Appointed Prebendary of Bristol, 1586. Returned to England, 1588. Rector of Wetheringselt, Suffolk, April 1590. Married, 1594 (?). Wife died, 1597 (?). Prebendary of Westminster, May 1602. Archdeacon, 1603. Chaplain of Savoy, 1604. Second marriage, March 1604. Interested in colony of Virginia, 1606. Died, in London, 23 Nov. 1616; buried in Westminster Abbey. *Works:* "Divers Voyages touching the Discovery of America" (under initials: R. H.), 1582; "The Principall Navigations, Voiages, and Discoveries of the English Nation," 1589 (enlarged edn., 3 vols., 1598-1600). *Posthumous:* "A Discourse concerning Western Planting," 1877 (written 1584). He *translated:* Laudonnière's "A Notable History," 1587; Ferdinand Soto's "Virginia richly Valued," 1609; and *edited:* Anglerius' "De Orbe Novo decades octo," 1587; Galvano's "Discoveries of the World," 1601.—SHARP, R. FARQUHARSON, 1897, *A Dictionary of English Authors, p.* 121.

Richard Hackluit was born of an ancient extract in this County*, whose Family hath flourished at . . . in good esteem. He was bred a Student in Christ Church in Oxford, and after was Prebendary of Westminster. His Genius inclined him to the Study of History, and especially to the Marine part thereof, which made him keep constant Intelligence with the most noted Seamen of Wapping, until the day of his death. He set forth a large Collection of the English Sea Voyages, Ancient, Middle, Modern, taken partly out of private Letters, which never were (or without his care had not been) printed; partly out of small Treatises, printed, and since irrecoverably lost, had not his providence preserved them. For some Pamphlets are produced, which for their cheapnesse and smalnesse men for the present neglect to buy, presuming they may procure them at their pleasure; which small Books, their first and last Edition being past (like some Spirits that appear but once) cannot afterwards with any price or pains be recovered. In a word, many of such useful Tracts of Sea Adventures, which before were scattered as several Ships, Mr. Hackluit hath embodied into a Fleet, divided into three Squadrons, so many several Volumes; a work of great honour to England; it being possible that many Ports and Islands in America, which, being base and barren, bear only a bare name for the present, may prove rich places for the future. And then these Voyages will be produced, and pleaded, as good Evidence of their belonging to England, as first discovered and denominated by English-men. Mr. Hackluit dyed in the beginning of King James's Reign, leaving a fair estate to an unthrift Son, who embezilled it, on this token, that he vanted, "that he

*Hereford-Shire.

cheated the covetous Usurer, who had given him spick and span new money, for the old Land of his Great Great Grandfather." —FULLER, THOMAS, 1662, *The Worthies of England, ed. Nichols, vol.* I, *p.* 453.

We have in our own language as good and as bad collections as ever were made; one instance of each may suffice. Mr. Hakluyt was an able, ingenious, diligent, accurate, and useful compiler; and his collections are as valuable as any thing in their kind; on the other hand, Purchas his Pilgrims are very voluminous, and for the most part a very trifling and insignificant collection.—HARRIS, JOHN, 1702, *Collection of Voyages and Travels, Introduction.*

Richard Hakluyt, the enlightened friend and able documentary historian of these commercial enterprises,* a man whose fame should be vindicated and asserted in the land which he helped to colonize. —BANCROFT, GEORGE, 1834–74, *History of the United States.*

Every reader conversant in the annals of our naval transactions, will cheerfully acknowledge the merit of Richard Hakluyt, who devoted his studies to the investigation of those periods of English history, which regard the improvement of navigation and commerce. He had the advantages of an academical education. He was elected student of Christ Church in Oxford, in 1570, and was therefore contemporary with Sidney at the University. To him we are principally indebted for a clear and comprehensive description of those noble discoveries of the English nation made by sea or overland to the most distant quarter of the earth. His incomparable industry was remunerated with every possible encouragement by Sir Francis Walsingham and Sir Philip Sidney. To the latter, as to a most generous promoter of all ingenious and useful knowledge, he inscribed his first collection of voyages and discoveries, printed in 1589. Thus animated and encouraged, he was enabled to leave to posterity the fruits of his unwearied labours—an invaluable treasure of nautical information preserved in volumes, which even at this day, affix to his name a brilliancy of reputation, which a series of ages can never efface or obscure. —ZOUCH, THOMAS, 1808, *Memoirs of the Life and Writings of Sir Philip Sidney.*

*Voyages to New England.

All hail to thee Richard Hakluyt! for thou wert a genius of no ordinary complexion. What, though the warmth of a prebendal stall in the Abbey of *Westminster* might have comforted thy limbs, and thy clerical duties in the rural shades of *Wetheringset* have occupied much of thy time, yet, behold this meritorious Divine stealing, "many a time and oft," to the then picturesque vicinity of *Wapping*;—holding discourse with sea-faring men: listening, with willing and greedy ears, to tales of adventure and high exploit: feeling the passion for visiting distant parts increasing daily within him; and influenced by the secret advice and urgent entreaty of that wise Minister Walsingham, gratifying this passion, in the collection of scarce and curious tracts, and in obtaining accurate notices relating to the growth and produce "of either Ind." —DIBDIN, THOMAS FROGNALL, 1824, *The Library Companion, p.* 377.

Much more is, indeed, offered to a refined and philosophic observer, though buried amid this unwieldy and unsightly mass, than was ever supposed by its original readers, or even its first compilers.—SMYTH, WILLIAM, 1840, *Lectures on Modern History, Lecture XXI.*

Alas for the readers of modern travels, who can no longer participate in the wild and awful sensations of the all-believing faith of "the home-bred wit" of the Elizabethan era,—the first readers of Hakluyt's immense collection!—DISRAELI, ISAAC, 1841, *Public Opinion, Amenities of Literature.*

The Prose Epic of the modern nation. They contain the heroic tales of the exploits of the great men in whom the new era was inaugurated. —FROUDE, JAMES ANTHONY, 1867, *England's Forgotten Worthies, Short Studies on Great Subjects.*

He might easily have made a name for himself as a writer, as an essayist or commentator, if he had not sacrificed this prospect for the sake of his lifelong work of research.—KER, W. P., 1893, *English Prose, ed. Craik, vol.* I, *p.* 516.

Hakluyt's "Principal Navigations, Voiages and Discoveries of the English Nation," 1589, with rare map, fine copy, in pigskin. Jadis, £26, 5s. Same copy, Duke of Hamilton (1884), £23.—WHEATLEY, HENRY B., 1898, *Prices of Books, p.* 219.

WILLIAM SHAKESPEARE

From Portrait by Martin Droeshout.

William Shakespeare

1564–1616

William Shakespeare, 1564–1616. Born, at Stratford-on-Avon, 22 or 23 April 1564. Educated at Stratford Grammar School, 1571–77 (?). Perhaps apprenticed to his father (a butcher), 1577. Married Ann Hathaway, 1582. To London, 1586; acted, and wrote for stage. Plays probably written between 1591 and 1611. Bought New Place, Stratford, May 1597. Bought a house in Blackfriars, 1613. Died, at Stratford-on-Avon, 23 April 1616. Buried in Stratford Church. *Works:* The following are known to have been printed in Shakespeare's lifetime: "Venus and Adonis," 1593; "Lucrece," 1594; "Richard III.," 1597; "Richard II.," 1597; "Romeo and Juliet," 1597; "Henry IV., Pt. I.," 1598; "Love's Labour's Lost," 1598; "Henry V.," 1600; "Midsummer Night's Dream," 1600; "Merchant of Venice," 1600; "Henry IV., Pt. II.," 1600; "Much Ado about Nothing," 1600; "Titus Andronicus," 1600; "Merry Wives of Windsor," 1602; "Hamlet," 1603; "King Lear," 1608; "Sonnets," 1609; "Troilus and Cressida," 1609. His "Comedies, Histories, and Tragedies," ed. by J. Heminge and H. Condell, were first published in 1623; his "Works," ed. by N. Rowe (7 vols.), 1709-10.—SHARP, R. FARQUHARSON, 1897, *A Dictionary of English Authors, p.* 253.

PERSONAL

GOOD FREND FOR IESVS SAKE FORBEARE,
TO DIGG THE DVST ENCLOASED HEARE:
BLESTE BE Y[E] MAN Y[T] SPARES THES STONES,
AND CVRST BE HE Y[T] MOVES MY BONES.
—*Inscription on the Tablet over Shakespeare's Grave, April* 25, 1616.

Base minded men al three of you, if by my miserie ye be not warned: for unto none of you (like me) sought those burres to cleave: those Puppits (I meane) that speake from our mouths, those Anticks garnisht in our colours. Is it not strange that I, to whom they al have beene beholding: is it not like that you, to whome they all have beene beholding, shall (were ye in that case that I am now) be both at once of them forsaken? Yes, trust them not: for there is an upstart Crow, beautified with our feathers, that with his *Tygers heart wrapt in a Players hide,* supposes he is as well able to bumbast out a blanke verse as the best of you: and being an absolute *Johannes fac totum,* is in his owne conceit the onely Shake-scene in a countrie. O that I might intreate your rare wits to be imployed in more profitable courses: & let these Apes imitate your past excellence, and never more acquaint them with your admired inventions. I know the best husband of you all will never prove an usurer and the kindest of them all wil never proove a kinde nurse: yet, whilst you may, seeke you better Maisters; for it is pittie men of such rare wits, should be subiect to the pleasures of such rude groomes.—GREENE, ROBERT, 1592, *A Groats-worth of Wit.*

About three moneths since died M. Robert Greene, leaving many papers in sundry Booke sellers hands, among other his Groats-worth of wit, in which, a letter written to diuers playmakers, is offensiuely by one or two of them taken, and because on the dead they cannot be auenged, they wilfully forge in their conceites a liuing author: and after tossing it to and fro, no remedy, but it must light on me. . . . With neither* of them that take offence was I acquainted, and with one† of them I care not if I neuer be: the other‡, whom at that time I did not so much spare, as since I wish I had, for that as I haue moderated the heate of liuing writers, and might haue vsed my owne discretion (especially in such a case) the author being dead, that I did not, I am as sory, as if the originall fault had beene my fault, because myselfe haue seene his demeanor no lesse ciuill than he exclent in the qualitie he professes: besides, diuers of worship haue reported his vprightness of dealing, which argues his honesty, and his facetious grace in writting, that aprooues his art.—CHETTLE, HENRY, 1592, *Kind-Hart's Dreame, ed. Rimbault, Preface, p.* iv.

?*Players*, I love yee, and your *Qualitie*,
As ye are Men, *that* pass time not abus'd:
And some I love for *painting, poesie*,
And say fell *Fortune* cannot be excus'd,
That hath for better *uses* you refus'd:
Wit, Courage, good shape, good partes, and all
    good,
As long as al these *goods* are no *worse* us'd,

*Marlowe and Shakespeare.
†Marlowe.
‡Shakespeare.

And though the *stage* doth staine pure gentle *bloud*,
Yet generous yee are in *minde* and *moode*.
—DAVIES, JOHN, OF HEREFORD, 1603, *Microcosmos, ed. Grosart.*

Renowned Spenser, lie a thought more nigh
To learned Chaucer; and rare Beaumont, lie
A little nearer Spenser; to make room
For Shakespeare in your three-fold four-fold tomb:
To lodge all four in one bed make a shift
Until Doomsday; for hardly will a fift,
Betwixt this day and that, by fate be slain,
For whom your curtains may be drawn again.
But if precedency in death doth bar
A fourth place in your sacred sepulchre,
Under this carvèd marble of thine own,
Sleep, rare tragedian, Shakspeare, sleep alone:
Thy unmolested peace, unsharèd cave,
Possess as lord, not tenant, of thy grave;
That unto us and others it may be
Honour hereafter to be laid by thee.
—BASSE, WILLIAM, 1616?, *Epitaph on Shakspeare.*

IVDICIO PYLIVM, GENIO SOCRATEM, ARTE MARONEM,
TERRA TEGIT, POPVLVS MÆRET, OLYMPVS HABET.

STAY PASSENGER, WHY GOEST THOV BY SO FAST?
READ IF THOV CANST, WHOM ENVIOVS DEATH HATH PLAST,
WITH IN THIS MONVMENT SHAKSPEARE WITH WHOME
QVICK NATVRE DIDE: WHOSE NAME DOTH DECK Y^S TOMBE
FAR MORE THEN COST: SIEH ALL, Y HE HATH WRITT,
LEAVES LIVING ART, BVT PAGE, TO SERVE HIS WITT.

OBIIT ANO DO^I 1616
ÆTATIS, 53. DIE 23 AP.

—*Inscriptions upon the Tablet under Shakespere's Bust, in the Chancel-north-wall of Stratford Church*, 1617–1622?

This Figure, that thou here seest put,
It was for gentle Shakespeare cut;
Wherein the Graver had a strife
With Nature, to out-doo the life:
O, could he but have drawne his Wit
As well in Brasse, as he hath hit
His Face; the Print would then surpasse
All, that was ever writ in Brasse.
But, since he cannot, Reader, looke
Not on his Picture, but his Booke.
—J(ONSON), B(EN), 1623, *Facing Droeshout's portrait of Shakespeare prefixed to the First Folio Edition of his Works.*

Mellifluous Shakespeare, whose enchanting quill
Commanded mirth or passion, was but *Will*.
—HEYWOOD, THOMAS, 1635, *The Hierarchy of the Blessed Angels.*

Shakspear had but two daughters, one whereof Mr. Hall, the physitian, married, and by her had on daughter married, to wit, the Lady Bernard of Abbingdon. I have heard that Mr. Shakspeare was a natural wit, without any art at all; hee frequented the plays all his younger time, but in his elder days lived at Stratford, and supplied the stage with two plays every year, and for itt had an allowance so large, that hee spent att the rate of 1,000*l.* a-year, as I have heard. Shakespeare, Drayton, and Ben Jonson, had a merie meeting, and itt seems drank too hard, for Shakespear died of a feavour there contracted. Remember to peruse Shakespeare's plays, and bee much versed in them, that I may not bee ignorant in that matter. Whether Dr. Heylin does well, in reckoning up the dramatick poets which have been famous in England, to omit Shakespeare.—WARD, REV. JOHN, 1648–78, *Diary, ed. Severn, p.* 183.

William Shakespeare was born at Stratford on Avon in this County*; in whom three eminent Poets may seem in some sort to be compounded. 1. Martial, in the warlike sound of his Surname (whence some may conjecture him of a Military extraction) *Hastivibrans*, or Shake-speare. 2. Ovid, the most naturall and witty of all Poets; and hence it was that Queen Elizabeth, coming into a Grammar-School, made this extemporary verse,

"*Persius* a Crab-staffe, Bawdy *Martial*, *Ovid* a fine Wag."

3. Plautus, who was an exact Comedian, yet never any Scholar, as our Shake-speare (if alive) would confess himself. Adde to all these, that though his Genius generally was jocular, and inclining him to festivity, yet he could (when so disposed) be solemn and serious, as appears by his Tragedies; so that Heraclitus himself (I mean if secret and unseen) might afford to smile at his Comedies, they were so merry; and Democritus scarce forbear to sigh at his Tragedies, they were so mournfull. He was an eminent instance of the

*Warwick.

truth of that Rule, "Poeta non fit, sed nascitur;" one is not made, but *born* a Poet. Indeed his Learning was very little, so that, as Cornish diamonds are not polished by any Lapidary, but are pointed and smoothed even as they are taken out of the Earth, so Nature itself was all the Art which was used upon him. Many were the Wet-combates betwixt him and Ben Jonson; which two I behold like a Spanish great Gallion and an English Man of War: Master Jonson (like the former) was built far higher in Learning; solid, but slow, in his performances. Shake-speare, with the English Man of War, lesser in bulk, but lighter in sailing, could turn with all tides, tack about, and take advantage of all winds, by the quickness of his Wit and Invention. —FULLER, THOMAS, 1662, *The Worthies of England, ed. Nichols, vol.* II, *p.* 414.

Mr. William Shakespear was borne at Stratford upon Avon in the county of Warwick. His father was a butcher, and I have been told heretofore by some of the neighbours, that when he was a boy he exercised his father's trade, but when he kill'd a calfe he would doe it in a high style, and make a speech. There was at that time another butcher's son in this towne that was held not at all inferior to him for a naturall witt, his acquaintance and coetanean, but dyed young. This William being inclined naturally to poetry and acting, came to London, I guesse, about 18; and was an actor at one of the playhouses, and did act exceedingly well (now B. Johnson was never a good actor, but an excellent instructor). He began early to make essayes at dramatique poetry, which at that time was very lowe; and his playes tooke well. He was a handsome, well-shap't man: very good company, and of a very readie and pleasant smooth witt.—AUBREY, JOHN, 1669-96, *Brief Lives, ed. Clark, vol.* II, *p.* 225.

He had, by a misfortune common enough to young fellows, fallen into ill company, and, amongst them, some that made a frequent practice of deer-stealing, engaged him more than once in robbing a park that belonged to Sir Thomas Lucy, of Charlecote, near Stratford. For this he was prosecuted by that gentleman, as he thought, somewhat too severely; and, in order to revenge that ill usage, he made a ballad upon him. And though this, probably the first essay of his poetry, be lost, yet it is said to have been so very bitter, that it redoubled the prosecution against him to that degree, that he was obliged to leave his business and family in Warwickshire, for some time, and shelter himself in London.—ROWE, NICHOLAS, 1709, *Some Account of the Life of William Shakespeare.*

Thou, soft-flowing Avon, by thy silver stream,
Of things more than Mortal sweet Shakespeare would dream,
The fairies by moonlight dance round his green bed,
For hallow'd the turf is which pillow'd his head.

. . . .

Flow on, silver Avon, in song ever flow,
Be the swans on thy waters whiter than snow,
Ever full be thy stream, like his name may it spread,
And the turf ever-hallow'd which pillow'd his head.

—GARRICK, DAVID, 1769, *Ode to Shakespeare.*

The tomb of Shakspeare is in the chancel. The place is solemn and sepulchral. Tall elms wave before the pointed windows, and the Avon, which runs at a short distance from the walls, keeps up a low perpetual murmur. A flat stone marks the spot where the bard is buried. There are four lines inscribed on it, said to have been written by himself, and which have in them something extremely awful. If they are indeed his own, they show that solicitude about the quiet of the grave, which seems natural to fine sensibilities and thoughtful minds. . . . As I crossed the bridge over the Avon on my return, I paused to contemplate the distant church in which the poet lies buried, and could not but exult in the malediction, which has kept his ashes undisturbed in its quiet and hallowed vaults. What honor could his name have derived from being mingled in dusty companionship with the epitaphs and escutcheons and venal eulogiums of a titled multitude? What would a crowded corner in Westminster Abbey have been, compared with this reverend pile, which seems to stand in beautiful loneliness as his sole mausoleum!—IRVING, WASHINGTON, 1819-48, *Stratford-On-Avon, Sketch Book.*

It was not without some pleasurable imaginations that I saw Stratford-upon-Avon, the very hills and woods which the boy Shakespeare had looked upon, the very church where his dust reposes, nay, the very house where he was born; the threshold over which his staggering footsteps carried him in infancy; the very stones where the urchin played marbles and flogged tops. . . . It is a small grim-looking house of bricks, bound, as was of old the fashion, with beams of oak intersecting the bricks which are built into it and fill up its interstices as the glass does in a window. The old tile roof is cast by age, and twisted into all varieties of curvature. Half the house has been modernised and made a butcher's shop. The street where it stands is a simple-looking, short, everyday village street, with houses mostly new, and consisting, like the Shakespeare house, of two low stories, or rather a story and a half. Stratford itself is a humble, pleasant-looking place, the residence as formerly of woolcombers and other quiet artisans, except where they have brought an ugly black canal into it, and polluted this classical borough by the presence of lighters or trackboats with famished horses, sooty drivers, and heaps of coke and coal. It seems considerably larger and less showy than Annan. Shakespeare, Breakspeare, and for aught I know sundry other spears, are still common names in Warwickshire. I was struck on my arrival at Birmingham by a sign not far from Badams's, indicating the abode of William Shakespeare, boot and shoe maker, which boots and shoes the modern Shakespeare also professed his ability to mend "cheap and neatly." Homer, I afterwards discovered, had settled in Birmingham as a button maker. —CARLYLE, THOMAS, 1824, *Letter to John Carlyle, Life, ed. Froude, vol.* I. *p.* 191.

Of William Shakspeare, whom, through the mouths of those whom he has inspired to body forth the modifications of his immense mind, we seem to know better than any human writer, it may be truly said that we scarcely know any thing. We see him, so far as we do see him, not in himself, but in a reflex image from the objectivity in which he was manifested: he is Falstaff and Mercutio and Malvolio and Jaques and Portia and Imogen and Lear and Othello; but to us he is scarcely a determined person, a substantial reality of past time, the man Shakspeare. The two greatest names in poetry are to us little more than names. If we are not yet come to question his unity, as we do that of "the blind old man of Scio's rocky isle," an improvement in critical acuteness doubtless reserved for a distant posterity, we as little feel the power of identifying the young man who came up from Stratford, was afterwards an indifferent player in a London theatre, and retired to his native place in middle life, with the author of Macbeth and Lear, as we can give a distinct historic personality to Homer. All that insatiable curiosity and unwearied diligence have hitherto detected about Shakspeare serves rather to disappoint and perplex us than to furnish the slightest illustration of his character. It is not the register of his baptism, or the draft of his will, or the orthography of his name, that we seek. No letter of his writing, no record of his conversation, no character of him drawn with any fulness by a contemporary, has been produced.—HALLAM, HENRY, 1837–39, *Introduction to the Literature of Europe, vol.* II, *pt.* ii, *ch.* vi, *par.* 34.

I can vouch, for the following form, all taken from writings of nearly the poet's own age. . . . Schaksper, Schakesper, Schakespeyr, Shagspere, Shaxper, Shaxpere, Shaxpeare, Shaxsper, Shaxspere, Shaxespere, Shakspere, Shakspear, Shakspeere, Shackspeare, Shackespeare, Shackespere, Shakspeyr, Shakesper, Shakespere, Shakeseper, Shakyspere, Shakespire, Shakespeire, Shakespear, Shakaspeare. They are all manifestly of the same type; and to these varieties others might be added. In two instances I have met with the name written *Saxpere*. . .

Shakespeare or Shakespear kept its ground as the received and proper orthography of the poet's name till the time of the two very eminent commentators Steevens and Malone. . . . A contemporary critic of inferior note in 1785 introduced another variation. In his hands the name became *Shakspere*, with the object, no doubt, of bringing back the orthography to the form in which the name is said to be found traced by the poet's own hand in his will and in other writings.—HUNTER, JOSEPH, 1845, *New Illustrations of the Life, Studies, and Writings of Shakespeare, vol.* I, *pp.* 4, 5.

As there is hardly a page in his writings which does not shed more light upon the biography of his mind, and bring us nearer to the individuality of the man, the antiquaries in despair have been compelled to abandon him to the psychologists; and the moment the transition from external to internal facts is made, the most obscure of men passes into the most notorious. For this personality and soul we call Shakespeare, the recorded incidents of whose outward career were so few and trifling, lived a more various life —a life more crowded with ideas, passions, volitions, and *events*—than any potentate the world has ever seen. Compared with his experience, the experience of Alexander or Hannibal, of Cæsar or Napoleon, was narrow and one-sided. He had projected himself into almost all the varieties of human character, and, in imagination, had intensely realized and *lived* the life of each. From the throne of the monarch to the bench of the village alehouse, there were few positions in which he had not placed himself, and which he had not for a time identified with his own.—WHIPPLE, EDWIN P., 1859–68, *The Literature of the Age of Elizabeth, p.* 33.

In April, 1664, it was a hundred years since Shakespeare was born. England was occupied in cheering loudly Charles II., who had sold Dunkirk to France for two hundred and fifty thousand pounds sterling, and in looking at something that was a skeleton and had been Cromwell, whitening under the north-east wind and rain on the gallows at Tyburn. In April, 1764, it was two hundred years since Shakespeare was born: England was contemplating the dawn of George III., a king destined to imbecility, who, at that epoch, in secret councils, and in somewhat unconstitutional asides with the Tory chiefs and the German Landgraves, was sketching out that policy of resistance to progress which was to strive, first against liberty in America, then against democracy in France, and which, only under the ministry of the first Pitt, had, in 1778, raised the debt of England to the sum of eighty millions sterling. In April, 1864, three hundred years since Shakespeare's birth, England raises a statue to Shakespeare. It is late, but it is well.—HUGO, VICTOR, 1864, *William Shakespeare, tr. Baillot, p.* 324.

The moral humility of Shakspere is equal to his intellectual grandeur. Mental wealth without pride—such is the example that he presents, both in theory and practice, to the most favoured son of genius.—HERAUD, JOHN A., 1865, *Shakspere, His Inner Life as Intimated in His Works, p.* 66.

To Stratford-on-the-Avon—And we passed
Thro' aisles and avenues of the princeliest trees
That ever eyes beheld. None such with us
Here in the bleaker North. And as we went
Through Lucy's park, the red day dropt i' the west;
A crimson glow, like blood in lovers' cheeks,
Spread up the soft green sky and passed away;
The mazy twilight came down on the lawns,
And all those huge trees seemed to fall asleep;
The deer went past like shadows. All the park
Lay round us like a dream; and one fine thought
Hung over us, and hallowed all. Yea, he,
The pride of England, glistened like a star,
And beckoned us to Stratford.

—LEIGHTON, ROBERT, 1869? *Stratford-on-Avon.*

Of Shakspeare all came from within—I mean from his soul and his genius; external circumstances contributed but slightly to his development. He was intimately bound up with his age; that is, he knew by experience the manners of country, court, and town; he had visited the heights, depths, the middle regions of the condition of mankind; nothing more. For the rest his life was commonplace; the irregularities, troubles, passions, successes through which he passed, were, on the whole, such as we meet with everywhere else.—TAINE, H. A., 1871, *History of English Literature, tr. Van Laun, vol.* I, *bk.* ii, *ch.* iv, *p.* 297.

The manner of his death is uncertain. His will, still preserved in the Prerogative Office, is dated March 25, 1616. The poet's handwriting, never very good, if we may judge from the few signatures that have been preserved, and fifty years more antiquated than that of Sir Thomas Lucy, is feeble, shaky, and imperfect; very little like what might have been expected from one whose practice in writing must have been considerable, and who had in his time filled many reams of manuscript. His death did not occur until the 23rd of April following. It would seem, therefore, that his death was far from sudden; and this alone would suffice to invalidate the tradition, circulated forty-five years after, that the poet died of a fever contracted at a merry meeting with Drayton and Ben Jonson. His bust in Stratford Church, his portrait by Droeshout prefixed to the first folio edition of his works, and the whole tenour of his life, contradict altogether the supposition that the poet was intemperate. If the opinion of competent judges may be taken, the bust was executed from a cast taken after death. It was certainly coloured after life, and until it was painted over by Malone — a greater crime to Shakspeare's memory than Mr. Gaskill's destruction of the famous mulberry tree—it represented the poet exactly as he appeared to his contemporaries. The eyes were a bright hazel, the hair and beard auburn; the doublet was scarlet, covered with a loose black sleeveless gown. As in Droeshout's portrait, the forehead is remarkably high and broad; in fact, the immense volume of the forehead is its most striking feature. The predominant characteristic of the whole is that of a composed, self-possessed, resolute, and vigorous Englishman, of a higher intellectual stamp than usual, but not so far removed from the general national type as we should have been inclined to expect from his writings.—BREWER, J. S., 1871-81, *English Studies, ed. Wace, p.* 235.

As in his dramatic world he embraces the widest variety of human experience, so in his personal character he may be said to have combined in harmonious union the widest range of qualities, including some apparently the most opposed. He was a vigilant and acute man of business, of great executive ability, with a power of looking into affairs which included a thorough mastery of tedious legal details. But with all his worldly prudence and foresight he was at the same time the most generous and affectionate of men, honored and loved by all who knew him, with the irresistible charm that belongs to simplicity and directness of character combined with thoughtful sympathy and real kindness of heart. And while displaying unrivalled skill, sagacity, and firmness in business transactions and practical affairs, he could promptly throw the whole burden aside, and in the exercise of his noble art pierce with an eagle's wing the very highest heaven of invention. That indeed was his native air, his true home, his permanent sphere, where he still rules with undisputed sway. He occupies a throne apart in the ideal and immortal kingdom of supreme creative art, poetical genius, and dramatic truth. — BAYNES, T. SPENCER, 1886, *Encyclopædia Britannica, Ninth ed., vol.* XXI, *p.* 803.

The folk who lived in Shakespeare's day
And saw that gentle figure pass
By London Bridge, his frequent way—
They little knew what man he was.
The pointed beard, the courteous mien,
The equal port to high and low,
All this they saw or might have seen—
But not the light behind the brow!
The doublet's modest gray or brown,
The slender sword-hilt's plain device,
What sign had these for prince or clown?
Few turned, or none, to scan him twice.
Yet 'twas the king of England's kings!
The rest with all their pomps and trains
Are mouldered, half-remembered things—
'Tis he alone that lives and reigns!

—ALDRICH, THOMAS BAILEY, 1890, *Guilielmus Rex.*

His literary practices and aims were those of contemporary men of letters, and the difference in the quality of his work and theirs was due not to conscious endeavour on his part to act otherwise than they, but to the magic and involuntary working of his genius. He seemed unconscious of his marvellous superiority to his professional comrades. The references in his will to his fellow-actors, and the spirit in which (as they announce in the First Folio) they approached the task of collecting his works after his death, corroborate the description of him as a sympathetic friend of gentle, unassuming mien. The later traditions brought together by Aubrey depict him as "very good company, and of a very ready and pleasant smooth wit," and there is much in other early posthumous references to suggest a genial, if not a convivial, temperament, linked to a quiet turn for good-humoured satire. But Bohemian ideals and modes of life had no genuine attraction for Shakespeare. His extant work attests his "copious" and continuous industry, and with his literary power and sociability there clearly went the shrewd capacity of a man of business. Pope had just warrant for the surmise that he

For gain not glory winged his roving flight,
And grew immortal in his own despite.

His literary attainments and successes were chiefly valued as serving the prosaic end of providing permanently for himself and his daughters. His highest ambition was to restore among his fellow-townsmen the family repute which his father's misfortunes had imperilled. Ideals so homely are reckoned rare among poets, but Chaucer and Sir Walter Scott, among writers of exalted genius, vie with Shakespeare in the sobriety of their personal aims and in the sanity of their mental attitude toward life's ordinary incidents.—LEE, SIDNEY, 1898, *A Life of William Shakespeare, p.* 278.

That must have been a momentous day in Shakespeare's life on which, after giving up his house in London, he mounted his horse and rode back to Stratford-on-Avon to take up his abode there for good. . . . Life lay behind him now. His hopes had been fulfilled in many ways; he was famous, he had raised himself a degree in the social scale, above all he was rich, but for all that he was not happy. The great town, in which he had spent the better part of a lifetime, had not so succeeded in attaching him to it that he would feel any pain in leaving it. There was neither man nor woman there so dear to him as to make society preferable to solitude, and the crowded life of London to the seclusion of the country and an existence passed in the midst of family and Nature. . . . The journey from London to Stratford took three days. He would put up at the inns at which he was accustomed to stay on his yearly journey to and fro, and where he was always greeted as a welcome guest, and given a bed with snow-white sheets, for which travellers on foot were charged an extra penny, but which he, as rider, enjoyed gratis. The hostess at Oxford, pretty Mistress Davenant, would give him a specially cordial greeting. The two were old and good friends. Little William, born in 1606, and now seven years old, possessed a certain, perhaps accidental, resemblance of feature to the guest. . . . It was the quietude of Stratford which attracted him, its leisure, the emptiness of its dirty streets, its remoteness from the busy world. What he really longed for was Nature, the Nature with which he had lived in such intimate companionship in his early youth, which he had missed so terribly while writing "As You Like It" and its fellow-plays, and from which he had so long been separated. Far more than human beings was it the gardens which he had bought and planted there which drew him back to his native town—the gardens and trees on which he looked from his windows at New Place.—BRANDES, GEORGE, 1898, *William Shakespeare, A Critical Study, vol.* II, *pp.* 389, 390, 392.

The Birthplace, as it is called, is a cottage of plaster and timber, two stories in height, with dormer windows, and a pleasant garden in the rear — all that remains of a considerable piece of land. It stands upon the street, and the visitor passes at once, through a little porch, into a low room, ceiled with black oak, paved with flags, and with a fireplace so wide that one sees at a glance what the chimney-corner once meant of comfort and cheer. On those seats, looking into the glowing fire, the imagination of a boy could hardly fail to kindle. A dark and narrow stair leads to the little bare room on the floor above in which Shakespeare was probably born. The place seems fitted, by its very simplicity, to serve as the starting-point for so great a career. There is a small fireplace; the low ceiling is within reach of the hand; on the narrow panes of glass which fill the casement names and initials are traced in irregular profusion. This room has been a place eagerly sought by literary pilgrims since the beginning of the century. The low ceiling and the walls were covered, in the early part of the century, with innumerable autographs. In 1820 the occupant, a woman who attached great importance to the privilege of showing the house to visitors, was compelled to give up that privilege, and, by way of revenge, removed the furniture and whitewashed the walls of the house. A part of the wall of the upper room escaped the sacrilegious hand of the jealous custodian, and names running back to the third decade of the last century are still to be found there. Other and perhaps more famous names have taken the places of those which were erased, and the walls are now a mass of hieroglyphs. Scott, Byron, Rogers, Tennyson, Thackeray, Dickens, have left this record of their interest in the room. No new names are now written on these blackened walls; the names of visitors are kept in a recordbook on the lower floor.—MABIE, HAMILTON WRIGHT, 1900, *William Shakespeare, Poet, Dramatist, and Man, p.* 35.

VENUS AND ADONIS

1585-7-1593

VENVS | AND ADONIS | *Vilia miretur vulgus: mihi flauus Apollo | Pocula Castalia plena ministret aqua.* | London | Imprinted by Richard Field, and are to be sold at | the signe of the white Greyhound in | Paules Church-yard. | 1593.—TITLE PAGE OF FIRST EDITION, 1593.

TO THE RIGHT HONOURABLE
HENRY WRIOTHESLY
EARL OF SOUTHAMPTON, AND BARON OF TICHFIELD.

Right Honourable,

I know not how I shall offend in dedicating my unpolished lines to your lordship, nor how the world will censure me for choosing so strong a prop to support so weak a burden: only, if your honour seem but pleased, I account myself highly praised, and vow to take advantage of all idle hours, till I have honoured you with some graver labour. But if the first heir of my invention prove deformed, I shall be sorry it had so noble a god-father, and never after ear so barren a land, for fear it yield me still so bad a harvest. I leave it to your honourable survey, and your honour to your heart's content; which I wish may always answer your own wish, and the world's hopeful expectation.

Your honour's in all duty,

—SHAKESPEARE, WILLIAM, 1593, *Dedication.*

This makes my mourning Muse resolve in teares,
This theames my heavie penne to plaine in prose;
Christ's thorne is sharpe, no head His garland weares;
Stil finest wits are 'stilling Venus' rose,
In Paynim toyes the sweetest vaines are spent;
To Christian workes few have their talents lent.

—SOUTHWELL, ROBERT, 1594? *Saint Peters Complaint, with other Poemes, The Authour to the Reader, ed. Grosart, p.* xii.

Let this duncified worlde esteeme of Spencer and Chaucer, I'le worshipp sweet Mr. Shakspeare, and to honoure him will lay his "Venus and Adonis" under my pillowe, as wee reade of one (I doe not well remember his name, but I am sure he was a kinge) slept with Homer under his bed's heade. Well, I'le bestowe a Frenche crowne in the faire writings of them out, and then I'le instructe thee about the delivery of them.—ANON, *The Return from Pernassus,* 1606, *pt,* i, *act.* iv, *sc.* i, *p.* 63.

But stay my Muse in thine owne confines keepe,
& wage not warre with so deere lov'd a neighbor,
But having sung thy day song, rest and sleepe
preserve thy small fame and his greater favor:
His Song was worthie merrit (*Shakspeare* hee)
sung the faire blossome, thou the withered tree
Laurell is due to him, his art and wit
hath purchast it, *Cypres* thy brow will fit.

—BARKSTEAD, WILLIAM, 1607, *Mirrha, the Mother of Adonis; or Lustes Prodegies, ed. Grosart,* 1876, *p.* 65.

Another (ah, Lord helpe) mee vilifies
With Art of Love, and how to subtilize,
Making lewd *Venus*, with eternall Lines,
To tye *Adonis* to her loves designes:
Fine wit is shew'n therein: but finer twere
If not attired in such bawdy Geare.
But be it as it will: the coyest Dames,
In private read it for their Closset-games:
For, sooth to say, the lines so draw them on,
To the venerian speculation,
That will they, nill they (if of flesh they bee)
They will thinke of it, sith *loose* Thought is free.

—DAVIES, JOHN, OF HEREFORD, 1611? *The Scourge of Folly and other Poems, Works, ed. Grosart, p.* 75.

In "Venus and Adonis," the poet, absolutely carried away by the voluptuous power of his subject, seems entirely to have lost sight of its mythological wealth. Venus, stripped of the prestige of divinity, is nothing but a beautiful courtesan, endeavouring unsuccessfully, by all the prayers, tears, and artifices of love, to stimulate the languid desires of a cold and disdainful youth. Hence arises a monotony which is not redeemed by the simple gracefulness and poetic merit of many passages, and which is augmented by the division of the poem into stanzas of six lines, the last two of which almost invariably present a *jeu d'esprit*. But a metre singularly free from irregularities, a cadence full of harmony, and a versification which had never before been equaled in England. —GUIZOT, FRANÇOIS PIERRE GUILLAUME, 1821-52, *Shakspeare and His Times, p.* 63.

It is difficult to say to what depths of bad taste the writer of certain passages in "Venus and Adonis" could not fall before his genius or his judgment was full-grown.—SWINBURNE, ALGERNON CHARLES, 1880, *A Study of Shakespeare, p.* 41.

"Venus and Adonis" brims over with poetry — erotic, lyrical, elegiac, and descriptive, — but of dramatic poetry there is none. . . . Shakespeare has been reproached with having debased and degraded the mythological riches of his subject in not presenting Venus as a goddess instead of as a mere beautiful amorous wanton; but the reproach is singularly wanting in perception, for it is precisely this that gives life to this picture. While rejecting the cold mythological verbiage of the Renaissance, he has kept the material and voluptuous spirit of its paganism, and produced this admirable picture of a woman, which has justly been compared to a painting by Titian for richness and depth of colour. — STAPFER, PAUL, 1880, *Shakespeare and Classical Antiquity, tr. Carey, pp.* 133, 135.

The Stratford boy hardly puts in his appearance in London before he presents Lord Southampton, as the "first heir of his invention," with—if not the most mature—at least the most carefully polished production that William Shakespeare's name was ever signed to; and, moreover, as polished, elegant, and sumptuous a piece of rhetoric as English letters has ever produced down to this very day.—MORGAN, APPLETON, 1881, *The Shakespearian Myth, p.* 41.

I think no author of his time could have treated the voluptuous story of "Venus and Adonis" as Shakespeare treated it. All through the hot air of its passion a fresh, pure breeze of something higher trembles, and I am astonished that more has not been made of this point by critics. —DALL, CAROLINE HEALEY, 1886, *What We Really Know about Shakespeare, p.* 98.

There were already many tuneful singers in 1593; but none of them except the master himself could raise such a pageant of voluptuous imagery, or accompany it with such a symphony of harmonious sound, as we find in "Venus and Adonis." No one except Spenser and Sackville evoked the rhyme-clangour of the stanza with such delicate art; no one except these two had portrayed such vivid pictures as the arrest of Adonis by Venus, the captivity of Mars, the portrait of herself by the goddess, the escape of the courser, the description of the boar and of the hare-hunt, the solitary night, the discovery of the foolish youth who has fled from Love's arms to those of Death. But while none, save these, of men living had done, or could have done, such work, there was much here which — whether either could have done it or not—neither had done. — SAINTSBURY, GEORGE, 1898, *A Short History of English Literature, p.* 317.

His careful, well-compacted, and thoroughly constructed poem.—MABIE, HAMILTON WRIGHT, 1900, *William Shakespeare, Poet, Dramatist, and Man, p.* 190.

In "Venus and Adonis" glows the whole fresh sensuousness of the Renaissance and of Shakespeare's youth. It is an entirely erotic poem, and contemporaries aver that it lay on the table of every light woman in London. The conduct of the poem presents a series of opportunities and pretexts for voluptuous situations and descriptions. The ineffectual blandishments lavished by Venus on the chaste and frigid youth, who, in his sheer boyishness, is as irresponsive as a bashful woman — her kisses, caresses, and embraces, are depicted in detail. It is as though a Titian or Rubens had painted a model in a whole series of tender situations, now in one attitude, now in another. Then comes the suggestive scene in which Adonis's horse breaks away in order to meet the challenge of a mare which happens to wander by, together with the goddess's comments thereupon. Then new advances and solicitations, almost inadmissibly daring, according to the taste of our day. An element of feeling is introduced in the portrayal of Venus's anguish when Adonis expresses his intention of hunting the boar. But it is to sheer description that the poet chiefly devotes himself—description of the charging boar, description of the fair young body bathed in blood, and so forth. There is a fire and rapture of colour in it all, as in a picture by some Italian master of a hundred years before. Quite unmistakable is the insinuating, luscious, almost saccharine quality of the writing, which accounts for the fact that, when his immediate contemporaries speak of Shakespeare's diction, honey is the similitude that first suggests itself to them. John Weever, in 1595, calls him "honey-tongued," and in 1598 Francis Meres uses the same term, with the addition of "mellifluous."—BRANDES, GEORGE, 1898, *William Shakespeare, A Critical Study, vol.* I, *p.* 68.

THE RAPE OF LUCRECE

1594

LVCRECE | LONDON. | Printed by Richard Field, for Iohn Harrison, and are | to be sold at the signe of the white Greyhound | in Paules Churh-yard. | 1594.—TITLE PAGE OF FIRST EDITION, 1594.

TO THE RIGHT HONOURABLE
HENRY WRIOTHESLY,
EARL OF SOUTHAMPTON, AND BARON OF TICHFIELD.

The love I dedicate to your lordship is without end; whereof this pamphlet, without beginning, is but a superfluous moiety. The warrant I have of your honourable disposition, not the worth of my untutored lines, makes it assured of acceptance. What I have done is yours; what I have to do is yours; being part in all I have, devoted yours. Were my worth greater, my duty would show greater; mean time, as it is, it is bound to your lordship, to whom I wish long life, still lengthened with all happiness.

Your Lordship's in all duty,

—SHAKESPEARE, WILLIAM, 1594, *Dedication.*

Lucrece, of whom proud Rome hath boasted long,
Lately reviv'd to live another age,
And here arriv'd to tell of Tarquin's wrong
Her chaste denial, and the Tyrant's rage,
Acting her passions on our stately stage;
She is remembered, all forgetting me,
Yet I as faire and chaste as e'er was she.

—DRAYTON, MICHAEL, 1594, *Matilda, s.* vi.

And Shakespeare, thou, whose hony flowing vaine,
(Pleasing the World) thy Praises doth containe;
Whose Venus, and whose Lucrece (sweet, and chast)
Thy name in Fame's immortall Booke have plac't.
Live ever you, at least in Fame live ever:
Well may the Body die, but Fame die never.

—BARNFIELD, RICHARD, 1605, *Remembrance of some English Poets.*

Who loves chaste life, there Lucrece for a teacher:
Who lis't read lust there's Venus and Adonis.

—FREEMAN, THOMAS, 1614, *Runne and a Great Cast.*

The two poems of Venus and Adonis and of Tarquin and Lucrece appear to us like a couple of ice-houses. They are about as hard, as glittering, and as cold. The author seems all the time to be thinking of his verses, and not of his subject—not of what his characters would feel, but of what he shall say; and as it must happen in all such cases, he always puts into their mouths those things which they would be the last to think of, and which it shows the greatest ingenuity in him to find out. The whole is laboured, uphill work. The poet is perpetually singling out the difficulties of the art to make an exhibition of his strength and skill in wrestling with them. He is making perpetual trials of them as if his mastery over them were doubted. . . A beautiful thought is sure to be lost in an endless commentary upon it. . . . There is, besides, a strange attempt to substitute the language of painting for that of poetry, to make us *see* their feelings in the faces of the persons.—HAZLITT, WILLIAM, 1817–69, *Characters of Shakespear's Plays, p.* 244.

The action is retarded by all manner of pretty ingenuities. Lucrece in her agony delivers *tirades* on Night, on Time, on Opportunity, as if they were theses for a degree in some academy of wit. Still the effect on a reader in the right mood is not that of frigid cleverness; the faults are faults of youth; the poet's pleasurable excitement can be perceived; nay at times we feel the energetic fervour of his heart. Now and again the poetry surprises, not by singularity, but as Keats has said that poetry ought to surprise, by a fine excess; sometimes a line is all gold seven times refined; and there is throughout such evidence of a rich, abounding nature in the writer that we are happy with him even while we recognize the idle errors of his nonage.—DOWDEN, EDWARD, 1880, *English Poets, ed. Ward, vol.* I, *p.* 437.

The strength of "Lucrece" lies in its graphic and gorgeous descriptions, and in its sometimes microscopic psychological analysis. For the rest, its pathos consists of elaborate and far-fetched rhetoric.

The lament of the heroine after the crime has been committed is pure declamation, extremely eloquent no doubt, but copious and artificial as an oration of Cicero's, rich in apostrophes and antitheses. The sorrow of "Collatine and his consorted lords" is portrayed in laboured and quibbling speeches. Shakespeare's knowledge and mastery are most clearly seen in the reflections scattered through the narrative.—BRANDES, GEORGE, 1898, *William Shakespeare, A Critical Study, vol.* I, *p.* 71.

If the "Venus" be a pageant of gesture, the "Lucrece" is a drama of emotion. You have the same wealth of imagery, but the images are no longer sunlit and sharply defined. They seem, rather, created by the reflex action of a sleepless brain—as it were fantastic symbols shaped from the lying report of tired eyes staring into darkness; and they are no longer used to decorate the outward play of natural desire and reluctance, but to project the shadows of abnormal passion and acute mental distress. — WYNDHAM, GEORGE, 1898, *ed. The Poems of Shakespeare, Introduction, p.* xcv.

A LOVER'S COMPLAINT

Of "A Lover's Complaint," marked as it is throughout with every possible sign suggestive of a far later date and a far different inspiration, I have only space or need to remark that it contains two of the most exquisitely Shakespearean verses ever vouchsafed to us by Shakespeare, and two of the most execrably euphuistic or dysphuistic lines ever inflicted on us by man.—SWINBURNE, ALGERNON, CHARLES, 1880, *A Study of Shakespare, p.* 61.

The framework of "A Lover's Complaint," its picturesqueness, versification, diction, repression, tenderness, and beauty, give to it a thoroughly Spenserian character, and convey the impression that we have here an early exercise in the Spenserian style; as such the poem links itself ultimately to the exquisite "Complaints" of Spenser's great master, Geoffrey Chaucer, with their ruthful burden:—*"Pitê is dede and buried in gentil herte."* — GOLLANCZ, ISRAEL, 1896, *ed. Temple Shakespeare, Preface to Lucrece, p.* vii.

If, as is possible, it be by Shakespeare, it must have been written in very early days.—LEE, SIDNEY, 1898, *A Life of William Shakespeare, p.* 91.

SONNETS

1592-1602-1609

SHAKE-SPEARES | Sonnets. | Neuer before Imprinted. | AT LONDON | By *G Eld* for *T. T.* and are | to be solde by *William Aspley.* | 1609.—TITLE PAGE OF FIRST SEPARATE EDITION, 1609.

TO THE ONLIE BEGETTER . OF
THESE INSVING SONNETS
MR. W H ALL HAPPINESSE
AND THAT ETERNITIE
PROMISED
BY
OVR EVER-LIVING POET
WISHETH
THE WELL-WISHING
ADVENTVRER IN
SETTING
FORTH T. T.

—DEDICATION OF FIRST EDITION, 1609.

Fugitive pieces which the poetic and sprightly grace of some lines would not have rescued from oblivion but for the curiosity which attaches to the slightest traces of a celebrated man. — GUIZOT, FRANÇOIS PIERRE GUILLAUME, 1821–52, *Shakspeare and His Times, p.* 65.

If any should be curious to discover
Whether to you I am a friend or lover,
Let them read Shakspeare's sonnets, taking thence
A whetstone for their dull intelligence
That tears and will not cut, or let them guess
How Diotima, the wise prophetess,
Instructed the instructor, and why he
Rebuked the infant spirit of melody
On Agathon's sweet lips, which as he spoke
Was as the lovely star when morn has broke
The roof of darkness, in the golden dawn,
Half-hidden and yet beautiful.

—SHELLEY, PERCY BYSSHE, 1822? *Studies for Epipsychidion, and Cancelled Passages, Poetical Works, ed. Forman, vol.* II, *p.* 392.

Scorn not the Sonnet; Critic, you have frowned,
Mindless of its just honours; with this key
Shakespeare unlocked his heart.

—WORDSWORTH, WILLIAM, 1827, *Sonnet.*

They contain such a quantity of profound thought as must astonish every reflecting reader; they are adorned by splendid and delicate imagery; they are sublime, pathetic, tender, or sweetly playful; while they delight the ear by their fluency and their varied harmonies of rhythm.—DYCE, ALEXANDER, 1833, *Specimens of English Sonnets, p.* 213

As a whole, however, these sonnets are no more to our poet's fame, than a snowball on the top of Olympus.—CAMPBELL, THOMAS, 1838, *ed. Shakspeare's Plays, Moxon ed., Life.*

They rise, indeed, in estimation, as we attentively read and reflect upon them; for I do not think that at first they give us much pleasure. No one ever entered more fully than Shakspeare into the character of this species of poetry, which admits of no expletive imagery, no merely ornamental line. . . . It is impossible not to wish that Shakspeare had never written them. There is a weakness and folly in all excessive and misplaced affection, which is not redeemed by the touches of nobler sentiments that abound in this long series of sonnets. But there are also faults of a merely critical nature. The obscurity is often such as only conjecture can penetrate; the strain of tenderness and adoration would be too monotonous, were it less unpleasing; and so many frigid conceits are scattered around, that we might almost fancy the poet to have written without genuine emotion, did not such a host of other passages attest the contrary. —HALLAM, HENRY, 1837–39, *Introduction to the Literature of Europe, vol.* III, *pt.* iii, *ch.* v, *par.* 48, 50.

There is nothing more remarkable or fascinating in English poetry. . . . We read them again and again, and find each time some new proof of his almost superhuman insight into human nature; of his unrivalled mastery over all the tones of love. We cannot bring ourselves to wish that "Shakspeare had never written them," or that the world should have wanted perhaps the most powerful and certainly the most singular, utterances of passion which Poetry has yet supplied.—PALGRAVE, FRANCIS TURNER, 1865, *ed. Songs and Sonnets by William Shakespeare, p.* 243.

We may look upon the Sonnets as a piece of music, or as Shakspere's pathetic sonata, each melody introduced, dropped again, brought in again with variations, but one full strain of undying love and friendship through the whole. . . . In the Sonnets we have the gentle Will, the melancholy mild-eyed man, of the Droeshout portrait. Shakspere's tender, sensitive, refined nature is seen clearly here, but through a glass darkly in the plays. . . . Still I think it is plain that Shakspere had become involved in an intrigue with a married woman, who threw him over for his friend Will. She was dark, had beautiful eyes, and was a fine musician, but false. . . . Sad as it may be to us to be forced to conclude that shame has to be cast on the noble name we reverence, yet let us remember that it is but for a temporary stain on his career, and that through the knowledge of the human heart he gained by his own trials we get the intensest and most valuable records of his genius. It is only those who have been through the mill themselves, that know how hard God's stones and the devil's grind.—FURNIVALL, FREDERICK JAMES, 1877, *ed. The Leopold Shakspere.*

With Wordsworth, Sir Henry Taylor, and Mr. Swinburne, with François-Victor Hugo, with Kreyssig, Ulrici, Gervinus, and Hermann Isaac, with Boaden, Armitage Brown, and Hallam, with Furnivall, Spalding, Rossetti, and Palgrave, I believe that Shakspere's Sonnets express his own feelings in his own person. To whom they were addressed is unknown. We shall never discover the name of that woman who for a season could sound, as no one else, the instrument in Shakspere's heart from the lowest note to the top of the compass. To the eyes of no diver among the wrecks of time will that curious talisman gleam.—DOWDEN, EDWARD, 1881, *ed. The Sonnets of William Shakspere.*

For our own part, we find it as difficult to believe that some of the Sonnets are autobiographical as that others are not; and all that has been written to prove that 1–126 are all addressed to the same person fails to convince us. It is clear enough that certain sets (like 1–17, for instance) form a regular series, but that all the poems are arranged in the order in which Shakespeare meant to have them is not so clear. There is no evidence that the edition of 1609 was supervised or even authorized by him. The enigmatical dedication is not his, but the publisher's; and the arrangement of the poems is probably that of the person who procured them for publication, whoever he may have been. The order seems to us more like that of a *collector*—one who knew something of their history, and was interested in getting them together for publication than that of the *author*. Possibly this collector had his own little theory as to the interconnection of some of them, like certain of the modern editors, no one of whom seems on the whole to have been any more successful in classifying them. We fear that both their order and the means by which the publisher got possession of them must continue to be among the insoluble problems of literature.—ROLFE, WILLIAM J., 1883–90, *ed. Shakespeare's Sonnets, Introduction, p.* 11.

These magnificent poems—magnificent notwithstanding many minor flaws—must always hold their high place, not only as the personal record of the greatest of our poets, but for the sake of their own consummate beauty and intellectual force.—SHARP, WILLIAM, 1886, *ed. Sonnets of This Century, p.* xlvii.

We have all tried to wring the heart out of that mystery. We have all felt the accent of acute passion alternating with the accent of what looks like artificial compliment—the inequality of style, the inequality of emotion, the inequality of artistic handling — in those unparalleled outpourings of a mighty poet's soul. We do not doubt their genuineness. We trace the outlines of a story in them, which it is not difficult to descipher, although the import may be painful. So far we are agreed. But when it comes to deciding whether Shakespeare intended a merely dramatic series of psychological lyrics, or whether he committed his own experience from day to day to paper in the sonnets, or whether he wrote them for a friend —who Mr. W. H was, and who the dark lady was—then at once we differ. As it seems to me, this is the point at which sound criticism diverges from criticism over-weighted with erudition or with subjective prepossession. — SYMONDS, JOHN ADDINGTON, 1890, *Essays Speculative and Suggestive, vol.* I, *p.* 117.

In literary value Shakespeare's sonnets are notably unequal. Many reach levels of lyric melody and meditative energy that are hardly to be matched elsewhere in poetry. The best examples are charged with the mellowed sweetness of rhythm and metre, the depth of thought and feeling, the vividness of imagery and the stimulating fervour of expression which are the finest proofs of poetic power. On the other hand, many sink almost into inanity beneath the burden of quibbles and conceits. In both their excellences and their defects Shakespeare's sonnets betray near kinship to his early dramatic work, in which passages of the highest poetic temper at times alternate with unimpressive displays of verbal jugglery.—LEE, SIDNEY, 1898, *A Life of William Shakespeare, p.* 87.

What is important is that Shakespeare has here caught up the sum of love and uttered it as no poet has before or since, and that in so doing he carried poetry—that is to say, the passionate expression in verse of the sensual and intellectual facts of life — to a pitch which it had never previously reached in English, and which it has never outstepped since. The coast-line of humanity must be wholly altered, the sea must change its nature, the moon must draw it in different ways, before that tide-mark is passed.—SAINTSBURY, GEORGE, 1898, *A Short History of English Literature, p.* 319.

Here, and here alone, we see Shakespeare himself, as distinct from his poetical creations, loving, admiring, longing, yearning, adoring, disappointed, humiliated, tortured. Here alone does he enter the confessional. Here more than anywhere else can we, who at a distance of three centuries do homage to the poet's art, feel ourselves in intimate communion, not only with the poet, but with the man. —BRANDES, GEORGE, 1898, *William Shakespeare, A Critical Study, vol.* I, *p.* 356.

Every person of culture who reads the Sonnets nowadays is pleased to find in most of them fertility of thought, beauty of imagery, and mellifluous versification, but having read them he is at a loss to know precisely what they are all about. Are they, he asks himself, a continuous poem, or so many isolated poems? Are they autobiographical or dramatic; or are they poems at all in the proper sense, and not enigmas, concealing under a poetic garb some deep and occult philosophy? Each of these questions has been answered affirmatively and negatively with equal zeal and ingenuity. In the complete editions of Shakespeare's "Works" the editors have tried their hands at solving the several difficulties, but not with much success; and bulky volumes have been prepared to prove various theories as to their design and significance, which carry no conviction with them beyond the immediate circle of authorship. These differences of opinion are largely due to a certain obscurity in the Sonnets themselves. . . . They allude to situations that have now passed entirely out of memory; they indulge in conceits and plays upon words which rather perplex than help the understanding of them; and often they admit locutions, which, if not wholly obsolete, are yet very different from our accepted forms. Indeed, in reading them, it sometimes happens that we come upon passages which at first seem clear and intelligible, but which on closer scrutiny, like the face of a dumb man, get indefinite and vague. —GODWIN, PARKE, 1900, *A New Study of the Sonnets of Shakespeare, pp.* 4, 6.

THE PASSIONATE PILGRIM

THE | PASSIONATE | PILGRIME | *By W. Shakespeare.* | AT LONDON | Printed for W. Iaggard, and are | to be sold by W. Leake, at the Grey- | hound in Paules Church-yard. | 1599. —TITLE PAGE OF FIRST EDITION, 1599.

Here likewise, I must necessarily insert a manifest injury done me in that worke, by taking the two Epistles of *Paris* to *Helen*, and *Helen* to *Paris*, and printing them in a lesse volume, under the name of another, which may put the world in opinion I might steale them from him; and hee to doe himselfe right, hath since published them in his owne name: but as I must acknowledge my lines not worthy his patronage, under whom he hath publisht them, so the Author I know much offended with M. *Jaggard* that (altogether unknowne to him) presumed to make so bold with his name. —HEYWOOD, THOMAS, 1612, *An Apology for Actors, Epistle.*

In "the Passionate Pilgrim," some critics find difficulty in tracing the hand of the poet; and we accidentally discover by the complaint of Heywood, a congenial dramatist, that there were two of his poems in one edition of this collection; and we know that there were also other poems by Marlowe and Barnefield and others. Heywood tells us that Shakespeare was greatly offended at this licentious use of his name; but he must have been inperturbably careless on such matters, otherwise he would not have suffered three editions of this spurious miscellany. —DISRAELI, ISAAC, 1841, *Shakespeare, Amenities of Literature.*

The worst active or positive blemish—and a most fearful and shameful blemish it is—to be found in this generally graceful and careful collection* will unluckily be found and cannot be overlooked on the fourth page; sixth on the list of selected poems is a copy of verse attributed to Shakespeare—of all men on earth!—by the infamous pirate, liar, and thief who published a worthless little volume of stolen and mutilated poetry patched up and padded out with dirty and dreary doggrel, under the senseless and preposterous title of "The Passionate Pilgrim." It is here more plausibly ascribed tho' on what authority I know not, to some scribbler—unknown to Shakespeare's contemporaries—who would seem to have signed himself Shakspere, and to have imagined that the gabble of geese or the chatter of apes was English and was verse. —SWINBURNE, ALGERNON CHARLES, 1891, *Social Verse, The Forum, vol.* 12, *p.* 173.

It contains twenty-one numbers, besides that lofty dirge, so unapproachably solemn, "The Phoenix and the Turtle." Of these, five are undoubtedly by Shakespeare. A sixth ("Crabbed age and youth"), if not by Shakespeare, is one of the loveliest lyrics in the language, and I for my part could give it to no other man. Note also that but for Jaggard's enterprise this jewel had been irrevocably lost to us, since it is known only through "The Passionate Pilgrim." Marlowe's "Live with me and be my love" and Barnefield's "As it fell upon a Day," make numbers seven and eight. And I imagine that even Mr. Swinburne cannot afford to scorn "Sweet rose, fair flower, untimely pluck'd soon vaded"—which again only occurs in "The Passionate Pilgrim." These nine numbers, with "The Phœnix and the Turtle," make up more than half the book. Among the rest we have the pretty and respectable lyrics; "If music and sweet poetry agree;" "Good night, good rest;" "Lord, how mine eyes throw gazes to the east;" "When as thine eye hath chose the dame," and the gay little song, "It was a Lording's daughter." There remain the "Venus and Adonis" sonnets and "My flocks feed not." Mr.

*"Lyra Elegantiarum," edited by Frederick Locker-Lampson.

Swinburne may call these "dirty and dreary doggrel," an he list, with no more risk than of being held a somewhat over-anxious moralist. But to call the whole book worthless is mere abuse of words. It is true, nevertheless, that one of the only two copies existing of the first edition was bought for three halfpence.—QUILLER-COUCH, A. T., 1895, *Adventures in Criticism, p.* 39.

THE PHŒNIX AND THE TURTLE
1601

To unassisted readers, it would appear to be a lament on the death of a poet, and of his poetic mistress. But the poem is so quaint, and charming in diction, tone, and allusions, and in its perfect metre and harmony, that I would gladly have the fullest illustration yet attainable. I consider this piece a good example of the rule, that there is a poetry for bards proper, as well as a poetry for the world of readers. This poem, if published for the first time, and without a known author's name, would find no general reception. Only the poets would save it.—EMERSON, RALPH WALDO, 1875, *Parnassus, Preface, p.* vi.

Priceless and unique.—GROSART, ALEXANDER B., 1878, *ed. Chester's Loves Martyr, Introduction.*

The contribution of the great dramatist is a remarkable poem in which he makes a notice of the obsequies of the phœnix and turtle-dove subservient to the delineation of spiritual union. It is generally thought that, in his own work, Chester meditated a personal allegory, but, if that be the case, there is nothing to indicate that Shakespeare participated in the design, nor even that he had endured the punishment of reading "Love's Martyr."—HALLIWELL-PHILLIPPS, J. O., 1881–86, *Outlines of the Life of Shakespeare, vol.* I, *p.* 173.

For ourself we agree with Malone, Emerson, Halliwell-Phillipps, and others, that the poem is clearly Shakespeare's. Aside from the internal evidence, the circumstances of its publication seem to us enough to settle the question. . . . The other poems he prints are all, we believe, acknowledged to be from the authors to whom he ascribes them. Why should we hesitate to accept "The Phœnix and the Turtle" as Shakespeare's, when Chester marks it as his, and when it is in no respect unworthy of him?—ROLFE, WILLIAM J., 1883, *Shakespeariana, Literary World, vol.* 14, *p.* 96.

The genuineness of the contribution with Shakespeare's name subscribed is now generally admitted, though no successful attempt has yet been made to explain the allegory, nor is any light thrown upon it by the other poems in the collection; among the contributors, in addition to Shakespeare, were Jonson, Chapman, and Marston. In all probability the occasion and subject of the whole collection, which has so long baffled patient research, will some day be discovered, and Shakespeare's meaning will be clear. It would seem from the title-page that the private family history of Sir John Salisbury ought to yield the necessary clue to the events. —GOLLANCZ, ISRAEL, 1896, *ed. Temple Shakespeare, Preface to Lucrece, p.* viii.

TITUS ANDRONICUS
(?) 1588–1600

The most lamenta- | ble Romaine Tragedie of *Titus* | *Andronicus.* | As it hath sundry times beene playde by the | Right Honourable the | Earle of Pembrooke, the | Earl of Darbie, the Earle of Sussex, and the | Lorde Chamberlaine theyr | Seruants. | AT LONDON, | Printed by I. R. for Edward White | and are to bee solde at his shoppe, at the little | North doore of Paules, at the signe of | the Gun. 1600.—TITLE PAGE OF FIRST EDITION, 1600

It is also agreed, that every man heere, exercise his owne Iudgement, and not censure by *Contagion*, or upon *trust*, from anothers voice, or face. . . . Hee that will sweare *Ieronimo* or *Andronicus* are the best playes yet, shall passe unexcepted at, heere, as a man whose Iudgement shewes it is constant, and hath stood still, these five and twentie, or thirtie yeeres. —JONSON, BEN, 1614, *Bartholomew Fayre, The Induction.*

I have been told by some anciently conversant with the stage, that it was not originally his, but brought by a private author to be acted, and he only gave some master-touches to one or two of the principal parts or characters.—RAVENSCROFT, EDWARD, 1678, *Titus Andronicus, Preface.*

All the editors and critics agree with Mr. Theobald in supposing this play spurious. I see no reason for differing from them; for the colour of the style is wholly different from that of the other plays, and there is an attempt at regular versification and artificial closes, not always inelegant, yet seldom pleasing. The barbarity of the spectacles, and the general massacre, which are here exhibited, can scarcely be conceived tolerable to any audience; yet we are told by Jonson, that they were not only born, but praised. That Shakspeare wrote any part, though Theobald declares it incontestible, I see no reason for believing.—JOHNSON, SAMUEL, 1768, *General Observations on Shakspeare's Plays.*

If those who reject this play as Shakespear's think it inferior to the rest of his productions, the doubt is easily cleared by recollecting that it was his first effort. There are certainly some things in it equal to his happiest sallies; and, as we know those are superior to the writings of any man who ever lived, the question to be asked is, and this will perpetually occur, if Shakespear did not write "Titus Andronicus," who did?—DIBDIN, CHARLES, 1795, *A Complete History of the Stage, vol.* III, *p.* 31.

If it be true that genius, even in its lowest abasement, gives forth some luminous rays to betray its presence; if Shakspeare, in particular, bore that distinctive mark which, in one of his sonnets, makes him say, in reference to his writings,

"That every word doth almost tell my name,"*

assuredly he had not to reproach himself with the production of that execrable accumulation of horrors which, under the name of "Titus Andronicus," has been fosted upon the English people as a dramatic work, and in which, Heaven be thanked! there is not a single spark of truth, or scintillation of genius, which can give evidence against him. — GUIZOT, FRANÇOIS PIERRE GUILLAUMAE, 1821-52, *Shakspeare and His Times, p.* 66.

"Titus Andronicus" is now by common consent denied to be, in any sense, a production of Shakspeare: very few passages, I should think not one, resemble his manner. — HALLAM, HENRY, 1837-39, *Introduction to the Literature of Europe, vol.* II, *pt.* ii, *ch.* vi, *par.* 35.

That, nevertheless, this drama is rich in isolated beauties, profound thougths, and striking peculiarities, Shakspearean imagery, which like lightning flashes over and illumines the whole piece, and that single scenes are even deeply affecting and highly poetical, is generally admitted, and requires no proof. It will be sufficient to call attention to the scenes of the shooting the arrows, and of the interview between Titus and Tamora, who announces herself to the old man, whom she believes to be mad, as the Goddess of Vengeance. —ULRICI, HERMANN, 1839, *Shakspeare's Dramatic Art, p.* 237.

Critics have vied with one another in loading this play with epithets of contempt; and indeed, as compared with the higher products of dramatic poetry, it has little to recommend it. But in itself, and for its times, it was very far from giving the indication of an unpoetical or undramatic mind. One proof of this is, that it was long a popular favorite on the stage. It is full of defects, but these are precisely such as a youthful aspirant, in an age of authorship, would be most likely to exhibit—such as the subjection to the taste of the day, good or bad, and the absence of that dramatic truth and reality which some experience of human passion, and observation of life and manners, can alone give the power to produce. — VERPLANCK, GULIAN CROMMELIN, 1844-47, *ed. The Illustrated Shakespeare, vol.* III.

After the first scene of "Andronicus," in which the author sets out with the stately pace of his time, we are very soon carried away, by the power of the language, the variety of the pause, and the especial freedom with which trochees are used at the ends of lines, to forget that the versification is not *altogether* upon the best Shaksperean model. There is the same instrument, but the performer has not yet thoroughly learnt its scope and its power.—KNIGHT, CHARLES, 1849, *Studies of Shakspere, bk.* ii, *ch.* i, *p.* 49.

In 1687 there was a tradition reported by Ravenscroft that this play was only touched by Shakespeare. Theobald, Johnson, Farmer, Steevens, Drake, Singer, Dyce, Hallam, H. Coleridge, W. S. Walker, reject it entirely. Malone, Ingleby, Staunton, think it was touched up by him. Capell, Collier, Knight, Gervinus, Ulrici, and many Germans, think it to be Shakespeare's; R. G. White, that it is a joint work of Greene, Marlowe, and

*Sonnet 76.

Shakespeare. . . . Is not Shakespeare's; it is built on the Marlowe blank-verse system, which Shakespeare in his early work opposed; and did not belong to Shakespeare's company till 1600.—FLEAY, FREDERICK GARD, 1859, *Shakespeare Manual, p.* 44.

Shakspere is the tragedy of Terror; this is the tragedy of Horror. . . . It reeks blood, it smells of blood; we almost feel that we have handled blood—it is so gross. The mental stain is not whitened by Shakspere's sweet springs of pity; the horror is not hallowed by that appalling sublimity with which he invested his chosen ministers of death. It is tragedy only in the coarsest material relationships.—MASSEY, GERALD, 1866, *Shakspere's Sonnets never before Interpreted, p.* 581, *Appendix D.*

That tragedy belongs to the pre-Shaksperian school of bloody dramas. If any portions of it be from Shakspere's hand, it has at least this interest—it shows that there was a period of Shakspere's authorship when the poet had not yet discovered himself, a period when he yielded to the popular influences of the day and hour; this much interest, and no more.—DOWDEN, EDWARD, 1875–80, *Shakspere, A Critical Study of His Mind and Art, p.* 48.

To me, as to Hallam and many others, the play declares as plainly as play can speak, "I am not Shakspere's; my repulsive subject, my blood and horrors, are not, and never were, his." I accept the tradition that Ravenscroft reports when he revived and altered the play in 1687, that it was brought to Shakspere to be touched up and prepared for the stage.—FURNIVALL, FREDERICK JAMES, 1877, *ed. The Leopold Shakspere.*

Nearly all the best critics, from Theobald downwards, are agreed that very little of this play was written by Shakespeare. And such is decidedly my own judgment now, though some thirty years ago, in "my salad days," I wrote and printed otherwise. . . . The question, by whom the main body of the play was written, is not so easily answered, and perhaps is hardly worth a detailed investigation. . . . I agree substantially with Mr. White and Mr. Fleay as to Marlowe's share in the workmanship.—HUDSON, HENRY N., 1880–81, *Harvard ed. Shakespeare, vol.* XIII, *pp.* 4, 5.

It is unnecessary to give any analysis of the play, which is simply a tissue of horrors. In no reader, however little educated, could it possibly excite the slightest emotion; all pity and all terror absolutely cease when the horrible is carried to such lengths, and its outrageous atrocity is even capable of provoking a fit of laughter.—STAPFER, PAUL, 1880, *Shakespeare and Classical Antiquity, tr. Carey, p.* 273.

It may at first seem strange that his name should have come to be associated with a work in which we find so few traces of his hand; but he may have improved the old play in other ways than by rewriting any considerable portion of it—by omissions, re-arrangement of scenes, and the like—and its great popularity in the revised form may have led to its being commonly known as "Shakespeare's *Titus Andronicus*" (in distinction from the earlier version, whosesoever it may have been), until at length it got to be generally regarded as one of his original productions. The verdict of the editors and critics is so nearly unanimous against the authenticity of the play that the burden of proof clearly rests with the other side.—ROLFE, WILLIAM J., 1883, *ed. Shakespeare's Tragedy of Titus Andronicus, Introduction, p.* 15.

As I re-read this play after coming straight from the study of Marlowe, I find again and again passages that, as it seems to me, no hand but his could have written. It is not easy in a question of this kind to set down in detail reasons for our belief. Marlowe's influence permeated so thoroughly the dramatic literature of his day, that it is hard sometimes to distinguish between master and pupil. When the master is writing at his best there is no difficulty, but when his work is hasty and ill-digested, or has been left incomplete and has received additions from other hands, then our perplexity is great. In our disgust at the brutal horrors that crowd the pages of "Titus Andronicus," we must beware of blinding ourselves to the imaginative power that marks much of the writing.—BULLEN, A. H., 1884, *ed. Works of Christopher Marlowe, Introduction, vol.* I, *p.* lxxvi.

It was no invention of Shakespeare's; it is not reconstructed upon Shakespeare's lines; but, as we see, characters were renamed, some of the matter was recast, crudities were struck out, here and there the writing was touched over, and some fresh lines were inserted. We find lines in which we feel young Shakespeare's touch, and while the whole construction of the play that Shakespeare worked upon is thoroughly unlike the inventions of Shakespeare himself, its crude horrors are, no doubt, felt the more intensely for his removal of absurdities in the first way of telling them, and for touches of his that gave more pomp of words and more force to the style, with now and then some small hint of a grace beyond the reach of the inventor and first writer of the play.—MORLEY, HENRY, 1893, *English Writers, vol.* X, *p.* 45.

Although, on the whole, one may certainly say that this rough-hewn drama, with its piling-up of external effects, has very little in common with the tone or spirit of Shakespeare's mature tragedies, yet we find scattered through it lines in which the most diverse critics have professed to recognise Shakespeare's revising touch, and to catch the ring of his voice. . . . It is quite unnecessary for any opponent of blind or exaggerated Shakespeare-worship to demonstrate to us the impossibility of bringing "Titus Andronicus" into harmony with any other than a barbarous conception of tragic poetry. But although the play is simply omitted without apology from the Danish translation of Shakespeare's works, it must by no means be overlooked by the student, whose chief interest lies in observing the genesis and development of the poet's genius. The lower its point of departure, the more marvellous its soaring flight. —BRANDES, GEORGE, 1898, *William Shakespeare, A Critical Study, vol,* I, *pp.* 40, 41.

Our loss is great indeed if an impertinent solicitude for Shakespeare's morals, an officious care for his reputation as a creator of character, lead us to pass over "Titus Andronicus."—WYNDHAM, GEORGE, 1898, *The Poems of Shakespeare, Introduction, p.* xvi.

LOVE'S LABOR'S LOST

1588–1598

A | Pleasant | Conceited Comedie | called, | Loues labors lost. | As it was presented before her Highnes | this last Christmas. | Newly corrected and augmented | *By W. Shakespere.* | Imprinted at London by W. W. | for *Cutbert Burby.* | 1598.—TITLE PAGE OF FIRST EDITION, 1598.

Love's Labour Lost I once did see, a Play
Y-cleped so, so called to my paine.
Which I to heare to my small Ioy did stay,
Giving attendance on my froward Dame:
My misgiving minde presaging to me ill,
Yet was I drawne to see it 'gainst my will,
. . . .
Each Actor plaid in cunning wise his part,
But chiefly Those entrapt in Cupids snare;
Yet All was fained, 't was not from the hart,
They seemde to grieve, but yet they felt no care:
'Twas I that Griefe (indeed) did beare in brest,
The others did but make a show in Iest.
—T(OFTE), R(OBERT), 1598, *Alba.*

I have sent and bene all thys morning huntyng for players Juglers & Such kinde of Creaturs, but fynde them harde to finde, wherfore Leavinge notes for them to seeke me, burbage ys come, & Sayes ther ys no new playe that the quene hath not seene, but they have Revyved an olde one, Cawled *Loves Labore lost,* which for wytt & mirthe he sayes will please her excedingly. And Thys ys apointed to be playd to Morowe night at my Lord of Sowthamptons, unless yow send a wrytt to Remove the Corpus Cum Causa to your howse in strande. Burbage ys my messenger Ready attendyng your pleasure. —COPE, SIR WALTER, 1604, *Letter "To the right honorable the Lorde Vycount Cranborne at the Courte." Historical MSS.* 1872, *p.* 148.

In this play, which all the editors have concurred to censure, and some have rejected as unworthy of our poet, it must be confessed that there are many passages mean, childish, and vulgar; and some which ought not to have been exhibited, as we are told they were, to a maiden queen. But there are scattered through the whole many sparks of genius; nor is there any play that has more evident marks of the hand of Shakspeare. —JOHNSON, SAMUEL, 1768, *General Observations on Shakspeare's Plays.*

"Love's Labour Lost" is numbered among the pieces of his youth. It is a humorsome display of frolic; a whole cornucopia of the most vivacious jokes is emptied into it. Youth is certainly perceivable in the lavish superfluity of labour in the execution: the unbroken succession of plays on words, and sallies of every description, hardly leave the spectator time to breathe; the sparkles of wit fly about in such profusion that they resemble a blaze of fireworks; while the dialogue, for the most part, is in the same hurried style in which the passing masks at a carnival attempt to banter each other.—SCHLEGEL, AUGUSTUS WILLIAM, 1809, *Dramatic Art and Literature, Lecture XII., tr. Black, rev. Morrison.*

If we were to part with any of the author's comedies, it should be this. Yet we should be loth to part with Don Adriano de Armado, that mighty potentate of nonsense; or his page, that handful of wit; with Nathaniel the curate, or Holofernes the schoolmaster, and their dispute after dinner, on "the golden cadences of poesy;" with Costard the clown, or Dull the constable. Biron is too accomplished a character to be lost to the world, and yet he could not appear without his fellow-courtiers and the king: and if we were to leave out the ladies, the gentlemen would have no mistresses. So that we believe we must let the whole play stand as it is, and we shall hardly venture to "set a mark of reprobation on it." Still we have some objections to the style, which we think savours more of the pedantic spirit of Shakespear's time than of his own genius; more of controversial divinity, and the logic of Peter Lombard, than of the inspiration of the Muse. It transports us quite as much to the manners of the court, and the quirks of courts of law, as to the scenes of nature, or the fairy-land of his own imagination.—HAZLITT, WILLIAM, 1817-69, *Characters of Shakespear's Plays, p.* 206.

If this juvenile drama had been the only one extant of our Shakspere, and we possessed the tradition only of his riper works, or accounts of them in writers who had not even mentioned this play—how many of Shakspere's characteristic features might we not still have discovered in "Love's Labour's Lost," though as in a portrait taken of him in his boyhood. I can never sufficiently admire the wonderful activity of thought throughout the whole of the first scene of the play, rendered natural, as it is, by the choice of the characters, and the whimsical determination on which the drama is founded.—COLERIDGE, SAMUEL TAYLOR, 1818, *Lectures and Notes on Shakspere, ed. Ashe, p.* 283.

Yet with all its diversity of characters, poetic beauties, wit, and sentences, "Love's Labour's Lost" is but little regarded. It is devoid of dramatic interest, and not even the fairest and freshest beauties of Shakspeare's genius can compensate for poverty of plot and deficiency of action. —SKOTTOWE, AUGUSTINE, 1824, *Life of Shakspeare, vol.* I, *p.* 254.

There is indeed little interest in the fable, if we can say that there is any fable at all; but there are beautiful coruscations of fancy, more original conception of character than in the "Comedy of Errors," more lively humor than in the "Gentlemen of Verona," more symptoms of Shakspeare's future powers as a comic writer than in either. Much that is here but imperfectly developed came forth again in his later plays, especially in "As you Like It," and "Much Ado about Nothing."—HALLAM, HENRY, 1837–39, *Introduction to the Literature of Europe, vol.* II, *pt.* ii, *ch.* vi, *par.* 38.

Both the characters and the dialogue are such as youthful talent might well invent, without much knowledge of real life, and would indeed be likely to invent, before the experience and observation of varied society. The comedy presents a picture, not of the true every-day life of the great or the beautiful, but exhibits groups of such brilliant personages as they might be supposed to appear in the artificial conversation, the elaborate and continual effort to surprise or dazzle by wit or elegance, which was the prevailing taste of the age, in its literature, its poetry, and even its pulpit; and in which the nobles and beauties of the day were accustomed to array themselves for exhibition, as in their state attire, for occasions of display. All this, when the leading idea was once caught, was quite within the reach of the young poet to imitate or surpass, with little or no personal knowledge of aristocratic—or what would now be termed fashionable—society.—VERPLANCK, GULIAN CROMMELIN, 1844-47, *ed. The Illustrated Shakespeare, vol.* II.

"Love's Labour's Lost" is not a favourite play with the general reader, but the cause of its modern unpopularity is to be sought for in the circumstance of its satire having been principally directed to fashions of language that have long passed away, and consequently little understood, rather than in any great deficiency of invention. When it has been deeply studied, there are few comedies that will afford more gratification. It abounds with touches of the highest humour; and the playful tricks and discoveries are conducted with so much dexterity, that, when we arrive at the conclusion, the chief wonder is how the interest could have been preserved in the development of so extremely meagre a plot. Rightly considered, this drama, being a satire on the humour of conversation, could not have been woven from a story involving much situation other than the merely amusing, or from any plot which invited the admission of the language of passion; for the free use of the latter would have been evidently inconsistent with the unity of the author's satirical design. — HALLIWELL-PHILLIPPS, J. O., 1855–79, *Memoranda on Love's Labour's Lost, p.* 18.

It is this foppery of delicate language, this fashionable plaything of his time, with which Shakespeare is occupied in "Love's Labours Lost." He shows us the manner in all its stages; passing from the grotesque and vulgar pedantry of Holofernes, through the extravagant but polished caricature of Armado, to become the peculiar characteristic of a real though still quaint poetry in Biron himself, who is still chargeable even at his best with just a little affectation. As Shakespeare laughs broadly at it in Holofernes or Armado, so he is the analyst of its curious charm in Biron; and this analysis involves a delicate raillery by Shakespeare himself at his own chosen manner. — PATER, WALTER, 1878, *Appreciations, p.* 171.

During certain scenes we seem almost to stand again by the cradle of new born comedy, and hear the first lisping and laughing accents run over from her baby lips in bubbling rhyme; but when the note changes we recognise the speech of gods. For the first time in our literature the higher key of poetic or romantic comedy is finely touched to a fine issue. The divine instrument fashioned by Marlowe for tragic purposes alone has found at once its new sweet use in the hands of Shakespeare. The way is prepared for "As You Like It" and the "Tempest;" the language is discovered which will befit the lips of Rosalind and Miranda. — SWINBURNE, ALGERNON CHARLES, 1880, *A Study of Shakespeare, p.* 47.

COMEDY OF ERRORS
1589–1623

After such sport, a "Comedy of Erorrs" (like to Plautus his Menechmus) was *played by the players;* so that night began and continued to the end, in nothing but confusion and errors; whereupon it was ever afterwards called the Night of Errors.—GESTA GRAYORUM, 1594.

As to the comic action which constitutes the chief bulk of this piece, if it be true that to excite laughter, awaken attention, and fix curiosity, be essential to its dramatic excellence, the "Comedy of Errors" cannot be pronounced an unsuccessful effort; both reader and spectator are hurried on to the close, through a series of thick-coming incidents, and under the pleasurable influence of novelty, expectation, and surprise; and the dialogue . . . is uniformly vivacious, pointed, and even effervescing. Shakspeare is visible, in fact, throughout the entire play, as well in the broad exuberance of its mirth, as in the cast of its more chastised parts, a combination of which may be found in the punishment and character of Pinch the pedagogue and conjurer, who is sketched in the strongest and most marked style of our author. If we consider, therefore, the construction of the fable, the narrowness of its basis, and that its powers of entertainment are almost exclusively confined to a continued deception of the external senses, we must confess that Shakspeare has not only improved on the Plautian model, but, making allowance for a somewhat too coarse vein of humour, has given to his production all the interest and variety that the nature and the limits of his subject would permit. — DRAKE, NATHAN, 1817, *Shakspeare and His Times, vol.* II, *p.* 288.

The myriad-minded man, our, and all men's, Shakspere, has in this piece presented us with a legitimate farce in exactest consonance with the philosophical principles and character of farce, as distinguished from comedy and from entertainments.—COLERIDGE, SAMUEL TAYLOR, 1818, *Lectures and Notes on Shakspere, ed. Ashe, p.* 292.

Until I saw it on the stage, (not mangled into an opera,) I had not imagined the extent of the mistakes, the drollery of them, their unabated continuance, till, at the end of the fourth act, they reached their climax with the assistance of Dr. Pinch, when the audience in their laughter rolled about like waves. . . . To the strange contrast of grave astonishment among the actors, with their laughable situations in the eyes of the spectators, who are let into the secret, is to be ascribed the irresistible effect.—BROWN, CHARLES ARMITAGE, 1838, *Shakespeare's Autobiographical Poems, pp.* 272, 273.

The "Comedy of Errors" is evidently one of Shakespeare's youthful works, and was probably written about 1591. This is supported not only by the frequent occurrence of rhymes and the long-drawn Alexandrines (doggerel verse) employed by the earlier English dramatists, but also by the greater carefulness and regularity of the language and versification. . . Another proof of its early origin is the fresh, youthful atmosphere of joke and jest which pervades the whole, a naïve pleasure in what is jocose and laughable for its own sake, and which, not being yet burdened by the weight of years, moves more lightly and more on the surface of things, and without that power and depth of humour which distinguishes the poet's maturer works.—ULRICI, HERMANN, 1839, *Shakespeare's Dramatic Art, tr. Schmitz.*

In this play Shakspere gayly confronts improbabilities, and requires the spectator to accept them. He adds to the twins Antipholus the twins Dromio. If we are in for improbability, let us at least be repaid for it by fun, and have that in abundance. Let the incredible become a twofold incredibility, and it is none the worse. We may conclude that, while Shakspere was ready to try his hand upon a farcical subject, a single experiment satisfied him that this was not his province, for to such subjects he never returned.—DOWDEN, EDWARD, 1875–80, *Shakspere, A Critical Study of His Mind and Art, p.* 50.

The "Comedy of Errors" not only surpasses the "Menæchmi" in the greater complexity of its plot, its greater variety of incident, but also in its more generous treatment of human nature. Not that elaborately wrought-out characters are to be sought in it; for this, it must be remembered, is Shakespeare's most absolutely comic, and almost farcical play, and in this particular class of work he never handled the incisive tool of an engraver, like Molière,—his pencil runs galloping over the canvas with a light fantastic touch; and this play is, moreover, one of his most youthful performances.—STAPFER, PAUL, 1880, *Shakespeare and Classical Antiquity, tr. Carey, p.* 150.

The reading of the play is like threading the mazes of a dream; where people and things are the same and not the same in the same moment. The mistakes, crosses, and vexations in the plot so rapidly succeed that to keep the course of events distinct in the mind is almost as desperate an achievement as following all the ramifications of a genealogical tree; and — may it be said? — about as useful. The piece, however, is amusing; and although our intellectual remuneration for the time expended is not remarkable, yet we should bear in mind that it is essentially a drama of *action* and circumstance; and if it could be effectually represented, the result would be infinitely ludicrous.—CLARKE, CHARLES COWDEN, 1881, *Shakespeare-Characters, Second Series, quoted by Rolfe.*

Act III, Scene i. seems to have been derived from the "Amphitruo" of Plautus; in the Latin comedy Mercury keeps the real Amphitruo out of his own house, while Jupiter, the sham Amphitruo, is within with Alcmena, the real Amphitruo's wife. The introduction of the twin Dromios is Shakespeare's own device; and all the pathos of the play is his: there is nothing in the Latin original suggestive of Ægeon's touching story at the opening of the play,—in Plautus, the father of the twins is already dead, and there is no reunion of husband, wife, and children. In spite, however, of this romanticising of Plautus, Shakespeare has maintained throughout the play the hallowed unities of time and place, "the necessary companions," according to Academic criticism, "of all corporal actions." From this point of view "The Comedy of Errors" may be regarded as the final triumph of the New Romantic Drama over its opponents; it carried the warfare into the enemy's camp, and scored the signal victory of harmonising Old and New, — the conventional canons of Latin Comedy and the pathos of Romanticism. —GOLLANCZ, ISRAEL, 1894, *ed. Temple Shakespeare, Preface to Comedy of Errors, p.* viii.

A MIDSUMMER NIGHT'S DREAM
1590–1600

A | Midsommer nights | dreame. | As it hath beene sundry times pub | *lickely acted, by the Right honoura* | ble, the Lord Chamberlaine his | *seruants.* | *Written by William Shakespeare.* | Imprinted at London, for *Thomas Fisher,* and are to | be soulde at his shoppe, at the Signe of the White Hart, | in *Fleetestreete.* 1600.—TITLE PAGE OF FIRST EDITION, 1600,

I say, as it is applausfully written, and commended to posterity, in the Midsummer-Night's Dream:—if we offend, it is with our good will: we came with no intent but to offend, and show our simple skill. —TAYLOR, JOHN, 1622, *Sir Gregory Nonsense, vol.* I.

There let Hymen oft appear
In saffron robe, with taper clear,
And pomp, and feast, and revelry,
With mask and antique pageantry;
Such sights as youthful Poets dream
On summer eves by haunted stream.

. . . .

Or sweetest Shakespeare, Fancy's child,
Warble his native wood-notes wild.
—MILTON, JOHN, 1633, *L'Allegro.*

September 29.—To the King's Theatre, where we saw "Midsummer's Night's Dream," which I had never seen before, nor shall ever again, for it is the most insipid ridiculous play that ever I saw in my life.—PEPYS, SAMUEL, 1662, *Diary and Correspondence.*

The Comical part of this Play, is printed separately in 4°. and used to be acted at *Bartholomew* Fair, and other Markets in the Country by Strolers, under the Title of "Bottom the Weaver."—LANGBAINE, GERARD, 1691, *An Account of the English Dramatick Poets, p.* 460.

Wild and fantastical as this play is, all the parts in their various modes are well written, and give the kind of pleasure which the author designed. Fairies in his time were much in fashion; common tradition had made them familiar, and Spenser's poem had made them great.—JOHNSON, SAMUEL, 1768, *General Observations on Shakspeare's Plays.*

It is astonishing that Shakespear should be considered, not only by foreigners, but by many of our own critics, as a gloomy and heavy writer, who painted nothing but "gorgons and hydras, and chimeras dire." His subtlety exceeds that of all other dramatic writers, insomuch that a celebrated person of the present day said that he regarded him rather as a metaphysician than a poet. His delicacy and sportive gaiety are infinite. In the "Midsummer Night's Dream" alone, we should imagine, there is more sweetness and beauty of description than in the whole range of French poetry put together. What we mean is this, that we will produce out of that single play ten passages, to which we do not think any ten passages in the works of the French poets can be opposed, displaying equal fancy and imagery.—HAZLITT, WILLIAM, 1817–69, *Characters of Shakespear's Plays, p.* 92.

It is, indeed, a fabric of the most buoyant and aerial texture, floating as it were between earth and heaven, and tinted with all the magic colouring of the rainbow.

"The earth hath bubbles as the water has,
And this is of them."

. . . . The canvas, it is true, which he has stretched, has been since expanded, and new groupes have been introduced; but the outline and the mode of colouring which he employed have been invariably followed. It is, in short, to his picture of the fairy world, that we are indebted for the "Nymphidia" of Drayton; the "Robin Goodfellow" of Jonson; the miniatures of Fletcher and Browne; the full-length portraits of Herrick; the sly allusions of Corbet, and the spirited and picturesque sketches of Milton. —DRAKE, NATHAN, 1817, *Shakspeare and His Times, vol.* II, *p.* 299, 353.

It evidently belongs to the earlier period of Shakspeare's genius; poetical, as we account it, more than dramatic; yet rather so because the indescribable profusion of imaginative poetry in this play overpowers our senses till we can hardly observe any thing else, than from any deficiency of dramatic excellence. For in reality the structure of the fable, consisting as it does of three if not four actions, very distinct in their subjects and personages, yet wrought into each other without effort or confusion, displays the skill, or rather instinctive felicity, of Shakspeare, as much as in any play he has written. . . . The "Midsummer Night's

Dream'' is, I believe, altogether original in one of the most beautiful conceptions that ever visited the mind of a poet,—the fairy machinery.—HALLAM, HENRY, 1837-39, *Introduction to the Literature of Europe, vol.* II, *pt.* ii, *ch.* vi, *par.* 39, 40.

Of all his works, the ''Midsummer Night's Dream'' leaves the strongest impression on my mind, that this miserable world must have, for once at least, contained a happy man. This play is so purely delicious, so little intermixed with the painful passions from which poetry distils her sterner sweets, so fragrant with hilarity, so bland and yet so bold, that I cannot imagine Shakspeare's mind to have been in any other frame than that of healthful ecstasy when the sparks of inspiration thrilled through his brain in composing it.—CAMPBELL, THOMAS, 1838, *ed. Shakspeare's Plays, Moxon ed., Life.*

This is, in several respects, the most remarkable composition of its author, and has probably contributed more to his general fame, as it has given a more peculiar evidence of the variety and brilliancy of his genius, than any other of his dramas. Not that it is in itself the noblest of his works, or even one of the highest order among them; but it is not only exquisite in its kind—it is also original and peculiar in its whole character, and of a class by itself.—VERPLANCK, GULIAN CROMMELIN, 1844-47, *ed. The Illustrated Shakespeare, vol.* II.

Bottom the weaver is the representative of the whole human race. His confidence in his own power is equally profound, whether he exclaims, ''Let me play the lion too; ''or whether he sings alone, ''that they shall hear I am not afraid; '' or whether, conscious that he is surrounded with spirits, he cries out, with his voice of authority, ''Where's Peasblossom?'' In every situation Bottom is the same,—the same personification of that self-love which the simple cannot conceal, and the wise can with difficulty suppress.—KNIGHT, CHARLES, 1849, *Studies of Shakspere, bk.* v, ch. ii, *p.* 209.

I know not any play of Shakespeare's in which the language is so uniformly unexceptionable as this. It is all poetry, and sweeter poetry was never written.—COLERIDGE, HARTLEY, 1849-51, *Essays and Marginalia, vol.* II, *p.* 138.

What a rich set of fellows those ''mechanicals'' are! and how individual are their several characteristics! Bully Bottom, the epitome of all the conceited donkeys that ever strutted and straddled on this stage of the world. . . . He is a choice arabesque impersonation of that colouring of conceit which, by the half-malice of the world, has been said to tinge the disposition of actors, as invariably as the rouge does their cheeks. Peter Quince, although the delegated manager of the company, fades into a shadow, a cipher, a nonentity before him.—CLARKE, CHARLES COWDEN, 1863, *Shakespeare-Characters, p.* 97.

''The Midsummer-Night's Dream'' is especially remarkable for its beauty as a composition. The theme throughout is treated with care as well as felicity. In structure, in diction, in characterisation, and poetical elegance, it is, we may boldly say, faultless. Nor is it less fitted for the stage than for the closet. However it may be acted, whether as a ballet with a favourite cantatrice in the part of Oberon, or otherwise as a Scandinavian legend with the faery monarch properly bearded, its histrionic representation is always charming. Its execution is as exquisite as its concept on is delicate.—HERAUD, JOHN A., 1865, *Shakspere, His Inner Life as Intimated in His Works, p.* 186.

In ''A Midsummer Night's Dream'' attains to a consummation which it had never before reached, either in our own, or in any other, dramatic literature. English romantic comedy, in a word, was now represented by an example, not of sudden (for nothing is sudden in literature), but of radiant perfection.—WARD, ADOLPHUS WILLIAM, 1875-99, *A History of English Dramatic Literature, vol.* II, *p.* 273.

In which some of his most delicate and sprightly verses have revelled. The whole play expresses humour on a revel, and brings into one human feeling the supernature, the caprice and gross mischance, the serious drift of life.—WEISS, JOHN, 1876, *Wit, Humor, and Shakspeare.*

Here each kind of excellence is equal throughout; there are here no purple patches on a gown of serge, but one seamless and imperial robe of a single dye. Of the lyric or the prosaic part, the counterchange of loves and laughters, of fancy fine as air and imagination high as heaven, what need can there be for any one to shame himself by the helpless attempt to say some word not utterly unworthy? Let it suffice us to accept this poem as the landmark of our first stage, and pause to look back from it on what lies behind us of partial or of perfect work. —SWINBURNE, ALGERNON CHARLES, 1880, *A Study of Shakespeare*, p. 49.

In no other of his works has Shakespeare more brilliantly shown that complete dominance of theme which is manifested in the perfect preservation of proportion. The strands of action are braided with astonishing grace. The fourfold story is never allowed to lapse into dulness or obscurity. There is caprice, but no distortion. The supernatural machinery is never wrested toward the production of startling or monstrous effects, but it deftly impels each mortal personage in the natural line of human development. The dream-spirit is maintained throughout, and perhaps it is for this reason, —that the poet was living and thinking and writing in the free, untrammelled world of his own spacious and airy imagination, and not in any definite sphere of this earth,—that "A Midsummer Night's Dream" is so radically superior to the other comedies written by him at about this period.—WINTER, WILLIAM, 1888, *Augustin Daly's Arrangement for Representation, Preface*, p. 12.

Here he gave his fancy the reins, and showed, as he created Titania and Oberon, and then, again, a Bottom, that nothing in the broad domain of poesy was to him impossible or unattainable. The moral maturity of the poet appears, however, most strikingly in the figure of Theseus, with his manly character, his delicacy of feeling, and his broad humanity. —TEN BRINK, BERNHARD, 1892-95, *Five Lectures on Shakespeare, tr. Franklin*, p. 78.

Enthralled by Shakespeare's art, and submissive to it, we accept without question every stroke of time's thievish progress, be it fast or slow; and, at the close, acknowledge that the promise of the opening lines has been redeemed. But if, in spite of all our best endeavours, our feeble wits refuse to follow him, Shakespeare smiles gently and benignantly as the curtain falls, and begging us to take no offence at shadows, bids us think it all as no more yielding than a dream.—FURNESS, HORACE HOWARD, 1895, *New Variorum Edition of Shakespeare, A Midsommer Nights Dreame, Preface*, p. xxxiv.

His first masterpiece is a masterpiece of grace, both lyrical and comic. . . . How is one to speak adequately of "A Midsummer Night's Dream?" It is idle to dwell upon the slightness of the character-drawing, for the poet's effort is not after characterisation; and, whatever its weak points, the poem as a whole is one of the tenderest, most original, and most perfect Shakespeare ever produced. It is Spenser's fairy-poetry developed and condensed; it is Shelley's spirit-poetry anticipated by more than two centuries. And the airy dream is shot with whimsical parody. The frontiers of Elf-land and Clown-land meet and mingle.—BRANDES, GEORGE, 1898, *William Shakespeare, A Critical Study*, vol. I, p. 76.

Shakespeare's joy in the possession of the poetic gift, and his earliest delight in life, found radiant expression in "A Midsummer Night's Dream," a masterpiece of poetic fancy, and the gayest and most beautiful of poetic comedies. Rich as this drama is in humorous effects, it is so essentially lyrical in spirit that it stands alone in English poetry; an exquisite expansion of the masque or festival poem into a drama of pure fancy and daring imagination.—MABIE, HAMILTON WRIGHT, 1900, *William Shakespeare, Poet, Dramatist, and Man*, p. 203.

TWO GENTLEMEN OF VERONA
1590-92

That this play is rightly attributed to Shakspeare, I have little doubt. If it be taken from him, to whom shall it be given? This question may be asked of all the disputed plays, except "Titus Andronicus;" and it will be found more credible, that Shakspeare might sometimes sink below his highest flights, than that any other should rise up to his lowest. —JOHNSON, SAMUEL, 1768, *General Observations on Shakspeare's Plays*.

The characters are drawn with strength and truth, and it is remarkable that in this play we have the first idea of what has been since called genteel comedy. The elegance, yet the contrast in Valentine and Protheus, is a very striking picture, not only of the etiquette, but the perfidy of polite life; for Protheus is more corrupted by education than nature, of which his remorse and his contrition are proofs, while Valentine has a mind so correctly inclined to rectitude that fashion and folly cannot corrupt it.—DIBDIN, CHARLES, 1795, *A Complete History of the Stage, vol.* III, *p.* 38.

This is little more than the first outline of a comedy loosely sketched in. It is the story of a novel dramatised with very little labour or pretension; yet there are passages of high poetical spirit, and of inimitable quaintness of humour, which are undoubtedly Shakespear's, and there is throughout the conduct of the fable a careless grace and felicity which marks it for his. —HAZLITT, WILLIAM, 1817–69, *Characters of Shakespear's Plays, p.* 187.

The "Two Gentlemen of Verona" ranks above the "Comedy of Errors," though still in the third class of Shakspeare's plays. It was probably the first English comedy in which characters are drawn from social life, at once ideal and true: the cavaliers of Verona and their lady-loves are graceful personages, with no transgression of the probabilities of nature; but they are not exactly the real men and women of the same rank in England. The imagination of Shakspeare must have been guided by some familiarity with romances before it struck out this comedy. It contains some very poetical lines.—HALLAM, HENRY, 1837–39, *Introduction to the Literature of Europe, pt.* ii, *ch.* vi, *par.* 37.

This play appears to me enriched with all the freshness of youth; with strong indications of his future matured poetical power and dramatic effect. It is the day-spring of genius, full of promise, beauty, and quietude, before the sun has arisen to its splendour. I can likewise discern in it his peculiar gradual developement of character, his minute touches, each tending to complete a portrait: and if these are not executed by the master-hand as shown in his later plays, they are by the same apprentice-hand, each touch of strength sufficient to harmonize with the whole.—BROWN, CHARLES ARMITAGE, 1838, *Shakespeare's Autobiographical Poems, p.* 231.

In parts, no doubt, the "Two Gentlemen of Verona" is sparkling with beauties, but as a whole it betrays a certain youthful awkwardness, and in execution a want of sustained power and depth. The composition is distinguished by the easy and harmonious flow of its language, by a peculiar freshness of view, by the *naïveté* of the particular thoughts, an unrestrained burst of wit and humour (*e. g.* in Speed and Launce), and by the delineation of the dramatic characters, which although but sketchily executed, is nevertheless striking, and invariably truthful. On the other hand, both the general view and the particular thought are deficient in depth; the parts do not readily round themselves off and combine into a whole; much is merely indicated which ought to have been more fully developed, and the conclusion especially is brought about too rapidly and without due preparation. —ULRICI, HERMANN, 1839, *Shakspeare's Dramatic Art, p.* 285.

The composition, as a whole, does not seem to have been poured forth with the rapid abundance of his later works; but, in its graver parts, bears evidence of the young author's careful elaboration, seldom daring to deviate from the habits of versification to which his muse had been accustomed, and fearful of venturing on any untried novelty of expression. . . . Upon the whole, the "Two Gentlemen of Verona," whatever rank of merit may be assigned to it by critics, will always be read and studied with deeper interest than it can probably excite as a mere literary performance, because it exhibits to us the great dramatist at a most interesting point in his career; giving striking, but imperfect and irregular, indications of his future powers.—VERPLANCK, GULIAN CROMMELIN, 1844–47, *ed. The Illustrated Shakespeare.*

The plot seems to have been, in the main, of our poet's own invention; though what relates to Proteus and Julia may have been suggested, mediately or immediately, by the story of Felix and Felismena in the Diana of Montemayor. Indeed the points of resemblance are such that I feel confident the poet must have been acquainted with that part of the Diana; and yet it was not translated till 1598. —KEIGHTLEY, THOMAS, 1867, *The Shakespeare-Expositor, p.* 22.

The "Two Gentlemen" is certainly far less beautiful in fancy than the "Dream," but it is a great advance on that play in dramatic construction.—FURNIVALL, FREDERICK JAMES, 1877, *ed. The Leopold Shakspere.*

There is an even sweetness, a simple equality of grace in thought and language which keeps the whole poem in tune, written as it is in a subdued key of unambitious harmony. In perfect unity and keeping the composition of this beautiful sketch may perhaps be said to mark a stage of advance, a new point of work attained, a faint but sensible change of manner, signalised by increased firmness of hand and clearness of outline. Slight and swift in execution as it is, few and simple as are the chords here struck of character and emotion, every shade of drawing and every note of sound is at one with the whole scheme of form and music.—SWINBURNE, ALGERNON CHARLES, 1880, *A Study of Shakespeare, p.* 48.

ROMEO AND JULIET

1591-3

AN | EXCELLENT | conceited Tragedie | OF | Romeo and Iuliet. | As it hath been often (with great applause) | plaid publiquely, by the right Ho | nourable the L. of *Hunsdon* | his Seruants. | LONDON, | Printed by Iohn Danter. | 1597.—TITLE PAGE OF FIRST EDITION, 1597.

Two households, both alike in dignity,
In fair Verona, where we lay our scene,
From ancient grudge break to new mutiny,
Where civil blood makes civil hands unclean.
From forth the fatal loins of these two foes
A pair of star-cross'd lovers take their life,
Whose misadventur'd piteous overthrows
Doth with their death bury their parents' strife.
The fearful passage of their death-mark'd love,
And the continuance of their parents' rage,
Which, but their children's end, nought could remove,
Is now the two hours' traffic of our stage;
The which if you with patient ears attend,
What here shall miss, our toil shall strive to mend.

—SHAKESPEARE, WILLIAM, 1597, *Romeo and Juliet, Prologue.*

March Ist.—To the Opera, and there saw "Romeo and Juliet," the first time it was ever acted; but it is a play of itself the worst that ever I heard in my life, and the worst acted that ever I saw these people do, and I am resolved to go no more to see the first time of acting, for they were all of them out more or less. —PEPYS, SAMUEL, 1662, *Diary and Correspondence.*

Shakespear show'd the best of his skill in his Mercutio, and he said himself, that he was forc'd to kill him in the third act, to prevent being kill'd by him. But, for my part, I cannot find he was so dangerous a person: I see nothing in him but what was so exceeding harmless, that he might have lived to the end of the play, and died in his bed, without offence to any man.—DRYDEN, JOHN, 1672, *The Conquest of Granada. Second Part. Defence of the Epilogue.*

"Romeo and Juliet" is best known by that copy of it which is generally performed, and in which Garrick has very judiciously done little more than make Shakespear alter his own play, fitting the catsatrophe to the original invention of the novelis . The two grand points that Garrick, by the advice of his friends, has insisted on, are the expunging the idea of Rosalind, and Romeo's sudden inconstancy on the first impression of Juliet's superior beauty, and heightening the catastrophe, by Romeo's first swallowing the poison, then in the extacy of finding Juliet survive, forgetting the desperate act he had committed, and flattering himself with a delusive hope of future happiness, and, again, the astonishment and delight of Juliet at recovering her lover, all which is instantly damped by a discovery that her fallacious hopes are to be but momentary. —DIBDIN, CHARLES, 1795, *A Complete History of the Stage, vol.* III, *p.* 43.

Who can repress a groan at the sight of an enlightened nation, that counts among its critics a Pope and an Addison, going into raptures over the description of an Apothecary in "Romeo and Juliet?" It is the most hideous and disgusting burlesque. True it is that a flash of lightning illumines it, as in all Shakspere's shadows. Romeo utters a reflection on the unfortunate wretch who clings so closely to life burdened though he be with every wretchedness. — CHATEAUBRIAND, FRANCOIS RENE, VICOMTE DE, 1801, *Shakspere ou Shakspeare.*

By the manner in which he has handled it, it has become a glorious song of praise on that inexpressible feeling which ennobles the soul and gives to it its highest sublimity, and which elevates even the senses themselves into soul, and at the same time is a melancholy elegy on its frailty from its own nature and external circumstances: at once the deification and the burial of love. It appears here like a heavenly spark that, descending to the earth, is converted into a flash of lightning, by which mortal creatures are almost in the same moment set on fire and consumed. Whatever is most intoxicating in the odour of a southern spring, languishing in the song of the nightingale, or voluptuous on the first opening of the rose, is breathed into this poem. But even more rapidly than the earliest blossoms of youth and beauty decay, it hurries on from the first timidly-bold declaration of love and modest return to the most unlimited passion, to an irrevocable union; then, amidst alternating storms of rapture and despair, to the death of the two lovers, who still appear enviable as their love survives them, and as by their death they have obtained a triumph over every separating power.—SCHLEGEL, AUGUSTUS WILLIAM, 1809, *Dramatic Art and Literature, tr. Black, Lecture XII.*

Of the truth of Juliet's story they* seem tenacious to a degree, insisting on the fact—giving a date (1303), and showing a tomb. It is a plain, open, and partly decayed sarcophagus, with withered leaves in it, in a wild and desolate conventual garden, once a cemetery, now ruined to the very graves. The situation struck me as very appropriate to the legend, being blighted as their love.—BYRON, LORD, 1816, *Letters.*

O! how shall I describe that exquisite ebullience and overflow of youthful life, wafted on over the laughing waves of pleasure and prosperity, as a wanton beauty that distorts the face on which she knows her lover is gazing enraptured, and wrinkles her forehead in the triumph of its smoothness! Wit ever wakeful, fancy busy and procreative as an insect, courage, an easy mind that, without cares of its own, is at once disposed to laugh away those of others, and yet to be interested in them—these and all congenial qualities, melting into the common *copula* of them all, the man of rank and the gentleman, with all its excellences and all its weaknesses, constitute the character of Mercutio!—COLERIDGE, SAMUEL TAYLOR, 1818, *Lectures and Notes on Shakspere, ed. Ashe, p.* 324.

*The Veronese.

What can be more truthful than the love of Romeo and Juliet, so young, so ardent, so unreflecting, full at once of physical passion and of moral tenderness, without restraint, and yet without coarseness, because delicacy of heart ever combines with the transports of the senses! There is nothing subtle or factitious in it, and nothing cleverly arranged by the poet; it is neither the pure love of piously exalted imaginations, nor the licentious love of palled and perverted lives; it is love itself—love complete, involuntary and sovereign, as it bursts forth in early youth, in the heart of man, at once simple and diverse, as God made it. "Romeo and Juliet" is truly the tragedy of love, as "Othello" is that of jealousy, and "Macbeth" that of ambition. . . . Wherever they are not disfigured by conceits, the lines in "Romeo and Juliet" are perhaps the most graceful and brilliant that ever flowed from Shakspeare's pen.—GUIZOT, FRANÇOIS PIERRE GUILLAUME, 1821-52, *Shakspeare and His Times, pp.* 167, 173.

I am inclined to think that the role of Friar Lawrence the Poet wrote for himself; in it is every variety of tone without its ever rising to the height of passionateness—golden words, part instructive, part soothing or consolatory; at last from these holy lips issue the sighs and the plaints of the unhappy lovers.—TIECK, JOHANN LUDWIG, 1826, *Dramaturgische Blatter, vol.* I.

Romeo and Juliet are not poetical beings placed on a prosaic back-ground; . . . but every circumstance, and every personage, and every shade of character in each tends to the developement of the sentiment which is the subject of the drama. The poetry, too, the richest that can possibly be conceived, is interfused through all the characters; the splendid imagery lavished upon all with the careless prodigality of genius; and the whole is lighted up into such a sunny brilliance of effect, as though Shakspeare had really transported himself into Italy, and had drunk to intoxication of her genial atmosphere. How truly it has been said, that "although Romeo and Juliet are in love, they are not love-sick!" What a false idea would anything of the mere whining amoroso, give us of Romeo, such as he really is in Shakspeare—the noble, gallant, ardent, brave, and witty!

And Juliet—with even less truth could the phrase or idea apply to her! . . . It is flushed with the genial spirit of the south: it tastes of youth, and of the essence of youth; of life, and of the very sap of life. We have indeed the struggle of love against evil destinies, and a thorny world; the pain, the grief, the anguish, the terror, the despair; the aching adieu; the pang unutterable of parted affection; and rapture, truth, and tenderness trampled into an early grave: but still an Elysian grace lingers round the whole, and the blue sky of Italy bends over all!—JAMESON, ANNA BROWNELL, 1832, *Characteristics of Women.*

The incidents in Romeo and Juliet are rapid, various, unintermitting in interest, sufficiently probable, and tending to the catastrophe. The most regular dramatist has hardly excelled one writing for an infant and barbarian stage. It is certain that the observation of the unity of time, which we find in this tragedy, unfashionable as the name of unity has become in our criticism, gives an intenseness of interest to the story, which is often diluted and dispersed in a dramatic history. No play of Shakspeare is more frequently represented, or honored with more tears.—HALLAM, HENRY, 1837-39, *Introduction to the Literature of Europe, pt.* ii, *ch.* vi, *par.* 43.

To eulogize this luxuriant drama would be like gilding refined gold.—CAMPBELL, THOMAS, 1838, *ed. Shakspeare's Plays, Moxon ed., Life.*

I consider Romeo designed to represent the character of an *unlucky* man—a man, who, with the best views and fairest intentions, is perpetually so unfortunate as to fail in every aspiration, and, while exerting himself to the utmost in their behalf, to involve all whom he holds dearest in misery and ruin. Had any other passion or pursuit occupied Romeo, he would have been equally unlucky as in his love. Ill-fortune has marked him for her own. From the beginning to end he intends the best; but his interfering is ever for the worst. . . . If we desire to moralize with the harsh-minded satirist, who never can be suspected of romance, we should join with him in extracting as a moral from the play—

"Nullum numen habes, si sit prudentia; nos te
Nos facimus, Fortuna, deam, caeloque locamus;"

and attribute the mishaps of Romeo, not to want of fortune, but of prudence. Philosophy and poetry differ not in essentials, and the stern censure of Juvenal is just. But still, when looking on the timeless tomb of Romeo, and contemplating the short and sad career through which he ran, we cannot help recollecting his mourning words over his dying friend, and suggest as an inscription over the monument of the luckless gentleman,

"I thought all for the best."

—MAGINN, WILLIAM, 1842-57, *Shakespeare Papers.*

While it has profoundly made use of all that is most true and deep in the innermost nature of love, the poet has imbued himself also with those external forms which the human mind had long before created in this domain of poetry. He preferred rather not to be original than to misconceive the form suitable; he preferred to borrow the expression and the style which centuries long had fashioned and developed, for in this the very test of their genuineness and durability lay; and thus the lyric love-poetry of all ages is, as it were, recognised in the forms, images, and expressions employed in this tragedy of love. — GERVINUS, G. G., 1845-62, *Shakespeare Commentaries, tr. Bunnètt, p.* 208.

Who does not recall those lovely summer nights in which the forces of nature seem eager for development, and constrained to remain in drowsy languor — a mingling of intense heat, superabundant energy, impetuous power, and silent freshness? The nightingale sings in the depths of the woods. The flower-cups are half closed. A pale lustre is shed over the foliage of the forests and upon the brow of the hills. The deep repose conceals, we are aware, a procreant force; the melancholy reserve of nature is the mask of a passionate emotion. Under the paleness and the coolness of the night, you divine restrained ardors, and flowers which brood in silence, impatient to shine forth. Such is the peculiar atmosphere with which Shakspeare has enveloped one of his most wonderful creations—"Romeo and Juliet." Not only the substance, but the forms of the language come from the South. Italy was the inventor of the tale: she drew it from her national memorials, her old family feuds, her annals filled with amorous and bloody intrigues. In its lyric accent, its blindness of passion, its blossoming and abundant vitality, in the brilliant imagery, in the bold composition, no one can fail to recognize Italy. Romeo utters himself like a sonnet of Petrarch, with the same refined choice and the same antitheses; there is the same grace and the same pleasure in versifying passion in allegorical stanzas. Juliet, too, is wholly the woman of Italy; with small gift of forethought, and absolutely ingenuous in her *abandon*, she is at once vehement and pure.—CHASLES, PHILARÈTE, 1851, *Etudes sur W. Shakspeare, Marie Stuart, et l'Arétin, pp.* 141, 142.

The language of the lovers often degenerates into quibbling; but what they feel with naivete they express with affectation. What they say is an idyll of the ball-room; what they feel is a most gracious and vivid picture of innocent love. And it is under this image that the two lovers remain graven on our imagination. All the world over, when two hearts, young and pure, fall in love with each other, if they are cultivated, they think of Romeo and Juliet; if they are uncultivated, they do better than think of them, they re-enact them.—GIRARDIN, SAINT-MARC, 1855, *Cours de Litterature Dramatique, vol.* III, *p.* 364.

"Romeo and Juliet" is a youthful work; if Shakespeare had written it later he would doubtless have lopped the *concetti* and the flowers of rhetoric, but he might perchance have drawn those passionate emotions with less ardor. Whoever touches the play under pretext of correcting it, cannot efface a blemish without erasing the brilliant colors of this youthful and burning poetry.—MÉZIÈRES, ALFRED, 1860, *Shakespeare ses. Œuvres et ses Critiques.*

In this first great dramatic work of Shakespeare we find: Invention, none; it is literally translated from an Italian novel: a vitiated taste, since the most scandalous obscenity usurps the place of that virgin purity which is as necessary to style as to love: a style in a great measure depraved by the Italian affectation of that age, when authors made jests in place of revealing what should have been the true and pure sentiments of the situations in which they placed their characters: pathos chilled by the false over-refinement of the expressions. Such are the defects of Shakespeare in this piece. But after this is admitted, and too well proved by the citations over which we have thrown the veil of omission, its beauties reveal a great genius, a splendid imagination, a soul full of pathos and a master of hearts. —LAMARTINE, ALPHONSE MARIE LOUIS DE, 1865, *Shakespeare et son Œuvre, p.* 132.

We found it a very old and time-worn edifice, built round an ample court, and we knew it, as we had been told we should, by the cap carven in stone above the interior of the grand portal. The family, anciently one of the principal in Verona, has fallen from much of its former greatness. . .

There was a great deal of stable litter, and many empty carts standing about in the court; and if I might hazard the opinion formed upon these and other appearances, I should say that old Capulet has now gone to keeping a hotel, united with the retail liquor business, both in a small way. —HOWELLS, WILLIAM DEAN, 1868, *Italian Journeys, p.* 306.

In two of the scenes we may say that the whole heart or spirit of "Romeo and Juliet" is summed up and distilled into perfect and pure expression; and these two are written in blank verse of equable and blameless melody. Outside the garden scene in the second act and the balcony scene in the third, there is much that is fanciful and graceful, much of elegiac pathos and fervid if fantastic passion; much also of superfluous rhetoric and (as it were) of wordy melody, which flows and foams hither and thither into something of extravagance and excess; but in these two there is no flaw, no outbreak, no superflux, and no failure. Throughout certain scenes of the third and fourth acts I think it may be reasonably and reverently allowed that the river of verse has broken its banks, not as yet through the force and weight of its gathering stream, but merely through the weakness of the barriers or boundaries found insufficient to confine it. —SWINBURNE, ALGERNON CHARLES, 1880, *A Study of Shakespeare, p.* 35.

There is in this play no scope for surmise, no possible misunderstanding of the chief characters or of the poet's purpose, such as there are in "Hamlet" and "Macbeth." The chill mists and vapours of the North seem to shroud these plays in an atmosphere of mystery, uncertainty, and gloom. But here all is distinct and luminous as the vivid sunshine, or the clear, tender moonlight of the South. You have but to throw your mind back into the history of the time, and to let your heart warm and your imagination kindle with the hot blood and quick-flashing fancies of the Italian temperament, and the whole tale of love and woe stands fully revealed before you. Still, to judge Juliet rightly, we must have clear ideas of Romeo, of her parents, and of all the circumstances that determined her conduct. —MARTIN, LADY (HELENA FAUCIT), 1881, *On Some of Shakespeare's Female Characters, p.* 192.

Is there a more delightful love-poem than "Romeo and Juliet?" yet it is full of conceits. . . . No one has drawn the true passion of love like Shakespeare. —TENNYSON, ALFRED, LORD, 1883, *Some Criticisms on Poets, Memoir by His Son, vol.* II, *p.* 291.

But though in *subject* Shakespeare follows Brooke, it need hardly be said that in its *spirit*—in its transfiguration of the story—the play altogether transcends the poem; a greater effort than Brooke's wearisome production would pale its uneffectual fire before the glowing warmth of this Song of Songs of Romantic Passion.—GOLLANCZ, ISRAEL, 1896, *ed. Temple Shakespeare, Romeo and Juliet, Preface, p.* x.

"Romeo and Juliet" is perhaps not such a flawless work of art as "A Midsummer Night's Dream." It is not so delicately, so absolutely harmonious. But it is an achievement of much greater significance and moment; it is the great and typical love-tragedy of the world. It soars immeasurably above all later attempts to approach it. The Danish critic who should mention such a tragedy as "Axel and Valborg" in the same breath with this play would show more patriotism than artistic sense. Beautiful as Oehlenschlager's drama is, the very nature of its theme forbids us to compare it with Shakespeare's. It celebrates constancy rather than love; it is a poem of tender emotions, of womanly magnanimity and chivalrous virtue, at war with passion and malignity. It is not, like "Romeo and Juliet," at once the pæan and the dirge of passion.—BRANDES, GEORGE, 1898, *William Shakespeare, A Critical Study, vol.* I, *p.* 92.

RICHARD II.

1593

THE | TRAGEDIE OF KING RI | CHARD THE SE | COND. | *As it hath beene publikely acted | by the right Honourable the | Lorde Chamberlaine his Ser | uants.* | LONDON | Printed by Valentine Simmes for Androw Wise, and | are to be sold at his shop in Paules church yard at | the signe of the Angel. | 1597.—TITLE PAGE OF FIRST EDITION, 1597.

This play is one of those which Shakspeare has apparently revised; but as success in works of invention is not always proportionate to labour, it is not finished at last with the happy force of some other of his tragedies, nor can be said much to affect the passions, or enlarge the understanding. — JOHNSON, SAMUEL, 1768, *General Observations on Shakspeare's Plays.*

We cannot suppose a more awful and affecting transaction, than a prince brought before his subjects, compelled to deprive himself of his royalty, and to resign his crown to the popular claimant, his near relation. This is a subject worthy the genius of Shakspeare; and yet, it must be confessed, he has fallen infinitely short of his usual powers to excite that tumult of passion which the action merited; he was ever too fond of quibble and conceit, but here he has indulged himself beyond his usual predilection for them; and I cannot help thinking, from this circumstance alone, that "Richard II" was written and acted much earlier than the date in the stationers books of 1597. —DAVIES, THOMAS, 1784, *Dramatic Micellanies, vol.* I, *p.* 169.

Certainly we cannot trace in it his usual force, either as to the characters or the language. The probability is that it was written in a hurry, which by the way is no excuse, and, as the circumstances are wholly taken from the historians and chroniclers of that day, many passages may have been literally transplanted from the history to the play. This having been done, the subject was found so unproductive that the author never thought it worth his while to finish it; and then the utmost we can say is that Shakespear was to blame for letting a play come forward unworthy of his reputation. — DIBDIN, CHARLES, 1795, *A Complete History of the Stage, vol.* III, *p.* 68.

In itself, and for the closet, I feel no hesitation in placing it as the first and most admirable of all Shakspere's purely historical plays. — COLERIDGE, SAMUEL TAYLOR, 1818, *Lectures and Notes on Shakspere, ed. Ashe, p.* 256.

He who had given old Lear, in his misery, so many noble and faithful friends, could not find one for Richard; the king had fallen, stripped and naked, into the hands of the poet, as he fell from his throne; and in himself alone the poet has been obliged to seek all his resources; the character of Richard II. is, therefore, one of the profoundest conceptions of Shakspeare.—GUIZOT, FRANCOIS PIERRE GUILLAUME, 1821–52, *Shakspeare and His Times, p.* 308.

It is this wonderful subjection of the poetical power to the higher law of truth —to the poetical truth, which is the highest truth, comprehending and expounding the historical truth—which must furnish the clue to the proper understanding of the drama of "Richard II." It appears to us that, when the poet first undertook

"to ope
The purple testament of bleeding war."—

to unfold the roll of the causes and consequences of that usurpation of the house of Lancaster which plunged three or four generations of Englishmen in bloodshed and misery — he approached the subject with an inflexibility of purpose as totally removed as it was possible to be from the levity of a partisan.—KNIGHT, CHARLES, 1849, *Studies of Shakspere, bk.* iv, *ch.* i, *p.* 152.

Beyond the scattered touches and the insinuations which denote the inability of the king, and his wavering between unseasonable power and weakness, the poet has chosen only one event for greater dramatic prominence, and with this the catastrophe of Richard's fate is united, namely, the knightly quarrel between Bolingbroke and Norfolk with which the play begins. . . . Shakespeare writes here an immortal lesson upon the royalty of God's grace and the law of inviolability. —GERVINUS, G. G., 1849–62, *Shakespeare Commentaries, tr. Bunnett, pp.* 284, 288.

"Richard II." is one of those plays of Shakespeare's which have never taken firm hold of the stage. Its exclusively political action and its lack of female characters are mainly to blame for this. But it is exceedingly interesting as his first attempt at independent treatment of a historical theme, and it rises far above the play which served as its model.—BRANDES, GEORGE, 1898, *William Shakespeare, A Critical Study, vol.* I, *p.* 143.

RICHARD III.

1594

The Tragedy of | King Richard the third. | Containing, | His treacherous Plots against his brother Clarence: | the pittiefull murther of his innocent nephewes: | his tyrannicall vsurpation: with the whole course | of his detested life, and most deserued death. | As it hath beene lately Acted by the | Right honourable the Lord Chamber- | laine his seruants. | AT LONDON | Printed by Valentine Sims, for Andrew Wise, | dwelling in Paules Chuch-yard, at the | Signe of the Angell. | 1597. — TITLE PAGE OF FIRST EDITION, 1597.

To him that impt my fame with Clio's quill,
Whose magick rais'd me from oblivion's den;
That writ my storie on the Muses hill,
And with my actions dignifi'd his pen:
He that from Helicon sends many a rill,
Whose nectared veines, are drunke by thirstie men;
Crown'd be his stile with fame, his head with bayes;
And none detract, but gratulate his praise.

—BROOKE, CHRISTOPHER, 1614, *The Ghost of Richard Third, pt.* ii, *st.* i, *ed. Grosart.*

Mine host was full of ale and history,
And in the morning when he brought us nigh
Where the two Roses join'd, you would suppose
Chaucer ne'er made the Romaunt of the Rose.
Hear him. See ye yon wood? There Richard lay
With his whole army. Look the other way,
And, lo! where Richmond in a bed of gorse
Encamp'd himself o'er night, and all his force:
Upon this hill they met. Why, he could tell
The inch where Richmond stood, where Richard fell,
Besides what of his knowledge he could say,
He had authentic notice from the play;
Which I might guess by 's must'ring up the ghosts,
And policies not incident to hosts;
But chiefly by that one perspicuous thing
Where he mistook a player for a king.
For when he would have said, King Richard died,
And call'd, A horse! a horse! he Burbage cried.

—CORBET, RICHARD, 1617, *Iter Boreale.*

This is one of the most celebrated of our author's performances; yet I know not whether it has not happened to him as to others, to be praised most, when praise is not most deserved. That this play has scenes noble in themselves, and very well contrived to strike in the exhibition, cannot be denied. But some parts are trifling, others shocking, and some improbable.—JOHNSON, SAMUEL, 1768, *General Observations on Shakspeare's Plays.*

One of the most prominent and detestable vices indeed, in Richard's character, his hypocrisy, connected, as it always is, in his person, with the most profound skill and dissimulation, has, owing to the various parts which it induces him to assume, most materially contributed to the popularity of this play, both on the stage, and in the closet. He is one who can

—"frame his face to all occasions,"

and accordingly appears, during the course of his career, under the contrasted forms of a subject and a monarch, a politician and a wit, a soldier and a suitor, a sinner and a saint; and in all with such apparent ease and fidelity to nature, that while to the explorer of the human mind he affords, by his penetration and address, a subject of peculiar interest and delight, he offers to the practised performer a study well calculated to call forth his fullest and finest exertions.—DRAKE, NATHAN, 1817, *Shakspeare and His Times, vol.* II, *p.* 374.

"Richard III." may be considered as properly a stage-play: it belongs to the theatre, rather than to the closet.—HAZLITT, WILLIAM, 1817-69, *Characters of Shakespear's Plays*, p. 160.

If we compare these speeches (of Edmund in Lear, and of Iago in Othello) with Richard's, and in like manner if we compare the way in which Iago's plot is first sown, and springs up and gradually grows and ripens in his brain, with Richard's downright enunciation of his projected series of crimes from the first, we may discern the contrast between the youth and the mature manhood of the mightiest intellect that ever lived upon earth, a contrast almost equally observable in the difference between the diction and metre of the two plays, and not unlike that between a great river rushing along turbidly in spring, bearing the freshly melted snows from Alpine mountains, with flakes of light scattered here and there over its surface, and the same river, when its waters have subsided into their autumnal tranquility, and compose a vast mirror for the whole landscape around them, and for the sun and stars and sky and clouds overhead.—HARE, A.W. AND J.C., 1827-48, *Guesses at Truth.*

This tragedy forms an epoch in the history of our poet and in that of dramatic poetry. In his preceding dramas he showed rather the suppleness than the knotted strength of his genius; but in the subtle cunning, the commanding courage, the lofty pride and ambition, the remorselessness of the third Richard, and in the whole sublime depravity of his character, he reminds us of the eulogium passed by Fuseli on Michael Angelo, who says, that Michael could stamp sublimity on the hump of a dwarf. So complete was this picture of human guilt, that Milton, in seeking for a guilty hero, was obliged to descend to the nether regions.—CAMPBELL, THOMAS, 1838, *ed. Shakspeare's Plays, Moxon ed., Life.*

"Richard III." is, and long has been—taking the stage and the closet together—the most universally and uninterruptedly popular of its author's works. Few of Shakespeare's plays passed through more than two or three editions, as they originally appeared, separately, in the customary form of quarto pamphlets. Of "Hamlet," which seems to have been the most popular of the other tragedies, there are but six of these editions; while of "Richard III.," between 1597 and 1634, we have, in addition to the copies in the first two folios, no less than eight separate editions, still preserved; and it is possible that there may have been yet another, no longer extant. There are also more references and allusions to it, in the writings of Shakespeare's contemporaries, and in those of the next generation of authors, than to any other of his works. For instance, Bishop Corbet, in his poems, Fuller, in his "Church History," and Milton, in one of his prose controversial tracts, all refer to it as familiar to their readers. It has kept perpetual possession of the stage, either in its primitive form, or as altered and adapted to the tastes of the times by Colley Cibber or by John Kemble. In one or other of these forms Richard III. has been the favourite character of all the eminent English tragedians, from Burbage, the original "Crookback," who was identified in his day, in the public mind, with the part, through the long succession of the monarchs of the English stage —Betterton, Cibber, Quin, Garrick, Henderson, Kemble, Cooke, Kean — down to our own days. Yet, in all the higher attributes of the poetic drama, "Richard III." bears no comparison with the poet's greater tragedies, or with the graver scenes of his more brilliant comedies. Intellectually and poetically, it must be assigned to a much lower class than "Romeo and Juliet," or "Othello;" than "Lear" or "Macbeth;" than the "Tempest" or the "Merchant of Venice."—VERPLANCK, GULIAN CROMMELIN, 1844–47, *ed. The Illustrated Shakespeare.*

If a portion of the bitterness and soured rage that lies in Richard's nature was rooted in this self-contempt of his outward appearance, his contempt of men on the other hand is grounded on the liberal gifts which nature has bestowed on his mind, and on the self-reliance which a comparison with the men around him inspired. Of consummate powers of speech, of animated mind and piercing wit, Shakespeare depicts him throughout in accordance with the Chronicle; in his hypocritical wooing of Anne, in his sarcasm, and in his equivocal language, this gift of a biting and malicious wit is called into play. He exhibits similar adroitness in his dealings with men; and here his contempt of all, scarcely to be dissembled even by this master of dissimulation, is clearly manifested. — GERVINUS, G. G., 1845–62, *Shakespeare Commentaries, tr. Bunnètt, p.* 264.

The drama is not so much a composition of co-operative characters, mutually developing and developed, as the prolonged yet hurried outcome of a single character, to which the other persons serve but as exponents and conductors; as if he were a volume of electricity disclosing himself by means of others, and quenching their active powers in the very process of doing so.—HUDSON, HENRY NORMAN, 1872–83, *Shakespeare: His Life, Art, and Characters, vol.* II, *p.* 156.

The references in this play to the three parts of "Henry VI." are so many as to make it impossible to deny the serial character and unity of the whole tetralogy, whatever questions may be raised as to the authorship of parts of it. The whole exhibits the fate of virtuous weakness in the face of unscrupulous strength, and concludes with the fate of this strength in the face of Providence. Henry VI. perishes by natural causes. The forces which destroy Richard III. are wholly supernatural. Three women are introduced whose curses are inevitable, like those of the Eumenides. Ghosts prophesy the event of a battle. Men's imprecations on themselves are literally fulfilled. Their destiny is made more to depend on their words than their actions; it is removed out of their hands, and placed in those of some unearthly power which hears prayer and judges the earth. As if the lesson of the poet was that there is human remedy where there are ordinary human motives, but that for power joined with Machiavellian policy the only remedy is patience dependent on Providence.—SIMPSON, RICHARD, 1874, *The Politics of Shakspere's Historical Plays, New Shakspere Society Transactions, p.* 396.

He typifies man contending against society, the individual defying by the strength of his own intellect and will all the forces naturally banded together against a rebellion such as his, and succumbing at last, like the boar caught in the toils of the huntsmen, who strike down the baffled lord of the forest like a rabid cur.—WARD, ADOLPHUS WILLIAM, 1875–99, *A History of English Dramatic Literature, vol.* II, *p.* 262.

The demonic intensity which distinguishes the play proceeds from the character of Richard as from its source and centre. As with the chief personages of Marlowe's plays, so Richard in this play rather occupies the imagination by audacity and force than insinuates himself through some subtle solvent, some magic and mystery of art. His character does not grow upon us; from the first it is complete. We are not curious to discover what Richard is, as we are curious to come into presence of the soul of Hamlet. We are in no doubt about Richard; but it yields us a strong sensation to observe him in various circumstances and situations; we are roused and animated by the presence of almost superhuman energy and power, even though that power and that energy be malign.— DOWDEN, EDWARD, 1875–80, *Shakspere, A Critical Study of His Mind and Art, p.* 161.

Villain as he is, he has the villain's coolness too. He never loses temper, except when he strikes the third messenger. As a general he is as skilful as Henry the Fifth, and looks to his sentinels; while, like Henry the Fourth, he is up and doing at the first notice of danger, and takes the right practical measures. Yet the conscience he ridicules, he is made to feel—

"there is no creature loves me;
And if I die, no soul shall pity me."

But we must note that this is only when his will is but half awake, half paralyzed by its weight of sleep. As soon as the man is himself again, neither conscience nor care for love or pity troubles him. The weakest part of the play is the scene of the citizens' talk; and the poorness of it, and the monotony of the women's curses, have given rise to the theory that in "Richard III." Shakspere was only re-writing an old play, of which he let bits stand. But though I once thought this possible, I have since become certain that it is not so. The wooing of Anne by Richard has stirred me, in reading it aloud, almost as much as any thing else in Shakspere. Note, too, how the first lines of the play lift you out of the mist and confusion of the "Henry VI." plays into the sun of Shakspere's genius.—FURNIVALL, FREDERICK JAMES, 1877, *ed. The Leopold Shakspere.*

This only of all Shakespeare's plays belongs absolutely to the school of Marlowe. The influence of the elder master, and that influence alone, is perceptible from end to end. Here at last we can see that Shakespeare has decidedly chosen his side. It is as fiery in passion, as single in purpose, as rhetorical often though never so inflated in expression, as "Tamburlaine" itself. It is doubtless a better piece of work than Marlowe ever did; I dare not say, that Marlowe ever could have done. — SWINBURNE, ALGERNON CHARLES, 1880, *A Study of Shakespeare, p.* 43.

In no other play of Shakespeare's, we may surely say, is the leading character so absolutely predominant as here. He absorbs almost the whole of the interest, and it is a triumph of Shakespeare's art that he makes us, in spite of everything, follow him with sympathy. This is partly because several of his victims are so worthless that their fate seems well deserved. Anne's weakness deprives her of our sympathy, and Richard's crime loses something of its horror when we see how lightly it is forgiven by the one who ought to take it most to heart. In spite of all his iniquities, he has wit and courage on his side—a wit which sometimes rises to Mephistophelean humour, a courage which does not fail him even in the moment of disaster, but sheds a glory over his fall which is lacking to the triumph of his coldly correct opponent. However false and hypocritical he may be towards others, he is no hypocrite to himself. He is chemically free from self-delusion, even applying to himself the most derogatory terms; and this candour in the depths of his nature appeals to us. It must be said for him, too, that threats and curses recoil from him innocuous, that neither hatred nor violence nor superior force can dash his courage. Strength of character is such a rare quality that it arouses sympathy even in a criminal. — BRANDES, GEORGE, 1898, *William Shakespeare, A Critical Study, vol.* I, *p.* 163.

HENRY VI., PART I
1590–92

Have certainly received what may be called a *thorough repair*. . . . I should conceive it would not be very difficult to feel one's way thro' these Plays, and distinguish every where the metal from the clay.—MORGANN, MAURICE, 1777–1827, *Essay on the Dramatic Character of Falstaff, p.* 49, *note.*

I am afraid that the defects of the play must necessarily affect my commentary; and I really cannot find one good passage to relieve the unavoidable dulness of minute criticism.—COURTENAY, THOMAS PEREGRINE, 1840, *Commentaries on the Historical Plays of Shakspeare, vol.* I, *p.* 213.

In Margaret we have a foreshadowing of Lady Macbeth finely contrasted with the meek and holy Henry, whose gentle lowliness of spirit is brought out with a prominence and beauty a good deal beyond what history alone would have suggested to the Poet; as even in the Lancastrian chronicles he appears unfitted for sovereignty, more from mere imbecility than from gentle virtues, unsuited to a station demanding "sterner stuff." Occasionally, too, as in the Cardinal's death, York's last scene, and many of Henry's speeches, appears a power of the pathetic and of the terrible, in which, however imperfectly developed, we cannot mistake the future author of "Lear" and "Macbeth." It is on that account that, while from the absence of that overflowing thought and quick-flashing fancy, which pervade the other histories, the paucity of those Shakespearian bold felicities of expression which fasten themselves upon the memory, and from the inferiority of the versification in freedom and melody, they can add nothing to the reputation of Shakespeare as a poet, they have nevertheless taken strong hold of the general mind, are familiar to all readers, and have certainly substituted their representations of the persons and incidents of the wars of York and Lancaster in popular opinion, alike to those of sober narratives of the chroniclers, and of the philosophic inferences of modern historians. — VERPLANCK, GULIAN CROMMELIN, 1844–47, *ed. The Illustrated Shakespeare, vol.* I.

If we separate all the scenes between York and Somerset, Mortimer and York, Margaret and Suffolk, and read them by themselves, we feel that we are looking upon a series of scenes which exhibit Shakespeare's style in his historical plays just in the manner in which we should have expected him to have written at the commencement of his career. We see the skilful and witty turn of speech and the germ of his figurative language; we perceive already the fine clever repartees and the more choice form of expression; in Mortimer's death-scene and in the lessons of his deeply-dissembled silent policy, which while dying he transmits to York, we see, with Hallam, all the genuine feeling and knowledge of human nature which belongs to Shakespeare in similar pathetic or political scenes in his other dramas; all . . . certainly in the germ which prefigures future perfection. These scenes contrast decidedly with the trivial, tedious war scenes and the alternate bombastic and dull disputes between Gloster and Winchester; they adhere to the common highway of historical poetry, though they have sufficient of the freshness of youthful art to furnish Schiller in his "Maid of Orleans" with many beautiful traits, and indeed with the principal idea of his drama. —GERVINUS, G. G., 1845–62, *Shakespeare Commentaries, tr. Bunn`tt, p.* 116.

There is a general agreement among cirtics in attributing to Shakspere the scene in which the white and red roses are plucked as emblems of the rival parties in the state; perhaps the scene of the wooing of Margaret by Suffolk if not written by Shakspere was touched by him. The general spirit of the drama belongs to an older school than the Shaksperian, and it is a happiness not to have to ascribe to our greatest poet the crude and hateful handling of the character of Joan of Arc, excused though to some extent it may be by the concurrence of view in our old English chronicles. — DOWDEN, EDWARD, 1877, *Shakspere, (Literature Primers), p.* 63.

It is broken and choppy to an intolerable degree. The only part of it to be put down to Shakspere is the Temple Garden scene of the red and white roses; and that has nothing specially characteristic in it, though the proportion of extra-syllabled lines in it forbids us supposing it is very early work. There must be at least three hands in the play, one of whom must have written — probably, only — the rhyme scenes of Talbot and his son. But poor as this play seems to us, we have Nash's evidence that it touched Elizabethan audiences.—FURNIVALL, FREDERICK JAMES, 1877, *ed. The Leopold Shakspere, Introduction, p.* xxxviii.

The authorship of the play in hand has been a theme of argument and controversy from the days of Theobald to the present time: some boldly maintaining that Shakespeare could have had no hand in it whatever; others supposing that he merely revised and improved it, and perhaps contributed a few scenes; while yet others hold the main body of it to be his, though an inferior hand may have had some share in the composition. The reasoning of the two former classes proceeds, I believe, entirely upon internal evidence, and seems to me radically at fault in allowing far too little for the probable difference between the boyhood and the manhood of Shakespeare's genius. The argument, branching out, as it does, into numerous details, and involving many nice points of critical inquiry, is much too long for rehearsal in this place; and, even if it were not so, a statement of it would hardly pay, as it is not of a nature to interest any but those who make a special study in matters of that kind. I have endeavored to understand the question thoroughly, and am not aware of any thing that should hinder my viewing it fairly; and I can but give it as my firm and settled judgment that the main body of the play is certainly Shakespeare's; nor do I perceive any clear and decisive reason for calling in another hand to account for any part of it. —HUDSON, HENRY NORMAN, 1880, *Harvard, ed. Shakespeare, vol.* VIII, *p.* 4.

HENRY VI., PART II

1594-5

Margaret of Anjou, as exhibited in these tragedies, is a dramatic portrait of considerable truth, and vigour, and consistency—but she is not one of Shakspeare's women. He who knew so well in what true greatness of spirit consisted—who could excite our respect and sympathy even for a Lady Macbeth, would never have given us a heroine without a touch of heroism; he would not have portrayed a high-hearted woman, struggling unsubdued against the strangest vicissitudes of fortune, meeting reverses and disasters, such as would have broken the most masculine spirit, with unshaken constancy, yet left her without a single personal quality which would excite our interest in her bravely endured misfortunes; and this too in the very face of history. He would not have given us, in lieu of the magnanimous queen, the subtle and accomplished French woman, a mere "Amazonian trull," with every coarser feature of depravity and ferocity; he would have redeemed her from unmingled detestation; he would have breathed into her some of his own sweet spirit—he would have given the woman a soul.—JAMESON, ANNA BROWNELL, 1832, *Characteristics of Women.*

I am certain that "Henry VI." is in the main not Shakespeare's, though here and there he may have put in a touch, as he undoubtedly did in "The Two Noble Kinsmen."—TENNYSON, ALFRED, LORD, 1883, *Some Criticisms on Poets, Memoir by His Son, vol.* II, *p.* 290.

Ah yes! Even Shakespeare is guilty of injustice towards this noble maiden who saved her country, and he treats her in an unfriendly and unloving manner, even if he does not proclaim himself her decided enemy. And even if she saved her country with the aid of hell, she still deserves respect and admiration. Or are the critics right, who hold that those passages in which the maid makes her appearance, as also *Parts II.* and *III.* of "Henry VI." are not by Shakespeare? They maintain that he only revised this trilogy which he took from older plays. I would gladly be of their opinion for the sake of the Maid of Orleans, but their arguments are untenable. In many parts these doubtful plays bear the full impress of Shakespeare's genius.—HEINE, HEINRICH, 1838-95, *Notes on Shakespeare Heroines, tr. Benecke, p.* 84.

HENRY VI., PART III

1594-5

From mere inferiority nothing can be inferred; in the productions of wit there will be inequality. Sometimes judgment will err, and sometimes the matter itself will defeat the artist. Of every author's works one will be the best, and one will be the worst. . . . Dissimilitude of style, and heterogeneousness of sentiment, may sufficiently show that a work does not really belong to the reputed author. But in these plays no such marks of spuriousness are found. The diction, the versification, and the figures, are Shakspeare's.—JOHNSON, SAMUEL, 1768, *General Observations on Shakspeare's Plays.*

Never attracting or affecting me quite as the other works of Shakespeare, nor indeed ever seeming to me to be his works, they had never been so perused as to engage me in spontaneous interpretation or restoration. Even up to the present hour too, of Shakespeare's close, bold, and subtle reasoning; his epigramatic play of words and ideas; his grace and dignity of dialogue; his psychological curiosity; his metaphorical prodigality; his disclosed fruits of pensive experience; his encased kernels of consolidated thought; his touches of human nature, here finely caught, there mysteriously inspired; his world-wide illustration; his magical imagery of outward things reflected from the innermost sense of them; all involved in a stream of melody whose onflow becomes in itself pathetic;—of these from the three parts of Henry the Sixth I still miss some sensible measure.—VAUGHAN, HENRY HALFORD, 1880, *New Readings and New Renderings of Shakespeare's Tragedies, vol.* II, *p.* v.

KING JOHN
1595

The tragedy of "King John," though not written with the utmost power of Shakspeare, is varied with a very pleasing interchange of incidents and characters. The lady's grief is very affecting; and the character of the bastard contains that mixture of greatness and levity which this author delighted to exhibit. — JOHNSON, SAMUEL, 1768, *General Observations on Shakspeare's Plays.*

I think its worth has been rather underrated. . . . In the order of Shakspeare's tragedies, I should place it immediately after Othello, Macbeth, Lear, Hamlet, Julius Cæsar, and Romeo and Juliet.—DAVIES, THOMAS, 1784, *Dramatic Micellanies, vol.* I, *p.* 114.

My idea of Constance is that of a lofty and proud spirit, associated with the most exquisite feelings of maternal tenderness, which is, in truth, the predominant feature of this interesting personage. The sentiments which she expresses, in the dialogue between herself, the King of France, and the Duke of Austria, at the commencement of the second act of this tragedy, very strongly evince the amiable traits of a humane disposition, and of a grateful heart. . . . The idea one naturally adopts of her qualities and appearance are, that she is noble in mind, and commanding in person and demeanour; that her countenance was capable of all the varieties of grand and tender expression, often agonized, though never distorted by the vehemence of her agitations. Her voice, too, must have been "propertied like the tuned spheres," obedient to all the softest inflections of maternal love, to all the pathos of the most exquisite sensibility, to the sudden burst of heart-rending sorrow, and to the terrifying imprecations of indignant majesty, when writhing under the miseries inflicted on her by her dastardly oppressors and treacherous allies. The actress whose lot it is to personate this great character should be richly endowed by nature for its various requirements; yet, even when thus fortunately gifted, much, very much, remains to be effected by herself; for in the performance of the part of Constance great difficulties, both mental and physical, present themselves.—SIDDONS, SARAH, 1831? *Life of Mrs. Siddons, by Campbell, ch.* V.

That which strikes us as the principal attribute of Constance is *power*—power of imagination, of will, of passion, of affection, of pride: the moral energy, that faculty which is principally exercised in self-control, and gives consistency to the rest, is deficient; or rather, to speak more correctly, the extraordinary development of sensibility and imagination, which lends to the character its rich poetical colouring, leaves the other qualities comparatively subordinate. Hence it is that the whole complexion of the character, notwithstanding its amazing grandeur, is so exquisitely feminine. The weakness of the woman, who by the very consciousness of that weakness is worked up to desperation and defiance, the fluctuations of temper and the bursts of sublime passion, the terrors, the impatience, and the tears, are all most true to feminine nature. The energy of Constance not being based upon strength of character, rises and falls with the tide of passion. Her haughty spirit swells against resistance, and is excited into frenzy by sorrow and disappointment; while neither from her towering pride, nor her strength of intellect, can she borrow patience to submit, or fortitude to endure. —JAMESON, ANNA BROWNELL, 1832, *Characteristics of Women.*

The prevailing characteristic both of the plot and of the chief personages in the play of "King John" is that of "craft." The poet, it is true, has taken —as he found it in the monkish record— the *historical* character of the king; but he has, with his own supreme genius, worked it out from the first scene to the last with undeviating consistency, and a revolting determination of purpose.— CLARKE, CHARLES COWDEN, 1863, *Shakespeare-Characters, p.* 319.

There is little in the play of "King John" which strengthens or gladdens the heart. In the tug of selfish power hither and thither, amidst the struggle of kingly greeds and priestly pride, amidst the sales of cities, the loveless marriage of princes, the rumors and confusion of the people, a pathetic beauty illumines the boyish figure of Arthur, so gracious, so passive, untouched by the adult rapacities and crimes of the others:

"Good, my mother, peace!
I would that I were low laid in my grave;
I am not worth this coil that's made for me."

The voice of maternal passion, a woman's voice, impotent and shrill, among the unheeding male forces, goes up also from the play. There is the pity of stern armed men for the ruin of a child's life. These, and the boisterous but genuine and hearty patriotism of Faulconbridge, are the only presences of human virtue or beauty which are to be perceived in the degenerate world depicted by Shakspere. — DOWDEN, EDWARD, 1875–80, *Shakspere, A Critical Study of His Mind and Art*, p. 153.

So long as John is the impersonator of England, of defiance to the foreigner, and opposition to the Pope, so long is he a hero. But he is bold outside only, only politically; inside, morally, he is a coward, sneak, and skunk. See how his nature comes out in the hints for the murder of Arthur, his turning on Hubert when he thinks the murder will bring evil to himself, and his imploring Falconbridge to deny it. His death ought, of course, dramatically to have followed from some act of his in the play, as revenge for the murder of Arthur, or his plundering the abbots or abbeys, or opposing the Pope. The author of "The Troublesome Raigne," with a true instinct, made a monk murder John out of revenge for his anti-Papal patriotism. But Shakspere, unfortunately, set this story aside, though there was some warrant for it in Holinshed, and thus left a serious blot on his drama which it is impossible to remove. The character which to me stands foremost in "John" is Constance, with that most touching expression of grief for the son she had lost. Beside her cry, the tender pleading of Arthur for his life is heard, and both are backt by the rough voice of Falconbridge, who, Englishman-like, depreciates his own motives at first, but is lifted by patriotism into a gallant soldier, while his deep moral nature shows itself in his heartfelt indignation at Arthur's supposed murder. The rhetoric of the earlier historical plays is kept up in "King John," and also Shakspere's power of creating situations, which he had possesst from the first.—FURNIVALL, FREDERICK JAMES, 1877, *ed. The Leopold Shakspere.*

Almost any prose can be cut up into blank verse, but blank verse becomes the finest vehicle of thought in the language of Shakespeare and Milton. As far as I am aware, no one has noticed what great Æschylean lines there are in Shakespeare, particularly in "King John."—TENNYSON, ALFRED, LORD, 1883, *Some Criticisms on Poets, Memoir by His Son, vol.* II, *p.* 289.

In this play, as in almost all the works of Shakespeare's younger years, the reader is perpetually amazed to find the finest poetical and rhetorical passages side by side with the most intolerable euphuistic affectations. And we cannot allege the excuse that these are legacies from the older play. On the contrary, there is nothing of the kind to be found in it; they are added by Shakespeare, evidently with the express purpose of displaying delicacy and profundity of thought.— BRANDES, GEORGE, 1898, *William Shakespeare, A Critical Study, vol.* I. *p.* 174.

MERCHANT OF VENICE
1596–98

THE | EXCELLENT | History of the Mer- | *chant of Venice.* | With the extreme cruelty of *Shylocke* | the Jew towards the said Merchant, in cut | *ting a just pound of his flesh. And the obtaining* | of *Portia* by the choyse *three Caskets.* | Written by W. SHAKESPEARE. | Printed by J. Roberts, 1600.— TITLE PAGE OF FIRST EDITION, 1600.

The Play it self, take it all together, seems to me to be one of the most finish'd of any of *Shakespear's*. The Tale indeed, in that Part relating to the Caskets, and the extravagant and unusual kind of Bond given by *Antonio*, is a little too much remov'd from the Rules of Probability: But taking the Fact for granted, we must allow it to be very beautifully written. There is something in the Friendship of *Antonio* to *Bassanio* very Great, Generous, and Tender. — ROWE, NICHOLAS, 1709, *Some Account of the Life &c., of Mr. William Shakespear*, *p.* xix.

With all my enthusiasm for Shakspeare, it is one of his plays that I like the least. The story of the caskets is silly, and except the character of Shylock, I see nothing beyond the attainment of a mortal: Euripides, or Racine or Voltaire, might have written all the rest. — WALPOLE, HORACE, 1788, *Letters, vol.* IX, *p.* 124.

I always consider the "Merchant of Venice" as concluding with the punishment of Shylock in the fourth Act; and a finer catastrophe does not occur in any drama, ancient or modern. The fifth act may be considered as a light afterpiece;

but it is an afterpiece by Shakespear, and in his best manner.—PYE, HENRY JAMES, 1807, *Comments on the Commentators on Shakespear, p.* 77.

"The Merchant of Venice" is one of Shakspeare's most perfect works: popular to an extraordinary degree, and calculated to produce the most powerful effect on the stage, and at the same time a wonder of ingenuity and art for the reflecting critic. Shylock, the Jew, is one of the inconceivable masterpieces of characterization of which Shakspeare alone furnishes us with examples. It is easy for the poet and the player to exhibit a caricature of national sentiments, modes of speaking, and gestures. Shylock however is everything but a common Jew: he possesses a very determinate and original individuality, and yet we perceive a light touch of Judaism in everything which he says and does. We imagine we hear a sprinkling of the Jewish pronunciation in the mere written words, as we sometimes still find it in the higher classes, notwithstanding their social refinement. In tranquil situations, what is foreign to the European blood and Christian sentiments is less perceivable, but in passion the national stamp appears more strongly marked. All these inimitable niceties the finished art of a great actor can alone properly express.—SCHLEGEL, AUGUSTUS WILLIAM, 1809, *Dramatic Art and Literature, tr. Black, Lecture XII.*

Portia is not a very great favourite with us; neither are we in love with her maid, Nerissa. Portia has a certain degree of affectation and pedantry about her, which is very unusual in Shakespear's women, but which perhaps was a proper qualification for the office of a "civil doctor," which she undertakes and executes so successfully. The speech about Mercy is very well; but there are a thousand finer ones in Shakespear. We do not admire the scene of the caskets: and object entirely to the Black Prince, Morocchius. We should like Jessica better if she had not deceived and robbed her father, and Lorenzo, if he had not married a Jewess, though he thinks he has a right to wrong a Jew. — HAZLITT, WILLIAM, 1817–69, *Characters of Shakespear's Plays, p.* 193.

Shylock is abhorred and execrated; but the skill of the poet has endued him with qualities which preserve him from contempt. His fierceness, cruelty, and relentlessness are dignified by intellectual vigour. His actions are deliberate, they are the emanations of his bold and masculine understanding. Let the art with which he negotiates his bond be contemplated; consider his coolness, his plausible exaggeration of the dangers to which Antonio's property is subjected; his bitter sarcasms and insulting gibes; all efforts of the mind to induce a belief of his indifference, and to disguise his real design: follow him into court, behold him maintaining his superiority in argument, unmoved by insult and unawed by power, till disappointment leaves him nothing to contend for and anguish stops his speech, and then let his claims to intellectual distinction be decided on. — SKOTTOWE, AUGUSTINE, 1824, *Life of Shakspeare, vol.* I, *p.* 325.

In the management of the plot, which is sufficiently complex without the slightest confusion or incoherence, I do not conceive that it has been surpassed in the annals of any theatre. . . . The variety of characters in the "Merchant of Venice," and the powerful delineation of those upon whom the interest chiefly depends, the effectiveness of many scenes in representation, the copiousness of the wit, and the beauty of the language, it would be superfluous to extol; nor is it our office to repeat a tale so often told as the praise of Shakspeare. In the language there is the commencement of a metaphysical obscurity which soon became characteristic; but it is perhaps less observable than in any later play. — HALLAM, HENRY, 1837–9, *Introduction to the Literature of Europe, vol.* II, *pt.* ii, *ch.* vi, *par.* 50.

When I saw this Play at Drury Lane, there stood behind me in the box a pale, fair Briton, who at the end of the Fourth Act, fell a-weeping passionately, several times exclaiming, "The poor man is wronged!" . . . When I think of those tears I have to rank "The Merchant of Venice" with the Tragedies, although the frame of the piece is decorated with the merriest figures of Masks, of Satyrs, and of Cupids, and the Poet meant the Play for a Comedy. . . . Wandering dream-hunter that I am, I looked round every where on the Rialto to see if I could not find Shylock. . . . But I found him nowhere on the Rialto, and I determined to seek my old acquaintance in the Synagogue. The Jews were then celebrating their day of Atonement. . . . Although I looked all round the Synagogue, I nowhere discovered the face of Shylock. I saw him not. But towards evening, when, according to Jewish belief, the gates of Heaven are shut, and no prayer can then obtain admittance, I heard a voice, with a ripple of tears that were never wept by eyes. It was a sob that could come only from a breast that held in it all the martyrdom which, for eighteen centuries, had been borne by a whole tortured people. It was the death-rattle of a soul sinking down dead-tired at heaven's gates. And I seemed to know the voice, and I felt that I had heard it long ago, when, in utter despair, it moaned out, then as now, "Jessica, my child!"—HEINE, HEINRICH, 1838–56?, *Sämmtliche Werke, vol.* V, *p.* 324.

One of the most popular, and, at the same time, noblest productions of our great master, unites all the charms and excellencies of Shakspeare's style. . . . But not merely does Shakspeare's wonderful skill in delineating character shine forth in this piece in the most brilliant light; the composition, arrangement, and unfolding of the intricate plot are equally wonderful. —ULRICI, HERMANN, 1839, *Shakspeare's Dramatic Art, pp.* 300, 301.

"The Merchant of Venice," in our opinion, was written neither to glorify friendship, nor to condemn the usurer, nor, finally to represent any moral idea, rich and manifold as are the moral allusions which the thougthful reader carries away with him, together with the æsthetic enjoyment of this work of Art. The essential and definite aspect of life here illustrated admonishes us that lasting success, sure, practical results can be secured only by a just estimate of things, by prudent use and calm endurance of given circumstances, equally far removed from violent resistance and cowardly concession. Strong feeling and clear, good sense holds the scales in the pervading character of the whole Drama; fortune helps the honest in so far as they boldly and wisely woo its favour; but rigid Idealism, although infinitely more amiable and estimable, shows itself as scarcely less dangerous than hard-hearted selfishness. —KREYSSIG, F., 1862, *Vorlesungen über Shakespeare, vol.* III, *p.* 381.

"The Merchant of Venice" marks the perfection of his development as a dramatist in the completeness of its stage effect, the ingenuity of its incidents, the ease of its movement, the poetic beauty of its higher passages, the reserve and self-control with which its poetry is used, the conception and development of character, and above all the mastery with which character and event are grouped round the figure of Shylock.—GREEN, JOHN RICHARD, 1874, *A Short History of the English People, ch.* vii, *sec.* vii.

I chose Shakespeare's Portia, then as now my ideal of a perfect woman,— . . . the wise, witty woman, loving with all her soul, and submitting with all her heart to a man whom everybody but herself (who was the best judge) would have judged her inferior; the laughter-loving, light-hearted, true-hearted, deep-hearted woman, full of keen perception, of active efficiency, of wisdom prompted by love, of tenderest unselfishness, of generous magnanimity; noble, simple, humble, pure; true, dutiful, religious, and full of fun; delightful above all others, the woman of women.—KEMBLE, FRANCES ANNE, 1876, *Old Woman's Gossip, Atlantic Monthly, vol.* 37, *p.* 713.

Shylock ranks as one of the most perfect characterizations in Shakespeare. How complete in every respect! How vividly does he rise up before us! Not merely his physical appearance, but his entire spiritual nature stands forth in the plainest lineaments. In fact, we feel as if we know him better than we could possibly have done in real life. The Poet has laid open the most hidden recesses of character, has portrayed him in the most diverse relations, with a truth and fulness unapproached and unapproachable. We ask ourselves—whence this completeness, this richness, this concreteness, of characterization? If we wish to see the infinite difference upon the same subjects, compare Shylock with the best efforts of other dramatists. Take *L'Avare*, by Molière. Placed by the side of Shylock, how meager and unsatisfactory! Can we get at the ground of this extraordinary superiority?—SNIDER, DENTON JAQUES, 1877, *Systems of Shakespeare's Dramas, vol.* I, *p.* 325.

But it is of little moment to consider how far away from Shakespeare has been the Portia of the English stage, as we gather from its annals. Rather should we try to form a clear and definite conception of her character, and of her influence upon the main incidents of the play, by a conscientious study of her in the leaves of the great master's "unvalued book." This, then, is how she pictures herself to my mind. I have always looked upon her as a perfect piece of Nature's handiwork. Her character combines all the graces of the richest womanhood with the strength of purpose, the wise helpfulness, and sustained power of the noblest manhood. Indeed, in this instance, Shakespeare shows us that it is the woman's keener wit and insight which see into and overcome the difficulty which has perplexed the wisest heads in Venice. For, without a doubt, as it seems to me at least, it is to her cultivated and bright intelligence, and not alone to the learned Bellario, her cousin, that Bassanio is indebted for the release of his friend Antonio.—MARTIN, LADY (HELENA FAUCIT), 1880, *On Some of Shakespeare's Female Characters, p.* 30.

The character of Shylock is one of Shakespeare's most perfect creations, even though he devotes comparatively little space to its elucidation. The conception of this figure is as grand as the perfection of art with which it appears upon the scene. The very first words he speaks are characteristic, and still more the manner in which he speaks them; and at each one of his utterances we seem to see the man before us, and we ourselves supply the gestures, the play of expression, which accompany his speech. As in his "Richard III." Shakespeare has here furnished the actor with a worthy and most grateful task. — TEN BRINK, BERNHARD, 1892–95, *Five Lectures on Shakespeare, tr. Franklin, p.* 185.

TAMING OF THE SHREW

1596–97

April 9.—To the King's house, . . . and there we saw "The Tameing of a Shrew," which hath some very good pieces in it, but generally is but a mean play; and the best part "Sawny," done by Lacy, hath not half its life, by reason of the words, I suppose, not being understood, at least by me. — PEPYS, SAMUEL, 1667, *Diary and Correspondence.*

"The Taming of the Shrew" is almost the only one of Shakespear's comedies that has a regular plot, and downright moral. — HAZLITT, WILLIAM, 1817-69, *Characters of Shakespear's Plays, p.* 219.

In the shape in which the piece lies before us it possesses the peculiarity of appearing at once perfect and imperfect. If we confine our attention to the principal part—the spectacle as it were within the spectacle—it seems no doubt complete and finished. On the other hand, the induction is left undeveloped and incomplete. —ULRICI, HERMANN, 1839, *Shakspeare's Dramatic Art, p.* 294.

He has stamped upon the comedy throughout, and especially in the Induction, the indelible and unquestionable marks of his own mind, by deliberately rejecting many passages of elaborate and even splendid imagery such as no poet of that age would have been ashamed of, to substitute other passages, and even scenes, of a higher and purer poetry and sweeter melody.—VERPLANCK, GULIAN CROMMELIN, 1844–47, *ed. The Illustrated Shakespeare.*

Shakspeare is quite as much at home in the sports afforded by birds of the air, as in the pursuit of beasts of chase; his knowledge of Falconry, or Hawking, so favourite a pastime with the noble and gentle of his day, is shown by numerous passages in his plays; and probably no writer on the Noble Science ever compressed so much technical information in a narrower compass than we find in eight lines in "The Taming of the Shrew," where Petruchio rejoices over the result of his treatment of the newly-married Katharine:—

"My falcon now is sharp, and passing empty, etc."

—FRENCH, GEORGE RUSSELL, 1868, *Shakspeareana Genealogica, Appendix, p.* 572.

The critics have been very warm in praise of Shakespeare's Induction, some, however, regretting that he did not keep it up till the end of the play, others suspecting that he did so keep it up, but that the continuation has been lost. I think otherwise decidedly, being convinced that in this as in other things the Poet was wiser than his critics. For the purpose of the Induction was but to start an interest in the play; and he probably knew that such interest, once started, would be rather hindered than furthered by any coming-in of other matter; that there would be no time to think of Sly amidst such a whirlwind of oddities and whimsicalities as he was going to raise. But the regret in question well approves the goodness of the thing; for, the better the thing, the more apt men are to think they have not enough until they have too much. — HUDSON, HENRY NORMAN, 1880, *ed. Harvard Shakespeare, vol.* II, *p.* 136.

The refined instinct, artistic judgment, and consummate taste of Shakespeare were perhaps never so wonderfully shown as in his recast of another man's work—a man of real if rough genius for comedy—which we get in the "Taming of the Shrew." Only the collation of scene with scene, then of speech with speech, then of line with line, will show how much may be borrowed from a stranger's material and how much may be added to it by the same stroke of a single hand. All the force and humour alike of character and situation belong to Shakespeare's eclipsed and forlorn precursor; he has added nothing; he has tempered and enriched everything. That the luckless author of the first sketch is like to remain a man as nameless as the deed of the witches in "Macbeth," unless some chance or caprice of accident should suddenly flash favouring light on his now impersonal and indiscoverable individuality, seems clear enough when we take into account the double and final disproof of his imaginary identity with Marlowe, which Mr. Dyce has put forward with such unanswerable certitude. He is a clumsy and coarse-fingered plagiarist from that poet, and his stolen jewels of expression look so grossly out of place in the homely setting of his usual style that they seem transmuted from real to sham. On the other hand, he is of all the Pre-Shakespeareans known to us incomparably the truest, the richest, the most powerful and original humourist; one indeed without a second on that ground, for "the rest are nowhere." —SWINBURNE, ALGERNON CHARLES, 1880, *A Study of Shakespeare, p.* 124.

It will be seen that the element of Intrigue, of Situation, predominates in this play, and its instrumentality is Disguise. The Romanic origin and coloring are observable in the Italian names, scenery, location, manners — in its Italian form generally. But the Teutonic element of character also makes a beginning. It is, however, rude and simple; it does not show the fine and detailed portraiture which will hereafter be developed; there is a single, dominant trait without relief. The product is unripe and uncouth in some respects, yet at the bottom the procedure is true—the retribution of the deed is the fundamental principle. The conviction and the method of the Master thus peer out in his earliest works. . . . The question whether it was written—wholly, partially, or not at all — by Shakespeare, is a matter of minor importance; the play remains exactly the same; hence a just criticism of it, as a whole, could not be changed by changing its authorship. There it stands in the book, there it belongs, and there it will remain, for it is an organic link in that series called the works of William Shakespeare.—SNIDER, DENTON JAQUES, 1887, *The Shakespearian Drama, The Comedies, pp.* 99, 100.

1.—If the author of "The Taming of a Shrew" was not William Shakespeare, he must have been a man acquainted with Stratford-on-Avon, with Wilmecote, with the Sly family, and with the tinker himself. Is it probable that two authors should exist having a cognizance of all these facts? 2.—If the author of the older comedy was not Shakespeare, the latter must have pirated an enormous quantity of lines and scenes from some other man, a fact which would not have escaped the notice of those who were ever ready to ridicule and censure him. But there is nothing on record to prove that he was ever criticised unfavorably for his production. 3. — Burby in 1606-7 sold three plays to Ling, all of which were then recognized as Shakespeare's, and one of them was the older comedy. Burby's transactions were honorable, and he would scarcely have foisted a counterfeit production upon his buyer. 4.—If the play as it now stands was not written before 1609 and after November 19th, 1607, all the contemporary evidence of Greene, Dekker, Henslowe, Kyd, Beaumont, Fletcher, and Rowlands must be considered as worthless; we must assign an earlier date to "Hamlet" than the one now usually received; and we must ignore the remarkable circumstance that Smethwick bought the old play in 1607, and lent the proprietors of the first Folio an improved version of it in 1622 or 1623.—FREY, ALBERT R., 1888, *Bankside Shakespeare, vol.* II, *Taming of the Shrew, Introduction, p.* 37.

He took very lightly this piece of task-work, executed, it would seem, to the order of his fellow-players. In point of diction and metre it is much less highly finished than others of his youthful comedies; but if we compare the Shakespearian play (in whose title the Shrew receives the definite instead of the indefinite article) point by point with the original, we obtain an invaluable glimpse into Shakespeare's comic, as formerly into his tragic, workshop. Few examples are so instructive as this.—BRANDES, GEORGE, 1898, *William Shakespeare, A Critical Study, vol.* I, *p.* 45.

HENRY IV., PART I
1596–97

The | History of | Henrie the | Fovrth; | With the battell at Shrewsburie, | *betweene the King and Lord* | Henry Percy, surnamed | Henrie Hotspur of | the North. | *With the humorous conceits of Sir* | John Falstalffe. | AT LONDON, | Printed by *P. S.* for *Andrew Wise*, dwelling | in Paules Churchyard, at the signe of | the Angell. 1598.—TITLE PAGE OF FIRST EDITION, 1598.

December 31.—In Paul's Church-yard I bought the play of "Henry the Fourth," and so went to the new Theatre and saw it acted; but my expectation being too great, it did not please me, as otherwise I believe it would; and my having a book, I believe did spoil it a little.—PEPYS, SAMUEL, 1660, *Diary and Correspondence.*

John Fastolfe, Knight. . . . The Stage hath been overbold with his memory, making him a Thrasonical Puff, and emblem of Mock-valour. True it is, Sir John Oldcastle did first bear the brunt of the one, being made the make-sport in all Plays for a Coward. It is easily known out of what purse this plack peny came; the Papists railing on him for a Heretick, and therefore he must also be a Coward, though indeed he was a man of arms, every inch of him, and as valiant as any in his age. Now as I am glad that Sir John Oldcastle is put out, so I am sorry that Sir John Fastolfe is put in, to relieve his memory in this base service, to be the anvil for every dull wit to strike upon. Nor is our Comedian excusable, by some alteration of his name, writing him Sir John Falstafe (and making him the property of pleasure for King Henry the Fifth, to abuse), seeing the vicinity of sounds intrench on the memory of that worthy Knight, and few do heed the inconsiderable difference in spelling of their name.—FULLER, THOMAS, 1662, *The Worthies of England, ed. Nichols, vol.* II, *p.* 131.

As to the Comical part, 'tis certainly our Author's own Invention; and the Character of Sir *John Falstaff*, is owned by Mr. *Dryden*, to be the best of Comical Characters: and the Author himself had so good an Opinion of it, that he continued it in no less than four Plays. This part used to be play'd by Mr. *Lacy*, and never fail'd of universal applause.—LANGBAINE, GERARD, 1691, *An Account of the English Dramatick Poets, p.* 456.

I cannot help thinking, there is more of contrivance and care in his execution of this play, than in almost any he has written. It is a more regular drama than his other historical plays, less charged with absurdities, and less involved in confusion. —MONTAGU, ELIZABETH, 1769, *Essay on the Writings and Genius of Shakespear, p.* 101.

He is a man at once young and old, enterprising and fat, a dupe and a wit, harmless and wicked, weak in principle and resolute by constitution, cowardly in appearance and brave in reality, a knave without malice, a liar without deceit, and a knight, a gentleman, and a soldier without either dignity, decency, or honor. This is a character which, though it may be decompounded, could not, I believe, have been formed, nor the ingredients of it duly mingled, upon any receipt whatever. It required the hand of Shakspeare himself to give to every particular part a relish of the whole, and of the whole to every particular part—alike the same incongruous, identical Falstaff, whether to the grave Chief-justice he vainly talks of his youth and offers to caper for a thousand, or cries to Mrs. Doll, "I am old!" "I am old!" although she is seated on his lap, and he is courting her for busses.—MORGANN, MAURICE, 1777–1825, *Essay on the Dramatic Character of Sir John Falstaff.*

It is confessed, by all the world, that there is an uncommon force and versatility in the mirth of Falstaff which is superior to all that dramatic poetry has hitherto invented. — DAVIES, THOMAS, 1784, *Dramatic Micellanies, vol.* I, *p.* 237.

If Shakespear's fondness for the ludicrous sometimes led to faults in his tragedies (which was not often the case) he has made us amends by the character of Falstaff. This is perhaps the most substantial comic character that ever was invented. Sir John carries a most portly presence in the mind's eye; and in him, not to speak it profanely, "we behold the fulness of the spirit of wit and humour bodily." We are as well acquainted with his person as his mind, and his jokes come upon us with double force and relish from the quantity of flesh through which they make their way, as he shakes his fat sides with laughter, or "lards the lean earth as he walks along." Other comic characters seem, if we approach and handle them, to resolves themselves into air, "into thin air;" but this is embodied and palpable to the grossest apprehension: it lies "three fingers deep upon the ribs," it plays about the lungs and diaphragm with all the force of animal enjoyment. His body is like a good estate to his mind, from which he receives rents and revenues of profit and pleasure in kind, according to its extent and the richness of the soil. Wit is often a meagre substitute for pleasurable sensation; an effusion of spleen and petty spite at the comforts of others, from feeling none in itself. Falstaff's wit is an emanation of a fine constitution; an exuberance of good-humour and good-nature; an overflowing of his love of laughter and good-fellowship; a giving vent to his heart's ease, and over-contentment with himself and others.—HAZLITT, WILLIAM, 1817–69, *Characters of Shakespear's Plays, p.* 133.

As an historical portrait, is not only unlike the original, but misleading and unjust in essential points of character.—TYLER, JAMES ENDELL, 1838, *Henry of Monmouth, vol.* I, *p.* 356.

"Henry IV. Part 1st," may challenge the world to produce another more original and rich in characters: the whole zodiac of theatrical genius has no constellation with so many bright and fixed stars of the first magnitude as are here grouped together.—CAMPBELL, THOMAS, 1838, *ed. Shakspeare's Plays, Moxon ed., Life.*

Shakespeare has indeed scarcely written another play of such fulness and diversity in fascinating and sharply delineated characters, bearing at the same time such a native stamp, and interwoven with a subject so national, and so universally interesting—a play, in fact, of such manifold and powerful force of attraction.—GERVINUS, G. G., 1849–62, *Shakespeare Commentaries, tr. Bunnètt, p.* 299.

This big pot-bellied fellow, a coward, a jester, a brawler, a drunkard, a lewd rascal, a pothouse poet, is one of Shakspeare's favourites. The reason is, that his manners are those of pure nature, and Shakspeare's mind is congenial with his own.—TAINE, H. A., 1871, *History of English Literature, tr. Van Laun, vol.* I, *bk.* ii, *ch.* iv, *p.* 323.

As to Hotspur, who can help liking him? With all his hot-headedness and petulance, his daring and his boasting, his humour with his wife, his scorn of that scented courtier, his lashing himself into a rage with Henry the Fourth, his keenness at a bargain (North-country to a T), his hatred of music, his love of his cropeared roan. Yet he is passion's slave, the thrall of every temper and whim. Himself and his own glory are really his gods, as at his death he says. What is his native land, what is England's weal, to him? Things to be sacrificed because his temper's crossed. One third to Wales, to England's foe, one third to himself, and but one third to Richard's rightful heir. In one sense, Hotspur is Kate the Shrew, in armour, and a man. But how he lives in the play, and starts from the printed page!—FURNIVALL, FREDERICK JAMES, 1877, *ed. The Leopold Shakspere.*

He was a great Artist, and, as such, distinguished between the temporary and permanent, between the non-essential and essential, traits of human character. Had his intention in creating Falstaff been solely to caricature a religious sect, Falstaff would have passed away with Puritanism. He still lives, and to-day is as perfect an impersonation of wit as ever, and appeals to our sense of humor as much as he did to that of Shakespeare's contemporaries. He will ever remain the most splendid manifestation of Shakespeare's genius in the realm of Comedy. —FLEMING, WILLIAM H., 1890, *Bankside Shakespeare, vol.* XII, *The First Part of Henry the Fourth, Introduction, p.* 9.

There is no such perfect conception of the selfish sensualist in literature, and the conception is all the more perfect because of the wit that lignts up the vice of Falstaff, a cold light without tenderness, for he was not a good fellow, though a merry companion. I am not sure but I should put him beside Hamlet, and on the same level, for the merit of his artistic completeness, and at one time I much preferred him, or at least his humor.—HOWELLS, WILLIAM DEAN, 1895, *My Literary Passions, p.* 72.

HENRY IV., PART II
1597–98

THE | Second part of Henrie | the fourth, continuing to his death, | *and coronation of Henrie* | the fift. | With the humours of sir Iohn Fal- | *staffe, and swaggering* | Pistoll. | *As it hath been sundrie times publikely* | acted by the right honourable, the Lord | Chamberlaine his seruants. | *Written by William Shakespeare.* LONDON | Printed by V. S. for Andrew Wise, and | William Aspley. | 1600.—TITLE PAGE OF FIRST EDITION, 1600.

I fancy every reader, when he ends this play, cries out with Desdemona, "O most lame and impotent conclusion!" . . . None of Shakspeare's plays are more read than the First and Second Parts of Henry the Fourth. Perhaps no author has ever in two plays afforded so much delight. The great events are interesting, for the fate of kingdoms depends upon them; the slighter occurrences are diverting, and, except one or two, sufficiently probable; the incidents are multiplied with wonderful fertility of invention, and the characters diversified with the utmost nicety of discernment, and the profoundest skill in the nature of man.—JOHNSON, SAMUEL, 1768, *General Observations on Shakspeare's Plays.*

It having been written, as the external and internal evidence concur in showing, not very long after the first part, when the author's mind was filled with the characters, story, and the spirit of that, the two together have the unity of a single drama. It is, however, inferior to its predecessor as a work of dramatic art, though, in my judgment, not at all so as a work of genius. It is not as perfect as the other as an historical tragi-comedy, as on its tragic side it has a less vivid and sustained interest, and approaches in those scenes more to the dramatized chronicle; in fact, adhering much more rigidly to historical authority, and deviating from it very little except in compressing into connected continuous actions events really separated by years.—VERPLANCK, GULIAN CROMMELIN, 1844–47, *ed. The Illustrated Shakespeare.*

The character of Sir John Falstaff is, I should think, the most witty and humorous combined that ever was portrayed. So palpably is the person presented to the mind's eye, that not only do we give him a veritable location in history, but the others, the real characters in the period, compared with him, appear to be the idealised people, and invented to be his foils and contrasts. As there is no romance like the romance of real life, so no real-life character comes home to our apprehensions and credulities like the romance of Sir John Falstaff. He is one grand identity. His body is fitted for his mind —bountiful, exuberant, and luxurious; and his mind was well appointed for his body—being rich, ample, sensual, sensuous, and imaginative. The very fatness of his person is the most felicitous correspondent to the unlimited opulence of his imagination.—CLARKE, CHARLES COWDEN, 1863, *Shakespeare-Characters, p.* 431.

MERRY WIVES OF WINDSOR
1598–99

A | Most pleasaunt and | excellent conceited Co- | medie, of Syr *John Falstaffe,* and the | merrie Wiues of *Windsor.* | Entermixed with sundrie | variable and pleasing humors of Syr *Hugh* | the Welch Knight, Iustice *Shallow,* and his | wise Cousin M. *Slender.* | With the swaggering vaine of Auncient | *Pistoll,* and Corporall *Nym.* | By *William Shakespeare.* | As it hath bene diuers times Acted by the right Honorable | my Lord Chamberlaines seruants Both before her | Maiestie, and elsewhere. | LONDON | Printed by T. C. for Arthur Iohnson; and are to be sold at | his shop in Powles Church-yard, at the signe of the | Flower de Leuse and the Crowne. | 1602.—TITLE PAGE OF FIRST EDITION, 1602.

But Shakespear's play in fourteen days was writ,
And in that space to make all just and fit,
Was an attempt surpassing human wit.
Yet our great Shakespear's matchless muse was such
None ever in so small time perform'd so much.

—DENNIS, JOHN, 1702, *The Comical Gallant.*

The conduct of this drama is deficient; the action begins and ends often before the conclusion, and the different parts might change places without inconvenience; but its general power, that power by which all works of genius shall finally be tried, is such, that perhaps it never yet had reader or spectator, who did not think it too soon at end. —JOHNSON, SAMUEL, 1768, *General Observations on Shakspeare's Plays.*

The "Merry Wives of Windsor" is no doubt a very amusing play, with a great deal of humour, character, and nature in it: but we should have liked it much better if any one else had been the hero of it, instead of Falstaff. We could have been contented if Shakespear had not been "commanded to show the knight in love." Wits and philosophers, for the most part, do not shine in that character; and Sir John himself by no means comes off with flying colours.—HAZLITT, WILLIAM, 1817–69, *Characters of Shakespear's Plays, p.* 229.

In the system of intrigued comedy, the "Merry Wives of Windsor" may be said to be almost perfect in its composition; it presents a true picture of manners; the *dénouement* is as piquant as it is well-prepared; and it is assuredly one of the merriest works in the whole comic repertory. —GUIZOT, FRANCOIS PIERRE GUILLAUME, 1821–52, *Shakspeare and His Times, p.* 85.

"The Merry Wives of Windsor" is the work of Shakspeare in which he has best displayed English manners; for though there is something of this in the historical plays, yet we rarely see in them such a picture of actual life as comedy ought to represent. . . . In this play the English gentleman in age and youth, is brought upon the stage, slightly caricatured in Shallow, and far more so in Slender. The latter, indeed, is a perfect satire, and I think was so intended, on the brilliant youth of the provinces, such as we may believe it to have been before the introduction of newspapers and turnpike roads; awkward and boobyish among civil people, but at home in rude sports, and proud of exploits at which the town would laugh, yet perhaps with more courage and good-nature than the laughers. No doubt can be raised that the family of Lucy is ridiculed in Shallow; but those who have recourse to the old fable of the deer-stealing, forget that Shakspeare never lost sight of his native county, and went, perhaps, every summer, to Stratford. It is not impossible that some arrogance of the provincial squires toward a player, whom, though a gentleman by birth and the recent grant of arms, they might not reckon such, excited his malicious wit to those admirable delineations.—HALLAM, HENRY, 1837–39, *Introduction to the Literature of Europe, pt.* iii, *ch.* vi, *par.* 38.

There is a prodigal and glorious throng of incident and character in this very admirable comedy: for variety, and broad, unceasing effect, it stands perhaps unrivalled. Each individual member of the breathing group—the Wives, the Husbands, the Doctor, Parson, mine Host of the Garter, Shallow, Slender; every character, in short, from Falstaff and his satellites to Simple and Rugby — stands out in the clearest light, and assists in reflecting the sunshine of the author's intellect for the delight and instruction of the reader or spectator. It has been said, and truly, that Falstaff, in this play, is not so unctuous and irresistible as in the two parts of "Henry IV.;" but if the Falstaff of Windsor must succumb to him of Gadshill and Shrewsbury, it should in fairness be added,

"Nought by himself can be his conqueror."

Even the gullibility of the unfortunate old boy (as drawn forth of him by the witcheries of the wicked wives) places him in an amiable point of view, and raises a new sensation in his favour. —VERPLANCK, GULIAN CROMMELIN, 1844–47, *The Illustrated Shakespeare, vol.* II.

That Queen Bess should have desired to see Falstaff making love proves her to have been, as she was, a gross-minded old baggage. Shakespeare has evaded the difficulty with great skill. He knew that Falstaff could not be in love; and has mixed but a little, a very little, *pruritus* with his fortune-hunting courtship. But the Falstaff of "The Merry Wives" is not the Falstaff of "Henry IV." It is a big-bellied impostor, assuming his name and style, or, at best, it is Falstaff in dotage. The Mrs. Quickly of Windsor is not mine hostess of the Boar's Head; but she is a very pleasant, busy, good-natured, unprincipled old woman, whom it is impossible to be angry with. Shallow should not have left his seat in Gloucestershire and his magisterial duties. Ford's jealousy is of too serious a complexion for the rest of the play. The merry wives are a delightful pair. Methinks I see them, with their comely, middle-aged visages, their dainty white ruffs and toys, their half-witch-like conic hats, their full farthingales, their neat though not over-slim waists, their housewifely keys, their girdles, their sly laughing looks, their apple-red cheeks, their brows the lines whereon look more like the work of mirth than years. And sweet Anne Page — she is a pretty little creature whom one would like to take on one's knee.—COLERIDGE, HARTLEY, 1849–51, *Essays and Marginalia, vol.* II, *pp.* 133, 134.

Is one of those delightfully happy plays of Shakespeare, beaming with sunshine and good humour, that makes one feel the better, the lighter, and the happier, for having seen or read it. — CLARKE, CHARLES COWDEN, 1863, *Shakespeare-Characters, p.* 141.

"The Merry Wives of Windsor" is a play written expressly for the barbarian aristocrats with their hatred of ideas, their insensibility to beauty, their hard efficient manners, and their demand for impropriety. The good folk of London liked to see a prince or a duke, and they liked to see him made gracious and generous. These royal and noble persons at Windsor wished to see the interior life of country gentlemen of the middle class, and to see the women of the middle class with their excellent *bourgeois* morals, and rough, jocose ways. The comedy of hearing a French physician and a Welsh parson speak broken English was appreciated by these spectators, who uttered their mother-tongue with exemplary accent. Shakspere did not make a grievance of his task. He threw himself into it with spirit, and despatched his work quickly —in fourteen days, if we accept the tradition. But Falstaff he was not prepared to recall from heaven or from hell. He dressed up a fat rogue, brought forward for the occasion from the back premises of the poet's imagination, in Falstaff's clothes; he allowed persons and places and times to jumble themselves up as they pleased; he made it impossible for the most laborious nineteenth-century critic to patch on "The Merry Wives" to "Henry IV." But the Queen and her court laughed as the buck-basket was emptied into the ditch, no more suspecting that its gross lading was not the incomparable jester of Eastcheap than Ford suspected the woman with a great beard to be other than the veritable Dame Pratt.—DOWDEN, EDWARD, 1875–80, *Shakspere, A Critical Study of His Mind and Art, p.* 329.

The task of presenting him so shorn of his beams, so much less than archangel (of comedy) ruined, and the excess of (humorous) glory obscured, would hardly, we cannot but think and feel, have spontaneously suggested itself to Shakespeare as a natural or eligible aim for the fresh exercise of his comic genius. To exhibit Falstaff as throughout the whole course of five acts a credulous and baffled dupe, one "easier to be played on than a pipe," was not really to reproduce him at all. The genuine Falstaff could no more have played such a part than the genuine Petruchio could have filled such an one as was assigned him by Fletcher in the luckless hour when that misguided poet undertook to continue the subject and to correct the moral of the next comedy in our catalogue of Shakespeare's. "The Tamer Tamed" is hardly less consistent or acceptable as a sequel to the "Taming of the Shrew" than the "Merry Wives of Windsor" as a supplement to "King Henry IV.:" and no conceivable comparison could more forcibly convey how broad and deep is the gulf of incongruity which divides them. — SWINBURNE, ALGERNON CHARLES 1880, *A Study of Shakespeare, p.* 116.

This play supplements the two parts of "King Henry IV." by showing what Falstaff stands for; the temptation of the flesh — the world, the flesh and the devil —backed to the uttermost with good wit and good humour, that have force to mislead our youth; here brought into relation with a simple, healthy womanhood. Mrs. Page and Mrs. Ford are not heroines with unexampled powers, but ordinary women, cheerful and right-minded, to whose minds Falstaff is as nothing. Quick parts, bent upon ill, fail in a wrestle with the mother-wit of plain folk who live loyally.—MORLEY, HENRY, 1893, *English Writers, vol.* X, *p.* 300.

It has failed to find favour with some, owing to a not ignoble dislike at seeing the degradation or discomfiture of Falstaff, but it must be remembered that Shakespeare, though never cruel with the morbid cruelty of the modern pessimist, is always perfectly awake to the facts of life. And, as a matter of fact, the bowls that Falstaff played involve the rubbers that are here depicted. It has also been a common saying that the play is little better than a farce. If so, it can only be said that Shakespeare very happily took or made the opportunity of showing how a farce also can pass under the species of eternity. How infinitely do the most farcical of the characters, such as Sir Hugh and Dr. Caius, excel the mere "Vices" of earlier playwrights! Who but Shakespeare had—we may almost say who but Shakespeare has — made an immortal thing of a mere ass, a mere puff-ball of foolish froth like Slender? If Chaucer had had the dramatic as he had the narrative faculty and atmosphere, he might have done Mrs. Quickly, who is a very near relative, in somewhat lower life, of the Wife of Bath, and rapidly ripening for her future experiences in Eastcheap. But Shallow is above even Chaucer, as are also the subtle differentiation between Mrs. Page and Mrs. Ford, and the half-dozen strokes which her creator judged sufficient for sweet Anne Page. As for Falstaff, it is mistaken affection which thinks him degraded, or "translated" Bottom-fashion. He is even as elsewhere, though under an unluckier star.—SAINTSBURY, GEORGE, 1898, *A Short History of English Literature, p.* 323.

HENRY V.

1599

THE | CRONICLE | History of Henry the fift, | With his battell fought at *Agin Court* in | France. Togither with *Auntient* | *Pistoll.* | *As it hath bene sundry times playd by the Right honorable* | *the Lord Chamberlaine his seruants.* | LONDON. | Printed by *Thomas Creede*, for Tho. Milling- | ton, and Iohn Busby. And are to be | sold at his house in Carter Lane, next | the Powle head. | 1600.—TITLE PAGE OF FIRST EDITION, 1600.

The popular and comic parts of the drama, although the originality of Falstaff's wit is absent, contains scenes of perfect natural gayety; and the Welshman Fluellen is a model of that serious, ingenious, inexhaustible, unexpected, and jocose military talkativeness, which excites at once our laughter and our sympathy. — GUIZOT, FRANCOIS PIERRE GUILLAUME, 1821–52, *Shakspeare and His Times, p.* 321.

This drama is full of singularly beautiful detached passages: for example, the reflections of the King upon ceremony,—the description of the deaths of York and Suffolk,—the glorious speech of the King before the battle, — the chorus of the fourth act,—remarkable illustrations of Shakspere's power as a descriptive poet. Nothing can be finer, also, than the commonwealth of bees in the first act. It is full of the most exquisite imagery and music. The art employed in transforming the whole scene of the hive into a resemblance of humanity is a perfect study—every successive object, as it is brought forward, being invested with its characteristic attribute. — KNIGHT, CHARLES, 1849, *Studies of Shakspere, bk.* iv, *ch.* iii, *p.* 185.

How popular after his old fashion, and at the same time how sublime, in his encouragement to the battle! How calm his last words to the French herald! How far is he from being over-hasty in giving credit to the victory! When he hears of the touching death of the noble York, how near is he to tears! and at the same moment, alarmed by a new tumult, how steeled to a bloody command! how impatiently furious at the last resistance! and at the moment when victory decides for him, how pious and how humble! And again, a short time after this solemn elevation of mind, he concludes his joke with Williams, careful even then that no harm should result from it. The poet has continued in the fifth act to show us to the very last the many-sided nature of the king. The terrible warrior is transformed into the merry bridegroom, the humorous vein again rises within him; yet he is not so much in love with his happiness, or so happy in his love, that in the midst of his wooing, and with all his jests and repartee, he would relax the smallest article of the peace which his policy had designed. —GERVINUS, G. G., 1849–62, *Shakespeare Commentaries, tr. Bunnètt, p.* 346.

As the noblest glories of England are presented in this play, so it presents Shakspere's ideal of active, practical, heroic manhood. If Hamlet exhibits the dangers and weakness of the contemplative nature, and Prospero, its calm and its conquest, Henry exhibits the utmost greatness which the active nature can attain. . . . In this play no character except Henry greatly interested Shakspere, unless it be the Welsh Fluellen, whom he loves (as Scott loved the Baron of Bradwardine) for his real simplicity underlying his apparatus of learning, and his touching faith in the theory of warfare. — DOWDEN, EDWARD, 1877, *Shakspere, (Literature Primers), pp.* 100, 101.

He proceeded to have a chronicle in hand to the close of his career, but he preserved for this class of work the laxity of evolution and lack of dramatic design which he had learned in his youth; and thus, side by side with plays the prodigious harmony of which Shakespeare alone could have conceived or executed, we have an epical fragment, like "Henry V.," which is less a drama by one particular poet, than a fold of the vast dramatic tapestry woven to the glory of England by the combined poetic patriotism of the Elizabethans. Is the whole of what we read here implicit Shakespeare, or did another hand combine with his to decorate this portion of the gallery? It is impossible to tell, and the reply, could it be given, would have no great critical value. "Henry V." is not "Othello." — GOSSE, EDMUND, 1897, *Short History of Modern English Literature, p.* 107.

"Henry V." is not one of Shakespeare's best plays, but it is one of his most amiable. He here shows himself not as the almost superhuman genius, but as the English patriot, whose enthusiasm is as beautiful as it is simple, and whose prejudices, even, are not unbecoming. The play not only points backward to the greatest period of England's past, but forward to King James, who, as the Protestant son of the Catholic Mary Stuart, was to put an end to religious persecutions, and who, as a Scotchman and a supporter of the Irish policy of Essex, was for the first time to show the world not only a sturdy England, but a powerful Great Britain.— BRANDES, GEORGE, 1898, *William Shakespeare, A Critical Study, vol.* I, *p.* 243.

MUCH ADO ABOUT NOTHING

1599

Much adoe about | Nothing. | *As it hath been sundrie times publickely* | acted by the right honourable, the Lord | Chamberlaine his seruants. | *Written by William Shakespeare.* | London | Printed by V. S. for Andrew Wise, and | William Aspley. | 1600.—TITLE PAGE OF FIRST EDITION, 1600.

This play is so witty, so playful, so abundant in strong writing, and rich humour, that it has always attracted universal applause. The beauties it contains are innumerable, they are a cluster, and are set so thick that they scarcely afford one another relief, and yet the best critic would find it difficult to say which of them ought to be displaced.—DIBDIN, CHARLES, 1795, *A Complete History of the Stage, vol.* III, *p.* 80.

Perhaps that middle point of comedy was never more nicely hit in which the ludicrous blends with the tender, and our follies, turning round against themselves in support of our affections, retain nothing but their humanity. — HAZLITT, WILLIAM, 1817-69, *Characters of Shakespear's Plays, p.* 214.

The interest in the plot is always in fact on account of the characters, not *vice versa,* as in almost all other writers; the plot is a mere canvas and no more. Hence arises the true justification of the same stratagem being used in regard to Benedick and Beatrice, — the vanity in each being alike. Take away from the "Much Ado About Nothing" all that which is not indispensable to the plot, either as having little to do with it, or, at best, like Dogberry and his comrades, forced into the service, when any other less ingeniously absurd watchmen and night-constables would have answered the mere necessities of the action;—take away Benedick, Beatrice, Dogberry, and the reaction of the former on the character of Hero,—and what will remain? In other writers the main agent of the plot is always the prominent character; in Shakspere it is so, or is not so, as the character is in itself calculated, or not calculated, to form the plot. Don John is the main-spring of the plot of this play; but he is merely shown and then withdrawn. —COLERIDGE, SAMUEL TAYLOR, 1818, *Lectures and Notes on Shakspere, ed. Ashe, p.* 239.

Shakspeare has exhibited in Beatrice a spirited and faithful portrait of the fine lady of his own time. The deportment, language, manners, and allusions, are those of a particular class in a particular age; but the individual and dramatic character which forms the groundwork, is strongly discriminated; and being taken from general nature, belongs to every age. In Beatrice, high intellect and high animal spirits meet, and excite each other like fire and air. In her wit, (which is brilliant without being imaginative,) there is a touch of insolence, not unfrequent in women when the wit predominates over reflection and imagination. In her temper, too, there is a slight infusion of the termagant; and her satirical humour plays with such an unrespective levity over all subjects alike, that it required a profound knowledge of women to bring such a character within the pale of our sympathy. But Beatrice, though wilful, is not wayward; she is volatile, not unfeeling. She has not only an exuberance of wit and gayety, but of heart, and soul, and energy of spirit; and is no more like the fine ladies of modern comedy,—whose wit consists in a temporary allusion, or a play upon words, and whose petulance is displayed in a toss of the head, a flirt of the fan, or a flourish of the pocket handkerchief—than one of our modern dandies is like Sir Philip Sidney. In Beatrice, Shakspeare has contrived that the poetry of the character shall not only soften, but heighten its comic effect.—JAMESON, ANNA BROWNELL, 1832, *Characteristics of Women.*

Our interest in Claudio is secured by this blending of the moral elements in his nature; but the foundation for a comedy and for a comic character does not appear to lie either in him or in the whole action in which Claudio is implicated. If we separate it from the rest, we shall retain a painful and not a cheerful impression. —GERVINUS, G. G., 1849–62, *Shakespeare Commentaries, tr. Bunnètt, p.* 414.

If it is proverbially impossible to determine by selection the greatest work of Shakespeare, it is easy enough to decide on the date and the name of his most perfect comic masterpiece. For absolute power of composition, for faultless balance and blameless rectitude of design, there is unquestionably no creation of his hand that will bear comparison with "Much Ado About Nothing." —SWINBURNE, ALGERNON CHARLES, 1880, *A Study of Shakspeare, p.* 153.

AS YOU LIKE IT

1600

Of this play the fable is wild and pleasing. I know not how the ladies will approve the facility with which both Rosiland and Celia give their hearts. To Celia much may be forgiven for the heroism of her friendship. The character of Jacques is natural and well preserved. The comic dialogue is very sprightly, with less mixture of low buffoonery than in some other plays; and the graver part is elegant and harmonious. By hastening to the end of his work, Shakspeare suppressed the dialogue between the usurper and the hermit, and lost an opportunity of exhibiting a moral lesson in which he might have found matter worthy of his highest powers. —JOHNSON, SAMUEL, 1768, *General Observations on Shakspeare's Plays.*

We make no scruple to affirm that "As You Like It" will afford considerable instruction from attentive perusal, with great addition of pleasure from adequate representation.—GENTLEMAN, FRANCIS, 1770, *Dramatic Censor, vol.* I, *p.* 478.

Shakespear has here converted the forest of Arden into another Arcadia, where they "fleet the time carelessly, as they did in the golden world." It is the most ideal of any of this author's plays. It is a pastoral drama, in which the interest arises more out of the sentiments and characters than out of the actions or situations. It is not what is done, but what is said, that claims our attention. Nursed in solitude, "under the shade of melancholy boughs," the imagination grows soft and delicate, and the wit runs riot in idleness, like a spoiled child, that is never sent to school. Caprice and fancy reign and revel here, and stern necessity is banished to the court The mild sentiments of humanity are strengthened with thought and leisure; the echo of the cares and noise of the world strikes upon the ear of those "who have felt them knowingly," softened by time and distance. "They hear the tumult, and are still. The very air of the place seems to breathe a spirit of philosophical poetry: to stir the thoughts, to touch the heart with pity, as the drowsy forest rustles to the sighing gale."—HAZLITT, WILLIAM, 1817–69, *Characters of Shakspear's Plays, p.* 214.

Rosalind is like a compound of essences, so volatile in their nature, and so exquisitely blended, that on any attempt to analyze them, they seem to escape us. To what else shall we compare her, all-enchanting as she is?—to the silvery summer clouds, which even while we gaze on them, shift their hues and forms, dissolving into air, and light, and rainbow showers?—to the May-morning, flush with opening blossoms and roseate dews, and "charm of earliest birds?"—to some wild and beautiful melody, such as some shepherd boy might "pipe to Amarillis in the shade?"—to a mountain streamlet, now smooth as a mirror in which the skies may glass themselves, and anon leaping and sparkling in the sunshine—or rather to the very sunshine itself? for so her genial spirit touches into life and beauty whatever it shines on!—JAMESON, ANNA BROWNELL, 1832, *Characteristics of Women.*

The sweet and sportive temper of Shakspeare, though it never deserted him, gave way to advancing years, and to the mastering force of serious thought. What he read we know but very imperfectly; yet, in the last years of this century, when five and thirty summers had ripened his genius, it seems that he must have transfused much of the wisdom of past ages into his own all-combining mind. In several of the historical plays, in the "Merchant of Venice," and especially in "As You Like It," the philosophic eye, turned inward on the mysteries of human nature, is more and more characteristic; and we might apply to the last comedy the bold figure that Coleridge has less appropriately employed as to the early poems, that "the creative power and the intellectual energy wrestle as in a war-embrace." In no other play, at least, do we find the bright imagination and fascinating grace of Shakspeare's youth so mingled with the thoughtfulness of his maturer age. . .

Few comedies of Shakspeare are more generally pleasing, and its manifold improbabilities do not much effect us in perusal. The brave, injured Orlando, the sprightly but modest Rosalind, the faithful Adam, the reflecting Jaques, the serene and magnanimous Duke, interest us by turns, though the play is not so well managed as to condense our sympathy, and direct it to the conclusion.—HALLAM, HENRY, 1837–39, *Introduction to the Literature of Europe, pt.* ii, *ch.* vi, *par.* 51.

The poet, in conceiving this fine work, first generated a lofty ideal. His aim was to set forth the power of patience as the panacea for earth's ills and the injustice of fortune, and self-command as the condition without which the power would be inoperative. Neither this power nor its condition can be easily illustrated in the life of courts; but the sylvan life such as the banished Duke and his companions live in Arden, is favourable to both. In the contrast between the two states of life lies the charm of the play, and the reconciliation of these formal opposites is the fulfilment of its ideal.—HERAUD, JOHN A., 1865, *Shakspere, His Inner Life as Intimated in his Works, p.* 235.

"As you Like It" is a caprice. Action there is none; interest barely; likelihood still less. And the whole is charming.—TAINE, H. A., 1871, *History of English Literature, tr. Van Laun, vol.* I, *bk.* ii, *ch.* iv, *p.* 343.

Nor can it well be worth any man's while to say or to hear for the thousandth time that "As You Like It" would be one of those works which prove, as Landor said long since, the falsehood of the stale axiom that no work of man's can be perfect, were it not for that one unlucky slip of the brush which has left so ugly a little smear in one corner of the canvas as the betrothal of Oliver to Celia; though, with all reverence for a great name and a noble memory, I can hardly think that matters were much mended in George Sand's adaptation of the play by the transference of her hand to Jaques. Once elsewhere, or twice only at the most, is any such other sacrifice of moral beauty or spiritual harmony to the necessities and traditions of the stage discernible in all the world-wide work of Shakespeare.—SWINBURNE, ALGERNON CHARLES, 1880, *A Study of Shakespeare, p.* 151.

Thus much may suffice to show that the Poet has here borrowed a good deal of excellent matter. With what judgment and art the borrowed matter was used by him can only be understood on a careful study of his workmanship. In no one of his comedies indeed has he drawn more freely from others; nor, I may add, is there any one wherein he has enriched his drawings more liberally from the glory of his own genius. To appreciate his wisdom as shown in what he left unused, one must read the whole of Lodge's novel. In that work we find no traces of Jaques, or Touchstone, or Audrey; nothing, indeed, that could yield the slightest hint towards either of those characters. It scarce need be said that these superaddings are enough of themselves to transform the whole into another nature; pouring through all its veins a free and lively circulation of the most original wit and humour and poetry. —HUDSON, HENRY NORMAN, 1880, *ed. Harvard Shakespeare, vol.* V, *p.* 6.

Much as I have written, I feel how imperfectly I have brought out all that this delightful play has been and is to me. I can but hope that I have said enough to show why I gave my heart to Rosalind, and found an ever new delight in trying to impersonate her.—MARTIN, LADY (HELENA FAUCIT), 1884, *On Some of Shakespeare's Female Characters, p.* 355.

One of the topmost things in Shakespeare, the masterpiece of romantic comedy, one of the great type-dramas of the world. —SAINTSBURY, GEORGE, 1898, *A Short History of English Literature, p.* 325.

TWELFTH NIGHT
1601

At our feast wee had a play called "Twelue Night, or What you Will," much like the Commedy of Errores, or Menechmi in Plautus, but most like and neere to that in Italian called *Inganni*. A good practise in it to make the Steward beleeve his Lady widdowe was in love with him, by counterfeyting a letter as from his Lady in generall termes, telling him what shee liked best in him, and prescribing his gesture in smiling, his apparaile, &c., and then when he came to practise making him beleeue they tooke him to be mad.—MANNINGHAM, JOHN, 1601, *Diary, Feb.* 2, *ed. Bruce, p.* 18.

January 6.—After dinner to the Duke's house, and there saw "Twelfth-Night" acted well, though it be but a silly play, and not related at all to the name or day. —PEPYS, SAMUEL, 1663, *Diary and Correspondence.*

This is justly considered as one of the most delightful of Shakspear's comedies. It is full of sweetness and pleasantry. It is perhaps too good-natured for comedy. It has little satire, and no spleen. It aims at the ludicrous rather than the ridiculous. It makes us laugh at the follies of mankind, not despise them, and still less bear any ill-will towards them.—HAZLITT, WILLIAM, 1817-69, *Characters of Shakspear's Plays, p.* 180.

We may walk into that stately hall and think,—Here Shakspere's "Twelfth Night" was acted in the Christmas of 1601; and here its exquisite poetry first fell upon the ear of some secluded scholar, and was to him as a fragrant flower blooming amidst the arid sands of his Bracton and his Fleta; and here its gentle satire upon the vain and the foolish penetrated into the natural heart of some grave and formal dispenser of justice, and made him look with tolerance, if not with sympathy, upon the mistakes of less grave and formal fellow-men; and here its ever-gushing spirit of enjoyment,—of fun without malice, of wit without grossness, of humour without extravagance,—taught the swaggering, roaring, overgrown boy, miscalled student, that there were higher sources of mirth than affrays in Fleet Street, or drunkenness in Whitefriars. Venerable Hall of the Middle Temple, thou art to our eyes more stately and more to be admired since we looked upon that entry in the Table-book of John Manningham! The Globe has perished, and so has the Blackfriars. The works of the poet who made the names of these frail buildings immortal need no associations to recommend them; but it is yet pleasant to know that there is one locality remaining where a play of Shakspere was listened to by his contemporaries; and that play, "Twelfth Night."—KNIGHT, CHARLES, 1849, *Studies of Shakspere, bk.* vii, *ch.* ii, *p.* 311.

Is the purest and merriest comedy which Shakespeare has written. . . . And the piece in truth is constituted throughout to make a strong impression of the maddest mirth. Rightly conceived and acted by players who even in caricature do not miss the line of beauty, it has an incredible effect.—GERVINUS, G. G., 1849-62, *Shakespeare Commentaries, tr. Bunnett, p.* 439.

The love of Viola is the sweetest and tenderest emotion that ever informed the heart of the purest and the most graceful of beings, with a spirit almost divine. Perhaps in the whole range of Shakespeare's poetry there is nothing which comes more unbidden into the mind, and always in connexion with some image of the ethereal beauty of the utterer, than Viola's celebrated speech to the Duke in her assumed garb of the page.—CLARKE, CHARLES COWDEN, 1863, *Shakespeare-Characters, p.* 196.

Of all Shakespeare's Comedies, perhaps "Twelfth Night" is the most richly woven with various hues of love, serious and mock-heroic. The amorous threads take warmer shifting colours from their neighbourhood to the unmitigated remorseless merry-making of the harum-scarum old wag Sir Toby and his sparkling captain in mischief, the "most excellent devil of wit," Maria. Beside their loud conviviality and pitiless fun the languishing sentiment of the cultivated love-lorn Duke stands out seven times refined, and goes with exquisite touch to the innermost sensibilities. —MINTO, WILLIAM, 1874–85, *Characteristics of English Poets, p.* 298.

"Twelfth Night" is perhaps the most graceful and harmonious comedy Shakespeare ever wrote. It is certainly that in which all the notes the poet strikes, the note of seriousness and of raillery, of passion, of tenderness, and of laughter, blend in the richest and fullest concord. It is like a symphony in which no strain can be dispensed with, or like a picture veiled in a golden haze, into which all the colours resolve themselves. The play does not overflow with wit and gaiety like its predecessor; we feel that Shakespeare's joy of life has culminated and is about to pass over into melancholy; but there is far more unity in it than in "As You Like It," and it is a great deal more dramatic.—BRANDES, GEORGE, 1898, *William Shakespeare, A Critical Study, vol.* I, *p.* 273.

ALL'S WELL THAT ENDS WELL
1601–2

I cannot reconcile my heart to Bertram; a man noble without generosity, and young without truth; who married Helen as a coward, and leaves her as a profligate; when she is dead by his unkindness, sneaks home to a second marriage, is accused by a woman whom he has wronged, defends himself by falsehood, and is dismissed to happiness. — JOHNSON, SAMUEL, 1768, *General Observations on Shakspeare's Plays.*

"All's Well That Ends Well" is one of the most pleasing of our author's comedies. The interest is however more of a serious than of a comic nature. The character of Helen is one of great sweetness and delicacy. She is placed in circumstances of the most critical kind, and has to court her husband both as a virgin and a wife: yet the most scrupulous nicety of female modesty is not once violated. There is not one thought or action that ought to bring a blush into her cheeks, or that for a moment lessens her in our esteem. Perhaps the romantic attachment of a beautiful and virtuous girl to one placed above her hopes by the circumstances of birth and fortune, was never so exquisitely expressed as in the reflections which she utters when young Rousillon leaves his mother's house, under whose protection she has been brought up with him, to repair to the French king's court. —HAZLITT, WILLIAM, 1817-69, *Characters of Shakspear's Plays, p.* 202.

The comic scenes, and the general graceful ease and fluency of its diction, give an air of lightness and variety to the play that are wanting in the novel. The mere story is not productive of more effect in one than in the other, and the drama makes no pretensions to rank in the first order of excellence. But a value is conferred upon Shakspeare's performance beyond its dramatic merit, by its being the repository of much sententious wisdom, and numerous passages of remarkable elegance. A single speech of the king may be referred to as an instance of both, and Helena's description of her hopeless passion may be selected as exquisitely beautiful. — SKOTTOWE, AUGUSTINE, 1824, *Life of Shakspeare, vol.* II, *p.* 142.

Helena, as a woman, is more passionate than imaginative; and, as a character, she bears the same relation to Juliet that Isabel bears to Portia. There is equal unity of purpose and effect, with much less of the glow of imagery and the external colouring of poetry in the sentiments, language and details. It is passion developed under its most profound and serious aspect; as in Isabella, we have the serious and the thoughtful, not the brilliant side of intellect. Both Helena and Isabel are distinguished by high mental powers, tinged with a melancholy sweetness; but in Isabella the serious and energetic part of the character is founded in religious principle; in Helena it is founded in deep passion. There never was, perhaps, a more beautiful picture of a woman's love, cherished in secret, not self-consuming in silent languishment—not pining in thought—not passive and "desponding over its idol"—but patient and hopeful, strong in its own intensity, and sustained by its own fond faith. . . . All the circumstances and details with which Helena is surrounded, are shocking to our feelings and wounding to our delicacy: and yet the beauty of the character is made to triumph over all.—JAMESON, ANNA BROWNELL, 1832, *Characteristics of Women.*

This play is seldom noticed, and perhaps little understood, unless there are many like Mrs. Jameson, who has ably analysed the character of Helen. It is called one of the poet's minor plays; and as far as it has no communion with the sublimer passions, the appellation is correct; in other respects it may rank with the best. That Dr. Johnson should have passed sentence on Bertram, according to his scholastic and abstract notions of perfection, instead of charitably considering the positive imperfections of our nature, is, at least, short-sighted.—BROWN, CHARLES ARMITAGE, 1838, *Shakespeare's Autobiographical Poems*, p. 266.

In Helena we clearly see the outlines of one of Shakespeare's great mediatorial women, but placed in a more trying situation than any of them. They all have and must have a common trait—a deeply reconciling spirit, which can see the lesser and surrender it for the greater; they disguise, prevaricate, fib openly, circumvent parent and even the law, to reach the higher end. Formal truth of every kind they immolate for their great ethical object, which is usually the healing of some disruption in the Family; in general, they sacrifice the Moral to the Institutional. All of them do thus—Portia, Rosalind, Viola, Iomgen, down to Anne Page; we follow them with delight and applaud in them just this strength which gives them mastery over their life's problem. But when we come to Helena we call a halt, and ask, Is not that which she sacrifices a higher spiritual good than the end attained? Is the price worth the purchase, and does not meditation for once cut off its own head?—SNIDER, D. J., 1887, *The Shakespearian Drama, The Comedies*, p. 207.

HAMLET

1602–3

The | Tragicall Historie of | HAMLET | *Prince of Denmarke* | By William Shakespeare. | As it hath beene diuerse times acted by his Highnesse ser- | uants in the Cittie of London: as also in the two V- | niuersities of Cambridge and Oxford, and else-where | At London printed for N. L. and John Trundell. | 1603.—TITLE PAGE OF FIRST EDITION, 1603.

It should be like the *Never-too-well read Arcadia*, where the *Prose* and *Verce* (*Matter* and *Words*) are like his *Mistresses* eyes, one still excelling another and without Corivall: or to come home to the vulgars *Element*, like *Friendly Shakespeare's Tragedies*, where the *Commedian* rides, when the *Tragedian* stands on Tip-toe: Faith it should please all, like Prince *Hamlet*. But in sadnesse, then it were to be feared he would runne mad: Insooth I will not be moone-sicke, to please: nor out of my wits though I displeased all.—SCOLOKER, ANTHONY, 1604, *Daiphantus, or the Passions of Love, Epistle to the Reader, Roxburghe Club reprint*, 1818.

September 5 (At "Serra Leona") I sent the interpreter, according to his desier, abord the Hector, whear he brooke fast, and after came abord mee, wher we gave the tragedie of Hamlett.—(Sept.) 30. Captain Hawkins dined with me, wher my companions acted Kinge Richard the Second.—31. I envited Captain Hawkins to a ffishe dinner, and had Hamlet acted abord me: wch I permitt to keepe my people from idlens and unlawfull games, or sleepe.—KEELING, CAPTAIN, 1607, *Narratives of Voyages towards the North-West in search of a Passage to Cathay and India*, 1496 *to* 1631, *ed. Rundall*, 1849, p. 231. *Journal of the Dragon.*

I saw "Hamlet Prince of Denmark" played, but now the old plays began to disgust this refined age, since his Majestie's being so long abroad.—EVELYN, JOHN, 1661, *Diary, Nov.* 26.

August 31.—To the Duke of York's playhouse, . . . and saw "Hamlet," which we have not seen this year before, or more; and mightily pleased with it, but above all, with Betterton, the best part, I believe, that ever man acted.—PEPYS, SAMUEL, 1668, *Diary and Correspondence.*

The scene represented by the Players is in wretched verse. This we may, without incurring the denomination of an ill-natured critic, venture to pronounce: that in almost every place where Shakespeare has attempted rhyme, either in the body of his plays, or at the ends of Acts or Scenes, he falls far short of the beauty and force of his blank verse. One would think they were written by two different persons. I believe we may justly take notice that rhyme never arrived at its true beauty, never came to its perfection, in England until long since Shakespeare's time.—HANMER, SIR THOMAS, 1736, *Some Remarks on the Tragedy of Hamlet, Prince of Denmark, p.* 39.

If the dramas of Shakspeare were to be characterized, each by the particular excellence which distinguishes it from the rest, we must allow to the tragedy of "Hamlet" the praise of variety. The incidents are so numerous that the argument of the play would make a long tale. The scenes are interchangeably diversified with merriment and solemnity; with merriment, that includes judicious and instructive observations; and solemnity, not strained by poetical violence above the natural sentiments of man. New characters appear from time to time in continual succession, exhibiting various forms of life and particular modes of conversation. The pretended madness of Hamlet causes much mirth, the mournful distraction of Ophelia fills the heart with tenderness, and every personage produces the effect intended, from the apparition, that in the first act chills the blood with horror, to the fop in the last, that exposes affectation to just contempt. The conduct is perhaps not wholly secure against objections. The action is indeed for the most part in continual progression, but there are some scenes which neither forward nor retard it. Of the feigned madness of Hamlet there appears no adequate cause, for he does nothing which he might not have done with the reputation of sanity.—JOHNSON, SAMUEL, 1768, *General Observations on Shakspeare's Plays.*

Englishmen believe in ghosts no more than the Romans did, yet they take pleasure in the tragedy of "Hamlet," in which the ghost of a king appears on the stage. Far be it from me to justify everything in that tragedy; it is a vulgar and barbarous drama, which would not be tolerated by the vilest populace of France, or Italy. Hamlet becomes crazy in the second act, and his mistress becomes crazy in the third; the prince slays the father of his mistress under the pretence of killing a rat, and the heroine throws herself into the river; a grave is dug on the stage, and the grave-diggers talk quodlibets worthy of themselves, while holding skulls in their hands; Hamlet responds to their nasty vulgarities in sillinesses no less disgusting. In the meanwhile another of the actors conquers Poland. Hamlet, his mother, and his father-in-law carouse on the stage; songs are sung at table; there is quarreling, fighting, killing.—one would imagine this piece to be the work of a drunken savage. But amidst all these vulgar irregularities, which to this day make the English drama so absurd and so barbarous, there are to be found in "Hamlet," by a *bizarrerie* still greater, some sublime passages, worthy of the greatest genius. It seems as though nature had mingled in the brain of Shakespeare the greatest conceivable strength and grandeur with whatsoever witless vulgarity can devise that is lowest and most detestable. It must be confessed that, amid the beauties which sparkle through this horrible extravagance, the ghost of Hamlet's father has a most striking theatrical effect. It always had a great effect upon the English,—I mean upon those who are the most highly educated, and who see most clearly all the irregularity of their old drama.—VOLTAIRE, FRANÇOIS MARIE AROUET, 1768, *Theatre Complet, vol.* II, *p.* 201.

"The time is out of joint; O cursed spite,
That ever I was born to set it right!"

In these words, I imagine, is the key to Hamlet's whole procedure, and to me it is clear that Shakespeare sought to depict a great deed laid upon a soul unequal to the performance of it. In this view I find the piece composed throughout. Here is an oak-tree planted in a costly vase, which should have received into its bosom only lovely flowers; the roots spread out, the vase is shivered to pieces. A beautiful, pure, and most moral nature, without the strength of nerve which makes the hero, sinks beneath a burden which it can neither bear nor throw off; every duty is holy to him,—this too hard. The impossible is required of him,—not the impossible in itself, but the impossible to him.

How he winds, turns, agonizes, advances, and recoils, ever reminded, ever reminding himself, and at last almost loses his purpose from his thoughts, without ever again recovering his peace of mind. . . . Hamlet is endowed more properly with sentiment than with a character; it is events alone that push him on; and accordingly the piece has somewhat the amplification of a novel. But as it is Fate that draws the plan, as the piece proceeds from a deed of terror, and the hero is steadily driven on to a deed of terror, the work is tragic in its highest sense, and admits of no other than a tragic end.—GOETHE, JOHANN WOLFGANG, 1778, *Wilhelm Meister*.

Hamlet cannot be said to have pursued his ends by very warrantable means; and if the poet, when he sacrificed him at last, meant to have enforced such a moral, it is not the worst that can be deduced from the play; for, as Maximus, in Beaumont and Fletcher's "Valentinian," says:—

"Although his justice were as white as truth,
His way was crooked to it; that condemns him."

The late Dr. Akinside once observed to me, that the conduct of Hamlet was every way unnatural and indefensible, unless he were to be regarded as a young man whose intellects were in some degree impaired by his own misfortunes; by the death of his father, the loss of expected sovereignty, and a sense of shame resulting from the hasty and incestuous marriage of his mother. I have dwelt the longer on this subject because Hamlet seems to have been hitherto regarded as a hero not undeserving the pity of the audience; and because no writer on Shakspeare has taken the pains to point out the immoral tendency of his character.—STEEVENS, GEORGE, 1778, *The Plays of William Shakspeare, vol.* X.

The character is consistent. Hamlet is exhibited with good dispositions, and struggling with untoward circumstances. The contest is interesting. As he endeavours to act aright we approve and esteem him. But his original constitution renders him unequal to the contest: he displays the weaknesses and imperfections to which his peculiar character is liable; he is unfortunate; his misfortunes are in some measure occasioned by his weakness: he thus becomes an object not of blame, but of genuine and tender regret.—RICHARDSON, WILLIAM, 1783, *Some of Shakespeare's Remarkable Characters*.

"Hamlet" was at first written by Shakespeare as a brief sketch; slowly, by degrees, it was amplified. With what love the poet did this, the work itself shows: it contains reflections upon life, the dreams of youth, partly philosophical, partly melancholy, such as Shakespeare himself (rank and situation put out of view) may have had. Every still soul loves to look into this calm sea in which is mirrored the universe of humanity, of time and eternity. The only piece, perhaps, which the pure *sensus humanitatis* has written, and yet a tragedy of Destiny, of dark, awful Fate.—HERDER, JOHANN GOTTFRIED, 1800? *Literatur und Kunst*.

"Hamlet" is single in its kind: a tragedy of thought inspired by continual and never satisfied meditation on human destiny and the dark perplexity of the events of this world, and calculated to call forth the very same meditation in the minds of the spectators. This enigmatical work resembles those irrational equations in which a fraction of unknown magnitude always remains, that will in no manner admit of solution. Much has been said, much written on this piece, and yet no thinking man who anew expresses himself on it will, in his view of the connection and the signification of all the parts, entirely coincide with his predecessors. . . . Respecting Hamlet's character, I cannot, according to the poet's views as I understand them, pronounce altogether so favourable a sentence as Goethe's.—SCHLEGEL, AUGUSTUS WILLIAM, 1809, *Dramatic Art and Literature, tr. Black*.

I see no reason to think that if the play of "Hamlet" were written over again by some such writer as Banks or Lillo, retaining the process of the story, but totally omitting all the poetry of it, all the divine features of Shakespeare, his stupendous intellect; and only taking care to give us enough of passionate dialogue, which Banks or Lillo were never at a loss to furnish; I see not how the effect could be much different upon an audience, nor how the actor has it in his power to represent Shakespeare to us differently from his representation of Banks or Lillo.—LAMB, CHARLES, 1810? *The Tragedies of Shakespeare*.

Hamlet is a name; his speeches and sayings but the idle coinage of the poet's brain. What then, are they not real? They are as real as our own thoughts. Their reality is in the reader's mind. It is *we* who are Hamlet. This play has a prophetic truth, which is above that of history. Whoever has become thoughtful and melancholy through his own mishaps or those of others; whoever has borne about with him the clouded brow of reflection, and thought himself "too much i' th' sun;" whoever has seen the golden lamp of day dimmed by envious mists rising in his own breast, and could find in the world before him only a dull blank with nothing left remarkable in it; whoever has known "the pangs of despised love, the insolence of office, or the spurns which patient merit of the unworthy takes;" he who has felt his mind sink within him, and sadness cling to his heart like a malady, who has had his hopes blighted and his youth staggered by the apparitions of strange things; who cannot be well at ease, while he sees evil hovering near him like a spectre; whose powers of action have been eaten up by thought, he to whom the universe seems infinite, and himself nothing; whose bitterness of soul makes him careless of consequences, and who goes to a play as his best resource to shove off, to a second remove, the evils of life by a mock representation of them —this is the true Hamlet. — HAZLITT, WILLIAM, 1817-69, *Characters of Shakespear's Plays, p.* 74.

I believe the character of Hamlet may be traced to Shakspere's deep and accurate science in mental philosophy. Indeed, that this character must have some connection with the common fundamental laws of our nature may be assumed from the fact, that Hamlet has been the darling of every country in which the literature of England has been fostered. — COLERIDGE, SAMUEL TAYLOR, 1818, *Lectures and Notes on Shakspere, ed. Ashe, p.* 343.

"Hamlet" is not the finest of Shakspeare's dramas; "Macbeth," and, I think, "Othello" also, are, on the whole, superior to it: but it perhaps contains the most remarkable examples of its author's most sublime beauties, as well as of his most glaring defects. Never has he unvailed with more originality, depth, and dramatic effect the inmost state of a mighty soul; never also, has he yielded with greater unrestraint to the terrible or burlesque fancies of his imagination, and to the abundant intemperance that is characteristic of a mind without any selection, and which delights to render them striking by a strong, ingenious, and unexpected expression without caring to give them a pure and natural form.—GUIZOT, FRANCOIS PIERRE GUILLAUME, 1821-52, *Shakspeare and His Times, p.* 174.

"Hamlet" is not the most admirable of Shakespeare's works; but Shakespeare is most admirable in "Hamlet." — BOERNE, L., 1829, *Gesammelte Schriften, Dram. Blätter, p.* 172.

Ophelia — poor Ophelia! O, far too soft, too good, too fair to be cast among the briers of this working-day world, and fall and bleed upon the thorns of life! What shall be said of her? for eloquence is mute before her! Like a strain of sad sweet music which comes floating by us on the wings of night and silence, and which we rather feel than hear—like the exhalation of the violet dying even upon the sense it charms—like the snow-flake dissolved in air before it has caught a stain of earth—like the light serf severed from the billow, which a breath disperses—such is the character of Ophelia: so exquisitely delicate, it seems as if a touch would profane it; so sanctified in our thoughts by the last and worst of human woes, that we scarcely dare to consider it too deeply. The love of Ophelia, which she never once confesses, is like a secret which we have stolen from her, and which ought to die upon our hearts as upon her own. Her sorrow ask not words but tears; and her madness has precisely the same effect that would be produced by the spectacle of real insanity, if brought before us: we feel inclined to turn away, and veil our eyes in reverential pity and too painful sympathy.—JAMESON, ANNA BROWNELL, 1832, *Characteristics of Women.*

If Shakespeare's "Hamlet" is to be characterized in a word, it is the tragedy of the *Nothingness of Reflection*, or, as even this phrase may be varied, it is the tragedy of the Intellect. . . . Next to "Faust," "Hamlet" is the profoundest, boldest, most characteristic tragedy that has ever been written.—GANS, EDUARD, 1834, *Vermischte Schriften, vol.* II, *p.* 270.

"Hamlet," that tragedy of maniacs, this *Royal Bedlam* in which every character is either crazy or criminal, in which feigned madness is added to real madness, and in which the grave itself furnishes the stage with the skull of a fool; in that Odeon of shadows and spectres where we hear nothing but reveries, the challenge of sentinels, the screeching of the night-bird and the roaring of the sea.—DE CHATEAUBRIAND, FRANÇOIS RENÉ, VISCOMTE, 1837, *Sketches of English Literature, vol.* I, *p.* 274.

If, in all Shakspeare's pieces, it is necessary to dig deep before we can reach to the lowest foundation on which the dramatic edifice is raised, this is the case especially in the present one. Every fresh commentator who studies and writes about "Hamlet," goes deeper and further than his predecessors, and thinks he has reached to the true foundation, which, nevertheless, lies all the while still deeper and far beyond his researches. This perhaps will be the fate also of my own speculations. However, I shall not be deterred by such a prospect, but comfort myself rather with the consoling certainty it affords of the surpassing fulness and the ever freshly-springing fertility of human genius.—ULRICI, HERMANN, 1839, *Shakspeare's Dramatic Art, p.* 213.

Yes, Germany is Hamlet! Lo!
  Upon her ramparts every night
There stalks in silence, grim and slow,
  Her buried Freedom's steel-clad sprite,
Beck'ning the warders watching there,
  And to the shrinking doubter saying:
"They've dropt fell poison in mine ear,
  Draw thou the sword! no more delaying!"
—FREILIGRATH, FERDINAND, 1844, *April, tr. Wister.*

There is no drama, as all the world knows, upon which so much has been written as Shakespeare's "Hamlet." Quick-witted heads (Herr Rötscher's excepted) have all had their say about it. After all sorts of fashions, lofty, profound, radical, superficial, polished, crude, desultory (Herr Rötscher's lucubrations not excepted), it has been æstheticised about, romanced about, dogmatized about, bemastered, berated, cut up, quibbled at, be-Hegeled, and be-Rötschered. A critical tower of Babel of amazing height and breadth has been reared, and for the same purpose as is in the Scripture: to scale celestial heights, and, as people see, with the same result. The celestial heights remain unscaled. A glib little sophomore (*Schulfuchs*) clambering up over the shoulders of Goethe, Gans, Tieck, and others, has reached the loftiest pinnacle of the tower, and there he is waving high in the air a school-programme with the device, "The Nothingness of Reflection," but showing only the nothingness of his own reflection; for his motto assumes that the all-powerful imagination of Shakespeare was impregnated by a miserable scholastic abstraction that has not virility enough to engender anything.—KLEIN, L., 1846, *Berliner Modenspiegel.*

No work of Shakespeare's is truly more clear in its design than this, although none, if we except the sonnets, has been so long and so entirely misunderstood. . . . The soliloquies of this "prince of speculative philosophy" are masterpieces of reflection, in which Shakespeare had recourse to the most profound depths of his wisdom; and the intricacies of his subtle thoughts mock the profundity of Scandinavian mysteries.—GERVINUS, G. G., 1849–62, *Shakespeare Commentaries, tr. Bunnètt, pp.* 550, 567.

From the rich troop of his heroes, Shakespeare has chosen Hamlet as the exponent, to the spectators and to posterity, of all that lay nearest to his own heart. It is Hamlet to whom Shakespeare has confided his confession of faith as an artist.—KREYSSIG, F., 1858, *Vorlesungen über Shakespeare, vol.* II, *p.* 235.

Two marvellous Adams, we have just said, are the man of Æschylus, Prometheus, and the man of Shakespeare, Hamlet. Prometheus is action. Hamlet is hesitation. In Prometheus, the obstacle is exterior; in Hamlet it is interior. In Prometheus, the will is securely nailed down by nails of brass and cannot get loose; besides, it has by its side two watchers, Force and Power. In Hamlet the will is more tied down yet; it is bound by previous meditation, the endless chain of the undecided. Try to get out of yourself if you can! What a Gordian knot is our reverie! Slavery from within, that is slavery indeed. Scale this enclosure, "to dream!" escape, if you can, from this prison, "to love!" the only dungeon is that which walls conscience in. Prometheus, in order to be free, has but a bronze collar to break and a god to conquer; Hamlet must break and conquer himself. Prometheus can raise himself upright, if he only lifts a mountain; to raise himself up, Hamlet must lift his own thoughts. If Prometheus plucks the vulture from his breast, all is said; Hamlet must tear Hamlet from his breast. Prometheus and Hamlet are two naked spleens; from one runs blood, from the other doubt. —HUGO, VICTOR, 1864, *William Shakespeare, tr. Baillot, p.* 195.

There would not be such a difference of opinion about this tragedy, and especially about the hero of it, were it only borne in mind that it is a tragedy written simply for the stage. But how has the poor prince been taken to task the last ten years! He could not help it that things went all askew in Germany in 1848. "Hamlet is Germany" in a most indubita ble sense, in that the German attempts at elucidating "Hamlet" are the contemporaneous history of the German mind in miniature.—HEBLER, C., 1864, *Aufstäze über Shakespeare, p.* 83.

If a dramatist wished to represent one of his persons as feigning madness, that assumed condition would be naturally desired by the writer to be as like as possible to the real affliction. If the other persons associated with him could at once discover that the madness was put on, of course the entire action would be marred, and the object for which the pretended madness would be designed would be defeated by the discovery. How consummate must be the poet's art who can have so skilfully described, to the minutest symptoms, the mental malady of a great mind as to leave it uncertain to the present day, even among learned physicians versed in such maladies, whether Hamlet's madness was real or assumed. —WISEMAN, NICHOLAS PATRICK STEPHEN, 1865, *William Shakespeare, p.* 41.

It is a curious fact that in this struggle "Hamlet," the very play the subject of which came to England from, or at least through, France, is always found in the vanguard. Whenever Shakespeare is spoken of, he is styled the author of "Hamlet," "Hamlet" being to a certain extent regarded as the embodiment not only of Shakespeare, but of the English drama in general. —ELZE, KARL, 1865, *Essays on Shakespeare, tr. Schmitz, p.* 194.

"Hamlet," which has never been fitly and perfectly played and never will be and never can be, "Hamlet" the intranslatable, "Hamlet" that twenty volumes of notes scarcely elucidate,—"Hamlet" is Shakespeare, as the "Misanthrope" is Molière. —CHASLES, PHILARÈTE, 1867, *Études Contemporaines, p.* 101.

Let us put aside altogether the idea that Hamlet, with his delays, was, in the mind of the poet, the type of the German race. In the first place, Hamlet is not German; he is a Dane, which is not the same thing; ask the Danes of the present day.—COURDAVEAUX, V., 1867, *Caractères et Talents. Études sur la Littérature Ancienne et Moderne, p.* 305.

Notwithstanding the wonderful manner in which Shakespeare has sublimated the material, the stuff of the old legend, there yet remains something of its original rudeness, and must always remain, because the fruit never can disown the soil out of which it has sprung.—BODENSTEDT, FRIEDRICH, 1870, *Introduction to Translation of Hamlet, p.* viii.

If we must draw a moral from Hamlet, it would seem to be, that Will is Fate, and that, Will once abdicating, the inevitable successor in the regency is Chance. Had Hamlet acted, instead of musing how good it would be to act, the king might have been the only victim. As it is, all the main actors in the story are the fortuitous sacrifice of his irresolution. We see how a single great vice of character at last draws to itself as allies and confederates all other weaknesses of the man, as in civil wars the timid and the selfish wait to throw themselves upon the stronger side.—LOWELL, JAMES RUSSELL, 1868–90, *Shakespeare Once More, Prose Works. Riverside ed., vol.* III, *p.* 91.

Hamlet is Shakspeare, and, at the close of this gallery of portraits which have all some features of his own, Shakspeare has painted himself in the most striking of all.—TAINE, H. A., 1871, *History of English Literature, tr. Van Laun, vol.* I, *bk.* ii, *ch.* iv, *p.* 340.

Shakespeare carefully avoids the appearance of everything sketchy, rectilineal, hurried. The branch ramifies. The situation is hollowed out.—LUDWIG, OTTO, 1872, *Shakespeare-Studien, p.* 138.

That it is not the piece itself particularly which impresses the public is evident from the fact, that for several decades the play has been given in different places in different shapes. Every one who has undertaken to alter the piece has picked out such parts as he considered especially effective, and left out other portions. . . . The fact that a piece has admitted of so many alterations shows how very loosely it is constructed.—BENEDIX, RODERICH, 1873, *Die Shakespearomanie, p.* 289.

In no other piece has Shakespeare employed in such measure all the means of his art. The earlier acts are among the most powerful in all dramatic literature. The epic *ductus* of the last two must not be considered as a defect. We find the same mode of composition in his other dramas.—GRIMM, HERMAN, 1875, *Hamlet, Preussische Jahrbücher, April, p.* 398.

In "Hamlet" alone, the most marvellously true as it is the most marvellously profound example of Shakspere's power of characterisation, the central character is conceived on a far broader basis than is furnished by the action of the play. In reading this tragedy, or seeing it acted on the stage, the plot is forgotten in the hero. It is as if Hamlet were pausing, not before the deed which he is in reality hesitating to perform — and which is neither a great nor a difficult one — but before action in general. This one necessity proves too heavy for Hamlet to bear; the acorn — to use Goethe's simile —bursts the vessel in which it has been planted; and Hamlet succumbs beneath the fardel which is imposed on all humanity.—WARD, ADOLPHUS WILLIAM, 1875–99, *A History of English Dramatic Literature, vol.* II, *p.* 294.

Not the faintest streak of Humor appears in this tragedy to reconcile us with the drift of it.—WEISS, JOHN, 1876, *Wit, Humor, and Shakespeare, p.* 159.

No one of mortal mould (save Him "whose blessed feet were nailed for our advantage to the bitter cross") ever trod this earth, commanding such absorbing interest as this Hamlet, this mere creation of a poet's brain. No syllable that he whispers, no word let fall by any one near him, but is caught and pondered as no words ever have been, except of Holy Writ. Upon no throne built by mortal hands has ever "beat so fierce a light" as upon that airy fabric reared at Elsinore. —FURNESS, HORACE HOWARD, 1877, *ed. New Variorum Shakespeare, Hamlet, p.* xii.

Every change in the text of "Hamlet" has impaired its fitness for the stage and increased its value for the closet in exact and perfect proportion. Now, this is not a matter of opinion—of Mr. Pope's opinion or Mr. Carlyle's; it is a matter of fact and evidence. Even in Shakespeare's time the actors threw out his additions; they throw out these very same additions in our own. The one especial speech, if any one such especial speech there be, in which the personal genius of Shakespeare soars up to the very highest of its height and strikes down to the very deepest of its depth, is passed over by modern actors; it was cut away by Hemings and Condell. We may almost assume it as certain that no boards have ever echoed — at least, more than once or twice—to the supreme soliloquy of Hamlet. Those words which combine the noblest pleading ever proffered for the rights of human reason with the loftiest vindication ever uttered of those rights, no mortal ear within our knowledge has ever heard spoken on the stage. A convocation even of all priests could not have been more unhesitatingly unanimous in its rejection than seems to have been the hereditary verdict of all actors. It could hardly have been found worthier of theological than it has been found of theatrical condemnation. Yet, beyond all question, magnificent as is that monologue on suicide and doubt which has passed from a proverb into a byword, it is actually eclipsed and distanced at once on philosophic and on poetical grounds by the later soliloquy on reason and resolution.—SWINBURNE, ALGERNON CHARLES, 1880, *A Study of Shakespeare, p.* 164.

Highly educated, possessed of a vivid imagination, his intellect is continually at war with his heart; and while the latter impels him to action, the stronger influence of his mind controls him, and he remains inert. . . . With him it is thought that produces doubt, and the idea of Shakspere as represented in "Hamlet" seems to be "the prevalence of thought over the faculty of action."—SALVINI, TOMMASO, 1881, *Impressions of Some Shaksperean Characters, Century Magazine, vol.* 23, *p.* 112.

"Hamlet" is the greatest creation in literature that I know of: though there may be elsewhere finer scenes and passages of poetry. Ugolino and Paolo and Francesca in Dante equal anything anywhere. It is said that Shakespeare was such a poor actor that he never got beyond his ghost in this play, but then the ghost is the most real ghost that ever was. The Queen did not think that Ophelia committed suicide, neither do I.—TENNYSON, ALFRED, LORD, 1883, *Some Criticisms on Poets, Memoir by His Son, vol.* II, *p.* 291.

"Hamlet" has given the name of Denmark a world-wide renown. Of all Danish men, there is only one who can be called famous on the largest scale; only one with whom the thoughts of men are for ever busied in Europe, America, Australia, aye, even in Asia and Africa, wherever European culture has made its way; and this one never existed, at any rate in the form in which he has become known to the world. Denmark has produced several men of note—Tycho Brahe, Thorvaldsen, and Hans Christian Andersen—but none of them has attained a hundredth part of Hamlet's fame. The "Hamlet" literature is comparable in extent to the literature of one of the smaller European peoples—the Slovaks, for instance.—BRANDES, GEORGE, 1898, *William Shakespeare, A Critical Study, vol.* II, *p.* 2.

"Hamlet" was the only drama by Shakespeare that was acted in his lifetime at the two Universities. It has since attracted more attnetion from actors, playgoers, and readers of all capacities than any other of Shakespeare's plays. Its world-wide popularity from its author's day to our own, when it is as warmly welcomed in the theatres of France and Germany as in those of England and America, is the most striking of the many testimonies to the eminence of Shakespeare's dramatic instinct. At a first glance there seems little in the play to attract the uneducated or the unreflecting. . . . It is the intensity of interest which Shakespeare contrives to excite in the character of the hero that explains the position of the play in popular esteem. The play's unrivalled power of attraction lies in the pathetic fascination exerted on minds of almost every calibre by the central figure—a high-born youth of chivalric instincts and finely developed intellect, who, when stirred to avenge in action a desperate private wrong, is foiled by introspective workings of the brain that paralyse the will.—LEE, SIDNEY, 1898, *A Life of William Shakespeare, pp.* 224, 225.

MEASURE FOR MEASURE
1603

Of this play, the light or comic part is very natural and pleasing, but the grave scenes, if a few passages be excepted, have more labour than elegance. The plot is rather intricate than artful. The time of the action is indefinite; some time, we know not how much, must have elapsed between the recess of the duke and the imprisonment of Claudio; for he must have learned the story of Mariana in his disguise, or he delegated his power to a man already known to be corrupted. The unities of action and place are sufficiently preserved.—JOHNSON, SAMUEL, 1768, *General Observations on Shakspeare's Plays.*

The noble virtue, the true greatness, and the feminine honour of Isabella, are every where conveyed through sentiments of responsive eloquence, and the great and commanding justice of the Duke, who learns the temper of his subjects to govern them, and who chuses for a wife the most amiable of those subjects, are dressed in language no less consonant.—DIBDIN, CHARLES, 1795, *A Complete History of the Stage, vol.* III, *p.* 314.

Yet, notwithstanding this agitating truthfulness, how tender and mild is the pervading tone of the picture! The piece takes improperly its name from punishment; the true significance of the whole is the triumph of mercy over strict justice, no man being himself so free from errors as to be entitled to deal it out to his equals. The most beautiful embellishment of the composition is the character of Isabella. . . . whose heavenly purity, amid the general corruption, is not stained with one unholy thought. In the humble robes of the novice she is a very angel of light.—SCHLEGEL, AUGUSTUS WILLIAM, 1809, *Dramatic Art and Literature.*

This play, which is Shakspere's throughout, is to me the most painful—say rather, the only painful—part of his genuine works. The comic and tragic parts equally border on the μισητον,—the one being disgusting, the other horrible; and the pardon and marriage of Angelo not merely baffles the strong indignant claim of justice — (for cruelty, with lust and damnable baseness, cannot be forgiven, because we cannot conceive them as being morally repented of;) but it is likewise degrading to the character of woman. Beaumont and Fletcher, who can follow Shakspere in his errors only, have presented a still worse, because more loathsome and contradictory, instance of the same kind in the "Night-Walker," in the marriage of Alathe to Algripe. Of the counterbalancing beauties of "Measure for Measure," I need say nothing; for I have already remarked that the play is Shakspere's throughout. — COLERIDGE, SAMUEL TAYLOR, 1818, *Lectures and Notes on Shakspere, ed. Ashe, p.* 299.

Is perhaps, after Hamlet, Lear, and Macbeth, the play in which Shakspeare struggles, as it were, most with the over-mastering power of his own mind the depths and intricacies of being, which he has searched and sounded with intense reflection, perplex and harass him; his personages arrest their course of action to pour forth, in language the most remote from common use, thoughts which few could grasp in the clearest expression; and thus he loses something of dramatic excellence in that of his contemplative philosophy. . . . I do not value the comic parts highly: Lucio's impudent profligacy, the result rather of sensual debasement than of natural ill disposition, is well represented; but Elbow is a very inferior repetition of Dogberry. In dramatic effect, "Measure for Measure" ranks high: the two scenes between Isabella and Angelo, that between her and Claudio, those where the Duke appears in disguise, and the catastrophe in the fifth act, are admirably written and very interesting; except so far as the spectator's knowledge of the two stratagems which have deceived Angelo may prevent him from participating in the indignation at Isabella's imaginary wrong, which her lamentations would excite. — HALLAM, HENRY, 1837–39, *Introduction to the Literature of Europe, pt.* iii, *ch.* vi, *par.* 40

"Measure for Measure" exhibits more clearly than any other piece the profound skill of Shakspeare, in giving intellectual depth and dramatic life to his traditional materials.—ULRICI, HERMANN, 1839, *Shakspeare's Dramatic Art, p.* 315.

No one of the high female characters of tragedy has been found more effective in representation than Isabella; while there is perhaps no composition of the same length in the language which has left more of its expressive phrases, its moral aphorisms, its brief sentences crowded with meaning, fixed in the general memory, and embodied by daily use in every form of popular eloquence, argument, and literature.—VERPLANCK, GULIAN CROMMELIN, 1844–47, *ed. The Illustrated Shakespeare.*

In "Measure for Measure," in contrast with the flawless execution of "Romeo and Juliet," Shakespeare has spent his art in just enough modification of the scheme of the older play to make it exponent of this purpose, adapting its terrible essential incidents, so that Coleridge found it the only painful work among Shakespeare's dramas, and leaving for the reader of to-day more than the usual number of difficult expressions; but infusing a lavish colour and a profound significance into it, so that under his touch certain select portions of it rise far above the level of all but his own best poetry, and working out of it a morality so characteristic that the play might well pass for the central expression of his moral judgments. It remains a comedy, as indeed is congruous with the bland, half-humorous equity which informs the whole composition, sinking from the heights of sorrow and terror into the rough scheme of the earlier piece; yet it is hardly less full of what is really tragic in man's existence than if Claudio had indeed "stooped to death." Even the humorous concluding scenes have traits of special grace, retaining in less emphatic passages a stray line or word of power, as it seems, so that we watch to the end for the traces where the nobler hand has glanced along, leaving its vestiges, as if accidentally or wastefully, in the rising of the style.—PATER, WALTER, 1874, *Appreciations, p.* 176.

Almost all that is here worthy of Shakespeare at any time is worthy of Shakespeare at his highest: and of this every touch, every line, every incident, every syllable belongs to pure and simple tragedy. The evasion of a tragic end by the invention and intromission of Mariana has deserved and received high praise for its ingenuity: but ingenius evasion of a natural and proper end is usually the distinctive quality which denotes a workman of a very much lower school than the school of Shakespeare. In short and in fact, the whole elaborate machinery by which the complete and completely unsatisfactory result of the whole plot is attained is so thoroughly worthy of such a contriver as "the old fantastical duke of dark corners" as to be in a moral sense, if I dare say what I think, very far from thoroughly worthy of the wisest and mightiest mind that ever was informed with the spirit or genius of creative poetry.—SWINBURNE, ALGERNON CHARLES, 1880, *A Study of Shakespeare, p.* 203.

He treated the subject as he did, because the interests of the theatre demanded that the woof of comedy should be interwoven with the severe and sombre warp of tragedy. But what a comedy! Dark, tragic, heavy as the poet's mood—a tragi-comedy, in which the unusually broad and realistic comic scenes, with their pictures of the dregs of society, cannot relieve the painfulness of the theme, or disguise the positively criminal nature of the action. One feels throughout, even in the comic episodes, that Shakespeare's burning wrath at the moral hypocrisy of self-righteousness underlies the whole structure like a volcano, which every moment shoots up its flames through the superficial form of comedy and the interludes of obligatory merriment. — BRANDES, GEORGE, 1898, *William Shakespeare, A Critical Study, vol.* II, *p.* 71.

Even in that unequal melody, "Measure for Measure," the great scene between Isabel and Claudio so far transcends anything that English, anything that European, drama had had to show for nearly two thousand years, that in this special point of view it remains perhaps the most wonderful in Shakespeare. Marlowe has nothing like it; his greatest passages, psychologically speaking, are always monologues; he cannot even attempt the clash and play of soul with soul that is so miraculously given here.—SAINTSBURY, GEORGE, 1898, *A Short History of English Literature, p.* 323.

JULIUS CÆSAR

1601-3

The many-headed multitude were drawne
By *Brutus* speech, that *Cæsar* was ambitious,
When eloquent *Mark Antonie* had showne
His vertues, who but *Brutus* then was vicious?
Mans memorie, with new, forgets the old,
One tale is good, untill another's told.

—WEEVER, JOHN, 1601, *The Mirror of Martyrs, s.* 4.

So I have seene, when Cesar would appeare,
And on the Stage at halfe-sword parley were,
Brutus and *Cassius*: oh how the Audience
Were ravish'd, with what new wonder they went thence,
When some new day they would not brooke a line
Of tedious (though well laboured) *Catiline*.

—DIGGES, LEONARD, 1640, *Upon Master William Shakespeare.*

This may shew with what indignity our poet treats the noblest Romans. But there is no other cloth in his wardrobe. Every one must wear a fool's coat that comes to be dressed by him; nor is he more civil to the ladies—Portia, in good manners, might have challenged more respect; she that shines a glory of the first magnitude in the gallery of heroic dames, is with our poet scarce one remove from a natural; she is the own cousin-german of one piece, the very same impertinent silly flesh and blood with Desdemona. Shakespear's genius lay for comedy and humour. In tragedy he appears quite out of his element; his brains are turned—he raves and rambles without any coherence, any spark of reason, or any rule to controul him, to set bounds to his phrenzy.—RYMER, THOMAS, 1693, *A Short View of the Tragedy of the Last Age.*

Of this tragedy many particular passages deserve regard, and the contention and reconcilement of Brutus and Cassius is universally celebrated; but I have never been strongly agitated in perusing it, and think it somewhat cold and unaffecting, compared with some other of Shakspeare's plays; his adherence to the real story, and to Roman manners, seems to have impeded the natural vigour of his genius.—JOHNSON, SAMUEL, 1768, *General Observations on Shakspeare's Plays.*

I know no part of Shakspere that more impresses on me the belief of his genius being superhuman, than this scene between Brutus and Cassius. In the Gnostic heresy, it might have been credited with less absurdity than most of their dogmas, that the Supreme had employed him to create, previously to his function of representing, characters. —COLERIDGE, SAMUEL TAYLOR, 1818, *Lectures and Notes on Shakspere, ed. Ashe, p.* 315.

Neither has he characters of insignificance, unless the phantom that stalks over the stage as Julius Cæsar, in the play of that name, may be accounted one. —LAMB, CHARLES, 1834, *Table-Talk.*

In "Julius Cæsar" Shakspere makes a complete imaginative study of the case of a man predestined to failure. . . . Brutus is an idealist. . . . Moral ideas and priuciples are more to him than concrete realities; he is studious of self-perfection. . . . Cassius, on the contrary, is by no means studious of moral perfection. He is frankly envious, and hates Cæsar. . . . Julius Cæsar appears in only three scenes of the play. In the first scene of the third act he dies. Where he does appear, the poet seems anxious to insist upon the weakness rather than the strength of Cæsar. . . . In the characters of the "Julius Cæsar" there is a severity of outline; they impose themselves with strict authority upon the imagination; subordinated to the great spirit of Cæsar, the conspirators appear as figures of life-size, but they impress us as no larger than life.—DOWDEN, EDWARD, 1875-80, *Shakspere, A Critical Study of His Mind and Art, pp.* 249, 251, 253, 272.

The style of "Julius Cæsar" is characterized by simplicity and breadth of touch, and each sentence is clear, easy, and flowing, with the thought clothed in perfect and adequate expression: the lines are as limpid as those of "Romeo and Juliet," but without their remains of rhyme and Italian conceits. Of all Shakespeare's works, none has greater purity of verse or transparent fluency. . . . Nothing perhaps in the whole roll of dramatic poetry equals the tenderness given by Shakespeare to Brutus, that tenderness of a strong nature which the force of contrast renders so touching and so beautiful. —STAPFER, PAUL, 1880, *Shakespeare and Classical Antiquity, tr. Carey, pp.* 317, 342.

It is afternoon, a little before three o'clock. Whole fleets of wherries are crossing the Thames, picking their way among the swans and the other boats, to land their passengers on the south bank of the river. Skiff after skiff puts forth from the Blackfriars stair, full of theatregoers who have delayed a little too long over their dinner and are afraid of being too late; for the flag waving over the Globe Theatre announces that there is a play to-day. The bills upon the street-posts have informed the public that Shakespeare's "Julius Cæsar" is to be presented, and the play draws a full house. People pay their sixpences and enter; the balconies and the pit are filled. Distinguished and specially favoured spectators take their seats on the stage behind the curtain. Then sound the first, the second, and the third trumpet-blasts, the curtain parts in the middle, and reveals a stage entirely hung with black. Enter the tribunes Flavius and Marullus; they scold the rabble and drive them home because they are loafing about on a week-day without their working-clothes and tools—in contravention of a London police regulation which the public finds so natural that they (and the poet) can conceive it as in force in ancient Rome. At first the audience is somewhat restless. The groundlings talk in undertones as they light their pipes. But the Second Citizen speaks the name Cæsar. There are cries of "Hush! hush!" and the progress of the play is followed with eager attention. It was received with applause, and soon became very popular.—BRANDES, GEORGE, 1898, *William Shakespeare, A Critical Study, vol.* I, *p* 357.

Brutus is one of the noblest and most consistent of Shakespearian creations; a man far above all self-seeking and capable of the loftiest patriotism; in whose whole bearing, as in his deepest nature, virtue wears her noblest aspect. But Brutus is an idealist, with a touch of the doctrinaire; his purposes are of the highest, but the means he employs to give those purposes effect are utterly inadequate; in a lofty spirit he embarks on an enterprise doomed to failure by the very temper and pressure of the age. "Julius Cæsar" is the tragedy of the conflict between a great nature, denied the sense of reality, and the world-spirit. Brutus is not only crushed, but recognizes that there was no other issue of his untimely endeavour.—MABIE, HAMILTON WRIGHT, 1900, *William Shakespeare, Poet, Dramatist, and Man, p.* 298.

OTHELLO

1604

THE | Tragœdy of Othello, | The Moore of Venice. | *As it hath beene diuerse times acted at the* | Globe, and at | Black-Friers, by | his Maiesties Seruants. | Written by VVilliam Shakespeare. | LONDON. | Printed by N. O. for *Thomas Walkley*, and are to be sold at his | shop, at the Eagle and Child, in Brittans Bursse. | 1622.—TITLE PAGE OF FIRST EDITION, 1622.

To set forth a booke without an Epistle, were like to the old English prouerbe, A blew coat without a badge, & the Author being dead, I thought good to take that piece of worke upon mee: To commend it, I will not, for that which is good, I hope euery man will commend, without intreaty: and I am the bolder, because the author's name is sufficient to vent his worke. Thus leauing euery one to the liberty of iudgement: I haue ventered to print this play, and leaue it to the generall censure.—WALKLEY, THOMAS, 1622, *The Stationer to the Reader, First Quarto ed.*

August 20.—To Deptford by water, reading "Othello, Moore of Venice," which I ever heretofore esteemed a mighty good play, but having so lately read "The Adventures of Five Houres," it seems a mean thing.—PEPYS, SAMUEL, 1666, *Diary and Correspondence.*

Whatever rubs or difficulty may stick on the bark, the moral use of this fable is very instructive. First, this may be a caution to all maidens of quality, how, without their parents' consent, they run away with blackamoors. Secondly, this may be a warning to all good wives, that they look well to their linen. Thirdly, this may be a lesson to husbands, that before their jealousy be tragical, the proofs may be mathematical. . . . Whence comes it then, that this is the top scene; the scene that raises "Othello" above all other tragedies at our theatres? It is purely from the *action;* from the mops and the mows, the grimace, the grins, and gesticulation. Such scenes as this have made all the world run after Harlequin and Scaramoucio. The several degrees of *action* were amongst the ancients distinguished by the cothurnus, the soccus, and the planipes. Had this scene been represented at Old Rome, Othello and Iago must have quitted their buskins; they must have played *barefoot:* for the spectators would not have been content without seeing their podometry; and the jealousy work out at the very toes of them. . . . There is in this play some burlesk, some humour, and ramble of comical wit, some shew, and some *mimicry* to divert the spectators; but the tragical part is clearly none other than a bloody farce, without salt or savour.—RYMER, THOMAS, 1693, *A Short View of the Tragedy of the Last Age.*

He whose genious has unfolded to him the knowledge of man's nature and the force of his passions; has taught him the causes by which the soul is moved to strong emotions, or calmed to rest; has enabled him not only to explain in words those emotions, but to exhibit them vividly to other eyes; thus ruling, exciting, distracting, soothing our feelings,—this man, however little aided by the discipline of learning, is, in my judgment, a philosopher of the highest rank. In this manner, in a single dramatic fable of our own Shakespeare, the passion of jealousy, its causes, progress, incidents, and effects, have been more truly, more acutely, more copiously, and more impressively delineated than has been done by all the disquisitions of all the philosophers who have treated on this dark argument.—LOWTH, ROBERT, 1753–63, *Prœlectiones de Sacra Poesi Hebrœorum.*

Cassio is brave, benevolent and honest, ruined only by his want of stubbornness to resist an insidious invitation. Roderigo's suspicious credulity, and impatient submission to the cheats which he sees practiced upon him, and which by persuasion he suffers to be repeated, exhibit a strong picture of a weak mind betrayed by unlawful desires to a false friend; and the virtue of Emilia is such as we often find worn loosely, but not cast off, easy to commit small crimes, but quickened and alarmed at atrocious villanies.—JOHNSON, SAMUEL, 1868, *General Observations on Shakspeare's Plays.*

The best play upon the whole of Shakespear, and saying this it naturally follows that it is the best the world can produce. —DIBDIN, CHARLES, 1795, *A Complete History of the Stage, vol.* III, *p.* 349.

Two shall be named, pre-eminently dear,—
The gentle Lady married to the Moor;
And heavenly Una with her milk-white Lamb.

—WORDSWORTH, WILLIAM, 1806, *Sonnet.*

Desdemona has espoused Othello; she has chosen him, as he is, out of a thousand others more worthy of her; she has left all for him; to all appearance she loves him; Iago himself does not doubt it; hardly have they received the nuptial benediction before they are separated; Othello sets out with Cassio—observe, with Cassio; Desdemona also departs for Cyprus; by accident the two parties, who had left Venice at different times arrive in Cyprus the same day, within half an hour of one another. To the knowledge and in the sight of all, Othello included, Cassio, the companion of his voyage, has not been able to speak to Desdemona more than ten minutes on the public road. And yet on the afternoon of this same day, in the midst of the first transports of a union which has been for so long a time retarded, Iago takes upon himself to persuade the amorous Othello that Desdemona, the gentle Desdemona, has betrayed him, before even she has belonged to him—that she has delivered up her heart and her person—to whom?—to Cassio, who has been able neither to see her nor to converse with her. And Iago speaks of his passion as a thing already ancient, and yet—and yet as a thing posterior to her marriage with Othello; for he represents Cassio as exclaiming,

"Cursed fate, that gave thee to the Moor!"

and Iago speaks of Cassio's intrigue with innumerable details and interminable explanations. Which is the greatest simpleton, the man who conceives such a project, or the man who allows himself to be entrapped by it? . . . The author is himself successful: but why? Because, such is the intensity and vivacity of his original conception, that the most revolting improbabilities, the most inconceivable absurdities, pass by unperceived; because no one is so ungracious, no one has the time to notice the stratagems of the drama. It is, however, another thing to offer these absurdities to be admired as merits.—GUIZOT, FRANCOIS PIERRE GUILLAUME, 1821–52, *Shakspeare and His Times, pp.* 279, 280.

Othello must not be conceived as a negro, but a high and chivalrous Moorish chief. Shakspere learned the spirit of the character from the Spanish poetry, which was prevalent in England in his time. Jealousy does not strike me as the point in his passion; I take it to be rather an agony that the creature, whom he had believed angelic, with whom he had garnered up his heart, and whom he could not help still loving, should be proved impure and worthless. It was the struggle *not* to love her. It was a moral indignation and regret that virtue should so fall:—"But yet the *pity* of it, Iago!—O Iago! the *pity* of it, Iago!" In addition to this, his honour was concerned: Iago would not have succeeded but by hinting that his honour was compromised. There is no ferocity in Othello; his mind is majestic and composed He deliberately determines to die; and speaks his last speech with a view of showing his attachment to the Venetian state, though it had superseded him. Schiller has the material Sublime; to produce an effect, he sets you a whole town on fire, and throws infants with their mothers into the flames, or locks up a father in an old tower. But Shakspere drops a handkerchief, and the same or greater effects follow. Lear is the most tremendous effort of Shakspere as a poet; Hamlet as a philosopher or meditator; and Othello is the union of the two. There is something gigantic and unformed in the former two; but in the latter, everything assumes its due place and proportion, and the whole mature powers of his mind are displayed in admirable equilibrium.—COLERIDGE, SAMUEL TAYLOR, 1822, *Table Talk, Dec.* 29.

Nothing in poetry has ever been written more pathetic than the scene preceding Desdemona's death; I confess I almost always turn away my eyes from the poor girl with her infinitely touching song of "Willow, willow, willow," and I would fain ask the Poet whether his tragic arrow, which always hits the mark, does not here pierce almost too deeply. I would not call the last word with which she dies a lie, or even a "noble" lie; this qualification has been wretchedly misused. The lie with which Desdemona dies is divine truth, too good to come within the compass of an earthly moral code.—HORN, FRANZ, 1823, *Shakespeare's Schauspiele erlautert, vol.* II.

"Othello" is perhaps the greatest work in the world. From what does it derive its power. From the clouds? From the ocean? From the mountains? Or from love strong as death, and jealousy cruel as the grave?—MACAULAY, THOMAS BABINGTON, 1824, *Essay on Dante.*

Emilia in this play is a perfect portrait from common life, a masterpiece in the Flemish style; and though not necessary as a contrast, it cannot be but that the thorough vulgarity, the loose principles of this plebian woman, united to a high degree of spirit, energetic feeling, strong sense, and low cunning, serve to place in brighter relief the exquisite refinement, the moral grace, the unblemished truth, and the soft submission of Desdemona.—JAMESON, ANNA BROWNELL, 1832, *Characteristics of Shakespeare's Women.*

It would settle the dispute as to whether Shakespeare intended Othello for a jealous character, to consider how differently we are affected towards him, and for Leontes in the "Winter's Tale." Leontes *is* that character. Othello's fault was simply credulity.—LAMB, CHARLES, 1834, *Table-Talk.*

"Othello" has always appeared to me the most fearful of all Shakspeare's tragedies, but truly in the sense of the Greek—δειυσταυο. My sympathies are as much repelled as attracted by it. The emotions it excites resemble those with which we regard the men who, while they irresistibly attract us by the powers and splendour of their genius, alienate us no less forcibly by their character and disposition. As often as I read it a ferment of conflicting thoughts and feelings takes possession of my mind, and it is only slowly that this deep commotion gives place to that soothing and calm elevation, which, in all the other tragedies of our author, so quickly succeeds the more painful impression.—ULRICI, HERMANN, 1839, *Shakspeare's Dramatic Art, p.* 183.

Were Othello but the spirited portrait of a half-tamed barbarian, we should view him as a bold and happy poetical conception, and, as such, the poet's work might satisfy our critical judgment; but it is because it depicts a noble mind, wrought by deep passion and dark devices to agonies such as every one might feel, that it awakens our strongest sympathies. We see in this drama a grand and true moral picture; we read in it a profound ethical lesson; for (to borrow the just image of the classical Lowth) while the matchless work is built up to the noblest height of poetry, it rests upon the deepest foundations of true philosophy.—VERPLANCK, GULIAN CROMMELIN, 1844-47, *ed. The Illustrated Shakespeare.*

Now what is Othello? He is night. An immense fatal figure. Night is amorous of day. Darkness loves the dawn. The African adores the white woman. Desdemona is Othello's brightness and frenzy! And then how easy to him is jealousy! He is great, he is dignified, he is majestic, he soars above all heads, he has as an escort bravery, battle, the braying of trumpets, the banner of war, renown, glory; he is radiant with twenty victories, he is studded with stars, this Othello: but he is black. And thus how soon, when jealous, the hero becomes monster, the black becomes the negro! How speedily has night beckoned to death! By the side of Othello, who is night, there is Iago, who is evil. Evil, the other form of darkness. Night is but the night of the world; evil is the night of the soul. How deeply black are perfidy and falsehood! To have ink or treason in the veins is the same thing. Whoever has jostled against imposture and perjury knows it. One must blindly grope one's way with roguery. Pour hypocrisy upon the break of day, and you put out the sun, and this, thanks to false religions, happens to God. Iago near Othello is the precipice near the landslip. "This way!" he says in a low voice. The snare advises blindness. The being of darkness guides the black. Deceit takes upon itself to give what light may be required by night. Jealousy uses falsehood as the blind man his dog. Iago the traitor, opposed to whiteness and candour, Othello the negro, what can be more terrible! These ferocities of the darkness act in unision. These two incarnations of the eclipse comprise together, the one roaring, the other sneering, the tragic suffocation of light.—HUGO, VICTOR, 1864, *William Shakespeare, tr. Baillot, p.* 208.

Actors do not comprehend that Shakespeare's greatest villains, Iago among them, have always a touch of conscience. You see the conscience working—therein lies one of Shakespeare's pre-eminencies. Iago ought to be acted as the "honest Iago," not the stage villain; he is the essentially jealous man, not Othello.—TENNYSON, ALFRED, LORD, 1883, *Some Criticisms on Poets, Memoir by His Son, vol.* II, *p.* 292.

Thus, too, we see one of the fundamental rules of Shakespeare vindicated—that man cannot escape his own deed; hence Othello is the author of his own fate, since by his guilt he has called up the avenger who will destroy him and his family; while, without the view above developed, he must appear as an innocent sufferer deceived by a malicious villain. It will, therefore, be seen that two things of the greatest importance have their sole explanation in this view, namely, the manner of Iago's revenge, and his knowledge of the assailable point in Othello's character. Here also we find the solution of the Moor's contradictory nature. He is, in general, unsuspecting; but, on account of his guilt, he is capable of one suspicion, namely, that wives may be faithless. The poet has thus added to the distinction of race—for which the Moor could not be blamed—a second motive, the criminal deed, of which he must take the responsibility. The military life of Othello will furnish the third principle—that of honour, which will impel him to destroy the wife whom he thinks to have violated it in its deepest and most tender part.—SNIDER, DENTON JAQUES, 1887, *The Shakespearian Drama, The Tragedies, p.* 107.

Surpasses all the others in the strength of its dramatic effects, culminating in the third act, which is indeed, dramatically, the most thrilling act in all his writings. —TEN BRINK, BERNHARD, 1892–95, *Five Lectures on Shakespeare, tr. Franklin, p.* 86.

Simple-minded critics have been of opinion that Shakespeare constructed Iago on the lines of the historic Richard III.—that is to say, found him in literature, in the pages of a chronicler. Believe me, Shakespeare met Iago in his own life, saw portions and aspects of him on every hand throughout his manhood, encountered him piecemeal, as it were, on his daily path, till one fine day, when he thoroughly felt and understood what malignant cleverness and baseness can effect, he melted down all these fragments, and out of them cast this figure. Iago—there is more of the grand manner in this figure than in the whole of "Macbeth." Iago—there is more depth, more penetrating knowledge of human nature in this one character than in the whole of "Macbeth." Iago is the very embodiment of the grand manner. He is not the principle of evil, not an old-fashioned, stupid devil; nor a Miltonic devil, who loves independence and has invented firearms; nor a Goethe's Mephistopheles, who talks cynicism, makes himself indispensable, and is generally in the right. Neither has he the magnificently foolhardy wickedness of a Cæsar Borgia, who lives his life in open defiance and reckless atrocity. Iago has no other aim than his own advantage.—BRANDES, GEORGE, 1898, *William Shakespeare, A Critical Study, vol.* II, *p.* 108.

MACBETH
1605–6

January 7.—To the Duke's house, and saw "Macbeth," which, though I saw it lately, yet appears a most excellent play in all respects, but especially in divertisement, though it be a deep tragedy; which is a strange perfection in a tragedy, it being most proper here, and suitable.—PEPYS, SAMUEL, 1666–7, *Diary and Correspondence.*

This play is deservedly celebrated for the propriety of its fictions, and solemnity, grandeur, and variety of its action, but it has no nice discriminations of character; the events are too great to admit the influence of particular dispositions, and the course of the action necessarily determines the conduct of the agents. The danger of ambition is well described; and I know not whether it may not be said, in defence of some parts which now seem improbable, that, in Shakspeare's time it was necessary to warn credulity against vain and illusive predictions.—JOHNSON, SAMUEL, 1768, *General Observations on Shakspeare's Plays.*

Macbeth wants no disguise of his natural disposition, for it is not bad; he does not affect more piety than he has: on the contrary, a part of his distress arises from a real sense of religion: which makes him regret that he could not join the chamberlains in prayer for God's blessing, and bewail that he has "given his eternal jewel to the common enemy of man." He continually reproaches himself for his deeds; no use can harden him: confidence cannot silence, and even despair cannot stifle, the cries of his conscience. By the first murder he put "rancours in the vessel of his peace:" and of the last he owns to Macduff, "My soul is too much charg'd with blood of thine already."—WHATELY, THOMAS, 1785–1839, *Remarks on Some Characters of Shakespere, p.* 89.

Who could exhaust the praise of this sublime work? Since "The Furies" of Æschylus, nothing so grand and terrible has ever been composed. The Witches are not, it is true, divine Eumenides, and are not intended to be so: they are ignoble and vulgar instruments of hell. A German poet therefore very ill understood their meaning, when he transformed them into mongrel beings a mixture of fates, furies, and enchantresses, and clothed them with tragical dignity. Let no man lay hand on Shakspeare's works to change anything essential in them; he will be sure to punish himself.—SCHLEGEL, AUGUSTUS WILLIAM, 1809, *Dramatic Art and Literature, tr. Black, Lecture XII.*

Macbeth is said to have been the last King of Scotland here buried; sixty preceded him, all doubtless as powerful in their day, but now unknown—*carent quia vate sacro.* A few weeks' labour of Shakspeare, an obscure player, has done more for the memory of Macbeth than all the gifts, wealth, and monuments of this cemetery of princes have been able to secure to the rest of its inhabitants.—SCOTT, SIR WALTER, 1814, *Iona, Diary, 28th August.*

"Macbeth" (generally speaking) is done upon a stronger and more systematic principle of contrast than any other of Shakespear's plays. It moves upon the verge of an abyss, and is a constant struggle between life and death. The action is desperate and the reaction is dreadful. It is a huddling together of fierce extremes, a war of opposite natures which of them shall destroy the other. There is nothing but what has a violent end or violent beginnings. The lights and shades are laid on with a determined hand; the transitions from triumph to despair, from the height of terror to the repose of death, are sudden and startling; every passion brings in its fellow-contrary, and the thoughts pitch and jostle against each other as in the dark. The whole play is an unruly chaos of strange and forbidden things, where the ground rocks under our feet. Shakespear's genius here took its full swing, and trod upon the farthest bounds of nature and passion. This circumstance will account for the abruptness and violent antitheses of the style, the throes and labour which run through the expression, and from defects will turn them into beauties.—HAZLITT, WILLIAM, 1817–69, *Characters of Shakespear's Plays, p.* 17.

How admirably Macduff's grief is in harmony with the whole play! It rends, not dissolves, the heart. "The tune of it goes manly." Thus is Shakspere always master of himself and of his subject,—a genuine Proteus:—we see all things in him, as images in a calm lake, most distinct, most accurate—only more splendid, more glorified. This is correctness in the only philosophical sense. But he requires your sympathy and your submission; you must have that recipiency of moral impression without which the purposes and ends of the drama would be frustrated, and the absence of which demonstrates an utter want of all imagination, a deadness to that necessary pleasure of being innocently—shall I say, deluded?—or rather, drawn away from ourselves to the music of noblest thought in harmonious sounds. Happy he, who not only in the public theatre, but in the labours of a profession, and round the light of his own hearth, still carries a heart so pleasure-fraught! —COLERIDGE, SAMUEL TAYLOR, 1818, *Lectures and Notes on Shakspere, ed. Ashe, p.* 379.

From my boyish days I had always felt a great perplexity on one point in "Macbeth." It was this:—The knocking at the gate which succeeds to the murder of Duncan produced to my feelings an effect for which I never could account. The effect was that it reflected back upon the murder a peculiar awfulness and a depth of solemnity; yet, however obstinately I endeavored with my understanding to comprehend this, for many years I never could see *why* it should produce such an effect. . . . At length I solved it to my own satisfaction; and my solution is this:—Murder, in ordinary cases, where the sympathy is wholly directed to the case of the murdered person, is an incident of coarse and vulgar horror; and for this reason,—that it flings the interest exclusively upon the natural but ignoble instinct by which we cleave to life: an instinct which, as being indispensable to the primal law of self-preservation, is the same in kind (though different in degree) amongst all living creatures. This instinct, therefore, because it annihilates all distinctions, and degrades the greatest of men to the level of the "poor beetle that we tread on," exhibits human nature in its most abject and humiliating attitude. Such an attitude would little suit the purposes of the poet. What then must he do? He must throw the interest on the murderer. Our sympathy must be with *him* (of course I mean a sypmathy of comprehension, a sympathy by which we enter into his feelings, and are made to understand them,—not a sympathy of pity or approbation). In the murdered person, all strife of thought, all flux and reflux of passion and of purpose, are crushed by one overwhelming panic; the fear of instant death smites him "with its petrific mace." But in the murderer, such a murderer as a poet will condescend to, there must be raging some great storm of passion, —jealousy, ambition, vengeance, hatred, —which will create a hell within him; and into this hell we are to look.—DE QUINCEY, THOMAS, 1823-60, *On the Knocking at the Gate in Macbeth, Collected Writings, ed. Masson, vol.* X, *pp.* 385, 391.

"'Macbeth,' said Goethe, "Is Shakespeare's best acting play, the one in which he shows most understanding with respect to the stage."—ECKERMANN, JOHN PETER, 1825, *Conversations of Goethe, Oct.* 15.

It was my custom to study my characters at night, when all the domestic cares and business of the day were over. On the night preceding that in which I was to appear in this part for the first time, I shut myself up, as usual, when all the family were retired, and commenced my study of Lady Macbeth. As the character is very short, I thought I should soon accomplish it. Being then only twenty years of age, I believed, as many others do believe, that little more was necessary than to get the words into my head; for the necessity of discrimination, and the development of character, at that time of my life, had scarcely entered into my imagination. But to proceed. I went on with tolerable composure, in the silence of the night (a night I can never forget), till I came to the assassination scene, when the horrors of the scene rose to a degree that made it impossible for me to get farther. I snatched up my candle, and hurried out of the room, in a paroxysm of terror. My dress was of silk, and the rustling of it, as I ascended the stairs to go to bed, seemed to my panic-struck fancy like the movement of a spectre pursuing me. At last I reached my chamber, where I found my husband fast asleep. I clapped my candlestick down upon the table, without the power of putting the candle out; and threw myself on my bed, without daring to stay even to take off my clothes. At peep of day I rose to resume my task; but so little did I know of my part when I appeared in it at night, that my shame and confusion cured me of procrastinating my business for the remainder of my life.—SIDDONS, SARAH, 1831? *Remarks on the Character of Lady Macbeth, Life of Mrs. Siddons by Campbell, vol.* II, *p.* 35.

In the mind of Lady Macbeth, ambition is represented as the ruling motive, an intense overmastering passion, which is gratified at the expense of every just and generous principle, and every feminine feeling. In the pursuit of her object, she is cruel, treacherous, and daring. She is doubly, trebly dyed in guilt and blood; for the murder she instigates is rendered more frightful by disloyalty and ingratitude, and by the violation of all the most sacred claims of kindred and hospitality. When her husband's more kindly nature shrinks from the perpetration of the deed of horror, she, like an evil genius, whispers him on to his damnation. The full measure of her wickedness is never disguised, the magnitude and atrocity of her crime is never extenuated, forgotten, or forgiven, in the whole course of the play. . . . Lady Macbeth's amazing power of intellect, her inexorable determination of purpose, her superhuman strength of nerve, render her as fearful in herself as her deeds are hateful; yet she is not a mere monster of depravity, with whom we have nothing in common, nor a meteor whose destroying path we watch in ignorant affright and amaze. She is a terrible impersonation of evil passions and mighty powers, never so far removed from our nature as to be cast beyond the pale of our sympathies; for the woman herself remains a woman to the last — still linked with her sex and with humanity.—JAMESON, ANNA BROWNELL, 1832, *Characteristics of Women.*

I regard the tragedy of "Macbeth," upon the whole, as the greatest treasure of our dramatic literature. We may look, as Britons, at Greek sculpture and at Italian paintings, with a humble consciousness that our native art has never reached their perfection; but, in the drama, we can confront Æschylus himself with Shakespeare; and of all modern theatres, *ours* alone can compete with the Greek in the unborrowed nativeness and sublimity of its superstition. In the grandeur of tragedy, "Macbeth" has no parallel, till we go back to the "Prometheus and the Furies" of the Attic stage. I could even produce, if it were not digressing too far from my subject, innumerable instances of striking similarity between the metaphorical mintage of Shakespeare's and of Æschylus's style,—a similarity, both in beauty and the fault of excess, that, unless the contrary had been proved, would lead me to suspect our great dramatist to have been a studious Greek scholar. But their resemblance arose only from the consanguinity of nature.—CAMPBELL, THOMAS, 1834, *Life of Mrs. Siddons, vol.* II, *p.* 6.

Kemble styles this the noblest of tragedies, and it is natural that he should prefer it to all others of Shakspeare, because, assuredly of the historical plays, and perhaps of all the plays, Othello alone excepted, it is the finest in representation. To read, I own that it is, in my opinion, inferior to some others, from the absence of the splendid and stately speeches which I have noticed in former plays.—COURTENAY, THOMAS PEREGRINE, 1840, *Commentaries on the Historical Plays of Shakspeare, vol.* II, *p.* 208.

This play has more the air of being a draft, if not unfinished, yet requiring to be retouched and written more in full by its author, than any other of his greater works. Full of incident as it is, it is still one of the shortest of the plays. Like "The Tempest" in this respect, we feel that it would be better if it were longer. We want more of the subdued and calm. There are also more passages than in other plays which seem to be carried beyond the just limits which part the true sublime from the inflated or the obscure,—passages which we may suppose to have been in the mind of Johnson when he said of the soaring genius of Shakespeare, "*sufflaminandus est.*" What might not "Macbeth" have been had the Poet been induced to sit down with the play, as it now is, before him, and to direct upon it the full force of his judgment and fine taste, removing here and there a too luxuriant expression, and giving us here and there a breadth of verdure on which the mind might find a momentary repose, and refresh itself amidst the multitude of exciting incidents which come in too rapid a succession upon us!—HUNTER, JOSEPH, 1845, *New Illustrations of the Life, Studies and Writings of Shakespeare, vol.* II, *p.* 158.

'Macbeth" seems inspired by the very genius of the tempest. This drama shows us the gathering, the discharge, and the dispelling of a domestic and political storm, which takes its peculiar hue from the individual character of the hero. It is not in the spirit of mischief that animates the "weird sisters," nor in the passionate and strong-willed ambition of Lady Macbeth, that we find the mainspring of this tragedy, but in the disproportioned though poetically tempered soul of Macbeth himself. A character like this, of extreme selfishness, with a most irritable fancy, must produce, even in ordinary circumstances, an excess of morbid apprehensiveness; which, however, as we see in him, is not inconsistent with the greatest physical courage, but generates of necessity the most entire moral cowardice. When, therefore, a man like this, ill enough qualified even for the honest and straight-forward transactions of life, had brought himself to snatch at an ambitious object by the commission of one great sanguinary crime, the new and false position in which he finds himself by his very success will but startle and exasperate him to escape, as Macbeth says, from "horrible imaginings" by the perpetration of greater and greater actual horrors, till inevitable destruction comes upon us amidst universal execration.—FLETCHER, GEORGE, 1847, *Studies of Shakespeare, p.* 109.

"Macbeth," the most awful creation of the poetic mind, is a study every way worthy of those to whom the storms of passion present the frequent cause of mental disease.—BUCKNILL, JOHN CHARLES, M. D., 1859-67, *The Mad Folk of Shakespeare, p.* 1.

It is, in fact, a powerful psychological study. Shakespeare depicts a state of mind not only novel, but highly dramatic. He has given us hardened villains, before, in his other pieces. But here he unveils the process by which the thought of crime penetrates a virtuous soul, the destruction it causes as soon as it gains lodgement there, and to what extremites it drags him who has not had strength enough to repel on its first appearance. Macbeth is not wicked like Iago, or Edmund in "Lear." He even begins well. He has defended his country and his king most zealously, and covered himself with glory on two battle-fields. His comrades in arms accord him ungrudging praise, and Duncan knows not how to recompense his deserts. But this brave soldier bears within him the germ of ambition; and, without as yet knowing the height of his aspirations, without even defining to himself his vague desires, he awakes to a simultaneous consciousness of his own power and the temptation to make trial of it.—MÉZIÈRES, A., 1860, *Shakespeare, ses Œuvres et ses Critiques.*

As regards wealth of thougth, "Macbeth" ranks far below "Hamlet;" it lacks the wide, free, historic perfection which in "Julius Cæsar" raises us above the horror of his tragic fall. It cannot be compared with "Othello" for completeness, depth of plot, or full, rich illustration of character. But, in our opinion, it excels all that Shakspeare, or any other poet, has created, in the simple force of the harmonious, majestic current of its action, in the transparency of its plan, in the nervous power and bold sweep of its language, and in its prodigal wealth of poetical coloring.—KREYSSIG, F., 1862, *Vorlesungen über Shakspeare, vol.* II, *p.* 346.

It is the prospective and retrospective representation of Macbeth's remorse that constitutes the element of horror in the play. Almost as much pity is felt for the murderer as for his victim. The true title of the tragedy might be, crime, remorse, and expiation. Lady Macbeth alone appears to stand outside of the pale of morality, but her life ends before the expiatory death of her husband, whose daring villainy, incapable of plotting or of enduring the crime, is unable to submit to its punishment. All the great crimes in Shakespeare are inspired by wicked women; men may execute, but cannot conceive them. The creature of sentiment is more depraved than the man of crime. The imagination of woman dallies more easily with crime than the hand of man is raised against his victim. We feel that in committing the murder Macbeth succumbed to a strength of depravity superior to his own. This strength of depravity is the ardent imagination of his wife. . . . Such is "Macbeth!" It is Crime! It is Remorse! It is the weakness of a strong man opposed to the seductions of a perverted and passionate woman! Above all, it is the immediate expiation of crime by the secret vengeance of God! Herein lies the invincible morality of Shakespeare. The Poet is in harmony with God.—LAMARTINE, ALPHONSE MARIE LOUIS DE, 1865, *Shakespeare et son Œuvre.*

The popular misunderstanding of the character of Macbeth is due, probably, to the description his wife gives of him in the first interview we have with her. . . . "Yet do I fear thy nature," etc. But it is obvious that so far as we see Macbeth in the play, nothing could be wider of the mark than this estimate of him. . . . For nothing can be farther from the truth than the popular view of Lady Macbeth. That wonderful characteristic of genius, which enables it to put on the character it conceives, reaches its highest manifestation in this marvellous portrait. . . . But all the truth and force of the delineation are lost when Lady Macbeth is regarded as a mere tempter and fiend. She is, in reality, nothing of the kind. Her part is simply that of a woman and a wife who shares her husband's ambition and supports him in it. So far from suggesting his crimes, she distinctly declares that he broke the enterprise to her. . . . We have seen that, before he saw his wife, Macbeth had made up his mind to this first step in his career of crime. All that she does is to back him in the execution of his own design.—CLAYDEN, P. W., 1867, *Macbeth and Lady Macbeth, Fortnightly Review, vol.* 8, *pp.* 163, 164.

The history of Macbeth is the story of a moral poisoning. Frank, sociable, and generous, though tainted from the first by base and ambitious thoughts, he is urged on to his ruin by the prophetic warnings of the witches, by golden opportunity, and the instigations of his wife. He has physical but lacks moral courage. The suggestion of a possible crown haunts him. He struggles, but he is a lion in the toils. He feels the resistless traction of fate, sees himself on the verge of an abyss, and his brain is filled with phantoms.—WELSH, ALFRED H., 1882, *Development of English Literature and Language, vol.* I, *p.* 384.

Macbeth is not, as is too often represented, a noisy swash-buckler; he is a full-furnished, ambitious man. In the scene with Duncan, the excess of courtesy adds a touch to the tragedy. It is like Clytemnestra's profusion to Agamemnon; who, by the way, always strikes me as uncommonly cold and haughty to his wife whom he had not seen for years.—TENNYSON, ALFRED, LORD, 1883, *Some Criticisms on Poets, Memoir by His Son, vol.* II, *p.* 292.

She would never have been the Lady Macbeth we see in Shakespeare's play if she had not been led to it by love for her husband, by her ambition in his interest. Her crime is not innate cruelty, but hardness of heart and unwomanly energy, though the former is even not strong enough to withhold her from tender feelings; and with a different husband she would have been a different wife.—LEO, F. A., 1885, *Shakespeare-Notes, p.* 68.

Stands alone by its grand simplicity of conception and the originality of its execution, giving us in a few bold strokes a consummate picture of the strange workings of a human soul.—TEN BRINK, BERNHARD, 1892–95, *Five Lectures on Shakespeare, tr. Franklin, p.* 87

I confess that this play seems to me one of Shakespeare's less interesting efforts; not from the artistic, but from the purely human point of view. It is a rich, highly moral melodrama; but only at occasional points in it do I feel the beating of Shakespeare's heart. My comparative coolness of feeling towards "Macbeth" may possibly be due in a considerable degree to the shamefully mutilated form in which this tragedy has been handed down to us. Who knows what it may have been when it came from Shakespeare's own hand! The text we possess, which was not printed till long after the poet's death, is clipped, pruned, and compressed for acting purposes. We can feel distinctly where the gaps occur, but that is of no avail. . . . Shakespeare has employed in the treatment of this subject a style that suits it—vehement to violence, compressed to congestion—figures treading upon each other's heels. —BRANDES, GEORGE, 1898, *William Shakespeare, A Critical Study, vol.* II, *pp.* 99, 101.

KING LEAR

1605–6

M. William Shak-speare: | HIS | True Chronicle Historie of the life | and death of King LEAR and his three | Daughters. | *With the vnfortunate life of* Edgar, *sonne* | and heire to the Earle of Gloster, and his | sullen and assumed humor of | Tom of Bedlam: | *As it was played before the Kings Maiestie at Whitehall vpon* | S. Stephans *night in Christmas Hollidayes.* | By his Maiesties seruants playing vsually at the Gloabe | on the Bancke-side. | LONDON. | Printed for *Nathaniel Butter*, and are to be sold at his shop in *Pauls* | Church-yard at the signe of the Pide Bull neere | S[t] *Austins* Gate. 1608.—TITLE PAGE OF FIRST EDITION, 1608.

Nothing but the Power of your Perswasion, and my Zeal for all the Remains of *Shakespear*, cou'd have wrought me to so bold an Undertaking. I found that the New-modelling of this Story, wou'd force me sometimes on the difficult Task of making the chiefest Persons speak something like their Character, on Matter whereof I had no Ground in my Author. *Lear's* real and *Edgar's* pretended Madness have so much of *extravagant Nature* (I know not how else to express it) as cou'd never have started but from our *Shakespear's* Creating Fancy. The Images and Language are so odd and surprizing, and yet so agreeable and proper, that whilst we grant that none but *Shakespear* cou'd have form'd such Conceptions; yet we are satisfied that they were the only Things in the World that ought to be said on those Occasions.—TATE, NAHUM, 1681, *The History of King Lear, Dedication.*

"King Lear" is an admirable tragedy . . . . as Shakespeare wrote it; but as it is reformed according to the chimerical notion of poetical justice, in my humble opinion it has lost half its beauty.—ADDISON, JOSEPH, 1711, *The Spectator, No.* 40, *April* 16.

Lear does not run mad till the third Act; yet his behaviour towards Cordelia in the first scene has all the appearance of a judgement totally depraved. . . . Lear banishes (Cordelia) his sight, consigns her over to want, and loads her with the deepest imprecations. What less than Phrenzy can inspire a rage so groundless, and a conduct so absurd? Lear, while in his senses, acts like a madman, and from his first appearance to his last seems to be wholly deprived of his reason. — LENNOX, CHARLOTTE, 1753-4, *Shakespear Illustrated, vol.* III, *p.* 287.

Can pity be more beautifully awakened than in the sufferings of the loyal and venerable Gloster, the miseries unnaturally inflicted on the tender, credulous, choleric, but noble Lear, or the unavailing filial piety of the angelic Cordelia? Can terror be more tremendously roused than by the wickedness of Goneril and Regan, or the blind adoption of Edmund by Gloster? Can delight be more legitimately gratified than by the conquest of struggling virtue over inordinate vice?—DIBDIN, CHARLES, 1795, *A Complete History of the Stage, vol.* III, *p.* 321.

We have here a plentiful crop of blunders. Kent talks, like a good Protestant, of *eating no fish;* and Gloster, of not standing in need of *spectacles.* We have *Turks, Bedlam* beggars, *child Roland, Saint Withold,* a *Marshal of France, steeples, dollars, paper, holy water,* and the *French disease.* There is an allusion to the old theatrical *moralities;* and *Nero,* who did not live till several hundred years after Lear, is mentioned by Edgar as an angler in the lake of darkness. — DOUCE, FRANCIS, 1807, *Illustrations of Shakspeare, vol.* II, *p.* 295.

Were Lear alone to suffer from his daughters, the impression would be limited to the powerful compassion felt by us for his private misfortune. But two such unheard of examples taking place at the same time have the appearance of a great commotion in the moral world: the picture becomes gigantic, and fills us with such alarm as we should entertain at the idea that the heavenly bodies might one day fall out of their regular orbits.—SCHLEGEL, AUGUSTUS WILLIAM, 1809, *Dramatic Art and Literature, tr. Black, Lecture XII.*

So to see Lear acted,—to see an old man tottering about the stage with a walking-stick, turned out of doors by his daughters in a rainy night, has nothing in it but what is painful and disgusting. We want to take him into shelter and relieve him. That is all the feeling which the acting of Lear ever produced in me. But the Lear of Shakespeare cannot be acted. The contemptible machinery by which they mimic the storm which he goes out in, is not more inadequate to represent the horrors of the real elements, than any actor can be to represent Lear; they might more easily propose to personate the Satan of Milton upon a stage, or one of Michael Angelo's terrible figures. The greatness of Lear is not in corporal dimension, but in intellectual: the explosions of passion are terrible as a volcano: they are storms turning up and disclosing to the bottom that sea his mind, with all its vast riches. It is his mind which is laid bare. This case of flesh and blood seems too insignificant to be thought on; even as he himself neglects it. On the stage we see nothing but corporal infirmities and weakness, the impotence of rage; while we read it, we see not Lear, but we are Lear, — we are in his mind, we are sustained by a grandeur which baffles the malice of daughters and storms; in the aberrations of his reason, we discover a mighty irregular power of reasoning, immethodized from the ordinary purposes of life, but exerting its powers, as the wind blows where it listeth, at will upon the corruptions and abuses of mankind.—LAMB, CHARLES, 1810? *On The Tragedies of Shakespeare.*

It is then the best of all Shakespear's plays, for it is the one in which he was the most in earnest. He was here fairly caught in the web of his own imagination. The passion which he has taken as his subject is that which strikes its root deepest into the human heart, of which the bond is the hardest to be unloosed; and the cancelling and tearing to pieces of which gives the greatest revulsion to the frame. This depth of nature, this force of passion, this tug and war of the elements of our being, this firm faith in filial piety, and the giddy anarchy and whirling tumult of the thoughts at finding this prop failing it, the contrast between the fixed, immoveable basis of natural affection, and the rapid, irregular starts of imagination, suddenly wrenched from all its accustomed holds and resting-places in the soul, this is what Shakespear has given, and what nobody else but he could give.—HAZLITT, WILLIAM, 1817-69, *Characters of Shakespear's Plays, p.* 108.

Of all Shakspere's plays "Macbeth" is the most rapid, "Hamlet" the slowest, in movement. "Lear" combines length with rapidity,—like the hurricane and the whirlpool, absorbing while it advances.

It begins as a stormy day in summer, with brightness; but that brightness is lurid, and anticipates the tempest.—COLERIDGE, SAMUEL TAYLOR, 1818, *Lectures and Notes on Shakspere, ed. Ashe, p.* 329.

The modern practice of blending comedy with tragedy, though liable to great abuse in point of practice, is undoubtedly an extension of the dramatic circle; but the comedy should be as in "King Lear," universal, ideal, and sublime. It is perhaps the intervention of this principle which determines the balance in favour of "King Lear" against "Œdipus Tyrannus" or the "Agamemnon," or, if you will, the trilogies with which they are connected; unless the intense power of the choral poetry, especially that of the latter, should be considered as restoring the equilibrium. "King Lear," if it can sustain this comparison, may be judged to be the most perfect specimen of the dramatic art existing in the world; in spite of the narrow conditions to which the poet was subjected by the ignorance of the philosophy of the drama which has prevailed in modern Europe. — SHELLEY, PERCY BYSSHE, 1822? *A Defence of Poetry, Works, ed. Forman, vol.* III, *p.* 114.

There is in the beauty of Cordelia's character an effect too sacred for words, and almost too deep for tears; within her heart is a fathomless well of purest affection, but its waters sleep in silence and obscurity,—never failing in their depth and never overflowing in their fulness. Every thing in her seems to lie beyond our view, and affects us in a manner which we feel rather than perceive. The character appears to have no surface, no salient points upon which the fancy can readily seize: there is little external development of intellect, less of passion, and still less of imagination. It is completely made out in the course of a few scenes, and we are surprised to find that in those few scenes there is a matter for a life of reflection, and materials enough for twenty heroines. If "Lear" be the grandest of Shakspeare's tragedies, Cordelia in herself, as a human being, governed by the purest and holiest impulses and motives, the most refined from all dross of selfishness and passion, approaches near to prefection; and in her adaptation, as a dramatic personage, to a determinate plan of action, may be pronounced altogether perfect. The character, to speak of it critically as a poetical conception, is not, however, to be comprehended at once, or easily; and in the same manner Cordelia, as a woman, is one whom we must have loved before we could have known her, and known her long before we could have known her truly.—JAMESON, ANNA BROWNELL, 1832, *Characteristics of Women.*

What "Lear" has in common with "Othello" is the soul of the Poet, dark, melancholy, deeply wounded, well-nigh shattered by the world; only here, in "Lear," still more than in "Othello," has he concentrated in his work, painted in burning colors, all the bitterness which the depravity of human nature must generate in a sensitive heart.—RAPP, MORITZ, 1843, *Shakspere's Schauspiele, Einleitung, p.* 7.

Lear's is a genuine case of insanity from the beginning to the end; such as we often see in aged persons. On reading it we cannot divest ourselves of the idea that it is a real case of insanity correctly reported. Still, we apprehend, the play, or *case*, is generally misunderstood. The general belief is, that the insanity of Lear originated solely from the ill-treatment of his daughters, while in truth he was insane before that, from the beginning of the play, when he gave his kingdom away, and banished, as it were, Cordelia and Kent, and abused his servants. The ill-usage of his daughters only aggravated the disease, and drove him to raving madness. Had it been otherwise, the case, as one of insanity, would have been inconsistent and very unusual.—BRIGHAM, A., M. D., 1844, *Shakespeare's Illustrations of Insanity, American Journal of Insanity, July.*

Goethe has pronounced the first scene absurd. More recent criticism, certainly in view of that judgment harsh, but not without reason, has defended it as unobjectionable, but yet hardly with a convincing, decisive result. . . . It appears to me that Shakespeare here, in giving motive and a dramatic form to the legend, is lacking in his usual care. This want is assuredly considerably alleviated by the excellent elucidations of the scenes that follow. But the satisfaction subsequently afforded to the understanding cannot be any compensation to us if the imagination has previously had just reason to be offended.—KREYSSIG, F., 1862, *Vorlesungen über Shakespeare, vol.* II, *p.* 316.

In "King Lear," with its ever-thickening gloom and deepening sorrows, we see the tragic fate which, as the world of man is constituted, too often waits on folly no less than on guilt, and involves the innocent alike with the guilty in the train of terrible consequences.—ARNOLD, THOMAS, 1862-87, *A Manual of English Literature, American ed., p.* 109.

"King Lear" is, indeed, the greatest single achievement in poetry of the Teutonic, or Northern, genius. By its largeness of conception and the variety of its details, by its revelation of a harmony existing between the forces of nature and the passions of man, by its grotesqueness and its sublimity, its own kinship with the great cathedrals of Gothic architecture. To conceive, to compass, to comprehend, at once in its stupendous unity and in its almost endless variety, a building like the cathedral of Rheims, or that of Cologne, is a feat which might seem to defy the most athletic imagination. But the impression which Shakspere's tragedy produces, while equally large — almost monstrous — and equally intricate, lacks the material fixity and determinateness of that produced by these great works in stone. Everything in the tragedy is in motion, and the motion is that of a tempest. — DOWDEN, EDWARD, 1875-80, *Shakspere, A Critical Study of His Mind and Art, p.* 229.

"King Lear" deals especially with the natural man as opposed to the artificial man. When the King saw Edgar, then a Tom o' Bedlam, in the great storm scene, he exclaims—"Is man no more than this? Consider him well. Thou owest the worm no silk, the beast no hide, the sheep no wool, the cat no perfume. Ha! here's three on 's (himself, the Fool, Kent) are sophisticated! Thou art the thing itself: unaccomodated man is no more but such a poor, bare, forked animal as thou art. Off, off, you lendings! Come; unbutton here." And he tears his clothes off him. And this bare-stripped figure, in that awful scene, may serve as an image of the society the play represents. It is a society with all its disguises torn off. The passions walk abroad, bold and confident. Greed lifts up its head unabashed; Lust scorns all holy ties; Wrath rages like a tempest. A fearful earth, indeed, if given over to such accursed powers! But it is not so. There is also the passion of Love, and throughout the play love is performing its secret ministry. Good and evil close in a fierce struggle, as always where there is life, and not mere death; and in the end good prevails, as in the end it must prevail: for evil has not only good to encounter, but it has to fight with itself: it is essentially self-consuming. So that in this play we have presented to us humanity in its purest and simplest elements — humanity unsophisticated, denuded of all its "lendings," with its natural impulses all unchecked and potent.—HALES, JOHN W., 1875-84, *Notes and Essays on Shakespeare, p.* 252.

Cordelia is as the sun above the deeps of hell shown in Goneril and Regan. One can hardly help wishing that Shakspere had followed the old story told by Layamon and other repeaters of Geoffrey of Monmouth, and made Cordelia set her father on the throne again, and reign after him for a while in peace. But the tragedian, the preacher of Shakspere's Third-Period lesson, did wisely for his art and meaning in letting the daughter and father lie in one grave.—FURNIVALL, FREDERICK JAMES, 1877, *ed. The Leopold Shakspere, Introduction to the Play.*

Of all Shakespeare's plays, "King Lear" is unquestionably that in which he has come nearest to the height and to the likeness of the one tragic poet on any side greater than himself whom the world in all its ages has ever seen born of time. It is by far the most Æschylean of his works; the most elemental and primæval, the most oceanic and Titanic in conception. He deals here with no subtleties as in "Hamlet," with no conventions as in "Othello:" there is no question of "a divided duty" or a problem half insoluble, a matter of country and connection, of family or of race; we look upward and downward, and in vain, into the deepest things of nature, into the highest things of providence; to the roots of life, and to the stars; from the roots that no God waters to the stars which give no man light; over a world full of death and life without resting-place or guidance.—SWINBURNE, ALGERNON CHARLES, 1880, *A Study of Shakespeare, p.* 170.

"King Lear" cannot possibly be acted, it is too titanic. At the beginning of the play Lear, in his old age, has grown half mad, choleric and despotic, and therefore cannot brook Cordelia's silence. This play shows a state of society where men's passions are savage and uncurbed. No play like this anywhere — not even the "Agamemnon"—is so terrifically human. —TENNYSON, ALFRED, LORD, 1883, *Some Criticisms on Poets, Memoir by His Son, vol.* II, *p.* 292.

It is in "King Lear" that the poet attains the summit of his tragic powers. . . . Higher than in "Lear" Shakespeare could not rise.—TEN BRINK, BERNHARD, 1892–95, *Five Lectures on Shakespeare, tr. Franklin, p.* 87.

"Lear" is the greatest problem Shakespeare had yet proposed to himself, all the agonies and horrors of the world compressed into five short acts. The impression of "Lear" may be summed up in the words: a world-catastrophe. Shakespeare is no longer minded to depict anything else. What is echoing in his ears, what is filling his mind, is the crash of a ruining world. — BRANDES, GEORGE, 1898, *William Shakespeare, A Critical Study, vol.* I, *p.* 283.

TROILUS AND CRESSIDA
1606–7

The | Famous Historie of | Troylus *and* Cresseid. | *Excellently expressing the beginning* | of their loues, with the conceited wooing | of *Pandarus* Prince of *Licia.* | *Written by* William Shakespeare. | LONDON | Imprinted by *G. Eld* for *R. Bonian* and *H. Walley*, and | are to be sold at the spred Eagle in Paules | Church-yeard, ouer against the | great North doore, | 1609. — TITLE PAGE OF FIRST EDITION, 1609.

A NEVER WRITER TO AN EVER READER. NEWS. Eternal reader, you have here a new play, never staled with the stage, never clapper-clawed with the palms of the vulgar, and yet passing full of the palm comical; for it is a birth of your brain, that never undertook anything comical vainly; and were but the vain names of comedies changed for the titles of commodities, or of plays for pleas, you should see all those grand censors, that now style them such vanities, flock to them for the main grace of their gravities; especially this author's comedies, that are so framed to the life, that they serve for the most common commentaries of all the actions of our lives, showing such a dexterity and power of wit, that the most displeased with plays are pleased with his comedies. . . . Amongst all there is none more witty than this: and had I time I would comment upon it, though I know it needs not (for so much as will make you think your testern well bestowed), but for so much worth as even poor I know to be stuffed in it. It deserves such a labour, as well as the best comedy in Terence or Plautus. And believe this, that when he is gone, and his comedies out of sale, you will scramble for them, and set up a new English Inquisition. Take this for a warning, and at the peril of your pleasures' loss and judgments, refuse not, nor like this the less for not being sullied with the smoky breath of the multitude; but thank fortune for the scape it hath made amongst you, since by the grand possessors' wills I believe you should have prayed for them rather than been prayed. And so I leave all such to be prayed for (for the states of their wit's healths) that will not praise it. Vale.—PREFACE TO FIRST EDITION, 1609.

Troy. Come, Cressida, my cresset light,
Thy face doth shine both day and night,
Behold, behold *thy garter blue*
Thy knight his valiant elbow wears,
That when he SHAKES his furious SPEARE,
The foe, in shivering fearful sort,
May lay him down in death to snort.
Cress. O knight, with valour in thy face,
Here *take my skreene*, wear it for grace;
Within thy helmet put the same,
Therewith to make thy enemies lame.
—ANON, 1603, *Histriomastix.*

The Poet Æschylus was held in the same veneration by the Athenians of after Ages as Shakespear is by us; . . . though the difficulties of altering are greater, and our reverence for Shakespear much more just, than that of the Grecians for Æschylus. . . . Yet it must be allowed to the present age, that the tongue in general is so much refined since Shakespear's time, that many of his words, and more of his phrases, are scarce intelligible. And of those which we understand, some are ungrammatical, others coarse; and his whole stile is so pestered with figurative expressions, that it is as affocted as it is obscure. It is true, that in his latter plays he had worn off somewhat of the rust; but the tragedy, which I have undertaken to correct, was in all probability one of his first endeavours on the stage. . . . Shakespeare (as I hinted), in the apprenticeship of his writing, modeled it into that play, which is now called by the name of "Troilus and Cressida;" but so lamely is it left to us, that it is not divided into acts; which fault I ascribe to the actors who printed it after Shakespear's death; and that too so carelesly, that a more uncorrect copy I never saw. For the play itself, the author seems to have begun it with some fire; the characters of Pandarus and Thersites are promising enough; but as if he grew weary of his task, after an entrance or two, he lets them fall: and the latter part of the tragedy is nothing but a confusion of drums and trumpets, excursions and alarms. The chief persons, who give name to the tragedy, are left alive: Cressida is false, and is not punished. Yet, after all, because the play was Shakespear's, and that there appeared in some places of it the admirable genius of the author, I undertook to remove that heap of rubbish under which many excellent thoughts lay wholly buried.—DRYDEN, JOHN, 1679, *Troilus and Cressida, Preface, Works, ed. Scott and Saintsbury, vol.* VI, *pp.* 254, 255.

This play, though miserably lame in its plan, has lines in which all the genius of Shakspeare burns out.—CARY, HENRY FRANCIS, 1797, *Memoirs, vol.* I, *p.* 108.

The historical play of "Troilus and Cressida" exhibits as full a specimen of the different styles in which this wonderful writer was qualified to excel, as is to be found in any of his works. . . . The great beauty of this play, as it is of all the genuine writings of Shakespear, beyond all didactic morality, beyond all mere flights of fancy, and beyond all sublime, a beauty entirely his own, and in which no writer ancient or modern can enter into competition with him, is that his men are men; his sentiments are living, and his characters marked with those delicate, evanescent, undefinable touches which identify them with the great delineations of nature. . . . The whole catalogue of the *dramatis personæ* in the play of "Troilus and Cressida," so far as they depend upon a rich and original vein of humour in the author, are drawn with a felicity which never was surpassed. The genius of Homer has been a topic of admiration to almost every generation of men since the period in which he wrote. But his characters will not bear the slightest comparison with the delineation of the same characters as they stand in Shakespeare.—GODWIN, WILLIAM, 1803, *Life of Geoffrey Chaucer, vol.* I, *pp.* 503, 505, 509.

Hector quotes *Aristotle;* Ulysses speaks of the bull-bearing *Milo,* and Pandarus of a man born in *April. Friday* and *Sunday* and even *minced-pies* with dates in them are introduced.—DOUCE, FRANCIS, 1807, *Illustrations of Shakspeare, vol.* II, *p.* 291.

This is one of the most loose and desultory of our author's plays: it rambles on just as it happens, but it overtakes, together with some indifferent matter, a prodigious number of fine things in its way. Troilus himself is no character: he is merely a common lover: but Cressida and her uncle Pandarus are hit off with proverbial truth.—HAZLITT, WILLIAM, 1817–69, *Characters of Shakespear's Plays.*

There is no one of Shakspere's plays harder to characterize. . . . I am half inclined to believe, that Shakspere's main object, or shall I rather say, his ruling impulse, was to translate the poetic heroes of paganism into the not less rude, but more intellectually vigorous, and more *featurely,* warriors of Christian chivalry—and to substantiate the distinct and graceful profiles or outlines of the Homeric epic into the flesh and blood of the romantic drama,—in short, to give a grand history-piece in the robust style of Albert Durer.—COLERIDGE, SAMUEL TAYLOR, 1818, *Lectures and Notes on Shakspere, ed. Ashe, pp.* 306, 308.

Would you see his mind unfettered, read "Troilus and Cressida," where he treats the materials of the "Iliad" in his own fashion.—ECKERMANN, JOHN PETER, 1825, *Conversations of Goethe.*

The play is, in all respects, a very remarkable and singular reproduction; and it has perplexed many a critic, not, as usual, by smaller difficulties of readings and interpretation, but by doubts as to the author's design and spirit. Its beauties are of the highest order. It contains passages fraught with moral truth and political wisdom — high truths, in large and philosophical discourse, such as remind us of the loftiest disquisitions of Hooker, or

Jeremy Taylor, on the foundations of social law. . . . Nor is there any drama more rich in variety and truth of character. . . . With all this, there is large alloy of inferior matter, such as Shakespeare too often permitted himself to use, in filling up the chasms of the scene, between loftier and brighter thoughts. More especially is there felt, by every reader, a sense of disappointment at the unsatisfactory effect of the whole, arising mainly from the want of unity in that effect, and in the interest of the plot—at the desultory and purposeless succession of incident and dialogue, all resembling (as Walter Scott well observes) "a legend, or a chronicle, rather than a dramatic composition."—VERPLANCK, GULIAN CROMMELIN, 1844–47, *ed. The Illustrated Shakespeare.*

"Troilus and Cressida" is Shakespeare's wisest play in the way of worldly wisdom. It is filled choke-full of sententious, and in most cases slightly satirical revelations of human nature, uttered with a felicity of phrase and an impressiveness of metaphor that make each one seem like a beam of light shot into the recesses of man's heart. . . . If we would know what Shakespeare thought of men and their motives after he reached maturity, we have but to read this drama; drama it is; but with what other character, who shall say? For, like the world's pageant, it is neither tragedy nor comedy, but a tragicomic history, in which the intrigues of amorous men and light-o'-loves and the brokerage of panders are mingled with the deliberations of sages and the strife and the death of heroes. —WHITE, RICHARD GRANT, 1877, *On Reading Shakespeare, Galaxy, vol.* 23, *pp.* 233, 235.

This is the most difficult of all Shakspere's plays to deal with, as well for date as position. . . . The play is evidently written in ill-humour with mankind; it is a bitter satire. Its purpose is not to show virtue her own feature, but contemptible weakness, paltry vanity, falsehood (like scorn), their own image. . . . Shakspere's treatment of Chaucer's heroine, Cressida, is, too, a shock to any lover of the early poet's work. To have the beautiful Cressida, hesitating, palpitating like the nightingale, before her sin; driven by force of hard circumstances which she could not control into unfaithfulness to her love; to have this Cressida, whom Chaucer spared for very ruth, set before us as a mere shameless wanton, making eyes at all the men she sees, and showing her looseness in the movement of every limb, is a terrible blow. But whatever may have been Shakspere's motive in this play, we certainly have in it his least pleasing production. There is no relief to the patchery, the jugglery, and the knavery, except the generous welcome of Nestor to Hector in the Grecian camp, and his frank praise of the gallant Trojan, who, labouring for Destiny, made cruel way through ranks of Greekish youth.—FURNIVALL, FREDERICK JAMES, 1877, *ed. The Leopold Shakspere.*

The point of special import and significance is that Shakespeare *always* shows a predilection for the Trojans, while the Greeks find but little favour in his sight. This undoubted bias on his part exhibits itself in an especially lively manner, and has widest scope, in "Troilus and Cressida." There are far grander works amongst Shakespeare's plays, but there is none more curious,—there is none that affords more matter for reflection and commentary in the realms, not only of learning and of history, but also of æsthetics, than does "Troilus and Cressida."—STAPFER, PAUL, 1880, *Shakespeare and Classical Antiquity, tr. Carey, p.* 157.

In spite of the admirable characterization in "Troilus and Cressida," and in spite of the host of imperishable sayings marked by a wealth of practical wisdom, there is no other drama of Shakespeare which appeals to us so little, which creates so unpleasing an impression.—TEN BRINK, BERNHARD, 1892–95, *Five Lectures on Shakespeare, tr. Franklin, p.* 93.

The effect of anti-climax and of all diminishing series is an unsatisfactory one. But the theme of the play is the *destruction* of *system* and *unity*, the factious disorganization of the Grecian camp; it is a picture of disorder and the overthrow of rule; and it is quite possible that the dramatist, whose genius was of the boldest and most innovating character, designedly left the picture without æsthetic totality in order to enhance the effect and deepen the impression made by the portrayal of principles which are the source of all imbecility.—RUGGLES, HENRY J., 1895, *The Plays of Shakespeare Founded on Literary Forms, p.* 399.

It was a curious coincidence that Shakespeare should lay hands on this material just at the most despondent period of his life; for nowhere could we well receive a deeper impression of modern crudeness and decadence, and never could we meet with a fuller expression of German-Gothic innate barbarism in relation to Hellenism than when we see this great poet of the Northern Renaissance make free with the poetry of the old world.—BRANDES, GEORGE, 1898, *William Shakespeare, A Critical Study, vol.* II, *p.* 206.

ANTONY AND CLEOPATRA
1606–7

The highest praise, or rather form of praise, of this play, which I can offer in my own mind, is the doubt which the perusal always occasion in me, whether the "Antony and Cleopatra" is not, in all exhibitions of a giant power in its strength and vigour of maturity, a formidable rival of "Macbeth," "Lear," "Hamlet," and "Othello." . . . Of all Shakspere's historical plays, "Antony and Cleopatra" is by far the most wonderful. There is not one in which he has followed history so minutely, and yet there are few in which he impresses the notion of angelic strength so much;—perhaps none in which he impresses it more strongly. This is greatly owing to the manner in which the fiery force is sustained throughout, and to the numerous momentary flashes of nature counteracting the historic abstraction. As a wonderful specimen of the way in which Shakspere lives up to the very end of this play, read the last part of the concluding scene. And if you would feel the judgment as well as the genius of Shakspere in your hearts' core, compare this astonishing drama with Dryden's "All For Love."—COLERIDGE, SAMUEL TAYLOR, 1818, *Lectures and Notes on Shakspere, ed. Ashe, pp.* 315, 316.

I have not the slightest doubt that Shakspeare's Cleopatra is the real historical Cleopatra—the "Rare Egyptian"—individualised and placed before us. Her mental accomplishments, her unequalled grace, her woman's wit and woman's wiles, her irresistible allurements, her starts of irregular grandeur, her bursts of ungovernable temper, her vivacity of imagination, her petulant caprice, her fickleness and her falsehood, her tenderness and her truth, her childish susceptibility to flattery, her magnificent spirit, her royal pride, the gorgeous Eastern colouring of the character; all these contradictory elements has Shakspeare seized, mingled them in their extremes, and fused them into one brilliant impersonation of classical elegance, Oriental voluptuousness, and gypsy sorcery.—JAMESON, ANNA BROWNELL, 1832, *Characteristics of Women.*

I am not aware that this play has been acted in modern times; nor do I believe it to be as great a favourite with readers in general as the high commendations of modern critics would lead me to expect. I know little of the histrionic art, but should imagine that Cleopatra, and Antony too, in good hands, would be exceedingly attractive on the stage; and there, perhaps, relying on the interest of the story, and the good acting, we should not so much miss that force and dignity of versification which captivate us in other plays, of which the plot and scenes are less interesting.—COURTENAY, THOMAS PEREGRINE, 1840, *Commentaries on the Historical Plays of Shakspeare, vol.* II, *p.* 275.

But independently of any other indications, it is certain that the ripe maturity of poetic mind pervades the whole tone of the tragedy, its diction, imagery, characters, thoughts. It exhibits itself everywhere, in a copious and varied magnificence, as from a mind and memory stored with the treasures acquired in its own past intellectual efforts, as well as with the knowledge of life and books, from all which the dramatic muse (to borrow the Oriental imagery which Milton has himself drawn from this very tragedy), like

> "the gorgeous East, with liberal hand,
> Showers on her kings barbaric pearl and gold."

Its poetry has as autumnal richness, such as can succeed only to the vernal luxuriance of genius, or its fiercer midsummer glow. We need no other proof than that which its own abundance affords, that this tragedy is the rich product of a mind where, as in Mark Antony's own Egypt, his "Nilus had swelled high," and

> "when it ebb'd, the seedsman
> Upon its slime and ooze scatter'd his grain,
> Which shortly came to harvest."

—VERPLANCK, GULIAN CROMMELIN, 1844–47, *ed. The Illustrated Shakespeare.*

The greatest monument of his dramatic subtlety is the tragedy of "Antony and Cleopatra." With all its noble bursts of passion and occasional splendour of description, this play has not perhaps the massive breadth of feeling and overpowering interest of the four great tragedies, "Macbeth," "Hamlet," "Lear," and "Othello;" but it is greater even than "Macbeth" and "Othello" in the range of its mastery over the fluctuations of profound passion: it is the greatest of Shakespeare's plays in the dramatist's greatest faculty. The conflict of motives in "Hamlet" is an achievement of genius that must always be regarded with wonder and reverence; but, to my mind, "Antony and Cleopatra" is the dramatist's masterpiece. One may have less interest in the final end of the subtle changes wrought in the hero and heroine: but in the pursuit and certain grasp of those changes, Shakespeare's dramatic genius appears at its supreme height. —MINTO, WILLIAM, 1874–85, *Characteristics of English Poets, p.* 318.

On "Antony and Cleopatra" Shakspere has poured out the glory of his genius in profusion, and makes us stand by, saddened and distressed, as the noble Antony sinks to his ruin, under the gorgeous colouring of the Eastern sky, the vicious splendour of the Egyptian queen; makes us look with admiring hate on the wonderful picture he has drawn, certainly far the most wonderful study of woman he has left us, of that Cleopatra of whom Enobarbus, who knew her every turn, said,

"Age cannot wither her, nor custom stale
Her infinite variety; other women
Cloy the appetites they feed, but she makes hungry
Where most she satisfies."

That in her, the dark woman of Shakspere's "Sonnets," his own fickle, serpent-like, attractive mistress, is to some extent embodied, I do not doubt. What a superbly sumptuous picture, as if painted by Veronese or Titian, is that where Cleopatra first met Antony upon the river of Cydnus! How admirably transferred from Plutarch's prose! And how that fatal inability to say "No" to woman shows us Antony's weakness and the cause of his final fall. —FURNIVALL, FREDERICK JAMES, 1877, *ed. The Leopold Shakspere, Introduction to the Play.*

The final impression left upon the mind by this woman, in whom there was no real goodness or grandeur of character, is that of grace and a fascination that never leave her from the beginning to the end, and in her last moments, that of majesty. As an example of the magic power of beauty and of poetry Shakespeare's Cleopatra stands alone. —STAPFER, PAUL, 1880, *Shakespeare and Classical Antiquity, tr. Carey, p.* 408.

In the later scenes Antony is still shown as a noble ruin. His dealing with Enobarbus, when deserted even by that once honest friend, is one clear indication of the generosity of Antony's large nature. He beats strong wings and lifts his head as if to soar, caught as an eagle in the toils. The strength of his desire towards Cleopatra is the weakness of Antony; the strength of her desire towards Antony is the whole strength of Cleopatra. Beyond that, her care in life is artifice of her profession as a beauty, who, at the age of thirty-eight, cannot afford to trust too simply to Nature. She has, in her own strength, pathetic traces at the last of that which might have been the glory of her womanhood, had not her thoughts been low.—MORLEY, HENRY, AND GRIFFIN, W. HALL, 1895, *English Writers, vol.* XI, *p.* 95.

Who knows! If he himself, William Shakespeare, had met her, who knows if he would have escaped with his life? And had he not met her? Was it not she whom in bygone days he had met and loved, and by whom he had been beloved and betrayed? It moved him strongly to find Cleopatra described as so dark, so tawny. His thoughts dwelt upon this. He too had stood in close relation to a dark, ensnaring woman—one whom in bitter moments he had been tempted to call a gipsy; "a right gipsy," as Cleopatra is called in this play, by those who are afraid of her or angry with her. She of whom he never thought without emotion, his black enchantress, his life's angel and fiend, whom he had hated and adored at the same time, whom he had despised even while he sued for her favour—what was she but a new incarnation of that dangerous, ensnaring serpent of the Nile! And how nearly had his whole inner world collapsed like a soap-bubble in his association with, and separation from, her! That would indeed have been the ruin of a world! How he had revelled and writhed, exulted and complained in those days! played ducks and drakes with his life, squandered his days and nights! Now he was a maturer man, a gentleman, a landed proprietor and tithe-farmer; but in him still lived the artist Bohemian, fitted to mate with the gipsy queen. —BRANDES, GEORGE, 1898, *William Shakespeare, A Critical Study, vol.* II, *p.* 144.

CORIOLANUS
1607–8

He was a man too full of passion and choler, and too much given over to self-will and opinion, as one of a high mind and great courage, that lacked the gravity and affability that is gotten with judgment of learning and reason, which only is to be looked for in a governor of State: and that remembered not how wilfulness is the thing of the world, which a governor of a commonwealth, for pleasing, should shun, being that which Plato called "solitariness;" as in the end, all men that are wilfully given to a self-opinion and obstinate mind, and who will never yield to other's reason but to their own, remain without company, and forsaken of all men. For a man that will live in the world must needs have patience, which lusty bloods make but a mock at. So Marcius, being a stout man of nature, that never yielded in any respect, as one thinking that to overcome always and to have the upper hand in all matters, was a token of magnanimity and of no base and faint courage, which spitteth out anger from the most weak and passioned part of the beast, much like the matter of an impostume: went home to his house, full freighted with spite and malice against the people.—NORTH, SIR THOMAS, 1579, *tr. Plutarch's Life of Coriolanus.*

The Tragedy of "Coriolanus" is one of the most amusing of our author's performances. The old man's merriment in Menenius; the lofty lady's dignity in Volumnia; the bridal modesty in Vergilia; the patrician and military haughtiness in Coriolanus; the plebian malignity and tribunitian insolence in Brutus and Sicinius, make a very pleasing and interesting variety; and the various revolutions of the hero's fortune, fill the mind with anxious curiosity. There is perhaps too much bustle in the first act, and too little in the last. —JOHNSON, SAMUEL, 1768, *General Observations on Shakespeare's Plays.*

To reduce the history of Coriolanus into a play was one of those labours, which our dramatic Hercules has achieved in a most wonderful manner; but after all, the labour is scarcely worth the pains, for, except the singularly noble character of Coriolanus, there is nothing correctly great in the piece.—DIBDIN, CHARLES, 1795, *A Complete History of the Stage, vol.* III, *p.* 340.

Shakespear has in this play shown himself well versed in history and state affairs. "Coriolanus" is a storehouse of political commonplaces. Any one who studies it may save himself the trouble of reading Burke's "Reflections," or Paine's "Rights of Man," or the Debates in both Houses of Parliament since the French Revolution or our own. The arguments for and against aristocracy or democracy, on the privileges of the few and the claims of the many, on liberty and slavery, power and the abuse of it, peace and war, are here very ably handled, with the spirit of a poet and the acuteness of a philosopher. Shakespear himself seems to have had a leaning to the arbitrary side of the question, perhaps from some feeling of contempt for his own origin; and to have spared no occasion of bating the rabble. What he says of them is very true: what he says of their betters is also very true, though he dwells less upon it. —HAZLITT, WILLIAM, 1817–69, *Characters of Shakespear's Plays, p.* 49.

In Volumnia, Shakspeare has given us the portrait of a Roman matron, conceived in the true antique spirit, and finished in every part. Although Coriolanus is the hero of the play, yet much of the interest of the action and the final catastrophe turn upon the character of his mother, Volumnia, and the power she exercised over his mind, by which, according to the story, "she saved Rome and lost her son." Her lofty patriotism, her patrician haughtiness, her maternal pride, her eloquence, and her towering spirit, are exhibited with the utmost power of effect; yet the truth of female nature is beautifully preserved, and the portrait, with all its vigour, is without harshness. —JAMESON, ANNA BROWNELL, 1832, *Characteristics of Women.*

The subject of "Coriolanus" is the ruin of a noble life through the sin of pride. If duty be the dominant ideal with Brutus, and pleasure of a magnificent kind be the ideal of Antony and Cleopatra, that which gives tone and colour to Coriolanus is an ideal of self-centred power. The greatness of Brutus is altogether that of the moral conscience; his external figure does not dilate upon the world through a golden haze like that of Antony, nor bulk massively and tower like that of Coriolanus. Brutus venerates his ideals, and venerates himself; but this veneration of self is in a certain sense disinterested. A haughty and passionate personal feeling, a superb egoism, are with Coriolanus the sources of weakness and of strength.—DOWDEN, EDWARD, 1875–80, *Shakspere: A Critical Study of his Mind and Art, p.* 282.

A loftier or a more perfect piece of man's work was never done in all the world than this tragedy of "Coriolanus."—SWINBURNE, ALGERNON CHARLES, 1880, *A Study of Shakespeare, p.* 188.

There is more unity in the tragedy of "Coriolanus" than in either of the other Roman plays; yet, grand and powerful as it is, its tragical interest is less than that of "Julius Cæsar," and its poetical merit less than that of "Antony and Cleopatra." There is something hard about it, both in sentiment and in style. The delineation of social and personal pride is not a subject to evoke much sympathy or emotion, and although it may in its course reach sublime heights, its sublimity is wholly independent of moral greatness. Of all Shakespeare's greater works, this is the most difficult to construe; the unintelligibility of several passages is doubtless due to some corruption of the text, but besides this, the general style is exceedingly obscure, and overloaded with metaphorical and elliptical expressions. Even the great scene between Coriolanus and his mother is not of uniform excellence.—STAPFER, PAUL, 1880, *Shakespeare and Classical Antiquity, tr. Carey, p.* 454.

"Coriolanus" was directly derived from Sir Thomas North's famous version of Plutarch's "Lives of the Noble Grecians and Romans," the book to which Shakespeare was indebted also for his "Julius Cæsar," "Antony and Cleopatra," and, to some extent, for "Timon of Athens," and which has been fittingly described as "most sovereign in its dominion over the minds of great men in all ages." North's monumental version is one of the masterpieces of English prose, and no better proof exists than a comparison of the play with its original. Shakespeare has borrowed North's very vocabulary, and many of his most striking effects; so closely does he follow the whole history that North's prose may actually assist in restoring a defective passage. —GOLLANCZ, ISRAEL, 1896, *ed. Temple Shakespeare, Coriolanus, Preface.*

TIMON OF ATHENS
1607–8

I am now to present your Grace with this History of *Timon*, which you were pleased to tell me you liked, and it is the more worthy of you, since it has the inimitable hand of *Shakespear* in it, which never made more Masterly strokes than in this. —SHADWELL, THOMAS, 1678, *The History of Timon of Athens, the Man-Hater, made into a play. Epistle Dedicatory.*

The play of Timon is a domestic tragedy, and therefore strongly fastens on the attention of the reader. In the plan there is not much art, but the incidents are natural, and the characters various and exact. The catastrophe affords a very powerful warning against that ostentatious liberality, which scatters bounty, but confers no benefits, and buys flattery, but not friendship. In this tragedy, are many passages perplexed, obscure, and probably corrupt, which I have endeavoured to rectify, or explain, with due dilligence; but, having only one copy, cannot promise myself that my endeavours shall be much applauded.—JOHNSON, SAMUEL, 1768, *General Observations on Shakspeare's Plays.*

"Timon of Athens" always appeared to us to be written with as intense a feeling of his subject as any one play of Shakespear. It is one of the few in which he seems to be in earnest throughout, never to trifle nor go out of his way. He does not relax in his efforts, nor lose sight of the unity of his design. It is the only play of our author in which spleen is the predominant feeling of the mind. It is as much a satire as a play: and contains some of the finest pieces of invective possible to be conceived, both in the snarling, captious answers of the cynic Apemantus, and in the impassioned and more terrible imprecations of Timon.—HAZLITT, WILLIAM, 1817–69, *Characters of Shakespeare's Plays, p.* 44.

"Timon of Athens" forms the beautiful close of Shakspeare's poetical career. It reflects more clearly than any other piece, the poet's consciousness of the nothingness of human life and nature in themselves, and a christian reliance on God, as the source of all that is abiding and per manent. We distinctly see him abandoning the trifling pursuits and contentions of this life, for calm heavenly meditation; but at the same time we see, that before he could arrive at this repose, his path had been crossed by many and heavy conflicts. Indeed, when we compare this tragedy with others which belong probably to his latest labours, the confession is forced from us that his view of the world and things, even in its *artistic* side, must have been somewhat troubled in the latter years of his career.—ULRICI, HERMANN, 1839, *Shakspeare's Dramatic Art, p*, 243.

The principle which we seek to establish, namely, that the "Timon of Athens" was a play originally produced by an artist very inferior to Shakspere, and which probably retained possession of the stage for some time in its first form; that it has come down to us not only re-written, but so far re-modelled that entire scenes of Shakspere have been substituted for entire scenes of the elder play; and lastly, that this substitution has been almost wholly confined to the character of Timon, and that in the development of that character alone, with the exception of some few occasional touches here and there, we must look for the unity of the Shaksperean conception of the Greek Misanthropos—the Timon of Aristophanes and Lucian and Plutarch—"the enemy to mankind," of the popular story books—of the "Pleasant Histories and excellent Novels," which were greedily devoured by the contemporaries of the boyish Shakspere.—KNIGHT, CHARLES, 1849, *Studies of Shakspere, bk.* ii, *ch.* iv, *p.* 70.

It certainly is not like the sepia sketch of a great master, perfect so far as it goes; nor yet like an unfinished picture which shews the basis of the artist's work; nor yet like those paintings of the old masters, in which the accessories were filled in by the 'prentice hands of their pupils, while the design and prominent figures indicated the taste and skill of high genius. It is rather an old painting, retouched perhaps in all its parts, and the prominent figures entirely remodeled by the hand of the great master, but designed and originally completed by a stranger. Of the type of Timon's character there can be no doubt. He is unmistakably of the family of Hamlet and Lear. The resemblance to Lear especially is close; like him at first, full of unreasoning confidence; like him at last, full of unreasoning hate.—BUCKNILL, JOHN CHARLES, M. D., 1859-67, *The Mad Folk of Shakespeare, p.* 236.

"Timon of Athens" unquestionably contains much matter from another hand. . . . The unShakespearian characters in the play are three Lords—Lucius, Lucullus, and Sempronius; three Servants—Flavius (Steward always in the Shakespeare part), Flaminius, and Servilius; three Strangers; three Creditors—Hortensius, Philotus, and 2d Varro; three Masquers; and the Soldier.—FLEAY, FREDERICK GARD, 1886, *Chronicle History of the Life and Work of William Shakespeare, pp.* 242, 243.

The play is, however, one of the less celebrated and less attractive among Shakespeare's works. The theme itself is not the most enticing, and its treatment must be pronounced to be in many respects unsatisfactory. The inequality of the execution will be acknowledged by every careful reader. Some parts are wrought out with great skill and completeness; others are hastily and rudely sketched, while certain necessary links seem to be omitted altogether. The versification is often a mystery, and the prose frequently appears to be written with exceeding carelessness. But the main characterisitc of the play is the dark coloring in which it portrays social life. Its speech is steeped in bitterness; it contains the most vindictive utterances against mankind to be found in Shakespeare. A noble, generous character is victimized to the last degree, and driven forward to suicide. Unselfishness apparently becomes tragic in a selfish world. Still, the other side is not neglected; this very unselfishness is seen to be at bottom selfish. Timon is guilty, and has to take the consequence of his deed. He turns misanthrope, full of vehement sarcasm and red-hot imprecation. The latter part of the play, in particular, is a bath of gall.—SNIDER, DENTON JAQUES, 1887, *The Shakespearian Drama, The Tragedies, p.* 13.

"Timon of Athens" has come down to us in a pitiable condition. The text is in a terrible state, and there are, not only between one scene and another, but between one page and another, such radical differences in the style and general spirit of the play as to preclude the possibility of its having been the work of one man. The threads of the story are often entirely disconnected, and circumstances occur (or are referred to) for which we were in no way prepared. The best part of the versification is distinctly Shakespearian, and contains all that wealth of thought which was characteristic of this period of his life; but the other parts are careless, discordant, and desperately monotonous. The prose dialogue especially jars, thrust as it is, with its long-winded straining after effect, into scenes which are otherwise compact and vigorous. All Shakespeare students of the present day concur in the opinion that "Timon of Athens," like "Pericles," is but a great fragment from the master-hand. —BRANDES, GEORGE, 1898, *William Shakespeare, A Critical Study, vol.* II. *p.* 254.

PERICLES
1608

THE LATE, | And much admired Play, | Called | Pericles, Prince | of Tyre, | With the true Relation of the whole Historie, aduentures, and fortunes of the said Prince: | As also, | The no lesse strange, and worthy accidents, | in the Birth and Life, of his Daughter | MARIANA. | As it hath been diuers and sundry times acted by | his Maiesties Seruants, at the Globe on | the Banck-side. | By William Shakespeare. | Imprinted at London for *Henry Gosson* | and are | to be sold at the Signe of the Sunne in | Paternoster Row. 1609. —TITLE PAGE OF THE FIRST EDITION, 1609.

And if it prove so happy as to please,
Weele say 'tis fortunate like *Pericles.*

—TAYLOR, ROBERT, 1614, *The Hogge hath lost his Pearle, Prologue.*

With Sophocles we may
Compare great Shakespeare: Aristophanes
Never like him his Fancy could display,
Witness the *Prince of Tyre, his Pericles.*

—SHEPPARD, SAMUEL, 1646, *The Times displayed in Six Sestyads.*

But Shakespeare, the plebeian driller, was
Founder'd in his Pericles, and must not pass.

—TATHAM, J., 1652, *In "Jovial Crew" by Richard Brome.*

We dare not charge the whole unequal play
Of Pericles on him; yet let us say,
As gold tho' mix'd with baser metal shines,
So do his bright inimitable lines
Throughout those rude wild scenes distinguish'd stand
And shew he touch'd them with no sparing hand.

—LILLO, GEORGE, 1738, *Marina, Prologue.*

This tragedy, I think, exhibits no equitable claim to be regarded as a work of Shakspeare's, any more than that with which it is most worthily associated, in the same volume, "Titus Andronicus." If one of these compositions is ludicrously shocking, the other is shockingly ludicrous; and the poet's reputation, I believe, would have been better consulted, by dismissing them both to contempt and oblivion. —SEYMOUR, E. H., 1805, *Remarks on Shakspeare, vol.* II, *p.* 436.

Many will be of opinion that it contains more that *he might have written* than either "Love's labour's lost," or "All's well that ends well."—DOUCE, FRANCIS 1807, *Illustrations of Shakspeare, vol.* II, *p.* 144.

However wild and extravagant the fable of "Pericles" may appear, if we consider its numerous choruses, its pageantry, and dumb shows, its continual succession of incidents, and the great length of time which they occupy, yet is it, we may venture to assert, the most spirited and pleasing specimen of the nature and fabric of our earliest romantic drama which we possess, and the more valuable, as it is the only one with which Shakspeare has favoured us. . . . From the extensive survey which has now been taken of the merits and supposed era of this early drama, the reader, it is probable, will gather sufficient data for concluding that by far the greater part of it issued from the pen of Shakspeare, that it was his first dramatic production, that it appeared towards the close of the year 1590, and that it deserves to be removed from the Appendix to the editions of Shakspeare, where it has hitherto appeared, and incorporated in the body of his works. —DRAKE, NATHAN, 1817, *Shakspeare and His Times, vol.* II, *pp.* 266–286.

Though it contains one fine scene and many scattered beauties, the play is a bad one; it is destitute of reality and art, and is entirely alien to Shakspeare's system:

it is interesting only as marking the point from which he started; and it seems to belong to his works as a last monument of that which he overthrew—as a remnant of that anti-dramatic scaffolding for which he was about to substitute the presence and movement of vitality.—GUIZOT, FRANCOIS PIERRE GUILLAUME, 1821–52, *Shakspeare and His Times, p.* 67.

It is generally believed that he had much to do with the tragedy of "Pericles," which is now printed among his works, and which external testimony, though we should not rely too much on that as to Shakspeare, has assigned to him; but the play is full of evident marks of an inferior hand.—HALLAM, HENRY, 1837–39, *Introduction to the Literature of Europe, pt.* ii, *ch.* vi, *par.* 35.

If it be the work of Shakspere, the foundations of it were laid when his art was imperfect, and he laboured somewhat in subjection to the influence of those ruder models for which he eventually substituted his own splendid examples of dramatic excellence. — KNIGHT, CHARLES, 1849, *Studies of Shakspere, bk.* ii, *ch.* ii, *p.* 53.

The work as it has come down to us is not in reality a drama at all, but an incompletely dramatised epic poem. . . . Thus the germs of all his latest works lie in this unjustly neglected and despised play, which has suffered under a double disadvantage: it is not entirely Shakespeare's work, and in such portions of it as are his own there exist, in the dark shadow cast by her hideous surroundings about Marina, traces of that gloomy mood from which he was but just emerging. But for all that, whether we look upon it as a contribution to Shakespeare's biography or as a poem, this beautiful and remarkable fragment, "Pericles," is a work of the greatest interest.—BRANDES, GEORGE, 1898, *William Shakespeare, A Critical Study, vol.* II, *pp.* 279, 295.

Great part of it *must* be Shakespeare's; there is perhaps no part that *might* not be; and the general characteristics of story-management and versification are a very odd mixture of his earliest and his latest manner — a "Love's Labour's Lost" blended with a "Winter's Tale."—SAINTSBURY, GEORGE, 1898, *A Short History of English Literature, p.* 327.

TWO NOBLE KINSMEN
1609

THE | TWO | NOBLE | KINSMEN: | Presented at the Blackfriers | by the Kings Maiesties servants, | with great applause: | Written by the memorable Worthies of their time; | { Mr John Fletcher, and Mr William Shakspeare. } Gent. | Printed at *London* by *Tho. Cotes,* for *Iohn Waterson:* | and are to be sold at the signe of the *Crowne* | in *Pauls* Church-yard. 1634.—TITLE PAGE OF FIRST EDITION, 1634.

This play is said to have been written by Shakespear and Fletcher, a circumstance which the editor of Beaumont and Fletcher seems to be greatly concerned about, probably out of tenderness for the reputation of Fletcher, but he need not have made himself in the smallest degree uneasy, for the play itself sufficiently proves that Shakespear had no hand in it. Indeed there is not much reputation to be claimed by any body, for the story is Chaucer's "Knights Tale," which we have seen already treated by Edwards to the great delight of queen Elizabeth. There is something, however, gaudy and fine in it; and, like most of the works of Beaumont and Fletcher, it resembles a parterre appearing so full of colours that form, and symmetry are not once thought of.—DIBDIN, CHARLES, 1795, *A Complete History of the Stage, vol.* III, *p.* 209.

I have no doubt whatever that the first act and the first scene of the second act of "The Two Noble Kinsmen" are Shakspere's."—COLERIDGE, SAMUEL TAYLOR, 1833, *Table-Talk, Feb.* 17.

Be the authorship whose it may, "The Two Noble Kinsmen" is undoubtedly one of the finest dramas in the volumes before us * It contains passages which, in dramatic vigour and passion, yield hardly to anything—perhaps to nothing—in the whole collection; while for gorgeousness of imagery, for delicacy of poetic feeling, and for grace, animation, and strength of language, we doubt whether there exists, under the names of our authors, any drama that comes near to it.—SPALDING, WILLIAM, 1847, *Dyce's Beaumont and Fletcher, Edinburgh Review, vol.* 86, *p.* 58.

For our own part, we wish that the question were as simple as in the case of

*Dyce's "Beaumont and Fletcher."

"Henry VIII.," but we do not find it so. We were at first ready to agree with Spalding and Hickson—with the latter rather than the former on the points as to which they differ—but on more careful study of the play, we find ourself wavering, as Spalding did, and coming to regard the problem as "really insoluble." Shakespeare perhaps had a share in the play; but, if so, it is impossible to decide just what it was, or how it came about.—ROLFE, WILLIAM J., 1883, *ed. The Two Noble Kinsmen, Introduction, p.* 21.

The play is of no particular value; it is far inferior to Fletcher's best work, and not to be compared with any of Shakespeare's completed dramas. Nevertheless, many eminent critics of this century have found distinct traces in this play of the styles of both greater and lesser poet.—BRANDES, GEORGE, 1898, *William Shakespeare, A Critical Study, vol.* II, *p.* 310.

THE TEMPEST
1610

If there bee never a *Servant-monster* i' the *Fayre*, who can helpe it? he sayes; nor a nest of *Antiques?* Hee is loth to make Nature afraid in his *Playes*, like those that beget *Tales*, *Tempests*, and such like *Drolleries*, to mixe his head with other mens heeles.—JONSON, BEN, 1614, *Bartholomew Fayre, Induction.*

November 7.—At noon resolved with Sir W. Pen to go see "The Tempest," an old play of Shakespeare's, acted, I hear, the first day. . . . The house mighty full; the King and Court there: and the most innocent play that ever I saw; and a curious piece of musique in an echo of half sentences, the echo repeating the former half, while the man goes on to the latter; which is mighty pretty. The play [has] no great wit, but yet good, above ordinary plays.—PEPYS, SAMUEL, 1667, *Diary and Correspondence.*

No man ever drew so many characters, or generally distinguished em' better from one another, excepting only *Johnson:* I will instance but in one, to show the copiousness of his invention; 'tis that of "Calyban," or the monster in "The Tempest." He seems there to have created a person which was not in Nature, a boldness which at first sight would appear intolerable; for he makes him a species of himself, begotten by an "Incubus" on a Witch; but this, as I have elsewhere prov'd, is not wholly beyond the bounds of credibility, at least the vulgar stile believe it. We have the separated notions of a spirit and of a witch; (and spirits, according to "Plato," are vested with a subtil body; according to some of his followers, have different sexes) therefore as from the distinct apprehensions of a horse, and of a man, Imagination has form'd a "Centaur," so from those of an "Incubus" and a "Sorceress," *Shakespear* has produc'd his Monster. Whether or no his generation can be defended, I leave to Philosophy; but of this I am certain, the Poet has most judiciously furnish'd him with a person, a language, and a character which will suit him both by Father's and Mother's side: he has all the discontents and malice of a Witch, and of a Devil; besides a convenient proportion of the deadly sins; Gluttony, Sloth, and Lust, are manifest; the dejectedness of a slave is likewise given him, and the ignorance of one bred up in a Desart Island. His person is monstrous, as he is the product of unnatural lust; and his language is as hobgoblin as his person; in all things he is distinguished from other mortals.—DRYDEN, JOHN, 1679, *Troilus and Cressida, Preface.*

This drama is one of the noblest efforts of that sublime and amazing imagination, peculiar to Shakspeare, which soars above the bounds of nature, without forsaking sense; or, more properly, carries nature along with him beyond her established limits.—WARBURTON, WILLIAM, 1747, *Shakspear Plays, with Comment and Notes.*

An Attempte To Rescue that Aunciente, English Poet, And Play-Wrighte, Maister Williaume Shakespere, from the Maney Errours, faulsely charged on him, by Certaine New-fangled Wittes; And To let him Speak for Himself, as right well he wotteth, when Freede from the many Careless Mistakeings, of The Heedless first Imprinters, of his Workes. By a Gentleman formerly of Greys-Inn.—HOLT, JOHN, 1749, *Title Page.*

But whatever might be Shakspeare's intention in forming or adopting the plot, he has made it instrumental to the production of many characters, diversified with boundless invention, and preserved with profound skill in nature, extensive knowledge of opinions, and accurate observation of life. In a single drama are here exhibited princes, courtiers, and sailors, all speaking in their real characters. There is the agency of airy spirits, and of an earthly goblin; the operations of magic, the tumults of a storm, the adventures of a desert island, the native effusion of untaught affection, the punishment of guilt, and the final happiness of the pair for whom our passions and reason are equally interested. — JOHNSON, SAMUEL, 1768, *General Observations on Shakspeare's Plays.*

The character of Caliban, in the "Tempest," is singularly original: but the almost animal figure, which his dress must give him, turns the attention from all that is philosophical in the conception of this part.—STAEL, MADAME DE, 1800, *The Influence of Literature upon Society, vol.* I, *p.* 271.

The "Tempest" is one of the most original and perfect of Shakespear's productions, and he has shown in it all the variety of his powers. It is full of grace and grandeur. The human and imaginary characters, the dramatic and the grotesque, are blended together with the greatest art, and without any appearance of it. Though he has here given "to airy nothing a local habitation and a name," yet that part which is only the fantastic creation of his mind has the same palpable texture, and coheres "semblably" with the rest. As the preternatural part has the air of reality, and almost haunts the imagination with a sense of truth, the real characters and events partake of the wildness of a dream.—HAZLITT, WILLIAM, 1817–69, *Characters of Shakespear's Plays, p.* 82.

None of his other plays are more amusing or more animated than this, and in none is a lively, and even waggish, gayety more naturally conjoined with serious interests, melancholy feelings, and touching affections. It is a fairy tale in all the force of the term, and in all the vivacity of the impressions which such a tale can impart.—GUIZOT, FRANCOIS PIERRE GUILLAUME, 1821–52, *Shakspeare and His Times, p.* 356.

The character of Miranda resolves itself into the very elements of womanhood. She is beautiful, modest, and tender, and she is these only; they comprise her whole being, external and internal. She is so perfectly unsophisticated, so delicately refined, that she is all but ethereal. Let us imagine any other woman placed beside Miranda—even one of Shakspeare's own loveliest and sweetest creations—there is not one of them that could sustain the comparison for a moment; not one that would not appear somewhat coarse or artificial when brought into immediate contact with this pure child of nature, this "Eve of an enchanted Paradise." What, then, has Shakspeare done?—"O wondrous skill and sweet wit of the man!"—he has removed Miranda far from all comparison with her own sex; he has placed her between the demi-demon of earth and the delicate spirit of air. The next step is into the ideal and supernatural; and the only being who approaches Miranda, with whom she can be contrasted, is Ariel. Beside the subtle essence of this ethereal sprite, this creature of elemental light and air, that "ran upon the winds, rode the curl'd clouds, and in the colours of the rainbow lived," Miranda herself appears a palpable reality, a woman, "breathing thoughtful breath," a woman, walking the earth in her mortal loveliness, with a heart as frail-strung, as passion-touched, as ever fluttered in a female bosom.—JAMESON, ANNA BROWNELL, 1832, *Characteristics of Women.*

Caliban has not yet been thoroughly fathomed. For all Shakspeare's great creations are, like works of nature, subject of inexhaustible study. It was this character of whom Charles I. and some of his ministers expressed such fervent admiration; and, among other circumstances, most justly they admired the new language almost with which he is endowed for the purpose of expressing his fiendish and yet carnal thoughts of hatred to his master. Caliban is evidently not meant for scorn, but for abomination mixed with fear and partial respect. He is purposely brought into contrast with the drunken Trinculo and Stephano, with an advantageous result. He is much more intellectual than either,—uses a more elevated language not disfigured by vulgarisms, and is not liable to the low passion for plunder, as they are. He is mortal, doubtless, as his "dam" (for Shakspeare will not call her mother) Sycorax. But he inherits from her such qualities of power as a witch could be supposed to bequeath. He trembles indeed before Prospero; but that is, as we are to understand, through the moral superiority of Prospero in Christian wisdom; for, when he finds himself in the presence of dissolute and unprincipled men, he rises at once into the dignity of intellectual power.—DE QUINCEY, THOMAS, 1838-63? *Shakspeare, Works, ed. Masson, vol.* IV, *p.* 85, *note.*

"The Tempest" is one of those works for which no other production of the author's prolific fancy could have prepared his readers. It is wholly of a different cast of temper, and mood of disposition, from those so conspicuous in his gayer comedies; while even the ethical dignity and poetic splendour of "The Merchant of Venice" could not well lead the critic to anticipate the solemn grandeur, the unrivalled harmony and grace, the bold originality, and the grave beauty of "The Tempest." — VERPLANCK, GULIAN CROMMELIN, 1844-47, *ed. The Illustrated Shakespeare.*

The thoughtful reader will find in the compact simplicity of its structure, and in the chastened grandeur of its diction and the lofty severity of its tone of thought, tempered although the one is with Shakespeare's own enchanting sweetness, and the other with that most human tenderness which is the peculiar trait of his mind, sufficient evidence that this play is the fruit of his genius in its full maturity.—WHITE, RICHARD GRANT, 1858, *ed. The Works of William Shakespeare, vol.* II, *p.* 7.

Shakespeare has combined all the resources of his wonderful imagination; and in it has with consummate skill displayed the vast variety of his powers. In this latter quality — that of his variety — the play may be pronounced the most original, as well as the most complete of his productions. It is at once instinct with grace and beauty, grandeur and sublimity, mirth, cheerfulness, and broad humour.— CLARKE, CHARLES COWDEN, 1863, *Shakespeare Characters, p.* 275.

Only one man resisted this universal current [i. e. the belief in witchcraft promulgated by James.] That man was Shakespeare. Shakespeare did not as did Reginald Scot. He did not reject the traditions of the Bible nor the legends; he engrafted them. He did not question the existence of the invisible world; he rehabilitated it. He did not deny man's supernatural power; he consecrated it. James the Sixth said: Accursed be spirits! Shakespeare says: Glory be to spirits! —HUGO, FRANÇOIS-VICTOR, 1865, *Œuvres Complètes de Shakespeare, vol.* II, *Introduction, p.* 87.

If I read it rightly, it is an example of how a great poet should write allegory,—not embodying metaphysical abstractions, but giving us ideals abstracted from life itself, suggesting an under-meaning everywhere, forcing it upon us nowhere, tantalizing the mind with hints that imply so much and tell so little, and yet keep the attention all eye and ear with eager, if fruitless, expectation. Here the leading characters are not merely typical, but symbolical,—that is, they do not illustrate a class of persons, they belong to universal Nature.—LOWELL, JAMES RUSSELL, 1868-90, *Shakespeare Once More, Prose Works, Riverside ed., vol.* III, *p.* 59.

"The Tempest" is not one of those plays whose interest consists in strong dramatic situations. The course of the action is revealed from the first. Prospero is too manifestly the controlling spirit to arouse much concern for his fortunes. Ferdinand and Miranda are soon put out of their pain, and Ariel lies beyond the limits of humanity. The action is simple and uniform, and all occurences are seen converging slowly towards their destined point. No play, perhaps, more perfectly combines intellectual satisfaction with imaginative pleasure. Above and behind the fascination of the plot and the poetry we behold Power and Right evenly paired and working together, and the justification of Providence producing that sentiment of repose and acquiescence which is the object and test of every true work of art.—GARNETT, RICHARD, 1887-90, *Henry Irving Shakespeare, vol.* VII, *p.* 188.

Is there, then, nothing to be said in favour of Caliban? Is there really and truly no print of goodness in him? Kindly Nature never wholly deserts her offspring, nor does Shakespeare. We may be very sure that he, who knew so well that there is always some soul of goodness in things evil, would not have abandoned even Caliban without infusing into his nature some charm which might be observingly distilled out. Why is it that Caliban's speech is always rhythmical? There is no character in the play whose words fall at times into sweeter cadences; if the Æolian melodies of the air are sweet, the deep bass of the earth is no less rhythmically resonant. We who see Caliban only in his prime and, a victim of heredity, full grown, are apt to forget the years of his childhood and of his innocency, when Prospero fondled him, stroked him, and made much of him, Miranda taught him to speak, and with the sympathetic instinct of young girlhood interpreted his thoughts and endowed his purposes with words.—FURNESS, HORACE HOWARD, 1892, *New Variorum Shakespeare, The Tempest, vol.* IX, *p.* iv.

There is little in Homer that is not true to nature, but there is no phase of nature that is not in Shakespeare. Analyze the components of a Shakespearian play, and you will see that I make no overstatement. "The Tempest," a romantic play, is as notable as any for poetic quality and varied conception. It takes elemental nature for its scenes and background, the unbarred sky, the sea in storm and calm, the enchanted flowery isle, so

"full of noises,
Sounds and sweet airs that give delight and hurt not."

The personages comprise many types, —king, noble, sage, low-born sailor, boisterous vagabond, youth and maiden in the heyday of their innocent love. To them are superadded beings of the earth and air, Caliban and Ariel, creations of the purest imagination. All these reveal their natures by speech and action, with a realism impossible to the tamer method of a narrative poem. Consider the poetic thought and diciton: what can excel Prospero's vision of the world's dissolution that shall leave "not a rack behind," or his stately abjuration of the magic art? Listen, here and there, to the songs of his tricksy spirit, his brave chick, Ariel: "Come unto these yellow sands," "Full fathom five thy father lies," "Where the bee sucks, there suck I." Then we have a play within a play, lightening and decorating it, the masque of Iris, Ceres, and Juno. I recapitulate these details to give a perfectly familiar illustration of the scope of the drama. True, this was Shakespeare, but the ideal should be studied in a masterpiece; and such a play as "The Tempest" shows the possibilities of invention and imagination in the most synthetic poetic form over which genius has extended its domain.—STEDMAN, EDMUND CLARENCE, 1892, *The Nature and Elements of Poetry, p.* 106.

That rich, fantastic wonder-poem, "The Tempest," on which Shakespeare concentrated for the last time all the powers of his mind. Everything here is ordered and concise, and so inspired with thought that we seem to be standing face to face with the poet's idea. In spite of all its boldness of imagination, the dramatic order and condensation are such that the whole complies with the severest rules of Aristotle, the action of the entire play occupying in reality only three hours.—BRANDES, GEORGE, 1898 *William Shakespeare, A Critical Study, vol.* II, *p.* 361.

The splendour of sunset in the "Tempest" can escape no one, and the sternest opponent of guesswork must admit the probable presence of a designed allegory in the figure of Prospero and the burying of the book, the breaking of the staff, at the close. Even if this be thought too fanciful, nowhere has Shakespeare been more prodigal of every species of his enchantment. The exquisite but contrasted grace of Miranda and Ariel, the wonderful creation of Caliban, the varied human criticism in Gonzalo and the bad brothers, the farce-comedy of Stephano and Trinculo, do not more show the illimitable fancy and creative power of the master in scene and character than the passages, not so much scattered as showered over the whole play, show his absolute supremacy in poetry. Both in the blank verse and the lyrics, in the dialogue and the set *tirades*, in long contexts and short phrases alike, he shows himself absolute, with nothing out of reach of his faculty of expression and suggestion, with every resource of verbal music and intellectual demonstration at his command.—SAINTSBURY, GEORGE, 1898, *A Short History of English Literature, p.* 328.

CYMBELINE

1610–12

This play has many just sentiments, some natural dialogues, and some pleasing scenes, but they are obtained at the expense of much incongruity. To remark the folly of the fiction, the absurdity of the conduct, the confusion of the names, and manners of different times, and the impossibility of the events in any system of life, were to waste criticism upon unresisting imbecility, upon faults too evident for detection, and too gross for aggravation.—JOHNSON, SAMUEL, 1768, *General Observations on Shakspeare's Plays.*

"Cymbeline" is one of the most delightful of Shakespear's historical plays. . . . We have almost as great an affection for Imogen as she had for Posthumus; and she deserves it better. Of all Shakespear's women she is perhaps the most tender and the most artless. Her incredulity in the opening scene with Iachimo, as to her husband's infidelity, is much the same as Desdemona's backwardness to believe Othello's jealousy. Her answer to the most distressing part of the picture is only, "My lord, I fear, has forgot Britain." Her readiness to pardon Iachimo's false imputations and his designs against herself, is a good lesson to prudes; and may show that where there is a real attachment to virtue, it has no need to bolster itself up with an outrageous or affected antipathy to vice. — HAZLITT, WILLIAM, 1817–69, *Characters of Shakespeare's Plays, pp.* 1–3.

On the whole, Imogen is a lovely compound of goodness, truth, and affection, with just so much of passion and intellect and poetry, as serve to lend to the picture that power and glowing richness of effect which it would otherwise have wanted; and of her it might be said, if we could condescend to quote from any other poet with Shakspeare open before us, that "her person was a paradise and her soul the cherub to guard it."—JAMESON, ANNA BROWNELL, 1832, *Characteristics of Women.*

This play is perhaps the fittest in Shakspeare's whole theatre to illustrate the principle, that great dramatic genius can occasionally venture on bold improbabilities, and yet not only shrive the offence, but leave us enchanted with the offender. I think I exaggerate not, in saying that Shakspeare has nowhere breathed more pleasurable feelings over the mind, as an antidote to tragic pain, than in "Cymbeline." — CAMPBELL, THOMAS, 1838, *ed. Shakspeare's Plays, Moxon ed., Life.*

The play of plays, which is "Cymbeline," remains alone to receive the last salute of all my love I think, as far as I can tell, I may say I have always loved this one beyond all other children of Shakespeare.—SWINBURNE, ALGERNON CHARLES, 1880, *A Study of Shakespeare, p,* 225.

Yet the play is not merely a series of beautiful pictures, or interesting episodes, such as we are accustomed to find in the productions of dramatists of less renown. Here, as elsewhere in Shakespeare, everything is subservient to the development of character. From this point of view every scene contributes its share to the dénouement, nor is there any falling off observable in the power of the artist; the master-hand is as discernible in these latest creations as in those of any earlier period. And he has put forth all his strength on the central figure of the drama, the matchless Imogen, to speak of whom is to sing one long pæan of praise, and whose very name is as full of music as her voice. In her is to be found everything that makes woman lovable, and there is no situation in which she is placed which does not reveal some fresh beauty in her character.—EVANS, H. A., 1887–90, *Henry Irving Shakespeare, vol.* VII, *p.* 86.

This play is peculiarly a play of regeneration, and shows in manifold characters the process by which the soul is to free itself of its weak, inadequate, sinful phases. We find here, even the unregenerate—Cloten and his mother, who persist in evil and perish, though they, too, have the same chance as the rest. They can not be mediated, they make the Inferno in this comedy, which, in certain respects, is Dantean. But the chief realm here is the Purgatory, which shows the erring man in the process of regeneration. Many forms he takes, from the demon Iachimo, through Posthumus, the King, Belarius; up to even the good ones, Imogen and Pisanio; all are going through the purgatorial discipline. Shakespeare's Purgatory, however, includes the guiltless and the guilty, in this being different from Dante's; the sinless have to suffer for and through the sinful, thereby attaining to completeness and passing from mere innocence to positive goodness. But we have also a touch of the primitive Paradise in the two youths and their mountain home. Theirs is the state of first innocence, without knowledge, but they thirst for experience, and quit their paradisaical abode, having the old Adam in them still. Thus the play completes the cycle of the human, if not of the divine, comedy.—SNIDER, DENTON JAQUES, 1887, *The Shakespearian Drama, The Comedies, p.* 542.

The skill of the dramatist in opening his story, and preparing by clear touches for effects to be produced as it draws near the close, is a marked feature in all plays of Shakespeare, and nowhere more marked than in "Cymbeline."—MORLEY, HENRY, AND GRIFFIN, W. HALL, 1895, *English Writers, vol.* XI, *p.* 139.

In depth and variety of colouring, in richness of matter, profundity of thought, and heedlessness of conventional canons, "Cymbeline" has few rivals among Shakespeare's plays. Fascinating as it is, however, this tragi-comedy has never been very popular on the stage. The great public, indeed, has neither studied nor understood it.—BRANDES, GEORGE, 1898, *William Shakespeare, A Critical Study, vol.* II, *p.* 323.

WINTER'S TALE

1611

He said Shakespeare wanted art and sometimes sense, for in one of his plays he brought in a number of men saying they had suffered shipwreck in Bohemia, where is no sea near by 100 miles.—DRUMMOND, WILLIAM, 1619, *Notes on Ben Jonson's Conversations.*

The novel has nothing in it half so low and improbable as this contrivance of the statue; and indeed wherever Shakespear has altered or invented, his "Winter's Tale" is greatly inferior to the old paltry story that furnished him with the subject of it. — LENNOX, CHARLOTTE, 1753-4, *Shakespear Illustrated.*

There is a scene in this play which is an exception to the rest, in being far more grand in exhibition than the reader will possibly behold in idea. This is the scene of the Statue, when Mrs. Siddons stands for Hermione.—INCHBALD, ELIZABETH, 1806-9, *British Theatre, vol.* XII.

The character of Hermione exhibits what is never found in the other sex, but rarely in our own—yet sometimes—dignity without pride, love without passion, and tenderness without weakness. To conceive a character in which there enters so much of the negative, required perhaps no rare and astonishing effort of genius, such as created a Juliet, a Miranda, or a Lady Macbeth; but to delineate such a character in the poetical form, to develop it through the medium of action and dialogue, without the aid of description; to preserve its tranquil, mild, and serious beauty, its unimpassioned dignity, and at the same time keep the strongest hold upon our sympathy and our imagination; and out of this exterior calm, produce the most profound pathos, the most vivid impression of life and internal power:—it is this which renders the character of Hermione one of Shakspeare's masterpieces. —JAMESON, ANNA BROWNELL, 1832, *Characteristics of Women.*

In this wild drama the comedy is excellent, the pastoral is exquisite; but of the scenes which carry on the plot, some appear to me to be harsh in the thought and infelicitous in diction:—Shakespeare throughout, but not always Shakespeare in a happy vein.—COLERIDGE, HARTLEY, 1849-51, *Essays and Marginalia, vol.* II, *p.* 148.

Accordingly the most remarkable stroke of genius in this play of Shakespeare is that he turned only into a comedy a subject which could furnish the most sombre of tragedies. He understood admirably that however violent and tragic were the acts, such a character would be necessarily comic. Indeed, so comic, that it is exactly the one which our Moliere has drawn in *Sganarelle, ou le Cocu imaginaire.* Leontes is formidable otherwise than the poor *bourgeois* of Molière, for his folly is supplied with far different means of action; but they are brothers, if not in rank yet in nature, and their souls plunge into the same grotesque element.—MONTÉGUT, EMILE, 1867, *Œuvres Complètes de Shakespeare, vol.* III.

The last complete play of Shakspere's as it is, the golden glow of the sunset of his genius is over it, the sweet country air all through it; and of few, if any of his plays, is there a pleasanter picture in the memory than of "Winter's Tale." As long as men can think, shall Perdita brighten and sweeten, Hermione ennoble, men's minds and lives. How happily, too, it brings Shakspere before us, mixing with his Stratford neighbours at their sheep-shearing and country sports, enjoying the vagabond pedlar's gammon and talk, delighting in the sweet Warwickshire maidens, and buying them "fairings," telling goblin stories to the boys, "There was a man dwelt by a churchyard,"—opening his heart afresh to all the innocent mirth, and the beauty of nature around him.—FURNIVALL, FREDERICK JAMES, 1877, *ed. The Leopold Shakspere, Introduction to the Play.*

The wild wind of the "Winter's Tale" at its opening would seem to blow us back into a winterier world indeed. And to the very end I must confess that I have in me so much of the spirit of Rachel weeping in Ramah as will not be comforted because Mamillius is not. It is well for those whose hearts are light enough, to take perfect comfort even in the substitution of his sister Perdita for the boy who died of "thoughts high for one so tender." Even the beautiful suggestion that Shakespeare as he wrote had in mind his own dead little son still fresh and living at his heart can hardly add more than a touch of additional tenderness to our perfect and piteous delight in him. And even in her daughter's embrace it seems hard if his mother should have utterly forgotten the little voice that had only time to tell her just eight words of that ghost story which neither she nor we were ever to hear ended.—SWINBURNE, ALGERNON CHARLES, 1880, *A Study of Shakespeare, p.* 222.

Besides the ripe comedy, characteristic of Shakespeare at his latest, which indeed harmonizes admirably with the idyl of love to which it serves as background, there is also a harsh exhibition, in Leontes, of the meanest of the passions, an insane jealousy, petty and violent as the man who nurses it. For sheer realism, for absolute insight into the most cobwebbed corners of our nature, Shakespeare has rarely surpassed this brief study, which, in its total effect, does but throw out in brighter relief the noble qualities of the other actors beside him, the pleasant qualities of the play they make by their acting.—SYMONS, ARTHUR, 1887–90, *Henry Irving Shakespeare, vol.* VII, *p.* 320.

"The Winter's Tale," with its interval for sixteen years between two acts, may be said, too, to mark the final overthrow of Time—the hallowed "Unity of Time"—by its natural adversary, the Romantic Drama. The play recalls Sir Philip Sidney's criticism, in his "Apologie for Poetrie," anent the crude romantic plays popular about 1580, when he outlined a plot somewhat analogous to that of "The Winter's Tale" as a typical instance of the abuse of dramatic decorum by lawless playwrights, who, contrary to academic rule, neglected both "time and place." "The Winter's Tale," perhaps the very last of Shakespeare's comedies, appropriately emphasises, as it were, the essential elements of the triumph of the New over the Old. Sidney could not foresee, in 1580, the glorious future in store for the despised Cinderella of the playhouses,

"Now grown in grace
Equal with wondering."

—GOLLANCZ, ISRAEL, 1894, *ed. Temple Shakespeare, Preface, p.* x.

HENRY VIII.

1613

Now let matters of state sleep, I will entertain you at the present with what happened at the Bankside. The king's players had a new play, called "All is True," representing some principal pieces of the reign of Henry VIII., which was set forth with many extraordinary circumstances of pomp and majesty, even to the matting of the stage; the knights of the Order, with their Georges and Garter, the guards with their embroidered coats and the like; sufficient, in Truth, within a while to make greatness very familiar if not ridiculous. Now King Henry making a masque at the Cardinal Wolsey's House, and certain canons being shot off at his entrance, some of the paper, or other stuff wherewith one of them was stopped, did light on the thatch, where being thought at first but an idle smoak, and their eyes more attentive to the show, it kindled inwardly and ran round like a train, consuming within less than an hour the whole House to the very grounds.—WOTTON, SIR HENRY, 1613, *Epistles.*

London this last of June 1613.

No longer since then yesterday, while Bourbege his companie were acting at ye Globe the play of Hen: 8, and there shooting of certayne chambers in way of triumph; the fire catch'd & fastened upon the thatch of ye house and there burned so furiously as it consumed the whole house & all in lesse then two houres (the people having enough to doe to save themselves).—LORKINS, THOMAS, 1613, *Letter to Sir Thomas Puckering. Harl. MS.* 7,002, *fo.* 268.

January 1.—Went to the Duke's house, the first play I have been at these six months, according to my last vowe, and here saw the so much cried-up play of "Henry the Eighth;" which, though I went with resolution to like it, is so simple a thing made up of a great many patches, that, besides the shows and processions in it, there is nothing in the world good or well done. —PEPYS, SAMUEL, 1663–4, *Diary and Correspondence.*

It was no easy task for an author to compose a dramatic piece which should comprehend several transactions of a monarch recently dead, who had rendered himself so odious to his subjects. To bring upon the stage, before the reigning queen, his daughter, a character so doubtful, at least, as her royal father; to present a strong resemblance of many of his most striking features, without alarming his sovereign, or disgusting the spectators; was an undertaking worthy the genius of Shakspeare; and in which, notwithstanding the apparent difficulty, he has admirably succeeded.—DAVIES, THOMAS, 1784, *Dramatic Micellanies, vol.* I, *p.* 338.

The character of Henry VIII. is drawn with great truth and spirit. It is like a very disagreeable portrait, sketched by the hand of a master. His gross appearance, his blustering demeanour, his vulgarity, his arrogance, his sensuality, his cruelty, his hypocrisy, his want of common decency and common humanity, are marked in strong lines. His traditional peculiarities of expression complete the reality of the picture. The authoritative expletive, "Ha!" with which he intimates his indignation or surprise, has an effect like the first startling sound that breaks from a thunder-cloud. He is of all the monarchs in our history the most disgusting: for he unites in himself all the vices of barbarism and refinement, without their virtues. —HAZLITT, WILLIAM, 1817–69, *Characters of Shakespear's Plays, p.* 170.

"Henry VIII" has for us a literary interest, on account of its style, which the poet has certainly been careful to bring into conformity with the language of the court, as spoken in his own time, or a few years previously. In no other of his works is the style so elliptical; the habits of conversation seem to introduce into the construction of its sentences that economy and abbreviation which, in English pronunciation, deprive words of nearly half their syllables. Moreover, we find in it scarcely any play upon words, and, excepting only in a few passages, very little poetry.—GUIZOT, FRANCOIS PIERRE GUILLAUME, 1821–52, *Shakspeare and His Times, p.* 340.

Poetical art perhaps never flattered a monster with such palpable likeness, and yet with such impalpable and cunning mitigation. He suborns his guilty love itself to seduce our sympathy by the beauty of its object.—CAMPBELL, THOMAS, 1838, *ed. Shakspeare's Plays, Moxon ed., Life.*

QUEEN KATHARINE. In spite of the great virtues which I have to acknowledge in her, I have an insurmountable dislike to this princess. As a married woman she was a pattern of social fidelity. As a queen she was most dignified and majestic. As a Christian she was virtue personified. But she inspired Dr. Samuel Johnson with a voice to sing her highest praise, and of all the women described by Shakespeare she is his special favourite. He mentions her with tender pathos . . . and this is insufferable. Shakespeare did his best to idealise the good woman but this is in vain, when we perceive that this beer-barrel Dr. Johnson is overcome by tender delight at her sight and runs over in her praise. Were she my wife I could make such praise a ground of separation.—HEINE, HEINRICH, 1838–95, *Notes on Shakespeare Heroines, tr. Benecke, p,* 100.

The opening . . . seemed to have the full stamp of Shakspere in his latest manner; the same close-packed expression; the same life and reality and freshness; the same rapid and abrupt turnings of thought, so quick that language can hardly follow fast enough; the same impatient activity of intellect and fancy, which, having once disclosed an idea, cannot wait to work it orderly out; the same daring confidence in the resources of language which plunges headlong into a sentence without knowing how it is to come forth; the same careless metre which disdains to produce its harmonious effects by the ordinary devices, yet is evidently subject to a master of harmony; the same entire freedom from book-language and commonplace.—SPEDDING, JAMES, 1850, *Who Wrote Shakspere's Henry VIII.? Gentleman's Magazine, August.*

In "Henry VIII." I think I see plainly the cropping out of the original rock on which his own finer stratum was laid. The first play was written by a superior, thoughtful man, with a vicious ear. I can mark his lines, and know well their cadence. See Wolsey's soliloquy, and the following scene with Cromwell, where instead of the metre of Shakspeare, whose secret is that the thought constructs the tune, so that reading for the sense will best bring out the rhythm,—here the lines are constructed on a given tune, and the verse has even a trace of pulpit eloquence. But the play contains through all its length unmistakable traits of Shakspeare's hand, and some passages, as the account of the coronation, are like autographs. What is odd, the compliment to Queen Elizabeth is in the bad rhythm.—EMERSON, RALPH WALDO, 1850–76, *Shakspeare; or, the Poet, Representative Men.*

We admit, then, that this play offers us in some not unimportant passages the single instance of a style not elsewhere precisely or altogether traceable in Shakespeare; that no exact parallel to it can be found among his other plays; and that if not the partial work it may certainly be taken as the general model of Fletcher in his tragic poetry. On the other hand, we contend that its exceptional quality might perhaps be explicable as a tentative essay in a new line by one who tried so many styles before settling into his latest; and that, without far stronger, clearer, and completer proof than has yet been or can ever be advanced, the question is not solved but merely evaded by the assumption of a double authorship.—SWINBURNE, ALGERNON CHARLES, 1880, *A Study of Shakespeare, p.* 93.

I have no doubt that much of "Henry VIII." also is not Shakespeare. It is largely written by Fletcher, with passages unmistakeably by Shakespeare, notably the two first scenes in the first Act, which are sane and compact in thought, expression and simile.—TENNYSON, ALFRED, LORD, 1883, *Some Criticisms on Poets, Memoir by his Son, vol.* II, *p.* 291.

If Katharine is a little disappointing, Anne is an unmitigated failure. . . . Turning to the character of Henry VIII. we find a showy figure, who plays his part of king not without effect. Looking deeper, we discover that there is nothing deeper to discover. The Henry of history is a puzzling character, but the Henry of a play should be adequately conceived and intelligibly presented. Whatever disguise he may choose to assume towards the men and women who walk beside him on the boards, to us he must be without disguise. As it is, we know no more than after reading Holinshed whether the Henry of the play believed or did not believe—or what partial belief he had—in those "scruples," for instance, to which he refers, not without a certain unction. He is illogical, insubstantial, the merely superficial presentment of a deeply interesting historical figure, who would, we may be sure, have had intense interest for Shakespeare, and to whom Shakespeare would have given his keenest thought, his finest workmanship.—SYMONS, ARTHUR, 1887–90, *Henry Irving Shakespeare, vol.* VIII, *pp.* 162, 163.

REJECTED PLAYS

Arden of Feversham

The speeches in "Arden of Feversham" have spirit and feeling; but there is none of that wit, that fertility of analogical imagery, which the worst plays of Shakspeare display. The language is also more plain and perspicuous than we ever find in him, especially on a subject so full of passion.—HALLAM, HENRY, 1842, *Introduction to the Literature of Europe, pt.* ii, *ch.* vi, *par.* 33, *note.*

The play, as a whole, is but a slovenly piece of work, and the characters carrying on its action are throughout either repulsive or uninteresting. There seems an intention to suggest in Arden's avarice a kind of poetic justification of his doom; but the hint is too slight to be of much effect. The character of the wife, hateful in itself, is invested with no adventitious charm or allurement; vice is painted as nakedly and blackly as it is by the chronicler. The personages of the hired ruffians are rather in Ben Jonson's style; but there is little humour to relieve the loathsomeness of the figures. On the other hand, "Arden of Feversham" contains one or two passages which strongly resemble Shakspere in manner.—WARD, ADOLPHUS WILLIAM, 1875–99, *A History of English Dramatic Literature, vol.* II, *p,* 218.

Either this play is the young Shakespeare's first tragic master-piece, or there was a writer unknown to us then alive and at work for the stage who excelled him as a tragic dramatist not less—to say the very least—than he was excelled by Marlowe as a narrative and tragic poet. . . . I cannot but finally take heart to say, even in the absence of all external or traditional testimony, that it seems to me not pardonable merely nor permissible, but simply logical and reasonable, to set down this poem, a young man's work on the face of it, as the possible work of no man's youthful hand but Shakespeare's.—SWINBURNE, ALGERNON CHARLES, 1880, *A Study of Shakespeare, pp.* 136, 141.

Has no similarities of versification, and does not, in its dealing with the murder of a husband by his wife and her base-born paramour, suggest Shakespeare's choice of subject, but is closer in some ways than any other play to his handling in character and psychological analysis.—SAINTSBURY, GEORGE, 1898, *A Short History of English Literature, p.* 329.

Highly as I esteem "Arden of Feversham," I cannot believe that Shakespeare wrote a single line of it. It was not like him to choose such a subject, and still less to treat it in such a fashion. The play is a domestic tragedy, in which a wife, after repeated attempts, murders her kind and forbearing husband, in order freely to indulge her passion for a worthless paramour. It is a dramatisation of an actual case, the facts of which are closely followed, but at the same time animated with great psychological insight. That Shakespeare had a distaste for such subjects is proved by his consistent avoidance of them, except in this problematical instance; whereas if he had once succeeded so well with such a theme, he would surely have repeated the experiment. The chief point is, however, that only in a few places, in the soliloquies, do we find the peculiar note of Shakespeare's style—that wealth of imagination, that luxuriant lyrism, which plays like sunlight over his speeches. In "Arden of Feversham" the style is a uniform drab.—BRANDES, GEORGE, 1898, *William Shakespeare, A Critical Study, vol.* I, *p.* 204.

Sir John Oldcastle

"Sir John Oldcastle" is certainly not worthy to be ranked among the works of Shakespear, and it is with great propriety that it has been generally rejected. It has, however, evident marks in places of strong and familiar genius, which might have arisen from his having improved it; but even then they appear to be the shadow of his writing rather than the writing itself.—DIBDIN, CHARLES, 1795, *A Complete History of the Stage, vol.* III, *p.* 77.

"Sir John Oldcastle" is the compound piecework of four minor playwrights, one of them afterwards and otherwise eminent as a poet—Munday, Drayton, Wilson, and Hathaway: a thin sample of poetic patchery cobbled up and stitched together so as to serve its hour for a season without falling to pieces at the first touch.—SWINBURNE, ALGERNON CHARLES, 1880, *A Study of Shakespeare, Appendix, p.* 232.

Cromwell

"Cromwell" is one of those plays rejected as Shakespear's, and certainly with great reason, for it has upon the whole less of those marks of his genius and judgment than any of those pieces that have been merely attributed to him. That he had some concern in it, however, cannot be doubted. The foot of Hercules can belong only to Hercules.—DIBDIN, CHARLES, 1795, *A Complete History of the Stage, vol.* III, *p.* 90.

"Thomas Lord Cromwell" is a piece of such utterly shapeless, spiritless, bodiless, soulless, senseless, helpless, worthless, rubbish, that there is no known writer of Shakespeare's age to whom it could be ascribed without the infliction of an unwarrantable insult on that writer's memory.—SWINBURNE, ALGERNON CHARLES, 1880, *A Study of Shakespeare, Appendix, p.* 232.

Yorkshire Tragedy

Is by some attributed to Shakespear; as however all his commentators, except Mr. Steevens, have agreed to reject it, to avoid unnecessary cavil, we will agree so far with them as to say that it seems to stand in a predicament something between "Pericles," and "Locrine;" for though there are evidently many images which appear to have emanated from the mind of Shakespear, those passages seem rather to have been written for the assistance of another than that the whole belonged to himself. Let the belief, however, rest either way, the merit of it cannot assist any more than the imperfections of it can diminish his reputation.—DIBDIN, CHARLES, 1795, *A Complete History of the Stage, vol.* III, *p.* 335.

For concentrated might and overwhelming weight of realism, this lurid little play beats "A Warning for Fair Women" fairly out of the field. It is and must always be (I had nearly said, thank heaven) unsurpassable for pure potency of horror; and the breathless heat of the action, its raging rate of speed, leaves actually no breathing-time for disgust; it consumes our very sense of repulsion as with fire. But such power as this, though a rare and a great gift, is not the right quality for a dramatist; it is not the fit property of a poet. Ford and Webster, even Tourneur and Marston, who have all been more or less wrongfully though more or less plausibly attacked on the score of excess in horror, have none of them left us anything so nakedly terrible, so terribly naked as this. Passion is here not merely stripped to the skin but stripped to the bones. I cannot tell who could and I cannot guess who would have written it. "'Tis a very excellent piece of work;" may we never exactly look upon its like again!—SWINBURNE, ALGERNON CHARLES, 1880, *A Study of Shakespeare, p.* 143.

AUTHORSHIP CONTROVERSY

Editors and commentators upon Shakspeare appear at every turn in all societies. In the club-house we meet three or four of a morning; in the park, see them meditating by the Serpentine, or under a tree in Kensington Gardens; no dinner table is without one or two; in the theatre you view them by dozens. Volume after volume is poured out in note, comment, conjecture, new reading, statement or mis-statement, contradiction, or variation of all kinds. Reviews, magazines, and newspapers, repeat these with so little mercy on the reader, as to give occasional emendations of their own. Some descant upon his sentiments, some upon his extravagancies, some upon his wonderful creations or flights of imagination, some upon his language or phraseology. Several suppose that he wrote more plays than he acknowledged; others, that he fathered more than he had written. While the last opinions are still more original and extraordinary—that his name is akin to a myth, and that he wrote no plays at all! Every new aspirant in this struggle for distinction aims to push his predecessor from his stool.—PRIOR, SIR JAMES, 1780–90, *Life of Edmund Malone, Editor of Shakspeare, p.* 47.

Alas, Shakespeare! Lethe is upon thee! But if it drown thee, it will give up and work the resurrection of better men and more worthy. Thou hast had thy century; they are about having theirs. . . . He was not the mate of the literary characters of his day, and none knew it better than himself. It is a fraud upon the world to thrust his surreptitious fame upon us. He had none that was worthy of being transmitted. The enquiry will be, who were the able literary men who wrote the dramas imputed to him? The plays themselves, or rather a small portion of them, will live as long as English literature is regarded as worth pursuit. The authorship of the plays is no otherwise material to us, than as a matter of curiosity, and to enable us to render exact justice; but they should not be assigned to Shakespeare alone, if at all.—HART, JOSEPH C., 1848, *The Ancient Lethe.*

Shall this crowning literary product of that great epoch, wherein these new ages have their beginning, vividly arranged in its choicest refinements, flashing everywhere on the surface with its costliest wit, crowded everywhere with its subtlest scholasticisms, betraying, on every page, its broadest, freshest range of experience, its most varied culture, its profoundest insight, its boldest grasp of comprehension—shall this crowning result of so many preceding ages of growth and culture, with its essential, and now palpable connection with the new scientific movement of the time from which it issues, be able to conceal from us, much longer, its history?—Shall we be able to accept in explanation of it, much longer, the story of the Stratford poacher?—BACON, DELIA, 1856, *William Shakespeare and his Plays, Putnam's Magazine, vol.* 7, *p.* 2.

I am sure that, if those who deny to Shakespeare the credit of writing his own dramas had thought of ascribing them to the judicious Hooker or the pious Bishop Andrews instead of Lord Bacon, they might have made a specious show of proof by carefully culled extracts from his writings. Nay, if

Jeremy Taylor, whose prose is so full of poetry, had not been born a generation too late, I would engage, in the same way, to put a plausible face on the theory that the plays of Shakespeare, except, perhaps, some passages wickedly interpolated, were composed by the eloquent and devout author of "Holy Living and Dead."—BRYANT, WILLIAM CULLEN, 1872, *Shakespeare, Occasional Addresses, vol.* II, *p.* 302.

It is not possible for me to feel the slightest interest in the sort of literary feat which I consider writing upon "Who wrote Shakespeare?" to be. I was very intimate with Harness, Milman, Dyce, Collier—all Shakespearian editors, commentators, and scholars—and this absurd theory about Bacon, which was first broached a good many years ago, never obtained credit for a moment with them; nor did they ever entertain for an instant a doubt that the plays attributed to William Shakespeare of Stratford-on-Avon were really written by him. Now I am intimately acquainted and in frequent communication with William Donne, Edward Fitzgerald, and James Spedding, all thorough Shakespeare scholars, and the latter a man who has just published a work upon Bacon, which has been really the labor of his life; none of these men, competent judges of the matter, ever mention the question of "Who wrote Shakespeare?" except as a ludicrous thing to be laughed at, and I think they may be trusted to decide whether it is or is not so. I have a slight feeling of disgust at the attack made thus on the personality of my greatest mental benefactor; and consider the whole thing a misapplication, not to say waste, of time and ingenuity that might be better employed. As I regard the memory of Shakespeare with love, veneration, and gratitude, and am proud and happy to be his countrywoman, considering it among the priviliges of my English birth, I resent the endeavor to prove that he deserved none of these feelings, but was a mere literary impostor. I wonder the question had any interest for you, for I should not have supposed you imagined Shakespeare had not written his own plays, Irish though you be. Do you remember the servant's joke in the farce of "High Life Below Stairs" where the cook asks, "Who wrote Shakespeare?" and one of the others answers, with, at any rate, partial plausibility, "Oh! why, Colley Cibber, to be sure!"—KEMBLE, FRANCES ANNE, 1874, *Further Records, A Series of Letters, p.* 53.

We may be told, at this stage, that such an extent of search and demonstration as I have devoted to these Baconian points is not necessary to dispose of a bubble which had never floated among the public with any amount of success; and we may be flippantly assured that the inexorable reasoning faculty of Time alone, would, of itself, dispel the fallacy; but such contemptuous treatment is not adequate to the destruction of a theory which has received the support of such minds as that of Lord Palmerston, in England, and such scholars and critics as Judge Holmes and General Butler in America. Bubbles thus patronized must be entirely exploded, or they will be sure to reappear whenever the world has a sick or idle hour, and delusions find their opportunity to strike. Moreover, nothing is lost by our inquiries, after all, beyond a little time; and I doubt not that all true admirers of our poet will agree, that one new ray of light which may thus be thrown upon the character and history of Shakespeare, will justify octavos of discussion.—WILKES, GEORGE, 1877, *Shakespeare from an American Point of View, p.* 457.

The critic has the same interest in the works of Miss Delia Bacon, Mr. W. H. Smith, and Judge Holmes, as the physician has in morbid anatomy. He reads them, not so much for the light which they throw on the question of authorship, as for their interest as examples of wrongheadedness. It is not at all a matter of moment whether Bacon, Raleigh, or another be the favorite on whom the works are fathered, but it is instructive to discover by what plausible process the positive evidences of Shakespeare's authorship (scanty as they are) are put out of court.—INGLEBY, CLEMENT MANSFIELD, 1877, *Shakespeare: The Man and the Book.*

When we ask whether it would have been easier for the author of the philosophy to have composed the drama, or the dramatic poet to have written the philosophy, the answer will depend upon which is the greater of the two. The greater includes the less, but the less can not include the greater. . . . Great as are the thoughts of the "Novum Organum," they are far inferior to that world of thought which is in the drama. We can easily conceive that Shakespeare, having produced in his prime the wonders and glories of the plays, should in his after leisure have developed the leading ideas of the Baconian philosophy. But it is difficult to imagine that Bacon, while devoting his main strength to politics, to law, to philosophy, should have, as a mere pastime for his leisure, produced in his idle moments the greatest intellectual work ever done on earth.—CLARKE, JAMES FREEMAN, 1881, *Did Shakespeare Write Bacon's Works? North American Review, vol.* 132, *p.* 171.

This work undertakes to demonstrate, not only that William Shakespeare did not, but that Francis Bacon did, write the plays and poems. It presents a critical view of the personal history of the two men, their education, learning, attainments, surroundings, and associates, the contemporaneousness of the writings in question, in prose and verse, an account of the earlier plays and editions, the spurious plays, and "the true original copies." It gives some evidence that Bacon was known to be the author by some of his contemporaries. It shows in what manner William Shakespeare came to have the reputation of being the writer. It exhibits a variety of facts and circumstances, which are strongly suggestive of Bacon as the real author. A comparison of the writings of contemporary authors in prose and verse, proves that no other writer of that age, but Bacon, can come into any competition for the authorship. . . . It is recognized that the evidence drawn from historical facts and biographical circumstances, are not in themselves alone entirely conclusive of the matter, however suggestive or significant as clearing the way for more decisive proofs, or as raising a high degree of probability; and it is conceded, that, in the absence of more direct evidence, the most decisive proof attainable is to be found in a critical and thorough comparison of the writings themselves, and that such a comparison will clearly establish the identity of the author as no other than Francis Bacon. —HOLMES, NATHANIEL, 1884, *The Authorship of Shakespeare, Bibliography of the Bacon-Shakespeare Controversy, ed. Wyman, p.* 28.

Bacon could no more have written the plays than Shakespeare could have prophesied the triumphs of natural philosophy.—CHURCH, RICHARD WILLIAM, 1884–88, *Bacon, p.* 218.

The ingenious critics who insist on merging the existence of Shakespeare in the philosophy of Bacon, are not entirely without excuse for their infatuation.—FRASER, JOHN, 1887, *Chaucer to Longfellow, p.* 311.

As to the actuality of the Cipher there can be but one conclusion. A long, continuous narrative, running through many pages, detailing historical events in a perfectly symmetrical, rhetorical, grammatical manner, and *always growing out of the same numbers, employed in the same way, and counting from the same, or similar, starting-points, cannot be otherwise than a pre-arranged arithmetical cipher.* Let those who would deny this proposition produce a single page of a connected story, eliminated, by an arithmetical rule, from any other work; in fact, let them find five words that will cohere, by accident, in due order, in any publication, where they were not first placed with intent and aforethought. I have never yet been able to find even three such. Regularity does not grow out of chaos. There can be no intellectual order without preëxisting intellectual purpose. The fruits of mind can only be found where mind is or has been.—DONNELLY, IGNATIUS, 1887, *The Great Cryptogram, Introduction, p.* v.

Some attempts have been recently made to extinguish Shakspeare's individuality in Bacon's. Any reader who intimately knows and sincerely loves both authors instinctively feels that the external evidence against Shakspeare's real existence is simply unworthy of critical consideration. Shakspeare's vast mind is in itself a sufficient puzzle for the critic and the metaphysician to explain; to blend it with Bacon's is to double the difficulties of the problem. Shakspeare and Bacon are both high above the ordinary range of even eminent intellects and souls; but to say that Bacon "wrote Shakspeare" is to introduce hopeless confusion into the philosophy of the human mind. Every critic who has the slightest discernment of spirits must know that the mental processes of Shakspeare and Bacon are fundamentally different,—a difference which goes deep down into vital sources of individual genius. Shakspeare individualizes the results of his knowledge; Bacon generalizes the results of his. The mind of Shakspeare *darts* to conclusions; the mind of Bacon *moves* to them with a gravity worthy of a lord chancellor. Both are men of large reason, large understanding, large imagination, large individuality; but they are different not only in degree, but in kind. It would be impossible for any intelligent critic to reconcile a really characteristic work of Shakspeare with a really characteristic work of Bacon. The mental processes of the two men are radically dissimilar. —WHIPPLE, EDWIN P., 1888, *Outlooks on Society, Literature and Politics, p.* 300.

The portrait, after all, that forms the frontispiece to the plays does not look like a perfect fool. It is not a bad nor a mean forehead, is it? If the person it represents did not do something remarkable, one cannot help wondering why not, with that great brain, and that speaking face. What did Ben Jonson mean by those verses of his, saying that this "was for the gentle Shakespeare cut"? Did he mean by gentle, silly? When he spoke of his wit, did he speak ironically? Or did Bacon buy up him too, and get him to write this lie? Joking apart, I think nothing more monstrous was ever conceived than this theory. It is too foolish even to be entitled to consideration.—STORY, WILLIAM WETMORE, 1890, *Conversations in a Studio, vol.* I, *p.* 173.

It is well known that in recent days a troop of less than half-educated people have put forth the doctrine that Shakespeare lent his name to a body of poetry with which he had really nothing to do—which he could not have understood, much less have written. Literary criticism is an instrument which, like all delicate tools, must be handled carefully, and only by those who have a vocation for it. Here it has fallen into the hands of raw Americans and fanatical women. Feminine criticism on the one hand, with its lack of artistic nerve, and Americanism on the other hand, with its lack of spiritual delicacy, have declared war to the knife against Shakespeare's personality, and have within the last few years found a considerable number of adherents. We have here another proof, if any were needed, that the judgment of the multitude, in questions of art, is a negligible quantity. Before the middle of this century, it had occurred to no human being to doubt that—trifling exceptions apart—the works attributed to Shakespeare were actually written by him. It has been reserved for the last forty years to see an ever-increasing stream of obloquy and contempt directed against what had hitherto been the most honoured name in modern literature.—BRANDES, GEORGE, 1898, *William Shakespeare, A Critical Study, vol.* I, *p.* 104.

The abundance of the contemporary evidence attesting Shakespeare's responsibility for the works published under his name gives the Baconian theory no rational right to a hearing; while such authentic examples of Bacon's effort to write verse as survive prove beyond all possibility of contradiction that, great as he was as a prose-writer and a philosopher, he was incapable of penning any of the poetry assigned to Shakespeare. Defective knowledge and illogical or casuistical argument alone render any other conclusion possible.—LEE, SIDNEY, 1898, *A Life of William Shakespeare, p.* 373, *Appendix.*

It appears that the author of the plays took little care for their preservation, while Bacon took the greatest pains to preserve his acknowledged writings, even when their publication must be postponed; that he was familiar with English poetry, songs and plays, both published and unpublished, some of the latter having no existence, probably, outside of the theatres, while there is nothing to show that Bacon had any knowledge of or taste for such writings, or that he could have had access to the unpublished plays, and in fact it seems probable that he despised them all; that Shakespeare was known and recognized as a poet from poems of conspicuous merit and undoubted authenticity, while Bacon produced no poem worthy of notice, and with a single exception was never spoken of by his contemporaries as a writer of poetry; that the author, moreover, shows an acquaintance with Warwickshire, the home of Shakespeare, and used names and language relating to habits, customs, sports, there prevalent, and to occupations with which Shakespeare was familiar, and also used provincialisms there current, while Bacon is not known ever to have visited that part of England; that he was also steeped in knowledge of rural life, and of the customs and habitual modes of speech of the lower classes, which Bacon would naturally have less acquaintance with; that the plays abound in anachronisms, historical errors, and obscurities and other peculiarities in the text, which Bacon was less likely than Shakespeare to fall into; and that the author was familiar with, and was full to repletion of allusions to, theatrical matters, and the habits and technical language of actors, which formed the daily life and speech of Shakespeare, while Bacon must have been less conversant if not entirely unacquainted with them. All of these circumstances tend in a greater or less degree to negative the theory of Baconian authorship; and the combined or cumulative force of so many detailed facts, all pointing in the same direction, is certainly a consideration of great weight.—ALLEN, CHARLES, 1900, *Notes on the Bacon-Shakespeare Question, p.* 237.

GENERAL

?And he, the man whom Nature selfe had made
To mock her selfe, and Truth to imitate,
With kindly counter under Mimick shade,
Our pleasant Willy, ah! is dead of late:
With whom all joy and jolly meriment
Is also deaded, and in dolour drent.
—SPENSER, EDMUND, 1591, *The Teares of the Muses, Spenser's Works, ed. Collier, vol.* iv, *p.* 335.

As the soul of Euphorbus was thought to live in Pythagoras: so the sweet witty soul of Ovid lives in mellifluous and honey-tongued Shakespeare. Witness his Venus and Adonis; his Lucrece; his sugared Sonnets, among his private friends; &c. As Plautus and Seneca are accounted the best for Comedy and Tragedy among the Latins: so Shakespeare among the English is the most excellent in both kinds for the stage. For Comedy: witness his Gentlemen of Verona; his (Comedy of) Errors; his Love's Labour's Lost; his Love's Labour's Won (? All's Well that Ends Well) his Midsummer Night's Dream; and his Merchant of Venice. For tragedy: his Richard II., Richard III., Henry IV., King John, Titus Andronicus, and his Romeo and Juliet. As Epius Stolo said that the Muses would speak with Plautus's tongue, if they would speak Latin: so I say that the Muses would speak with Shakespeare's fine filed phrase; if they would speak English.—MERES, FRANCIS, 1598, *Palladis Tamia.*

Honie-tong'd Shekespeare when I saw thine issue,
I swore Apollo got them and none other,
Their rosie-tainted features cloth'd in tissue,
Some heaven born goddesse said to be their mother:
Rose-cheekt Adonis with his amber tresses,
Faire fire-hot Venus charming him to love her,
Chaste Lucretia virgine-like her dresses,
Proud lust-stung Tarquine seeking still to prove her.
Romea, Richard, more whose names I know not,
Their sugred tongues and power attractive beuty
Say they are Saints, althogh that Sts. they shew not
For thousands vowes to them subjective dutie:
They burn in love, thy children Shakespear het thē,
Go, wo thy Muse, more Nymphish brood beget them.
—WEEVER, JOHN, 1599, *Epigrammes in the Oldest Cut and Newest Fashion.*

Our English Terence.—DAVIES, JOHN, OF HEREFORD, 1611, *The Scourge of Folly, Works, ed. Grosart, p.* 26

Soule of the Age!
The applause! delight! the wonder of our Stage!
My *Shakespeare*, rise; I will not lodge thee by
Chaucer, or *Spenser*, or bid *Beaumont* lye
A little further, to make thee a roome:
Thou art a Moniment, without a tombe,
And art alive still, while thy Booke doth live,
And we have wits to read, and praise to give.
That I not mixe thee so, my braine excuses;
I meane with great, but disproportion'd *Muses:*
For, if I thought my judgement were of yeeres,
I should commit thee surely with thy peeres,
And tell, how farre thou didstst our *Lily* outshine,
Or sporting *Kid*, or *Marlowes* mighty line.
And though thou hadst small *Latine*, and lesse *Greeke*,
From thence to honour thee, I would not seeke
For names; but call forth thund'ring *Æschilus*,
Euripides, and *Sophocles* to us,
Paccuvius, *Accius*, him of *Cordova* dead,
To life againe, to heare thy Buskin tread,
And shake a Stage: Or, when thy Sockes were on,

Leave thee alone, for the comparison
Of all, that insolent *Greece*, or haughtie *Rome*
sent forth, or since did from their ashes come.

. . . .

He was not of an age, but for all time!
And all the *Muses* still were in their prime,
When like *Apollo* he came forth to warme
Our eares, or like a *Mercury* to charme!
Nature her selfe was proud of his designes,
And joy'd to weare the dressing of his lines!
Which were so richly spun, and woven so fit,
As, since, she will vouchsafe no other Wit.

. . . .

Sweet Swan of *Avon!*

. . . .

Shine forth, thou Starre of *Poets*, and with rage,
Or influence, chide, or cheere the drooping Stage;
Which, since thy flight frō hence, hath mourn'd like night,
And despaires day, but for thy Volumes light.

—JONSON, BEN, 1623, *Shakespeare's Works, Preface.*

And though you be a Magistrate of wit, and sit on the Stage at *Black-Friers*, or the *Cock-pit*, to arraigne Playes dailie, know, these Playes have had their triall alreadie, and stood out all Appeales; and do now come forth quitted rather by a Decree of Court, then any purchas'd Letters of commendation. It had bene a thing, we confesse, worthie to have bene wished, that the Author himselfe had liv'd to have set forth, and overseen his owne writtings; But since it hath bin ordain'd otherwise, and he by death departed from that right, we pray you do not envie his Friends, the office of their care, and paine, to have collected & publish'd them; and so to have publish'd them, as where (before) you were abus'd with diverse stolne, and surreptitious copies, maimed, and deformed by the frauds and stealthes of injurious impostors, that expos'd them: even those, are now offer'd to your view cur'd, and perfect of their limbes; and all the rest, absolute in their numbers, as he conceived thē. Who, as he was a happie imitator of Nature, was a most gentle expresser of it. His mind and hand went together: And what he thought, he uttered with that easinesse, that wee have scarse received from him a blot in his papers. But it is not our province, who onely gather his works, and give them you, to praise him. It is yours that reade him. And there we hope, to your divers capacities, you will finde enough, both to draw, and hold you: for his wit can no more lie hid, then it could be lost. Reade him, therefore; and againe, and againe: And if then you doe not like him, surely you are in some manifest danger, not to understand him. And so we leave you to other of his Friends, whom if you need, can bee your guides: if you neede them not, you can leade your selves, and others. And such Readers we wish him.—HEMINGE, JOHN, AND CONDELL, HENRIE, 1623, *First Folio Edition of Shakespeare's Works, Address to the Reader.*

Those hands, which you so clapt, go now, and ring
You *Britaines* brave; for done are *Shakespeares* dayes:
His dayes are done, that made the dainty Playes,
Which make the Globe of heav'n and earth to ring.
Dry'de is that veine, dry'd is the *Thespian* Spring,
Turn'd all to teares, and *Phœbus* clouds his rayes:
That corp's, that coffin now besticke those bayes,
Which crown'd him *Poet* first, then *Poets* King.

—HOLLAND, HUGH, 1623, *Prefixed to the First Folio Edition of Shakespeare's Works.*

Shakespeare thou hadst as smooth a Comicke vaine,
Fitting the socke, and in thy natural braine,
As strong conception, and as Cleere a rage,
As any one that trafiqu'd with the stage.

—DRAYTON, MICHAEL, 1627, *Of Poets and Poesie.*

I *remember*, the Players have often mentioned it as an honour to *Shakespeare*, that in his writing, (whatsoever he penn'd) hee never blotted out line. My answer hath beene, would he had blotted a thousand. Which they thought a malevolent speech. I had not told posterity this, but for their ignorance, who choose that circumstance to commend their friend by, wherein he most faulted. And to justifie mine owne candor, (for I lov'd the man, and doe honour his memory (on this side Idolatry) as much as any.) Hee was (indeed) honest, and of an open, and free nature: had an excellent *Phantsie;* brave notions, and gentle expressions: wherein hee flow'd with that facility, that sometime it was necessary he should be stop'd: *Sufflaminandus erat;* as *Augustus* said of *Haterius*. His wit was in his owne power; would the rule of it had beene so too.

Many times hee fell into those things, could not escape laughter: As when hee said in the person of *Cæsar*, one speaking to him; *Cæsar thou dost me wrong.* Hee replyed: *Cæsar did never wrong, but with just cause:* and such like; which were ridiculous. But hee redeemed his vices, with his vertues. There was ever more in him to be praysed, then to be pardoned. —JONSON, BEN, 1630–37, *Timber, or Discoveries.*

What neede my *Shakespeare* for his honour'd bones,
The labour of an Age, in piled stones
Or that his hallow'd Reliques should be hid
Under a starre-ypointing Pyramid?
Dear Sonne of Memory, great Heire of *Fame*,
What needst thou such dull witnesse of thy Name?
Thou in our wonder and astonishment
Hast built thy selfe a lasting Monument:
For whil'st to th' shame of slow-endevouring Art
Thy easie numbers flow, and that each part,
Hath from the leaves of thy unvalued Booke,
Those Delphicke Lines with deepe Impression tooke
Then thou our fancy of her selfe bereaving,
Dost make us Marble with too much conceiving,
And so Sepulcher'd in such pompe dost lie
That Kings for such a Tombe would wish to die.

—MILTON, JOHN, 1630, *An Epitaph on the admirable Dramaticke Poet, W. Shakespeare.*

In a Conversation between Sir John Suckling, Sir William D'Avenant, Endymion Porter, Mr. Hales of Eaton, and Ben Johnson, Sir John Suckling, who was a profess'd admirer of Shakespear, had undertaken his Defence against Ben Johnson with some warmth; Mr. Hales, who had sat still for some time, hearing Ben frequently reproaching him with the want of Learning, and Ignorance of the Antients, told him at last, "That if Mr. Shakespear had not read the Antients, he had likewise not stollen any thing from 'em; [a fault the other made no Conscience of] and that if he would produce any one Topick finely treated by any of them, he would undertake to shew something upon the same Subject at least as well written by Shakespear."—HALES, JOHN, OF ETON, c 1633, *Some Account of the Life of Mr. William Shakespear, prefixed to the edition of his Works by Nicholas Rowe,* 1709, *vol.* I, *p.* xiv.

Thy Muses sugred dainties seeme to us
Like the fam'd Apples of old *Tantalus:*
For we (admiring) see and heare thy straines,
But none I see or heare, those sweets attaines.

—BANCROFT, THOMAS, 1639, *Two Bookes of Epigrammes, and Epitaphs, No.* 118.

One asked another what Shakespeares workes were worth, all being bound together? hee answered, not a farthing: not worth a farthing, said he, why so? He answered, that his playes were worth a great deale of money, but he never heard that his workes were worth anything at all. —CHAMBERLAIN, ROBERT, 1640, *Jocabella, or a Cabinet of Conceits.*

In speaking of this we entred Loves Library, which was very spacious, and compleatly filled with great variety of Bookes of all faculties, and in all kindes of Volumes. . . . There was also *Shakespeere*, who (as *Cupid* informed me) creepes into the womens closets about bed time, and if it were not for some of the old out-of-date Grandames (who are set over the rest as their tutoresses) the young sparkish Girles would read in *Shakespeere* day and night, so that they would open the Booke or Tome, and the men with a Fescue in their hands should point to the Verse.—JOHNSON, JOHN, 1641, *The Academy of Love, pp.* 96-99.

The Sweetest Swan of Avon, to y[e] faire
And Cruel Delia, passionatelie Sings:
Other mens weakenesses and follies are
Honour and witt in him; each Accent brings
A Sprig to Crowne him Poet; and Contrive
A Monument, in his owne worke, to live.

—DANIEL, GEORGE, 1647, *Vindication of Poesie, ed. Grosart.*

Shakespeare to thee was dull, whose best jest lyes
I' th Ladies questions, and the Fooles replyes;
Old fashion'd wit, which walkt from town to town
In turn'd Hose, which our fathers call'd the Clown;
Whose wit our nice times would obsceanness call,
And which made Bawdry pass for Comicall:
Nature was all his Art, thy veine was free
As his, but without his scurility.

—CARTWRIGHT, WILLIAM, 1647, *Upon the Dramatick Poems of Mr. John Fletcher.*

I wonder how that person you mention in your letter, could either have the conscience, or confidence to dispraise *Shakespear's* playes, as to say they were made up onely with clowns, fools, watchmen, and the like; but to answer that person, though *Shakespear's* wit will answer for himself, I say, that it seems by his judging, or censuring, he understands not playes, or wit. . . . 'Tis harder, and requires more wit to express a jester, than a grave statesman; yet *Shakespear* did not want wit, to express to the life all sorts of persons, of what quality, profession, degree, breeding, or birth soever; nor did he want wit to express the divers and different humours, or natures, or several passions in mankind; and so well he hath express'd in his playes all sorts of persons, as one would think he had been transformed into every one of those persons he hath described; and as sometimes one would think he was really himself the clown or jester he feigns, so one would think, he was also the king, and privy-councillor; also as one would think he were really the coward he feigns, so one would think he were the most valiant and experienced souldier.—CAVENDISH, MARGARET, 1664, *CCXI Sociable Letters written by the Lady Marchioness of Newcastle, Letter CXXIII.*

But *Shakespear's* magic could not copyed be;
Within that circle none durst walk but he.
—DRYDEN, JOHN, 1669, *The Tempest, Prologue.*

His comoedies will remaine witt as long as the English tongue is understood, for that he handles *mores hominum.* Now our present writers reflect so much upon particular persons and coxcombeities, that twenty yeares hence they will not be understood. Though, as Ben: Johnson sayes of him, that he had but little Latine and lesse Greek, he understood Latine pretty well, for he had been in his younger yeares a schoolmaster in the countrey.—from Mr. . . . Beeston.—AUBREY, JOHN, 1669–96, *Brief Lives, ed. Clark, vol.* II, *p.* 227.

Shakespeare, who many times has written better than any poet, in any language, is yet so far from writing wit always, or expressing that wit according to the dignity of the subject, that he writes, in many places, below the dullest writers of ours, or any precedent age. Never did any author precipitate himself from such height of thought to so low expressions, as he often does. He is the very Janus of poets; he wears almost everywhere two faces; and you have scarce begun to admire the one, ere you despise the other. . . . Let us therefore admire the beauties and the height of Shakespeare, without falling after him into a carelessness, and, as I may call it, a lethargy of thought, for whole scenes together.—DRYDEN, JOHN, 1672, *An Essay on the Dramatic Poetry of the Last Age, Works, ed. Scott and Saintsbury, vol.* IV, *pp.* 236, 242.

William Shakespeare, the glory of the English stage, whose nativity at Stratford upon Avon, is the highest honour that town can boast of: from an actor of tragedies and comedies, he became a maker; and such a maker, that though some others may perhaps pretend to a more exact decorum and œconomie, especially in tragedy, never any expressed a more lofty and tragic height; never any represented nature more purely to the life, and where the polishments of art are most wanting, as probably his learning was not extraordinary, he pleaseth with a certain wild and native elegance; and in all his writings hath an unvulgar style, as well in his "Venus and Adonis," his "Rape of Lucrece," and other various poems, as in his dramatics.—PHILLIPS, EDWARD, 1675, *Theatrum Poetarum Anglicanorum, ed. Brydges, p.* 240.

Shakespear was the first that opened this vein upon our stage, which has run so freely and so pleasantly ever since, that I have often wondered to find it appear so little upon any others, being a subject so proper for them; since humour is but a picture of particular life, as comedy is of general.—TEMPLE, SIR WILLIAM, 1680–90, *Of Poetry, Works, vol.* III, *p.* 412,

Our *Shakespear* wrote too in an age as blest,
The happiest poet of his time, and best,
A gracious Prince's favour chear'd his Muse,
A constant Favour he ne'er fear'd to lose.
Therefore he wrote with Fancy unconfin'd,
And Thoughts that were Immortal as his Mind.
And from the Crop of his luxuriant Pen
E'er since succeeding Poets humbly glean.
—OTWAY, THOMAS, 1680, *History and Fall of Caius Marius, Prologue.*

I confess I cou'd never yet get a true account of his Learning, and am apt to think it more than Common Report allows him. I am sure he never touches on a Roman Story, but the Persons, the Passages, the Manners, the Circumstances, the Ceremonies, all are Roman. And what Relishes yet of a more exact Knowledge, you do not only see a Roman in his Heroe, but the particular Genius of the Man, without the least mistake of his Character, given him by their best Historians. You find his Anthony in all the Defects and Excellencies of his Mind, a Souldier, a Reveller, Amorous, sometimes Rash, sometimes Considerate, with all the various Emotions of his Mind. His Brutus agen has all the Constancy, Gravity, Morality, Generosity, Imaginable, without the least Mixture of private Interest or Irregular Passion. He is true to him, even in the imitation of his Oratory, the famous Speech which he makes him deliver, being exactly agreeable to his manner of expressing himself; of which we have this account, *Facultas ejus erat Militaris & Bellicis accommodata Tumultubus.* But however it far'd with our Author for Book-Learning, 'tis evident that no man was better studied in Men and Things, the most useful Knowledge for a Dramatic Writer. He was a most diligent Spie upon Nature, trac'd her through her darkest Recesses, pictur'd her in her just Proportion and Colours; in which Variety 'tis impossible that all shou'd be equally pleasant, 'tis sufficient that all be proper.—TATE, NAHUM, 1680, *The Loyal General, a Tragedy, Address to Edward Tayler.*

Shackspear whose fruitfull Genius, happy Wit
Was fram'd and finisht at a lucky hit
The Pride of Nature, and the shame of Schools,
Born to Create, and not to Learn from Rules.
—SEDLEY, SIR CHARLES, 1693, *The Wary Widow, by Henry Higden, Prologue.*

Besides some laudable Attempts which have been made with tolerable Success, of late years, towards a just manner of Writing, both in the heroick and familiar Style; we have older Proofs of a right Disposition in our People towards the moral and instructive Way. Our old dramatick Poet, Shakespear, may witness for our good Ear and manly Relish. Notwithstanding his natural Rudeness, his unpolish'd Style, his antiquated Phrase and Wit, his want of Method and Coherence, and his Deficiency in almost all the Graces and Ornaments of this kind of Writings; yet by the Justness of his Moral, the Aptness of many of his *Descriptions,* and the plain and natural Turn of several of his *Characters,* he pleases his Audience, and often gains their Ear, without a single Bribe from Luxury or Vice.—SHAFTESBURY, ANTHONY, EARL OF, 1710, *Advice to an Author, Characteristics, Works, vol.* I, *p.* 275.

And yet in Shakespeare something still I find,
That makes me less esteem all human kind;
He made one nature, and another found,
Both in his page with master strokes abound:
His witches, fairies, and enchanted isle,
Bid us no longer at our nurses smile;
Of lost historians we almost complain,
Nor think it the creation of his brain,
Who lives, when his Othello's in a trance?
With his great Talbot too he conquer'd France.
—YOUNG, EDWARD, 1712, *An Epistle to Lord Lansdowne.*

Among the English [who have introduced fairies, witches, &c.] Shakespeare has incomparably excelled all others. That noble extravagance of fancy, which he had in so great perfection, thoroughly qualified him to touch this weak, superstitious part of his reader's imagination; and made him capable of succeeding where he had nothing to support him besides the strength of his own genius. There is something so wild, and yet so solemn, in the speeches of his ghosts, fairies, witches, and the like imaginary persons, that we cannot forbear thinking them natural, though we have no rule by which to judge of them, and must confess, if there are such beings in the world, it looks highly probable they should talk and act as he has represented them.—ADDISON, JOSEPH, 1712, *Spectator, No.* 419, *July.* 1.

If ever any author deserved the name of an *original,* it was Shakespear. Homer himself drew not his art so immediately from the fountains of Nature; it proceeded through Egyptian strainers and channels, and came to him not without some tincture of the learning, or some cast of the models, of those before him. The poetry of Shakespear was inspiration indeed; he is not so much an imitator as an instrument of Nature; and it is not so just to say that he speaks from her, as that she speaks through him. His *characters* are so much Nature herself, that 'tis a sort of injury to call them by so distant a name as copies of her. Those of other poets have a constant resemblance, which shows that they received them from one another, and were but multipliers of the same image; each picture, like a mock rainbow, is but the reflection of a reflection. But every single character in Shakespear is as much an individual as those in life itself; it is as impossible to find any two alike; and such as from their relation or affinity in any respect appear most to be twins, will upon comparison be found remarkably distinct. To this life and variety of character we must add the wonderful preservation of it, which is such throughout his Plays, that, had all the speeches been printed without the very names of the persons, I believe one might have applied them with certainty to every speaker. The *power* over our *passions* was never possess'd in a more eminent degree, or displayed in so different instances. Yet all along there is seen no labour, no pains to raise them; no preparation to guide or guess to the effect, or be perceiv'd to lead towards it; but the heart swells, and the tears burst out, just at the proper places. We are surprised at the moment we weep; and yet upon reflection find the passion so just, that we should have been surprised if we had not wept, and wept at that very moment.—POPE, ALEXANDER, 1725, *ed. Shakspear's Plays, Preface, Works, ed. Elwin and Courthope, vol.* X, *p.* 534.

For lofty sense,
Creative fancy, and inspection keen
Through the deep windings of the human heart,
Is not wild Shakespeare thine and Nature's boast?

—THOMSON, JAMES, 1727, *The Seasons, Summer, v.* 1563–6.

Some ladies have shewn a truly public spirit in rescuing the admirable, yet almost forgotten Shakspeare, from being totally sunk in oblivion:—they have contributed to raise a monument to his memory, and frequently honoured his works with their presence on the stage:—an action which deserves the highest encomiums, and will be attended with an adequate reward; since, in preserving the fame of the dead bard, they add a brightness to their own, which will shine to late posterity.—HAYWOOD, ELIZA, 1745, *The Female Spectator, vol.* I, *p.* 259.

There have been some ages in which providence seemed pleased in a most remarkable manner to display it self, in giving to the world the finest genius's to illuminate a people formerly barbarous. After a long night of Gothic ignorance, after many ages of priestcraft and superstition, learning and genius visited our Island in the days of the renowned Queen Elizabeth. It was then that liberty began to dawn, and the people having shook off the restraints of priestly austerity, presumed to think for themselves. At an Æra so remarkable as this, so famous in his story, it seems no wonder that the nation should be blessed with those immortal ornaments of wit and learning, who all conspired at once to make it famous.—This astonishing genius, seemed to be commissioned from above, to deliver us not only from the ignorance under which we laboured as to poetry, but to carry poetry almost to its perfection.—CIBBER, THEOPHILUS, 1753, *Lives of the Poets, vol.* I, *p.* 123.

Far from the sun and summer gale,
In thy green lap was Nature's darling laid,
What time, where lucid Avon stray'd,
To him the mighty mother did unveil
Her awful face; the dauntless child
Stretch'd forth his little arms and smiled,
"This pencil take" (she said) "whose colours clear
Richly paint the vernal year;
Thine too these golden keys, immortal Boy!
This can unlock the gates of joy;
Of horror that, and thrilling fears,
Or ope the sacred source of sympathetic tears."

—GRAY, THOMAS, 1755, *The Progress of Poesy.*

Things of the noblest kind his genius drew,
And look'd through Nature at a single view:
A loose he gave to his unbounded soul,
And taught new lands to rise, new seas to roll;
Call'd into being scenes unknown before,
And passing Nature's bounds, was something more.

—CHURCHILL, CHARLES, 1761, *The Rosciad, v.* 264–70.

If Shakspere be considered as a Man, born in a rude age, and educated in the lowest manner, without any instruction, either from the world or from books, he may be regarded as a prodigy; if represented as a poet, capable of furnishing a proper entertainment to a refined or intelligent audience, we must abate much of this eulogy. In his compositions, we regret that many irregularities, and even absurdities, should so frequently disfigure the animated and passionate scenes intermixed with them; and, at the same time, we perhaps admire the more those beauties, on account of their being surrounded with such deformities. A striking peculiarity of sentiment, adapted to a single character, he frequently hits, as it were, by inspiration; but a reasonable propriety of thought he cannot for any time uphold. Nervous and picturesque expressions as well as descriptions abound in him; but it is in vain we look either for purity or simplicity of diction. His total ignorance of all theatrical art and conduct, however material a defect, yet, as it affects the spectator rather than the reader, we can more easily excuse, than that want of taste which often prevails in his productions, and which gives way only by intervals to the irradiations of genius. A great and fertile genius he certainly possessed, and one enriched equally with a tragic and comic vein; but he ought to be cited as a proof, how dangerous it is to rely on these advantages alone for attaining an excellence in the finer arts. And there may even remain a suspicion that we overrate, if possible, the greatness of his genius; in the same manner as bodies often appear more gigantic, on account of their being disproportioned and misshapen.—HUME, DAVID, 1754–62, *History of England, Reign of James I., Appendix.*

This therefore is the praise of Shakspeare, that his drama is the mirror of life; that he who has mazed his imagination, in following the phantoms which other writers raise up before him, may here be cured of his delirious ecstasies, by reading human sentiments in human language, by scenes from which a hermit may estimate the transactions of the world, and a confessor predict the progress of the passions. . . . The force of his comic scenes has suffered little diminution from the changes made by a century and a half, in manners or in words. As his personages act upon principles arising from genuine passion, very little modified by particular forms, their pleasures and vexations are communicable at all times and to all places; they are natural, and therefore durable; the adventitious peculiarities of personal habits are only superficial dyes, bright and pleasing for a little while, yet soon fading to a dim tinct, without any remains of former lustre; but the discriminations of true passion are the colours of nature; they pervade the whole mass, and can only perish with the body that exhibits them. The accidental compositions of heterogeneous modes are dissolved by the chance which combined them; but the uniform simplicity of primitive qualities neither admits increase, nor suffers decay. The sand heaped by one flood is scattered by another, but the rock always continues in its place. Time, which is perpetually washing away the dissoluble fabrics of other poets, passes, without *injuring* the adamant of Shakspeare.—JOHNSON, SAMUEL, 1768, *ed. Shakspeare's Works, Preface.*

Shakspeare . . . that first genius of the world. . . . I hold a perfect comedy to be the perfection of human composition, and I firmly believe that fifty Iliads and Æneids could be written sooner than such a character as Falstaff's. . . . Shakspeare, who was superior to all mankind, wrote some whole plays that are as bad as any of our present writers. . . . Annibal Caracci himself could not paint like our Raphael poet! . . . Milton and . . . Shakspeare, the only two mortals I am acquainted with who ventured beyond the visible diurnal sphere, and preserved their intellects. . . . Was Raphael himself as great a genius in his art as the author of "Macbeth?"—WALPOLE, HORACE, 1776–90, *Letters, vol.* VI, *pp.* 394, 395, VII, 135, 373, VIII, 160, IX, 254.

The first object which presents itself to us on the English theatre, is the great Shakspeare. Great he may be justly called, as the extent and force of his natural genius, both for tragedy and comedy, are altogether unrivalled. But, at the same time, it is genius shooting wild; deficient in just taste, and altogether unassisted by knowledge or art. Long has he been idolized by the British nation; much has been said, and much has been written concerning him; criticism has been drawn to the very dregs, in commentaries upon his words and witticisms; and yet it remains, to this day, in doubt, whether his beauties, or his faults, be greatest. Admirable scenes, and passages without number, there are in his plays; passages beyond what are to be found in any other dramatic writer; but there is hardly any one of his plays which can be called altogether a good one, or which can be read with uninterrupted pleasure from beginning to end. Besides extreme irregularities in conduct, and grotesque mixtures of serious and comic in one piece, we are often interrupted by unnatural thoughts, harsh expressions, a certain obscure bombast, and a play upon words which he is fond of pursuing; and these interruptions to our pleasure too frequently occur, on occasions when we would least wish to meet with them. All these faults, however, Shakspeare redeems, by two of the greatest excellencies which any tragic poet can possess; his lively and diversified paintings of character; his strong and natural expressions of passion. These are his two chief virtues; on these his merit rests.—BLAIR, HUGH, 1783, *Lectures on Rhetoric and Belles Lettres, ed. Mills.*

Shakespear whose writings are the offspring of an intuition that mocks description, that shames the schools, and that ascertains sublimity; whose knowledge of human nature was profound, penetrating and infallible; whose morality and philosophy confirm all that was good and wise in the ancients; whose words are in our mouths, and their irresistible influence in our hearts; whose eulogium may be felt but cannot be expressed, and whose own pen alone was equal to the composition of his epitaph: this Shakespear in the mouths of his fellow creatures is more known for a few inconsiderable blemishes, sprung from redundant fancy and indispensable conformity, than for innumerable beauties, delightful as truth, and commanding as inspiration.—DIBDIN, CHARLES, 1795, *A Complete History of the Stage, vol.* III, *p.* 15.

I proceed now to the mention of Shakespear, a writer whom no ingenuous English reader can recollect without the profoundest esteem and the most unbounded admiration. His gigantic mind enabled him in a great degree to overcome the fetters in which the English language was at that period bound. In him we but rarely trace the languid and tedious formality which at that time characterised English composition. His soul was too impetuous, and his sympathy with human passions too entire, not to instruct him in the shortest road to the heart. But Shakespear for the most part is great only, when great passions are to be expressed. In the calmer and less turbid scenes of life his genius seems in a great degree to forsake him. His wit is generally far fetched, trivial and cold. His tranquil style is perplexed, pedantical, and greatly disfigured with conceits.—GODWIN, WILLIAM, 1797, *Of English Style, The Enquirer, p.* 388.

There are beauties of the first order to be found in Shakspeare, relating to every country and every period of time. His faults are those which belonged to the times in which he lived. . . . If he excelled in exciting pity; what energy appeared in his terror! It was from the crime itself that he drew dismay and fear. It may be said of crimes painted by Shakspeare, as the Bible says of Death, that he is the KING OF TERRORS. . . . One of the greatest faults which Shakspeare can be accused of, is his want of simplicity in the intervals of his sublime passages. When he is not exalted, he is affected; he wanted the art of sustaining himself, that is to say, of being as natural in his scenes of transition, as he was in the grand movements of the soul.—STAEL, MADAME DE, 1800, *The Influence of Literature upon Society, ch.* xiii.

The admirers of the tragic and comic genius of the English poet seem to me to be much deceived when they applaud the *naturalness of his style.* Shakspeare is natural in his sentiments and ideas, never in his expressions, except in those fine scenes where his genius rises to its highest flight; yet in those very scenes his language is often affected; he has all the faults of the Italian writers of his time; he is eminently wanting in simplicity. His descriptions are inflated, distorted; they betray the badly-educated man, who, not knowing the gender, nor the accent, nor the exact meaning of words, introduces poetic expressions at hap-hazard into the most trivial situations.—CHATEAUBRIAND, FRANCOIS RENE, VICOMTE DE, 1801, *Shakspere on Shakspeare.*

The claims of this great poet on the admiration of mankind are innumerable, but rhythmical modulation is not one of them; nor do I think it either wise or just to hold him forth as supereminent in every quality which constitutes genius. Beaumont is as sublime, Fletcher as pathetic, and Jonson as nervous. Nor let it be accounted poor or niggard praise to allow him only an equality with these extraordinary men in their peculiar excellencies, while he is admitted to possess many others, to which they made no approaches. Indeed if I were asked for the discriminating quality of Shakespeare's mind, that by which he is raised above all competition, above all prospect of rivalry, I should say it was WIT.—GIFFORD, WILLIAM, 1805–13, *Plays of Massinger, Introduction.*

In regard to the pathos, Shakespear is greatly inferior to many dramatic poets. In the terrific and sublime he is unequalled, but he does not possess the power of Otway, and many inferior poets, in exciting pity. He is pre-eminent in "unlocking the gates of horror and thrilling fears," but not so "in opening the sacred source of sympathetic tears."—PYE, HENRY JAMES, 1807, *Comments on the Commentators on Shakespear, p.* xii.

Let princes o'er their subject kingdoms rule,
'Tis Shakespeare's province to command the soul!
To add one leaf, oh, Shakespeare! to thy bays,
How vain the effort, and how mean my lays!
Immortal Shakespeare! o'er thy hallow'd page,
Age becomes taught, and youth is e'en made sage.

—BONAPARTE, PRINCE LUCIEN, 1810, *Written in the Visitors' Book at Stratford.*

Let any one compare the prodigious variety, and wide-ranging freedom of Shakespeare, with the narrow round of flames, tempests, treasons, victims, and tyrants, that scantily adorn the sententious pomp of the French drama, and he will not fail to recognise the vast superiority of the former, in the excitement of the imagination, and all the diversities of poetical delight.—JEFFREY, FRANCIS, 1811–44, *Ford's Works, Contributions to the Edinburgh Review, vol.* II, *p.* 297.

. . . the magic of that name
Defies the scythe of time, the torch of flame.

—BYRON, LORD, 1812, *Address Spoken at the Opening of Drury Lane Theatre.*

The English stage might be considered equally without rule and without model when Shakspeare arose. The effect of the genius of an individual upon the taste of a nation is mighty; but that genius, in its turn, is formed according to the opinions prevalent at the period when it comes into existence. Such was the case with Shakspeare. With an education more extensive, and a taste refined by the classical models, it is probable that he also, in admiration of the ancient Drama, might have mistaken the form for the essence, and subscribed to those rules which had produced such masterpieces of art. Fortunately for the full exertion of a genius as comprehensive and versatile as intense and powerful, Shakspeare had no access to any models of which the commanding merit might have controlled and limited his own exertions. He followed the path which a nameless crowd of obscure writers had trodden before him; but he moved in it with the grace and majestic step of a being of a superior order; and vindicated for ever the British theatre from a pedantic restriction to classical rule. Nothing went before Shakspeare which in any respect was fit to fix and stamp the character of a national Drama; and certainly no one will succeed him capable of establishing, by mere authority, a form more restricted than that which Shakspeare used.—SCOTT, SIR WALTER, 1814–23, *Essay on the Drama, Prose Works.*

If intelligence and penetrating depth of observation, as far as they are necessary to the characterizing of life, were the first of poetic qualities, hardly any other poet could enter into competition with him. Others have sought to transport us, for a moment, to an ideal condition of humanity: he presents us with a picture of man, in the depths of his fall and moral disorganization, with all his doings and sufferings, his thoughts and desires, with a painful minuteness. In this respect he may almost be called a satirist; and well might the complicated enigma of existence, and of man's degradation, as set forth by him, produce a deeper and more lasting impression than is made by a host of splenetic caricaturists, who are called satiric poets. But throughout his works there is a radiant reminiscence of man's pristine dignity and elevation, from which immorality and meanness are an abnormal apostasy: and on every occasion this reminiscence, united to the poet's own nobility of soul and tender feeling, beams forth in patriotic enthusiasm, sublime philanthrophy, and glowing love. . . . In the works of Shakspere a whole world is unfolded. Whosoever has comprehended this, and been penetrated with the spirit of his poetry will hardly allow the seeming want of form, or, rather, the form peculiar to his mighty genius, nor even the criticism of those who have misconceived the poet's meaning, to disturb his admiration; as he progresses he will, rather, approve the form as both sufficient and excellent in itself, and in harmonious conformity with the spirit and essence of his art. Shakspere's poetry is, upon the whole, near akin to the German spirit: hence he is appreciated in Germany more than any other foreign poet, and regarded with almost native affection.—SCHLEGEL, FREDERICK, 1815–59, *Lectures on the History of Literature, pp.* 274, 276.

It is the peculiar excellence of Shakespear's heroines, that they seem to exist only in their attachment to others. They are pure abstractions of the affections. We think as little of their persons as they do themselves, because we are let into the secrets of their hearts, which are more important. We are too much interested in their affairs to stop to look at their faces, except by stealth and at intervals. No one ever hit the true perfection of the female character, the sense of weakness leaning on the strength of its affections for support, so well as Shakespear: no one ever so well painted natural tenderness free from affectation and disguise: no one else ever so well showed how delicacy and timidity, when driven to extremity, grow romantic and extravagant.—HAZLITT, WILLIAM, 1817–69, *Characters of Shakespear's Plays, p.* 3.

. . divinest Shakespere's might
Fills Avon and the world with light
Like omniscient power which he
Imaged 'mid mortality.

—SHELLEY, PERCY BYSSHE, 1818, *Lines written among the Euganean Hills.*

Merciful, wonder-making Heaven! what a man was this Shakspere! Myriad-minded, indeed, he was!—COLERIDGE, SAMUEL TAYLOR, 1818, *Lectures and Notes on Shakspere, ed. Ashe, p.* 251.

Regardless of immortalizing his name, he who had penetrated the most hidden stores of Nature; he who had studied man in all his various capacities and failings; he to whom the retrospect of all that had been seemed familiar, and who, as it were, looked into the very soul of time, and read futurity, yet would not see his own greatness beyond mortality, but suffered the hand of ignorance to plant sickly weeds among his ever-blooming flowers, and which the unabated exertions of genius, for more than a century, have not been able totally to destroy.—JACKSON, ZACHARIAH, 1819, *Shakspeare's Genius Justified, Preface, p.* v.

Shakespeare is of no age. He speaks a language which thrills in our blood in spite of the separation of two hundred years. His thoughts, passions, feelings, strains of fancy, all are of this day, as they were of his own—and his genius may be contemporary with the mind of every generation for a thousand years to come. He, above all poets, looked upon men, and lived for mankind. His genius, universal in intellect and sympathy, could find, in no more bounded circumference, its proper sphere. It could not bear exclusion from any part of human existence. Whatever in nature and life was given to man, was given in contemplation and poetry to him also, and over the undimmed mirror of his mind passed all the shades of our mortal world. Look through his plays, and tell what form of existence, what quality of spirit, he is most skilful to delineate? Which of all the manifold beings he has drawn, lives before our thoughts, our eyes, in most unpictured reality? Is it Othello, Shylock, Falstaff, Lear, the Wife of Macbeth, Imogen, Hamlet, Ariel? In none of the other great dramatists do we see any thing like a perfected art. In their works, everything, it is true, exists in some shape or other, which can be required in a drama taking for its interest the absolute interest of human life and nature; but, after all, may not the very best of their works be looked on as sublime masses of chaotic confusion, through which the elements of our moral being appear? It was Shakespeare, the most unlearned of all our writers, who first exhibited on the stage perfect models, perfect images of all human characters, and of all human events. We cannot conceive any skill that could from his great characters remove any defect, or add to their perfect composition. Except in him, we look in vain for the entire fulness, the self-consistency, and self-completeness of perfect art. All the rest of our drama may be regarded rather as a testimony of the state of genius—of the state of mind of the country, full of great poetical disposition, and great tragic capacity and power—than as a collection of the works of an art. Of Shakespeare and Homer alone it may be averred, that we miss in them nothing of the greatness of nature. In all other poets we do; we feel the measure of their power, and the restraint under which it is held; but in Shakespeare and in Homer, all is free and unbounded as in nature; and as we travel along with them, in a car drawn by celestial steeds, our view seems ever interminable as before, and still equally far off the glorious horizon.—WILSON, JOHN, 1819, *A Few Words on Shakespeare, Works, vol.* VII, *p.* 420.

Ever since I have been able to think and feel, I have recognized Shakspere as the first among all poets; the richest and deepest, the most instructive and delightful, the most mysterious and the clearest, and to whom I devoted myself with ever new reverence and love. . . . In Shakspere, poetry, virtue, truth, life, and history is altogether one: he is therefore not only a great poet in the usual sense of the word, but also for every thinking being an instructive author; the best expounder of the scriptural text, "the earth is everywhere the Lord's."—HORN, FRANZ, 1822, *Shakspeere's Schauspiele Erläutert, Prefaces.*

O mighty poet! Thy works are not, as those of other men, simply and merely great works of art, but are also like the phenomena of nature—like the sun and the sea, the stars and the flowers, like frost and snow, rain and dew, hail-storm and thunder, which are to be studied with entire submission of our own faculties, and in the perfect faith that in them there can be no too much or too little, nothing useless or inert, but that, the further we press in our discoveries, the more we shall see proofs of design and self-supporting arrangement where the careless eye had seen nothing but accident!—DE QUINCEY, THOMAS, 1823–60, *On The Knocking at the Gate in Macbeth, Works, ed. Masson, vol.* X, *p.* 393.

"A dramatic talent of any importance," said Goethe, "could not forbear to notice Shakspeare's works, nay, could not forbear to study them. Having studied them, he must be aware that Shakspeare has already exhausted the whole of human nature in all its tendencies, in all its heights and depths, and that, in fact, there remains for him, the aftercomer, nothing more to do. And how could one get courage only to put pen to paper, if one were conscious in an earnest appreciating spirit, that such unfathomable and unattainable excellences were already in existence! It fared better with me fifty years ago in my own dear Germany. I could soon come to an end with all that then existed; it could not long awe me, or occupy my attention. I soon left behind me German literature, and the study of it, and turned my thoughts to life and to production. So on and on I went in my own natural development, and on and on I fashioned the productions of epoch after epoch. And at every step of life and development, my standard of excellence was not much higher than what at such step I was able to attain. But had I been born an Englishman, and had all those numerous masterpieces been brought before me in all their power, at my first dawn of youthful consciousness, they would have overpowered me, and I should not have known what to do. I could not have gone on with such fresh light-heartedness, but should have had to bethink myself, and look about for a long time, to find some new outlet."—ECKERMANN, JOHN PETER, 1824, *Conversations of Goethe, tr. Oxenford, v.* I, *p.* 114.

While he abandons himself to the impulse of his imagination, his compositions are not only the sweetest and the most sublime, but also the most faultless that the world has ever seen. But as soon as his critical powers come into play, he sinks to the level of Cowley, or rather he does ill what Cowley did well. All that is bad in his works is bad elaborately, and of malice aforethought. The only thing wanting to make them perfect was, that he should never have troubled himself with thinking whether they were good or not. Like the angels in Milton, he sinks "with compulsion and laborious flight." His natural tendency is upwards. That he may soar, it is only necessary that he should not struggle to fall. He resembled the American cacique, who, possessing in unmeasured abundance the metals which in polished societies are esteemed the most precious, was utterly unconscious of their value, and gave up treasures more valuable than the imperial crowns of other countries, to secure some gaudy and far-fetched but worthless bauble, a plated button, or a necklace of coloured glass.—MACAULAY, THOMAS BABINGTON, 1826, *Dryden, Edinburgh Review, Critical and Miscellaneous Essays.*

. . . An immortal man,—
Nature's chief darling, an illustrious mate,
Destined to foil old Death's oblivious plan,
And shine untarnished by the fogs of Fate,
Time's famous rival till the final date!

—HOOD, THOMAS, 1828, *The Plea of the Midsummer Fairies, S. cv.*

I rejoice that the name of no one woman is popularly identified with that of Shakspeare. He belongs to us all!—the creator of Desdemona, and Juliet, and Ophelia, and Imogen, and Viola, and Constance, and Cornelia, and Rosalind, and Portia, was not the poet of one woman, but the POET OF WOMANKIND.—JAMESON, ANNA BROWNELL, 1829, *The Loves of the Poets, vol.* I, *p.* 248.

O thou divine human creature—greater name than even divine poet or divine philosopher—and yet thou wast all three—a very spring and vernal abundance of all fair and noble things is to be found in thy productions! They are truly a second nature. We walk in them, with whatever society we please; either with men, or fair women, or circling spirits, or with none but the whispering airs and leaves. Thou makest worlds of green trees and gentle natures for us, in thy forests of Arden, and thy courtly retirements of Navarre. Thou bringest us amongst the holiday lasses on the green sward; layest us to sleep among fairies in the bowers of midsummer; wakest us with the song of the lark and the silver-sweet voices of lovers: bringest more music to our ears, both from earth and from the planets; anon settest us upon enchanted islands, where it welcomes us again, from the touching of invisible instruments; and after all, restorest us to our still desired haven, the arms of humanity. Whether grieving us or making us glad, thou makest us kinder and happier. The tears which thou fetchest down, are like the rains of April, softening the times that come after them. Thy smiles are those of the month of love, the more blessed and universal for the tears.—HUNT, LEIGH, 1833, *The Indicator, ch.* xxxvi.

Great poet, 'twas thy art,
To know thyself, and in thyself to be
Whate'er love, hate, ambition, destiny,
Or the firm fatal purpose of the heart,
Can make of Man. Yet thou wert still the same,
Serene of thought, unhurt by thy own flame.

—COLERIDGE, HARTLEY, 1833, *To Shakespeare.*

The piece which he* composed upon what he called "the old English model," lay by him some thirty years, and was not published till towards the close of his life. He was the only person in those days who ventured to follow our old dramatists; for the revival of Shakespeare's plays upon the stage produced no visible effect upon contemporary play-wrights. But when Garrick had made the name of Shakespeare popular, a race of Shakespearean commentators arose, who introduced a sort of taste for the books of Shakespeare's age; and as they worked in the rubbish, buried treasures, of which they were not in search, were brought to light, for those who could understand their value. Thus, though in their cumbrous annotations, the last labourer always added more rubbish to the heaps which his predecessors had accumulated, they did good service by directing attention to our earlier literature. The very homage which they paid to Shakespeare tended to impress the multitude with an opinion of the paramount importance of his works, and a belief in excellencies of which they could have no perception. They who had any books for show considered Shakespeare, from this time, as a necessary part of the furniture of their shelves. Even the Jubilee, and its after representation at the theatres, contributed to confirm this useful persuasion. Thousands who had not seen one of his plays, nor read a line of them, heard of Shakespeare, and understood that his name was one of those of which it became Englishmen to be proud.—SOUTHEY, ROBERT, 1835, *Life of Cowper, vol.* I, *p.* 338.

But the high spirit that sleepeth here below,
More than all beautiful and stately things,
Glory to God, the mighty Maker, brings;
To whom alone 'twas given the bounds to know
Of human action, and the secret springs
Whence the deep streams of joy and sorrow flow.

—ALFORD, HENRY, 1837, *Stratford-upon-Avon.*

*Mason.

Shakspere was, and is, beyond all comparison, the greatest Poet that the world has ever seen. He is greatest in general power, and greatest in style, which is a symbol or evidence of power. . . . He was not a mere poet in the vulgar sense of the term. . . . On the contrary, he was a man eminently acute, logical, philosophical. His reasoning faculty was on a par with his imagination, and pervaded all his works as completely. . . . We hold him to have been not one, but legion; and we think that in all the cases where critics have attempted to distinguish him by any one particular excellence of intellect, they have failed. . . . His great merit, as it appears to us, is that he had no peculiar, no prominent merit: his mind was so well constituted, so justly and admirably balanced, that it had nothing in excess.—PROCTER, BRYAN WALLER, 1838, *ed. Works of Ben Jonson, Preface.*

Even as Jesus Christ impressed this son of Hamonia, so am I impressed by William Shakespeare. I grow desperate when I reflect that after all he is an Englishman, belonging to that most odious nation which God in his anger created.—HEINE, HEINRICH, 1838–95, *Notes on Shakespeare Heroines, tr. Benecke, p.* 9.

Shakspeare's learning, whatever it was, gave him hints as to sources from which classical information was to be drawn. The age abounded in classical translations; it also teemed with public pageants, and Allegory itself might be said to have walked the streets. He may have laughed at the absurdity of many of those pageants, but still they would refresh his fancy. Whether he read assiduously or carelessly, it should be remembered that reading was to him not of the vulgar benefit that it is to ordinary minds. Was there a spark of sense or sensibility in any author, on whose works he glanced, that spark assimilated to his soul, and it belonged to it as rightfully as the light of heaven to the eye of the eagle.—CAMPBELL, THOMAS, 1838, *ed. Shakspeare's Plays, Moxon ed., Life.*

This poet, so often sneered at as a frantic and barbarous writer is, above all, remarkable for a judgment so high, so firm, so uncompromising, that one is almost tempted to impeach his coldness, and to find in this impassible observer something that may be almost called cruel towards the human race. In the historical pieces of Shakspere, the picturesque, rapid, and vehement genius which has produced them seems to bow before the superior law of a judgment almost ironical in its clear-sightedness. Sensibility to impressions, the ardent force of imagination, the eloquence of passion—these brilliant gifts of nature, which would seem destined to draw a poet beyond all limits, are subordinated in this extraordinary intelligence to a calm and almost deriding sagacity, which pardons nothing and forgets nothing. Thus, the dramas of which we speak are painful as real history. Æschylus exhibits to us Fate hovering over the world; Calderon opens to us heaven and hell as the last words of the enigma of life; Voltaire renders his drama an instrument for asserting his own peculiar doctrines;—but Shakspere seeks *his* Fate in the hearts of men, and when he makes us see them so capricious, so bewildered, so irresolute, he teaches us to contemplate, without surprise the untoward events and sudden changes of fortune. In the purely poetical dramas to which this great poet has given so much verisimilitude, we console ourselves in believing that the evils which he paints are imaginary, and that their truth is but general. But the dramatic chronicles which Shakspere has sketched are altogether real.—CHASLES, PHILARÈTE, 1838, *Dictionnaire de la Conversation et de la Lecture, vol.* XLX.

The protagonist on the great arena of modern poetry, and the glory of the human intellect. . . . After this review of Shakspeare's life, it becomes our duty to take a summary survey of his works, of his intellectual powers, and of his station in literature,—a station which is now irrevocably settled, not so much (which happens in other cases) by a vast overbalance of favourable suffrages, as by acclamation; not so much by the *voices* of those who admire him up to the verge of idolatry, as by the *acts* of those who everywhere seek for his works among the primal necessities of life, demand them, and crave them as they do their daily bread; not so much by eulogy openly proclaiming itself, as by the silent homage recorded in the endless multiplication of what he has bequeathed us; not so much by his own compatriots, who, with regard to almost every other author, compose the total amount of his *effective* audience, as by the unanimous "All hail!" of intellectual Christendom; finally, not by the hasty partisanship of his own generation, nor by the biassed judgment of an age trained in the same modes of feeling and of thinking with himself, but by the solemn award of generation succeeding to generation, of one age correcting the obliquities or peculiarities of another; by the verdict of two hundred and thirty years, which have now elapsed since the very *latest* of his creations, or of two hundred and forty-seven years if we date from the earliest; a verdict which has been continually revived and reopened, probed, searched, vexed, by criticism in every spirit, from the most genial and intelligent, down to the most malignant and scurrilously hostile which feeble heads and great ignorance could suggest when co-operating with impure hearts and narrow sensibilities; a verdict, in short, sustained and countersigned by a longer series of writers, many of them eminent for wit or learning, than were ever before congregated upon any inquest relating to any author, be he who he might, ancient or modern, Pagan or Christian.—DE QUINCEY, THOMAS, 1838-63, *Shakspeare, Works, ed. Masson, vol.* IV, *pp.* 17, 69.

Amid the sights and tales of common things,
Leaf, flower, and bird, and wars, and deaths
 of kings—
Of shore and sea, and Nature's daily round,
Of life that tills, and tombs that load the
 ground,
His visions mingle, swell, command, pace by,
And haunt with living presence, heart and
 eye.
And tones from him by other bosoms caught
Awaken flush and stir of mounting thought;
And the long sigh, and deep, impassioned
 thrill
Rouse custom's trance, and spur the faltering
 will.
Above the goodly land, more his than ours,
He sits supreme, enthroned in skyey towers,
And sees the heroic brood of his creation
Teach larger life to his ennobled nation.
—STERLING, JOHN, 1839, *Shakespeare.*

Here, I say, is an English King, whom no time or chance, Parliament or combination of Parliaments, can dethrone! This King Shakespeare, does not he shine, in crowned sovereignty, over us all, as the noblest, gentlest, yet strongest of rallying signs; indestructible; really more valuable in that point of view than any other means or appliance whatsoever? We can fancy him as radiant aloft over all the Nations of Englishmen a thousand years hence. From Paramatta, from New York, wheresoever, under what sort of Parish-Constable soever, English men and women are, they will say to one another: "Yes, this Shakespeare is ours; we produced him, we speak and think by him; we are of one blood and kind with him."—CARLYLE, THOMAS, 1840, *The Hero as Poet, Heroes and Hero-Worship.*

It is hard to speak of Shakespeare; these measures of the statures of common poets fall from our hands when we seek to measure him: it is harder to praise him. Like the tall plane-tree which Xerxes found standing in the midst of an open country, and honoured inappropriately with his "barbaric pomp," with bracelets and chains and rings suspended on its branches, so has it been with Shakespeare. A thousand critics have commended him with praises as unsuitable as a gold ring to a plane-tree. A thousand hearts have gone out to him, carrying necklaces.—BROWNING, ELIZABETH BARRETT, 1842-63, *The Book of the Poets, p.* 151.

If it be said that Shakspere wrote perfect historical plays on subjects belonging to the preceding centuries, I answer, that they *are* perfect plays just because there is no care about centuries in them, but a life which all men recognise for the human life of all time; and this it is, not because Shakspere sought to give universal truth, but because, painting honestly and completely from the men about him, he painted that human nature which is, indeed, constant enough,—a rogue in the fifteenth century being, *at heart*, what a rogue is in the nineteenth and was in the twelfth; and an honest or knightly man being, in like manner, very similar to other such at any other time. And the work of these great idealists is, therefore, always universal; not because it is *not portrait*, but because it is *complete* portrait down to the heart, which is the same in all ages: and the work of the mean idealists is *not* universal, not because it is portrait, but because it is *half* portrait,—of the outside, the manners and the dress, not of the heart. Thus Tintoret and Shakspere paint, both of them, simply Venetian and English nature as they saw it in their time, down to the root; and it does for *all* time; but as for any care to cast themselves into the particular ways and tones of thought, or custom, of past time in their historical work, you will find it in neither of them, nor in any other perfectly great man that I know of.—RUSKIN, JOHN, 1843–60, *Modern Painters, pt.* iv, *ch.* vii.

It is a relief to read some true book, wherein all are equally dead,—equally alive. I think the best parts of Shakespeare would only be enhanced by the most thrilling and affecting events. I have found it so. And so much the more, as they are not intended for consolation.—THOREAU, HENRY DAVID, 1843, *Familiar Letters, ed. Sanborn, p.* 50.

There Shakespeare, on whose forehead climb
The crowns o' the world: O eyes sublime
With tears and laughter for all time!

—BROWNING, ELIZABETH BARRETT, 1844, *A Vision of Poets.*

Others abide our question. Thou art free.
We ask and ask—Thou smilest and art still,
Out-topping knowledge. For the loftiest hill,
Who to the stars uncrowns his majesty,
Planting his steadfast footsteps in the sea,
Making the heaven of heavens his dwelling-place,
Spares but the cloudy border of his base
To the foil'd searching of mortality;
And thou, who didst the stars and sunbeams know,
Self-school'd, self-scann'd, self-honour'd, self-secure,
Didst tread on earth unguess'd at.—Better so!
All pains the immortal spirit must endure,
All weakness which impairs, all griefs which bow,
Find their sole speech in that victorious brow.

—ARNOLD, MATTHEW, 1848, *Shakespeare.*

Our poet's mask was impenetrable. You cannot see the mountain near. It took a century to make it suspected; and not until two centuries had passed, after his death, did any criticism which we think adequate begin to appear. It was not possible to write the history of Shakspeare till now; for he is the father of German literature: it was with the introduction of Shakspeare into German, by Lessing, and the translation of his works by Wieland and Schlegel, that the rapid burst of German literature was most intimately connected. It was not until the nineteenth century, whose speculative genius is a sort of living Hamlet, that the tragedy of Hamlet could find such wondering readers. Now, literature, philosophy and thought, are Shakspearized. His mind is the horizon beyond which, at present, we do not see. Our ears are educated to music by his rhythm. . . . Shakspeare is the only biographer of Shakspeare; and even he can tell nothing, except to the Shakspeare in us, that is, to our most apprehensive and sympathetic hour. . . . He was a full man, who liked to talk; a brain exhaling thoughts and images, which, seeking vent, found the drama next at hand. Had he been less, we should have had to consider how well he filled his place, how good a dramatist he was,—and he is the best in the world. . . . He wrote the airs for all our modern music: he wrote the text of modern life; the text of manners: he drew the man of England and Europe; the father of the man in America; he drew the man, and described the day, and what is done in it: he read the hearts of men and women, their probity, and their second thought and wiles; the wiles of innocence, and the transitions by which virtues and vices slide into their contraries: he could divide the mother's part from the father's part in the face of the child, or draw the fine demarcations of freedom and of fate: he knew the laws of repression which make the police of nature: and all the sweets and all the terrors of human lot lay in his mind as truly but as softly as the landscape lies on the eye. And the importance of this wisdom of life sinks the form, as of Drama or Epic, out of notice. 'Tis like making a question concerning the paper on which a king's message is written. No recipe can be given for the making of a Shakspeare; but the possibility of the translation of things into song is demonstrated.—EMERSON, RALPH WALDO, 1850–76, *Shakspeare; or, the Poet; Representative Men, Works, Riverside ed., vol.* IV, *pp.* 194, 198, 200, 201, 204.

I have read and studied our great dramatist for nearly half a century; and if I could read and study him for half a century more, I should yet be far from arriving at an accurate knowledge of his works, or an adequate appreciation of his worth. He is an author whom no man can read enough, nor study enough.—COLLIER, JOHN PAYNE, 1853, *Notes and Emendations to the Text of Shakespeare's Plays, Introduction.*

. . . like Shakespeare . . .
To reach the popular heart through open ways;
To speak for all men; to be wise and true,
Bright as the noon-time, clear as morning dew,
And wholesome in the spirit and the form.

—MACKAY, CHARLES, 1855, *Mist.*

. . wide as Shakespeare's soul, . . .

—DOBELL, SYDNEY, 1855, *Sonnets of the War.*

I doubt whether Shakspeare ever had any thougth at all of making his personages speak characteristically. In most instances, I conceive,—probably in all,—he drew characters correctly because he *could not avoid it;* and would never have attained, in that department, such excellence as he has, if he had made any studied efforts for it. And the same, probably, may be said of Homer, and of those other writers who have excelled the most in delineating characters. Shakspeare's peculiar genius consisted chiefly, I conceive, in his forming the same distinct and consistent idea of an imaginary person that an ordinary man forms of a real and well-known individual. We usually conjecture pretty accurately, concerning a very intimate acquaintance, how he would speak or act on any supposed occasion; if any one should report to us his having done or said something quite out of character, we should at once be struck with the inconsistency; and we often represent to ourselves, and describe to others, without any conscious effort, not only the substance of what he would have been likely to say, but even his characteristic phrases and looks. Shakspeare *could* no more have endured an expression from the lips of Macbeth inconsistent with the character originally conceived, than an ordinary man could contribute to his most respectable acquaintance the behaviour of a ruffian, or to a human being the voice of a bird, or to a European the features and hue of a negro. Merely from the vividness of the original conception, characteristic conduct and language spontaneously suggested themselves to the great dramatist's pen. He called his personages into being, and left them, as it were, to speak and act for themselves. . . . Slender, and Shallow, and Aguecheek, as Shakspeare has painted them, though equally fools, resemble one another no more than Richard, and Macbeth, and Julius Cæsar.—WHATELY, RICHARD, 1856, *Bacon's Essays.*

We have the country justice of the time (Shallow); the small country gentlemen (Ford and Page); the young country gull (Aguecheek); the fool (Touchstone); the town gallant (Mercutio); the court gallant (Benedict); the waiting-woman (Maria); the steward (Malvolio); the serving-man (Peter); the page (Robin); the housekeeper (Mrs. Quickly); the statesman (Polonius); the fop (Osrick); the tinker (Sly); the pedlar (Autolycus); the weaver (Bottom); the merchant (Antonio); the village pedant (Holofernes); the malcontent (Jacques); the usurer (Shylock); the tavern wit (Falstaff); the disbanded soldier (Parolles); the town doctor (Caius); the hedge priest (Sir Oliver); the landlord (of the Garter); the drawer (Francis); besides 'prentices, cooks, musicians, nurses, thieves, carriers,—all of the age in which he lived. He quotes the ballads of his day: "Jephtha and his Daughter;" "The King and the Beggar;" "The Humour of Forty Fancies;" "Fire, fire, Jack boy, ho boy." His domestic scenery is that of his own house: the rushes are strewed, the jacks and jills cleaned, the carpets laid, and the serving-men in new fustian and white stockings,—their blue coats brushed, and their hair sleek combed: he has ivory coffers with Turkey cushions bossed with pearl, arras of purple, and valance of Venice.—THORNBURY, GEORGE WALTER, 1856, *Shakspere's England, vol.* II, *p.* 36.

. . . th' accepted King
Of all earthly minstrelling
Crowned with homely Avon lilies,
As his regal way and will is.

—ARNOLD, SIR EDWIN, 1856, *Alla Mano Della Mia Donna.*

The influence of Shakespeare on the French stage touches at a multitude of points; it appears, not in a simple sketch of the authors who have imitated or translated Shakespeare, not in a dry list of names, but by an accurate analysis of it; that is to say, by a philosophic history of whatsoever has helped to diffuse it, or of whatsoever has been inspired by it; a vast subject, doubtless, since the example of Shakespeare has prompted, whether directly or indirectly, almost all the theories and almost all the works of the modern drama. The analysis, therefore, of the influence of Shakespeare comprises *the history both of the form* and *of the theory of the Drama*, and, up to a certain point, *the history of dramatic criticism* in France during nearly two centuires; two centuries fruitful, indeed, in attempts and results, and thè subject opens and spreads the farther we advance. . . . The theatre of Shakespeare is the most perfect that the world has yet seen. It will continue to be a study for dramatic authors of all ages, and all will find in it the very nutriment for an artistic education—an education which will be developed unconsciously, so to speak, by the study of all the emotions that can stir the heart, of all the loftiest thoughts that can elevate the soul. The influence of Shakespeare upon the French stage has been profoundly salutary.—LACROIX, ALBERT, 1856, *Historie de l'Influence de Shakespeare sur le Théatre Français, p.* 338.

Only Shakespeare wrote comedy and tragedy with truly ideal elevation and breadth. Only Shakespeare had that true sense of humor which, like the universal solvent sought by the alchemists, so fuses together all the elements of a character, (as in Falstaff,) that any question of good or evil, of dignified or ridiculous, is silenced by the apprehension of its thorough humanity. Rabelais shows gleams of it in Panurge; but, in our opinion, no man ever possessed it in an equal degree with Shakespeare, except Cervantes; no man has since shown anything like an approach to it, (for Molière's quality was comic power rather than humor,) except Sterne, Fielding, and perhaps Richter. Only Shakespeare was endowed with that healthy equilibrium of nature whose point of rest was midway between the imagination and the understanding,—that perfectly unruffled brain which reflected all objects with almost inhuman impartiality, —that outlook whose range was ecliptical, dominating all zones of human thought and action,—that power of veri-similar conception which could take away Richard III. from History, and Ulysses from Homer,—and that creative faculty whose equal touch is alike vivifying in Shallow and in Lear. He alone never seeks in abnormal and monstrous characters to evade the risks and responsibilities of absolute truthfulness, not to stimulate a jaded imagination by Caligulan horrors of plot.—LOWELL, JAMES RUSSELL, 1858-64–90, *Library of Old Authors, Prose Works, Riverside ed., p.* 278.

Shakespeare, indeed, in his transcendently beautiful embodiments of feminine excellence, the most exquisite creations in literature, passed into a region of sentiment and thought, of ideals and of ideas, altogether higher and more supernatural than that region in which he shaped his delicate Ariels and his fairy Titanias. The question has been raised whether sex extends to soul. However this may be decided, here is a soul, with its records in literature, who is at once the manliest of men, and the most womanly of women; who can not only recognize the feminine element in existing individuals, but discern the idea, the pattern, the radiant genius, of womanhood itself, as it hovers unseen by other eyes, over the living representatives of the sex. Literature boasts many eminent female poets and novelists; but not one has ever approached Shakespeare in the purity, the sweetness, the refinement, the elevation, of his perceptions of feminine character,—much less approached him in the power of embodying these perceptions in persons. These characters are so thoroughly domesticated on the earth, that we are tempted to forget the heaven of invention from which he brought them. The most beautiful of spirits, they are the most tender of daughters, lovers, and wives. They are "airy shapes," but they "syllable men's names." Rosalind, Juliet, Ophelia, Viola, Perdita, Miranda, Desdemona, Hermione, Portia, Isabella, Imogen, Cordelia, —if their names do not call up their natures, the most elaborate analysis of criticism will be of no avail.—WHIPPLE, EDWIN P., 1859–68, *The Literature of the Age of Elizabeth, p.* 80.

Faith thus dislodged from ancient schools
and creeds,
Question to question, doubt to doubt succeeds—
Clouds gathering flame for thunders soon to
be,
And glass'd on Shakespeare as upon a sea.
Each guess of others into worlds unknown
Shakespeare revolves, but guards conceal'd
his own—
As in the Infinite hangs poised his thought,
Surveying all things, and asserting nought.
—LYTTON, EDWARD, LORD, 1860, *St. Stephen's.*

Of the several works of Shakespere—plays and poems—there were prior to 1616 in circulation, in all, no fewer than between sixty and sixty-five editions. Some of these reached as many as six editions within a period of not more than twenty-one years. This argues of itself an extensive popularity, especially when we reflect on the small number of the reading public of his day. If we take the lowest estimate of the editions (sixty), and suppose each issue to have consisted of the lowest possible paying number (300 say), we should have in circulation no fewer than 18,000 copies of the productions of the great dramatist in print during his lifetime.—NEIL, SAMUEL, 1861, *Shakespere, A Critical Biography*, p. 59.

He stands, in his relations to English literature, in the same position that the great Greek sculptors stood with respect to ancient art, embodying conceptions of humanity in its various attributes with indescribable skill, and with an exquisite agreement to nature.—DRAPER, JOHN WILLIAM, 1861–76, *History of the Intellectual Development of Europe, vol.* II, *p.* 249.

Nor even in his plays is Shakspeare merely a dramatist. Apart altogether from his dramatic power he is the greatest poet that ever lived. His sympathy is the most universal, his imagination the most plastic, his diction the most expressive, ever given to any writer. His poetry has in itself the power and varied excellences of all other poetry. While in grandeur, and beauty, and passion, and sweetest music, and all the other higher gifts of song he may be ranked with the greatest,—with Spenser, and Chaucer, and Milton, and Dante, and Homer,—he is at the same time more nervous than Dryden, and more sententious than Pope, and more sparkling and of more abounding conceit, when he chooses, than Donne, or Cowley, or Butler. In whose handling was language ever such a flame of fire as it is in his? His wonderful potency in the use of this instrument would alone set him above all other writers.—CRAIK, GEORGE L., 1861, *A Compendious History of English Literature and of the English Language, vol.* I, *p.* 591.

Although the dialect of Shakespeare does not exhibit the same relative superiority as that of Chaucer over all older and contemporaneous literature, its absolute superiority is, nevertheless, unquestionable. I have before had occasion to remark that the greatest authors very often confine themselves to a restricted vocabulary, and that the power of their diction lies, not in the multitude of words, but in skilful combination and adaptation of a few. This is strikingly verified by an examination of the stock of words employed by Shakespeare. He introduces, indeed. terms borrowed from every art and every science, from all theoretical knowledge and all human experience; but his entire vocabulary little exceeds fifteen thousand words, and of these a large number, chiefly of Latin origin, occur but once or at most twice in his pages. The affluence of his speech arises from variety of combination, not from numerical abundance. And yet the authorized vocabulary of Shakespeare's time probably embraced twice or thrice the number of words which he found necessary for his purposes; for though there were at that time no dictionaries which exhibit a great stock of words, yet in perusing Hooker, the old translators, and the early voyagers and travellers, we find a verbal wealth, a copiousness of diction, which forms a singular contrast with the philological economy of the great dramatist. In his theory of dramatic construction, Shakespeare owes little—in his conception of character, nothing—to earlier or contemporary artists; but in his diction, everything except felicity of selection and combination. The existence of the whole copious English vocabulary was necessary, in order that his marvellous gift of selection might have room for its exercise.—MARSH, GEORGE P., 1862, *Origin and History of the English Language, etc., p.* 569.

In Shakespeare we admire the mighty power with which, after a brief introduction, he throws excitement in the way of his heroes and impels them swiftly in rapid upward stages to a momentous height. His method of leading the action and the characters beyond the climax, in the first half of the play, may also serve as a model to us. And in the second half, the catastrophe itself is planned with the sureness and scope of genius, with no attempt at overwhelming effect, without apparent effort, with concise execution, a consequence of the play, following as a matter of course. But the great poet does not always have success with the forces of the falling action, between climax and catastrophe, the part which fills about the fourth act of our plays. In this important place, he seems too much restrained by the customs of his stage. In many of the greatest dramas of his artistic time, the action is divided up, in this part, into several little scenes, which have an episodical character and are inserted only to make the connection clear. The inner conditions of the hero are concealed, the heightening of effects and the concentration so necessary here fails. It is so in "Hamlet," in "King Lear," in "Macbeth," somewhat so in "Antony and Cleopatra." Even in "Julius Cæsar," the return action contains, indeed, that splendid quarrel scene and the reconciliation between Brutus and Cassius, and the appearance of the ghost; but what follows is again much divided, fragmentary. In "Richard III.," the falling action is indeed drawn together into several great impulses; but yet these do not in a sufficient degree correspond in stage effect to the immense power of the first part.—FREYTAG, GUSTAV, 1863–94, *Technique of the Drama, tr. MacEwan, p.* 185.

We are more intimate with Shakespeare's men and women than we are with our contemporaries, and they are, on the whole, better company. They are more beautiful in form and feature, and they express themselves in a way that the most gifted strive after in vain. What if Shakespeare's people could walk out of the playbooks and settle down upon some spot of earth and conduct life there! There would be found humanity's whitest wheat, the world's unalloyed gold. The very winds could not visit the place roughly. No king's court could present you such an array. Where else could we find a philosopher like Halmet? a friend like Antonio? a witty fellow like Mercutio? where else Imogen's piquant face? Portia's gravity and womanly sweetness? Rosalind's true heart and silvery laughter? Cordelia's beauty of holiness? These would form the centre of the court, but the purlieus, how many-coloured! Malvolio would walk mincingly in the sunshine there; Autolycus would filch purses. Sir Andrew Aguecheek and Sir Toby Belch would be eternal boon companions. And as Falstaff sets out homeward from the tavern, the portly knight leading the revellers like a three-decker a line of frigates, they are encountered by Dogberry, who summons them to stand and answer to the watch as they are honest men.—SMITH, ALEXANDER, 1863, *Dreamthorp, p.* 283.

Not only is Shakespeare the closest of all reasoners, but the web of his argument is always of a golden tissue. . . . The very sweepings of his genius are virgin gold.—CLARKE, CHARLES COWDEN, 1863, *Shakespeare-Characters, pp.* 23, 119.

Given a shadow, Shakspere had the power to place himself so, that that shadow became his own—was the correct representation as shadow, of his form coming between it and the sunlight. And this is the highest dramatic gift that a man can possess. But we feel at the same time, that this is, in the main, not so much art as inspiration.—MACDONALD, GEORGE, 1863, *The Imagination and Other Essays, p.* 161.

This player was a prophet from on high,
Thine own elected. Statesman, poet, sage,
For him thy sovereign pleasure passed them by;
Sidney's fair youth, and Raleigh's ripened age,
Spenser's chaste soul, and his imperial mind
Who taught and shamed mankind.
—HOLMES, OLIVER WENDELL, 1864, *Shakespeare Tercentennial Celebration.*

If I preach about Shakspere, and the method of treatment should be somewhat unusual in your ear, I hope you will remember that this is the very thing which I am set to do. Why, then, I would ask, have we just cause to celebrate with a jubilee the fact that three hundred years ago Shakspere was born; or, in other words, why do we thank God that such a man has been among us? What is there we have read in his writings to render them an enduring benefit to us,—a possession forever,—such as we feel makes us richer, wiser, and, using it aright, better than we should have been without them? It is this question which we propose to discuss. Those who mould a nation's life should be men acquainted with God's scheme of the universe, cheerfully working in their own appointed sphere the work which has been assigned them, accepting God's world because it is His, with all its strange riddles and perplexities, with all the burdens which it lays upon each one of us:—not fiercely dashing and shaking themselves like imprisoned birds against the bars of their prison house, or moodily nourishing in their own hearts, and in the hearts of others, thoughts of discontent, revolt, and despair. Such a poet, I am bold to affirm, we possessed in Shakspere.—TRENCH, RICHARD CHENEVIX, 1864, *Sermon, Tercentenary of Shakspere, Stratford-upon-Avon, April* 23.

In order to deal fairly with this former part of our investigation, it is necessary to remark, in the first instance, that, while the *whole contents* and *general language* of the Bible would be known to our poet from translations previously in use, in regard to particular *words* and *modes of speech*, it is probable that our translators of 1611 owed to Shakspeare as much as, or rather far more than, he owed to them. . . . Take the entire range of English Literature; put together our best authors, who have written upon subjects not professedly religious or theological, and we shall not find, I believe, in them *all united*, so much evidence of the Bible having been read and used, as we have found in Shakspeare *alone*. This is a *phenomenon* which admits of being looked at from several points of view; but I shall be content to regard it solely in connection with the undoubted fact, that of all our authors, Shakspeare is also, by general confession, the greatest and the best. —WORDSWORTH, CHARLES, 1864–80, *Shakspeare's Knowledge and Use of the Bible, pp.* 9, 345.

Homer, Job, Æschylus, Isaiah, Ezekiel, Lucretius, Juvenal, St. John, St. Paul, Tacitus, Dante, Rabelais, Cervantes, Shakespeare. That is the avenue of the immoveable giants of the human mind. The men of genius are a dynasty. Indeed there is no other. They wear all the crowns, even that of thorns. Each of them represents the sum total of absolute that man can realize. We repeat it, to choose between these men, to prefer one to the other, to mark with the finger the first among these first, it cannot be. All are the Mind. Perhaps, in an extreme case—and yet every objection would be legitimate—you might mark out as the highest summit among those summits, Homer, Æschylus, Job, Isaiah, Dante, and Shakespeare. It is understood that we speak here only in an Art point of view, and in Art, in the literary point of view. Two men in this group, Æschylus and Shakespeare, represent specially the drama. . . . His poetry has the sharp perfume of honey made by the vagabond bee without a hive. Here prose, there verse; all forms, being but receptacles for the idea, suit him. This poetry weeps and laughs. The English tongue, a language little formed, now assists, now harms him, but everywhere the deep mind gushes forth translucent. Shakespeare's drama proceeds with a kind of distracted rhythm; it is so vast that it staggers; it has and gives the vertigo; but nothing is so solid as this excited grandeur. Shakespeare, shuddering, has in himself the winds, the spirits, the philters, the vibrations, the fluctuations of transient breezes, the obscure penetration of effluvia, the great unknown sap. Thence his agitation, in the depth of which is repose. It is agitation in which Goethe is wanting, wrongly praised for his impassiveness, which is inferiority. This agitation, all minds of the first order have it. It is in Job, in Æschylus, in Alighieri. This agitation is humanity.—HUGO, VICTOR, 1864, *William Shakespeare, tr. Baillot, pp.* 66, 185.

He combines in one individual, and harmonizes, qualities apparently incongruous, his genius revealing to him their affinities. —WHITE, RICHARD GRANT, 1865, *ed., The Works of William Shakespeare, an Essay on Shakespeare's Genius, vol.* I, *p.* ccxxxii.

Morning and night meet, as in Nature, in the poet's writings—the comic and the tragic In the full flush and luxuriance of his powers he rises upon us bright, lively, and jocund as the dawn; we know not where he will lead us in the abundance of his poetical caprice, what stores of mirth and wanton wiles, what brilliant and ever-changing hues will sparkle, dazzle, and allure us in his ambrosial course. But that bright morning—unlike the morning of many of the poet's contemporaries —goes down in a solemn and glorious sunset, canopied with clouds of gold and purple.—BREWER, JOHN SHERREN, 1871–81, *English Studies, ed. Wace, p.* 249.

His was one of those delicate souls which, like a perfect instrument of music, vibrate of themselves at the slightest touch. . . . He had a sympathetic genius; I mean that naturally he knew how to forget himself and become transfused into all the objects which he conceived. . . . Shakspeare imagines with copiousness and excess; he spreads metaphors profusely over all he writes; every instant abstract ideas are changed into images; it is a series of paintings which is unfolded in his mind. He does not seek them, they come of themselves; they crowd within him, covering his arguments; they dim with their brightness the pure light of logic. He does not labour to explain or prove; picture on picture, image on image, he is forever copying the strange and splendid visions which are engendered one within another, and are heaped up within him. . . . Shakspeare never sees things tranquilly. All the powers of his mind are concentrated in the present image or idea. He is buried and absorbed in it. With such a genius, we are on the brink of an abyss; the eddying water dashes in headlong, devouring whatever objects it meets, bringing them to light again, if at all, transformed and mutilated. We pause stupefied before these convulsive metaphors, which might have been written by a fevered hand in a night's delirium, which gather a pageful of ideas and pictures in half a sentence, which scorch the eyes they would enlighten. . . . The most immoderate of all violators of language, the most marvellous of all creators of souls, the farthest removed from regular logic and classical reason, the one most capable of exciting in us a world of forms, and of placing living beings before us.—TAINE, H. A., 1871, *History of English Literature, tr. Van Laun, vol.* I, *bk.* ii, *ch.* iv, *pp.* 303, 307, 309, 310.

An imagination so creative, a reason so vigorous, a wisdom so clear and comprehensive, taking views of life and character and duty so broad and just and true, a spirit so fiery and at the same time so gentle, such acuteness of observation and such power of presenting to other minds what is observed—such a combination of qualities seems to afford us, as we contemplate it, a glimpse of what, in certain respects, the immortal part of man shall be, when every cause that dims its vision or weakens its energy or fetters its activity or checks its expansion shall be wholly done away, and that subtler essence shall be left to the full and free exercise of the powers with which God endowed it. —BRYANT, WILLIAM CULLEN, 1872, *Shakspeare, Orations and Addresses, p.* 372.

Here, in his right, he stands!
No breadth of earth-dividing seas can bar
The breeze of morning, or the morning star,
From visiting our lands:
His wit, the breeze, his wisdom, as the star,
Shone where our earliest life was set, and blew
To freshen hope and plan
In brains American,—
To urge, resist, encourage, and subdue!
He came, a household ghost we could not ban:
He sat, on winter nights, by cabin fires;
His summer fairies linked their hands
Along our yellow sands;
He preached within the shadow of our spires;
And when the certain Fate drew nigh, to cleave
The birth-cord, and a separate being leave,
He, in our ranks of patient-hearted men,
Wrought with the boundless forces of his fame,
Victorious, and became
The Master of our thought, the land's first Citizen!

—TAYLOR, BAYARD, 1872, *Shakespeare's Statue, Central Park, New York, May* 23.

There is no room for comparison between him and any other man in Europe, from Chaucer before to Milton after, nor then, again (we hold,) till we reach Sterne and three or four writers of this century.—PALGRAVE, FRANCIS TURNER, 1872, *Thomas Watson The Poet, North American Review, vol.* 114, *p.* 89.

A vision as of crowded city streets,
With human life in endless overflow;
Thunder of thoroughfares; trumpets that blow
To battle; clamor, in obscure retreats,
Of sailors landed from their anchored fleets;
Tolling of bells in turrets, and below
Voices of children, and bright flowers that throw
O'er garden-walls their intermingled sweets!
This vision comes to me when I unfold
The volume of the Poet paramount,
Whom all the Muses loved, not one alone;—
Into his hands they put the lyre of gold,
And, crowned with sacred laurel at their fount,
Placed him as Musagetes on their throne.

—LONGFELLOW, HENRY WADSWORTH, 1873, *A Book of Sonnets.*

By common consent his is one of the greatest names in literature. We recognize the following points in his intellectual supremacy:—1. His profound philosophical insight; his knowledge of human nature enabling him to seize unerringly upon the governing principle or master passion of a man or class of men. 2.—The creativeness of his imagination; exemplified in the multitude of striking characters, embodiments of the laws his intuition has detected. He names more than a thousand, each of whom expresses the thought or sentiment in fitting language and conduct. 3.—The skillful grouping of characters, arrangement of scenes, construction and development of plots. 4.—His style; that marvellous copiousness and felicity conjoined, whereby is brought down to our midst the Shakespearian world, as perceived by an eye at once telescopic and microscopic, by an ear keenly sensitive to all harmonies and discords, by a mind at once the most piercing and the most comprehensive, by a heart tenderer than a mother's, yet stouter than that of Leonidas. 5.—His wit and humor. Falstaff is the most comic character in literature; yet he is but one of a multitude. 6.—His power of portraying deep emotion. Others may have equalled him in single instances, but their successes in this particular are few to his.—SPRAGUE, HOMER B., 1874–8, *Masterpieces in English Literature, p.* 107.

To praise Shakespeare is unnecessary, at least in countries of Germanic language. It would be rudeness to suppose any cultivated man or woman to be ignorant of the works of the greatest poet of all times who shows the whole world and mankind as in a glass. . . . The high, lasting, and in some sense unique position Shakespeare occupies in the literature of the world has thus been acknowledged; but it would be wrong and foolish to exalt him above all other great poets; as has been done by some, in Germany especially. Shakespeare is indeed a poet "for all time;" but every great poet is that. We cannot understand why he should have a superior privilege to Homer, Æschylus, Aristophanes, Dante, Cervantes, Molière, Goethe, Byron. Shakespeare was an Englishman of the Elizabethan era, every inch of him, sharing the prejudices and superstitions of his time and of his countrymen. . . . We see that the true criterion for judging Shakespeare is his own time. Looking upon him in that light we shall be truly just to him. The form of his works, which is undoubtedly faulty at times, belongs to his time and to his country. The spirit of his poetry is and remains the precious possession of mankind, among whose teachers and prophets he will always occupy the front rank.—SCHERR, J., 1874, *A History of English Literature, pp.* 73, 83, 84.

He is not certainly a religionist; he is not a moralist. He neither fashions precepts, nor makes it his business directly or indirectly to enforce them. Is he therefore immoral? Then is nature immoral, human history and the record of daily life; for it is these that Shakespeare reproduces. If he does not so construct his plot, so manipulate his characters, as to give peculiar and brilliant light to moral issues, no more does he pervert and cover them up. He allows the moral forces, among other real natural forces, to flow on with events, to exercise their own share of control over them, and to come out, from time to time, in terrific thunder shocks of retribution. He merely fails, as a showman, to arrest the spectacle, invite attention and rehearse the unmistakable lesson. At bottom, Shakespeare, instead of being an immoral, is a moral writer; because he handles powerfully and truthfully natural, real forces; those which in the world shape character, control its development, gather up its issues. . . . Shakespeare is the poet of natural religion, because he cannot otherwise present nature.—BASCOM, JOHN, 1874, *Philosophy of English Literature, pp.* 124, 129.

The general public were really the first to recognise Shakespeare: no literary potentate bailed him out of obscurity.—MINTO, WILLIAM, 1874-85, *Characteristics of English Poets, p.* 266.

Engrossed though he is with stirring events and thrilling emotions and powerful human characters, it is wonderful how many are the side-glances that he and his characters cast at the Nature that surrounds them. And these glances are like everything else in him, rapid, vivid, and intense. . . . There is hardly one of his plays in which the season and the scene is not flashed upon the mind by a single stroke more vividly than it could be by the most lengthened description.—SHAIRP, JOHN CAMPBELL, 1877, *On Poetic Interpretation of Nature, p.* 174.

Another of the characteristics of Shakspere is his unerring common sense; his feeling of congruity, whether in manners or morals, in taste or in feeling. With all his inexhaustible wealth of imagination, and his daring use of it, he has always the fear of the ridiculous before his eyes, and never gets upon stilts. His imagery may be colossal, it is never disproportioned. . . . Closely connected with Shakespeare's artistic moderation and common sense is his moral uprightness, rectitude of judgment, and soundness of feeling.—SIMPSON, RICHARD, 1878, *The School of Shakspere, vol.* II, *pp.* 396, 397.

Nor is it quite sound and sober criticism to say, of Shakspeare: "He was altogether, from end to end, an artist, and the greatest artist the modern world has known." Or again: "In the unchangeableness of pure art-power Shakspeare stands entirely alone." There is a peculiarity in Mr. Stopford Brooke's use of the words *art, artist.* He means by an artist one whose aim in writing is not to reveal himself, but to give pleasure; he says most truly that Shakspeare's aim was to please, that Shakspeare "made men and women whose dramatic action on each other and towards a catastrophe was intended to please the public, not to reveal himself." This is indeed the true temper of the artist. But when we call a man emphatically *artist*, a *great artist*, we mean something more than this temper in which he works; we mean by art, not merely an aim to please, but also, and more, a law of pure and flawless workmanship. As living always under the sway of *this* law, and as, therefore, a perfect artist, we do not conceive of Shakspeare. His workmanship is often far from being pure and flawless.

Till that Bellona's bridegroom, lapp'd in proof,
Confronted him with self-comparisons—

There is but one name for such writing as that, if Shakspeare had signed it a thousand times,—it is detestable. And it is too frequent in Shakspeare. . . . We ought not to speak of Shakspere as "altogether, from end to end, an artist;" as "standing entirely alone in the unchangeableness of pure art-power." He is the richest, the most wonderful, the most powerful, the most delightful of poets; he is not altogether, nor even eminently an artist.—ARNOLD, MATTHEW, 1879, *A Guide to English Literature, Mixed Essays, pp.* 193, 194.

The universality and inexhaustible versatility of our own Shakespeare are unique in all literature. But the very richness of his qualities detracts from the symmetry and directness of the dramatic impression. For this reason neither is Lear, nor Othello, nor Macbeth, nor Hamlet (each supreme as an imaginative creation) so typically perfect a tragedy as the Agamemnon. In each of the four there are slight incidents which we could spare without any evident loss.—HARRISON, FREDERIC, 1879–86, *The Choice of Books and other Literary Pieces, p.* 30.

The drama is undoubtedly the most characteristic expression of the Renaissance. . . . Everybody wrote a play, either a tragedy or a comedy: among the writers are many names, which singly were great enough to have thrown lustre over any country—Beaumont and Fletcher, Ford and Massinger, "rare Ben Jonson." But they all pale before Shakespeare: they are so infinitely below him, that they hardly seem to belong to the same race. And yet this brilliant flower sprang into being all at once. There is no hidden growth long enough to account for such a perfect development. Like Provençal poetry in the eleventh, like Dante's poetry in the fourteenth century, it was born full grown. We have seen that Shakespeare drew his plots from the classic ballads and from old stories; but where did he learn to make so many characters, each one of whom would be sufficient for an ordinary writer,—to pierce the motives of every action,—to create living beings?—POOR, LAURA ELIZABETH, 1880, *Sanskrit and its Kindred Literatures; Studies in Comparative Mythology, p.* 426.

The Bible apart, Shakespeare's dramas are, by general consent, the greatest classic and literary treasure of the world. His text, with all the admitted imperfections on its head, is nevertheless a venerable and sacred thing, and must nowise be touched but under a strong restraining sense of pious awe. Woe to the man that exercises his critical surgery here without a profound reverence for the subject! All glib ingenuity, all shifty cleverness, should be sternly warned off from medling with the matter.—HUDSON, HENRY NORMAN, 1880, *ed. Harvard Shakespeare, vol.* I, *Preface, p.* xxi.

Not if men's tongues and angels' all in one
Spake, might the word be said that might speak Thee.
Streams, winds, woods, flowers, fields, mountains, yea, the sea,
What power is in them all to praise the sun?
His praise is this,—he can be praised of none.
Man, woman, child, praise God for him; but he
Exults not to be worshipped, but to be.
He is; and, being, beholds his work well done.
All joy, all glory, all sorrow, all strength, all mirth,
Are his: without him, day were night on earth.
Time knows not his from time's own period.
All lutes, all harps, all viols, all flutes, all lyres,
Fall dumb before him ere one string suspires.
All stars are angels; but the sun is God.
—SWINBURNE, ALGERNON CHARLES, 1882, *William Shakespeare, Tristram of Lyonesse and Other Poems, p.* 280.

"How weak are words—to carry thoughts like mine!"
Saith each dull daughter round the much bored Nine.
Yet words sufficed for Shakespeare's suit, when he
Woo'd Time, and won instead Eternity.
—WATSON, WILLIAM, 1884, *Epigrams.*

Shakespeare!—To such name's sounding, what succeeds
Fitly as silence? Falter forth the spell,—
Act follows word, the speaker knows full well,
Nor tampers with its magic more than needs.
Two names there are: That which the Hebrew reads
With his soul only: if from lips it fell,
Echo, back thundered by earth, heaven and hell,
Would own "Thou didst create us!" Naught impedes
We voice the other name, man's most of might,
Awesomely, lovingly: let awe and love
Mutely await their working, leave to sight
All of the issue as—below—above—
Shakespeare's creation rises: one remove,
Though dread—this finite from that infinite.
—BROWNING, ROBERT, 1884, *The Names.*

The perfect model of the perfect mind!
Within the spheric fullness of his sense,
Within his kingly soul's circumference,
The image of the universe was shrined;
In lofty utterance, his tongue outlined
The golden orb of all intelligence;
He touched the circle of omnipotence,
Defining things no other ere defined.
God made but one! the rack of centuries,
The rolling chariot of resistless years,
Leaves unbedimmed the amaranth he wears;
His fame is co-eternal with the skies,
His words are fadeless as our memories,
His influence as deathless as our tears.
—MATTHEWS, JAMES NEWTON, 1884, *Shakespeare.*

Dante may over-top Milton, but Shakespeare surpasses both. He is our finest achievement; his plays our noblest possession; the things in the world most worth thinking about. To live daily in his company, to study his works with minute and loving care—in no spirit of pendantry searching for double endings, but in order to discover their secret, and to make the spoken word tell upon the hearts of man and woman—this might have been expected to produce great intellectual if not moral results.—BIRRELL, AUGUSTINE, 1884, *Obiter Dicta, p.* 146.

Shakspere's pre-eminence consists chiefly in this, that he did supremely well what all were doing. His touch on life was so unerringly true that the most diverse objects took shape and place together naturally in his atmosphere of art; even as in the full rich sunlight of a summer afternoon the many-moving crowds, the river, bridges, buildings, parks, and domes of a great city stand distinct but harmonised. No theatre is so rich in countless and contrasted types of womanhood. Shakespere's women have passed into a proverb.—SYMONDS, JOHN ADDINGTON, 1884, *Shakspere's Predecessors in the English Drama, p.* 58.

His was the nectar of the gods of Greece,
The lute of Orpheus, and the Golden Fleece
Of grand endeavour; and the thunder-roll
Of words majestic, which, from pole to pole,
Have borne the tidings of our English tongue.
He gave us Hamlet; and he taught us more
Than schools have taught us; and his fairy-lore
Was fraught with science; and he called from death
Verona's Lovers, with the burning breath
Of their great passion that has filled the spheres.
He made us know Cordelia, and the man
Who murder'd sleep, and baleful Caliban;
And, one by one, athwart the gloom appear'd
Maidens and men and myths who were revered
In olden days, before the earth was sad.
Aye! this is true. It was ordained so;
He was thine own, three hundred years ago;

But ours to-day; and ours till earth be red
With doom-day splendour for the quick and dead,
And days and nights are scattered like the leaves.
It was for this he lived, for this he died:
To raise to Heaven the face that never lied,
To lean to earth the lips that should become
Fraught with conviction when the mouth was dumb,
And all the firm, fine body turn'd to clay.

—MACKAY, ERIC, 1886, *Love Letters of a Violinist and Other Poems*, p. 107

The plays in the *Globe* edition contain just a thousand closely-printed pages. I do not think that there are fifty in all, perhaps not twenty—putting scraps and patches together—in which the Shakesperian touch is wanting, and I do not think that that touch appears outside the covers of the volume once in a thousand pages of all the rest of English literature.—SAINTSBURY, GEORGE, 1887, *History of Elizabethan Literature*, p. 173.

The rough workmanship in Shakespeare puts me out and often quite repels me, whereas in the great Latin, French, and Italian writers, as in our own Milton, there is usually a high degree of finish in the literary workmanship itself which attracts me, and gives me a profound and unfailing satisfaction.—HAMERTON, PHILIP GILBERT, 1887, *Books Which Have Influenced Me*, p. 63.

Shakespeare has served me best. Few living friends have had upon me an influence so strong for good as Hamlet or Rosalind. The last character, already well beloved in the reading, I had the good fortune to see, I must think, in an impressionable hour, played by Mrs. Scott Siddons. Nothing has ever more moved, more delighted, more refreshed me; nor has the influence quite passed away. Kent's brief speech over the dying Lear had a great effect upon my mind, and was the burden of my reflections for long, so profoundly, so touchingly generous did it appear in sense, so overpowering in expression. — STEVENSON, ROBERT LOUIS, 1887, *Books Which Have Influenced Me*, p. 4.

When I was fifteen, Dicks's Shakespeare was published in penny weekly numbers. I had never read any of his plays, and as I have never to this day witnessed the performance of any stage play, I was then in absolute ignorance of what "Shakespeare" meant. The first number contained two plays, "Hamlet" and "Othello," at a halfpenny each. I shall never forget the shock—the bewildering shock—which I received from the last scene in "Hamlet." So invariably had novelists, and even romantic poets like Scott, brought their heroes and heroines happily together before they left the stage, that it was some time before I could realise that in "Hamlet" all was different. The death of Ophelia had startled me; that was irretrievable, no doubt; but Hamlet might still be saved. But when at last death swept the board, and the curtain fell on a universal shambles, I was dazed, angry, and incredulous. I read the play over again, not for the story this time; and then read "Othello." It was one of the turning-points of my life. I was fascinated. Every week, until the series were complete, I devoured the two new plays contained in each number. They enormously widened the horizon of life; they added new and vivid colour to existence, and they intensified my perception of the tragic issues of love and of death that are bound up in every human heart. But that was not all; Shakespeare was to me the key to all literature. In this way, in my enthusiasm for Shakespeare I greedily devoured criticisms of his plays wherever I found them.—STEAD, W. T., 1887, *Books Which Have Influenced Me*, p. 28.

It remained for Shakspere to combine the idealism with the realism of Love in proper proportions. The colours with which he painted the passion and sentiment of modern Love are as fresh and as true to life as on the day when they were first put on his canvas. Like Dante, however, he was emotionally ahead of his time, as an examination of contemporary literature in England and elsewhere shows. . . . It is in the works of Shakspere that the various motives and emotions which constitute Love—sensuous, æsthetic intellectual—are for the first time mingled in proper proportions. Shakspere's Love is Modern Love, full-fledged, and therefore calls for no separate analysis.—FINCK, HENRY T., 1887, *Romantic Love and Personal Beauty*, vol. I, pp. 3, 178.

It is said that ten thousand different essays, pamphlets and books have been printed and published concerning the life and writings of William Shakespeare. This is something unparalleled in the history of literature. No other name among men of letters has created such an interest. What an amazing attraction, what a boundless fascination, must people find in the life and character of this man! Men of every nation, of every rank, are captivated by him. . . . People of foreign nations are so much interested in him, that they learn English merely to read his works in the original; and there is hardly a language capable of literary expression into which these works have not been again and again translated. He is called the father of German literature, and even at the present day is more read and studied in Germany than any native author. His birthplace, now the property of the English nation, has become a Mecca to which pilgrims from the four corners of the world resort; the relation and explanation of the events of his life form one of the great problems of modern times; and societies for the study and elucidation of his writings have been organized in every part of the civilized world. He is the glory of the English-speaking race, and every member of that race, from one end of the world to the other, is more or less indebted to him for what he is, for what culture or enlightenment he possesses, for what largeness of view, superior power of expression, or increased social and intellectual advantages he enjoys; indeed, I may say that mankind is indebted to him for a richer and more copious speech, a larger social and intellectual life, and a more abundant fund of rational amusement, than it ever possessed before. —WATERS, ROBERT, 1888, *William Shakespeare Portrayed by Himself, pp.* 1, 2.

Superb and inimitable as all is, it is mostly an objective and physiological kind of power and beauty the soul finds in Shakspere—a stlye supremely grand of the sort, but in my opinion stopping short of the grandest sort, at any rate for fulfilling and satisfying modern and scientific and democratic American purposes. Think, not of growths as forests primeval, or Yellowstone geysers, or Colorado ravines, but of costly marble palaces, and palace rooms, and the noblest fixings and furniture, and noble owners and occupants to correspond—think of carefully built gardens from the beautiful but sophisticated gardening art at its best, with walks and bowers and artificial lakes, and appropriate statue-groups and the finest cultivated roses and lilies and japonicas in plenty—and you have the tally of Shakspere. The low characters, mechanics, even the loyal henchmen—all in themselves nothing—serve as capital foils to the aristocracy. The comedies (exquisite as they certainly are) bringing in admirably portray'd common characters, have the unmistakable hue of plays, portraits, made for the divertisement only of the elite of the castle, and from its point of view. The comedies are altogether non-acceptable to America and Democracy. But to the deepest soul, it seems a shame to pick and choose from the riches Shakspere has left us—to criticise his infinitely royal, multiform quality—to gauge, with optic glasses, the dazzle of his sun-like beams.—WHITMAN, WALT, 1888, *November Boughs, p.* 56.

For my part, I believe that Shakespeare wrote his plays, like the conscientious playwright that he was, to fill the theatre and make money for his fellow-actors and for himself; and I confess to absolute scepticism in reference to the belief that in these dramas Shakespeare's self can be discovered (except on the broadest lines,) or that either his outer or his inner life is to any discoverable degree reflected in his plays; it is because Shakespeare is *not* there that the characters are so perfect, —the smallest dash of the author's self would mar to that extent the truth of the character, and make of it a mask.—FURNESS, HORACE HOWARD, 1890, *ed. New Variorum Edition of Shakespeare, As You Like It, Introduction, p.* viii.

So large a space did the great dramatist fill in the delightsome journey we were to make together, down through the pleasant country of English letters, that he seemed not so much a personality as some great British stronghold, with outworks, and with pennons flying—standing all athwart the Elizabethan Valley, down which our track was to lead us. From far away back of Chaucer, when the first Romances of King Arthur were told, when glimpses of a King Lear and a Macbeth appeared in old chronicles—this great monument of Elizabethan times loomed high in our front; and go far as we may down the current of English letters, it will not be out of sight, but loom up grandly behind us. And now that we are fairly abreast of it, my fancy still clings to that figure of a great castle—brimful of life—with which the lesser poets of the age contrast like so many out-lying towers, that we can walk all round about, and measure, and scale, and tell of their age, and forces, and style; but this Shakesperean hulk is so vast, so wondrous, so peopled with creatures, who are real, yet unreal—that measure and scale count for nothing. We hear around it the tramp of armies and the blare of trumpets; yet these do not drown the sick voice of poor distraught Ophelia. We see the white banner of France flung to the breeze, and the English columbine nodding in clefts of the wall; we hear the ravens croak from turrets that lift above the chamber of Macbeth, and the howling of the rainstorms that drenched poor Lear; and we see Jessica at her casement, and the Jew Shylock whetting his greedy knife, and the humpbacked Richard raging in battle, and the Prince boy—apart in his dim tower—piteously questioning the jailer Huburt, who has brought "hot-irons" with him. Then there is Falstaff, and Dame Quickly, and the pretty Juliet sighing herself away from her moonlit balcony. These are all live people to us; we know them; and we know Hamlet, and Brutus, and Mark Antony, and the witty, coquettish Rosalind; even the poor Mariana of the moated grange.—MITCHELL, DONALD G., 1890, *English Lands Letters and Kings, From Elizabeth to Anne, p.* 57.

Herein Chaucer stands at the opposite pole from Shakspeare. The work of the latter abounds in coarse allusions, in filthy conceits, in double meanings. But these passages in the great dramatist's writings are supremely uninteresting. They are as tedious as they are vile. They cannot be called innocent, but they are innocuous, owing to the saving grace of stupidity. When Shakspeare appeals to the lower nature, he does it largely through the agency of verbal quibbles, which are, if possible, more execrable intellectually than they are morally. To trace the allusions contained in them, to unravel the obscurities inwrapped in them, involve a degree of labor which few are willing to bestow, or a previous acquaintance with human nastiness that few have qualified themselves to possess. The result is that these things are constantly passed over unnoticed. There is little attraction in the pursuit of knowledge peculiarly difficult to acquire, and with which, when obtained, the acquirer is more disgusted than pleased.—LOUNSBURY, THOMAS R., 1891, *Studies in Chaucer, vol.* III, *p.* 364.

I seldom refer to Shakespeare in these lectures, since we all instinctively resort to him as to nature itself; his text being not only the chief illustration of each phrase that may arise, but also, like nature, presenting all phases in combination. It displays more of clear and various beauty, more insight, surer descriptive touches,—above all, more human life,—than that of any other poet; yes, and more art, in spite of a certain constructive disdain,—the free and prodigal art that is like nature's own. Thus he seems to require our whole attention or none, and it is as well to illustrate a special quality by some poet more dependent upon it. Yet if there is one gift which sets Shakespeare at a distance even from those who approach him on one or another side, it is that of his imagination. As he is the chief of poets, we infer that the faculty in which he is supereminent must be the greatest of poetic endowments. Yes: in his wonderland, as elsewhere, imagination is king. There is little doubt concerning the hold of Shakespeare upon future ages. I have sometimes debated whether, in the change of dramatic ideals and of methods in life and thought, he may not become outworn and alien. But the purely creative quality of his imagination renders it likely that its structures will endure. . . . Shakespeare's imagination is still more independent of discovery, place, or time. It is neither early nor late, antiquated nor modern; or, rather, it is always modern and abiding.—STEDMAN, EDMUND CLARENCE, 1892, *The Nature and Elements of Poetry, pp.* 229, 230.

Shakespeare is the first among the great Engish poets since the Old English period in whom the Teutonic spirit again overpoweringly asserts itself, and presses into its service all those elements of foreign culture which were assimilated by the national character. In him we find again that soul-stirring note of deep feeling, that simple boldness of poetic expression, which plunges us, without preparation or mediation,—apparently without any effort at artistic effect,—into the very heart of the subject; in short, he has that genuineness of sentiment which is a chief characteristic of Germanic poesy.—TEN BRINK, BERNHARD, 1892-95, *Five Lectures on Shakespeare, tr. Franklin, p.* 33.

Shakespeare loved his England and so sounded her praises. The imagination of the poet seized upon the skeleton of the chroniclers and clothed them with flesh and blood. From King John to Henry VIII., from Magna Charta to the Reformation, whether conscious or not of the splendid scope of his achievement, the poet historian has sung an immortal epic of the English nation, having for its dominant note the passing of feudalism and the rise of the common people. The germ of this development has never died out of the souls of that hardy race whose forefathers crept across the gray waste of the German ocean in their frail boats of wood and hide, to grapple with unknown foes upon unknown shores, and to lay the cornerstone of that great and free nation, of whose best life Shakespeare was the poet, chronicler, and seer. — WARNER, BEVERLEY E., 1894, *English History in Shakespeare's Plays, p.* 15.

Probably no dramatist ever needed the stage less, and none ever brought more to it. There have been few joys for me in life comparable to that of seeing the curtain rise on Hamlet, and hearing the guards begin to talk about the ghost; and yet how fully this joy imparts itself without any material embodiment! It is the same in the whole range of his plays: they fill the scene, but if there is no scene they fill the soul. They are neither worse nor better because of the theatre. They are so great that it cannot hamper them; they are so vital that they enlarge it to their own proportions and endue it with something of their own living force. They make it the size of life, and yet they retire it so wholly that you think no more of it than you think of the physiognomy of one who talks importantly to you. I have heard people say that they would rather not see Shakespeare played than to see him played ill, but I cannot agree with them. He can better afford to be played ill than any other man that ever wrote. Whoever is on the stage it is always Shakespeare who is speaking to me, and perhaps this is the reason why in the past I can trace no discrepancy between reading his plays and seeing them.—HOWELLS, WILLIAM DEAN, 1895, *My Literary Passions, p.* 75.

We cannot lay our hand on anything and say for certain that it was spoken by Shakespeare out of his own personality. He created men and women whose dramatic action on each other, and towards a chosen end, was intended to please the public, not to reveal himself. Frequently failing in fineness of workmanship, having, but far less than the other dramatists, the faults of the art of his time, he was yet in all other points—in creative power, in impassioned conception and execution, in truth to universal human nature, in intellectual power, in intensity of feeling, in the great matter and manner of his poetry, in the welding together of thought, passion, and action, in range, in plenteousness, in the continuance of his romantic feeling—the greatest poet our modern world has known. Like the rest of the greater poets, he reflected the noble things of his time, but refused to reflect the base.—BROOKE, STOPFORD A., 1896, *English Literature, p.* 140.

The first poet who recognised insanity as a disease and painted it as such is Shakespeare, whose fine power of observation far outstripped his age. He who could paint the world in all its truth and reality, who was able to reproduce the most diverse characters, unfalsified and true to Nature, succeeded also in painting in a mastery way mental derangements in all their typical phenomena, just as we observe them to-day, and this at a time at which science was far from a correct recognition of physical disorders. In Shakespeare, the derangements of King Lear, Hamlet, and Lady Macbeth are photographic reproductions of pure objective experience. They fill out certainly the world of the poet who painted all human passions with minute fidelity in his plays, and therefore undertook also to paint according to his observation the human mind under morbid obscuration. In these characters, therefore, we have neither the embodiment of any particular conception of the universe nor an artistic dressing up of any moral or doctrine.—HIRSCH, WILLIAM, 1896, *Genius and Degeneration, p.* 321.

He is an author whom, however we read him, we can hardly read amiss. Yet, just because of this fact, which we may misunderstand as implying that any reading of Shakspere is as good as any other, we are in danger of approaching him in a way to shut up our sympathies and imaginations, and so cut ourselves off from the main avenues of his power. The earnest student, who sees the libraries that have grown up about the works of Shakspere, can hardly escape the inference that the great dramatist is properly an object only of study. Yet never was there conclusion that Shakspere himself would sooner have repudiated. What was the audience for whom Shakspere wrote his plays? Exclusively an audience that gathered to be amused. Entertainment, not instruction, was Shakspere's aim. Shakspere does teach us in a myriad ways, and may properly be made the object of almost innumerable kinds of study; but the fact remains that, until we have read his plays, or, still better, have seen them acted, with no other purpose than pure enjoyment, we have not yet known Shakspere.—KOOPMAN, HARRY LYMAN, 1896, *The Mastery of Books*, p. 24.

In Shakespeare an heroic epoch culminates; he is the commanding peak of a vast group of mountains. It is therefore vain to consider him as though he stood alone, a solitary portent in a plain. More than any other of the greatest poets of the world, he rises, by insensible degrees, on the shoulders and the hands of a crowd of precursors, yet so rapidly did this crowd collect that our eyes are scarcely quick enough to perceive the process. . . . Of those whose inestimable privilege it was to meet Shakespeare day by day, we have no evidence that one perceived the supremacy of his genius. The case is rather curious, for it was not that anything austere or arrogant in himself or his work repelled recognition, or that those who gazed were blinded by excess of light. On the contrary, it seemed to his own friends that they appreciated his amiable, easy talent at its proper value; he was "gentle" Shakespeare to them, and they loved both the man and his poetry. But that he excelled them all at every point, as the oak excells the willow, this, had it been whispered at the Mermaid, would have aroused smiles of derision. . . . For another century the peak of the mountain was shrouded in mists, although its height was vaguely conjectured. Dryden, our earliest modern critic, gradually perceived Shakespeare's greatness, and proclaimed it in his "Prefaces." Meanwhile, and on until a century after Shakespeare's death, this most glorious of English names had not penetrated across the Channel, and was absolutely unrecognised in France. Voltaire introduced Shakespeare to French readers in 1731, and "Hamlet" was translated by Ducis in 1769. Here at home, in the generations of Pope and Johnson, the magnitude of Shakespeare became gradually apparent to all English critics, and with Garrick his plays once more took the stage. Yet into all the honest admiration of the eighteenth century there entered a prosaic element; the greatness was felt, but vaguely and painfully. At the end of the age of Johnson a generation was born to whom, for the first time, Shakespeare spoke with clear accents. Coleridge and Hazlitt expounded him to a world so ready to accept him, that in regarding the great Revival of 1800 Shakespeare seems almost as completely a factor in it as Wordsworth himself. In the hands of such critics, for the first time, the fog cleared away from the majestic mountain, and showed to the gaze of the world its varied and harmonious splendour.—GOSSE, EDMUND, 1897, *Short History of Modern English Literature*, pp. 100, 108.

Strictly speaking, there is no literary fame worth envying, save Shakespeare's —and Shakespeare's amounted to this, that Addison wrote "An Account of the Greatest English Poets" in which his name deos not appear; and that, of the people one meets in the streets of any city, the majority will not even have heard of him. — HIGGINSON, THOMAS WENTWORTH, 1897, *Favorites of a Day, Book and Heart*, p. 78.

Shakespeare is a well-spring of characters which are saturated with the comic spirit; with more of what we will call blood-life than is to be found anywhere out of Shakespeare; and they are of this world, but they are of the world enlarged to our embrace by imagination, and by great poetic imagination.—MEREDITH, GEORGE, 1897, *An Essay on Comedy and the Uses of the Comic Spirit*, p. 16.

I have not intended to compare the poetry of Shakespeare with the poetry of the Bible. Shakespeare has neither the eloquence of Isaiah nor the sublimity of Job. What Shakespeare does not profess to do, Job and Isaiah do profess to do—namely, to teach of God and duty. Nor have I intended to compare the merits of the great uninspired poets, or to call one greater and another less. It is better to call each great in his peculiar sphere. But in the creation of character Shakespeare so far surpasses all others, that by common consent we have come to regard him as the greatest secular poet of the world. Will the world ever see a poet who shall surpass him? It can only be by adding Dante's vision of God and Wordsworth's vision of nature to Shakespeare's vision of humanity. Until some inspired bard shall touch all these several strings with simultaneous and equal mastery, we may well content ourselves with Shakespeare. —STRONG, AUGUSTUS HOPKINS, 1897, *The Great Poets and Their Theology, p.* 219.

Shakespeare's spirit is not to be assimilated; this is impossible to a man of our time: one can but dress oneself up in the cast-off garment which served as a covering to his genius. This garment does not suit us,—it is either too long or too short, or both together. One dresses up as Shakespeare for an hour, and resembles the great man about as much as a lawyer's clerk, masquerading *en mousquetaire*, resembles d'Artagnan, or as the Turk of carnival time resembles the genuine Turk smoking his pipe outside his cafè in Stamboul. This tremendous model, all whose aspects we cannot see because it goes beyond the orbit of our perspective glass, oppresses and paralyses our intelligence: did one understand it, one would not be much the better off. It would be sheer folly to wish the modern English dramatist not to read his Shakespeare, for it is in Shakespeare that he will find the English character in all its length and breadth; let him absorb and steep himself in Shakespeare by all means: but let him then forget Shakespeare and be of his own time, let him not walk our streets of to-day in the doublet and hose of 1600. The choice has to be made between Shakespeare and life, for in literature, as in morals, it is not possible to serve two masters. It is possible that Shakespeare has been, and is still, the great obstacle to a free development of a national drama. Nor is there anything to be astonished at in this. The Shakespeare whom we know could not have been born when he was had there been another Shakespeare two and a half centuries before.—FILON, AUGUSTIN, 1897, *The English Stage, tr. Whyte, p.* 175.

The first edition of Shakespeare's Plays (folio, 1623) has been rising in price from the commencement of the nineteenth century; but the enormous prices now paid do not date further back than 1864, when a specially fine copy was bought by the Baroness Burdett-Coutts at George Daniel's sale for £716, 2s. This amount was paid on account of the height of the book and of its great beauty, and possibly the circumstance of the year being the tercentenary of Shakespeare's birth had something to do with it, but this sale had the effect of raising the price of all copies permanently. . . . The following is a list of some of the copies which have been sold since the famous Daniel copy:—In 1882 Beresford-Hope's copy, with verses inlaid, title repaired, in morocco by Clarke, fetched £238; and Ouvry's sound copy, in red morocco by Clarke and Bedford, sold for £420. The Earl of Gosford's copy, perfect, with title and verses mounted, and margins of leaves slightly mended, was sold in 1884 for £470. Hartley's copy was in poor condition, although very tall ($13\frac{3}{8}$ by $8\frac{3}{4}$), title with portrait wanting, page with verses mutilated, and some leaves mended. It sold in 1887 for £255. Hartley gave £500 for it to those who had bought it at a knock-out for £75. The Earl of Aylesford's copy, wanting title, with verses from second edition, and five leaves stained, sold in 1888 for £200. In 1889 F. Perkins's copy, with title and verses mounted, sold for £415; and Halliwell Phillipps's poor copy, with portrait, verses, preliminary and last leaf in facsimile, for £95. W. H. Crawford's imperfect copy, with title, verses, prefatory matter, and "Cymbeline" reprinted in facsimilie, sold in 1891 for £16, 10s. In this same year Brayton Ives's copy, perfect, but rather short, was sold in New York for 4,200 dollars (£840).—WHEATLEY, HENRY B., 1898, *Prices of Books, pp.* 223, 228.

The monarch of mankind! they are proud words those, but they do not altogether over-estimate the truth. He is by no means the only king in the intellectual world, but his power is unlimited by time or space. From the moment his life's history ceases his far greater history begins. We find its first records in Great Britain, and consequently in North America; then it spread among the German-speaking peoples and the whole Teutonic race, on through the Scandinavian countries to the Finns and the Sclavonic races. We find his influence in France, Spain, and Italy; and now, in the nineteenth century, it may be traced over the whole civilised world. His writings are translated into every tongue and all the languages of the earth do him honour. . . . All the real intellectual life of England since his day has been stamped by his genius, all her creative spirits have imbibed their life's nourishment from his works. Modern German intellectual life is based, through Lessing, upon him. Goethe and Schiller are unimaginable without him. His influence is felt in France through Voltaire, Victor Hugo, and Alfred de Vigny. Ludovic Vitet and Alfred de Musset were from the very first inspired by him. Not only the drama in Russia and Poland felt his influence, but the inmost spiritual life of the Sclavonic story-tellers and brooders is fashioned after the pattern of his imperishable creations. From the moment of the regeneration of poetry in the North he was reverenced by Ewald, Oehlenschläger, Bredahl, and Hauch, and he is not without his influence upon Björnson and Ibsen.—BRANDES, GEORGE, 1898, *William Shakespeare, A Critical Study, vol.* II, *p.* 411.

No estimate of Shakespeare's genius can be adequate. In knowledge of human character, in wealth of humour, in depth of passion, in fertility of fancy, and in soundness of judgment he has no rival. It is true of him, as of no other writer, that his language and versification adapt themselves to every phase of sentiment, and sound every note in the scale of felicity. Some defects are to be acknowledged, but they sink into insignificance when measured by the magnitude of his achievement. Sudden transitions, elliptical expressions, mixed metaphors, indefensible verbal quibbles, and fantastic conceits at times create an atmosphere of obscurity. The student is perplexed, too, by obsolete words and by some hopelessly corrupt readings. But when the whole of Shakespeare's vast work is scrutinised with due attention, the glow of his imagination is seen to leave few passages wholly unillumined.—LEE, SIDNEY, 1898, *A Life of William Shakespeare, p.* 355.

Shakespeare could be idealistic when he dreamed, as he could be spiritual when he reflected. The spectacle of life did not pass before his eyes as a mere phantasmagoria. He seized upon its principles; he became wise. Nothing can exceed the ripeness of his seasoned judgment, or the occasional breadth, sadness, and terseness of his reflection. The author of "Hamlet" could not be without metaphysical aptitude; "Macbeth" could not have been written without a sort of sibylline inspiration, or the Sonnets without something of the Platonic mind. It is all the more remarkable, therefore, that we should have to search through all the works of Shakespeare to find half a dozen passages that have so much as a religious sound, and that even these passages, upon examinations, should prove not to be the expression of any deep religious conception. If Shakespeare had been without metaphysical capacity, or without moral maturity, we could have explained his strange insensibility to religion; but as it is, we must marvel at his indifference and ask ourselves what can be the causes of it. For, even if we should not regard the absence of religion as an imperfection in his own thought, we must admit it to be an incompleteness in his portrayal of the thought of others.—SANTAYANA, GEORGE, 1900, *Interpretations of Poetry and Religion, p.* 153.

As the Spokesman of a race to which has fallen a large share of the government of the modern world, and as the chief exponent in literature of the fundamental conception of life held by the Western world at a time when the thought of the East and the West are being brought into searching comparison, Shakespeare must be studied in the near future with a deeper recognition of the significance of his work and its value as a source of spiritual culture.—MABIE, HAMILTON WRIGHT, 1900, *William Shakespeare, Poet, Dramatist, and Man, Preface, p.* vii.

Beaumont and Fletcher

Plays published in their lifetime under the joint names of Francis Beaumont and John Fletcher, or attributed to them: "The Woman Hater" (anon.), 1607; "The Knight of the Burning Pestle," 1613; "Cupid's Revenge" (published in Fletcher's name), 1615; "The Scornful Ladie," 1616; "A King and no King," 1619; "The Maid's Tragedy" (anon.), 1619; "Phylaster," 1620 (performed 1611); "Tragedy of Thierry, King of France" (anon., possibly by Fletcher alone), 1621. *Posthumous:* "The Elder Brother" (published in Fletcher's name), 1637; "The Bloody Brother" (published under initials: B. J. F.), 1639; "Wit Without Money" (probably by Fletcher alone), 1639; "Comedies and Tragedies" (containing the following plays, some of which were subsequently published separately: "The Mad Lover," "The Spanish Curate," "The Little French Lawyer," "The Custome of the Countrey," "The Noble Gentleman," "The Captaine," "The Beggar's Bush," "The Coxcombe," "The False One," "The Chances," "The Loyall Subject," "The Lawes of Candy," "The Lover's Progresse," "The Island Princesse," "The Humorous Lieutenant," "The Nice Valour," "The Maid in the Mill," "The Prophetesse," "Bonduca," "The Sea Voyage," "The Double Marriage," "The Pilgrime," "The Knight of Malta," "The Woman's Prize," "Love's Cure," "The Honest Man's Fortune," "The Queene of Corinth," "Women Pleas'd," "A Wife for a Moneth," "Wit at severall Weapons," "Valentinian," "The Fair Maide of the Inne," "Love's Pilgrimage," "The Masque of the Gentlemen of Grayes Inne, etc.," "Four Plays or Moral Representations in One"), 1647; "The Wild-Goose Chase" (probably by Fletcher alone), 1652. *Collected Works:* ed. with memoir, by Dyce (11 vols.), 1843–46.—SHARP, R. FARQUHARSON, 1897, *A Dictionary of English Authors, p.* 21.

PERSONAL

He [Fletcher] had an excellent wit, which, the back-friends to Stage-plays will say, was neither idle, nor well imploy'd; for he and Francis Beaumont Esquire, like Castor and Pollux (most happy when in conjunction) raised the English to equal the Athenian and Roman Theater: Beaumont bringing the ballast of judgement, Fletcher the sail of phantasie; both compounding a Poet to admiration.—FULLER, THOMAS, 1662, *The Worthies of England, ed. Nichols, vol.* II, *p.* 168.

Mr. Francis Beaumont was the son of Judge Beaumont. There was a wonderful consimility of phansey between him and Mr. John Fletcher, which caused that dearnesse of friendship between them. I thinke they were both of Queen's College in Cambridge. I have heard Dr. John Earles (since bishop of Sarum), who knew them, say that his maine businesse was to correct the overflowings of Mr. Fletcher's witt. They lived together on the Banke side, not far from the Play-house, both batchelors; lay together—from Sir James Hales, etc.; had one wench in the house between them, which they did so admire; the same cloathes and cloake, &c., betweene them.—AUBREY, JOHN, 1669–96, *Brief Lives, ed: Clark, vol.* I, *p.* 95.

How happens it, the reader may ask, that this collection of plays, although not a third part ascribed to Beaumont, should be called "Beaumont and Fletcher" instead of "Fletcher and Beaumont?" A question of mere curiosity rather than of moment fortunately demands no better answer than I have to give—another conjecture. Beaumont, we find reason to believe, was a very precocious writer, published works, and made acquaintances among the Wits, before Fletcher did, who appears in the light of a late genius comparatively. Thus Fletcher would have joined Beaumont, as it were, not Beaumont Fletcher; and Beaumont would have been the paramount name, the one most spoken of at the "Mermaid" among choice spirits. Besides, from the very superior excellence of their earlier joint-essays, "Philaster," &c., a presumption arises that Beaumont contributed the weightier share of them; else, why did not Fletcher reach the same perfection in some of those many works we know to be by him alone? This also might explain wherefore Beaumont's name took precedence of Fletcher's, which it kept afterwards from habit. Or that very simple solution of numberless phenomena, which philosophers puzzle themselves stupid otherwise to account for, may probably resolve the present enigma better than any chain of profound causes we could tie together—videlicet, *accident.*—DARLEY, GEORGE, 1840, *ed. Works of Beaumont and Fletcher, Introduction, vol.* I, *p.* xxv.

FRANCIS BEAUMONT

It is somewhat remarkable respecting the Siamese Twins in literature (Beaumont and Fletcher) that although they were both descended from honourable families, and had both received a liberal and collegiate education, the record of their lives does not extend beyond a few unimportant, and mayhap even these not authentic, anecdotes, with a catalogue of their literary compositions.—CLARKE, CHARLES COWDEN, 1871, *On the Comic Writers of England, Gentleman's Magazine, n. s., vol.* 7, *p.* 27.

A student of physiognomy will not fail to mark the points of likeness and of difference between the faces of the two friends; both models of noble manhood, handsome and significant in feature and expression alike;—Beaumont's the statelier and serener of the two, with clear thoughtful eyes, full arched brows, and strong aquiline nose; a grave and beautiful mouth, with full and finely curved lips; the form of face a long pure oval, and the imperial head with its "fair large front" and clustering hair set firm and carried high with an aspect at once of quiet command and kingly observation: Fletcher's a more keen and fervid face, sharper in outline every way, with an air of bright ardour and glad fiery impatience; sanguine and nervous, suiting the complexion and colour of hair; the expression of the eager eyes and lips almost recalling that of a noble hound in act to break the leash it strains at;—two heads as lordly of feature and as expressive of aspect as any gallery of great men can show.—SWINBURNE, ALGERNON CHARLES, 1894, *Studies in Prose and Poetry, p.* 59.

GENERAL

Great are their faults, and glorious is their flame.
In both our English genius is expressed;
Lofty and bold, but negligently dressed.
—WALLER, EDMUND, 1645? *The Maid's Tragedy, Prologue.*

Whom but to mention is to throw a cloud upon all former names, and benight posterity; this book being, without flattery, the greatest monument of the scene that time and humanity have produced, and must live, not only the crown and sole reputation of our own, but the stain of all other nations and languages. . . . Infinitely more might be said of these rare copies; but let the ingenuous reader peruse them, and he will find them so able to speak their own worth, that they need not come into the world with a trumpet, since any one of these incomparable pieces, well understood, will prove a preface to the rest; and if the reader can taste the best wit ever trod our English stage, he will be forced himself to become a breathing panegyric to them all.—SHIRLEY, JAMES, 1647, *ed. Works of Beaumont and Fletcher, To the Reader.*

. . . You were both for both; not semi-wits,
Eace piece is wholly two, yet never splits:
Ye are not two faculties, and one soul still,
He th' understanding, thou the quick free-will;
Not as two voices in one song embrace,
Fletcher's keen treble, and deep Beaumont's base,
Two, full, congenial souls; still both prevail'd;
His muse and thine were quarter'd, not impaled:
Both brought your ingots, both toil'd at the mint,
Beat, melted, sifted, till no dross stuck in't;
Then in each other's scales weigh'd every grain,
Then smooth'd and burnish'd, then weigh'd all again;
Stampt both your names upon't at one bold hit,
Then, then 'twas coin, as well as bullion-wit.
—BERKENHEAD, J., 1647, *On the Happy Collection of Mr. Fletcher's Works.*

. . . Here's a magazine of purest sense,
Cloth'd in the newest garb of eloquence:
Scenes that are quick and sprightly, in whose veins
Bubbles the quintessence of sweet high strains.
Lines, like their authors, and each word of it
Does say, 'twas writ by a gemini of wit.
—BROME, ALEXANDER, 1647, *On the Plays of Beaumont and Fletcher.*

Their plots were generally more regular than Shakespeare's, especially those which were made before Beaumont's death; and they understood and imitated the conversation of gentlemen much better; whose wild debaucheries, and quickness of wit in repartees, no poet before them could paint as they have done. Humour, which Ben Jonson derived from particular persons, they made it not their business to describe: they represented all the passions very lively, but above all, love. I am apt to believe the English language in them arrived to its highest perfection; what words have since been taken in, are rather superfluous than ornamental. Their plays are now the most pleasant and frequent entertainments of the stage; two of theirs being acted through the year for one of Shakespeare's or Jonson's: the reason is, because there is a certain gaiety in their comedies, and pathos in their more serious plays, which suits generally with all men's humours. Shakespeare's language is likewise a little obsolete, and Ben Jonson's wit comes short of theirs.—DRYDEN, JOHN, 1668-93, *An Essay of Dramatic Poesy, Works, ed. Scott and Saintsbury, vol.* XV, *p.* 345.

Of witty Beaumont's poetry, and Fletcher's,
Who for a few misprisions of wit,
Are charged by those who ten times worse
commit;
And for misjudging some unhappy scenes,
Are censured for't with more unlucky sense;
When all their worst miscarriages delight,
And please more, than the best that pedants
write.

—BUTLER, SAMUEL, c 1680, *Upon Critics who judge of modern plays precisely by the rules of the ancients.*

To speak first of Mr. *Beaumont,* he was Master of a good Wit, and a better Judgment; he so admirably well understood the Art of the Stage, that even *Johnson* himself thought it no disparagement to submit his Writings to his Correction. . . . Mr. *Fletcher's* Wit was equal to Mr. *Beaumont's* Judgment, and was so luxuriant, that like superfluous Branches, it was frequently prun'd by his Judicious Partner. These Poets perfectly understood Breeding, and therefore successfully copy'd the Conversation of Gentlemen. They knew how to describe the Manners of the Age; and *Fletcher* had a peculiar tallent in expressing all his thoughts, with Life and Briskness. No Man ever understood, or drew the Passions more lively than he; and his witty Raillery was so drest, that it rather pleas'd than disgusted the modest part of his Audience. In a word, *Fletcher's* Fancy, and *Beaumont's* Judgment combin'd, produc'd such Plays, as will remain Monuments of their Wit to all Posterity. Nay, Mr. *Fletcher* himself after Mr. *Beaumont's* Decease, compos'd several Dramatick Pieces, which were well worthy the Pen of so great a Master.—LANGBAINE, GERARD, 1691, *An Account of the English Dramatick Poets, p.* 204.

Beaumont and Fletcher, with many fair pretensions to theatrical reputation, never could fix a foundation solid enough to establish that sort of fame which commands legitimate suffrage upon the spot, and challenges the award of posterity. They were rather amateurs than writers, rather gentlemen than professors; yet has the stage many obligations to them.—DIBDIN, CHARLES, 1795, *A Complete History of the Stage, vol.* III, *p.* 203.

After all, Beaumont and Fletcher were but an inferior sort of Shakespeares and Sidneys.—LAMB, CHARLES, 1808, *Specimens of Dramatic Poets.*

Beaumont and Fletcher were in fact men of the most distinguished talents; they scarcely wanted any thing more than a profounder seriousness of mind, and that artistic sagacity which every where observes a due measure, to rank beside the greatest dramatic poets of all nations. They possessed extraordinary fecundity and flexibility of mind, and a facility which, however, too often degenerated into carelessness. The highest perfection they have hardly ever attained; and I should have little hesitation in affirming that they had not even an idea of it: however, on several occasions they have approached quite close to it. And why was it denied them to take this last step? Because with them poetry was not an inward devotion of the feeling and imagination, but a means to obtain brilliant results. Their first object was effect, which the great artist can hardly fail of attaining if he is determined above all things to satisfy himself.—SCHLEGEL, AUGUSTUS WILLIAM, 1809, *Dramatic Art and Literature.*

Beaumont and Fletcher have still a high poetical value. If character be sometimes violated, probability discarded, and the interest of the plot neglected, the reader is, on the other hand, often gratified by the most beautiful description, the most tender and passionate dialogue; a display of brilliant wit and gaiety, or a feast of comic humour. These attributes had so much effect on the public, that, during the end of the seventeenth and the beginning of the eighteenth centuries, many of Beaumont and Fletcher's plays had possession of the stage, while those of Shakspeare were laid upon the shelf.—SCOTT, SIR WALTER, 1814-23, *Essay on the Drama*

In Beaumont and Fletcher you have descriptions of characters by the poet rather than the characters themselves; we are told and impressively told, of their being; but we rarely or never feel that they actually are. Beaumont and Fletcher are the most lyrical of our dramatists. I think their comedies the best part of their works, although there are scenes of very deep tragic interest in some of their plays. I particularly recommend Monsieur Thomas for good pure comic humour. There is, occasionally, considerable license in their dramas; and this opens a subject much needing vindication and sound exposition, but which is beset with such difficulties for a Lecturer, that I must pass it by.—COLERIDGE, SAMUEL TAYLOR, 1818, *Notes on Jonson, Beaumont, Fletcher, and Massinger, ed. Ashe, p.* 401.

There are such extremes of grossness and magnificence in their drama, so much sweetness and beauty interspersed with views of nature either falsely romantic, or vulgar beyond reality; there is so much to animate and amuse us, and yet so much that we would willingly overlook, that I cannot help comparing the contrasted impressions which they make, to those which we receive from visiting some great and ancient city, picturesquely but irregularly built, glittering with spires and surrounded with gardens, but exhibiting in many quarters the lanes and hovels of wretchedness. They have scenes of wealthy and high life which remind us of courts and palaces frequented by elegant females and high-spirited gallants, whilst their noble old martial characters, with Caractacus in the midst of them, may inspire us with the same sort of regard which we pay to the rough-hewn magnificence of an ancient fortress. Unhappily, the same simile, without being hunted down, will apply but too faithfully to the *nuisances* of their drama. Their language is often basely profligate. Shakspeare's and Jonson's indelicacies are but casual blots; whilst theirs are sometimes essential colours of their painting, and extend, in one or two instances, to entire and offensive scenes. This fault has deservedly injured their reputation; and, saving a very slight allowance for the fashion and taste of their age, admits of no sort of apology.—CAMPBELL, THOMAS, 1819, *An Essay on English Poetry.*

Beaumont and Fletcher, with all their prodigious merits, appear to me the first writers who in some measure departed from the genuine tragic style of the age of Shakspeare. They thought less of their subject, and more of themselves, than some others. They had a great and unquestioned command over the stores both of fancy and passion; but they availed themselves too often of common-place extravagances and theatrical trick. . . . Beaumont and Fletcher were the first also who laid the foundation of the artificial diction and tinselled pomp of the next generation of poets, by aiming at a profusion of ambitious ornaments, and by translating the commonest circumstances into the language of metaphor and passion.—HAZLITT, WILLIAM, 1820, *Lectures on the Literature of the Age of Elizabeth, pp.* 107, 110.

Will you let Vincent bring me another volume of "Beaumont and Fletcher?" for I have read two-thirds of the one I have, and suspect I shall not be able to resist going all through with them. Am astonished at what they would have said to you, had you been at their side, insisting upon advance of story, non-superfluities, &c. Am more astonished (ever) at the amazing coarseness they mingle with their delicacies, and the true love they mingle with their false; am delighted with their wit, poetry, and high gentlemanly style, &c. &c. But Lord! what a gentleman, after all, was Shakspeare, even to *their* gentlemen! &c. &c. &c. &c. The woolstapler's son, by some divine right of love on the part of father and mother, or whatsoever mystery it was, was a born prince compared with the bishop's and judge's sons.—HUNT, LEIGH, 1835, *Correspondence, ed. Thornton Hunt, vol.* I, *p.* 282.

Of all our early dramatic poets, none have suffered such mangling by the printer as Beaumont and Fletcher. Their style is generally elliptical, and not very perspicuous; they use words in peculiar senses; and there seems often an attempt at pointed expression, in which its meaning has deserted them. But, after every effort to comprehend their language, it is continually so remote from all possibility of bearing a rational sense, that we can only have recourse to one hypothesis,—that of an extensive and irreparable corruption of the text. . . . The comic talents of these authors far exceeded their skill in tragedy. In comedy they founded a new school, at least in England, the vestiges of which are still to be traced in our theatre. Their plays are at once distinguishable from those of their contemporaries by the regard to dramatic effect which influenced the writer's imagination. Though not personally connected with the stage, they had its picture ever before their eyes. Hence their incidents are numerous and striking; their characters sometimes slightly sketched, not drawn, like those of Jonson, from a preconceived design, but preserving that degree of individual distinctness which a common audience requires, and often highly humorous without extravagance; their language brilliant with wit; their measure, though they do not make great use of prose, very lax and rapid, running frequently to lines of thirteen and fourteen syllables. Few of their comedies are without a mixture of grave sentiments or elevated characters; and, though there is much to condemn in their indecency and even licentiousness of principle, they never descend to the coarse buffoonery not unfrequent in their age.—HALLAM, HENRY, 1837-39, *Introduction to the Literature of Europe, pt.* iii, *ch.* vi, *pars.* 62, 86.

The verse of Beaumont and Fletcher has often more freedom and variety of rhythm than that of Shakspeare, but seldom do they display an equal mastery over accents and pauses. They have not his precision, his dignity, and breadth. Their variations of rhythm are of a kind to change the heroic verse into a blank verse metre of a different kind, which may nevertheless be admirably suited to passages of a wild and joyous character, or to convey emotions of excessive and ungovernable passion. But they use it on all occasions, and this weakens the effect of their versification,—the variation almost becoming the metre, and therefore *no* variation.—HORNE, R. H., 1841, *Chaucer's Poems Modernized, Introduction, p.* lix.

It is generally conceded that Beaumont and Fletcher are more effeminate and dissolute than the band of dramatic authors to which they must be still considered to belong. Their minds had not the grasp, tension, insight, and collected energy, which characterized others who possessed less fertility. Their tragic Muse carouses in crime, and reels out upon us with bloodshot eyes and dishevelled tresses. From this relaxation of intellect and looseness of principle comes, in a great degree, their habit of disturbing the natural relations of things in their representations of the sterner passions. The atmosphere of their tragedy is too often hot, thick, and filled with pestilential vapors. They pushed every thing to excess. Their weakness is most evident when they strain the fiercest after power. Their strength is flushed, bloated, spasmodic, and furious. They pitch every thing in a high key, approaching to a scream.—WHIPPLE, EDWIN P., 1846, *North American Review, vol.* 63, *p.* 77, *Essays and Reviews, vol.* II, *p.* 59.

Their comic characters, though generally very unnatural, and devoid of that rich *internal* humour—that *luce di dentro*, as the Italian artists phrase it—which makes Shakspeare's so admirable, are written with a droll extravagance and fearless *verve* which seldom fail to excite a laugh.—SHAW, THOMAS B., 1847, *Outlines of English Literature, p.* 128.

We may once for all tell the uninitiated that more beastly, elaborate, and incessant filth and obscenity are not to be found in all literature, than in the plays of these three* dramatists; and that we, at least, could only read one or two of them through. They repelled us by the strong shock of disgust, and we have never since been able to understand of what materials the men are made who have read and reread them, paused and lingered over them, dwelt fondly on their beauties, and even ventured to compare them to the plays of Shakspeare; the morality of which, considering his age, is as wonderful as the genius.—GILFILLAN, GEORGE, 1855, *A Third Gallery of Portraits, p.* 186.

The names of the dramatic writers of the present period that hold rank the nearest to Shakspeare still remain to be mentioned. Those of Beaumont and Fletcher must be regarded as indicating one poet rather than two, for it is impossible to make anything of the contradictory accounts that have been handed down as to their respective shares in the plays published in their conjoint names, and the plays themselves furnish no evidence that is more decisive. . . . They have

*Including Massinger.

given us all sorts of writing, good, bad, and indifferent, in abundance. Without referring in particular to what we now deem the indecency and licentiousness which pollutes all their plays, but which, strange to say, seems not to have been looked upon in that light by anybody in their own age, simply because it is usually wrapped in very transparent *double entendre*, they might, if judged by nearly one half of all they have left us, be held to belong to almost the lowest rank of our dramatists instead of to the highest. There is scarcely one of their dramas that does not bear marks of haste and carelessness, or of a blight in some part or other from the playhouse tastes or compliances to which they were wont too easily to give themselves up when the louder applause of the day and the town made them thoughtless of their truer fame. But fortunately, on the other hand, in scarcely any of their pieces is the deformity thus occasioned more than partial: the circumstances in which they wrote have somewhat debased the produce of their fine genius, but their genius itself suffered nothing from the unworthy uses it was often put to. It springs up again from the dust and mud, as gay a creature of the element as ever, soaring and singing at heaven's gate as if it had never touched the ground. Nothing can go beyond the flow and brilliancy of the dialogue of these writers in their happier scenes, it is the richest stream of real conversation, edged with the fire of poetry. —CRAIK, GEORGE L., 1861, *A Compendious History of English Literature and of the English Language, vol.* I, *pp.* 600, 601.

There is much fine writing in these plays; but they are marred even for reading, much more for acting, by their utter want of measure and sobriety; a defect partly due, perhaps, to the predilection of the authors for Spanish plots.—ARNOLD, THOMAS, 1862–87, *A Manual of English Literature, p.* 114.

Beaumont and Fletcher are generally allowed to have made a nearer approach to Shakespeare than did any other dramatist either before or after. This may be true in general. No doubt in the construction of their plays, the smoothness, correctness, and general richness of their language, the reckless abundance of their fancy, and the occasional depth of passion, they do often remind one of the unapproachable master; as they likewise do by the occasional cropping out of an everlasting thought divinely worded. Still, the intelligent reader must feel that their dramas are characterized by weakness, crudeness, want of strength and point, and a certain effeminate softness often not unpleasing. Nearly all their productions bear the marks of haste and carelessness; they seem to have revelled in composition, to have delighted in throwing off drama after drama, giving themselves little trouble about perfection in details. — KELTIE, JOHN SCOTT, 1870, *Works of the British Dramatists, p.* 238.

They were endowed with an imperial command of language, an almost unlimited gift of imagination, a remarkable store of fancy as associated with wit and humour, not so high a judgment in connecting and conducting the plots of their dramas, a quick but extravagant vision in the perception and delineation of character, and little or very moderate power in forming creations of dramatic fancy beyond the confines of their world at the Mermaid or the Actors' Society at Lincoln's Inn; and the tradition exists that at their club-meeting the conversations of the two brother-friends were wont to be as entertaining as "comedies." They, however, who search for, expecting to find, grand aphorisms of human experience or quintessential drops of human wisdom, cordials of thought and sentiment that quicken the pulse and make us gladder and better men as often as we revert to and reflect upon them, will return from their travail with Beaumont and Fletcher lightly laden.—CLARKE, CHARLES COWDEN, 1871, *On the Comic Writers of England, Gentleman's Magazine, n. s., vol.* 7, *p.* 48.

The dramas of Beaumont and Fletcher stand higher than those even of Ben Jonson, and, of all the dramatic writings of that day, come nearest to the magic circle which encloses Shakespeare. Their wonderful knowledge of stage effect doubtless helped their popularity. They catered also, to some extent, to the low taste of the age, by introducing licentious scenes and expressions which exclude their plays both from the stage and from the domestic circle at the present day. At the same time, they abound in striking beauties, both of thought and language, and the general tone of their works is of an elevating character.—HART, JOHN S., 1872, *A Manual of English Literature, p.* 91.

I am not aware that any of Fletcher's unassisted plays are in some respect more devoid of "judgment" than certain of those in which Beaumont is held to have taken part; while on the other hand I doubt whether any of the joint plays surpass in cleverness of construction some in which Fletcher worked alone. Cavils of this kind might be multiplied; but I am at a loss to see in what respect it would prove possible to show that the co-operation of Beaumont either enhanced or impeded the creative powers of Fletcher. Doubtless their joint productions are not disfigured by such offences against a high standard of dramatic morality as those which disfigure certain plays written independently by Fletcher only; but he would be a rash judge who, with some of the joint plays before him, should conclude Beaumont to have acted in this respect as a "check" upon his friend. For all we know to the contrary, Beaumont and Fletcher were alike dramatic poets of so high an ability as to be able to work on terms of equality, and to conceive in thorough harmony with one another what in certain resepcts of form they may have to a great degree executed independently; while it is evident that neither of them was possessed of creative powers with which capabilities of an inferior order could under no circumstances be fused in authorship.—WARD, ADOLPHUS WILLIAM, 1875–99, *A History of English Dramatic Literature, vol.* II, *p.* 660.

Beaumont and Fletcher are great names in the English Drama, but the demands commonly made by critics in their favour hardly seem to be justified if we are to apply to them the canons derived from the works of admitted masters of the stage. That Beaumont at least was a great poet his exquisite lyrics—hardly below Shakspere's own—abundantly testify. In romantic tragedy, too, the joint work of these great men was assuredly of the highest class, but I find little in their comedy-writings which is fit to stand on a level with their "Philaster," or their "Maid's Tragedy." Their comic method at its best was Jonson's method, but their work in this line will bear no sort of comparison with Jonson's. . . . The reader of the comedies of Beaumont and Fletcher is for ever brought up by bits of coarse, rough, gross, or careless handiwork, far below the standard of the best work of the period.—CRAWFURD, OSWALD, 1883, *ed. English Comic Dramatists, p.* 58.

Here we meet with Beaumont and Fletcher, inventors of heroical romance, gifted with inexhaustible resources in the rhetoric of tragical and comical situations, abounding in exquisite lyrical outpourings of unpremeditated song.—SYMONDS, JOHN ADDINGTON, 1887, *Marlowe, (Mermaid Series), General Introduction on the Drama, p.* xxv.

Beaumont and Fletcher kept the stage —kept it constantly and triumphantly— till almost, if not quite, within living memory; while since the seventeenth century, and since its earlier part, I do not know that any play of Dekker's or Middleton's, of Webster's or of Ford's, has been presented to an English audience. This of itself constituted at the great revival of interest in Elizabethan literature something of a prejudice in favour of *les oubliés et les dédaignes*, and this prejudice has naturally grown stronger since all alike have been banished from the stage. The Copper Captain and the Humorous Lieutenant, Bessus and Monsieur Thomas, are no longer on the boards to plead for their authors. The comparative depreciation of Lamb and others is still on the shelves to support their rivals. . . . It used to be fashionable to praise their "young men," probably because of the agreeable contrast which they present with the brutality of the Restoration hero; but their girls are more to my fancy. . . . Of the highest and most terrible graces, as of the sweetest and most poetical, Beaumont and Fletcher may have little to set beside the masterpieces of some other men; for accomplished, varied, and fertile production, they need not fear any competition. —SAINTSBURY, GEORGE, 1887, *History of Elizabethan Literature, pp.* 254, 257, 266.

But whatever helping touches or of outside journey-work may have been contributed to that mass of plays which bears name of Beaumont and Fletcher, it is certain that they hold of right that brilliant reputation for deft and lively and winning dramatic work which put their popularity before Jonson's, if not before Shakespeare's.—MITCHELL, DONALD G., 1890, *English Lands Letters and Kings, From Elizabeth to Anne, p.* 95.

In short, I am inclined to think Fletcher the more poet of the two. Where there is pathos or humor, I am in doubt whether they belong to him or his partner, for I find these qualities both in the plays they wrote together and in those which are wholly his. In the expression of sentiment going far enough to excite a painless æsthetic sympathy, but stopping short of tragic passion, Beaumont is quite the equal of his friend. In the art of heightening and enriching such a sentiment by poetical associations and pictorial accessories, Fletcher seems to me the superior. Both, as I have said, have the art of being pathetic, and of conceiving pathetic situations; but neither of them had depth enough of character for that tragic pathos which is too terrible for tears; for those passionate convulsions when our human nature, like the sea in earthquake, is sucked away deep down from its habitual shores, leaving bare for a moment slimy beds stirring with loathsome life, and weedy tangles before undreamed of, and instantly hidden again under the rush of its reaction. Theirs are no sudden revelations, flashes out of the very tempest itself, and born of its own collisions; but much rather a melancholy Ovidian grace like that of the Heroic Epistles, conscious of itself, yet not so conscious as to beget distrust, and make us feel as if we had been cheated of our tenderness. If they ope the sacred source of sympathetic tears, it is not without due warning and ceremonious preparation. I do not mean to say that their sentiment is not real because it is pensive, and not passionate. It is real, but it is never heart-rending. I say it all in saying that their region is that of fancy. . . . Of the later dramatists, Beaumont and Fletcher, I think, rank next to Shakespeare in the amount of pleasure they give, though not in the quality of it, and in fanciful charm of expression. In spite of all their coarseness, there is a delicacy, a sensibility, an air of romance, and above all a grace, in their best work that make them forever attractive to the young, and to all those who have learned to grow old amiably.—LOWELL, JAMES RUSSELL, 1891–92, *Beaumont and Fletcher, Harper's Magazine, vol.* 85, *pp.* 758, 761.

The perfect union in genius and in friendship which has made one name of the two names of these great twin brothers in song is a thing so admirable and so delightful to remember, that it would seem ungracious and unkindly to claim for either a precedence which we may be sure he would have been eager to disclaim. But if a distinction must be made between the Dioscuri of English poetry, we must admit that Beaumont was the twin of heavenlier birth. Only as Pollux was on one side a demigod of diviner blood than Castor can it be said that on any side Beaumont was a poet of higher and purer genius than Fletcher; but so much must be allowed by all who have eyes and ears to discern in the fabric of their common work a distinction without a difference. Few things are stranger than the avowal of so great and exquisite a critic as Coleridge that he could trace no faintest line of demarcation between the plays which we owe mainly to Beaumont and the plays which we owe solely to Fletcher. To others this line has always appeared in almost every case unmistakable. . . . The genius of Beaumont was deeper, sweeter, nobler than his elder's: the genius of Fletcher more brilliant, more supple, more prodigal and more voluble than his friend's. Without a taint or a shadow on his fame of such imitative servility as marks and degrades the mere henchman or satellite of a stronger poet, Beaumont may fairly be said to hold of Shakespeare in his tragedy, in his comedy of Jonson; in each case rather as a kinsman than as a client, as an ally than as a follower: but the more special province of Fletcher was a land of his own discovering, where no later colonist has ever had power to settle or to share his reign.—SWINBURNE, ALGERNON CHARLES, 1894, *Studies in Prose and Poetry, pp.* 61, 70.

The aims which actuated Beaumont and Fletcher were so lofty, and their actual performance so huge in extent, and uniformly ambitious in effort, that we are bound to judge them by no standard less exacting than the highest. Their resolute intention was to conquer a place in the very forefront of English literature, and for a time they seemed unquestionably to have succeeded in so doing. For a generation after the death of Fletcher, it might reasonably be mooted whether any British writer of poetry had excelled them. After the Restoration, although their popularity continued, their reputation with the critics began to decline, and no one will again name them with poets of the first class. They take, and will retain, an honourable position in the second rank, but in the first they can never again be placed. The conditions of their time seriously affected them. The highest point of poetic elevation had been reached, and the age, brilliant as it was, was one of decadence. It would have been possible to Beaumont and Fletcher—as still later on, when the incline was still more rapid, it yet was to Milton—to resist the elements of decay, to be pertinaciously distinguished, austere, and noble. But they had not enough strength of purpose for this; they gave way to the stream, and were carried down it, contenting themselves with flinging on it, from full hands, profuse showers of lyrical blossoms. They had to deal with a public which had cultivated a taste for the drama, and liked it coarse, bustling, and crude. They made it their business to please this public, not to teach or lead it, and the consequence was that they sacrificed to the whimsies of the pit all the proprieties, intellectual, moral, and theatrical. —GOSSE, EDMUND. 1894, *The Jacobean Poets*, p. 83.

Francis Beaumont

1584–1616

Francis Beaumont, 1584–1616. Born, at Grace-Dieu, Leicestershire, 1584. Matriculated at Broadgates Hall (now Pembroke College, Oxford), 1597. Left University without degree, April 1598, on death of father. Admitted to Inner Temple, 3 Nov. 1600. First verses published, 1602. Early intimacy with John Fletcher. Wrote dramas with him, 1605–14. Lived in London, with occasional visits to Grace-Dieu. Married Ursula Isley, 1613 (?). Had two daughters. Died, 6 March 1616. Buried in Westminster Abbey. *Works:* For plays written with John Fletcher, [*see* Beaumont and Fletcher]. Verse prefixed to Sir John Beaumont's "Metamorphosis of Tobacco," 1602; "Salmacis and Hermaphroditus" (anon.; authorship not certain), 1602; "The Masque of the Gentlemen of Grayes Inne and the Inner Temple" (anon.), (1613); contrib. to "Certain Elegies, done by sundrie excellent Wits," 1618. *Posthumous:* "Poems," 1640.—SHARP, R. FARQUHARSON, 1897, *A Dictionary of English Authors*, p. 20.

PERSONAL

Thou should'st have followed me, but Death, to blame,
Miscounted years, and measured age by fame;
So dearly hast thou bought thy precious lines—
Their praise grew swiftly, so thy life declines:
Thy Muse, the hearer's queen, the reader's love,
All ears, all hearts—but Death's—could please and move.

—BEAUMONT, SIR JOHN, 1616? *An Epitaph on My Deare Brother, Francis Beaumont.*

That Francis Beaumont loved too much himself and his own verses.—DRUMMOND, WILLIAM, 1619, *Conversations of Ben Jonson.*

Excellent Beaumont, in the foremost rank
Of the rarest wits, was never more than *Frank.*

—HEYWOOD, THOMAS, 1635, *The Hierarchy of the Blessed Angels.*

There, on the margin of a streamlet wild,
Did Francis Beaumont sport, an eager child;
There, under shadow of the neighbouring rocks,
Sang youthful tales of shepherds and their flocks;
Unconscious prelude to heroic themes,
Heart-breaking tears, and melancholy dreams
Of slighted love, and scorn, and jealous rage,
With which his genius shook the buskined stage.

—WORDSWORTH, WILLIAM, 1811, *Inscription for a Seat in the Groves of Coleorton.*

Of Beaumont's character it is for obvious reasons less easy to form a definite conception than of his friend's. But though a genuine popularity may naturally have attached to a young man of rank and fortune moving on terms of friendly equality among those with whom the pursuit of an art was a question of bread as well as of honour—though a halo of admiring regrets naturally surrounded the memory of one who died young in the midst of his fame—and though, lastly, it is probable that the surviving Fletcher, in especial, assiduously proclaimed his friend's merits to a willing audience—yet we need not undervalue the agreement among his contemporaries that in him was lost one "in the foremost rank of the rar'st Wits" of his age. Tradition has handed down the "judiciousness" of Beaumont as his most memorable characteristic in his relations to two men, neither of whom he can have equalled in creative power—Ben Jonson and Fletcher. And whatever judgment may be formed concerning his claim to the laurels of which he is popularly allowed an equal share, he must assuredly have deserved the esteem with which he seems to have been regarded by so many of his contemporaries, the friendship with which he was honoured by Ben Jonson, and the fraternal affection inspired by him in Fletcher.—WARD, ADOLPHUS WILLIAM, 1875-99, *A History of English Dramatic Literature, vol.* II, *p.* 652.

GENERAL

The strongest marble fears the smallest rain;
The rusting canker eats the purest gold.
Honour's best dye dreads envy's blackest stain;
The crimson badge of beauty must wax old:
But this fair issue of thy fruitful brain,
Nor dreads age, envy, cankering rust, or rain.
—FLETCHER, JOHN, 1610, *To Beaumont on his Poems.*

How I do love thee, Beaumont and thy Muse,
That unto me dost such religion use!
How I do fear myself, that am not worth
The least indulgent thought thy pen drops forth!
At once thou mak'st me happy and unmak'st;
And giving largely to me more thou tak'st!
What fate is mine, that so itself bereaves?
What art is thine, that so thy friend deceives?
When even there, where most thou praisest me,
For writing better, I must envy thee.
—JONSON, BEN, 1616, *To Francis Beaumont, Epigrams.*

Oh, when I read those excellent things of thine,
Such strength, such sweetness, couch'd in every line,
Such life of fancy, such high choice of brain,
Nought of the vulgar wit or borrow'd strain,
Such passion, such expressions meet my eye,
Such wit untainted with obscenity,
And these so unaffectedly express'd,
All in a language purely-flowing drest;
And all so born within thyself, thine own,
So new, so fresh, so nothing trod upon,
I grieve not now, that old Menander's vein
Is ruin'd, to survive in thee again;
Such in his time was he, of the same piece,
The smooth, even, natural wit, and love of Greece.
—EARLE, JOHN, 1616-47? *On Mr. Beaumont.*

He that hath such acuteness and such wit,
As would ask ten good heads to husband it;
He that can write so well, that no man dare
Refuse it for the best, let him beware:
Beaumont is dead, by whose sole death appears,
Wit's a disease consumes men in few years.
—CORBET, RICHARD, 1616? *On Mr. Francis Beaumont, Then Newly Dead.*

Had, with the advantage of Shakespeare's wit, which was their precedent, great natural gifts, improved by study; Beaumont especially being so accurate a judge of plays, that Ben Jonson, while he lived, submitted all his writings to his censure, and 'tis thought, used his judgment in correcting, if not contriving, all his plots. What value he had for him, appears by the verses he writ to him; and therefore I need speak no further of it. —DRYDEN, JOHN, 1668-93, *An Essay of Dramatic Poesy, Works, ed. Scott and Saintsbury, vol.* XV *p.* 345.

The tradition runs that his chief business was to correct the overflowings of Fletcher's fancy, and hold its volatile creativeness in check. Everybody of that age commended his judgment, and even Ben Jonson is said to have consulted him in regard to his plots. The plays in which he had a main hand exhibit a firmer hold upon character, a more orderly disposition of the incidents, and greater symmetry in the construction, than the others. His verse is also simpler, sweeter, more voluble, than Fletcher's, with few of the latter's double and triple endings and harsh pauses. . . . After, however, awarding to Beaumont all that he can properly claim, he must still be placed below Fletcher, not merely in fertility, but in force and variety of genius.—WHIPPLE, EDWIN P., 1859-68, *The Literature of the Age of Elizabeth, pp.* 161, 165.

Compare with Beaumont's admirable farce of Bessus the wretched imitation of it attempted after his death in the "Nice Valour" of Fletcher; whose proper genius was neither for pure tragedy nor broad farce, but for high comedy and heroic romance—a field of his own invention; witness "Monsieur Thomas" and "The Knight of Malta:" while Beaumont has approved himself in tragedy all but the worthiest disciple of Shakespeare, in farce beyond all comparison the aptest pupil of Jonson. He could give us no "Fox" or "Alchemist;" but the inventor of Bessus and Calianax was worthy of the esteem and affection returned to him by the creator of Morise and Rabbi Busy.—SWINBURNE, ALGERNON CHARLES, 1880, *A Study of Shakespeare, p.* 89, *Note.*

The history of the English drama from 1611 to 1642 may serve, when it is written, to illustrate the statement that, so far as this great national product had any single source, it sprang originally from the spirit of united patriotism; and the claim of Francis Beaumont to consideration in such a history would be partly at least the fact that he was more than any other man the link between the earlier and the later generation.—MACAULAY, G. C., 1883, *Francis Beaumont, A Critical Study, p.* 194.

Beaumont's successive "elegies" and minor poems, written at various times, are in aggregate inexplicably poor and unequal. Even with the "sole daughter" of a Sidney to inspire him, his "mourning" verse is mechanical. It is alone as a dramatic poet that he lives.—GROSART, A. B., 1885, *Dictionary of National Biography, vol.* IV, *p.* 55.

There was no lack of difference, especially of a metrical nature, about their styles. As far as we can judge, Beaumont's was the gift for tragedy; he had less wit and less skill than Fletcher, but he was more genuinely inspired, richer in feeling, and more daring in invention than his brother poet. His noble head is encircled by a halo of sadness, for, like Marlowe and Shelley, two of England's greatest poets, he died before he had completed his thirtieth year.—BRANDES, GEORGE, 1898, *William Shakespeare, A Critical Study, vol.* II, *p.* 298.

Sir John Napier

1550–1617

Born at Merchiston, near Edinburgh, 1550: died there, April 4, 1617. A Scottish mathematician, famous as the inventor of logarithms. He was the eldest son of Archibald, the seventh Napier of Merchiston, hereditary justice-general of Scotland. He matriculated at St. Salvator's College, St. Andrews, in 1563, and probably completed his education at the University of Paris. His "Mirifici logarithmorum canonis descriptio," in which his discovery was announced, appeared in 1614. Napier's bones or rods, constructed to simplify multiplication and division, were introduced in the "Rabdologia" (1617). The "Constructio," or method by which the canon was constructed, was published in 1619 by his son Robert, edited by Henry Briggs.—SMITH, BENJAMIN E., *ed.* 1894–97, *The Century Cyclopedia of Names, p.* 721.

This admirable invention added to the ingenious algorithm of the Indians, by reducing to a few days the labour of several months, doubles—if we may so speak—the life of astronomers, and spares them the errors and disgust inseparable from long calculations; an invention, too, which is the more satisfying to the human mind from its having been entirely deduced from its own resources. In the arts man makes use of the materials and the forms of nature to increase his powers; but in this case it is all his own work.—LAPLACE, PIERRE SIMON, 1796, *Systême du Monde,* liv, v, *ch.* iv.

Many inventions have been eclipsed or obscured by new discoveries, or they have been so altered by subsequent improvements that their original form can hardly be recognized, and, in some instances, has been entirely forgotten. This has almost always happened to the discoveries made at an early period in the progress of science, and before their principles were fully unfolded. It has been quite otherwise with the invention of logarithms, which came out of the hands of the author so perfect that it has never yet received but one material improvement—that which it derived, as has just been said, from the ingenuity of his friend in conjunction with his own. Subsequent improvements in science, instead of offering anything that could supplant this invention, have only enlarged the circle to which its utility extended. Logarithms have been applied to numberless purposes which were not thought of at the time of their first construction. Even the sagacity of the author did not see the immense fertility of the principle he had discovered: he calculated his tables merely to facilitate arithmetical, and chiefly trigonometrical computation; and little imagined that he was at the same time constructing a scale whereon to measure the density of the strata of the atmosphere and the heights of mountains, that he was actually computing the areas and the lengths of innumerable curves, and was preparing for a calculus which was yet to be discovered many of the most refined and most valuable of its resources. Of Napier, therefore, if of any man, it may safely be pronounced, that his name will never be eclipsed by any one more conspicuous, or his invention be superseded by anything more valuable.—PLAYFAIR, JOHN, 1816–19, *Dissertation on the Progress of Mechanical and Physical Science, Encyclopædia Britannica.*

The invention of logarithms is one of the rarest instances of sagacity in the history of mankind; and it has been justly noticed as remarkable, that it issued complete from the mind of its author, and has not received any improvement since his time.—HALLAM, HENRY, 1837–39, *Introduction to the Literature of Europe, pt.* III, *ch.* viii, *par.* 4.

We have few examples, indeed, of truly great men pursuing simultaneously their own peculiar studies and the critical examination of the Scriptures. The most illustrious have been the ornaments of our own land, and England may well be proud of having had Napier, and Milton, and Locke, and Newton, for the champions both of its faith and its Protestantism. —BREWSTER, SIR DAVID, 1855, *Memoirs of the Life and Writings of Sir Isaac Newton, vol.* II, *p.* 355.

Napier's great invention of logarithms has from his own day to the present hour been one of the most active and efficient servants of all the sciences dependent upon calculation; nor could those of them in which the most splendid triumphs have been achieved have possibly been carried to the height they have reached without its assistance.—CRAIK, GEORGE L., 1861, *A Compendious History of English Literature, etc., vol.* II, *p.* 143.

The more one considers the condition of science at the time, and the state of the country in which the discovery took place, the more wonderful does the invention of logarithms appear. When algebra had advanced to the point where exponents were introduced, nothing would be more natural than that their utility as a means of performing multiplications and divisions should be remarked; but it is one of the surprises in the history of science that logarithms were invented as an arithmetical improvement years before their connexion with exponents was known. It is to be noticed also that the invention was not the result of any happy accident.—GLAISHER, J. W. L., 1884, *Encyclopædia Britannica, Ninth ed., vol.* XVII, *p.* 183.

Napier appears, in the fragmentary records that have survived, as a man both just in his dealings with his neighbours and firmly resolved to obtain like justice from them. In his disputes with his father, his step-brothers, the Grahams of Boquhopple, and the magistrates of Edinburgh, he seems invariably to have carried his point. He was a strict Calvinist, and a resolute opponent of papal aggression. His powerful intellect and determined will are best indicated in his prolonged and successful efforts to facilitate numerical calculation which resulted in his discovery of logarithms. The advantage of a table of logarithms are that by its employment multiplication and division can be performed by simple addition and substraction, the extraction of the roots of numbers by division, and the raising of them to any power by multiplication. By these simple processes the most complicated problems in astronomy, navigation, and cognate sciences can be solved by an easy and certain method. The invention necessarily gave a great impulse to all the sciences which depend for their progress on exact computation. Napier's place among great originators in mathematics is fully acknowledged, and the improvements that he introduced constitute a new epoch in the history of the science. He was the earliest British writer to make a contribution of commanding value to the progress of mathematics.—MACDONALD, W. RAE, 1894, *Dictionary of National Biography. vol.* XL, *p.* 64.

Sir Walter Raleigh

1552–1618

Walter Raleigh, born at Hayes, near Budleigh, in Devonshire, in 1552, entered Oriel College, Oxford, in 1568, went as a volunteer to France in 1569, and served in the continental wars for several years. Received with favour at Court, he was knighted, and took part in expeditions for planting colonies in North America. Raleigh distinguished himself in various engagements with the Spanish Armada in 1588. In 1595 he sailed in search of the fabulous El Dorado, and having made some conquests in South America, on his return in 1595 published an account of his voyage, under the title "The Discovery of the Large, Rich, and Beautiful Empire of Guiana." He distinguished himself at the capture of Cadiz in 1596, and took Fayal in 1597; but on the death of Elizabeth he fell out of favour, and was tried for high treason at Winchester, and found guilty in Spetember, 1603. Though reprieved, he remained a prisoner in the Tower thirteen years, during which time he wrote the fragment of "The History of the World," published in 1614. Having obtained his release, he sailed for Guiana in 1617, and on his return to England in July, 1618, was arrested at the instigation of the Spaniards, whose possessions in the new world he had assailed. On the 28th of October, 1618, the sentence was passed upon him, and he was beheaded, Oct. 29.—TOWNSEND, GEORGE H., 1870, *The Every-Day Book of Modern Literature, vol.* I, *p.* 183.

PERSONAL

Good Mr. Vice Chamberlaine;—As soon as I came on boarde the Carick on Wednesday at one of clock, with the rest of Her Majesty's commissioners, within one halfe houre Sir Walter Ralegh arrived with hys keper Mr. Blunt; I assure you, Sir, hys poore servants, to the number of 140 goodly men, and all the mariners, came to him with such shouts and joy as I never saw a man more troubled to quiet them in my life. But his hart is broken, for he is very extreamly pensive longer than he is busied, in w^h he can toil terribly. But if you dyd heare him rage at the spoiles, finding all the short wares utterly devoured, you would laugh, as I do w^n I can not choose. The meeting betweene him and Sir John Gilbert, was with teares on Sr John's part; and he, belike finding it is knowen he hath a keper, whensoever he is saluted with congratulations for liberty, he doth answer no, I am stylle ye Queen of England's poore captive. I wished him to conceale it, because here it diminisheth his credite, w^h I do vowe to you before God is greater amongst the mariners than I thoght for: I do grace him as much as I may, for I find him marveilously greedy to do any thing to recover ye conceit of his brutish offence. —CECYLL, ROBERT, 1592, *Letter, Sept.* 21, *State Paper Office.*

Sir Walter Ralegh did (in my judgment) no man better; and his artillery [had] most effect. I never knew the gentleman till this time: and I am sorry for it, for there are in him excellent things, besides his valour. And the observation he hath in this voyage used with my Lord of Essex hath made me love him.—STANDEN, SIR ANTHONY, 1596, *Letter to Lord Burghley, Cadiz, July* 5*th. MS. Harl.*, 6845, *fol.* 101, *verso.* (*British Museum.*)

We see that theas two gallants, having onc chosen to converse *inter* αμφιβία, . . . devide their provinces at this day, touching traffick of the State, with so great artifice, as, if the Peac goo forward, COBHAM prospers by his industri; if it doo not, RAWLIE by his opposition. In matter of intelligence COBHAM is commended as most secret; in matter of action RAWLIE blazed as most sufficient. COBHAM in discoursing hath holden a kind of privelege to vent his passions; RAWLY, to temporize. COBHAM must have the rough hand of ESAU, in exeqution of rigor; RAWLIE, the softe voic of JACOB in courtlye hypocrisy. COBHAM must delight, seconde, inveigle, and possesse the Queene's opinion,—by improving dangers, casting figurs, and contrivinge invectives against the Scottish hopes, pretensions, and actions. RAWLY must insinuat his own affection, applaud their expectations, and concurr with them. COBHAM must in all things tender the consirvation of the present State, to maintayn his owne tenur. RAWLIE must perswad anticipation, for prouf of knowne destini. COBHAM must exclayme against

SIR WALTER RALEIGH

From Engraving by Phillibrown,
Painting by Zucchero.

SIR THOMAS WYATT

From Engraving by H. Robinson,
Painting by Holbein.

HENRY HOWARD
EARL OF SURREY

From Painting by Titian.

the small account and reckininge that is made of noblemen. RAWLIE must in all discoursis hold them to bee fooles, and therby unsufficient for charge; or cowhards, and therefore uncapable of lieutenancye. COBHAM must relate, and gain the credit of the Queen's satisfaction; RAWLY must inspir and romanc; secur from justification. COBHAM must be the block almighte, that gives oracles; RAWLIE must (be) the cogginge spirit that still prompteth it.—HOWARD, HENRY, LORD, 1602, *Letter to Secretary Sir R. Cecil; Edwards' Life of Raleigh, vol.* II, *p.* 441.

Cecil dothe beare no love to Raleighe, as you well understande, in the matter of Essex. I wyste not that he hathe evyll desygn, in pointe of faithe or relygion. As he hath often discoursede to me wyth moch lernynge, wysdom, and freedome, I knowe he dothe somewhat dyffer in opynyon from some others; but I thynke alsoe his hearte is welle fixed in everye honeste thynge, as farre as I can looke into hym. He seemethe wondrouslie fitted, bothe by arte and nature, to serve the state, especiallie as he is versede in foraign matters, his skyll theryn being alwaies estimable and prayse-worthie. In relygion, he hathe showne (in pryvate talke) great depthe and goode readynge, as I once experyencede at hys owne howse, before manie lernede men.—HARINGTON, SIR JOHN, 1603, *Letter to John Still, Nugæ Antiquæ, vol.* I.

I will prove you the notoriest Traitor that ever came to the bar. . . . Thou art a monster; thou hast an English face, but a Spanish heart. . . . We have to deal to-day with a man of wit. . . Thou hast a Spanish heart, and thyself art a Spider of Hell.—COKE, SIR EDWARD, 1603, *Trial of Sir Walter Raleigh, Cobbett's Collection of State Trials, vol.* II, *No.* 74.

For myself, I am left of all men that have done good to many. All my good turns forgotten; all my errors revived and expounded to all extremity of ill. All my services, hazards, and expenses for my country—plantings, discoveries, fights, councils, and whatsoever else—malice hath now covered over. I am now made an enemy and traitor by the word of an unworthy man. He hath proclaimed me to be a partaker of his vain imaginations, notwithstanding the whole course of my life hath approved the contrary, as my death shall approve it. Woe, woe, woe be unto him by whose falsehood we are lost. He hath separated us asunder. He hath slain my honor; my fortune. He hath robbed thee of thy husband, thy child of his father, and me of you both. O God! thou dost know my wrongs. Know, then, thou my wife, and child;—know, then, thou my Lord and King, that I ever thought them too honest to betray, and too good to conspire against.—RALEIGH, SIR WALTER, 1603, *Letter to Lady Raleigh; Edwards' Life of Raleigh, vol.* II, *p.* 384.

No man denies but he had many sufficiencies in him; but what were these but so many weapons of practice and danger against the state, if he escaped? being so deeply tainted in so many points of discontent, dishonesty, and disloyalty. He knew, as he had written, that as in nature, so in policy, *a privatione ad habitum not fit regressio*. And therefore being desperate of any fortune here, agreeable to the height of his mind, who can doubt but he would have made up his fortune elsewhere, upon any terms against his sovereign and country?—STUCLEY, SIR LEWIS, 1618, *Petition to the King.*

MY KIND DOGGE, If I have any power or credit with you, I pray you let me have a trial of it, at this time, in dealing sincerely and ernestly with the King that Sir WALTER RALEGH'S life may not be called in question. If you do it so that the success answer my expectation, assure yourself that I will take it extraordinarily kindly at your hands; and rest one that wisheth you well, and desires you to continew still, as you have been, a true servant to your Master.—ANNE, QUEEN OF DENMARK, 1618, *Letter to the Marquess of Buckingham, Edwards' Life of Ralegh, vol.* II, *p.* 487.

I was commaunded by the Lords of the Counsayle to be with him, both in prison and att his death, and so sett downe the manner of his death as nere as I could. . . . He was the most fearlesse of death that ever was knowen; and the most resolute and confident, yet with reverence and conscience. When I begann to incourage him against the feare of death, he seemed to make so light of itt, that I wondered att him, and when I told him, that the deare servants of God, in better causes than his, had shrunke backe and trembled a litle, he denyed not, but yet gave God thankes, he never feared death, and much lesse then, for it was but an opinion and imagination; and the manner of death though to others might seeme greevous, yet he had rather dye so then of a burning fever. . . . He was very cheerefull that morning he dyed, eate his breakefast hertily, and tooke tobacco, and made no more of his death, then if he had bene to take a journey, and left a great impression in the minds of those that beheld him, inasmuch that Sir Lewis Stukely and the French man grow very odious. This was the newes a weeke since: but now it is blowen over, and he allmost forgotten.—TOUNSON, REV. ROBERT, 1618, *Letter to Sir John Isham, Nov. 9, Hearne's Hemingforde, App., vol.* I.

Sir Walter Ralegh had the favour to be beheaded at Westminster, where he died with great applause of the beholders, most constantly, most Christianly, most religiously.—PYM, JOHN, 1618, *Memorable Accidents.*

A man known and well deserving to be known; a man endued not with common endowments, being stored with the best of nature's furniture; taught much by much experience, experienced in both fortunes so feelingly and apparently, that it may truly be controverted whether he were more happy or miserable; yet behold in him the strange character of a mere man, a man subject to as many changes of resolution as resolute to be the instrument of change; politic, and yet in policy so unsteady, that his too much apprehension was the foil of his judgment.—FORD, JOHN, 1620, *A Line of Life, Works, ed. Gifford and Dyce, vol.* III, *p.* 399.

Sir Walter Rawleigh was one, that (it seems) Fortune had pickt out of purpose, of whom to make an example, or to use as her Tennis-Ball, thereby to shew what she could doe; for she tost him up of nothing, and too and fro to greatnesse, and from thence down to little more than to that wherein she found him, (a bare Gentleman). Not that he was lesse, for he was well descended, and of good alliance, but poor in his beginnings. . . . He had in the outward man, a good presence, in a handsome and well compacted person, a strong naturall wit, and a better judgement, with a bold and plausible tongue, whereby he could set out his parts to the best advantage; and to these he had the adjuncts of some generall Learning, which by diligence he enforced to a great augmentation, and perfection; for he was an indefatigable Reader, whether by Sea or Land, and none of the least observers both of men and the times.—NAUNTON, SIR ROBERT, 1630? *Fragmenta Regalia, ed. Arber, pp.* 47, 48.

Shall I not add, as parallel to this, a wonder and example of our own; such as if that old philosopher* were yet living, without dishonour he might acknowledge as the equal of his virtue? Take it in that—else unmatched—fortitude of our RALEIGH! the magnanimity of his sufferings, that large chronicle of fortitude! All preparations that are terrible were presented to his eye; guards and officers were about him, the scaffold and the executioner, the axe, and the more cruel expectation of his enemies. And what did all this work on the resolution of our Raleigh? Made it an impression of weak fear, or a distraction of his reason? Nothing so little did that great soul suffer. He gathered only the more strength and advantage; his mind became the clearer, as if already it had been freed from the cloud and oppression of the body; and such was his unmoved courage and placid temper, that while it changed the affection of the enemies who had come to witness it and turned their joy to sorrow, it filled all men else with admiration and emotion, leaving with them only this doubt, whether death were more acceptable to him or he more welcome unto death. —ELIOT, SIR JOHN, 1632? *Monarchy of Man, (MS.) Brit. Mus. Harleian, Coll.* 2228.

I have heard his enemies confess, that he was one of the weightiest and wisest men that this island ever bred; Mr. Nath. Carpenter, a learned and judicious author, was not in the wrong when he gave this discreet character of him, "Who hath not known or read of this prodigy of wit and fortune, sir Walter Rawleigh, a man infortunate in nothing else but in the greatness of his wit and advancement, whose eminent worth was such, both in domestic policy, forren expeditions, and discoveries in arts and literature, both practic and contemplative, that it might seem at once to conquer example and imitation."—HOWELL, JAMES, 1645, *Letter to Carew Raleigh, Raleigh's Works, vol.* VIII.

*Canius.

I dare not then so blast thy memory
As say I do lament or pity thee.
Were I to choose a subject to bestow
My pity on, he should be one as low
In spirit as desert; that durst not die,
But rather were content by slavery
To purchase life: or I would pity those,
Thy most industrious and friendly foes,
Who, when they thought to make thee scandal's story,
Lent thee a swifter flight to heaven and glory;
That thought, by cutting off some withered days
Which thou could'st spare them, to eclipse thy praise;
Yet gave it brighter foil; made thy ag'd fame
Appear more white and fair than foul their shame;
And did promote an execution
Which, but for them, nature and age had done.

—KING, BISHOP HENRY, 1657, *Poems, Elegies, Paradoxes and Sonnets, p.* 97.

Coming to the Court, found some hopes of the Queen's favours reflecting upon him. This made him write in a glasse window, obvious to the Queen's eye,—"Fain would I climb, yet fear I to fall." Her Majesty, either espying or being shown it, did under-write—"If thy heart fails thee, climb not at all." . . . Captain Raleigh, coming out of Ireland to the English court in good habit (his cloaths being then a considerable part of his estate), found the Queen walking till meeting with a *plashy place*, she seemed to scruple going thereon. Presently Raleigh cast and spread his new plush cloak on the ground; whereon the Queen trod gently, rewarding him afterwards with many *suits*, for his so free and seasonable tender of so fair a *foot-cloath*. Thus an advantageous admission into the first notice of a Prince is more than half a degree to preferment.—FULLER, THOMAS, 1662, *Worthies of England, ed. Nichols, vol.* I.

He was a tall, handsome, and bold man: but his naeve was that he was damnable proud. Old Sir Robert Harley of Brampton-Brian Castle, who knew him, would say 'twas a great question who was the proudest, Sir Walter, or Sir Thomas Overbury, but the difference that was, was judged on Sir Thomas' side. . . . His beard turnd up naturally.—I have heard my grandmother say that when she was young, they were wont to talke of this rebus, viz.,

The enemie to the stomack, and the word of disgrace,
Is the name of the gentleman with a bold face.

. . . Old Sir Thomas Malett, one of the justices of the King's Bench tempore Caroli I et II, knew Sir Walter; and I have heard him say that, notwithstanding his so great mastership in style and his conversation with the learnedst and politest persons, yet he spake broad Devonshire to his dyeing day. His voice was small, as likewise were my schoolfellowes', his grandnephewes. . . . Sir Walter Ralegh was a great chymist; and amongst some MSS. receipts, I have seen some secrets from him. He studyed most in his sea-voyages, where he carried always a trunke of bookes along with him, and had nothing to divert him. . . . Memorandum:—he made an excellent cordiall, good in feavers, etc.; Mr. Robert Boyle haz the recipe, and makes it and does great cures by it. . . . A person so much immerst in action all along and in fabrication of his owne fortunes, (till his confinement in the Tower) could have but little time to study, but what he could spare in the morning. He was no slug; without doubt, had a wonderfull waking spirit, and great judgment to guide it.—AUBREY, JOHN, 1669–96, *Brief Lives, ed. Clark, vol.* II, *p.* 182.

Jealous of virtue that was so sublime,
His country damn'd his merit as a crime.
The traitor's doom did on the patriot wait;
He sav'd—and then he perish'd by the state.

—PACK, RICHARDSON, 1719, *Dr. Sewell's Tragedy of Sir Walter Raleigh, Prologue.*

He shone in the senate as a patriot, and the remains we have of his speeches, leave us in doubt which we ought most to admire, the beauty of his eloquence, or the strength of his understanding. . . . In regard to his private life, a beneficent master, a kind husband, an affectionate father; and, in respect to the world, a warm friend, a pleasant companion, and a fine gentleman. In a word, he may be truly styled the English Xenophon; for no man of his age did things more worthy of being recorded, and no man was more able to record them than himself; insomuch, that we may say of him, as Scaliger did of Cæsar, "that he fought, and wrote, with the same inimitable spirit." And thus I take my leave of one, whom it is impossible to praise enough.—CAMPBELL, JOHN, 1742–44, *History and Lives of the British Admirals, vol.* I.

He was accused by Cobham alone, in a sudden fit of passion, upon hearing that

Raleigh, when examined, had pointed out some circumstances, by which Cobham's guilt might be known and ascertained. This accusation Cobham afterwards retracted; and soon after he retracted his retraction. Yet upon the written evidence of this single witness, a man of no honour or understanding, and so contradictory in his testimony, not confronted with Raleigh, not supported by any concurring circumstance, was that great man, contrary to all law and equity, found guilty by the jury. His name was at that time extremely odious in England; and every man was pleased to give sentence against the capital enemy of Essex, the favourite of the people.—HUME, DAVID, 1754–62, *The History of England, vol.* IV, *ch.* xlv.

The character of sir Walter Ralegh is a combination of so many eminent qualities, of the statesman, the commander both at sea and land, and the writer; and the course of his life was so full of remarkable and interesting scenes at home and abroad, and of all the varieties of fortune, which could shew the extent and vigour of his mind in every situation; that, had he flourished in the earlier ages of the world, the history of him would unquestionably have been the choice of the Roman Nepos and the Grecian Plutarch; nor could that latter have found juster parallels to him, than two of the most illustrious names of antiquity, Xenophon and Cæsar, who were, like him, equal masters of the sword and the pen, and equally capable of performing the greatest actions, and recording them with dignity.—BIRCH, THOMAS, 1760? *Life of Sir Walter Ralegh, Ralegh's Works, Oxford ed., vol.* I, *p.* 571.

In this mighty genius there lies an unsuspected disposition, which requires to be demonstrated, before it is possible to conceive its reality. From his earliest days, probably by his early reading of the romantic incidents of the first Spanish adventurers in the New World, he himself betrayed the genius of an *adventurer*, which prevailed in his character to the latest; and it often involved him in the practice of mean artifices and petty deceptions; which appear like folly in the wisdom of a sage; like ineptitude in the profound views of a politician: like cowardice in the magnanimity of a hero; and degrade by their littleness the grandeur of character which was closed by a splendid death, worthy the life of the wisest and the greatest of mankind!—DISRAELI, ISAAC, 1791–1824, *Secret History of Sir Walter Rawleigh, Curiosities of Literature.*

The character of Raleigh was not without dark shades; nor had his conduct in the prosperous and active part of his career been free from the blemishes of pride towards his inferiors, immoderate adulation towards the princess whose smile had called him forth from obscurity, a rapacious desire of wealth and power, and an unhesitating employment of the courtly arts of intrigue and corruption. But a genius, equally comprehensive and lofty, had redeemed him from these unworthinesses. . . . His piety, which had been rashly called in question by persons incapable of making allowance for any deviation from popular opinions, shone forth in the last solemn scene in admirable union with manly courage and philosophical composure.—AIKIN, LUCY, 1822, *Memoirs of the Court of King James the First, vol.* II, *p.* 103.

Raleigh, the soldier, the sailor, the scholar, the courtier, the orator, the poet, the historian, the philosopher, sometimes reviewing the queen's guards, sometimes giving chase to a Spanish galleon, then answering the chiefs of the country party in the House of Commons, then again murmuring one of his sweet love-songs too near the ears of her highness's maids of honour, and soon after poring over the Talmud, or collating Polybius with Livy.—MACAULAY, THOMAS BABINGTON, 1832, *Nares's Memoirs of Burghley, Critical and Miscellaneous Essays.*

The name of Raleigh stands highest among the statesmen of England who advanced the colonization of the United States. . . . In his civil career he was jealous of the honor, the prosperity, and the advancement of his country. In parliament he defended the freedom of domestic industry. When, through unequal legislation, taxation was a burden upon industry rather than wealth, he argued for a change; himself possessed of a lucrative monoply, he gave his voice for the repeal of all monoplies; he used his influence with his sovereign to mitigate the severity of the judgments against the non-conformists, and as a legislator he resisted the sweeping enactment of persecuting laws. In the career of discovery, his perseverance was never baffled by losses. . . . After a lapse of nearly two centuries, the state of North Carolina, in 1792, revived in its capital "THE CITY OF RALEIGH," in grateful commemoration of his name and fame.—BANCROFT, GEORGE, 1834–82, *History of the United States, vol.* I. *ch.* V.

The versatility of Raleigh's genius and pursuits were strikingly exemplified in his acquaintance with the mechanical arts, and his addiction to experimental inquiries. His discourses on shipbuilding, the navy, and naval tactics, are, we believe, the earliest productions of the kind in the English language. We never have been able to account for his great knowledge of seamanship, in which he had but little practical training, nor had he made many considerable voyages. His favour at court, his captures at sea, and his brilliant courage, procured him the rank of admiral, and employment as such on several important occasions; for naval rank was not yet regulated by any fixed rules of promotion; but, in point of fact, he rose to a reputation as a seaman not surpassed by any man of his day. After Drake and Hawkins disappeared from the scene, he seems, indeed, to have enjoyed a preeminence over all his contemporaries. Strong native predilections, and a wonderfully versatile mind, can alone explain his extraordinary proficiency in maritime affairs. —NAPIER, MACVEY, 1840–53, *Lord Bacon and Sir Walter Raleigh, p.* 223.

MY DEAR N.,—I have now read your Raleigh with great pleasure, and I hope profit. I do not think you have quite escaped the common snare of biographers, partiality and over-admiration of your hero, whom I think you very satisfactorily make out to have been both a traitor and a pirate—*au reste, très honnête homme.* I think you overpraise his History too, considering how much of it is a mere *réchauffé* of biblical trash. However, he was a dashing fellow, no doubt, and would probably have been a better man in a better age. What I can least forgive in him is being truly loved by nobody, with all his gifts and graces.—JEFFREY, FRANCIS, LORD, 1840, *Correspondence of Macvey Napier, p.* 320.

The abominable injustice of executing a man for political purposes, was not without many parallels in the reigns of his predecessors; but the singular and peculiar baseness of prostrating the law of England to the will of a foreign power, of delivering the sword of English Justice into the hand of the King of Spain, to enable him to wreak his vengeance on an English subject, and destroy one of the most distinguished men of the age, was reserved for a monarch so mean and pusillanimous as James the First.—JARDINE, DAVID, 1847, *Criminal Trials, vol.* I, *p.* 520.

Near Elizabeth's Armory is the dungeon of Sir Walter Raleigh. There he was confined twelve years, and within those dark walls he wrote his "History of the World." Gallant Raleigh! I crept into the cell, and touched with reverence the cold stones upon which that noble head had so often rested.—LE VERT, OCTAVIA WALTON, 1853–57, *Souvenirs of Travel, vol.* I, *p.* 42.

In all the everyday affairs of life, he remains without a blot; a diligent, methodical, prudent man, who, though he plays for great stakes, ventures and loses his whole fortune again and again, yet never seems to omit the "doing the duty which lies nearest him;" never gets into mean money scrapes; never neglects tenants or duty; never gives way for one instant to "the eccentricities of genius." If he had done so, be sure that we should have heard of it.—KINGSLEY, CHARLES, 1859, *Sir Walter Raleigh and his Time, Miscellanies, p.* 23.

His fame was rising, instead of falling. Great ladies from the court cast wistful glances at his room. Men from the streets and ships came crowding to the wharf whence they could see him walking on the wall. Raleigh was a sight to see; not only for his fame and name, but for his picturesque and dazzling figure. Fifty-one years old; tall, tawny, splendid; with the bronze of tropical suns on his leonine cheek, a bushy beard, a round moustache, and a ripple of curling hair, which his man Peter took an hour to dress. Appareled as became such a figure, in scarf and band of the richest color and costliest stuff, in cap and plume worth a ransom, in jacket powdered with gems; his whole attire, from cap to shoe-strings, blazing with rubies, emeralds, and pearls; he was allowed to be one of the handsomest men alive.—DIXON, WILLIAM HEPWORTH, 1869, *Her Majesty's Tower, p.* 254.

Few greater men have ever lived in England, or anywhere else, than Raleigh. No man contributed more, if so much, towards the earliest American Colonization.—WINTHROP, ROBERT C., 1873–78, *Addresses and Speeches on Various Occasions, vol.* III, *p.* 270.

Ralegh combined in his own person the aspirations of the age in a most vivid manner. He was ambitious, fond of show, with high aims, deeply engaged in the factions of the court; but at the same time he had a spirit of noble enterprise, was ingenious and thoughtful. In everything new that was produced in the region of discoveries and inventions, of literature and art, he played the part of a fellow worker: he lived in the circle of universal knowledge, its problems and its progress. In his appearance he had something that announced a man of superior mind and nature.—RANKE, LEOPOLD VON, 1875, *A History of England, vol.* I, *p.* 338.

He went to his trial a man so unpopular that he was hooted and pelted on the road; he came out an object of general pity and admiration, and has held his place ever since as one of England's favorite and representative heroes; and yet, if we except his gallant bearing and splendid abilities (which were no new revelations), there was nothing in his case which could have tended either to excite popular sympathy or to command popular respect; nor has anything been discovered since that enables us to explain his connection with the plot in a way at all favorable to his character. By his own showing he had been in intimate and confidential relation with a man whom nobody liked or respected, and who was secretly seeking help from the hated Spaniard in a plot to dispossess James in favor of the Lady Arabella. By his own admission he had at least listened to an offer of a large sum of money,—certainly Spanish, and therefore presumably in consideration of some service to be rendered to Spain. And though it is true that we do not know with what purposes he listened, how much he knew, how far he acquiesced, or what he intended to do, it is impossible to believe that his intentions (whether treasonable or not) were, or were then supposed to be, either popular or patriotic. He did not himself attempt to put any such color upon his proceedings; declaring only that he did not know of the plot in which his confidential friends were engaged. His blindest advocates have not succeeded in doing it for him. And those who, though partial, have taken pains to examine and felt bound to respect the evidence, have scarcely succeeded even in believing him innocent.—SPEDDING, JAMES, 1878, *An Account of the Life and Times of Francis Bacon, vol.* I, *p.* 436.

God has made nobler heroes, but he never made a finer gentleman than Walter Raleigh.—STEVENSON, ROBERT LOUIS, 1881, *Virginibus Puerisque and Other Papers.*

The New World's sons, from England's breasts we drew
Such milk as bids remember whence we came;
Proud of her Past, wherefrom our Present grew,
This window we inscribe with Raleigh's name.

—LOWELL, JAMES RUSSELL, 1882, *Inscription, Raleigh Memorial Window.*

Sir Walter Raleigh, in whose honour this window is given, was not one of the world's simple, blameless characters, like William Caxton of whom we spoke so recently. Men of splendid physique and genius, children of a splendid and passionate age, have temptations more intense and terrible than we who live our small humdrum lives in the petty routine of commonplace. Our faults may be as bad as theirs, though they are meaner and smaller faults. Their sins show large in the largeness of their lives, and in the fierce light which beats upon them. . . . If Walter Raleigh, in some things, sinned greatly, God loved him so well that he also suffered greatly and out of much tribulation washed his robes white in the blood of the Lamb. . . . Remember also that he must be ranked forever among the benefactors of his race, and that there are very few of us who have not done worse deeds than he, and have never done as good ones. It is strange to me that one paltry tablet should hitherto have been almost the only memorial of such a man. Great nations should have more pride in their few great sons. I think that Americans will rejoice with us that, after more than 280 years, he should have a worthier memorial of his immortal deeds in the Church under whose altar lies his headless corpse.—FARRAR, FREDERICK W., 1882, *Sermon Preached at the unveiling of the Raleigh Window, Westminster, the gift of American citizens.*

It is difficult for us at this distance of time to realise the feelings with which Raleigh was regarded by the great mass of his contemporaries. To us he is the man who had more genius than all the Privy Council put together. At the first mention of his name, there rises up before us the remembrance of the active mind, the meditative head, and the bold heart, which have stamped themselves indelibly upon the pages of the history of two continents. Above all, we think of him as the victim of oppression, sobered down by the patient endurance of an undeserved imprisonment, and as finally passing into his bloody grave, struck down by an unjust sentence. To the greater number of the men amongst whom he moved, he was simply the most unpopular man in England. Here and there were to be found a few who knew his worth. Those who had served under him, like his faithful Captain Keymis, and those who, like Sir John Harington, merely met him occasionally in social intercourse, knew well what the loyal heart of the man really was. But by the multitude, whom he despised, and by the grave statesmen and showy courtiers with whom he jostled for Elizabeth's favour, he was regarded as an insolent and unprincipled wretch, who feared neither God nor man, and who would shrink from no crime if he could thereby satisfy his ambitious desires. There can be no doubt that these charges, frivolous as they must seem to those who know what Raleigh's true nature was, had some basis in his character Looking down as he did from the eminence of genius upon the actions of lesser men, he was too apt to treat them with the arrogance and scorn which they seldom deserved, and which it was certain that they would resent. —GARDINER, SAMUEL R., 1883, *History of England from the Accession of James I. to the Outbreak of the Civil War, vol.* I, *p.* 88.

There is a proposal now in the United States to erect a monument to Sir Walter Raleigh. . . . Such a man, such principles, such a career, ought not to be given to the youth of the American republic as ideally correct and æsthetically beautiful. Raleigh was a man of versatile talents, possessing in a high degree the gifts of courtiership; fond of power, of land, of money, of luxury, of adventure; unscrupulous, of low standard of morality, and in many respects more like our Aaron Burr than like the Bayard of France, without fear and without reproach. That the great empire of America is under the least obligation to him is not susceptible of proof. His motive in sending an expedition out here was purely commercial and selfish, so far as the proofs go. He was actuated by the same motives in going to Ireland. He was no worse a man than his time and the standards of the age in which he lived made it inevitable that he should be.—SULLIVAN, MARGARET F., 1884, *Concerning Sir Walter Raleigh, Catholic World, vol.* 39, *p.* 636

In all the pictures we have of him there is almost nothing to suggest the typical Englishman, burly and robust. About six feet in height, he is rather thin than corpulent, and in the vivacity of expression and the nervous cast of his features he resembles rather the modern New-Englander than the old-time Englishman. There was a peculiar fascination in his address, and it is certain from all accounts that the Queen was thoroughly taken with him from the very first.—TARBOX, INCREASE N., 1884, *Sir Walter Ralegh and His Colony in America, p.* 25.

He was essentially an acrid and despotic nature. Among the eminent men of his day he scarcely had a true friend, and it is painful to read in the letters of his contemporaries how frequent were the disparaging remarks his petulent and grasping disposition called forth. Yet, in spite of the faults and vices of his character, the name of Raleigh is one which the history of this island will never attempt to erase from its list of celebrities. The man was, in every sense of the word, a true patriot, confident in the prowess of his country, and keenly sensitive as to her honour. It was the staunchness of his English instincts that made him wax so wroth when he saw a miserable creature, like our first James truckle to foreign Powers and drag the flag of England through the mire of a base servility.—EWALD, ALEXANDER CHARLES, 1885, *Studies Re-studied, p.* 204.

His face had neither the ethereal beauty of Sidney's nor the intellectual delicacy of Spenser's; it was cast in a rougher mould than theirs. The forehead, it is acknowledged, was too high for the proportion of the features, and for this reason, perhaps, is usually hidden in the portraits by a hat. We must think of Raleigh . . . as a tall, somewhat bony man, about six feet high, with dark hair and a high colour, a facial expression of great brightness and alertness, personable from the virile force of his figure, and illustrating these attractions by a splendid taste in dress. His clothes were at all times noticeably gorgeous; and to the end of his life he was commonly bedizened with precious stones to his very shoes. When he was arrested in 1603 he was carrying 4,000*l.* in jewels on his bosom, and when he was finally captured on August 10, 1618, his pockets were found full of the diamonds and jacinths which he had hastily removed from various parts of his person. —GOSSE, EDMUND, 1886, *Raleigh*, (*English Worthies*), *p.* 20.

When I consider his busy and brilliant and perturbed life, with its wonderful adventures, its strange friendships, its toils, its quiet hours with Spenser upon the Mulla shore, its other hours amidst the jungles of the Orinoco, its lawless gallantries in the court of Elizabeth, its booty snatched from Spanish galleons he has set ablaze, its perils, its long captivities—it is the life itself that seems to me a great Elizabethan epic, with all its fires, its mated couples of rhythmic sentiment, its poetic splendors, its shortened beat and broken pauses and blind turns, and its noble climacteric in a bloody death that is without shame and full of the largest pathos.—MITCHELL, DONALD G., 1890, *English Lands Letters and Kings, From Elizabeth to Anne*, *p.* 18.

It will scarcely be denied that there has always been room for a new presentment of Ralegh's personality. That the want has remained unsatisfied after all the efforts made to supply it is to be imputed less to defects in the writers, than to the intrinsic difficulties of the subject. Ralegh's multifarious activity, with the width of the area in which it operated, is itself a disturbing element. It is confusing for a biographer to be required to keep at once independent and in unison the poet, statesman, courtier, schemer, patriot, soldier, sailor, freebooter, discoverer, colonist castle-builder, historian, philosopher, chemist, prisoner, and visionary. The variety of Ralegh's powers and tendencies, and of their exercise, is the distinctive note of him, and of the epoch which needed, fashioned, and used him. A whole band of faculties stood ready in him at any moment for action. Several generally were at work simultaneously. For the man to be properly visible, he should be shown flashing from more facets than a brilliant. Few are the pens which can vividly reflect versatility like his. . . . Never surely was there a career more beset with insoluble riddles and unmanageable dilemmas. At each step, in the relation of the most ordinary incidents, exactness of dates, or precision of events, appears unattainable. Fiction is ever elbowing fact, so that it might be supposed contemporaries had with one accord been conspiring to disguise the truth from posterity. The uncertainty is deepened tenfold when motives have to be measured and appraised. Ralegh was the best hated personage in the kingdom.—STEBBING, WILLIAM, 1891, *Sir Walter Ralegh*, *p.* 7.

One of the finest answers given in an examination was that of the boy who was asked to repeat all he knew of Sir Walter Raleigh. This was it: "He introduced tobacco into England, and while he was smoking he exclaimed, 'Master Ridley, we have this day lighted such a fire in England as shall never be put out.' " Can that, with any sort of justice, be styled a blunder?—WHEATLEY, HENRY B., 1893, *Literary Blunders*, *p.* 171

During the reign of Queen Elizabeth no Englishman lived a more complete life than Sir Walter Ralegh. Country gentleman, student, soldier, sailor, adventurer, courtier, favorite and spoilsman, colonizer, fighter, landlord, agriculturist, poet, patron of letters, state prisoner, explorer, conqueror, politician, statesman, conspirator, chemist, scholar, historian, self-seeker, and ultimately a martyr to patriotism, he acquired through the latter half of Elizabeth's reign the most comprehensive experience ever known to an Englishman.—WENDELL, BARRETT, 1894, *William Shakspere*, *p.* 404.

Probably his persuasive eloquence was one of his greatest gifts, and his personal fascination must have been marvellous; for when he chose, which in his arrogance he rarely did, he could bring even those who hated him to his side. He took no care, however, to be popular, for he always scorned and contemned the people, and on the death of Elizabeth he was probably the best hated man in England. —HUME, MARTIN A. S., 1897, *Sir Walter Ralegh (Builders of Greater Britain)*, *p.* 31.

Spain drank a deep draught of revenge when the hero of Cadiz and Fayal was beheaded in the Palace Yard at Westminster; a scene fit to have made Elizabeth turn in her grave in the Abbey hard by. A fouler judicial murder never stained the annals of any country.—FISKE, JOHN, 1897, *Old Virginia and Her Neighbours, vol.* I, *p.* 200.

POEMS

For dittie and amourous *Ode* I finde Sir *Walter Rawleyghs* vayne most loftie, insolent, and passionate.—PUTTENHAM, GEORGE, 1589, *The Arte of English Poesie, ed. Arber, p.* 77.

And there that shepheard of the Ocean is,
That spends his wit in loves consuming smart:
Full sweetly tempred is that Muse of his,
That can empierce a Princes mightie hart.
—SPENSER, EDMUND, 1595, *Colin Clouts Come Home Againe, Spenser's Works, ed. Collier, vol.* V, *p.* 47.

The English poems of Sir Walter Raleigh . . . are not easily to be mended.—BOLTON, EDMUND, 1624, *Hypercritica.*

Sir Walter Raleigh, a person both sufficiently known in history and by his "History of the World," seems also by the character given him by the author of the "Art of English Poetry" to have exprest himself more a poet than the little we have extant of his poetry seems to import.—PHILLIPS, EDWARD, 1675, *Theatrum Poetarum Anglicanorum, ed. Brydges, p.* 285.

Do I pronounce Raleigh a poet? Not, perhaps, in the judgment of a severe criticism. Raleigh, in his better days, was too much occupied in action to have cultivated all the powers of a poet, which require solitude and perpetual meditation, and a refinement of sensibility, such as intercourse with business and the world deadens! . . . The production of an *Heroic Poem* would have nobly employed this illustrious Hero's mighty faculties, during the lamentable years of his unjust incarceration. But how could He delight to dwell on the tale of Heroes, to whom the result of Heroism had been oppression, imprisonment, ruin, and condemnation to death? We have no proof that Raleigh possessed the copious, vivid, and creative powers of Spenser; nor is it probable that any cultivation would have brought forth from him fruit equally rich. But even in the careless fragments now presented to the reader, I think we can perceive some traits of attraction and excellence which, perhaps, even Spenser wanted. If less diversified than that gifted bard, he would, I think, have sometimes been more forcible and sublime; his images would have been more gigantic, and his reflections more daring. With all his mental attention keenly bent on the best state of existing things in political society, the range of his thoughts had been lowered down to practical wisdom; but other habits of intellectual exercise, excursions into the ethereal fields of fiction, and converse with the spirits which inhabit those upper regions, would have given a grasp and a colour to his conceptions as magnificent as the fortitude of his soul.—BRYDGES, SAMUEL EGERTON, 1813, *ed. The Poems of Sir Walter Raleigh, pp.* 43, 46.

For amatory sweetness, and pastoral simplicity, few efforts will be found to surpass the poems distinguished as "Phillida's Love-Call," "The Shepherd's Description of Love," the "Answer to Marlow," and "The Silent Lover."—DRAKE, NATHAN, 1817, *Shakspeare and his Times, vol.* I, *p.* 640.

A higher strain of compliment cannot well be conceived than this, [sonnet] which raises your idea even of that which it disparages in the comparison, and makes you feel that nothing could have torn the writer from his idolatrous enthusiasm for Petrarch and his Laura's tomb, but Spenser's magic verses and diviner "Faëry Queen"—the one lifted above mortality, the other brought from the skies!—HAZLITT, WILLIAM, 1820, *Lectures on the Literature of the Age of Elizabeth, p.* 177.

As a poet, Sir Walter Raleigh appears not to be appreciated as he deserves to be. . . . Had Raleigh cultivated his talent for Poetry, there can be no doubt that he would have attained a high rank among the bards of that poetical age; but his genius was too universal to admit of being confined to any one particular pursuit.—RYAN, RICHARD, 1826, *Poetry and Poets, vol.* I, *p.* 40.

Spenser's friend Raleigh left us so excellent a sonnet on the "Faerie Queene," that it makes us wish he had written a thousand; or rather, that he had devoted his whole life to poetry, instead of the pursuits that ruined him. . . . His pen was very like a sword. You see, in this one little sonnet, what possession he takes of the whole poetical world, in favor of the sovereignity of his friend Spenser. He was not exactly in the right; but when did conquerors consider the right? The sonnet is of the least artistical order, as to construction, consisting only of the three elegiac quatrains and a couplet; and it has the fault of monotonous assonance in the rhymes; yet it flows with such nerve and will, and is so dashing and sounding in the rest of its modulation, that no impression remains upon the mind but that of triumphant force.—HUNT, LEIGH, 1859?-67, *An Essay on the Sonnet, ed. Lee, vol.* I. *p.* 75.

The biographers and editors of Raleigh have been sorely puzzled by finding that a poem, usually called "The Silent Lover," and assigned to Raleigh, was attributed in one of the Ashmolean MSS. (No. 781, p. 143) to *Lo. Walden.* In the index to the MSS. they are called "*Lo Walden's verses;*" and Ritson, on the authority of this name only, inserts Lord Walden (afterwards Earl of Suffolk) in his "Bibliotheca Poetica," p. 383. Park goes even farther; for, upon the strength of the Ashm. MS. and Ritson, he actually converts Lord Walden into one of his "Royal and Noble Authors," and writes his life accordingly. What is the fact? The reader will hardly require it to be pointed out. "The Silent Lover" is unquestionably by Raleigh; but at the time it was written, or got abroad, its author was Lord Warden, *i. e.* Lord Warden of the Stannaries; and because Lord Warden was miswritten Lo. Walden, an attempt has been made to deprive the real owner of his undoubted property. Our neighbours of Edinburgh have not scrupled, not merely to rob Raleigh of a lovely addition to his few poetical remains, but to attribute the poem to their countryman Sir Robert Aytoun, in an edition of his works published in 1844. For "Lord Walden" we have only to read Lord *Warden* and the difficulty is at an end—a curious instance of the important consequence of a very slight corruption.—COLLIER, JOHN PAYNE, 1862, *Works of Spenser, Life, vol.* I, *p.* lxii, *note.*

I am persuaded that he wrote "The Lie;" for I do not believe that any one then living, except Shakspeare, was so capable of having written it.—ARNOLD, THOMAS, 1862-87, *A Manual of English Literature, p.* 95.

For a long time Raleigh's claim to this poem* seemed unusually doubtful; it is now established at least as conclusively as in the case of any of his poems. We have the direct testimony of two contemporary MSS., and the still stronger evidence of at least two contemporary answers, written during Raleigh's lifetime, and reproaching him with the poem by name or implication. An untraced and unauthorized story, that he wrote the poem the night before his death, is contradicted by the dates—it was printed ten years before that time, in 1608; and it can be found in MSS. more than ten years earlier still, in 1596, 1595, or 1593. But the question of the authorship is not touched by the refutation of the legend, when so many independent witnesses assert the one without the other. There are five other claimants, but not one with a case that will bear the slightest examination. For the claim of Richard Edwards we are indebted to a mere mistake of Ellis's; for that of F. Davison to a freak of Ritson's; that of Lord Essex is only known from the correspondence of Percy, who did not believe it; and those of Sylvester and Lord Pembroke are sufficiently refuted by the mutilated character of the copies which were printed among their posthumous writings.—HANNAH, JOHN, 1870, *The Courtly Poets from Raleigh to Montrose, p.* 220.

Raleigh was a master in the art of verse, though his superiority in other respects has somewhat detracted from his fame in this. . . . Stately and vigorous is his language, bearing the impress of an unbending will, a will that did not quail when the block even was in view. Many poems which were once associated with his name have been discovered not to be his workmanship, but those which remain, and which have been unquestionably authenticated, bear witness to the variety of his gifts. He was certainly a writer

* "The Lie"

of *vers de société*, but being naturally a man of a grave and strong spirit, rather than a laughing and volatile one, his verse is now and again heavy and sententious.—SMITH, GEORGE BARNETT, 1875, *English Fugitive Poets, Poets and Novelists, pp.* 379, 380.

As a matter of fact, no poem ["Cynthia"] of the like ambition had been written in England for a century past, and if it had been published, it would perhaps have taken a place only second to its immediate contemporary, "The Faery Queen."—GOSSE, EDMUND, 1886, *Raleigh, (English Worthies), p.* 47.

His poetry, which is not so commonly read as it deserves to be, is a striking testimony both of the social habits of the time, and of the character of the man himself. It is conspicuous for amatory sweetness coupled with pastoral simplicity. Raleigh was the most polished courtier who ever adorned the precincts of English royalty; fond perhaps, as Macaulay says, of whispering his love sonnets too near to the willing ears of Elizabeth's maids of honour, but too innately refined to relapse into vulgar debauchery. In fact, the Court of the maiden Queen was one of the least dissolute of any monarch in the history of England. Raleigh's sonnets are an admirable reflection of the manners of the society in which he lived.—UNDERHILL, GEORGE F., 1887, *Literary Epochs, p.* 94.

His fancy could inspire in his "Pilgrimage" one of the loftiest appeals in all literature to Heaven from the pedantry of human justice or injustice. . . . The Court spoilt him for a national poet, as it spoilt Cowley; as it might, if it had been more generous, have spoilt Dryden. He desired to be read between the lines by a class which loved to think its own separate thoughts, and express its own separate feelings in its own diction, sometimes in its own jargon. He hunted for epigrams, and too often sparkled rather than burned. He was afraid not to be witty, to wrangle, as he himself has said,

In tickle points of niceness.

Often he refined instead of soaring. In place of sympathising he was ever striving to concentrate men's regards on himself. —STEBBING, WILLIAM, 1891, *Sir Walter Ralegh, p.* 78.

Himself one of the noblest of Elizabethan courtly singers, rivalling Sidney, even approaching Shakespeare in his sonnets, perhaps the greatest service he rendered to English poetry was in snatching from obscurity the poet Spenser, and promoting the publication of the "Faerie Queen."—HUME, MARTIN A. S., 1897, *Sir Walter Ralegh (Builders of Greater Britain), p.* 104.

Though his imagery is vivid and metaphorical, it is often homely; his thought is very plain and direct, and his poetry breathes a spirit of high disdain and fierce indignation, mixed with a strong feeling of religion, evidently the result of personal experience. . . . Though the authorship ["The Lie"] has been questioned, is certainly Raleigh's.—COURTHOPE, W. J., 1897, *A History of English Poetry, vol.* II, *pp.* 310, 311.

HISTORY OF THE WORLD
1614

That Sir W. Raughley esteemed more of fame than conscience. The best wits of England were employed for making his Historie. Ben himself had written a piece to him of the Punick warre, which he had altered and set in his booke.—DRUMMOND, WILLIAM, 1619, *Notes of Ben Jonson's Conversations, ed. Laing, p.* 15.

Recreate yourself with Sir Walter Raleigh's "History;" it is a body of history, and will add much more to your understanding than fragments of stones.—CROMWELL, OLIVER, 1650, *Letter to Richard Cromwell.*

How memorable an instance has our age afforded us of an eminent person to whose imprisonment we are all obliged, besides many philosophical experiments, for that noble "History of the World" now in our hands! The court had his youthful and freer years, and the Tower his latter age; the Tower reformed the courtier in him, and produced those worthy monuments of art and industry, which we should have in vain expected from his freedom and jollity.—HALL, BISHOP JOSEPH, 1652, *Balm of Gilead.*

Sir Walter Ralegh is never to be mentioned without honour.—HOWELL, WILLIAM, 1662, *Universal History, Preface.*

His booke sold very slowly at first, and the bookeseller complayned of it, and told him that he should be a looser by it, which put Sir W. into a passion, and sayd that since the world did not understand it, they should not have his second part, which he tooke and threw into the fire, and burnt before his face.—AUBREY, JOHN, 1669–96, *Brief Lives, ed.Clark, vol.* II, *p.* 191.

Sir Walter Ralegh's "History of the World" is a work of so vast a compass, such endless variety, that no genius, but one adventurous as his own, durst have undertaken that great design. I do not apprehend any great difficulty in collecting and common-placing an universal history from the whole body of historians; that is nothing but mechanic labour. But to digest the several authors in his mind; to take in all their majesty, strength, and beauty; to raise the spirit of meaner historians, and to equal all the excellencies of the best; this is sir Walter's peculiar praise. His style is the most perfect, the happiest, the most beautiful of the age he wrote in; majestic, clear, and manly; and he appears every where so superior rather than unequal to his subject, that the spirit of Rome and Athens seems to be breathed into his work.—FELTON, HENRY, 1711, *Dissertation on Reading the Classics.*

His grand labour, I mean that ocean of history, wherein he has outdone all that went before him, and given such lights to futurity as must ever be grateful. . . . No work, of any author in England, has been so often reprinted that is of equal size and antiquity. . . . Besides his own learning, knowledge, and judgment, which many would have thought sufficient for any undertaking, he, with that caution wherewith we have beheld so many others of his great enterprises tempered, would suffer no part of this "History" to pass his own hand, before some of the most able scholars, whom he assembled, it seems, for this purpose, had debated the parts he was most doubtful of, and they most conversant in, before him. Thus in the Mosaic and Oriental antiquities, or fainter and more remote footsteps of time, he would sometimes consult the learned Dr. Robert Burhill. In all parts of chronology, geography, and other branches of mathematical science, he wanted not the opinions of the learned Hariot, and the earl of Northumberland's three magi, long his neighbours in the Tower; and wherever he scrupled any thing in the phrase or diction, he would hear the acute and ingenious sir John Hoskyns, sometime also resident in these confines; who viewed and reviewed the said "History," as we are told, before it went to the press, and whom Ben Johnson, proud of calling others his sons, could gratify that humour in calling father. Thus having spared for no labour, and neglected no means to bring this work to the perfection wherein we behold it, it is no wonder that some scribbler or other should, upon finding it so universally read, endeavour to raise himself a little profit or credit from it, by pretending that the world needed an abridgment of its history, as if that wherewith sir Walter Ralegh has presented us, either is or was intended for any thing more.—OLDYS, WILLIAM, 1730, *Life of Sir Walter Ralegh, Oxford ed., vol.* I, *pp.* 448, 450.

The attempt of Raleigh is deservedly celebrated for the labour of his researches, and the elegance of his style; but he has endeavoured to exert his judgment more than his genius, to select facts, rather than to adorn them; and has produced an historical dissertation, but seldom risen to the majesty of history.—JOHNSON, SAMUEL, 1751, *The Rambler, No.* 122.

If the reader of Raleigh's "History" can have the patience to wade through the Jewish and Rabbinical learning which compose the half of the volume, he will find, when he comes to the Greek and Roman story, that his pains are not unrewarded. Raleigh is the best model of that ancient style which some writers would affect to revive at present.—HUME, DAVID, 1754–62, *History of England, Appendix.*

The great historians of this period, who condescended to use their native tongue, were Raleigh, Hayward, Knolles, Bacon, and Daniel, writers who in this province still hold no inferior rank among the classics of their country. The "History of the World," by Sir Walter, exhibits great strength of style and much solidity of judgment.—DRAKE, NATHAN, 1817, *Shakspeare and his Times, vol.* I, *p.* 476.

The appearance of this work turned every eye once more upon him. Men had hitherto considered him as an adventurer and a courtier; they now stood in astonishment at his multifarious acquirements, his deep research, his chronological knowledge, and his various acquaintance with the Grecian and rabbinical writers; though in reality that acquaintance appears to have been derived from versions in the Latin language. Admiration for his talents begot pity for his fate.—LINGARD, JOHN, 1819–30, *A History of England, vol.* IX, *ch.* iii, *p.* 165.

That great work which will be as permanent as the English language. . . . An extraordinary monument of human labour and genius, and which, in the vastness of its subject, its research and learning, the wisdom of its political reflections, and the beauties of its style, has not been equalled by any writer of this, or perhaps of any other country. This will appear the more wonderful if we recollect the circumstances under which it was completed. . . . It is laborious without being heavy, learned without being dry, acute and ingenious without degenerating into the subtile but trivial distinctions of the schoolmen. . . . Perhaps its most striking feature is the sweet tone of philosophic melancholy which pervades the whole. Written in prison during the quiet evening of a tempestuous life, we feel, in its perusal, that we are the companions of a superior mind, nursed in contemplation, and chastened and improved by sorrow, in which the bitter recollection of injury, and the asperity of resentment, have passed away, leaving only the heavenly lesson, that all is vanity.—TYTLER, PATRICK FRASER, 1833, *Life of Sir Walter Raleigh, pp.* 312, 333, 346, 347.

There is little now obsolete in the words of Raleigh, nor, to any great degree, in his turn of phrase; the periods, when pains have been taken with them, show that artificial structure which we find in Sidney and Hooker; he is less pedantic than most of his contemporaries, seldom low, never affected.—HALLAM, HENRY, 1837–39, *Introduction to the Literature of Europe, pt.* iii, *ch.* vii, *par.* 32.

James I. put to death the famous Sir Walter Raleigh, whose Universal History is still read for Sir Walter's own sake. If there are books which keep alive the names of the authors, there are authors whose names keep alive their books.—CHATEAUBRIAND, FRANÇOIS RENÉ, VICOMTE DE, 1837, *Sketches of English Literature, vol.* I, *p.* 343.

It is to the Greek and Roman story that we would direct the attention of any one wishing to acquaint himself with Raleigh's peculiar merits. The narrative is clear, spirited, and unembarrassed; replete with remarks disclosing the mind of the soldier and the statesman; and largely sprinkled and adorned with original, forcible, and graphic expressions. But this portion of the work has a still more remarkable distinction, when considered as the production of an age not yet formed to any high notions of international morality, from its invariable reprehension of wars of ambition, and its entire freedom from those illusions which have biassed both historians and their readers in regard to the perfidies and cruelties exhibited in ancient, particularly Roman history. In this respect, he appears to us to stand honourably distinguished from all preceding authors; but while he thus endeavours to moderate our admiration of the Romans by awakening us to a strong perception of their national crimes, he never fails to do justice to their manly virtues, their energy of character, and their public affections.—NAPIER, MACVEY, 1840-53, *Lord Bacon and Sir Walter Raleigh, p.* 213

The vigour of Raleigh's mind, and the extent and the application of his intellectual acquirements, not only enabled him to support this long endurance in a prison, but to consider it as his home. "His mind to him a kingdom was;" nay more, it was to him the whole world; for there he composed that extraordinary "History of the World," which was looked upon as a model of the English language, unparalleled at the time for conciseness and perspicuity of style; superior even to that of Bacon, being free from the overwhelming verbosity of this great man, by which the sense is sometimes obscured. —BARROW, JOHN, 1845, *Memoirs of the Naval Worthies of Queen Elizabeth's Reign, p.* 415.

The style of the history is excellent,—clear, sweet, flexible, straightforward and business-like, discussing the question of the locality of Paradise as Raleigh would have discussed the question of an expedition against Spain at the council-table of Elizabeth.—WHIPPLE, EDWIN P., 1859–68, *The Literature of the Age of Elizabeth, p.* 276.

Raleigh's "History," as a record of facts, has long been superseded; the interest it possesses at the present day is derived almost entirely from its literary merits, and from a few passages in which the author takes occasion to allude to circumstances that have fallen within his own experience. Much of it is written without any ambition of eloquence; but the style, even where it is most careless, is still lively and exciting, from a tone of the actual world which it preserves, and a certain frankness and heartiness coming from Raleigh's profession and his warm and impetuous character. It is not disfigured by any of the petty pedantries to some one or other of which most of the writers of books in that day gave way more or less, and it has altogether comparatively little of the taint of age upon it; while in some passages the composition, without losing anything of its natural grace and heartiness, is wrought up to great rhetorical polish and elevation.—CRAIK, GEORGE L., 1861, *A Compendious History of English Literature and of the English Language, vol.* I, *p.* 618.

A fine antique eloquence flows from his pen, enriched with a deep learning, which excites wonder when displayed by Raleigh. The soldier, the sailor, or the courtier is hardly the man from whom we expect profound philosophy or deep research; yet Raleigh showed by this achievement a power of wielding the pen, at least not inferior to his skill with sword or compass. That part of the History which he was able to complete, opening with the Creation, closes with the second Macedonian war, about one hundred and sixty-eight years before Christ. A deep tinge of melancholy, caught from the sombre walls that were ever frowning on his task, pervades the pages of the great book.—COLLIER, WILLIAM FRANCIS, 1861, *History of English Literature, p.* 152.

Ralegh's long confinement in the Tower had the effect to gain him a high reputa tion for learning, and, judging from what he has left us, he was one of the best scholars of the age in which he lived. His great work, "The History of the World," is indeed a great monument to his memory, as it is equally a monument to his want of judgment in the choice of a subject.—DRAKE, SAMUEL G., 1862, *A Brief Memoir of Sir Walter Ralegh, p.* 17.

It must not be forgotten that Ben Jonson claimed a share in the great "History," both for himself and for others. The probable amount of Raleigh's obligations has been fairly stated by Oldys, exaggerated by D'Israeli, and again reduced to reasonable dimensions by Mr. Tytler, Mr. Macvey Napier, and Mr. Edwards.—HANNAH, JOHN, 1870, *The Courtly Poets from Raleigh to Montrose, p.* 229.

Only the preface and the conclusion have much literary value; they are among the finest remains of Elizabethan prose.—MINTO, WILLIAM, 1872–80, *Manual of English Prose Literature, p.* 233.

It is regarded as a model of style, and the pioneer of the great English school of historical writers.—HART, JOHN S., 1873, *A Short Course in Literature, p.* 41.

A work of great merit for his time.—SCHERR, J., 1874, *A History of English Literature, p.* 48, *note.*

What a remarkable work would it have been, had Walter Ralegh himself recorded the history of his time. . . . The history of the world which Walter Ralegh had leisure to write in his prison, is an endeavour to put together the materials of Universal History as they lay before him from ancient times, and so make them more intelligible. He touches on the events of his age only in allusions, which excited attention at the time, but remain obscure to posterity.—RANKE, LEOPOLD VON, 1875, *A History of England, vol.* I, *p.* 453.

Both in style and matter, this celebrated work is vastly superior to all the English historical productions which had previously appeared. Its style, though partaking of the faults of the age in being frequently stiff and inverted, has fewer of these defects than the diction of any other writer of the time.—CHAMBERS, ROBERT, 1876, *Cyclopædia of English Literature, ed. Carruthers*

The sentences may sometimes strike us as long and cumbersome, but they are in the main easy and flowing; they impress the ear with a feeling of completeness. Occasionally he rises to real elouqence, especially when describing battles. His account of the Punic War is one of the most striking parts of the book. It is when he is dealing with men and their doings that he is at his best; it is then that we seem to see Ralegh's real character much more than when he indulges in philosophical speculations.—CREIGHTON, LOUISE, 1877, *Life of Sir Walter Ralegh.*

A work which for simple majesty of subject and style is hardly to be surpassed in prose.—MACDONALD, GEORGE, 1883, *The Imagination and Other Essays, p.* 105.

Will compare favorably in style, exhaustiveness of research, freedom from bias, and depth of judgment, with many of our more brilliant and pretentious historical works. . . . On account of the imperfect scientific knowledge of his times, there is much material in this history that is now considered crude; but many of his digressions upon government, wars and treaties, battles, and the characters of great men, are very interesting and instructive even to the student of to-day.—SMITH, M. W., 1882, *Studies in English Literature, p.* 104.

His masterpiece, the famous "History of the World," is made up of short passages of the most extraordinary beauty, and long stretches of monotonous narration and digression, showing not much grace of style, and absolutely no sense of proportion or skill in arrangement. The contrast is so strange that some have sought to see in the undoubted facts that Raleigh, in his tedious prison labours, had assistants and helpers (Ben Jonson among others), a reason for the superior excellence of such set pieces as the Preface, the Epilogue, and others, which are scattered about the course of the work. But independently of the other fact that excellence of the most varied kind meets us at every turn, though it also deserts us at every turn, in Raleigh's varied literary work, and that it would be absurd to attribute all these passages to some "affable familiar ghost," there is the additional difficulty that in none of his reported helpers' own work do the peculiar graces of the purple passages of the "History" occur. The immortal descant on mortality with which the book closes, and which is one of the highest achievements of English prose, is not in the least like Jonson, not in the least like Selden, not in the least like any one of whose connection with Raleigh there is record. Donne might have written it; but there is not the smallest reason for supposing that he did, and many for being certain that he did not. Therefore, it is only fair to give Raleigh himself the credit for this and all other passages of the kind.—SAINTSBURY, GEORGE, 1887, *History of Elizabethan Literature, p.* 212

A great reservoir of facts, stated with all grace and dignity, but which, like a great many heavy, excellent books, is never read. The matter-of-fact young man remembers that Sir Walter Raleigh first brought potatoes and (possibly) tobacco into England; but forgets his ponderous "History."—MITCHELL, DONALD G., 1890, *English Lands Letters and Kings, From Elizabeth to Anne, p.* 13.

This huge composition is one of the principal glories of seventeenth century literature, and takes a very prominent place in the history of English prose. As before, so here we find Raleigh superior to the ornaments and oddities of the Euphuists. He indites a large matter, and it is in a broad and serious style. The Preface, perhaps, leads the reader to expect something more modern, more entertaining than he finds. It is not easy to sympathise with a historian who confutes Steuchius Eugubinus and Goropius Becanus at great length, especially as those flies now exist only in the amber of their opponent. But the narrative, if obsolete and long-winded, possesses an extraordinary distinction, and, in its brighter parts, is positively resplendent. The book is full of practical wisdom, knowledge of men in the mass, and trenchant study of character. It is heavy and slow in movement, the true historical spirit, as we now conceive it, is absent, and it would probably baffle most readers to pursue its attenuated thread of entertainment down to the triumph of Emilius Paulus. But of its dignity there can be no two opinions, and in sustained power it easily surpassed every prose work of its own age.—GOSSE, EDMUND, 1893, *English Prose, ed. Craik.*

The design and style of Ralegh's "History of the World" are instinct with a magnanimity which places the book among the noblest literary enterprises. Throughout it breathes a serious moral purpose. —LAUGHTON, J. K., AND LEE, SIDNEY, 1896, *Dictionary of National Biography. vol.* XLVII, *p.* 203.

That delightful "History of the World" which is one of the glories of English prose literature.—FISKE, JOHN, 1897, *Old Virginia and Her Neighbours, vol.* I, *p.* 197.

GENERAL

To thee, that art the sommers Nightingale,
Thy soveraine Goddesses most deare delight,
Why doe I send this rusticke Madrigale,
That may thy tunefull eare unseason quite?
Thou onely fit this Argument to write,
In whose high thoughts Pleasure hath built her bowre,
And dainty love learnd sweetly to endite.
My rimes I know unsavory and sowre,
To tast the streames that, like a golden showre,
Flow from thy fruitfull head, of thy love's praise;
Fitter, perhaps, to thonder Martiall stowre,
When so thee lift thy lofty Muse to raise:
Yet, till that thou thy Poeme wilt make knowne,
Let thy faire Cinthias praises be thus rudely showne.
—SPENSER, EDMUND, 1589, *Sonnets Addressed to Various Noblemen, &c., The Faerie Queene, bk.* i.

Sir Walter Raleigh, not to be contemned, either for judgment or style.—JONSON, BEN, 1630–7, *Timber*, LXXIX.

Many years in my hands, ["Cabnet Council"] and finding it lately by chance among other books and papers, upon reading thereof I thought it a kind of injury to withhold longer the work of so eminent an author from the public.—MILTON, JOHN, 1658, *Introduction to The Cabnet-Council.*

There was some time in the Library of Sir *Kenelm Digby*, a Manuscript History of the Life and Death of the Conqueror, said to have been written by *Sir Walter Raleigh.*—NICOLSON, WILLIAM, 1696–1714, *English Historical Library.*

In talking over the design for a dictionary, that might be authoritative for our English writers; Mr. Pope rejected Sir Walter Raleigh twice, as too affected. —POPE, ALEXANDER, 1743–44, *Spence's Anecdotes, p.* 235.

A writer more learned than Shakespear, more polished by the varieties of human intercourse, and that with persons of the highest eminence and station, than Hooker. —GODWIN, WILLIAM, 1797, *The Enquirer.*

The diction of Raleigh is more pure and perspicuous, and more free from inversions, than that of any other writer of the age of Elizabeth or James the First.—DRAKE, NATHAN, 1804, *Essays Illustrative of the Tatler, Spectator, and Guardian, vol.* II, *p.* 14.

Upon maritimal concerns he published no fewer than eight treatises, being, as he proudly announced, the first writer either ancient or modern that had treated on this subject. These works are written with great perspicuity, and, although the practices recommended in them be now obsolete, and the improvements and plans suggested, superseded by the rapid strides of modern science, they are interesting, as all compositions dictated by good sense and experience must ever be; and curious, as illustrating the comparative progress of navigation, and of the arts connected with it.—THOMSON, KATHERINE, 1830, *Memoirs of the Life of Sir Walter Ralegh, p.* 259.

Raleigh was, beyond all doubt, one of the most eminent persons in an age which was extraordinarily prolific of great men. He is equally distinguished in the naval and in the literary history of his country. —SOUTHEY, ROBERT, 1837, *Lives of the British Admirals, vol.* IV, *p.* 440.

The thoughts of Sir Walter Raleigh on moral prudence are few, but precious.—HALLAM, HENRY, 1837–39, *Introduction to the Literature of Europe, pt.* iii, *ch.* iv, *par.* 37.

Looking at the activity of his life, his wars, his voyages, his parliamentary duties, one is astonished at the amount of work which he did. But this work was not all. Some of the ablest state papers of the time were drawn up by him. In history, politics, philosophy, science, and poetry, his mind was also employed; and his pen productive of memorable works. His writings are voluminous. He wrote, besides his great history, on the Prerogatives of Parliament; on Trade; on Shipping; on the State of Spain; on the Life and Death of Mahomet; on the Life and Death of William the Conqueror; on Mines and Trials of Minerals; on almost every subject interesting to man.—LANGFORD, JOHN ALFRED, 1861, *Prison Books and Their Authors, p.* 91.

A writer of magnificent prose, itself full of religion and poetry both in thought and expression. . . . It would be very unfair to judge Sir Walter by his verse. His prose is infinitely better, and equally displays the devout tendency of his mind —a tendency common to all the great men of that age. The worst I know of him is the selfishly prudent advice he left behind for his son. No doubt he had his faults, we must not judge a man even by what he says in an over-anxiety for the prosperity of his child.—MACDONALD, GEORGE, 1868, *England's Antiphon, pp.* 71, 76.

When the vigour of debate passed from Parliament to the Press, no deceased writer rendered truer service to Britain than did Ralegh in supporting and lighting up the policy which is truly liberal, just because it builds upon old foundations, appeals to old instincts, and brings out what is true and vital in the national traditions. A passionate and untiring energy is not more characteristic of Ralegh the man, than a clinging to political development, rather than political construction, is the distinctive mark of Ralegh the publicist. Hence it is, as I believe, that his name figures so saliently and so continually in the political literature of the eighteenth century. In the seventeenth, his deeds and his endeavours were continually rising before the minds of men who were still fighting under the same banner and against the same enemies. Not a few of them had been the contemporaries of his closing years. In the eighteenth, all the outward circumstances of the political conflict had changed. New men are seen in the arena. The party combinations are new. The impulses and the aims of the strife are new. Yet Ralegh's writings are even more frequently appealed to. A large volume might be made of the quotations which were pressed into service during the bitter contests of the Georgian reigns, and of the commentaries which grew out of the quotations.—EDWARDS, EDWARD, 1868, *The Life of Sir Walter Ralegh, vol.* I, *p.* 718.

The "Discovery" is a matter-of-fact record of his own voyage, his dealings with the natives, and his impressions of the scenery. It was much ridiculed at the time by his jealous enemies, but there is nothing incredible in what he professes to have seen, though he was too sanguine in his beliefs as to the splendour of the parts of the empire that he had not seen. As regards the style, he "neither studied phrase, form, nor fashion;" yet at times he shows his natural power of graphic description —MINTO, WILLIAM, 1872–80, *Manual of English Prose Literature, p.* 233.

He loved letters intensely, and was one of those bountiful protectors of literature in this age who gave without a thought of patronage or any desire but to help upward the aspiring intellect.—LAWRENCE, EUGENE, 1878, *English Literature, Romance Period, p.* 95.

This restless spirit, who seemed, in his ceaseless occupations, to have lived only for his own age and his own pleasure, was the true servant of posterity, who hail him as also one of the founders of literature. —WELSH, ALFRED H., 1882, *Development of English Literature and Language, vol.* I, *p.* 357.

This ["A Discourse on War"] may be recommended to the modern reader as the most generally pleasing of Raleigh's prose compositions, and the one in which, owing to its modest limits, the peculiarities of his style may be most conveniently studied. The last passage of the little book forms one of the most charming pages of the literature of that time, and closes with a pathetic and dignified statement of Raleigh's own attitude towards war.—GOSSE, EDMUND, 1886, *Raleigh, (English Worthies), p.* 185.

Undoubtedly Bacon (Shakespeare in his person as he lived being in the main *nominis umbra*) is the grandest figure of the age; but Raleigh is the most fascinating. Of the versatility and daring of the Elizabethans he remains the chief representative. In a larger sense than that in which the words were afterwards applied, he was "not one but all mankind's epitome." Soldier, courtier, philosopher, and poet, he had carried the spirit of Sidney into the field, and discussed metres and myths with Spenser when it was won. Drake was his only master among the kings of the sea; Bacon himself his only superior in the work of the "Instauratio Magna." Known abroad as the champion of the Indians, as the great intercessor for civil and religious liberty at home, he could turn from writing verses, only surpassed in grace by the lyrics of the later Cavaliers, to study "the learning of the Egyptians," or what passed for such before the reign of criticism, and record with an equal credulity and eloquence the annals of antiquity as then accepted. Early among the pioneers of European civilisation in the New World, he was the first modern historian of the Old.—NICHOL, JOHN, 1888, *Francis Bacon, His Life and Philosophy, pt.* i, *p.* 170.

This ["Discovery of Guiana"] was a work of high importance in the development of English prose, the most brilliant and original contribution to the literature of travel which had been made during the reign of Elizabeth, rich as that had been in work of the same class. Hume, who spurned the "Discovery" from him as "full of the grossest and most palpable lies," showed an eighteenth-century blindness to the truth which lay under the magnificent diction of Raleigh's narrative, but it is strange that the conduct of that narrative itself could win no word of praise from such a critic.—GOSSE, EDMUND, 1893, *English Prose, ed. Craik, vol.* I, *p.* 528.

Ralegh makes amazing show of systematic arrangement; but the analysis is often arbitrary and inexact. On the one hand this poor analysis, on the other his utterly unwieldy and elephantine periods, make him an exceedingly bad paragraphist.—LEWIS, EDWIN HERBERT, 1894, *The History of the English Paragraph, p.* 89.

Of Raleigh's voluminous writings the advice to his son, or, as he entitles it, "Instructions to his Son and to Posterity," is one of the few which still maintains its interest.—COLLINS, JOHN CHURTON, 1895, *Lord Chesterfield's Letters, Essays and Studies, p.* 231.

His mental calibre cannot be fairly judged, nor his versatility fully realised, until his achievements in poetry, in history, and political philosophy have been taken into account. However impetuous and rash was he in action, he surveyed life in his writings with wisdom and insight, and recorded his observations with dignity and judicial calmness. It is difficult to reconcile the religious tone of his writings with the reputation for infidelity which attached to Ralegh until his death, and was admitted to be justifiable by Hume. The charges brought against Ralegh and Marlowe in 1593 were repeated in general terms within four months after his execution by Archbishop Abbot, who attributed the catastrophe to his "questioning" of "God's being and omnipotence." (Abbot to Sir Thomas Roe, 19 Feb. 1618-19). Such a charge seems confuted on almost every page of his "History of the World," in which he follows in his early chapters the Old Testament narrative with most confiding literalness, and earnestly insists throughout on God's beneficence. A similar sentiment finds repeated expression in his political essays. . . . Nothing actually inconsistent with these views can be detected in two works in which he dealt with metaphysical speculation.—LAUGHTON, J. K., AND LEE, SIDNEY, 1896, *Dictionary of National Biography, vol.* XLVII, *pp.* 200, 201.

He could dangle at Court and bandy compliments as well as the most empty-headed fine gentlemen; but he gave up only five hours of the twenty-four to sleep, and spent every hour he could snatch in study. His reading must have been omnivorous, for his breadth of view, his depth of knowledge, and his profundity of thought—far in advance of his contemporaries—prove him to have been perhaps the most universally capable Englishman that ever lived—a fit contemporary of Shakspeare and Bacon.—HUME, MARTIN A. S., 1897, *Sir Walter Ralegh (Builders of Greater Britain), p.* 39.

Joshua Sylvester

1563–1618

Joshua Sylvester: author; born in England in 1563; became eminent as a linguist; was a member of the Company of Merchant Adventurers at Stade, Holland. Died at Middelburg, Holland, Sept. 28, 1618. He is best known as the translator into English of Du Bartas's "Divine Weekes and Workes" (1605; 7th ed. 1641). The original was by a French Huguenot nobleman; Sylvester's version had great popularity among the Puritans of Old and New England, and was one of the sources of inspiration to Milton when writing "Paradise Lost." The quaint "conceited" style of Du Bartas was, if anything, exaggerated in the translation. In 1615 Sylvester published a singular anti-tobacco tract—"Tobacco Battered and the Pipes Shattered," etc.—intended to please James I., who hated the weed.—BEERS, HENRY A., 1897, *Johnson's Universal Cyclopædia, vol.* VII, *p.* 861.

Thus to aduenture forth, and re-conuay
The best of treasures, from a Forraine Coast,
And take that wealth wherin they gloried most,
And make it Ours by such a gallant pray,
And that without in-iustice; doth bewray
The glory of the Worke, that we may boast
Much to haue wonne, and others nothing lost
By taking such a famous prize away.
As thou industrious Sylvester hast wrought,
And heere enritch'd us with th'immortall store
Of others sacred lines: which from them brought
Comes by thy taking greater then before:
So hast thou lighted from a flame deuout,
As great a flame, that neuer shall goe out.

—DANIEL, SAMUEL, 1606, *To my Good Friend, M. Syluester, Daniel's Works, ed. Grosart, vol.* I, *p.* 281.

That Silvester's translation of Du Bartas was not well done; and that he wrote his verses before it, ere he understood to conferr.—DRUMMOND, WILLIAM, 1619, *Notes on Ben Jonson's Conversation, ed. Laing.*

And Silvester, who from the French more weak
Made Bartas of his six days' labour speak
In natural English, who, had he there stay'd
He had done well, and never had bewray'd
His own invention to have bin so poor,
Who still wrote less in striving to write more.

—DRAYTON, MICHAEL, c 1627, *Of Poets and Poesie.*

The English Translator of Du Bartas his Poem of the six Daies work of Creation, by which he is more generally fam'd, (for that poem hath ever had many great admirers among us) than by his own poems commonly printed therewith.—PHILLIPS, EDWARD, 1675, *Theatrum Poetarum Anglicanorum, ed. Brydges, p.* 277.

Queen Elizabeth had a great respect for him, King James I. a greater, and Prince Henry greatest of all, and so much valued by him that he made him his first Poet-Pensioner.—WOOD, ANTHONY, 1691–1721, *Athenæ Oxonensis, vol.* I, *p.* 594.

As a whole, in its general structure and execution, it is insufferably heavy and tedious, nor will a reader, in the present day, be easily found, who shall possess perseverance and patience adequate to its complete perusal. In this mass of deterring materials, however, and which abounds with quaintnesses, puerilities, and vulgarisms, of almost every description, are to be discovered beauties of no common kind.—DRAKE, NATHAN, 1798, *Literary Hours, vol.* III, *p.* 82.

This person, who in his day obtained the name of "Silver-tongued Sylvester," was educated by his uncle, W. Plumb, esq. and is reported to have been a merchant-adventurer. Queen Elizabeth is said to have had a respect for him, and her successor a greater, and Prince Henry greater than his father. His moral conduct, his piety, and his courage and patience in adversity, were highly celebrated: and he was so accomplished in languages as to understand French, Spanish, Dutch, Italian, and Latin. But his forwardness to correct the vices of the age, exposed him to a powerful resentment; and his country is said to have treated him with ingratitude.—BRYDGES, SAMUEL EDGERTON, 1800, *ed. Phillips' Theatrum Poetarum Anglicanorum, p.* 277.

Thoughts and expressions there certainly are in Milton, which leave his acquaintance with Sylvester hardly questionable; although some of the expressions quoted by Mr. Dunster, which are common to them both, may be traced back to other poets older than Sylvester. The entire amount of his obligations, as Mr. Dunster justly admits, cannot detract from our opinion of Milton. If Sylvester ever stood high in his favour, it must have been when he was very young. The beauties which occur so strangely intermixed with bathos and flatness in Sylvester's poem, might have caught the youthful discernment, and long dwelt in the memory, of the great poet. But he must have perused it with disgust at Sylvester's general manner. Many of his epithets and happy phrases were really worthy of Milton; but by far the greater proportion of his thoughts and expressions have a quaintness and flatness more worthy of Quarles and Wither.—CAMPBELL, THOMAS, 1819, *An Essay on English Poetry.*

The principal poem of Du Bartas, which is a history of the Creation, was written in a sufficiently inflated style; but this was exaggerated by Sylvester, who added many peculiarities of his own, such, among others, as compound, or rather agglutinated, words made up of half a dozen radicals. Its poetical merit is slender, but the translation is not without philological interest, because it contains a considerable number of words and forms, of which examples are hardly to be met with elsewhere, and there are passages which serve as commentaries and explanations of obscure expressions in Shakespeare, and other dramatic authors of the time. It is, however, difficult to understand how an age that produced a Shakespeare could bestow such unbounded applause on a Du Bartas and a Sylvester.—MARSH, GEORGE P., 1862, *Origin and History of the English Language, etc., p.* 548.

Sylvester, though starting, as we see, as a Merchant-adventurer, became in time so mere a literary adventurer and translating drudge, that we cannot feel much interest about him or his unoriginal works.—COLLIER, JOHN PAYNE, 1865, *A Bibliographical and Critical Account of the Rarest Books in the English Language, vol.* II, *p.* 410.

Joshua Sylvester is one of those men of letters whom accident rather than property seems to have made absurd. He has existed in English literature chiefly as an Englisher of the Frenchman Du Bartas, whom an even greater ignorance has chosen to regard as something grotesque. Du Bartas is one of the grandest, if also one of the most unequal, poets of Europe, and Joshua Sylvester, his translator, succeeded in keeping some of his grandeur if he even added to his inequality. His original work is insignificant compared with his translation; but it is penetrated with the same qualities. —SAINTSBURY, GEORGE, 1887, *History of Elizabethan Literature, p.* 289.

Another transitional figure is that of Joshua Sylvester, whom few historians of literature have deigned to mention. He was, however, an active producer of successful verse in his own age, and he wielded, moreover, by means of his famous translation, a prodigious influence. . . . Sylvester was ambitious of high distinction, but he was dragged down by poverty and by a natural turbidity of style. His original sonnets and lyrics are constantly striking, but never flawless; his translations, as poems, are full of force and colour, but crude. His talent was genuine, but it never ripened, and seems to be turning sour when it should be growing mellow. He does not fear to be tiresome and grotesque for pages at a time, and in Du Bartas he unhappily found a model who, in spite of his own remarkable qualities, sanctioned the worst errors of Sylvester. Milton was, however, attracted to Du Bartas, and approached him, almost unquestionably, through Sylvester, whose version was extremely popular until the middle of the century. Sylvester's vocabulary was very extensive, and he revelled in the pseudo-scientific phraseology of his French prototype.—GOSSE, EDMUND, 1894, *The Jacobean Poets, p.* 14.

Du Bartas has not shared Spenser's immortality; but few books have won a wider popularity than Sylvester's translation obtained in the Puritan homes of England. The author, a French Huguenot who had fought for Henry of Navarre, left behind him at his death, in 1590, a long descriptive poem entitled "The Divine Weeks and Works." The first part, which alone was complete, gave an account of the days of the Creation, founded on the biblical record; and the second "week" carried on the Scripture story to the reign of David, where it abruptly terminated. This poem was translated into English by Joshua Sylvester, himself a poet of some ability, in 1605, and passed through several editions in rapid succession. Its scriptural basis secured for it a welcome in Puritan households, and as the publisher's office was in Bread Street, an early copy would certainly find its way to the Spread Eagle. Sylvester's uncouth imagery and quaintly-structured verse is not without a certain attractiveness even now, but they have a higher claim to remembrance as an influence of Milton's childhood, out of which was destined to grow, in the fulness of time, "Paradise Lost." — MASTERMAN, J. HOWARD B., 1897, *The Age of Milton, p.* 3.

Though no exact scholar (his rendering is indeed far more of a paraphrase than a translation), he had some pre-eminent qualifications for the task he had undertaken. His religious sympathy with his original was profound, and he had a native quaintness that well reflected the curious phraseology of Du Bartas. His enthusiasm overflowed in embellishments of his own, in which he is often at his best.—SECCOMBE, THOMAS, 1898, *Dictionary of National Biography, vol.* IV, *p.* 261.

Samuel Daniel

1562–1619

Born, near Taunton (?), 1562. At Magdalen Hall, Oxford, (1579–82?). Possibly with Lord Stafford on an embassy to France, 1586. Visit to Italy, about 1588 or 1589. Tutor to William Herbert, son of Earl of Pembroke; lived at Wilton, Salisbury. Some sonnets of his first printed in 1591 edn. of Sidney's "Astrophel and Stella." This being done without his knowledge, he published fifty sonnets, under title "Delia," in 1592. Tutor to Anne Clifford, daughter of Countess of Cumberland, about 1598 (?), at Skipton, Yorkshire. Possibly succeeded Spenser as poet laureate, 1599. Considerable literary activity and reputation. Masques by Daniel performed before royalty at Hampton Court, 1604; at Oxford, 1605; at Whitehall, 1610; in London, 1614. Controller of the Children of the Revels to the Queen, 1604–18. Groom of the Queen's Privy Chamber, 1607–19. Removed from London to a farm near Beckington, Wilts, about 1603 (?). Died there, Oct. 1619. Probably married. *Works:* "Delia," 1592 (2nd edition same year); "Cleopatra," 1594; "First Fowre Bookes of the Civile Wars," 1595; 5th, 1595; 6th, 1601; 7th and 8th, 1609; "Musophilus," 1599; "A Letter from Octavia," 1599; "Poeticall Essayes," 1599; "Works . . . augmented," 1601 (with new title-page, 1602); "The Defence of Rhyme," 1602; "A Panegyricke Congratulatorie," 1603; "The Vision of the Twelve Goddesses," 1604; "The Queenes Arcadia" (anon), 1605; "Philotas" 1605; "Ulisses and the Syren," 1605; "Certaine Small Poems," 1605; "Certaine Small Workes," 1607; "Tethys Festival," 1610 (also issued with "The Order and Solemnitie of the Creation," 1610); "The Collection of the Historie of England," pt. i., 1612; pt. ii., 1617; "Hymen's Triumph," 1615. He *translated:* P. Giovio's "Imprese," 1585; and contrib. verses to the 1611 and 1613 editions of Florio's "Montaigne." *Collected Works:* ed. by his brother, John Daniel, 1623.—SHARP, R. FARQUHARSON, 1897, *A Dictionary of English Authors, p.* 72.

PERSONAL

HERE LYES EXPECTINGE THE SECOND COMMING OF OUR LORD & SAUIOUR JESUS CHRIST Y^E DEAD BODY OF SAMUELL DANYELL ESQ THAT EXCELLENT POETT AND HISTORIAN WHO WAS TUTOR TO THE LADY ANNE CLIFFORD IN HER YOUTH SHE THAT WAS SOLE DAUGHTER AND HEIRE TO GEORGE CLIFFORD ÆARLE OF CV̄BERLAND WHO IN GRATITUDE TO HIM ERECTED THIS MONUMENT IN HIS MEMORY A LONG TIME AFTER WHEN SHE WAS COUNTESSE DOWAGER OF PEMBROKE DORSETT & MOV̄TGOMERY. HE DYED IN OCTOBER 1619.—*Inscription on Mural Monument, Beckington Church.*

Samuel Daniel was a good honest man, had no children; but no poet.—DRUMMOND, WILLIAM, 1619, *Notes on Ben Jonson's Conversations, ed. Laing.*

He was a Servant in Ordinary to Queen Anne, who allowed him a fair Salary. As the Tortoise burieth himself all the Winter in the ground, so Mr. Daniel would lye hid at his Garden-house in Old-street, nigh London, for some months together (the more retiredly to enjoy the Company of the Muses); and then would appear in publick, to converse with his Friends, whereof Dr. Cowel and Mr. Camden were principal. Some tax him to smak of the Old Cask, as resenting of the Romish Religion; but they have a quicker Palate than I, who can make any such discovery. In his old age he turn'd Husbandman, and rented a Farm in Wiltshire nigh the Devises. I can give no account how he thrived thereupon; for, though he was well vers'd in Virgil, his Fellow Husbandman-Poet, yet there is more required to make a rich Farmer, than only to say his Georgicks by heart. . . . Besides, I suspect that Mr. Daniel's fancy was too fine and sublimated, to be wrought down to his private profit. However, he had neither a bank of wealth, or lank of want; living in a competent condition. By Justina his wife he had no child; and I am unsatisfied both in the place and time of death; but collect the latter to be about the end of the Reign of King James.—FULLER, THOMAS, 1662, *The Worthies of England, ed. Nichols, vol.* II, *p.* 288.

His Geny being more, more prone to easier and smoother studies, than in pecking and hewing at logic, he left the university without the honour of a degree, and exercised it much in English history and poetry, of which he then gave several ingenious specimens.—WOOD, ANTHONY, 1691–1721, *Athenæ Oxonienses, vol.* I., *p.* 447.

He has touches of tenderness as well as fancy; for *he* was in earnest, and the object of his attachment was real, though disguised under the name of Delia. She resided on the banks of the river Avon, and was unmoved by the poet's strains. Rank with her outweighed love and genius.—JAMESON, ANNA BROWNELL, 1829, *The Loves of the Poets, vol.* I. *p.* 265.

Though he rejected it and called out upon it, "gentle" remains Lamb's constant epithet. And, curiously enough, in the gentleness and dignified melancholy of his life, Daniel stands nearer to Lamb than any other English writer, with the possible exception of Scott. His circumstances were less gloomily picturesque. But I defy any feeling man to read the scanty narrative of Daniel's life and think of him thereafter without sympathy and respect. . . . Now there is but one answer to this—that a man of really strong spirit does not suffer himself to be "put out of that sense which nature had made my part." Daniel's words indicate the weakness that in the end made futile all his powers; they indicate a certain "donnish" timidity (if I may use the epithet), a certain distrust of his own genius. Such a timidity and such a distrust often accompany very exquisite faculties: indeed, they may be said to imply a certain exquisiteness of feeling. But they explain why, of the two contemporaries, the robust Ben Jonson is to-day a living figure in most men's conception of those times, while Samuel Daniel is rather a fleeting ghost. And his self-distrust was even then recognised as well as his exquisiteness. He is indeed "well-languaged Daniel," "sweet honey-dropping Daniel," "Rosamund's trumpeter, sweet as the nightingale," revered and admired by all his compeers.—QUILLER-COUCH, A. T., 1895, *Adventures in Criticism, pp.* 51, 54.

DELIA
1592

Kisse Delia's hand for her sweet Prophets sake,
  Whose, not affected but well couched, teares
Have power, have worth a marble minde to shake;
  Whose fame no Iron-age or time out weares:
Then lay you downe in Phillis lappe and sleepe,
Untill she weeping read, and reading weepe.
—LODGE, THOMAS, 1593, *Phillis.*

And thou, the sweet Museus of these times,
Pardon my rugged and unfiled rymes,
Whose scarce invention is too meane and base,
When Delias glorious Muse dooth come in place.
—DRAYTON, MICHAEL, 1594, *Endimion and Phœbe.*

As Parthenius Nicæus excellently sang the praises of Arete: so Daniel hath divinely sonnetted the matchless beauty of Delia.—MERES, FRANCIS, 1598, *Palladis Tamia.*

The publication of Daniel's sonnets in 1592 is an epoch in the history of the English Sonnet. This was the first body of sonnets written in what is sometimes called by pre-eminence the English form—three independent quatrains closed in a couplet. Daniel also set an example to Shakespeare in treating the sonnet as a stanza, connecting several of them together as consecutive parts of a larger expression. Apart from their form, there is not very much interest in the sonnets to Delia. They have all Daniel's smoothness and felicity of phrase, and are pervaded by exceedingly sweet and soft sentiment. Though they rouse no strong feelings, they may be dwelt upon by a sympathetic reader with lively enjoyment. One of them, with somewhat greater depth of feeling than most of the others, the sonnet beginning—"Care-charmer Sleep, son of the sable Night," is ranked among the best sonnets in the language. But their most general interest is found in their relation to Shakespeare's sonnets, several of which seem to have been built up from ideas suggested by the study of those to Delia.—MINTO, WILLIAM, 1874-85, *Characteristics of English Poets, p.* 192.

In a certain tender swing of movement, attained by great art in the selection of words presenting sounds upon which the tongue and ear can linger, and which at the same time suavely melt into each other with the true liquid flow of genuine poetic sequences, Daniel must be esteemed the greatest English artist.—LANIER, SIDNEY, 1880, *A Forgotten English Poet, Music and Poetry, p.* 127.

It is when we open Daniel's "Delia" that we recognise close kinship. The manner is the same, though the master proves himself of tardier imagination and less ardent temper. Diction, imagery, rhymes, and, in sonnets of like form, versification distinctly resemble those of Shakspere. Malone was surely right when he recognised in Daniel the master of Shakspere as a writer of sonnets—a master quickly excelled by his pupil. And it is in Daniel that we find sonnet starting from sonnet almost in Shakspere's manner, only that Daniel often links poem with poem in more formal wise, the last or the penultimate line of one poem supplying the first line of that which immediately follows.—DOWDEN, EDWARD, 1881, *ed. The Sonnets of William Shakspere, Introduction, p.* xlix.

He was an estimable man, and was a good poet, according to the standard of his day, which was more tolerant of tediousness than ours. That he was a lover is not evident from his sonnets, which are not without a certain tenderness and elegance, and which may be read as exercises of fancy with considerable pleasure. . . . The highest compliment that can be paid them is to say that two or three of them might have been written by Shakspere, who seems to have had them in mind while writing his own sonnets.—STODDARD, RICHARD HENRY, 1881, *The Sonnet in English Poetry, Scribner's Monthly, vol.* 22, *p.* 910.

I do not suppose it is likely now that we shall ever know who "Delia" was. But I for one recognize in these Sonnets a human passion, and not mere "sportive wit" or "idle play." The grief grows o'times monotonous and even grotesque, but ever and anon there comes the genuine "cry" of a man's heart in suspensive anguish. He is by no means a strong man—contrariwise reveals a good deal of valetudinarian sentimentalism; yet is there reality of "love," and not simply rhyme-craft.—GROSART, ALEXANDER B., 1885, *ed. The Complete Works of Samuel Daniel, Memorial-Introduction, vol.* I, *p.* xvii.

As a sonneteer Daniel deserves the highest praise. His sonnets are formed by three elegiac verses of alternate rhyme concluding with a couplet. For sweetness of rhythm, delicate imagery, and purity of language they nearly surpass Shakespeare's efforts. Daniel's corrections are usually for the better, and show him to have been an exceptionally slow and conscientious writer.—LEE, SIDNEY, 1888, *Dictionary of National Biography, vol.* XIV, *p.* 34.

THE COMPLAINT OF ROSAMOND
1592

Some dul-headed diuines deeme it no more cunninge to write an exquisite Poem, than to preach pure Caluin, or distill the juice of a Commentary in a quarter sermon. . . . You shall finde there goes more exquisite paines and puritie of wit, to the writing of one such rare Poem as "Rosamond" than to a hundred of your dunsticall Sermons.—NASHE, THOMAS, 1592, *Piers Penilesse.*

Why thither speeds not Rosamond's trumpeter,
Sweet as the nightingale?
—PEELE, GEORGE, 1593, *The Honor of the Garter.*

As every one mourneth, when he heareth of the lamentable plangors of Thracian Orpheus for his dearest Euridyce: so every one passionateth, when he readeth the afflicted death of Daniel's distressed *Rosamond.*—MERES, FRANCIS, 1598, *Palladis Tamia.*

Samuel Daniel's "Complaint of Rosamond," with its seven-line stanza (1592), stood to "Lucrece" in even closer relation than Lodge's "Scilla," with its six-line stanza, to "Venus and Adonis." The pathetic accents of Shakespeare's heroine are those of Daniel's heroine purified and glorified.—LEE, SIDNEY, 1898, *A Life af William Shakespeare, p.* 76.

THE CIVILE WARS
1595–1623

And Daniell, praised for thy sweet-chast verse:
Whose Fame is grav'd on Rosamond's blacke Herse:
Still mayst thou live, and still be honoured,
For that rare worke, the White Rose and the Red.
—BARNFIELD, RICHARD, 1605, *Remembrance of some English Poets.*

Daniel wrott "Civill Warres," and yett hath not one batle in all his book.—DRUMMOND, WILLIAM, 1619, *Notes on Ben Jonson's Conversations, ed. Laing.*

Samuel Daniel the historian, is unpoetical; but has good sense often.—POPE, ALEXANDER, 1728–30, *Spence's Anecdotes, p.* 17.

Gravely sober on all ordinary affairs, & not easily excited by any—yet there is one, on which his Blood boils—whenever he speaks of English valour exerted against a foreign Enemy. Do read over

—but some evening when we are quite comfortable, at your fireside. . . . He must not be read piecemeal. Even by leaving off & looking at a stanza by itself, I find the loss.—COLERIDGE, SAMUEL TAYLOR, 1808, *Letter to Charles Lamb, The Lambs, ed. Hazlitt, p.* 222.

Sound morality, prudential wisdom, and occasional touches of the pathetic, delivered in a style of then unequalled chastity and perspicuity, will be recognised throughout his work; but neither warmth, passion, nor sublimity, nor the most distant trace of enthusiasm can be found to animate the mass.—DRAKE, NATHAN, 1817, *Shakspeare and his Times, vol.* I, *p.* 611.

Faithfully adhering to truth, which he does not suffer so much as an ornamental episode to interrupt, and equally studious to avoid the bolder figures of poetry, it is not surprising that Daniel should be little read. It is, indeed, certain that much Italian and Spanish poetry, even by those whose name has once stood rather high, depends chiefly upon merits which he abundantly possesses,—a smoothness of rhythm, and a lucid narration in simple language. But that which from the natural delight in sweet sound is enough to content the ear in the Southern tongues, will always seem bald and tame in our less harmonious verse. It is the chief praise of Daniel, and must have contributed to what popularity he enjoyed in his own age, that his English is eminently pure, free from affectation of archaism and from pedantic innovation, with very little that is now obsolete. Both in prose and in poetry, he is, as to language, among the best writers of his time, and wanted but a greater confidence in his own power, or, to speak less indulgently, a greater share of it, to sustain his correct taste, calm sense, and moral feeling.—HALLAM, HENRY, 1837–39, *Introduction to the Literature of Europe, pt.* iii, *ch.* v, *par.* 43.

His epic on the civil wars is a failure as a poem.—LEE, SIDNEY, 1888, *Dictionary of National Biography, vol.* XIV, *p.* 30.

DEFENCE OF RHYME
1602–07

His "Defence of Rhyme," written in prose (a more difficult test than verse), has a passionate eloquence that reminds one of Burke, and is more light-armed and modern than the prose of Milton fifty years later.—LOWELL, JAMES RUSSELL, 1875–90, *Spenser, Prose Works, Riverside ed., vol.* IV, *p.* 282.

Daniel's criticism is very reasonable, and adequately exposed Campion's absurd argument.—LEE, SIDNEY, 1888, *Dictionary of National Biography, vol.* XIV, *p.* 27.

It must be confessed that a careful reading of Daniel's "Defence of Ryme" will leave a better impression of the real weight of that able and thoughtful author than too continued a perusal of much of his "chaste and correct" poetry.—SCHELLING, FELIX E., 1891, *Poetic and Verse Criticism of the Reign of Elizabeth, p.* 91.

HISTORY OF ENGLAND
1612–17

He was also a judicious Historian; witness his "Lives of our English Kings, since the Conquest, until King Edward the Third;" wherein he hath the happiness to reconcile brevity with clearnesse, qualities of great distance in other Authours; a work since commendably continued (but not with equal quicknesse and judgment) by Mr. Trussell.—FULLER, THOMAS, 1662, *The Worthies of England, ed. Nichols, vol.* II, *p.* 288.

Samuel Daniel, an author of good note and reputation in King James his reign; whose History of the II first Kings of England from the Norman Conquest, though it be of all the rest of his works most principally sought after and regarded, yet are not his poetical writings totally forgotten.—PHILLIPS, EDWARD, 1675, *Theatrum Poetarum Anglicanorum, ed. Brydges, p.* 258.

However his Genius was qualified for Poetry, I take his History of *England* to be the *Crown* of all his Works.—LANGBAINE, GERARD, 1691, *An Account of the English Dramatick Poets, p.* 104.

Is deserving of some attention on account of its language. . . . It is true that the merits of Daniel are chiefly negative; he is never pedantic or antithetical or low, as his contemporaries were apt to be: but his periods are ill-constructed; he has little vigor or elegance; and it is only by observing how much pains he must have taken to reject phrases which were growing obsolete, that we give him credit for having done more than follow the common stream of easy writing. A slight tinge of archaism, and a certain majesty of expression, relatively to colloquial usage, were thought by Bacon and Raleigh congenial to an elevated style: but Daniel, a gentleman of the king's household, wrote as the court spoke; and his facility would be pleasing if his sentences had a less negligent structure. As an historian, he has recourse only to common authorities; but his narration is fluent and perspicuous, with a regular vein of good sense, more the characteristic of his mind, both in verse and prose, than any commanding vigor.—HALLAM, HENRY, 1837–39, *Introduction to the Literature of Europe, pt.* iii, *ch.* vii, *par.* 33.

As a branch of literature, English history in the new shape which we have noted began in the work of the poet Daniel. The chronicles of Stowe and Speed, who preceded him, are simple records of the past, often copied almost literally from the annals they used, and utterly without style or arrangement; while Daniel inaccurate and superficial as he is, gave his story a literary form, and embodied it in a pure and graceful prose.—GREEN, JOHN RICHARD, 1874, *A Short History of the English People, ch.* VII, *sec.* V.

GENERAL

And there is a new shepherd late up sprong,
The which doth all afore him far surpass:
Appearing well in that well-tuned song,
Which late he sung unto a scornful Lass.
Yet doth his trembling Muse but lowly fly,
As daring not too rashly mount on height,
And doth her tender plumes as yet but try
In love's soft lays and looser thoughts' delight.
Then rouse thy feathers quickly, Daniel,
And to what course thou please thyself advance:
But most, me seems, thy accent will excel
In tragic plaints and passionate mischance.

—SPENSER, EDMUND, 1595, *Colin Clout's Come Home Again.*

Let other countries (sweet Cambridge) envie (yet admire) my Virgil, thy Petrarch, divine *Spenser*. And unlesse I erre (a thing easie in such simplicitie) deluded by dearlie beloved *Delia*, and fortunatelie fortunate *Cleopatra*, Oxford thou maist extoll thy court-deare verse happie *Daniell*, whose sweete refined Muse, in contracted shape, were sufficient amongst men, to gaine pardon of the sinne to *Rosamond*, and euer-living praise to her loving Delia.—CLARKE, WILLIAM, 1595, *Polimanteia.*

The sweetest song-man of all English Swains.—CHETTLE, HENRY, 1603, *Englands Mourning Garment.*

Sweet hony dropping *Daniell* doth wage
Warre with the proudest big Italian,
That melts his heart in sugred sonneting.
Onely let him more sparingly make use
Of others wit, and use his owne the more:
That well may scorne base imitation.

—*Anon.*, 1606, *The Return from Parnassus, Act* I, *Sc.* 2.

I know I shall be read among the rest
So long as men speak English, and so long
As verse and virtue shall be in request,
Or grace to honest industry belong.

—DANIEL, SAMUEL, 1607, *Prefatory Verses to Edition of Poems.*

Well-languaged Daniel.—BROWNE, WILLIAM, 1613, *Britannia's Pastorals.*

The works of Samuel Daniel containe somewhat aflat, but yet withal a very pure and copious English, and words as warrantable as any mans, and fitter perhaps for prose than measure.—BOLTON, EDMUND, 1624, *Hypercritica.*

Amongst these Samuel Daniel, whom if I
May speak of, but to censure do deny,
Only have heard some wise men him rehearse,
To be too much historian in verse:
His rimes were smooth, his metres well did close,
But yet his manner better fitted prose.

—DRAYTON, MICHAEL, C 1627, *Of Poets and Poesie.*

Mr. *Daniel's* Works are very various, and consist of History, Plays, and Poems; in all which he appears to me a Person of great Good-Sense, and unbiass'd Integrity; both Clear, and Concise in his Expression; rather too simple and void of Ornament, and not comparable in his Numbers either to *Fairfax* or *Spencer;* But, on the whole, highly worthy of Esteem and Reputation.—COOPER, ELIZABETH, 1737, *The Muses' Library, p.* 382.

The Atticus of his day.—HEADLEY, HENRY, 1787, *Select Beauties of Ancient English Poetry, vol.* I, *p.* xlii.

Daniel's sonnets are very beautiful. His "Civil Wars" are rather distinguished by elegance than sublimity of expression; but they contain many curious and some highly poetical passages. His prose "History of England" was once much esteemed for the purity and conciseness of its style. Headley considers him as the Atticus of his day.—ELLIS, GEORGE, 1790-1845, *Specimens of the Early English Poets, vol.* II, *p.* 278.

Daniel is "*somewhat* a-*flat*," as one of his contemporaries said of him, but he had more sensibility than Drayton, and his moral reflection rises to higher dignity. —CAMPBELL, THOMAS, 1819, *An Essay on English Poetry.*

In Daniel's Sonnets there is scarcely one good line; while his "Hymen's Triumph," of which Chalmers says not one word, exhibits a continued series of first-rate beauties in thought, passion, and imagery, and in language and metre is so faultless, that the style of that poem may without extravagance be declared to be imperishable English.—COLERIDGE, SAMUEL TAYLOR, 1820, *Miscellanies, p.* 293.

Certainly an unconquerable Alp of weariness, his tragedies would have delighted Voltaire: they are a good deal worse than "Cato."—BEDDOES, THOMAS LOVELL, 1824, *Letters, p.* 5.

Daniel frequently wrote below his subject and his strength, but always in a strain of tender feeling, and in language as easy and natural as it is pure. For his diction alone he would deserve to be studied by all students or lovers of poetry, even if his works did not abound with passages of singular beauty. Thoughtful, grateful, right-minded and gentle-hearted, there is no poet in our language of whom it may be affirmed with more certainty, from his writings, that he was an amiable and wise and good man.—SOUTHEY, ROBERT, 1831, *Select Works of the British Poets from Chaucer to Jonson.*

Daniel was unquestionably one of the most skilful versifiers of his day, and in general his pen was guided by good taste, and by just if not strong feeling.—COLLIER, JOHN PAYNE, 1831, *History of English Dramatic Poetry, vol.* III, *p.* 249.

If he avoided the pedantry and quaintness which were too apt to vitiate the style of the period, and wrote what might be called modern English, it has still been found that modern Englishmen cannot be coaxed into reading what is so lucidly written. His longest work, a versified History of the Civil Wars, dispassionate as a chronicle and unimpassioned as a poem, is now only read by those critics in whom the sense of duty is victorious over the disposition to doze. The best expressions of his pensive, tender, and thoughtful nature are his epistles and his sonnets. Among the epistles, that to the Countess of Cumberland is the best. It is a model for all adulatory addresses to women; indeed, a masterpiece of subtile compliment; for it assumes in its object a sympathy with whatever is noblest in sentiment, and an understanding of whatever is most elevated in thought.—WHIPPLE, EDWIN P., 1859-68, *The Literature of the Age of Elizabeth, p.* 223.

His verse, too, always careful and exact, is in many passages more than smooth; even in his dramatic writings (which, having nothing dramatic about them except the form, have been held in very small estimation) it is frequently musical and sweet, though always artificial. The highest quality of his poetry is a tone of quiet, pensive reflection in which he is fond of indulging, and which often rises to dignity and eloquence, and has at times even something of depth and originality. . . . In his narrative poetry, Daniel is in general wire-drawn, flat, and feeble. He has no passion, and very little descriptive power. His "Civil Wars" has certainly as little of martial animation in it as any poem in the language.—CRAIK, GEORGE L., 1861, *A Compendious History of English Literature and of the English Language, vol.* I, *pp.* 557, 558.

He did indeed refine our tongue, and deserved the praise his contemporaries concur in giving him of being "well-languaged." Writing two hundred and fifty years ago, he stands in no need of a glossary, and I have noted scarce a dozen words, and not more turns of phrase, in his works, that have become obsolete. This certainly indicates both remarkable taste and equally remarkable judgment. There is a conscious dignity in his thought and sentiment such as we rarely meet. His best poems always remind me of a table-land, where, because all is so level, we are apt to forget on how lofty a plane we are standing. I think his "Musophilus" the best poem of its kind in the language. The reflections are natural, the expression condensed, the thought weighty, and the language worthy of it. But he also wasted himself on an historical poem, in which the characters were incapable of that remoteness from ordinary associations which is essential to the ideal. Not that we can escape into the ideal by *merely* emigrating into the past or the unfamiliar. As in the German legend the little black Kobold of prose that haunts us in the present will seat himself on the first load of furniture when we undertake our flitting, if the magician be not there to exorcise him. No man can jump off his own shadow, nor, for that matter, off his own age, and it is very likely that Daniel had only the thinking and languaging parts of a poet's outfit, without the higher creative gift which alone can endow his conceptions with enduring life and with an interest which transcends the parish limits of his generation.—LOWELL, JAMES RUSSELL, 1875–90, *Spenser, Prose Works, Riverside ed., vol.* IV, *p.* 280.

A better instance could not be chosen than this "Cleopatra," to prove the impotence in England of the pseudo-classic style. Daniel's tragedy bore points of strong resemblance to the work of contemporary French playwrights. But it hardly needed the fierce light from Cleopatra's dying hours in Shakspere's play to pale its ineffectual fires.—SYMONDS, JOHN ADDINGTON, 1884, *Shakspere's Predecessors in the English Drama, p.* 223.

The poetical value of Daniel may almost be summed up in two words—sweetness and dignity. He is decidedly wanting in strength, and, despite "Delia," can hardly be said to have had a spark of passion. Even in his own day it was doubted whether he had not overweighted himself with his choice of historical subjects, though the epithet of "well-languaged," given to him at the time, evinces a real comprehension of one of his best claims to attention. No writer of the period has such a command of pure English, unadulterated by xenomania and unweakened by purism, as Daniel. Whatever unfavourable things have been said of him from time to time have been chiefly based on the fact that his chaste and correct style lacks the fiery quaintness, the irregular and audacious attraction of his contemporaries. Nor was he less a master of versification than of vocabulary. His "Defence of Rhyme" shows that he possessed the theory: all his poetical works show that he was a master of the practice. He rarely attempted and probably would not have excelled in the lighter lyrical measures. But in the grave music of the various elaborate stanzas in which the Elizabethan poets delighted, and of which the Spenserian, though the crown and flower, is only the most perfect, he was a great proficient, and his couplets and blank verse are not inferior.—SAINTSBURY, GEORGE, 1887, *History of Elizabethan Literature.*

Daniel's writings show, by many a touch, that he was well read in Italian. He has a refinement that rejects extravagant conceits, but to the finer influences of Italian literature he owes much of his grace. Restraint from prevalent excess brought Daniel's verse nearer to the style of a later generation that was deliberately putting such excess away.—MORLEY, HENRY, 1893, *English Writers, vol.* X, *p.* 307.

The almost unrelieved excision of all ornament and colour, the uniform stateliness, the lack of passion, which render Daniel admirable and sometimes even charming in a short poem, weary us in his long productions, and so invariably sententious is he that we are tempted to call him a Polonius among poets.—GOSSE, EDMUND, 1894, *The Jacobean Poets, p.* 13.

Such stories . . . prove Warner to have had a true, pathetic vein of poetry. His English is not how ever so good as that of "well-languaged Daniel," who, among tragedies and pastoral comedies, the noble series of sonnets to Delia and poems of pure fancy, wrote "The Complaint of Rosamond," far more poetical than his steadier, even prosaic "Civil Wars of York and Lancaster." Spenser saw in him a new "shepherd of poetry who did far surpass the rest," and Coleridge says that the style of his "Hymen's Triumph" may be declared "imperishable English." —BROOKE, STOPFORD A., 1896, *English Literature, p.* 121.

Pure in utterance, refined and meditative, and typical minor master of the closet lyric.—CARPENTER, FREDERIC IVES, 1897, *English Lyric Poetry,* 1500-1700, *Introduction, p.* xliv.

A most accomplished and conscientious artist in verse, who had a genuine, but mild, poetic nature. The care he took to revise his work is evidence of his conscience as a workman, and the fact that his changes were commonly for the better is proof of his judgment. It is mainly the beauty of his English which will cause him to be read for ever among the rest.—HANNAY, DAVID, 1898, *The Later Renaissance, p.* 215.

John Barclay

1582-1621

John Barclay, author of the "Argenis," was born in 1582, at Pont-a-Mousson in Lorraine, where his father, a Scot, was professor of Law. Owing, it is said, to persecution by the Jesuits, he came with his father to England about 1603, and either then or in 1605 published his "Euphormionis Satyricon," a politico-satirical romance, chiefly directed against the Jesuits, supplements to which were the second part (1607), the "Apologia" (1611,) and the "Icon Animorum" (1614). In 1616 he went to Rome, where he died, a good Catholic, in 1621. In the same year appeared his Latin political allegory, "Argenis," according to Cowper the "best romance that ever was written." There are three English versions, the last by Clara Reeve in 1772.—PATRICK AND GROOME, *eds.*, 1897, *Chambers's Biographical Dictionary, p.* 67.

In it the various forms of government are investigated, the causes of faction detected, and the remedies pointed out for most of the evils that can arise in a state. . . . It affords such a variety of entertainment, that every kind of reader may find in it something suitable to his own taste and disposition: the statesman, the philosopher, the soldier, the lover, the citizen, the friend of mankind, each may gratify his favourite propensity, while the reader who comes for his amusement only, will not go away disappointed.—REEVE, CLARA, 1772, *tr. The Phœnix, or the History of Polyarchus and Argenis, Preface.*

It is interesting in a high degree; richer in incident than can be imagined, full of surprises, which the reader never forestalls, and yet free from all entanglement and confusion. The style too appears to me to be such as would not dishonour Tacitus himself.—COWPER, WILLIAM, 1787, *Letter to Samuel Rose.*

The "Argenis" of Barclay, a son of the defender of royal authority against republican theories, is a Latin romance, superior perhaps to those after Cervantes, which the Spanish or French language could boast. It has indeed always been reckoned among political allegories. That the state of France in the last years of Henry III. is partially shadowed in it, can admit of no doubt: several characters are faintly veiled either by anagram or Greek translation of their names; but whether to avoid the insipidity of servile allegory, or to excite the reader by perplexity, Barclay has mingled so much of mere fiction with his story, that no attempts at a regular key to the whole work can be successful; nor in fact does the fable of this romance run in any parallel stream with real events. His object seems, in great measure, to have been the discussion of political questions in feigned dialogue. But, though in these we find no want of acuteness or good sense, they have not at present much novelty in our eyes; and though the style is really pleasing, or, as some have judged, excellent, and the incidents not ill contrived, it might be hard to go entirely through a Latin romance of 700 pages, unless indeed we had no alternative given but the perusal of the similar works in Spanish or French.—HALLAM, HENRY, 1837-39, *Introduction to the Literature of Europe, pt.* iii, *ch.* vii, *par.* 56.

We may be permitted to remind classical critics of the recorded opinion of Grotius:

"Gente Caledonius, Gallus natalibus hic est,
Romam Romano qui docet ore loqui."
"A Scot by blood,—and French by birth,—this man
At Rome speaks Latin as no Roman can."

—ALLIBONE, S. AUSTIN, 1854-58, *Dictionary of English Literature, vol.* I. *p.* 117.

Barclay is a writer of the highest merit, who has adapted the style of Petronius, elevated by the assiduous study of more dignified models, with signal success to the requirements of his own day. His "Satyricon" shows how completely at an early age he had appropriated the fascinating elegance of Petronius, while good taste or good morals kept his matter singularly pure considering his age and his vocation as a satirist. There is more of youthful vigour in the "Satyricon," more weight and finish in the "Argenis," which enjoys the further advantages of an interesting plot and a serious purpose. The "Satyricon" is partly autobiographical, partly based on his father's adventures, and one main object is the ridicule of persons individually obnoxious to him, such as the Duke of Lorraine, who figures under the name of Callion. The jesuits are attacked under the collective designation of Acignii; and the puritans, whom Barclay hardly liked better, are impersonated under the figure of Catharinus. In the "Argenis," though most of the characters are real personages, the merely personal element is less conspicuous; the author's purpose is graver, and his scope wider. He designed to admonish princes and politicians, and above all to denounce political faction and conspiracy, and show how they might be repressed. The League and the Gunpowder plot had evidently made a strong impression on his youthful mind. The valour and conduct of Archombrotus and Poliarchus (both representing Henry IV), the regal dignity and feminine weakness of Hyanisbe (Elizabeth), the presumptuous arrogance of Radirobanes (Philip II), are powerfully depicted. As a story, the work occasionally flags, but the style and the thoughts maintain the reader's interest. . . . His adherence to the catholic religion was probably the result of a sincere preference, but his writings are by no means those of a zealot. —GARNETT, RICHARD, 1885, *Dictionary of National Biography, vol.* III, *pp.* 163, 164.

The one remarkable romance of the period that may be claimed for England is the "Argenis" (1621), by John Barclay. Born in France of Scotch father and French mother, Barclay lived in France and in England, and finally migrated to Italy, where he wrote the "Argentis" in Latin. He is thus a real example of the man without a country. His romance was at once diffused through Europe in five Latin editions, and translations into English, French, Spanish, Italian, and Dutch. It is a medley. It resembles the "Arcadia" in its shipwrecks, pirates, and disguises. In its weighty parts, which recommended it to the learned, it discusses the problems of statecraft, and is thus affiliated to the "Utopia." But what gives it a date in the development of fiction is that it is "a stately fable in manner of a history." In it Barclay extends to prose romance the allegorical method of Spenser's "Faery Queen." . . . Barclay opened the way for a long line of French romances, which, beginning about 1625, extended through the following fifty years.—GROSS, WILBUR L., 1899, *Development of the English Novel, pp.* 14, 15.

Sir Henry Savile

1549-1622

Born at Bradley near Halifax, became fellow of Merton College, Oxford, travelled on the Continent (1578), was Queen Elizabeth's tutor in Greek and mathematics, became Warden of Merton in 1585, and Provost of Eton in 1596, and was knighted in 1604. In 1619 he founded chairs of Geometry and Astronomy at Oxford. His principal works are "Rerum Anglicarum Scriptores" (1596), containing the works of William of Malmesbury, Henry of Huntingdon, Roger Hoveden, and "Ingulph": "Commentaries concerning Roman Warfare" (1598); "Fower Bookes of the Histories" and the "Agricola" of Tacitus (1581); and a magnificent edition of St. Chrysostom (1610-13).—PATRICK AND GROOME, *eds.*, 1897, *Chambers's Biographical Dictionary, p.* 825.

The magasine of all learning.—MONTAGU, RICHARD, 1621, *Diatribæ.*

He was bred in Oxford, and at last became Warden of Merton Colledge, and also Provost of Eaton. Thus this skilfull Gardiner had at the same time a Nurcery of young Plants, and an Orchard of grown Trees, both flourishing under his carefull inspection. This worthy Knight carefully collected the best Copies of Saint Chrysostome, and imployed learned men to transcribe and make Annotations on them; which done, he fairly set it forth, on his own cost, in a most beautifull Edition; a burden which he underwent without stooping under it, though the weight thereof would have broken the back of an ordinary person. But the Papists at Paris had their Emissaries in England, who surreptitiously procured this Knight's learned labours, and sent them over weekly by the Post into France, schedatim, sheet by sheet, as here they passed the Press. Then Fronto Duceus (a French Cardinall as I take it) caused them to be printed there with implicite faith and blind obedience, letter for letter, as he received them out of England, onely joyning thereunto a Latine translation and some other inconsiderable Additions. Thus two Editions of Saint Chrysostome did together run a race in the world, which should get the speed of the other in publique sale and acceptance. Sir Henry's Edition started first by the advantage of some Months. But the Parisian Edition came up close to it, and advantaged with the Latine Translation (though dearer of price) out-stript it in quickness of sale; but of late the Savilian Chrysostome hath much mended its pace, so that very few are left of the whole impression.—FULLER, THOMAS, 1662, *The Worthies of England, ed. Nichols, vol.* II, *p.* 516.

Many are the encomiums given of him by divers authors, which, if I should enumerate, may make a manual. . . . Aubrey also informs us that he was an extraordinary handsome man; no lady had a finer complexion. — WOOD, ANTHONY, 1691–1721, *Athenæ Oxonienses.*

We may justly deem him the most learned Englishman, in profane literature, of the reign of Elizabeth. . . . No edition of a Greek author published in the first part of the seventeenth century is superior, at least in magnificence, to that of "Chrysostom" by Sir Henry Savile. This came forth, in 1612, from a press established at Etòn by himself, provost of that college. He had procured types and pressmen in Holland, and three years had been employed in printing the eight volumes of this great work; one which, both in splendour of execution and in the erudition displayed in it by Savile, who had collected several manuscripts of "Chrysostom," leaves immeasurably behind it every earlier production of the English press.—HALLAM, HENRY, 1837–39, *Introduction to the Literature of Europe, pt.* ii, *ch.* i, *par.* 50, *pt.* iii, *ch.* i, *par.* 8.

Almost the only great work in the department of ancient scholarship that appeared in England in the reigns of James I. and Charles I. was the magnificent edition of Chrysostom.—CRAIK, GEORGE L., 1861, *A Compendious History of English Literature and of The English Language, vol.* II, *p.* 85

William Camden

1551–1623

William Camden, son of Samson Camden, a paper-stainer, was born in London, 2nd May 1551. He was educated at Christ's Hospital and at St. Paul's School; and in 1566 proceeded to Magdalen College, Oxford. He successively removed to Broadgate Hall (Pembroke College) and Christ Church, was refused a bachelor's degree when he left the university in 1570, but took it on his return to Oxford in 1573. In 1575 he became second master of Westminster School. Soon after this Camden began to collect materials for a great work on the antiquities of England, which resulted, in 1586, in the publication of his "Britannia." He became head-master of Westminster in March 1593, an office which he resigned in 1597 on being made Clarenceux King-at-Arms. In 1603 he published at Frankfort a collection of the works of the ancient English historians. In 1607 a fall from his horse invalided him for many months, and in 1609 his health was further impaired by a dangerous indisposition. In spite of these and successive severe illnesses, Camden continued his indefatigable labours. In 1622 he founded the Camden professorship of Ancient History at Oxford. He died in his house at Chiselhurst, in Kent, on 9th November 1623, and was buried with full heraldic honours in Westminster Abbey.—CRAIK, HENRY, 1893, *ed., English Prose, vol.* I, *p.* 499.

GENERAL

Cambden! the nourice of antiquitie
  And lanterne unto late succeeding age,
To see the light of simple veritie
  Buried in ruinse, through the great outrage
  Of her own people led with warlike rage:
Cambden! though Time all moniments obscure,
Yet thy just labours ever shall endure.

—SPENSER, EDMUND, 1591, *The Ruines of Time.*

The rat is not so contemptible but he may help the lion, at a pinch, out of those nets wherein his strength is hampered; and the words of an inferior may often carry matter in them to admonish his superior of some important consideration; and surely, of what account soever I might have seemed to this learned man, yet, in respect to my profession and courteous offer, (I being an officer-of-arms, and he then but a schoolmaster), might well have vouchsafed the perusal of my notes. . .

His incongruity in his principles of heraldry—for which I challenge him!—for depriving some nobles of issue to succeed them, who had issue, of whom are descended many worthy families: denying barons and earls that were, and making barons and earls of others that were not; mistaking the son for the father, and the father for the son; affirming legitimate children to be illegitimate, and illegitimate to be legitimate; and framing incestuous and unnatural marriages, making the father to marry the son's wife, and the son his own mother.—BROOKE, RALPH, 1625–1724? *Second Discovery of Errors.*

He lies buried in the South cross-aisle of Westminster Abbey, his effigies ½ on an altar, with this inscription:—

Qui fide antiqua et opera assidua
Britannicam antiquitatem indagavit
Simplicitatem innatam
honestis studiis excoluit
Animi solertiam candore illustravit
Gulielmus Camdenius
ab Elizabetha regina ad regis armorum
(Clarentii titulo) dignitatem evocatus
Hic
Spe certa resurgendi in Christo
S. E.
Qui obiit anno Domini 1623, 9 Novembris,
Aetatis suae 74:

in his hand a booke, on the leaves whereof is writt BRITANNIA.—AUBREY, JOHN, 1669–96, *Brief Lives, ed. Clark, vol.* I, *p.* 145.

The glory of this queen's reign, as well as her successor's, and the prince of our English antiquaries, was Mr. Camden, whose life has been written at large by Dr. Smith, Mr. Wood, and Dr. Gibson. So that I need not here mention any of its particulars. His Britannia is the book which chiefly respects the subject of this chapter; and may honestly be stiled the common sun, whereat our modern writers have all lighted their little torches.—NICOLSON, WILLIAM, 1696–1714, *English Historical Library, ch.* i.

Camden's "History of Queen Elizabeth" may be esteemed good composition, both for style and matter. It is written with simplicity of expression, very rare in that age, and with a regard to truth. It would not, perhaps, be too much to affirm, that it is among the best historical productions which have yet been composed by any Englishman. It is well known that the English have not much excelled in that kind of literature.—HUME, DAVID, 1755–62, *The History of England, James I., Appendix.*

This English Pausanius, as he has been called, took unwearied pains to celebrate all that was worthy, valiant, and great in the annals of his country; and, at the same time he excited emulation in young minds, he formed them for great undertakings; for he was master of Westminster school, whence have issued so many divines, lawyers, warriors, and statesmen. His opinions were proudly looked up to, and his learning, his judgment, his universal knowledge, and the discharge of his professional duties, procured him the protection of his sovereign, the association of the great, and the admiration of the literari, who dignified him by the appellation of the great Camden.—DIBDIN, CHARLES, 1795, *A Complete History of the Stage, vol.* III, *p.* 139.

Camden possessed one of those strongly directed minds which early in life plan some vast labour, while their imagination and their industry feed on it for many successive years; and they shed the flower and sweetness of their lives in the preparation of a work which at its maturity excites the gratitude of their nation. His passion for our national antiquities discovered itself even in his school-days, grew up with him at the University; and, when afterwards engaged in his public duties as master at Westminster school, he there composed his "Britannia," "at spare hours, and on festival days." To the perpetual care of his work, he voluntarily sacrificed all other views in life, and even drew himself away from domestic pleasures; for he refused marriage and preferments, which might interrupt his beloved studies! The work at length produced, received all the admiration due to so great an enterprise; and even foreigners, as the work was composed in the universal language of learning, could sympathise with Britons, when they contemplated the stupendous labour. Camden was honoured by the titles (for the very names of illustrious genius become such), of the Varro, the Strabo, and the Pausanias of Britain.—DISRAELI, ISAAC, 1812–13, *Camden and Brooke, Quarrels of Authors.*

William Camden, now scarcely thought of except as an antiquary, was in truth a trained and ripe scholar, and an intelligent student of history. England has more reason to be proud of him than of many whose names are more familiar to our ears. The man who won the friendship of the president De Thou, and corresponded on equal terms with that eminent historian, as also with Casaubon and Lipsius abroad, and Usher and Spelman at home, must have possessed solid and extraordinary merits. . . . In 1604 he published his "Reliquiæ Britannicæ," a treatise on the early inhabitants of Britain. In this work, undeterred by the sham array of authorities which had imposed upon Holinshed, he "blew away sixty British kings with one blast." Burleigh, the great statesman of the reign of Elizabeth, the Cavour of the sixteenth century, singled out Camden as the fittest man in all England to write the history of the first thirty years of the Queen's reign, and intrusted to him, for that purpose, a large mass of state papers. Eighteen years elapsed before Camden discharged the trust. At last, in 1615, his "History, or Annals of England during the Reign of Queen Elizabeth" made its appearance. . . . His history must be taken as a vindication, but in a more moderate tone than was then usual, of the Protestant policy of England since the accession of Elizabeth. Its value would be greater than it is, but for his almost uniform neglect to quote his authorities for the statements he makes. This fact, coupled to the discovery, in our own times, of many new and independent sources of information, to him unknown, has caused his labours to be much disregarded.—ARNOLD, THOMAS, 1868–75, *Chaucer to Wordsworth, pp.* 125, 126.

Camden, who has been described as the Strabo of England, is charged by Birch with suppressing and colouring the events of Elizabeth's reign; but Camden's high reputation as a historian requires no vindication against the false statements of the Puritan, Thomas Birch. If Camden is not always correct, he certainly has not made any intentional misrepresentation of facts.—BURKE, S. HUBERT, 1883, *Historical Portraits of the Tudor Dynasty and the Reformation Period, vol.* IV, *p.* 97.

Camden appears to have been of a peculiarly happy temperament. His gentleness of disposition made and kept him many friends. He was active in body, of middle height, of a pleasant countenance, and as his portraits, taken when he was well advanced in life, present him, of a ruddy complexion. He was careless of ordinary personal distinction, and refused knighthood. "I never made suit to any man," he writes in his letter to Ussher in 1618 (ep. 195), "no, not to his majesty, but for a matter of course, incident to my place; neither, God be praised, I needed, having gathered a contented sufficiency by my long labours in the school." And again, his own words, "My life and my writings apologise for me" (ep. 194), might have been adopted as his motto. Among his intimate friends Smith enumerates Sir Robert Cotton, Bishop Godwin, Matthew Sutcliffe, Sir Henry Savile, Sir Henry Wotton, Archbishop Ussher, Sir Henry Bourghchier, Sir Henry Spelman, and John Selden. In addition, his printed correspondence connects him with Thomas Savile, who died early (1592), Degory Wheare, John Johnstone of St. Andrews, Sir William Beecher the diplomatist, and many other Englishmen; and Ortelius, James Gruter, the librarian of the Elector Palatine, the historian and statesman, Jaques de Thou, Casaubon, Peter Sweerts, Peiresc, Jean Hotman, once Leicester's secretary, and others.—THOMPSON, E. MAUNDE, 1886, *Dictionary of National Biography, vol.* VIII, *p.* 283.

Yet although Camden is one of the glories of Oxford, of Westminster, and of all England, it does not appear that he can very safely be claimed as one of the glories of English prose. In a work like the present, which deals rather with the development of English prose style than with anything else, it may indeed be doubtful whether an Englishman who wrote splendidly, but wrote almost exclusively in Latin, has any claim to appear at all. If we give him a small niche here, it is mainly complimentary, and to avoid the apparent solecism of entirely omitting him. . . . Very little can be conjectured from the fragments of Camden as to the manner in which he would have used the English language if he had chosen to make it the habitual instrument for his thought.—GOSSE, EDMUND, 1893, *English Prose, ed. Craik, vol.* I. *pp.* 499, 500.

Giles Fletcher

1588?-1623

(Brother of Phineas Fletcher.) Born, probably in London, about 1588. Probably educated at Westminster School. To Cambridge, 1602 (?). Scholar of Trinity College, Cambridge, 12 April 1605; B. A., 1606; Minor Fellow of Trinity College, 17 Sept. 1608. Reader in Greek Grammar, 1615; Reader in Greek Language, 1618. Ordained, 1618. Rector of Alderton, Suffolk. Died, 1623. *Works:* "Christ's Victorie and Triumph," 1610; "The Reward of the Faithfull," 1623; "Licia" (anon.), (1593). *Collected Poems:* ed. by A.B. Grosart, 1868.—SHARP, R. FARQUHARSON, 1897, *A Dictionary of English Authors, p.* 100.

The Spenser of this age.—QUARLES, FRANCIS, 1633, *Poems.*

Equally beloved of the muses and graces.—WOOD, ANTHONY, 1691-1721, *Athanæ Oxonensis.*

A poem ["Christ's Victory"] rich and picturesque, and on a much happier subject than that of his brother, yet unenlivened by personification.—HEADLEY, HENRY, 1787, *Select Beauties of Ancient English Poetry.*

Giles, inferior as he is to Spenser and Milton, might be figured, in his happiest moments, as a link of connection in our poetry between those congenial spirits, for he reminds us of both, and evidently gave hints to the latter in a poem on the same subject with "Paradise Regained."—CAMPBELL, THOMAS, 1819, *Specimens of the British Poets.*

Giles seems to have more vigor than his elder brother, but less sweetness, less smoothness, and more affectation in his style. This indeed, is deformed by words neither English nor Latin, but simply barbarous; such as *elamping, eblazon, deprostrate, purpured, glitterand,* and many others. They both bear much resemblance to Spenser. Giles sometimes ventures to cope with him, even in celebrated passages, such as the description of the Cave of Despair. And he has had the honor, in turn, of being followed by Milton, especially in the first meeting of our Saviour with Satan, in the "Paradise Regained." Both of these brothers are deserving of much praise: they were endowed with minds eminently poetical, and not inferior in imagination to any of their contemporaries. But an injudicious taste, and an excessive fondness for a style which the public was rapidly abandoning,—that of allegorical personification, — prevented their powers from being effectively displayed.—HALLAM, HENRY, 1837-39, *Introduction to the Literature of Europe, pt.* iii.

His poem of "Christ's Victory and Triumph," in parts almost sublime, in parts almost puerile, is a proof that imaginative fertility may exist in a mind with little imaginative grasp. Campbell, however, considers him a connecting link between Spenser and Milton.—WHIPPLE, EDWIN P., 1859-68, *The Literature of the Age of Elizabeth, p.* 222.

The intensity of the Poets' own Love and Faith, Hope and Graciousness lies over his Poem—like a bar of sunlight—as one has seen such shattering itself in dazzling glory against a heath-purpled mountain-side. In unexpected turns, in equally unexpected places, you are reminded that you have no mere Singer working artistically but a "Saint"—in the Bible not Mediæval-Papistical meaning—pouring out the glad Worship of his whole nature—a nature rich of faculty in itself and enriched with celestial riches. This inworking into the very "stuff" of his Poem, of his own personality—imparts a tender humanness to it: and came of that brave self-estimate or in another sense fine naturalness, which belongs to the greatest of our great names among those who have insight, — SHAKESPEARE, and touchingly BACON, MILTON, SIR THOMAS BROWNE. Approve or condemn, accept or reject, it is something to feel as you read that a man's own warm blood, not the mere ink of his pen, flows and thrills through his book.—GROSART, ALEXANDER B., 1869, *ed. Poems of Phineas Fletcher, Essay on the Poetry of the Fletchers, vol.* I, *p.* clxxiv.

There is a massive grandeur and earnestness about "Christ's Victory" which strikes the imagination.—CHAMBERS, ROBERT, 1876, *Cyclopædia of English Literature, ed. Carruthers.*

Giles Fletcher is eminently a religious poet—in the technical sense of the word, as happily also in the more general sense. He deals with Christian themes: "Christ's

Victory in Heaven," "Christ's Victory on Earth," "Christ's Triumph over Death," "Christ's Triumph after Death;" and it is his special distinction, that in handling such themes he does not sink into a mere rhyming dogmatist, but writes with a genuine enthusiasm and joy. . . Giles Fletcher's success as a "religious" poet, so far as he succeeds, is due first to the selection of themes which he makes, and secondly to the genuine religious ardour that inspired him. He delighted to contemplate the career of the central Hero of his Christian faith and love—His ineffable self-sacrifice, His leading captivity captive, His complete and irreversible triumph. That career he conceived and beheld vividly and intensely with a pure unalloyed acceptance; it thrilled and inspired him with a real passion of worship and delight. So blissfully enthralled and enraptured, what else could he sing of? His heart was hot within him; while he was musing, the fire burned; then spake he with his tongue. It was the tongue of one highly cultured and accomplished, of a rich and clear imagination, with a natural gift of eloquence, with a fine sense of melody, and metrical skill to express it.—HALES, JOHN W., 1880, *English Poets, ed. Ward, vol.* II, *pp.* 104, 105.

Fletcher tells the story of Christ's life with many digressions, and concludes with an affectionate reference to the poetic work of his brother Phineas, whom he calls "Young Thyrsilis." His admiration of Spenser is very apparent. Allegorical descriptions of vices and virtues abound in his poem. There is a wealth of effective imagery, with which the occasional simplicity of some passages descriptive of natural scenery contrasts attractively. But exaggerated Spenserian characteristics mar the success of the work as a whole.—LEE, SIDNEY, 1889, *Dictionary of National Biography, vol.* XIX, *p.* 302.

"Licia" is what a typical sonnet-cycle ought to be, a delicate and almost intangible thread of story on which are strung the separate sonnet-pearls. In this case the jewels have a particular finish. Fletcher has adopted the idea of a series of quatrains, often extending the number to four, and a concluding couplet, which he seems fond of utilising to give an epigrammatic finish to the ingenious incident he so often makes the subject of the sonnet. He is fully in the spirit of the Italian mode, however, acknowledging in his title page his indebtedness to poets of other nationalities than his own.—CROW, MARTHA FOOTE, 1896, *ed. Elizabethan Sonnet-Cycles, Licia, p.* 82.

He was the author of the finest religious poem produced in English literature between the "Vision of Piers Plowman" and "Paradise Lost." In several passages of his fourfold "Christ's Victory and Truimph" (1610) Giles Fletcher solved the difficult problem of how to be at once gorgeous and yet simple, majestic and yet touching. At his apogee he surpasses his very master, for his imagination lifts him to a spiritual sublimity. In the beatific vision in his fourth canto we are reminded of no lesser poem than the "Paradiso." It is right to say that these splendours are not sustained, and that Giles Fletcher is often florid and sometimes merely trivial. The sonorous purity and elevation of Giles Fletcher at his best give more than a hint of the approaching Milton, and he represents the Spenserian tradition at its very highest.—GOSSE, EDMUND, 1897, *Short History of Modern English Literature, p.* 121.

Thomas Lodge

1558?-1625

Born, in London, 1558(?). At Merchant Taylors' School, March, 1570 to 1573(?). To Trinity College, Oxford, as Servitor, 1573(?); B. A., 8 July 1577; M. A., 3 Feb. 1581. Student of Lincoln's Inn, 26 April 1578. Devoted himself to literature. Married (i.) Joan——, 1583. Tragedy, "The Wounds of Civill War," produced, 1587(?); "A Looking Glasse for London and England" (written with Greene), produced 8 March 1592. Possibly wrote other plays with Greene. Visited Canaries, 1588–89(?); South America, 1591–93. Moved from London to Low Leyton, Essex, 1596; began to study medicine. M. D., Avignon, 1600. M. D., Oxford, 25 Oct., 1602. Licentiate, College of Physicians, 1610. Practised in London. Travelled frequently on Continent. Married (ii.) Jane Aldred. Died, in London, Sept. (?) 1625. *Works:* "Defence of Plays," 1580(?); "An Alarum against Usurers," 1584; "Scillaes Metamorphysis," 1589 (later edn., called: "A most pleasant historie of Glaucus and Scilla," 1610); "Rosalynde" (anon.), 1590; "Robert, second Duke of Normandy," 1591; "Catharos" (anon.), 1591; "Euphues Shadow" (anon.), 1592; "Phillis," 1593; "Life and death of William Longbeard" (anon.), 1593; "The Wounds of Civill War," 1594; "A Looking Glasse for London" (with Greene), 1594; "A Fig for Momus" (anon.), 1595; "The Divel Conjured" (anon.), 1596; "A Margarite of America," 1596; "Wits Miserie," 1596; "Prosopopeia," 1596; "Paradoxes" (anon.), 1602; "A Treatise of the Plague," 1603. He *translated:* Josephus' Works, 1602; Seneca's Works, 1614; "A Learned Summary of Du Bartas," 1625. *Collected Works:* ed. by E. Gosse, with *memoir*, 1878-82.—SHARP, R. FARQUHARSON, 1897, *A Dictionary of English Authors, p.* 172.

ROSALYNDE
1590

Placing Lodge's novel by the side of other productions of the same class, we cannot hesitate to declare it a very amusing and varied composition, full of agreeable and graceful invention (for we are aware of no foreign authority for any of the incidents), and with much natural force and simplicity in the style of the narrative. That it is here and there disfigured by the faults of the time, by forced conceits, by lowness of allusion and expression, and sometimes by inconsistency and want of decorum in the characters, cannot be denied. These are errors which the judgment and genius of Shakespeare taught him to avoid; but the admitted extent and nature of his general obligations to Lodge afford a high tribute to the excellence of that "original," which Steevens pronounced "worthless."—COLLIER, JOHN PAYNE, 1843, *Shakespeare's Library, Introduction to Lodge's Rosalynd, vol.* I.

The last work of fiction of any importance which distinctly bears the impress of euphuism. . . . It is probably the only work of fiction of Elizabeth's time which could be read through at the present day without impatience.—TUCKERMAN, BAYARD, 1882, *A History of English Prose Fiction, p.* 88.

Lodge was a true poet, though his path was on the lower slopes of Parnassus, and his "Rosalynde" has much natural beauty that is in some sense heightened by the artifices of its style.—MORLEY, HENRY, 1893, *English Writers, vol.* X, *p.* 61.

If Sidney had no followers in the line of ideal fiction, he had at least a rival with the novel readers of the time in the person of Thomas Lodge. The latter's "Rosalind," which appeared about the same time as the "Arcadia," resembles the latter in its essence, being an attempt to fuse in one narrative the best features of the heroic and pastoral school of fiction. It is possible that Lodge may have received some useful hints from the efforts of Sidney, but at all events his story is more compact, more logical, and consequently more readable. Certain situations of the romances of chivalry are here repeated and the pastoral notion of the heroine's disguise in man's dress plays a prominent part in the plot.—WARREN, F. M., 1895, *A History of the Novel Previous to the Seventeenth Century, p.* 338.

Lodge's (Thomas) "Rosalynde," 1598. Longman (1815), £20 (imperfect). Heber, £5, 10s. Ouvry (1882), £63.—WHEATLEY, HENRY B., 1898, *Prices of Books, p.* 219

GENERAL

To the Gentlemen Readers, Health. Gentlemen, after many of mine owne labours that you have courteouslie accepted, I present you with *Euphues shadowe*, in the behalfe of my absent friend, M. Thomas Lodge, who at his departure to sea upon a long voyage, was willing, as a generall farewell to all courteous Gentlemen, to leave this his worke to the view, which if you grace with your favours eyther as his affected meaning, or the worthe of the worke requires, not onely I for him shall rest yours, but what laboures his Sea studies affords, shall be, I dare promise, offered to your sight, to gratifie your courtesies, and his pen, as himselfe every waye yours for ever. Farewell.—GREENE, ROBERT, 1592, *ed. Euphues Shadow.*

And thou, my Goldey, which in Sommer dayes
Has feasted us with merry roundelayes;
And, when my Muse scarce able was to flye,
Didst imp her wings with thy sweete Poesie.

—DRAYTON, MICHAEL, 1594, *Endimion and Phœbe.*

Lodge for his oare in every paper boate,
He that turns over *Galen* every day,
To sit and simper *Euphues* legacy.

—ANON., 1606, THE RETURN FROM PARNASSUS, *Act* 1, *Sc.* 2.

Lodge and Greene are the only imitators of Lyly who have atoned for affectation of style by any felicity of genius or invention.—DUNLOP, JOHN, 1814-45, *The History of Fiction.*

As a poet, Lodge is to be placed in a rank superior to Greene, and in some respects inferior to Kyd. Greene's love of natural beauty was overlaid by a mass of affectation and conceit, which rarely allowed it to appear, and to a certain degree he was imitated by Lodge, with whom he was intimate, and with whom he wrote one dramatic performance. The love of natural beauty in Lodge, however, breaks through the fanciful allusions and artificial ornaments with which he endeavoured to adapt himself to the taste of the time. —COLLIER, JOHN PAYNE, 1831, *History of English Dramatic Poetry, vol.* III, *p.* 213.

One of the best poets of the age.—HALLAM, HENRY, 1842, *Introduction to the Literature of Europe, pt.* ii, *ch.* vi, *par.* 33, *note.*

His lines ["Wounds of Civil War"] possess not the slightest approach to flexibility; they invariably consist of ten syllables, with a pause at the end of every line—"each alley like its brother;" the ocasional use of the triplet is the only variety. Lodge's tragedy has the appearance of a most correct and laboured performance; and the result is that of insufferable tediousness.—KNIGHT, CHARLES, 1849, *Studies of Shakspere, bk.* i, *ch.* vi, *p.* 30.

In considering Lodge's literary character, it may be remarked that he belongs to a class of writers, the Greenes, Lylys, Marlowes, and Peeles, displaying poetical and dramatic genius, not indeed of the highest order, but from the versatility of their talents, and the early period in which they flourished, as the precursors of our greater English dramatists, not likely to be soon forgotten.—LAING, DAVID, 1853, *ed. A Defence of Poetry, etc., Introduction, p.* lviii.

Lodge's love-poems have an exquisite delicacy and grace: they breathe a tenderer and truer passion than we find in any of his contemporaries. His sonnets are more loose and straggling, slighter and less compactly built, than Constable's or Daniel's; but they have a wonderful charm of sweet fancy and unaffected tenderness. His themes are the usual praises of beauty and complaints of unkindness; but he contrives to impart to them a most unusual air of sincere devotion and graceful fervour. None of his rivals can equal the direct and earnest simplicity and grace of his adoration of Phyllis, and avowal of faith in her constancy. . . . There is a seeming artlessness in Lodge's sonnets, a winning directness, that constitutes a great part of their charm. They seem to be uttered through a clear and pure medium straight from the heart: their tender fragrance and music come from the heart itself. If the poet's design was to assume a pastoral innocence and simplicity, he has eminently succeeded. There are many conceits in his sonnets, but they are expressed so simply and naturally that they take on the semblance of half-earnest beliefs. . . . It may, however, be acknowledged that Lodge's nature was not specially fitted for the sonnet form of composition; he was not sufficiently patient and meditative to elaborate intricate stanzas. His lines have on them the dewy freshness of an impulsive gush,—a freshness off which the dew has not been brushed by the travail of thought; and the opening of his sonnets in many cases leads us to expect better things than we find as we proceed when the leading idea has been hammered out into a quatorzain. . . . Lodge's "Fig for Momus" is often amusing, but the satire is not very pungent. He was much too good-natured a man to be a satirist: he was not capable even of smiling spite, much less of bitter derision.—MINTO, WILLIAM, 1874-85, *Characteristics of English Poets, pp.* 198, 199, 202.

All the sonnets in the "Phillis," a work of the most tantalizing inequality, suffer more or less from Lodge's caprices of style; so that while only a necessary discretion is exercised in limiting the selection to a single sonnet, it has been too frequently at a sacrifice of beauties which one would fain pluck from their commonplace environment.—MAIN, DAVID M., 1879, *A Treasury of English Sonnets, p.* 260.

Lodge was the least boisterous of the noisy group of learned wits who, with

Greene and Marlowe at their head, invaded London from the universities during the close of Elizabeth's reign. . . . In some respects Lodge is superior to most of the lyrical poets of his time. He is certainly the best of the Euphuists, and no one rivalled him in the creation of a dreamy scene, "out of space, out of time," where the loves and jousts of an ideal chivalry could be pleasantly tempered by the tending of sheep. His romances, with their frequent interludes of fine verse, are delightful reading, although the action flags, and there is simply no attempt at characterisation. A very courtly and knightly spirit of morality perfumes the stately sentences, laden with learned allusion and flowing imagery; the lovers are devoted beyond belief, the knights are braver, the shepherds wiser, the nymphs more lovely and more flinty-hearted than tongue can tell. . . . Among all the Elizabethans, no one borrowed his inspiration more directly from the Italians than Lodge. . . . As a satirist Lodge is weak and tame; as a dramatist he is wholly without skill; as a writer of romances we have seen that he is charming, but thoroughly artificial. It is by his lyrical poetry that he preserves a living place in literature. His best odes and madrigals rank with the finest work of that rich age. In short pieces of an erotic or contemplative character he throws aside all his habitual languor, and surprises the reader, who has been toiling somewhat wearily through the forest of Arden, by the brilliance and rapidity of his verse, by the *elan* of his passion, and by the bright turn of his fancy. In his best songs Lodge shows a command over the more sumptous and splendid parts of language, that reminds the reader of Marlowe's gift in tragedy; and of all the Elizabethans Lodge is the one who most frequently recalls Shelley to mind.—GOSSE, EDMUND, 1880, *English Poets, ed. Ward, vol.* I, *pp.* 424, 425.

. . . Lodge, flushed from lyric bowers.
—SWINBURNE, ALGERNON CHARLES, 1882, *The Many.*

Lodge, indeed, as it seems to me, was one of the not uncommon persons who can always do best with a model before them. He euphuised with better taste than Lyly, but in imitation of him; his tales in prose are more graceful than those of Greene, whom he copied; it at least seems likely that he out-Marlowed Marlowe in the rant of the "Looking-Glass for London," and the stiffness of the "Wounds of Civil War," and he chiefly polished Sidney in his sonnets and madrigals. It is not to be denied, however, that in three out of these four departments he gave us charming work.—SAINTSBURY, GEORGE, 1887, *History of Elizabethan Literature, p.* 109.

If Lodge cannot be considered a man of genius, he is certainly a writer of very remarkable gifts.—JUSSERAND, J. J., 1890, *The English Novel in the Time of Shakespeare, p.* 204.

Of all Lodge's multifarious writings, his contributions to the drama form the least valuable portion.—COLLINS, JOHN C., 1895, *Essays and Studies, p.* 177.

For this name or ideal, or whatever Phillis represented in the poet's thought, he has poured forth a passion that has an air of sincerity, an artless freshness, a flute-like clearness of tone, as rare as delightful. It is the very voice of the oaten pipe itself, thin, clear, and pure. The touches of seriousness are impossible to mistake. . . . In spite of its defects, the lax structure of the sonnet-form, the obscurities and needless blurring, and the disappointing inequalities, "Phillis" takes a high place among the sonnet-cycles. —CROW, MARTHA FOOTE, 1896, *ed. Elizabethan Sonnet-Cycles, Phillis, pp.* 9, 10.

Lodge has suffered the fate of all poets who have thought of their style before their subject. He had a graceful fancy, a fine taste, and a tuneful ear, but his mind was not possessed by any idea of universal interest. He was first inspired to write by the atmosphere of prevailing Euphuism; most of his compositions—plays, novels, histories, sonnets, and satires—are steeped in this fashionable manner. For many of the subjects he attempted he had no turn. His dramas are written with a heavy hand; his satires are of that general kind which awakens no fear, and therefore no interest. The sonnet had long ceased to yield any fresh store of conceits; and the only novelties that Lodge could introduce into it for the glorification of his Phillis were double rhymes and fresh mechanical combinations of sound.—COURTHOPE, W. J., 1897, *A History of English Poetry, vol.* II, *p.* 322.

John Fletcher

1579–1625

Born, at Rye, Dec. 1579. Possibly "pensioner" of Corpus Coll., Camb., 1591; Bible-Clerk, 1593. Early intimacy with Francis Beaumont. Collaborated with him, 1605-14. Died, in London, Aug. 1625; buried at St. Saviour's Southwark, 29 Aug. *Works:* [For plays published under the joint names of Francis Beaumont and John Fletcher, *see supra:* Beaumont and Fletcher.] "The Faithful Shepherdess" [1609?]; "The Tragedy of Thierry, King of France" (anon.; possibly by Fletcher), 1621. *Posthumous:* "The Two Noble Kinsmen" (published in names of Fletcher and Shakespeare; probably by Fletcher [and Massinger?]), 1634; "The Elder Brother" (published in Fletcher's name; probably written with Beaumont), 1637; "Monsieur Thomas," 1639; "Wit Without Money" (published in Beaumont and Fletcher's names; probably by Fletcher), 1639; "Rule a Wife and Have a Wife," 1640; "The Coronation" (anon.), 1640; "The Night Walker" (with Shirley?), 1640.—SHARP, R. FARQUHARSON, 1897, *A Dictionary of English Authors, p.* 100.

PERSONAL

Meeting once in a Tavern, to contrive the rude draught of a Tragedy, Fletcher undertook to kill the King therein; whose words being overheard by a listener (though his Loyalty not to be blamed herein), he was accused of High Treason; till, the mistake soon appearing, that the plot was only against a Dramatick and Scenical King, all wound off in merriment. Nor could it be laid to Fletcher's charge, what Ajax doth to Ulysses:

> . . . Nihil hic *Diomede* remoto.
> "When *Diomede* was gone,
> He could do nought alone."

For, surviving his Partner, he wrote good Comedies himself, though inferiour to the former; and no wonder, if a single thread was not so strong as a twisted one. —FULLER, THOMAS, 1662, *The Worthies of England, ed. Nichols, vol.* II, *p.* 168.

Mr. John Fletcher, poet: in the great plague, 1625, a knight of Norfolk (or Suffolke) invited him into the countrey. He stayed but to make himself a suite of cloathes, and while it was makeing, fell sick of the plague and dyed. This I had (1688) from his tayler, who is now a very old man, and clarke of St. Mary Overy's. —AUBREY, JOHN, 1669–96, *Brief Lives, ed. Clark, vol.* I, *p.* 254.

Oldwit.—I knew Fletcher, my friend Fletcher, and his maid Joan; I shall never forget him; I have supped with him at his house on the Bankside; he loved a fat loin of pork of all things in the world; and Joan, his maid, had her beer-glass of sack, and we all kissed her; faith, and were as merry as passed.—SHADWELL, THOMAS, 1689, *Bury Fair, Act* i, *Scene* i.

A few years ago Fletcher's name and the date of his death were engraved upon a stone in the pavement of the choir of St. Saviour's, although the exact spot where his bones lie is not recorded.—HUTTON, LAURENCE, 1885, *Literary Landmarks of London, p.* 108.

THE FAITHFUL SHEPHERDESS

1609

> I, that am glad thy innocence was thy guilt,
> And wish that all the Muses' blood were spilt
> In such a martyrdom, to vex their eyes,
> Do crown thy murder'd poem: which shall rise
> A glorifièd work to time, when fire,
> Or moths shall eat what all these fools admire.

—JONSON, BEN, 1610, *To my worthy Author, Mr. John Fletcher upon his Faithful Shepherdess* .

If all the parts of this delightful pastoral had been in unison with its many innocent scenes and sweet lyric intermixtures, it had been a poem fit to vie with "Comus" or the "Arcadia," to have been put into the hands of boys and virgins, to have made matter for young dreams, like the loves of Hermia and Lysander. But a spot is on the face of this Diana. Nothing short of infatuation could have driven Fletcher upon mixing with this "blessedness" such an ugly deformity as Cloe, the wanton shepherdess! Coarse words do but wound the ears; but a character of lewdness affronts the mind. Female lewdness at once shocks nature and morality. If Cloe was meant to set off Clorin by contrast, Fletcher should have known that such weeds by juxtaposition do not set off but kill sweet flowers.—LAMB, CHARLES, 1808, *Specimens of Dramatic Poets.*

JOHN FLETCHER

From Engraving by H. Robinson.

The author has in it given a loose to his fancy, and his fancy was his most delightful and genial quality, where, to use his own words:—

"He takes most ease, and grows ambitious
Thro'his own wanton fire and pride delicious."

The songs and lyrical descriptions throughout are luxuriant and delicate in a high degree. He came near to Spenser in a certain tender and voluptuous sense of natural beauty; he came near to Shakespeare in the playful and fantastic expression of it. The whole composition is an exquisite union of dramatic and pastoral poetry; where the local descriptions receive a tincture from the sentiments and purposes of the speaker, and each character, cradled in the lap of Nature, paints "her virgin fancies wild" with romantic grace and classic elegance.—HAZLITT, WILLIAM, 1820, *Lectures on the Literature of the Age of Elizabeth, p.* 115.

"The Faithful Shepherdess," deservedly among the most celebrated productions of Fletcher, stands alone in its class, and admits of no comparison with any other play. . . . It is impossible to withhold our praise from the poetical beauties of this pastoral drama. Every one knows that it contains the germ of "Comus:" the benevolent Satyr, whose last proposition to "stray in the middle air, and stay the sailing rack, or nimbly take hold of the moon," is not much in the character of those sylvans, has been judiciously metamorphosed by Milton to an attendant spirit; and a more austere as well as more uniform language has been given to the speakers. But Milton has borrowed largely from the imagination of his predecessor; and, by quoting the lyric parts of the "Faithful Shepherdess," it would be easy to deceive any one not accurately familiar with the songs of "Comus." They abound with that rapid succession of ideal scenery, that darting of the poet's fancy from earth to heaven, those picturesque and novel metaphors, which distinguish much of the poetry of this age, and which are ultimately, perhaps, in great measure referable to Shakspeare.—HALLAM, HENRY, 1837–39, *Introduction to the Literature of Europe, p.* iii, *ch.* vi, *pars.* 76, 77.

Fletcher's volubility is against more than his metre: he seems often to throw his words at thoughts in the hope of hitting them off by hazard, but he misses them altogether. His light-headed shafts fall short of their mark. When they do touch, however, it is with the irradiating effect if not the force of thunderbolts: this has an inexpressible charm. After all we have heard of "The Faithful Shepherdess," a fine English Pastoral Drama remains to be written.—DARLEY, GEORGE, 1840, *ed. Works of Beaumont and Fletcher, Introduction, vol.* I, *p.* lii.

The melody, the romantic sweetness of fancy, the luxuriant and luxurious descriptions of nature, and the true lyric inspiration, of large portions of this drama, are not more striking than the deliberate desecration of its beauty by the introduction of impure sentiments and images. The hoof-prints of unclean beasts are visible all over Fletcher's pastoral paradise; and they are there by design. Why they are there is a question which can be answered only by pointing out the primal defect of Fletcher's mind, which was an incapacity to conceive or represent goodness and innocence except as the ideal opposites of evil and depravity. He took depravity as the positive fact of life, and then framed from fancy a kind of goodness out of its negation.—WHIPPLE, EDWIN P., 1859–68, *The Literature of the Age of Elizabeth, p.* 175.

All the qualities of his dramatic verse, its delightful ease and grace, and its overflowing fancifulness, come out in the lyrical speeches of the "Faithful Shepherdess." Milton himself, though he put a greater volume of imagination and sound into the measure, never gave it such an airy lightness; and we must look onwards to Shelley's "Ariel to Miranda" for an echo to these lyrics, still sweeter than their melody, and to his "Music, when soft voices die" for a fellow to "Weep no more."—BRADLEY, ANDREW CECIL, 1880, *English Poets, ed. Ward, vol.* II, *p.* 44.

GENERAL

Fletcher the Muses darling, and choice love
Of Phœbus, the delight of every Grove;
Upon whose head the Laurel grew, whose wit
Was the Times wonder, and example yet.

—SHIRLEY, JAMES, 1640, *The Sisters, Prologue.*

Though when all Fletcher writ, and the entire
Man was indulged unto that sacred fire,
His thoughts and his thoughts' dress, appear'd both such
That 'twas his happy fault to do too much:

Who therefore wisely did submit each birth
To knowing Beaumont, ere it did come forth,
Working again until he said 'twas fit,
And made him the sobriety of his wit.
Though thus he call'd his judge into his fame,
And for that aid allow'd him half the name,
'Tis known that sometimes he did stand alone,
That both the sponge and pencil were his own;
That himself judged himself, could singly do,
And was at last Beaumont and Fletcher too.

—CARTWRIGHT, WILLIAM, 1647, *Upon the Dramatical Poems of Mr. John Fletcher.*

Yet what from Jonson's oil and sweat did flow,
Or what more easy Nature did bestow
On Shakespeare's gentler Muse, in the full grown
Their graces both appear; yet so, that none
Can say, here Nature ends and Art begins.
But mix'd like the elements, and born like twins;
So interweaved, so like, so much the same,
None this mere Nature, that mere Art can name:
'Twas this the ancients meant; Nature and Skill
Are the two tops of their Parnassus' hill.

—DENHAM, SIR JOHN, 1647, *On Mr. John Fletcher's Works.*

None writes love's passion in the world, like thee.

—HERRICK, ROBERT, 1648, *Upon Master Fletcher's incomparable Plays.*

John Fletcher, one of the happy triumvirate (the other two being Jonson and Shakespear) of the chief dramatic poets of our nation in the last foregoing age, among whom there might be said to be a symmetry of perfection, while each excelled in his peculiar way: Ben Jonson, in his elaborate pains and knowledge of authors; Shakespear, in his pure vein of wit, and natural poesy height; Fletcher, in a courtly elegance and genteel familiarity of style, and withal a wit and invention so overflowing, that the luxuriant branches thereof were frequently thought convenient to be lopped off by his almost incomparable companion Francis Beaumont.—PHILLIPS, EDWARD, 1675, *Theatrum Poetarum Anglicanorum.*

In easy dialogue is Fletcher's praise;
He moved the mind, but had not power to raise.

—DRYDEN, JOHN, 1693, *Epistle to my dear friend, Mr. Congreve, on his Comedy called The Double Dealer.*

Fletcher's ideas moved slow; his versification, though sweet, is tedious, it stops at every turn; he lays line upon line, making up one after the other, adding image to image so deliberately, that we see their junctures. Shakespeare mingles everything, runs line into line, embarrasses sentences and metaphors; before one idea has burst its shell, another is hatched and clamorous for disclosure. Another striking difference between Fletcher and Shakespeare, is the fondness of the former for unnatural and violent situations. He seems to have thought that nothing great could be produced in an ordinary way. The chief incidents in some of his most admired tragedies show this. Shakespeare had nothing of this contortion in his mind, none of that craving after violent situations, and flights of strained and improbable virtue which I think always betrays an imperfect moral sensibility. The wit of Fletcher is excellent like his serious scenes, but there is something strained and far-fetched in both. He is too mistrustful of Nature, he always goes a little on one side of her. Shakespeare chose her without a reserve.—LAMB, CHARLES, 1808, *Specimens of Dramatic Poets.*

The sentiments and style of Fletcher, where not concealed by obscurity, or corruption of the text, are very dramatic. We cannot deny that the depths of Shakspeare's mind were often unfathomable by an audience: the bow was drawn by a matchless hand; but the shaft went out of sight. All might listen to Fletcher's pleasing, though not profound or vigorous, language; his thoughts are noble, and tinged with the ideality of romance, his metaphors vivid, though sometimes too forced; he possesses the idiom of English without much pedantry, though in many passages he strains it beyond common use; his versification, though studiously irregular, is often rhythmical and sweet. Yet we are seldom arrested by striking beauties; good lines occur in every page, fine ones but rarely: we lay down the volume with a sense of admiration of what we have read, but little of it remains distinctly in the memory. Fletcher is not much quoted, and has not even afforded copious materials to those who cull the beauties of ancient lore.—HALLAM, HENRY, 1837–39, *Introduction to the Literature of Europe, pt.* iii, *ch.* vi, *par.* 83.

No art in the poet, nor accomplishment in the performers, will again restore "A King and No King," "Philaster," or "The Faithful Shepherdess" to the répertoire of acting plays. But in proportion as Fletcher departed from the schools of Shakespeare and Jonson, he acquired a lower but more natural tone, and, with less ambition, was really more successful. He was an artist of the second order, constrained to unnatural and spasmodical movements while he remained in the higher regions of art, but moving gracefully and spontaneously when he descended to the lower.—DONNE, WILLIAM BODHAM, 1850–58, *Essays on the Drama, p.* 66.

Of Fletcher, indeed, it is difficult to convey an adequate idea, without running into some of his own extravagance, and without quoting passages which would shock all modern notions of decency. He most assuredly was not a great man nor a great poet. He lacked seriousness, depth, purpose, principle, imaginative closeness of conception, imaginative condensation of expression. He saw everything at one remove from its soul and essence, and must be ranked with poets of the second class. But no other poet ever had such furious animal spirits, a keener sense of enjoyment, a more perfect abandonment to whatever was uppermost in his mind at the moment. There was no conscience in his rakish and dissolute nature. Nothing in him—wit, humor, fancy, appetite, sentiment, passion, knowledge of life, knowledge of books, all his good and all his bad thoughts—met any impediment of taste or principle when rushing into expression. His eyes flash, his cheeks glow, as he writes; his air is hurried and eager; the blood that tingles and throbs in his veins flushes his words; and will and judgment, taken captive, follow with reluctant steps and half-averted faces the perilous lead of the passions they should direct. As there was no reserve in him, there was no reserved power. Rich as were the elements of his nature, they were never thoroughly organized in intellectual character; and as no presiding personality regulated the activity of his mind, he seems hardly to be morally responsible for the excesses into which he was impelled. Composition, indeed, sets his brain in a whirl. He sometimes writes as if inspired by a satyr; he sometimes writes as if inspired by a seraph; but neither satyr not seraph had any hold on his individuality, and neither could put fetters on his caprice. There is the same gusto in his indecencies as in his refinements. Though an Englishman, he has no morality, except that morality which is connected with generous instincts, or which is awakened by the sense of beauty.—WHIPPLE, EDWIN P., 1859-68, *The Literature of the Age of Elizabeth, p.* 165.

Fletcher was a man of good society from his birth; his gentlemen therefore are all "of the right race." They commit no solecisms in behaviour; and the garb of their conversations is of gold tissue. He lived in a whitened-sepulchre age, and when it mattered very little how uncleanly was the inside of the cup, provided the exterior did not offend the nostrils of the skin-deep propriety of its aristocracy. They were of "outward show elaborate, of inward less exact."—CLARKE, CHARLES COWDEN, 1871, *On the Comic Writers of England, Gentleman's Magazine, n. s., vol.* 7, *p.* 48.

Fletcher is seen at his best in his comedies. Few poets have been endowed with a larger share of wit and fancy, freshness and variety. Such plays as the "Wildgoose-Chase" and "Monsieur Thomas" are a feast of mirth from beginning to end. The "Faithful Shepherdess" is (not excepting Ben Jonson's "Sad Shepherd") the sweetest of English pastoral plays; and some of the songs scattered in profusion through Fletcher's works are hardly surpassed by Shakespeare. In tragedy he does not rank with the highest. "Bonduca" and "Valentinian" are impressive works, but inferior to the tragedies that he wrote with Beaumont, the "Maid's Tragedy" and "A King and No King."—BULLEN, A. H., 1889, *Dictionary of National Biography, vol.* XIX, *p.* 310.

His crown of praise is to have created a wholly new and wholly delightful form of mixed comedy or dramatic romance, dealing merely with the humours and sentiments of men, their passions and their chances; to have woven of all these a web of emotion and event with such gay dexterity, to have blended his colours and combined his effects with such exquisite facility and swift light sureness of touch, that we may return once and again from those heights and depths of poetry to which access was forbidden him, ready as ever to enjoy as of old the fresh incomparable charm, the force and ease and grace of life, which fill and animate the radiant world of his romantic invention. Neither before him nor after do we find, in this his special field of fancy and of work, more than shadows or echos of his coming or departing genius.—SWINBURNE, ALGERNON CHARLES, 1894, *Studies in Prose and Poetry, p.* 70.

Sir John Davies

1569–1626

Born at Tisbury, Wiltshire, 1569 (baptized April 16): died Dec. 8, 1626. An English poet. He was called to the bar in 1595, disbarred in 1598, and readmitted in 1601. In that year he was returned to Parliament for Corfe Castle. In 1603 he was made solicitor-general for Ireland, and in 1606 succeeded to the position of attorney-general for Ireland. In 1614 he was member of Parliament for Newcastle-under-Lyme. For the last ten years of his life he was a sergeant-at-law in England. He was made chief justice in 1626, but died before taking possession of the office. Among his works are "Orchestra" (on dancing, 1596), "Nosce Teipsum" (1599), "Hymns to Astræa" (1599), acrostics to Queen Elizabeth.—SMITH, BENJAMIN E., *ed.* 1894-97, *The Century Cyclopedia of Names, p.* 311.

PERSONAL

Sir John Davis, the learned and well accomplisht father of a no less learned and accomplished daughter, the present Countess Dowager of Huntington: his poem "Nosce Teipsum" (besides which and his "Orchestra," publisht together with it, both the products of his younger years, I remember to have seen from the hands of the Countess, a judicious metaphrase of several of David's psalms) is said to have made him first known to Queen Elizabeth, and afterwards brought him in favor with King James, under whose auspices, addicting himself to the study of the Common Law of England, he was made the King's first Serjeant, and afterwards his Attorney General in Ireland. —PHILLIPS, EDWARD, 1675, *Theatrum Poetarum Anglicanorum, ed. Brydges, p.* 271.

Sometimes called of the Inner Temple, was a contemporary of Montagu, with a less brilliant, yet more singular career. He was a young fellow who was not only addicted to much hearing of the chimes at midnight, but who roused the slumbering students by riotous noises of his own and his boon companions, making night hideous in "the wee sma' hours ayont the twal." Davies was expelled for this irregular course of life, and immediately availed himself of the opportunity afforded him by this enforced leisure to compose, what no other expelled student had ever thought of doing, a poem on the immortality of the soul! It is a work which shows that, however much the author may have loved the ways that moral students should avoid, he had also rendered himself familiar with the better paths, and could walk therein with dignity. This poem saved him from ruin, and ultimately raised him to a fortune which culminated in the poet—now the able lawyer—being raised to the Chief Justiceship of the Court of King's Bench. There, however, Sir John Davies never took his seat, for he was mortally stricken by apoplexy before he could be sworn in. This once riotous Templar of Montagu's early days, who wrote a noble work on the immortality of the soul in the very hey-day of his young blood, who afterwards became famous for his gravity as a judge, his wisdom as a politician, and his soundness as a statesman, terminated his literary career as the author of a poem in praise of dancing.—MANCHESTER, DUKE OF, 1864, *Court and Society from Elizabeth to Anne, vol.* I, *p.* 289.

NOSCE TEIPSUM

1599

Davies's "Nosce Teipsum" is an excellent poem, in opening the nature, faculties, and certain immortality of man's soul.—BAXTER, RICHARD, 1681, *Poetical Fragments, Prefatory Address.*

His poem on the "Immortality of the Soul" is a noble monument of his learning, acuteness, command of language, and facility of versification.—ELLIS, GEORGE, 1790-1845, *Specimens of the Early English Poets, vol.* II, *p.* 329.

Davies carried abstract reasoning into verse with an acuteness and felicity which have seldom been equalled. His reasons, undoubtedly, with too much labour, formality, and subtlety, to afford uniform poetical pleasure. The generality of his stanzas exhibit hard arguments interwoven with the pliant materials of fancy, so closely, that we may compare them to a texture of cloth and metallic threads, which is cold and stiff, while it is splendidly curious. There is this difference, however, between Davies and the commonly styled metaphysical poets, that *he* argues like a hard thinker, and *they*, for the most part, like madmen. If we conquer the drier parts of Davies's poem, and bestow a little attention on thoughts which were meant, not to gratify the indolence, but to challenge the activity of the mind, we shall find in the entire essay fresh beauties at every perusal: for in the happier parts we come to logical truths so well illustrated by ingenious similes, that we know not whether to call the thoughts more poetically or philosophically just. The judgment and fancy are reconciled, and the imagery of the poem seems to start more vividly from the surrounding shades of abstraction.—CAMPBELL, THOMAS, 1819, *An Essay on English Poetry.*

Perhaps no language can produce a poem, extending to so great a length, of more condensation of thought, or in which fewer languid verses will be found. Yet, according to some definitions, the "Nosce Teipsum" is wholly unpoetical, inasmuch as it shows no passion and little fancy. If it reaches the heart at all, it is through the reason. But, since strong argument in terse and correct style fails not to give us pleasure in prose, it seems strange that it should lose its effect when it gains the aid of regular metre to gratify the ear and assist the memory. Lines there are in Davies which far outweigh much of the descriptive and imaginative poetry of the last two centuries, whether we estimate them by the pleasure they impart to us, or by the intellectual vigor they display. — HALLAM, HENRY, 1837-39, *Introduction to the Literature of Europe, pt.* ii, *ch.* v, *par.* 70.

It is a wonderful instance of what can be done for metaphysics in verse, and by means of imagination or poetic embodiment generally. — MACDONALD, GEORGE, 1868, *England's Antiphon, p.* 105.

Its stanzas of elegiac verse were so well packed with thought, always neatly contained within the limit of each stanza, that we shall afterwards have to trace back to this poem the adoption of its measure as, for a time, our "heroic stanza."—MORLEY, HENRY, 1873, *First Sketch of English Literature, p.* 459.

For the history of philosophy it is of great significance, as it enables the student to understand the psychology and philosophy which were current before the introduction of the philosophies of Descartes on the one hand and of Hobbes and Locke on the other. The versification is uncommonly successful. It may be regarded as a triumph of diction in the expression of subtle thought in concise and fluent verse. It is by no means free from the conceits which were current in all the versification of its time, but it is remarkable in the history of literature for the skill with which it conducts philosophical discussion in the forms, and with somewhat of the spirit of elevated poetry.—UEBERWEG, FRIEDRICH, 1873, *History of Philosophy, tr. Morris, vol.* II, *p.* 352.

It is vain indeed to make definitions of poetry which would deprive any poet of his well-won title. Whatever may be said as to what poetry should be, the fact remains that the author of "Nosce Teipsum" is a poet. In the kingdom of poetry, as has been said, are many mansions, and undoubtedly one of these belongs to Sir John Davies, however we may describe it, however we may censure its style and arrangement. Far be from us any such critical or scholastic formulæ as would prevent us from all due appreciation of such refined, imaginative thought and subtle, finished workmanship, as mark the first notable philosophical poem of our literature.—HALES, JOHN W., 1876-93, *Folia Litteraria, p.* 163.

With considerable appositeness of argument, and clearness of exposition, Sir John Davies sets forth his thoroughly spiritualistic psychology, and develops numerous considerations tending to establish the doctrine of the soul's immortality, all founded on the best philosophy the world had produced, and pervaded by an obvious breath of sincere and independent conviction; this, too, in spite of the apparent over-confidence (and very mediocre poetry) of the concluding stanza. . . . The poem may stand as a document to prove what was the thoughtful faith of the best type of English gentlemen in his day.—MORRIS, GEORGE S., 1880, *British Thought and Thinkers, pp.* 67, 68.

It is a strange performance, and is to be admired rather for the measure of victory it obtains over unfavourable conditions, than for any absolute poetical merits. . . . Expression of this high and tender quality is not to be looked for in "Nosce Teipsum." The poem deals with an eternally poetic subject, the longings, griefs, and destiny of the soul, in such a way as to furnish one more illustration of the futility of "philosophical poetry,"—of the manner in which the attempt to combine poetry and science extracts all pathos and all influence from the most pathetic and the most potent of themes.—WARD, MARY A., 1880, *English Poets, ed. Ward, vol.* I, *pp.* 549, 550.

GENERAL

Acute *Iohn Davis*, I affect thy rymes,
That ierck in hidden charmes these looser times:
Thy plainer verse, thy vnaffected vaine,
Is grac'd with a faire (end and sooping traine.)

—ANON, 1606, *The Return from Parnassus, ed. Macray, Act* i, *Sc.* 2, *p.* 85.

Davies and Wither, by whose Muse's power
A natural day to me seems but an hour,
And could I ever hear their learned lays,
Ages would turn to artificial days.

—BROWNE, WILLIAM, 1613, *Britannia's Pastorals, bk.* ii, *song* ii.

Left behind Him more valuable Witnesses of his Merit, than all the Titles that Heraldry can invent, or Monarchs bestow: The joint Applauses of *Cambden*, Sir *John Harington, Ben Johnson, Selden, Donn, Corbet, &c.!* These are great, and unquestionable Authorities in Favour of this Author; and I shall only presume to add, That, in my humble Opinion, no Philosophical Writer, I have met with, ever explain'd their Ideas more clearly, or familiarly even in Prose; or any so beautifully or harmoniously in Verse. There is a peculiar Happiness in his Similies, being introduc'd to illustrate, more than adorn; which renders them as useful, as entertaining; and distinguishes his from those of every other Author.—COOPER, ELIZABETH, 1737, *The Muses' Library, p.* 332.

It is usual among critics, even such critics as Hallam and Campbell, to decide that the imaginative power of the poem on the "Immortality of the Soul" consists in the illustration of the arguments rather than in the perception of the premises. But the truth would seem to be that the author exhibits his imagination more in his insight than in his imagery. The poetic excellence of the work comes from the power of clear, steady beholding of spiritual facts with the spiritual eye,—of beholding them so clearly that the task of stating, illustrating, and reasoning from them is performed with masterly ease.—WHIPPLE, EDWIN P., 1859-1868, *The Literature of the Age of Elizabeth, p.* 239.

This vivid, sprightly, and melodious Poem, ["Orchestra"] was Sir John's earliest "venture" of any extent: and it is important to remember this, as spurious capital for blame, has been found in the supposition that it was his latest.—GROSART, ALEXANDER B., 1869, *ed. Sir John Davies' Complete Poems, Memorial-Introduction, p.* 11.

The "Hymns to Astræa," . . . may be ranked as one of the most readable and freely written expressions of that complex sentiment toward the Queen of which each considerable Elizabethan poet became in turn the mouthpiece.—WARD, MARY A., 1880, *English Poets, ed. Ward, vol.* I, *p.* 548.

Founded as it ["Orchestra"] is on a mere conceit—the reduction of all natural phenomena to a grave and regulated motion which the author calls dancing—it is one of the very best poems of the school of Spenser, and in harmony of metre (the seven-lined stanza) and grace of illustration is sometimes not too far behind Spenser himself.—SAINTSBURY, GEORGE, 1887, *History of Elizabethan Literature, p.* 294.

Sir John Davies, whose philosophical poems were among the most original and beautiful literary productions of the close of Elizabeth's reign. . . . He was eminently a writer before his time. His extremely ingenious "Orchestra," a poem on dancing, has much in it that suggests the Fletchers on one side and Donne on the other, while his more celebrated *magnum opus* of the "Nosce Teipsum" is the general precursor of all the school of metaphysical ingenuity and argumentative imagination. In Davies there is hardly a trace of those qualities which we have sought to distinguish as specially Elizabethan, and we have difficulty in obliging ourselves to remember that his poems were given to the public during the course of the sixteenth century. To the exquisite novelty and sweetness of his "Hymns of Astræa," critical justice has never yet been done.—GOSSE, EDMUND, 1894, *The Jacobean Poets*, p. 8.

Lancelot Andrews

1555-1626

Lancelot Andrews, or Andrewes: a learned English theologian; one of the most illustrious of English prelates; born in London, Sept. 25, 1555; educated at Cambridge and Oxford. He was one of the chaplains of Queen Elizabeth, who appointed him Dean of Westminster. He was one of the divines selected to translate the Bible under the auspices of James I., and became Bishop of Chichester in 1605. In 1609 he was translated to the see of Ely, and appointed a privy councilor; was considered the most learned English theologian of his time, except Ussher, and had a high reputation as a pulpit orator. His works, though uncritically edited and but fragmentary, place him in the front rank of English theologians. He became Bishop of Winchester in 1618; he was the author of religious works, among which was a "Manual of Private Devotions and Meditations for Every Day in the Week." In polemics he assailed Bellarmine in his "Responsio ad Apologiam," a treatise never answered. On Nov. 23, 1600, Andrews preached at Whitehall his memorable sermon on justification, maintaining the evangelical view as opposed to the Sacerdotal. Andrews, in the Lambeth Articles, which mark an epoch in English Church history, adopted the doctrine of St. Augustine as modified by Aquinas. Died in London, Sept. 25, 1626.—PERRY, W. S., 1897, *Johnson's Universal Cyclopædia, vol.* I, *p.* 211.

He was an unimitable Preacher in his way; and such Plagiaries who have stolen his Sermons could never steal his Preaching, and could make nothing of that whereof he made all things as he desired. Pious and pleasant Bishop Felton (his Contemporary and Colleague) indevoured in vain in his Sermon to assimilate his style; and therefore said merrily of himself, "I had almost marr'd my own natural Trot, by endeavouring to imitate his artifical Amble."—FULLER, THOMAS, 1662, *The Worthies of England, ed. Nichols, vol.* II, *p.* 66.

Old Mr. Sutton, a very learned man of those dayes, of Blandford St. Maries, Dorset, was his school fellowe, and sayd that Lancelot Andrewes was a great long boy of 18 yeares old at least before he went to the university. . . . His great learning quickly made him known in the university, and also to King James, who much valued him for it, and advanced him, and at last made him bishop of Winchester, which bishoprick he ordered with great prudence as to government of the parsons, preferring of ingeniose persons that were staked to poore livings and did *dilitescere*. . . . He had not that smooth way of oratory as now. It was a shrewd and severe animadversion of a Scotish lord, who, when king James asked him how he liked bp. A.'s sermon, sayd that he was learned, but he did play with his text, as a Jack-an-apes does, who takes up a thing and tosses and playes with it, and then he takes up another, and playes a little with it. Here's a pretty thing, and there's a pretty thing!—AUBREY, JOHN, 1669-96, *Brief Lives, ed. Clark, vol.* I, *pp.* 29, 30, 31.

Indeed, he was the most apostolical and primitive-like divine, in my opinion, that ever wore a rochet, in his age; of a most venerable gravity, and yet most sweet in all commerce; the most devout that ever I saw when he appeared before God; of such a growth in all kinds of learning, that very able clerks were of low stature to him. . . . In the pulpit, a Homer among preachers.—HACKET, BISHOP JOHN, 1693, *Scrinia Reserta: the Life of Archbishop Williams*.

A man far more learned in patristic theology than any of the Elizabethan bishops, or perhaps than any of his English contemporaries except Usher.—HALLAM, HENRY, 1837-39, *Introduction to the Literature of Europe, pt.* iii, *ch.* ii, *par.* 10.

The sermons of Bishop Andrews exemplify, very pertinently, the chief defects in style that have been attributed to the writers of his period; while to these they add other faults, incident to the effusions of a mind poor in fancy, coarse in taste, ingeniously rash in catching at trivial analogies, and constantly burying good thoughts under a heap of useless phrases. Yet, though they were corrupt models, and dangerous in proportion to the fame of the author, it is not surprising that they made the extraordinary impression they did. They contain, more than any other works of their kind and time, the unworked materials of oratory; and of oratory, too, belonging to the most severe and powerful class. There is something Demosthenic in the impatient vehemence, with which the pious bishop showers down his short, clumsy, harsh sentences; and the likeness becomes still more exact, when we hear him alternating stern and eager questions with sad or indignant answers. His Latin quotations, though incessant, are always brief: his field of erudite illustration is prudently confined; and his multiplied divisions and subdivisions, being quite agreeable to the growing fashion, may have helped to increase the respect of the hearers for the great strength and ingenuity of thought which the preacher so often showed. There is often much aptness in the parallels which it is his besetting fault to accumulate so thickly, and to overdraw so grotesquely; and an overpowering effect must sometimes have been produced by the dexterous boldness with which, anticipating an adverse opinion or feeling, he throws it back in the teeth of those who were likely to entertain it.—SPALDING, WILLIAM, 1852-82, *A History of English Literature, p.* 219.

The Church of England contains no name more truly venerable than that of this good prelate. For polish and suavity of manners he was excelled by no gentleman of the court; in piety, by no anchorite of better times and purer days. In the discharge of all the duties of religion, he so walked as to be an illustrious exemplar to his flock and to the church of God. James I. had so high an opinion of his abilities, that he employed him to answer Bellarmine's Treatise against his own Defence of the Right of Kings. He was also a favourite with Charles I. Casaubon, Cluverius, Vossius, Grotius, Peter du Moulin, Barclay, and Erpenius were among his correspondents. Lord Clarendon regrets that he was not raised to the primacy on the death of Archbishop Bancroft. Thus respected in life, he was not less honoured at his death, by a Latin elegy from the author of "Paradise Lost." —ALLIBONE, S. AUSTIN, 1854-58, *Dictionary of English Literature, vol.* I, *p.* 61.

Each sermon of Bishop Andrewes might furnish a diffuse writer matter for an entire treatise. No one can read them without being fairly bewildered and astonished at the vast stores of thought and learning which are poured out almost recklessly before him. But with regard to manner the case is different. Bishop Andrewes's manner is in the highest degree peculiar. He tortures, twists, and twirls his subject about, so that one can hardly imagine that he could have been listened to with becoming gravity. Sometimes he indulges in puns and curious plays on words; sometimes by an extraordinary jumbling together of English, Latin, and Greek words, he produces the most curious effect; so that we are tempted to say that as these sermons are the richest and most copious in matter, so are they the worst in style and manner of any that have ever obtained a more than passing celebrity. We feel persuaded that the Bishop of Winchester must have been "followed" by many of the courtiers not for edification but for amusement; that his oddities must have furnished them with a stock of good stories, and that King James often enjoyed a hearty laugh over these congenial *facetiæ*. . . . There are few more eminent names in our Church history than that of Bishop Andrewes. . . . For more than twenty years regarded as without question the leading divine of the Church of England.—PERRY GEORGE G., 1861, *History of the Church of England, vol.* I, *pp.* 54, 354, 355.

Both the learning and ability of Andrews, indeed, are conspicuous in everything he has written; but his eloquence, nevertheless, is to a modern taste grotesque enough. In his more ambitious passages he is the very prince of verbal posture-masters,—if not the first in date, the first in extravagance, of the artificial, quibbling, syllable-tormenting school of our English pulpit rhetoricians; and he undoubtedly contributed more to spread the disease of that manner of writing than any other individual. . . . Many a "natural trot" Andrews no doubt was the cause of spoiling in his day, and long after it. This bishop is further very notable, in the history of the English Church, as the first great asserter of those semi-popish notions touching doctrines, rites, and ecclesiastical government with which Laud afterwards blew up the establishment. Andrews, however, was a very different sort of person from Laud,—as superior to him in sense and policy as in learning and general strength and comprehensiveness of understanding.—CRAIK, GEORGE L., 1861, *A Compendious History of English Literature and of the English Language, vol.* I, *p.* 610.

Lancelot Andrewes, the most devout and, at the same time, the most honest of the nascent High Church party of that period, lamented alike by Clarendon and by Milton, was Dean for five years. Under his care, probably in the Deanery, met the Westminster Committee of the Authorised Version of James I., to which was confided the translation of the Old Testament, from Genesis to Kings, and of the Epistles in the New. In him the close connection of the Abbey with the School reached its climax.—STANLEY, ARTHUR PENRHYN, 1867, *Historical Memorials of Westminster Abbey, p.* 413.

In redundant display of learning he goes beyond even Jeremy Taylor; and his word-play is after the manner we have illustrated from Ascham and Lyly.—MINTO, WILLIAM, 1872-80, *Manual of English Prose Literature, p.* 252.

Andrewes was eminent in three capacities: (1) As a prelate. Few men have more happily combined the various qualities which contribute to make a great prelate than Andrewes. His principles were most distinct and definite, and from these principles he never swerved. He was a thorough English churchman, as far removed from Romanism on the one hand, as from puritanism on the other. He never interfered in public affairs, either as a privy councillor or in any other capacity, except when the spiritual interests of the church seemed to him to be at stake; and then, in spite of his constitutional modesty, he spoke out boldly and to the point. His learning was unequalled. From his childhood to his death he was an indefatigable student; his multifarious business as a public man was never allowed to interfere with his studies. He made a rule of not being interrupted, except for public or private prayer, before dinner-time (12 o'clock); when he was intruded upon, he would say "he was afraid he was no true scholar who came to see him before noon." The result was that he made himself master of fifteen languages, if not more, while his knowledge of patristic theology was quite unrivalled. . . . (2) As a preacher, Andrewes was generally held to be the very "stella prædicantium," an "angel in the pulpit." . . . (3) As a writer. Andrewes published but little in his lifetime, though his works now fill eight 8vo volumes in the "Library of Anglo-Catholic Theology."—OVERTON, J. H., 1885, *Dictionary of National Biography, vol.* I, *pp.* 402, 403, 404.

I must not, however, pass from this topic without some attempt to do justice to the signal benefit which Newman conferred by his admirable translation of Bishop Andrewes's "Private Devotions." It was indeed an invaluable boon, for which all of us, but the clergy especially, cannot be too thankful. O! that he had clung to Bishop Andrewes as his guide not only *orandi*, but *credendi!*—WORDSWORTH, CHARLES, 1890, *Annals of My Early Life,* 1806–1846, *p.* 345.

Andrewes may be said with truth to have been one of the most learned and holy men by whom the Church has ever been ruled. His sermons—quaint, erudite, humorous, and spiritual—were the delight of his own age. His prayers have been constantly brought out in new editions, and have been the companions of the piety of two centuries. His controversial writings laid the foundation of the Anglican position as it was expressed and defended by the divines of the rest of the century. The special characteristic of his work was its appeal to primitive antiquity and the resort for interpretation to the historical formularies of the undivided Church. The strength of the appeal which he made to the intelligence of his own and the next age lay in the fact that he spoke to the heart no less than to the head.—HUTTON, WILLIAM HOLDEN, 1895, *Social England, ed. Traill, vol.* IV, *p.* 25.

Francis Bacon

1561-1626

Francis Bacon, Baron Verulam, 1561-1626. Born, at York House, 22 Jan. 1561. At Trinity Coll., Cambridge, April 1573 to March 1575. Admitted at Gray's Inn, 27 June 1575; called to Bar, 27 June 1582. With Sir Amias Paulet's embassy to France, 1576. M. P. for Melcombe Regis, 1584. M. P. for Taunton, 1586. Bencher of Gray's Inn, 1586. M. P. for Liverpool, 1589. Friendship with Earl of Essex begun, 1591. M. P. for Middlesex, 1593. Employed as Learned Counsel to Queen, 1594. M. A., Cambridge, 27 July 1594. "Essays" published, 1597. M. P. for Southampton, 1597. Arrested for debt, Sept. 1598. Took part in trials of Earl of Essex, 5 June 1600 and 19 Feb. 1601. Knighted, 23 July 1603. Appointed on Commission to discuss Union, 1604. Pension of £60 granted as Counsel to the King, Aug. 1604. Married Alice Barnham, 10 May 1606. Speech in Parliament in favour of Union proposals, 17 Feb. 1607. Solicitor-General, 25 June 1607. Attorney-General, 27 Oct. 1613. Prosecutor in Earl of Somerset's trial, 25 May 1616. Privy Councillor, 9 June 1616. Lord Keeper, 7 March 1617. Lord Chancellor, 7 Jan. 1618. Created Baron Verulam, 12 July 1618. Prosecution of Sir Walter Raleigh, 1618; of Earl of Suffolk, 1619; of Sir Henry Yelverton, 1620. "Novum Organum" published, Oct. 1620. Created Viscount St. Alban, 27 Jan. 1621. Tried for bribery, and sentenced to deprivation of office, fine of £40,000 and imprisonment in Tower, 3 May 1621. Partial mitigation of sentence by King, Sept. 1621. Died, 9 April 1626. Buried at St. Michael's Church, St. Albans. *Works:* "Essays," 1597; "Declaration of the practises and treasons attempted . . . by Robert late Earle of Essex" (anon.), 1601; "Apologie of the Earle of Essex. . . . Penned by himself" (or rather, by Bacon), 1603; "Brief Discourse touching the happie Union of the Kingdomes of England and Scotland" (anon.), 1603; "Apologie in certaine imputations concerning the late Earle of Essex," 1604; "Certaine considerations touching the better pacification . . of the Church of England" (anon), 1604; "Of the Proficience and Advancement of Learning," 1605; "De Sapientia Veterum," 1609; "Charge Concerning Duels," 1614; "Instauratio Magna" ("Novum Organum"), 1620; "Historie of the Raigne of King Henry the Seventh," 1622; "Historia Naturalis et Experimentalis ad condendam Philosophiam" ("Historia Ventorum"), 1622; "De Dignitate et Augmentis Scientiarum," 1623; "Historia Vitæ et Mortis," 1623; "Translation of Certaine Psalmes," 1625; "Apophthegmes new and old," 1625. *Posthumous:* "Sylva Sylvarum," 1627; "Considerations touching a warre with Spaine," 1629; "The Use of the Law" (anon.) in "The Lawyers' Light. . . . By I. D.," 1629; "Certaine Miscellany Works," 1629; "Operum Moralium et Civilium tomus," 1638; "The Elements of the Common Lawes of England," 1640; "A Wise and Moderate Discourse concerning Church Affaires" (anon.), 1641; "Remaines," 1648; "The Felicity of Queen Elizabeth," 1651; "Scripta in Naturali et Universali Philosophia," 1653; "The Mirrour of State and Eloquence," 1656; "Resuscitatio," 1657: "Opuscula varia posthuma," 1658; "New Atlantis," 1660; "Opera Omnia," 1665; "Letters," 1702; "A Conference of Pleasure," 1870; "The Promu of Formularies and Elegancies," 1883.—SHARP, R. FARQUHARSON, 1897, *A Dictionary of English Authors, p.* 13.

PERSONAL

FRANCISCUS BACON, BARO DE VERULAM, S^T. ALBANI VIC^MES,
Seu Notioribus Titulis
Scientiarum Lumen, Facundiæ Lex
Sic Sedebat:
Qui Postquam Omnia Naturalis Sapientiæ
Et Civilis Arcana Evolvisset,
Naturæ Decretum Explevit.
Composita Solvantur.
AN. DNI. M. DC. XXVI.
AETAT^IS LXVI.

—WOTTON, SIR HENRY, *Inscription on Bacon's Monument.*

She* did acknowledge you had a great wit and an excellent gift of speech, and much other good learning. But in the law she rather thought you could make *show* to the utmost of your knowledge than that you were *deep.*—ESSEX, EARL OF, *Letter to Francis Bacon.*

I have found an alderman's daughter, a handsome maiden to my liking.—BACON, FRANCIS, 1606, *Letter to Sir Robert Cecil, May.*

*Queen Elizabeth.

FRANCIS BACON

From Engraving by Francis Hall, after an old Print, by Simon Puss.

Sir Francis Bacon was married yesterday to his young wench in Maribone Chapel. He was clad from top to toe in purple, and hath made himself and his wife such store of fine raiments of cloth of silver and gold that it draws deep into her portion. The dinner was kept at his father-in-law Sir John Packington's lodging, over against the Savoy, where his chief guests were the three knights, Cope, Hicks, and Beeston; and upon this conceit (as he said himself), that since he could not have my Lord of Salisbury in person, which he wished, he would have him at least in his representative body. —CARLETON, SIR DUDLEY, 1606, *Letter, May 11th.*

Haile, happie Genius of this antient pile!
How comes it all things so about thee smile?
The fire, the wine, the men, and in the midst
Thou stand'st, as if some mystery thou did'st!
Pardon, I read it in thy face, the day
For whose returnes, and many, all these pray:
And so doe I. This is the sixtieth year,
Since Bacon, and thy Lord, was borne and here;
Son to the grave, wise Keeper of the Seale,
Fame and foundation of the English weale:
What then his father was, that since is he,
Now with a title more to the degree.
England's High Chancellor! the destined heire
In his soft cradle to his father's chair;
Whose even thred the Fates spinne round and full,
Out of their choycest and their whitest woole.
'Tis a brave cause of joy; let it be knowne,—
For 'twere a narrow gladnesse, kept thine owne.
Give me a deep-crowned bowle, that I may sing,
In raysing him, the wysdome of my King.

—JONSON, BEN, 1620, *Lord Bacon's Birth Day.*

You found me of the Learned Counsel Extraordinary, without patent or fee—a kind of *individuum vagum.* You established me, and brought me into *Ordinary.* Soon after, you placed me *Solicitor,* where I served seven years. Then your majesty made me your *Attorney,* or *Procurator General.* Then *Privy Counsellor,* while I was attorney—a kind of miracle of your favor that had not been in many ages. Thence *Keeper of your Seal;* and because that was a kind of planet and not fixed, *Chancellor.* And when your majesty could raise me no higher, it was your grace to illustrate me with beams of honor: first making me *Baron Verulam,* and now *Viscount St. Albans.* So this is the eighth rise or reach, a diapason in music, even a good number and accord for a close. And so I may without superstition be buried in St. Alban's habit or vestment.—BACON, FRANCIS, 1621, *Letter to King James.*

The Chancellor being convicted of bribery, pretends, as if being weary of honour, he would resign his place, being much loaded with calumnies.—CAMDEN, WILLIAM, 1603-23, *Annales Jacobi Reges, Annals of King James.*

There happened in my time one noble speaker, who was full of gravity in his speaking. His language (where he could spare or pass by a jest) was nobly censorious. No man ever spake more neatly, more pressly, more weightily, or suffered less emptiness, less idleness, in what he uttered. No member of his speech, but consisted of his own graces. His hearers could not cough, or look aside from him, without loss. He commanded where he spoke; and had his judges angry and pleased at his devotion. No man had their affections more in his power. The fear of every man that heard him was, lest he should make an end. . . . My conceit of his person was never increased toward him by his place, or honours: but I have and do reverence him, for the greatness that was only proper to himself, in that he seemed to me ever, by his work, one of the greatest men, and most worthy of admiration, that had been in many ages. In his adversity I ever prayed, that God would give him strength; for greatness he could not want. Neither could I condole in a word or syllabel for him, as knowing no accident could do harm to virtue, but rather help to make it manifest.—JONSON, BEN, *Timber, or Discoveries,* 1630-37, lxxviii, lxxx, *Works, ed. Gifford and Cunningham, vol.* IX, *pp.* 163, 165.

Pity it was he was not entertained with some liberal salary, abstracted from all affairs, both of court and judicature, and furnished with sufficiency both of means and helps for the going on of his design; which, had it been, he might have given us such a body of Natural Philosophy, and made it so subservient to the public good, that neither Aristotle nor Theophrastus amongst the Ancients nor Paracelsus, or the rest of our latest chymists, would have been considerable.—HEYLIN, PETER, 1644–71, *The Life and Death of Archbishop Laud.*

His great spirit was brought low, and this humiliation might have raised him again, if his offences had not been so weighty as to keep him down. . . . He was a fit jewel to have beautified and adorned a flourishing kingdom, if his flaws had not disgraced the lustre that should have set him off.—WILSON, ARTHUR, 1653, *The History of Great Britain; being the Life and Reign of King James I.*

None can character him to the life, save himself. He was in parts more than a man; who in any liberal profession might be whatsoever he would himself: a great honourer of ancient authors, yet a great deviser and practiser of new ways in learning: privy counsellor, as to king James, so to nature itself, diving into many of her abstruse mysteries. New conclusions he would dig out with mattocks of gold and silver; not caring what his experience cost him, expending on the trials of nature all and more than he got by the trials at the bar; posterity being the better for his—though he the worse for his own—dear experiments. He and his servants had all in common; the men never wanting what their master had; and thus what came flowing in unto him was sent flying away from him, who, in giving of rewards, knew no bounds but the bottom of his own purse. Wherefore, when king James heard that he had given ten pounds to an under-keeper, by whom he had sent him a buck, the king said merrily, "I and he shall both die beggars;" which was condemnable prodigality in a subject. He lived many years after; and in his books will ever survive: in the reading whereof, modest men commend him in what they do—condemn themselves in what they do not—understand, as believing the fault in their own eyes, and not in the object.—FULLER, THOMAS, 1655, *The Church Historg of Britain, ed. Nichols, vol.* III, *bk.* X, *par.* 22, *p.* 290.

His meals were reflections of the ear as well as of the stomack: like the *Noctes Atticæ* or *Convivia Deipno Sophistarum,* wherein a man might be refreshed in his mind and understanding no less than in his body. And I have known some of no mean parts, that have professed to make use of their note-books, when they have risen from his table. In which conversations and otherwise, he was no dashing man, as some men are; but ever a countenancer and fosterer of another man's parts. Neither was he one, that would appropriate the speech wholly to himself or delight to out-vie others, but leave a liberty to the co-assessors to take their turns. Wherein he would draw a man on, and allure him to speak upon such a subject as wherein he was peculiarly skilful and would delight to speak: and for himself he contemned no man's observations, but would light his torch at every man's candle. . . . Neither was he, in his time, less gracious with the subject than with his Sovereign. . . . He was free from malice, which (as he said himself) he never bred, nor fed. He was no revenger of injuries, which if he had minded he had both opportunity and place high enough, to have done it. He was no heaver of men out of their places, as delighting in their ruin and undoing. He was no defamer of any man to his Prince.—RAWLEY, WILLIAM, 1657-61, *Life of Bacon, Resuscitatio.*

His decrees were generally made with so much equity, that, though gifts rendered him suspected for injustice, yet never any decree made by him was reversed as unjust.—RUSHWORTH, JOHN, 1659-1701, *Historical Collections, vol.* I.

He was so excellent, so agreeable a speaker, that all who heard him were uneasy if he was interrupted, and sorry when he concluded. . . . Now this general knowledge he had in all things husbanded by his wit, and dignified by so majestical a carriage, he was known to own, struck such an awful reverence in those he questioned, that they durst not conceal the most intrinsic part of their mysteries from him, for fear of appearing ignorant or saucy: all of which rendered him no less necessary than admirable at the Council-table, where in reference to impositions, monopolies, &c., where the meanest manufactures were a usual argument; and, as I have heard, did in this baffle the Earl of Middlesex, that was born and bred a Citizen; yet without any great, (if at all,) interrupting his other studies, as is not hard to be imagined of a quick apprehension, in which he was admirable. —OSBORN, FRANCIS, 1659, *Miscellaneous Works.*

Shortly after the king dissolved the Parliament, but never restored that matchless lord to his place, which made him then to wish the many years he had spent in state policy and law study had been solely devoted to true philosophy: for (said he) the one, at the best, doth but comprehend man's frailty in its greatest splendour; but the other the mysterious knowledge of all things created in the six days' work.—BUSHEL, THOMAS, 1660, *Extract of the Lord Bacon's Philosophical Theory in Mineral Prosecutions.*

Methinks in this one man I do at once find enough occasion to admire the strength of human wit, and to bewail the weakness of a mortal condition; for is it not wonderful, that he who had run through all the degrees of that profession which usually takes up men's whole time, who had studied, and practised, and governed the Common Law, who had always lived in the crowd, and borne the greatest burden of civil business, should yet find leisure enough for these retired studies, to excel all those men who separate themselves for this very purpose? He was a man of strong, clear, powerful, imagination; his genius was searching and invincible, and of this I need give no other proof than his style itself; which, as, for the most part, it describes men's minds as well as pictures do their bodies, so it did his above all men living; the course of it vigorous and majestic; the wit, bold and familiar; the comparisons, fetched out of the way, and yet the most easy; in all, expressing a soul equally skilled in men and nature.—SPRAT, THOMAS, 1667, *History of the Royal Society of London.*

All that were *great and good* loved and honoured him. . . . He was ἀ ηαιδεραστης. His Ganimeds and favourites tooke bribes; but his lordship alwayes gave judgement *secundum aequum et bonum.* His decrees in Chancery stand firme, i. e. there are fewer of his decrees reverst then of any other Chancellor. . . . He had a delicate, lively hazel eie; Dr. Harvey told me it was like the eie of a viper. . . . Mr. Hobbs told me that the cause of his lordship's death was trying an experiment: viz., as he was taking the aire in a coach with Dr. Witherbone (a Scotchman, Physitian to the King) towards High-gate, snow lay on the ground, and it came into my lord's thoughts, why flesh might not be preserved in snow, as in salt. They were resolved they would try the experiment presently. They alighted out of the coach, and went into a poore woman's howse at the bottome of Highgate hill, and bought a hen, and made the woman exenterate it, and then stuffed the bodie with snow, and my lord did help to doe it himselfe. The snow so chilled him, that he immediately fell so extremely ill, that he could not returne to his lodgings (I suppose then at Graye's Inne), but went to the earle of Arundell's house at Highgate, where they putt him into a good bed warmed with a panne, but it was a damp bed that had not been layn-in in about a yeare before, which gave him such a cold that in 2 or 3 dayes, as I remember he told me, he dyed of suffocation.—AUBREY, JOHN, 1669-96, *Brief Lives, ed. Clark, vol.* I, *pp.* 70, 71, 72, 75.

Who can forbear to observe and lament the weakness and infirmity of human nature? To see a man so far exalted above the common level of his fellow-creatures, to sink so far below it; to see a man who, like Seneca, gave admirable rules for the conduct of life, and condemning the avaricious pursuit after riches, and, what is unlike Seneca, condemning them in his own person, and yet be defiled thereby. —STEPHENS, ROBERT, 1702, *ed. Letters of Lord Bacon, Introduction.*

I was infinitely pleased to find among the works of this extraordinary man a prayer of his own composing, which, for the elevation of thought, and greatness of expression, seems rather the devotion of an angel than a man. . . . In this prayer, at the same time that we find him prostrating himself before the great mercy seat, and humbled under afflictions which at that time lay heavy upon him, we see him supported by the sense of his integrity, his zeal, his devotion, and his love to mankind; which give him a much higher figure in the minds of thinking men, than that greatness had done from which he was fallen.—ADDISON, JOSEPH, 1710, *The Tatler, No.* 267.

If Parts allure thee, think how Bacon shined,
The wisest, brightest, meanest of mankind!
—POPE, ALEXANDER, 1734, *Essay on Man, Epistle IV, v.* 281–2.

A man universally admired for the greatness of his genius, and beloved for the courteousness and humanity of his behaviour. He was the great ornament of his age and nation; and nought was wanting to render him the ornament of human nature itself, but that strength of mind which might check his intemperate desire of preferment, that could add nothing to his dignity, and might restrain his profuse inclination to expense, that could be requisite neither for his honour nor entertainment. His want of economy, and his indulgence to servants, had involved him in necessities; and, in order to supply his prodigality, he had been tempted to take bribes, by the title of presents, and that in a very open manner, from suitors in chancery. . . . The Lords insisted on a particular confession of all his corruptions. He acknowledged twenty-eight articles; and was sentenced to pay a fine of forty thousand pounds, to be imprisoned in the Tower during the King's pleasure, to be for ever incapable of any office, place, or employment, and never again to sit in Parliament, or come within the verge of the court. This dreadful sentence, dreadful to a man of nice sensibility to honour, he survived five years; and, being released in a little time from the Tower, his genius, yet unbroken, supported itself amidst involved circumstances and a depressed spirit, and shone out in literary productions, which have made his guilt or weaknesses be forgotten or overlooked by posterity.—HUME, DAVID, 1754–62, *History of England, James I., Appendix.*

Nature had designed him to rule a master spirit in the world of letters; but ambition led him to crouch at court in search of wealth and preferment. Neither did he fail in his object: industry and perseverance enabled him to overcome the jealousy of Elizabeth, the favouritism of James, and the intrigues of his competitors. He was not only in possession of the great seal; in addition to the rank of baron, he had recently obtained, as a new proof of the royal favour, the title of viscount St. Alban's. But, if he found the ascent to greatness slow and toilsome, his fall was sudden and instantaneous. . . . Of his guilt there was no doubt: but, had he submitted with patience to his fate, had he devoted to literary pursuits those intellectual powers which made him the prodigy of the age, he might have redeemed his character, and have conferred immortal benefits on mankind. He revised, indeed, his former works, he procured them to be translated into the Latin language, and he wrote a life of Henry VII.; but these were unwelcome tasks, suggested to him from authority, and performed with reluctance. He still looked back to the flesh pots of Egypt, the favours of the court; and in addition to the restoration to liberty, and the remission of his fine, boons which were granted, he solicited with unceasing importunity both a pension and employment. With this view he continued to harass the king, the prince, and the favourite, with letters; he pleaded his former services, he sought to move pity by prayers the most abject, and to win favour by flattery the most blasphemous. But his petitions were received with coldness, and treated with contempt; the repeated failure of his hopes soured his temper and impaired his health; and he died, the victim of mistaken and disappointed ambition, in the fifth year after his disgrace.—LINGARD, JOHN, 1819-30, *History of England, vol.* IX, *pp.* 183, 185.

This chancellor was peculiarly eminent as a patron of distinguished churchmen and men of letters; and few persons of his day received a larger share of learned incense.—AIKIN, LUCY, 1822, *Memoirs of the Court of King James the First, vol.* I, *p.* 109.

A more pious mind never existed. There is scarcely a line of his works in which a deep, awful, religious feeling is not manifested. . . . He was of a temperament of the most delicate sensibility: so excitable, as to be affected by the slightest alterations in the atmosphere. It is probable that the temperament of genuis may much depend upon such pressibility, and that to this cause the excellencies and failures of Bacon may frequently be traced. His health was always delicate. . . . The extent of his views was immense. He stood on a cliff, and surveyed the whole of nature. . . . His powers were varied and in great perfection. His senses were exquisitely acute. . . . His imagination was fruitful and vivid; but he understood its laws, and governed it with absolute sway. He used it as a philosopher. . . . He so mastered and subdued his mind as to counteract disinclination to study; and he prevented fatigue by stopping in due time: by a judicious intermission of studies, and by never plodding upon books; for, although he read incessantly, he winnowed quickly. . . . As a lawyer he looked with microscopic eye into its subtleties, and soon made great proficience in the science. He was active in the discharge of his professional duties: and published various works upon different parts of the law. . . . As a Judge, it has never been pretended that any decree made by him was ever reversed as unjust. . . . As a Statesman he was indefatigable in his public exertions. . . . His love of reform, his master passion, manifested itself both as a statesman and as a lawyer.—MONTAGU, BASIL, 1834, *The Life of Francis Bacon*,

The moral qualities of Bacon were not of a high order. We do not say that he was a bad man. He was not inhuman or tyrannical. He bore with meekness his high civil honours, and the far higher honours gained by his intellect. He was very seldom, if ever, provoked into treating any person with malignity and insolence. No man more readily held up the left cheek to those who had smitten the right. No man was more expert at the soft answer which turneth away wrath. He was never accused of intemperance in his pleasures. His even temper, his flowing courtesy, the general respectability of his demeanour, made a favourable impression on those who saw him in situations which do not severally try the principles. His faults were—we write it with pain—coldness of heart and meanness of spirit. He seems to have been incapable of feeling strong affection, of facing great dangers, of making great sacrifices.—MACAULAY, THOMAS BABINGTON, 1834, *Lord Bacon, Edinburgh Review, Critical and Miscellaneous Essays.*

Bacon, in all the misfortunes of his life, was the victim of his ignorance of the value of money. He brought himself to distress and degradation by wasteful negligence, and allowed himself to be robbed and ruined in his fortune and reputation by his servants. His life should be a moral lesson, and his genius is an intellectual guide, to all mankind.—MACKINTOSH, SIR JAMES, 1835, *History of England, by Wallace and Bell, vol.* IV, *p.* 312.

Though Bacon was quite as bad a public man as he* represents, his vices were not the consequences of a weak and servile temperament, but of the same profound and subtle mind that he evinced in letters. He chose his means according as they could bring success to his ends. And it is remarkable . . . that his worst and meanest acts *invariably succeeded* in their object,—nay, that they were the only means by which his objects *could* have been gained. Thus his ingratitude to Essex was his great stepping-stone to his after distinctions, and his cowardly submission on the detection of his corruption, not only saved his head, but restored him to liberty, wealth, and rank. I could show, too, from Bacon's letters that Macaulay is mistaken as to his religious sincerity. As Bacon himself says, he wrapped up his physic in sweets for the priests to swallow. In fact, he was not a weak, irresolute actor in politics, but a consummate and masterly hypocrite, trained in the rules of Italian statesmanship.—BULWER, EDWARD LYTTON, 1837, *Correspondence of Macvey Napier, p.* 194.

He idolized state and magnificence in his own person; the brilliancy of his robes and the blaze of his equipage his imagination seemed to feed on; he loved to be gazed on in the streets, and to be wondered at in the cabinet: but, with this feminine weakness, this philosopher was still so philosophic as to scorn the least prudential care of his fortune; so that, while he was enamoured of wealth, he could not bring himself down to the love of money. Participating in the corruptions of the age, he was himself incorruptible: the Lord Chancellor never gave a partial or unjust sentence; and Rushworth has told us, that not one of his decrees was ever reversed. Such a man was not made to crouch and to fawn, to breathe the infection of a corrupted court, to make himself the scapegoat in the mysterious darkness of court-intrigues; but he was this man of wretchedness!—DISRAELI, ISAAC, 1841, *Bacon, Amenities of Literature.*

Has the world's meanness and cunning engrafted into his intellect, and remains smooth, serene, unenthusiastic, and in some degree base, even with all his sincere devotion and universal wisdom; bearing, to the end of life, the likeness of a marble

*Macaulay.

palace in the street of a great city, fairly furnished within, and bright in wall and battlement, yet noisome in places about the foundations.—RUSKIN, JOHN, 1843-60, *Modern Painters, pt.* v, *ch.* xx, *The Mountain Glory, p.* 354.

There is in this Lord Keeper an appetite, not to say a ravenousness, for earthly promotion and the envy of surrounding flunkies, which seems to me excessive. Thou knowest him, O reader: he is that stupendous Bacon who discovered the new way of discovering truth,—as has been very copiously explained for the last half century,—and so made men of us all. Undoubtedly a most hot seething, fermenting piece of Life with liquorish viper eyes; made of the finest elements, a beautiful kind of man, if you will; but of the earth, earthy; a certain seething, ever-fermenting prurience which prodigally burns up things:—very beautiful, but very clayey and tereene every thing of them;—not a great soul, which he seemed so near being, ah no!—CARLYLE, THOMAS, 1844-49-98, *Historical Sketches of Notable Persons and Events in the Reigns of James I. and Charles I., p.* 131.

Among his good qualities it ought to be mentioned, that he had no mean jealousy of others, and he was always disposed to patronise merit. Feeling how long he himself had been unjustly depressed from unworthy motives, he never would inflict similar injustice on others, and he repeatedly cautions statesmen to guard against this propensity. "He that plots to be a figure among ciphers is the decay of a whole age." He retained through life his passion for planting and gardening, and, when Chancellor, he ornamented Lincoln's Inn Fields with walks and groves, and gave the first example of an umbrageous square in a great metropolis. . . . He was of a middling stature,—his limbs well formed, though not robust,—his forehead high, spacious, and open,—his eye lively and penetrating; there were deep lines of thinking in his face;—his smile was both intellectual and benevolent;—the marks of age were prematurely impressed upon him;—in advanced life, his whole appearance was venerably pleasing, so that a stranger was insensibly drawn to love before knowing how much reason there was to admire him. . . . Notwithstanding all the money he had received, duly and unduly,—such was his love of expense, and his neglect of his affairs, that upon his death his estate appears to have been found insolvent. All the six executors whom he named in his will refused to act, and on the 13th of July, 1627, administration with the will annexed was granted to Sir Thomas Meautys, and Sir Robert Rich, a Master in Chancery, as two of his creditors.—No funds were forthcoming for the foundation of his lecture-ships.—CAMPBELL, LORD, 1845-56, *Lives of the Lord Chancellors and Keepers of the Great Seal of England, vol.* II.

No one lapse is known to have blurred the beauty of his youth. No rush of mad young blood ever drives him into brawls. To men of less temper and generosity than his own—to Devereux and Montjoy, to Percy and Vere, to Sackville and Bruce—he leaves the glory of Calais sands and Marylebone Park. If he be weak on the score of dress and pomp; if he dote like a young girl on flowers, on scents, on gay colors, on the trappings of a horse, the ins and outs of a garden, the furniture of a room; he neither drinks nor games, nor runs wild and loose in love. Armed with the most winning ways, the most glozing lip at court, he hurts no husband's peace, he drags no woman's name into the mire. He seeks no victories like those of Essex; he burns no shame like Raleigh into the cheek of one he loves. No Lady Rich, as in Sydney's immortal line, has cause

To blush when *he* is named.

When the passions fan out in most men, poetry flowers out in him. Old when a child, he seems to grow younger as he grows in years. Yet with all his wisdom he is not too wise to be a dreamer of dreams; for while busy with his books in Paris he gives ear to a ghostly intimation of his father's death. All his pores lie open to external nature. Birds and flowers delight his eye; his pulse beats quick at the sight of a fine horse, a ship in full sail, a soft sweep of country; everything holy, innocent, and gay acts on his spirits like wine on a strong man's blood. Joyous, helpful, swift to do good, slow to think evil, he leaves on every one who meets him a sense of friendliness, of peace and power.—DIXON, WILLIAM HEPWORTH, 1860-61, *Personal History of Lord Bacon, p.* 14.

Even the peerage of Francis Bacon was conferred, not for his merits, but for his demerits, for acts of servile baseness to that hideous court that have left behind them a stain as immortal as his name.—BISSET, ANDREW, 1864, *Omitted Chapters of the History of England, vol.* I, *p.* 3.

Francis Bacon was endowed by nature with the richest gifts and most extraordinary powers. His mother was a learned woman in those days when learning for either sex implied a knowledge of the Greek and Latin classics. . . . His father was not only Lord Keeper of the Great Seal, but an eminent scholar and a patron of learning and art, who had the reputation of uniting in himself "the opposite characters of a witty and a weighty speaker." . . . An original thinker always; a curious explorer into every branch, and a master in nearly all parts, of human learning and knowledge; a brilliant essayist, an ingenious critic, a scientific inventor, a subtle, bold, and all-grasping philosopher; an accurate and profound legal writer, a leading orator and statesman, a counsellor of sovereigns and princes, a director in the affairs of nations, and, in spite of all faults, whether his own, or of his time, or of servants whose rise was his fall, "the justest Chancellor that had been in the five changes since Sir Nicholas Bacon's time."—HOLMES, NATHANIEL, 1866, *The Authorship of Shakespeare, pp.* 110, 600.

The meanness of Bacon, spoken of in the bitterest line of one of the bitterest poets, contrasts so strangely with the elevation of Bacon's genius, that even they who cannot get rid of the impression left upon their minds by his conduct to Essex remain perplexed by the apparent enigma. . . . That much of Bacon's advice seems, in itself, intrinsically mean, we do not for a moment deny; but what we feel very strongly is, that until we can place ourselves in the peculiar focus of his own familiar position, and of the personal relations of the great family of statesmen who then lived round the English throne, occupied by an able, crafty, and conceited—a vacillating and dangerous woman, whose word could and did decide the fate of any one or more of them, we cannot rightly judge the exact standard of Bacon's worldly wisdom.—CRACROFT, BERNARD, 1868, *Essays, Political and Miscellaneous.*

His natural gifts were formed by the simple addition of those of his mother to those of his father. It is doubtful whether or no he was very precocious, but Queen Elizabeth certainly took delight in his boyish wit, gravity, and judgment.—GALTON, FRANCIS, 1869, *Hereditary Genius, p.* 200.

I am persuaded for my own part that, if he had died before Christmas 1620, his example and authority upon all questions of business, politics, administration, legislation, and morals, would have stood quite as high and been as much studied and quoted, and with quite as good reason, as it has upon questions purely intellectual. All his life he had been studying to know and to speak the truth; and I doubt whether there was ever any man whose evidence upon matters of fact may be more absolutely relied on, or who could more truly say with Kent, in Lear,—

All my reports go with the modest truth;
Nor more, nor clipp'd; but so.

. . . All the evidence shows that he was a very sensitive man, who felt acutely both kindness and unkindness, but that he was at the same time remarkably free from the ordinary defect of sensitive natures,—irritability and aptness to take offense. . . Bacon's record is unusully full, and as his life presented to himself many doubtful problems for action, it has left to us many questionable actions for criticism; and among them not a few which he would not himself have repeated or attempted to justify. One thing, however, must be admitted to his advantage. Of the contemporaries whose opinion of him is known to us, those who saw him nearest in his private life give him the best character.—SPEDDING, JAMES, 1878, *An Account of the Life and Times of Francis Bacon, vol.* II, *pp.* 521, 642, 654.

View him only as a thinker, and all the qualities that attract reverence for intellectual greatness—enthusiastic ardour in the pursuit of truth, penetrating and prophetic insight, grasp and comprehensiveness of mind, and a certain noble audacity of speculation and irrepressible confidence in human progress—meet the eye. View him only as an actor on the stage of public life, at one of the most corrupt periods of England's political history, and it is possible to see in him only a clever, pliant man of the world, inspired with a somewhat vulgar ambition for the good things of life, yielding to the contaminating influences of the time, cold and somewhat faithless in his friendships, identifying himself with the measures of rulers conspicuous for their meanness, duplicity, and cruelty, and sacrificing his own self-respect, if not for worldly gain, at least to serve the ends of people who were not worthy, and whom he must have known not to be worthy, to untie his shoe-latchet. Such, or something like this, are the materials from which it has been possible to produce the picture, full of coarsely-drawn contrasts, of glaring lights and ink-black shadows, Hyperion and Satyr combined, which popular writers have offered to us as the faithful representation of the character of Bacon. Even were it nearer the truth than it is, it is difficult to understand the strange zest which these writers seems to feel in exposing the weaknesses and inconsistencies of a great nature, and in ferreting out every obscure and doubtful detail by which the proof of his supposed infamy can be strengthened. There are those, indeed, who can find consolation for their own littleness in the failings of an exalted mind, and whose delight in this sort of morbid anatomy is not to be wondered at; but surely for those who, by their own acknowledgment, find in Bacon "the most exquisitely constructed intellect that has ever been bestowed on any of the children of men," the worthier attitude would be, instead of airing one's wit and fancy and fine-writing over the inconsistencies of greatness, if possible, to ignore and forget them, if not, to speak of them with a regret too profound for flippancy.—CAIRD, JOHN, 1880–98, *University Addresses, p.* 129.

He was anything rather than "mean." On the other hand, he was generous, open-hearted, affectionate, peculiarly sensitive to kindnesses, and equally forgetful of injuries. The epithet of "great," which has been so ungrudgingly accorded to him as a writer, might, without any singular impropriety, be applied to him also as a man. The story of his life, it must be confessed, is not altogether what the reader of his works would have desired, but the contrast has been so exaggerated as to amount to a serious and injurious misrepresentation. — FOWLER, THOMAS, 1881, *Bacon, (English Philosophers), p.* 28.

The vast intellect of "high-browed Verulam" commands our respectful admiration, but it is icy and ungenial; we cannot bring ourselves to love the man, however much we may venerate the writer. —NICOLL, HENRY J., 1882, *Landmarks of English Literature, p.* 94.

If James had been capable of appreciating Bacon's genius, the name of the prophet of natural science might have come down to us as great in politics as it is in philosophy. The defects in his character would hardly have been known, or, if they had been known, they would have been lost in the greatness of his achievements.—GARDINER, SAMUEL R., 1883, *History of England, vol.* I, *p.* 164.

The life of Francis Bacon is one which it is a pain to write or to read. It is the life of a man endowed with as rare a combination of noble gifts as ever was bestowed on a human intellect; the life of one with whom the whole purpose of living and of every day's work was to do great things to enlighten and elevate his race, to enrich it with new powers, to lay up in store for all ages to come a source of blessings which should never fail or dry up; it was the life of a man who had high thoughts of the ends and methods of law and government, and with whom the general and public good was regarded as the standard by which the use of public power was to be measured; the life of a man who had struggled hard and successfully for the measure of prosperity and opulence which makes work easy and gives a man room and force for carrying out his purposes. All his life long his first and never-sleeping passion was the romantic and splendid ambition after knowledge, for the conquest of nature and for the service of man; gathering up in himself the spirit and longings and efforts of all discoverers and inventors of the arts, as they are symbolised in the mythical Prometheus. He rose to the highest place and honour; and yet that place and honour were but the fringe and adornment of all that made him great. It is difficult to imagine a grander and more magnificent career; and his name ranks among the few chosen examples of human achievement. And yet it was not only an unhappy life; it was a poor life. . . . When he is a lawyer, he seems only a lawyer. If he had not been the author of the "Instauratio," his life would not have looked very different from that of any other of the shrewd and supple lawyers who hung on to the Tudor and Stuart Courts, and who unscrupulously pushed their way to preferment. . . . Both in his philosophical thinking, and in the feelings of his mind in the various accidents and occasions of life, Bacon was a religious man, with a serious and genuine religion. . . . It is not too much to say that in temper, in honesty, in labour, in humility, in reverence, he was the most perfect example that the world had yet seen of the student of nature, the enthusiast for knowledge. That such a man was tempted and fell, and suffered the Nemesis of his fall, is an instance of the awful truth embodied in the tragedy of "Faust."—CHURCH, RICHARD WILLIAM, 1884-88, *Bacon (English Men of Letters), pp.* 1, 78, 222, 225.

What a great failure Bacon was, whenever he was tried! Poor Essex, hunted to death merely for "getting up a row," and Bacon sacrificing him without compunction, and without seeing that he was probably made a tool of, merely to serve his personal advantage! Then the poetical justice, as they call it,—very prosaic justice,—of his own destruction, by a bolt out of a clear sky, which an enemy was adroit enough to direct to his ruin. And poor Bacon with conscience enough to feel that he deserved it, but not spirit enough to make a fight. No, if Pope's fling was undeserved, as you say, it was because of the mean and ignoble set around him. Almost and pitiable and tragic in its way, pitiable in its true sense, was the upshot of Bacon's higher and nobler life, conceiving vaguely and laboring all his days over that which he was unable and incompetent to bring to the birth. His memory reaping a great reward of fame for a century or so, and then the conclusion reluctantly reached that nothing tangible in the advancement of Natural Science can be attributed to him. Altogether, what a solemn sermon! It might be preached from the pulpit of St. Paul's.—GRAY, ASA, 1884, *Letters, vol.* II, *p.* 749.

Probably in consenting to contribute to the destruction of his friend, Bacon was acting under, what must have seemed to him, considerable pressure. If he had refused the task assigned to him by the Crown, he must have given up all chance of the Queen's favour and with it all hope of promotion. Very inferior men have made as great, or greater, sacrifices; but Bacon was not the man to make such a sacrifice. . . . Bacon had a keen sense of the value of fortune, of the possibilities of a learned léisure, of the importance of his own colossal plans for the benefit of the human race; on the other hand he had a very dull sense of the claims of honour and friendship. Forced to choose between prosperity and friendship, he preferred to be prosperous even at the cost of facilitating the ruin of a friend for whom ruin, in any case, was ultimately inevitable. . . . One of the strongest helps that a man can have in the time of trouble seems to have been denied to Bacon. No record in any letter or document hitherto has attested that his wife sympathised with his pursuits, or shared any of his aspirations. Her name is scarcely mentioned in his voluminous correspondence, except in a letter indicating that her convenience, as well as his own, required that York House should be retained.—ABBOTT, EDWIN ABBOTT, 1885, *Francis Bacon, An Account of His Life and Works, pp.* 81, 82, 308.

The great Lord Bacon, who has come down to us in Pope's epigrammatic judgment as "wisest, brightest, meanest of mankind," finds in Mr. Dixon a brilliant advocate against the charges of treachery to his patron, Essex, and receiving bribes as a judge. The sum of this defence seems to be that in Bacon's day all judges took bribes and all courtiers were ungrateful. This is equivalent to saying that Bacon was no worse than his contemporaries. The answer to this is that his contemporaries, at all events, seemed to think it wrong for a judge to take bribes, and punished Bacon for so doing. Therefore, Bacon was undeniably inferior in moral sense to his contemporaries. Indeed, he did not attempt to excuse the act except by saying that he never sold justice, that his judgments were always conscientious, although he might have received a present from one party to the suit. In respect to Essex, there can be no doubt that Bacon was disloyal to his benefactor. Bacon was a selfish man, a time-server, waiting on courts, and intent on his own fortunes. That posterity to whose judgment the great man committed his reputation has done his unparalleled genius full justice; but there are spots on the sun, and there are these distinct blemishes on Bacon's character.—BROWNE, IRVING, 1885, *Iconoclasm and Whitewash, p.* 12.

Bacon was full of crotchets, so to speak. In spring, he would go out for a drive in an open coach while it rained, to receive "the benefit of irrigation," which, he contended, was "most wholesome because of the nitre in the air, and the universal spirit of the world." He had extraordinary notions and indulged them freely, such as dosing himself with chemicals, rhubarb, nitre, saffron, and many other medicines. At every meal his table was abundantly strewn with flowers and sweet herbs.—BALLOU, MATURIN M., 1886, *Genius in Sunshine and Shadow, p.* 57, *note.*

Bacon's conduct to Essex has been the subject of more vituperation than perhaps any other single act of any other single man. It has been denounced as mean and treacherous, dark, mournful, and shameful; it has been used to point half the morals and adorn half the tales against ingratitude for the last two centuries. Mr. Spedding has devoted a whole volume to this theme, and arranged the documents relating to the question in a manner which calls for a modification of the popular judgment similar if not equal to that achieved by Carlyle's commentary on the letters of Cromwell. In an age when a good courtier has come to be considered as the reverse of a good citizen, men will continue to wish that Bacon had acted differently; but he must be acquitted of anything like treachery.—NICHOL, JOHN, 1888, *Francis Bacon, His Life and Philosophy, Part* i, *p.* 46.

Francis Bacon, Sir Francis Bacon, Baron Verulam, Viscount St. Albans,—these represent one individuality; but *Lord* Bacon is demonstrably a fictitious personage who never had any real existence on our planet. Lord Verulam, Lord St. Albans is somebody we can recognize; but Lord Bacon is an individual unknown to the British peerage. Hardwicke, Brougham, and Macaulay selected their family names when they were made nobles; but who would speak of Chesterfield as Lord Stanhope, or Chatham as Lord Pitt? Bacon deliberately chose to be Lord Verulam and Lord St. Albans rather than Lord Bacon. Why should everybody, including scores of men who know better, still persist in calling him "Lord" Bacon? . . . Whatever may be our opinion of him as a practical statesman, we all feel, in reading him, that we are in communion with an intellect which is essentially lordly. His "Method of Induction," which some men of science ostentatiously celebrate but practically disregard, is demonstrably inadequate to explain the progress of modern invention and discovery. By his Method he never discovered anything himself; and certainly by his Method nothing has ever been discovered by those who rank themselves among his disciples. Still, he keeps his position as a kind of autocrat by the sheer force of a certain grandeur in his intelligence. It is useless to show that he misconceived the object of science, and was ignorant of its processes; he is still "Lord" Bacon even to such men as Whewell, Herschel, Comte, Mill, Huxley, Lewes, and Herbert Spencer. Every tyro in science can expose the errors of his Method; every eminent scientist persists in calling him "Lord," and persists in calling him Bacon. Verulam is a grander title; but it has never forced itself either into popular or scientific speech.—WHIPPLE, EDWIN PERCY, 1888, *Outlooks on Society, Literature and Politics, pp.* 301, 303.

Here was a great mind—a wonderful intellect which everyone admired, and in which everyone of English birth, from Royalty down took—and ever will take—a national pride; but, withal, few of those amiabilities ever crop out in this great character which make men loved. He can see a poor priest culprit come to the rack without qualms; and could look stolidly on, as Essex, his special benefactor in his youth, walked to the scaffold; yet the misstatement of a truth, with respect to physics, or any matter about which truth or untruth was clearly demonstrable, affected him like a galvanic shock. His biographers, Montagu and Spedding, have padded his angularities into roundness; while Pope and Macaulay have lashed him in the grave. I think we must find the real man somewhere between them; if we credit him with a great straight-thinking, truth-seeking brain, and little or no capacity for affection, the riddle of his strange life will be more easily solved. . . . Indeed his protestations of undying friendship to all of high station, whom he addresses unctuously, are French in their amplitude, and French, too, in their vanities. He presses sharply always toward the great end of self-advancement—whether by flatteries, or cajolement, or direct entreaty. He believed in the survival of the fittest; and that the fittest should struggle to make the survival good —no matter what weak ones, or timid ones, or confiding ones, or emotional ones should go to the wall, or the bottom, in the struggle.—MITCHELL, DONALD G., 1889, *English Lands Letters and Kings, From Celt to Tudor, pp.* 250, 253.

The dispassionate mind that his philosophy required, Bacon applied somewhat too coldly to the philosophy of life. Without hatreds or warm affections, preferring always a kind course to an unkind one, but yielding easily to stubborn facts in his search for prosperity, Bacon, I have said, failed as a man, although he had no active evil in his character, for want of a few generous enthusiasms,—MORLEY, HENRY, AND GRIFFIN, W. HALL, 1895, *English Writers, vol.* XI, *p.* 22.

Bacon, with his brilliant intellectual equipment and his consciousness of his great powers, is not to be set down as simply a bad man. But his heart was cold, and he had no greatness of soul. He was absorbed, to a quite unworthy degree, in the pursuit of worldly prosperity. Always deeply in debt, he coveted above everything fine houses and gardens, massive plate, great revenues, and, as essential preliminaries, high offices and employments, titles and distinctions, which he might well have left to men of meaner worth. He passed half his life in the character of an office-seeker, met with one humiliating refusal after another, and returned humble thanks for the gracious denial. Once and once only, in his early days in Parliament, did he display some independence and rectitude; but when he saw that it gave offence in the highest places, he repented as bitterly as though he had been guilty of a sin against all political morality, and besought her Majesty's forgiveness in terms that might have befitted a detected thief.—BRANDES, GEORGE, 1898, *William Shakespeare, A Critical Study, vol.* I, *p.* 309.

ESSAYS
1597–1625

Sir Francis Bacon hath set out new Essays, where, in a chapter of *Deformity*, the world takes notice that he paints out his little cousin [Robert Cecil, Earl of Salisbury] to the life.—CHAMBERLAIN, NICHOLAS, 1612, *Letter to Sir Dudley Carleton, Dec.* 17. *Court and Times of James I., vol.* I, *p.* 214.

The virtue of these "Essays" is too well allowed to require any comment. Without the elegance of Addison, or the charming egotism of Montaigne, they have acquired the widest circulation: and if Bacon had written no more, they would have bequeathed his name undying to posterity. Burke preferred them to the rest of his writings, and Dr. Johnson observed that "their excellence and value consists in their being the observations of a strong mind operating upon life, and, in consequence, you will find there what you seldom find in other books."—MALONE, EDMUND, 1794, *Life of Sir Joshua Reynolds.*

No book contains a greater fund of useful knowledge, or displays a more intimate acquaintance with human life and manners. The style, however, is not pleasing; it is devoid of melody and simplicity, and the sentences are too short and antithetic.—DRAKE, NATHAN, 1804, *Essays Illustrative of the Tatler, Spectator, and Guardian, vol.* II, *p.* 20.

The small volume to which he has given the title of "Essays," the best known and the most popular of all his works. It is one of those where the superiority of his genius appears to the greatest advantage; the novelty and depth of his reflections often receiving a strong relief from the triteness of the subject. It may be read from beginning to end in a few hours; and yet after the twentieth perusal one seldom fails to remark in it something overlooked before. This, indeed, is a characteristic of all Bacon's writings, and is only to be accounted for by the inexhaustible ailment they furnish to our own thoughts, and the sympathetic activity they impart to our torpid faculties.—STEWART, DUGALD, 1815-21, *First Preliminary Dissertation, Encyclopædia Britannica.*

For style, they are rich and venerable —for thinking, incorrect and fanciful.—CARLYLE, THOMAS, 1817, *Early Letters, ed. Norton, p.* 61.

The Essays, which are ten in number, abound with condensed thought and practical wisdom, neatly, pressly, and weightily stated, and, like all his early works, are simple, without imagery. They are written in his favourite style of aphorisms, although each essay is apparently a continued work; and without that love of antithesis and false glitter to which truth and justness of thought is frequently sacrificed by the writers of maxims.—MONTAGU, BASIL, 1834, *The Life of Francis Bacon, p.* xxxvii.

It is by the "Essays" that Bacon is best known to the multitude. The "Novum Organum" and the "De Augmentis" are much talked of, but little read. They have produced indeed a vast effect on the opinions of mankind; but they have produced it through the operations of intermediate agents. They have moved the intellects which have moved the world. It is in the "Essays" alone that the mind of Bacon is brought into immediate contact with the minds of ordinary readers. There, he opens an exoteric school, and he talks to plain men in language which everybody understands, about things in which everybody is interested. He has thus enabled those who must otherwise have taken his merits on trust to judge for themselves; and the great body of readers have, during several generations, acknowledged that the man who has treated with such consummate ability questions with which they are familiar, may well be supposed to deserve all the praise bestowed on him by those who have sat in his inner school.—MACAULAY, THOMAS BABINGTON, 1834, *Lord Bacon, Edinburgh Review, Critical and Miscellaneous Essays.*

The transcendent strength of Bacon's mind is visible in the whole tenor of these "Essays," unequal as they must be from the very nature of such compositions. They are deeper and more discriminating than any earlier, or almost any later, work in the English language, full of recondite observation, long matured and carefully sifted. . . . Few books are more quoted; and, what is not always the case with such books, we may add, that few are more generally read. In this respect they lead the van of our prose literature: for no gentleman is ashamed of owning that he has not read the Elizabethan writers: but it would be somewhat derogatory to a man of the slightest claim to polite letters, were he unacquainted with the "Esasys" of Bacon. It is, indeed, little worth while to read this or any other book for reputation's sake; but very few in our language so well repay the pains, or afford more nourishment to the thoughts. —HALLAM, HENRY 1837–39, *Introduction to the Literature of Europe, pt.* iii, *ch.* iv, *par.* 34.

Bacon's "Essays" are the portrait of an ambitious and profound calculator,—a great man of the vulgar sort. Of the upper world of man's being they speak few and faint words.—EMERSON, RALPH WALDO, 1838–93, *Milton, Works, Riverside ed., vol.* XII, *p.* 152.

His English Essays and Treatises will be read and admired by the Anglo-Saxon race all over the world, to the most distant generations; while since the age which immediately succeeded his own, only a few recondite scholars have penetrated and relished the admirable good sense enveloped in his crabbed Latinity. —CAMPBELL, JOHN, LORD, 1845–56, *Lives of the Lord Chancellors and Keepers of the Great Seal of England, vol.* II.

There is scarcely a volume in the whole prose literature of England, which is, more emphatically, at once a product of the English intellect, and an agency in the history of English practical ethics. The style of the "Essays" is very attractive, though never pedantically exact, and often even negligent, in its observance of the rules of grammatical concord and regimen; but though many Latinized words are introduced, even its solecisms are English, and it is, in all probability, a fair picture of the language used at that time by men of the highest culture, in the conversational discussion of questions of practical philosophy, or what the Germans call *world-wisdom* —MARSH, GEORGE P., 1862, *The Origin and History of the English Language, etc., p.* 549.

Bacon's sentence bends beneath the weight of his thought, like a branch beneath the weight of its fruit. Bacon seems to have written his essays with Shakespeare's pen. . . . He writes like one on whom presses the weight of affairs, and he approaches a subject always on its serious side. He does not play with it fantastically. He lives amongst great ideas, as with great nobles, with whom he dare not be too familiar. In the tone of his mind there is ever something imperial. When he writes on building, he speaks of a palace with spacious entrances, and courts, and banqueting-halls; when he writes on gardens, he speaks of alleys and mounts, waste places and fountains, of a garden "which is indeed prince-like."—SMITH, ALEXANDER, 1863, *Dreamthorp, pp.* 31, 32.

Stands confessedly at the head of all works of this class in English literature. It is in a sense properly taken as a model for all, and is one of the wisest and most thoughtful books for men of every condition and every age.—PORTER, NOAH, 1870, *Books and Reading, ch.* xix.

The style of these brief essays, in which every sentence was compact with thought and polished in expression until it might run alone through the world as a maxim, had all the strength of euphuism and none of its weakness. The sentences were all such as it needed ingenuity to write; but this was the rare ingenuity of wisdom. Each essay, shrewdly discriminative, contained a succession of wise thoughts exactly worded.—MORLEY, HENRY, 1873, *First Sketch of English Literature, p.* 465.

His "Essays" are not at all sceptical, like the French essays, from which he may have borrowed this appellation: they are thorouhgly dogmatic. . . . They are extremely instructive for the internal relations of English society. They show wide observation and calm wisdom, and, like his philosophical works, are a treasure for the English nation, whose views of life have been built upon them.—RANKE, LEOPOLD VON, 1875, *A History of England, vol.* I, *p.* 459.

I venture to affirm that Bacon's greatest and most characteristic work is not the "De Augmentis," or the "Novum Orgnaum," or any of his purely scientific writings, but the "Essays," and that even of his more ambitious works the most valuable element is the many incidental remarks and suggestions which constitute a kind of practical worldly wisdom or philosophy of common life.—CAIRD, JOHN, 1880, *University Addresses, p.* 135.

The essays of Bacon contain the classicalism of the Renaissance combined with the practical moral sense of the Englishman.—MORRIS, GEORGE S., 1880, *British Thought and Thinkers, p.* 128.

Nothing can be more loose than the structure of the essays. There is no art, no style, and, except in a few, the political ones, no order: thoughts are put down and left unsupported, unproved, undeveloped. In the first form of the ten, which composed the first edition of 1597, they are more like notes of analysis or tables of contents; they are austere even to meagreness. But the general character continues in the enlarged and expanded ones of Bacon's later years. . . . But these short papers say what they have to say without preface, and in literary undress, without a superfluous word, without the joints and bands of structure: they say it in brief, rapid sentences, which come down, sentence after sentence like the strokes of a great hammer.—CHURCH, RICHARD WILLIAM, 1884-88, *Bacon, (English Men of Letters), p.* 273.

In certain features they stand alone in this field of writing. There is nothing of the gay paradox of Montaigne, the sounding verbiage of Seneca, or the witty sophistry of Rochefoucauld. They express the "practical reason" of the English mind. Each sentence is beaten gold. One of his observations on men and manners is like a chalk outline by Michael Angelo. And as a model of English style, the "Essays" are unrivalled, although I think they have less of stately eloquence than the "Advancement of Learning."—WASHBURN, EMELYN W., 1884, *Studies in Early English Literature, p.* 202.

The literature of aphorism contains one English name of magnificent and immortal lustre—the name of Francis Bacon. Bacon's essays are the unique masterpiece in our literature of this oracular wisdom of life, applied to the scattered occasions of men's existence.—MORLEY, JOHN, 1887-90, *Aphorisms, Studies in Literature, p.* 73.

Of this book Hallam said, that it "leads the van of our prose literature." In saying this, he did but formulate the impression of educated men in his day, but that was before the upper course of the stream had been adequately explored. As English prose it is indeed a very remarkable book, especially as it lets us see through the now prevailing and rampant Classicism to some select retreat where the true English tradition flourishes with its native vigour.—EARLE, JOHN, 1890, *English Prose, p.* 442.

Less than seventy years after the death of Bacon his "Essays" were so completely forgotten that when extracts from them were discovered in the common-place book of a deceased lady of quality, they were supposed to be her own, were published and praised by people as clever as Congreve, went through several editions, and were not detected until within the present century.—GOSSE, EDMUND, 1892, *Tennyson—and After, Questions at Issue, p.* 190.

This work secured for ever Bacon's fame as a writer of rare wisdom, who expressed his vigorous and original thought in a style marked by compressed fulness of meaning, calm strength, and the utmost felicity of diction. The book is a triumph of literary skill, a combination of almost perfect excellence of matter and form.—SANDERSON, EDGAR, 1893, *History of England and the British Empire, p.* 511.

Their dignity, wealth of fancy, masculine grasp of ethical questions, language all compact, produce an effect, not of warmth and friendliness, but of intellectual activity. Bacon called himself "a bell-ringer who is up first to call others to church."—GEORGE, ANDREW J., 1898, *From Chaucer to Arnold, Types of Literary Art, p.* 631.

Certainly no other prose work of its size is so often used in quotation.—RAFFETY, FRANK W., 1899, *Books Worth Reading, p.* 45.

ADVANCEMENT OF LEARNING
1605

His character of the schoolmen is perhaps the finest philosophical sketch that ever was drawn.—HAZLITT, WILLIAM, 1820, *Lectures on the Literature of the Age of Elizabeth, p.* 217.

Neither the most liberal of the professions, nor even the wider field of politics and legislation, could supply to the genius of Bacon a sufficient sphere of activity; and turning aside for a short space from the career of worldly ambition, in which he had many competitors, to that in which he marched unrivalled and alone, he completed and gave to the world in 1605 his immortal work on the "Advancement of Learning." . . . The experience of ages has shown, that he who assumes the character of a reformer in the art of reasoning, an expositor of the errors of the schools, soars above the region of popular applause only to excite the alarms, or encounter the hostility, of the learned; whose pride, whose prejudices and whose interests he offends or threatens. Thus, whilst a few inquisitive and enlightened spirits, such as Jonson and Wotton and Raleigh, hailed with delight and awe the discoveries of their great contemporary, born to establish an era in the progress of the human mind, the erudite disciples of ancient error busied themselves in depreciating and decrying what they would not or could not understand.—AIKIN, LUCY, 1822, *Memoirs of the Court of King James the First, vol.* I, *pp.* 193, 195.

The work is dedicated to King James the First, and its introduction inspires a mingled sentiment of admiration of the boldness and grandeur of the design which it announces, and of heart-ache at the depth of degradation to which it sinks in the servile adulation with which it besmears the king. . . . The stupendous magnitude of this undertaking, the courtly cunning, ingenuity, and meanness of suggesting it to the King as if it was an enterprise of his own, the lofty consciousness of its sublimity, and the sly implied disclaimer of it as anything more on the part of the author than a mere speculative whim to be moulded into form and substance, are all deserving of profound meditation—of more than I can give. He proceeds then to enumerate and to refute the objections against learning—of divines, of politicians, as arising from the fortunes, manners, or studies of learned men. He discusses the diseases of learning—the peccant humors which have not only given impediment to the proficiency of learning, but have given occasion to the traducement thereof. And he closes the book with a copious and cheering exhibition of the dignity of learning—a theme upon which I follow him with delight. The style is a continuous and perpetual citation of classical and scriptural quotations.—ADAMS, JOHN QUINCY, 1844, *Diary, July* 19, *Memoirs, ed. C. F. Adams, vol.* XII, *p.* 72.

Marked the first decisive appearance of the new philosophy. . . . He did not thoroughly understand the older philosophy which he attacked. His revolt from the waste of human intelligence which he conceived to be owing to the adoption of a false method of investigation blinded him to the real value of deduction as an instrument of discovery; and he was encouraged in his contempt for it as much by his own ignorance of mathematics as by the non-existence in his day of the great deductive sciences of physics and astronomy. Nor had he a more accurate prevision of the method of modern science.—GREEN, JOHN RICHARD, 1874, *Short History of the English People, ch.* ix.

The two finest prose essays in the English language are Lord Bacon's "Essay on the Advancement of Learning," and Milton's tract on "The Freedom of the Press." And these are also interesting to that degree that, having once read them, you will never forget them.—CLARKE, JAMES FREEMAN, 1880, *Self-Culture, p.* 321.

In the philosophical and historical works there is no want of attention to the flow and order and ornament of composition. When we come to the "Advancement of Learning," we come to a book which is one of the landmarks of what high thought and rich imagination have made of the English language. It is the first great book in English prose of secular interest; the first book which can claim a place beside the "Laws of Ecclesiastical Polity." . . . It contains some of his finest writings.—CHURCH, RICHARD WILLIAM, 1884–88, *Bacon, (English Men of Letters), pp.* 275, 276.

The "Advancement" is written, or finished at least, obviously in too great haste; the Second Book is sometimes almost slovenly, and the close of it leaves us nowhere. But the opening part, in which Bacon sums up first the discredits and then the dignity of learning, defending wisdom, and justifying it to its sons, remains one of the great performances of the seventeenth century. The matter of it is obsolete, human knowledge having progressed so far forwards and backwards since 1605; and something dry and unripe in Bacon's manner—which mellowed in later life—diminishes our pleasure in reading what is none the less a very noble work, and one intended to be the prologue to the author's vast edifice of philosophical inquiry. At this point, however, he unluckily determined to abandon English brick for Latin stone.—GOSSE, EDMUND, 1897, *Short History of Modern English Literature, p.* 131.

NOVUM ORGANUM
1620

I have received, from many parts beyond the seas, testimonies touching that work, much beyond what I could have expected at the first in so abstruse an argument.—BACON, FRANCIS, 1622, *Epistle to Bishop Andrewes, prefixed to An Advertisement touching on Holy War.*

I have received three copies of that work, wherewith your Lordship hath done a great and everlasting benefit to all the children of Nature, and to Nature herself in her utmost extent and latitude, who never before had so true an Interpreter, or so inward a Secretary of her Cabinet.—WOTTON, SIR HENRY, 1622, *Letter to Bacon, Reliquiæ Wottonianæ.*

The most singular, and the least of all his pieces, is that which, at this time, is most useless and least read, I mean his "Novum Scientiarum Organum." This is the scaffold with which the new philosophy was raised; and when the edifice was built, part of it at least, the scaffold was no longer of service. The lord Bacon was not yet acquainted with nature, but then he knew, and pointed out, the several paths that led to it.—VOLTAIRE, FRANCOIS MARIE ARONET, 1732? *Letters on the English Nation.*

He saw and taught his contemporaries and future ages, that reasoning is nothing worth, except as it is founded on facts. . . . Most valuable of all his works, and by him most highly valued. It is written in a plain unadorned style in aphorisms, invariably stated by him to be the proper style for philosophy, which, conscious of its own power, ought to go forth "naked and unarmed;" but, from the want of symmetry and ornament, from its abstruseness, from the novelty of its terms, and from the imperfect state in which it was published, it has, although the most valuable, hitherto been too much neglected; but it will not so continue. The time has arrived, or is fast approaching, when the pleasures of intellectual pursuit will have so deeply pervaded society, that they will, to a considerable extent, form the pleasures of our youth; and the lamentation in the "Advancement of Learning" will be diminished or pass away.—MONTAGU, BASIL, 1834, *The Life of Francis Bacon, pp.* cclxxxiii, ccxcvii. *Bacon's Complete Works.*

If Bacon constructed a method to which modern science owes its existence, we shall find its cultivators grateful for the gift, and offering the richest incense at the shrine of a benefactor whose generous labours conducted them to immortality. No such testimonies, however, are to be found. Nearly two hundred years have gone by, teeming with the richest fruits of human genius, and no grateful disciple has appeared to vindicate the rights of the alleged legislator of science. Even Newton, who was born and educated after the publication of the "Novum Organon," never mentions the name of Bacon or his system; and the amiable and indefatigable Boyle treated him with the same disrespectful silence. When we are told, therefore, that Newton owed all his discoveries to the method of Bacon, nothing more can be meant than that he proceeded in that path of observation and experiment which had been so warmly recommended in the "Novum Organon;" but it ought to have been added, that the same method was practised by his predecessors; that Newton possessed no secret that was not used by Galileo and Copernicus; and that he would have enriched science with the same splendid discoveries if the name and the writings of Bacon had never been heard of.—BREWSTER, SIR DAVID, 1855, *Memoirs of the Life, Writings, and Discoveries of Sir Isaac Newton, vol.* II, *p.* 402.

There is no book which gives me such a sense of greatness; because the sayings are like keys which turn every way and *fit* whichever chamber of truth you want to turn into,—physical, mental, and moral science alike.—GREENWELL, DORA, 1860, *Memoirs, ed. Dorling, p.* 47

The Lord Chancellor, with his titles of honour, is almost forgotten when the author of the "Novum Organum" rises in our view. . . . The pains which Bacon took to make it worthy of his fame may be judged from the fact, that he copied and corrected it twelve times before he gave it to the world.—COLLIER, WILLIAM FRANCIS, 1861, *History of English Literature, p.* 158.

Bacon the magnificent might be fit to lay down the chart of all knowledge; Bacon the despised seems fitter to guide patient and foot-sore pilgrims through tangled roads, amidst dangers arising from their own presumption, into a region of light. And this is, at last, the true glory of the "Novum Organum."—MAURICE, FREDERICK DENISON, 1862, *Moral and Metaphysical Philosophy, vol.* II, *p.* 233.

His acquaintance* with Bacon was probably slight, and what he knew of his Latin works was, we suspect, what he had picked up in conversation from Bolingbroke and Clarke. No man who had read the "Novum Organum" would speak of it as Voltaire speaks of it in his Twelfth Letter.—COLLINS, JOHN CHURTON, 1868, *Bolingbroke, A Historical Study; and Voltaire in England, p.* 260.

When we take in hand the "Novum Organum," it is not wholly out of place to remember that Bacon took a bribe. So much we should expect an editor of that treatise to remind us of. But we should hardly wish to have him detail, in his introduction to it, the history of Bacon's corruption, his black behaviour to Essex, the murder of Raleigh, the torture of Peacham.—PATTISON, MARK, 1872-89, *Pope and his Editors, Essays, vol.* II, *p.* 383.

In spite however of his inadequate appreciation either of the old philosophy or the new, the almost unanimous voice of later ages has attributed, and justly attributed, to the "Novum Organum" a decisive influence on the development of modern science.—GREEN, JOHN RICHARD, 1874, *Short History of the English People, ch.* ix.

And now at last the "Novum Organum," the fragmentary relic of that grand scheme for the restoration of the sciences which had floated before his youthful imagination in the days when he boasted that he had "taken all knowledge for his province," had passed through the press. For the reception with which it met, he cared but little: Coke might recommend him with a snarl to restore the justice and the laws of England before he meddled with the doctrines of the old philosophers; James might meet him with the silly jest that the book was like the peace of God, because it passed all understanding. It was for posterity that he worked, and for the judgment of posterity he was content to wait. . . . As a practical book, addressed to practical men, it was as complete a failure as was the commercial policy of its writer. . . . That which

*Voltaire.

gives to the author of the "Novum Organum" a place apart amongst "those who know," is, that being, as he was, far behind some of his contemporaries in scientific knowledge, and possessing scarcely any of the qualifications needed for scientific investigation, he was yet able, by a singular and intuitive prescience, to make the vision of the coming age his own, and not only to point out the course which would be taken by the stream even then springing into life, but to make his very errors and shortcomings replete with the highest spirit of that patient and toilsome progress from which he himself turned aside. —GARDINER, SAMUEL R., 1883, *History of England, vol.* III, *pp.* 394, 395.

HISTORY OF HENRY VII.

1622

But this good Work was the most effectually undertaken and compleated by the Incomparable Sir Francis Bacon, who has bravely surmounted all those difficulties, and pass'd over those Rocks and Shallows, against which he took such Pains to caution other less experienc'd Historians. He has perfectly put himself into King Henry's own Garb and Livery, giving as sprightly a View of the Secrets of his Council, as if himself had been President in it. Not trivial Passages, such as are below the Notice of a Statesman, are mix'd with his Sage Remarks: Nor is any thing of Weight or Moment slubber'd over with that careless Hast and Indifferency which is too common in other Writers. No Allowances are given to the Author's own Conjecture or Invention; where a little Pains and Consideration will serve to set the Matter in its proper and true Light. No Impertinent Digressions, nor fanciful Comments, distract his Readers: But the whole is written in such a Grave and Uniform Style, as becomes both the Subject and the Artificer.—NICOLSON, WILLIAM, 1696-1714, *English Historical Library.*

Thus ignominious was the fall of the famous Bacon! despicable in all the active parts of life, and only glorious in the contemplative. Him the rays of knowledge served but to embellish, not enlighten; and philosophy itself was degraded by a conjunction with his mean soul: we are told that he often lamented that ambition and vain glory had diverted him from spending his whole time in the manner worthy of his extensive genius; but there is too much reason to believe, from his conduct, that these sentiments arose from the weight of his mortifications, and not from the conviction of his judgment. He preferred mean applications to James, and continued to flatter him so far, as to paint his grandfather, Henry the Seventh, in an amiable light. —MACAULAY, CATHERINE, 1763-83, *History of England, vol.* I.

The only two pieces of history we have, in any respect to be compared with the ancient, are, the reign of Henry the Seventh by my lord Bacon, and the history of our civil wars in the last century by your noble ancestor my lord chancellor Clarendon.—BOLINGBROKE, HENRY ST. JOHN, VISCOUNT, 1751? *Works, vol.* II, *p.* 246.

Bacon's "Henry the VIIth" betrays too much of the apologist for arbitrary power, but it is otherwise of great value; it is written from original, and now lost, materials, with vigour and philosophical acuteness.—DRAKE, NATHAN, 1817, *Shakspeare and His Times, vol.* I, *p.* 476.

Of all his works, this gave the least satisfaction to the public; and after recently again perusing it, I must confess that it is hardly equal to Sir Thomas More's "History of Richard III.," or to Camden's of Queen Elizabeth,—leaving the reproach upon our literature of being lamentably deficient in historical composition, till the days of Hume, Robertson, and Gibbon. Some have accounted for Bacon's failure by supposing a decline in his faculties; but he afterwards showed that they remained in their pristine vigour to the very close of his career.—CAMPBELL, JOHN, LORD, 1845-56, *Lives of the Lord Chancellors and Keepers of the Great Seal of England, vol.* II.

Is in many ways a masterly work. With the true philosophic temper, he seeks, not content with a superficial narrative of events, to trace out and exhibit their causes and connections; and hence he approaches to the modern conception of history, as the record of the development of peoples, rather than of the actions of princes and other showy personages.—ARNOLD, THOMAS, 1862-87, *Manual of English Literature, p.* 128.

In one respect Bacon's History is in strong contrast to Macaulay's. In relating the schemes and actions of such a king as Henry, Macaulay would have overlaid the narrative with strong expressions of approval or disapproval. Bacon writes calmly, narrating facts and motives without any comment of a moral nature. Sometimes, indeed, he criticises, but it is from the point of view of a politician, not of a moralist; a piece of cruelty or perfidy is either censured only as being injudicious, or not commented upon at all. On this ground he is visited with a sonorous declamation by Sir James Mackintosh—as if his not improving the occasion were a sign that he approved of what had been done. Bacon wrote upon a principle that is beginning to be pretty widely accepted as regards personal histories claiming to be impartial—namely, that "it is the true office of history to represent the events themselves together with the counsels, and to leave the observations and conclusions thereupon to the liberty and faculty of every man's judgment." He does not seek to seal up historical facts from the useful office of "pointing a moral;" he only held that the moralising should not interfere with the narrative.—MINTO, WILLIAM, 1872–80, *Manual of English Prose Literature, p.* 249.

A work which, done under every advantage, would have been a rare specimen of skill, diligence, and spirit in the workman; but for which, begun as it was immediately after so tremendous an overthrow, and carried on in the middle of so many difficulties in the present and anxieties for the future, it would be hard to find a parallel. Though not one of his works which stand highest either in reputation or popularity with later times,—being neither generally read (an accident which it shares with most of the others) nor generally supposed to be of great value (in which it is more singular),—it has done its work more effectually perhaps than any of them. None of the histories which had been written before conveyed any idea either of the distinctive character of the man or the real business of his reign. Every history which has been written since has derived all its light from this, and followed its guidance in every question of importance; and the additional materials which come to light from time to time, and enable us to make many corrections in the history of the events, only serve to confirm and illustrate the truth of its interpretation of them.—SPEDDING, JAMES, 1878, *An Account of the Life and Times of Francis Bacon, vol.* II, *p.* 542.

The government of the first Tudor, though by no means one of the worst, was a government of usurpation. Its most efficient means of accomplishing its ends was the secret court of Star Chamber. This court kept no records, and was not responsible for its acts. Whatever was necessary for the firmer establishment of the new line was done probably without question and without scruple. Very little documentary evidence was left. But even what little existed in Bacon's time seems not to have been used by the historian. From the beginning to the end of his work, Bacon has given only one reference to an authority, and even that reference is so indefinite as almost to justify the suspicion that it was meant to mislead. The value of the history as a record of truth, therefore, rests solely upon the nature of the habits then prevailing in the investigation of knowledge, and on the character of the historian for veracity. Unfortunately, neither of these foundations is trustworthy. Bacon was not born till more than fifty years after the death of the king whose history he undertook to write. Three important and turbulent reigns had intervened. Bacon had every interest in giving to the facts, as he narrated them, a certain color. Unfortunately, we are debarred from believing that he would be overscrupulous in his searches after exact knowledge, even if exact knowledge were accessible. But it was not. It is therefore but simple truth to say that no court in any civilized community would accept of Bacon's testimony as a basis on which to build up any judicial decision whatever. Historical evidence, in order to be conclusive, must be of the same general nature as all other evidence. The conclusion to which we are brought is obvious. The book teaches us something of Bacon; it teaches us possibly something of the way in which Bacon regarded Henry VII.; it teaches us still more of the way in which Bacon desired his readers to regard his opinions of Henry VII.; but of Henry VII. himself, or of his reign, it teaches us very little indeed. —ADAMS, CHARLES KENDALL, 1881–88, *A Manual of Historical Literature, p.* 8.

Stands confessedly amongst the choicest first-fruits of the long harvest of English historical literature.—GARDINER, SAMUEL R., 1883, *History of England, vol.* IV, *p.* 132.

Is a model of clear historical narration, not exactly picturesque, but never dull; and though not exactly erudite, yet by no means wanting in erudition, and exhibiting conclusions which, after two centuries and a half of record-grubbing, have not been seriously impugned or greatly altered by any modern historian. In this book, which was written late, Bacon had, of course, the advantage of his long previous training in the actual politics of a school not very greatly altered since the time he was describing, but this does not diminish the credit due to him for formal excellence. —SAINTSBURY, GEORGE, 1887, *History of Elizabethan Literature, p.* 209.

PHILOSOPHY

No man* made more observations, or caused more to be made, to the end, that at last some notions of natural things, more sound and pure than those commonly received, might be collected; for which reason he admired the genius, and approved the design of that great Chancellor of England, Sir Francis Bacon.—GASSENDI, PIERRE, 1641? *Life of Peiresc, book* vi, *p.* 207.

You formerly wrote me, that you knew persons who were willing to labour for the advancement of the sciences, at the cost of all sorts of observations and experiments: now, if any one who is inclined this way, could be prevailed upon to undertake a history of the appearances of the heavenly bodies, to be drawn up according to the Verulamian method, without the admixture of hypothesis; such a work as this would prove of great utility, and would save me a great deal of trouble in the prosecution of my inquiries.—DESCARTES, RENE, 1650? *Letter to Father Mersenne, Vie de M. Descartes, vol.* I, *p*, 148.

The Patriarch of experimental philosophy.—POWER, HENRY, 1664, *Experimental Philosophy, p.* 82.

It is certain that Lord Bacon's way of experiment, as now prosecuted by sundry English gentlemen, affords more probabilities of glorious and profitable fruits, than the attempts of any other age or nation whatsoever.—HAVERS, G., 1664, *Philosophical Conferences, Preface.*

*Peiresc.

The Royal Society was a work well becoming the largeness of Bacon's wit to devise, and the greatness of Clarendon's prudence to establish.—SPRAT, THOMAS, 1667, *History of the Royal Society of London.*

Bacon at last, a mighty man, arose, . . .
And boldly undertook the injur'd pupil's cause.
Bacon, like Moses, led us forth at last,
The barren wilderness he pas'd;
Did on the very border stand
Of the bles'd promised land;
And, from the mountain's top of his exalted wit,
Saw it himself, and shew'd us it.
—COWLEY, ABRAHAM, 1667? *Ode to the Royal Society.*

When our renowned Lord Bacon had demonstrated the methods for a perfect restoration of all parts of real knowledge, the success became on a sudden stupendous, and effective philosophy began to sparkle, and even to flow into beams of bright shining light all over the world.—OLDENBURG, HENRY, 1672, *Preface to Philosophical Transactions of the Royal Society.*

Though there was bred in Mr. Bacon so early a dislike of the Physiology of Aristotle, yet he did not despise him with that pride and haughtiness with which youth is wont to be puffed up. He has a just esteem of that great master of learning, greater than that which Aristotle expressed himself towards the philosophers that went before him; for he endeavoured (some say) to stifle all their labours, designing to himself an universal monarchy over opinions, as his patron Alexander did over men. Our hero owned what was excellent in him, but in his inquiries into nature he proceeded not upon his principles. He began the work anew, and laid the foundation of philosophic theory in numerous experiments.—TENISON THOMAS, 1674–79, *Baconiana.*

It was owing to the sagacity and freedom of Lord Bacon that men were then pretty well enabled both to make discoveries and to remove the impediments that had hitherto kept physics from being useful.—BOYLE, ROBERT, 1683, *New Experiments and Observations Touching Cold.*

The late most wise Chancellor of England was the chief writer of our age, and carried as it were the standard that we might press forward, and make greater discoveries in Philosophic matters, than any of which hitherto our schools had rung. So that if in our time any great improvements have been made in Philosophy, there has been not a little owing to that great man.—PUFFENDORF, SAMUEL, 1694? *Specimen Controversies, cap.* i.

By standing up against the Dogmatists, he emancipated and set free philosophy, which had long been a miserable captive, and which hath ever since made conquest in the territories of Nature.—EVELYN, JOHN, 1697, *Numismata.*

Though I give on this occasion, a preference to Bacon and to Locke over Des Cartes and the author of the logic of Port-royal, it is not from so mean and contemptible a motive as this would be, that they were Englishmen. The advancement of knowledge, and the improvement of reason are of common concern to all rational creatures. We are all of the same country in these respects: and he who thinks and acts otherwise is a promoter of faction in the great commonwealth of learning. As much as I admire these two philosophers, I am not blind to their errors; for even I, who have no telescopical eyes, can discern spots in these suns. I can discern a tincture, and sometimes more than a tincture, in Bacon, of those false notions which we are apt to imbibe as men, as individuals, as members of society, and as scholars, and against which he himself is very solicitous to put us on our guard.—BOLINGBROKE, HENRY ST. JOHN, VISCOUNT, 1751? *Essays on Human Knowledge, Works, vol.* III, *p.* 319.

Never did two men, gifted with such genius, recommend paths of inquiry so widely different. Descartes aspired to deduce an explanation of the whole system of things by reasoning *a priori* upon assumed principles: Bacon, on the contrary, held that it was necessary to observe Nature thoroughly before attempting to explain her ways; that we must ascend to principles through the medium of facts; and that our conclusions must be warrented by what we observe. Descartes reasoned about the World, as if the laws which govern it had not yet been established, as if every thing were still to create. Bacon considered it as a vast edifice, which it was necessary to view in all directions, to explore through all its recesses and windings, before any conjecture even could be safely formed as to the principles of its construction, or the foundations on which it rests. Thus, the philosophy of Bacon, by recommending the careful observation of Nature, still continues to be followed, whilst that of Descartes, whose essence lay in hypothesis, has wholly disappeared.—BAILLY, JEAN SYLVAIN, 1775-87, *Histoire de l' Astronomie Moderne, vol.* II, liv. 4, § 2.

The influence of Bacon's genius on the subsequent progress of physical discovery, has been seldom duly appreciated; by some writers almost entirely overlooked, and by others considered as the sole cause of the reformation in science which has since taken place. Of these two extremes, the latter certainly is the least wide of the truth; for, in the whole history of letters, no other individual can be mentioned, whose exertions have had so indisputable an effect in forwarding the intellectual progress of mankind. On the other hand, it must be acknowledged, that before the era when Bacon appeared, various philosophers in different parts of Europe had struck into the right path; and it may perhaps be doubted, whether any one important rule with respect to the true method of investigation be contained in his works, of which no hint can be traced in those of his predecessors. His great merit lay in concentrating their feeble and scattered lights; fixing the attention of philosophers on the distinguishing characteristics of true and of false science, by a felicity of illustration peculiar to himself, seconded by the commanding powers of a bold and figurative eloquence. —STEWART, DUGALD, 1802-3, *Account of the Life and Writings of Thomas Reid, sect.* II.

This mighty genius ranks as the father of modern physics, inasmuch as he brought back the spirit of investigation from the barren verbal subtleties of the schools to nature and experience: he made and completed many important discoveries himself, and seems to have had a dim and imperfect foresight of many others. Stimulated by his capacious and stirring intellect, experimental science extended her boundaries in every direction: intellectual culture, nay, the social organization of modern Europe generally, assumed a new shape and complexion.—SCHLEGEL, FREDERICK, 1815, *Lectures on the History of Literature, p.* 286.

Bacon's grand distinction, considered as an improver of physics, lies in this, that he was the first who clearly and fully pointed out the rules and safeguards of right reasoning in physical inquiries. Many other philosophers, both ancient and modern, had referred to observation and experiment in a cursory way, as furnishing the materials of physical knowledge; but no one, before him, had attempted to systematize the true method of discovery; or to prove that the *inductive*, is the *only* method by which the genuine office of philosophy can be exercised, and its genuine ends accomplished. It has sometimes been stated, that Galileo was, at least in an equal degree with Bacon, the father of the Inductive Logic; but it would be more correct to say, that his discoveries furnished some fortunate illustrations of its principles. To explain these principles was no object of his; nor does he manifest any great anxiety to recommend their adoption, with a view to the general improvement of science.—NAPIER, MACVEY, 1818-53, *Lord Bacon and Sir Walter Raleigh*, *p*. 14.

The opinion so prevalent during the last thirty years, that Lord Bacon introduced the art of experimental inquiry on physical subjects, and that he devised and published a method of discovering scientific truth, called the method of induction, appears to me to be without foundation, and perfectly inconsistent with the history of science. This heresy, which I consider as most injurious to the progress of scientific inquiry, seems to have been first propagated by D'Alembert, and afterwards fostered in our University by Mr. Stewart and Mr. Playfair, three men of great talent, but not one of whom ever made a single discovery in physics. . . . It has been said, however, by the admirers of Bacon, that though a few philosophers knew the secret of making advances in science, yet the great body were ignorant of it, and that Paracelsus, Van Helmont, and many others, were guided in their inquiries by very inferior methods. . . . It seems quite clear that Bacon, who knew nothing either of Mathematics or Physics, conceived the ambitious design of establishing a general method of scientific inquiry. This method, which he has explained at great length, is neither more nor less than a crusade against Aristotle, with the words *experiment and observation* emblazoned on his banner. . . . The method given by Bacon is, independent of all this, quite useless, and in point of fact has never been used in any successful inquiry. A collection of facts, however skilfully they may be conjured with, can never yield general laws unless they contain that master-fact in which the discovery resides, or upon which the law mainly depends.—BREWSTER, SIR DAVID, 1824, *Letter, April* 26, *The Home Life of Sir David Brewster*, *pp*. 128, 129, 130.

It is no proof of a solid acquaintance with Lord Bacon's philosophy, to deify his name as the ancient schools did those of their founders, or even to exaggerate the powers of his genius. Powers they were surprisingly great, yet limited in their range, and not in all respects equal; nor could they overcome every impediment of circumstance. Even of Bacon it may be said, that he attempted more than he has achieved, and perhaps more than he clearly apprehended. His objects appear sometimes indistinct, and I am not sure that they are always consistent. In the "Advancement of Learning," he aspired to fill up, or at least to indicate, the deficiencies in every department of knowledge: he gradually confined himself to philosophy, and at length to physics. But few of his works can be deemed complete, not even the treatise "De Augmentis," which comes nearer to this than most of the rest. Hence the study of Lord Bacon is difficult, and not, as I conceive, very well adapted to those who have made no progress whatever in the exact sciences, nor accustomed themselves to independent thinking.—HALLAM, HENRY, 1837-39, *Introduction to the Literature of Europe*.

He is one of the men to whom I owe most, though I have never followed him into the domain of physical science, where his method is most strikingly exhibited. What little physics I know, is almost purely theoretical. But the least knowledge of the history of science, coupled with a knowledge of the state of philosophy in Bacon's day, is sufficient to enable me to appreciate the wonderful depth and comprehensiveness of his views, and to see how, to use Macaulay's language, "he dug deep, that after ages might pile high." —LEWES, GEORGE HENRY, 1843, *Correspondence of Macvey Napier*, *p*. 445.

It was as a philosopher that Bacon conquered immortality, and here he stands superior to all who went before and to all who have followed him. If he be not entitled to a place in the interior of the splendid temple which he imagined for those who, by inventing arts, have embellished life, his statue ought to appear in the more honourable position of the portico, as the great master who has taught how arts are to be invented . . . He accomplished more for the real advancement of knowledge than any of those who spent their lives in calm meditation under sequestered porticos or amidst academic groves.—CAMPBELL, JOHN, LORD, 1845–56, *Lives of the Lord Chancellors and Keepers of the Great Seal of England, vol.* II.

Lord Bacon has the English duality. His centuries of observations on useful science, and his experiments, I suppose, were worth nothing. One hint of Franklin, or Watt, or Dalton, or Davy, or any one who had a talent for experiment, was worth all his lifetime of exquisite trifles. But he drinks of a diviner stream, and marks the influx of idealism into England. Where that goes, is poetry, health and progress. —EMERSON, RALPH WALDO, 1856-84, *English Traits, Works, Riverside ed., vol.* V, *p.* 227.

Bacon has been likened to the prophet who from Mount Pisgah surveyed the Promised Land, but left it for others to take possession of. Of this happy image perhaps part of the felicity was not perceived by its author. For though Pisgah was a place of large prospect, yet still the Promised Land was a land of definite extent and known boundaries, and moreover it was certain that after no long time the chosen people would be in possession of it all. And this agrees with what Bacon promised to himself and to mankind from the instauration of the sciences. . . . In this respect, then, as in others, the hopes of Francis Bacon were not destined to be fulfilled. It is neither to the technical part of his method nor to the details of his view of the nature and progress of science that his great fame is justly owing. His merits are of another kind. They belong to the spirit rather than to the positive precepts of his philosophy.—ELLIS, ROBERT LESLIE, 1857, *Bacon's Philosophical Works, General Preface, vol.* I, *pp.* 63, 64.

With the audacity of ignorance, he presumed to criticise what he did not understand, and, with a superb conceit, disparaged the great Copernicus. . . . The more closely we examine the writings of Lord Bacon, the more unworthy does he seem to have been of the great reputation which has been awarded to him. The popular delusion to which he owes so much originated at a time when the history of science was unknown. They who first brought him into notice knew nothing of the old school of Alexandria. This boasted founder of a new philosophy could not comprehend, and would not accept, the greatest of all scientific doctrines when it was plainly set before his eyes. It has been represented that the invention of the true method of physical science was an amusement of Bacon's hours of relaxation from the more laborious studies of law and duties of a court. His chief admirers have been persons of a literary turn, who have an idea that scientific discoveries are accomplished by a mechanico-mental operation. Bacon never produced any great practical results himself, no great physicist has ever made any use of his method. He has had the same to do with the development of modern science that the inventor of the orrery has had to do with the discovery of the mechanism of the world. . . . No man can envent an organon for writing tragedies and epic poems. . . . Few scientific pretenders have made more mistakes than Lord Bacon. He rejected the Copernican system, and spoke insolently of its great author; he undertook to criticise adversely Gilbert's treatise "De Magnete;" he was occupied in the condemnation of any investigation of final causes, while Harvey was deducing the circulation of the blood from Aquapendente's discovery of the valves in the veins; he was doubtful whether instruments were of any advantage, while Galileo was investigating the heavens with the telescope. Ignorant himself of every branch of mathematics, he presumed that they were useless in science, but a few years before Newton achieved by their aid his immortal discoveries. It is time that the sacred name of philosophy should be severed from its long connexion with that of one who was a pretender in science, a time-serving politician, an insidious lawyer, a corrupt judge, a treacherous friend, a bad man.—DRAPER, JOHN WILLIAM, 1861-76, *History of the Intellectual Development of Europe, vol.* II, *pp.* 258, 259, 260.

The actual and undeniable facts that when compared with the writings of the Italian natural philosophers those of Bacon breathe more of the modern spirit, and yet that he ignores the discoveries which have proved themselves to be most fruitful for susbequent times, and even their originators (Copernicus, Galileo, Gilbert, Harvey, and others), or at least is less able to appreciate them than the former,—that, further, in spite of his praise of natural science he has exerted on its development no influence worthy of the name—(facts which in recent times have led to such different verdicts on Bacon), can only be harmonised (but then easily harmonised) when we do not attribute to Bacon the position of the initiator of modern philosophy, but see in him the close of the philosophy of the Middle Ages. He has left behind him the standpoint from which natural science subjected itself to dogma and in which she contended against it. Therefore he stands higher and nearer to modern times. But this advance refers only to the relation of the doctrines of natural science to religion and the Church. . . . Measured by the standard of the Middle Ages Bacon appears modern, by that of modern times he appears mediæval. But to say this implies that his merit is no small one.—ERDMANN, JOHANN EDUARD, 1865-76, *A History of Philosophy, tr. Hough, vol.* I, *pp.* 682, 683.

The first practical effect of Bacon's writing was produced in this country in the department of physics. Meetings were held in the rooms of Dr. Wilkins, at Oxford, for the purpose of cultivating natural science and making experiments. Out of these meetings sprang the Royal Society (1638, chartered 1662); and the more important members, Wallis, Wilkins, Childrey, Boyle, Sprat, Digby, all recognised Bacon as practically their founder. —ANGUS, JOSEPH, 1865, *The Handbook of English Literature, p.* 364.

He certainly never made utility the sole object of science, or at least never restricted utility to material advantages. He asserted in the noblest language the superiority of abstract truth to all the fruits of invention, and would never have called those speculations useless which form the intellectual character of an age. Yet, on the other hand, it must be acknowledged that the general tone of his writings, the extraordinary emphasis which he laid upon the value of experiments, and above all upon the bearing of his philosophy on material comforts, represents a tendency which was very naturally developed into the narrowest utilitarianism. — LECKY, WILLIAM EDWARD HARTPOLE, 1865, *Spirit of Rationalism in Europe, vol.* I, *ch.* iv, *pt.* i.

Bacon of Verulam stripped off from natural philosophy the theosophical character which it bore during the Transitional Period, and limited it in its method to experiment and induction. The fundamental traits of this method he made apart of the philosophic consciousness of mankind, as emancipated in its investigations from the restriction to any particular department of natural science. He thus became the founder—not, indeed, of the empirical method of natural investigation, but—of the empirical line of modern philosophers.—UEBERWEG, FRIEDRICH, 1871-73, *A History of Philosophy, tr. by Morris, vol.* II, *p.* 33.

As a philosophical author, Bacon shows that he possessed a thorough knowledge of all the learning of his time. . . . The powerful and lasting influence which this philosophical realism exercised on the civilizaiton of England may be traced down to the present day.—SCHERR, J., 1874, *A History of English Literature, pp.* 41, 42.

The whole endeavor of Bacon in science is to attain the fact, and to ascend from particular facts to general. He turned away with utter dissatisfaction from the speculating *in vacuo* of the Middle Ages. His intellect demanded positive knowledge; he could not feed upon the wind. From the tradition of philosophy and from authority he reverted to nature. Between faith and reason Bacon set a great and impassable gulf. Theology is something too high for human intellect to discuss. Bacon is profoundly deferential to theology, because, as one cannot help suspecting, he was profoundly indifferent about it. The schoolmen for the service of faith had summoned human reason to their aid, and Reason, the ally, had in time proved a dangerous antagonist. Bacon, in the interest of science, dismissed faith to the unexceptionable province of supernatural truths. To him a dogma of theology was equally credible whether it possessed an appearance of reasonableness or appeared absurd. The total force of intellect he reserved for subjugating to the understanding the world of positive fact.—DOWDEN, EDWARD, 1875-80, *Shakespere, A Critical Study of His Mind and Art, p.* 16.

Had Locke not yet made acquaintance with the writings of Bacon, which could hardly have been beyond the understanding of such a student? or did he regard Bacon rather as the great herald and pioneer of the new philosophy than as himself a great philosopher? There would be some warrant for that view, and though Locke's philosophical debt to Bacon was a great one, Descartes was evidently a more attractive teacher for one situated and constituted as Locke was.—BOURNE, H. R. FOX, 1876, *The Life of John Locke, vol.* I, *p.* 62.

Certainly, more than any man of his time, Bacon seems to have realized that he was standing at the vestibule of a new age, and was charged with the mission of showing the insufficiency of the past and the bright hopes of the future.—BROWNING, OSCAR, 1881, *An Introduction to the History of Educational Theories.*

I get driven out of all patience by Spedding's special pleading for him. He seems to me to have done no *work,* to have shown no example of what he calls his method. But his imagination was his great faculty, and all that is most valuable in him is due to the prescient instinctive insight with which he looked on the possibilities of knowledge; the enthusiasm of a seer, not of a philosopher who had measured, and weighed, and compared, and done what Mozley calls the underground work of solid thinking. Galileo, as you say, and Pascal *did* what Bacon talked about without knowing how to do it, and they talked *after* they had touch of the realities of a hunt after physical truth.—CHURCH, RICHARD WILLIAM, 1883, *Letter to Dr. Asa Gray, Life and Letters of Dean Church, p.* 376.

Was this not the very time when Bacon stood out before Europe the herald, if not the leader, of the great scientific movement of modern days, and to his own land set an example of sober practical thinking which the English mind has never since forgotten? If Hobbes, in the last years of Bacon's life, was gradually working his way through scholarly studies to the position of a philosophical thinker, under whose influence but Bacon's could the development proceed? From whom but the first of English modern philosophers should the second, being in actual contact with him, learn to think with the freedom of a modern, and the practical purpose of an Englishman?—ROBERTSON, GEORGE CROOM, 1886, *Hobbes* (*Philosophical Classics*), *p.* 18.

No delusion is greater than the notion that method and industry can make up for lack of motherwit, either in science or in practical life; and it is strange that, with his knowledge of mankind, Bacon should have dreamed that his, or any other, "via inveniendi scientias" would "level men's wits" and leave little scope for that inborn capacity which is called genius. As a matter of fact, Bacon's "via" has proved hoplessly impracticable; while the "anticipation of nature" by the invention of hypotheses based on incomplete inductions, which he specially condemns, has proved itself to be a most efficient, indeed an indispensable, instrument of scientific progress. Finally, that transcendental alchemy—the superinducement of new forms on matter—which Bacon declares to be the supreme aim of science, has been wholly ignored by those who have created the physical knowledge of the present day. Even the eloquent advocacy of the Chancellor brought no unmixed good to physical science. It was natural enough that the man who, in his better moments, took "all knowledge for his patrimony," but, in his worse, sold that birthright for the mess of pottage of Court favour and professional success, for pomp and show, should be led to attach an undue value to the practical advantages which he foresaw, as Roger Bacon and, indeed, Seneca had foreseen, long before his time, must follow in the train of the advancement of natural knowledge.—WARD, THOMAS HUMPHRY, 1887, *The Reign of Queen Victoria, vol.* II, *p.* 325.

Bacon is the *bête noire* and butt of Specialists, the modern Schoolmen, who resent his insufficient view of their little worlds. Mere politicians complain that he was neither a Whig nor a Tory: Mere theologians see that, with all his orthodox protestations, Religion was on the fringe of his system: Mere physicists, led by Harvey, who begins the attack in his dictum that he "wrote like a Lord Chancellor," dislike or distrust his metaphysics, and dwell, as Baron Liebig does, with acrimonious exclusiveness on his defects. Their comments are narrowly correct; but, like those of mere dryasdust philologists on the classics of literature, so one-sided as to be impertinent. The inaccuracies inevitable to universal views, must be conceded to the ingratitude of those prone to bite the hand that feeds them.—NICHOL, JOHN, 1889, *Francis Bacon, His Life and Philosophy, Part* ii, *p.* 242.

It is an exaggeration of Bacon's merit to regard him as the creator of the experimental method and of modern science. On the contrary, Bacon was the product of the scientific revival of the sixteenth century, and his manifesto is but the conclusion, or as we might say the moral, which English common-sense draws from the scientific movement. But though he cannot be said to have originated the experimental method, we must at least concede to him the honor of having raised it from the low condition to which scholastic prejudice had consigned it, and of having insured it a legal existence, so to say, by the most eloquent plea ever made in its favor. It is no small matter to speak out what many think, and no one dares to confess even to himself. Nay, more. Though experimental *science* and its methods originated long before the time of the great chancellor, Bacon is none the less the founder of experimental *philosophy*, the father of modern positivistic philosophy, in so far as he was the first to affirm, in clear and eloquent words that true philosophy and science have common interests, and that a *separate* metaphysics is futile.—WEBER, ALFRED, 1892-96, *History of Philosophy, tr. Thilly, p.* 298.

The stately tropes and metaphors; the magnificent promises and heraldings of what the new science is to give us; the cunningly adjusted scraps of classical or biblical phrase; the pithy apophthegms; the shrewd commonsense; the suggestion that seems even more pregnant than it is; the masterful employment of a learning which is perhaps more thoroughly at command than extensive or profound—all these notes of "topmost Verulam" are well known. Unjust to his predecessors, hasty and even superficial in his grasp of sciences and philosophies, rhetorical, casuistical, almost shallow, delusive in his mighty promises, hollow in his cunning schemes and methods—all these unfavorable labels have been at different times attached to Bacon, and for some at least of them the Devil's Advocate may make out a strong case. But the magnificence of his literature, and his imagination in the directions where he was imaginative, is undeniable; and he was perhaps, to those who look at literature as it affects and is affected by the social history of England, the best mouthpiece and embodiment of that side of the late Renaissance which retained the hopes of an all-embracing *philosophia prima*, supporting them on the treacherous struts and props that seemed to be lent by the new learning in physics as well as by the study of the ancients.—SAINTSBURY, GEORGE, 1895, *Social England, ed. Traill, vol.* IV, *p.* 105.

Bacon was neither a retired and patient nor an accurate thinker—the desire to apply and make his learning useful led him away from the "sapientum templa serena" into the forum of life: in his own experience, as well as in his writings, he anticipated many of the dangers which beset modern culture—the love of premature application, and the haste for practical results and achievements.—MERZ, JOHN THEODORE, 1896, *A History of European Thought in the Nineteenth Century, vol.* I, *p.* 94.

Diderot's is a scientific mind, notably predisposed to experimental sciences. He is a mathematician, and particularly a naturalist; his master, however, is not the geometrician, Descartes, but the physician, Bacon, to whom he has more than once rendered abundant homage.—PELLISSIER, GEORGES, 1897, *The Literary Movement in France During the Nineteenth Century, tr. Brinton, p.* 36.

GENERAL

Crown of all modern authors.—SANDYS, GEORGE, 1621-26, *Ovid's Metamorphosis, English ed., notes.*

Lewis Elzevir wrote me lately from Amsterdam, that he was designed to begin shortly an edition in *quarto*, of all the works of Lord Bacon; and he desired my advice and any assistance I could give him; to the end that, as far as possible, these works might come abroad with advantage, which have been long received with the kindest eulogies, and with the most attested applause of the learned world.—GRUTER, ISAAC, 1652, *Letter to William Rawley, Tenison's Baconiana.*

If there were a beam of knowledge derived from God upon any man, in these modern times, it was upon him. For though he was a great reader of books, yet he had not his knowledge from books, but from some grounds or notions from within himself; which notwithstanding, he vented with great caution and circumspection. His book of "Instauratio Magna" (which, in his own account, was the chiefest of his works) was no slight imagination or fancy of his brain; but a settled and concocted notion: the production of many years' labour and travail. I myself have seen at the least twelve copies of the "Instauration" revised, year by year, one after another; and every year altered and amended in the frame thereof; till, at the last, it came to that model, in which it was committed to the press: as many living creatures do lick their young ones till they bring them to their strength of limbs. In the composing of his books he did rather drive at a masculine and clear expression than at any fineness or affectation of phrases; and would often ask if the meaning were expressed *plainly enough.* As being one that accounted words to be but subservient or ministerial to matter, and not the principal: and if his style were polite, it was because he could do no otherwise. Neither was he given to any light conceits, or descanting upon words: but did ever, purposely and industriously, avoid them. For he held such things to be but digressions or diversions from the scope intended, and to derogate from the weight and dignity of the style.—RAWLEY, WILLIAM, 1657-61, *Life of Bacon, Resuscitatio.*

Fell into a dislike of Aristotle's Philosophy, as barren and jejune, inabling some to dispute, more to wrangle, few to find out trueth, and none, if confining themselves to his principles. Hence it was that afterwards he traded so largely in Experiments; so that, as Socrates is said to be the first who stooped towering Speculations into practical Morality, Sir Francis was one of the first, who reduced notional to real and scientifical Philosophy. . . . . His abilities were a clear confutation of two vulgar errors, (libells on learned men); First, that Judgement, Wit, Fancy, and Memory, cannot eminently be in conjunction in the same person; whereas our Knight was a rich Cabinet, fill'd with all four, besides a golden key to open it, Elocution. Secondly, "That he who is something in all, is nothing in any one Art;" whereas he was singular in *singulis*, and, being in-at-all, came off with credit. Such as condemn him for pride, if in his place, with the fifth part of his parts, had been ten times prouder themselves. . . . He may be said to have left nothing to his Executors, and all to his Heirs, under which notion the Learned of all ages may be beheld.—FULLER, THOMAS, 1662, *The Worthies of England, ed. Nichols, vol.* II, *pp.* 110, 111.

Who knows not how Herbary had been improved by Theophrastus, Dioscorides, the Arabians, and other Peripatetics? who can deny that Physic, in every part of it, was improved by Galen and others, before the Lord Bacon ever sucked? and what accessionals had not Chemistry received by the cultivation of the Aristotlians, before his House of Solomon was dreamed of? Let us, therefore, not be concluded by the aphorisms of this Lord. Let his *insulse adherents* buy some salt, and make use of more than one grain when they read him; and let us believe better of the ancients, than that their methods of science were so unfruitful.—STUBBE, HENRY, 1671, *Lord Bacon's Relation of the Sweating Sickness Examined, Preface, p.* 5.

A man who, for the greatness of genius, and compass of knowledge, did honour to his age and country; I could almost say to human nature itself. He possessed at once all these extraordinary talents which were divided amongst the greatest authors of antiquity. He had the sound, distinct, comprehensive knowledge of Aristotle, with all the beautiful lights, graces, and embellishments of Cicero. One does not know which to admire most in his writings, the strength of reason, force of style, or brightness of imagination.—ADDISON, JOSEPH, 1710, *The Tatler, No.* 267.

Lord Bacon was the greatest genius that England (or perhaps any country) ever produced.—POPE, ALEXANDER, 1734-36, *Spence's Anecdotes, p.* 128.

Lord Bacon is the first author who has attempted any style that can be relishable to the present age.—BOYLE, JOHN, (Lord Orrery), 1751, *Remarks on the Life and Writings of Dr. Jonathan Swift, p.* 234.

Allowing as much sense to Sir Philip* as his warmest admirers can demand for him, surely this country has produced many men of far greater abilities, who have by no means met with a proportionate share of applause. It were a vain parade to name them—take Lord Bacon alone, who I believe of all our writers, except Newton, is most known to foreigners, and to who Sir Philip was a puny child in genius.—WALPOLE, HORACE, 1758, *Letter to David Hume, July* 15. *Letters, vol.* III, *p.* 151.

The great glory of literature in this island, during the reign of James, was Lord Bacon. . . . If we consider the variety of talents displayed by this man; as a public speaker, a man of business, a wit, a courtier, a companion, an author, a philosopher; he is justly the object of great admiration. If we consider him merely as an author and philosopher, the light in which we view him at present, though very estimable, he was yet inferior to his contemporary Galileo, perhaps even to Kepler. Bacon pointed out at a distance the road to true philosophy: Galileo both pointed it out to others, and made himself considerable advances in it. The Englishman was ignorant of geometry: the Florentine revived that science, excelled in it, and was the first that applied it, together with experiment, to natural philosophy. The former rejected, with the most positive disdain, the system of Copernicus; the latter fortified it with new proofs, derived both from reason and the senses. Bacon's style is stiff and rigid; his wit, though often brilliant, is also often unnatural and far-fetched; and he seems to be the original of those pointed smiles and long-spun allegories which so much distinguish the English authors; Galileo is a lively and agreeable, though somewhat a prolix writer. But Italy not united in any single government, and perhaps satiated with that literary glory which it has possessed both in ancient and modern times, has too much neglected the renown which it has acquired by giving birth to so great a man. That national spirit which prevails among the English, and which forms their great happiness, is the cause why they bestow on all their eminent writers, and on Bacon among the rest, such praises and acclamations as may often appear partial and excessive.—HUME, DAVID, 1754-62, *History of England, James I., Appendix.*

*Sir Philip Sidney.

The English language is the only object in his great survey of art and of nature, which owes nothing of its excellence to the genius of Bacon.—DISRAELI, ISAAC, 1791-1824, *Of Lord Bacon at Home, Curiosities of Literature.*

Who is there, that, upon hearing this name does not instantly recognise everything of genius the most profound, everything of literature the most extensive, everything of discovery the most penetrating, everything of observation on human life the most distinguishing and refined? All these must be instantly recognised, for they are all inseparably associated with the name of Lord Veralum.—BURKE, EDMUND, 1794, *Speech on the Impeachment of Warren Hastings, May* 28.

If it be true that the compositions of Bacon are scarcely at all read in his native country, I could not devise a more effectual charm to revive a taste which ought never to have declined, than a just translation of the "Cogitata et Visa." When Hume denied this author the praise of eloquence, he must either have forgot that such a work issued from his pen; or that profound observations, clothed with enlarged sentiments and the images of a copious and exquisite fancy, will fully compensate the want of idiomatic purity, or a rhetorical structure of periods.—HORNER, FRANCIS, 1801, *Journal, Memoirs and Correspondence, vol.* I, *p.* 168.

That the composition of Lord Bacon, especially in his scientific works, was in general perspicuous, will not be denied; but that he reached the acme of our language, and exhibited the graces of Cicero, is surely hyperbolical praise.—DRAKE, NATHAN, 1804, *Essays Illustrative of the Tatler, Spectator, and Guardian, vol.* II, *p.* 18.

The vigour of his mind did not sink with his fall from power. For a while, indeed, it was broken and disturbed by the rock on which he had dashed; but soon his thoughts, bursting into a new channel, flowed onward with their accustomed, full, and majestic course.—BURNETT, GEORGE, 1807, *Specimens of English Prose Writers, vol.* II, *p.* 344.

He has in general inspired a fervour of admiration which vents itself in indiscriminate praise, and is very adverse to a calm examination of the character of his understanding, which was very peculiar, and on that account described with more than ordinary imperfection, by that unfortunately vague and weak part of language which attempts to distinguish the varieties of mental superiority. . . . It is easy to describe his transcendent merit in general terms of commendation; for some of his great qualities lie on the surface of his writings. But that in which he most excelled all other men, was the range and compass of his intellectual view and the power of contemplating many and distant objects together without indistinctness or confusion, which he himself has called "discursive" or "comprehensive" understanding. This wide ranging intellect was illuminated by the brightest Fancy that ever contented itself with the office of only ministering to Reason: and from this singular relation of the two grand faculties of man, it has resulted, that his philosophy, though illustrated still more than adorned by the utmost splendour of imagery, continues still subject to the undivided supremacy of Intellect. . . No man ever united a more poetical style to a less poetical philosophy. One great end of his discipline is to prevent mysticism and fanaticism from obstructing the pursuit of truth.—MACKINTOSH, SIR JAMES, 1816-46, *On the Philosophical Genius of Lord Bacon and Mr. Locke.*

His character was then an amazing insight into the limits of human knowledge and acquaintance with the landmarks of human intellect, so as to trace its past history or point out the path to future inquiries, but when he quits the ground of contemplation of what others have done or left undone to project himself into future discoveries, he becomes quaint and fantastic, instead of original. His strength was in reflection, not in production; he was the surveyor, not the builder, of the fabric of science. He had not strictly the constructive faculty. He was the principal pioneer in the march of modern philosophy, and has completed the education and discipline of the mind for the acquisition of truth, by explaining all the impediments or furtherances that can be applied to it or cleared out of its way. In a word, he was one of the greatest men this country has to boast, and his name deserves to stand, where it is generally placed, by the side of those of our greatest writers, whether we consider the variety, the strength, or splendour of his faculties, for ornament or use.—HAZLITT, WILLIAM, 1820, *Lectures on the Literature of the Age of Elizabeth, p.* 215.

In his historical authorities, is often inaccurate. I could give half a dozen instances from his Apophthegms only.—BYRON, LORD, 1821, *Poetical Works, vol.* IX, *p.* 448, *note.*

It is scarcely possible to read a page of his works without seeing that the love of knowledge was his ruling passion; that his real happiness consisted in intellectual delight. How beautifully does he state this when enumerating the blessings attendant upon the pursuit and possession of knowledge.—MONTAGU, BASIL, 1834, *The Life of Francis Bacon, p.* ccclxxviii.

His eloquence, though not untainted with the vicious taste of his age, would alone have entitled him to a high rank in literature. He had a wonderful talent for packing thought close and rendering it portable. In wit, if by wit he meant the power of perceiving analogies between things which appear to have been nothing in common, he never had an equal—not even Cowley—not even the author of "Hudibras." Indeed, he possessed this faculty, or rather this faculty possessed him, to a morbid degree—MACAULAY, THOMAS BABINGTON, 1834, *Lord Bacon, Edinburgh Review, Critical and Miscellaneous Essays.*

That Shakespeare's appearance upon a soil so admirably prepared was neither marvellous nor accidental is evidenced even by the corresponding appearance of such a contemporary as Bacon. Scarcely can anything be said of Shakespeare's position generally with regard to mediæval poetry which does not also bear upon the position of the renovator Bacon with regard to mediæval philosophy. Neither knew nor mentioned the other, although Bacon was almost called upon to have done so in his remarks upon the theatre of his day. It may be presumed that Shakespeare liked Bacon but little, if he knew his writings and life, that he liked not his ostentation, which, without on the whole interfering with his modesty, recurred too often in many instances; that he liked not the fault-finding which his ill-health might have caused, nor the narrow-mindedness with which he pronounced the histrionic art to be infamous, although he allowed that the ancients regarded the drama as a school for virtue; nor the theoretic precepts of worldly wisdom which he gave forth; nor, lastly, the practical career which he lived. Before his mind, however, if he had fathomed it, he must have bent in reverence. For just as Shakespeare was an interpreter of the secrets of history and of human nature, Bacon was an interpreter of lifeless nature.—GERVINUS, G. G., 1849–62, *Shakespeare Commentaries, tr. Bunnett, p.* 884.

No English writer has surpassed him in fervor and brilliancy of style, in force of expression, or in richness of magnificence of imagery. Keen in discovering analogies where no resemblance is apparent to common eyes, he has sometimes indulged, to excess, in the exercise of this talent. But in general his comparisons are not less clear and apposite than full of imagination and meaning. He has treated of philosophy with all the splendor, yet none of the vagueness, of poetry. Sometimes, too, his style possesses a degree of conciseness very rarely to be found in the compositions of the Elizabethan age.—MILLS, ABRAHAM, 1851, *The Literature and the Literary Men of Great Britain and Ireland, vol.* I, *p.* 388.

If I were asked to describe Bacon as briefly as I could, I should say that he was the liberator of the hands of knowledge.—HUNT, LEIGH, 1851, *Table Talk, p.* 84.

I refer to him, because I fancy that many have a notion of his books on the Interpretation of Nature as very valuable for scientific men, and his books on Morals and Politics as very wise for statesmen and men of the world, but not as friends. They form this notion because they suppose, that the more we know of Bacon himself, the less sympathy we should have with him. I should be sorry to hold this opinion, because I owe him immense gratitude; and I could not cherish it if I thought of him, even as the sagest of book-makers and not as a human being. I should be sorry to hold it, because if I did not find in him a man who deserved reverence and love, I should not feel either the indignation or the sorrow which I desire to feel for his misdoings.—MAURICE, FREDERICK DENISON, 1856-74, *The Friendship of Books and Other Lectures, ed. Hughes, p.* 11.

Many thanks for the Bacon which you found in the Barrow. It all amounts to wondrous little, if, as you say, Bacon was known to the Cambridge men generally. How could Bacon be so little quoted? The conceits of which that age was fond were taken out of puerility by him, and made into wit and covered with taste. And yet they knew nothing of him to speak of. Newton's silence is emphatic. When I have time and opportunity I intend to work out the thesis, "That Newton was more indebted to the Schoolmen than to Bacon, and probably better acquainted with them."—DE MORGAN, AUGUSTUS, 1858, *Memoir, Letter to the Rev. Dr. Whewell, Oct.* 10, *p.* 296.

Newton was anything but illiterate. He *knew* Bacon. His silence is most marked. How could he avoid every possible amount of mention of Bacon on every possible subject? I never said he did not *know* Bacon; I only said he could not be *proved* to have known of his existence. Nor can he. I think he has taken such pains not to be known to know him as cannot be attributed to accident. —DE MORGAN, AUGUSTUS, 1861, *Memoir, Letter to the Rev. Dr. Whewell, Jan.* 20, *p.* 305.

What is true of Shakespeare is true of Bacon. Bacon thought in parables. Of the astounding versatility of his thought, of the universality of its reach, the subtlety of its discrimination, the practical Machiavellian omniscience of motive good and evil, it is difficult by words to convey any adequate idea. But the plasticity of his thought is always the humble servant of his omnipresent imagination. His intellect is always at the mercy of his fancy for a clothing. All his intellectual facts are wrapt in visions of beautiful illustration.—CRACROFT, BERNARD, 1868, *Essays, Political and Miscellaneous, vol.* II, *p.* 218.

Except it be Milton's, there is not any prose fuller of grand poetic embodiments than Lord Bacon's.—MACDONALD, GEORGE, 1868, *England's Antiphon, p.* 93.

Of Bacon, more than of any other writer, it may be said that "in the very dust of his writings there is gold."—FARRAR, FREDERIC WILLIAM, 1869–73, *Families of Speech.*

There is nothing in English prose superior to his diction.—TAINE, H. A., 1871, *History of English Literature, tr. Van Laun, vol.* I, *bk.* ii, *ch.* i, *p.* 216.

Read a page of Macaulay, and you exhaust the thought at a single perusal. Read a page of Bacon twenty times, and at each reading you will discover new meanings, unobserved before. That haze which the naked eye could not penetrate is found by the telescope to be a nebula, composed of innumerable distinct stars. The one writer informs, the other stimulates, the mind. The one enlightens, the other inspires. The first communicates facts and opinions; the second floods and surcharges you with mental life.—MATHEWS, WILLIAM, 1872, *Getting on in the World, p.* 245.

Bacon's range of subjects was wide, and his command of words within that range as great as any man could have acquired. He took pains to keep his vocabulary rich. From some private notes that have been preserved, we see that he had a habit of jotting down and refreshing his memory with varieties of expression on all subjects that were likely to occur for discussion. He uses a great many more obsolete words than either Hooker or Sidney. To be sure, the language of the feelings and the language of theology have changed less than the language of science. But in his narrative and in his "Essays," as well as in his scientific writings, Bacon shows a decided preference now and then for "inkhorn terms."—MINTO, WILLIAM, 1872–80, *Manual of English Prose Literature, p.* 241.

His utterances are not infrequently marked with a grandeur and solemnity of tone, a majesty of diction, which renders it impossible to forget, and difficult even to criticise them. . . . There is no author, unless it be Shakespeare, who is so easily remembered or so frequently quoted. . . . The terse and burning words, issuing, as it were, from the lips of an irresistible commander.—FOWLER, THOMAS, 1881, *Francis Bacon, (English Philosophers), p.* 202.

In the matter of diction he uses more obsolete words than either Hooker or Sidney, but he is immeasurably superior to them both in the perspicuity of his sentences which, though occasionally involved, as a rule allow us to see into his thoughts with great distinctness. The aphoristic style of his essays is worthy of all praise, and he may be considered the first English master of antithesis: it was perhaps his work in this direction which gave his peculiar bent to the literature of the early part of the 17th century.—FLETCHER, C. R. L., 1881, *The Development of English Prose Style, p.* 10.

Bacon was always much more careful of the value of aptness of a thought than of its appearing new and original. Of all great writers he least minds repeating himself, perhaps in the very same words; so that a simile, an illustration, a quotation pleases him, he returns to it—he is never tired of it; it obviously gives him satisfaction to introduce it again and again.—CHURCH, RICHARD WILLIAM, 1884–88, *Bacon, (English Men of Letters), p.* 29.

Imagination is a compound of intellectual power and feeling. The intellectual power may be great, but if it is not accompanied with feeling, it will not minister to feeling; or it will minister to many feelings by turns, and to none in particular. As far as the intellectual power of a poet goes, few men have excelled Bacon. He had a mind stored with imagery, able to produce various and vivid illustrations of whatever thought came before him; but these illustrations touched no deep feeling; they were fresh, original, racy, fanciful, picturesque, a play of the head that never touched the heart. The man was by nature cold; he had not the emotional depth or compass of an average Englishman. Perhaps his strongest feeling of an enlarged or generous description was for human progress, but it did not rise to passion; there was no fervour, no fury in it. Compare him with Shelley on the same subject, and you will see the difference between meagreness and intensity of feeling. What intellect can be, without strong feeling, we have in Bacon; what intellect is, with strong feeling, we have in Shelley. The feeling gives the tone to the thoughts; sets the intellect at work to find language having its own intensity, to pile up lofty and impressive circumstances; and then we have the poet, the orator, the thoughts that breathe, and the words that burn. Bacon wrote on many impressive themes—on Truth, on Love, on Religion, on Death, and on the Virtues in detail; he was always original, illustrative, fanciful; if intellectual means and resources could make a man feel in these things, he would have felt deeply; yet he never did.—BAIN, ALEXANDER, 1884, *Practical Essays, p.* 16.

Bacon's style varied almost as much as his handwriting; but it was influenced more by the subject-matter than by youth or old age. Few men have shown equal versatility in adapting their language to the slightest shade of circumstance and purpose. His style depended upon whether he was addressing a king, or a great nobleman, or a philosopher, or a friend; whether he was composing a State paper, pleading in a State trial, magnifying the Prerogative, extolling Truth, discussing studies, exhorting a judge, sending a New Year's present, or sounding a trumpet to prepare the way for the Kingdom of Man over Nature. It is a mistake to suppose that Bacon was never florid till he grew old. On the contrary, in the early "Devices," written during his connection with Essex, he uses a rich exuberant style and poetic rhythm; but he prefers the rhetorical question of appeal to the complex period. On the other hand. in all his formal philosophical works, even in the "Advancement of Learning," published as early as 1605, he uses the graver periodic structure, though often illustrated with rich metaphor. . . . In his estimation, literary style was a snare quite as often as a help.—ABBOTT, EDWIN ABBOTT, 1885, *Francis Bacon, An Account of His Life and Works, pp.* 447, 453.

Illustrious beyond all others except Shakespeare in his intellect, and, with whatever infirmities, still not less than noble in his moral mind.—TAYLOR, SIR HENRY, 1885, *Autobiography, vol.* I, *p.* 195.

In Bacon, as far as was possible in one man, the learning of the age met and mingled. All the Romance—*i. e.*, at that date all the literary—languages of Europe, were part of his province. In his pages all the classics—save Homer and the Greek dramatists—are rifled to enrich the "Globus Intellectualis." All the philosophies of the West and most of the little then known of science, come within his ken. His criticisms of history are generally sound, as are his references to the dicta and methods of previous authors, and his quotations, though somewhat overlaid, are always illuminating. He had no pretension to the minute scholarship of a Casaubon or a Scaliger; but his grasp of the Latin tongue was firm, and his use of it facile.—NICHOL, JOHN, 1888, *Francis Bacon, His Life and Philosophy, Part* i, *p.* 18.

The highest literary merit of Bacon's "Essays" is their combination of charm and of poetic prose with conciseness of expression and fulness of thought. But the oratorical and ideal manner in which, with his variety, he sometimes wrote, is best seen in his "New Atlantis," that imaginary land in the unreachable seas. —BROOKE, STOPFORD A., 1896, *English Literature, p.* 109.

In his English works, considered alone, we have to confess a certain poverty. He who thought it the first distemper of learning, that men should study words and not matter, is now in the singular condition of having outlived his matter, or, at least, a great part of it, while his words are as vivid as ever. We could now wish that he could have been persuaded to "hunt more after choiceness of the phrase, and the round and clear composition of the sentence, and the sweet falling of the clauses," qualities which he had the temerity to profess to despise. —GOSSE, EDMUND, 1897, *Short History of Modern English Literature, p.* 130.

In Bacon's sentences we may often find remarkable condensation of thought in few words. One does not have to search for two grains of wheat hid in two bushels of chaff. . . . His work abounds in illustrations, analogies, and striking imagery.—HALLECK, REUBEN POST, 1900, *History of English Literature, pp.* 124, 125.

John Webster

Fl. 1620

John Wesbter, *fl.* 1620. No details of life known. Said to have been clerk of St. Andrew's, Holborn, and to have belonged to the Merchant Taylors' Company. Perhaps an actor as well as dramatist. *Works* (several lost): "The History of Sir Thomas Wyatt" (with Dekker), 1607; "Westward-Hoe" (with Dekker), 1607; "Northward-Hoe" (with Dekker), 1607; "The White Divel," 1612; "A Monumental Columne erected tò the living Memory of . . . Henry, late Prince of Wales," 1613; "The Devil's Law-Case," 1623; "The Tragedy of Dutchesse of Malfy," 1623; "The Monument of Honour," 1624; "Appius and Virginia," 1654; "A Cure for a Cuckold" (with Rowley), 1661; "The Thracian Wonder" (with Rowley), 1661. *Collected Works:* ed. by A. Dyce (4 vols.), 1830; new edn., 1857.—SHARP, R. FARQUHARSON, 1897, *A Dictionary of English Authors, p.* 296.

PERSONAL

Seldom has the biographer greater cause to lament a deficiency of materials than when engaged on the life of any of our early dramatists. Among that illustrious band John Webster occupies a distinguished place; and yet so scanty is our information concerning him, that in the present essay I can do little more than enumerate his different productions, and adduce proof that he was not the author of certain prose-pieces which have been attributed to him.—DYCE, ALEXANDER, 1830–57, *ed. The Works of John Webster, p.* ix.

The abrupt withdrawal of Webster from writing for the stage—a step which he seems to have taken when he was little over thirty years of age—points to a sense of a want of harmony between his genius and the theatre. . . . If it were not absolutely certain that he flourished between 1602 and 1612, we should be inclined to place the period of his activity at least ten years earlier. Although in fact an exact contemporary of Beaumont and Fletcher, and evidently much Shakespeare's junior, a place between Marlowe and those dramatists seems appropriate to him, so primitive is his theatrical art, so ingenuous and inexperienced his notion of the stage. . . . Webster is an impressive rather than a dexterous playwright; but as a romantic poet of passion he takes a position in the very first rank of his contemporaries.—GOSSE, EDMUND, 1894, *The Jacobean Poets, pp.* 172, 173.

THE WHITE DEVIL

1612

THE | WHITE DIVEL, | or | The Tragedy of *Paulo Giordano* | *Vrsini*, Duke of *Brachiano*, | With | The Life and Death of Vittoria | Corombona the famous | *Venetian* Curtizan. | *Acted by the Queenes Majesties Seruants.* | Written by John Webster. | LONDON, | Printed by N. O. for *Thomas Archer*, and are to be sold | at his Shop in Popeshead Pallace neere the | Royall Exchange 1612.—TITLE PAGE OF FIRST EDITION.

To those who report I was a long time in finishing this tragedy, I confesse I do not write with a goose-quill winged with two feathers; and, if they will needs make it my fault, I must answer them with that of Euripides to Alcestides, a tragick writer: Alcestides objecting that Euripides had onely in three daies composed three verses, whereas himself had written three hundredth; Thou telst truthe (quoth he), but heres the difference, thine shall onely be read for three daies, whereas mine shall continue three ages.—WEBSTER, JOHN, 1612, *The White Devil, Preface.*

Methinks a very poor play.—PEPYS, SAMUEL, 1661, *Diary.*

I never saw anything like the funeral dirge in this play, for the death of Marcello, except the ditty which reminds Ferdinand of his drowned father in the "Tempest." As that is of the water, watery; so this is of the earth, earthy. Both have that intenseness of feeling, which seems to resolve itself into the element which it contemplates.—LAMB, CHARLES, 1808, *Specimens of Dramatic Poets.*

Although I cannot agree with those who regard this tragedy as the masterpiece of its author, it is beyond all doubt a most remarkable work. . . . The personages of this tragedy—above all that of the heroine—are conceived with the most striking original power and carried out with unerring consistency; but we crave—and crave in vain—some relief to the almost sickening combinations of awe and loathing created by such characters and motives as this drama presents.—WARD, ADOLPHUS WILLIAM, 1875-99, *A History of English Dramatic Literature, vol.* III, *pp.* 56, 57.

One of the most glorious works of the period. Vittoria is perfect throughout, and in the justly-lauded trial scene she has no superior on any stage. Brachiano is a thoroughly life-like portrait of the man who is completely besotted with an evil woman. Flamineo I have spoken of, and not favourably; yet in literature, if not in life, he is a triumph; and above all the absorbing tragic interest of the play, which it is impossible to take up without finishing, has to be counted in. But the real charm of "The White Devil" is the wholly miraculous poetry in phrases and short passages which it contains. Vittoria's dream of the yew-tree, almost all the speeches of the unfortunate Isabella, and most of her rival's, have this merit. But the most wonderful flashes of poetry are put in the mouth of the scoundrel Flamineo, where they have a singular effect.—SAINTSBURY, GEORGE, 1887, *History of Elizabethan Literature, p.* 275.

In 1612 John Webster stood revealed to the then somewhat narrow world of readers as a tragic poet and dramatist of the very foremost rank in the very highest class. "The White Devil," also known as "Vittoria Corombona," is a tragedy based on events then comparatively recent—on a chronicle of crime and retribution in which the leading circumstances were altered and adapted with the most delicate art and the most consummate judgment from the incompleteness of incomposite reality to the requisites of the stage of Shakespeare. By him alone among English poets have the finest scenes and passages of this tragedy been ever surpassed or equalled in the crowning qualities of tragic or dramatic poetry—in pathos and passion, in subtlety and strength, in harmonious variety of art and infallible fidelity to nature.—SWINBURNE, ALGERNON CHARLES, 1894, *Studies in Prose and Poetry, p.* 50.

The sketchiness of this play, which is not divided into acts and scenes, and progresses with unaccountable gaps in the story, and perfunctory makeshifts of dumb show, has been the wonder of critics. But Webster was particularly interested in his own work as a romantic rather than a theatrical poet, and it must be remembered that after a long apprenticeship in collaboration, "The White Devil" was his first independent play. It reads as though the writer had put in only what interested him, and had left the rest for a coadjutor, who did not happen to present himself, to fill up. The central figure of Vittoria, the subtle, masterful, and exquisite she-devil, is filled up very minutely and vividly in the otherwise hastily painted canvas; and in the trial-scene, which is perhaps the most perfectly sustained which Webster has left us, we are so much captivated by the beauty and ingenuity of the murderess that, as Lamb says in a famous passage, we are ready to expect that "all the court will rise and make proffer to defend her in spite of the utmost conviction of her guilt."—GOSSE, EDMUND, 1894, *The Jacobean Poets, p.* 169.

Webster's genius did not find full expression until he wholly freed himself from the trammels of partnership with men of powers inferior to his own. At an unascertained date between 1607 and 1612 he for the first time wrote a play singlehanded, and there evinced such command of tragic art and intensity as Shakespeare alone among Englishmen has surpassed.—LEE, SIDNEY, 1899, *Dictionary of National Biography, vol.* LX, *p.* 121.

DUTCHESSE OF MALFY
1623

THE | TRAGEDY | OF THE DVTCHESSE | OF MALFY. | *As it was Presented Priuatly, at the Black* | *Friers; and publiquely at the Globe, By the* | Kings Maiesties Seruants | The perfect and exact Coppy, with diuerse | *things Printed, that the length of the Play would* | not beare in the Presentment | Written by *John Webster.* | LONDON: | Printed by Nicholas Okes, for Iohn | Waterson, and are to be sold at the | signe of the Crowne, in *Paules* | Church-yard 1623.—TITLE PAGE OF FIRST EDITION.

Crown him a poet, whom nor Rome nor
    Greece
Transcend in all their's for a masterpiece;
In which, whiles words and matter change,
    and men
Act one another, he, from whose clear pen,

They all took life, to memory hath lent
A lasting fame to raise his monument.

—FORD, JOHN, 1623, *To the Reader of the Author, and His "Duchess of Malfi."*

I never saw thy Duchess till the day
That she was lively bodied in thy play:
How'er she answer'd her low-rated love
Her brother's anger did so fatal prove,
Yet my opinion is, she might speak more,
But never in her life so well before.

—ROWLEY, WILLIAM, 1623, *To His Friend, Mr. John Webster, upon his "Duchess of Malfi."*

All the several parts of the dreadful apparatus with which the death of the Duchess is ushered in, the waxen images which counterfeit death, the wild masque of madmen, the tombmaker, the bellman, the living person's dirge, the mortification by degrees,—are not more remote from the conceptions of ordinary vengeance, than the strange character of suffering which they seem to bring upon their victim is out of the imagination of ordinary poets. As they are not like inflictions of this life, so her language seems not of this world. She has lived among horrors till she is become "native and endowed unto that element." She speaks the dialect of despair; her tongue has a smatch of Tartarus and the souls in bale. To move a horror skilfully, to touch a soul to the quick, to lay upon fear as much as it can bear, to wean and weary a life till it is ready to drop, and then step in with mortal instruments to take its last forfeit: this only a Webster can do. Inferior geniuses may "upon horror's head horrors accumulate" but they cannot do this. They mistake quantity for quality; they "terrify babes with painted devils;" but they know not how a soul is to be moved. Their terrors want dignity, their affrightments are without decorum.—LAMB, CHARLES, 1808, *Specimens of Dramatic Poets.*

"The Duchess of Malfy" abounds more in the terrible than "The White Devil." It turns on the mortal offence which the lady gives to her two proud brothers, Ferdinand, Duke of Calabria, and a cardinal, by indulging in a generous, though infatuated passion, for Antonio, her steward. This passion, a subject always most difficult to treat, is managed in this case with infinite delicacy; and, in a situation of great peril for the author, she condescends, without being degraded, and declares the affection with which her dependant has inspired her, without losing anything of dignity and respect.—MILLS, ABRAHAM, 1851, *The Literature and the Literary Men of Great Britain and Ireland, vol.* I, *p.* 345.

The "Duchess of Malfi" is certainly in a pure and loftier strain; but in spite of the praise which has been lavished on her, we must take the liberty to doubt whether the poor Duchess is "a person" at all. General goodness and beauty, intense though pure affection for a man below her in rank, and a will to carry out her purpose at all hazards, are not enough to distinguish her from thousands of other women; but Webster has no such purpose. What he was thinking and writing of was, not truth, but effect; not the Duchess, but her story; not her brothers, but their rage; not Antonio, her major-domo and husband, but his good and bad fortunes; and thus he has made Antonio merely insipid, the brother merely unnatural, and the Duchess, (in the critical moment of the play,) merely forward. That curious scene, in which she acquaints Antonio with her love for him, and makes him marry her, is, on the whole, painful. Webster himself seems to have felt that it was so; and, dreading lest he had gone too far, to have tried to redeem the Duchess at the end by making her break down in two exquisite lines of loving shame: but he has utterly forgotten to explain or justify her love, by giving to Antonio, (as Shakspeare would probably have done,) such strong specialties of character as would compel, and therefore excuse his mistress's affection. He has plenty of time to do this in the first scenes,—time which he wastes on irrelevant matter; and all that we gather from them is that Antonio is a worthy and thoughtful person. If he gives promise of being more, he utterly disappoints that promise afterwards. In the scene in which the Duchess tells her love, he is far smaller, rather than greater than the Antonio of the opening scene, though (as there) altogether passive. He hears his mistress's declaration, just as any other respectable youth might; is exceedingly astonished, and a good deal frightened; has to be talked out of his fears till one naturally expects a revulsion on the Duchess's part into something like scorn or shame, (which might have given a good opportunity for calling out sudden strength in Antonio:) but so busy is Webster with his business of drawing mere blind love, that he leaves Antonio to be a mere puppet, whose worthiness we are to believe in only from the Duchess's assurance to him that he is perfection of all that man should be; which, as all lovers are of the same opinion the day before the wedding, is not of much importance.—KINGSLEY, CHARLES, 1859, *Plays and Puritans, Sir Walter Raleigh and His Time*, *p.* 102.

The total impression left upon the mind by the tragic action of "The Duchess of Malfi" is unsurpassed in depth by anything else known to have been achieved by Webster; nor is the hope unreasonable that so masterly a work may permanently recover possession of the English stage. —WARD, ADOLPHUS WILLIAM, 1875–99, *A History of English Dramatic Literature*, *vol.* III, *p.* 60.

Webster's "Duchess of Malfi" teaches both the triumphs and the dangers of the dramatic fury. The construction runs riot; certain characters are powerfully conceived, others are wild figments of the brain. It is full of most fantastic speech and action; yet the tragedy, the passion, the felicitious language and imagery of various scenes, are nothing less than Shakespearean. To comprehend rightly the good and bad qualities of this play is to have gained a liberal education in poëtic criticism.—STEDMAN, EDMUND CLARENCE, 1892, *The Nature and Elements of Poetry*, *p.* 249.

Webster's masterpiece is "The Duchess of Malfy," of which it may confidently be alleged that it is the finest tragedy in the English language outside the works of Shakespeare. . . . It is curious that in a writer so distinguished by care in the working out of detail, we should find so lax a metrical system as marks "The Duchess of Malfy." Here, again, Webster seems to be content to leave the general surface dull, while burnishing his own favourite passages to a high lustre. . . . The horrible dumb shows of "The Duchess of Malfy"—the strangled children, the chorus of maniacs, the murder of Cariola, as she bites and scratches, the scuffling and stabbing in the fifth act, are, it appears to me—with all deference to the eminent critics, who have applauded them—blots on what is notwithstanding a truly noble poem, and what, with more reserve in this respect, would have been one of the first tragedies of the world.—GOSSE, EDMUND, 1894, *The Jacobean Poets*, *pp.* 166, 167, 169.

Was first printed in the memorable year which witnessed the first publication of his collected plays. This tragedy stands out among its compeers as one of the imperishable and ineradicable landmarks of literature. All the great qualities apparent in "The White Devil" reappear in "The Duchess of Malfy," combined with a yet more perfect execution, and utilized with a yet more consummate skill. No poet has ever so long and so successfully sustained at their utmost heighth and intensity the expressed emotions and the united effects of terror and pity. The transcendent imagination and the impassioned sympathy which inspire this most tragic of all tragedies save "King Lear" are fused together in the fourth act into a creation which has hardly been excelled for unflagging energy of impression and of pathos in all the dramatic or poetic literature of the world. — SWINBURNE, ALGERNON CHARLES, 1894, *Studies in Prose and Poetry*, *p.* 51.

THE DEVIL'S LAW-CASE

1632

THE DEUILS LAW-CASE. | or, | When Women goe to Law, the | Deuill is full of Businesse, | *A new Tragecomœdy.* | *The true and perfect Copie from the Originall.* | As it was approouedly well Acted | by her Maiesties Seruants | Written by Iohn Webster. | London, | Printed by *A. M.* for *Iohn Grismand*, and are | to be sold at his Shop in Pauls Alley at the | Signe of the Gvnne. 1623.—TITLE PAGE OF FIRST EDITION.

Despite fine passages, a mere "salmagundi."—SAINTSBURY, GEORGE, 1887, *History of Elizabethan Literature*, *p.* 274.

If the playwright took a step forwards in his Roman play, he took several backwards in his incoherent tragi-comedy of "The Devil's Law-Case." Here no charm attaches to the characters; the plot moves around no central interest; the structure of the piece, from a stage point of view, is utterly at fault. None the less, this strange play will always have its readers, for Webster's literary faculty is nowhere exhibited to greater perfection, and the poetry of the text abounds in verbal felicities.—GOSSE, EDMUND, 1894, *The Jacobean Poets, p.* 171.

APPIUS AND VIRGINIA
1654

In "Appius and Virginia," printed in 1654, probably after its author's death, we may consider ourselves justified in recognising a work of his later manhood, if not of his old age. The theme is indeed one which might readily be supposed to have commended itself to Webster's love of the terrible; but he has treated it without adding fresh effects of his own invention to those which he found ready to his hand. Yet the play has genuine power; and were it not that the action seems to continue too long after the death of Virginia, this tragedy might be described as one of the most commendable efforts of its class. The evenness, however, of its execution, and the absence (except in the central situation) of any passages of a peculiarly striking or startling character, exclude "Appius and Virginia" from the brief list of Webster's most characteristic productions.—WARD, ADOLPHUS WILLIAM, 1875–99, *A History of English Dramatic Literature, vol.* III, *p.* 62.

While the romantic and literary glow of language is severely restrained, there is here a very noticeable advance in every species of dramatic propriety, and "Appius and Virginia" is by far the best constructed of Webster's plays. . . . The scenes are largely set, the characters, especially those of Virginius and of Appius, justly designed and well contrasted, while the stiffness of Roman manners, as seen through a Jacobean medium, is not in this case sufficient to destroy the suppleness of the movement nor the pathos of the situation. "Appius and Virginia," as a poem, will never possess the attractiveness of the two great Italian romances, but it is the best-executed of Webster's dramas.—GOSSE, EDMUND, 1894, *The Jacobean Poets, pp.* 170, 171.

A work which would alone have sufficed to perpetuate the memory of its author among all competent lovers of English poetry at its best.—SWINBURNE, ALGERNON CHARLES, 1894, *Studies in Prose and Poetry, p.* 51.

"Appius and Virginia" differs largely from the other plays in diction and figure. It is more rhetorical and declamatory, it contains fewer striking and original similitudes; and with a sort of dramatic propriety its language is more latinized and conventional. The attempt is obviously in another vein than the Italianate tragedies of "The White Devil" and "The Duchess of Malfi."—CARPENTER, FREDERIC IVES, 1895, *Metaphor and Simile in the Minor Elizabethan Drama, p.* 80.

GENERAL

An Author that liv'd in the Reign of King *James* the First; and was in those Days accounted an Excellent Poet. He joyn'd with *Decker*, *Marston*, and *Rowley*, in several Plays; and was likewise Author of others, which have even in our Age gain'd Applause. . . . Mr. *Philips* has committed a great Mistake, in ascribing several Plays to our Author, and his Associate Mr. *Decker;* One of which belong to another Writer, whose Name is annexed, and the rest are Anonymous.—LANGBAINE, GERARD, 1691, *An Account of the English Dramatick Poets, pp.* 508, 510.

In his pictures of wretchedness and despair, he has introduced touches of expression which curdle the very blood with terror, and make the hair stand erect. Of this, the death of The Dutchesse of Malfy, with all its preparatory horrors, is a most distinguishing proof. The fifth act of his "Vittoria Corombona" shows, also, with what occasional skill he could imbibe the imagination of Shakspeare, particularly where its features seem to breathe a more than earthly wildness.—DRAKE, NATHAN, 1817, *Shakspeare and his Times, vol.* II, *p.* 565.

Webster has a gloomy force of imagination, not unmixed with the beautiful and pathetic. But it is "beauty in the lap of horror:" he caricatures the shapes of terror, and his Pegasus is like a nightmare.—CAMPBELL, THOMAS, 1819, *An Essay on English Poetry.*

His "White Devil" and "Dutchess of Malfi," upon the whole, perhaps, come the nearest to Shakspeare of any thing we have upon record: the only drawback to them, the only shade of imputation that can be thrown upon them, "by which they lose some colour," is, that they are too like Shakspeare, and often direct imitations of him, both in general conception and individual expression.—HAZLITT, WILLIAM, 1820, *Lectures on the Literature of the Age of Elizabeth, Lecture III.*

"Westward Ho" and "Northward Ho" . . . are full of life and bustle, and remarkable for the light they throw on the manners and customs of the time. Though by no means pure, they are comparatively little stained by that grossness from which none of our old comedies are entirely free. In them the worst things are always called the worst names: the licentious and the debauched always speak most strictly in character; and the rake, the bawd, and the courtezan, are odious in representation as they would be if actually present. —DYCE, ALEXANDER, 1830-57, *ed. The Works of John Webster, p.* xiii.

Is one of the best of our ancient dramatists.—SCOTT, SIR WALTER, 1831, *Letter to Rev. A. Dyce, March* 31. *Lockhart's Scott, ch.* lxxix.

He possessed very considerable powers, and ought to be ranked, I think, the next below Ford. With less of poetic grace than Shirley, he had incomparably more vigor; with less of nature and simplicity than Heywood, he had a more elevated genius and a bolder pencil. But the deep sorrows and terrors of tragedy were peculiarly his province.—HALLAM, HENRY, 1837-39, *Introduction to the Literature of Europe, pt.* iii, *ch.* vi, *par.* 100.

Webster was formed upon Shakspere. He had no pretensions to the inexhaustible wit, the all-penetrating humour, of his master; but he had the power of approaching the terrible energy of his passion, and the profoundness of his pathos, in characters which he took out of the great muster-roll of humanity and placed in fearful situations and sometimes with revolting imaginings almost beyond humanity. . . . It is clear what dramatic writers were the objects of Webster's love. He did not aspire to the "full and heightened style of Master Chapman," nor would his genius be shackled by the examples of "the laboured and understanding works of Master Jonson." He belonged to the school of the romantic dramatists.—KNIGHT, CHARLES, 1842-67, *William Shakspere: A Biography.*

John Webster, a mighty and funereal genius, is the next author we shall mention. We can compare his mind to nothing so well as to some old Gothic cathedral, with its arches soaring heavenward, but carved with monsters and angels, with saints and fiends, in grotesque confusion. Gleams of sunlight fall here and there, it is true, through the huge window, but they are coloured with the sombre dies of painted glass, bearing records of human pride and human nothingness, and they fall in long slanting columns, twinkling silently with motes and dusty splendour, upon the tombs of the mighty; lighting dimly up now the armour of a recumbent Templar or the ruff of some dead beauty, and now feebly losing themselves amid the ragged coffins and scutcheons in the vaults below. His fancy was wild and powerful, but gloomy and monstrous, dwelling ever on the vanities of earthly glory, on the nothingness of pomp, not without many terrible hints at the emptiness of our trust, and many bold questionings of human hopes of a hereafter.—SHAW, THOMAS B., 1847, *Outlines of English Literature, p.* 130.

Wesbter's most famous works are "The Duchess of Malfy" and "Vittoria Corombona," but we are strongly inclined to call "The Devil's Law-Case" his best play. The two former are in a great measure answerable for the "spasmodic" school of poets, since the extravagances of a man of genius are as sure of imitation as the equable self-possession of his higher moments is incapable of it. Webster had, no doubt, the primal requisite of a poet, imagination, but in him it was truly untamed, and Aristotle's admirable distinction between the *Horrible* and the *Terrible* in tragedy was never better illustrated and confirmed than in the "Duchess" and "Vittoria." His nature had something of the sleuth-hound quality in it, and a plot, to keep his mind eager on the trail, must be sprinkled with fresh blood at every turn. . . . He has not the condensing power of Shakespeare, who squeezed meaning into a phrase with an hydraulic press, but he could carve a cherry-stone with any of the *concettisti,* and abounds in imaginative quaintnesses that are worthy of Donne, and epigrammatic tersenesses that reminds us of Fuller. Nor is he wanting in poetic phrases of the purest crystallization.—LOWELL, JAMES RUSSELL, 1858-64-90, *Library of Old Authors, Prose Works, Riverside ed., vol.* I, *p.* 279, 281.

Webster was one of those writers whose genius consists in the expression of special moods, and who, outside of those moods, cannot force their creative faculties into vigorous action. His mind by instinctive sentiment was directed to the contemplation of the darker aspects of life. He brooded over crime and misery until his imagination was enveloped in their atmosphere, found a fearful joy in probing their sources and tracing their consequences, became strangely familiar with their physiognomy and psychology, and felt a shuddering sympathy with their "deep groans and terrible ghastly looks." There was hardly a remote corner of the soul, which hid a feeling capable of giving mental pain, into which this artist in agony had not curiously peered. . . . He is such a spendthrift of his stimulants, and accumulates horror on horror, and crime on crime, with such fatal facility, that he would render the mind callous to his terrors, were it not that what is acted is still less than what is suggested, and that the souls of his characters are greater than their sufferings or more terrible than their deeds. The crimes and the criminals belong to Italy as it was in the sixteenth century, when poisoning and assassination were almost in the fashion; the feelings with which they are regarded are English; and the result of the combination is to make the poisoners and assassins more fiendishly malignant in spirit than they actually were.—WHIPPLE, EDWIN P., 1859–68, *The Literature of the Age of Elizabeth*, *pp.* 139, 141.

A sombre man, whose thoughts seem incessantly to be haunting tombs and charnel-houses. . . . No one has equalled Webster in creating desperate characters, utter wretches, bitter misanthropes, in blackening and blaspheming human life, above all, in depicting the shameless depravity and refined ferocity of Italian manners.—TAINE, H. A., 1871, *History of English Literature, tr. Van Laun, vol.* I, *bk.* ii, *ch.* ii, *p.* 252.

In passing onward to John Webster, we come into the presence of a poet to whom a foremost place has been rarely denied among the later writers of the great age of our drama, and in whom it is impossible not to recognise a genius of commanding originality, though apparently of not very versatile powers. It is most unfortunate that but few plays should have been preserved of which he was the sole author; for it is in these that his most distinctive gifts stand forth with incomparably the greatest clearness, and, as is pointed out by the most adequate of his modern critics, he seems, like Shakspere and Jonson, to have preferred to work alone. . . . Webster's most powerful plays and scenes are characterised by something besides their effective appeal to the emotion of terror. He has a true insight into human nature, and is capable of exhibiting the operation of powerful influences upon it with marvellous directness. He is aware that men and women will lay open the inmost recesses of their souls in moments of deep or sudden agitation; he has learnt that on such occasions unexpected contrasts—an impulse of genuine compassion in an assassin, a movement of true dignity in a harlot—are wont to offer themselves to the surprised observer; he is acquainted with the fury and the bitterness, the goad and the after-sting of passion, and with the broken vocabulary of grief. All these he knows and understands, and is able to reproduce, not continually or wearisomely, but with that unerring recognition of supremely fitting occasions which is one of the highest, as it is beyond all doubt one of the rarest, gifts of true dramatic genius.—WARD, ADOLPHUS WILLIAM, 1875–99, *History of English Dramatic Literature, vol.* III, *pp.* 51, 63.

He* becomes the best critic, almost the discoverer, of Webster, a dramatist of genius so sombre, so heavily coloured, so *macabre*.—PATER, WALTER, 1878–89, *Appreciations*, *p.* 110.

Thunder: the flesh quails, and the soul bows down.
 Night: east, west, south, and northward, very night.
 Star upon struggling star strives into sight,
Star after shuddering star the deep storms drown.
The very throne of night, her very crown,
 A man lays hand on, and usurps her right.
 Song from the highest of heaven's imperious height
Shoots, as a fire to smite some towering town.
Rage, anguish, harrowing fear, heart-crazing crime,
Make monstrous all the murderous face of Time

*Charles Lamb.

Shown in the spheral orbit of a glass
Revolving. Earth cries out from all her graves,
Frail, on frail rafts, across wide-wallowing waves,
Shapes here and there of child and mother pass.

—SWINBURNE, ALGERNON CHARLES, 1882, *John Webster.*

John Webster excelled in the delineation of strange and fantastic horrors. He was pre-eminently the dramatist of Death. But his works abound in passages of surprising tenderness and beauty. The vices and crimes which he delighted to paint have, notwithstanding their extravagance, an appearance of terrible reality; and he had the wonderful faculty of surmising and looking into the inmost thoughts and springs of action in the human mind. He was an artist of the highest type.—BALDWIN, JAMES, 1882, *English Literature and Literary Criticism, English Poetry, p.* 238.

Of all these later dramatists, the most Shakespearean is Webster, an artist of agony.—WELSH, ALFRED H., 1882, *Development of English Literature and Language, vol.* I*, p.* 422.

John Webster, one of Shakspere's dramatic disciples, delighted in nothing so much as in full-length studies of tragic female figures. There are indeed wonderful creations in his plays beside these—sinister and cynical faces of men apparent in the gloom. But in his greatest dramas all exists for the sake of the one woman after whom each drama is named—the Duchess of Malfi, Webster's lady of sorrow, and his White Devil, Vittoria Corombona, on whom, splendid in her crime, he turns a high light of imagination that dazzles while we gaze.—DOWDEN, EDWARD, 1887, *Transcripts and Studies, p.* 341.

Webster rises to Shakespeare's shoulder by his sincerity, nobility, and unerring truth to life in its most thrilling moments. —SYMONDS, JOHN ADDINGTON, 1887, *Marlowe, (Mermaid Series), General Introduction on the Drama, p.* xxv.

There are, indeed, wondrous flashes of dramatic power; by whiles, too, there are refreshing openings-out to the light or sinlessness of common day—a lifting of thought and consciousness up from the great welter of crime and crime's entanglements; but there is little brightness, sparse sunshine, rare panoply of green or blooming things; even the flowers are put to sad offices, and

"do cover
The friendless bodies of unburied men."

When a man's flower culture gets reduced to such narrow margin as this it does not carry exhilarating odors with it. —MITCHELL, DONALD G., 1890, *English Lands Letters and Kings, From Elizabeth to Anne, p.* 90.

This poet's morbid imagination affects us like that touch of the dead man's hand in one of the hideous scenes of his own most famous play.—WATSON, WILLIAM, 1893, *Excursions in Criticism, p.* 13.

Nothing so much as a close and careful study of his imagery can bring home to one the extraordinary originality and power of Webster in his particular sphere. Webster worked consciously, deliberately, and with a thorough command of his materials. His pages are strewn with tropes, and, in spite of their profusion, such is the keenness of his marvelous "analogical instinct" and the dramatic force of his imagination that scarcely ever do they seem forced or out of keeping. Language here seems to reach the extreme of ruthless and biting intensity. There is scarcely any faded imagery, and there are very few conventional tags; everything stands out in sharp lines, as if etched. The characteristic fault of Webster's imagery, the defect of his peculiar quality, is that he errs if anything on the side of the bizarre, or even of the grotesque. This criticism could be enforced by many citations. . . . The acrid nature of Webster's genius is everywhere felt in his pungent use of similitudes. The sardonic character of Flamineo in "The White Devil" is heightened by the irony of his incessant similes. So in "The Duchess of Malfi" Antonio's rather colorless virtues are artfully depicted through his fondness for sententious comparisons. —CARPENTER, FREDERIC IVES, 1895, *Metaphor and Simile in the Minor Elizabethan Drama, pp.* 75, 77.

Greater in some respects than any but Shakespeare, is John Webster, who requires but a closer grasp of style and a happier architecture to rank among the leading English poets. . . . Webster has so splendid a sense of the majesty of death, of the mutability of human pleasures, and of the velocity and weight of destiny, that he rises to conceptions which have an Æschylean dignity; but, unhappily, he grows weary of sustaining them, his ideas of stage-craft are rudimentary and spectacular, and his single well-constructed play, "Appius and Virginia," has a certain disappointing tameness.—GOSSE, EDMUND, 1897, *Short History of Modern English Literature, pp.* 118, 119.

Webster lacked Shakespeare's sureness of touch in developing character, and his studies of human nature often suffer from over-elaboration. With a persistence that seems unjustifiable in a great artist, Webster, moreover, concentrated his chief energies on repulsive themes and characters; he trafficked with an obstinate monotony in fantastic crimes. Nevertheless he had a true artistic sense. . . . Is rarely coarse. In depicting the perversities of passion he never deviated into pruriency, and handled situations of conventional delicacy with dignified reticence.—LEE, SIDNEY, 1899, *Dictionary of National Biography, vol.* LX, *p.* 124.

Nicholas Breton

1545?–1626?

Little is known of his life save that he studied at Oriel College, Oxford; and almost less of his forty-two pastorals, satires, &c., in verse and prose, which were edited by Dr. Grosart in 1877 and 1893.—PATRICK AND GROOME, *eds.*, 1897, *Chambers's Biographical Dictionary, p.* 131.

Thou, that wouldst find the habit of true passion,
And see a mind attir'd in perfect strains
. . . .
Look here on Breton's work, the master print:
Where such perfections to the life do rise.
—JONSON, BEN, 1600, *In Authorem prefacing Breton's "Melacolike Humours."*

Nicholas Breton, a writer of pastoral, sonnets, canzons and madrigals, in which kind of writing he keeps company with several other contemporary æmulators of Spencer and Sir Philip Sidny, in a publist collection of selected odes of the chief pastoral sonnetteers, &c. of that age.—PHILLIPS, EDWARD, 1675, *Theatrum Poetarum Anglicanorum, ed. Brydges, p.* 319.

The ballad of "Phillida and Corydon," reprinted by Percy, is a delicious little poem; and if we are to judge from this specimen, his poetical powers, for surely he must have had the powers of a poet, were distinguished by a simplicity, at once easy and elegant.—BRYDGES, SAMUEL EDGERTON, 1800, *ed. Phillips's Theatrum Poetarum Anglicanorum, p.* 321.

His happiest vein is in little pastoral pieces. In addition to the long roll of his indifferent works which are enumerated in the "Biographia Poetica," the "Censura Literaria" imputes to him a novel of singular absurdity, in which the miseries of the heroine of the story are consummated by having her nose bit off by an aged and angry rival of her husband.—CAMPBELL, THOMAS, 1819, *Specimens of the British Poets.*

A man of no ordinary genius, writing in his more inspired moments with tenderness and delicacy.—DYCE, ALEXANDER, 1831–61, *Dramatic and Poetical Works of Robert Greene, p.* 25.

As a literary man Breton impresses us most by his versatility and his habitual refinement. He is a satirical, religious, romance, and pastoral writer in both prose and verse. But he wrote with exceptional facility, and as a consequence he wrote too much. His fertile fancy often led him into fantastic puerilities. It is in his pastoral lyrics that he is seen at his best. The pathos here is always sincere; the gaiety never falls into grossness, the melody is fresh and the style clear.—LEE, SIDNEY, 1886, *Dictionary of National Biography, vol.* VI, *p.* 276.

If we could take as his the charming lullaby of "The Arbour of Amorous Devices" he would stand (if only as a kind of "single-speech") high as a poet. But I fear that Dr. Grosart's attribution of it to him is based on little external and refuted by all internal evidence. His best certain thing is the pretty "Phillida and Corydon" idyll, which may be found in "England's Helicon" or in Mr. Ward's "Poets." But I own that I can never read this latter without thinking of two lines of Fulke Greville's in the same metre and on no very different theme—

"O'er enamelled meads they went,
Quiet she, he passion-rent,"

which are simply worth all the works of Breton's prose and verse, unless we count the "Lullaby," put together. In the *mots rayonnants*, the *mots de lumière*, he is sadly deficient. But his work (which is nearly as plentiful in verse as in prose) is, as has been said, very interesting to the literary student, because it shows better perhaps than anything else the style of literature which a man, disdaining to condescend to burlesque or bawdry, not gifted with any extraordinary talent, either at prosé or verse, but possessed of a certain literary faculty, could then produce with a fair chance of being published and bought. It cannot be said that the result shows great daintiness in Breton's public. The verse, with an improvement in sweetness and fluency, is very much of the doggerel style which was prevalent before Spenser; and the prose, though showing considerable faculty, if not of invention, yet of adroit imitation of previously invented styles, is devoid of distinction and point. . . . The pervading characteristics are Breton's invariable modesty, his pious, and, if I may be permitted to use the word, gentlemanly spirit, and a fashion of writing which, if not very pointed, picturesque, or epigrammatic, is clear, easy, and on the whole rather superior in observance of the laws of grammar and arrangement to the work of men of much greater note in his day. —SAINTSBURY, GEORGE, 1887, *History of Elizabethan Literature, pp.* 239, 240.

Nicholas Breton was an Elizabethan primitive, who went on publishing fresh volumes until after the death of James I., but without having modified the sixteenth-century character of his style. . . . Of these short productions "The Passionate Shepherd" is by far the best, and ranks very high among Breton's contributions to poetry. It is a collection of pastoral lyrics, in a variety of measures, very lightly, liquidly, and innocently thrown off, with no sense of intellectual effort and no great attention to style. Breton has a very pleasant acquaintance with nature. . . . Breton had the root of poetry in him, but he was no scholar, inartistic, and absolutely devoid of the gift of self-criticism. A small posy has been selected by Mr. Bullen from the wilderness of his overgrown garden.—GOSSE, EDMUND, 1894, *The Jacobean Poets, pp.* 15, 17.

There is a naturalness, an easy flow, and gaiety, a tenderness and purity about Breton that ought to restore him to fame. —SCHELLING, FELIX E., 1895, *A Book of Elizabethan Lyrics, p.* 226.

As fresh as Nash, as copious as Lodge, but endowed with a finer artistic feeling, and altogether captivating in his ready grace and buoyancy.—CARPENTER, FREDERIC IVES, 1897, *English Lyric Poetry,* 1500–1700, *Introduction, p.* xliii.

Sir John Beaumont

1583–1627

Was the second son of Judge Francis Beaumont, and an elder brother of Francis, the celebrated dramatic poet. He was entered a gentleman commoner of Broadgates' Hall, (now Pembroke College,) Oxford, in 1596. After some attention to the study of law, he retired to the family seat at Grace-Dieu, Leicestershire. Anth. Wood ascribes to him the "Crown of Thorns," a poem in 8 books, never printed. His son gave his father's writings to the world, under the title of "Bosworth Field, with a Taste of the Variety of Other Poems," 1629. Pages 181-2 are missing in all copies.—ALLIBONE, S. AUSTIN, 1854–8, *Dictionary of English Literature, vol.* I, *p.* 151.

This book will live; it hath a genius; this
Above his reader, or his praiser, is.

—JONSON, BEN, 1629, *Verses Prefixed to Bosworth Field.*

Thy care for that, which was not worth thy breath,
Brought on too soon thy much-lamented death.
But Heav'n was kind, and would not let thee see
The plagues that must upon this nation be,
By whom the Muses have neglected been,
Which shall add weight and measure to their sin.

—DRAYTON, MICHAEL, 1629? *To Sir John Beaumont.*

The former part of his life he successfully employed in poetry, and the latter he as happily bestowed on more serious and beneficial studies; And had not death untimely cut him off in his middle age, he might have prov'd a patriot, being accounted at the time of his death a person of great knowledge, gravity, and worth. —WOOD, ANTHONY, 1691–1721, *Athenæ Oxonienses, vol.* I, *p.* 524.

Herbert is lower than Crashaw, Sir John Beaumont higher, and Donne, a good deal so.—POPE, ALEXANDER, 1728–30, *Spence's Anecdotes, p.* 17.

"Bosworth Field" may be compared with Addison's "Campaign," without a high compliment to either. Sir John has no fancy, but there is force and dignity in some of his passages; and he deserves notice as one of the earliest polishers of what is called the heroic couplet.—CAMPBELL, THOMAS, 1819, *Specimens of the British Poets.*

The commendation of improving the rhythm of the couplet is due also to Sir John Beaumont, author of a short poem on the battle of Bosworth Field. It was not written, however, so early as the "Britannia's Pastorals" of Browne. In other respects, it has no pretensions to a high rank.—HALLAM, HENRY, 1837–39, *Introduction to the Literature of Europe.*

From high up in the seventeenth century careful students have detected a tendency towards the smoother and correcter, but tamer prosody. I do not think that the beginnings of the classical heroic couplet in England can be explored with advantage earlier than in the works of Sir John Beaumont, who, dying in 1627, left behind him a very carefully written historical poem of "Bosworth Field."—GOSSE, EDMUND, 1897, *Short History of Modern English Literature, p.* 157.

Beaumont's son and heir, Sir John, piously prepared and published in 1629 his father's poems for the first time under the title: "Bosworth Field, with a Taste of the Variety of other Poems, left by Sir John Beaumont, Baronet, deceased: Set forth by his Sonne, Sir John Beaumont, Baronet: and dedicated to the Kings most excellent Maiestie." "Bosworth Field" is written in heroic couplets of ten syllables. The preserving fragrance of the book must be looked for, not in his secular, but in his sacred poems. Very strong religious feeling is apparent in many of his poems, especially in his "In Desolation," "Of the Miserable State of Man," and "Of Sinne."—GROSART, ALEXANDER B., 1885, *Dictionary oj National Biography, vol.* IV, *p.* 59.

Thomas Middleton

1570?-1627

Thomas Middleton, 1570[?]-1627. Born, in London, 1570[?]. Student at Gray's Inn, 1593[?]. Began to write plays about 1600. Wrote a number of plays and masques. Married (i.) Mary Morbeck, 1603[?]. After her death he married (ii.) Magdalen ——, 1627 [?]. Appointed City Chronologer, 6 Sept. 1620. Died, at Newington Butts, July 1627; buried in parish church, 4 July. *Works:* "The Wisdom of Solomon Paraphrased," 1597; "Microcynion" (under initials: T. M.; attrib. to Middleton), 1559; "Master Constable Blurt" (anon.), 1602; "The Blacke Booke" (under initials: T. M.; attrib. to Middleton), 1604; "Father Hubburd's Tales" (under pseud. "Oliver Hubburd"), 1604; "Michaelmas Terme" (anon.) 1607; "The Phœnix" (anon.), 1607; "A Trick to Catch the Old-One" (under initials: T. M.), 1608; "The Famelie of Love" (anon.), 1608; "Your Five Gallants" [1608]; "A Mad World, my Masters" (under initials: T. M.), 1608; "Sir Robert Sherley," 1609; "The Roaring Girle" (with Dekker), 1611; "The Triumphs of Truth," 1613; "Civitatis Amor" (anon.), 1616; "The Tryumphs of Honor and Industry" (under initials: T. M.), 1617; "A Faire Quarrell" (with Rowley), 1617; "The Peacemaker" (anon.; attrib. to Middleton), 1618; "The Inner Temple Masque," 1619; "The Triumphs of Love and Antiquity," 1619; "The World Tost at Tennis" (with Rowley), 1620; "The Sunne in Aries," 1621; "The Triumphs of Honor and Virtue," 1622; "The Triumphs of Integrity," 1623; "A Game at Chess" (anon. [1624], 3rd. edn. same year); "The Triumphs of Health and Prosperity,"

1626. *Posthumous:* "A Chast Mayd in Cheape-side," 1630; "The Widdow" (with Jonson and Fletcher), 1652; "The Changeling" (with Rowley), 1653; "The Spanish Gipsie" (with Rowley), 1653; "The Old Law" (with Massinger and Rowley), 1656; "No Wit, No Help like a Woman's," 1657; "Two new playes; viz., More Dissemblers besides Women;" "Women Beware Women," 1657; "The Mayor of Quinborough," 1661; "Anything for a Quiet Life," 1662; "The Witch," 1778. *Collected Works:* ed. by Dyce, 1840; by A. H. Bullen, 1885-86.—SHARP, R. FARQUHARSON, 1897, *A Dictionary of English Authors, p.* 196.

PERSONAL

Jacconot. Well said, Master Middleton —a merry devil and a long-lived one run monkey-wise up your back-bone! May your days be as happy as they're sober, and your nights full of applause! May no brawling mob pelt you, or your friends, when throned, nor hoot down your plays when your soul's pinned like a cockchafer on public opinion! May no learned or unlearned calf write against your knowledge and wit, and no brother paper-stainer pilfer your pages, and then call you a general thief!—HORNE, R. H., 1837, *The Death of Marlowe.*

Was born about 1570, and was the son of a gentleman settled in London, whose wife likewise sprang from a London family. It is highly probable that he was at one time a member of one of the Universities,—Cambridge as it would seem, to whose life and ways he frequently refers in his plays with the easy but not unconscious familiarity of the old University man. He may safely be identified with one of the two Thomas Middletons who were admitted to Gray's Inn in 1593 and 1596 respectively,—with the former of these for choice. Thus he passed through the social experiences habitual to young gentlemen of his day before settling down to the labours of his life; and, apart from the evidence of his portrait, it will, I think, be allowed that his dramatic works are, notwithstanding their frequent coarseness, distinguished by a general flavour of good-breeding from those of such authors as Jonson, Dekker, or Marston.—WARD, ADOLPHUS WILLIAM, 1875-99, *A History of English Dramatic Literature, vol.* II, *p.* 493.

A GAME OF CHESS

1624

I doubt not but you have heard of our famous play of Gondomar, which hath been followed with extraordinary curiosity, and frequented by all sorts of people, old and young, rich and poor, masters and servants, papists, wise men, &c., churchmen and Scotsmen, as Sir Henry Wotton, Sir Albert Morton, Sir Benjamin Rudyard, Sir Thomas Lake, and a world besides. The Lady Smith would have gone if she could have persuaded me to go thither. I am not so sour ncr so severe but that I would willingly have attended her, but I could not sit so long, for we must have been there before one o'clock at farthest to find any room. They counterfeited his person to the life, with all his graces and faces, and had gotten, they say, a cast suit of his apparel for the purpose, and his letter, wherein the world says there lacked nothing but a couple of asses to carry it, and Sir George Petre or Sir Tobie Matthew to bear him company. But the worst is, playing him, they played somebody else, for which they are forbidden to play that or any other play till the King's further pleasure be known; and they may be glad if they can so escape Scot-free. The wonder lasted but nine days, for so long they played it.—CHAMBERLAIN, NICHOLAS, 1624, *Letter to Sir Dudley Carleton. Court and Times of James I., vol.* II, *p.* 472.

The literary merits of this dramatic allegory are by no means of a high order, and the political views shadowed forth in it are, so far as it is possible to judge, of that reckless sort which usually result from an endeavour to suit the current humour of popular sentiment. But while the historical student will not fail to observe with what strength public opinion must have run in the direction of the sentiments of this piece, for its author to have ventured upon producing it,—and for it to have passed the censorship of the Master of the Revels,—neither will literary criticism pass by unheeded so singular a composition. This play, which Ben Jonson is hardly unjust in alluding to as "poor," is in fact the solitary work with which the Elisabethan drama fairly attempted to match the political comedies of Aristophanes. No literary species can spring out of the earth in a single day.—WARD, ADOLPHUS WILLIAM, 1875-99, *A History of English Dramatic Literature, vol.* II, *p.* 536.

"A Game at Chess" contains some very caustic satire against Gondomar (the black Knight), whose fair seeming hypocrisy is exposed with masterly power, while his bodily infirmities are ridiculed with provoking persistence. The satirist's lash falls heavily on the apostate Bishop of Spalato (the Fat Bishop), who is represented as a swag-bellied monster of gluttony—and lecherous withal. There is abundant evidence to show that the satire was keenly appreciated. Three editions—without date, but probably printed in 1624—have come down, and Collier possessed a title-page of an edition dated 1625.—BULLEN, A. H., 1885, *ed. The Works of Thomas Middleton, vol.* I, *p.* lxxxiv.

The play which brought Middleton into prison, and earned for the actors a sum so far beyond parallel as to have seemed incredible till the fullest evidence was procured, is one of the most complete and exquisite works of artistic ingenuity and dexterity that ever excited or offended, enraptured or scandalized an audience of friends or enemies: the only work of English poetry which may properly be called Aristophanic. It has the same depth of civic seriousness, the same earnest ardour and devotion to the old cause of the old country, the same solid fervour of enthusiasm and indignation, which animated the third great poet of Athens against the corruption of art by the sophistry of Euripides and the corruption of manhood by the sophistry of Socrates. The delicate skill of the workmanship can only be appreciated by careful and thorough study.—SWINBURNE, A. C., 1886, *Thomas Middleton, The Nineteenth Century, vol.* 19, *p.* 146.

THE CHANGELING

The character of De Flores in this play has in it a strangeness of iniquity, such as we think is hardly paralleled in the whole range of the Elizabethan drama. The passions of this brute-imp are not human. They are such as might be conceived of as springing from the union of animal with fiendish impulses, in a nature which knew no law outside of its own lust, and was as incapable of a scruple as of a sympathy.—WHIPPLE, EDWIN P., 1859-68, *The Literature of the Age of Elizabeth, p.* 125.

Regarded as an artistic whole, "The Changeling" cannot challenge comparison with "The Maid's Tragedy," "The Broken Heart," or "The Duchess of Malfi." It has not the sustained tragic interest of those masterpieces; but there is one scene in "The Changeling" which, for appalling depth of passion, is not merely unsurpassed, but, I believe, unequalled outside Shakespeare's greatest tragedies.—BULLEN, A. H., 1885, *ed., The Works of Thomas Middleton, Introduction, vol.* I, *p.* lx.

WOMEN BEWARE WOMEN

Livia the "good neighbor" is as real a creature as one of Chaucer's characters. She is such another jolly Housewife as the Wife of Bath.—LAMB, CHARLES, 1808, *Specimens of Dramatic Poets.*

Middleton's style was not marked by any peculiar quality of his own, but was made up, in equal proportions, of the faults and excellences common to his contemporaries. In his "Women beware Women" there is a rich marrowy vein of internal sentiment, with fine occasional insight into human nature and cool cutting irony of expression. He is lamentably deficient in the plot and *dénouement* of the story.—HAZLITT, WILLIAM, 1820, *Literature of the Age of Elizabeth.*

A drama which shows a deep study of the sources of human frailty, considerable skill in exhibiting the passions in their consecutive, if not in their conflicting action, and a firm hold upon character; but it lacks pathos, tenderness, and humanity; its power is out of all proportion to its geniality; the characters, while they stand definitely out to the eye, are seen through no visionary medium of sentiment and fancy.—WHIPPLE, EDWIN P., 1859-68, *Literature of the Age of Elizabeth.*

Middleton fails to show himself capable of true tragic self-control; and though his aim is undoubtedly moral, he is unable by lofty sentiment to furnish any relief to the grossness of the situations, while the humorous characters are revoltingly coarse. He lacked, in short, both delicacy of feeling and sustained earnestness; and this tragedy, though it has received high praise, seems to me to indicate that his most distinctive dramatic powers lay in a different direction.—WARD, ADOLPHUS WILLIAM, 1875-99, *A History of English Dramatic Literature, vol.* II, *p.* 514.

The tragedy of "Women beware Women," whether or not it be accepted as the masterpiece of Middleton, is at least an excellent example of the facility and fluency and equable promptitude of style which all students will duly appreciate and applaud in the riper and completer work of this admirable poet. It is full to overflowing of noble eloquence, of inventive resource and suggestive effect, of rhetorical affluence and theatrical ability. The opening or exposition of the play is quite masterly: and the scene in which the forsaken husband is seduced into consolation by the temptress of his wife is worthy of all praise for the straightforward ingenuity and the serious delicacy by which the action is rendered credible and the situation endurable. But I fear that few or none will be found to disagree with my opinion that no such approbation or tolerance can be reasonably extended so as to cover or condone the offences of either the underplot or the upshot of the play. The one is repulsive beyond redemption by elegance of style, the other is preposterous beyond extenuation on the score of logic or poetical justice.—SWINBURNE, ALGERNON CHARLES, 1886, *Thomas Middleton, The Nineteenth Century, vol.* 19, *p.* 148.

This is no doubt the most powerful single play of Middleton's. The main plot is worked out with great mastery, the leading characters are most vividly drawn, and, unattractive as they all are, strikingly illustrate what Middleton could achieve by sheer dramatic force.—HERFORD, CHARLES H., 1894, *Dictionary of National Biography, vol.* XXXVII, *p.* 361.

A FAIR QUARRELL

High above all the works yet mentioned there stands and will stand conspicuous while noble emotion and noble verse have honour among English readers the pathetic and heroic play so memorably appreciated by Charles Lamb, "A Fair Quarrel." It would be the vainest and emptiest impertinence to offer a word in echo of his priceless and imperishable praise. The delicate nobility of the central conception on which the hero's character depends for its full relief and development should be enough to efface all remembrance of any defect or default in moral taste, any shortcoming on the æsthetic side of ethics, which may be detected in any slighter or hastier example of the poet's invention. —SWINBURNE, ALGERNON CHARLES, 1886, *Thomas Middleton, The Nineteenth Century, vol.* 19, *p.* 145.

THE WITCH

Though some resemblance may be traced between the charms in Macbeth, and the incantations in this play, which is supposed to have preceded it, this coincidence will not detract much from the originality of Shakespeare. His witches are distinguished from the witches of Middleton by essential differences. These are creatures to whom man or woman, plotting some dire mischief, might resort for occasional consultation. Those originate deeds of blood, and begin bad impulses to men. From the moment that their eyes first meet with Macbeth's, he is spellbound. That meeting sways his destiny. He can never break the fascination. These witches can hurt the body, those have power over the soul. Hecate in Middleton has a son, a low buffoon: the hags of Shakespeare have neither child of their own, nor seem to be descended from any parent. They are foul anomalies, of whom we know not whence they are sprung, nor whether they have beginning or ending. As they are without human passions, so they seem to be without human relations. They come with thunder and lightning, and vanish to airy music. This is all we know of them. Except Hecate, they have no *names;* which heightens their mysteriousness. The names, and some of the properties, which the other author has given to his hags, excite smiles. The Weird Sisters are serious things. Their presence cannot co-exist with mirth. But, in a lesser degree, the witches of Middleton are fine creations. Their power too is, in some measure, over the mind. They raise jars, jealousies, strifes, "like a thick scurf" over life.—LAMB, CHARLES, 1808, *Specimens of Dramatic Poets.*

The hags of Middleton are drawn with a bold and creative pencil, and seem to take a middle station between the terrific sisterhood of Shakspeare, and the traditonary witch of the country-village. They are pictures full of fancy, but not kept sufficiently aloof from the ludicrous and familiar. — DRAKE, NATHAN, 1817, *Shakspeare and His Times, vol.* II, *p.* 566.

The commentators would have everything, in Shakspeare and everybody else, to be borrowed or stolen: they have the genius and the zeal of thief-catchers in ferreting out and exposing all transferences among writers, real and imaginary, of thoughts, words, and syllables; and in the present case, as in many others, their professional ardor seems to have made a great deal out of very little.—CRAIK, GEORGE L., 1861, *A Compendious History of English Literature and of the English Language, vol.* I, *p.* 596.

Middleton's name has of late been revived in connection with the authorship of "Macbeth." It has been conjectured, on the ground of certain slight coincidences between Middleton's play and the witch scenes, that Middleton had a hand in the composition of "Macbeth." The supposition is about as groundless as any ever made in connection with Shakespeare, which is saying a good deal. Even if either author borrowed the words of the song from the other, that is no evidence of further co-operation. The plays are wholly different in spirit. "The Witch" is by no means one of Middleton's best plays. The plot is both intricate and feeble; and the witches, in spite of Charles Lamb's exquisite comparison of them with Shakespeare's, are, as stage creations, essentially comic and spectacular. With their ribald revelry, their cauldrons, their hideous spells and wierd incantations, they are much more calculated to excite laughter than fear as exhibited on the stage, however much fitted to touch the chords of superstitious dread when transported by the imagination to their native wilds. The characters of the play do not treat them with sufficient respect to command the sympathy of the audience for them.—MINTO, WILLIAM, 1874-85, *Characteristics of English Poets, p.* 349.

Has received, owing to its Shakespearean interest, more attention than it deserves on its own merits. It is strangely ill-constructed and is not by any means one of Middleton's finest works, though uncritical writers have absurdly advanced it to the first place.—BULLEN, A. H., 1885, *ed., The Works of Thomas Middleton, Introduction, vol.* I, *p.* lii.

There is poetry enough in "The Witch" to furnish forth a whole generation of poeticules: but the construction or composition of the play, the arrangement and evolution of event, the distinction or development of character, would do less than little credit to a boy of twelve; who at any rate would hardly have thought of patching up so ridiculous a reconciliation between intending murderers and intended victims as here exceeds in absurdity the chaotic combination of accident and error which disposes of inconvenient or superfluous underlings.—SWINBURNE, ALGERNON CHARLES, 1886, *Thomas Middleton, The Nineteenth Century, vol.* 19, *p.* 147.

GENERAL

Quicke are your wits, sharp your conceits,
  Short and more sweete your layes:
Quicke, but no wit, sharpe no conceit,
  Short and less sweete my praise.

—WEEVER, JOHN, 1599, *Epigrammes in the Oldest Cut and Newest Fashion.*

He was Contemporary with those Famous Poets *Johnson, Fletcher, Massinger,* and *Rowley,* in whose Friendship he had a large Share; and tho' he came short of the two former in parts, yet like the *Ivy* by the Assistance of the *Oak,* (being joyn'd with them in several Plays) he clim'd up to some considerable height of Reputation.—LANGBAINE, GERARD, 1691, *An Account of the English Dramatick Poets, p.* 370.

Humour, wit, and character, though in a degree inferior to that which distinguishes the preceding poets, are to be found in the comedy of Middleton; and, occasionally a pleasing interchange of elegant imagery and tender sentiment. His tragedy is not devoid of pathos, though possessing little dignity or elevation; but there is, in many of his plays, and especially in the tragi-comedy of "The Witch," a strength and compass of imagination which entitle him to a very respectable rank among the cultivators of the *Romantic* drama.—DRAKE, NATHAN, 1817, *Shakspeare and His Times, vol.* II, *p.* 565.

Middleton belongs to this lower class of dramatic writers: his tragedy entitled "Women beware Women" is founded on the story of Bianca Cappello; it is full of action, but the characters are all too vicious to be interesting, and the language does not rise much above mediocrity. In comedy, Middleton deserves more praise. "A Trick to catch the Old One," and several others that bear his name, are amusing and spirited.—HALLAM, HENRY, 1837-39, *Introduction to the Literature of Europe, pt.* iii, *ch.* vi, *par.* 103.

Middleton partakes of the poetry and sweetness of Decker, but not to the same height: and he talks more at random. You hardly know what to make of the dialogue or stories of some of his plays. But he has more fancy: and there is one character of his (De Flores in the "Changeling") which, for effect at once tragical, probable, and poetical, surpasses anything I know of in the drama of domestic life. —HUNT, LEIGH, 1844, *Imagination and Fancy*, *p.* 198.

Chiefly remarkable for a few striking ideas imperfectly wrought out.—SPALDING, WILLIAM, 1852-82, *A History of English Literature*, *p.* 265.

With less fluency of diction, less skill in fastening the reader's interest to his fable, harsher in versification, and generally clumsier in construction, the best plays of Thomas Middleton are still superior to Heywood's in force of imagination, depth of passion, and fulness of matter. It must, however, be admitted that the sentiments which direct his powers are not so fine as Heywood's. He depresses the mind, rather than invigorates it. The eye he cast on human life was not the eye of a sympathizing poet, but rather that of a sagacious cynic. His observation, though sharp, close, and vigilant, is somewhat ironic and unfeeling. His penetrating, incisive intellect cuts its way to the heart of a character as with a knife; and if he lays bare its throbs of guilt and weakness, and lets you into the secrets of its organization, he conceives his whole work is performed.—WHIPPLE, EDWIN P., 1859-68, *The Literature of the Age of Elizabeth*, *p.* 123.

Middleton has not Dekker's lightness of touch and etherial purity of tenderness, but there are qualities in which he comes nearer than any contemporary dramatist to the master mind of the time. There is a certain imperial confidence in his use of words and imagery, a daring originality and impatient force of expression, an easy freedom of humour, wide of range yet thoroughly well in hand, such as we find in the same degree even in the age of giants in no Elizabethan saving only Shakespeare. . . . Regarded as wholes, Middleton's tragedies fall very far short of the dignity of Shakespeare's. His heroes and heroines are not made of the same noble stuff, and their calamities have not the same grandeur. The characters are all so vile that the pity and terror pronounced by their death is almost wholly physical. But in the expression of incidental moments of passion, Middleton often rises to a sublime pitch of energy. —MINTO, WILLIAM, 1874-85, *Characteristics of English Poets*, *p.* 347.

The modesty with which Middleton himself appears to have abstained from any endeavour to assert his claims to fame or eminence of any kind pleads in his favour, and it may be asserted without fear of objection that he possessed not a few among the many qualities which constitute a dramatist of the order next to the highest. . . . More than ordinarily successful in romantic comedy, at times even here very felicitous in his choice of subjects, he seems to exhibit his full powers when in contact with his native soil. His imagination seems to have been strong enough to penetrate into regions of abnormal passion and of impulses such as seem to swallow up the whole being of man; but, upon the whole, his comedies dealing with the national life of his own age seem most congenial to his gifts, while constituting as a whole the truest dramatic representation of the sphere within which they move. . . . For his whole genius was free from any tendency to exaggeration, while of his moral aim there is no reason whatever to doubt. It may be questioned whether he was cast in a sufficiently strong mould to impress his age with the purpose which animated his satire; but there is no hollowness about his principles as to the conduct of life, and no unreality about his method of enforcing them. In brilliancy and, regarding his works as a whole, in depth of either pathos or humour he falls below many of his fellow-dramatists; but in lightness, vivacity, and sureness of touch it would be difficult—with one exception always—to name his superior.—WARD, ADOLPHUS WILLIAM, 1875-99, *A History of English Dramatic Literature*, *vol.* II, *pp.* 538, 539, 540.

A wild moon riding high from cloud to cloud,
  That sees and sees not, glimmering far beneath,
  Hell's children revel along the shuddering heath
With dirge-like mirth and raiment like a shroud;
A worse fair face than witchcraft's, passion-proud,

With brows blood-flecked behind their bridal wreath,
And lips that bade the assassin's sword find sheath
Deep in the heart whereto love's heart was vowed;
A game of close contentious crafts and creeds
Played till white England bring black Spain to shame;
A son's bright sword and brighter soul, whose deeds
High conscience lights for mother's love and fame;
Pure gypsy flowers, and poisonous courtly weeds:
Such tokens and such trophies crown thy name.

—SWINBURNE, ALGERNON CHARLES, 1882, *Thomas Middleton.*

There are critics who station poets in order of merit as a schoolmaster ranges his pupils in the classroom. This process I do not intend to adopt with Middleton. The test of a poet's real power ultimately resolves itself into the question whether he leaves a permanent impression on the mind of a capable reader. . . . Middleton may be charged with extravagance and coarseness. True: but he could make the blood tingle; he could barb his words so that they pierce the heart through and through. If "The Changeling," "Women beware Women," "The Spanish Gipsy," and "A Fair Quarrel" do not justify Middleton's claims to be considered a great dramatist, I know not which of Shakespeare's followers is worthy of the title. —BULLEN, A. H., 1885, *ed., The Works of Thomas Middleton, Introduction, vol.* I, *pp.* xcii, xciii.

Middleton has a faculty almost peculiar to himself of carrying, it might almost be said of hustling, the reader or spectator along, so that he has no time to stop and consider defects. His characters are extremely human and lively, his dialogue seldom lags, his catastrophes, if not his plots, are often ingenious, and he is never heavy. The moral atmosphere of his plays is not very refined,—by which I do not at all mean merely that he indulges in loose situations and loose language. All the dramatists from Shakespere downwards do that; and Middleton is neither better nor worse than the average. But in striking contrast to Shakespere and to others, Middleton has no kind of poetical morality in the sense in which the term poetical justice is better known. He is not too careful that the rogues shall not have the best of it; he makes his most virtuous and his vilest characters hobnob together very contentedly; and he is, in short, though never brutal, like the post-Restoration school, never very delicate. The style, however, of these works of his did not easily admit of such delicacy, except in the infusion of a strong romantic element such as that which Shakespere almost always infuses. Middleton has hardly done it more than once—in the charming comedy of "The Spanish Gipsy," —and the result there is so agreeable that the reader only wishes he had done it oftener.—SAINTSBURY, GEORGE, 1887, *History of Elizabethan Literature, p.* 268.

There is, unfortunately, too much of Middleton in existence; a single volume might be selected which would give readers an exceedingly high impression of his genius. He had no lyrical gift, and his verse, although it is enlivened by a singularly bright and unexpected diction, is not in itself of any great beauty.—GOSSE, EDMUND, 1894, *The Jacobean Poets, p.* 126.

Unlike his successor, Jonson, Middleton evidently gave high satisfaction in his function of "city chronologer," and his pageants were admired by his city patrons. He seems also to have been popular with the play going public both before and after the civil war. None of his pieces is known to have failed on the stage. But before the revolution he had fallen, in common with all but one or two of his dramatic contemporaries, into a neglect from which he has been seen among the last to recover. This is partly due to his striking inequality. A facile and inventive writer, he could turn out an abundance of sufficiently effective work with little effort; but he had little sustained inspiration; he is very great only in single scenes. . . . His habitual occupation with depraved types becomes an artistic method; he creates characters which fascinate without making the smallest appeal to sympathy, tragedy which harrows without rousing either pity or terror, and language which disdains charm, but penetrates by remorseless veracity and by touches of strange and sudden power.—HERFORD, CHARLES H., 1894, *Dictionary of National Biography, vol.* XXXVII, *p.* 359.

Few of the lyrics of Middleton are altogether satisfactory; in all his work, like

Massinger and some others, Middleton seems to inhabit that dangerous limbo that lies between the realms of the highest genius and the ordinary levels of a work-a-day world; making, it is true, an occasional flight into the former, but more usually contentedly trudging along the highways of the latter.—SCHELLING, FELIX E., 1895, *A Book of Elizabethan Lyrics, p.* 264, *note.*

Cyril Tourneur

1575?-1626?

Cyril Tourneur, a dramatist of whom we know only that he served in the Low Countries, and died in Ireland, Feb. 28, 1626, leaving his widow destitute. In 1600 he published his "Transformed Metamorphosis" (discovered in 1872), a satirical poem, marred by pedantic affectations; in 1609 a "Funereal Poem" on Sir Francis Vere; in 1613 an "Elegy" on Prince Henry. His fame rests on two plays, the "Revenger's Tragedy," printed in 1607, and the (earlier and poorer) "Atheist's Tragedy," printed in 1611. The "Revenger's Tragedy," a tangled web of lust and blood, shows tragic intensity, condensed passion, fiery strength of phrase, cynical and bitter mockery. Fleay thinks it the work of Webster. There is a complete edition by Churton Collins (1878); and of the two plays, with two of Webster's, by J. A. Symonds (1888).—PATRICK AND GROOME, *eds.*, 1897, *Chambers's Biographical Dictionary, p.* 922.

The reality and life of the dialogue, ["Revenger's Tragedy"] in which Vindici and Hippolito first tempt their mother, and then threaten her with death for consenting to the dishonour of their sister, passes any scenical illusion I ever felt. I never read it but my ears tingle, and I feel a hot blush overspread my cheeks, as if I were presently about to proclaim such malefactions of myself as the brothers here rebuke in their unnatural parent, in words more keen and dagger-like than those which Hamlet speaks to his mother. Such power has the passion of shame truly personated, not only to strike guilty creatures unto the soul, but to "appal" even those that are "free."—LAMB, CHARLES, 1808, *Specimens of Dramatic Poets.*

Tourneur was far from having the breadth and the weight of Webster's genius: he does not take so deep a hold of the being of his personages. Yet he is entitled to a high and unique place among the Elizabethan dramatists. There is a piercing intelligence in his grasp of character, a daring vigour and fire in his expression. His two plays show no elaborate study of variety of character; but he burns the chief moods of his principal characters deep into the mind.—MINTO, WILLIAM, 1874-85, *Characteristics of English Poets, p.* 357.

"The Revenger's Tragedy," printed in 1607, had been uniformly assigned to Tourneur, until Mr. Fleay threw doubts on the correctness of the assumption. I cannot, however, consider this scepticism warranted. Undoubtedly, the distance is considerable between the style of this play and that of its predecessor; and although the reflexion of Shakspere is still constantly cast upon the troubled waters, the writer has acquired a power of condensed expression of his own which he owes to no example or model. The versification, again, differs essentially from that of "The Atheist's Tragedy;" the structure of the verse is strong, and its peculiar effect seems to me to gain from the frequent use of rime. One can only conclude that the order of sequence between the two plays according to the dates of publication known to us must be reversed, and that "The Revenger's Tragedy," in its original form, was composed several years before its successor. . . . It has been thought possible to find in such a play "the noblest ardour of moral emotion," and "the most fervent passion of eager and indignant sympathy with all that is best and abhorrence of all that is worst in women or in men." Beyond dispute, however, it contains evidence of high tragic power, and of a gift of diction matching itself with extraordinary fitness to demands such as few if any of our dramatists have ever made upon their powers. Passages in this tragedy are illuminated by an imagery of singular distinctness as well as intensity. And if, as we are not prepared to doubt, "The Revenger's Tragedy" was Tourneur's work, it is with a sense of amazement that we turn from this solitary monument of his genius as a tragic poet of unmistakable distinction. —WARD, ADOLPHUS WILLIAM, 1875–99, *A History of English Dramatic Literature, vol.* III, *pp.* 69, 70.

A great poet, who has stamped deep on every page he has written the expression of a powerful, anomalous, unique genius. . . . High among Tourneur's distinctive merits must also be ranked his singular mastery over the element of language. In graphic intensity of magical expression, he is second only to Shakespeare and Webster. He wields at will subtle, poignant phrase, curt, irritable turn, searching epithet, pregnant epigram, or, again lucid, copious and expansive speech, rising and falling in easy and exquisite harmony with the thought it expresses. In words which burn like fire and brand like vitriol, Vindici clothes his scoffs and mockery; in words which melt like music, Castabella mourns her young lover or pleads with her unnatural step-father. His versification also is, like Shakespeare's on which it is carefully formed, much wider in its range and varied in its mould than is usual with his contemporaries, whose styles are, so far at least as essential attributes are concerned, comparatively uniform and manneristic. . . . Tourneur's great defect as a dramatic poet is undoubtedly the narrowness of his range of vision—of his insight and sympathies—and this is evident in the sketchy and abstract nature of many of his subordinate characters.—COLLINS, JOHN CHURTON, 1878, *ed., Plays and Poems of Cyril Tourneur, Introduction, vol.* I, *pp.* xiii, xlvii, lii.

Addressed himself to the most ferocious school of sub-Marlovian tragedy, and to the rugged and almost unintelligible satire of Marston. . . . The concentration of gloomy and almost insane vigour in "The Revenger's Tragedy," the splendid poetry of a few passages which have long ago found a home in the extract books, and the less separable but equally distinct poetic value of scattered lines and phrases, cannot escape any competent reader. But, at the same time, I find it almost impossible to say anything for either play as a whole, and here only I come a long way behind Mr. Swinburne in his admiration of our dramatists. The "Atheist's Tragedy" is an inextricable imbroglio of tragic and comic scenes and characters, in which it is hardly possible to see or follow any clue; while the low extravagance of all the comedy and the frantic rant of not a little of the tragedy combine to stifle the real pathos of some of the characters. "The Revenger's Tragedy" is on a distinctly higher level; the determination of Vindice to revenge his wrongs, and the noble and hapless figure of Castiza, could not have been presented as they are presented except by a man with a distinct strain of genius, both in conception and execution. But the effect, as a whole, is marred by a profusion of almost all the worst faults of the drama of the whole period from Peele to Davenant. The incoherence and improbability of the action, the reckless, inartistic, butcherly prodigality of blood and horrors, and the absence of any kind of redeeming interest of contrasting light to all the shade, though very characteristic of a class, and that no small one, of Elizabethan drama, cannot be said to be otherwise than characteristic of its faults. —SAINTSBURY, GEORGE, 1887, *History of Elizabethan Literature, p.* 285.

Enough has already been cited to prove beyond all chance of cavil from any student worthy of the name that the place of Cyril Tourneur is not among minor poets, nor his genius of such a temper as naturally to attract the sympathy or arouse the enthusiasm of their admirers; that among the comrades or the disciples who to us may appear but as retainers or satellites of Shakespeare his rank is high and his credentials to that rank are clear. . . . If the noblest ardour of moral emotion, the most fervent passion of eager and indignant sympathy with all that is best and abhorrence of all that is worst in women or in men—if the most absolute and imperial command of all resources and conquest of all difficulties inherent in the most effective and the most various instrument ever yet devised for the poetry of the tragic drama—if the keenest insight and the sublimest impulse that can guide the perception and animate the expression of a poet whose line of work is naturally confined to the limits of moral or ethical tragedy—if all these qualities may be admitted to confer a right to remembrance and a claim to regard, there can be no fear and no danger of forgetfulness for the name of Cyril Tourneur.—SWINBURNE, ALGERNON CHARLES, 1887, *Cyril Tourneur, The Nineteenth Century, vol.* 21, *pp.* 426, 427.

Tourneur was a fierce and bitter spirit. The words in which he unpacked his heart are vitalised with passion. He felt so keenly that oftentimes his phrase is the offspring of the emotion, so terse and vigorous and apt, so vivid and so potent and eager, it appears. . . . Tourneur is not a great tragic. "The Atheist's Tragedy" is but grotesquely and extravagantly horrible; its personages are caricatures of passion; its comedy is inexpressibly sordid; its incidents are absurd when they are not simply abominable. But it is written in excellent dramatic verse and in a rich and brilliant diction, and it contains a number of pregnant epithets and ringing lines and violent phrases. And if you halve the blame and double the praise you will do something less than justice to that "Revenger's Tragedy" which is Tourneur's immortality. After all its companion is but a bastard of the loud, malignant, antic muse of Marston; the elegies are cold, elaborate, and very tedious; the "Transformed Metamorphosis" is better verse but harder reading than "Sordello" itself. But the "Revenger's Tragedy" has merit as a piece of art and therewith a rare interest as a window on the artist's mind. The effect is as of a volcanic landscape. An earthquake has passed, and among grisly shapes and blasted aspects here lurks and wanders the genius of ruin. —HENLEY, WILLIAM ERNEST, 1890, *Views and Reviews, pp.* 106, 107.

His two lurid tragedies surpass in horror of iniquity and profusion of ghastly innuendo all other compositions of their time. Cyril Tourneur is prince of those whose design is "to make our flesh creep," and occasionally he still succeeds.—GOSSE, EDMUND, 1897, *A Short History of Modern English Literature, p.* 119.

Cyril Tourneur is only really memorable on account of two plays. . . . Tourneur's reputation mainly rests on his "Revenger's Tragædie." The "Atheists Tragedie," of which the crude plot owes something to the "Decameron" (VII. 6), is childishly grotesque, and, in spite of some descriptive passages of a certain grandeur, notably the picture of the hungry sea lapping at the body of a drowned soldier, is so markedly inferior to "The Revenger's Tragædie" as to have given rise to some fanciful doubts as to a common authorship. "The Revenger's Tragædie" displays a lurid tragic power that Hazlitt was the first to compare with that of Webster. . . . Mr. Swinburne's estimate of Tourneur's genius is unduly enthusiastic. Great as is his tragic intensity, Tourneur luxuriates in hideous forms of vice to an extent which almost suggests moral aberration, and sets his work in a category of dramatic art far below the highest. Whether his choice of topics was due to a morbid mental development, or merely to a spirit of literary emulation in the genre of Ford and Webster, a more extended knowledge of Tourneur's life might possibly enable us to ascertain.—SECCOMBE, THOMAS, 1899, *Dictionary of National Biography, vol.* LVII, *pp.* 87, 88, 89.

Sir Fulke Greville

Lord Brooke

1554—1628

Born, at Beauchamp Court, Warwickshire, 1554. To Shrewsbury School, 17 Oct. 1564. Friendship with Philip Sidney begun. Matric. at Jesus Coll., Cambridge, 20 May 1568. Held post in Court of Marches, 1576-77. In favour at Elizabeth's court. To Heidelberg with Sidney, Feb. 1577. Accompanied diplomatic mission to Flanders, 1578. To Germany again, 1579. Secretary for Principality of Wales, 20 April 1583; held office till death. Served in Normandy under Henry of Navarre, 1591. M. P. for Warwickshire, 1592-93, 1597, 1601, 1620. Estate of Wedgnock Park granted him by Queen, 1597. Knight of the Bath, Oct. 1597. Treasurer of the Wars, March 1598; Treasurer of the Navy, Sept. 1598. Castle of Warwick granted him, 1605. Chancellor of the Exchequer, Oct. 1614 to Jan. 1621. Created Baron Brooke, 29 Jan. 1621. Took seat in House of Lords, 15 Nov. 1621. On Council of War, 1624; on Council of Foreign Affairs, 1625. Died, from wound inflicted by a servant, 30

Sept. 1628. Buried in St. Mary's Church, Warwick. *Works:* Contributions to "The Phœnix Nest," 1593; to Bodenham's "Belvedere," 1600; to "Englands Helicon," 1600; "The Tragedy of Mustapha" (anon.), 1609. *Posthumous* "Certaine Learned and Elegant Workes of the Rt. Hon. Fulke, Lord Brooke," 1633; "The Life of the Renowned Sir Philip Sidney," 1625; "The Remains of Sir Fulk Grevill," 1670. *Collected Works:*—ed. by Grosart, with *memoir*—(4 vols.), 1870.—SHARP, R. FARQUHARSON, 1897, *A Dictionary of English Authors, p.* 119.

The English poems of sir Walter Raleigh, of John Donne, of Hugh Holland, but especially of sir Foulk Grevile in his matchless "Mustapha," are not easily to be mended."—BOLTON, EDMUND, 1624, *Hypercritica.*

He had the longest lease, and the smoothest time without rub, of any of her* Favorites. . . . He was a brave Gentleman, and honourably descended. . . . Neither illiterate; for . . . there are of his now extant, some fragments of his Poem, and of those times, which doe interest him in the Muses; and which shews, the Queen's election had ever a noble conduct, and its motions more of virtue and judgment, than of fancy.—NAUNTON, SIR ROBERT, 1630? *Fragmenta Regalia, ed. Arber, p.* 50.

January 1st. Dined with my Lord Crew, with whom was Mr. Browne, Clerk of the House of Lords, and Mr. John Crew. Here was mighty good discourse, as there is always: and among other things my Lord Crew did turn to a place in the "Life of Sir Philip Sidney," wrote by Sir Fulke Greville, which do fortell the present condition of this nation, in relation to the Dutch, to the very degree of a prophecy; and is so remarkable that I am resolved to buy one of them, it being, quite throughout, a good discourse. . . . Jan. 2d. To Westminister Hall, and there staid a little: and then home, and by the way did find with difficulty the "Life of Sir Philip Sydney." . . . And the bookseller told me that he had sold four within this week or two, which is more than ever he sold in all his life of them; and he could not imagine what should be the reason of it: but I suppose it is from the same reason of people's observing of this part therein, touching his prophesying our present condition here in England in relation to the Dutch, which is very remarkable.—PEPYS, SAMUEL, 1667-8, *Diary.*

Was a good witt, and had been a good poet in his youth. He wrote a poeme in folio which he printed not till he was old, and then, (as Sir W.† said) with too much judgment and refining, spoyld it, which was at first a delicate thing.—AUBREY, JOHN, 1669-96, *Brief Lives, ed. Clark, vol.* I, *p.* 205.

Sir Fulke Grevill, Lord Brooke, a man of great note in his age, hath a poem lately printed (1670) for subject's liberty, which I greatly wonder this age could bear.—BAXTER, RICHARD, 1681, *Poetical Fragments, Prefatory Address.*

Alabam, a Tragedy printed in Folio 1633. This Play Seems an Imitation of the Ancients. The Prologue is spoken by a Ghost, one of the Old Kings of *Ormus*, (an Island Scituate at the Entrance of the *Persian* Gulf) where the Scene of the Dramma lies. This Spectre gives an Account of each Character; which is possibly done in Imitation of *Euripides*, who usually introduced one of the chief Actors, as the Prologue: whose business was to explain all those Circumstances which preceded the opening of the Stage. The Author has been so careful in observing the Rules of *Aristotle* and *Horace*, that whereas *Horace* says

. . . *nec quarta loqui persona laboret.*

He has in no Scene throughout introduc'd above two Speakers; except in the Chorus between each Act: and even there he observes all the Rules laid down by that great Master, in the Art of Poetry.—LANGBAINE, GERARD, 1691, *An Account of the English Dramatick Poets, p.* 38.

I don't know whether a Woman may be acquitted for endeavouring to sum up a Character so various, and important as his Lordship's.—But, if the Attempt can be excus'd, I don't desire to have it pass for a decisive Sentence.—Perhaps few Men that dealt in Poetry had more Learning, or real Wisdom than this Nobleman, and yet his Stile is sometimes so dark, and mysterious, I mean it appears so to me, that one would imagine he chose rather to conceal, than illustrate his Meaning.—At other Times again His Wit breaks out with an uncommon Brightness,

*Elizabeth.

†Davenant.

and Shines, I had almost said, without an Equal.—'Tis the same Thing with his Poetry, sometimes so harsh, and uncouth, as if he had no Ear for Musick, at others so smooth and harmonious, as if He was Master of all its Powers.—COOPER, ELIZABETH, 1737, *The Muses' Library, p.* 216.

A man of much note in his time, but one of those admired wits who have lost much of their reputation in the eyes of posterity. A thousand accidents of birth, court-favour, or popularity, concur sometimes to gild a slender proportion of merit. —WALPOLE, HORACE, 1758, *A Catalogue of the Royal and Noble Authors.*

The two tragedies of Lord Brooke, printed among his poems, might with more propriety have been termed political treatises than plays. Their author has strangely contrived to make passion, character, and interest, of the highest order, subservient to the expression of stage dogmas and mysteries. He is nine parts Machiavel and Tacitus, for one part Sophocles or Seneca. In this writer's estimate of the powers of the mind, the understanding must have held a most tyrannical pre-eminence. Whether we look into his plays, or his most passionate love-poems, we shall find all frozen and made rigid with intellect. The finest movements of the human heart, the utmost grandeur of which the soul is capable, are essentially comprised in the actions and speeches of Cælica and Camena. Shakespeare, who seems to have had a peculiar delight in contemplating womanly perfection, whom for his many sweet images of female excellence all women are in an especial manner bound to love, has not raised the ideal of the female character higher than Lord Brooke, in these two women, has done. But it requires a study equivalent to the learning of a new language to understand their meaning when they speak.—LAMB, CHARLES, 1808, *Specimens of Dramatic Poets.*

As to Fulke Greville, he is like nothing but one of his own "Prologues spoken by the ghost of an old king of Ormus," a truly formidable and inviting personage: his style is apocalyptical, cabalistical, a knot worthy of such an apparition to untie; and for the unravelling a passage or two, I would stand the brunt of an encounter with so portentious commentator. —HAZLITT, WILLIAM, 1821–22, *Table Talk.*

Another philosophical poet, Sir Fulke Greville. . . . The titles of Lord Brooke's poems, "A Treatise of Human Learning," "A Treatise of Monarchy," "A Treatise of Religion," "An Inquisition upon Fame and Honor," lead us to anticipate more of sense than fancy. In this we are not deceived: his mind was pregnant with deep reflection upon multifarious learning; but he struggles to give utterance to thoughts which he had not fully endowed with words, and amidst the shackles of rhyme and metre, which he had not learned to manage. Hence of all our poets he may be reckoned the most obscure; in aiming at condensation, he becomes elliptical beyond the bounds of the language; and his rhymes, being forced for the sake of sound, leave all meaning behind. Lord Brooke's poetry is chiefly worth notice as an indication of that thinking spirit upon political science which was to produce the riper speculations of Hobbes and Harrington and Locke.—HALLAM, HENRY, 1837–39, *Introduction to the Literature of Europe, pt.* iii, *ch.* v, *par.* 35.

Had deep thoughts enough to accomplish ten poets of these degenerate days, though because of some obscurity in their expression you would find some twenty critics "full of oaths" by the pyramids, that they all meant nothing.—BROWNING, ELIZABETH BARRETT, 1842–63, *The Book of the Poets, p.* 142.

"A Treatise on Religion," in which, if the reader do not find much of poetic form, he will find at least some grand spiritual philosophy, the stuff whereof all highest poetry is fashioned. It is one of the first poems in which the philosophy of religion, and not either its doctrine, feeling, or history, predominates. It is, as a whole, poor, chiefly from its being so loosely written. There are men, and men whose thoughts are of great worth, to whom it never seems to occur that they may utter very largely and convey very little; that what is clear to themselves is in their speech obscure as a late twilight. Their utterance is rarely articulate: their spiritual mouth talks with but half-movements of its lips; it does not model their thoughts into clear-cut shapes, such as the spiritual ear can distinguish as they enter it. Of such is Lord Brooke.—MACDONALD, GEORGE, 1868, *England's Antiphon, p.* 89.

Even as the tragedies stand, they fail to do justice to the original design of the writer, who informs us that he had at first intended the "treatises," now printed separately and extending to much the same length as the tragedies themselves, to serve as choruses to the several acts of the latter, in addition no doubt to the choruses proper, for the most part tolerably lengthy in themselves, already appended to them. On the difficult style and the profundity of meaning which characterise the treatises there is no need for descanting here; but even in the tragedies as they stand, in the dialogue as well as in the purely didactic—they cannot be called lyric—excursuses, the language is extremely obscure. This is the result, not of ambiguity or vagueness of diction, but of a closeness as well as abstruseness of thought to which to all intents and purposes no reader will prove equal unless he approaches these so-called dramas as a student addresses himself to a set of long series of problems. It is this peculiarity of style—a peculiarity extending to almost everything that he has left behind him in verse—which must continue to leave Lord Brooke's tragedies unread except by a resolute few. Seneca and Euripides, whom he generally though not slavishly follows as his dramatic models, are not responsible for what is the reverse of a rhetorical, and only as it were incidentally a sententious, style. It should be added that there are to be found in these strange compositions not only characters as strongly conceived as they are subtly worked out, but situations full of awe and pathos; but everything, to recur to Lamb's inimitable phraseology, is "frozen and made rigid with intellect."—WARD, ADOLPHUS WILLIAM, 1875-99, *A History of English Dramatic Literature, vol.* II, *p.* 614.

Even "Cœlica" is very unlikely to find readers as a whole, owing to the strangely repellent character of Brooke's thought, which is intricate and obscure, and of his style, which is at any rate sometimes as harsh and eccentric as the theories of poetry which made him compose verse-treatises on politics. Nevertheless there is much nobility of thought and expression in him, and not unfrequent flashes of real poetry, while his very faults are characteristic. . . . He has but the ore of poetry, not the smelted metal. —SAINTSBURY, GEORGE, 1887, *History of Elizabethan Literature, pp.* 99, 100.

Brooke writes in his discursive memoir of Sidney with reference to his tragedies: "For my own part I found my creeping genius more fixed upon the images of life than the images of wit." This is a just criticism of all Brooke's literary work. To "elegancy of style" or "smoothness of verse" he rarely aspires. He is essentially a philosopher, cultivating "a close, mysterious, and sentenious way of writing," which is commonly more suitable to prose than poetry. His subjects are for the most part incapable of imaginative treatment. In his collection of love poems, which, though written in varied metres, he entitles sonnets, he seeks to express passionate love, and often with good lyrical effects; but the understanding seems as a rule to tyrannise over emotion, and all is "frozen and made rigid with intellect." Sidney's influence is very perceptible, and some of Brooke's stanzas harshly echo passages from "Astrophel" and "Stella."—LEE, SIDNEY, 1890, *Dictionary of National Biography, vol.* XXIII, *p.* 162.

Lord Brooke's verse is unsympathetic and unattractive, yet far too original and well-sustained to be overlooked. He is like one of those lakes, which exist here and there on the world's surface, which are connected with no other system of waters, and by no river contribute to the sea. Lord Brooke's abstruse and acrid poetry proceeded from nowhere and influenced no one. It is a solitary phenomenon in our literature, and the author a kind of marsupial in our poetical zoology. —GOSSE, EDMUND, 1894, *The Jacobean Poets, p.* 194.

The lyrics of that most interesting and "difficult" of poets, Fulke Greville . . . are the more remarkable in their frequent grace of fancy, uncommon wit, originality, and real music of expression in that they are the sister products of the obscure and intricate musings and the often eccentric didacticism of "Mustapha" and "Alaham." . . . It is not Donne, but Greville, that is the Elizabethan Browning. For substantiation of this I would recommend a comparative reading of "Alaham" and "Sordello."—SCHELLING, FELIX E., 1895, *A Book of Elizabethan Lyrics, pp.* xxiii, 222.

Samuel Purchas

1575?-1628

Born at Thaxted, studied at St. John's College, Cambridge, and became vicar of Eastwood in 1604, and in 1614 rector of St. Martin's, Ludgate. His great works were "Purchas his Pilgrimage, or Relations of the World in all Ages" (1613; 4th ed. enlarged, 1626), and "Hakluytus Posthumus, or Purchas his Pilgrimes" (based on the papers of Hakluyt, 1625). Another work is "Purchas his Pilgrim; Microcosmus, or the History of Man" (1619).— PATRICK AND GROOME, *ed.* 1897, *Chambers's Biographical Dictionary, p.* 767.

This my *first Voyage* of Discoverie, besides mine owne pore stocke laide thereon, hath made mee indebted to *above twelve hundred Authours*, of one or other kinde, in I know not how many hundredths of their Treatises, Epistles, Relations, and Histories, of divers Subjectes and Languages, borrowed by my selfe; besides what (for want of the Authors themselves) I have taken upon trust of other men's goods in their hands.—PURCHAS, SAMUEL, 1626, *Dedication to Archbishop Abbot, 4th ed.*

This worthy divine, who is by some stiled our English-Ptolemy . . . being desirous to forward his natural geny he had to the collecting and writing of voyages, travels, and pilgrimages, left his cure to his brother.—WOOD, ANTHONY, 1691–1721, *Fasti Oxonienses.*

Is not only valuable for the various instruction and amusement contained in it, but is also very estimable on a national and, I may add, a religious account.—GRANGER, JAMES, 1769-1824, *Biographical History of England, vol.* II, *p.* 68.

These vast and valuable collections are an honour to the reigns of Elizabeth and James, and, notwithstanding the industry and research of the moderns, have not yet been superseded.—DRAKE, NATHAN, 1817, *Shakspeare and his Times, vol.* I, *p.* 477.

The "Pilgrimes and Pilgrimage" of Purchas . . . exhibit a monument of care, diligence, and research, that, of its kind, can hardly be surpassed.—DIBBIN, THOMAS FROGNALL, 1824, *The Library Companion, p.* 381.

Imbued by nature, like Hakluyt, with a strong bias towards geographical studies, after having formed an extensive library in that department, and consulted, as he professes, above 1,200 authors, published the first volume of his "Pilgrim," a collection of voyages in all parts of the world, 1613: four more followed in 1625. The accuracy of this useful compiler has been denied by those who have had better means of knowledge, and probably is inferior to that of Hakluyt; but his labor was far more comprehensive. The "Pilgrim" was, at all events, a great source of knowledge to the contemporaries of Purchas.—HALLAM, HENRY, 1837–39, *Introduction to the Literature of Europe, pt.* iii, *ch.* ix, *par.* 31.

But the work by which alone Purchas's name is now known is "Hakluytus Posthumus, or Purchas his Pilgrimes, contayning a History of the World in Sea Voyages and Land-Trauells by Englishmen and others. . . . ," with portrait on the title-page, ætat. 48 (4 vols. 4to, 1625; the fourth edition of the "Pilgrimage" being exactly the same size, is frequently catalogued as the fifth volume of the "Pilgrimes;" it is really a totally different work). This work has never been reprinted, and its rarity, still more than its interest, has given it an exaggerated value to book collectors. The intrinsic value of the book is due rather to its having preserved some record of early voyages otherwise unknown, than to the literary skill or ability of the author. It may fairly be supposed that the originals of many of the journals entrusted to him, of which he published an imperfect abstract, were lost through his carelessness; so that the fact that the "Pilgrimes" contains the only extant account of some voyages is by his fault, not by his merit. A comparison of what he has printed with such originals as remain shows that he was very far indeed from a faithful editor or a judicious compiler, and that he took little pains to arrive at an accurate knowledge of facts. He inherited many of the manuscripts of Richard Hakluyt, but the use he made of them was widely different from Hakluyt's.—LAUGHTON, J. K., 1896, *Dictionary of National Biography, vol.* XLVII, *p.* 45.

John Speed

1552?-1629

Antiquary; born at Farrington, Cheshire, England, in 1542; was a tailor in London until late in life, but at the same time was amassing an extensive knowledge of English antiquities, and was enabled by Sir Fulke Greville to publish a costly and valuable series of works. He published anonymously about 1590 a treatise on the "Genealogies of the Scriptures," afterwards prefixed to the first edition of King James's Bible (1611), but his first appearance as an author was in 1608, when he printed fifty-four maps of various countries and cities, and engravings of antiquities of England and Wales, which were incorporated into "The Theatre of the Empire of Great Britain" (folio, 1611). In the same year he published his "History of Great Britain under the Conquests of the Romans, Saxons, Danes, and Normans." Died in London, July 28, 1629.—ADAMS, CHARLES KENDALL. *ed.* 1897, *Johnson's Universal Cyclopædia, vol.* VII, *p.* 661.

He was first bred to a handicraft, and as I take it to a Taylor. I write not this for his but my own disgrace, when I consider how far his industry hath outstript my ingenuous education. Sir Fulk Grevill, a great favourer of Learning, perceiving how his wide soul was stuffed with too narrow an occupation, first wrought his inlargement as the said Author doth ingenuously confess, "Whose merits to me-ward I do acknowledge, in setting this hand free from the daily imployments of a manuall Trade, and giving it his liberty thus to express the inclination of my mind, himself being the procurer of my present estate." This is he who afterwards designed the Maps and composed the History of England, though much helped in both (no shame to crave aid in a work too weighty for any one's back to bear) by Sir Robert Cotton, Master Camden, Master Barkham, and others. He also made the usefull Genealogies preposed formerly to English Bibles in all Volumes, having a Patent granted him from King James, in reward of his great labours, to receive the benefit thereof to him and his. This was very beneficiall unto them, by composition with the Company of Stationers, until this licentious age, neglecting all such ingenious helps to understand Scripture, and almost levelling (if not prevented) the propriety of all Authors of Books. He dyed in London, anno 1629; and was buried in Saint Giles without Criplegate, in the same Parish with Master John Fox; so that no one Church in England containeth the corps of two such usefull and voluminous Historians. Master Josias Shute preached his Funerall Sermon: and thus we take our leaves of Father Speed, truly answering in name, in both the acceptions thereof, for celerity and success.—FULLER, THOMAS, 1662, *The Worthies of England, ed. Nichols, vol.* I, *p.* 190.

John Speed must be acknowledged to have had a head the best disposed towards history of any of our writers; and would certainly have outdone himself, as far as he has gone beyond the rest of his profession, if the advantages of his education had been answerable to those of his natural genius. But what could be expected from a taylor? However, we may boldly say, that his chronicle is the largest and best we have hitherto extant. It begins with the first inhabitants of the island, and ends with the union of the kingdoms under king James, to whom it is dedicated. Though some say he spent twice seven years in compiling the whole, he himself owns he made more haste than he ought to have done; and that he was forced to trust a deal of his work in the hands of his friends and journeymen. And the truth of this honest acknowledgment and confession is obvious enough to a discerning reader; who will easily find a mighty difference in the style, as well as matter of several of the reigns.—NICOLSON, WILLIAM, 1696? *Burnett's Specimens of English Prose Writers, vol.* II.

Dec. 9. *Arch. A. Bodl.* 89. "A Chronology from the Floud to our Saviour," folio. 'Twas formerly Mr. Tho. Underhill's, A. M. who gave it here. It cost him, as appears at the beginning, 3 *libs.* 6*s.* 8*d.* In the register it is expressed, that the author was Hugh Broughton. Upon which having recourse to Mr. Broughton's works, before which there is put a preface, giving some account of his life, by Dr. Lightfoot; I find there, that

Dr. Lightfoot tells us, that the first book which made Mr. Broughton known to the world was his publishing his book called, "A Concent of Scripture," which came out 1588. Mr. John Speed, a man well known, was overseer of the press for its printing, a taylor by trade, but by acquaintance with Mr. Broughton, grown very studious in the scriptures, and by his directions grown very skillfull in them. While this was printing, Mr. Speed, by Mr. Broughton's direction, gathered all the genealogies of the Bible into one view, and at last they were published under his name, in the form we have them before our Bibles. But it was Mr. Broughton that directed and digested them, and there are yet fair manuscripts of them to be shewed (amongst which this in the Bodlejan library I take to be one, being a very fair neat book,) some whereof have the names in Hebrew and Greek, and some in the Latin letter, and in some of them Mr. Broughton's own hand. And one that attended him, Dorman, or Dalman, or of such a name, had made such a collection, by the direction of his master, before Mr. Speed had collected his *one view.* Yet notwithstanding this, when the "Genealogie" came to be published, because the bishops would not suffer Mr. Broughton's name to be prefixed, Mr. Speed went away with all the credit and profit.—HEARNE, THOMAS, 1705, *Reliquiæ Hearnianæ, ed. Bliss, vol.* I, *p.* 80.

His maps were very justly esteemed, and his "History of Great Britain" was, in its kind, incomparably more complete than all the histories of his predecessors put together.—GRANGER, JAMES, 1769–1824, *Biographical History of England, vol.* III, *p.* 147.

In every respect, a work of very great merit.—DRAKE, NATHAN, 1817, *Shakspeare and his Times, vol.* I, *p.* 476.

These various works of Stow and Speed rank among the head sources or fountains of our knowledge in the department of national antiquities.—CRAIK, GEORGE L., 1861, *A Compendious History of English Literature and of the English Language, vol.* I, *p.* 620.

He was the first to reject the fables of preceding chroniclers concerning the origin of the Britons, and to exercise a just discrimination in the selection of authorities. . . . This collection was superior to any other that had appeared.—CHAMBERS, ROBERT, 1876, *Cyclopædia of English Literature, ed. Carruthers.*

Gabriel Harvey

1545?-1630

An excellent English and Latin poet, equally well known as the friend of Spenser and as the enemy of Nash, was educated at Christ's College and at Pembroke Hall, Cambridge, and in 1585 became Doctor of Laws. The following are his principal English publications:—"Three proper and wittie Familiar Letters: lately passed betweene two Vniuersitie Men," Lon., 1580, 4to. . . . The University men were himself and Edmund Spenser. 2. "Fovre Letters and certaine Sonnets," 1592, 4to. . . . This contains many literary notices of his contemporaries, and is therefore of great value to the antiquary. 3. "Pierces Supererogation; or, a new Prayse of the Old Asse," 1593, 4to. 4. "A New Letter of Notable Contents," 1593.—ALLIBONE, S. AUSTIN, 1854–58, *Dictionary of English Authors, vol.* I, *p.* 796.

To the Worshipfull his Very Singular Good Friend, Maister G. H. . . . Good Master G. I perceiue by your most curteous and frendly Letters your good will to be no lesse in deed, than I alwayes esteemed. In recōpence whereof, think I beseech you, that I wil spare neither speech, nor wryting, nor aught else, whensoeuer, and wheresoeuer occasion shal be offred me: yea, I will not stay, till it be offred, but will seeke it, in al that possibly I may. And that you may perceiue how much your Counsel in al things preuaileth with me, and how altogither I am ruled and ouer-ruled thereby: I am now determined to alter mine owne former purpose, and to subscribe to your aduizemet: being nothwithstāding resolued stil, to abide your farther resolution.—SPENSER, EDMUND, 1579, *Letter to Gabriel Harvey, ed. Grosart, Harvey's Works, vol.* I, *p.* 5.

Now I trust, M. Harvey, that upon sight of your speciall frends and fellow

Poets doings, or els for envie of so many unworthy Quidams, which catch at the garlond which to you alone is dewe, you will be perswaded to pluck out of the hateful darknesse those so many excellent English poemes of yours which lye hid, and bring them forth to eternall light. Trust me, you doe both them great wrong, in depriving them of the desired sonne; and also your selfe, in smoothering your deserved prayses; and all men generally, in withholding from them so divine pleasures, which they might conceive of your gallant English verses, as they have already doen of your Latine Poemes, which, in my opinion, both for invention and Elocution are very delicate and superexcellent. And thus againe I take my leave of my good Mayster Harvey: from my lodging at London thys 10. of Aprill, 1579.—KIRKE, EDWARD? 1579, *Spenser's Shepheards Calender, Epistle to Gabriell Harvey.*

Therefore wyll I aduenture to sette them together, as two of the rarest witts, and learnedst masters of Poetrie in England. Whose worthy and notable skyl in this faculty, I would wysh if their high dignities and serious businesses would permit, they would styll graunt to bee a furtheraunce to that reformed kinde of Poetry, which Master *Haruey* did once beginne to ratify: and surely in mine opinion, if hee had chosen some grauer matter, and handled but with halfe that skyll, which I knowe he could haue doone, and not powred it foorth at a venture, as a thinge betweene iest and earnest, it had taken greater effect then it did.—WEBBE, WILLIAM, 1586, *A Discourse of English Poetrie, ed. Arber, p.* 36.

A proverb it is, as stale as sea-biefe, save a thief from the gallows and hee'le be the first to shew thee the way to Saint Gilesesse. Harvey I manifestly saved from the knot under the eare: Verily, he had hanged him selfe had I gone forwards in my vengeance; but, I know not how, upon his prostrate intreatie, I was content to give him a short Psalme of mercy. Now, for reprieving him when he was ripe for execution, thus he requites me. Sixe and thirty sheets of mustard-pot paper since that hath he published against me. . . . Some few crummes of my booke hath he confuted: all the rest of his invention is nothing but an oxe with a pudding in his bellie. . . . Maister Lillie, poore deceasses Kit Marlow, reverent Doctor Perne, with a hundred other quiet senselesse carcasses before the Conquest departed, in the same worke he hath most notoriously and vilely dealt with; and, to conclude, he hath proved him selfe to be the only Gabriel Grave-digger under heaven.—NASHE, THOMAS, 1594, *Christ's Teares over Jerusalem.*

This person, who made a great noise in his time, was born at Saffron-walden in Essex; and tho' his father was a rope-maker as Thomas Nash, a great scoffer, and his antagonist, tells us, yet he had rich kindred and was nearly allied to Sir Thomas Smith, the great statesman in Queen Elizabeth's reign.—WOOD, ANTHONY, 1691–1721, *Fasti Oxonienses, vol.* I, *p.* 128.

Of this writer, so well known in his time, the author of many respectable works, and of no inferior accomplishments in learning or talents, very imperfect accounts are to be found in any of our biographical compilations. He certainly deserves a place among the national records of his countrymen.—BELOE, WILLIAM, 1807, *Anecdotes of Literature and Scarce Books, vol.* II, *p.* 197.

An author of considerable rank. . . . Harvey was a pedant, but pedantry was part of the erudition of an age when our national literature was passing from its infancy; he introduced hexameter verses into our language, and pompously laid claim to an invention which, designed for the reformation of English verse, was practised till it was found sufficiently ridiculous. His style was infected with his pedantic taste; and the hard outline of his satirical humour betrays the scholastic cynic, not the airy and fluent wit. He had, perhaps, the foibles of a man who was clearing himself from obscurity; he prided himself on his family alliances, while he fastidiously looked askance on the trade of his father—a rope-manufacturer. He was somewhat rich in his apparel, according to the rank in society he held; and, hungering after the notice of his friends, they fed him on soft sonnet and relishing dedication, till Harvey ventured to publish a collection of panegyrics on himself—and thus gravely stepped into a niche erected to Vanity.—DISRAELI, ISAAC, 1812–13, *Literary Ridicule, Calamities of Authors.*

He was a profound scholar, and no inelegant composer of verses: some of his productions evince great learning and research; and though it is impossible to admire his hobbling English hexameters (of which he pompously proclaimed himself the inventor), we cannot read his lines prefixed to "The Faerie Queene" without acknowledging their beauty.—DYCE, ALEXANDER, 1831–61, *ed. Dramatic and Poetical Works of Robert Greene, p.* 63.

A dry hard student, full of caustic wit, but not lacking, when the humor took him, grace and tenderness. He hurled fierce, stinging words in profusion at any one with whom he chanced to be offended, but to all who pleased him he was a warm and helpful friend. His genius was wasted in his efforts to naturalize the hexameter and other classical metres in English, and of this idle attempt he claimed to be the originator.—BOURNE, H. R. FOX, 1862, *A Memoir of Sir Philip Sidney, p.* 44.

He did not become a great man, or what he called "a megalander;" we may, if we will, class him with what is fossil or extinct in literature—its megatherium or dodo. But in his day he worked hard, aspired nobly, and left witness to his labour and his aspiration. Perhaps we do not care, for his own sake, to read the evidence, but set him aside as one of the small matters, if any there be, in which it is not worth while to be just. Then let him have the advantage of being not merely Gabriel Harvey, although to him that was something, but also Spenser's Hobbinol, which is to us more. He was, during some important years of Spenser's life, the poet's "long-approved and singular good friend" and counsellor. The counsel was outgrown, but not the friendship. To our credence as well as Harvey's, Spenser has left what he once called "the eternal memory of our everlasting friendship, the inviolable memory of our unspotted friendship, the sacred memory of our vowed friendship;" and it is a little due perhaps to Spenser that we should ascertain how much credit is due to the commentators who would have us think that he wrote in this way to a conceited pedant seven years older than himself.—MORLEY, HENRY, 1869, *Spenser's "Hobbinol," Fortnightly Review,* N. S. *vol.* 5, *p.* 274.

Harvey is a remarkable instance of the refining influence of classical studies. Amid the pedantic farrago of his omnisufficiency (to borrow one of his own words) we come suddenly upon passages whose gravity of sentiment, stateliness of movement, and purity of diction remind us of Landor. These lucid intervals in his overweening vanity explain and justify the friendship of Spenser. Yet the reiteration of emphasis with which he insists on all the world's knowing that Nash had called him an ass, probably gave Shakespeare the hint for one of the most comic touches in the character of Dogberry.—LOWELL, JAMES RUSSELL, 1875–90, *Spenser, Prose Works, Riverside ed., vol.* IV, *p.* 285, *note.*

Except to students of Elizabethan literary history, he has become an utterly obscure personage; and he has not usually been spoken of with much respect.—CHURCH, RICHARD WILLIAM, 1879, *Spenser, (English Men of Letters), p.* 18.

Of no contemporary of equal notoriety in men's mouths over so many years, do we know so little as of him. The Damascus blade of Thomas Nashe wounded him mortally. He was speedily forgotten—though he lived on to an unusual age; and no one seems to have cared to rescue his memory from its swift and inexorable oblivion. Even his academic course is obscure and dateless. We have had to wait for these long centuries to learn the chief facts of it contained in his (so-called) "Letter-Book."—GROSART, ALEXANDER B., 1884, *ed. Works of Gabriel Harvey, Memorial-Introduction, vol.* I, *p.* ix.

He was emphatically of Mr. Carlyle's "acrid-quack" genus.—SAINTSBURY, GEORGE, 1887, *History of Elizabethan Literature, p.* 232.

He was a man of arrogant and censorious spirit, far too conscious of his own considerable abilities, while but little disposed to recognise the merits and claims of others. . . . An overweening estimate of his own attainments and abilities, conjoined with disappointed ambition, seems to have rendered Harvey singularly sensitive and quarrelsome; and to his contemporaries he was best known by the scurrilous paper warfare in which he became involved with the writers Nashe and Greene.—MULLINGER, J. BASS, 1891, *Dictionary of National Biography, vol.* XXV, *pp.* 83, 84.

John Smith

1579–1631

Born at Willoughby, Lincolnshire, in Jan., 1579: died at London, June 21, 1631. An English adventurer, president of the colony of Virginia 1608–09. He was the eldest son of George Smith, a tenant farmer. Little is known of his life, except through his own writings, which are largely eulogistic of himself and of questionable authority. . . . He wrote "A True Relation" (1608), "A Map of Virginia" (1612), "A Description of New England (1616), "New England's Trials" (1620), "The Generall Historie of Virginia, New England and the Summer Isles" (1624), "An Accidence for Young Seamen" (1626), "The True Travels" (1630), and "Advertisements for the Inexperienced Planters of New England" (1631).—SMITH, BENJAMIN E., *ed.* 1894–97, *The Century Cyclopedia of Names, p.* 940.

PERSONAL

He spent the most of his life in Foraign parts. First in Hungary, under the Emperour, fighting against the Turks; three of which he himself killed in single duells; and therefore was authorized by Sigismund King of Hungary to bear three Turks-heads, as an augmentation to his Armes. Here he gave intelligence to a besieged City in the night, by significant Fire-works formed in the aire, in legible characters, with many strange performances, the scene whereof is laid at such a distance, they are cheaper credited then confuted. From the Turks in Europe he passed to the Pagans in America, where, towards the latter end of the Raign of Queen Elizabeth, such his perills, preservations, dangers, deliverances, they seem to most men above belief, to some beyond truth. Yet have we two witnesses to attest them, the Prose and the Pictures, both in his own Book; and it soundeth much to the diminution of his deeds, that he alone is the Herauld to publish and proclaim them. . . . Moderate men must allow Captain Smith to have been very instrumentall in settling the Plantation in Virginia, whereof he was Governour, as also Admiral of New-England. He led his old age in London, where his having a Prince's mind imprisoned in a poor man's purse rendered him to the contempt of such who were not ingenuous. Yet he efforted his spirits with the remembrance and relation of what formerly he had been, and what he had done. He was buried in Sepulchre's-Church Quire, on the South-side thereof, having a ranting Epitaph inscribed in a table over him, too long to transcribe.—FULLER, THOMAS, 1662, *The Worthies of England, ed. Nichols, vol.* I, *p.* 189.

Wherever upon this continent the English language is spoken, his deeds should be recounted and his memory hallowed. His services should not only be not forgotten, but should be "freshly remembered." His name should not only be honored by the silent canvas and the cold marble, but his praises should dwell living upon the lips of men, and should be handed down by fathers to their children. Poetry has imagined nothing more stirring and romantic than his life and adventures, and History, upon her ample page, has recorded few more honorable and spotless names.—HILLARD, GEORGE S., 1834, *Life of Captain John Smith, Sparks's American Biography, vol.* II, *p.* 397.

Captain John Smith united the strongest spirit of adventure with eminent powers of action. Full of courage and self-possession, he was fertile in expedients, and prompt in execution. He had a just idea of the public good, and clearly discerned that it was not the true interest of England to seek in Virginia for gold and sudden wealth. "Nothing," said he, "is to be expected thence but by labor;" and as a public officer he excelled in its direction. The historians of Virginia have with common consent looked to him as the preserver of their commonwealth in its infancy; and there is hardly room to doubt that, but for his vigor, industry, and resolution, it would have been deserted like the Virginia of the north, and with better excuse.—BANCROFT, GEORGE, 1834–82, *History of the United States, vol.* I, *ch.* vi.

"His body was deposited in Sepulchre's Church choir, on the south side thereof," with a rather florid epitaph, of which the following are the first and last lines:

"Here lies one conquer'd that hath conquer'd kings!
Oh, may his soul in sweet Elysium sleep!"

The verses, some by men of mark, which accompany his "Generall Historie" and others of his works, are highly eulogistic of his private character and public deeds. Edward Robinson addresses him as

"Thou that to passe the world's four parts
dost deeme
No more than 'twere to go to bed or drinke;"

and Thomas Carlton relieves us of the fear that he was wont, soldier and sailor like, to "drinke" too easily, by the assertion,

"I never knew a Warryer yet, but thee,
From wine, tobacco, debts, dice, oaths, so
free."

—ALLIBONE, S. AUSTIN, 1870, *Dictionary of English Literature, vol.* II, *p.* 2145.

He was perhaps the last professional knight-errant that the world saw; a free lance, who could not hear of a fight going on anywhere in the world without hastening to have a hand in it; a sworn champion of the ladies also, all of whom he loved too ardently to be guilty of the invidious offence of marrying any one of them; a restless, vain, ambitious, overbearing, blustering fellow, who made all men either his hot friends or his hot enemies; a man who down to the present hour has his celebrity in the world chiefly on account of alleged exploits among Turks, Tartars, and Indians, of which exploits he alone has furnished the history—never failing to celebrate himself in them all as the one resplendent and invincible hero.—TYLER, MOSES COIT, 1878, *A History of American Literature, vol.* I, *p.* 18.

The truth of this story [of Smith's Rescue by Pocahontas], was never doubted till 1866, when the eminent antiquary, Dr. Charles Deane of Cambridge, Mass., in reprinting Smith's first book, the "True Relation" of 1609, pointed out that it contains no reference to this hairbreadth escape. Since then many American historians and scholars have concluded that it never happened at all; and, in order to be consistent, they have tried to prove that Smith was a blustering braggadocio, which is the very last thing that could in truth be said of him. The rescue of a captive doomed to death by a woman is not such an unheard-of thing in Indian stories. If the truth of this deliverance be denied, how then did Smith come back to James Town loaded with presents, when the other three men were killed, George Cassen in particular, in a most horrible manner? And how is it, supposing Smith's account to be false, that Pocahontas afterwards frequently came to James Town, and was next to Smith himself, the salvation of the colony? The fact is, nobody doubted the story in Smith's lifetime, and he had enemies enough.—ARBER, EDWARD, 1887, *Encyclopædia Britannica, Ninth ed., vol.* XXII, *p.* 175.

The romantic life of Captain John Smith is too well known to need retelling. His character, too, needs no new light shed upon it. We must acknowledge that he was inordinately vain, fond of boasting, impetuous, imperious, restless, yet we know that his shrewdness, his indomitable courage, and his sound judgment more than once saved the Virginia Colony from ruin.—PATTEE, FRED LEWIS, 1896, *A History of American Literature, p.* 16.

Much controversy has arisen as to the truth of the stories published by Smith about his own adventures. But the modern historian, while recognising the extravagance of the details of many of the more picturesque of Smith's self-recorded exploits, is bound to give full weight to his record of his more prosaic achievements—in laying the solid foundations of the prosperity of the new settlement of Virginia.—DOYLE, J. A., 1898, *Dictionary of National Biography, vol.* LIII, *p.* 72.

GENERAL

His style is simple and concise, his narratives bear the stamp of truth, and his descriptions are free from false ornament.—TOCQUEVILLE, ALEXIS DE, 1835, *Democracy in America, tr. Reeve, vol.* I, *p.* 274.

I made acquaintance with brave Captain Smith, as a boy in my grandfather's library at home, where I remember how I would sit at the good old man's knees, with my favourite volume on my own, spelling out the exploits of our Virginian hero. I loved to read of Smith's travels, sufferings, captivities, escapes, not only in America, but Europe.—THACKERAY, WILLIAM MAKEPEACE, 1859, *Henry Warrington in The Virginians, ch.* XXX.

As students of literature we shall be drawn to Captain John Smith as belonging to that noble type of manhood of which the Elizabethan period produced so many examples—the man of action who was also a man of letters, the man of letters who was also a man of action: the wholsomest type of manhood anywhere to be found; body and brain both active, both cultivated; the mind not made fastidious and morbid by too much bookishness, nor coarse and dull by too little; not a doer who is dumb, not a speech-maker who cannot do; the knowledge that comes of books widened and freshened by the knowledge that comes of experience; the literary sense fortified by common sense; the bashfulness and delicacy of the scholar hovering as a finer presence above the forceful audacity of the man of the world; at once bookman, penman, swordsman, diplomat, sailor, courtier, orator. . . . . As a writer his merits are really great—clearness, force, vividness, picturesque and dramatic energy, a diction racy and crisp. He had the faults of an impulsive, irascible, egotistic, and imaginative nature; he sometimes bought human praise at too high a price; but he had great abilities in word and deed; his nature was upon the whole generous and noble; and during the first two decades of the seventeenth century he did more than any other Englishman to make an American nation and an American literature possible.—TYLER, MOSES COIT, 1878, *A History of American Literature, vol.* I, *pp.* 19, 38.

For twenty years he was a voluminous writer, working off his superfluous energy in setting forth his adventures in new forms. . . . He seldom writes a book, or a tract, without beginning it or working into it a résumé of his life.—WARNER, CHARLES DUDLEY, 1881, *Captain John Smith, p.* 278.

His zeal was greater than his discretion, and his industry was often fruitless; but as an explorer and describer of American men, soil, and possibilities, his service to the nascent colonies was unquestionable. This bald list of his adventures, discoveries, and doings explains his prominence in the American history of the seventeenth century. His voluminous writings deserve but a humble place in literature. Strictly speaking, they are a part of English, not American literature, for Smith's continuous residence on American soil was a matter of but two years' lasting; and, all told, he was in the New World but two years and eight months. It is uncertain what share Smith had in the writing of the works passing under his name; some of his assertions (as the famous legend of the rescue of his life by Pocahontas) are questionable, and others demonstrably false. At their best, his books lack high literary merit, and are material for the historian rather than the critic.—RICHARDSON, CHARLES F., 1887, *American Literature*, 1607-1885, *vol.* I, *p.* 64.

Captain Smith's writings have small literary value apart from the interest of the events which they describe and the diverting but forcible personality which they unconsciously display. They are the rough-hewn records of a busy man of action, whose sword was mightier than his pen.—BEERS, HENRY A., 1895, *Initial Studies in American Literature, p.* 14.

John Smith was the most picturesque figure in the early history of America; and his writings are like him—bold, free, highly colored.—MATTHEWS, BRANDER, 1896, *An Introduction to the Study of American Literature, p.* 16.

Smith's earliest book, "A True Relation of Virginia," was printed in London in 1608, the year of Milton's birth. It is a hurried, semi-official document, giving a sketchy account of the first year of the colony. When we read of the young captain's own busy doings in those critical months, building forts and palisadoes, planting, exploring, fighting, sojourning among the Indians, now as captive, now as guest, trading blue beads for corn and venison, we wonder that he found the moments in which to jot down his news at all. Yet heedless of art, all rough-and-ready as the headlong narrative is, the vigor of the man, and the reality of the situation make it graphic.—BATES, KATHARINE LEE, 1897, *American Literature, p.* 8.

Smith was a prolific and, no doubt, a rapid writer; but, like Sir Walter Raleigh, he made authorship merely an incident in a life crowded with dangers and brave deeds. As we might expect, he is not a finished writer; but his books are graphic and entertaining, and full of the vigor and power of the man. If his love of "brave adventure" and the spirit of the artist made him occasionally draw upon his imagination to heighten the interest, at least some of his readers will secretly be thankful for the romance, and pardon the trifling lapses from truth.—PANCOAST, HENRY S., 1898, *An Introduction to American Literature, p.* 39.

Michael Drayton

1563–1631

Michael Drayton, 1563–1631. Born, at Hartshill, Warwickshire, 1563. Probably page in household of Sir Henry Goodere of Powlesworth. First work published (and suppressed), 1591. Wrote many poetical works. Wrote for stage, 1597–1602. Esquire to Sir Walter Aston, 1603. Probably not married. Died, 1631. Buried in Westminster Abbey. *Works*: "The Harmonie of the Church," 1591 (suppressed; reissued as "A Heavenly Harmonie," 1610); "Idea," 1593; "The Legend of Piers Gaveston," 1593; "Matilda," 1594; "Endymion and Phœbe" [1594]; "Ideas Mirrour," 1594; "Mortimeriados," 1596 (reissued as "The Barrons' Wars," 1603); "Poemes Lyrick and Pastorall" [1605?]; "England's Heroicall Epistles," 1597; "The first part of the . . . Life of Sir John Oldcastle" (probably by Munday, Drayton, and others), 1600; "To the Majestie of King James," 1603; "A Pæan Triumphall," 1604; "The Owle," 1604; "Moyses in a Map of his Miracles," 1604; "Poems," 1605; "Poems Lyrick and Pastorall: Odes, Eglogs, etc." [1606?]; "The Historie of the Life and Death of the Lord Cromwell," 1609; "Poly-Olbion," pt. i. [1612]; pt. ii, 1622; "Poems," 1619;" "Certain Elegies" (anon., with Beaumont and others), 1620; "The Battaile of Agincourt, etc.," 1627; "The Muses Elizium," 1630; "Noah's Floud" (anon.), 1630. He contrib. verses to Morley's "First Book of Ballets," 1595; Middleton's "Legend of Duke Humphrey," 1600; DeSerres' "Perfect Use of Silk-wormes," 1607; Davies' "Holy Rood," 1609; Murray's "Sophonisba," 1611; Tuke's "Discourse against Painting . . . of Women," 1616; Chapman's "Hesiod," 1618; Munday's "Primaleon of Greece," 1619; Vicars' "Manuductio" [1620?]; Holland's "Naumachia," 1622; Sir J. Beaumont's "Bosworth Field," 1629. *Collected works*: in 1 vol., 1748; in 4 vols., 1753; ed. by J. P. Collier, 1856.—SHARP, R. FARQUHARSON, 1897, *A Dictionary of English Authors*, p. 87.

PERSONAL

As Aulus Persius Flaccus is reported, among all writers to (have) been of an honest life and upright conversation: so Michael Drayton, *quem toties honoris et amoris causa nomino*, among scholars, soldiers, poets, and all sorts of people, is held for a man of virtuous disposition, honest conversation, and well governed carriage: which is almost miraculous among good wits in these declining and corrupt times; when there is nothing but roguery in villainous man, and when cheating and craftiness are counted the cleanest wit and soundest wisdom.—MERES, FRANCIS, 1598, *Palladis Tamia*.

Drayton feared him; and he esteemed not of him.—DRUMMOND, WILLIAM, 1619, *Notes on Ben Jonson's Conversations*.

It hath been question'd, Michael, if I be
A friend at all; or, if at all, to thee:
Because, who made the question, have not seen
Those ambling visits pass in verse, between
Thy Muse and mine, as they expect: 'tis true,
You have not writ to me, nor I to you.
And though I now begin, 'tis not to rub
Haunch against haunch, or raise a riming club
About the town; this reckoning I will pay
Without conferring symbols; this, my day.
—JONSON, BEN, 1627, *A Vision on the Muses of his friend, Michael Drayton*.

He was a pious Poet, his conscience having always the command of his fancy; very temperate in his life, slow of speech, and inoffensive in company. He changed his Laurel for a Crown of Glory, anno 1631; and is buried in Westminster-Abby, near the South door, with this Epitaph:

"Doe, pious Marble, let thy Readers know,
What they and what their children owe
To Draiton's name, whose sacred dust
We recommend unto thy trust.
Protect his memory, and preserve his story,
Remain a lasting Monument of his glory:
And when thy ruins shall disclaime
To be the Treasurer of his name;
His name that cannot fade, shall be
An everlasting Monument to thee."
—FULLER, THOMAS, 1662, *The Worthies of England, ed. Nichols, vol.* II, *p.* 415.

Drayton was never married, and little is known of his private life. He loved a lady of Conventry, to whom he promises an immortality he had not been able to confer.—JAMESON, ANNA BROWNELL, 1829, *The Loves of the Poets, vol.* I, *p.* 263.

Next followed—such was the inequality of fortune—Drayton, of whom, after the lapse of not much more than a hundred years, Goldsmith, in his visit to the Abbey, could say, when he saw his monument, "Drayton! I never heard of him before."

Indeed, it was the common remark of London gossips—"Drayton, with half a nose, was next, whose works are forgot before his monument is worn out." But at the time the "Polyolbion" was regarded as a masterpiece of art. It is uncertain whether he was buried in the Nave, or in this spot. But his bust was erected here by the same great lady who raised that to Spenser. Fuller, in his quaint manner, again revives their joint connexion with the grave of their predecessor:—"Chaucer lies buried in the south aisle of St. Peter's, Westminster, and now hath got the company of Spenser and Drayton, a pair of royal poets, enough almost to make passengers' feet to move metrically, who go over the place where so much poetical dust is interred." How little the verdict of Goldsmith was then anticipated appears from the fine lines on Drayton's monument, ascribed both to Ben Jonson and to Quarles, which, in invoking "the pious marble" to protect his memory, predict that when its

> Ruin shall disclaim
> To be the treasurer of his fame,
> His name, that cannot fade, shall be
> An everlasting monument to thee.

—STANLEY, ARTHUR PENRHYN, 1867-96, *Historical Memorials of Westminster Abbey.*

In person, he was a swart little man, full of energy and an enthusiastic sense of his own powers; erudite, laborious, versatile; noted for the respectability of his life, and distinguished by the ardour of his orthodox and patriotic sentiments. I doubt whether he had any special call to poetry beyond the contagion of circumstances; ambition made his verses. . . . Drayton has a suspicious pride in the exercise of his gift: originality and versatility are the two qualities that he boasts of, as if he had overmastered the muse by intellectual force rather than won her by natural affinity.—MINTO, WILLIAM, 1875-85, *Characteristics of English Poets, p.* 206.

Drayton was buried in Westminster Abbey, according to Fuller "in the south aisle near to Chaucer's grave and Spenser's, where his monument stands;" but Dean Stanley believes that he lies near the small north door of the nave. Mr. Marshall, the stonecutter in Fetter Lane, told Aubrey that the lines on his "pious marble were writ by Francis Quarles, a very good man." They declare that his name cannot fade; and yet when Goldsmith read them, a century later, he confessed that he had never heard the name before.—HUTTON, LAURENCE, 1885, *Literary Landmarks of London, p.* 91.

IDEA
1593

The sixty-three sonnets, varied in different editions of Drayton's "Idea," are among the most puzzling of the whole group. Their average value is not of the very highest. Yet there are here and there the strangest suggestions of Drayton's countryman, Shakespere, and there is one sonnet, No. 61, beginning, "Since there's no help, come let us kiss and part," which I at least find it impossible to believe to be Drayton's, and which is Shakespere all over. That Drayton was the author of "Idea" as a whole is certain, not merely from the local allusions, but from the resemblance to the more successful exercises of his clear, masculine, vigorous, fertile, but occasionally rather unpoetical style. The sonnet just referred to is itself one of the very finest existing —perhaps one of the ten or twelve best sonnets in the world. — SAINTSBURY, GEORGE, 1887, *History of Elizabethan Literature, p.* 114.

BARONS' WARS
1596-1603

Though not very pleasing, however, in its general effect, this poem, "The Barons' Wars," contains several passages of considerable beauty, which men of greater renown, especially Milton, who availed himself largely of all the poetry of the preceding age, have been willing to imitate.—HALLAM, HENRY, 1837-39, *Introduction to the Literature of Europe, pt.* ii, *ch.* v, *par.* 69.

His "Barons' Wars" are not tame or prosaic, they are full of action and strife; swords flash and helmets rattle on every page. But unfortunately, Mortimer, the hero of the poem, the guilty favourite of Edward II.'s queen, is a personage in whom we vainly endeavour to get up an interest. There is much prolixity of description in this poem, due, it would seem, to imitation of Spenser, whose influence on Drayton's mind and style are conspicuous. But it is one thing to be prolix in a work of pure imagination, when the poet detains us thereby in that magic world of unearthly beauty in which his own spirit habitually dwells, and quite another thing to be prolix in a poem founded upon and closely following historical fact. . . . If Drayton had known, like Tasso, how to associate imaginary Clorindas and Erminias with his historical personages, he might have been as discursive as he pleased. But this was "a grace beyond the reach" of his art; and the "Barons' Wars" remain, therefore, incurably uninteresting.—ARNOLD, THOMAS, 1868-75, *Chaucer to Wordsworth, pp.* 95, 96.

Setting aside "The Faerie Queene" and Shakespeare's plays, Drayton's "Barons' Wars" must take rank as the best heroic poem written in the reign of Queen Elizabeth. The poet sought in all ways to give to the treatment of his subject epic dignity. The action is one great in itself and in its consequences, national, and associated with first principles of civil polity. There is greatness in the persons, and for the chief person Drayton uses all arts of the poet to enlarge and raise the character of Mortimer. The thoughts are noble, and associated clearly with the action. There is a strong passion of love well blended with strong passion of war. There is care to maintain the level of heroic thought in treatment of mere trivial incidents. There is even some suggestion of an episode of the past in the description of Edward's glance over the chronicle of reigns of predecessors that he found, before his murder, in the prison. If there could have been a clearer view of greatness in the consequence of the action, that could have been presented to us by an episode of the future, this heroic poem, though without epic "machinery," would rank among our epics. But it is enough to say that Drayton, with an eye towards epic, did achieve the writing of a true heroic poem, laboured carefully in the first writing, and twice revised.—MORLEY, HENRY, 1893, *English Writers, vol.* X, *p.* 318.

ENGLAND'S HEROICAL EPISTLES

1597

Michael Drayton's Heroical Epistles are well worth the reading also for the purpose of our subject, which is to furnish an English historian with choice and copy of tongue.—BOLTON, EDMUND, 1624, *Hypercritica.*

The style is flowing, fiery, and energetic, and withal extremely *modern;* it seems to anticipate the "full resounding line" of Dryden, and to rebuke the presumption of the poets of the Stuart age, who chose to say that English had never been properly and purely written till Waller and Denham arose.—ARNOLD, THOMAS, 1868-75, *Chaucer to Wordsworth, p.* 96.

POLY-OLBION

1612–22

As Joannes Honterus, in Latin verse, wrote three books of Cosmography, with geographical tables; so Michael Drayton is now in penning in English verse, a poem called Poly-olbion [which is] geographical and hydrographical of all the forests, woods, mountains, fountains, rivers, lakes, floods, baths [spas], and springs that be in England.—MERES, FRANCIS, 1598, *Palladis Tamia.*

That Michael Drayton's "Polyolbion," if (he) had performed what he promised to writte (the deeds of all the Worthies) had been excellent: His long verses pleased him not.—DRUMMOND, WILLIAM, 1619, *Notes on Ben Jonson's Conversations.*

When I first undertook this Poem, or, as some very skilful in this kind have pleased to term it, this Herculean labour, I was by some virtuous friends persuaded, that I should receive much comfort and encouragement therein; and for these reasons: First, that it was a new, clear, way, never before gone by any; then, that it contained all the Delicacies, Delights, and Rarities of this renowned Isle, interwoven with the Histories of the Britans, Saxons, Normans, and the later English: And further that there is scarcely any of the Nobility or Gentry of this land, but that he is some way or other by his Blood interested therein. But it hath fallen out otherwise; for instead of that comfort, which my noble friends (from the freedom of their spirits) proposed as my due, I have met with barbarous ignorance, and base detraction; such a cloud hath the Devil drawn over the world's judgment, whose opinion is in few years fallen so far below all ballatry, that the lethargy is incurable. . . . And as for those cattle whereof I spake before, *Odi profanum vulgus, et arceo,* of which I account them, be they never so great, and so I leave them. To my friends, and the lovers of my labours, I wish all happiness.—DRAYTON, MICHAEL, 1622, *Poly-Olbion, The Second Part, ed. Hooper, Preface, pp.* ix, x.

Affords a much truer account of this kingdom, and the dominion of Wales, than could well be expected from the pen of a poet.—NICOLSON, WILLIAM, 1696-1714, *English Historical Library.*

Drayton, sweet ancient Bard, his Albion sung,
With their own praise her echoing Valleys rung;
His bounding Muse o'er ev'ry mountain rode,
And ev'ry river warbled where he flow'd.
—KIRKPATRICK, JAMES, 1750, *Sea-Piece, Canto* ii.

His "Poly-Olbion" is one of the most singular works this country has produced, and seems to me eminently original. The information contained in it is in general so acute, that he is quoted as an authority both by Hearne and Wood. His perpetual allusions to obsolete traditions, remote events, remarkable facts and personages, together with his curious genealogies of rivers, and his taste for natural history, have contributed to render his work very valuable to the antiquary.—HEADLEY, HENRY, 1787, *Select Beauties of Ancient English Poetry.*

His "Polyolbion" is certainly a wonderful work, exhibiting, at once, the learning of an historian, an antiquary, a naturalist, and a geographer, and embellished by the imagination of a poet.—ELLIS, GEORGE, 1790-1845, *Specimens of the Early English Poets.*

He has treated the subject with such topographical and minute detail as to chain his poetry to the map; and he has unfortunately chosen a form of verse which, though agreeable when interspersed with other measures, is fatiguing in long continuance by itself: still it is impossible to read the poem without admiring the richness of his local associations, and the beauty and variety of the fabulous allusions which he scatters around him. Such, indeed is the profusion of romantic recollections in the Poly-olbion, that a poet of taste and selection might there find subjects of happy description, to which the author who suggested them had not the power of doing justice; for Drayton started so many remembrances, that he lost his inspiration in the effort of memory.—CAMPBELL, THOMAS, 1819, *Specimens of the British Poets.*

A work once famous, though now scarcely known except by its uncouth name. . . . It is, indeed, one of the most learned and ingenious poems in the language, and unique in literature; being a treasure-house of topographic, antiquarian, and traditional lore, which the heavy versification alone was sufficient to sink into neglect, even if public taste had not changed since the age of garrulity which it was written to instruct and entertain.—MONTGOMERY, JAMES, 1833, *Lectures on General Literature, Lecture IV.*

Next to Daniel in time, and much above him in reach of mind, we place Michael Drayton. . . . Drayton's "Polyolbion" is a poem of about 30,000 lines in length, written in Alexandrine couplets; a measure, from its monotony, and perhaps from its frequency in doggerel ballads, not at all pleasing to the ear. It contains a topographical description of England, illustrated with a prodigality of historical and legendary erudition. Such a poem is essentially designed to instruct, and speaks to the understanding more than to the fancy. . . . The style of Drayton is sustained, with extraordinary ability, on an equable line, from which he seldom much deviates, neither brilliant nor prosaic: few or no passages could be marked as impressive, but few are languid or mean. The language is clear, strong, various, and sufficiently figurative; the stories and fictions interspersed, as well as the general spirit and liveliness, relieve the heaviness incident to topographical description. There is probably no poem of this kind, in any other language, comparable together in extent and excellence to the "Polyolbion;" nor can any one read a portion of it without admiration for its learned and highly gifted author. Yet perhaps no English poem, known as well by name, is so little known beyond its name; for, while its immense length deters the common reader, it affords, as has just been hinted, no great harvest for selection, and would be judged very unfairly by partial extracts.—HALLAM, HENRY, 1837-39, *Introduction to the Literature of Europe, pt.* iii, *ch.* v, *par.* 44.

Huge in length, as well as injudicious in purpose, Drayton's work has seldom perhaps been read from beginning to end; but no one susceptible of poetic beauty can look into any part of it, without being fascinated and longing to read more. There is not in existence any instance so signal, of fine fancy and feeling, and great command of pure and strong language, thrown almost utterly away. Beautiful natural objects, striking national legends, recent facts, and ingenious allegorical and mythological inventions, are all lavished on this thankless design.—SPALDING, WILLIAM, 1852-82, *A History of English Literature, p.* 278.

The essential difficulty with the "Poly-Olbion" is, that, with all its merits, it is unreadable. The poetic feeling, the grace, the freshness, the pure, bright, and vigorous diction, which characterize it, appear to more advantage in the poet's minor pieces, where his subjects are less unwieldy, and the vivacity of his fancy makes us forget his lack of high imagination.—WHIPPLE, EDWIN P., 1859-68, *The Literature of the Age of Elizabeth, p.* 227.

A miracle of industry and sustained enthusiasm.--MINTO, WILLIAM, 1875–85, *Characteristics of English Poets, p.* 207.

That very little read Drayton, whose great "Polyolbion" seems as if it might have filled the place of "Bradshaw's Guide" to tourists of the *Arcadia* stamp. Let me tell you that you will find a great deal of very good poetry in that same "Polyolbion" if you venture to face it.—NORTHCOTE, HENRY STAFFORD, 1885, *Desultory Reading, p.* 56.

Who now reads the "Polyolbion," that river epic, which imitates its theme in its quaintly meandering course? Here and there may be seen a rapt angler for fine passages, scantily dotted along its banks, and there is no better angling in British poetry.—LE GALLIENNE, RICHARD, 1893-95, *Retrospective Reviews, vol.* II, *p.* 55.

Full of quaint and minute learning, local knowledge, and romantic touches, the poem, strange as it is, is singularly interesting. If it reaches no great height it sinks to no depth; we move, so to speak, with a kind of swinging motion along a lofty tableland where fresh, healthy breezes blow; we note the varying scenery, we watch the fish in the clear streams, and learn their names; we cull the flowers, we linger within the woods, or are present at the wedding of a Thames with an Isis.—MORLEY, HENRY, AND GRIFFIN, W. HALL, 1895, *English Writers, vol.* XI, *p.* 321.

A huge British gazetteer in broken-backed twelve-syllable verse, is a portent of misplaced energy.—GOSSE, EDMUND, 1897, *A Short History of Modern English Literature, p.* 121.

BATTLE OF AGINCOURT
1627

His ode on the Battle of Agincourt is, perhaps, his masterpiece.—MINTO, WILLIAM, 1875-85, *Characteristics of English Poets, p.* 207.

It runs, it leaps, clashing its verses like swords upon bucklers, and moves the pulse to a charge.—LOWELL, JAMES RUSSELL, 1875-90, *Spenser, Prose Works, Riverside ed., vol.* IV, *p,* 280.

The Agincourt ballad,

"Fair stood the wind for France."

is quite at the head of its own class of verse in England—Campbell's two masterpieces, and the present poet-laureate's direct imitation in the "Six Hundred," falling, the first somewhat, and the last considerably, short of it. The sweep of the metre, the martial glow of the sentiment, and the skill with which the names are wrought into the verse, are altogether beyond praise.—SAINTSBURY, GEORGE, 1887, *History of Elizabethan Literature, p.* 141.

By far the best of the odes, however, is the noble "Battle of Agincourt," which is Drayton's greatest claim to the recognition of posterity, and the most spirited of all his lyrics.—GOSSE, EDMUND, 1894, *The Jacobean Poets, p.* 96.

NYMPHIDIA

Elegant simplicity, so necessary in Bucolic poetry, was no characteristic of the author of the "Fairy Queen." In every requisite for this province of his divine art, he has been much excelled by Drayton, whose "Nymphidia" may be considered as one of the best specimens we have of the pastoral eclogue.—DRAKE, NATHAN, 1798, *Literary Hours, vol.* I, *No.* XVI.

The fairy poem of "Nymphidia" is one of the most graceful trifles in the language, possessing a dancing movement and a felicitous choice of imagery and language which triumphantly avoid the trivial on the one hand, and the obviously burlesque on the other.—SAINTSBURY, GEORGE, 1887, *History of Elizabethan Literature, p.* 142.

GENERAL

Drayton is termed "golden-mouthed," for the purity and preciousness of his style and phrase.—MERES, FRANCIS, 1598, *Palladis Tamia.*

The Peeres of heav'n kept a parliament,
And for Wittes-mirrour Philip Sidney sent:
To keepe another when they doe intend,
Twentie to one for Drayton they will send,
Yet bade him leave his learning; so it fled
And vow'd to live with thee since he was dead.

—WEEVER, JOHN, 1599, *Epigrammes in the Oldest Cut and Newest Fashion.*

And Drayton, whose well-written Tragedies,
And sweet Epistles, soare thy fame to skies,
Thy learned Name is equall with the rest,
Whose stately Numbers are so well addrest.

—BARNFIELD, RICHARD, 1605, *Remembrance of Some English Poets.*

Draytons sweete muse is like a sanguine dy, Able to rauish the rash gazers eye. How euer he wants one true note of a Poet of our times, and that is this, hee cannot swagger it well in a Tauerne, nor domineere in a hot house.—ANON, 1606, *The Return from Parnassus, ed. Macray, Act I, Sc.* 2, *p.* 85.

Our second Ovid, the most pleasing Muse
That heav'n did e'er in mortal's brain infuse,
All-lovèd Drayton, in soul-raping strains,
A genuine note, of all the nymphish trains
Began to tune; on it all ears were hung,
As sometime Dido's on Æneas' tongue.

—BROWNE, WILLIAM, 1616, *Britannia's Pastorals, bk.* ii, *song* ii.

Draiton is sweet and Smooth; though not exact,
Perhaps, to stricter Eyes; yet he shall live
Beyond their Malice.

—DANIEL, GEORGE, 1647, *A Vindication of Poesy.*

Michael Drayton, contemporary of Spencer and Sir Philip Sydney, and for fame and renown in poetry, not much inferior in his time to either: however, he seems somewhat antiquated in the esteem of the more curious of these times, especially in his "Polyalbion," the old fashion'd kind of verse whereof, seem somewhat to diminish that respect which was formerly paid to the subject, as being both pleasant and elaborate, and thereupon thought worthy to be commented upon by that once walking library of our nation, Selden; his "England's Heroical Epistles," are more generally lik'd; and to such as love the pretty chat of nymphs and shepherds, his Nymphals and other things of that nature, cannot be unpleasant.—PHILLIPS, EDWARD, 1675, *Theatrum Poetarum Anglicanorum, ed. Brydges, p.* 262.

As we walked along to a particular part of the temple, there, says the gentleman, pointing with his finger, that is the poet's corner; there you see the monuments of Shakspeare, and Milton, and Prior, and Drayton. Drayton! I replied, I never heard of him before.—GOLDSMITH, OLIVER, 1762, *A Citizen of the World, Letter* XIII.

Of Drayton the best parts are pastoral, and these are indeed truly excellent; his "Legends," however, his "Heroical Epistles" and his "Barons Warres," contain many pathetic passages; but his most elaborate work the "Poly-Olbion" exhibits much more of the Antiquary than of the Poet. Drayton is frequently a pleasing but never a great poet.—DRAKE, NATHAN, 1798, *Literary Hours, No.* xxviii.

The excellent fable of the maddening rain I have found in Drayton's "Moon Calf," most miserably marred in the telling! vastly inferior to Benedict Fay's Latin exposition of it, and that is no great thing. *Vide* his Lucretian Poem on the Newtonian System. Never was a finer tale for a satire, or, rather, to conclude a long satirical poem of five or six hundred lines.—COLERIDGE, SAMUEL TAYLOR, 1805, *Anima Poetæ, p.* 130.

The language of Drayton is free and perspicuous. With less depth of feeling than that which occasionally bursts from Cowley, he is a less excruciating hunter of conceits, and in harmony of expression is quite a contrast to Donne. A tinge of grace and romance pervades much of his poetry: and even his pastorals, which exhibit the most fantastic views of nature, sparkle with elegant imagery. . . . On a general survey, the mass of his poetry has no strength or sustaining spirit adequate to its bulk. There is a perpetual play of fancy on its surface; but the impulses of passion, and the guidance of judgment give it no strong movements nor consistent course. In scenery or in history he cannot command selected views, but meets them by chance as he travels over the track of detail. His great subjects have no interesting centre, no shade for uninteresting things. Not to speak of his dull passages, his description is generally lost in a flutter of whimsical touches. His muse has certainly no strength for extensive flights, though she sports in happy moments on a brilliant and graceful wing.—CAMPBELL, THOMAS, 1819, *Specimens of the British Poets.*

Michael Drayton's "Poly-Olbion" is a work of great length and of unabated freshness and vigour in itself, though the monotony of the subject tires the reader. He describes each place with the accuracy of a topographer, and the enthusiasm of a poet, as if his Muse were the very *genius loci*. His "Heroical Epistles" are also excellent. He has a few lighter pieces, but none of exquisite beauty or grace. His mind is a rich marly soil that produces an abundant harvest, and repays the husbandman's toil, but few flaunting flowers, the garden's pride, grow in it, nor any poisonous weeds.—HAZLITT, WILLIAM, 1820, *Lectures on the Literature of the Age of Elizabeth, p.* 192.

Drayton wrote well in every metre which he attempted: but what he thus says of the Italian stanza may be more truly said of the English one invented by Spenser, and used by him in one of the noblest works of human genius. And he committed a great error when he fixed upon the Alexandrine as the measure in which to write his "Polyolbion"; for of all measures it is that which, in our language, admits the least variety.—SOUTHEY, ROBERT, 1835, *Life of Cowper, p.* 300.

It was at one time a question in the mind of Tyrwhitt, whether the date of the "Nymphidia" was prior to that of the "Midsummer Night's Dream;" but his decision in favour of the priority of the latter was determined by observing that Don Quixote, which did not make its appearance till five years after Shakspeare's drama, is cited in Drayton's poem.—HIPPISLEY, J. H., 1837, *Chapters on Early English Literature, p.* 313, *note.*

It was the misfortune of Drayton not to have been a popular poet; which we may infer from his altercations with his booksellers, and from their frequent practice of prefixing new title pages, with fresher dates, to the first editions of his poems. That he was also in perpetual quarrel with his Muse, appears by his frequent alteration of his poems. He often felt that curse of an infelicitous poet, that his diligence was more active than his creative power. Drayton was a poet of volume; but his genius was peculiar: from an unhappy facility in composition, in reaching excellence he too often declined into mediocrity. A modern reader may be struck by the purity and strength of his diction: his strong descriptive manner lays hold on the fancy; but he is always a poet of reason, and never of passion. He cannot be considered as a poet of mediocrity, who has written so much above that level; nor a poet who can rank among the highest class, who has often flattened his spirit by its redundance.—DISRAELI, ISAAC, 1841, *Drayton, Amenities of Literature.*

Hail to thee Michael! true, pains-taking wight,
So various that 'tis hard to praise thee right;
For driest fact and finest faery fable
Employ'd thy genius indefatigable.
What bard more zealous of our England's glory,
More deeply versed in all her antique story,
Recorded feat, tradition quaint and hoary?
What muse like thine so patiently would plod
From shire to shire in pilgrim sandal shod,
Calling to life and voice, and conscious will,
The shifting streamlet and the sluggish hill?
Great genealogist of earth and water,
The very Plutarch of insensate matter.

—COLERIDGE, HARTLEY, 1849, *Drayton, Sketches of English Poets, Poems, vol.* II, *p.* 294.

The market-value, both of his poetry and virtue, was small, and he seems to have been always on bad terms with the booksellers. His poems, we believe, were the first which arrived at second editions by the simple process of merely reprinting, with additions, the title-pages of the first,—a fact which is ominous of his bad success with the public. The defect of his mind was not the lack of materials, but the lack of taste to select, and imagination to fuse, his materials.—WHIPPLE, EDWIN P., 1859-68, *The Literature of the Age of Elizabeth, p.* 226.

Drayton eminently suits a "Selection" such as ours, since his parts are better than his whole.—GILFILLAN, GEORGE, 1860, *Specimens with Memoirs of the Less-Known British Poets, vol.* I, *p.* 230.

The genius of Drayton is neither very imaginative nor very pathetic; but he is an agreeable and weighty writer, with an ardent if not a highly creative, fancy. From the height to which he occasionally ascends, as well as from his power of keeping longer on the wing, he must be ranked, as he always has been, much before both Warner and Daniel. He has greatly more elevation than the former, and more true poetic life than the latter.—CRAIK, GEORGE L., 1861, *A Compendious History of English Literature and of the English Language, vol.* I, *p.* 563.

The "Polyolbion" is nothing less than a versified gazetteer of England and Wales,—fortunately Scotland was not yet annexed, or the poem would have been even longer, and already it is the plesiosaurus of verse. Mountains, rivers, and even marshes are personified, to narrate historical episodes, or to give us geographical lectures. There are two fine verses in the seventh book, where, speaking of the cutting down some noble woods, he says,—

"Their trunks like aged folk now bare and naked stand,
As for revenge to heaven each held a withered hand;"

and there is a passage about the sea in the twentieth book that comes near being fine; but the far greater part is mere joiner-work. Consider the life of man, that we flee away as a shadow, that our days are as a post, and then think whether we can afford to honor such a draft upon our time as is implied in these thirty books all in alexandrines! Even the laborious Selden, who wrote annotations on it, sometimes more entertaining than the text, gave out at the end of the eighteenth book. Yet Drayton could write well, and had an agreeable lightsomeness of fancy, as his "Nymphidia" proves.—LOWELL, JAMES RUSSELL, 1875-90, *Spenser, Prose Works, Riverside, ed. vol.* IV, *p.* 279.

Drayton's jewels five words long are of the rarest, and their sparkle when they do occur is not of the brightest or most enchanting lustre. But considering his enormous volume, he is a poet of surprisingly high merit. Although he has written some fifty or sixty thousand lines, the bulk of them on subjects not too favourable to poetical treatment, he has yet succeeded in giving to the whole an unmistakably poetical flavour, and in maintaining that flavour throughout. The variety of his work, and at the same time the unfailing touch by which he lifts that work, not indeed into the highest regions of poetry, but far above its lower confines, are his most remarkable characteristics.—SAINTSBURY, GEORGE, 1880, *English Poets, ed. Ward, vol.* I, *p.* 526.

Drayton's touch is less delicate than Daniel's, and his poetry is of a heavier character; it is dull.—STODDARD, RICHARD HENRY, 1881, *The Sonnet in English Poetry, Scribner's Monthly, vol.* 22, *p.* 910.

His poetry won him applause from many quarters. He is mentioned under the name of "Good Rowland" in Barnfield's "Affectionate Shepheard," 1594, and he is praised in company with Spenser, Daniel, and Shakespeare in Barnfield's "A Remembrance of some English Poets," 1598. Lodge dedicated to him in 1595 one of the epistles in "A Fig for Momus." In 1596 Fitzgeoffrey, in his poem on Sir Francis Drake, speaks of "golden-mouthed Drayton musicall." A very clear proof of his popularity is shown by the fact that he is quoted no less than a hundred and fifty times in "England's Parnassus," 1600. Drummond of Hawthornden was one of his fervent admirers. . . . His poetry was little to the taste of eighteenth-century critics. From a well-known passage of Goldsmith's "Citizen of the World" it would seem that his very name had passed into oblivion. Since the days of Charles Lamb and Coleridge his fame has revived, but no complete edition of his works has yet been issued.—BULLEN, A. H., 1888, *Dictionary of National Biography, vol.* XVI, *p.* 12.

Lyrical sweetness, fertility of invention, richness of descriptive power, are Drayton's most characteristic qualities, but along with these he has the great style of an heroic time. He has, perhaps, little of the dramatic gift, as usually understood, though, as Mr. Symonds has admonished us, much of the so-called dramatic work of the Elizabethans is really lyrical. Besides, Drayton had one essential of the dramatic gift: he could at least make single figures live and move before us. . . . Drayton seems to have exercised no selection upon his materials, but to have followed the chronicler almost slavishly from point to point.—LE GALLIENNE, RICHARD, 1893-95, *Retrospective Reviews, vol.* II, *pp.* 50, 52.

During the eighteenth century, at least, no non-dramatic poet of our period was so much read or so often reprinted as

Drayton. Joseph Hunter expressed no opinion shocking to his generation when he claimed for Drayton a place in the first class of English poets. His ease, correctness, and lucidity were attractive to our elder critics, and outweighed the lack of the more exquisite qualities of style. If Drayton can no longer be awarded such superlative honours as were formerly paid to him, he is nevertheless a poet of considerable originality and merit, whose greatest enemy has been his want of measure. His works form far too huge a bulk, and would be more gladly read if the imagination in them were more concentrated and the style more concise. Drayton attempted almost every variety of poetic art, and his aim was possibly a little too encyclopædic for his gifts.—GOSSE, EDMUND, 1894, *The Jacobean Poets, p.* 93.

Has left some Pastorals, so quick and airy in touch, so attractive in feeling, that it is vexing to find how completely the landscape which he saw and must have enjoyed was silenced or exiled from his poetry by the mere conventionalities of pseudo-classicalism.—PALGRAVE, FRANCIS TURNER, 1896, *Landscape in Poetry, p.* 146.

Grave-minded, with the ethical poet's fuller ambition, and touched with the new and deeper lyric feeling that utters itself most perfectly in Shakespeare's sonnets. —CARPENTER, FREDERIC IVES, 1897, *English Lyric Poetry,* 1500-1700, *Introduction, p.* xliv.

Sir Robert Cotton

1570–1631

Was a distinguished antiquary and collector of manuscripts. He assisted Camden in his labours on the "Britannia." On the accession of James I. he was knighted, and frequently consulted by the Privy Council on constitutional points. He was one of those who suggested to James I. the idea of creating baronets, and was himself raised to this rank in 1611. Sir Robert wrote numerous antiquarian tracts and pamphlets. But his chief title to remembrance is due to the magnificent manuscript library he collected, which passed to his heir intact, and was acquired by the nation in 1706. After being partly destroyed by fire in 1731, it was placed in the British Museum in 1757.—LOW AND PULLING, *eds.*, 1884, *Dictionary of English History, p.* 318.

Sir Robert Cotton was the author of various historical, political, and antiquarian works, which are now of little interest, except to men of kindred tastes. His name is remembered chiefly for the benefit which he conferred upon literature, by saving his valuable library of manuscripts from dispersion. After being considerably augmented by his son and grandson, it became, in 1706, the property of the public, and in 1757 was deposited in the British Museum. One hundred and eleven of the manuscripts, many of them highly valuable, had before this time been unfortunately destroyed by fire. —CHAMBERS, ROBERT, 1876, *Cyclopædia of English Literature, ed. Carruthers.*

His collection of coins and medals was one of the earliest. Very many languages were represented in his library. His rich collection of Saxon charters proved the foundation of the scholarly study of pre-Norman-English history, and his Hebrew and Greek manuscripts greatly advanced biblical criticism. Original authorities for every period of English history were in his possession. His reputation was European. De Thou was one of his warmest admirers, and Gruterus, in his edition of Cicero, describes him as one of the most learned men of the age. Duchesne, Bourdelet, Puteanus all acknowledged obligations to him. Bishop Montague calls him "the magazine of history," and among his own countrymen, besides Camden, Speed, Selden, and Raleigh, . . . Spelman, Dugdale, Sir Henry Savile, Knolles, Gale, Burnet, Strype, and Rymer, the compiler of the "Fœdera," all drew largely on his collections. Cotton wrote nothing that adequately represented his learning, and it is to be regretted that he did not concentrate his attention on some great historical work. His English style is readable, although not distinctive, and his power of research was inexhaustible. —LEE, SIDNEY, 1887, *Dictionary of National Biography, vol.* XII, *p.* 312.

John Donne

1573–1631

Born, in London, 1573. Privately educated. Matric. Hart Hall, Oxford, 23 Oct. 1584. Took no degree. Probably travelled abroad, 1588-91. Admitted to Lincoln's Inn, 6 May 1592. With Earl of Essex to Cadiz, June 1596. Secretary to Sir Thomas Egerton, Aug. 1596 to 1601. Wrote many poems and satires. Married secretly Anne More, niece of Lady Egerton, Dec. [?] 1600. Dismissed from secretaryship when marriage was discovered. Lived at a friend's house at Pyrford till 1604; then with brother-in-law, Sir Thomas Grymes, at Peckham; and subsequently lived at Mitcham. Gradually obtained favour at Court of James I. Degree of M. A., Oxford, conferred, 10 Oct. 1610. To Germany, France and Belgium with Sir Robert Drury, Nov. 1611 to Aug. 1612. Studied theology. Ordained, Jan. 1615, and appointed Chaplain to King. Degree of D. D., Cambridge, granted at King's request, March 1615. Rector of Keyston, Hants, Jan. 1616; of Sevenoaks, July 1616. Divinity Reader to Lincoln's Inn, Oct. 1616 to Feb. 1622. Wife died, 15 Aug. 1617. To Germany with Lord Doncaster, as Chaplain, April 1619. Dean of St. Paul's, 27 Nov. 1621. Prolocutor to Convocation, 1623 and 1624. Rector of Blunham, Beds, 1622; Vicar of St. Dunstan's-in-the-West, 1623. Died, in London, 31 March 1631. Buried in St. Paul's Cathedral. *Works:* "Pseudo-Martyr," 1610; "Conclave Ignatii," 1610 [?] (only two copies known); an English version of preceding, "Ignatius his Conclave" (anon.), 1611; "An Anatomy of the World" (anon.), 1611; "The Progress of the Soule" (anon.), 1621; "A Sermon" [on Judges xx. 15], 1622; "A Sermon" [on Acts i. 8], 1622; "Encænia," 1623; "Devotions upon Urgent Occasions," 1624 (2nd edn. same year); "The first Sermon preached to King Charles," 1625; "A Sermon preached to the King's M^tie," 1626; "Four Sermons," 1625; "A Sermon of Commemoration of the Lady Dāvers," 1627; "Death's Duell," 1630. *Posthumous:* "Poems by J. D.," 1633; "Juvenilia," 1633; "Six Sermons," 1634; "LXXX Sermons," 1640; "βιαθανατος," 1644; "Poems," 1649; "Fifty Sermons," 1649; "Essays in Divinity," 1651; "Letters to Several Persons of Honour," 1651; "Paradoxes, Problemes, Essayes, etc.," 1652; "Fasciculus Poematum" (mostly spurious), 1652; "Six and twenty Sermons," 1660; "A Collection of Letters," 1660; "Donne's Satyr," 1662. *Collected Works:* "Poetical Works," ed. by Izaak Walton (3 vols.), 1779;(?) "Poems," ed. by Hannah, 1843; "Unpublished Poems," ed. by Sir John Simeon, [1856]; "Poems," ed. by Sir John Simeon, 1858; "Works," ed. by Alford, 1839; "Poems," ed. by Grosart (2 vols.), 1872-73. *Life:* by Walton, ed. by Causton, 1855.—Sharp, R. Farquharson, 1897, *A Dictionary of English Authors*, p. 84.

PERSONAL

JOHANNES DONNE,
Sac. Theol. Profess.
Post Varia Studia, Quibus Ab Annis
Tenerrimis Fideliter, Nec Infeliciter
Incubuit;
Instinctu Et Impulsu Sp. Sancti, Monitu
Et Hortatu
Regis Jacobi, Ordines Sacros Amplexus,
Anno Sui Jesu, MDCXIV. Et Suæ Ætatis
XLII.
Decanatu Hujus Ecclesiæ Indutus,
XXVII. Novembris, MDCXXI
Exutus Morte Ultimo Die Martii,
MDCXXXI.
Hic Licet In Occiduo Cinere, Aspicit Eum
Cujus Nomen Est Oriens.

—*Inscription on Monument.*

To have liv'd eminent, in a degree
Beyond our lofti'st flights, that is, like Thee
Or t' have had too much merit, is not safe;
For such excesses find no Epitaph.
At common graves we have Poetic eyes
Can melt themselves in easy Elegies. . . .
But at Thine, Poem, or Inscription
(Rich soul of wit, and language) we have
none.
Indeed, a silence does that tomb befit,
Where is no Herald left to blazon it.

—King, Henry, 1631? *To the Memory of My Ever desired Friend Doctor Donne.*

He was of stature moderately tall; of a straight and equally-proportioned body, to which all his words and actions gave an unexpressible addition of comeliness. The mleancholy and pleasant humour were in him so contempered, that each gave advantage to the other, and made his company one of the delights of mankind. His fancy was unimitably high, equalled only by his great wit; both being made useful by a commanding judgment. His aspect was cheerful, and such as gave a

JOHN DONNE

From a Portrait ascribed to Cornelius Jansen, in the Dyce Collection, South Kensington Museum.

JOHN FOXE

From Engraving from The Acts and Monuments of the Church.

THOMAS SACKVILLE

From Lodge's Portraits of Illustrious Personages.

silent testimony of a clear knowing soul, and of a conscience at peace with itself. His melting eye shewed that he had a soft heart, full of noble compassion; of too brave a soul to offer injuries, and too much a Christian not to pardon them in others. . . . He was by nature highly passionate, but more apt to reluct at the excesses of it. A great lover of the offices of humanity, and of so merciful a spirit, that he never beheld the miseries of mankind without pity and relief.—WALTON, IZAAK, 1639, *The Life of Dr. John Donne.*

Mr. John Dunne, who leaving Oxford, lived at the Innes of Court, not dissolute, but very neat; a great Visitor of Ladies, a great frequenter of Playes, a great writer of conceited Verses; until such times as King James taking notice of the pregnancy of his Wit, was a means that he betook him to the study of Divinity, and thereupon proceeding Doctor, was made Dean of Pauls; and became so rare a Preacher, that he was not only commended, but even admired by all who heard him. —BAKER, SIR RICHARD, 1641, *A Chronicle of the Kings of England.*

This is that Dr. Donne, born in London, (but extracted from Wales,) by his mother's side, great great-grandchild to Sir Thomas More, whom he much resembled in his endowments; a great traveller; first, secretary to the lord Egerton, and after, by the persuasion of king James and encouragement of bishop Morton, entered into Orders, made doctor of divinity, (of Trinity College in Cambridge,) and dean of St. Paul's.—FULLER, THOMAS, 1655, *The Church History of Britain, vol.* III, *bk.* X, *par.* 17, *p.* 324.

Dr. Donne, . . . a laureate wit; neither was it impossible that a vulgar soul should dwell in such promising features.—HACKET, JOHN, 1693, *Life of Archbishop Williams,* § 74.

The life of Donne is more interesting than his poetry.—CAMPBELL, THOMAS, 1819, *Specimens of the British Poets.*

Dr. Donne, once so celebrated as a writer, now so neglected, is more interesting for his matrimonial history, and for one little poem addressed to his wife, than for all his learned, metaphysical, and theological productions. —JAMESON, ANNA BROWNELL, 1829, *The Loves of the Poets, vol.* II, *p.* 94.

The knowledge of Donne's immense learning, the subtlety and capacity of his intellect, the intense depth and wide scope of his thought, the charm of his conversation, the sadness of his life, gave a vivid meaning and interest to his poems . . . circulated among his acquaintances, which at this distance of time we cannot reach without a certain effort of imagination. . . . Dr. Donne is one of the most interesting personalities among our men of letters. The superficial facts of his life are so incongruous as to be an irresistible provocation to inquiry. What are we to make of the fact that the founder of a licentious school of erotic poetry, a man acknowledged to be the greatest wit in a licentious Court, with an early bias in matters of religion towards Roman Catholicism, entered the Church of England when he was past middle age and is now numbered among its greatest divines? Was he a convert like St. Augustine, or an indifferent worldling like Talleyrand? Superficial appearances are rather in favour of the latter supposition. —MINTO, WILLIAM, 1880, *John Donne, The Nineteenth Century, vol* 7, *p.* 849.

Against the wall of the south choir aisle in the Cathedral of St. Paul is a monument which very few of the thousands who visit the church daily observe, or have an opportunity of observing, but which, once seen, is not easily forgotten. It is the long, gaunt, upright figure of a man, wrapped close in a shroud, which is knotted at the head and feet, and leaves only the face exposed—a face wan, worn, almost ghastly, with eyes closed as in death. This figure is executed in white marble, and stands on an urn of the same, as if it had just arisen therefrom. The whole is placed in a black niche, which, by its contrast, enhances the death-like paleness of the shrouded figure. Above the canopy is an inscription recording that the man whose effigy stands beneath, though his ashes are mingled with western dust, looks towards Him whose name is the Orient. . . . It was not such a memorial as Donne's surviving friends might think suitable to commemorate the deceased, but it was the very monument which Donne himself designed as a true emblem of his past life and his future hopes.—LIGHTFOOT, J. B., 1895, *Historical Essays, pp.* 221, 223.

His graceful person, vivacity of conversation, and many accomplishments secured for him the *entrée* at the houses of the nobility and a recognised position among the celebrities of Queen Elizabeth's court. He was conspicuous as a young man of fortune who spent his money freely, and mixed on equal terms with the courtiers, and probably had the character of being richer than he was. . . . The young man, among his other gifts, had the great advantage of being able to do with very little sleep. He could read all night and be gay and wakeful and alert all day. He threw himself into the amusements and frivolities of the court with all the glee of youth, but never so as to interfere with his duties. The favourite of fortune, he was too the favourite of the fortunate—the envy of some, he was the darling of more. Those of his contemporaries who knew him intimately speak of him at all times as if there was none like him; the charm of his person and manners were irresistible. He must have had much love to give, or he could never had so much bestowed upon him.—JESSOPP, AUGUSTUS, 1897, *John Donne, Sometime Dean of St. Paul's, pp.* 13, 18.

History presents us with no instance of a man of letters more obviously led up to by the experience and character of his ancestors than was John Donne. As we have him revealed to us, he is what a genealogist might wish him to be. Every salient feature in his mind and temperament is foreshadowed by the general trend of his family, or by the idiosyncrasy of some individual member of it. . . . The greatest preacher of his age. . . . No one, in the history of English literature, as it seems to me, is so difficult to realise, so impossible to measure, in the vast curves of his extraordinary and contradictory features. Of his life, of his experiences, of his opinions, we know more now than it has been vouchsafed to us to know of any other of the great Elizabethan and Jacobean galaxy of writers, and yet how little we fathom his contradictions, how little we can account for his impulses and his limitations. Even those of us who have for years made his least adventures the subject of close and eager investigation must admit at last that he eludes us. He was not the crystal-hearted saint that Walton adored and exalted. He was not the crafty and redoubtable courtier whom the recusants suspected. He was not the prophet of the intricacies of fleshly feeling whom the young poets looked up to and worshipped. He was none of these, or all of these, or more. What was he? It is impossible to say, for, with all his superficial expansion, his secret died with him. We are tempted to declare that of all great men he is the one of whom least is essentially known. Is not this, perhaps, the secret of his perennial fascination?—GOSSE, EDMUND, 1899, *The Life and Letters of John Donne. vol.* I, *pp.* 3, 11, *vol.* II, *p.* 290.

SERMONS

A preacher in earnest; weeping sometimes for his auditory, sometimes with them; always preaching to himself, like an angel from a cloud, but in none; carrying some, as St. Paul was, to heaven in holy raptures; and enticing others by a sacred art and courtship to amend their lives: here picturing a Vice so as to make it ugly to those that practised it; and a Virtue so as to make it beloved, even by those who loved it not; and all this with a most particular grace and an unexpressible addition of comeliness.—WALTON, IZAAK, 1639, *The Life of Dr. John Donne.*

The sermons of Donne have sometimes been praised in late times. They are undoubtedly the productions of a very ingenious and a very learned man; and two folio volumes by such a person may be expected to supply favorable specimens. In their general character, they will not appear, I think, much worthy of being rescued from oblivion. The subtility of Donne, and his fondness for such inconclusive reasoning as a subtle disputant is apt to fall into, runs through all of these sermons at which I have looked. His learning he seems to have perverted in order to cull every impertinence of the fathers and schoolmen, their remote analogies, their strained allegories, their technical distinctions; and to these he has added much of a similar kind from his own fanciful understanding.—HALLAM, HENRY, 1837-39, *Introduction to the Literature of Europe, pt.* iii, *ch.* ii, *par.* 70.

Donne's published sermons are in form nearly as grotesque as his poems, though they are characterized by profounder qualities of heart and mind. It was his misfortune to know thoroughly the works of fourteen hundred writers, most of them necessarily worthless; and he could not help displaying his erudition in his discourses. Of what is now called taste he was absolutely destitute. His sermons are a curious mosaic of quaintness, quotation, wisdom, puerility, subtilty, and ecstasy. The pedant and the seer possess him by turns, and in reading no other divine are our transitions from yawning to rapture so swift and unexpected. He has passages of transcendent merit, passages which evince a spiritual vision so piercing, and a feeling of divine things so intense, that for the time we seem to be communing with a religious genius of the most exalted and exalting order; but soon he involves us in a maze of quotations and references, and our minds are hustled by what Hallam calls "the rabble of bad authors" that this saint and sage has always at his skirts, even when he ascends to the highest heaven of contemplation.—WHIPPLE, EDWIN P., 1859-68, *The Literature of the Age of Elizabeth, p.* 237.

The sermons of Donne, while they are superior in style, are sometimes fantastic, like his poetry, but they are never coarse, and they derive a touching interest from his history.—BOTTA, ANNE C. LYNCH, 1860, *Hand-Book of Universal Literature, p.* 476.

In Donne's sermons, an intellectual epicure not too fastidious to read sermons will find a delicious feast. Whether these sermons can be taken as patterns by the modern preacher is another affair. It will not be contended that any congregation is equal to the effort of following his subtleties. In short, as exercises in abstract subtlety, fanciful ingenuity, and scholarship, the sermons are admirable. Judged by the first rule of popular exposition, the style is bad—a bewildering maze to the ordinary reader, much more to the ordinary hearer.—MINTO, WILLIAM, 1872-80, *Manual of English Prose Literature, p.* 253.

During this year, 1622, Donne's first printed sermon appeared. It was delivered at Paul's Cross on 15 Sept. to an enormous congregation, in obedience to the king's commands, who had just issued his "Directions to Preachers," and had made choice of the dean of St. Paul's to explain his reasons for issuing the injunctions. The sermon was at once printed; copies of the original edition are rarely met with. Two months later Donne preached his glorious sermon before the Virginian Company. . . . Donne's Sermon struck a note in full sympathy with the larger views and nobler aims of the minority. His sermon may be truly described as the first missionary sermon printed in the English language. The original edition was at once absorbed. The same is true of every other sermon printed during Donne's lifetime; in their original shape they are extremely scarce. The truth is that as a preacher at this time Donne stood almost alone. Andrewes's preaching days were over (he died in September 1626), Hall never carried with him the conviction of being much more than a consummate gladiator, and was rarely heard in London; of the rest there was hardly one who was not either ponderously learned like Sanderson, or a mere performer like the rank and file of rhetoricians who came up to London to air their eloquences at Paul's Cross. The result was that Donne's popularity was always on the increase, he rose to every occasion, and surprised his friends, as Walton tells us, by the growth of his genius and earnestness even to the end—JESSOPP, AUGUSTUS, 1888, *Dictionary of National Biography, vol.* XV, *p.* 229.

GENERAL

One thing more I must tell you; but so softly, that I am loth to hear myself: and so softly, that if that good lady were in the room, with you and this letter, she might not hear. It is, that I am brought to a necessity of printing my poems, and addressing them to my Lord Chamberlain. This I mean to do forthwith; not for much public view, but at mine own cost, a few copies. I apprehend some incongruities in the resolution; and I know what I shall suffer from many interpretations; but I am at an end, of much considering that; and, if I were as startling in that kind, as I ever was, yet in this particular, I am under an unescapable necessity, as I shall let you perceive when I see you. By this occasion I am made a rhapsodist of mine own rags, and that cost me more diligence, to seek them, than it did to make them. This made me ask to borrow that old book of you, which it will be too late to see, for that use, when I see you; for I must do this as a valediction to the world, before I take orders. But this is it, I am to ask you: whether you ever made any such use of the letter in verse, *à nostre comtesse chez vous*, as that I may not put it in, amongst the rest to persons of that rank; for I desire it very much, that something should bear her name in the book, and I would be just to my written words to my Lord Harrington to write nothing after that. I pray tell me as soon as you can, if I be at liberty to insert that: for if you have by any occasion applied any pieces to it, I see not, that it will be discerned, when it appears in the whole piece. Though this be a little matter, I would be sorry not to have an account of it, within as little after New Year's-tide, as you could.—DONNE, JOHN, 1614, *Letter to Sir Henry Goodyere, Dec.* 20, *Alford, vol.* VI, *p.* 367.

Donne, the delight of Phœbus and each Muse,
Who, to thy one, all other brains refuse;
Whose every work of thy most early wit
Came forth example, and remains so yet;
Longer a-knowing than most wits do live,
And which no affection praise enough can give!
To it, thy language, letters, arts, best life,
Which might with half mankind maintain a strife;
All which I meant to praise, and yet I would;
But leave, because I cannot as I should!
—JONSON, BEN, 1616, *To John Donne.*

That Done's Anniversarie was profane and full of blasphemies: that he told Mr. Done, if it had been written of the Virgin Marie it had been something; to which he answered, that he described the Idea of a Woman, and not as she was. That Done, for not keeping of accent, deserved hanging. . . . He esteemeth John Done the first poet in the world in some things: his verses of the "Lost Chaine" he heth by heart; and that passage of the "Calme," *That dust and feathers doe not stirr, all was so quiet.* Affirmeth Done to have written all his best pieces ere he was 25 years old.—DRUMMOND, WILLIAM, 1619, *Notes on Ben Jonson's Conversations.*

The Muses' garden, with pedantic weeds
O'erspread, was purg'd by thee, the lazie seeds
Of servile imitation throwne away,
And fresh invention planted; thou didst pay
The debts of our penurious banquerout age:
. . . . . . whatsoever wrong
By ours was done the Greek or Latin tongue,
Thou hast redeem'd, and opened as a mine
Of rich and pregnant fancie . . .
. . . to the awe of thy imperious wit
Our troublesome language bends, made only fit,
With her tough thick-rib'd hoopes, to gird about
Thy gyant fancy.
—CAREW, THOMAS, 1631? *An Elegie upon the Death of Doctor Donne, Works, ed. Hazlitt, pp.* 93, 94.

. . . all the softnesses,
The Shadow, Light, the Air, and Life, of Love;
The Sharpness of all Wit; ev'n bitterness
Makes Satire Sweet; all wit did God improve,
'Twas flamed in him, 'Twas but warm upon
His Embers; He was more; and it is Donne.
—DANIEL GEORGE, 1647, *A Vindication of Poesy.*

Would not Donne's satires, which abound with so much wit, appear more charming, if he had taken care of his words, and of his numbers? But he followed Horace so very close, that of necessity he must fall with him; and I may safely say it of this present age, that if we are not so great wits as Donne, yet, certainly, we are better poets.—DRYDEN, JOHN, 1692, *Essay on Satire, Works ed. Scott and Saintsbury, vol.* XIII, *p.* 109.

If it be true that the purport of poetry should be to please, no author has written with such utter neglect of the rule. It is scarce possible for a human ear to endure the dissonance and discord of his couplets, and even when his thoughts are clothed in the melody of Pope, they appear to me hardly worth the decoration.—DRAKE, NATHAN 1798, *Literary Hours, No.* XXVIII.

Donne had not music enough to render his broken rhyming couplets sufferable, and neither his wit, nor his pointed satire, were sufficient to rescue him from that neglect which his uncouth and rugged versification speedily superinduced.—WHITE, HENRY KIRKE, 1806, *Melancholy Hours, Remains, ed. Southey, vol.* II, *p.* 286.

Since Dryden, the metre of our poets leads to the sense: in our elder and more genuine bards, the sense, including the passion, leads to the metre. Read even Donne's satires as he meant them to be read, and as the sense and passion demand, and you will find in the lines a manly harmony.—COLERIDGE, SAMUEL TAYLOR, 1818, *Notes on Beaumont and Fletcher, ed. Ashe, p.* 427.

Nothing could have made Donne a poet, unless as great a change had been worked in the internal structure of his ears, as was wrought in elongating those of Midas. —SOUTHEY, ROBERT, 1807, *Specimens of the Later English Poets, vol.* I, *p.* xxiv.

Donne was the "best good-natured man, with the worst natured Muse." Aromantic and uxorious lover, he addresses the object of his real tenderness with ideas that outrage decorum. He begins his own epithalamium with most indelicate invocation to his bride. His ruggedness and whim are almost proverbially known. Yet there is a beauty of thought which at intervals rises from his chaotic imagination, like the form of Venus smiling on the waters. —CAMPBELL, THOMAS, 1819. *An Essay on English Poetry.*

Donne is the most inharmonious of our versifiers, if he can be said to have deserved such a name by lines too rugged to seem metre. Of his earlier poems, many are very licentious; the later are chiefly devout. Few are good for much; the conceits have not even the merit of being intelligible: it would perhaps be difficult to select three passages that we should care to read again.—HALLAM, HENRY, 1837-39, *Introduction to the Literature of Europe, pt.* iii, *ch.* v, *par.* 39.

Having a dumb angel, and knowing more noble poetry than he articulates.—BROWNING, ELIZABETH BARRETT, 1842-63, *The Book of the Poets, vol,* II, *p.* 50.

With verses gnarl'd and knotted, hobbled on.
—LANDOR, WALTER SAVAGE, 1846, *Satirists.*

Of stubborn thoughts a garland thought to twine;
To his fair Maid brought cabalistic posies,
And sung quaint ditties of metempsychosis;
"Twists iron pokers into true love-knots,"
Coining hard words, not found in polyglots,
—COLERIDGE, HARTLEY, 1849, *Donne, Sketches of English Poets, Poems, vol.* II, *p.* 295.

With vast learning, with subtile and penetrating intellect, with a fancy singularly fruitful and ingenious, he still contrived to disconnect, more or less, his learning from what was worth learning, his intellect from what was reasonable, his fancy from what was beautiful. His poems, or rather his metrical problems, are obscure in thought, rugged in versification, and full of conceits which are intended to surprise rather than to please; but they still exhibit a power of intellect, both analytical and analogical, competent at once to separate the minutest and connect the remotest ideas. This power, while it might not have given his poems grace, sweetness, freshness, and melody, would still, if properly directed, have made them valuable for their thoughts; but in the case of Donne it is perverted to the production of what is *bizarre* or unnatural, and his muse is thus as hostile to use as to beauty. The intention is, not to idealize what is true, but to display the writer's skill and wit in giving a show of reason to what is false. The effect of this on the moral charcter of Donne was pernicious. A subtile intellectual scepticism, which weakened will, divorced thought from action and literature from life, and made existence a puzzle and a dream, resulted from this perversion of his intellect. He found that he could wittily justify what was vicious as well as what was unnatural; and his amatory poems, accordingly, are characterized by a cold, hard, labored, intellectualized sensuality, worse than the worst impurity of his contemporaries, because it has no excuse of passion for its violations of decency.—WHIPPLE, EDWIN P., 1859-68, *The Literature of the Age of Elizabeth, p.* 231.

Donne, altogether, gives us the impression of a great genius ruined by a false system. He is a charioteer run away with by his own pampered steeds. He begins generally well, but long ere the close, quibbles, conceits, and the temptation of shewing off recondite learning, prove too strong for him, and he who commenced following a serene star, ends pursuing a will-o'-wisp into a bottomless morass. Compare, for instance, the ingenious nonsense which abounds in the middle and the close of his "Progress of the Soul" with the dark, but magnificent stanzas which are the first in the poem. In no writings in the language is there more spilt treasure—a more lavish loss of beautiful, original, and striking things than in the poems of Donne.—GILFILLAN, GEORGE, 1860, *Specimens with Memoirs of the Less-Known British Poets, vol.* I, *p.* 203.

On a superficial inspection, Donne's verses look like so many riddles. They seem to be written upon the principle of making the meaning as difficult to be found out as possible,—of using all the resources of language, not to express thought, but to conceal it. Nothing is said in a direct, natural manner; conceit follows conceit without intermission; the most remote analogies, the most far-fetched images, the most unexpected turns, one after another, surprise and often puzzle the understanding; while things of the most opposite kinds—the harsh and the harmonious, the graceful and the grotesque, the grave and the gay, the pious and the profane—meet and mingle in the strangest of dances. But, running through all this bewilderment, a deeper insight detects not only a vein of the most exuberant wit, but often the sunniest and most delicate fancy, and the truest tenderness and depth of feeling.—CRAIK, GEORGE L., 1861, *A Compendious History of English Literature and of the English Language, vol.* I, *p.* 579.

There is indeed much in Donne, in the unfolding of his moral and spiritual life, which often reminds us of St. Augustine. I do not mean that, noteworthy as on many accounts he was, and in the language of Carew, one of his contemporaries,

"A king who ruled as he thought fit
The universal monarchy of wit."

he at all approached in intellectual or spiritual stature to the great Doctor of the Western Church. But still there was in Donne the same tumultuous youth, the same final deliverance from them; and then the same passionate and personal grasp of the central truths of Christianity, linking itself as this did with all that he had suffered, and all that he had sinned, and all through which by God's grace he had victoriously struggled.—TRENCH, RICHARD CHENEVIX, 1868, *A Household Book of English Poetry, p.* 403.

The central thought of Dr. Donne is nearly sure to be just: the subordinate thoughts by means of which he unfolds it are often grotesque, and so wildly associated as to remind one of the lawlessness of a dream, wherein mere suggestion without choice or fitness rules the sequence. As some of the writers of whom I have last spoken would play with words, Dr. Donne would sport with ideas, and with the visual images or embodiments of them. Certainly in his case much knowledge reveals itself in the association of his ideas, and great facility in the management and utterance of them. True likewise, he says nothing unrelated to the main idea of the poem; but not the less certainly does the whole resemble the speech of a child of active imagination, to whom judgment as to the character of his suggestions is impossible, his taste being equally gratified with a lovely image and a brilliant absurdity: a butterfly and a shining potsherd are to him similarly desirable. Whatever wild thing starts from the thicket of thought, all is worthy game to the hunting intellect of Dr. Donne, and is followed without question of tone, keeping, or harmony. In his play with words, Sir Philip Sidney kept good heed that even that should serve the end in view; in his play with ideas, Dr. John Donne, so far from serving the end, sometimes obscures it almost hopelessly: the hart escapes while he follows the squirrels and weasels and bats. It is not surprising that, their author being so inartistic with regard to their object, his verses themselves should be harsh and unmusical beyond the worse that one would imagine fit to be called verse. He enjoys the unenviable distinction of having no rival in ruggedness of metric movement and associated sounds. This is clearly the result of indifference; and indifference, however, which grows very strange to us when we find that he *can* write a lovely verse and even an exquisite stanza.—MACDONALD, GEORGE, 1868, *England's Antiphon, p.* 114.

A pungent satirist, of terrible crudeness, a powerful poet, of a precise and intense imagination, who still preserves something of the energy and thrill of the original inspiration. But he deliberately abuses all these gifts, and succeeds with great difficulty in concocting a piece of nonsense. . . . Twenty times while reading him we rub our brow, and ask with astonishment, how a man could so have tormented and contorted himself, strained his style, refined on his refinement, hit upon such absurd comparisons?—TAINE, H. A., 1871, *History of English Literature, tr. Van Laun, vol.* I, *bk.* ii, *ch.* i, *pp.* 203, 204.

His reputation as a poet, great in his own day, low during the latter part of the seventeenth and the whole of the eighteenth centuries, has latterly revived. In its days of abasement, critics spoke of his harsh and rugged versification, and his leaving nature for conceit. It seems to be now acknowledged that, amidst much bad taste, there is much real poetry, and that of a high order, in Donne.—CHAMBERS, ROBERT, 1876, *Cyclopœdia of English Literature, ed. Carruthers.*

Better and truer verse none ever wrote . . .
Than thou, revered and magisterial Donne!
—BROWNING, ROBERT, 1878, *The Two Poets of Croisic.*

Donne's contemporary reputation as a poet, and still more as a preacher, was immense; and a glance at his works would suffice to show that he did not deserve the contempt with which he was subsequently treated. But yet his chief interest is that he was the principal founder of a school which especially expressed and represented a certain bad taste of his day. Of his genius there can be no question; but it was perversely directed. One may almost invert Jonson's famous panegyric on Shakespeare, and say that Donne was not for all time but for an age. . . . His natural gifts were certainly great. He possesses a real energy and fervour. He loved, and he suffered much, and he writes with a passion which is perceptible through all his artificialities.—HALES, JOHN W., 1880, *English Poets, ed. Ward, vol.* I, *pp.* 558, 560.

We find little to admire, and nothing to love. We see that farfetched similes, extravagant metaphors, are not here occasional blemishes, but the substance. He should have given us simple images, simply expressed; for he loved and suffered much: but fashion was stronger than nature.—WELSH, ALFRED, 1882, *Development of English Literature and Language, vol.* I, *p.* 413.

Donne's poems were first collected in 1633: they cover an extraordinary range in subject, and are throughout marked with a strange originality almost equally fascinating and repellent. It is possible that his familiarity with Italian and Spanish literatures, both at that time deeply coloured by fantastic and far-fetched thought, may have in some degree influenced him in that direction. His poems were probably written mainly during youth. There is a strange solemn passionate earnestness about them, a quality which underlies the fanciful "conceits" of all his work.—PALGRAVE, FRANCIS T., 1889, *The Treasury of Sacred Song, note, p.* 333.

In him the Jacobean spirit, as opposed to the Elizabethan, is paramount. His were the first poems which protested, in their form alike and their tendency, against the pastoral sweetness of the Spenserians. Something new in English literature begins in Donne, something which proceeded, under his potent influence, to colour poetry for nearly a hundred years. The exact mode in which that influence was immediately distributed is unknown to us, or very dimly perceived. To know more about it is one of the great desiderata of literary history. The imitation of Donne's style begins so early, and becomes so general, that several critics have taken for granted that there must have been editions of his writings which have disappeared. . . . The style of Donne, like a very odd perfume, was found to cling to every one who touched it, and we observe the remarkable phenomenon of poems which had not passed through a printer's hands exercising the influence of a body of accepted classical work. In estimating the poetry of the Jacobean age, therefore, there is no writer who demands more careful study than this enigmatical and subterranean master, this veiled Isis whose utterances outweigh the oracles of all the visible gods.—GOSSE, EDMUND, 1894, *The Jacobean Poets, pp.* 47, 48.

After he had taken holy orders Donne seldom threw his passions into verse; even his "Divine Poems" are, with few exceptions, of early date; the poet in Donne did not cease to exist, but his ardour, his imagination, his delight in what is strange and wonderful, his tenderness, his tears, his smiles, his erudition, his intellectual ingenuities, were all placed at the service of one whose desire was that he might die in the pulpit, or if not die, that he might take his death in the pulpit, a desire which was in fact fulfilled. . . . Donne as a poet is certainly difficult of access. . . . He sometimes wrote best, or thought he wrote best, when his themes were wholly of the imagination. Still it is evident that Donne, the student, the recluse, the speculator on recondite problems, was also a man who adventured in pursuit of violent delights which had violent ends. . . . In whatever sunny garden, and at whatever banquet Donne sits, he discerns in air the dark Scythesman of that great picture attributed to Orcagna. An entire section of his poetry is assigned to death.—DOWDEN, EDWARD, 1895, *New Studies in Literature, pp.* 90, 91, 107, 117.

As in the case of the pastoral fashion, there were other currents of lyrical production, less directed by the conventionalities of the moment. Spenser aside, whose elaborated state does not lend itself readily to the shorter lyric, and whose singing robes are stiff with tissue of gold, wrought work, and gems inlaid, and Shakespeare, also, whose non-dramatic Muse is dedicated to thoughtful sonnet and mournful threnody, as well as to the sprightlier melodies of love, wine, and merriment, the most important poetical influence of this decade is that of that grave and marvelous man, Dr. John Donne. I would respectfully invite the attention of those who still persist with Dr. Johnson in regarding this great poet as the founder of a certain "Metaphysical School of Poetry," a man all but contemporary with Cowley, and a writer harsh, obscure, and incomprehensible in his diction, first to an examination of facts which are within the reach of all, and, secondly, to an honest study of his works. . . . Just as Shakespeare touched life and man at all points, and, absorbing the light of his time, gave it forth a hundredfold, so Donne, withdrawn almost wholly from the influences affecting his contemporaries, shone and glowed with a strange light all his own. . . . It seems to me that no one, excepting Shakespeare, with Sidney, Greville, and Jonson in lesser measure, has done so much to develop intellectualized emotion in the Elizabethan lyric as John Donne.—SCHELLING, FELIX E., 1895, *A Book of Elizabethan Lyrics, pp.* xxi, xxii, xxiii.

There is hardly any, perhaps indeed there is not any, English author on whom it is so hard to keep the just mixture of personal appreciation and critical measure as it is on John Donne. It is almost necessary that those who do not like him should not like him at all; should be scarcely able to see how any decent and intelligent human creature can like him. It is almost as necessary that those who do like him should either like him so much as to speak unadvisedly with their lips, or else curb and restrain the expression of their love for fear that it should seem on that side idolatry. But these are not the only dangers. Donne is eminently of that kind which lends itself to sham liking, to coterie worship, to a false enthusiasm; and here is another weapon in the hands of the infidels, and another stumbling-block for the feet of the true believers. . . . In Donne's case the yea-nay fashion of censorship which is necessary and desirable in the case of others is quite superfluous. His faults are so gross, so open, so palpable, that they hardly require the usual amount of critical comment and condemnation. But this very peculiarity of theirs constantly obscures his beauties even to not unfit readers. They open him; they are shocked, or bored, or irritated, or puzzled by his occasional nastiness (for he is now and then simply and inexcusably nasty), his frequent involution and eccentricity, his not quite rare indulgence in extravagances which go near to silliness; and so they lose the extraordinary beauties which lie beyond or among these faults. . . . For those who have experienced, or who at least understand, the ups-and-downs, the ins-and-outs of human temperament, the alternations not merely of passion and satiety, but of passion and laughter, of passion and melancholy reflection, of passion earthly enough and spiritual rapture almost heavenly, there is no poet and hardly any writer like Donne. —SAINTSBURY, GEORGE, 1896, *Poems of John Donne, Introduction, vol.* I, *pp.* xi, xxxi, xxxii.

"The Will of John Donne" is probably the wittiest and the bitterest lyric in our language. Donne's love passages and their record in verse were over before the author was of age. His wit then turned into metaphysical sermon-writing and theological polemics, and his bitterness into a despairing austerity.—CRAWFURD, OSWALD, 1896, *Lyrical Verse from Elizabeth to Victoria, p.* 426.

Donne is a thoroughly original spirit and a great innovator; he is thoughtful, indirect, and strange; he nurses his fancies, lives with them, and broods over them so much that they are still modern in all their distinction and ardour, in spite of the strangeness of their apparel—a strangeness no greater perhaps than that of some modern poets, like Browning, as the apparel of their verse will appear two hundred years hence. Ingenuity, allusiveness, the evocation of remote images and of analogies that startle the mind into a more than half acquiescence, phantoms of deep thoughts, and emotions half-sophisticated and wholly intense: these things mark the poetry of Donne. His lyric is original and taking, but it lacks simple thoughts; it does not sing. It is ascetic and sometimes austere; the sense of sin, the staple of contemporary tragedy, enters the lyric with Donne. He is all for terseness and meaning; and his versification accords with his thought and is equally elliptical.—CARPENTER, FREDERIC IVES, 1897, *English Lyric Poetry*, 1500-1700, *Introduction, p.* lviii.

One of the most enigmatical and debated, alternately one of the most attractive and most repellent, figures in English literature.—HANNAY, DAVID, 1898, *The Later Renaissance, p.* 220.

In one way he has partly become obsolete because he belonged so completely to the dying epoch. The scholasticism in which his mind was steeped was to become hateful and then contemptible to the rising philosophy; the literature which he had assimilated went to the dust-heaps; preachers condescended to drop their doctorial robes; downright common-sense came in with Tillotson and South in the next generation; and not only the learning but the congenial habit of thought became unintelligible. Donne's poetical creed went the same way, and if Pope and Parnell perceived that there was some genuine ore in his verses and tried to beat it into the coinage of their own day, they only spoilt it in trying to polish it. But on the other side, Donne's depth of feeling, whether tortured into short lyrics or expanding into voluble rhetoric, has a charm which perhaps gains a new charm from modern sentimentalists. His morbid or "neurotic" constitution has a real affinity for latter-day pessimists. If they talk philosophy where he had to be content with scholastic theology the substance is pretty much the same. He has the characteristic love for getting pungency at any price; for dwelling upon the horrible till we cannot say whether it attracts or repels him; and can love the "intense" and supersublimated as much as if he were skilled in all the latest æsthetic canons. —STEPHEN, LESLIE, 1899, *John Donne, The National Review, vol.* 34, *p.* 613.

Was the mind of the dialectician, of the intellectual adventurer; he is a poet almost by accident, or at least for reasons with which art in the abstract has but little to do. He writes verse, first of all, because he has observed keenly, and because it pleases the pride of his intellect to satirise the pretensions of humanity. Then it is the flesh which speaks in his verse, the curiosity of woman, which he has explored in the same spirit of adventure; then passion, making a slave of him for love's sake, and turning at last to the slave's hatred; finally, religion, taken up with the same intellectual interest, the same subtle indifference, and, in its turn, passing also into passionate reality. A few poems are inspired in him by what he has seen in remote countries; some are marriage songs and funeral elegies, written for friendship or for money. But he writes nothing "out of his own head," as we say; nothing lightly, or, it would seem, easily; nothing for the song's sake. He speaks, in a letter, of "descending to print anything in verse"; and it is certain that he was never completely absorbed by his own poetry, or at all careful to measure his achievements against those of others. He took his own poems very seriously, he worked upon them with the whole force of his intellect; but to himself, even before he became a divine, he was something more than a poet. Poetry was but one means of expressing the many-sided activity of his mind and temperament. Prose was another, preaching another; travel and contact with great events and persons scarcley less important to him, in the building up of himself.—SYMONS, ARTHUR, 1899, *John Donne, Fortnightly Review, n s., vol.* 66, *p.* 735.

John Donne is of interest to the student of literature chiefly because of the influence which he exerted on the poetry of the age. His verse teems with forced comparisons and analogies between things remarkable for their dissimilarity. An obscure likeness and a worthless conceit were as important to him as was the problem of existence to Hamlet.—HALLECK, REUBEN POST, 1900, *History of English Literature, p.* 186.

George Herbert

1593–1633

Born, at Montgomery Castle, 3 April 1593. At Westminster School, 1605 [?]-09; King's Scholar, 5 May 1609. Matric., Trin. Coll., Camb., 18 Dec. 1609; B. A., 1613; M. A., 1616; Minor Fellow, 3 Oct. 1614; Major Fellow, 15 March 1616; Prelector in School of Rhetoric, 1618; Deputy Public Orator, 21 Oct. 1619; Public Orator, 18 Jan. 1619 to 1627. Contrib. to "Cambridge Elegies," 1612, 1619. Prebend. of Layton Ecclesia, 1625. Married Jane Danvers, 5 March 1629. Rector of Fugglestone-with-Bemerton, Wilts, April 1630. Died, at Bemerton, 3 March 1633. Buried in Bemerton church. *Works:* "Parentalia," 1627; "Oratio, qua . . . Principis Caroli Reditum ex Hispaniis celebravit Georgius Herbert," 1623. *Posthumous:* "The Temple" (prvi. ptd.; only one copy known), 1633 (two other edns., publicly ptd., same year); "Jacula Prudentum," 1651 (originally pubd. in "Witt's Recreation," 1640, as "Outlandish Proverbs"); "Herbert's Remains," 1652; "Musæ Responsoriæ ad Andreæ Melvini Scoti Anti-Tami-Cami-Categoriam" (pubd. as appendix to Vivian's "Ecclesiastes Solomonis"), 1662. He *translated:* Cornaro's "Treatise of Temperance," 1634; J. de Valdes' "Hundred and Ten Considerations," 1638.—SHARP, R. FARQUHARSON, 1897, *A Dictionary of English Authors*, p. 132.

PERSONAL

Mr. George Herbert, Esq. Parson of Fuggleston and Bemerton, was buried 3d day of March, 1632.—*Parish Register of Bemerton.*

So pious his life, that, as he was a copy of primitive, he might be a pattern of Sanctity to posterity. To testifie his independency on all others, he never mentioned the name of Jesus Christ, but with this addition, "My Master." Next God the Word, he loved the Word of God; being heard often to protest, "That he would not part with one leaf thereof for the whole world."—FULLER, THOMAS, 1662, *The Worthies of England, ed. Nichols, vol.* II, *p.* 601.

He was buryed (according to his owne desire) with the singing service for the buriall of dead, by the singing men of Sarum. Fr(ancis) Sambroke (attorney) then assisted as a chorister boy; my uncle, Thomas Danvers, was at the funerall. Vide in the Register booke at the office when he dyed, for the parish register is lost. Memorandum:—in the chancell are many apt sentences of the Scripture. . . . When he was first maried he lived a yeare or better at Dantesey house. H. Allen, of Dantesey, was well acquainted with him, who has told me that he had a very good hand on the lute, and that he sett his own lyricks or sacred poems. 'Tis an honour to the place, to have had the heavenly and ingeniose contemplation of this good man, who was pious even to prophesie;—e. g.

"Religion now on tip-toe stands,
Ready to goe to the American strands."

—AUBREY, JOHN, 1669–96, *Brief Lives, ed. Clark, vol.* I, *pp.* 309, 310.

He was for his person of a stature inclining towards tallness; his body was very straight, and so far from being cumbered with too much flesh, that he was lean to an extremity. His aspect was cheerful, and his speech and motion did both declare him a gentleman; for they were all so meek and obliging, that they purchased love and respect from all that knew him. . . . Brought most of his parishioners, and many gentlemen in the neighbourhood, constantly to make a part of his congregation twice a day: and some of the meaner sort of his parish did so love and reverence Mr. Herbert, that they would let their plough rest when Mr. Herbert's Saint's-bell rung to prayers, that they might also offer their devotions to God with him; and would then return back to their plough. And his most holy life was such, that it begot such reverence to God, and to him, that they thought themselves the happier, when they carried Mr. Herbert's blessing back with them to their labour. Thus powerful was his reason and example to persuade others to a practical piety and devotion.—WALTON, ISAAC, 1670, *The Life of Mr. George Herbert.*

His face as the face of a spirit, dimly bright.—BROWNING, ELIZABETH BARRETT, 1842-63, *The Book of the Poets, vol.* II, *p.* 50.

What was said of the late venerable Dr. John Brown, of Edinburgh, that "his face was a sermon for Christ," holds of the thought-lined, burdened-eyed, translucent as if transfigured face of Herbert. There is a noble "ivory palace" for the meek and holy soul there; brow steep rather than wide; lips tremulous as with music; nose pronounced as Richard Baxter's; cheeks worn and thin; hair full and flowing as in younger days: altogether a face which one could scarcely pass without note—all the more that there are lines in it which inevitably suggest that if George Herbert mellowed into the sweet lovingness and gentleness of John "whom Jesus loved," it was of grace, and through masterdom of a naturally lofty, fiery spirit. After all, these are the men of God who leave the deepest mark on their generation. —GROSART, ALEXANDER B., 1873, *George Herbert, Leisure Hour, vol.* 22, *p.* 455.

He was buried at Bemerton, where a new church has been built in his honor. It may be found on the high-road leading west from Salisbury, and only a mile and a half away; and at Wilton—the carpet town—which is only a fifteen minutes' walk beyond, may be found that gorgeous church, built not long ago by another son of the Pembroke stock (the late Lord Herbert of Lea), who perhaps may have had in mind the churchly honors due to his poetic kinsman; and yet all the marbles which are lavished upon this Wilton shrine are poorer, and will sooner fade than the mosaic of verse builded into "The Temple" of George Herbert.—MITCHELL, DONALD G., 1890, *English Lands Letters and Kings, From Elizabeth to Anne, p.* 119.

At Bemerton he lived, as he wrote, the ideal life of "A Priest to the Temple." While his simple sermons and his life of goodness won his people to a good life, he was writing poems which should catch the hearts of the next generation and enlist men's sentiment and sympathy in the restoration of the Church. Herbert's life was itself the noblest of his poems, and while it had the beauty of his verses it had their quaintnesses as well. Those exquisite lines of his, so characteristic of his age and his style, give a picture suggestive of his own character:—

"Sweet day, so cool, so calm, so bright,
The bridal of the earth and sky."

—HUTTON, WILLIAM HOLDEN, 1895, *Social England, ed. Traill, vol.* IV, *p.* 34.

THE TEMPLE
1633

Sir, I pray deliver this little book to my dear brother Farrer, and tell him, he shall find in it a picture of the many spiritual conflicts that have passed betwixt God and my soul, before I could subject mine to the will of Jesus my Master: in whose service I have now found perfect freedom. Desire him to read it; and then, if he can think it may turn to the advantage of any dejected poor soul: let it be made public; if not let him burn it; for I and it are less than the least of God's mercies.—HERBERT, GEORGE, 1632, *To Mr. Duncon, Walton's Life of Herbert.*

A book, in which by declaring his own spiritual conflicts, he hath comforted and raised many a dejected and discomposed soul, and charmed them into sweet and quiet thoughts: a book, by the frequent reading whereof, and the assistance of that Spirit that seemed to inspire the Author, the Reader may attain habits of Peace and Piety, and all the gifts of the Holy Ghost and Heaven: and may, by still reading, still keep those sacred fires burning upon the altar of so pure a heart, as shall free it from the anxieties of this world, and keep it fixed upon things that are above.—WALTON, ISAAC, 1639, *Life of Dr. John Donne, p.* 97.

I find more substantial comfort now in pious George Herbert's "Temple," which I used to read to amuse myself with his quaintness, in short, only to laugh at, than in all the poetry since the poems of Milton. —COLERIDGE, SAMUEL TAYLOR, 1818, *Lectures and Notes on Shakspere.*

Its poetical merit is of a very rare, lofty, and original order. It is full of that subtle perception of analogies which is competent only of high poetical genius. . . . Altogether, there are few places on earth nearer Heaven, filled with a richer and holier light, adorned with chaster and nobler ornaments, or where our souls can worship with a more entire forgetfulness of self, and a more thorough realisation of the things unseen and eternal, than in "The Temple" of George Herbert.—GILFILLAN, GEORGE, 1853, *ed. The Poetical Works of George Herbert, pp.* xxi, xxvi.

His poetry is the *bizarre* expression of a deeply religious and intensely thoughtful nature, sincere at heart, but strange, farfetched, and serenely crotchety in utterance. Nothing can be more frigid than the conceits in which he clothes the great majority of his pious ejaculations and heavenly ecstasies. Yet every reader feels that his fancy, quaint as it often is, is a part of the organism of his character; and that his quaintness, his uncouth metaphors and comparisons, his squalid phraseology, his holy charades and pious riddles, his inspirations crystallized into ingenuities, and his general disposition to represent the divine through the exterior guise of the odd, are vitally connected with that essential beauty and sweetness of soul which give his poems their wild flavor and fragrance. Amateurs in sanctity, and men of fine religious taste, will tell you that genuine emotion can never find an outlet in such an elaborately fantastic form; and the proposition, according, as it does, with the rules of Blair and Kames and Whately, commands your immediate assent; but still you feel that genuine emotion is there, and, if you watch sharply, you will find that Taste, entering holy George Herbert's "Temple," after a preliminary sniff of imbecile contempt, somehow slinks away abashed after the first verse at the "Church-porch." . . . One of the profoundest utterances of the Elizabethan age, George Herbert's lines on Man.—WHIPPLE, EDWIN P., 1859-68, *The Literature of the Age of Elizabeth, pp.* 247, 248.

"The Temple" is the enigmatical history of a difficult resignation; it is full of the author's baffled ambition and his distress, now at the want of a sphere for his energies, now at the fluctuations of spirit, the ebb and flow of intellectual activity, natural to a temperament as frail as it was eager. There is something a little feverish and disproportioned in his passionate heart-searchings. The facts of the case lie in a nutshell. Herbert was a younger son of a large family; he lost his father early, and his mother, a devout, tender, imperious woman, decided, partly out of piety and partly out of distrust of his power to make his own way in the world, that he should be provided for in the Church. When he was twenty-six he was appointed Public Orator at Cambridge, and hoped to make this position a stepping-stone to employment at court. After eight years his patrons and his mother were dead, and he made up his mind to settle down with a wife on the living of Bemerton, where he died after a short but memorable incumbency of three years. The flower of his poetry seems to belong to the two years of acute crisis which preceded his installation at Bemerton or to the Indian summer of content when he imagined that his failure as a courtier was a prelude to his success in the higher character of a country parson.—SIMCOX, GEORGE AUGUSTUS, 1880, *English Poets, ed. Ward, vol.* II, *p.* 193.

It is a book to be taken as a friend to be loved, rather than as a performance to be criticised. As a manual of devotion it is as though a seraph covered his face with his wings in rapturous adoration; as a poem it is full of that subtle perception of analogies to be found only in works of genius; while the passage on "Man" shows how the poets in their loftiest moods may sometimes anticipate some of the most wonderful discoveries of science and some of the sublimest speculations of philosophy.—BROWN, JOHN, 1890, *The Parson of Bemerton, Good Words, vol.* 31, *p.* 697.

GENERAL

The first, that with any effectual success attempted a diversion of this foul and overflowing stream, was the blessed man, Mr. George Herbert, whose holy life and verse gained many pious converts—of whom I am the least—and gave the first check to a most flourishing and admired wit of his time.—VAUGHAN, HENRY, 1650, *Silex Scintillans, Preface.*

But I must confess, after all, that, next the Scripture Poems, there are none so savoury to me as Mr. George Herbert's and Mr. George Sandys'. I know that Cowley and others far exceed Herbert in wit and accurate composure; but as Seneca takes with me above all his contemporaries, because he speaketh things by words, feelingly and seriously, like a man that is past jest; so Herbert speaks to God like one that really believeth a God, and whose business in the world is most with God. Heart-work and Heaven-work make up his books.—BAXTER, RICHARD, 1681, *Poetical Fragments, Prefatory Address.*

A writer of the same class, though infinitely inferior to both Quarles and Crashaw. His poetry is a compound of enthusiasm without sublimity, and conceit without either ingenuity or imagination. . . . When a man is once reduced to the impartial test of time,—when partiality, friendship, fashion, and party, have withdrawn their influence,—our surprise is frequently excited by past subjects of admiration that now cease to strike. He who takes up the poems of Herbert would little suspect that he had been public orator of an university, and a favourite of his sovereign; that he had received flattery and praise from Donne and from Bacon; and that the biographers of the day had enrolled his name among the first names of his country.—HEADLEY, HENRY, 1787, *Select Beauties of Ancient English Poetry.*

His beauties of thought and diction are so overloaded with far-fetched conceits and quaintnesses; low, and vulgar, and even indelicate imagery; and a pertinacious appropriation of Scripture language and figure, in situations where they make a most unseemly exhibition, that there is now very little probability of his ever regaining the popularity which he has lost. That there was much, however, of the real Poetical temperament in the composition of his mind, the following lines, although not free from his characteristic blemishes, will abundantly prove:

"Sweet Day! so cool, so calm, so bright," &c.
—NEELE, HENRY, 1827, *Lectures on English Poetry.*

Even the friendly taste of Mr. Keble was offended by the constant flutter of his fancy, forever hovering round and round the theme. But this was a peculiarity which the most gifted writers admired. Dryden openly avowed that nothing appeared more beautiful to him than the imagery in Cowley, which some readers condemned. It must, at least, be said, in praise of this creative playfulness, that it is a quality of the intellect singularly sprightly and buoyant; it ranges over a boundless landscape, pierces into every corner, and by the light of its own fire—to adopt a phrase of Temple—discovers a thousand little bodies, or images in the world, unseen by common eyes, and only manifested by the rays of that poetic sun.—WILLMOTT, ROBERT ARIS, 1854, *ed. The Works of George Herbert, Introduction.*

Herbert was an intimate friend of Donne, and no doubt a great admirer of his poetry but his own has been to a great extent preserved from the imitation of Donne's peculiar style, into which it might in other circumstances have fallen, in all probability by its having been composed with little effort or elaboration, and chiefly to relieve and amuse his own mind by the melodious expression of his favorite fancies and contemplations. His quaintness lies in his thoughts rather than in their expression, which is in general sufficiently simple and luminous.—CRAIK, GEORGE L., 1861, *A Compendious History of English Literature and of the English Language, vol.* II, *p.* 19.

Here comes a poet indeed! and how am I to show him due honour? With his book humbly, doubtfully offered, with the ashes of the poems of his youth fluttering in the wind of his priestly garments, he crosses the threshold. Or rather, for I had forgotten the symbol of my book, let us all go from our chapel to the choir, and humbly ask him to sing that he may make us worthy of his song. In George Herbert there is poetry enough and to spare: it is the household bread of his being. . . . With a conscience tender as a child's, almost diseased in its tenderness, and a heart loving as a woman's, his intellect is none the less powerful. Its movements are as the sword-play of an alert, poised, well-knit, strong-wristed fencer with the rapier, in which the skill impresses one more than the force, while without the force the skill would be valueless, even hurtful, to its possessor. There is a graceful humour with it occasionally, even in his most serious poems adding much to their charm.—MACDONALD, GEORGE, 1886, *England's Antiphon, pp* 174, 176.

Although later generations have moderated the lavish praise bestowed upon Herbert by his contemporaries, the final judgment seems strongly in favor of the poet's claims to lasting recognition. His poems are at times overloaded with conceits and quaint imagery—the great fault of that age—but this cannot destroy the vein of true, devotional poetry running through them all.—HART, JOHN S., 1872, *A Manual of English Literature, p.* 76.

The place of George Herbert among the sacred poets of England may be safely pronounced as secure as that of the greatest of his contemporaries. By this we do not at all mean to claim for him such quality or quantity of genius as belongs to these "greatest;" nor indeed would we even put him on a level with Henry Vaughan the Silurist, or Richard Crashaw. But we do mean that his fame is as true and catholic, and covetable and imperishable, as that of any. We could as soon conceive of the skylark's singing dying out of our love, or the daisy of the "grene grasse" ceasing to be "a thing of beauty," as of the verse-Temple built fully two centuries and a half ago being now suffered to go to ruin or to take stain. Myriads treasure in their heart of hearts the poems of George Herbert who know little and do not care to know more of the mighty sons of song.—GROSART, ALEX. B., 1873, *George Herbert, Leisure Hour, vol.* 22, *p.* 325.

Herbert is the psalmist dear to all who love religious poetry with exquisite refinement of thought. So much piety was never married to so much wit. Herbert identifies himself with Jewish genius, as Michael Angelo did when carving or painting prophets and patriarchs, not merely old men in robes and beards, but with the sanctity and the character of the Pentateuch and the prophecy conspicuous in them. His wit and his piety are genuine, and are sure to make a lifelong friend of a good reader.—EMERSON, RALPH WALDO, 1875, *Parnassus, Preface, p.* vi.

It is to another literature that we must look for much that is peculiar to George Herbert; and this will not only account for many of his faults, but will explain by what side of his character this scholar and gentleman was attracted to country life, and could find contentment in the talk and ways of villagers. The writings to which we allude are those of the moralists of the silver age or later, pagans of the decline, or, at best, but demi-Christians, whose works seem to us so trite and dull, but on which our forefathers, unspoiled by excitement, and not yet exigent in literary style, ruminated with a quiet delight such as we seldom feel. It is from the writings of these authors in many cases that they formed the proverbs which they esteemed as the highest axioms of practical wisdom, and which George Herbert has treasured so fondly in his "Jacula Prudentum."—WEBSTER, WENTWORTH, 1882, *The Academy, vol.* 22, *p.* 22.

It may be confessed without shame and without innuendo that Herbert has been on the whole a greater favourite with readers than with critics, and the reason is obvious. He is not prodigal of the finest strokes of poetry. To take only his own contemporaries, and undoubtedly pupils, his gentle moralising and devotion are tame and cold beside the burning glow of Crashaw, commonplace and popular beside the intellectual subtlety and, now and then, the inspired touch of Vaughan. But he never drops into the flatness and the extravagance of both these writers, and his beauties, assuredly not mean in themselves, and very constantly present, are both in kind and in arrangement admirably suited to the average comprehension. He is quaint and conceited; but his quaintnesses and conceits are never beyond the reach of any tolerably intelligent understanding. He is devout, but his devotion does not transgress into the more fantastic regions of piety. He is a mystic, but of the more exoteric school of mysticism. Thus he is among sacred poets very much (though relatively he occupies a higher place) what the late Mr. Longfellow was among profane poets. He expresses common needs, common thoughts, the everyday emotions of the Christian, just sublimated sufficiently to make them attractive. The fashion and his own taste gave him a pleasing quaintness, which his good sense kept from being ever obscure or offensive or extravagant. —SAINTSBURY, GEORGE, 1887, *History of Elizabethan Literature, p.* 372.

Herbert's imagery shows much over-elaboration, after the manner of Donne, who had been a close friend of his mother, and of his own youth: but his verses are free from the dulness of most of Vaughan's poems and the extravagance of many of Crashaw's. He is the poet of a meditative and sober piety that is catholic alike in the wideness of its appeal and in its love of symbol and imagery.—MASTERMAN, J. HOWARD B., 1897, *The Age of Milton, p.* 108.

Vaughan's intellectual debt to Herbert revolves itself into somewhat less than nothing; for in following him with zeal to the Missionary College of the Muses, he lost rather than gained, and he is altogether delightful and persuasive only where he is altogether himself. Nevertheless, a certain spirit of conformity and filial piety towards Herbert has betrayed Vaughan into frequent and flagrant imitations.—GUINEY, LOUISE IMOGEN, 1894, *Henry Vaughan, A Little English Gallery, p.* 95.

Herbert has an extraordinary tenderness, and it is his singular privilege to have been able to clothe the common aspirations, fears, and needs of the religious mind in language more truly poetical than any other Englishman. He is often extravagant, but rarely dull or flat; his greatest fault lay in an excessive pseudo-psychological ingenuity, which was a snare to all these lyrists, and in a tasteless delight in metrical innovations, often as ugly as they were unprecedented. He sank to writing in the shape of wings and pillars and altars. On this side, in spite of the beauty of their isolated songs and passages, the general decadence of the age was apparent in the lyrical writers. There was no principle of poetic style recognised, and when the spasm of creative passion was over, the dullest mechanism seemed good enough to be adopted.—GOSSE, EDMUND, 1897, *Short History of Modern English Literature, p.* 147.

George Abbot

1562-1633

Born at Guildford, Surrey, Oct. 29, 1562: died at Croydon, Aug. 4, 1633. An English prelate, appointed archbishop of Canterbury in Feb., 1611. He was graduated at Oxford (Balliol College), where he was tutor until 1593, and became master of University College in 1597, dean of Winchester in 1600, vice-chancellor of Oxford University in 1600 (and again in 1603 and 1605), bishop of Coventry and Lichfield in May, 1609, and bishop of London in Feb., 1610. He was a firm Protestant, and was influential in state affairs during the reign of James I. He was one of the translators of the New Testament in the King James version.—SMITH, BENJAMIN E., *ed.*, 1894-97, *The Century Cyclopedia of Names, p.* 2.

A grave man in his conversation, and unblamable in his life. Indeed, it is charged on him that *non amavit gentem nostram*, "he loved not our nation;" forsaking the birds of his own feather to fly with others, and generally favouring the laity above the clergy, in all cases brought before him. But this he endeavoured to excuse to a private friend, by protesting he was himself so severe to the clergy on purpose to rescue them from the severity of others, and to prevent the punishment of them from lay judges, to their greater shame. I also read in a nameless author, that towards his death he was not only discontented himself, but his house was the rendezvous of all malcontents in church and state; making midnight of noonday, by constant keeping of candles light in his chamber and study; as also such visitants as repaired unto him, called themselves Nicodemites, because of their secret addresses. But a credible person, and one of his nearest relations, knew nothing thereof; which, with me, much shaketh the probability of the report. And thus we leave the archbishop, and the rest of his praises, to be reported by the poor people of Guildford, in Surrey, where he founded and endowed a fair almshouse in the town of his nativity.—FULLER, THOMAS, 1655, *The Church History of Britain, vol.* III, *bk.* xi, *par.* 53-5, *p.* 350.

Archbishop Abbot was borne in the howse of old Flemish building, timber and brick, now an alehouse, the signe "Three Mariners," by the river's side by the bridge on the north side of the street in St. Nicholas parish on the right hand as you goe out of the towne northwards. Old Nightingale was his servant, and weepes when he talkes of him. Every one that knew, loved him. He was sometimes cholerique. He was borne the first howse over the bridge on the right hand in St. Nicholas parish (Guildford). He was the sonne of a sherman. His mother, with child of him, longed for a jack, and dream't that if shee could eate a jack, her son should be a great man. The next morning, goeing to the river, which runs by the howse (which is by the bridge) with her payle to take up some water, a good jack came into her payle. Which shee eat up, all, her selfe. This is gener'lly received for a trueth.—AUBREY, JOHN, 1669-96, *Brief Lives, ed. Clark, vol.* I, *p.* 24.

He was also a learned man, and had his erudition all of the old stamp. The things that he hath written . . . shew him to be a man of parts, learning, vigilancy, and unwearied study, tho' overwhelmed with business.—WOOD, ANTHONY, 1691–1721, *Athenæ Oxonienses, vol.* I, *f.* 584.

His character was of a negative, not to say neutral, cast. He was neither deficient in piety, morality, talents, or learning, but he exercised them only with a decency so cold and sober that it had an air even of selfishness. He was an example calculated for a village, not for a kingdom. In the spiritual concerns of his great office he was obstinate without zeal, and in the temporal haughty without dignity. His understanding, though strong, was of an order too coarse and mechanical to be applied to the niceties of state affairs, and an ungracious temper, together with a rough unbending honesty, rendered him almost a stranger to the Court. It is natural to ask how such a man could have arisen to the highest station within the reach of a subject?—Simply by good fortune.—LODGE, EDMUND, 1821-34, *Portraits of Illustrious Personages of Great Britain, vol.* III.

A sincere but narrow-minded Calvinist, he was equally opposed to Catholics and to heretics. . . . He was charitable, and far less obsequious to the kingly will than most of his compeers. His closing years were clouded by an accident, the shooting of a gamekeeper (1621); and during the last six he was almost superseded by Laud.—PATRICK AND GROOME, *eds.*, 1897, *Chambers's Biographical Dictionary, p.* 5.

Anthony Munday

1553–1633

Poet-Laureate of the City of London, was concerned in writing fourteen plays,—"Sir John Oldcastle," 1600; "The Death of Robert, Earl of Huntington," 1601, &c.; trans. "Amadis de Gaul," "Palmerin of England," and other romances, and pub. a number of political and poetical pieces. Among the best-known of the latter are: 1. "Banquet of Daintie Conceits," 1588, 4to. . . . 2. "The Fountayne of Fame," 1580, 4to. 3. "Pain of Pleasure," 1586, 4to.—ALLIBONE, S. AUSTIN, 1870, *Dictionary of English Literature, vol.* II, *p.* 1386.

An earnest traueller in this arte, and in whose name I have seene very excellent workes, among which surely, the most exquisite vaine of a witty poeticall heade is shewed in the sweete sobs of "Sheepheardes and Nymphes:" a worke well worthy to be viewed, and to bee esteemed as very rare Poetrie.—WEBBE, WILLIAM, 1586, *A Discourse of English Poetrie.*

Of the versions of honest Anthony, one of the most indefatigable translators of romance in the reign of Elizabeth, not much can be said either in point of style or fidelity. Labouring for those who possessed an eager and indiscriminating appetite for the marvellous, he was not greatly solictitous about the preservation of the manners and costume of his original, but rather strove to accommodate his authors to the taste of the majority of his readers. To enumerate the various romances which he attempted to naturalise, would be tedious and unprofitable.—DRAKE, NATHAN, 1817, *Shakspeare and His Times, vol.* I, *p.* 54.

There is nothing in Munday's compositions above the tamest mediocrity, and he is worth mentioning only as a specimen of the literary journeyman of the time.—MINTO, WILLIAM, 1874-85, *Characteristics of English Poets, p.* 253.

Munday was in his versatility an epitome of his age. Ready to turn his hand to any occupation, he was a man of letters little more than a compiler, destitute of originality or style; yet, apart from such names as Shakespeare and Marlowe, there are few Elizabethan writers who occupied a greater share of public attention, or contributed more largely to popular information and amusement.—SECCOMBE, THOMAS, 1894, *Dictionary of National Biography, vol.* XXXIX, *p.* 294.

An obscure and fertile literary hack, reeling out volume after volume of ordinary verse and yet more ordinary prose, yet reaching once or twice a rare level, which shall preserve his name from oblivion.—SCHELLING, FELIX E., 1895, *A Book of Elizabethan Lyrics, p.* xxix.

George Chapman

1559?-1634

Born, near Hitchin, 1559(?). Educated at Trinity College, Oxford(?). First poems printed, 1594. First part of Homer translation pub., 1598. Prolific writer for stage. Died, in London, 12 May 1634. Buried in churchyard of St. Giles-in-the-Fields. *Works:* "Σκια Νυκτος" (under initials: G. W. Gent.), 1594; "Ovid's Banquet of Sence" (anon.), 1595; Completion of Marlowe's "Hero and Leander," 1598; "The Blind Beggar of Alexandria," 1598; "Seaven Bookes of the Iliades of Homere," translated, 1598; "Achilles' Shield" translated, 1598; "An Humorous Dayes Mirth" (under initials: G. C.), 1599; "Eastward Hoe" (with Jonson and Marston), 1605; "All Fools," 1605; "The Gentleman Usher," 1606; "Monsieur d'Olive," 1606; "Sir Gyles Goosecappe" (anon.), 1606 (performed 1601); "Bussy d'Ambois" (anon.), 1607; "The Tragedie of Cæsar and Pompey" (anon.), 1607; "The Conspiracie and Tragedie of Charles, Duke of Byron," 1608 (performed 1605); "Euthymiæ Raptus," 1609; "The Iliades of Homer" (complete), [1611]; "May Day," 1611; "The Widowes Teares" ("by Geor. Chap."), 1612; Translation of Petrarch's "Seven Penitentiall Psalms," 1612; "An Epicede" (anon.), 1612; "The Revenge of Bussy d'Ambois," 1613; "Memorable Masque," 1614; "Eugenia," 1614; "Andromeda Liberata," 1614; "Twenty Four Bookes of Homere's Odisses translated," 1614; Iliad and Odyssey translations together, 1616; "Divine Poem" of Musæus translated, 1617; Hesiod's "Georgicks" translated, 1618; "Two Wise Men," (anon.), 1619; "Pro Vere Autumni Lachrymæ," 1622; "A Justification of a Strange Action of Nero," 1629; Homer's "Batrachomyomachia" translated, 1624; "The Warres of Pompey and Cæsar" (anon.), 1631. *Posthumous:* "The Ball" (with Shirley), 1639 (acted 1632); "The Tragedy of Chabot" (with Shirley), 1639 (acted 1635); "The Tragedy of Alphonsus, Emperor of Germany," 1654; "Revenge for Honour," 1654. He contributed verses to: Jones's "Nennio," 1595; Jonson's "Sejanus," 1605, and "Volpone," 1606; Fletcher's "Faithful Shepherdesse," 1610 (?); "Parthenia," 1611; Field's "A Woman is a Weathercock," 1612. *Collected Works:* in 3 vols., 1874–75.—SHARP, R. FARQUHARSON, 1897, *A Dictionary of English Authors, p.* 52.

PERSONAL

'Tis true that Chapman's reverend ashes must
Lye rudely mingled with the vulgar dust,
'Cause carefull heyers the wealthy only have,
To build a glorious trouble o're the grave.
Yet doe I not despaire some one may be
So seriously devout to poesie,
As to translate his reliques, and find roome
In the warme church to build him up a tombe,
Since Spenser hath a stone.
—HABINGTON, WILLIAM, 1634, *Castara.*

Not the meanest of the English poets of his time; who dying the 12th of May 1634, aged 77 years, was buried in the yard on the south side of the Church of S. Giles's in the Fields near London. Over his grave, near to the south wall of the church, was soon after a monument erected, built after the way of the old Romans, by the care and charge of his beloved friend Inigo Jones the King's Archatect; whereon is engraven this, *Georgius Chapmannus Poeta Homericus, Philosophus verus (etsi Christianus Poeta) plusquam celebris,* &c.—WOOD, ANTHONY, 1691–1721, *Athenæ Oxonienses.*

In Chapman scholarship appears to have exerted its best traditional influences, instead of its wine being turned to vinegar by any infusion of vanity or jealousy. He seems to have been esteemed by patrons of the highest rank and eminence—Bacon was one of their number—and to have enjoyed in an exceptional degree the good-will of his fellow-poets. Jonson "loved" Chapman, knew a piece of his "Iliads" by heart, and averred that, next himself, "only Fletcher and Chapman could make a masque." Marston and Shirley were associated with him as playwrights. Webster speaks of him with what may be described as an excess of enthusiasm; for he seems to place him at the head of contemporary dramatists. This general esteem, in which the younger growth of lovers of letters seems to have shared, was probably due to the dignity of Chapman's character as well as to the reputation which his learning and talents had secured him.—WARD, ADOLPHUS WILLIAM, 1875–99, *A History of English Dramatic Literature, vol.* II, *p.* 413.

HERO AND LEANDER
1598

Chapman was a true and excellent poet, in some respects Marlowe's superior, but altogether different from him in lines of thought and modes of expression, and labouring besides under the immense disadvantage of singing as it were in falsetto, by endeavouring to work in the style and spirit of another man's performance.—CUNNINGHAM, LT. COL. FRANCIS, 1870, *ed. The Works of Christopher Marlowe, Introduction, p.* xvii.

In Chapman's continuation, as in everything that Chapman wrote, there are fine passages in abundance; but the reader is wearied by tedious digressions, dull moralising, and violent conceits. There are couplets in the "Tale of Teras" (Fifth Sestiad) that for purity of colour and perfection of form are hardly excelled by anything in the first two sestiads; such passages, however, are few.—BULLEN, A. H., 1884, *ed. The Works of Christopher Marlowe, Introduction, vol.* I, *p.* lii.

Marlowe died before he had completed the poem; it was finished by George Chapman, and no stronger proof of the greatness of Marlowe's genius can be furnished than the contrast between the work of the two men. Chapman did not write without inspiration; but whereas Marlowe's style . . . is all flame, his successor's, even in his most brilliant moments, is half smoke.—COURTHOPE, W. J., 1897, *A History of English Poetry, vol.* II, *p.* 327.

TRANSLATION OF HOMER
1598–1616

I must confess that, to mine own ear, those continual cadences of couplets used in long continued poems are very tiresome and unpleasing, by reason that still methinks they run on with a sound of one nature, and a kind of certainty which stuffs the delight rather than entertains it. But yet, notwithstanding, I must not of my own daintiness condemn this kind of writing, which peradventure to another may seem most delightful; and many worthy compositions we see to have passed with commendation in that kind. Besides methinks sometimes to beguile the ear with a running out and passing over the rhyme, as no bound to stay us in the line where the violence of the matter will break through, is rather graceful than otherwise. Wherein I find my Homer-Lucan, as if he gloried to seem to have no bounds albeit he were confined within his measures, to be in my conceit most happy; for so thereby they who care not for verse or rhyme may pass it over without taking any notice thereof, and please themselves with a well-measured prose.—DANIEL, SAMUEL, 1603, *A Defence of Rhyme.*

Then in the strain beyond an Oaten Quill
The learned shepherd of fair Hitching Hill
Sung the heroic deeds of Greece and Troy,
In lines so worthy life, that I employ
My Reed in vain to overtake his fame.
All praiseful tongues do wait upon that name.

—BROWNE, WILLIAM, 1613, *Britannia's Pastorals, bk.* ii, *song* ii.

If all the vulgar tongues that speak this day
Were ask'd of thy discoveries; they must say,
To the Greek coast thine only knew the way.
Such passage hast thou found, such returns made,
As now of all men, it is call'd thy trade,
And who make thither else, rob or invade.

—JONSON, BEN, 1618, *To my worthy and honoured friend, Master George Chapman.*

Brave language are Chapman's Iliads.—BOLTON, EDMUND, 1624, *Hypercritica.*

He hath been highly celebrated among men for his brave language in his translation of Homer's Iliads, those I mean which are translated into Tessaradecasyllabons, or lines of fourteen syllables.—WOOD, ANTHONY, 1691-1721, *Athenæ Oxonienses, vol.* II, *f.* 378.

That which is to be allowed him, and which very much contributed to cover his defects, is a daring fiery spirit that animates his translation, which is something like what one might imagine Homer himself would have writ before he arrived at years of discretion.—POPE, ALEXANDER, 1715–20, *The Iliad of Homer, Preface.*

He has by no means represented the dignity or the simplicity of Homer. He is sometimes paraphrastic and redundant, but more frequently retrenches or impoverishes what he could not feel and express. In the meantime, he labours with the inconvenience of an aukward, inharmonious, and unheroic measure, imposed by custom, but disgustful to modern ears. Yet he is not always without strength or spirit. He has enriched our languages with many compound epithets, so much in the manner of Homer, such as the *silver-footed* Thetis, the *silver-throned* Juno, the *triple-feathered* helme, the *high-walled* Thebes, the *faire-haired* boy, the *silver-flowing* floods, the *hugely-peopled* towns, the Grecians *navy-bound*, the *strong-winged* lance, and many more which might be collected. Dryden reports, that Waller never could read Chapman's Homer without a degree of transport. Pope is of opinion, that Chapman covers his defects "by a daring fiery spirit that animates his translation, which is something like what one might imagine Homer himself to have writ before he arrived to years of discretion." But his fire is too frequently darkened, by that sort of fustian which now disfigured the diction of our tragedy.—WARTON, THOMAS, 1778-81, *History of English Poetry, sec.* lix.

Chapman I have sent in order that you might read the "Odyssey;" the "Iliad" is fine, but less equal in the translation, as well as less interesting in itself. What is stupidly said of Shakspeare is really true and appropriate of Chapman: "mighty faults counterpoised by mighty beauties." . . . It is as truly an original poem as the "Faery Queen;"—it will give you small idea of Homer, though a far truer one than Pope's epigrams, or Cowper's cumbersome most anti-Homeric Miltonism. For Chapman writes and feels as a poet,—as Homer might have written had he lived in England in the reign of Queen Elizabeth. In short, it is an exquisite poem, in spite of its frequent and perverse quaintnesses and harshnesses, which are, however, amply repaid by almost unexampled sweetness and beauty of language, all over spirit and feeling.—COLERIDGE, SAMUEL TAYLOR, 1807, *Letter to Wordsworth* (?), *Coleridge's Literary Remains.*

He would have made a great epic poet, if indeed he has not abundantly shown himself to be one; for his Homer is not so properly a translation as the stories of Achilles and Ulysses re-written. The earnestness and passion which he has put into every part of these poems, would be incredible to a reader of mere modern translations. His almost Greek zeal for the glory of his heroes can only be paralleled by that fierce spirit of Hebrew bigotry, with which Milton, as if personating one of the zealots of the old law, clothed himself when he sat down to paint the acts of Samson against the uncircumcised. The great obstacle to Chapman's translations being read, is their unconquerable quaintness. He pours out in the same breath the most just and natural, and the most violent and crude expressions. He seems to grasp at whatever words come first to hand while the enthusiasm is upon him, as if all other must be inadequate to the divine meaning. But passion (the all in all in poetry) is everywhere present, raising the low, dignifying the mean, and putting sense into the absurd. He makes his readers glow, weep, tremble, take any affection which he pleases, be moved by words, or in spite of them, be disgusted and overcome their disgust.—LAMB, CHARLES, 1808, *Specimens of Dramatic Poets.*

Much have I travell'd in the realms of gold,
And many goodly states and kingdoms seen;
Round many western islands have I been
Which bards in fealty to Apollo hold.
Oft of one wide expanse had I been told
That deep-brow'd Homer ruled as his demesne;
Yet did I never breathe its pure serene
Till I heard Chapman speak out loud and bold:
Then felt I like some watcher of the skies
When a new planet swims into his ken;
Or like stout Cortez when with eagle eyes
He stared at the Pacific—and all his men
Look'd at each other with a wild surmise—
Silent, upon a peak in Darien.

—KEATS, JOHN, 1815, *On First Looking into Chapman's Homer.*

Chapman often caught the ideas of Homer, and went on writing Homerically, at once the translator and the original.—DISRAELI, ISAAC, 1841, *Predecessors and Contemporaries of Shakspeare, Amenities of Literature.*

The Homer of Chapman, whatever its defects, alone of all English versions has this crowning merit of being, where it is most successful, thoroughly alive. He has made for us the best poem that has yet been Englished out of Homer, and in so far gives us a truer idea of him.—LOWELL, JAMES RUSSELL, 1858-64-90, *Library of Old Authors, Prose Works, Riverside ed., vol.* I, *p.* 290.

His greatest performance, and it was a gigantic one, was his translation of

Homer, which, in spite of obvious faults, excels all other translations in the power to rouse and lift and inflame the mind. Some eminent painter, we believe Barry, said that, when he went into the street after reading it, men seemed ten feet high. Pope averred that the translation of the Iliad might be supposed to have been written by Homer before he arrived at years of discretion; and Coleridge declares the version of the Odyssey to be as truly an original poem as the "Faery Queen."—WHIPPLE, EDWIN P., 1859-68, *The Literature of the Age of Elizabeth, p.* 148.

Between Chapman and Homer there is interposed the mist of the fancifulness of the Elizabethan age, entirely alien to the plain directness of Homer's thought and feeling. . . . Chapman's style is not artificial and literary like Pope's, nor his movement elaborate and self-retarding like the Miltonic movement of Cowper. He is plain-spoken, fresh, vigorous, and to a certain degree, rapid; and all these are Homeric qualities. I cannot say that I think the movement of his fourteen-syllable line, which has been so much commended, Homeric. . . . But as eminently as Homer is plain, so eminently is the Elizabethan literature in general, and Chapman in particular, fanciful. . . . Homer expresses himself like a man of adult reason, Chapman like a man whose reason has not yet cleared itself. . . . The Elizabethan poet fails to render Homer because he cannot forbear to interpose a play of thought between his object and its expression.—ARNOLD, MATTHEW, 1861, *Lectures on Homer, pp.* 11, 22, 24, 25, 29.

It bears from first to last the impress of a genius worthy even of the great task which the English poet set himself and carried through with indomitable devotion. As a translation proper it inevitably suffered from the influence of later schools of poetry, as well as from its own undeniable defects in the way of scholarly accuracy. But the neglect which befell Chapman's "Homer" by reason of the success of the version by Pope and his coadjutors, produced the reaction in its favour represented by Charles Lamb, Coleridge and Keats. They judged it, again to quote Mr. Swinburne, by the standard of original work rather than of pure translation,—not that this latter is the criterion by which "Pope's Homer" itself can claim to stand or fall. Of more recent critics, none worthy of the name has refused Chapman's "Homer" the praise due to its vigour and passion, qualities without which Homer can never be fitly reproduced. But it is equally true that Chapman's style has characteristics which are partly proper to himself, partly shared by him with the literary age to which he belonged; and that these characteristics are entirely foreign to other Homeric qualities,—above all to those of simplicity and directness.—WARD, ADOLPHUS WILLIAM, 1875-99, *A History of English Dramatic Literature, vol.* II, *p.* 411.

The more he admired Homer, the more Chapman felt bound to dress him up in the height of rhetorical conceit. He excused himself by the argument, that we have not the epics as Homer imagined them, that "the books were not set together by Homer." He probably imagined that, if Homer had had his own way with his own works, he would have produced something much more in the Chapman manner, and he kindly added, ever and anon, a turn which he fancied Homer would approve. The English reader must be on his guard against this custom of Chapman's, and must remember, too, that the translator's erudition was exceedingly fantastic. . . . Chapman has another great fault, allied indeed to a great excellence. In his speed, in the rapidity of the movement of his lines, he is Homeric. The last twelve books of the "Iliad" were struck out at a white heat, in fifteen weeks. Chapman was carried away by the current of the Homeric verse, and this is his great saving merit. Homer inspires him, however uncouth his utterance, as Apollo inspired the Pythoness.—LANG, ANDREW, 1880, *English Poets, ed. Ward, vol.* I, *pp.* 514, 515.

Chapman's Homer is one of the great achievements of the Elizabethan age, a monument of skill and devotion. The mistranslations are many and grievous, and it is clear that Chapman's knowledge of Greek was not profound; but through the whole work there breathes a spirit of sleepless energy that amply atones for all crudities and conceits.—BULLEN, A. H., 1887, *Dictionary of National Biography, vol.* X, *p.* 49.

The greatest of English translators.

His version, with all its faults, outlived the popularity even of Pope, was for more than two centuries the resort of all who, unable to read Greek, wished to know what the Greek was, and, despite the finical scholarship of the present day, is likely to survive all the attempts made with us. I speak with all humility, but as having learnt Homer from Homer himself, and not from any translation, prose or verse. I am perfectly aware of Chapman's outrageous liberties, of his occasional unfaithfulness (for a libertine need not necessarily be unfaithful in translation), and of the condescension to his own fancies and the fancies of his age, which obscures not more perhaps than some condescensions which nearness and contemporary influences prevent some of us from seeing the character of the original. But at the same time, either I have no skill in criticism, and have been reading Greek for thirty years to none effect, or Chapman is far nearer Homer than any modern translator in any modern language. —SAINTSBURY, GEORGE, 1887, *History of Elizabethan Literature, pp.* 185, 189.

The literalists will never like him, of course; he drops words that worry him—whole lines indeed with which he does not choose to grapple; he adds words, too—whole lines, scenes almost; there is vulgarity sometimes, and coarseness; he calls things by their old homely names; there is no fine talk about the chest or the abdomen, but the Greek lances drive straight through the ribs or to the navel, and if a cut be clean and large—we are not told of crimson tides—but the blood gurgles out in great gouts as in a slaughter-house; there may be over-plainness, and over-heat, and over-stress; but nowhere weakness; and his unwieldy, staggering lines—fourteen syllables long—forge on through the ruts which the Homeric chariots have worn, bouncing and heaving and plunging and jolting, but always lunging forward with their great burden of battle, of brazen shields, and ponderous war-gods.—MITCHELL, DONALD G., 1889, *English Lands Letters and Kings, From Celt to Tudor, p.* 266.

Chapman's aim was to reproduce the *sense* of his original. Having chosen the long ballad-metre as his vehicle of translation, he stuck so closely to the text that, though translating paraphrastically, he rendered the Greek in an even smaller number of English lines. No material thought is omitted in his version; none is added; by his literal fidelity, and (it must be added) by his own genuine poetical feeling, he catches something of the greatness of his author, but his metre is not equal to the epic dignity of the subject, and his verses are devoid of grace, proportion, and harmony.—COURTHOPE, WILLIAM JOHN, 1889, *Life of Alexander Pope, Pope's Works, vol.* V, *p.* 162.

To render the comparatively unknown Homer into good English verse was an achievement worthy of the acknowledgments Chapman received. His translation is to this day, in spite of its faults, the best that England possesses. . . . Even in his fine translation of Homer, he is unable to forego his tendency to obscurity, and constrained and inflated expression. It is universally admitted that even a translation must take some colouring from its translator, and no man in England was less Hellenic than Chapman. Swinburne has rightly observed that his temperament was more Icelandic than Greek, that he handled the sacred vessels of Greek art with the substantial grasp of the barbarian, and when he would reproduce Homer he gave rather the stride of a giant than the step of a god.—BRANDES, GEORGE, 1898, *Shakespeare, A Critical Study, vol.* II, *pp.* 204, 206.

Chapman secures an animated swiftness of movement, but not the easy, rapid, varied flowingness of Homer. At its worst Chapman's movement is a ponderous bear-trot; and at its best a resonant, clanking swiftness, aglow with fire. But even this broken or jarring rapidity, in place of the fluid one of Homer, is gained at the loss of plainness of idea, of simplicity in expression, and of nobleness of manner. His style is loose, tortuous, and archaic, and its ideas are often curious, fantastic, and irrational. But, condemn this version as we may, it is the one mature students like best, as young students do Pope's.—GENTNER, PHILIP, 1899, *Introduction to Pope's Iliad, p.* iii.

GENERAL

Detraction is the sworne friend to ignorance: For mine owne part I have ever truly cherisht my good opinion of other mens worthy Labours, especially of that full and haightned stile of maister *Chapman.*—WEBSTER, JOHN, 1612, *The White Divel, Dedication.*

Reverent Chapman, who hath brough to us
Musæus, Homer, and Hesiodus
Out of the Greek, and by his skill hath rear'd
Them to that height and to our tongue endear'd
That, were those poets at this day alive,
To see their books thus with us to survive,
They would think, having neglected them so long,
They had bin written in the English tongue.
—DRAYTON, MICHAEL, c 1627, *Of Poets and Poesie.*

George Chapman, a poetical writer, flourishing in the reigns of Queen Elizabeth and King James, in that repute for his translations both of "Homer," and "Hesiod," and what he wrote of his own proper genius, that he is thought not the meanest of English poets of that time, and particularly for his Dramatic writings.—PHILLIPS, EDWARD, 1675, *Theatrum Poetarum Anglicanorum, ed. Brydges, p.* 250.

A dwarfish thought ["Bussy d'Ambois"], dressed up in gigantic words, repetition in abundance, looseness of expression, and gross hyperboles; the sense of one line expanded prodigiously into ten; and, to sum up all, uncorrect English, and a hideous mingle of false poetry and true nonsense.—DRYDEN, JOHN, 1681, *The Spanish Friar, Dedicatory Epistle; Dryden's Works, ed. Scott and Saintsbury, vol.* VI, *p.* 404.

I can give him no greater Commendation, than that he was so intimate with the famous *Johnson*, as to engage in a Triumvirate with Him, and *Marston* in a Play called "Eastward-Hoe;" a Favour which the haughty *Ben* could seldome be perswaded to. —LANGBAINE, GERARD, 1691, *An Account of the English Dramatick Poets, p.* 57.

Of all the English play-writers, perhaps approaches nearest to Shakespeare in the descriptive and didactic, in passages which are less purely dramatic. Dramatic imitation was not his talent. He could not go out of himself, as Shakespeare could shift at pleasure, to inform and animate other existences, but in himself he had an eye to perceive and a soul to embrace all forms and modes of being.—LAMB, CHARLES, 1808, *Specimens of Dramatic Poets.*

His diction is chiefly marked by barbarous ruggedness, false elevation, and extravagant metaphor. The drama owes him very little; his "Bussy D'Ambois" is a piece of frigid atrocity, and in the "Widow's Tears," where his heroine Cynthia falls in love with a sentinel guarding the corpse of her husband, whom she was bitterly lamenting, he has dramatized one of the most puerile and disgusting legends ever fabricated for the disparagement of female constancy.—CAMPBELL, THOMAS, 1819, *Specimens of the British Poets.*

His "Bussy d'Ambois," though not without interest or some fancy, is rather a collection of apophthegms or pointed sayings in the form of a dialogue than a poem or a tragedy. In his verses the oracles have not ceased. Every other line is an axiom in morals—a libel on mankind, if truth is a libel. He is too stately for a wit, in his serious writings—too formal for a poet.—HAZLITT, WILLIAM, 1820, *Lectures on the Literature of the Age of Elizabeth.*

Chapman, who assisted Ben Jonson and some others in comedy, deserves but limited praise for his "Bussy d'Amboise." The style in this and in all his tragedies is extravagantly hyperbolical: he is not very dramatic, nor has any power of exciting emotion except in those who sympathize with a tumid pride and self-confidence. Yet he has more thinking than many of the old dramatists; and the praise of one of his critics, though strongly worded, is not without some foundation, that we "seldom find richer contemplations on the nature of man and the world."—HALLAM, HENRY, 1837-39, *Introduction to the Literature of Europe, pt.* iii, *ch.* vi, *par.* 103.

His mastery of English is something wonderful even in an age of masters, when the language was still a mother-tongue, and not a contrivance of pedants and grammarians.—LOWELL, JAMES RUSSELL, 1858-64-90, *Library of Old Authors, Prose Works, Riverside ed., vol.* I, *p.* 290.

Chapman was a man with great elements in his nature, which were so imperfectly harmonized that what he was found but a stuttering expression in what he wrote and did. There were gaps in his mind; or, to use Victor Hugo's image, "his intellect was a book with some leaves torn out." His force, great as it was, was that of an Ajax, rather than that of an Achilles. Few dramatists of the time afford nobler passages of description and reflection. Few are wiser, deeper, manlier in their strain of thinking. But when we turn to the dramas from which these grand things have been detached, we find extravagance, confusion, huge thoughts lying in helpless heaps, sublimity in parts conducing to no general effect of sublimity, the movement lagging and unwieldy, and the plot urged on to the catastrophe by incoherent expedients. His imagination partook of the incompleteness of his intellect. Strong enough to clothe the ideas and emotions of a common poet, it was plainly inadequate to embody the vast, half-formed conceptions which gasped for expression in his soul in its moments of poetic exaltation. Often we feel his meaning, rather than apprehend it. The imagery has the indefiniteness of distant objects seen by moonlight. There are whole passages in his works in which he seems engaged in expressing Chapman to Chapman, like the deaf egotist who only placed his trumpet to his ear when he himself talked.—WHIPPLE, EDWIN P., 1859-68, *The Literature of the Age of Elizabeth, p.* 150.

George Chapman is conspicuous among the mob of easy and precocious writers in his generation for his late entrance into the service of the Muses, and his loudly proclaimed enthusiasm and strenuous labours in that service. He made no secret of the effort that it cost him to climb Parnassus, or of his fiery resolution to reach the top; he rather exaggerated his struggles and the vehemence of his ambition. He refrained from publication till he was thirty-five years old, and then burst upon the world like a repressed and accumulated volcano. The swelling arrogance and lofty expectations with which he had restrained his secret labours display themselves without reserve in the "Shadow of Night"—his first contribution to print. . . . Chapman's designs were always ambitious; but he was guided more like a pedant by authoritative models than like a genuine artist by a clear judgment and sure instinct of his own. He had, undoubtedly, immense power; but his sail was a great deal prouder and fuller than his ship.—MINTO, WILLIAM, 1874-85, *Characteristics of English Poets, pp.* 325, 331.

Although destitute of a knowledge of dramatic effect neither in the tragic nor in the comic branch of the playwright's art, it would almost seem as if Chapman had lacked the power, when working alone, of fully developing a character by means of dramatic action; certainly none of the comedies or tragedies written by him alone are as stage-plays comparable to "Eastward Hoe" and "Chabot" respectively. But though falling short of this power, he is happy in the invention of character in both tragedy and comedy, —in the latter more particularly, as his Monsieur d'Olive would alone suffice to prove. . . . The strength of Chapman lies in particular passages rather than in his plays as a whole. . . . Like Shakspere, he is able at times to reveal by these sudden flashes of poetic power depths of true feeling as well as of true wisdom. His observation is strikingly original as well as apt, and there is often something proverbial or gnomic about these passages, in which the physical as well as the moral world is called into play, and of which (if there be any profit in anthologies) it would be well worth while to attempt a complete list. . . . Chapman's style is unmistakably influenced by his classical learning; but he cannot be pronounced pedantically fond of displaying it.—WARD, ADOLPHUS WILLIAM, 1875-99, *A History of English Dramatic Literature, vol.* II, *pp.* 447, 448, 449.

He enters the serene temples and handles the holy vessels of Hellenic art with the stride and the grasp of a high-handed and high-minded barbarian. . . . The name of Chapman should always be held great; yet must it always at first recall the names of greater men. For one who thinks of him as the author of his best play or his loftiest lines of gnomic verse, a score will at once remember him as the translator of Homer or the continuator of Marlowe.—SWINBURNE, ALGERNON CHARLES, 1875, *George Chapman's Poetical and Dramatic Works, Preface.*

Few writers were more culpably Alexandrian than George Chapman. The spirit of Callimachus or of Lycophron seems at times to have come upon him, as the *lutin* was supposed to whisper ideas extraordinarily good or evil, to Corneille. When under the influence of this possession, Chapman displayed the very qualities and unconsciously translated the language of Callimachus. He vowed that he detested popularity, and all that can please "the commune reader." He inveighed against the "invidious detractor" who became a spectre that dogged him in every enterprise. He hid his meaning in a mist of verbiage, within a labyrinth of conceits, and himself said, only too truly, about the "sweet Leander" of Marlowe,

"I in floods of ink
Must drown thy graces."

It is scarcely necessary to justify these remarks by illustrations from Chapman's works. Every reader of the poems and the prefaces finds barbarism, churlish temper, and pedantry in profusion. In spite of unpopularity, Chapman "rested as resolute as Seneca, satisfying himself if but a few, if one, or if none like" his verses. Why then is Chapman, as it were in his own despite, a poet still worthy of the regard of lovers of poetry? The answer is partly to be found in his courageous and ardent spirit, a spirit bitterly at odds with life, but still true to its nobility, still capable, in happier moments, of divining life's real significance, and of asserting lofty truths in pregnant words. In his poems we find him moving from an exaggerated pessimism, a pessimism worthy of a Romanticist of 1830, to more dignified acquiesence in human destiny.—LANG, ANDREW, 1880, *English Poets, ed. Ward, vol.* I, *p.* 510.

Ponderous Chapman, smouldering into flame by flashes.—SYMONDS, JOHN ADDINGTON, 1887, *Marlowe,* (*Mermaid Series*), *General Introduction on the Drama, p.* xxv.

It is rash to differ from Lamb, but I am bound in mere sincerity to admit that I find nothing even remotely Shakespearian in plays that seem bombastic, loose, and incoherent to the last extreme, and in which the errors of the primitive Elizabethans, due mainly to inexperience, are complacently repeated and continued through the noblest years of perfected art, in which Shakespeare, Jonson, and Fletcher held the stage. Chapman was an admirable and sometimes even a great poet, but it is hard to admit that he was ever a tolerable playwright.—GOSSE, EDMUND, 1894, *The Jacobean Poets, p.* 40.

George Chapman, despite the geniune force and genius that must always secure him a high place among the great names of his age, discloses in his works, to a surprising degree, the confusion of imagery, the prolixity of thought and the tedious diffuseness, if beauty, of expression which characterized the poetic school of his youth and the later, lesser Spenserians. —SCHELLING, FELIX E., 1895, *A Book of Elizabethan Lyrics, p.* 251.

A remarkable dramatist, a poet of merit, and an altogether admirable translator.—SAINTSBURY, GEORGE, 1895, *Social England, ed. Traill, vol.* III, *p.* 523.

In general Chapman is characterized by abundant and highly conscious and literary use of metaphor and simile. He loves to amplify and pursue his tropes. This tendency, however, does not prevent frequent obscurity in the illustration, due to his theory of style in part, and partly also to the naturally involved and abstract character of his genius. Hardly any writer has a manner so personal to himself and so unmistakable as Chapman in his original tragedy style. His range is very wide and miscellaneous but he is also remarkable for a certain stock of favorite illustrations and metaphors which are repeated from play to play, often with only slight variations.—CARPENTER, FREDERIC IVES, 1895, *Metaphor and Simile in the Minor Elizabethan Drama, p.* 104.

He illuminated the age of Elizabeth by the first part of his translation of Homer; he lived on into the reign of Charles I. His poems (of which the best are his continuation of Marlowe's "Hero and Leander," and "The Tears of Peace") are extreme examples of the gnarled, sensuous, formless, and obscure poetry of which Dryden cured our literature. His plays are of a finer quality, especially the five tragedies taken from French history. They are weighty with thought, but the thought devours their action, and they are difficult and sensational. Inequality pervades them. His mingling of intellectual violence with intellectual imagination, of obscurity with a noble exultation and clearness of poetry, is a strange compound of the earlier and later Elizabethans. He, like Marlowe, but with less of beauty, "hurled instructive fire about the world." —BROOKE, STOPFORD A., 1896, *English Literature, p.* 143.

There is little doubt that Shakespeare found Chapman personally antipathetic. His style was unequalled for arrogance and pedantry; he was insufferably vain of his learning, and not a whit less conceited of the divine inspiration he, as poet, must necessarily possess. Even the most ardent of his modern admirers admits that his own poems are both grotesque and wearisome, and Shakespeare must certainly have suffered under the miserable conclusion Chapman added to Marlowe's beautiful "Hero and Leander," a poem that Shakespeare himself so greatly admired. Take only the fragment of introductory prose which prefaces his translation of Homer, and try to wade through it. Short as it is, it is impossible. Read but the confused garrulity and impossible imagery of the dedication in 1598, and could a more shocking collection of mediæval philology be found outside the two pages he writes about Homer?—BRANDES, GEORGE, 1898, *Shakespeare, A Critical Study, vol.* II, *p.* 205.

John Marston

1575?-1634

John Marston, 1575[?]-1634. Born, at Coventry[?], 1575[?]. Matric. Brasenose Coll., Oxford, 4 Feb. 1592; B. A., 6 Feb. 1594. Wrote plays, 1599-1607. Ordained Rector of Christ-church, Hampshire, Oct. 1616 to Sept. 1631. Married Mary Wilkes. Died, in London, 25 June 1634; buried in Temple Church. *Works:* "The Metamorphosis of Pygmalion's Image" (under initials: W. K.), 1598; "The Scourge of Vilanie" (under pseud: W. Kinsayder), 1598; "The History of Antonio and Mellida" (under initials: J. M.), 1602; "Antonio's Revenge," 1602; "The Malcontent," 1604; "Eastward Hoe" (with Jonson and Chapman), 1605; "The Dutch Courtezan," 1605; "Parasitaster," 1606; "The Wonder of Women," 1606; "What You Will," 1607; "Histriomastix" (anon.; probably partly by Marston), 1610; "The Insatiate Countess," 1613; "Jack Drum's Entertainment" (anon.; probably by Marston), 1616; "Tragedies and Comedies" (anon.), 1633 (another edn., with his name, same year). *Collected Works:* ed. by J. O. Halliwell (3 vols.), 1856; by A. H. Bullen (3 vols.), 1887. —SHARP, R. FARQUHARSON, 1897, *A Dictionarg of English Authors, p.* 186.

PERSONAL

Mr. Henslowe, at the Rose on the Bankside. If you like my playe of Columbus, it is verie well, and you shall give me noe more than twentie poundes for it, but If nott, lett me have it by the Bearer againe, as I know the kinges men will freelie give me as much for it, and the profitts of the third daye moreover.—MARSTON, JOHN, 1599, *Letter to Henslowe.*

He had many quarrells with Marston, beat him, and took his pistol from him, wrote his "Poetaster" on him; the beginning of them were, that Marston represented him in the stage, in his youth given to venerie.—DRUMMOND, WILLIAM, 1619, *Notes on Ben Jonson's Conversations.*

Of all the dramatists of the time, the most disagreeable in disposition, though by no means the least powerful in mind, was John Marston. The time of his birth is not known; his name is entangled in contemporary records with that of another John Marston; and we may be sure that his mischief-loving spirit would have been delighted could he have anticipated that the antiquaries, a century after his death, would be driven to despair by the difficulty of discriminating one from the other.—WHIPPLE, EDWIN P., 1859-68, *The Literature of the Age of Elizabeth, p.* 125.

THE MALCONTENT

1604

THE MALCONTENT. | Augmented by Marston. | With the Additions played by the *Kings* | *Maiesties Servants.* | Written | By IOHN WEBSTER. | At London: Printed by U. S. for William Aspley, and are | to be sold at his shop in Paules Church-yard. 1604. | TITLE PAGE OF FIRST EDITION.

We have accordingly no warrant for refusing to Marston the credit of any of the most striking passages in this play, which seems to me almost unapproached by his other productions in its occasional condensed vigour of expression, however greatly we may be tempted to attribute some at least among them to Webster. And there is at all events one example of truly powerful writing not forming part of the additions, and thus undoubtedly the property of Marston, which illustrates the difficulty of trusting too implicitly to instinct in seeking to discriminate between the touch or manner of different poets.—WARD, ADOLPHUS WILLIAM, 1875-99, *A History of English Dramatic Literature, vol.* II, *p.* 483.

Though not free from Marston's two chief vices of coarseness and exaggerated cynicism, it is a play of great merit, and much the best thing he has done, though the reconciliation, at the end, of such a husband and such a wife as Piero and Aurelia, between whom there is a chasm of adultery and murder, again lacks veriimilitude.—SAINTSBURY, GEORGE, 1887, *History of Elizabethan Literature, p.* 198.

Sad and stern, not unhopeful or unloving, the spirit of this poem is more in harmony with that of Webster's later tragedies than with that of Marston's previous plays; its accent is sardonic rather than pessimistic, ironical rather than despondent. The plot is neither well conceived nor well constructed; the catastrophe is little less than absurd, especially from the ethical or moral point of view; the characters are thinly sketched, the situations at once forced and conventional; there are few sorrier or stranger figures in serious fiction than is that of the penitent usurper when he takes to his arms his repentant wife, together with one of her two paramours, in a sudden rapture of forgiving affection; the part which gives the play its name is the only one drawn with any firmness of outline, unless we except that of the malignant and distempered old parasite; but there is a certain interest in the awkward evolution of the story, and there are scenes and passages of singular power and beauty which would suffice to redeem the whole work from condemnation or oblivion, even though it had not the saving salt in it of an earnest and evident sincerity.—SWINBURNE, ALGERNON CHARLES, 1888, *John Marston, The Nineteenth Century, vol.* 24, *p.* 536.

GENERAL

When Fuscus first had taught his Muse to scold,
He gloried in her rugged vaine so much,
That every one came to him heare her should,
First Victor, then Cinna; nor did he grutch
To let both players and artificers
Deale with his darling, as if confident
None of all these he did repute for lechers,
Or thought her face would all such lusts prevent.
But how can he a bawdes surname refuse,
Who to all sorts thus prostitutes his Muse?
—GUILPIN, EDWARD, 1598, *Skialetheia.*

Marston, thy Muse enharbours Horace vaine,
Then, some Augustus give thee Horace merit;
And thine, embuskin'd Johnson, doth retaine
So rich a stile and wondrous gallant spirit,
That if to praise your Muses I desired,
My Muse would muse. Such wittes must be admired.
—WEEVER, JOHN, 1599, *Epigrammes in the Oldest Cut and Newest Fashion.*

Methinks he is a ruffian in his style;
Withouten bands' or garters' ornament,
He quaffs a cup of Frenchmen's helicon,
Then royster doyster in his oily terms,
Cuts, thrusts, and foins at whomsoe'er he meets,
And shews about Ram-alley meditations.
. . . .
Aye, there is one that backs a paper steed
And manageth a pen knife gallantly;
Strikes his poinado at a button's breadth,
Brings the great battering-ram of terms to towns,
And at first volley of his cannon shot
Batters the walls of the old fusty world.
—ANON, 1606, *The Return from Parnassus, act* i, *sc.* 2.

Marston wrott his Father-in-lawes preachings, and his Father-in-law his Commedies. —DRUMMOND, WILLIAM, 1619, *Notes on Ben Jonson's Conversations.*

A Tragic and Comic Writer, not of the meanest rank, among our English Dramatics.—PHILLIPS, EDWARD, 1675, *Theatrum Poetarum Anglicanorum, ed. Brydges p.* 234.

It is Marston's misfortune, that he can never keep clear of the impurities of the brothel. His stream of poetry, if sometimes bright and unpolluted, almost always betrays a muddy bottom. The satirist who too freely indulges himself in the display of that licentiousness which he means to proscribe, absolutely defeats his own design. He inflames those passions which he professes to suppress, gratifies the depravations of a prurient curiosity, and seduces innocent minds to an acquaintance with ideas which they might never have known.—WARTON, THOMAS, 1778-81, *History of English Poetry, sec.* lxv.

Marston having consulted regularity and correctness in the conduct of his plays, and besides having written them naturally, and both with humour and pathos, must rank before Decker, and essentially, upon a par with Chapman and Heywood, especially when we are told that his poems rendered him still more celebrated than his plays. Being, however, a severe satirist, his contemporaries were not willing to allow him his due portion of praise, and posterity cannot properly judge of his whole merit. What we know of him, however, ranks him very respectfully as a writer.—DIBDIN, CHARLES, 1795, *A Complete History of the Stage, vol.* III, *p.* 263.

The most scurrilous, filthy, and obscene writer of his time.—GIFFORD, WILLIAM, 1816, *ed. The Works of Ben Jonson.*

Marston, better known in the drama than in satire, was characterized by his contemporaries for his ruffian style. He has more will than skill in invective. "He puts in his blows with love," as the pugilists say of a hard but artless fighter; a degrading image, but on that account not the less applicable to a coarse satirist. —CAMPBELL, THOMAS, 1819, *An Essay on English Poetry.*

Marston is a writer of great merit, who rose to tragedy from the ground of comedy, and whose *forte* was not sympathy, either with the stronger or softer emotions, but an impatient scorn and bitter indignation against the vices and follies of men, which vented itself either in comic irony or in lofty invective. He was properly a satirist. He was not a favourite with his contemporaries, nor they with him. He was first on terms of great intimacy, and afterwards at open war, with Ben Jonson; and he is most unfairly criticized in "The Return from Parnassus," under the name of Monsieur Kinsayder, as a mere libeller and buffoon.—HAZLITT, WILLIAM, 1820, *Lectures on the Literature of the Age of Elizabeth.*

Marston is a tumid and ranting tragedian, a wholesale dealer in murders and ghosts.—HALLAM, HENRY, 1837-39, *Introduction to the Literature of Europe, pt.* iii, *ch.* vi, *par.* 103.

Marston is chiefly remarkable for a fine tone of moral satire.—SHAW, THOMAS B., 1847, *Outlines of English Literature, p.* 131.

Of the dramatic works of Marston and Lilly it is enough to say that they are truly *works* to the reader, but in no sense dramatic, nor, as literature, worth the paper they blot. . . . We think that we have sustained our indictment of Mr. Halliwell's text with ample proof. The title of the book should have been, "The Works of John Marston, containing all the Misprints of the Original Copies, together with a few added for the First Time in this Edition, the whole carefully let alone by James Orchard Halliwell, F.R.S., F.S.A." It occurs to us that Mr. Halliwell may be also a Fellow of the Geological Society, and may have caught from its members the enthusiasm which leads him to attach so extraordinary a value to every goose-track of the Elizabethan formation. It is bad enough to be, as Marston was, one of those middling poets whom neither gods nor men nor columns (Horace had never seen a newspaper) tolerate; but, really, even they do not deserve the frightful retribution of being reprinted by a Halliwell.—LOWELL, JAMES RUSSELL, 1858-64-90, *Library of Old Authors, Prose Works, Riverside ed., vol.* I, *pp.* 254, 271.

Marston's plays, whether comedies or tragedies, all bear the mark of his bitter and misanthropic spirit,—a spirit that seemed cursed by the companionship of its own thoughts, and forced them out through a well-grounded fear that they would fester if left within. . . . Marston is not without sprightliness, but his sprightliness is never the sprightliness of the kid, though it is sometimes that of a hyena, and sometimes that of the polecat. . . . His tragedies, indeed, though not without a gloomy power, are extravagant and horrible in conception and conduct. Even when he copies, he makes the thing his own by caricaturing it.—WHIPPLE, EDWIN P., 1859-68, *The Literature of the Age of Elizabeth, pp.* 127, 128.

He is to be classed with Sackville and Chapman, as having more poetical than dramatic genius; although he has given no proof of a creative imagination equal to what is displayed in the early poetry of the former, and the best of Chapman's is instinct with a diviner fire. But he is, nevertheless, a very imposing declaimer in verse.—CRAIK, GEORGE L., 1861, *A Compendious History of English Literature and of the English Language, vol.* I, *p.* 597.

John Marston is the Skelton or Swift of the Elizabethan period. Like them, he wrote in denunciation and derision of what seemed to him vicious or weakly sentimental; and like them, he impatiently carried a passion for directness of speech to the extremes of coarseness. He was for no half-veiled exposure of vices. . . . Marston's plays are very remarkable and distinctive productions. They are written with amazing energy—energy audacious, defiant, shameless, yet, when viewed in the totality of its manifestations, not unworthy to be called Titanic. They make no pretence to dramatic impartiality; they are written throughout in the spirit of his satires; his puppets walk the stage as embodiments of various ramifications of deadly sins and contemptible fopperies, side by side with virtuous opposites and indignant commenting censors. His characters, indeed, speak and act with vigorous life: they are much more forcible and distinct personalities than Chapman's characters. But though Marston brings out his characters sharply and clearly, and puts them in lifelike motion, they are too manifestly objects of their creator's liking and disliking: some are caricatured, some are unduly black, and some unduly stainless. From one great fault Marston's personages are exceedingly free: they may be overdrawn, and they may be coarse, but they are seldom dull—their life is a rough coarse life, but life it is. And all his serious creations have here and there put into their mouths passages of tremendous energy.—MINTO, WILLIAM, 1874-85, *Characteristics of English Poets*, *pp.* 332, 335.

Shakspere in particular shines through the seams of most of Marston's plays. His literary ambition was manifestly very great; and opposition vexed him to the quick. But though his ambition was sustained by many acquirements, and by the powers of occasional pathos and fluent humour, while at times he could rise to poetic beauty of expression, yet there is a false ring about most of his efforts, and a want of sustained force in nearly all. He sought to excel in various dramatic species, but can hardly be said to have reached excellence unless in the depiction of the abnormal excesses of contemporary manners; and even here he fails in concentration of effect. Thus I remain in doubt whether on the whole he deserves to be ranked among the great dramatists. with whose names his own is habitually associated, as having like them adorned our dramatic literature with creations of original genius.—WARD, ADOLPHUS WILLIAM, 1875-99, *A History of English Dramatic Literature, vol.* II, *p.* 492.

The foulness of Marston's fancy is often loathsome, even to a critic without squeamishness. It is still a long step in development, if not in time, from him to the ideal tragedy of Hamlet or Othello; to mistake these "preludings" for his music is like the blunder of the Siamese amateur at the opera, who thanked the orchestra on the tuning of their instruments.—WASHBURN, EMELYN W., 1884, *Studies in Early English Literature, p.* 137.

Marston, that biting satirist and tense sententious builder of blank verse.—SYMONDS, JOHN ADDINGTON, 1887, *Marlowe, (Mermaid Series), General Introduction on the Drama, p.* xxv.

That he was an ill-tempered person with considerable talents, who succeeded, at any rate for a time, in mistaking his ill-temper for *sæva indignatio*, and his talents for genius, is not, I think, too harsh a description of Marston. In the hotbed of the literary influences of the time, these conditions of his produced some remarkable fruit. But when my friend Professor Minto attributes to him "amazing and almost Titanic energy," mentions "life" several times over as one of the chief characteristics of his personages (I should say that they had as much life as violently-moved marionettes), and discovers "amiable and admirable characters" among them, I am compelled not, of course, to be positive that my own very different estimate is right, but to wonder at the singularly different way in which the same things strike different persons, who are not as a rule likely to look at them from very different points of view. —SAINTSBURY, GEORGE, 1887, *History of Elizabethan Literature, p.* 196.

Two of the epithets which Ben Jonson, in his elaborate attack on Marston, selected for ridicule as characteristically grotesque instances of affected and infelicitous innovation—but which nevertheless have taken root in the language, and practically justified their adoption—describe as happily as any that could be chosen to describe the better and the worse quality of his early tragic and satiric style. These words are "strenuous" and "clumsy." It is perpetually, indefatigably, and fatiguingly strenuous; it is too often vehemently, emphatically, and laboriously clumsy. But at its best, when the clumsy and ponderous incompetence of expression which disfigures it is supplanted by a strenuous felicity of ardent and triumphant aspiration, it has notes and touches in the compass of its course not unworthy of Webster or Tourneur or even Shakespeare himself. Its occasionally exquisite delicacy is as remarkable as its more frequent excess of coarseness, awkwardness, or violent and elaborate extravagance. No sooner has he said anything especially beautiful, pathetic, or sublime, than the evil genius must needs take his turn, exact as it were the forfeit of his bond, impel the poet into some sheer perversity, deface the flow and form of the verse with some preposterous crudity or flatulence of phrase which would discredit the most incapable or the most fantastic novice. And the worst of it all is that he limps or stumbles with either foot alternately. At one moment he exaggerates the license of artificial rhetoric, the strain and swell of the most high-flown and hyperbolical poetic diction; at the next, he falls flat upon the naked level of insignificant or offensive realism.—SWINBURNE, ALGERNON CHARLES, 1888, *John Marston, The Nineteenth Century, vol.* 24, *p.* 531.

In 1602 came from the press the "History of Antonio and Mellida. The First Part," 4to, and "Antonio's Revenge. The Second Part," 4to, both acted by the Children of Paul's. These plays had been entered in the Stationers' Register on 24 Oct. 1601, and in the same year had been held up to ridicule by Ben Jonson in the "Poetaster." The writing is uneven; detached scenes are memorable, but there is an intolerable quantity of fustian. Frequently we are reminded of Seneca's tragedies, which Marston had closely studied. The "Malcontent," 1604, 4to, reissued in the same year, with additions by Webster, is more skilfully constructed, and shows few traces of the barbarous diction that disfigured "Antonio and Mellida."—BULLEN, A. H., 1893, *Dictionary of National Biography, vol.* XXXVI, *p.* 257.

He preferred to scold at his contemporaries in verse which is as pleasant to read as charcoal would be to eat, and to lecture an imaginary world made up of vices which he took at second hand from Latin books, in a style which raises the image of ancient Pistol unpacking his heart with curses.—HANNAY, DAVID, 1898, *The Later Renaissance, p.* 222.

Sir Edward Coke

1552–1634

Born at Mileham, Norfolk, England, Feb. 1, 1552: died at Stoke Pogis, Sept. 3, 1634. A noted English jurist. He was speaker of the House of Commons 1592–93, attorney-general 1593–94, chief justice of the Common Pleas 1606, and chief justice of the King's Bench 1613. He came into conflict with the king and Bacon on matters touching the royal prerogative, especially the right of granting commendams, and was removed from the bench Nov. 15, 1616. Among the noted cases which he conducted as prosecutor are those of Essex and Southampton in 1601, of Sir Walter Raleigh in 1603 (in which he disgraced himself by the brutality of his language), and of the gunpowder plotters in 1605. In the later part of his life he rendered notable service, in Parliament, to the cause of English freedom, his last important speech being a direct attack on Buckingham. His chief works are his "Reports" (1600-15) and his "Institutes," which consist of a reprint and translation of Littleton's "Tenures" with a commentary (popularly known as "Coke upon Littleton"); the text of various statutes from Magna Charta to the time of James I., with a commentary; a treatise on criminal law; and a treatise on the jurisdiction of the different law-courts.—SMITH, BENJAMIN E., *ed.* 1894–97, *The Century Cyclopedia of Names, p.* 265.

Five sorts of people he used to foredesign to misery and poverty; Chemists, Monopolizers, Concelers, Promoters, and Rythming Poets. For three things he would give God solemn thanks; that he never gave his body to physick, nor his heart to cruelty, nor his hand to corruption. In three things he did much applaud his own success; in his fair fortune with his Wife, in his happy study of the Laws, and in his free coming by all his Offices, *nec prece, nec pretio*, neither begging nor bribing for preferment. His parts were admirable: he had a deep judgment, faithful memory, active fancy; and the jewel of his mind was put into a fair case, a beautiful body, with a comely countenance; a case, which he did wipe and keep clean, delighting in good cloaths, well worne; and being wont to say, "that the outward neatness of our bodies might be a Monitor of purity to our souls." In his pleadings, discourse, and judgements, he declined all circumlocutions, usually saying, "The matter lies in a little room." In all places, callings, and jurisdictions, he commended modesty and sobriety within their boundaries, saying, "If a River swells beyond its Banks, it loseth its own Channel." If any adverse party crossed him, he would patiently reply, "If another punish me, I will not punish myself." In the highest Term of business, he made Vacation to himself at his Table; and would never be persuaded privately to retract what he had publikely adjudged, professing, he was a Judge in a Court, and not in a Chamber. . . . His most learned and laborious works on the Laws will last to be admired by the judicious posterity whilst Fame hath a trumpet left her, and any breath to blow therein.—FULLER, THOMAS, 1662, *The Worthies of England, ed. Nichols, vol.* II, *pp.* 129, 130.

Sir Edward Coke—that great oracle of our law.—BURKE, EDMUND, 1790, *Reflections on the Revolution in France.*

Coké was "the oracle of law" but, like too many great lawyers, he was so completely one as to have been nothing else. Coke has said, "the common law is the absolute perfection of all reason;" a dictum which might admit of some ridicule. Armed with law, he committed acts of injustice; for in how many cases, passion mixing itself with law, *summum jus* becomes *summa injuria.* Official violence brutalized, and political ambition extinguished, every spark of nature in this great lawyer, when he struck at his victims, public or domestic. His solitary knowledge, perhaps, had deadened his judgment in other studies; and yet his narrow spirit could shrink with jealousy at the celebrity obtained by more liberal pursuits than his own. The errors of the great are as instructive as their virtues; and the secret history of the outrageous lawyer may have, at least, the merit of novelty, although not of panegyric.—DISRAELI, ISAAC, 1791–1824, *Domestic History of Sir Edward Coke, Curiosities of Literature.*

He was a man of strong though narrow intellect; confessedly the greatest master of English law that had ever appeared, but proud and overbearing, a flatterer and tool of the court till he had obtained his ends, and odious to the nation for the brutal manner in which, as attorney-general, he had behaved towards sir Walter Raleigh on his trial.—HALLAM, HENRY, 1827–46, *The Constitutional History of England, ch.* vi.

Fierce with dark keeping, his mind resembled some of those gloomy structures where records and muniments are piled to the exclusion of all higher or nobler matters. For genius he had no love: with philosophy he had no sympathy.—MONTAGU, BASIL, 1834, *The Life of Bacon.*

Pedant, bigot, and savage as he was, he had qualities which bore as strong, though a very disagreeable resemblance to some of the highest virtues which a public man can possess. He was an exception to a maxim which we believe to be generally true, that those who trample on the helpless are disposed to cringe to the powerful. He behaved with gross rudeness to his juniors at the bar, and with execrable cruelty to prisoners on trial for their lives. But he stood up manfully against the king and the king's favourites. No man of that age appeared to so little advantage when he was opposed to an inferior, and was in the wrong. But, on the other hand, it is but fair to admit, that no man of that age made so creditable a figure when he was opposed to a superior, and happened to be in the right. On such occasion, his half-suppressed insolence and his impracticable obstinacy had a respectable and interesting appearance, when compared with the abject servility of the bar and of the bench.—MACAULAY, THOMAS BABINGTON, 1834, *Lord Bacon, Edinburgh Review, Critical and Miscellaneous Essays.*

The leviathan of the common law, and the sublime of common sense,—a man who could have been produced only by the slow gestation of centuries, English in bone and blood and brain. Stout as an oak, though capable of being yielding as a willow; with an intellect tough, fibrous, holding with a Titanic clutch its enormity of acquisition; with a disposition hard, arrogant, obstinate, just; and with a heart avaricious of wealth and power, scorning all weak and most amiable emotions, but clinging, in spite of its selfish fits and starts of servility, to English laws, customs, and liberties, with the tenacity of mingled instinct and passion; the man looms up before us, rude, ungenerous, and revengeful, as when he insulted Bacon in his abasement, and roared out "spider of hell" to Raleigh in his unjust impeachment, yet rarely losing that stiff, daring spirit which drafted the immortal "Petition of Right," and that sour and sullen honesty which told the messenger of James I., who came to command him to prejudge a case in which the king's prerogative was concerned "when the case happens, I shall do that which will be fit for a judge to do."—WHIPPLE, EDWIN P., 1866, *The English Mind, Character and Characteristic Men, p.* 184.

The lustre which, in the eye of the jurist, gathers around the name of Coke, as one of the fathers in his profession, is tarnished when memory recalls his brutal ferocity in the trial of Raleigh.—HAWKS, FRANCIS L., 1856, *History of North Carolina, vol.* I, *p.* 47.

Coke also has a place in literature. His reports are, even at the present day, known without his name simply as "The Reports," and his "Institutes" is one of the most learned works which this age produced. It is rather a collection provided with notes, but is instructive and suggestive from the variety of and the contrast of its contents. Coke traced the English laws to the remotest antiquity; he considered them as the common production of the wisest men of earlier ages, and at the same time as the great inheritance of the English people, and its best protection against every kind of tyranny, spiritual or temporal. Even the old Norman French, in which they were to a great extent composed, he would not part with, for a peculiar meaning attached itself, in his view, to every word.—RANKE, LEOPOLD VON, 1875, *A History of England, vol.* I, *p.* 455.

The ablest, and also the most truculent and unscrupulous of English lawyers.—CHURCH, RICHARD WILLIAM, 1884-88, *Bacon, (English Men of Letters), p.* 36.

The height of Coke's legal fame has overshadowed his other claims to greatness. . . . Of Coke as a lawyer it is difficult to speak without attaching either too great or too little weight to his vast reputation. In avoiding the indiscriminate laudation with which he has been injured there is a danger of falling into the still more unbecoming error of speaking without due respect of a great man who has exercised a really profound influence on English law.—MACDONELL, G. P., 1887, *Dictionary of National Biography, vol.* XI, *pp.* 239, 240.

With Coke—the victim, it was said at the time, of "pride, prohibitions, præmunire, and prerogative"—no one who has read the trials of Raleigh, or noted how the vaunted champion of national rights veered in his view of them according to the place he happened to hold, can have any personal sympathy. A pedant and a boor, the assertion of his own undignified dignity, rather than any larger motive, determined his attitude. On the other hand, it must be admitted that he was sometimes in the right, and that his attempt to make his court an *imperium in imperio* foreran the assertion of the important principle that law has a place in the realm altogether apart from politics.—NICHOL, JOHN, 1888, *Francis Bacon, His Life and Philosophy, Part* I, *p.* 140.

Edward Fairfax

C 1580-1635

Translator of Tasso, was a son (perhaps a natural son) of Sir Thomas Fairfax of Denton in Yorkshire. His life was spent in literary pursuits at Fewston, near Otley; and his translation of Tasso's "Gerusalemme Liberata" (1600) has been universally praised. His "Discourse of Witchcraft" (1621) was published by Monckton Milnes in the "Miscellanies" of the Philobiblon Society (1858-59).—PATRICK AND GROOME, *eds.,* 1897, *Chambers's Biographical Dictionary, p.* 353.

One of the most judicious, elegant, and haply in his time, most approved of English Translatours, both for his choice of so worthily extoll'd a heroic poet as Torquato Tasso; as for the exactness of his version, in which he is judg'd by some to have approved himself no less a poet than in what he hath written of his own genius.—PHILLIPS, EDWARD, 1675, *Theatrum Poetarum Anglicanorum, ed. Brydges, p.* 191.

Milton has acknowledged to me, that Spenser was his original; and many besides myself have heard our famous Waller own, that he derived the harmony of his numbers from "Godfrey of Bulloigne," which was turned into English by Mr. Fairfax.—DRYDEN, JOHN, 1700, *Preface to the Fables, Works, ed. Scott and Saintsbury, vol.* XI, *p.* 210.

A Gentleman of so much Merit, that he eminently deserves to be rank'd among the First of our *English* Writers; yet has He hitherto been treated with so much Neglect, to say no Worse, That no one Author has afforded us a tolerable Sketch of his Life; or given Themselves even the Trouble to make the slightest Enquiry after Him. *Philips* so far overlooks him, that he was forc'd to crowd him into his Supplement, and his Transcriber *Winstanly*, does, in a Manner, the same, by postponing him till after the Earl of *Rochester*. Sir *Thomas Pope Blunt* makes no mention of him at all: And Mr. *Jacob* informs us he wrote in the Reign of King *Charles* the *First;* tho' He dedicates his Translation of *Tasso* to Queen *Elizabeth:* Indeed all that name him, do him the Justice to allow he was an accomplish'd Genius; but then 'tis in so cool, and careless a Manner, as plainly indicates they were very little acquainted with the Merit they prais'd. . . . In Fact, this Gentleman is the only Writer down to *D'Avenant,* that needs no Apology to be made for him, on Account of the Age he lived in.—His Diction being, generally speaking, so pure, so elegant, and full of Graces, and the Turn of his Lines so perfectly Melodious, that I hardly believe the Original *Italian* has greatly the Advantage in either: Nor could any Author, in my Opinion, be justify'd for attempting *Tasso* anew, as long as his Translation can be read.—COOPER, ELIZABETH, 1737, *The Muses' Library, pp.* 342, 343.

Fairfax has translated Tasso with an elegance and ease, and at the same time with an exactness, which, for that age, are surprising.—HUME, DAVID, 1754-62. *The History of England, James I., Appendix.*

I question whether any late attempt to naturalize the beautiful epic of Tasso can be considered as superior, either in energy or fidelity, to this old but admirable version. In many places the diction of Fairfax is peculiarly pleasing; and he greatly excels in transfusing the rural imagery of his author, and which sometimes receives even improvement from his colouring.—DRAKE, NATHAN, 1798, *Literary Hours, No.* XXVIII.

His translation of the Jerusalem was published when he was a young man, was inscribed to Queen Elizabeth, and forms one of the glories of her reign.—CAMPBELL, THOMAS, 1819, *Specimens of the British Poets.*

Of Fairfax, the elegant translator of Tasso, it is enough to say that he is styled by Dryden "the poetical father of Waller," and quoted by him, in conjunction with Spenser, as "one of the great masters of our language."—PRESCOTT, WILLIAM HICKLING, 1831, *Italian Narrative Poetry, Biographical and Critical Miscellanies.*

If it does not represent the grace of its original, and deviates also too much from its sense, is by no means deficient in spirit and vigor. It has been considered as one of the earliest works, in which the obsolete English, which had not been laid aside in the days of Sackville, and which Spenser affected to preserve, gave way to a style not much differing, at least in point of single words and phrases, from that of the present age. But this praise is equally due to Daniel, to Drayton, and to others of the later Elizabethan poets. The translation of Ariosto by Sir John Harrington, in 1591, is much inferior.—HALLAM, HENRY, 1837-39, *Introduction to the Literature of Europe, pt.* ii, *ch.* v, *par.* 74.

Fairfax employs the *ottava rima* in his translation of Tasso's "Jerusalem Delivered;" and great as is the poetical merit of this translation, the reader soon tires of the rhyme-scheme.—CORSON, HIRAM, 1892, *A Primer of English Verse, p.* 90.

Fairfax's worst blunders, or seeming blunders, in translation do little damage to the spirit of his text.—MORLEY, HENRY, 1893, *English Writers, vol.* X, *p.* 460.

Richard Corbet

1582–1635

Poet-bishop, the son of a gardener at Ewell, Surrey, from Westminster School passed to Broadgates Hall, Oxford, and thence to Christ Church. He had been vicar of Cassington, Oxfordshire, and Stewkley, Bucks, as well as a prebendary of Salisbury, when in 1620 he was made Dean of Christ Church. In 1624 he was consecrated to the see of Oxford, and in 1632 translated to Norwich. Corbet's "Poems" (1647; ed. by Gilchrist, 1807) reflect the jovial temper of the man. His longest piece is "Iter Boreale," a holiday-tour of four students; the best and best-known is the "Fairies' Farewell."—PATRICK AND GROOME, *eds.*, 1897, *Chambers's Biographical Dictionary*, *p.* 246.

He had a good interest with great men, as you may find in his poems, and with the then great favourite, the duke of Bucks; his excellent witt was lettres of recommendation to him. I have forgott the story, but at the same time that Dr. (Samuel) Fell thought to have carried it, Dr. Corbet putt a pretty trick on (him) to lett him take a journey on purpose to London for it, when he had already the graunt of it. . . . His conversation was extreme pleasant. Dr. Stubbins was one of his cronies; he was a jolly fatt Dr. and a very good house-keeper; parson of (Ambrosden) in Oxfordshire. As Dr. Corbet and he were riding in Lob-lane, in wett weather, ('tis an extraordinary deepe dirty lane) the coach fell; and Dr. Corbet sayd that Dr. Stubbins was up to the elbowes in mud, he was up to the elbowes in Stubbins. . . . One time, as he was confirming, the country people pressing in to see the ceremonie, sayd he "*Beare-off there, or I'le confirme yee with my staffe.*" Another time being to lay his hand on the head of a man very bald, he turns to his chaplaine (Lushington) and sayd, "*Some dust, Lushington,*" (to keepe his hand from slipping).—AUBREY, JOHN, 1669-96, *Brief Lives, ed. Clark, vol.* I, *pp.* 185, 186.

Esteemed one of the most celebrated wits in the university, as his poems, jests, romantic fancies and exploits, which he made and perform'd extempore, shew'd. —WOOD, ANTHONY, 1691-1721, *Athenæ Oxonienses, vol.* I, *f.* 600.

The anecdotes of this facetious bishop, quoted by Headley from the Aubrey MSS., would fill several pages of a jest-book. It is more to his honour to be told, that though entirely hostile in his principles to the Puritans, he frequently softened, with his humane and characteristic pleasantry, the furious orders against them which Laud enjoined him to execute.—CAMPBELL, THOMAS, 1819, *Specimen of the British Poets.*

One of the most remarkable among the clerical poets of this earlier half of the seventeenth century was Dr. Richard Corbet. . . . Corbet's poetry is a mixture of alternation of gravity and drollery. But it is the subject or occasion, rather than the style or manner, that makes the difference; he never rises to anything higher than wit; and he is as witty in his elegies as in his ballads. As that ingredient, however, is not so suitable for the former as for the latter, his graver performances are worth very little. Nor is his merriment of a high order; when it is most elaborate it is strained and fantastic, and when more natural it is apt to run into buffoonery. But much of his verse, indeed, is merely prose in rhyme, and very indifferent rhyme for the most part.—CRAIK, GEORGE L., 1861, *A Compendious History of English Literature and of the English Language, vol.* II, *p.* 21.

Corbet's work is of that peculiar class which is usually, though not always, due to "university wits," and which only appeals to people with a considerable appreciation of humour, and a large stock of general information. It is always occasional in character, and rarely succeeds so well as when the treatment is one of distinct *persiflage.*—SAINTSBURY, GEORGE, 1887, *History of Elizabethan Literature, p.* 383.

Corbet's poems are for the most part in a rollicking satiric vein, and are always very good-humoured, with the single exception of his verses "upon Mrs. Mallet, an unhandsome gentlewoman that made love to him." The well-known "Fairies Farewell," a graceful and fanciful piece of verse, is his most serious production. —LEE, SIDNEY, 1887, *Dictionary of National Biography, vol.* XII, *p.* 204.

Thomas Randolph

1605-1635

Born at Houghton, Daventry, Northamptonshire, 1605: died 1634. An English poet and dramatist. He was educated at Westminster and Cambridge, and was also incorporated at Oxford. Ben Jonson adopted him as one of his "sons." He wrote "Aristippus," "The Muses' Looking-Glass, a Comedy," "Amyntas, or the Impossible Dowry," "The Conceited Pedlar," "The Jealous Lovers," "Down with Knavery" (from the "Plutus" of Aristophanes), etc.; also a number of minor poems.—SMITH, BENJAMIN E., *ed.*, 1894-97, *The Century Cyclopedia of Names, p.* 842.

His wit and learning endeared him to Ben Jonson, who owned him, like Cartwright, as his adopted son in the Muses. Unhappily he followed the taste of Ben not only at the pen, but at the bottle; and he closed his life in poverty, at the age of twenty-nine,—a date lamentably premature, when we consider the promises of his genius. His wit and humour are very conspicuous in the Puritan characters, whom he supposes the spectators of his scenes in the "Muse's Looking-Glass." Throughout the rest of that drama (though it is on the whole his best performance) he unfortunately prescribed to himself too hard and confined a system of dramatic effect.—CAMPBELL, THOMAS, 1819, *Specimens of the British Poets.*

Randolph has a good deal of fancy, and his verse flows very melodiously; but his poetry has in general a bookish and borrowed air. Much of it is on subjects of love and gallantry; but the love is chiefly of the head, or, at most, of the senses,—the gallantry, it is easy to see, that merely of a fellow of a college and a reader of Ovid.—CRAIK, GEORGE L., 1861, *A Compendious History of English Literature and of the English Language, vol.* II, *p.* 20.

It seems probable that in the premature death of Randolph, English literature underwent a very heavy loss. . . . Intellect and imagination Randolph possessed in full measure, but as he does not seem to have been born to excel in play-writing or in song-writing, and as he died too early to set his own mark on literature, we are left to speculate down what groove such brilliant and energetic gifts as his would finally have proceeded. Had he lived longer his massive intelligence might have made him a dangerous rival or a master to Dryden, and as he shows no inclination towards the French manner of poetry, he might have delayed or altogether warded off the influx of the classical taste. He showed no precocity of genius; he was gradually gathering his singing-robes about him, having already studied much, yet having still much to learn. There is no poet whose works so tempt the critic to ask, "what was the next step in his development?" He died just too soon to impress his name on history.—GOSSE, EDMUND, 1880, *English Poets, ed. Ward, vol,* II, *p.* 219.

Sons born of many a loyal Muse to Ben,
All true-begotten. . . .
Prince Randolph, nighest his throne of all his men,
Being highest in spirit and heart who hailed him then
King, nor might other spread so blithe a sail.

—SWINBURNE, ALGERNON CHARLES, 1882, *The Tribe of Benjamin.*

The most gifted (according to general estimate rather than to specific performance) of the Tribe of Ben. . . . There is no doubt that Randolph's work gives the impression of considerable power. At the same time it is fair to remember that the author's life was one very conducive to precocity, inasmuch as he underwent at once the three stimulating influences of an elaborate literary education, of endowed leisure to devote himself to what literary occupations he pleased. . . . It may be plausibly argued that, good as what Randolph's first thirty years gave is, it ought to have been better still if it was ever going to be of the best. —SAINTSBURY, GEORGE, 1887, *History of Elizabethan Literature, pp.* 413, 414.

Randolph achieved a wide reputation in his own day, and was classed by his contemporaries among "the most pregnant wits of his age." Fertile in imagination, he could on occasion express himself with rare power and beauty. But his promise, as might be expected from his irregular life and premature death, was greater than his performance.—LEE, SIDNEY, 1896, *Dictionary of National Biography, vol.* XLVII, *p.* 282.

BEN JONSON

From Engraving by H. Robinson, from Picture by Gerard Honthorst.

Ben Jonson

1573?-1637

Born, in Westminster (?), 1573(?). Educated at St.-Martin's-in-the-Fields Parish School; and at Westminster School. Worked as a bricklayer for a short time; afterwards served with English troops in Flanders. Returned to England about 1592; married soon afterwards. First acted, and wrote for stage, about 1595. Imprisoned for killing a fellow-actor in a duel, 1598. Became a Roman Catholic, same year. "Every Man in His Humour," produced at Globe Theatre, 1598. Wrote plays for Henslowe's company, 1599-1602. "Sejanus," produced at Globe Theatre, 1603. Prolific writer of plays; and of Masques, for Court performance, 1605-30. Imprisoned for a short time in connection with political allusions in play "Eastward Ho," 1605. In France, as tutor to son of Sir W. Raleigh, 1613. Journey to Scotland, on foot, 1618. Elected Burgess of Edinburgh, Sept. 1618. Visited Drummond of Hawthornden. Returned to England, spring of 1619. Visit to Oxford, 1620; received Hon. M. A. degree. Ill-health began, 1626. Chronologer to City of London, Sept. 1628; deprived of Salary, 1631; restored to post, Sept. 1634. Died, in London, 6 Aug. 1637. Buried in Westminster Abbey. *Works:* "Every Man Out of His Humour," 1600 (2nd edn. same year); "Cynthia's Revels," 1600; "Every Man in his Humour," 1601; "Poëtaster," 1602; Additions to "Jeronymo," 1602; "A Particular Entertainment," 1603; "Part of King James his . . . Entertainment," 1604; "Sejanus," 1605; "Eastward Ho" (with Chapman and Marston), 1605 (3rd edn. same year); "Hymenæi," 1606; "Volpone," 1607; "Description of the . . . Masque" at Viscount Hadington's Marriage (1608); "Epicœne," 1609; "The Character of two royall Masques," 1609; "Ben Jonson, his Case is Altered," 1609; "The Masque of Queenes," 1609; "Cateline his Conspiracy," 1611; "The Alchemist," 1612; "Certayne Masques," 1615; "Works" (2 vols.), 1616-40; "Lovers Made Men" (known as "The Masque of Lethe;" anon.), 1617; "The Masque of Augures," 1621; "Neptune's Triumph" (anon.), [1623]; "The Fortunate Isles" [1624]; "Love's Triumph through Callipolis," 1630; "Chloridia" [1630?]; "The New Inne," 1631. *Posthumous:* "The Bloody Brother, by B. J. F." (mainly by Fletcher; perhaps part by Jonson), 1639; "Underwoods," 1640; "Excreation against Vulcan," 1640; "The English Grammar," 1640; "The Widow" (with Fletcher and Middleton), 1652; "The Fall of Mortimer" (anon.: completed by another hand), 1771; "The Sad Shepherd," ed. by F. G. Waldron, 1783. He *translated:* "Horace his Art of Poetrie," 1640. *Collected Works:* in one vol., 1692; in 7 vols., ed. by Whalley, 1756; ed. by Gifford, 1816.—SHARP, R. FARQUHARSON, 1897, *A Dictionary of English Authors*, p. 152.

PERSONAL

Sence you weare with me I have lost one of company, which hurteth me greatly, that is Gabrill, for he is slayen in Hogesden fylldes (Hoxton Fields) by the hands of Bengemen Jonson, bricklayer, therefore I wold fayne have a littell of your counsell yf I would.—HENSLOWE, PHILIPS, 1598, *Letter to Edward Alleyne, Sept.* 26, *Collier's Memoirs of Edward Alleyne.*

At Leith I found my long approved and assured good friend Master Benjamin Jonson, at one Master John Stuart's house. I thank him for his great kindness; for, at my taking leave of him, he gave me a piece of gold of two-and-twenty shillings' value, to drink his health in England.—TAYLOR, JOHN, 1618, *Pennylesse Pilgrimage.*

A great lover and praiser of himself; a contemner and scorner of others; given rather to losse a friend than a jest; jealous of every word and action of those about him (especiallie after drink, which is one of the elements in which he liveth); a dissembler of ill parts which raigne in him, a bragger of some good that he wanteth; thinketh nothing well bot what either he himself or some of his friends and countrymen hath said or done; he is passionately kynde and angry; careless either to gaine or keep; vindicative, but, if he be well answered, at himself. . . . For any religion, as being versed in both. Interpreteth best sayings and deeds often to the worst. Oppressed with fantasie, which hath ever mastered his reason, a generall disease in many Poets. His inventions are smooth and easie; but above all he excelleth in a Translation.—DRUMMOND, WILLIAM, 1619, *Notes on Ben Jonson's Conversations.*

Come, leave the loathèd stage,
And the more loathsome age;
Where pride and impudence, in faction knit,
Usurp the chair of wit!
Indicting and arraigning every day
Something they call a play.
Let their fastidious, vain
Commission of the brain
Run on and rage, sweat, censure and condemn;
They were not made for thee, less thou for them.

—JONSON, BEN, c 1629, *Ode to Himself.*

And famous Jonson, though his learned pen
Be dipt in Castaly, is still but *Ben.*

—HEYWOOD, THOMAS, 1635, *The Hierarchy of the Blessed Angels.*

Sir:—I was invited yesternight to a solemn Supper, by *B. J.*, where you were deeply remembered; there was good company, excellent cheer, choice wines, and jovial welcome: One thing intervened, which almost spoiled the relish of the rest, that *B.* began to engross all the discourse, to vapour extremely by himself, and, by vilifying others, to magnify his own *Muse.* *T. Ca.* buzzed me in the ear, that though *Ben* had barrelled up a great deal of knowledge, yet it seems he had not read the *Ethiques*, which, among other precepts of Morality, forbid self-commendation, declaring it to be an ill-favoured solecism in good manners. . . . But for my part, I am content to dispense with the *Roman* infirmity of *B.*, now that time hath snowed upon his *pericranium.* You know *Ovid*, and (your) *Horace* were subject to this humour, the first bursting out into

Jamq; opus exegi, quod nec Jovis ira nec ignis, &c.

The other into

Exegi monumentum ære perenniùs, &c.

As also *Cicero*, while he forced himself into this hexameter: "O fortunatam natam, me consule Romam!" There is another reason that excuseth *B.*, which is, that if one be allowed to love the natural issue of his Body, why not that of his Brain, which is of a spiritual and more noble extraction?—HOWELL, JAMES, 1636, *Letter to Sir Thomas Hawk, April 5th.*

The first that broke silence was good old Ben,
Prepared before with Canary wine,
And he told them plainly he deserved the bays,
For his were called works where others were but plays.
. . . .
Apollo stopped him there, and bad him not go on,
'T was merit, he said, and not presumption,
Must carry 't; at which Ben turned about,
And in great choler offered to go out.

—SUCKLING, SIR JOHN, 1637, *A Sessions of the Poets.*

Ah Ben!
Say how, or when
Shall we thy guests
Meet at those lyric feasts,
Made at the Sun,
The Dog, the Triple Tun?
Where we such clusters had
As made us nobly wild, not mad;
And yet each verse of thine
Outdid the meat, outdid the frolic wine.
My Ben!
Or come again,
Or send to us,
Thy wit's great overplus;
But teach us yet
Wisely to husband it,
Lest we that talent spend;
And having once brought to an end
That precious stock, the store
Of such a wit the world should have no more.

—HERRICK, ROBERT, 1637? *An Ode for Him.*

Though I cannot with all my industrious inquiry find him in his cradle, I can fetch him from his long coats. When a little child, he lived in Harts-horn-lane near Charing-cross, where his Mother married a Bricklayer for her second husband. . . . He help'd in the building of the new structure of Lincoln's Inn, when, having a trowell in his hand, he had a book in his pocket. Some gentlemen, pitying that his parts should be buried under the rubbish of so mean a calling, did by their bounty manumise him freely to follow his own ingenious inclinations. Indeed his parts were not so ready to run of themselves, as able to answer the spur; so that it may be truly said of him, that he had an elaborate wit wrought out by his own industry. He would sit silent in learned company, and suck in (besides wine) their several humors into his observation. What was ore in others, he was able to refine to himself.—FULLER, THOMAS, 1662, *The Worthies of England, ed. Nichols, vol.* II, *p.* 112.

His mother, after his father's death, married a bricklayer; and 'tis generally sayd that he wrought sometime with his father-in-lawe (and particularly on the gardenwall of Lincoln's Inne next to Chancery-lane—from old parson [Richard]

Hill, of Stretton, Hereff., 1646), and that . . . . , a knight, a bencher, walking thro' and hearing him repeat some Greeke verses out of Homer, discoursing with him, and finding him to have a witt extraordinary, gave him some exhibition to maintaine him at Trinity college in Cambridge, where he was . . . . (quaere). Then he went into the Lowe-countreys, and spent some time (not very long) in the armie, not to the disgrace of . . . , as you may find in his Epigrammes. Then he came over into England, and acted and wrote, but both ill, at the Green Curtaine, a kind of nursery or obscure playhouse, somewhere in the suburbes (I thinke towards Shoreditch or Clarkenwell)—from J. Greenhill. Then he undertooke againe to write a playe, and did hitt it admirably well, viz. "Every man . . . ." which was his first good one. . . . He was (or rather had been) of a clear and faire skin; his habit was very plaine. I have heard Mr. Lacy, the player, say that he was wont to weare a coate like a coachman's coate, with slitts under the arme-pitts. He would many times exceed in drinke (Canarie was his beloved liquour): then he would tumble home to bed, and, when he had thoroughly perspired, then to studie. I have seen his studyeing chaire, which was of strawe, such as old woemen used, and as Aulus Gellius is drawen in. . . . He lies buryed in the north aisle in the path of square stone (the rest is lozenge), opposite to the scutcheon of Robertus de Ros, with this inscription only on him, in a pavement square, of blew marble, about 14 inches square,

O RARE BENN IOHNSON

which was donne at the chardge of Jack Young (afterwards knighted) who, walking there when the grave was covering, gave the fellow eighteen pence to cutt it.—AUBREY, JOHN, 1669-96, *Brief Lives, ed. Clark, vol.* II, *pp.* 11, 12, 13.

Ben Johnson's name can never be forgotten, having by his very good learning, and the severity of his nature and manners, very much reformed the Stage; and indeed the English poetry itself; his natural advantages were, judgment to order and govern fancy, rather than excess of fancy, his productions being slow and upon deliberation, yet then abounding with great wit and fancy, and will live accordingly; and surely as he did exceedingly exalt the English language in eloquence, propriety, and masculine expressions; so he was the best judge of, and fittest to prescribe rules to Poetry and Poets, of any man who had lived with, or before him, or since; if Mr. Cowley had not made a flight beyond all men, with that modesty yet, to ascribe much of this, to the example and learning of Ben. Johnson. His conversation was very good, and with the men of most note; and he had for many years an extraordinary kindness for Mr. Hyde, till he found he betook himself to business, which he believed ought never to be preferred before his company: he lived to be very old, and till the palsy made a deep impression upon his body, and his mind.—CLARENDON, EDWARD, LORD, 1674–1760, *Life, vol.* I, *p.* 23.

He was a Man of a very free Temper, and withal blunt, and somewhat haughty to those that were either Rivals in *Fame*, or Enemies to his Writings: (witness his "Poetaster," wherein he falls upon *Decker*, and his answer to Dr. *Gill*, who writ against his "Magnetick Lady,") otherwise of a good Sociable Humor, when amongst his Sons and Friends in the *Apollo*.—LANGBAINE, GERARD, 1691, *An Account of the English Dramatick Poets, p.* 283.

Each true Briton is to Ben so civil,
He swears the Muses met him at the Devil.
—POPE, ALEXANDER, 1733, *First Epistle of the Second Book of Horace.*

Jonson hath been often represented as of an envious, arrogant, overbearing temper, and insolent and haughty in his converse; but these ungracious drawings were the performance of his enemies; who certainly were not solicitous to give a flattering likeness of the original. But considering the provocations he received, with the mean and contemptible talents of those who opposed him, what we condemn as vanity or conceit, might be only the exertions of conscious and insulted merit. . . . In his studies Jonson was laborious and indefatigable: his reading was copious and extensive; his memory so tenacious and strong that, when turned of forty, he could have repeated all that he ever wrote: his judgment was accurate and solid; and often consulted by those who knew him well, in branches of very curious learning, and far remote from the flowery paths loved and frequented by the muses.—WHALLEY, PETER, 1756, *ed. Jonson's Works, Life of Jonson, p.* lv.

Notwithstanding the remarks which will be found scattered over the succeeding volumes, respecting the alleged hostility of Jonson to Shakspeare, it appears to me that I should but imperfectly discharge my duty unless I presented the reader with a concentrated view of a part of the proofs by which the accusation is supposed to be made good. Our dramatic literature has been absolutely poisoned by the malice of Jonson's persecutors. Whoever brought forward an old poet offered up a victim to his fame, and this victim was invariably our author: but while it was generously admitted that the rest of his contemporaries felt his malignity only at intervals, it was universally affirmed that his abuse of Shakspeare was unremitted. Neither writer nor reader ever dreamed of questioning the accuracy of this statement; and nothing could be more amusing than the complacent simplicity with which it was handed down from Mr. Malone to Mr. Weber, from Mr. G. Chalmers to Mr. Stephen Jones. It is to the praise of Mr. Gilchrist that he was the first person who, amidst the general outcry against Jonson, evinced sufficient honesty to investigate the truth, and sufficient courage to declare it. His little Publication startled the critics, though it could not silence them. His triumph, however, was complete; for he had justice on his side: and there is something ludicrous in the half-concessions which the force of his facts occasionally elicits from his opponents.—GIFFORD, WILLIAM, 1816, *ed. Works of Ben Jonson, vol.* I, *p.* cxciii.

O Ben, my rare Friend, is this in very deed thou? There in the body, with thy rugged sagacities and genialities; with thy rugged Annandale face and unquenchable laughing eyes;—like a rock hiding in it perennial limpid wells! My rare friend, there is in thee something of the lion, I observe:—thou art the rugged Stonemason, the harsh, learned Hodman; yet hast strains too of a noble softness, melodious as the voice of wood-doves, fitfully thrilling as the note of nightingales, now and then! Rarer union of rough clumsy strength with touches of an Ariel beauty I have not met with. A sterling man, a true Singer-heart,—born of my native Valley too: to whom and to which be all honour!—CARLYLE, THOMAS, 1844-49-98, *Historical Sketches of Notable Persons and Events in the Reigns of James I. and Charles I., p.* 74.

In spite, therefore, of his faults, both as a man and as an author—his arrogance, his intemperance, his sarcastic and sometimes coarse humour, his pedantry and his pride —we must ever hold him to have been a great and good man; grateful, generous, valiant, free spoken, with something of the old Roman spirit in him, a mighty artist, and a man of a gigantic and cultivated genius; and we may reverently echo the beautiful words of the epitaph which long remained inscribed upon his grave—

"O rare Ben Jonson!"

—SHAW, THOMAS B., 1847, *Outlines of English Literature, p.* 125.

How Decker's hearers must have appreciated every allusion to the arrogant Ben the Poet; with the fierce mouth and small beard; his face marked with small pox; his hollow cheeks; his speaking through his nose; his sour face when he reads his own songs; his stamping on the stage as if he was treading mortar. The audience all knew Master Jonson had once killed a man in a duel, and had left brick-making to make rails; they knew he took months writing a play, and that he despised the opinion of his audience, and they laughed accordingly.—THORNBURY, GEORGE WALTER, 1856, *Shakspere's England, vol.* II, *p.* 13.

This man, Ben Jonson, commonly stands next to Shakespeare in a consideration of the dramatic literature of the age of Elizabeth; and certainly if the "thousand-souled" Shakespeare may be said to represent mankind, Ben as unmistakably stands for English-kind. He is "Saxon" England in epitome,—John Bull passing from a name into a man,—a proud, strong, tough, solid, domineering individual, whose intellect and personality cannot be severed, even in thought, from his body and personal appearance. Ben's mind, indeed, was rooted in Ben's character; and his character took symbolic form in his physical frame. He seemed built up, mentally as well as bodily, out of beef and sack, mutton and Canary; or, to say the least, was a joint product of the English mind and the English larder, of the fat as well as the thought of the land, of the soil as well as the soul of England. The moment we attempt to estimate his eminence as a dramatist, he disturbs the equanimity of our judgment by tumbling head-foremost into the imagination as a big, bluff, burly, and quarrelsome man, with "a mountain belly and a rocky face." He is a very pleasant boon companion as long as we make our idea of his importance agree with his own; but the instant we attempt to dissect his intellectual pretensions, the living animal becomes a dangerous subject, — his countenance flames, his great hands double up, his thick lips begin to twitch with impending invective, and, while the critic's impression of him is thus all the more vivid, he is checked in its expression by a very natural fear of the consequences. There is no safety but in taking this rowdy leviathan of letters at his own valuation; and the relation of critics towards him is as perilous as that of the jurymen towards the Irish advocate, who had an unpleasant habit of sending them the challenge of the duellist whenever they brought in a verdict against any of his clients. There is, in fact, such a vast ainmal force in old Ben's self-assertion, that he bullies posterity as he bullied his contemporaries; and, while we admit his claim to rank next to Shakespeare among the dramatists of his age, we beg our readers to understand that we do it under intimidation.—WHIPPLE, EDWIN P., 1859-68, *The Literature of the Age of Elizabeth, p.* 85.

According to the local tradition, he asked the King (Charles I.) to grant him a favour. "What is it?" said the King—"Give me eighteen inches of square ground." "Where?" asked the King.—"In Westminster Abbey." This is one explanation given of the story that he was buried standing upright. Another is that it was in view to his readiness for the Resurrection. . . . This stone * was taken up when, in 1821, the Nave was repaved, and was brought back from the stoneyard of the clerk of the works, in the time of Dean Buckland, by whose order it was fitted into its present place in the north wall of the Nave. Meanwhile, the original spot had been marked by a small triangular lozenge, with a copy of the old inscription. When, in 1849, Sir Robert Wilson was buried close by, the loose sand of Jonson's grave (to use the expression of the clerk of the works who superintended the operation) "rippled in like a quicksand," and the clerk "saw the two leg-bones of Jonson, fixed bolt upright in the sand, as though the body had been buried in the upright position; and the skull came rolling down among the sand, from a position above the leg-bones, to the bottom of the newly-made grave. There was still hair upon it, and it was of a red colour." It was seen once more on the digging of John Hunter's grave; and "it had still traces of red hair upon it. The world long wondered that he should lie buried from the rest of the poets and want a tomb." This monument, in fact, was to have been erected by subscription soon after his death, but was delayed by the breaking-out of the Civil War. The present medallion in Poets' Corner was set up in the middle of the last century by "a person of quality, whose name was desired to be concealed." By a mistake of the sculptor, the buttons were set on the left side of the coat. Hence this epigram—

O rare Ben Jonson—what a turncoat grown!
Thou ne'er wast such, till clad in stone:
Then let not this disturb thy sprite,
Another age shall set thy buttons right.

—STANLEY, ARTHUR PENRHYN, 1867-96, *Historical Memorials of Westminster Abbey, pp.* 288, 289.

*Covering his grave.

A vigorous, heavy and uncouth person; a wide and long face, early marred by scurvy, a square jaw, enormous cheeks; his animal organs as much developed as those of his intellect; the sour aspect of a man in a passion or on the verge of a passion; to which add the body of an athlete, about forty years of age, "mountain belly, ungracious gait." Such was the outside, and the inside is like it. He is a genuine Englishman, big and coarsely framed, energetic, combative, proud, often morose, and prone to strange splenetic imaginations.—TAINE, H. A., 1871, *History of English Literature, tr. Van Laun, vol.* I, *bk.* ii, *ch.* iii, *p.* 268.

Jonson's person was not built on the classical type of graceful or dignified symmetry: he had the large and rugged dimensions of a strong Borderland river, swollen by a sedentary life into huge corpulence. Although in his later days he jested at his own "mountain belly and his rocky face," he probably bore his unwieldy figure with a more athletic carriage than his namesake the lexicographer. Bodily as well as mentally he belonged to the race of Anak. His position among his contemporaries was very much what Samuel Johnson's might have been had he been contradicted and fought against by independent rivals, jealous and resentful of his dictatorial manner. Ben Jonson's large and irascible personality could not have failed to command respect; but his rivals had too much respect for them selves to give way absolutely to his authority. They refused to be as grasshoppers in his sight. We should do wrong, however, to suppose that this disturbed the giant's peace of mind.—MINTO, WILLIAM, 1874-85, *Characteristics of English Poets, p.* 338.

Besides being a born critic, Jonson was possessed of both a generous heart and a robust intellect; and there is a ludicrous incongruity with the transparent nature of the man in the supposition that it was poisoned by a malignant hatred of Shakspere and his fame. The difference between the two poets was indeed extremely great, and reflects itself in almost everything left to us from their respective hands. But it is not a whit less absurd to look upon Jonson and Shakspere as the heads of opposite schools or tendencies in literature, than to suppose the one writer to have personally regarded the other with a jealous feeling of rivalry. . . . Ben Jonson was a genuine scholar, whose chief pride was his library, afterwards destroyed by a fire which inflicted an irreparable loss upon our literature. His love of reading must have been insatiable; of his book-learning numberless illustrations are furnished by his plays, in one of which he bears testimony to it with pardonable self-sufficiency. But to the canary-sack must be ascribed part of the boastfulness which made him tell Drummond that "he was better versed, and knew more in Greek and Latin, than all the Poets in England, and"—here Drummond appears to have imperfectly understood the author of the "English Grammar" — "quintessence their brains."—WARD, ADOLPHUS WILLIAM, 1875-99, *A History of English Dramatic Literature, vol.* II, *pp.* 297, 314.

He goes there,* or to other like places, very often. He is a friend no doubt of the landlady; he is a friend, too, of all the housemaids, and talks university chaff to them; a friend, too, of all such male frequenters of the house as will listen to him, and will never dispute him; otherwise he is a slang-whanger and a bear.—MITCHELL, DONALD G., 1889, *English Lands Letters and Kings, From Celt to Tudor, p.* 295.

A man of extreme convivial and decidedly undomestic turn, he was accessible to everyone at the taverns he frequented, and besides the group of "Sons," which is famous, and included all the more noted men of letters of the second half of our period, he seems to have had a wide circle of *protégés* and clients extending, as later traditions more or less dimly indicate, all over the kingdom. This semi-Falstaffian gift of tavern-kingship, however, could not have availed of itself to give Jonson the position he held. But his more solid claims to literary respect were usually great. Although it is very doubtful whether he belonged to either University in any but an honorary capacity, scholars of the strictest academic sufficiency like Selden, Farnaby, and others, admitted his scholarship; he was the honoured friend of Raleigh and Bacon; and it is impossible for any reader, himself possessing the slightest tincture of classical learning, not to recognise in every work of Jonson's—be it play, poem, or prose—the presence of reading which never obscured, though it sometimes stiffened and hardened, the creative faculties of the author.—SAINTSBURY, GEORGE, 1895, *Social England, ed. Traill, vol.* IV, *p.* 113.

Ben Jonson was an awfully unguarded man; he struck out right and left, and straight from the arm-pits. He hit hard; all his life was a fight. He seems to have loved fighting. Turbulent, glorious old whirlwind of a man: so honest, so bitter, so keen, so bluff, so hearty and kind, so fierce and uncompromising! He was a Scotchman by his ancestry, and he had a good deal of the *perfervidum genus* stowed away in the capacious receptacle of his brawny breast.—BROWN, T. E., 1896, *Ben Jonson, The New Review, vol.* 14, *p.* 514.

He was strong and massive in body, racy and coarse, full of self-esteem, and

*The Mermaid.

combative instincts, saturated with the conviction of the scholar's high rank and the poet's exalted vocation, full of contempt for ignorance, frivolity, and lowness, classic in his tastes, with a bent towards careful structure and leisurely development of thought in all that he wrote, and yet a true poet in so far as he was not only irregular in his life and quite incapable of saving any of the money he now and then earned, but was, moreover, subject to hallucinations: once saw Carthaginians and Romans fighting on his great toe, and, on another occasion, had a vision of his son with a bloody cross on his brow, which was supposed to forbode his death. . . . With all his weaknesses, however, he was a sturdy, energetic, and high-minded man, a commanding, independent, and very comprehensive intelligence, and from 1598, when he makes his first appearance on Shakespeare's horizon, throughout the rest of his life, he was, so far as we can see, the man of all his contemporaries whose name was oftenest mentioned along with Shakespeare's. . . . Though his society may have been somewhat fatiguing, it must nevertheless have been both instructive and stimulating to Shakespeare, since Ben was greatly his superior in historical and linguistic knowledge, while as a poet he pursued a totally different ideal.—BRANDES, GEORGE, 1898, *William Shakespeare, A Critical Study, vol.* I, *pp.* 385, 388.

He was a loyal and affectionate father, and a constant if not an adoring husband; he described his wife many years after his marriage as "a shrew, yet honest."—MABIE, HAMILTON WRIGHT, 1900, *William Shakespeare, Poet, Dramatist, and Man, p.* 280.

EVERY MAN IN HIS HUMOUR
1597–98

"Every Man in his Humour" is founded on such follies and passions as are perpetually incident to, and connected with, man's nature; such as do not depend upon local custom or change of fashion; and, for that reason, will bid fair to last as long as many of our old comedies. The language of Jonson is very peculiar; in perspicuity and elegance he is inferior to Beaumont and Fletcher, and very unlike the masculine dialogue of Massinger. It is almost needless to observe that he comes far short of the variety, strength, and natural flow, of Shakspeare. To avoid the common idiom, he plunges into stiff, quaint, and harsh, phraseology: he has borrowed more words, from the Latin tongue, than all the authors of his time. However, the style of this play, as well as that of the "Alchemist" and "Silent Woman," is more disentangled and free from foreign auxiliaries than the greatest part of his works. Most of the characters are truly dramatic.—DAVIES, THOMAS, 1783, *Dramatic Micellanies, vol.* II, *p.* 53.

"Every Man in his Humour" is perhaps the earliest of European domestic comedies that deserves to be remembered; for even the Mandragora of Machiavel shrinks to a mere farce in comparison. A much greater master of comic powers than Jonson was indeed his contemporary, and, as he perhaps fáncied, his rival; but, for some reason Shakspeare had never yet drawn his story from the domestic life of his countrymen. Jonson avoided the common defect of the Italian and Spanish theatre, the sacrifice of all other dramatic objects to one only, a rapid and amusing succession of incidents: his plot is slight and of no great complexity; but his excellence is to be found in the variety of his characters, and in their individuality, very clearly definded, with little extravagance.—HALLAM, HENRY, 1837-39, *Introduction to the Literature of Europe, pt.* ii, *ch.* vi, *par.* 53.

Neither my duly unqualified love for the greater poet nor my duly qualified regard for the less can alter my sense that their mutual relations are in this one case inverted; that "Every Man in his Humour" is altogether a better comedy and work of higher art than the "Merry Wives of Windsor."—SWINBURNE, ALGERNON CHARLES, 1880, *A Study of Shakespeare, p.* 121.

The success of "Every Man in his Humor" will surprise no one who has followed the varied and yet simple action of this lively comedy. It is written with all Jonson's precision and in his peculiar manner; but it lacks that rigidity which his manner afterwards assumed. Though the parts of the knavish servant and his young master remind us of the Roman theatre, Jonson has recast them in accordance with English character and custom. His erudition, indeed, in this play makes itself less prominently felt than in some of his later masterpieces. Kitely, as the jealous husband, deserves a place beside Ford in Shakespeare's "Merry Wives of Windsor."—SYMONDS, JOHN ADDINGTON, 1886, *Ben Jonson, (English Worthies)*.

EVERY MAN OUT OF HIS HUMOUR
1599

I fear no mood stamp'd in a private brow,
When I am pleased t' unmask a public vice.
I fear no strumpet's drugs, nor ruffian's stab,
Should I detect their hateful luxuries.
—JONSON, BEN, 1599, *Every Man out of his Humour, Prologue.*

If the reader would see the extravagance of building dramatic manners on abstract ideas, in its full light, he needs only turn to B. Johnson's "Every Man out of his Humour;" which under the name of a *play of character* is in fact, an unnatural, and, as the painters call it, *hard* delineation of a group of simply existing passions, wholly chimerical, and unlike to anything we observe in the commerce of real life. Yet this comedy has always had its admirers. And *Randolph* in particular, was so taken with the design, that he seems to have formed his *muse's looking-glass* in express imitation of it.—HURD, RICHARD, 1757, *A Dissertation on the Several Provinces of the Drama, vol.* I, *p.* 266.

In aim the comedy is truly moral; and if in many passages the author displays no small measure of self-complacency, he must be allowed to have done enough and more than enough to warrant the satisfaction with which he evidently regarded what is one of the masterpieces of English comic literature. The learning of Ben Jonson is very amply exhibited in this play, which abounds with reminiscences from the classics and from Erasmus.—WARD, ADOLPHUS WILLIAM, 1875-99, *A History of English Dramatic Literature, vol.* II, *p.* 349.

The fervour and intensity of the verse which expresses his loftier mood of intolerant indignation, the studious and implacable versatility of scorn which animates the expression of his disgust at the viler or crueller examples of social villainy then open to his contemptuous or furious observation, though they certainly cannot suffice to make a play, suffice to make a living and imperishable work of the dramatic satire which passes so rapidly from one phase to another of folly, fraud, or vice.—SWINBURNE, ALGERNON CHARLES, 1889, *A Study of Ben Jonson, p.* 16.

He is above everything a satirist of vice: he hates it, and he lashes it with a whip of scorpions. Listen to Asper—clearly Jonson himself—in the introduction to "Every Man Out of His Humour." It is very scathing; but it is very splendid. As a mere question, of language, how nervous it is, how like the very best and strongest utterings of our own time! Contempt is the most frequent note; but sometimes it swells to defiance, and becomes gratuitously, recklessly insulting. —BROWN, T. E., 1896, *Ben Jonson, The New Review, vol.* 14, *p.* 522.

CYNTHIA'S REVELS
1600

However we may respect Jonson's sterling qualities as man and poet, we cannot read the prologue and epilogue to "Cynthia's Revels" without resenting its strain of self-laudation. The three characters, used by him as masks in the three "Comical Satires," namely, Asper, Crites, Horace, make us justly angry. We cannot stomach the writer who thus dared to praise and puff himself.—SYMONDS, JOHN ADDINGTON, 1886, *Ben Jonson, (English Worthies), p.* 35.

The most noticeable point in this studiously wayward and laboriously erratic design is that the principle of composition is as conspicuous by its absence as the breath of inspiration: that the artist, the scholar, the disciple, the student of classic models, is as indiscoverable as the spontaneous humourist or poet. The wildest, the roughest, the crudest offspring of literary impulse working blindly on the passionate elements of excitable ignorance was never more formless, more incoherent, more defective in structure, than this voluminous abortion of deliberate intelligence and conscientious culture.—SWINBURNE, ALGERNON CHARLES, 1889, *A Study of Ben Jonson, p.* 20.

THE POETASTER
1601

This Roman play seems written to confute those enemies of Ben in his own days and ours, who have said he made a pedantical use of his learning. He has here revived the whole Court of Augustus, by a learned spell. We are admitted to the society of the illustrious dead. Virgil,

Horace, Ovid, Tibullus, converse in our own tongue more finely and poetically than they were used to express themselves in their native Latin. Nothing can be imagined more elegant, refined, and courtlike, than the scenes between this Louis the Fourteenth of antiquity and his literati. The whole essence and secret of that kind of intercourse is contained therein. The economical liberality by which greatness, seeming to waive some part of its prerogative, takes care to lose none of the essentials; the prudential liberties of an inferior, which flatter by commanded boldness and soothe with complimentary sincerity.—LAMB, CHARLES, 1808, *Specimens of Dramatic Poets.*

"Poetaster" is Jonson's acknowledged reply to the numerous attacks that had been made upon him during a period of three years. . . . So far as Jonson was concerned "The War of the Theatres" was ended, although peace was not declared. —PENNIMAN, JOSIAH H., 1897, *The War of the Theatres, p.* 118.

SEJANUS
1603

The more we reflect and examine, examine and reflect, the more astonished shall we be at the immense superiority of Shakspere over his contemporaries:—and yet what contemporaries!—giant minds indeed! Think of Jonson's erudition, and the force of learned authority in that age; and yet in no genuine part of Shakspere's works is there to be found such an absurd rant and ventriloquism as this, and too, too many other passages ferruminated by Jonson from Seneca's tragedies and the writings of the later Romans. I call it ventriloquism, because Sejanus is a puppet, out of which the poet makes his own voice appear to come.—COLERIDGE, SAMUEL TAYLOR, 1818, *Notes on Ben Jonson, ed. Ashe, p.* 414.

Whatever this tragedy may want in the agitating power of poetry, it has a strength and dramatic skill that might have secured it, at least, from the petulant contempt with which it has been too often spoken of. Though collected from the dead languages, it is not a lifeless mass of antiquity, but the work of a severe and strong imagination, compelling shapes of truth and consistency to rise in dramatic order from the fragments of Roman eloquence and history; and an air not only of life but of grandeur is given to those curiously adjusted materials.—CAMPBELL, THOMAS, 1819, *Specimens of the British Poets.*

In 1603, he produced his weighty tragedy of "Sejanus," at Shakespeare's theatre, The Globe,—Shakespeare himself acting one of the inferior parts. Think of Shakespeare laboriously committing to memory the blank verse of Jonson! Though "Sejanus" failed of theatrical success, its wealth of knowledge and solid thought made it the best of all answers to his opponents. It was as if they had questioned his capacity to build a ship, and he had confuted them with a man-of-war.—WHIPPLE, EDWIN P., 1859-68, *The Literature of the Age of Elizabeth, p.* 102.

Although "Sejanus his Fall" may not have received on its appearance the credit or the homage due to the serious and solid merit of its composition and its execution, it must be granted that the author has once more fallen into the excusable but nevertheless unpardonable error of the too studious and industrious Martha. He was careful and troubled about many things absolutely superfluous and supererogatory; matters of no value or concern whatever for the purpose or the import of a dramatic poem: but the one thing needful, the very condition of poetic life and dramatic interest, he utterly and persistently overlooked.—SWINBURNE, ALGERNON CHARLES, 1889, *A Study of Ben Jonson, p.* 27.

Was not very successful, but it succeeded better after he had recast it in part and made it all his own. It was printed in 1605, and the small criticisms of a pedantic age Ben Jonson forestalled by footnotes citing the authority for all that he had worked into harmonious and very noble play. Because the footnotes were there, and looked erudite, the superficial thing to do was to pronounce the play pedantic. But it is not pedantic. Jonson was no pedant. He had carried on for himself the education received at Westminster School, was a good scholar, delighted in his studies, and accumulated a large library, which, in or about the year 1622, was burnt. But he was true poet and true artist.—MORLEY, HENRY, AND GRIFFIN, W. HALL, 1895, *English Writers, vol.* XI, *p.* 219.

VOLPONE, OR THE FOX

1605-06

. . . the art which thou alone
Hast taught our tongue, the rules of time,
of place,
And other rites, delivered with the grace
Of comic style, which only, is far more
Than any English stage hath known before.
—BEAUMONT, FRANCIS, 1607? *To My Dear Friend, Master Ben Jonson, upon his "Fox."*

In the comedy of "The Fox," there is not much to be censured, except the language, which is so pedantic and struck so full of Latinity, that few, except the learned, can perfectly understand it. "Jonson," says Dr. Young, "brought all the antients upon his head: by studying to speak like a Roman, he forgot the language of his country."—DAVIES, THOMAS, 1783, *Dramatic Micellanies, vol.* II, *p.* 97.

This admirable, indeed, but yet more wonderful than admirable, play is from the fertility and vigour of invention, character, language, and sentiment the strongest proof, how impossible it is to keep up any pleasurable interest in a tale, in which there is no goodness of heart in any of the prominent characters. After the third act, this play becomes not a dead, but a painful weight on the feelings.—COLERIDGE, SAMUEL TAYLOR, 1818, *Notes on Ben Jonson, ed. Ashe, p.* 414.

The revolting aspects of life exhibited in this comedy are likely to prevent full justice being rendered its merits by most modern readers. Yet it long retained its hold over the national stage, while—which is less to be wondered at—the central character continued for generations to express to the popular mind the incarnation of a most loathsome variety of the vast *genus* hypocrite. Everybody knows how, at a critical stage of events in the reign of Queen Anne, Dr. Sacheverell in his notorious sermon pointed an attack upon the Whig leaders as representatives of revolution principles, by alluding to the Lord Treasurer Godolphin under the nickname of the Old Fox or Volpone.—WARD, ADOLPHUS WILLIAM, 1875-99, *A History of English Dramatic Literature, vol.* II, *p.* 363.

We, however, who are far removed from the literary discords of those times, can peruse with calmness and enjoy the manly eloquence of that great dedication to the Sister Universities which forms the preface to "Volpone." Bating some personalities and blustering defiances which impair the dignity of the oration. This high-built edifice of ceremonious language deserves to rank with Milton's sublime periods upon the poet's priesthood, and with Sidney's lofty vindication of the poet's claim to prophecy. Unhappily, the piece, which ought to find its honoured place in every anthology of English prose, is both too long to quote in full, and also too closely wrought to bear abstraction of its well-weighed sentences without the risk of mutilation.—SYMONDS, JOHN ADDINGTON, 1886, *Ben Jonson, (English Worthies), p.* 31.

No other of even his very greatest works is at once so admirable and so enjoyable. The construction or composition of "The Alchemist" is perhaps more wonderful in the perfection and combination of cumulative detail, in triumphant simplicity of process and impeccable felicity of result: but there is in "Volpone" a touch of something like imagination, a savour of something like romance, which gives a higher tone to the style and a deeper interest to the action. The chief agents are indeed what Mr. Carlyle would have called "unspeakably unexemplary mortals:" but the serious fervour and passionate intensity of their resolute and resourceful wickedness give somewhat of a lurid and distorted dignity to the display of their doings and sufferings, which is wanting to the less gigantic and heroic villainies of Subtle, Dol, and Face.—SWINBURNE, ALGERNON CHARLES, 1889, *A Study of Ben Jonson, p.* 35.

Ben Jonson added a cubit to his literary stature by producing his noble comedy of "Volpone or the Fox."—GOSSE, EDMUND, 1894, *The Jacobean Poets, p.* 24.

EPICOENE, OR THE SILENT WOMAN

1610

When his play of a "Silent Woman" was first acted, ther was found verses after on the stage against him, concluding that that play was well named the "Silent Woman," ther was never one man to say Plaudite to it.—DRUMMOND, WILLIAM, 1619, *Notes on Ben Jonson's Conversations.*

This is to my feelings the most entertaining of old Ben's comedies, and, more than any other, would admit of being brought out anew, if under the management of a judicious and stage-understanding play-wright; and an actor, who had studied Morose, might make his fortune.—COLERIDGE, SAMUEL TAYLOR, 1818, *Notes on Ben Jonson, ed. Ashe, p.* 415.

The plot is a distasteful one to my own feelings: it is coarse in design, coarse in its improbability, and, in short, is a direct contradiction of the author's own theory as to that which should characterise *legitimate* comedy; for the play of "Epicene" is little better than a hoydening farce. The character of Morose himself is certainly well sustained, although in it an extreme case is put throughout; and enormous demands are made upon the credulity of the audience that such a man could be supposed to exist at all, with so morbid a sensitiveness to noise as to poison his whole existence.—CLARKE, CHARLES COWDEN, 1871, *On the Comic Writers of England, Gentleman's Magazine,* N. S. *vol.* 6, *p.* 643.

"Epicoene" would be properly described as an elaborate farce. . . . Of its kind "Epicoene" is without a rival, unless we turn to the writings of a comic dramatist worthy to rank as Jonson's peer—I speak of course of Molière. The briskness of the fun in the dialogue—only here and there lapsing into Jonson's favourite weakness for lengthy analyses of character—is even less remarkable than the fecundity of invention displayed in a series of effective situations. Instead of flagging, the play grows more and more amusing from act to act; the fourth, with the catastrophe of the two timid fools—one of the most laughable comic situations ever invented—surpasses all that has preceded it; but the fifth is even better, with its inimitable consultation on the question of Divorce, and its final surprise.—WARD, ADOLPHUS WILLIAM, 1875-99, *A History of English Dramatic Literature, vol.* II, *p.* 365.

Of "The Silent Woman" it is not easy to say anything new and true. Its merits are salient and superb: the combination of parts and the accumulation of incidents are so skilfully arranged and so powerfully designed that the result is in its own way incomparable—or comparable only with other works of the master's hand while yet in the fullness of its cunning and the freshness of its strength. But a play of this kind must inevitably challenge a comparison, in the judgment of modern readers, between its author and Molière: and Jonson can hardly, on the whole, sustain that most perilous comparison. It is true that there is matter enough in Jonson's play to have furnished forth two or three of Molière's: and that on that ground—on the score of industrious intelligence and laborious versatility of humour—"The Silent Woman" is as superior to the "Misanthrope" and the "Bourgeois Gentilhomme" as to "Twelfth Night" and "Much Ado about Nothing." But even when most dazzled by the splendour of studied wit and the felicity of deliberate humour which may even yet explain the extraordinary popularity or reputation of this most imperial and elaborate of all farces, we feel that the author could no more have rivalled the author of "Twelfth Night" than he could have rivalled the author of "Othello." The Nemesis of the satirist is upon him: he cannot be simply at ease: he cannot be happy in his work without some undertone of sarcasm, some afterthought of allusion, aimed at matters which Molière would have reserved for a slighter style of satire, and which Shakespeare would scarcely have condescended to recognise as possible objects of even momentary attention. His wit is wonderful—admirable, laughable, laudable—it is not in the fullest and the deepest sense delightful. It is radically cruel, contemptuous, intolerant; the sneer of the superior person—Dauphine or Clerimont—is always ready to pass into a snarl: there is something in this great classic writer of the bull-baiting or bear-baiting brutality of his age.—SWINBURNE, ALGERNON CHARLES, 1889, *A Study of Ben Jonson, p.* 50.

THE ALCHEMIST

1610

To say, this comedy pleased long ago,
Is not enough to make it past you now.
Yet, gentlemen, your ancestors had wit;
When few men censured, and when fewer writ.
And Jonson, of those few the best, chose this,
As the best model of his masterpiece.
Subtle was got by our Albumazar,
That Alchymist by this Astrologer;
Here he was fashion'd, and we may suppose
He liked the fashion well, who wore the clothes.
But Ben made nobly his what he did mould;

**What was another's lead becomes his gold:
Like an unrighteous conqueror he reigns,
Yet rules that well, which he unjustly gains.**
—DRYDEN, JOHN, 1668, *Albumazar, Prologue.*

This comedy, which was laudably written to ridicule a prevailing folly, must, no doubt, have been greatly successful originally, since we have seen it very much followed and admired during the time Garrick ornamented the stage. His incomparable performance, however, of Abel Drugger was a considerable drawback from the proper reputation of the author, and in great measure the cause of the success of the play; at the same time it must be confessed that the best acting can do nothing without good materials, with which certainly the "Alchymist" abounds.—DIBDIN, CHARLES, 1795, *A Complete History of the Stage, vol.* III, *p.* 295.

The judgment is perfectly overwhelmed by the torment of images, words, and book-knowledge, with which Epicure Mammon (Act 2, Scene 2) confounds and stunts his incredulous hearer. They come pouring out like the successive falls of Nilus. They "doubly redouble strokes upon the foe." Description outstrides proof. We are made to believe effects before we have testimony for their causes. If there is no one image which attains the height of the sublime, yet the confluence and assemblage of them all produces a result equal to the grandest poetry. The huge Xerxean army contervails against single Achilles. Epicure Mammon is the most determined offspring of its author. It has the whole "matter and copy of the father—eye, nose, lip, the trick of his frown." It is just such a swaggerer as contemporaries have described old Ben to be. Meercraft, Bobadil, the Host of the New Inn, have all his image and superscription. But Mammon is arrogant pretension personified. Sir Samson Legend, in "Love for Love," is such another lying, overbearing character, but he does not come up to Epicure Mammon. What a "towering bravery" there is in his sensuality! he affects no pleasure under a Sultan. It is as if "Egypt with Assyria strove in luxury."—LAMB, CHARLES, 1808, *Specimens of Dramatic Poets.*

Jonson here escaped his usual pitfall of the unsympathetic, for the vices and follies he satirises are not loathsome, only contemptible at worst, and not always that. He found an opportunity of exercising his extraordinary faculty of concentration as he nowhere else did, and has given us in Sir Epicure Mammon a really magnificent picture of concupiscence, of sensual appetite generally, sublimed by heat of imagination into something really poetic.—SAINTSBURY, GEORGE, 1887, *History of Elizabethan Literature, p.* 181.

The steadfast and imperturbable skill of hand which has woven so many threads of incident, so many shades of character, so many changes of intrigue, into so perfect and superb a pattern of incomparable art as dazzles and delights the reader of "The Alchemist" is unquestionably unique—above comparison with any later or earlier example of kindred genius in the whole range of comedy, if not in the whole world of fiction. The manifold harmony of inventive combination and imaginative contrast—the multitudinous unity of various and concordant effects—the complexity and the simplicity of action and impression, which hardly allow the reader's mind to hesitate between enjoyment and astonishment, laughter and wonder, admiration and diversion—all the distinctive qualities which the alchemic cunning of the poet has fused together in the crucible of dramatic satire for the production of a flawless work of art, have given us the most perfect model of imaginative realism and satirical comedy that the world has ever seen; the most wonderful work of its kind that can ever be run upon the same lines.—SWINBURNE, ALGERNON CHARLES, 1889, *A Study of Ben Jonson, p.* 36.

Remains, in spite of its proved unfittedness for the stage, and its antiquated interests, one of the most splendid compositions written by an English hand. Lamb, with unerring instinct, hit upon the central jewel of the whole splendid fabric when he selected for special praise the long scene in Subtle's house, where Epicure Mammon boasts what rare things he will do when he obtains the philosopher's stone. Here Jonson, running and leaping under the tremendous weight of his own equipment, perfectly overwhelms the judgment "by the torrent of images, words, and book-knowledge with which Mammon confounds and stuns" us.—GOSSE, EDMUND, 1894, *The Jacobean Poets, p.* 28.

CATILINE

1611

Thy labours shall outlive thee; and, like gold
Stampt for continuance, shall be current, where
There is a sun, a people, or a year.

—FLETCHER, JOHN, 1611? *To my worthy friend, Ben Jonson, on his Catiline.*

Whose inspirations, if great Rome had had,
Her good things had been bettered, and her bad
Undone; the first for joy, the last for fear,
That such a Muse should spread them, to our ear.
But woe to us then! for thy laureat brow
If Rome enjoyed had, we had wanted now.
. . . .
Each subject thou, still thee each subject raises,
And whosoe'er thy book, himself dispraises.

—FIELD, NATHANIEL, 1611? *To his Worthy and Beloved Friend, Master Ben Jonson, on his "Catiline."*

With strenuous, sinewy words that Catiline swells,
I reckon it not among men—miracles.
How could that poem well a vigour lack,
When each line oft cost Ben a cup of sack.

—R. BARON, 1650, *Pocula Castalia, p.* 113.

"Catiline" is only less interesting than "Sejanus," because it presents no such difficult problem of characterisation as Tiberius. Within the limits of his subject, however, Jonson has fully availed himself of his opportunities. Each of the characters, notably those of the conspirators, stands out distinctly from the rest; perhaps in his effort to draw distinctly, the dramatist has, after his manner, rather overdrawn the humours, thereby impairing the humanity, of his personages,—the visionary imbecility of Lentulus, the braggadocio of Cethegus, the savage ferocity of Catiline. On the other hand, the oratorical expansiveness of Cicero is delicately, though copiously illustrated; the danger is avoided of rendering him ridiculous, although both his love of speech and his respect for his own achievements are allowed ample expression. Of Cæsar and of Cato enough is hardly made; the key to the double-handed policy of the former is not clearly revealed, while the latter appears too generally as the mere echo of Cicero. The female characters of the play are drawn with a humour nothing less than exuberant.—WARD, ADOLPHUS WILLIAM, 1875-99, *A History of English Dramatic Literature, vol.* II, *p.* 341.

BARTHOLOMEW FAIR

1614

This strange play, out of which might be framed the humour of half a dozen farces, is fuller, perhaps, of comic characters than any thing that ever appeared on the stage. We are given to understand that Jonson wrote it purposely to ridicule the age in which he lived, for the prevalent preference given to low wit, instead of polished and refined writing. If this was his motive he has outwitted himself, for there is more nature in "Bartholomew Fair" than in any one of his other works; but yet, being as it is, crammed full of extraneous and heterogeneous incidents, he has as much overshot the mark as he had come short of it in his "Catiline," which this play was written purposely to defend; that tragedy having nothing interesting in it, on account of its dullness and declamation; and this comedy, on account of its wildness and extravagance.—DIBDIN, CHARLES, 1795, *A Complete History of the Stage, vol.* III, *p.* 297.

Absolutely original, so far as is known, in both conception and construction, it abounds with the most direct kind of satire and with the broadest fun.—WARD, ADOLPHUS WILLIAM, 1875-99, *A History of English Dramatic Literature, vol.* II, *p.* 370.

A pure farce, conceived in the spirit of rollicking mirth, and executed with colossal energy. It is no satire either of manners or of individuals, but a broad Dutch painting of the humours of a London Carnival. . . . The personages are admirably studied and grouped together with consummate insight into dramatic effect. The proctor, with his pretty wife and puritanical mother-in-law; the sleek minister from Banbury, who woos the widow; the squire from Harrow, and his watchful attendant.—SYMONDS, JOHN ADDINGTON, 1886, *Ben Jonson, (English Worthies), p.* 111.

There is no dramatic work in English at all comparable in its own kind with this brilliant and bewildering presentment of a comic turmoil, and, by a curious chance, it is exactly here, where it might be expected that the dramatist would be peculiarly tempted to subordinate all attempt at character-painting to the mere embodiment of humours, that one of Ben Jonson's few really living and breathing creatures is found in the person of the Puritan, Rabbi Zeal-of-the Land.—GOSSE, EDMUND, 1894, *The Jacobean Poets, p.* 32.

THE SAD SHEPHERD
1637

In his unfinished pastoral drama of the "Sad Shepherd," his biographer traces one bright and sunny ray that broke through the gloom of his settling days.—CAMPBELL, THOMAS, 1819, *Specimens of the British Poets.*

Fletcher's pastoral, blasted as it is in some parts by fire not from heaven, is still a green and leafy wilderness of poetical beauty; Jonson's, deformed also by some brutality more elaborate than anything of the same sort in Fletcher, is at the best but a trim garden, and, had it been ever so happily finished, would have been nothing more.—CRAIK, GEORGE L., 1861, *A Compendious History of English Literature and of the English Language, vol.* I, *p.* 605.

A very charming fragment; so sweet and gentle, that it stands alone in conspicuous beauty amidst the rough and stalwart productions of his dramatic Muse.—CLARKE, CHARLES COWDEN, 1871, *On the Comic Writers of England, Gentleman's Magazine,* N. S., *vol.* 6, *p.* 649.

The "Sad Shepherd" is not quite complete; but, though not without a few blots and stains, it contains some of Jonson's finest poetry. The shepherdess Amie is such a sweet creation that one is indignant at the dramatist for the vulgar and wholly superfluous immodesty of one of her expressions in her first confession of unrest: to the pure all things are pure, but it exposes the simple shepherdess to unnecessary ridicule from the ordinary reader. One is surprised to find such sympathy with simple innocence in rare but rough Ben—all the more that the "Sad Shepherd" was written in his later years, when he was exacerbated by failure and poverty.—MINTO, WILLIAM, 1874-85, *Characteristics of English Poets, p.* 343.

In "The Sad Shepherd" he has with singular freshness caught the spirit of the greenwood. If this pastoral is more realistic in texture than either Spenser's or Milton's efforts in the same direction, the result is due, partly to the character of the writer, partly to the circumstance that Jonson's "shepherds" are beings of a definite age and country.—WARD, ADOLPHUS WILLIAM, 1875-99, *A History of English Dramatic Literature, vol.* II, *p.* 385.

Jonson, stout and rugged as he was undoubtedly, Dryasdust as some conceive him, had yet an exquisite sense of rural beauty. This he showed in the fine fragment of his "Sad Shepherd."—SYMONDS, JOHN ADDINGTON, 1884, *Shakspere's Predecessors in the English Drama, p.* 350.

GENERAL

Our English Horace.—CHETTLE HENRY, 1603, *Englands Mourning Garment.*

Not onely give you the Idea, but the soule of the acting Idea; as well could, if so he would, the elaborate English Horace, that gives number, weight and measure to every word, to teach the reader by his industries, even our Lawreat, worthy Benjamen, whose Muze approves him with (our mother) the Ebrew signification to bee the elder Sonne, and happely to have been the childe of Sorrow.—SMITHES, SIR THOMAS, 1605, *Voiage and Entertainment in Rushia.*

A meere Empyrick, one that getts what he hath by obseruation, and makes onely nature priuy to what he indites, so slow an Inuentor that he were better betake himselfe to his old trade of Bricklaying, a bould whorson, as confident now in making a booke, as he was in times past in laying of a brick.—ANON, 1606, *The Return from Parnassus, ed. Macray, Act I, Sc.* 2, *p.* 87.

The labored and understanding works of Master Jonson.—WEBSTER, JOHN, 1612, *The White Devil, Preface.*

Johnson, whose full of merit to reherse
Too copious is to be confined in verse;
Yet therein only fittest to be known,
Could any write a line which he might own.
One, so judicious; so well-knowing; and
A man whose least worth is to understand;
One so exact in all he doth prefer
To able censure; for the theatre
Not Seneca transcends his worth of praise;
Who writes him well shall well deserve the bays.

—BROWNE, WILLIAM, 1613, *Britannia's Pastorals, bk.* ii, *song* ii.

If that thy lore were equall to thy wit,
Thou in Apollo's chaire might justly sit.

—GAMAGE, WILLIAM, 1613, *Linsi-woolsie, or Two Centuries of Epigrammes.*

For lyric sweetness in an ode, or sonnet,
To Ben the best of wits might vail their bonnet.
—Hodgson, William, 1616, *Commendatory Verses on Ben Jonson.*

If I should declare mine own rudeness rudely, I should then confess, that I never tasted English more to my liking, nor more smart, and put to the height of use in poetry, than in that vital, judicious, and most practicable language of Benjamin Jonson's poems.—Bolton, Edmund, 1624, *Hypercritica.*

Next these, learn'd Jonson in this list I bring,
Who had drunk deep of the Pierian spring,
Whose knowledge did him worthily prefer,
And long was lord here of the theater:
Who in opinion made our learn'd to stick
Whether in poems rightly dramatic
Strong Seneca or Plautus, he or they,
Should bear the buskin and the sock away.
—Drayton, Michael, c 1627, *Of Poets and Poesie.*

He better loves Ben Jonson's book of plays,
But that therein of wit he finds such plenty
That he scarce understands a jest of twenty.
—Lenton, Francis, 1629, *The Young Gallant's Whirligig.*

Let others glut on the extorted praise
Of vulgar breath, trust thou to after days;
Thy labour'd works shall live, when time devours
Th' abortive offspring of their hasty hours . . .
. . . let this suffice—
The wiser world doth greater thee confess
Than all men else, than thyself only less.
—Carew, Thomas, 1631? *To Ben Jonson.*

If Jonson's learned sock be on.
—Milton, John, 1633, *L'Allegro.*

That when we hear but once of Jonson's name,
Whose mention shall make proud the breath of fame,
We may agree, and crowns of laurel bring
A justice unto him the poets' king.
—Shirley, James, 1637, *The Alchemist, Prologue.*

What are his faults (O Envy!) that you speake
English at Court, the learned Stage acts Greeke?
That Latine Hee reduc'd, and could command
That which your *Shakespeare* scarce could understand?
—Ramsay, H., 1638, *Upon the Death of Benjamin Jonson.*

Drawn to the life of every line and limb,
He (in his truth of art, and that in him)
Lives yet, and will, while letters can be read;
The loss is ours; now hope of life is dead.
Great men, and worthy of report, must fall
Into their earth, and sleeping there sleep all:
Since he, whose pen in every strain did use
To drop a verse, and every verse a muse,
Is vow'd to heaven; as having with fair glory,
Sung thanks of honour, or some nobler story.
The court, the university, the heat
Of theatres, with what can else beget
Belief, and admiration, clearly prove
Our Poet first in merit, as in love:
Yet if he do not at his full appear,
Survey him in his Works, and know him there.
—Ford, John, 1638, *On the best of English Poets, Ben Jonson, Deceased.*

The Muses' fairest light in no dark time;
The wonder of a learned age; the line
Which none can pass; the most proportion'd wit,
To Nature, the best judge of what was fit;
The deepest, plainest, highest, clearest pen;
The voice most echo'd by consenting men;
The soul which answer'd best to all well said
By others, and which most requital made;
Tuned to the highest key of ancient Rome,
Returning all her music with his own,
In whom with nature, study claimed a part,
And yet who to himself owed all his art:
Here lies Ben Jonson! Every age will look
With sorrow here, with wonder on his book.
—Cleveland, John, 1638, *To the Memory of Ben Jonson.*

And now, since Jonson's gone, we well may say,
The stage hath seen her glory and decay.
Whose judgment was't refined it? or who
Gave laws, by which hereafter all must go,
But solid Jonson? from whose full strong quill,
Each line did like a diamond drop distil,
Though hard, yet clear.
—Feltham, Owen, 1638, *To the Memory of Immortal Ben.*

Mirror of poets! mirror of our age!
—Waller, Edmund, 1638, *Upon Ben Jonson.*

Look up! where Seneca and Sophocles,
Quick Plautus and sharp Aristophanes,
Enlighten yon bright orb! doth not your eye,
Among them, one far larger fire descry,
At which their lights grow pale? 'Tis Jonson.
—Habington, William, 1638, *Upon the Death of Ben Jonson.*

Thou great refiner of our poesy,
Who turn'st to gold that which before was lead,
Then with that pure elixir raised the dead!
Nine sisters who (for all the poets' lies)

Had been deemed mortal, did not Jonson rise
And with celestial sparks (not stol'n) revive
Those who could erst keep winged fame alive.
—BEAUMONT, SIR JOHN, 1638, *To the Memory of him who can never be Forgotten, Master Benjamin Jonson.*

To compare our English Dramatick Poets together (without taxing them) *Shakespear* excelled in a natural Vein, *Fletcher* in Wit, and *Johnson* in Gravity and ponderousness of Style; whose onely fault was, he was too elaborate; and had he mixt less erudition with his Playes, they had been more pleasant and delightful than they are. Comparing him with *Shakespear*, you shall see the difference betwixt Nature and Art; and with *Fletcher*, the difference between Wit and Judgement: Wit being an exuberant thing, like *Nilus*, never more commendable then when it overflowes; but Judgement a stayed and reposed thing, alwayes containing it self within its bounds and limits.—FLECKNOE, RICHARD, c 1660-64, *A Short Discourse of the English Stage.*

He was paramount in the Dramatique part of Poetry, and taught the Stage an exact conformity to the laws of Comedians. His Comedies were above the Volge (which are only tickled with downright obscenity), and took not so well at the first stroke as at the rebound, when beheld the second time; yea they will endure reading, and that with due commendation, so long as either ingenuity or learning are fashionable in our Nation. If his later be not so spriteful and vigorous as his first pieces, all that are old will, and all that desire to be old should, excuse him therein.—FULLER, THOMAS, 1662, *The Worthies of England, ed. Nichols, vol.* II, *p.* 112.

As for Jonson, to whose character I am now arrived, if we look upon him while he was himself (for his last plays were but his dotages), I think him the most learned and judicious writer which any theatre ever had. He was a most severe judge of himself, as well as others. One cannot say he wanted wit, but rather that he was frugal of it. In his works you find little to retrench or alter. Wit and language, and humour also in some measure, we had before him; but something of art was wanting to the drama, till he came. He managed his strength to more advantage than any who preceded him. You seldom find him making love in any of his scenes, or endeavouring to move the passions; his genius was too sullen and saturnine to do it gracefully, especially when he knew he came after those who had performed both to such an height. Humour was his proper sphere; and in that he delighted most to represent mechanic people. He was deeply conversant in the ancients, both Greek and Latin, and he borrowed boldly from them: there is scarce a poet or historian among the Roman authors of those times, whom he has not translated in "Sejanus" and "Catiline." But he has done his robberies so openly, that one may say he fears not to be taxed by any law. He invades authors like a monarch; and what would be theft in other poets, is only victory in him. With the spoils of these writers he so represents old Rome to us, in its rites, ceremonies, and customs, that if one of their poets had written either of his tragedies, we had seen less of it than in him. If there was any fault in his language, it was, that he weaved it too closely and laboriously, in his comedies especially: perhaps, too, he did a little too much Romanize our tongue, leaving the words which he translated almost as much Latin as he found them: wherein, though he learnedly followed their language, he did not enough comply with the idiom of ours. If I would compare him with Shakespeare, I must acknowledge him the more correct poet, but Shakespeare the greater wit. Shakespeare was the Homer, or father of our dramatic poets; Jonson was the Virgil, the pattern of elaborate writing; I admire him, but I love Shakespeare. To conclude of him; as he has given us the most correct plays, so in the precepts which he has laid down in his "Discoveries," we have as many and profitable rules for perfecting the stage, as any wherewith the French can furnish us.—DRYDEN, JOHN, 1668-93, *An Essay of Dramatic Poesy; Works, ed. Scott and Saintsbury, vol.* XV, *p.* 346.

Benjamin Jonson, the most learned, judicious, and correct, generally so accounted, of our English Comedians, and the more to be admired for being so, for that neither the height of natural parts, for he was no Shakespeare, nor the cost of extraordinary education, for he is reported but a bricklayer's son, but his own proper industry and addiction to books advanced him to this perfection. In three of his comedies, namely, "The Fox," "Alchymist," and "Silent Woman," he may be compared in the judgment of learned men, for decorum, language, and well humouring of the parts, as well with the chief of the ancient Greek and Latin comedians, as the prime of modern Italians, who have been judged the best of Europe for a happy vein in comedies; nor is his "Bartholomew Fair" much short of them. As for his other comedies, "Cynthia's Revels," "Poetaster," and the rest, let the name of Ben Johnson protect them against whoever shall think fit to be severe in censure against them. The truth is, his tragedies, "Sejanus" and "Catiline," seem to have in them more of an artificial and inflate, than of a pathetical and naturally tragic height.—PHILLIPS, EDWARD, 1675, *Theatrum Poetarum Anglicanorum, ed. Brydges, p.* 241.

Too nicely Jonson knew the critic's part;
Nature in him was almost lost in art.

—COLLINS, WILLIAM, 1743, *Epistle to Sir Thomas Hanmer.*

Then Jonson came, instructed from the school,
To please in method, and invent by rule;
His studious patience and laborious art,
By regular approach assail'd the heart:
Cold approbation gave the lingering bays,
For those, who durst not censure. scarce could praise.
A mortal born, he met the general doom,
But left, like Egypt's kings, a lasting tomb.

—JOHNSON, SAMUEL, 1747, *Prologue, spoken by Mr. Garrick at the opening of the Theatre Royal, Drury Lane.*

Jonson possessed all the learning which was wanting to Shakspeare, and wanted all the genius of which the other was possessed. Both of them were equally deficient in taste and elegance, in harmony and correctness. A servile copyist of the ancients, Jonson translated into bad English the beautiful passages of the Greek and Roman authors, without accommodating them to the manners of his age and country. His merit has been totally eclipsed by that of Shakspeare, whose rude genius prevailed over the rude art of his contemporary.—HUME, DAVID, 1754-62, *The History of England, James I., Appendix.*

His nature was severe and rigid, and this in giving a strength and manliness, gave at times too, an intemperance to his satyr. His taste for ridicule was strong but indelicate, which made him not over curious in the choice of his *topics*. And lastly, his *style* in picturing characters, tho' masterly, was without that elegance of *hand*, which is required to correct and allay the force of so bold a colouring. Thus, the biass of his nature leading him to Plautus rather than Terence for his model, it is not to be wondered that his wit is too frequently caustic; his raillery coarse; and his humour excessive.—HURD, RICHARD, 1757, *A Dissertation on the Several Provinces of the Drama, vol.* I, *p.* 306.

The book of man he read with nicest art,
And ransack'd all the secrets of the heart;
Exerted penetration's utmost force,
And traced each passion to its proper source;
Then, strongly mark'd, in liveliest colours drew
And brought each foible forth to public view:
The coxcomb felt a lash in every word,
And fools, hung out, their brother fools deterr'd.
His comic humour kept the world in awe,
And laughter frighten'd Folly more than Law.

—CHURCHILL, CHARLES, 1761, *The Rosciad, v.* 275–284.

He was as defective in tragedy, as he was excellent in comedy; and that excellence is confined to a few of his works. In Shakspeare, we see the force of genius; in Jonson, the power of industry. He is frequently deficient in the harmony, and sometimes even in the measure, of his verses. What appears to be facility in his compositions is generally the effect of uncommon labour. — GRANGER, JAMES, 1769-1824, *Biographical History of England, vol.* II, *p.* 125.

Jonson gave an early example of metaphysical poetry; indeed, it was the natural resource of a mind amply stored with learning, gifted with a tenacious memory and the power of constant labour, but to which was denied that vivid perception of what is naturally beautiful, and that happiness of expression, which at once conveys to the reader the idea of the poet. . . . In reading Shakspeare, we often meet passages so congenial to our nature and feelings, that, beautiful as they are, we can hardly help wondering they did not occur to ourselves; in studying Jonson, we have often to marvel how his conceptions could have occurred to any human being. The one is like an ancient statue, the beauty of which, springing from the exactness of proportion, does not always strike at first sight, but rises upon us as we bestow time in considering it; the other is the representation of a monster, which is at first only surprising, and ludicrous or disgusting ever after.—SCOTT, SIR WALTER, 1805, *Life of John Dryden.*

He endeavoured to form an exact estimate of what he had on every occasion to perform; hence he succeeded best in that species of the drama which makes the principal demand on the understanding and with little call on the imagination and feeling,—the comedy of character. He introduced nothing into his works which critical dissection should not be able to extract again, as his confidence in it was such, that he conceived it exhausted everything which pleases and charms us in poetry. He was not aware that in the chemical retort of the critic what is most valuable, the volatile living spirit of a poem, evaporates. His pieces are in general deficient in soul, in that nameless something which never ceases to attract and enchant us even because it is indefinable. In the lyrical pieces, his Masques, we feel the want of a certain mental music of imagery and intonation, which the most accurate observation of difficult measures cannot give. He is everywhere deficient in those excellencies which, unsought, flow from the poet's pen, and which no artist who purposely hunts for them can ever hope to find. We must not quarrel with him, however, for entertaining a high opinion of his own works, since whatever merits they have he owed, like acquired moral properties, altogether to himself. The production of them was attended with labour, and unfortunately it is also a labour to read them. They resemble solid and regular edifices, before which, however, the clumsy scaffolding still remains, to interrupt and prevent us from viewing the architecture with ease and receiving from it a harmonious impression.—SCHLEGEL, AUGUSTUS WILLIAM, 1809, *Dramatic Art and Literature.*

With such extraordinary requisites for the stage, joined to a strain of poetry always manly, frequently lofty, and sometimes almost sublime, it may, at first, appear strange that his dramas are not more in vogue; but a little attention to his peculiar modes and habits of thinking will, perhaps, enable us in some measure to account for it. The grace and urbanity which mark his lighter pieces he laid aside whenever he approached the stage, and put on the censor with the stock. This system (whether wise or unwise,) naturally led to circumstances which affect his popularity as a writer; he was obliged, as one of his critics justly observes, "to hunt down his own characters," and, to continue the metaphor, he was frequently carried too far in the chase.—GIFFORD, WILLIAM, 1816, *ed. The Works of Ben Jonson, Memoir, vol.* I.

Ben Jonson is original; he is, indeed, the only one of the great dramatists of that day who was not either directly produced, or very greatly modified, by Shakspere. In truth, he differs from our great master in everything—in form and in substance—and betrays no tokens of his proximity. He is not original in the same way as Shakspere is original; but after a fashion of his own, Ben Jonson is most truly original. . . . Ben Jonson exhibits a sterling English diction, and he has with great skill contrived varieties of construction; but his style is rarely sweet or harmonious, in consequence of his labour at point and strength being so evident. In all his works, in verse or prose, there is an extraordinary opulence of thought; but it is the produce of an amassing power in the author, and not of a growth from within. Indeed a large proportion of Ben Jonson's thoughts may be traced to classic or obscure modern writers, by those who are learned and curious enough to follow the steps of this robust, surly, and observing dramatist.—COLERIDGE, SAMUEL TAYLOR, 1818, *Notes on Jonson, Beaumont, Fletcher, and Massinger, ed. Ashe, pp.* 396, 397.

There are people who cannot take olives: and I cannot much relish Ben Jonson, though I have taken some pains to do it, and went to the task with every sort of good will. I do not deny his power or his merit; far from it; but it is to me a repulsive and unamiable kind. He was a great man in himself, but one cannot readily sympathize with him. His works, as the characteristic productions of an individual mind, or as records of the manners of a particular age, cannot be valued too highly; but they have little charm for the mere general reader.—HAZLITT, WILLIAM, 1819, *Lectures on the English Comic Writers.*

In the regular drama he certainly holds up no romantic mirror to nature. His object was to exhibit human characters at once strongly comic and severely and instructively true; to nourish the understanding, while he feasted the sense of ridicule. He is more anxious for verisimilitude than even for comic effect. He understood the humors and peculiarities of his species scientifically, and brought them forward in their greatest contrasts and subtlest modifications. If Shakspeare carelessly scattered illusion, Jonson skillfully prepared it. This is speaking of Jonson in his happiest manner. There is a great deal of harsh and sour fruit in his miscellaneous poetry. It is acknowledged that in the drama he frequently overlabours his delineation of character, and wastes it tediously upon uninteresting humours and peculiarities. He is a moral painter, who delights overmuch to show his knowledge of moral anatomy.—CAMPBELL, THOMAS, 1819, *An Essay on English Poetry.*

I do not think that his Poetical merits are yet properly appreciated. I cannot consent that the palm of humour alone shall be given to him; while in wit, feeling, pathos, and Poetical diction, he is to be sunk fathoms below Fletcher and Massinger. In the last particular, I think that he excels them both, and, indeed, all his contemporaries, excepting Shakspeare. —NEELE, HENRY, 1828, *Lectures on English Poetry; Lecture III.*

There is nothing in his own entire plays equalling in pathetic beauty some of his contributions to "The Spanish Tragedy." —COLLIER, JOHN PAYNE, 1831, *History of English Dramatic Poetry, vol.* III, *p.* 205, *note.*

If asked to give our opinion of Ben Jonson's powers in general, we should say that he was a poet of a high order, as far as learning, fancy, and an absolute rage of ambition, could conspire to make him one; but that he never touched at the highest, except by violent efforts, and during the greatest felicity of his sense of success. The material so predominated in him over the spiritual,—the sensual over the sentimental,—that he was more social than loving, and far more wilful and fanciful than imaginative. Desiring the strongest immediate effect, rather than the best effect, he subserved by wholesale in his comedies to the grossness and commonplace of the very multitude whom he hectored; and in love with whatsoever he knew or uttered, he set learning above feeling in writing his tragedies, and never knew when to leave off, whether in tragedy or comedy. His style is more clear and correct than impassioned, and only rises above a certain level at remarkable intervals, when he is heated by a sense of luxury or domination. He betrays what was weak in himself, and even a secret misgiving, by incessant attacks upon the weakness and envy of others; and, in his highest moods, instead of the healthy, serene, and good-natured might of Shakspeare, has something of a puffed and uneasy pomp, a bigness instead of greatness, analogous to his gross habit of body: nor, when you think of him at any time, can you well separate the idea from that of the assuming scholar and the flustered man of taverns.—HUNT, LEIGH, 1839, *Men, Women, and Books, vol.* II.

Ben Jonson was a man of the *new* age, and the *new* direction of mind; he was that half of Shakspeare which reached forward into the future, but in a more eminent degree. His chief strength was in the very excess of his one-sidedness. With the immense force of his intellectual, reflective, and critical powers, he knocked down everything in his own way —but overthrew the good together with the bad. His first principle was, to have definite palpable reasons for everything: he wished at every point *to know* what ought to be done or left undone. The clearness of the reflecting *consciousness* was the standard to which he referred everything; but of that immediate creative faculty of fancy and feeling which is properly artistic, he possessed scarcely a germ. On this account the other half of Shakspeare's character, which, like the whole of the English national theatre, belonged to the romantic middle ages, was to him hateful, inconceivable, and worthless.—ULRICI, HERMANN, 1839, *Shakspeare's Dramatic Art, pp.* 81, 82.

Jonson's intense observation was microscopical when turned to the minute evolutions of society, while his diversified learning at all times bore him into a nobler sphere of comprehension. This taste for reality, and this fullness of knowledge on whatever theme he chose, had a reciprocal action; and the one could not go without the other. Our poet doggedly set to "a humour" through its slightest anomalies, and, in the pride of his comic art, expanded his prototype. Yet this was but half the labor which he loved: his mind was stored with the most burdensome knowledge; and to the scholar the various erudition which he had so diligently acquired threw a more permanent light over those transient scenes which the painter of manners had so carefully copied.—DISRAELI, ISAAC, 1841, *The "Humours" of Jonson, Amenities of Literature.*

O rare Ben Jonson, let us have thy songs, rounded each with a spherical thought, and the lyrics from thy masques alive with learned fantasy, and thine epigrams keen and quaint, and thy noble epitaphs, under which the dead seem stirring! . . . At Jonson's name we stop perforce, and do salutation in the dust to the impress of that "learned sock." He was a learned man, as everybody knows; and as everybody does not believe, not the worse for his learning. His material, brought laboriously from East and West, is wrapt in a flame of his own. If the elasticity and abandonment of Shakespeare and of certain of Shakespeare's brothers, are not found in his writings, the reason of the defects need not be sought out in his readings. His genius, high and verdant as it grew, yet belonged to the hard woods: it was lance-wood rather than bow-wood—a genius rather noble than graceful—eloquent, with a certain severity and emphasis of enunciation.—BROWNING, ELIZABETH BARRETT, 1842-63, *The Book of the Poets.*

With this basis of sound English sense, Jonson has fancy, humor, satire, learning, a large knowledge of men and motives, and a remarkable command of language, sportive, scornful, fanciful, and impassioned. One of the fixed facts in English literature, he is too strongly rooted ever to be upset. He stands out from all his contemporaries, original, peculiar, leaning on none for aid, and to be tried by his own merits alone. Had his imagination been as sensitive as that of many of his contemporaries, or his self-love less, he would probably have fallen into their conscious or unconscious imitation of Shakespeare; but, as it was, he remained satisfied with himself to the last, delving in his own mine.—WHIPPLE, EDWIN P., 1846, *Old English Dramatists, Essays and Reviews, vol.* II, *p.* 26.

A mighty and solid genius, whose plays bear an impress of majestic art and slow but powerful elaboration, distinguishing them from the careless ease and unpremeditated abundance so strongly characterising the drama of this period. . . . He was undoubtedly one of the most learned of this or indeed any age of English literature.—SHAW, THOMAS B., 1847, *Outlines of English Literature, ch.* vii.

We of this age, a little too careless perhaps of learned labor, would give a whole wilderness of Catilines and Poetasters, and even of Alchemists and Volpones, for another score of the exquisite lyrics which are scattered carelessly through the plays and masques which—strange contrast with the rugged verse in which they are imbedded—seem to have burst into being at a stroke, just as the evening primrose flings open her fair petals at the close of the day. Lovelier songs were never written than these wild and irregular ditties.—MITFORD, MARY RUSSELL, 1851, *Recollections of a Literary Life, ch.* xix.

He read the best Latin books, and the commentaries which illustrated them; he wrote two plays on subjects taken from Roman history. Very striking subjects they were. The hero of one was Catiline, who tried to overthrow the social order of the Republic; the hero of the other was Sejanus, who represents, by his grandeur and his fall, the very character and spirit of the Empire in the days of Tiberius. In dealing with these subjects, Ben Jonson had the help of two of the greatest Roman authors, both of them possessing remarkable powers of narration, one of them a man of earnest character, subtle insight, deep reflection. Though few men in his day understood these authors, and the government and circumstances of Rome, better than Jonson, though he was a skilful and experienced play-writer, most readers are glad when they have got Catiline and Sejanus fairly done with. They do not find that they have received any distinct impressions from them of Roman life; to learn what it was they must go to the authors whom he has copied.—MAURICE, FREDERICK DENISON, 1856-74, *The Friendship of Books and Other Lectures, ed. Hughes, p.* 8.

Ben Jonson was a conscientious and intelligent workman, whose plays glow, here and there, with the golden pollen of that poetic feeling with which his age impregnated all thought and expression; but his leading characteristic, like that of his great namesake, Samuel, was a hearty common sense, which fitted him rather to be a great critic than a great poet. He had a keen and ready eye for the comic in situation, but no humor.—LOWELL, JAMES RUSSELL, 1858-64-90, *Library of Old Authors, Prose Works, Riverside ed., vol.* I, *p.* 277.

Shakespeare had permanently near him one envious person, Ben Jonson, an indifferent comic poet, whose *début* he assisted.—HUGO, VICTOR, 1864, *William Shakespeare, tr. Baillot, p.* 23.

Few writers have laboured more, and more conscientiously; his knowledge was vast, and in this age of great scholars he was one of the best classics of his time, as deep as he was accurate and thorough, having studied the minutest details of ancient life. It was not enough for him to have stored himself from the best writers, to have their whole works continually in his mind, to scatter his pages, whether he would or no, with recollections of them. . . . A still greater proof of his force is, that his learning in nowise mars his vigour; heavy as is the mass with which he loads himself, he carries it without stooping. This wonderful compound of reading and observation suddenly begins to move, and falls like a mountain on the overwhelmed reader. . . . A genuine literary Leviathan, like the war elephants which used to bear towers, men, weapons, machines on their backs, and ran as swiftly under the freight as a nimble steed.—TAINE, H. A., 1871, *History of English Literature, tr. Van Laun, vol.* I, *bk.* ii, *ch.* iii, *pp.* 270, 271.

Ben Jonson has been regarded as the first person who has done much in settling the "*grammar* of the English language." This merit is duly awarded to him, and Pope gives him the credit of having brought critical learning into vogue; also of having instructed both actors and spectators in what was the proper province of the dramatic Muse. His prose style, however, is a transcript of his laborious and painstaking mind, ostentatiously correct, and frequently forcible, with commonly a satisfactory felicity of epithet; but his sentences never appear to be extemporaneous, but always studied, and as being one result of the primæval curse, for he seems to have produced both his thoughts and his language "by the sweat of his brow."—CLARKE, CHARLES COWDEN, 1871, *On the Comic Writers of England, Gentleman's Magazine,* N. S., *vol.* 6, *p.* 633.

One grave defect in all his creations is what may be called their monotony. There is no flexibility of disposition, no free play of nature. Moreover, his works exhibit too plainly the travail and effort with which they were composed. One seems to be taken into his workshop, and see him toiling and groaning, and, in the very act of elaboration, shaping now this limb and now that.—HALES, JOHN W., 1873, *Notes and Essays on Shakespeare, p.* 66.

His comedy is no genial reflection of life as it is, but a moral, satirical effort to reform manners. It is only his wonderful grace and real poetic feeling that lighten all this pedantry. He shares the vigor and buoyancy of life which distinguished the school from which he sprang. His stage is thronged with figures. In spite of his talk about correctness, his own extravagance is only saved from becoming ridiculous by his amazing force. If he could not create characters, his wealth of striking details gave life to the types which he substituted for them. His poetry, too, is of the highest order; his lyrics of the purest, lightest fancy; his masques rich with gorgeous pictures; his pastoral, "The Sad Shepherd," fragment as it is, breathes a delicate tenderness.—GREEN, JOHN RICHARD, 1874, *A Short History of the English People, ch.* vii, *sec.* vii.

Ben Jonson had a mind of immense force and pertinacious grasp; but nothing could be wider of the truth than the notion maintained with such ferocity by Gifford, that he was the father of regular comedy, the pioneer of severe and correct taste. Jonson's domineering scholarship must not be taken for more than it was worth: it was a large and gratifying possession in itself, but he would probably have written better plays and more poetry without it. It is a sad application of the mathematical method to the history of our literature to argue that the most learned playwright of his time superseded the rude efforts of such untaught mother-wits as Shakespeare with compositions based on classical models. What Jonson really did was to work out his own ideas of comedy and tragedy, and he expressly claimed the right to do so. The most scrupulous adherence to the unity of time, and the most rigid exclusion of tragic elements from comedy, do not make a play classical. Ben Jonson conformed to these externals; but there was not a more violently unclassical spirit than his among all the writers for the stage in that generation.—MINTO, WILLIAM, 1874-85, *Characteristics of English Poets, p.* 337.

To the modern reader, Ben Jonson's plays have lost their old attraction; but his occasional poems are full of heroic thought, and his songs are among the best in the language.—EMERSON, RALPH, WALDO, 1875, *Parnassus, Preface, p.* vi.

Broad-absed, broad-fronted, bounteous, multiform,
With many a valley impleached with ivy and vine,
Wherein the springs of all the streams run wine,
And many a crag full-faced against the storm,
The mountain where thy Muse's feet made warm
Those lawns that revelled with her dance divine,
Shines yet with fire as it was wont to shine
From tossing torches round the dance a-swarm.
Nor less, high-stationed on the gray grave heights,
High-thoughted seers with heaven's heart-kindling lights
Hold converse: and the herd of meaner things
Knows or by fiery scourge or fiery shaft
When wrath on thy broad brows has risen, and laughed,
Darkening thy soul with shadow of thunderous wings.

—SWINBURNE, ALGERNON CHARLES, 1882, *Ben Jonson.*

Ben Jonson stands at the head of that school of dramatists who take for their *Dramatis Personæ* not individuals but conventional types, and who somewhat ignore the complexities of human nature. No argument is wanted to show that Shakspere's method of truly holding the mirror up to nature is the higher, the greater, and the truer method, but Jonson has ancient tradition in favour of his view of the dramatic art. . . . Seldom departs from the strict tradition: his cowardly braggarts are most inveterate cowards and braggarts, his knaves most arrant knaves, his fools have no redeeming touch of good sense, and his misers are grasping and avaricious beyond all human precedent and possibility. Nevertheless, the magnificent genius of the man—chiefly a literary genius—takes the reader's judgment by storm; and if the reader's, how much more would the hearer be captivated by the broad persistent humor of Bobadill and the mordant cynicism of Mosca and Volpone!—CRAWFURD, OSWALD, 1883, *ed. English Comic Dramatists, p.* 12.

His racy representations of the follies and oddities, and, as he would call them, the humours, of the day, are balanced by the classical representations which led Milton to speak of "Jonson's learned sock," though there are indeed some of his works which rise almost to the dignity of the buskin. "The Alchemist," "The Fox," and "Every Man in his Humour" have made themselves well known. Let me commend to you a less real drama, "Catiline," in which the story of the great conspiracy is finely told, partly through noble paraphrases of Cicero and Sallust, and partly through the play of the dialogue between the conspirators. If any of you should be tempted to read it, let him take note of the delicious piece of partly personal, partly political, gossip among the Roman ladies, which leads to the betrayal of the plot. There is another clever Roman play, "The Poetaster," which would have been a rather appropriate subject for discussion to-night, for it tells the old old tale of the struggle between father and son, when the one enjoins the study of the law and the other flies resolutely to his studies in poetry.—NORTHCOTE, HENRY STAFFORD, 1885, *Desultory Reading, p.* 54.

His literary influence was very great, and with Donne he determined the whole course of English literature for many years and retained a great name even in the comparative eclipse of the "Giant Race" after the Restoration. It was only when the study of Shakespere became a favourite subject with persons of more industry than intelligence in the early eighteenth century, that a singular fabric of myth grew up round Ben Jonson. He was pictured as an incarnation of envy, hatred, malice, and all uncharitableness, directed in the first place towards Shakespere, and then towards all other literary craftsmen. William Gifford, his first competent editor, set himself to work to destroy this, and undoubtedly succeeded. But the acrimony with which Gifford tinctured all his literary polemic perhaps rather injured his treatment of the case; even yet it may be doubted whether Ben Jonson has attained anything like his proper place in English literary history. . . . His lovely "Masques" are probably unread by all but a few scores, if so many, in each generation. His noble sinewy prose is, for the most part, unattractive in subject. His minor poems, though not a few of them are known even to smatterers in literature, are as a whole (or at least it would seem so) unknown. Yet his merits are extraordinary.—SAINTSBURY, GEORGE, 1887, *History of Elizabethan Literature, pp.* 176, 177.

The more I read of the literary history of those days the more impressed I am by the predominance of Ben Jonson;—a great, careless, hard-living, hard-drinking, not ill-natured literary monarch. His strength is evidenced by the deference shown him—by his versatility; now some musical masque sparkling with little dainty bits which a sentimental miss might copy in her album or chant in her boudoir; and this, matched or followed by some labored drama full of classic knowledge, full of largest wordcraft, snapping with fire-crackers of wit, loaded with ponderous nuggets of strong sense, and the whole capped and booted with prologue and epilogue where poetic graces shine through proudest averments of indifference—of scorn of applause—of audacious self-sufficiency. — MITCHELL, DONALD G., 1890, *English Lands Letters and Kings, From Elizabeth to Anne, p.* 26.

Too few read Ben Jonson's plays.—STEDMAN, EDMUND CLARENCE, 1892, *The Nature and Elements of Poetry, p.* 170.

He repels his admirers, he holds readers at arm's length. He is the least sympathetic of all the great English poets, and to appreciate him the rarest of literary tastes is required,—an appetite for dry intellectual beauty, for austerity of thought, for poetry that is logical, and hard, and lusty. Yet he did a mighty work for the English language. At a time when it threatened to sink into mere prettiness or oddity, and to substitute what was non-essential for what was definite and durable, Jonson threw his massive learning and logic into the scale, and forbade Jacobean poetry to kick the beam. He was rewarded by the passionate devotion of a tribe of wits and scholars; he made a deep mark on our literature for several generations subsequent to his own, and he enjoys the perennial respect of all close students of poetry.—GOSSE, EDMUND, 1894, *The Jacobean Poets, pp.* 37, 38.

Jonson's pages are not so thickly sown with metaphor as are Chapman's and those of many others. His language is too realistic for that. There are almost no prolonged similes and few prolonged metaphorical passages. Short similes, however, are very frequently employed.—CARPENTER, FREDERIC IVES, 1895, *Metaphor and Simile in the Minor Elizabethan Drama, pp.* 127, 132.

Jonson, whose splendid scorn took to itself lyric wings in the two great Odes to Himself, sang high and aloof for a while, then the frenzy caught him, and he flung away his lyre to gird himself for deeds of mischief among nameless and noteless antagonists. . . . He lost the calm of his temper and the clearness of his singing voice, he degraded his magnanimity by allowing it to engage in street-brawls, and he endangered the sanctuary of the inviolable soul.—RALEIGH, WALTER, 1897, *Style, pp.* 68, 71.

The comic of Jonson is a scholar's excogitation of the comic.—MEREDITH, GEORGE, 1897, *An Essay on Comedy and the Uses of the Comic Spirit, p.* 16.

It was Jonson who first revealed to the age the literary possibilities of the masque, and lesser men were not slow to follow in the path which he had marked out. Had it not been for Jonson, it is hardly too much to say that the masque would today be the exclusive property of the Court chronicler and the antiquarian, and of no more significance to literature than a tilting match or a Christmas gambol. —EVANS, HERBERT ARTHUR, 1897, *English Masques, Introduction, p.* xi.

Sir Robert Ayton

1570-1638

A scottish poet and courtier, knighted by James I. in 1612. He was one of the first Scotsmen who wrote in English with any degree of elegance and purity. "I do confess thou'rt smooth and fair," and the prototype of "Auld Lang Syne," have been ascribed to him, but on scant authority.—PATRICK AND GROOME, *eds.*, 1897, *Chambers's Biographical Dictionary p.* 55.

Sir Robert Aiton, knight;—he lies buried in the south aisle of the choire of Westminster abbey where there is erected to his memory an elegant marble and copper monument and inscription. . . . That Sir Robert was one of the best poets of his time—Mr. John Dreyden says he has seen verses of his, some of the best of that age, printed with some other verses—quaere. He was acquainted with all the witts of his time in England. He was a great acquaintance of Mr. Thomas Hobbes of Malemsbury, whom Mr. Hobbes told me he made use of (together with Ben Johnson) for an Aristarchus, when he made his Epistle Dedicatory to his translation of Thucydides.—AUBREY, JOHN, 1669-96, *Brief Lives, ed. Clark, vol.* I.

Aytoun's poems are not numerous, nor of sustained effort, but they show much perfection in the art of poetry, and a Horatian elegance of style and turn of thought becoming their semi-lyrical character. He himself possibly placed more value upon his Latin Poems, which appeared in the "Delitiae Poetarum Scotorum," than on his English Poems, for they appeared in all sorts of ways, scattered here and there, and were only first collected in 1844, on the occasion of a manuscript copy having come into the hands of Dr. Charles Rogers, who had them printed for private circulation.—ROSS, J., 1884, *The Book of Scottish Poems, p.* 358.

Connected with several of the wits of that period; and Jonson averred to Drummond that "Sir R. Ayton loved him dearly." He was evidently a man of sprightly talents, as well as an elegant scholar: his Latin poems, which occur in the "Delitiæ Poetarum Scotorum," have been highly commended by Borrichius; and his English poems, although inconsiderable for their number and length, are sufficient to evince that he was capable of higher efforts.—IRVING, DAVID, 1861, *The History of Scottish Poetry, ed. Carlyle, pp.* 554, 555.

To whom is commonly attributed the well-known song, "I do confess thou'rt smooth and fair," and who is also the author of a considerable number of other similar effusions, many of them of superior polish and elegance.—CRAIK, GEORGE L., 1861, *A Compendious History of English History and of the English Language, vol.* II, *p.* 288.

The literary repute of Sir Robert Aytoun is as much of a paradox as Sir Edward Dyer's. His Latin productions are stilted and unmellifluous, mere echoes of the iron age of classic Latinity, and simply grotesque beside Buchanan's and Johnston's. Sir John Scot of Scotstarvet indeed gives him a relatively large space in his "Delitiæ Poet. Scot.," but simply from his contemporary repute. Among his Latin poems appear several epitaphs and epigrams celebrating eminent contemporaries. The latest event to which any of them refers is the death of Buckingham in 1628, commemorated in elegiacs. Aytoun's "Diophantus and Charidora" has a certain interest as having been among the earlier writing in English by a Scot, but it is poor in substance. His "Inconstancy Upbraided" has a ring of truthfulness and touches of music. Such praise as is due to the elegant trifles of an accomplished man of the world is all that can be allowed his poems. If it could be proved that he wrote "I do confess thou'rt smooth and fair," of which Burns gave a Scottish version, it would not be necessary to modify this estimate; and it is all but certain that Sir Robert Aytoun did not write it.—GROSART, ALEXANDER B., 1885, *Dictionary of National Biography, vol.* II, *p.* 301.

Aytoun long preserved a considerable reputation for the grace and delicacy of his verse; but, unhappily a doubt hangs over his most admired compositions, and it is not certain that we possess, as his, the verses which Dryden pronounced "some of the best of that age."—GOSSE, EDMUND, 1894, *The Jacobean Poets, p.* 106.